Real Estate Encyclopedia

Canadian Edition

Real Estate Encyclopedia

Education for the Professional

Canadian Edition

International Standard Book Number: 1-894726-00-6

June, 2002

Original Copyright:
Ontario Real Estate Association
99 Duncan Mill Road
Don Mills, ON   M3B 1Z2

Canadian Edition:
Amended and reprinted for national circulation by the Alliance for Canadian Real Estate Education with permission, based on the original text titled *Real Estate Encyclopedia* (Ontario Real Estate Association, September 2000).

Learning System: © Acronamic Learning Systems Inc.
Editing, Formatting, and Design: Automation Plus Ltd.
Printing and Binding: MediaLinx Print & Graphic Solutions Inc.

Acknowledgements

The Alliance for Canadian Real Estate Education would like to acknowledge the significant contribution made by the Ontario Real Estate Association in developing the publication titled *Real Estate Encyclopedia* (Ontario Real Estate Association, September 2000) without which this product would not have been possible. ACRE wishes to thank the Association for its generous permission to reprint the text with selected changes to accommodate national circulation in the interest of furthering real estate knowledge across Canada.

A special note of thanks is also extended to the various Ontario government ministries, Canada Mortgage and Housing Corporation, and the Real Estate Council of Ontario for providing materials and illustrations in the production of the original OREA text. These contributions remain a vital element in the amended publication.

Disclaimer

Preface

Real estate, as with any profession, is built on a firm foundation of knowledge driven by widely accepted practices, procedures, and terminologies. Salespeople and brokers require convenient access to vital information and prospective practitioners want a one-stop reference guide for their new careers. On a grander scale, the profession as a whole needs a reliable resource for the future advancement of real estate. The *Real Estate Encyclopedia, Canadian Edition* is a dynamic *work in progress* designed to keep pace with a continuously changing marketplace and represents a diligent effort to bring structure to an otherwise fragmented body of knowledge.

The encyclopedia is not a past event, but a future happening. The digital revolution is breaking down traditional barriers. Consumers and practitioners now routinely access thousands of real estate listings across Canada with a simple electronic search. Given this rapid pace of information sharing, reference documents and learning materials will soon lag far behind if significant steps were not taken. This publication is not only needed, but essential for both paper-based and electronic reference purposes, as standardization ultimately paves the way for greater strides in any business or profession.

The *Real Estate Encyclopedia, Canadian Edition* consolidates information within a systematic framework for the benefit of practitioners throughout Canada. This edition is intended for use in conjunction with provincial reference manuals to provide a broad perspective on real estate issues, procedures, and requirements.

This publication is designed for quick and expedient access to desired information. The compendium of facts, descriptions, illustrations, and examples empowers the reader to grasp both the vitality and complexities of the real estate marketplace. Individuals who want to discover and understand a truly exciting segment of the Canadian economy will find this book invaluable.

Table of Contents

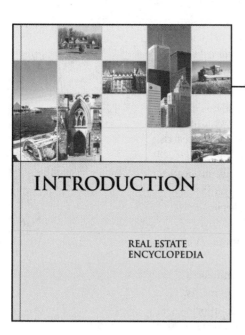

INTRODUCTION

REAL ESTATE
ENCYCLOPEDIA

A–Z REFERENCE

REAL ESTATE
ENCYCLOPEDIA

APPENDIX

REAL ESTATE
ENCYCLOPEDIA

INDEX

REAL ESTATE
ENCYCLOPEDIA

INTRODUCTION

REAL ESTATE
ENCYCLOPEDIA

Reference Design

The *Real Estate Encyclopedia, Canadian Edition* is a unique reference text for salespeople and brokers:

- **A–Z Reference** Alphabetic ordering of national and international terms, phrases, and widely-accepted procedures and practices.
- **Appendix** Selected tables and guidelines.
- **Index** Summary listing of topics.

This product, originally developed by the Ontario Real Estate Association, is designed for use by other provinces to promote consistency in real estate brokerage across Canada. The *Real Estate Encyclopedia, Canadian Edition* should be read in conjunction with applicable provincial materials to provide a full description of topics contained within this publication.

This text forms part of an integrated learning system* for classroom and self-directed (online and correspondence) modes of delivery. The learning system meets and exceeds national standards as set out in the *National Code of Real Estate Education*, advances labour mobility provisions pursuant to the *Agreement on Internal Trade* for reduction of barriers to education certification throughout Canada, and aligns with curriculum standards established by the *Alliance for Canadian Real Estate Education*.

How to Search in the Encyclopedia

Step 1: Check the A–Z Reference
- Guide words are provided at the top of each page.
- *Info Links* for national references are situated at the front of each letter.
- Cross-references are included for other **A–Z Reference** materials or the **Appendix**, as applicable.
- Where appropriate, the reader is directed to provincial materials for additional information.

Step 2: Check the Index
The detailed index provides a quick search mechanism for both the **A–Z Reference** and the **Appendix**.

Step 3: Refer to Provincial Reference Materials
Topics requiring further provincial specifics are identified as follows:

Provincial See applicable reference materials.

Provincial content and its integration with this publication will vary. Selected provinces have published or are currently developing provincial reference manuals to complement the encyclopedia, while emphasizing province-specific materials. The texts, when used in concert, form a national/provincial resource for all salesperson and broker licensing programs.

*Copyright: 2002, Acronamic Learning Systems Inc.

Guidelines

Info Links

National *Info Links* are located at the front of each alphabetic section to highlight significant federal government initiatives and national agencies/ organizations. References include address, contact numbers, and/or web sites. Provincial references are included where federal/provincial jurisdictional areas overlap.

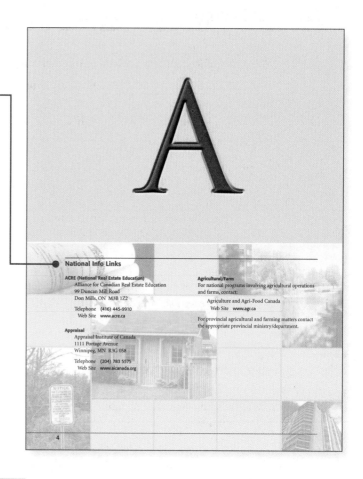

National Info Links

ACRE (National Real Estate Education)
Alliance for Canadian Real Estate Education
99 Duncan Mill Road
Don Mills, ON M3B 1Z2

Telephone (416) 445-9910
Web Site www.acre.ca

Appraisal
Appraisal Institute of Canada
1111 Portage Avenue
Winnipeg, MN R3G 0S8

Telephone (204) 783 5575
Web Site www.aicanada.org

Agricultural/Farm
For national programs involving agricultural operations and farms, contact:

Agriculture and Agri-Food Canada
Web Site www.agr.ca

For provincial agricultural and farming matters contact the appropriate provincial ministry/department.

4

BEAM

or outfitting of office space. The *bay depth* refers to the measurement from the inside wall (tenant's side), of a corridor wall to the exterior wall or glass. Bay depth is important in deriving the most efficient use of space.

Example   Bay Depth
Tenant Savard is considering lease premises in a newly-constructed office building. The bay depth is 38 feet and an interior six-foot corridor is planned. Accordingly, sufficient room is available for exterior and interior office areas with equal depth measurements of 16 feet each. Obviously, the importance of bay depth is directly related to the type of tenants involved. In this instance, Savard wants individual offices to accommodate associates in her software development business. Larger tenants, such as a legal firm, will pay close attention to bay depth to ensure adequate sizing of outer offices, combined with sufficient room for support staff in interior or open office areas.

BEAM

A long structural component, typically made of wood (solid or built-up), plywood, or steel designed to carry floor and wall loads horizontally to the foundation.

Application   The structural integrity of beams is important in any building. Undersized or over-spanned beams may sag or crack and lead to the ultimate failure of an entire framing system. Over-spanned wood beams can be readily identified and are usually remedied with the addition of posts, enlarged beams, or effected through some type of load reduction.

Beams can suffer mechanical damage and be weakened by notching, cutting, or drilling. The amount of weakening is a function of where the damage occurs on the beam, how significant the damage is, and how far it is from the supports. Steel beams can be much stronger than wood beams and are more resistant to rot, termites, and mechanical damage, but are more expensive, heavier, difficult to handle and are susceptible to rust.

Fire is an obvious concern with both wood and steel beams. Interestingly, a steel beam will lose its strength in a fire earlier than a wood beam, although a wood beam actually burns. Steel loses its strength after being exposed to temperatures of 1,000°F for about four minutes. Figure B.6 illustrates beam construction.

BEARINGS
(SEE METES AND BOUNDS)

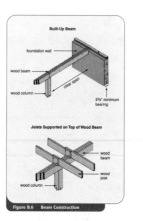

Built-Up Beam

foundation wall
wood beam
wood column
clear span
3⅜" minimum bearing

Joists Supported on Top of Wood Beam

wood beam
wood joist
wood column

Figure B.6   Beam Construction

BERM

Contoured landscaped areas, normally found on commercial or industrial properties that act as a buffer within the site plan for that particular enterprise. Berms often form part of a landscaping design for hotels, resorts, and restaurant facilities. Figure B.7 illustrates a typical berm situated on a commercial property.

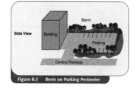

Side View
Building
Berm
Parking
Central Parkway

Figure B.7   Berm on Parking Perimeter

70

Guide Words

Guide words appear in the appropriate upper-right or upper-left corner of the page to facilitate faster searches. The upper-left reference indicates the first new topic on the page. The upper-right reference aligns with the last topic on the page.

Topic Headings

Topic headings are bolded with graphic underline for quick identification. Sub-topics are afforded special colour treatment for ease of reference.

Topic Descriptions

Topics include descriptive definitions from a real estate perspective. Most contain direct applications relating to the real estate profession. Complex topics are ordered either alphabetically or logically to promote ease of readership. *Applications* are focused on procedures and practical examples applying to the listing and selling of real estate.

Page Tabs

Step-down tabs are visible at the edge of the page for quick reference.

Topic Table of Contents

Selected complex topics include a detailed Table of Contents to assist in researching subject matter.

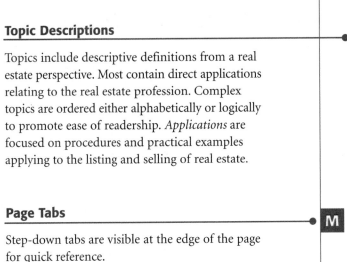

MORE OR LESS

A term often found in a property description, intended to cover slight, unimportant, or unsubstantial inaccuracies of which both parties are willing to assume the risk.

MORTGAGE

A charge on land as security for the payment of a debt with certain remedies for nonpayment. A mortgage is a claim or encumbrance upon the real property given by the owner of the property to the lender as security for money borrowed and typically registered in the applicable provincial land registration system.

The two parties to a mortgage transaction are referred to as the *mortgagor* (borrower) and the *mortgagee* (lender). The lender *gives* or lends the money and registers the mortgage against the property. In return, the borrower

398

gives the mortgage as security for the loan, receives the funds, makes the required payments, and maintains possession of the property. The borrower has a right to have the mortgage discharged from the title once the debt is paid off.

Assignment

The assigning of a mortgagee's rights, ownership and interest in a mortgage to a new mortgagee. The mortgage is an interest in land and can be sold, transferred, or assigned without the consent of the mortgagor. The mortgagor is given notice in writing of the assignment and thereafter makes his/her payments to the assignee. The assignee acquires all the rights of the mortgagee and can exercise these against the mortgagor. This individual acquires only the rights that the mortgagee had and no agreement between the mortgagee and the assignee changes any rights that the mortgagor already has, nor can it impose any additional burden on the mortgagor.

The assignee takes the mortgage subject to the state of accounts between the mortgagee and mortgagor. If, for example, due to a prepayment privilege, the mortgagor had made an additional payment off the principal of which the assignee was not aware, the assignee would have no claim on the mortgagor. After the mortgagor is expressly notified of the assignment and if he or she continues to make payments to the original mortgagee, the assignee can take legal action against the mortgagor to collect the money.

> **Example   Mortgage–Assignment**
> Investor Thompson holds a mortgage on property owned by Smith. Thompson assigns the mortgage as of February 1, 20xx to ABC Investments Ltd. and formally notifies Smith. The mortgage amount is $24,512 as at February 1, 20xx and the mortgage payment date is the fifteenth of each month. Thompson's interest of $24,512 is transferred to ABC Investments Ltd. Smith's February payment is apportioned using the February 1, 20xx date. All future payments should be made to ABC Investments Ltd. Smith is liable to ABC following that date even if he inadvertently keeps forwarding payments to Thompson. As a protection, the new assignee may require a guarantee of the mortgage by the original mortgagee and an indemnification agreement to further support his/her position in the event that the original mortgagor defaults.

Provincial   See applicable reference materials. The ability to assign or transfer a mortgage along with appropriate procedures is regulated by provincial statutory provisions.

Assumption

Existing mortgage financing may be assumed by the buyer provided that the mortgagee agrees and, in most instances,

---

CALCULATING BREAK-EVEN

STEP 1
Determine the Value of the Revenue Unit

= Adjusted Gross Income ÷ # of Units
= $1,093,740 ÷ 536
= $2,041

EXPENSE ANALYSIS SUMMARY	FIXED	VARIABLE	TOTAL
Total Commission Expense		713,414	
• Total Advertising Expense	29,540	+ 40,669	
• Total Personnel Expense	+ 78,125		
• Total Communication Expense	+ 12,989	+ 9,221	
• Total Occupancy Expense	+ 30,189		
• Total Operating Expense		+ 29,179	
• Total General Expense	+ 32,843		
= TOTAL EXPENSES	= 183,686	+ 792,483	976,169

NET INCOME BEFORE TAXES		TOTAL
ADJUSTED GROSS INCOME (from Income Analysis)		1,093,740
– TOTAL EXPENSES (from Expense Analysis)		– 976,169
= NET INCOME BEFORE TAXES		= 117,571

STEP 2
Determine the Variable Cost Factor

= Variable Expenses ÷ Revenue Units
= $792,483 ÷ 536
= $1,479

STEP 3
Determining the Break-Even Factor
= STEP 1 – Variable Cost Factor
= $2,041 – $1479
= $562

STEP 4
Determine Number of Units to Break-Even
= Fixed Costs ÷ Break-Even Factor
= $183,686 ÷ $562
= 327 units (rounded)

Figure B.16   Break-Even

BUFFER ZONE

An area of land specifically set aside, or otherwise identified, that separates two distinct land uses and commonly identified as areas of vacant land that separate different land uses, e.g., residential and commercial, and often zoned as open space.

Buffer zones are typically found within site plan agreements. These areas are not zoned as such, but are identified as landscaped areas including berms that *buffer* the use in relation to adjacent property. Practitioners refer to buffer zones in relation to actual uses, e.g., a heavy area of multi-residential buildings are viewed as a buffer between commercial property on an arterial road and single-family residential housing.

BUILD TO SUIT
(SEE ALSO DESIGN BUILD)

An agreement, typically between a landlord and a new tenant, whereby the landlord assumes the obligation of *fitting up* the demised space to tenant specifications within established building standards. The tenant takes possession when the space is completed.

> **Example   Build to Suit**
> Acme Manufacturing Inc. is seeking an industrial site in Anycity. Anycity Developments Inc. owns suitable property currently zoned for industrial use. Acme provides the specifications for the new building to a tenant representative (salesperson) employed by ABC Realty Inc. The salesperson negotiates with Anycity and develops a lease agreement that is subsequently signed by the parties. Anycity as the landlord, proceeds to build a structure to suit the tenant's specifications.

The example provided is not intended to narrowly focus build to suit arrangements within lease situations. Build to suit can involve combinations including owned or leased property as well as sale/leaseback arrangements. During the past decade, the term *design build* has gradually replaced *build to suit* when referencing such arrangements.

BUILDER'S/CONTRACTOR'S LIEN

A claim against a property that is filed by a person or corporation in the provincial land registry or land titles office for labour, services, or materials supplied in the performance of contractual work.

Provincial   See applicable reference materials.

88

Figures

Illustrations are included in figure boxes and are numbered in ascending order by alphabetic section, e.g., **Figure B.16** (Letter B, Figure 16).

Illustrations emphasize such items as construction layouts, detailed calculations, topic flow charts, and forms.

Examples

Examples expand descriptive text in relation to common real estate activities. Titles parallel topic headings and may include sub-headings where applicable.

Examples, primarily focused on scenarios, may include portions of forms, mathematical formulae, and selected graphics to assist the reader.

Cross-References

A–Z Cross-References are situated immediately below the main topic heading and are identified as either *see* (topic description is located elsewhere), or *see also* (additional information is provided elsewhere). Where appropriate, references are placed in the descriptive text (distinctively high-lighted, e.g. see **Goods and Services Tax**).

Provincial references direct the reader to access applicable provincial materials.

The **Appendix** includes multi-page reference materials relating to selected topics. Cross-references are included where applicable, e.g., see **Mortgage Payment Factors** in the **Appendix**.

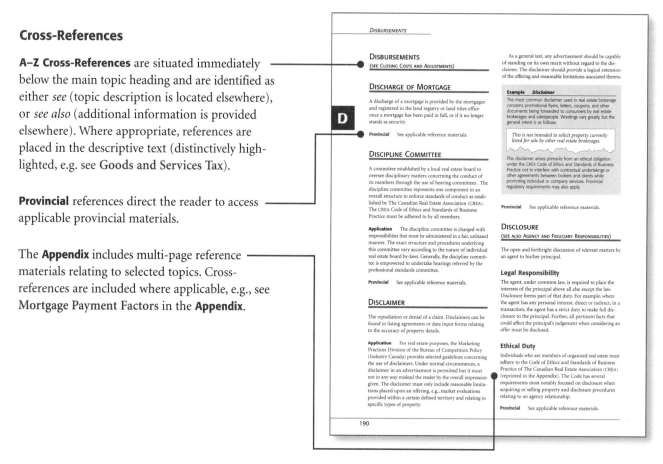

Index

Cross-references are provided to other topics for additional descriptions, e.g., See interest adjustment date.

Page numbers in bold indicate major treatment of topic, e.g., **26–27**.

Topic nesting is used for ease of reference.

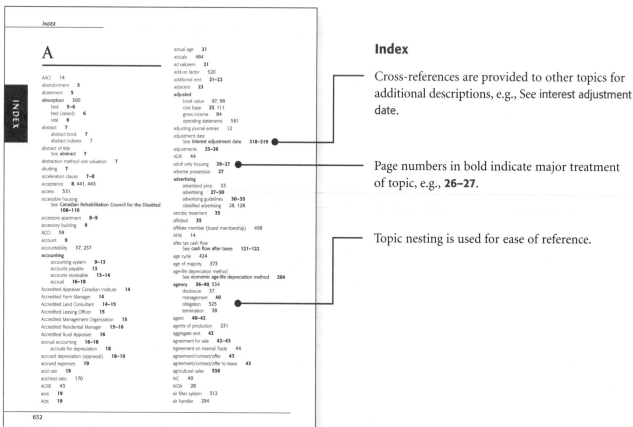

Editorial Comments

Researching Real Estate Topics

In a perfect world, real estate would be easily contained in one publication. However, the reality is a complex mix of federal and provincial authorities, responsibilities, and procedures that often defy classification. The *Real Estate Encyclopedia, Canadian Edition* represents the first attempt to consolidate national topics as a centralized access point to complement provincial reference materials, learning products, and related activities.

The need for both national and provincial perspectives is best made by way of examples. Consider mortgaging, a fundamental element in most real estate transactions. While the topic contains national/international principles, procedures, and descriptions, most day-to-day activity is driven by provincial legislation. For example, while the term *prepayment privilege* is nationally recognized and impacted by Canadian case law, provincial statutory requirements can affect its use. To compound matters, mortgage financing overlaps traditional federal/provincial boundaries. Canada Mortgage and Housing Corporation pursues both primary and secondary Canadian mortgage markets. Banks are national in scope and accordingly governed under the federal *Bank Act* and also regulated by the *Interest Act* in regard to blended mortgage payments. At the same time, mortgage brokers and mortgages are regulated by provincial statute. Given these complexities, this publication details common terms, mortgage market descriptions, and financial calculations. The appropriate provincial materials concentrate on mortgage legislation.

Similar complexities are found in other topic areas. Matters regarding federal taxation and the acquisition, ownership, and disposition of property are found in this publication, e.g., capital cost allowance, capital gain, and goods and services tax. Real property assessment/taxation, along with land transfer tax, appropriately fall to provincial domain. Brokerage management also poses challenges. A real estate brokerage, as with any business, operates in terms of sound business practices that transcend provincial jurisdictions and are appropriately found in this encyclopedia. However, brokerages also fall under provincial regulatory guidelines and statutes. Once again, the need for distinct treatment is evident.

Terminology

Acronyms

A range of acronyms are typical for any profession and real estate is no exception. Only widely used and accepted acronyms are found in this publication.

Agent/Broker

The term *agent* is generally applied to discussions concerning agency law, e.g., duties/responsibilities of an agent to a principal, while the term *broker* refers to a person meeting qualifications of a broker pursuant to provincial licensing law. It is acknowledged that *agent* is used in selected provinces, e.g., Alberta, but *broker* still predominates in most Canadian jurisdictions.

Agreement/Contract

Provincial jurisdictions use differing terminologies for pre-printed forms involving the purchase of real property, e.g., agreement of purchase and sale, offer to purchase, contract of purchase and sale, and purchase contract. The term *agreement/contract* is typically inserted for such references. However, the singular words *agreement* or *contract* are occasionally used to improve readability. All associated forms are referenced by generic terms, e.g., notices, waivers, and mutual releases.

Associate Broker

The term *broker* is normally associated with a principal broker or owner of a real estate brokerage. Provincial regulatory bodies may include additional terms referring to individuals who meet broker qualification levels, but do not own the brokerage, e.g., *associate broker*. Such terms are not used in this publication.

Broker/Brokerage

Provincial legislation typically requires the registration of the real estate brokerage as well as the principal broker/owner and commonly refers to both as *brokers* because each must meet broker licensing requirements. To avoid confusion, all references to sole proprietorships, partnerships, and corporations registered as real estate brokers are referred to as *brokerages* or *real estate brokerages* unless context dictates otherwise.

Definitions/Descriptions

All topics are described from a real estate perspective and do not address other meanings and applications found in the marketplace, e.g., depreciation describes loss of value only relating to real estate, investment analysis centres on income properties (as opposed to stocks or other investments), and accounting/taxation issues focus solely on real estate brokerages and salespeople. Descriptions are neither authoritative nor definitive in nature, but included as summary statements and explanatory text to advance general knowledge. The reader should always access appropriate source documents and seek expert advice as required.

Design Marks/Certification Marks

REALTOR® is a design mark licensed by The Canadian Real Estate Association pursuant to a Trademark License and International Affiliate Agreement with the National Association of REALTORS® (NAR). MLS®, Multiple Listing Service® and the MLS design mark are certification marks registered and owned by The Canadian Real Estate Association.

Licensed/Registered

The term *licensed/registered* is used when referring to brokers or salespersons authorized pursuant to the applicable provincial statute. Historically, most individuals received *licences* but the trend has moved toward *registrations*. Legal implications relating to this conversion go beyond the present publication.

Ministry/Department

The term *ministry/department* is used when referring to provincial ministries or departments owing to differing terminologies and provincial government structures throughout Canada.

Provinces/Territories

References to *provinces* or *provincial* are deemed to include *territory* or *territorial* as appropriate.

Salesperson

The term *salesperson* refers to any individual authorized by a registered broker (agent) pursuant to provincial real estate legislation to act on behalf of the broker in the trading of real estate. The scope of responsibilities, methods of employment, and registration requirements are set out in applicable provincial materials.

Usage/Spelling

The English language is a dynamic medium that defies precise correctness. Historically, usage and spelling could be distinguished by social status, but lines became blurred as democratic societies blossomed and the world witnessed an explosion of printed matter. The digital revolution has only compounded the situation, particularly given software spell checking devices notoriously geared to *American English*. The painful fact is that the English language is bombarded by countless international variations, prone to regional or provincial differences, and directly influenced by business jargon and industry-specific terms.

Canadian English, while elusive, does exist together with subtle differences from either *English* or *American English*. Canadians staunchly defend *colour* in the face of *color*, insist on the noun *licence* instead of *license*, but actively endorse the verb *licensing*, not *licencing* (although some provincial jurisdictions disagree on this point). Our municipalities pass *by-laws*, not *bylaws*, and plumbers install *faucets* not *taps*. Unfortunately, most dictionaries are either *English* or *American English*, with little appreciation for the Canadian perspective. Given these limitations, accepted authorities on standard Canadian usage prevail wherever possible unless, as frequently happens, they disagree. In the absence of agreement, preference files are continuously updated and applied as the need arises.

Illustrations

Adapted from illustrations provided by Canada Mortgage and Housing Corporation

A–Z REFERENCE

REAL ESTATE
ENCYCLOPEDIA

A

National Info Links

ACRE (National Real Estate Education)
Alliance for Canadian Real Estate Education
99 Duncan Mill Road
Don Mills, ON M3B 1Z2

Telephone   (416) 445-9910
 Web Site   **www.acre.ca**

Appraisal
Appraisal Institute of Canada
1111 Portage Avenue
Winnipeg, MN R3G 0S8

Telephone   (204) 783 5575
 Web Site   **www.aicanada.org**

Agricultural/Farm
For national programs involving agricultural operations
and farms, contact:

Agriculture and Agri-Food Canada
 Web Site   **www.agr.ca**

For provincial agricultural and farming matters contact
the appropriate provincial ministry/department.

ABANDONMENT

To give up or discontinue any further interest in something. For real estate purposes, abandonment refers to the relinquishment or surrender of property rights. In leased property, abandonment involves the voluntary surrender of the premises by a tenant before the lease expires, without consent of the owner. In legal terms, abandonment refers to the general intention to relinquish along with the physical act of abandoning.

Abandonment is not fully effected and the obligations of the abandoning person are not rescinded until the other party accepts the relinquishment.

Application   In the case of an agreement/contract involving real estate, the buyer must give proper notice of intention to cancel and the seller must accept such notice, thereby terminating the agreement. However, assuming that the sale in question is valid and binding, abandonment by the buyer does not relieve contractual obligations—the seller must specifically release the buyer. Real estate practitioners encounter abandonment when a mortgagor is unable to make stipulated mortgage payments and vacates the premises. The mortgagee then takes control and may exercise options concerning the disposition of the property. When the mortgagor is in default, various legal remedies are available including foreclosure, judicial sale, power of sale, and quit claim deed.

Provincial   See applicable reference materials.

Example   *Abandonment*

Owner Smith leased a retail commercial space to Tenant Jones. Rents due and payable under the lease were remitted promptly for the first six months, however, Smith did not receive rent during the seventh and eighth month. On visiting the property near the end of the eighth month, Smith discovered that Jones had abandoned the premises. This action did not relieve Jones of obligations associated with the lease and Smith took appropriate legal action as set out in the lease document. He entered the premises to seize any remaining assets of Jones pursuant to his right of distrain. He also took legal action against Jones for the deficiency and leased the space, following selected renovations, to a new tenant.

Abandonment is also referenced in commercial leases. Lease wordings will differ but, generally, once abandonment has taken place, the entire amount of rent owing under the lease is due and payable. The landlord is permitted to enter and seize the assets remaining on the premises to assist in satisfying outstanding amounts.

ABATEMENT

Most frequently associated with a reduction of rent, interest, or amount due. However, the term can apply to any reduction, for example, noise abatement (the placing of highway sound barrier walls adjacent to residential areas), and pollution abatement (control of smokestack emissions), governed by provisions of the *Canadian Environmental Protection Act* or applicable provincial environmental legislation. In the case of rent, a landlord may be unable to complete various improvements with a resulting delay for the tenant in gaining possession. This circumstance could give rise to an abatement of rent.

Example   *Abatement*

In residential sales, a situation might arise where Buyer Jones' solicitor discovers unpaid amounts by Seller Smith at closing. Jones, in making such payments on behalf of Smith, would normally receive an abatement (credit) that would appear on a statement of adjustments at the point of closing.

An observed defect in the property or title to that property may also warrant an abatement and be subject to negotiations between buyer and seller. In commercial leases, Landlord Smith and Tenant Jones might agree that an abatement of ten days' rent is reasonable, given construction delays in preparing the unit for occupancy. Based on a monthly rent of $1,500, the abatement of $500 would be one-third ($\frac{1}{3}$) of that rent, assuming a 30-day rental period.

ABSORPTION BED

One component of a disposal system normally built using two or more rows of buried distribution pipe. Regulations concerning the exact layout of such beds are overseen by the provincial ministry/department involved with environmental issues. In particular, certain percolation specifications apply, as well as detailed construction requirements.

Various types of absorption beds (also known as *leaching beds*), are found in Canada, ranging from the small septic tank system that contains a tank and leaching bed constructed below existing terrain levels, to the more complex and newer versions of raised absorption beds with special sand filtering systems. These raised beds are designed to operate within smaller defined clearances and areas, resulting in special construction requirements.

See Figure A.1 for an illustration of a residential sewage system including septic tank, absorption bed, and a cross-sectional view of the distribution pipe along with stone and backfill layers.

Provincial   See applicable reference materials.

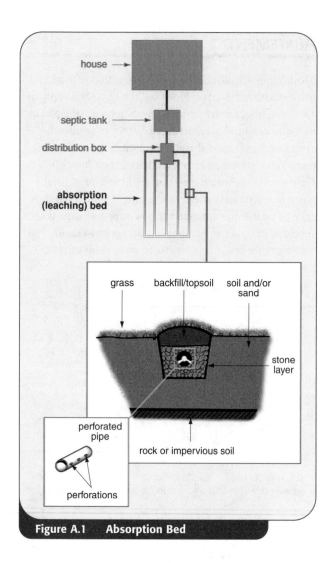

house

septic tank

distribution box

absorption (leaching) bed

grass backfill/topsoil soil and/or sand

stone layer

perforated pipe

rock or impervious soil

perforations

Figure A.1   Absorption Bed

ABSORPTION BED (RAISED)

A leaching bed constructed on or above the existing terrain as part of a waste disposal system using imported soil and/ or special filters approved by the appropriate provincial ministry/department.

Application   Practitioners encounter differing provincial terminologies and requirements. In some provinces, such beds are referred to as *mounds*.

Given special absorption qualities of approved filter sand, the overall leaching bed size is reduced in comparison to conventional leaching beds used with a waste disposal system (e.g., septic tank system). Clearances from adjacent wells and structures are increased by an amount equal to two units horizontal for each unit vertical height of the surface of the leaching bed above natural grade. For example, if the clearance to a well was 15 metres for a standard leaching bed, a raised absorption bed might require a minimum clearance of 30 metres or more.

Raised absorption beds are frequently encountered where there is a lack of soil depth to accommodate a standard leaching system, such as in rocky terrain typical in many recreational areas. Raised absorption beds have a life expectancy of between 25 and 35 years, as is the case with standard leaching beds, however, this can vary depending on circumstances.

Raised absorption beds are regulated by the provincial ministry/department responsible for environmental matters. Published material is available concerning their installation and minimum distribution pipe clearances from structures, property lines, wells, and other water sources such as a lake, river, pond, stream, or reservoir.

Provincial   See applicable reference materials.

ABSORPTION RATE

A rate usually expressed in square feet (or its metric equivalent), referring to the total amount of space that has been leased or sold within a specified period.

Example 1   *Absorption Rate*

The City of Anycity has a current office space inventory of 52,068,985 sq. ft. The supply of new office space, included in that total, was 4,432,000 sq. ft. during the preceding 12-month period, with a corresponding absorption of 3,187,719 sq. ft. for the same period. Accordingly, the absorption rate for office space during that period was:

$$3,187,719 \div 4,432,000$$
$$= .7193 \text{ or } 71.93\%$$

Example 2   *Absorption Rate*

Builder Anderson forecasts total construction of single-family residential homes at 1,247 units for the upcoming year with an absorption of 950 for the same period. Accordingly, he is estimating an absorption rate of .7618 or 76.18%. If he builds 50 homes, Anderson expects that approximately 38 (50 x 76.18% = 38.09) of those homes will sell during the period based on the estimated absorption rate.

Application   Commercial brokerages often express absorption in terms of ratios or rates. The most common reference involves an absorption rate that describes the relationship between amount of vacant space consumed and total space available for a particular property type. Absorption, together with total available space, provides a useful indicator of activity within a specific segment of the marketplace, e.g., office, retail, and industrial space. Absorption rates are also referenced in residential real estate, particularly relating to new homes.

ABSTRACT

A written history of the title, but not assurance of good title, to a parcel of real estate as recorded in a land registry or land titles office. Abstracts (abstract pages) include a condensed history of the title to individual parcels of land and include a synopsis of all recorded instruments affecting the title, e.g., deeds/transfers of land, mortgages, discharges of mortgages, encumbrances, easements, and restrictive covenants. Abstract pages have undergone modifications in format, information required, and method of recording within provincial jurisdictions utilizing the registry system.

Provincial   See applicable reference materials.

ABSTRACT BOOK

Represents the central reference source within a registry system. Historically, these books (also referred to as *abstract indexes*), began as a compilation of patented lots in numeric order by lot and concession, but ultimately expanded to include a variety of books including sub-divisions and condominiums. Individual ownership was detailed by way of abstract pages within a wide range of abstract books. During the past decade, cumbersome abstract books and associated manual recording systems have given way to computerized record keeping.

Application   The recording of interests in real estate varies by individual province. The terms *abstract* and *abstract book* are most commonly associated with the registry system (as opposed to terms such as *parcel registers* found in land titles). Currently, both the registry and land titles systems are used in Ontario and the Maritime Provinces. Registry is non-existent in Saskatchewan, Alberta, and British Columbia. Manitoba still retains selected registry records related primarily to railroad properties.

Provincial   See applicable reference materials.

ABSTRACT OF TITLE
(SEE ABSTRACT)

ABSTRACTION METHOD–SITE VALUATION

A method of appraising property by separating the value of structures and physical improvements from the overall value of the total property to arrive at a value of the site alone. This approach is often used in establishing the value of a specific site when vacant comparable sites cannot be obtained and is also referred to as the *allocation* or *extraction* method.

Example	Abstraction Method–Site Valuation
A developer is marketing new homes as a package that includes the lot and improvements. The buyer wants to establish how much the site is worth at the time of acquiring the property. The site value could be determined as follows:	
Total Purchase Price	$187,500
Value of Improvements (includes house, landscaping, services, etc.)	–125,000
Value of Site	**$ 62,500**

Abstraction is one of four methods typically used in site valuation. The others are **Comparative Sales Method, Land Development Method,** and **Land Residual Method.**

ABUTTING

A term referring to the existence of a common boundary between two parcels of land. Abutting should be clearly differentiated from the word *adjacent* that refers to properties in close proximity, but not necessarily sharing a common boundary. See **Figure A.2.**

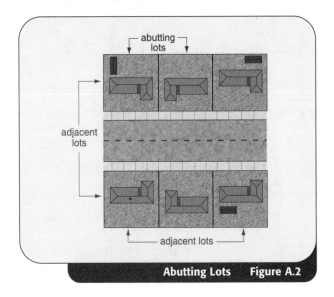

Abutting Lots   Figure A.2

ACCELERATION CLAUSE

A clause in a mortgage that causes the mortgage to become immediately due and payable (full principal amount *plus* all accrued interest), upon default by the mortgagor.

Application This clause has the net effect of accelerating the maturity date and providing the mortgagee all remedies within the document. At the point of acceleration, the mortgagor's equity of redemption can be accessed and the mortgagee can take action to foreclose. A sample clause follows:

> *Upon default, the indebtedness shall, at the option of the chargee, immediately become payable and the remedies on default given by this mortgage may be exercised forthwith.*

Acceleration clauses are not limited to mortgages and can also be found in installment contracts. In the broader legal sense, an acceleration clause represents any provision within an agreement that prematurely accelerates a party's rights and/or interests.

Example   *Acceleration Clause*

Owner Smith has a mortgage on his residence with a payment schedule based on amortized amounts containing both principal and interest. Smith, as the mortgagor, makes the 11th payment but defaults on the 12th. The mortgagee, Lender Inc., takes legal action immediately and accelerates the mortgage making it due immediately. The amount owing as of the date on which the 12th payment was due would consist of an outstanding balance of $49,767.94 plus all interest accruing. Typically additional time would be required to collect the outstanding balance. All interest accruing during that later period is the responsibility of the mortgagor.

Mortgage Payment Schedule				
PAYMENT #	TOTAL PAYMENT	INTEREST	PRINCIPAL	BALANCE
01	586.94	567.01	19.93	49,980.07
02	586.94	566.79	20.15	49,959.92
03	586.94	566.56	20.38	49,939.54
04	586.94	566.33	20.61	49,918.93
05	586.94	566.09	20.85	49,898.08
06	586.94	565.86	21.08	49,877.00
07	586.94	565.62	21.32	49,855.68
08	586.94	565.38	21.56	49,834.12
09	586.94	565.13	21.81	49,812.31
10	586.94	564.88	22.06	49,790.25
11	**586.94**	**564.63**	**22.31**	**49,767.94**
12	586.94	564.38	22.56	49,745.38
13	586.94	564.13	22.81	49,722.57
14	586.94	563.87	23.07	49,699.50
15	586.94	563.61	23.33	49,676.17
16	586.94	563.34	23.60	49,652.57

ACCEPTANCE

The act of agreeing to take or receive something that is offered.

Application As a rule, the act of acceptance must be communicated back to the person who made the offer before the agreement/contract is complete. Provincial jurisdictions encourage the use of a standard agreement/contract for the sale of real estate and specific requirements must be followed to ensure the written acceptance of both buyer and seller. The agreement/contract is signed by both buyer and seller, sealed, dated in the presence of a witness(es), and both parties must acknowledge receipt of the accepted agreement/contract. Exact procedures regarding acceptance, distribution of copies, and acknowledgement of receipt will vary by province.

Generally, acceptance must be:

- Unconditional, that is, all the terms of the contract must be accepted without alteration;
- Communicated to the party who made the offer or that party's agent;
- Made in the manner required by the offer; and
- Made within the time required by the offer, or within a reasonable time if no time is stated.

Acceptance must be unconditional by the other party without any change with respect to the terms of the offer. Should any change be made, then acceptance has not occurred, but rather a counter offer is made and the original offeror may accept or refuse. Acceptance, after communication of that acceptance, cannot be revoked.

Provincial See applicable reference materials.

ACCESSIBLE HOUSING
(SEE CANADIAN REHABILITATION COUNCIL FOR THE DISABLED)

ACCESSORY APARTMENT

A residential unit, other than the primary residential unit, located within the main structure. Currently, no universally accepted definition exists regarding such units and descriptions will vary based on local zoning by-laws. Safety issues are usually a major concern from a municipal perspective. Consequently, fire and building codes normally address regulations concerning the construction and occupation of accessory residential units in houses. Electrical inspections are also typically required.

The term *in-law suite* is used in various parts of Canada to denote the occupancy of an accessory apartment by a direct relative. In-law suites are sometimes exempted under selected municipal regulations (e.g., zoning), given the family relationship, but procedures vary by province.

Regardless, such suites must normally comply with health and safety requirements.

Application   Concerns regarding accessory units relate to egress (means of exit), fire separation and related requirements, and adherence to specified legislation.

Example   *Accessory Apartment*

Owner Smith received approval from the local municipality to add a second residential unit within his single-family detached home. The municipality has various requirements concerning the construction of the unit. In particular, Smith must comply with all items as set out in the applicable fire code concerning smoke alarms, fire separation between dwelling units, means of escape, and electrical wiring. Smith is visited by representatives of the electrical utility and the fire department. Following the fire department inspection, Smith is advised that he must improve the fire separations between the two units within a specified time period.

Provincial   See applicable reference materials.

ACCESSORY BUILDING

A building, other than the main structure, that is best described as an outbuilding, e.g., garage, pump house, poolside heater building, or utility shed. No precise or uniform guidelines exist regarding what constitutes an accessory building. As a general rule, any significant outside structure would be included.

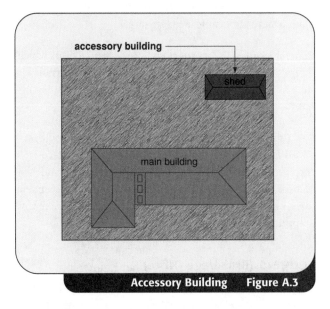

Accessory Building   Figure A.3

Application   When listing property, practitioners must be careful to detail all outside structures and specifically highlight any distinguishing features of such structures,

e.g., a garage with an enclosed workshop. For appraisal purposes, all significant accessory buildings should be described if they are material in nature. In other words, if such structures add to or detract from the value of the subject property. Such structures are identified on a sketch and further outlined within the appraisal report. See Figure A.3. In some instances, appraisal report forms lack sufficient space to describe such buildings within the standard format. An addendum should be attached.

ACCOUNT
(SEE ALSO CHART OF ACCOUNTS)

A record used to summarize all increases and decreases in a particular asset, liability, shareholder (owner) equity, revenue, or expense category in a set of accounting books. An account is a detailed record of receipts and payments of money or of trade transactions that have taken place between two or more persons.

Application   A common example within the brokerage involves the statutory trust account. The real estate trust account has an accompanying brokerage real estate trust ledger that sets out in detail the deposits and disbursements from that trust account.

Provincial   See applicable reference materials.

ACCOUNTING

The process is best described as the identifying, measuring, communicating, and interpreting of financial activity of a business, together with the theory and system of setting up and maintaining the books of an organization including the analysis of a business operation through the study of income and expenses.

ACCOUNTING SYSTEM

Accounting involves the transferral of information from various journals to the general ledger for the production of financial statements. Accounting should not be confused with bookkeeping which simply focuses on recording entries, maintaining journals, issuing cheques, and producing basic reports usual to the day-to-day operation of the brokerage. An accounting system consists of source documents, journals, and a general ledger that in turn leads to a trial balance and financial statements for the applicable business operation.

See **Figure A.4** for a double-entry recording framework used to process various transactions and events through the accounts for financial statement preparation.

Provincial   See applicable reference materials.

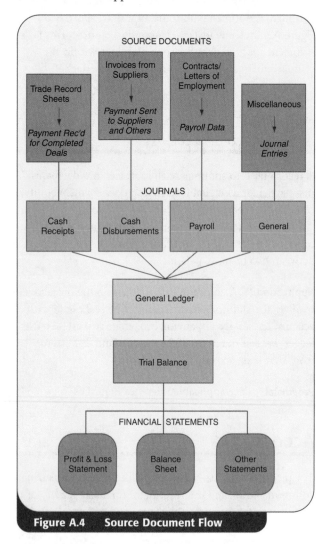

Figure A.4   Source Document Flow

Assumptions

An accounting system is generally founded on the following assumptions.

- Assets are recorded at cost.
- Depreciation corresponds to economic life and is recorded separately.
- The costs concerning intangible assets are amortized and applied against income over the benefit period.
- Fair and reasonable disclosure is provided to avoid misleading the typical investor.
- The principle of consistency is applied.
- The matching principle is utilized with all expenses and revenues.
- Generally accepted accounting principles are used.

Journalizing

Each transaction is initially recorded by way of a journal entry in the appropriate journal using source documents such as trade record sheets, cheques received and issued, and payroll data. A typical journal entry format follows:

Date	Account	DR	CR
Feb. 2	Office Supplies	$250.53	
	Cash		$250.53
	To record the purchase of office supplies.		

The journal provides a format where transactions, or summaries of similar transactions, are recorded based on chronological order as they occur, resulting in a financial record of all events for the business. The journal is often referred to as the *book of original entry* as all transactions enter the accounting system at this point. The term *general* in this area of accounting denotes that specialized journals may be required.

Journals (Brokerage Office)

Cash Receipts Journal   Records all cash and cheques received and deposited to the bank. See **Figure A.5**.

Cash Disbursements Journal   Records all payments issued by the brokerage. See **Figure A.6**.

Payroll Journal   Records, by employee, all monies paid by way of salaries or commission and source deductions made where applicable. See **Figure A.7**.

General Journal   Records non-routine transactions which do not align with the parameters of the other journals, such as bad debts and year end closing entries. See **Figure A.8**.

Real Estate Trust Synoptic/Journal   In selected provinces, a Real Estate Trust Synoptic/Journal is maintained in addition to the Real Estate Trust Ledger. This journal records, in chronological order, the receipt and disbursement of all trust money. See provincial reference materials if applicable.

Ledgers (Brokerage Office)

A group of organized accounts where the individual unit is the *account*. Usually one ledger account is assigned for each balance sheet and profit and loss statement account. Examples include cash, accounts receivable, accounts payable, equipment, accumulated depreciation, tax payable, commission revenue, office supplies, rent, etc.

CASH RECEIPTS JOURNAL

Date	Description	Cash DR	Commission Receivable CR	Referral Receivable CR	Salesperson Receivable CR	Miscellaneous Accounts CR
Feb. 2	3826 Harold Dr. Tr. 347 Transfer from Trust #911	3,460.00	3,460.00			
Feb. 5	319 Maple Lane Tr. 338 Rec'd from ABC Realty Inc.	450.00		450.00		
Feb. 8	Salesperson Lee Rec'd Payment on Acct.	729.10			729.10	
Feb. 10	Anycity Bank Interest Earned on GIC	126.00				126.00

Cash Receipts Journal   Figure A.5

CASH DISBURSEMENTS JOURNAL

Date	Cheq. #	Description	Cash CR	Other Brokers DR	Advertising DR	Telephone DR	Office Supplies DR	Business Promotion DR
Feb. 2	3726	Telephone	1,533.89			1,533.89		
Feb. 2	3727	ABC Realty Ltd. (Tr. 341)	3,255.00	3,255.00				
Feb. 2	3728	Best Office Supply	381.50				381.50	
Feb. 3	3729	XYZ Awards Ltd.	355.00					355.00
Feb. 5	3730	Local Gazette	372.45		372.45			

Cash Disbursements Journal   Figure A.6

PAYROLL JOURNAL

EMPLOYEE: Salesperson Lee

Date	Cheq. #	Gross Payable	CPP Deduct	EI Deduct	Tax Deduct	Misc. Deduct	Expenses Deduct	Net Payable
Feb. 15	3750	2,248.13	38.41	52.83	323.53	150.00	25.50	1,657.86
Feb. 28	3769	1,593.18	31.86	37.44	228.58		25.50	1,269.80
Feb. 28	3770	2,024.55	40.49	47.58	290.49		64.50	1,581.49

Payroll Journal   Figure A.7

GENERAL JOURNAL
December, 20xx

Date	Account Name	Account #	DR	CR
Dec. 31	Insurance Expenses	8300	134.11	
	Prepaid Expenses	1800		134.11
	To write off December portion of building insurance			
Dec. 31	Allowance for Doubtful Accounts	8101	15,000.00	
	Commissions Receivable	1100		15,000.00
	To allow for deals not closing until next year–S612 and S800			
Dec. 31	Salaries Expense	9000	50,000.00	
	Accrued Bonuses	2800		50,000.00
	To accrue for 20xx management bonuses			
Dec. 31	Corporate Income Tax Expense	9999	19,800.00	
	Corporate Income Tax Payable	2950		19,800.00
	To set up 20xx taxes payable			
Dec. 31	Less: Accumulated Amortization—Office Equipment	1471		311.56
	Less: Accumulated Amortization—Furniture	1441		2,096.88
	Less: Accumulated Amortization—Computer/Software	1501		3,811.97
	Depreciation and Amortization	5550	6,220.41	
	To record depreciation for 20xx			

Figure A.8   General Journal

General Ledger   All financial data of the business can be found in the general ledger. Entries are cross-referenced back to the originating journal so that, if necessary, an entry can be traced to the original documentation. Every account in the general ledger has a separate sheet. Each account has a debit, credit, or nil balance. Adding up all the debits and credits should result in equal totals. The books are then said to be in balance. At the end of each month, a trial balance is prepared using the general ledger. All brokerages maintain a general ledger as well as subsidiary ledgers. An example of a subsidiary ledger is the real estate trust ledger.

Real Estate Trust Ledger   This ledger chronologically records, for each transaction, the trust money received and disbursed indicating:

- From where the money was received;
- To whom it was disbursed;
- The reason for each disbursement; and
- Any unexpended balance.

Procedures concerning real estate trust ledgers will vary by province including trade numbering systems, required information to be entered, methods and recording of disbursements from the trust, and supporting journals (if applicable). Figure A.9 reflects entries for a typical real estate trust ledger illustrating usual entries.

Posting

Totalled transactions entered in the journals are posted (entered) to individual accounts in the general ledger at periodic intervals, e.g., weekly. Journalizing of additional subsidiary ledgers may also be required.

Adjusting Journal Entries

Errors detected on the trial balance must be corrected using adjusting journal entries. Such entries are necessary to accurately measure all activity during the accounting period, e.g., an adjusting entry would be required to record depreciation expense during the period.

Most corrections and adjustments are recorded by making the appropriate entry in the general journal, and posting to the individual general ledger accounts. Preparation of another trial balance will ensure equality of debits and credits.

Trial Balance

A listing of the general ledger accounts with respective balances. All accounts with *debit* balances are totalled separately from accounts with *credit* balances. The two should be equal. Trial balances are taken as a partial check of mathematical accuracy of posted entries. The trial balance demonstrates solely the mathematical correctness of the general ledger but does not guarantee the accuracy of recorded items, nor does it ensure that such

REAL ESTATE TRUST LEDGER		October–December, 20xx			
Date	Description	Trade No.	Deposits (CR)	Cheques (DR)	Explanation
Oct. 3 Dec. 2 Dec. 2	J.R. Smith—buyer—re: 64 Pearl St. Cheque #6—to Wm. Gordon Transferred as full commission to Gen. Acc., Ch #7	1	750.00	250.00 500.00	Transaction closed. Commission transferred to Gen. Acc. Balance to seller.
Nov. 13	E.R. Holway—buyer—re: 1270 Bloor St.	2	1,200.00		Pending (open) transaction
Nov. 14	R. Hall—buyer—re: 17 Floral Dr. Deposit of $1,000.00 is held by vendor (H.J. Valley)	3			Entry (DR/CR) not required; deposit held by seller.
Dec. 1	H. Thompson—buyer—re: 70 Shield Ave.	4	1,500.00		Pending (open) transaction.
Dec. 2 Dec. 26	D. Jones—buyer—re: 29 Craven Rd. Transferred as part Commission to Gen. Acc., Ch #9	5	500.00	500.00	Transaction closed. Partial commission to Gen. Acc.
Dec. 12 Dec. 20	G. Peters—buyer—re: 2 Taylor Dr. Cheque #8—cancelled—deposit returned to purchaser	6	600.00	600.00	Transaction aborted. Mutual release obtained and deposit returned to buyer.
Dec. 15 Dec. 31	A. Davey—buyer—27 Nomad St. Additional deposit from purchaser	7	1,200.00 1,000.00		Pending (open) transaction. Note additional deposit.
Dec. 21 Dec. 28 Dec. 28	C.A. King—buyer—re: 276 Queen St. Cheque #10 to seller (K. Patterson) Transferred as full commission to Gen. Acc., Ch #11	8	1,000.00	200.00 800.00	Transaction closed. Full commission transferred to Gen. Acc.— balance to seller.
Dec. 25	H.F. Edward—buyer—re: "Gold" Beauty Shop, Deposit of $2,000.00 is held by R. Egon Real Estate Ltd.	9			Entry not required, deposit held by selling brokerage.

Real Estate Trust Ledger   Figure A.9

items have been properly entered. For example, discrepancies may exist if a transaction was (a) never entered, (b) posted twice, or (c) posted in reverse. **Figure A.10** depicts a trial balance within the overall accounting system for a brokerage prior to the preparation of financial statements.

ACCOUNTS PAYABLE

A liability arising from the purchase of goods or services on credit. The person to whom the account payable is owed is called a creditor.

ACCOUNTS RECEIVABLE

An asset arising from the rendering of services or sale of products/goods to consumers, with payment due some time in the future. Accounts receivable is normally viewed as a *current asset* in most accounting systems.

Application   Accounts receivable (real estate commission), is normally one of the largest assets in a real estate brokerage with a substantial portion of such monies owed to the salespeople involved with real estate transactions. The brokerage must ensure that receivables being assigned

ABC REALTY INC.
Trial Balance
December 31, 20x1

	DEBIT	CREDIT
Bank	$ 4,500	$
Commission Receivable	5,700	
Office Furniture and Equipment	2,400	
Automobile	5,000	
Accumulated Depreciation		1,900
Bank Loan		3,000
Accrued Liabilities		900
Accounts Payable		1,100
Payroll Deductions Payable		300
Loan Payable (due 20x2)		5,000
Shareholder Drawings		15,000
Capital		1,300
Commission Income		102,000
Management Fees	15,000	
Commission Expense	64,000	
Advertising	10,000	
Bank Charges and Interest	700	
Rent	4,200	
Insurance and Taxes	800	
Office Salaries and Benefits	11,000	
Office Supplies and Expenses	1,600	
Utilities	3,200	
Accounting and Legal	1,000	
Depreciation Expense	1,400	
	$130,500	$130,500

Trial Balance   Figure A.10

A

as assets for purposes of brokerage loans only represent those amounts specifically due to the brokerage and not those monies owed to the salespeople.

ACCREDITED APPRAISER CANADIAN INSTITUTE
(SEE ALSO APPRAISAL INSTITUTE OF CANADA)

Acronym: AACI   The Appraisal Institute of Canada (AIC) awards the AACI designation. The AACI designation denotes fully accredited membership in the Institute and may be used by the holder for the appraisal of a full range of real property. The Institute grants the AACI upon successful completion of the following.

- Course Series 1000;
- Course Series 2000 and 3000 (based on an urban or agricultural option);
- Demonstration Appraisal Report meeting AACI requirements;
- Article and attain three years (600 days) of appraisal experience; and
- Review by the National/Provincial Admissions Committee of current work samples, followed by a verbal interview by the Committee.

Effective January 1, 1998, candidates applying for new membership and former members seeking reinstatement must hold a university degree from an accredited university in order to attain use of the AACI designation.

Reference   The national office of the Appraisal Institute of Canada is located at 1111 Portage Avenue, Winnipeg, MN R3G 0S8.

The above information was summarized from detailed materials provided by the Institute with no representation concerning its accuracy or completeness. Contact AIC for current requirements.

ACCREDITED FARM MANAGER

Acronym: AFM   A real estate designation offered by The American Society of Farm Managers and Rural Appraisers, Inc. (ASFMRA) located in the United States. The applicant, must meet various requirements including:

- Five years of farm management experience for a fee or salary for which the applicant has submitted written, signed reports;
- Submission of a demonstration report;

- Submission of a management plan (if one has not been submitted within the last three years or for the M–20 course);
- Complete and pass the required ASFMRA courses as outlined in the current education catalogue;
- Complete the application form and pass the final accrediting examination which consists of a written exam, case study problems, and a verbal exam; and
- Have a college degree or equivalent.

Reference   The American Society of Farm Managers and Rural Appraisers, Inc. can be contacted at Suite 408, 950 S. Cherry Street, Denver, CO 80222-2664.

The above information was summarized from detailed materials provided by ASFMRA with no representation concerning its accuracy or completeness. Contact ASFMRA for current requirements.

ACCREDITED LAND CONSULTANT

Acronym: ALC   The REALTORS Land Institute (RLI) awards the ALC designation. To become an ALC candidate, you must:

- Be an RLI member in good standing;
- Belong to a local board as a member or Institute Affiliate member;
- Submit an application for candidacy with an application fee or other fee as may be required;
- Pay additional National RLI dues assessment (plus chapter dues);
- Submit a resume of professional, business, and civic background;
- Know that a current designated member may challenge a candidate's approval for candidacy; and
- Successfully complete the required RLI Land University courses under one of two options.

Option 1   Applies to members with less than five years of real estate experience or less than $5 million sales production within the last five years as defined.

- Candidates are required to take seven RLI Land University courses.
- Candidates may petition to the designation committee to submit up to four REALTOR/REALTOR Affiliate courses for the required seven courses.

Option 2   Applies to members with five years or more of real estate brokerage experience and $5 million or more of documented non-residential real estate sales or sales supervision within the five years prior to candidacy.

- Candidates must take three of the seven courses and document five years of real estate brokerage experience with a minimum of $5 million non-residential (residential is 1–4 family) real estate sales or sales supervision in lieu of other courses. All sales must be documented.
- Candidates must fulfill other requirements as set out by the RLI.

Reference   For details regarding the ALC program, contact the REALTORS Land Institute, 430 North Michigan Avenue, Chicago, IL, 60611.

The above information was summarized from detailed materials provided by RLI with no representation concerning its accuracy or completeness. Contact RLI for current requirements.

ACCREDITED LEASING OFFICER
(SEE ALSO REAL ESTATE INSTITUTE OF CANADA)

Acronym: ALO   The ALO designation is awarded by the Real Estate Institute of Canada (REIC) and is focused on individuals who negotiate leases or are involved in space planning, lease administration, and the acquisition/disposal of space by lease. To earn the ALO designation, the applicant must:

- Achieve candidacy status;
- Be active in commercial leasing;
- Have at least one year of creditable experience, as defined by REIC;
- Be a high school graduate or equivalent;
- Complete and submit the candidacy application form to REIC with the application fee; and
- Be endorsed by the local REIC Chapter.

Once a candidate, the individual must remain as a candidate for a minimum of one year with a maximum of five years to meet requirements for ALO membership. As an ALO candidate, a series of core and specialty courses are required. To achieve ALO membership, the individual must:

- Successfully complete the ALO core courses;
- Successfully complete the ALO specialty courses;
- Have three years of creditable experience, as defined by REIC;
- Abide by the REIC Code of Professional Standards;
- Be a candidate for a minimum of one year; and
- Be affiliated with and endorsed by the local REIC chapter.

Reference   For details regarding the ALO program, contact the Real Estate Institute of Canada, 5407 Eglinton Avenue West, Suite 208, Etobicoke, ON M9C 5K6.

The above information was summarized from detailed materials provided by REIC with no representation concerning its accuracy or completeness. Contact REIC for current requirements.

ACCREDITED MANAGEMENT ORGANIZATION

Acronym: AMO   The AMO is the only designation awarded by the Institute of Real Estate Management (IREM) to firms.

To become an AMO firm, the organization must meet the following qualifications:

- Have been in the real estate management business for at least three years;
- Have a CPM member in charge of the firm's real estate management operation who has completed Course 701 or equivalent;
- Meet specific insurance requirements;
- Be subjected to and pass a credit investigation;
- Submit six letters of reference;
- Agree to comply with the AMO Code of Ethics;
- Formally apply and pay the application fee;
- Be endorsed by the local IREM chapter; and
- Be approved by the National AMO Committee and the Governing Council of the Institute.

Reference   For details regarding the AMO program, contact the Institute of Real Estate Management at 430 North Michigan Avenue, Chicago, IL 60611-4090. IREM's affiliate in Canada serves the educational/certification needs of Canadian real estate professionals. The IREM Division of the Real Estate Institute of Canada (REIC) is located at Suite 208, 5407 Eglinton Avenue West, Etobicoke, ON M9C 5K6.

The above information was summarized from detailed materials provided by IREM with no representation concerning its accuracy or completeness. Contact REIC for current requirements.

ACCREDITED RESIDENTIAL MANAGER

Acronym: ARM   The Institute of Real Estate Management (IREM) in the United States awards the ARM designation to site managers specializing in residential real estate. Attainment of the ARM award is based on achieving high

A

standards in the areas of education, experience, and commitment to the ARM Code of Ethics. The Real Estate Institute of Canada (REIC) administers the Accredited Residential Manager program in Canada through the IREM Division.

To achieve the ARM award, applicants are required to successfully complete an in-depth course on residential site management. The course focuses on proven multi-housing management skills, and provides detailed coverage of such subjects as marketing techniques, equal opportunity compliance, analyzing vacancy factors, budgeting, and the selection and management of service contractors. In addition to meeting these education and ethical requirements, ARM participants must meet specific experience standards and other qualifications.

To earn the ARM service award, individuals must:

- Complete the ARM application form and send it to REIC National with the application fee;
- Be of legal age;
- Be a high school graduate or equivalent; and
- Be actively managing residential property, which means (a) managing a minimum portfolio of 30 units, (b) performing at least 10 of the 22 functions REIC uses to define a residential manager.

Once an applicant, to achieve the ARM service award, the individual must:

- Successfully complete Course 101, Successful Site Management;
- Perform, or supervise those who perform, residential management functions as defined by the IREM Division of the Real Estate Institute of Canada;
- Meet ARM cumulative experience requirements; and
- Be endorsed by the local REIC/IREM chapter.

Reference   For details regarding the ARM program, contact the IREM Division of the Real Estate Institute of Canada (REIC) at Suite 208, 5407 Eglinton Avenue West, Etobicoke, ON M9C 5K6.

The above information was summarized from detailed materials provided by IREM and REIC with no representation concerning its accuracy or completeness. Contact REIC for current requirements.

ACCREDITED RURAL APPRAISER

Acronym: ARA   The ARA designation is offered by The American Society of Farm Managers and Rural Appraisers, Inc. (ASFMRA) located in the United States. The applicant must meet various requirements including:

- Five years of rural appraisal experience for a fee or salary for which the applicant has submitted written and signed reports;
- Submission of a demonstration narrative rural appraisal report (if one has not been submitted within the last three years to advance to the Professional level);
- Complete and pass the required ASFMRA courses as outlined in the current education catalogue;
- Complete the application form and pass the final accrediting exam which consists of a two-part written exam and a verbal exam; and
- Have a college degree or equivalent.

Reference   The American Society of Farm Managers and Rural Appraisers, Inc. can be contacted at Suite 408, 950 S. Cherry Street, Denver, CO 80222-2664.

The above information was summarized from detailed materials provided by ASFMRA with no representation concerning its accuracy or completeness. Contact ASFMRA for current requirements.

ACCRUAL ACCOUNTING

An accounting method where each item of revenue or expense is recorded based on the date such an event occurred without concern for the *actual date* of receipt or payment. Net income is measured as the difference between revenues and expenses rather than the difference between cash received and cash disbursed.

Application   When applying accrual accounting in a brokerage office, revenue must be viewed in terms of contingencies and unique qualities associated with a real estate trade. Two methods of recording income are used:

- *Trade Written* (Option A): Date the trade is written.
- *Trade Closed* (Option B): Date the trade closes.

Option B is more prevalent, given the uncertainties associated with the completion of real estate transactions, e.g., unfulfilled conditions, fall-throughs, and closing delays. However, both approaches should be seriously evaluated with consideration for prevailing practices in the particular market area, any specific provincial requirements, and appropriate guidance from an accounting expert.

Figure A.11 provides a simplified scenario for the flow of recorded entries involving both trade written and trade closed options over a five-month period commencing with an agreement signed on January 15, 20xx and closing on April 15, 20xx.

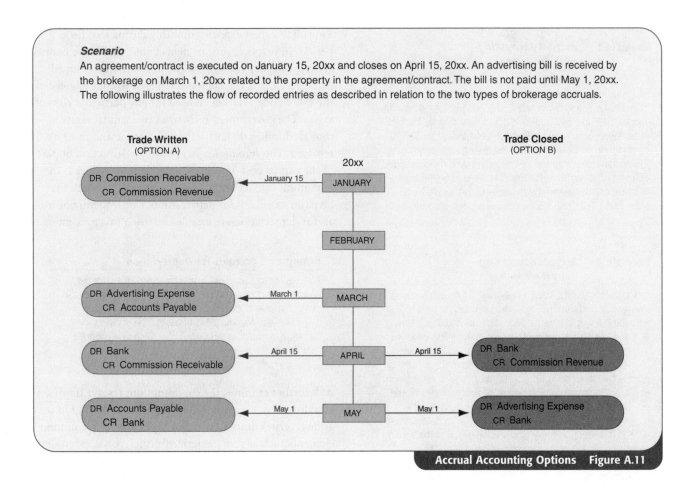

Scenario

An agreement/contract is executed on January 15, 20xx and closes on April 15, 20xx. An advertising bill is received by the brokerage on March 1, 20xx related to the property in the agreement/contract. The bill is not paid until May 1, 20xx. The following illustrates the flow of recorded entries as described in relation to the two types of brokerage accruals.

Accrual Accounting Options   Figure A.11

Trade Written (Option A)

The income from a real estate trade (transaction) is recorded when the trade occurs. The major disadvantage is that the brokerage may pay taxes on income that has not yet been received. In addition, tax may be paid on trades that in fact do not close. However, a sole proprietor has four months after the calendar year end (a corporation has six months after the fiscal year end), in which to file a return. Therefore, appropriate adjustments could be made prior to final statements being submitted for tax purposes.

Trade Closed (Option B)

The brokerage records income from a trade (transaction) when it actually closes, thereby minimizing year end adjustments.

No simple answer exists as to which approach is most appropriate regarding the recording of revenue. The prevailing trend in most provinces remains *trade closed* as proponents claim this system produces a more accurate cash flow picture, avoids extensive adjustments, and properly addresses the uncertainties of future trades. At year end, accruals are set-up for trades that have closed but monies have not yet been received. Brokerages are encouraged to seek professional assistance to critically evaluate which approach is most suitable.

Accrual *vs.* Cash Accounting

Two methods of computing income are permitted from a tax perspective—cash or accrual. Cash accounting, referred to as a *single entry system*, requires that the taxpayer record any cash received during the year along with monies expended in the same period. The difference for that particular taxation year is the profit or loss.

According to the *Income Tax Act*, the cash method can only be used by commissioned salespeople, farmers, and fishermen, and no longer applies to a business or profession (Section 1020, *Income Tax Act*).

A real estate brokerage is held to be a profession and must apply the accrual method of computing expenses and revenue (subject to considerations as discussed regarding trade written/trade closed). Accrual accounting requires a double set of entries, hence the reference to double entry system. Accrual accounting makes use of debits and credits with two accounting entries for any single transaction: a debit and a credit. Often described as the accounts payable/receivable method, revenue and expenses are entered as they are incurred and not when paid/received. **Figure A.12** describes the accrual method regarding an expense that flows over a two-year period.

A

Example 1   *Accrual Accounting—*
Cash Accounting

Cash accounting tracks actual income received and expenses paid at the time each occurs. For example, if a commission salesperson received a printing bill one month ago for $49 and paid it during the current month, his/her personal records would reflect the debt today. Similarly, if a commission of $2,000 is received during the current month for a sale effected last month, it would be recorded during the current month. The difference between the revenue ($2,000) and the expense ($49) would be a profit of $1,951, with tax computed on that amount.

Example 2   *Accrual Accounting—*
Accrual Accounting

In accrual accounting, using the details of the cash accounting example and assuming the invoice is received by a broker-age, the bill would have appeared in last month's journal, as the expense was incurred at that point. If the expense represented a considerable amount, it could be prorated over three or four subsequent months to more accurately portray the expense in relation to the rate of consumption. Similarly, the commission cheque deposited today would not be reflected in the current month's income (if the brokerage had elected to report income on a date written basis). This revenue entry would appear during the month the deal was accepted (perhaps 60 days ago), as a credit to an accounts receivable account.

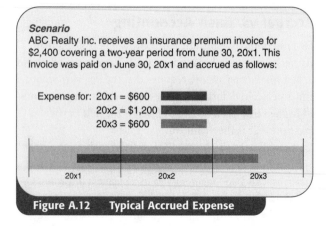

Scenario
ABC Realty Inc. receives an insurance premium invoice for $2,400 covering a two-year period from June 30, 20x1. This invoice was paid on June 30, 20x1 and accrued as follows:

Expense for: 20x1 = $600
20x2 = $1,200
20x3 = $600

20x1   20x2   20x3

Figure A.12   Typical Accrued Expense

ACCRUALS FOR DEPRECIATION

Frequently associated with accounting procedures relating to the recapture provisions involving capital invested in improvements over their remaining economic life.

Application   For purposes of accounting, accruals for depreciation are sometimes referred to as *future depreciation,* given that the amount is set aside at the start of a fiscal period for future allocation relating to a particular item.

This total is then *expensed* monthly during that fiscal period. In practice, various items falling under the same general category (class of assets) are normally grouped together. Canada Customs and Revenue Agency establishes the rate of depreciation allowed for any particular class of assets. The government recognizes that capital assets, though durable, do have a limited lifetime and must be replaced. The *Income Tax Act* permits a deduction of part of the capital cost of assets. Capital cost allowance is the maximum rate set under the *Income Tax Act* which the taxpayer can claim for depreciation. Consequently, accruals for depreciation are established using this maximum.

Example   *Accruals for Depreciation*

ABC Realty Inc. acquires a specific piece of equipment. Assume that the undepreciated value is $12,000 for the current year and the maximum rate for depreciation is 10% per year for that class of asset. The accruals for depreciation for that year would be $1,200, expensed monthly at the rate of $100.

As a further example, the condominium reserve fund established by a condominium corporation is used to set aside (accrue) money for major replacement of common elements such as roofs, exterior finishes, roads, sidewalks, electrical and plumbing systems, and recreational facilities. To ensure that appropriate amounts are available in contemplation of these replacements, the corporation may initiate, or be required by statute to complete, a reserve fund study for the building.

Typically, a technical audit is undertaken to assess the current condition and future life expectancy of various component parts of the common elements. Based on this analysis, a reserve fund study is prepared that contains a schedule outlining a 20 to 30-year projection of anticipated common element replacements. The schedule sets out each year along with the opening balance in the reserve fund, the annual contribution to meet anticipated replacements (costed in future dollars), interest earned on monies in the fund, and a closing balance. The reserve fund study normally makes two overall assumptions:

- The interest rate on funds held in reserve; and
- The inflation rate for determining future costs of replacement.

ACCRUED DEPRECIATION (APPRAISAL)

A loss of value, measured as of the date of appraisal, indicating the difference between reproduction cost new (RCN) or replacement cost of improvements, and the present worth of those improvements. Accrued depreciation is sometimes referred to as *diminished utility*. This loss of value or diminished utility of the improvements to real property can be caused by many different factors. Using one or more of these methods, a schedule of accrued depreciation can be developed for the appraised property through several integrated steps.

Various methods are used by appraisers including Observed Condition (Breakdown) Method, Economic Age-Life Depreciation Method, and Economic Age-Life Depreciation Method (Modified).

Application   Figure A.13 illustrates a typical schedule of accrued depreciation prepared by an appraiser when applying the cost approach to value. This involves estimating the reproduction cost less deductions for various forms of depreciation leading to a depreciated cost of the building and improvements, which is added to the site value to arrive at the final estimate of value.

ACCRUED EXPENSES
(SEE ALSO ACCRUAL ACCOUNTING)

Incurred expenses that are payable at a future date. In accrual accounting (often described as the accounts payable/accounts receivable method), revenue and expenses are entered as they are incurred and not when paid or received.

ACID RAIN/LAKE ACIDITY

The influx of airborne acids entering bodies of water through precipitation and ground water runoff. Such acids can directly impact vegetation, fish, and the entire ecosystem. Acid sensitivity refers to the ability of any lake to overcome acidic deposits that occur as a result of acid rain.

Application   Acidity in lakes is measured using a pH scale that ranges from 0 to 14; the lower the pH, the greater the acidity. In selected provinces, the ministry/department responsible for environmental matters conducts surveys of lakes and categorizes the results based on the lake's ability to neutralize a certain amount of acid. In Ontario the Ministry of the Environment has established the rating system that follows.

Level 1   Lakes have zero or negative alkalinity and have already become acidic.

Level 2   Lakes have very low alkalinity and are sensitive to heavy acid loadings by way of precipitation (or such things as spring run off).

Level 3   Lakes are moderately sensitive to heavy acid loadings.

Level 4   Lakes are of low sensitivity, but have experienced some damage due to acid rain.

Level 5   Lakes are not sensitive to acid loadings.

Reference   Contact the offices of Environment Canada and provincial ministries/departments responsible for information on current initiatives, measurement guidelines, and regulations concerning acid rain.

Provincial   See applicable reference materials.

ACRE

An imperial unit of measure equaling 43,560 square feet or 4,840 square yards, .4 hectares, ten square chains, or 160 square rods. In metric terms, one acre equals .405 hectares and one hectare equals 2.471 acres. Figure A.14 illustrates an acre in comparison to a hectare.

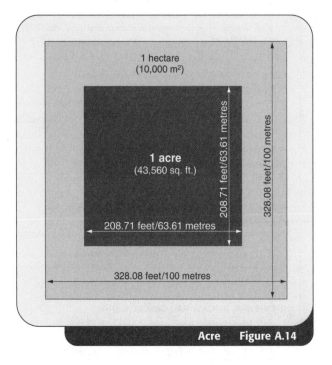

1 hectare
(10,000 m²)

1 acre
(43,560 sq. ft.)

208.71 feet/63.61 metres

328.08 feet/100 metres

208.71 feet/63.61 metres

328.08 feet/100 metres

Acre   Figure A.14

ACTS

A range of provincial and federal statutes impact the sale of real estate. Applicable federal legislation is included in this publication under the appropriate title. Provincial legislation will vary. Refer to applicable provincial reference materials.

A

Schedule of Estimate of Accrued Depreciation

Estimated Value of Site		$77,000
Estimated Reproduction Cost New	$71,750	
Less Estimated Accrued Depreciation:		

1. PHYSICAL DETERIORATION

Curable Physical Deterioration	RCN	Cost to Cure	
Painting Interior	1,600	1,700	
Eaves & Downspouts	500	650	
Doors	400	450	
	2,500	2,800	
Curable Physical Deterioration			$ 2,800

Incurable Physical Deterioration	RCN	Eff. Age	Life Exp.	Dep. $	
Short-Lived					
Heating	1,400	15	20	1,050	
Kitchen Built-In	1,500	15	20	1,125	
Tiled Floors	400	9	12	300	
Hardwood Floors	800	15	20	600	
Exterior Painting	1,000	1	4	250	
Roof Covering	1,000	15	20	750	
Electric Fixtures	600	15	20	450	
Hot Water Heater	350	15	20	263	
	7,050			4,788	
Short-Lived Incurable Physical Deterioration					+4,788

Long-Lived		
RCN	71,750	
Less Physical Curable RCN	−2,500	
Less Physical Incurable (short-lived) RCN	−7,050	
Total Long-Lived	62,200	
Long-Lived Incurable Physical Deterioration		
[Eff. Age 10 yrs; Economic Life 50 yrs. (10 ÷ 50 x 62,200)]	12,440	+12,440

TOTAL PHYSICAL DETERIORATION	20,028

2. FUNCTIONAL OBSOLESCENCE

Curable Functional Obsolescence		
Modernization of cupboards	2,000	
Less Depreciation Costs of Existing Cupboards	−685	
Curable Functional Obsolescence	1,315	1,315

Incurable Functional Obsolescence		
Monthly Rent Loss x Monthly Rental Factor ($10 X 180)	1,800	1,800

TOTAL FUNCTIONAL OBSOLESCENCE	+3,115

3. EXTERNAL (LOCATIONAL) OBSOLESCENCE

Monthly Rent Loss x Monthly Rental Factor: $5 X 180 = 900
Ratio of Land to Building: 1:3

TOTAL EXTERNAL (LOCATIONAL) OBSOLESCENCE (3/4 of $900)	+675

Total Depreciation (All Causes)		−23,818
Depreciated Cost of Building	47,932	
Plus Depreciated Cost of Outside Improvements	+1,800	
Total Depreciated Cost of All Improvements		+49,732
ESTIMATED VALUE BY COST APPROACH		**$126,732**

Figure A.13   Accrued Depreciation Schedule

ACTUAL AGE

The actual number of years that have passed since a structure was built; also referred to as the *chronological age*. The actual age of a structure must be differentiated from its effective age for appraisal purposes.

Figure A.15 illustrates the difference between actual age and related terms.

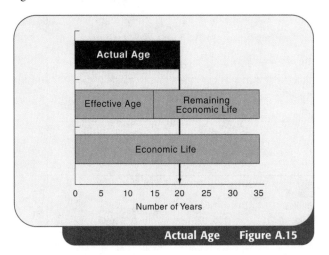

Actual Age   Figure A.15

AD VALOREM

According to value [Latin]. Tax levied against property according to the value of that property. This term is generally used in reference to the calculation of real property taxes. Once established, the assessed value becomes the basis for realty tax calculation.

Application   A municipality will determine its financial needs and establish an appropriate budget. The total budget is then divided by the assessed value of all properties to arrive at a multiplier (tax rate) or mill rate (the traditional rate used by municipalities). This rate is applied in relation to individual property assessments to arrive at the current realty taxes payable by the owner of that property.

The mill or tax rate charged normally varies by type of property. For instance, the rate for commercial property will usually differ from residential. Methods for calculating rates vary by provincial jurisdiction. In Ontario the mill rate has been replaced with a tax rate. Tax rates are established by the municipality for various property classes, e.g., residential, multi-residential, commercial, and industrial. The tax rate is simply a percentage rather than a mill rate that is expressed in tenths of a cent. The change from mill rate to a percentage tax rate was intended to simplify the process for property owners including explanations on tax notices.

Example   *Ad Valorem (Using Mill Rate)*

Each year Anycity's elected civic officials determine the city budget for the upcoming year. When required revenue is established in line with the budget process, this amount is divided by the total taxable assessments and a figure called a mill rate is struck. A mill is the unit of taxation applied to taxable assessed value. One mill amounts to $1.00 of tax for every $1,000 of assessed value. In the simplest scenario, if the city budget requires $7,500,000 and the total assessment is $750,000,000, then the calculation is:

$$\$7,500,000 \div \$750,000,000$$
$$= 10 \text{ mills (or } 0.01 \text{ or } 1\% \text{ in Ontario)}$$

This means that for every $1,000 of assessment, a property owner pays $10.00 in municipal taxes. John and Mary Smith live in Anycity and their home, according to the value of the property, has been assessed at $185,000. With a mill rate of 10, the Smiths' taxes are:

$$\$185,000 \div 1,000 \times 10$$
$$= \$1,850.00$$

In Ontario, the tax rate for purposes of this example is 1%. The Smiths' taxes are as follows:

$$\$185,000 \times 0.01 \ (1\%)$$
$$= \$1,850.00$$

Provincial   See applicable reference materials.

ADDITIONAL RENT

The amount owed by a commercial tenant in addition to base rent that represents the proportionate share of operating costs as defined within the lease document.

Application   Additional rent, commonly found in office and retail store leases, is typically estimated at the commencement of any fiscal or calendar year for the building with the tenant paying equal monthly installments in advance throughout the period for which the estimate is made. However, if the taxing authority (municipality) requires the full payment of realty taxes over the first portion of a year, the tenant in most leases is obligated to pay the entire taxes during that portion of the year.

The sum of base rent and additional rent constitutes the rent. In most leases, amounts above the base rent are referred to as *additional rent* and are usually made up of operating costs, property taxes, and utilities. Arrangements will vary depending on the specific lease.

The landlord normally estimates the tenant's proportionate share as a percentage using the tenant's rentable area as numerator and rentable area of the building as denominator. The landlord typically provides a statement of actual amounts payable by the tenant along with supporting details following the fiscal or calendar year end. If monies are owed, the tenant remits the deficiency; any surplus is credited to the tenant's account. Figure A.16 illustrates a typical statement that a landlord would provide to a commercial tenant concerning additional rent due on leased premises.

ANYCITY REAL ESTATE MANAGERS LTD.
BILLING FOR BUILDING EXPENSES
FOR 20X1

135 Industrial Drive

Westgate Industries Ltd.
Suite 501

March 7, 20x2   Invoice No. 0078105

Proportionate Share of Operating Expenses	(suite) / (building)	1,521 / 155,102	**= .009806** (or 0.9806%)
Proportionate Share of Property Tax Expenses	(suite) / (net building)	1,521 / 130,760	**= .011632** (or 1,1632%)
Occupancy Adjustment—# of days		365 / 365	**= 1** (or 100%)
Property Tax Expenses = Building Assessed Value x Tax Rate (Net of ground and second floor)		1,240,985 x 0.520570	**= $646,019.56**

Building Expenses	Operating Expenses	Property Taxes	
Total Expenses for 20x1	$671,273.00	$646,019.56	
Proportionate Share of Expenses (from above)	0.9806%	1.1632%	
Expenses Related to Premises (from above)	6,582.50	7,514.50	
Occupancy Adjustment (from above)	100.00%	100.00%	
Your Share of Expenses	6,582.50	7,514.50	
Less: Installments Billed in 20x1	(6,012.96)	(7,596.00)	
Net Amount of Expense due from(to) tenant	$569.54	($81.50)	$488.04
GST (R123456789)			34.16
TOTAL AMOUNT DUE FROM (TO) TENANT			**$522.20**

Figure A.16   Statement of Additional Rent

ADJACENT

Lying near to, but not necessarily abutting, the property. An adjacent property does not share a common boundary as is the case with abutting properties. See Figure A.17.

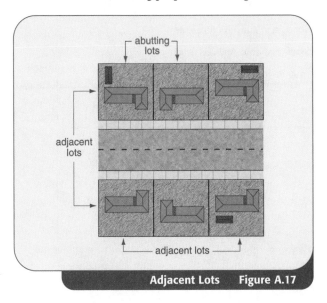

Adjacent Lots   Figure A.17

ADJUSTED COST BASE

For purposes of real estate investment analysis, the acquisition price of a property subject to adjustments for deductions and additions pursuant to the *Income Tax Act.*

Application   The adjusted cost base is used in determining the gain or capital gain arising from the disposition of property. The gain or capital gain is subsequently applied in calculations leading to *tax liability on sale* and ultimately the *sale proceeds after taxes. Sale proceeds after taxes* is a necessary component in calculating the internal rate of return for a property from an after tax perspective. Often referred to as the *adjusted cost base at sale*, this calculation requires forecasting operations cash flow and sale proceeds cash flow for a specified holding period to point of sale.

Example	*Adjusted Cost Base*	
Acquisition Price		$379,500
Less: Soft Costs Allocated		−7,930
Plus: Capitalized Items		+0
Plus: Unamortized Soft Costs		+12,500
Less: Partial Sales		−0
Adjusted Cost Base at Sale		**$384,070**

ADJUSTMENT DATE
(SEE INTEREST ADJUSTMENT DATE)

ADJUSTMENTS

Normally refers to those items requiring apportionment as of the date of closing a transaction. Such adjustments include rent, mortgage interest, realty tax, local improvement rates, unmetered public or private utility charges, and non-metered cost of fuel. Adjustments are apportioned and allowed to the day of completion, the day of completion itself to be charged to the buyer. Terminology concerning *day of completion* will vary by province—in some instances, the term *closing date* is used.

Standard agreements/contracts in various provinces contain a clause concerning adjustments as of the date of closing. A typical wording is included relating to a residential transaction.

> *Any rents, mortgage interest, realty taxes including local improvement rates and unmetered public or private utility charges, and unmetered cost of fuel, as applicable, shall be apportioned and allowed to the day of completion, the day of completion itself to be apportioned to Purchaser.*

Figure A.18 illustrates a *Statement of Adjustments* for a typical residential property.

Fuel

If metered and a reading is taken on closing, no adjustment is required. In the case of tanks, the seller fills the tank and the buyer pays for a full tank at closing.

Insurance

The buyer arranges new coverage and no adjustment is required as per the agreement. The *Agreement of Purchase and Sale* used in Ontario specifically states:

> *...No insurance shall be transferred on completion...*

Procedures may vary by province and special provisions could apply in regard to condominiums.

STATEMENT OF ADJUSTMENTS

SELLER	James Earl Jones and Judy Wilma Jones
BUYER	Mary Rose Smith and John Michael Smith
PROPERTY	123 Main Street, Anycity
ADJUSTED AS OF	June 30, 20xx

PURCHASE PRICE $238,000.00

DEPOSIT $20,000.00

REALTY TAXES

Realty taxes for 20xx	$2,428.46	
Amount paid by Seller	2,428.46	
Less Sellers' share	−1,197.60	
Allow Sellers	$1,230.86	1,230.86

FUEL OIL

Full Tank 909 (gallons/litres)

Allow Vendor 909 x $0.419 per unit	$380.87	380.87

UTILITIES

Meters to be read on closing.
No adjustment.

INSURANCE

Buyer to arrange new insurance.
No adjustment.

BALANCE DUE ON CLOSING   219,611.73

Payable by Certified Cheque(s)

TOTALS $239,611.73 $239,611.73

E. & O. E.

Figure A.18   Statement of Adjustments

Interest on Assumed Mortgages

The seller makes regular payments until closing as mortgages are paid in arrears. The principal balance is determined after the last payment is made by the seller. Interest is calculated on a per diem basis and credited to the buyer, and he/she makes the next regular payment. Interest due on the mortgage for the actual closing day is the responsibility of the buyer.

> **Example** *Adjustments–*
> *Interest on Assumed Mortgages*
>
> A buyer is assuming a mortgage with a balance of $46,593.34 as of closing December 18th. The seller paid the mortgage payment for December 1st of $546.31. The interest portion of the payment that will be paid by the buyer on January 1st is $493.21. The buyer is responsible for the period December 18th through the 31st. The daily interest payable is $15.91.
>
> = 17 days x $15.91
> = $270.47
>
> This amount is owed by the seller and the buyer will be credited for $270.47 on the statement of adjustments.

Rent

The buyer should be given credit for prepaid rent accruing from the closing date to the next rent due date.

> **Example** *Adjustments–Rent*
>
> If rent of $900 is paid on the first day of the month, the buyer gets credit for one day if the deal closes on June 30th, i.e., 1/30th of $900 or $30. The adjustment includes, where applicable, a credit of any deposit paid by the tenant for the last month's rent along with interest on that amount. If this residential tenant took possession on January 1st and paid a deposit of $900, there will be a credit to the buyer of $900 and approximately $27 in accrued interest (assuming a statutory 6% interest rate on rent deposits).

Taxes/Local Improvements

As a general statement, the adjustment is calculated on the proportionate share of taxes borne by the buyer and seller in relation to the closing date. However, fluctuations in payments to the municipality during the year can result in more complex calculations. The situation is complicated due to municipal budgeting processes. Municipalities must determine in advance what the anticipated taxes will be for the upcoming year. As councils are frequently elected in the fall, the final budget is not determined until the spring. Consequently, municipalities must estimate taxes and distribute interim tax bills. Sellers remit taxes based on these interim bills with adjustments made

coincident with the final tax notice. Further, all taxes for the year are usually paid in advance of the year end. Consequently, the seller's position in regard to taxes paid can vary significantly depending on when the sale occurs during the year.

> **Example 1** *Adjustments–*
> *Taxes/Local Improvements*
>
>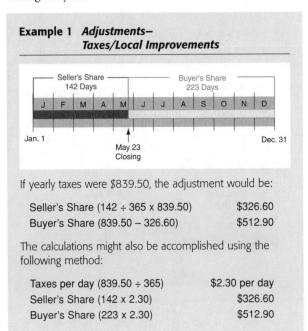
>
> If yearly taxes were $839.50, the adjustment would be:
>
> | | |
> |---|---|
> | Seller's Share (142 ÷ 365 x 839.50) | $326.60 |
> | Buyer's Share (839.50 – 326.60) | $512.90 |
>
> The calculations might also be accomplished using the following method:
>
> | | |
> |---|---|
> | Taxes per day (839.50 ÷ 365) | $2.30 per day |
> | Seller's Share (142 x 2.30) | $326.60 |
> | Buyer's Share (223 x 2.30) | $512.90 |

> **Example 2** *Adjustments–*
> *Taxes/Local Improvements*
>
> The tax year in Anycity is the same as the calendar year, but municipal taxes are payable in full by June 30th of each year. When a house is sold during the tax year, an adjustment is made between the seller and the buyer.
>
> *Scenario 1*
> Assume that a sale in Anycity is completed July 15th and annual realty taxes of $839.50 were paid by the seller on June 30th. The seller is responsible for the taxes from January 1st to July 14th, or 195 days inclusive, and the buyer is responsible for the balance, i.e., from July 15th to December 31st. The seller's portion of the taxes is:
>
> = 195 ÷ 365 x $839.50
> = $448.50
>
> The buyer's portion is the remainder or $391.00 and this amount will be credited to the seller at closing.
>
> *Scenario 2*
> Assume that the sale is completed May 1st and taxes of $839.50 have not been paid. The buyer will pay the taxes when due in June; however, the seller owes the buyer taxes for the period January 1st to April 30th, or 120 days. The seller's portion of the taxes is:
>
> = 120 ÷ 365 x $839.50
> = $276.00
>
> This amount will be credited to the buyer at closing as it is money that the seller owes the buyer. The buyer then pays the taxes in full on June 30th.

Taxes/Local Improvements (New Mortgage)

When property is sold, the tax apportionment is relatively straightforward. If the sale is completed on May 23rd, the seller will pay the taxes for 142 days and the buyer will pay taxes for 223 days (including day of completion—the day the buyer takes legal responsibility for the property).

However, if a new mortgage is placed on the property, the mortgage lender wants to ensure that enough monies are collected to pay taxes for the full year.

Example   Adjustments–
Taxes/Local Improvements
(New Mortgage)

Assume that the lender must forward the full tax payment of 839.50 by June 30th.

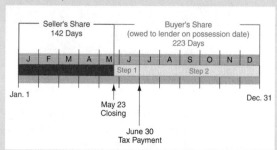

Step One: Taxes to June 30
Taxes collected by PIT (principal, interest, and taxes) payment: 9 days in May plus 30 days in June = 39 days.

Amount of Taxes Collected (39 ÷ 365 x 839.50) $89.70

Step Two: Taxes for Balance of Year
Obviously, the lender will be short 184 days (July–December) on June 30th. Therefore, the buyer must pay the lender on completion day.

Taxes for Balance of Year (184÷ 365 x 839.50) $423.20

Some lenders demand payment at completion date, while others will increase the monthly tax payment due in order to recover the deficiency over the next year.

Taxes (Assuming a PIT Mortgage)

When assuming a PIT mortgage, monies accumulated in the tax account remain with the mortgage, since the lender will not return the funds to the seller. The buyer will re-imburse the seller through an adjustment on the *Statement of Adjustments*.

Water/Utilities

Typically, the seller will order a meter reading to coincide with the date of closing. Consequently no adjustment is required. Some areas within provincial jurisdictions may

---

Example   Adjustments–
Taxes (Assuming A PIT Mortgage)

Using the preceding example with a completion date of May 23rd, the lender collects an estimated amount for taxes from the seller since July 1st of the previous year. Assume the seller paid $70 per month tax, the account would be:

July (previous year) up to and including
May (current year) (11 months x 70) $770.00

The lender would have paid July to December (previous year) taxes during the prior year. Therefore, the seller owes taxes for the period January 1st to May 22nd (buyer pays for completion date). Therefore, the seller's share of taxes is:

MONTH	DAYS	MONTH	DAYS
January	31	April	30
February	28	May	22
March	31	Total	142

Seller's Share (142 ÷ 365 x 839.50) = $326.60

Since the tax account totals $770.00, the buyer owes the seller $770.00 − 326.60 = $443.40. This money is credited to the seller on closing. The tax account with the mortgage lender stays intact and the lender has adequate funds to pay taxes on June 30th as the buyer's taxes are, in effect, paid to December 31st.

Example   Adjustments–
Water/Utilities

If a seller paid $100.00 on January 1st as a flat charge for water usage during the calendar year, the credit allowed to the seller is $49.32 (180 ÷ 365 days x $100.00) for a June 30th completion date. If the amount has not been prepaid by the seller, the buyer will receive a credit for the seller's share (on the statement of adjustments), and the buyer will pay the full amount when billed.

---

have bulk charges for services provided to residents. An example is provided concerning an adjustment for this type of situation.

Provincial   See applicable reference materials.

ADULT ONLY HOUSING

Provincial legislation was amended in most provinces to comply with the *Canadian Charter of Rights and Freedom* making *adult only* housing illegal. In Ontario, the *Ontario Human Rights Code* contained an exemption (Sec. 20.4) allowing adult only accommodation. However, in 1986, the government passed omnibus legislation amending the *Human Rights Code* to comply with the *Canadian*

Charter of Rights and Freedom. In the process, the exemption was removed and all *adult only* buildings (condominium or rental) became illegal. In June 1990, the Ontario Human Rights Commission ruled that adult only buildings discriminate on the basis of family status. Applicable legislation will vary by province.

Provincial   See applicable reference materials.

ADVERSE POSSESSION

When an individual, not the owner, takes possession of the property, hostile to, and without the consent of the owner and remains in exclusive possession using the land like an owner and ignoring the claims of other persons including the owner. It is possible, by adverse possession, for an occupier of land to extinguish the title of the owner. The possessor then becomes, in effect, the owner of the land.

Title by adverse possession began in medieval times, given the number of large estates and the fact that absentee landowners and squatters often entered and stayed on those lands for long periods. With the introduction of more accurate surveys, the number of squatters has become smaller. Under common law, a person can acquire possessory title to lands under certain circumstances by taking possession of the lands for a period of time as set out in the applicable provincial law of limitations. The possession must be open, exclusive, and continuous for a period, without the consent of the owner, but with the owner's knowledge. Adverse possession ceases to be effective if interrupted by the owner before the limitation period has elapsed, or if the adverse possessor abandons the land before the limitation period has expired, as the law considers that possession has returned to the owner.

Application   Practitioners must exercise caution in all matters regarding adverse possession. As background, possessory title in Ontario is only granted under the *Registry Act.* No title by adverse possession can occur under land titles. In provinces still under the registry system (i.e., Maritime Provinces and parts of Manitoba and Ontario), statutes set out limitation periods beyond which an owner loses the right to regain possession of his/her land. In Ontario, for those areas under the registry system, the period is ten years as set out in the *Limitations Act.* In Nova Scotia, the statutory period is set out in the *Limitations of Actions Act* and is for a period of 20 years; if the holder of the legal title is outside the province, the period is 40 years. The onus of proof rests with the individual claiming adverse possession. Expert legal advice is strongly recommended regarding such matters.

The principle behind the law of limitations is that a person who has a right of action against another must pursue it within a time period or lose the right. He/she must not keep the other party in indefinite jeopardy of being sued. No title by adverse possession can occur in British Columbia, Alberta, Saskatchewan, and those parts of Manitoba and Ontario which are under the land titles systems. All of these jurisdictions have provided by statute that the title of the registered owner cannot be extinguished by adverse possession.

Example   *Adverse Possession*

Buyer Jones acquires a one acre rural lot in Ontario based on measurements and a survey provided by Seller Smith. Without precisely measuring the property, both parties assume that the lot includes a small laneway on the westerly edge of the lot. The abutting neighbour, next to the laneway, is also under the same impression and consequently no formal consent is required as everyone assumes that Smith owns the property in question. In fact, the laneway is not owned by Smith, but by the neighbour. A few days following closing, Jones erects a fence between the lane and the neighbour. Under common law, the lands in question might be acquired by Jones through adverse possession if such possession was open, exclusive, and continuous for a time period as set out in provincial legislation, without the consent of the owner but with the owner's knowledge.

Provincial   See applicable reference materials.

ADVERTISING

Generally viewed as anything that influences people favourably and is composed of various tools and techniques to convey a specific message. The topic is often narrowly perceived but is actually quite broad. An advertisement includes any verbal, written, or graphic representation, in a newspaper, magazine, flyer, handbill, or other written form, billboard, sign, or electronic media.

Application   Unfortunately, many real estate salespersons speak of advertising when they are actually referring to promotion that relates more to the attainment of specific goals as opposed to day-to-day advertising tools and techniques, e.g., the advancement of an idea, support of a product, or the delivery of a certain image. Promotion can entail personal publicity, institutional material to bolster an image, maintenance of a particular marketing plan, and the advancement of specific properties.

Promotion is the sum of favourable communication delivered by specific advertising tools. In turn, promotion is tied to marketing strategies that embody a mix of activities to achieve pre-determined organizational or personal goals. While advertising tools and promotional goals are important, a marketing strategy will take into account consumer wants and needs, pricing, supply and demand, research expenditures, product development, and distribution factors in the marketplace.

Standards

Advertising standards for real estate brokers (agents) and salespeople arise from four primary sources:

- Provincial legislation and/or standards established by an appropriate provincial regulatory body;
- Federal statutes (in particular, the *Competition Act*);
- The Canadian Real Estate Association (CREA) Code of Ethics and Standards of Business Practice; and
- Office policy manuals designed by individual brokerages or franchise organizations providing services to those brokerages.

Provincial   See applicable reference materials.

Classifications

Advertising is generally grouped into two categories:

- *Institutional advertising* is directed toward the overall advancement of a specific person or brokerage. It is designed to promote goodwill and instill a pre-determined impression in the public's mind through the use of logos, corporate slogans, and specific themes to advance a market or niche position.
- *Specific advertising* is focused on individual products and services. The most popular advertising medium for real estate is the classified section of the newspaper. Features and benefits are a priority, with overall brokerage image being secondary.

Institutional Advertising

A form of real estate advertising that is not directed to the sale of a particular property, but rather the promotion of a service, person, or brokerage to the general public. Institutional advertising by real estate brokers (agents) and salespeople falls under the general requirements set out for all advertising.

Classified Advertising

Performs various functions usually reaching a specific market, satisfying the needs of seller clients, promoting sales staff, and building company image. The majority of readers who respond, in all probability, will not be qualified prospects and this fact should be kept in mind when constructing an ad for a specific property. Frequently, the property does not sell as a direct result of that advertising.

Rather, classified advertising is designed to get the telephone to ring. One of the most effective means of developing a good ad is the **AIDA** formula.

- Get the prospect's **A**ttention by creating a unique and interesting heading and related lead line(s).
- Continue to create **I**nterest by outlining the benefits and amenities.
- Build **D**esire for the prospect to live in that property or community by describing a way of life.
- Prompt the caller to take **A**ction by calling the office as a result of the copy used.

Heading

The heading must have instant reader appeal. The best headings seem to appeal to reader self-interest, introduce new ideas or features, and arouse curiosity. Most studies agree that the number one item of interest is location of the property. Ranking close behind as number two are price and financial terms. Always write the heading so that readers are persuaded to examine the rest of the ad.

Body Copy

Once interest is gained, body copy should complement the heading and induce the reader to look for additional facts. The real objective of body copy is to get the reader from desire to point of action.

- Use active words and phrases that cut sharply, register quickly, and are easily grasped by the reader.
- Be truthful and vivid, but don't exaggerate.
- Avoid abbreviations that can cause confusion.
- Resist long body copy to avoid losing the reader's attention.
- Always include the price and/or financial terms.
- Use fresh words and avoid tired adjectives (e.g., nice, big, and beautiful).
- Keep language direct and informative.

As with any form of selling, some type of close is required—a request for action is necessary. Make certain the reader is asked to take some action. When the ad is complete the following questions should be reviewed:

- Does the ad start with an attention getter?
- Is the ad written from the prospect's viewpoint?
- Were the strongest appeals selected?
- Are secondary appeals fully utilized?
- Does the ad select and qualify prospects?
- Does the ad provide a clear picture of the property?
- Has the ad been properly edited?
- Does the ad make it easy for prospects to inquire?
- Does the ad *ask for the order*?

A man was recently moving from Vancouver to Toronto. He had two cars and wanted one driven to Toronto, so he ran an advertisement in the local newspaper:

Dependable individual wanted to drive my car to Toronto—expenses paid.

After a week, only a few replies were received and these proved unsatisfactory. He decided to run the ad one more time and changed just two words. The new ad generated a flood of calls:

Responsible individual wanted to drive my Jaguar to Toronto—expenses paid.

Costs

Advertising represents a significant cost to real estate brokerages and salespeople. Historically, it was common to find brokers (agents) providing rough guidelines for salespeople concerning advertising expenses. Brokerages now establish one or a combination of the following: preset limits; advertising restrictions based on individual salesperson production; or expense obligations defined contractually by allocating part or all advertising expenses to the salesperson(s).

Sales production is the result of advertising and not the reverse. A weighting factor is largely based on individual judgement and would vary from one marketplace to another. The overall weighting allocation does not seriously disrupt the basic business pattern. In the example provided, 72% of sales volume is forecasted by the end of August, while 76% of advertising dollars will be consumed at that time.

Ethical Responsibilities

The Canadian Real Estate Association (CREA) Code of Ethics and Standards of Business Practice addresses advertising standards. Article 18 outlines the requirement for accurate portrayals in advertising and proper identification of the salesperson and brokerage.

REALTORS shall ensure a true presentation in all advertising. Properties and services shall not be advertised without identifying the firm or, where applicable, the individual practitioner, in accordance with provincial licensing legislation.

Example   *Advertising–Costs*

ABC Realty Inc. is attempting to place reasonable controls on advertising expenses based on seasonal fluctuations within the local market. Broker/Owner Johnson budgeted $50,000 for advertising during the upcoming year. Johnson then breaks the budgeted dollars into monthly allocations according to MLS statistics and percentage of business written during each successive month based on the year's experience. As a final step, he reallocates the advertising dollars weighting the allocation slightly in advance of peak activity periods.

MONTH	% OF TOTAL YEAR ACTIVITY	DOLLAR ALLOCATION	WEIGHTED ALLOCATION
January	5%	$2,500	$3,500
February	7%	3,500	4,500
March	10%	5,000	6,500
April	15%	7,500	7,500
May	15%	7,500	6,500
June	10%	5,000	4,000
July	5%	2,500	2,000
August	5%	2,500	3,500
September	10%	5,000	5,500
October	10%	5,000	3,500
November	5%	2,500	2,000
December	3%	1,500	1,000
TOTAL	100%	$50,000	$50,000

Interpretations of this Article reveal further requirements. The following is adapted from the *Interpretations of the Standards of Business Practice.* A REALTOR should:

- Ensure that contents of all advertising accurately and properly reflect property or services being advertised;
- Not advertise any properties in a manner that is contrary to provincial legislation requirements;
- Not advertise any property owned by himself/herself or owned by another member without identifying the member as a real estate practitioner. Such identification shall be in the manner required by the applicable regulatory legislation; and
- Refrain from advertising any seemingly derogatory statements about competitors, their businesses, or their business practices. Such advertising may form the basis of an ethics charge only if the statements are false or misleading within the meaning of the *Competition Act*, are otherwise prohibited by law, or relate to information that was restricted from use at the request of the seller.

Reference   The *Code of Ethics* and *Standards of Business Practice* of The Canadian Real Estate Association applies to members of organized real estate in all provinces and has been reproduced in its entirety in the **Appendix**.

Provincial Requirements

In various provinces, the real estate profession is either self-regulated or co-regulated. Accordingly, the regulating body may have established various standards and rules/procedures that address advertising requirements as well as other trading practices.

In some provinces the provincial regulatory body has instituted a Code of Ethics that applies to all salespersons and brokers. The Code assists registrants/licensees in understanding ethical conduct expected, and in understanding principles upon which such conduct is based.

Provincial   See applicable reference materials.

Office Policies

Written brokerage policies that contain advertising guidelines to assist salespeople.

Most office policies are found in manuals designed to define and explain procedures adopted by the brokerage for the conduct of business. Often, advertising policies are referred to both in the office policy manual and within individual salesperson contracts.

Example 1   *Advertising–Office Policies*

Salesperson Jamieson has recently joined XYZ Real Estate Ltd. The cost of all advertising is borne by the individual salesperson, beyond a prescribed contribution by the brokerage. A co-operative advertising fund also exists to facilitate institutional advertising for the brokerage as a whole. The specific clause in Jamieson's independent contractor agreement reads as follows:

The salesperson agrees to pay the applicable co-operative advertising fee as set out in Schedule A [attached to this agreement]. *The salesperson shall be responsible for all expenses relating to real estate listings and sales except as specifically excluded herein. Without restricting the generality of the foregoing, the salesperson agrees to pay for travel, entertainment, conventions, education programs, all advertising including classified newspaper and any and all personal promotion, real estate board fees, annual fees for registration, listing books, business cards, and repair and maintenance of an automobile. Any foregoing expenses paid by the brokerage on behalf of the salesperson shall be paid to the brokerage as set out in this agreement.*

Example 2   *Advertising–Office Policies*

ABC Realty Inc. has a detailed advertising policy that ranges from sign requirements to the handling of ad calls by the receptionist. In addition, the brokerage pays for certain classified advertising provided it meets specific standards. Policies are abbreviated for illustration purposes.

- All ads must not exceed 35 words (excluding heading and telephone number), with headings no longer than 14 characters. If limits are exceeded, the ad will be counted as two ads.

- Each ad must bear the brokerage name in large type along with address and telephone number unless contained within a multiple ad copy under the brokerage's banner.

- All ads must be given to the receptionist in accordance with preset deadlines.

- Display ads and out-of-town advertisements must have management approval.

- Management must review ads prior to publication.

ADVERTISING GUIDELINES

The standard of honesty and accuracy in advertising impacts the professionalism of practitioners. Advertising should be in good taste, factual, and clear in its implication. Standards of acceptable advertising are established by statute at provincial and federal levels. The *Competition Act* imposes requirements in terms of misleading advertising and deceptive marketing practices, as do provincial regulatory bodies.

Provincial   See applicable reference materials.

Provincial Requirements

Advertising requirements and guidelines will vary by provincial jurisdiction, i.e., the real estate profession is either self-regulated or co-regulated. Accordingly, the regulating body may have established various standards and rules/procedures that address advertising requirements as well as other trading practices.

Federal Requirements (*Competition Act*)

The *Competition Act*, while enforcing various matters, prohibits misleading advertising and deceptive business practices in the promotion of a service or the supply/use of a product. Industry Canada is responsible for the Act with enforcement and administration undertaken by the Competition Bureau. An excerpt of the *Competition Act* is provided as **Figure A.19**.

False and Misleading Advertising–*Competition Act*

The *Competition Act*, although dictating procedures on a number of trading activities, is particularly broad in its approach to false or deceptive advertising practices. In particular, Section 52 of the *Competition Act* should be noted:

52 (1) "No person shall, for the purpose of promoting, directly or indirectly, the supply or use of a product or for the purpose of promoting, directly or indirectly, any business interest, by any means whatever, knowingly or recklessly make a representation to the public that is false or misleading in a material respect."

The following are three important factors involving offences under this statute.

- The term *material* refers to any information which could affect a purchasing decision. In other words, any representation that might influence a consumer in the marketplace can fall under the Act. Consequently, the *Competition Act* touches upon practically every activity involving the day-to-day trading of real estate and related purchasing decisions.

- Proof of intention to deceive is not necessarily a prerequisite for charges under this statute. In fact, it is not a proper defence to argue that the misrepresentation was never intended. However, Subsection 60 (2) does state that a proper defence can be *due diligence* to correct the error.

- The definition of "misleading" is deliberately expanded to include non-literal impressions given by the advertisements. This is commonly referred to as the *general impression test*.

52 (4) "In any prosecution for a contravention of this section, the general impression conveyed by the representation as well as the literal meaning thereof shall be taken into account in determining whether or not the representation is false or misleading in a material respect."

The actual wording of an advertisement may be technically correct, but the general impression can still be false.

Excerpt—Competition Act   Figure A.19

Canadian Real Estate Association (CREA)

The Canadian Real Estate Association publishes an informative booklet with particular emphasis on false and misleading advertising, deceptive marketing practices, and enforcement of applicable portions of the *Competition Act* by the Marketing Practices Branch of the Bureau of Competition Policy. The publication titled *Guidelines for Real Estate Advertising, Marketing and Promotion Practices* (CREA, 2000) also provides useful guidance for advertising by CREA for the purpose of trading in real estate.

An excerpt from this publication has been reprinted in Figure A.20 for information purposes only. Individual brokerage policies and procedures vary by provincial jurisdiction. This material was developed based upon publications, interpretations, and opinions current at time of publication and is subject to change. Individuals are advised to access current information from appropriate authorities, the broker, and/or legal counsel, prior to the development of any marketing materials. Various provinces are either self-regulated or co-regulated and may have established appropriate standards concerning advertising practices.

General Parameters

The issues of accuracy and clarity are fundamental to all advertising. Selected topics are discussed for guidance.

Abbreviations   The cost of classified advertising is a primary rationale for the use of abbreviations. Also, a host of codes and contractions are used when completing MLS listing forms. Consequently, abbreviations are becoming more widespread in advertising. As a general rule, those found in local trading areas are acceptable provided that they do not confuse or mislead.

**Example   *Advertising Guidelines–
General Parameters–
Abbreviations***

A reader in Toronto would understand the DVP as the Don Valley Parkway, and a buyer would correctly decipher *3 BR TH* as a three-bedroom townhouse. However, *ASSUME 1ST, 2ND, MIN DN, QUALF.* could present problems. Abbreviations should be avoided whenever uninformed or innocent parties could misunderstand. This is particularly true when describing property uses, zoning, mortgaging, or other specific attributes of a property.

Misleading Leadlines and Similar Claims*

◆ *Appraisal at No Obligation, Professional Estimate, and Similar Terms*
Some members advertise their services using such terms as above. Caution should be used in offering this service if the true intention of the member is merely to provide an estimate of value for the purpose of inducing the owner to decide whether or not to offer the property for sale. If a property owner mistakenly assumes that the member's estimate of value is, in fact, a valid property appraisal and relies on it for another purpose, and as a result of such reliance suffers loss, then the person supplying the information may be guilty of misleading advertising and may also be liable for damages. Members are advised to specify the purpose for which evaluations of property are provided.

◆ *Cash Buyers Waiting*
This phrase and variations of it could be grossly misleading if it cannot be substantiated that cash buyers are, in fact, available to the advertiser and are ready to purchase at current market values.

◆ *Single Family Area*
Care should be taken in the use of this phrase to determine that, in fact, multiple family development is not liable to take place in the area concerned.

◆ *Near School, Close to Transportation*
These phrases beg the question of interpretation as to the meaning of *near* and *close.* To avoid misunderstanding, it would be more desirable to include the actual number of blocks or miles to the facility, and certainly some indication, in the case of a school, as to the type of school.

◆ *Bargain*
If this term is used, it should only be used if the property clearly is a bargain when compared with similar properties in the relevant market which are available for purchase or have recently been sold.

◆ *Building Lot*
A lot should only be described in this manner if it is a lot which either has been or will be approved for the erection of a house. (In some areas, checker-board development has led to the establishment of certain lots on which the municipality will not issue a building permit in the foreseeable future).

◆ *Future Investment*
Future Investment is a highly vague and potentially misleading term which could cause a possible purchaser to believe financial gain was likely to be realized when, in fact, it might well not be. Especially in the residential market, use of this phrase should probably be avoided.

◆ *Future Subdivision Land, Future Development Land*
Avoid reference to the possibilities for the future use which may not be realized, unless you can clearly identify specific plans and the conditions under which they might come to fruition.

◆ *Private*
This word should not be used by a real estate agent because it indicates a sale by the vendor direct to the purchaser. This would include the home of a licensed agent.

◆ *New*
New is an absolute term and, therefore, should not be used unless the facts support its use. A roof that is one and a half years old may be new, in as much as it replaces the original roof on the house, but it is not *new.* It is better to describe it as a roof, one and a half years old.
This same practice applies to major appliances, basic plumbing and wiring and other features which you might otherwise be tempted to describe as new, if they have been recently installed or renovated.

◆ *Estate Sale*
The implication of this term is that the property is being sold by a trustee liquidating an estate and, therefore, might be obtained somewhat more cheaply. This can be seriously misleading if the property is being sold as a normal sale having no connection with the settling of an estate.

◆ *Easy Terms*
Care must be taken with the use of the phrase *easy terms.* The phrase is relative and, if the meaning is not fully explained, could well be misleading. For example, easy terms for a family with moderate to high annual household income are certainly not easy terms for a family with low annual household income.

◆ *Stop Renting*
Although a leadline like *Stop Renting* is unobjectionable where the cost of buying the home (including mortgage obligations) is generally within the reach of renters in the relevant market, the phrase can be misleading where the price or purchase terms do not support its use.

*Text modified to accommodate publishing format.

Advertised Price   Subsection 58(3) of the *Competition Act* does permit *sales above the advertised price* in the case of private real estate transactions. Specifically, the actual reference in the Act excludes *the sale of a product by or on behalf of the person who is not engaged in the business of dealing in that product (e.g., private real estate sales).*

However, other representations concerning price come under scrutiny. Any reduction or other alteration of price should be clearly identified and not be materially misleading. Further, the suggestion of a *bargain* that is not substantiated can have legal ramifications. Consider the following case involving a property listed below market value.

Example   *Advertising Guidelines–*
General Parameters–
Advertised Price (Hypothetical)

The accused (a house builder in Anycity), promoting the sale of new homes in a brochure, stated that his homes were priced $10,000 below market value, and published the prices of homes recently sold in the market area for comparison purposes. An investigation revealed that the builder's homes were not priced below market value and that the comparison homes differed from those of the accused in several respects. The accused pleaded guilty to one charge under Subsection 52(1) of the *Competition Act* was convicted and fined $10,000.

Human Rights Code   Provincial jurisdictions have passed human rights legislation that impacts advertising. A salesperson, in advertising a property, cannot set out preferences for a specific class or group of individuals that are specifically forbidden under provincial legislation, e.g., colour, race, ethnic origin, or religion. The issue of preferences also extends into the area of commercial and residential tenancies.

Provincial   See applicable reference materials.

Contests   The *Competition Act* outlines basic rules for the operation of contests. Section 59 focuses primarily on adequate and fair disclosure of certain key facts:

- Approximate number and value of prizes included in the contest.
- Allocation of prizes by region, if applicable.
- Chances of winning (if it is within the knowledge of the advertiser).
- Whether or not a skill testing question is required to win the contest.
- Place where the contest rules may be obtained.
- The closing date of the contest.
- Any unusual restrictions or conditions relating to the promotional contest.

Practitioners are strongly encouraged to seek expert advice in the development of contests, particularly those involving games of chance, to ensure compliance with the lottery provisions of the *Criminal Code*, and other applicable provincial and federal statutes.

Coupons/Market Evaluation Certificates   Certificates and coupons, must clearly identify the service being provided. Disclaimers and limiting conditions should be consistent with the overall impression conveyed.

Distribution   During the past few years, considerable discussion has centered on the issues of interference, solicitation, and the distribution of promotional materials in the marketplace with a particular focus on the mailing and/or delivery of promotional materials to listed properties. During 1995, The Canadian Real Estate Association provided *Solicitation Guidelines* to all real estate boards for their consideration and possible adoption. A direct quote from the overall guidelines specifically addresses the distribution of materials:

The above-mentioned rules [letter also addresses recommended procedures concerning related activities] *do not preclude Members from making general announcements, messages or advertisements (hereinafter referred to as "general announcements" or "announcement") to prospective clients describing their services and the terms of their availability even though some recipients may have entered into representation agreements with another Member, provided such general announcements include a clear, prominent and emphasized statement that the announcement is not intended to cause or induce breach of an exiting listing agreement. A general canvass, general mailing or distribution addressed to all prospective clients in a given geographical area or in a given profession, business, club or organization, or other classification or group, is deemed "general" for the purposes of this rule if it is a mass-produced announcement in identical form to the general public, or an identifiable group of the public, whether communicated by radio, television, newspaper, flyers, form letters (even though personally addressed), or computerized telephone messages.*

Reference   See *Boards/Associations Dispatch 95-15* issued by The Canadian Real Estate Association.

Fine Print/Disclaimers   Classified advertising and other types of promotional material often contain additional information in small print that either qualifies or otherwise expands the message being conveyed. Real estate practitioners, in order to save space, may relegate certain information to the *fine print*. Generally, this text will not

A

arouse concern if it is additive and complementary to the main message. However, if the fine print in any way contradicts or otherwise limits the general impression conveyed by the main message, then a violation under the *Competition Act* may arise.

Disclaimers are frequently found in fine print. As a rule, such disclaimers should not contain information that materially limits or contradicts the main text or have any significant effect on the general impression being conveyed in the ad. The *Canadian Code of Advertising Standards,* Clause 1(d) provides guidance on the issues of disclaimers and asterisked *fine print* information.

> *Disclaimers or asterisked information must not contradict more prominent aspects of the message and should be located and presented in such a manner as to be clearly visible.*

Source: November, 1990, revision to The Canadian Code of Advertising Standards as quoted in *Misleading Advertising Bulletin,* Issue 4, 1990 published by Industry Canada.

The size of the fine print has also come under scrutiny by the Director of Investigation and Research of the Competition Bureau. Fine print should be clearly visible, readable, and relative to the print size used throughout other portions of the advertisement, and take into account the needs of the targeted audience (e.g., age of reader and ability to read). While *general impression* remains the ultimate test, the Director has indicated the acceptability of *7 point print size* as a minimum.

This sentence is printed in 7 point Formata Regular.

However, such a minimum measurement is subject to the qualifiers mentioned above.

Free Offerings   If a product or service is advertised as *free*, then such an offering shall not include any condition or other requirement that the prospective customer would be unable to comply with. The Director of Investigation and Research also addresses the *two for one* offerings by citing the following example as a false representation: *Buy one real estate lot receive your next choice absolutely free*, where the price of the first lot is inflated to cover the cost of the *free* lot.

Multiple Listing Agreements   All MLS listings are viewed as advertisements and consequently fall under the *Competition Act.* All members must ensure that listing information is accurate and correct.

As a rule, real estate practitioners are advised to include nothing on a listing agreement that cannot be verified by source documentation. Information concerning items such as lot size, legal description, mortgage financing, taxes, chattels and fixtures, current zoning, and rentals, to mention a few, come under scrutiny. In fact, inaccurate representations are normally not only actionable under the federal statute but also under common law as either innocent or fraudulent misrepresentation.

The importance of accurate listing information and representations relating thereto is obviously a major factor in broker liability in the marketplace. Although lacking definitive Canadian research at this time, statistical information from the United States underscores the legal entanglements between buyers and brokers that undoubtedly arise from matters pertaining to the accuracy and adequacy of listing information. In fact, the majority of claims involve the buyer as claimant.

Personal Identification   Guidelines, procedures, and specific wordings within applicable legislation will vary concerning personal identification of salespeople and brokers (agents) in relation to promotional materials.

Provincial legislation or trading practices set out by regulatory bodies require that salespeople clearly be identified as the employee and that the broker is the employer. Practitioners should be careful not to falsely identify services, position, or areas of specialty. Provincial requirements will vary.

Pictures/Illustrations   No erroneous impression can be conveyed when a picture or illustration accompanies and forms part of an overall advertisement. For example, if homes are being sold in the $100,000–$150,000 price range, and the house pictured in the advertisement is a model other than that offered, an offence could arise under the *Competition Act.* Further, the fine print in such advertisements requires careful wording.

In the case of illustrations, it is common to see various *asterisked statements* in new home sales such as:

> *Illustrations are artist's concept only, prices and specifications subject to change without notice.*
>
> *Limited quantities available in some price ranges.*
>
> *Illustration only. Prices and specifications subject to change without notice, E. & O. E.*

If a complaint is lodged under provisions of the *Competition Act*, the content of such statements including the respective sizes, and locations in relation to other advertised information would all be taken into consideration by the Director of Investigation and Research.

Promotional Claims   Real estate practitioners must be careful to correctly represent any claims concerning personal performance levels. As with many other areas of advertising, the general impression of the marketing piece and the actual text must agree, and the statement must be accurate and not misleading.

Caution is strongly advised when contemplating claim statements such as:

> *The best....in the area,*
> *The first....in production,*
> *The most popular choice for...,*
> *The most...respected.......,*
> *The largest..., etc.*

While such claims may be substantiated, the Director of Investigation and Research will regard each case on its own merits. Ensure that performance claims are correct and accurate. Consider the following decision under the *Competition Act*:

The accused, in promoting a real estate service, made the following representation in newspaper advertisements: *For maximum exposure and results...over 90% of* [Name of Broker (Agent)] *Realty team listings have sold in 12 days or less.* Investigation revealed that the representation was untrue. Fine: $500.

If testimonials are utilized in promotional material, ensure that any statements printed are accurate, not taken out of context from a larger statement, and that the person providing such statement has in fact received the services outlined in the testimonial. As a matter of policy, the signed statements of individuals should be kept on file in case their authenticity is ever questioned.

Summary

Advertising has become an increasingly complicated facet of real estate trading. Salespeople must consider legal issues and statutory regulations that surround the presentation of property and the provision of services in the marketplace. In the future, the industry will undoubtedly develop additional guidelines and utilize more complex disclosure forms to address the needs of an expanding, sophisticated consumer market.

A conscious move toward more definition in all stages of real estate negotiations has also appeared, be it the listing process, promotion of property, representations made to both buyer and seller during negotiations, and the drafting of complete terms to fully document agreements between parties. This demand for accuracy is neither isolated to real estate sales nor solely directed to salespersons' activities. Many brokerages have introduced seller disclosure forms to ensure accurate information when obtaining listing information from a principal. Listing forms, once a half-page document, now consume two pages or more. Proper disclaimers and qualifiers, once the exception, are now commonplace in all types of print advertising.

The future undoubtedly will demand even clearer delineation of facts, responsibilities, and representations in the interest of fair marketing practices and consumer protection. Regulatory bodies are already confronting new issues surrounding private versus public information, direct mail and telephone canvassing procedures, increasingly detailed disclosure forms, and precise statements of agency responsibilities and duties. Ironically, for all the complexities of modern laws, be they decreed by parliament or declared in courts, the practitioner looking to the future will be best served by following the simple, unencumbered guidelines already established in codes of ethics designed by organized real estate and provincial regulatory bodies.

AEROBIC TREATMENT

A system of treating waste that involves the pumping of air into sewage to accelerate the breakdown.

Application   Aerobic treatment is one of several waste disposal systems identified and grouped by classes within provincial jurisdictions. Waste disposal classifications are part of an overall regulatory structure administered by the appropriate provincial environmental ministry/department. Practitioners selling rural and recreational properties routinely encounter issues concerning the installation and maintenance of such systems.

Provincial   See applicable reference materials.

AFFIDAVIT

A voluntary statement or declaration reduced to writing and sworn to, or affirmed before, an officer who is authorized to administer an oath or affirmation, for example, a notary public or commissioner for taking affidavits. An affidavit of service is a sworn statement that a notice has been served properly.

AFTER TAX CASH FLOW
(SEE CASH FLOW AFTER TAXES)

AGE-LIFE DEPRECIATION METHOD
(SEE ECONOMIC AGE-LIFE DEPRECIATION METHOD)

AGENCY

Application   An agency relationship arises in a real estate transaction when a person, wishing to sell his/her home, seeks the assistance of a real estate brokerage through discussions with a real estate broker or salesperson employed by that brokerage. The principal is the seller of the property and the brokerage is the agent. Alternatively, the brokerage may be engaged by a buyer to assist in the purchase of a property. In this situation, the buyer is the principal and the brokerage is the agent. The agency relationship, in either case, exists between the brokerage and the buyer or seller despite the fact that a broker or salesperson actually secures the agency agreement/contract.

Agency has grown into a complex topic beyond traditional seller agency because of the evolution of client/customer relationships. To complicate matters, agency practices and associated disclosure procedures currently vary by province as well as within brokerages and real estate boards across Canada. Further, terminologies differ based on individual provincial registration requirements.

Many situations involve agency relationships, e.g., executors acting as agents for estates, guardians acting as agents for minors, union representatives acting as agents for worker members, and salespeople, brokers (agents), and brokerages acting as agents for buyers and sellers.

NOTE All references to real estate brokerage assume that a real estate brokerage is a legal entity licensed or registered under the appropriate provincial jurisdiction. Brokers (agents) and salespersons are employed or otherwise appointed by that brokerage. The term *brokerage* for this publication refers to the real estate brokerage (be it a sole proprietorship, partnership, or corporation), in addition to individuals registered as either brokers (agents) or salespersons.

Provincial   See applicable reference materials.

Creation

The relationship between principal and agent, wherein an agent is authorized by the principal to act on the principal's behalf in business transactions with a third party. The agency relationship results from mutual consent between the principal and agent. Formalities, such as compensation or a written agreement are not necessary to create agency; nor does agency have to be intended, it can be created accidentally.

Agency can be established through various methods.

By Express Agreement   The most common method of creating an agency relationship. An express agreement should set out the definite understanding of client and brokerage (principal and agent), regarding the relationship. Common law does not require the agency relationship to be expressed in writing; however, it is obviously better for both principal and agent that a written agreement/contract exists. In the real estate profession the practice of written authority is commonplace through the use of listing and buyer agency forms.

By Ratification   Agency is created by ratification if the principal accepts the benefits of an agent's previously unauthorized act. For example, Seller Smith, adopts the actions of ABC Realty Inc., although the actions of ABC Realty Inc. were carried out without the express authority of Smith.

Ratification can occur when a salesperson is attempting to obtain listings and the homeowner will not sign an agreement/contract but advises the salesperson that if he/she has interested buyers to *bring them over*. When the salesperson does introduce a buyer and secures a sale, the seller has accepted the benefits and liabilities of that sale and thereby becomes the principal. When the agent expects to create agency retroactively, the agent must act on behalf of the principal even before agency has been ratified.

By Estoppel or Conduct   Occurs when a principal gives the impression to a third person that another person is acting on his/her behalf as an agent. For example, Smith, by deeds or conduct authorizes Jones, to act as his/her agent. Smith is then prevented from denying the existence of Jones' agency to a third party who dealt with Jones on the basis of Smith's words and conduct. In real estate, if a seller indicates to prospective buyers that they should contact a specific salesperson about the purchase of the seller's home, the seller may be legally barred from denying that the agency existed, even though a listing was not signed.

Agency may also be created when an agent gives the impression to a third party that the agent is protecting and promoting the interests of the third party.

By Operation of Law (By Necessity)   Occurs when an emergency situation exists whereby the agent has the authority to bind his/her principal, although under normal circumstances this right would not exist. For example, an agent might be required to save goods of a client in his/her absence when unable to reach the principal for a decision given the need for immediate action. This type of circumstance could occur to the master of a ship or carrier of perishable produce, but is unlikely to happen in matters surrounding real estate transactions.

By Implied Authority   The authority to act on behalf of another may be implied, under certain circumstances. For example, if Smith had given ABC Realty Inc. express authority to do something, the courts would imply (in the absence of evidence to the contrary), that Smith has also given ABC Realty Inc. the authority to do those things necessary to carry out the express authority.

Disclosure

Agency disclosure has become complex with the advent of various agency relationships. While agents owe principals the duty of good faith and full disclosure, more precise guidelines were required in addition to common law requirements. Consequently, codes of ethics and provincial regulatory procedures and controls have been developed requiring specific disclosure procedures concerning the role and nature of agency services.

Most disclosure requirements, above those dictated by common law, concentrate on the timing and completeness of disclosure along with the informed consent of the client. Disclosure requirements are detailed in the national code established by organized real estate and in codes for individual provincial jurisdictions.

Code of Ethics: The Canadian Real Estate Association
Members of organized real estate are required to fully disclose the existence and nature of a member's agency relationship. Effective January 1, 1995, the CREA Code of Ethics was revised with a subsequent change in April 1995.

> *The REALTOR shall fully disclose in writing to, and is advised to seek written acknowledgement of disclosure from, all parties to a transaction regarding the role and the nature of service the REALTOR will be providing to the client versus the customer or other party to the transaction. The REALTOR shall also disclose his or her role to other REALTORS involved in the transaction.*

Article 3 now reads:

Real Estate Act/Regulations   Agency disclosure requirements have been established for licensees/registrants in a number of provincial jurisdictions.

Provincial   See applicable reference materials.

Duties

The agent is considered in law to represent the principal and to bring the principal into legal relationships with other parties. The needs of individuals are so complex that, to a large extent, such needs are fulfilled not by their own efforts but by the efforts of others on their behalf. If someone acts on behalf of another, he/she is considered in law to be an extension of that person. The law governing relations between these individuals and other persons is referred to as the *law of agency*.

Agents owe principals (e.g., clients) their primary allegiance, including such duties as good faith and full disclosure, competence, obedience, and accounting. Classifications and terminology regarding these duties, generally fall under the term *fiduciary responsibilities* and vary somewhat in printed materials. Fiduciary duties are best explained using the following six categories.

Disclosure   The agent must disclose to his/her principal any information relevant to the transaction in which the agent has been engaged to assist. This includes any facts affecting the value or desirability of the property and all known relevant and material information.

Competence   The agent must exercise a degree of competence when representing his/her principal such as would be expected from an average person in that occupation or profession. In all agency relationships, the law sees the agent as an extension of the principal. Thus, the principal is liable for the agent's actions. Therefore, the agent will be under a duty to use superior skill and knowledge while pursuing the principal's affairs. An agent who claims to be a specialist must exercise competence in that specialty.

Obedience   An agent is obligated to obey the principal's lawful and reasonable instructions, even if the agent doesn't agree with them.

Accountability   An agent is obligated to account for all monies or property entrusted to his/her care that belongs to the principal, i.e., safeguard any money or documents relative to the principal's transactions or affairs.

Confidentiality   An agent must not use information acquired as the principal's agent for any purpose that is likely to cause the principal harm or to interfere with the principal's business, now or in the future. The duty of confidentiality should not be confused with a real estate professional's responsibility to disclose known material facts about the property to non-principals. The obligation to disclose such facts, including defects, is based on the professional's duty to treat all persons fairly and honestly.

Loyalty   The most important duty an agent has toward the principal is loyalty. The agent must place the interests of the principal above all else except the law in carrying out his/her functions as an agent.

Agents owe third parties (e.g., customers) the ethical duty to be honest, the legal duty not to misrepresent, and the responsibility to exercise due care when answering inquiries or giving information. In real estate, the agency relationship can be established between the agent and either the buyer or the seller. The relationship can arise out of an agreement either expressed or implied, or written or oral. Agency relationships should be in writing and real estate brokerages should ensure that all activities fall within the limits of that authority. Agency will be implied when agents treat customers as principals (clients), even though no written agreement/contract exists.

Termination

The act of terminating a relationship between principal and agent will not affect any rights of either party that arose during the agency relationship. Several methods can be used to terminate an agency relationship.

Mutual Consent   Since the agency relationship is created by an agreement/contract between parties, it is clear that the relationship can be terminated by the parties if they agree to do so.

Revocation   Generally, a principal has the absolute right to revoke any authority given to an agent at any time. However, in the majority of real estate scenarios, the principal has agreed to certain obligations until a specific date. The principal is not required to contract with anyone as a consequence of the agency agreement/contract and may remove the property from the market by refusing to enter into any agreement. However, the principal may be liable for damages for breach of the agency, if the terms of that agency agreement are satisfied. Similarly, an agent may terminate the agency agreement, but may remain liable for damages for breach of the agreement if there was a fixed expiry date.

Expiry   The agency relationship will terminate at the date agreed to by the parties, i.e., the expiry date set out in the listing or buyer agency agreement/contract. This may be replaced by either a new or renewal agreement and a true copy of this agreement must be given to the seller. The agreement may continue for purposes of commission resulting from a sale in a holdover period as provided in the listing agreement or buyer agency agreement.

Completion/Performance   When the agent completes what was agreed to and the ultimate purpose is achieved, the relationship will terminate. The parties hope that the relationship will end with the successful completion of an agreement/contract, e.g., the sale of the principal's property or the acquisition of property by the buyer.

Impossibility   Termination will occur if the agreement/contract involves material that no longer exists, e.g. a building destroyed by fire. A listing agreement may provide for a continuation to permit the sale of the vacant land. An agency agreement concerning the sale of property may also be disrupted if the property is expropriated or foreclosed and neither commission nor damages may be payable, depending on the terms of the agency arrangement.

Death, Mental Incapacity, or Bankruptcy   The agency agreement/contract will be terminated in the event of the death, bankruptcy, or mental incapacity of either the agent or the principal. Limited circumstances may exist where the agency agreement will continue despite the principal's death. For that reason, agreements may provide for an irrevocable provision and the requirement that such agreements be binding on the estate of the principal.

Licence/Registration Cancellation   Termination of agency will result if the agency agreement/contract becomes void due to the cancellation of a brokerage's licence/registration.

Types of Agency

Buyer Agency

A real estate brokerage representing the interests of the buyer. Buyer agency can be established by implication, as well as a written agreement/contract. Buyers seeking exclusive representation usually do so through an agency agreement. This relationship is the counterpart of seller agency with the same agency principles and practices applying.

A representative of the buyer must use professional negotiation skills, seek appropriate properties that meet the buyer's needs, describe the merits and defects of any selected property, keep information confidential concerning the buyer, and generally act in the buyer's best interests. The hallmarks of this relationship are good faith, full disclosure, competence, obedience, and accounting. The buyer and the brokerage will enter into a signed buyer agency agreement that details their relationship. The exact title of the buyer agency agreement will vary by provincial jurisdiction, e.g., *Buyer Agency Agreement* and *Exclusive Buyer's Brokerage Contract*.

The seller usually pays all commission to the listing brokerage who, in turn, forwards the appropriate portion to the buyer's brokerage. Alternatively, the buyer's brokerage can be paid directly by the buyer and, therefore, this amount does not form part of the sale proceeds. In most transactions, the commission to the buyer's brokerage is paid via the listing brokerage from the proceeds of the sale. Payment procedures for the payment of commission will vary by provincial jurisdiction.

Dual Agency

The same brokerage has an agency relationship with both the buyer and the seller in a real estate transaction. Dual agency also occurs when different salespeople represent buyer and seller, and are employed by the same brokerage, including those who work in different branch offices. The brokerage or its representatives must advise the seller and the buyer of the dual aspect of representation and must be impartial when representing both parties. Both buyer and seller must give their informed consent to this form of representation.

> *The law does not allow a person to assume relations so essentially inconsistent and repugnant to each other without the authority and consent of both principals.*

Source: Mr. Justice Hughes, New Brunswick Court of Appeals, Cec MacManus Realty Ltd. vs. Bray, 1979.

Extreme care must be exercised if a brokerage practises dual agency representation. If a dispute develops and remains unresolved, the brokerage and its representatives cannot continue to act for both parties. In the simplest situation, dual agency involves the seller signing a listing agreement/contract with the brokerage and a buyer authorizing a buyer agency agreement with the same brokerage, with both parties understanding the inherent duality of function being performed by the brokerage. While legally permissible, the Canadian Real Estate Association has traditionally discouraged this practice. Dual agency can be awkward and potentially dangerous both legally and ethically for a brokerage and its representatives.

> *The Canadian Real Estate Association (CREA) has taken the position that it does not encourage the practice of dual agency representation. Therefore, CREA has not developed materials (clauses, forms, and procedures) for dealing with unique situations that might necessitate the practice. Therefore, check with management before committing the brokerage to any situation that might contemplate dual agency representation.*

Source: *Sample Office Policy Manual*, CREA

Proponents of dual agency advocate that full and complete disclosure, precise guidelines for conduct in a dual agency situation, and proper documentation will all but eliminate any risks. However, a strong cautionary note must be voiced.

> *Although disclosed dual agency relationships are technically lawful, there are compelling reasons real estate brokers (agents) should avoid creating them.*

Source: *Who is My Client? A REALTORS Guide to Compliance with the Law of Agency*, NATIONAL ASSOCIATION OF REALTORS.

Implied (Unintended) Dual Agency   The real danger with dual agency lies not so much with expressed agency, which can be largely remedied through proper procedures, but rather with implied dual agent relationships. In an expressed, fully disclosed relationship, the brokerage and its representatives can, in fact, represent both buyer and seller if the terms and responsibilities are clearly understood and agreed to by both parties in advance, through informed consent. With unintended dual agency, no formal document exists. Such duality arises when a brokerage or salesperson inadvertently represents two parties or unwittingly works on both sides of the transaction.

Limited Dual Agency   Procedures, including variations found in provincial jurisdictions and individual brokerages, have generated considerable discussion. Most concerns centre on the issue of confidentiality and loyalty owed to the seller that conflicts with the same duties owed to the buyer. In some jurisdictions, rules and procedures have been imposed by legislation and/or the appropriate regulatory body limiting duties owed to both buyer and seller under such circumstances. Generally, *limited dual agency* sets out procedures regarding:

- Non-disclosure of the price that either party is prepared to pay the other.
- Non-disclosure of the motivation of either buyer or seller.
- Non-disclosure of the terms of competing offers.
- Not disclose personal or financial information unless authorized.
- Not represent the interest of the buyer over the seller (or vice versa).

Undisclosed Dual Agency   This situation arises when a professional is found to be acting in an agency role for conflicting interests without prior approval, understanding, and agreement of the parties. The results may have serious consequences including forfeiture of commission, discipline by a local board or regulatory body, punitive or exemplary damages, and possibly the loss of salesperson or broker licence/registration. The broker and/or manager who is responsible for the activities of the sales force may also be at risk.

Seller Agency

Establishes a relationship in which the brokerage and its salespeople represent the interests of the seller exclusively.

Sellers typically give authority to a brokerage to sell their property by signing a listing agreement/contract that establishes a formal agency relationship between the seller and the real estate brokerage. This agreement/contract sets out what the seller instructs the brokerage to do and what services are provided under seller agency. Further, it provides that representatives of the seller will use their professional negotiation skills to seek qualified buyers and generally promote the listed property, while keeping information concerning the seller confidential and always acting in the seller's best interests. The hallmarks of this relationship are good faith, full disclosure, competence, obedience, and accounting. The seller has traditionally paid a commission directly to the agent. The listing agency then pays any brokers or salespeople within its employ and, if applicable, any co-operating brokerages involved in the transaction.

Single Agency

A relationship between a seller or buyer and an agent wherein the agent is considered in law to represent only the principal.

Agents owe principals their primary allegiance, including good faith and full disclosure, competence, obedience, and accounting. Single agency is to be differentiated from dual agency in which the same agent has an agency relationship with both the seller and the buyer in the same real estate transaction. With the rise of buyer agency, the term *single agency* is sometimes used to refer to brokerages that only work with either buyers or sellers. For example, a brokerage dealing only with buyers and not offering agency services to sellers is referenced in certain jurisdictions as being a single buyer brokerage.

Sub-Agency

An agency relationship whereby an individual is empowered by an agent to act on behalf of a principal of that agent.

The sub-agency concept extends to the authorization of co-operating brokerages to work on behalf of the seller. Traditionally, Multiple Listing Services were based on the automatic offering of sub-agency by the listing broker to all other members of the real estate board. The use of sub-agency has gradually diminished given the growing popularity of buyer agency.

AGENCY MANAGEMENT

The management of a residential or commercial property by a person or other entity authorized by the owner. Agency management is one of three common types of property management (also known as *fee management*).

Agency Management   Occurs when the owner(s) of a building hire a professional management company to administer the property or properties. The property manager is an employee or owner of the management firm. Fees are usually based on a percentage of property income.

In-House Management   Generally preferred by organizations with large property portfolios, where sufficient revenues allow the owners to employ a full-time property manager. This frees them from day-to-day management responsibilities and permits an expanded role in management decisions.

Owner/Self Management   This form of management is prevalent among owners of small buildings.

AGENT

One who is authorized by a principal to represent that principal in business transactions with another party. An agent acts on behalf of a principal as an extension of that person, and can bring the principal into legal relationships with others.

Role

The agent must obey the principal's lawful instructions, although not necessarily subject to detailed and direct control or supervision as to how work is to be done. In many cases, an agent is authorized to bring the principal into contractual relations with other persons referred to as third parties. A typical example is the relationship between an owner of real estate and the real estate broker engaged to sell the property.

An agent in a real estate transaction is a special class of agent who may negotiate contracts for the principal, while not entrusted with the possession of the title documents or the sale article. To assist in understanding the role of an agent, the relationship may be compared with two variations, namely that of master and servant, and of employer and independent contractor. All three relationships are easier to define in theory than to identify in practice. In modern business, each may assume complicated and overlapping forms.

Real estate agency is somewhat different from the traditional agent/principal relationship. For example, the seller exercises much less control over the agent than might be the case in other agency arrangements. In fact, the brokerage has various principals (buyers and sellers) to which it owes fiduciary duties at the same time. Further, the brokerage is not entrusted with the property, but rather only the marketing of the home. As a result, brokerage agency is often viewed as a special class of agent given the uniqueness associated with buying and selling real estate.

Delegation of Duties

As a rule of law, agents are expected to carry out their duties personally, since the principal expects them to accomplish allotted tasks for which they were engaged. However, exceptions to the rule apply to real estate brokerage.

Express Authority

The most common form of delegation is granted in a typical multiple listing agreement/contract, where the principal authorizes the listing broker to co-operate with other brokers in marketing the property. If a co-operating broker acts as a sub-agent, the duties of the agent to the principal are delegated to the sub-agent.

Implied Consent

The second form of delegation is by way of implication. If an agent is involved in a profession in which it is common public knowledge that delegation of duties is necessary and standard practice, then it may be argued that the principal has given implied consent to delegate, e.g., the listing of a property.

Traditionally, the listing brokerage was the agent and a co-operating brokerage was the sub-agent owing the same duties to the seller as the listing brokerage. Recently, the co-operating brokerage has taken on the role of a buyer agent in which allegiance is owed to the buyer while allegiance of the listing brokerage is owed to the seller. Consequently, the above example has limited applicability in the current marketplace.

Statutory

The final form of delegation whereby real estate brokerages are permitted to delegate duties to licensed/registered salespeople under the applicable provincial legislation. Therefore, if ABC Realty Inc. hires a salesperson who is registered under the Act, then that salesperson can work on behalf of the brokerage to secure listings and sell property for the brokerage.

The typical real estate transaction in most provinces involves listing brokerage that is the agent for the seller and any co-operating brokerages are assumed to be agents for the buyer unless otherwise agreed to. Thus, the co-operating brokerage's allegiance is toward the buyer and the listing brokerage's allegiance is toward the seller with both commissions being paid from the proceeds of the sale.

Duties to the Principal

A real estate agent under the law has numerous responsibilities to the principal including general duties at common law and specific provisions of provincial statutes. The fundamental duties of an agent to a principal are:

- Good faith and full disclosure;
- Competence;
- Obedience;

- Accountability;
- Confidentiality; and
- Loyalty.

The agent has an obligation to perform all duties personally unless otherwise authorized by express consent, by implication, or by statute. If an agent does not carry out his/her duties, the principal has remedies that include dismissal, damages, action to recover property, action for an accounting, action to resist payment, prosecution, and indemnity.

Duties to Third Parties

When the agent represents a client, that principal is owed complete loyalty. However, where do the brokerage and its salespeople stand in relation to the third party when there is no client relationship with that individual?

Legally, the brokerage and salespeople have specific duties failing which liability for damages can result.

- Make no misrepresentation regarding the property to the third party.
- Be fair and ethical.
- Take care in answering third party inquiries to ensure complete and accurate information.

Example *Agent–Duties to Third Parties*

Buyer Jones advised Salesperson Martin that she could afford a monthly mortgage payment of $1,000. Martin knew that Jones was relying on her expertise and advice. The MLS listing showed a mortgage at 7% with monthly payments of $1,032.34, amortized over 25 years, but due in one year. Martin did not explain to Jones that the interest rate might change the following year and in fact stated that the rate would apply for the full term of the mortgage. The buyer assumed that the term was 25 years and Martin said nothing to correct this assumption.

At renewal date, nine months following closing, the rate increased to 8.5%. Jones sued Martin and the judge held that Martin and the brokerage were negligent for failing to confirm and fully explain the listing information relating to the mortgage. The judge stated that an agent is under a duty to avoid negligent misrepresentations.

AGGREGATE RENT

The total or gross rent amount for a lease term. Given wide divergences of lease arrangements, the aggregate rent can be made up of several components. Typically, in commercial office leasing, the aggregate represents the sum of the base rent and additional rent. In a retail complex, the aggregate or total rent may consist of the base rent (often referred to as the *minimum rent*), additional rent (often referred

to in a commercial lease as *The Tenant's Proportionate Share of Landlord's Costs*), and a percentage rent involving gross sales in excess of a stated dollar volume for each rental year.

Example *Aggregate Rent*

A commercial office tenancy has a rentable area of 1,520 square feet and a base monthly rent of $380 based on an annual rate of $3.00 per square foot for the rentable area. The total building rentable area is 155,102 square feet. Consequently, the tenant's proportionate share is:

$$1,520 \div 155,102 = .0098 \text{ or } 0.98\%$$

Assuming estimated total operating expenses and taxes for the year are $1,368,000. Tenant's annual proportionate share would be:

$$\$1,368,000 \times .0098 = \$13,406.40 \text{ or } \$8.82 \text{ p.s.f.}$$

If the expenses and property taxes were equally distributed throughout the year, the monthly additional rent is:

$$\$13,406.40 \div 12 = \$1,117.20$$

The aggregate or gross rent (assuming no further adjustments were required concerning additional rent following year end), would be based on $11.82 per square foot ($3.00 + $8.82). The yearly aggregate is therefore $17,966.40 ($11.82 x 1,520).

AGREEMENT FOR SALE

An agreement for the purchase of real property wherein the seller retains title to the property while permitting the buyer to occupy the premises without becoming the owner. Title is not conveyed until some future stipulated date or until some future event occurs.

- When payment for the property is made in full.
- When sufficient payments are made to pay the difference between the price and the existing mortgage.
- When the buyer has built up sufficient downpayment and the seller feels comfortable in taking back a mortgage on the property.

Until one of these occurrences takes place, the buyer is said to have a contractual interest in the property. If payment default occurs, the buyer immediately relinquishes any right to the property. The seller has no need to foreclose as title still rests with that individual.

Application In most provincial jurisdictions, no standard form exists for an agreement for sale to be used by real estate practitioners, but forms are provided by legal publishers. An agreement for sale is infrequently used but could be viewed as a financing alternative for a buyer with limited downpayment when the seller is seeking the best possible security. This agreement should be clearly differentiated from the preprinted agreement/contract that is commonly used in the transacting of real estate. In such agreements, title passes on the payment of the purchase price.

The agreement for sale can be used in various circumstances: where existing mortgages cannot be discharged for a specified period, when the deposit is small, or where it is impractical to have a sale with a mortgage back to the seller.

Example *Agreement for Sale*

Buyer Jones agrees to pay $3,000 downpayment with 12 installment payments of $3,000 and takes possession of the property. Upon receipt of the full $39,000, Seller Smith takes back the balance of the purchase price as a seller-take-back mortgage. Once Jones has made all payments in full, he will get the normal transfer/deed. If Jones defaults in payment prior to receiving the full sum of $39,000, Seller Smith can terminate the agreement and proceed with eviction, unless a court orders the reinstatement of the agreement.

AGREEMENT/CONTRACT/OFFER

A written document by which one party agrees to sell and another agrees to purchase and title passes upon the payment of an agreed purchase price.

Application Formats and wordings vary by provincial jurisdiction. For example, in Ontario and Nova Scotia, the residential agreement form is referred to as an *Agreement of Purchase and Sale*; in Manitoba the comparable form is an *Offer to Purchase*, while in Saskatchewan, the document is called a *Contract of Purchase and Sale*.

In some provincial jurisdictions, no law exists requiring that an offer involving real estate be drafted on a preprinted form; in others, certain forms are mandatory. In Ontario, while not mandatory, the OREA *Agreement of Purchase and Sale* has gained wide-scale acceptance within organized real estate. In selected jurisdictions, distinct agreements have been designed for commercial, condominium, and other specialty properties.

Provincial See applicable reference materials.

AGREEMENT/CONTRACT/OFFER TO LEASE

An agreement/contract/offer designed for either commercial or residential properties by which one party, the lessor,

agrees to lease to another party, the lessee, certain premises as set out in the agreement. Formats and wordings will vary by provincial jurisdiction.

Provincial See applicable reference materials.

AGRICULTURAL SALES
(SEE RURAL, RECREATIONAL, AND AGRICULTURAL SALES)

AIR RIGHTS

A fractional interest within a fee simple estate relating to the rights to use space above the physical surface of the land. Land can actually be divided into three horizontal spaces: sub-surface, surface, and air rights. Air rights, as with other fractional interests, can become a separate unit of real property and consist of fee rights that can be sold or leased. The rights associated with the interest relate to the use, control, and regulation of that space.

Application Air rights are normally acquired to permit the construction of bridge approaches, piers, elevated streets and sidewalks, and in some cases, entire building structures. From appraisal and brokerage perspectives, air rights are marketable and can be valued in the marketplace. Air rights can have substantial value depending on the highest and best use attributable to that space, e.g., construction of a skyscraper or multi-level building above an existing use such as a railroad. However, if such use is limited to a ground level parking lot or pedestrian promenade, the air rights may be of limited value.

ALLIANCE FOR CANADIAN REAL ESTATE EDUCATION

Acronym: ACRE The Alliance for Canadian Real Estate Education is a partnership of provincial and territorial real estate associations working together to develop and produce education materials. ACRE, which includes representatives of provincial and territorial real estate association staff responsible for education, reports to the provincial/territorial association executive officers and presidents.

The alliance, officially formed in January 1999, enables real estate educators and regulatory agencies across Canada to work together more closely, while increasing efficiency and reducing duplication of programs and efforts.

Mandate

ACRE is accountable to the provincial/territorial associations for the following:

- Researching and developing real estate education core curricula blueprints.
- Developing, maintaining, and monitoring national standards to guide the administration and delivery of real estate education in Canada.
- Facilitating co-operation among the provinces/territories, thereby enhancing efficiencies and reducing duplication of development and delivery costs.
- Liaising with regulatory bodies on issues concerning licensing education requirements.

National Code of Real Estate Education

The Alliance has been instrumental in the development of, and refinements to, the National Code of Real Estate Education. During the early 1980s, an informal group of provincial directors of education met with the objective of exchanging information and sharing materials related to real estate education. The first project of this group, then known as the Education Directors National Work Group (EDNWG), was a skills analysis for residential real estate salespeople. This research, validated by education directors, provided learning outcomes that were integrated into the national code. Skills analysis of industrial, commercial, and investment salespeople, brokers, and property managers followed. National core curricula were subsequently created as blueprints for course development.

The National Code of Real Estate Education embodies these blueprints along with detailed procedures involving governance, administration, and quality control in program management. The code is a work in progress currently containing two volumes: Volume 1: The Code, and Volume 2: Recommendations. This document is designed to develop and maintain quality programs based on a common set of educational standards.

Agreement on Internal Trade

The Alliance, along with its predecessor (the EDNWG), has been actively involved in compliance issues concerning the *Agreement on Internal Trade (AIT)*, signed by the federal, provincial, and territorial governments. The AIT contains a labour mobility objective requiring that:

Provincial/territorial regulatory bodies are obligated to reconcile differences in licensing standards and to recognize the qualifications of other provinces/ territories.

The Alliance is a leader in this process for real estate education. The National Code of Real Estate Education now includes a provision that all real estate licensing education programs must adhere to the spirit of the agreement by reducing barriers to educational certification for real estate practitioners in other jurisdictions. The AIT requires that Canadian regulatory bodies assess occupations being regulated for similarities and differences, agree to recognize qualifications of workers from other jurisdictions in areas of sufficient similarity, conduct occupational analysis and implement mechanisms when significant differences exist, and document the recognition and conciliation process for filing with the Labour Mobility Co-ordinator, Ministry of Labour. The majority of ACRE activities either directly or indirectly contribute to this objective.

Canadian Regulators

ACRE, in carrying out its mandate, provides assistance to provincial regulatory agencies throughout Canada in the development and maintenance of real estate education standards. ACRE also assists regulators in achieving mutual objectives. Canadian regulatory bodies are members of the Association of Real Estate License Law Officials (ARELLO) headquartered in the United States. ARELLO was established to assist in the administration and enforcement of licence laws throughout Canada and the United States.

Reference   For additional information, contact the Alliance for Canadian Real Estate Education, 99 Duncan Mill Road, Don Mills, ON M3B 1Z2.

ALTERNATE BROKER
(SEE AUTHORIZED OFFICIAL)

ALTERNATIVE DISPUTE RESOLUTION

Acronym: ADR   A process involving a facilitated negotiator acting as a neutral third party to resolve a controversy between two or more parties. ADR has gained widespread popularity as a viable option to resolving disputes that might otherwise proceed to regulatory hearings or legal action.

Application   For real estate purposes, provincial regulatory bodies may utilize this technique as a possible option in disputes involving registrants and consumers. Real estate boards may also apply ADR techniques in member-to-member disagreements relating to matters that fall within their respective jurisdictions.

Provincial   See applicable reference materials.

AMENDMENT TO AGREEMENT/CONTRACT/OFFER

An amending document that formalizes any mutual agreement between buyer and seller, affects an original agreement, and which is acceptable to both parties.

Application   Amendments are used when a binding agreement concerning the lease or sale of property has been signed, sealed, and delivered, and a situation arises requiring modifications and formal documentation in regard to such amendments. The amendment may be a single document, e.g., in Ontario, this form is referred to as an *Amendment to Agreement*. In Saskatchewan, the *Amendment to Contract of Purchase and Sale and/or Notice to Remove Conditions* provides for amendments as well as notice concerning the removal of conditions.

Amendments also apply to binding listing agreements. For example, the listing has been signed by both parties and true copies delivered but, a subsequent situation arises requiring an amendment to the agreement. Amending forms will vary by provincial jurisdiction and/or local real estate board.

Provincial   See applicable reference materials.

AMENITIES

Features that are agreeable or pleasing. In real estate, items of a beneficial nature arising from the location of, or improvements to, a property.

Application   For real estate purposes, amenities normally refer to features and conditions on the property, e.g., landscaping and surrounding the property as in the case of schools, parks, and access to transportation. In condominiums, amenities refer to selected common elements that benefit all unit owners such as recreational facilities including squash courts, indoor swimming pools, weight training facilities, exercise equipment, billiards, saunas, whirlpools, and lighted outdoor tennis courts. The facilities might also include close access to transportation, nearby yacht clubs, landscaped open areas, public parks, bicycle pathways, and outdoor party areas.

AMENITY AREA

An outside area designed and used for passive or active recreational purposes. More specifically in relation to a property on which a house is situated, an amenity area usually refers to the outdoor area intended for recreational use or aesthetic purposes and may include landscaped areas, patios, and decks.

> **Example**   *Amenity Area*
>
> Buyer Savard has recently acquired a building lot in the Municipality of Anycity. The bylaws of this particular city detail various side and rear yard setbacks and minimum square footage requirements for a single-family detached structure. Further, at least 30% of the total lot area must be used as amenity area, namely, for passive or active recreational purposes including lawns, landscaped areas, decks, and patios, but specifically excluding driveways, walkways, and accessory buildings.

AMORTIZATION

The gradual retirement of a debt by means of periodic partial payments of principal and interest.

Application   Amortized loans are commonplace both for residential and commercial properties. Detailed printouts assist in explaining the gradual retirement of the debt through periodic payments of principal and interest. The amortized mortgage provides for a blended payment (weekly, bi-weekly, monthly, semi-monthly, or other periodic installments during the loan term). Amortized loans, through the use of a blended payment, provide a steadily declining interest portion along with an increasing principal portion for each successive payment. In combination, these blended payments result in the gradual reduction in the mortgage balance over the amortization period. See the example on the following page.

AMORTIZATION PERIOD
(SEE ALSO MORTGAGE PAYMENT FACTORS)

The time period required to completely retire the debt through scheduled payments of principal and interest.

Application   Real estate practitioners commonly use mortgage payment factors to calculate principal and interest payments based on varying loan amounts and amortization periods. Mortgage payment factors (per $1,000 of loan amount for selected interest rates), are detailed in the **Appendix**. While payment factors are commonly referred to regarding monthly time periods, weekly, bi-weekly, and semi-monthly payment factors are also provided.

Example 1   *Amortization Period*

Using the mortgage payment factors (see the **Appendix**), consider an 8% mortgage in the amount of $125,500 with blended monthly payments and an amortization period of 25 years. The payment would be:

$$125.5 \text{ (000's)} \times 7.632135 = \$957.83$$

NOTE   Mortgage payment factors are expressed as a factor per $1,000 of loan amount.

If the borrower made a monthly payment of $957.83 for a period of 25 years, the mortgage amount of $125,500 including all interest charged at 8% would be paid and the debt retired.

Example 2   *Amortization*

Buyer Wong has agreed to a mortgage based on an initial sum of $50,000 amortized over 25 years with blended principal and interest monthly payments of $586.94. Wong requires a report detailing the principal and interest portions of each payment along with the balance for the first two years. Salesperson Lane, of ABC Realty Inc., obtains a computer printout of the amortization schedule. The printout shows the gradual reduction of principal through successive payments. Wong can analyze the interest and principal portions of each payment and successive balances during the 24-month period. If all payments were made for the full amortization period, the debt would be completely paid.

PAYMENT NUMBER	TOTAL PAYMENT	INTEREST	PRINCIPAL	BALANCE
01	586.94	567.01	19.93	49,980.07
02	586.94	566.79	20.15	49,959.92
03	586.94	566.56	20.38	49,939.54
04	586.94	566.33	20.61	49,918.93
05	586.94	566.09	20.85	49,898.08
06	586.94	565.86	21.08	49,877.00
07	586.94	565.62	21.32	49,855.68
08	586.94	565.38	21.56	49,834.12
09	586.94	565.13	21.81	49,812.31
10	586.94	564.88	22.06	49,790.25
11	586.94	564.63	22.31	49,767.94
12	586.94	564.38	22.56	49,745.38
13	586.94	564.13	22.81	49,722.57
14	586.94	563.87	23.07	49,699.50
15	586.94	563.61	23.33	49,676.17
16	586.94	563.34	23.60	49,652.57
17	586.94	563.07	23.87	49,628.70
18	586.94	562.80	24.14	49,604.56
19	586.94	562.53	24.41	49,580.15
20	586.94	562.25	24.69	49,555.46
21	586.94	561.97	24.97	49,530.49
22	586.94	561.69	25.25	49,505.24
23	586.94	561.40	25.54	49,479.70
24	**586.94**	**561.11**	**25.82**	**49,453.87**

AMORTIZED MORTGAGE

A mortgage loan in which the principal and interest are repayable in monthly or other periodic installments during the loan period.

ANAEROBIC TREATMENT

The use of bacteria that can survive without oxygen in the breakdown of sewage within a waste disposal system, as distinguished from an *aerobic* system in which oxygen is used to accelerate breakdown.

Provincial   See applicable reference materials.

ANCHOR TENANT

A key or major tenant, usually in reference to a commercial shopping centre, that will attract other businesses as well as consumers.

Application   Anchor tenants generally consist of commercial operations such as department stores, major fashion outlets, drug stores, and supermarkets. Large commercial centres will normally have more than one anchor tenant. This category of tenant will frequently employ personnel such as in-house solicitors specializing in leases and lease negotiations, real estate managers, and construction and research/design departments.

Typically, anchor tenants require their particular form of lease document in negotiations with the landlord. The landlord may agree to the lease form given the potential subsequent draw of other tenants and the value of having an anchor tenant for mortgaging and sale purposes.

Anchor tenants can also exercise significant control within the centre. For example, they may require the landlord not to make construction additions without their consent. In instances where the centre is only partially completed, the anchor tenant(s) may require that:

- A certain parking ratio be maintained.
- Their vista be kept clear to ensure visual impact.
- No *high parking* requirement tenants (e.g., movie cinemas) be permitted without their consent.

Research on anchor tenants indicates that rental rates of smaller tenants are in part affected by the presence of an anchor tenant. The loss of such a tenant can impact remaining tenants owing to the declining drawing power of the shopping centre. This often translates into reduced sales that affect percentage rents being paid to the landlord and may also pose collection problems from existing tenants if store revenues falter. Consequently, the value of the shopping centre can also diminish given income lost from the departing anchor tenant and ramifications of that loss on other tenants. The loss may also extend to the municipality through erosion of the tax base.

Example   *Anchor Tenant*

Developer Reed is constructing a retail mall containing 25 units ranging in size from 1,000 to 4,000 square feet. Reed has provision for a 35,000 square foot food store that hopefully will become a local grocery outlet for the neighbourhood. The grocery store will be the anchor tenant in this retail mall and is expected to generate additional traffic to the site, promote interest in the project from other potential tenants, represent a stable income source as other tenants are gradually recruited, and represent a key element in obtaining base rent rates in the range of $15.00 to $18.00 per square foot.

ANNEXATION

Land annexation normally refers to the attachment or incorporation of one parcel of land within an adjacent municipality, e.g., a city annexing a defined area from an abutting township. Annexation usually occurs when a metropolitan area requires additional property for growth. In doing so, public debates often arise over the real or perceived threat concerning loss of autonomy, lack of control of various services, and an inability to control long-term taxation policy for the immediate area.

ANNIVERSARY DATE

The same point in time during each calendar year. Anniversary dates are commonly associated with salesperson registration, employment, leases, and mortgages. In the case of a mortgage, the first anniversary date normally occurs one year from the date mortgage interest commences.

Example   *Anniversary Date (Mortgage)*

A mortgage is given by an owner to a lender as security for monies loaned to the owner. The interest runs from the date of the advance of those monies. A typical mortgage with a five-year term will provide a specific date for the interest to commence, called the interest adjustment date. If the interest adjustment date is January 1, 20x1, payments of principal and interest will commence one month later on February 1, 20x1 and continue for five years. The last regular payment will be due on December 1, 20x6.

ANNUAL REPORTING (BROKERAGE)

The reporting of financial operations on an annual basis.

Application   Real estate legislation in selected provinces requires brokerages to report various matters concerning financial operations, trust funds, and trust accounts to the appropriate authority. A typical wording is included for illustration purposes.

Every broker shall, annually, within four months after the end of his or her financial year, furnish to the Registrar a report of (a) a chartered accountant; (b) a member of some professional accounting organization recognized by the Commission; or a person approved by the Commission; in the form set out in Schedule A as to compliance by the broker with subsection 26(1) of the Act and with this regulation.

Source: Real Estate Brokers Act, Manitoba

Provincial   See applicable reference materials.

ANNUAL STATEMENTS
(SEE ALSO ACCOUNTING SYSTEM AND FINANCIAL STATEMENTS)

A fully detailed and annotated set of financial statements pertaining to all income and expenses (profit or loss statement), statement of assets and liabilities (balance sheet), and the disposition and application of net funds for the applicable period (statement of changes in financial position).

ANNUITY

A regular stream of payments payable at stated intervals for a fixed period of time, often for the recipient's lifetime in the case of insurance or pension. For investment calculations, an annuity can be viewed either in terms of compounding (the future value of a series of regular payments), or discounting (the present value of a series of future regular payments).

Application   A mortgage is a good example of an annuity in the real estate marketplace. While the borrower's perspective is one of repaying a debt, the lender's point of view focuses on investing in an annuity. The initial loan advanced by the lender becomes an investment made today with the legal right to receive equal payments at predetermined intervals in the future.

The relevance of annuities and regular stated payments is limited for real estate practitioners as most real estate investments generate uneven cash flows throughout the holding period. Compounding and discounting of irregular cash flows is an integral aspect of real estate investment analysis. Commercial practitioners routinely examine, critically assess, and forecast cash flows of investment-grade properties for clients. Fortunately, modern financial calculators and software programs handily address irregular operations and sale proceeds cash flows that lead to investment comparisons and valuation. Cash flows are not only determinative of value in revenue-producing real estate, but also form the basis for meaningful comparison of investment options.

ANTICIPATION, PRINCIPLE OF

(SEE PRINCIPLES (APPRAISAL))

APARTMENT

A separate residential unit consisting of a combination of rooms or a single room used as a dwelling and normally located in the same structure as other occupancies (commercial, residential, or otherwise). A grouping of apartments in one structure is frequently referred to as a *residential complex* or *residential apartment building*.

APARTMENT BUILDING

A building designed for the separate housing of three or more families, where mutual services are supplied for comfortable and convenient occupancy. Buildings with separate housing and mutual services for two families are normally referred to as *duplexes*. The definition of, and specific requirements for, an apartment building may vary by provincial jurisdiction through statutory definitions and descriptions, and by local municipality through zoning and related by-laws.

APPRAISAL

The act or process of estimating value. The resulting opinion of value derived from the appraisal may be informal, transmitted verbally, or it may be formal, presented in written form. Usually, it is a written statement setting forth an opinion of the value of an adequately described property as of a specified date, supported by the presentation and analysis of relevant data.

Appraisal Date

The date to which the valuation applies, sometimes referred to as the effective date of the appraisal.

> **Example   *Appraisal–Appraisal Date***
>
> An appraiser, when preparing an appraisal report, will identify the appraisal date in discussing the purpose of the appraisal, e.g., *This appraisal is to estimate the market value of the subject property as of November 30th, 20xx for sale purposes.*
>
> The appraisal date is also found in the final estimate of value, e.g., *Based on the above data and analysis, it is my opinion that the estimated market value of the subject property, as described in this report, is $225,000 as of November 30, 20xx.*

Appraisal Process

A systematic analysis of factors that bear upon the value of real estate. An orderly process by which the task (e.g., estimating market value as at a specified date), is established, the work necessary to solve the problem is planned, and the data involved is acquired, classified, analyzed, and interpreted into an estimate of value.

Appraisal Purpose

The purpose of the appraisal refers to the use that will be made of the value estimate. Five major purposes or reasons are outlined for which an appraisal may be required.

Transfer of Ownership   Involves the buying, selling, and exchanging of real estate.

Extension of Credit   Normally relates to mortgage lending or other financing and an estimate of value to establish the loan amount.

Compensation for Damage or Loss   Usually involves insurance claims or expropriation.

Taxation   Includes municipal assessment for property taxes and income tax on capital gains.

Land Use Studies or Feasibility Studies   Largely carried out for developers and investors interested in establishing the highest and best use of a particular parcel of land. This process typically involves a number of estimates of value for different forms of development, e.g., freehold detached homes as compared to condominium townhouses.

It is essential that the purpose be established at the very beginning of the assignment and be clearly stated in the appraisal report.

The purpose is often simply stated as follows:

This appraisal is to estimate the market value of the subject property as of November 30th, 20xx, for sale purposes.

Appraisal Report

A written summary estimating the value of property and the conditions and limitations at the time of appraisal.

Two recognized types of appraisal reports are found in the marketplace.

The Narrative Report

Takes a logical, systematic, and detailed approach by presenting theory, facts, analysis, application of methodology, and finally conclusions. Narrative reports must be written in sufficient detail and in such a way that a reader will easily understand the appraiser's reasoning and justifications for the conclusions and estimates reached.

The Form Report

Consists primarily of preprinted information that is checked off or details are inserted where relevant. Space is provided for brief additional comments. The form report allows for a reasonably brief, but systematic and precise presentation of information and analysis. Provincial jurisdictions that participate in the *MVA–Residential Designation* program use this report format or a variation thereof.

Provincial   See applicable reference materials.

Report Content

The appraisal is an orderly process with a methodical outline covering the necessary steps in estimating the value of a property. Eight commonly accepted steps, referred to as the appraisal process, establish the basis for report content as illustrated in **Figure A.22**.

Report Outline

An appraisal plan or outline is recommended when the appraisal activity involves the production of a complex narrative report. This plan or outline should be established prior to the commencement of work and could include tentative lists of tables, charts, diagrams, and maps needed and headings/subheading for sections within the report.

Appraisal outlines will vary considerably. **Figure A.21** represents an outline for illustration purposes only. Practitioners should develop a basic outline prior to undertaking the full appraisal report.

REPORT OUTLINE

Introduction
Title Page
Letter of Transmittal
Photographs of Subject Property
Summary of Salient Facts about the Property
Assumptions and Limiting Conditions
Certification of Appraiser
Definition of the Appraisal Problem
Analysis:
- Property/Neighbourhood Description
- Site Description
- Description of Improvements/Exterior
- Description of Improvements/Interior

Methods of Valuation:
- Cost Approach to Value
- Market Data Approach to Value (Direct Comparison Approach)

Reconciliation and Final Estimate
Addenda:
- Neighbourhood Map and Site Comparables
- Site Plan
- Floor Plan
- Comparable Property Sales

Appraisal Report Outline   Figure A.21

APPRAISAL INSTITUTE OF CANADA

Acronym: AIC   The Appraisal Institute of Canada, founded in 1938, is the national society of professional real estate appraisers. The Institute is dedicated to serving the public interest by advancing high standards for members of the appraisal profession through the granting of the CRA and AACI designations.

Practising members provide reasoned valuations widely respected by courts, chartered banks, real estate corporations, trust companies, mortgage and lending institutions, all levels of government, and private individuals. Members are governed by a Code of Ethics and Uniform Standards of Professional Appraisal Practice that establish minimum standards of performance in the rendering of professional services. The Institute's education program is available through most of its provincial associations and chapters. Certain universities and colleges also offer the program on a full-time basis.

Reference   The national office of the Appraisal Institute of Canada is located at 1111 Portage Avenue, Winnipeg, MN R3G 0S8. Provincial offices are maintained in all provinces.

THE APPRAISAL PROCESS

Step 1
Define the Problem

Identify the property to be appraised, the property rights involved, the purpose of the appraisal, type of value required, the date of the appraisal, identify any assumptions and limiting conditions, and reach an agreement with the client.

Step 2
Preliminary Inspection and Planning the Work

A preliminary survey determines the highest and best use, type and sources of data needed to support the analysis, determines the value approaches to be used, provides the design for the research program, and outlines the appraisal report. An appraisal plan is then established.

Step 3
Data Collection and Analysis

Involves the acquisition of relevant data concerning market trends, neighbourhood and site analysis, and the inspection/analysis of the property's improvements.

Step 4
Apply the Cost Approach

Estimate the site value through an acceptable method, estimate reproduction or replacement cost for the improvements, estimate accrued depreciation, and complete the necessary calculations to arrive at value by the cost approach.

Step 5
Apply the Direct Comparison Approach

Detail the five steps in this approach consisting of selection of comparables, data collection, analysis of relevant data, comparisons with subject property together with appropriate adjustments, and reconciliation to arrive at value estimate.

Step 6
Apply the Income Approach

Estimate the annual gross income, total annual operating expenses, and the net operating income (or cash flow), select the appropriate capitalization rate, and convert the income into a value estimate.

Step 7
Reconciliation and Final Estimate

Provide final reconciliation by reviewing the approaches to value and arriving at a final estimate.

Step 8
Write the Appraisal Report

Prepare the final report (narrative, form, or letter of opinion), along with certification and necessary appendices.

Figure A.22   Eight Steps in the Appraisal Process

APPRAISAL SPECIALTY

Real estate practitioners routinely face the challenges of estimating the value of property. Most information studied is understandably related to appraisals. The process of evaluating or appraising is complex due to many physical, political, economic, and social factors that affect the value of any parcel of real estate. Information such as estates in land, the rights of ownership, and limitations on those rights obviously affect value. In addition, knowledge of the improvements upon the land (e.g., main structure and outbuildings), and the variety of uses based on such improvements is vital to the process.

In addition to listing and selling requirements, many owners of real property often require the services of an appraisal specialist. A true appraisal specialist is a professional who has dedicated years to study, has combined this knowledge with extensive practical experience, and is engaged full time in the practice of appraisal.

Application   A professional appraiser is a researcher who has mastered the techniques and procedures to be applied in the appraisal of different types of property. The most common appraisal approach for residential property involves the research and analysis of market data on previous sales of similar properties in order to arrive at a conclusion concerning the value of the subject property. In appraising income properties, the approach usually includes the analysis of financial statements, the reconstruction of an operating statement, and the capitalization of a potential income stream into a value for the property. Lastly, the cost approach estimates the value of land based on market data, the reproduction or replacement cost of the improvements less depreciation, and adding these two components to arrive at a final value.

Professional appraisers are often referred to as *fee appraisers* who market services on the basis of cost for time, expertise, and effort required to arrive at a value estimate. Other appraisers may work for large corporations engaged in the development of properties for various levels of government. Unlike real estate sales, the appraisal profession involves relatively set work hours for inspection of properties and preparation of reports. Many professional appraisers have earned some form of designation from a creditable institution.

APPRAISER

A professional who estimates value and possesses the necessary qualifications, ability, and experience to execute or direct the appraisal of real and/or personal property.

APPRECIATION

An increase in value brought about by any factor.

Example   *Appreciation*

Three urban ravine lots were currently listed at $175,000 each. Lots 1 and 2 sold, and homes were immediately constructed. The owner temporarily removed Lot 3 from the market. During that period, new municipal legislation was passed forbidding the creation of any additional lots on ravines within that community, save and except for existing approved lots. Lot 3 is now in greater demand and consequently appreciates in value. The sale price of this land during the subsequent building season is $250,000. The appreciation in value ($75,000) results from increasing scarcity of lots owing primarily to the restrictive nature of the new legislation.

APPROACHES TO VALUE
(SEE ALSO COST APPROACH, DIRECT COMPARISON APPROACH AND INCOME APPROACH)

Methods employed by an appraiser to estimate the value of real property.

APPROVED LENDERS

Lending institutions whose mortgages may qualify for insurance against default from Canada Mortgage and Housing Corporation (CMHC) or from a private mortgage insurance company such as GE Capital Mortgage Insurance Canada.

APPURTENANCE

Rights that go with a property. Something that is outside the real property, but belongs to the land, is joined thereto, and adds to greater enjoyment of the land.

Application   A right-of-way is one example of an appurtenance that allows access over a property. Most commonly, a right-of-way involves one landowner that has access over another, usually adjacent, property. In **Figure A.23**, the owner of Lot 1 has been granted a right-of-way over Lot 2 in order to access the lake.

Appurtenance can also apply to other rights that are outside the property but add to greater enjoyment, for example, riparian rights or access to dock facilities in the case of recreational properties.

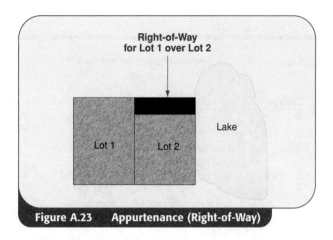

Figure A.23   Appurtenance (Right-of-Way)

AQUATIC PLANT CONTROL

Aquatic plants are a natural and important part of the eco-system and include cattails, bulrushes, pondweed, pond lilies, etc. Such plants provide excellent habitat for fish, insects, and terrestrial wildlife. They do not attract leeches or act as breeding grounds for mosquitoes, but are an important food source for muskrats and moose. Aquatic plants assist in preventing cloudy water by stabilizing lake sediments and reducing silt. They also protect shorelines from excessive erosion by absorbing the force of wave action. Such plants use large amounts of nutrients thereby reducing the amount available for algae growth and absorb poten-tially toxic substances, such as mercury and lead.

However, excessive growth of aquatic plants in recre-ational water and drinking water reservoirs can create problems including swimming nuisances, boating diffi-culties, less appealing drinking water, and less dissolved oxygen in the water for fish habitat. Dense aquatic plant growth in small streams and drains can impede water flow and contribute to the flooding of nearby areas. Concentration of aquatic plants may be an indicator of water quality problems, such as too much nitrogen and phosphorus from fertilizers, sewage, grey water, pet feces, cleaning products, and shoreline erosion.

Application   Real estate practitioners marketing recre-ational properties often address questions concerning the temporary control of aquatic plants on shorelines. Control may be achieved by removing plants manually from beach-front areas or, on a large-scale basis, through the use of harvesting equipment. Chemicals are also an attractive control alternative due to ease of use but pose hazards in terms of environmental and ecosystem damage. Their use, if permitted at all, is generally controlled in provincial jurisdictions by appropriate environmental legislation.

Provincial   See applicable reference materials.

ARBITRATION

The process of determining a resolution to a controversy involving two or more parties. The parties often choose the person(s) to make such determination or agree to be bound by person(s) statutorily or otherwise authorized to conduct the arbitration process.

Application   In brokerage activities, organized real estate provides a structure for the use of arbitration involving disputes between REALTORS as members of local real estate boards. The Canadian Real Estate Association (CREA) Code of Ethics provides for arbitration in Article 27 of the *Standards of Business Practice*:

> *In the event of a dispute between REALTORS associated with different firms of the same local Board/Association regarding the fee or commission earned or to be earned in connection with a real estate transaction, the dispute shall be submitted for arbitration in accordance with the By-laws, Rules and Regulations of their Real Estate Board/Association.*

The Code clearly states that a REALTOR must place such matters before the appropriate committee for resolution in accordance with the rules/regulations of the board. The requirement to arbitrate commission disputes is therefore a board matter since the by-laws and rules/regulations are a contract between the Board and its Members. See the Appendix for the CREA *Code of Ethics*.

ARBITRATION AND MEDIATION INSTITUTE OF CANADA

Acronym: AMIC   The AMIC is a not-for-profit institute founded in 1974 for the purposes of increasing profession-alism in the dispute resolution field through training and certification of arbitrators and mediators, public education, and the provision of National Rules for Commercial Arbitration and Rules for Commercial Mediation. Two designations are awarded by AMIC.

Chartered Arbitrator (C.Arb)   Experienced arbitrators who have demonstrated a certain level of education in the field and experience as arbitrators.

Chartered Mediator (C.Med)   Experienced mediators who have demonstrated a certain level of education in the field and experience as mediators.

Reference   Arbitration and Mediation Institute of Canada, 232-329 March Road, Kanata, ON   K2K 2E1.

ARCHITECT

A professional engaged in designing buildings and other structures, including the supervision of construction to ensure conformance to plans and specifications.

ARCHITECTURAL DRAWINGS

Drawings include architectural contractual materials relating to lot plans, floor plans, elevations, sections, details, schedules, any incidental architectural diagrams and specifications, and specialized data normally handled by consultants to the architect or owner.

Example *Architectural Drawings*

Buyer McKay is considering the purchase of a new home. While the listing provides a sketch, McKay wants to review the plans in detail, particularly the exterior appearance. Salesperson Jamieson, of XYZ Real Estate Ltd., obtains the architectural drawings from the builder. depicting the front and rear elevations of the new home including detailed measurements and specifications.

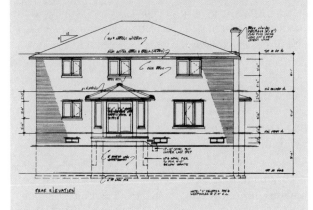

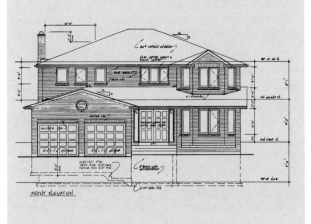

ARM'S LENGTH

A transaction freely arrived at in the open market, unaffected by abnormal pressure or by factors limiting competitive negotiations, as might be the case in a transaction between related parties.

Application Arm's length transactions are important in appraisals to reflect fair market value when making adjustments under the direct comparison approach and arriving at the estimated value of a subject property. These sales are also very important for various taxation matters relating to the purchase and sale of real estate.

A sale involving a nominal purchase price, which is transacted between family members, would not be considered at arm's length. Further, a disposition of property through transfer of title from both spouses to one spouse in a divorce settlement would not normally be conducted at arm's length.

Transactions through the Multiple Listing Service (MLS) are usually conducted at arm's length as the parties are typically unknown to each other, no abnormal pressure exists, and free market forces prevail.

ARREARS
(SEE ALSO DEFAULT)

The circumstance of being behind in payments. The term is commonly used with respect to delinquent payments under a mortgage document.

Example *Arrears*

Seller Smith has a $50,000 mortgage amortized over 25 years with regular monthly payments of $586.94 to include principal and interest. He has not made any payments on the mortgage for a period of three months. Accordingly, he is in arrears to the amount of (3 x 586.94) $1,760.82 plus interest.

ASBESTOS

Asbestos, a mineral fibre located in rock, is found in a variety of products including household and building supplies. Asbestos was widely used in construction from the early 1900s until the 1970s and is best known for its strengthening characteristics, thermal and acoustical insulation qualities, and fire retardant capabilities. The product is most frequently encountered in roofing materials, wall and pipe coverings, floor tiles, appliances, ceilings, patching compounds, textured paints, and door gaskets of stoves, furnaces, and ovens.

Chrysotile makes up about 90% of world asbestos production and trade. In Canada, chrysotile is the only type of asbestos mined. Canada accounts for about 20 percent of world chrysotile asbestos production and exports more than half a million tonnes of asbestos products (worth more than $300 million), to 60 countries every year. The chrysotile industry employs some 2,500 people, mainly in a 100-km strip in Québec's Eastern Townships extending from the town of Asbestos (site of the western world's largest known deposit), to East Broughton in the east. The industry also accounts for approximately 6,500 indirect jobs, the vast majority of which are in rural communities depending on a prosperous chrysotile asbestos industry.

Since 1979, Canada has been the champion of the *controlled-use* approach to asbestos. This approach is based on risk assessment and prohibits specific uses, such as asbestos-spraying, where workers cannot be protected. Several countries have supported Canada's position and the International Labour Organization and the World Health Organization have either adopted or supported this approach.

Classification

Asbestos is classified as friable and non-friable and is described as follows.

Friable   Material that is easily crumbled, pulverized, or reduced to powder by hand pressure. Friable material can be disrupted during renovation, repairs, cleaning, or related activities. Asbestos is most commonly seen in the form of a fluffy, spray-on material for fireproofing and insulating walls and ceilings. Another form is the fibrous grey paper used to wrap pipes and boilers for heat insulation. Lastly, asbestos can be found with a cement-like plaster appearance that was used for soundproofing and fire retardance.

Friable asbestos is dangerous as it can release fibres into the air that are not collected by furnace filters or vacuum cleaners. Inhalation of these airborne fibres can cause an accumulation in the lungs creating problems such as lung cancer or asbestosis, a degenerative lung disease.

Non-Friable   Asbestos may be found in pre-fabricated products typically containing bonding agents (e.g., painted cement sheets used around wood-burning stoves), that prevent any airborne dispersion of fibres unless the product is physically altered through sanding, drilling, or cutting. Non-friable asbestos comes in the form of wallboard (that looks like gypsum), and in exterior cladding for structures. These products only release hazardous fibres when broken or altered.

Detection/Measurement

Health studies indicate that asbestos fibre, once airborne, can become a serious health threat. Provincial responses to the detection and measurement of asbestos vary.

- In Ontario, exposure limits are currently being revised to align with the American Conference of Governmental Industrial Hygenists.
- In Nova Scotia, the acceptable level set out in the *Occupational Health and Safety Act* (administered by the Department of Labour), is 0.2 fibres per cubic centimetre.
- In Manitoba, the Workplace Health Hazard Regulation defines the occupational exposure limit of a designated material (asbestos is designated as such), as being the level close to zero as is reasonably practicable. For asbestos, the Workplace Safety and Health Division of the Manitoba Department of Labour utilizes 0.1 fibres per cubic centimetre of air as being *as close to zero as reasonably practicable.*
- In the United States, 0.2 fibres per cubic centimetre has been set as the permissible exposure limit over an eight-hour period.

Many provinces have classified asbestos as a hazardous product and passed strict regulations governing its removal and disposal. Asbestos testing and removal of asbestos-containing material is a specialized area of environmental management and should be conducted by suitably qualified environmental experts.

Application   Most difficulties in real estate arise from renovations undertaken in older buildings (usually pre-1980 structures). If alterations are contemplated, try to determine if the material contains asbestos. A qualified asbestos inspector should make the determination, however, failing this approach, plumbing, building, and heating contractors can often make a reasonable judgement. As a last resort, laboratory analysis is necessary.

An experienced contractor trained in the removal of asbestos is best. Asbestos analysis may be required to determine if asbestos in a friable condition is present within an on-site facility. If asbestos is confirmed in a friable condition, removal should be accomplished under a plan developed by an asbestos abatement specialist and any removal in compliance with the plan should be verified.

Asbestos in itself is not hazardous and is only a health risk when airborne. Given proper building maintenance and avoidance of unwarranted asbestos removal, the problem need not be exaggerated. However, friable forms of asbestos, e.g., crumbling insulation around plumbing pipes, can pose a real danger. Stringent guidelines exist for the removal of such material.

The use of asbestos in buildings has been banned in most provinces. In fact, many suppliers ceased using the product in 1973, coinciding with the ban on all spray applications during that same year.

Real estate practitioners may encounter this substance in various residential and commercial properties built prior to that date. Friable asbestos is the most dangerous. Here are a few items to look for:

- Insulated water pipes that are deteriorating (asbestos insulating materials for water pipes appeared in 1920 to the early 1970s).
- Ceiling or wall materials that are crumbling due to water damage.
- Old stove, oven, and furnace door gaskets.
- Homes built between 1930 and the mid-1950s may have insulation manufactured with asbestos.
- Dated fluffy sprayed-on materials may contain asbestos.
- Older homes (pre-1980), may have asbestos and should be more closely inspected (recommend a home inspection).

Persons contemplating renovation work may have problems with the removal of asbestos. Practitioners should be prepared to generally discuss the issue of friable and non-friable asbestos with consumers.

ASSEMBLAGE

(SEE ALSO PLOTTAGE)

The combining of two or more abutting parcels of land into one ownership or use for the purpose of greater utility.

Application   The assembly of land is most commonly associated with suburban developments in which large tracts of land are acquired and merged for residential subdivisions. However, assemblage is an ongoing process in a variety of locations as existing residential neighbourhoods are redeveloped. Smaller parcels of land are combined to form the basis for new commercial ventures, and downtown core areas undergo transformations from small buildings to larger structures requiring greater land areas.

Practitioners occasionally confuse *assemblage* with *plottage value*. Plottage value refers to an incremental value owing to the merging process. Assemblage is merely the process of combining properties and could result in either an increase in value (plottage value), or a decrease in unit value owing to the creation of excess land. Presumably, most assembly activities proceed on the basis that plottage value will occur.

Example   *Assemblage*

Seller Smith wishes to acquire the extra lot abutting his residential site for the purpose of building a larger, irregular shaped swimming pool at the same time his new home is being constructed. The increased pool size will not add substantial value. In fact, the merged property will create excess land with no economic benefit as a whole. This form of assemblage is referred to as *excess land*. If the owner had acquired the adjacent property to build a larger home, the value of the entire lot and house, as a total entity, might well increase and the assemblage can be referred to as *plottage*.

ASSESSMENT

Property assessment is a measure of *current* or *market value* [provincial terminology will vary somewhat], established for the purpose of apportioning local taxes within a municipality. Assessment is used to determine the property owner's share of taxes.

Application   Practitioners are routinely asked questions regarding taxation issues in relation to listed properties and must be capable of explaining calculations, the assessment process, and rights of appeal.

Calculation   Municipalities raise money to provide services such as garbage pick-up, sewers, new roads and repairs, police, and education. Most of this funding comes from property taxes. Property taxes are calculated based on a tax rate (typically a percentage factor, but mill rates are still used in some jurisdictions).

The tax rate is established by dividing the budget for the current year by the total assessment. Different rates are applied to various classifications of property, e.g., residential, multi-unit residential, industrial, commercial, and farmland. The property classification structure varies by province but the intent is the same.

Assessed Value   The value of a property according to the tax rolls. Market value and assessed value do not necessarily coincide although assessed value is usually based on market valuation using sales of comparable properties. Assessment authorities update assessed values on a periodic basis to ensure fair valuation.

Assessment Process   The ongoing process of inspections, reviews, and statutory general reassessments. The assessment roll is the official record of real property assessments and may be revised each year. The roll normally contains a roll number (numeric identifier), name(s) of the owner(s), municipal address and legal description, assessed value of land and improvements, and applicable codes. An assessment notice is then sent out to each owner shown on the roll during a general assessment. If revisions to the official assessment roll are required between general assessments, notification by way of an assessment notice is sent to the property owner. An assessment notice is not a demand for payment of taxes, but merely sets out the assessed value of the property for the ensuing year. The total of the assessed value of all the individual properties on the roll provides the base for property taxation.

Improvements   One of the anomalies of a tax on real property is that, in theory, critics argue it discourages the improvement of property. The basis for assessment is the fair *current* or *market value* of the property. If value goes up, the taxes may increase. Additions or installations can affect property assessment to the extent that they increase the fair market value of the property as calculated by the assessor, e.g., the addition of a sunroom or an outdoor swimming pool, extensive remodelling, the addition/ enlargement of a garage, or the creation of a recreation room. Not all improvements to a property are assessed for taxation purposes, for example, normal repair and maintenance, landscaping, lawns, shrubs, fencing, private sidewalks, or private driveways.

In planning personal finances, the actual or prospective owner of a home that requires extensive improvements should allow not only for installments on any loan required to finance work but also for the possible increase in municipal taxes as a result of that work.

Appeal   Municipalities forward assessment notices in the early part of the applicable taxation year. Property owners who feel the assessment is incorrect or unfair may appeal to the applicable provincial appeal board. Generally, taxpayers cannot dispute taxes, only the assessment on the property. In most provinces, the appeal process is commenced by completing and forwarding the appropriate section of the assessment notice within a specified time limit.

Typically, the appeal is first assigned to an assessor who contacts the property owner to review the assessment and address matters of concern. This may result in either an increasing or decreasing adjustment, along with an amended assessment notice; or the appeal may be withdrawn once the assessment is fully explained to the property owner's satisfaction. If the owner is dissatisfied, the appeal is forwarded to an appeal board. Appeal boards in Canada are established as impartial, quasi-judicial bodies that have the responsibility to hear assessment appeals with regard to assessed value.

Provincial   See applicable reference materials.

ASSET

Any physical property or right that is owned and has a monetary value, generally appearing as one of the major categories on a financial balance sheet.

Assets are economic resources that are owned by a business and are expected to benefit future operations. They may have definite physical form such as buildings, equipment, or office furniture, or be intangible such as accounts receivable, investments in government bonds, or a patent.

Example   *Asset*

Buyer Patton, a registered real estate broker, is analyzing the assets from the balance sheet of ABC Realty Inc., a local real estate operation currently listed for sale. As the illustration reveals, the corporation has total assets of $408,013 consisting of $131,613 in current assets and $276,400 in fixed assets.

Patton, in the review process, will have many other factors to consider in the decision-making process; e.g., listing inventory, number of salespeople, and volume of sales.

ABC Realty Inc.
Balance Sheet
as at December 31, 20xx

Assets

Current Assets		
Cash	$71,500	
Commissions Receivable	41,328	
Prepaid Expenses	3,785	
Short Term Deposit	15,000	
Total Current Assets		$131,613
Fixed Assets		
Office Building	270,000	
Computer Equipment	18,500	
Office Equipment	25,000	
Less Accumulated Amortization	(37,100)	
Total Fixed Assets		276,400
TOTAL ASSETS		**$408,013**
Liabilities and Equity		
Current Liabilities		
Expenses Payable	2,200	
Commissions Due	31,234	
Accounts Payable	21,242	
Taxes Payable (Fed. and Prov.)	432	
Total Current Liabilities		55,108
Long Term Liabilities		
Mortgage	106,500	
Notes Payable	10,000	
Total Long Term Liabilities		116,500
Equity		
Retained Earnings		236,405
TOTAL LIABILITIES AND EQUITY		**$408,013**

ASSET LEASING

Assets can be purchased outright, financed through a loan, or leased by a financial or operating lease. The difference between the two leases revolves around cancellation provisions. A financial lease cannot be cancelled at any time and must confer ownership within a reasonable period, or be of such a length that the lessee will derive all the benefits of ownership from its useful lifespan. An operating lease may be terminated provided that proper notice is given. Often, an operating lease is referred to as a *rental lease*, a good example of which is telephone equipment within a brokerage office.

Application The decision on leasing or purchasing assets will depend on a variety of factors. Considerations are illustrated in Figure A.24. The effect of inflation has not been addressed.

ASSET MANAGEMENT

A sophisticated form of property management under which the managing agent organizes and operates the total real estate venture and whose concern extends beyond net operating income.

ASSIGNEE

An individual or firm that takes the right or title of another by assignment. The assignee's rights are found in common law, however, provincial statutes may impact such rights, e.g., tenancies and mortgages. In residential tenancy legislation for example, landlords cannot typically refuse an assignment on an arbitrary or unreasonable basis.

ADVANTAGES	DISADVANTAGES
Purchasing the Asset Outright	
• Purchase price is known.	• Outright purchase may seriously affect cash flow.
• Buyer may negotiate a better deal by paying cash.	• Technology may change before the value of the asset has been fully recovered.
• No monthly payments.	• Registered loan may affect ability to arrange other financing.
• Item is owned and reflected as an asset on financial statements.	
• Asset may be pledged as security.	
• Capital cost allowance can be claimed.	
Financing the Asset	
• Purchase price may be negotiable.	• Monthly payment obligation.
• Set interest rate may be negotiable.	• Chattel mortgage usually registered.
• No large capital outlay.	• Owner may be required to make a substantial downpayment from personal funds.
• Asset is owned subject to the lien.	• Asset cannot be pledged as security until the loan is fully paid.
• Interest is deductible.	
Financial Lease	
• Avoids the risks of obsolescence. If the original cost of the asset is completely amortized during the lease, then the risk is passed on to the business.	• Unless written into the lease agreement, the residual value of the asset (if any) passes back to the lessor at the end of the term.
• Can acquire the asset without a downpayment.	• Interest cost of leasing is typically higher than the interest cost of debt.
• Lease payments are 100% tax deductible.	• Lessee is responsible for all lease payments under the terms of the contract and, if problems arise, may be forced to buy-out the lease.
• Lease obligation doesn't appear on the balance sheet as a debt and can have a favourable effect when calculating financial ratios.	

Asset Acquisition vs. Lease   Figure A.24

A

Example   *Assignee*

Thompson is actively involved in mortgage investments. McKay is the mortgagee for a first mortgage in the amount of $25,000 bearing interest at 8% and due in four years. McKay prefers to have the cash and wishes to assign all rights under the mortgage to Thompson in return for a cash payment. Accordingly, Thompson pays McKay $21,000 for the mortgage and McKay signs over all rights.

ASSIGNMENT

The transfer of rights in a contract, usually in writing, to another party. The general rule of law is that all contracts are assignable with certain rare exceptions, e.g., personal service contracts are not generally assignable.

Assignment of Mortgage

A frequent assignment situation in real estate involves mortgages. The original mortgagee, may decide to sell the mortgage to another lender by way of an assignment document. This transfer assigns the registered mortgage as well as all rights to collect outstanding amounts due under the mortgage. The amount payable for an assignment will vary depending on how favourable the terms of the original mortgage are in comparison with market conditions at point of sale.

If the current rates are higher than the stated rate on the mortgage, then the mortgagee will probably have to discount the mortgage face value to make the offering attractive to potential assignees. The discount has the net effect of raising the overall yield. Conversely, an investor might pay additional monies to the mortgagee if the mortgage has an interest rate substantially higher than current rates.

Assignment of Agreement/Contract

An assignment may also occur in an agreement/contract involving the sale of real estate. If a buyer contemplates the assignment of rights to a corporation or other party prior to closing, a possible clause in the agreement/contract might be:

The buyer shall have the right at any time prior to closing, to assign the within offer to any person, persons or corporation, and upon delivery to the seller of notice of such assignment, together with the assignee's covenant in favour of the seller to be bound hereby as buyer, the buyer hereinbefore named shall stand released from all further liability hereunder.

The seller must carefully consider this type of assignment as no recourse against the original buyer is possible. This clause should not be used when the agreement/contract involves a *seller-take-back* mortgage. An alternate wording to better protect the seller follows:

The buyer covenants and agrees that he or she shall in no way directly or indirectly assign, rent, lease, convey, list or in any way advertise for sale, sell, or otherwise transfer his or her rights under this Agreement prior to the completion date to any other person without the express written consent of the seller. Such consent may be granted or withheld at the seller's sole option.

Liabilities *vs.* Rights

As a general rule, liabilities under a contract cannot be assigned by the party obligated, so as to compel the other party to accept performance by an unrelated third party. However, liability can be assigned if there is express consent or an implied intention of the parties to permit the assignment. The courts may hold that such an intention was implied if the obligation does not involve a special personal qualification, and if it was immaterial that the obligation was performed by someone other than the person originally liable.

Rights, as opposed to liabilities, under a contract can generally be assigned except where, for reasons of confidence between the parties or personal qualifications, such action would increase or change the obligations. For example, in a seller take-back mortgage, the court will not imply an intention to permit an assignment without the consent of that seller.

ASSIGNMENT OF LEASE
(SEE LEASE)

ASSIGNMENT OF MORTGAGE
(SEE MORTGAGE)

ASSIGNOR

An individual or firm who transfers or assigns rights or title to another. The assignor's rights are found in common law, however, provincial legislation may impact such rights, e.g., tenancies and mortgages.

ASSOCIATE OF CANADIAN CONDOMINIUM INSTITUTE

Acronym: ACCI   The Canadian Condominium Institute (CCI) awards the ACCI designation. CCI, formed in 1982, is an independent, non-profit organization with chapters throughout Canada. A person seeking the ACCI designation must be a member in good standing of the CCI Chapter through which application is made. To qualify for the designation, the individual must have five years' experience selling condominiums, have contributed to the condominium community at large, be professionally recognized, and have signed the Code of Ethics. Approval procedures do not require course attendance, however, recommendation from the CCI local chapter to write the examination, which covers all aspects of condominium knowledge and the *Condominium Act*, is required.

Reference   The Canadian Condominium Institute can be contacted at Suite 310, 2175 Sheppard Avenue East, North York, ON M2J 1W8.

Information furnished was summarized from detailed materials provided by the Institute with no representation concerning its accuracy or completeness. Contact CCI for current chapter locations and requirements.

ASSUMPTION OF MORTGAGE

(SEE MORTGAGE)

AUCTIONEER

An individual who conducts a public sale of property and/or goods to the highest bidder, which may be subject to restrictions by the seller. Real estate brokers may conduct auctions of real property provided they comply with local municipal regulations and applicable provincial real estate legislation.

Legislative control of auctioneers and exemptions under applicable legislation varies by province. In Ontario, auctioneers are exempted under the *Real Estate and Business Brokers Act (REBBA)* and may conduct sales of real property under certain circumstances. Section 5 of REBBA reads as follows:

> *Registration shall not be required in respect of any trade in real estate by,…(b) an auctioneer where the trade is made in the course of and as part of the auctioneer's duties as auctioneer. (REBBA, R.S.O. 1990 c. R-4.)*

In certain provinces, the auctioneer is exempted from registration provided that he/she is performing duties at an auction sale, since the auctioneer is only seeking the highest bid and is not actually selling the property. Any offers or deposits obtained after the highest bidder has been ascertained by the auctioneer falls beyond the scope of the auctioneer unless he/she is licensed under the applicable provincial real estate act.

Application   Auctioneers point to various benefits of auctioning real estate, but generally emphasize the competitive bidding environment, the removal of an artificial ceiling on the asking price, and the immediate binding contract that can flow from an auction. Normally, the auctioneer operates under an auction authority that is an agreement between the seller and auctioneer. This document sets out the conditions under which a fee is earned and the length of the agreement.

In addition, auctioneers usually prepare an auctioning plan or strategy regarding advertising and promotion, the type of information to be contained in the bidder's information package, the plan for showings, and auction location. A substantial number of resources are available for practitioners contemplating auctioning activities such as the National Auctioneers Association and the Certified Auctioneers Institute (both US organizations).

Generally, three types of auctions exist in the real estate marketplace:

- The *absolute auction* is without a minimum reserve bid for the seller. This type of auction normally attracts the widest interest since a sale is virtually guaranteed with no restrictions or limitations on the final selling price.
- The *minimum bid* auction provides a safety net for the seller. He/she can establish the minimum acceptable sale price. Obviously, the amount of interest in the sale is many times directly related to the minimum bid. A minimum well below market value should attract proportionately more interest.
- The *auction by confirmation* permits the seller to reject any final high bid price.

Provincial   See applicable reference materials.

AUDIT

Independent examination of the accounting records and other evidence relating to a business to support the expression of an impartial expert opinion about the fairness and reliability of financial statements. Upon completion of an audit, an auditor's report is issued that accompanies the financial statements of a business. This report from the auditor attests that the auditing steps taken during the verification of accounting records meet the approved standards of auditing practice and that the financial statements are prepared in conformity with generally accepted accounting principles.

AUTHORITY

The legal power or right given by a principal and accepted by the agent to act on the principal's behalf in business transactions with a third party.

Application   The listing agreement is the most common form of authority delegated to real estate brokerages. Wordings for this authority vary as no standard form prevails throughout Canada. However, most set out similar basic responsibilities concerning the marketing of the property, payment of commission for its sale, lease, exchange or option, and authority to co-operate with other brokerages.

A typical introductory wording for an exclusive listing authority is provided:

> *I [the seller] hereby give you the exclusive and irrevocable right to act as my agent to lease or sell the Property until 11:59 p.m. on the __ day of _____, 20xx for the price of _____ Canadian Dollars ($Can), and upon the terms particularly set out herein, or at such other price or terms acceptable to me. It is understood that the price set out above is at my personal request, after full discussion with your representative regarding potential market value of the property.*

Most listing forms then detail various responsibilities and obligations flowing from this authority, such as:

- Commission payable for the marketing of property on terms and conditions as set out in the listing or as otherwise accepted.
- Agency relationship including the right to co-operate with any other brokerage.
- Referral of inquiries by the seller from any source whatsoever to the brokerage.
- Permission to show prospective purchasers and market the property including the placement of a *for sale* sign.

Provincial   See applicable reference materials.

AUTHORIZED OFFICIAL

The applicable provincial real estate act/regulations may identify certain licensees/registrants or others employed or appointed by the broker who are authorized to act on behalf of the brokerage. Most commonly, authorization is extended to a branch manager employed by the brokerage and registered under the applicable real estate legislation to act on behalf of the brokerage.

An authorized official is typically appointed and employed by a broker and does not receive a registration certificate, but is named on the employing broker's certificate. The existence of an authorized official is not generally found in Canada and is specific to the Province of Manitoba. Other similar arrangements may exist in other provinces.

Provincial   See applicable reference materials.

AUTOMATIC RENEWAL CLAUSE

A provision commonly associated with a commercial lease provision that automatically ensures renewal of the lease unless either the tenant or the landlord notifies the other party of a desire to terminate the agreement.

An automatic renewal clause should not be confused with a renewal option. The latter provides the right, but not the obligation, to continue the lease on terms and conditions as set out in that option.

Example   *Automatic Renewal Clause*

Tenant Jones wants to ensure a continued commercial tenancy and Landlord Smith is interested in minimum involvement with the property. The parties conclude that they will essentially agree until they disagree concerning the property. Consequently, an automatic renewal clause is inserted in the lease agreement. A typical wording follows:

> *The lessee, when not in default hereunder, shall have the right to an automatic renewal of the lease for successive one year periods commencing at the first anniversary date of the lease unless written notice of termination is provided by either party to the other sixty (60) days prior to the anniversary date of the lease in any particular year. Upon such notice, vacant possession of the property shall be granted to the lessor by the lessee as of that particular anniversary date.*

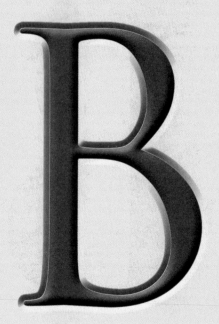

National Info Links

Building Codes

For national model building codes and related research, contact:

    Institute for Research in Construction
      Web Site   www.nrc.ca

For details regarding provincial regulations contact the appropriate provincial ministry/department.

Building Management

    BOMI Canada
    415 Yonge Street, Suite 901
    Toronto, ON M5B 2E7

    Telephone   (416) 977-8700
     Web Site   www.bomi-edu.org

Business Financial and Management Services

    Business Development Bank of Canada
    BDC Building
    5 Place Ville Marie
    Montreal, PQ H3B 5E7

    Telephone   (514) 283 7515
                    (800) 463 6232
    Web Site   www.bdc.ca

BACTERIOLOGICAL ANALYSIS

(SEE ALSO WATER)

A service normally provided by provincial governments or contracted agencies to establish the coliform and fecal counts present in water. Methods and standards for bacteriological analysis vary by provincial jurisdiction.

Provincial   See applicable reference materials.

BALANCE DUE ON COMPLETION

(SEE ALSO ADJUSTMENTS)

The amount of money that the buyer is required to pay the seller to complete the purchase of real estate after all adjustments have been made, and trust deposits (if applicable) have been deducted; frequently referred to as balance due on closing.

BALANCE, PRINCIPLE OF

(SEE PRINCIPLES (APPRAISAL))

BALANCE SHEET

(SEE ALSO FINANCIAL STATEMENTS)

A statement of the financial position of a business at a specific date by summarizing assets, liabilities, and shareholder's (owner's) equity. The balance sheet provides information concerning the resources of a corporation including claims against those resources and is grouped under three categories. **Figure B.1** illustrates a typical brokerage balance sheet.

Assets   Resources acquired from which future benefit may be obtained and ordered based on decreasing liquidity. Items least capable of being converted into cash are listed last.

Liabilities   Obligations arising from past transactions, typically ordered based on time of maturity with the longest dates listed last. However, exceptions apply.

Shareholder's (Owner's) Equity   Remaining interest of the owner after all liabilities are deducted from assets. Equity items are usually listed in terms of permanency; in other words, capital contribution amounts are listed prior to accumulated earnings.

ABC Realty Inc.
Balance Sheet
as at December 31, 20xx

Assets

Current Assets		
Cash	$71,500	
Commissions Receivable	41,328	
Prepaid Expenses	3,785	
Short Term Deposit	15,000	
Total Current Assets		$131,613
Fixed Assets		
Office Building	270,000	
Computer Equipment	18,500	
Office Equipment	25,000	
Less Accumulated Amortization	(37,100)	
Total Fixed Assets		276,400
TOTAL ASSETS		**$408,013**

Liabilities and Equity

Current Liabilities		
Expenses Payable	2,200	
Commissions Due	31,234	
Accounts Payable	21,242	
Taxes Payable (Fed. and Prov.)	432	
Total Current Liabilities		55,108
Long Term Liabilities		
Mortgage	106,500	
Notes Payable	10,000	
Total Long Term Liabilities		116,500
Equity		
Retained Earnings		236,405
TOTAL LIABILITIES AND EQUITY		**$408,013**

Balance Sheet   Figure B.1

BALLOON PAYMENT

A final payment on a mortgage at its maturity date to pay off the debt in full. See **Figure B.2** for a typical five-year Canadian mortgage in which a balance is due on the 60th payment amounting to $48,887.41.

BAND OF INVESTMENT

(SEE ALSO CAPITALIZATION)

A means of estimating the value of property through the use of an overall capitalization rate (or a discount rate), that represents the weighted average of selected components of the property being valued.

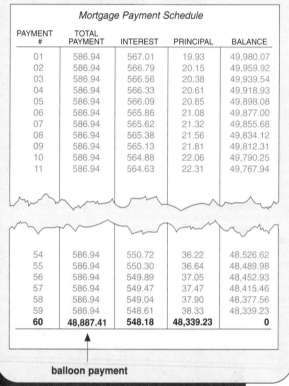

Scenario

A mortgage of $50,000 is calculated semi-annually not in advance at a rate of 14% per annum with a 25-year amortization and a 5-year term. The mortgagor is required to make 59 payments of $586.94. At the end of the term, the balloon payment required to fully retire the debt is $48,887.41.

Mortgage Payment Schedule

PAYMENT #	TOTAL PAYMENT	INTEREST	PRINCIPAL	BALANCE
01	586.94	567.01	19.93	49,980.07
02	586.94	566.79	20.15	49,959.92
03	586.94	566.56	20.38	49,939.54
04	586.94	566.33	20.61	49,918.93
05	586.94	566.09	20.85	49,898.08
06	586.94	565.86	21.08	49,877.00
07	586.94	565.62	21.32	49,855.68
08	586.94	565.38	21.56	49,834.12
09	586.94	565.13	21.81	49,812.31
10	586.94	564.88	22.06	49,790.25
11	586.94	564.63	22.31	49,767.94
54	586.94	550.72	36.22	48,526.62
55	586.94	550.30	36.64	48,489.98
56	586.94	549.89	37.05	48,452.93
57	586.94	549.47	37.47	48,415.46
58	586.94	549.04	37.90	48,377.56
59	586.94	548.61	38.33	48,339.23
60	**48,887.41**	**548.18**	**48,339.23**	**0**

balloon payment

Figure B.2   Balloon Payment

The band of investment technique is most frequently associated with mortgage/equity and land/building components, although other approaches are possible. For example, in recent years, risk and probability theorists have applied the band of investment concept to arrive at a weighted average discount rate when discounting future cash flows to arrive at an estimate of present value. The discount rate is constructed based on the probability of various events occurring in the marketplace.

Application   For real estate practitioners, the band of investment method is typically used with equity and mortgage components to arrive at an overall capitalization rate. The formula applied is:

$$R_o = (M \times R_m) + (1-M)(R_e)$$

Where: R_o = Overall Capitalization Rate
M = Mortgage Ratio
R_m = Mortgage Capitalization Rate (Constant)
R_e = Equity Capitalization Rate

Salesperson Lane is estimating the value of a multi-residential property based on equity and mortgage components. Her research indicates that an equity capitalization rate of 12% (.12) and a mortgage capitalization rate (mortgage constant) of 8.97% (.0897) is appropriate. Properties of this type normally have an equity to mortgage ratio of 25/75. Therefore, the overall capitalization rate is:

$$R_o = (M \times R_m) + (1-M)(R_e)$$
$$= (.75 \times .0897) + (.25 \times .12)$$
$$= .097275 \text{ (rounded to .0973 or 9.73\%)}$$

If the net operating income of this property is $39,872, then the estimate of value would be:

$$\$39,872 \div .0973 = \$409,784 \text{ (rounded to \$410,000)}$$

BANK PARTITION

A form of space divider usually made of steel and glass and extending approximately five to six feet up from the floor, rather than completely extended to the ceiling.

Application   Bank partitions are most commonly found in commercial office space and are designed to provide a form of privacy for work areas while not significantly impairing air circulation and maintaining some degree of open concept within an overall floor layout.

BANK RECONCILIATION

An accounting of the items that make up the difference between the balance shown on a bank statement and the balance of cash according to the depositor's records. The purpose of reconciling the bank statement is to provide assurances that the bank and the depositor are in agreement concerning the amount of money on deposit. A bank statement total may vary from a brokerage's book total due to issued cheques which have been recorded but not cashed and deposits which have been recorded but have not been received by the bank. Reconciliation is necessary because the bank and the depositor are maintaining independent records of the bank account activity and differences must be accounted for (*reconciled*).

Application   Real estate brokerages are required to perform a monthly reconciliation of their real estate trust account(s). The format will vary by provincial jurisdiction, but most dictate a reconciliation containing the following elements.

- A balance as per the bank statement less any outstanding cheques which are usually recorded by date, cheque number, and amount.
- The addition of outstanding deposits which are normally recorded by date, trade number, address, and amount.
- The calculation of balance per bank statement, less outstanding cheques, plus outstanding deposits to arrive at the reconciled bank balance that must equal the balance for the bank account according to the brokerage books of account.

Example *Bank Reconciliation*

A typical bank reconciliation is provided for ABC Realty Inc. outlining two schedules: Schedule A represents the reconciliation of the bank account, and Schedule B outlines the list of client deposits currently held by the brokerage. The illustration complies with provincial requirements for the Province of Ontario as set out in the *Real Estate and Business Brokers Act*. Provincial requirements will vary.

ABC Realty Inc.
Bank Reconciliation of Real Estate Trust Account
As at May, 20xx

Schedule A: Reconciliation of Bank Account

Balance as per Bank Statement May 31, 20xx		$105,800
Less: Outstanding Cheques:		
Cheque #00839	$9,000	
Cheque #00842	5,000	
Cheque #00847	3,000	
Total Outstanding Cheques		−17,000
Add: Outstanding Deposits		
May 31, 20xx Trade #152 389 Leslie	7,600	
Total Outstanding Deposits		+7,600
Reconciled Bank Balance as at May 31, 20xx		**$96,400**

ABC Realty Inc.
Bank Reconciliation of Real Estate Trust Account
As at May, 20xx

Schedule B: List of Client Deposits

Trade #128	3648 Dundas St. W.	$10,000
Trade #136	825 Martindale Road	15,000
Trade #137	260 Donald Street	20,000
Trade #138	2838 Valley Cres.	13,000
Trade #141	360 Mason Ave.	10,000
Trade #148	1931 Burlington Ave.	5,000
Trade #149	123 Main Street	10,800
Trade #150	791 Westcott Street	5,000
Trade #152	389 Leslie Street	7,600
Total List of Client Deposits		**$96,400**

- A schedule of all client deposits now held in the trust account must agree with the reconciled bank balance. Client deposits are normally recorded by date, trade (transaction) number, address of property, and amount.
- Signature of the broker attesting that the reconciliation is correct.

Provincial   See applicable reference materials.

BANKED ELEVATORS

A group of elevators adjacent to each other located within a specific demised enclosure.

Application   The location of banked elevators will vary based on intended use. Elevators in commercial buildings are normally situated in a centre-core or side-core area. *Core* refers to the area that houses elevators, mechanical systems, electrical services, housekeeping facilities, and washrooms. The centre-core structure appears most efficient for multiple tenant floor plans while the side-core provides more open space for a large, single tenant. The side-core arrangement is proving popular with the growing use of regional/national distribution and call centres in which large groups of employees are concentrated within an open landscaped arrangement.

BANKRUPTCY

A circumstance in which a debtor is unable to meet financial obligations to creditors or when liabilities exceed realizable assets. A debtor, unable to satisfy valid financial claims against himself/herself, may seek the protection of bankruptcy laws. Alternatively, the creditors of that debtor may also sue a debtor in court, obtain a judgment, and seek to satisfy the judgment by having the debtor's assets seized.

Application   The *Bankruptcy and Insolvency Act* applies to individuals as well as limited companies, partnerships, and individual proprietors who carry on business in Canada. Bankruptcy is assigned to the jurisdiction of the federal Parliament under the *Constitution Act* and, accordingly, the *Bankruptcy and Insolvency Act* is a federal statute.

The *Bankruptcy and Insolvency Act* sets out various types of conduct that constitute an act of bankruptcy by a debtor.

- Assignment of assets to a trustee where the repayment arrangement is unsatisfactory to the creditors.
- Fraudulent transfer of assets to a third party other than a trustee in anticipation of bankruptcy.

B

- Fraudulent preference or payment by a debtor that has the effect of settling the claim of one creditor in preference to the valid claims of other creditors.
- An attempt by the debtor to abscond.
- A failure to redeem goods seized under an execution issued against the debtor.
- Presentation at a meeting of creditors of a statement of assets and liabilities disclosing the debtor's insolvency or a written admission by the debtor that he/she is unable to pay debts.
- Any attempt to remove or hide property.
- Notice to any of the creditors that the debtor is suspending payment of debts.
- Default in any proposal that the debtor has previously persuaded the creditors to accept as a means of forestalling bankruptcy proceedings.
- A failure to meet liabilities as they become due.

The *Bankruptcy and Insolvency Act* performs three main tasks for debtors and creditors.

- Establishes a uniform practice in bankruptcy proceedings throughout the country.
- Provides for an equitable distribution of the debtor's assets among creditors.
- Provides for the release or discharge of an honest, but unfortunate, debtor from obligations to permit the resumption of business activities subject to certain stipulations.

Provincial   See applicable reference materials. Bankruptcy procedures are highly technical and complex. Seek information from appropriate legal counsel and/or a licensed trustee.

BANKRUPTCY TRANSMISSION

Under bankruptcy, assets of the debtor vest in the name of the trustee in bankruptcy.

Application   Every conveyance by a trustee in bankruptcy requires first that title to the land be vested in the name of the trustee. A transmission application is used in conjunction with an affidavit of the trustee and a certified copy of the assignment of receiving order. These documents are filed in the land registry or land titles office depending on the province. Upon the assignment being filed with an official receiver, the bankrupt person ceases to have any capacity to dispose of or otherwise deal with his/her property.

BARE LAND CONDOMINIUM UNIT

A condominium corporation in which the condominium plan shows only the boundaries of the property without buildings, and registration of the condominium can be effected prior to construction of any buildings.

Provincial   See applicable reference materials. The existence, terms, and procedures concerning bare land (also referred to as *vacant land condominiums*), will vary by provincial jurisdiction.

BASE LEASE

A contract, i.e., lease agreement, setting out minimum tenancy requirements applicable to all tenants. Base leases are used in both residential and commercial properties.

Application   A base lease typically contains minimum rents, services provided, allocation of common areas, and other items common to all tenants. While precise wordings vary, certain elements are present in all leases. As with an agreement/contract or a mortgage, the lease must contain specific information, the lack of which could render the agreement invalid. The elements are:

- Names of all parties;
- Description of the leased premises;
- Statement of consideration;
- Legality of use;
- Commencement and expiration dates; and
- Rights and obligations of the parties, e.g., restrictions, additional costs, and exclusive covenants as governed by the particular circumstances.

Failure to specify the above in sufficient detail and clarity can result in problems irrespective of legal issues surrounding the drafting of a lease.

The base lease is best described as a general form of agreement designed to suit as many tenants and requirements as is practical given the specific nature of the property being leased. Special tailoring of the base lease is necessary, particularly in the commercial field, for tenants with diverse demands and amendments. In a multi-tenancy complex, i.e., office building, the base lease normally includes a multi-page document and various schedules.

Figure B.3 illustrates the major topics addressed in a typical shopping centre lease. The table of contents refers to four schedules common to many commercial leases. A brief description of each follows.

Schedule A–Premises

A large scale building plan or floor plan shows the exact configuration of the leased premise, together with all mechanical details. The plan is typically required by the tenant's interior designer or architect as the basis for detailed interior construction plans for submission to, and approval by, the landlord.

Schedule B–Land (Site Plan)

A plot plan or site plan showing the overall lands, dimensions, access and egress systems, boundary roads or highways, parking, loading facilities, and the building located thereon, together with common areas. The demised or leased premises will be outlined on the site plan.

Schedule C–Landlord's and Tenant's Work

A detailed breakdown of work to be completed, based on drawings by the tenant and approved by the landlord.

Generally, the landlord's work relates to structural items while the tenant's work focuses on the leased area and the installation of mechanical and structural improvements. Special requirements and provisions of the landlord are normally outlined in this schedule. The scope of landlord and tenant work will vary significantly as terms are subject to negotiations between the parties concerning the lease.

Schedule D–Rules and Regulations

The detailing of rules and regulations governing the operation of the complex including maintenance requirements (e.g., keeping interior/exterior clean, maintaining mechanical apparatus, and refraining from undue accumulation of garbage and packing boxes), and agreeing not to undertake certain activities (e.g., kitchen facilities, maintaining stipulated hours of operation, and adhering to various property management requirements).

BASE LINE
(SEE ALSO MERIDIAN LINE)

A line running in an east-west direction used by surveyors in conjunction with a north-south line (meridian) to locate and describe property. Base and meridian lines are used in rectangular surveys common to Western Canada in which all land descriptions relate the north-south meridian line to its east-west base line.

Base Lease Components
Shopping Centre

Intent of Lease	Signs and Advertising
Premises	Landlord's Signs
Shopping Centre	Painting, Decorating, and Displays
Term	
Deferment of Opening	Changes and Additions to the Shopping Centre
Failure to Open	
Specifications	Scaffolds
Allocation of Utilities	Damage to Premises
Heating and Air-conditioning	Damage to the Shopping Centre
Tenant's Repairs	Architects Certificate
Waste or Nuisance	Expropriation
Landlord's Repairs	Inspections by Landlords
Tenant to Notify	Advertising
Alterations by Tenant	Time of Essence
Injuries and Damage	Entire Agreement
Indemnity	Interpretation

Schedules

Schedule A—Premises
Schedule B—Lands
Schedule C—Landlord's and Tenant's Work
Schedule D—Rules and Regulations

Base Lease Components   Figure B.3

BASE RENT
(SEE ALSO ADDITIONAL RENT)

The minimum rent payable by the tenant under a lease as distinguished from additional rents associated with operating costs and from percentage rent.

Application   In commercial property, base rent was often referred to as a *net/net/net lease* or a *triple net lease*. Such terms proved confusing in the marketplace as net and net/net arrangements were also used. Real estate practitioners now commonly refer to such rent as simply *base rent* or *minimum rent*. Base rent is an amount payable based on the rentable square foot/square metre area of the demised premises. Base rent should not be confused with additional rents that typically involve other expenses borne by the tenant in relation to the overall maintenance and operation of the building. A typical lease wording for base rent involving an office complex follows:

B

The tenant will throughout the term pay to the landlord at its head office, or at any other place designated by the landlord, in Canadian funds, without demand and without deduction, abatement, or compensation, as Base Rent, the annual sum of $48,000 payable in equal consecutive monthly installments of $4,000 each in advance on the first day of each calendar month. The Base Rent is calculated by applying the annual rate of $4.00 per square foot to the rentable area of the premises.

It is also customary, when describing the base or minimum rent in a lease, to set out provisions for pro-rating any partial month, postdated cheques in each consecutive year of the lease term, and a penalty for any cheques that are not honoured when presented.

BASE YEAR

The year of a lease term (or other point in time), used as the standard or benchmark when applying an escalator clause or some form of an index to calculate incremental changes in lease payments.

Application   Typically, an escalator clause sets out the year for comparison (base year) and then provides for annual rental adjustments based on a formula using the Consumer Price Index (CPI) or a comparable inflation measurement. The formula stipulated in the lease also provides for the frequency of adjustment and any limitations or ceilings for such calculations using the base year. The base year can also be used to establish expense limits paid by the landlord, with subsequent amounts being the tenant's responsibility.

Example   *Base Year*

Lessor Wong owns a small commercial plaza and leased a 2,000 square foot office to ABC Realty Inc. The parties agreed that the rental would be $17.00 per square foot per year for a 5-year term subject to increases based on the Consumer Price Index (CPI). Therefore, the base year rent for calculation purposes is:

$17.00 x 2,000 = $34,000 (total yearly rent payable)

In the following year, assuming that the CPI increases by 1.7% (0.017), rent per square foot for that year would be:

$17.00 + ($17.00 x 0.017) = $17.29 (rounded)

The total yearly rent would then be:

$17.29 x 2,000 = $34,580

BASEMENT
(SEE ALSO DAMP-PROOFING)

That part of a building that is either wholly or partially below ground level.

Design

Building codes set out requirements for structural components, including basements, to ensure sufficient structural capacity and integrity that will effectively handle anticipated loads and influences. Most building codes specifically refer to the foundation. Generally, the foundation is intended to be sufficiently strong so that any yielding will occur first in the superstructure, unless the design of a particular building provides otherwise.

Leakage

Basement leakage is an issue routinely addressed by real estate practitioners as this problem is often found at some point in the life of a basement. In the vast majority of cases, the leakage is not structurally significant and can be controlled relatively inexpensively. Most basement leaks tend to be intermittent—it may only be wet during or after periods of rain or melting snow. Homeowners must monitor the situation and take action based on the frequency and extent of the leakage.

Basement leakage can often be identified by repairs on interior or exterior walls. Repairs may include patching, cement parging, or the use of various water-proofing products. A freshly excavated area or new sod along the edge of a house may indicate that remedial work has been undertaken. Efflorescence, a whitish mineral deposit, on interior walls is also an indication as it remains after water has evaporated. Many other signs may be present: rusty nails in base-boards; rusted electrical boxes near floor level; rusted support posts on appliances; mould or mildew; crumbling plaster or drywall at floor level; peeling paint; water stains; warped boards; or sagging cardboard boxes stored on the floor.

Most leakage problems can be corrected or eliminated by improvements to exterior grading and proper performance of eavestroughs and downspouts. The ground immediately adjacent to the foundation should slope away from the structure at a rate of one inch per foot, for at least the first six feet. If the general topography is such that water is directed toward the structure, further measures to divert water may be required. Practitioners are always cautioned regarding basement leakage. While many situations can be addressed and resolved, certain properties may have water problems that require significant modifications, and even then, may not be successfully resolved. At all times, direct buyers and sellers to appropriate experts for guidance on leakage matters.

Wall Construction

Basement walls are normally built using poured concrete or concrete block, however, other materials have been introduced into the marketplace, e.g., wood foundations. They are the load-bearing component of the structure and transfer the weight of the roof and floors down to the footing. Building codes set out requirements concerning damp-proofing and water-proofing of exterior walls below ground level (or any slab in contact with the ground). A typical basement wall constructed with concrete blocks is depicted including other components such as the footing, damp-proofing and parging. See Figure B.4.

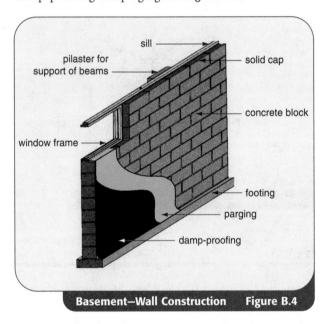

Basement—Wall Construction   Figure B.4

Insulation

The typical insulated wall consists of below grade damp-proofing, batt insulation, a vapour barrier, and a finished interior wall usually consisting of drywall or panelling.

Building codes establish insulation requirements for basement walls in new homes. Insulation in older homes is relatively inexpensive, easy to do, and cost effective, but certain risks exist. If the basement has chronic moisture areas, correction of the external problem must be completed. Second, interior insulation could cause frost damage to the foundation walls, as the walls will be significantly colder after installing the insulation. Third, obstructions such as electrical panels and plumbing must be accommodated. Figure B.5 illustrates a typical insulated basement wall including a vapour barrier and possible finishings, e.g., plywood or drywall.

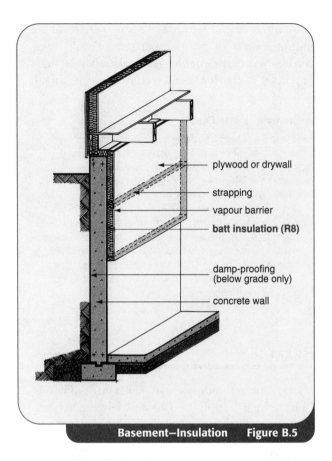

Basement—Insulation   Figure B.5

BASIS POINT

A basis point is $1/100$ of 1%.

Application For real estate purposes, basis points are most commonly referenced in regard to mortgage rates. For example, if the three-year mortgage rate rises from 7.25% to 7.50%, the increase amounts to 25 basis points.

BAY

An unfinished area located between a row of columns and the bearing wall. A bay is usually the smallest area into which a building floor can be partitioned.

BAY DEPTH

Bay depth generally refers to the distance from the bearing wall to a row of columns within a building.

Application Bay depth is an important consideration in the layout of office, retail, and industrial buildings. In retail office leasing, the term takes on a precise meaning when referring to bay measurements in the construction or outfitting of office space. The *bay depth* refers to the measurement from the inside wall (tenant's side), of a corridor wall to the exterior wall or glass. Bay depth is important in deriving the most efficient use of space.

Example   *Bay Depth*

Tenant Savard is considering lease premises in a newly-constructed office building. The bay depth is 38 feet and an interior six-foot corridor is planned. Accordingly, sufficient room is available for exterior and interior office areas with equal depth measurements of 16 feet each. Obviously, the importance of bay depth is directly related to the type of tenants involved. In this instance, Savard wants individual offices to accommodate associates in her software development business. Larger tenants, such as a legal firm, will pay close attention to bay depth to ensure adequate sizing of outer offices, combined with sufficient room for support staff in interior or open office areas.

BEAM

A long structural component, typically made of wood (solid or built-up), plywood, or steel designed to carry floor and wall loads horizontally to the foundation.

Application   The structural integrity of beams is important in any building. Undersized or over-spanned beams may sag or crack and lead to the ultimate failure of an entire framing system. Over-spanned wood beams can be readily identified and are usually remedied with the addition of posts, enlarged beams, or effected through some type of load reduction.

Beams can suffer mechanical damage and be weakened by notching, cutting, or drilling. The amount of weakening is a function of where the damage occurs on the beam, how significant the damage is, and how far it is from the supports. Steel beams can be much stronger than wood beams and are more resistant to rot, termites, and mechanical damage, but are more expensive, heavier, difficult to handle and are susceptible to rust.

Fire is an obvious concern with both wood and steel beams. Interestingly, a steel beam will lose its strength in a fire earlier than a wood beam, although a wood beam actually burns. Steel loses its strength after being exposed to temperatures of 1,000°F for about four minutes. Figure B.6 illustrates beam construction.

BEARINGS
(SEE METES AND BOUNDS)

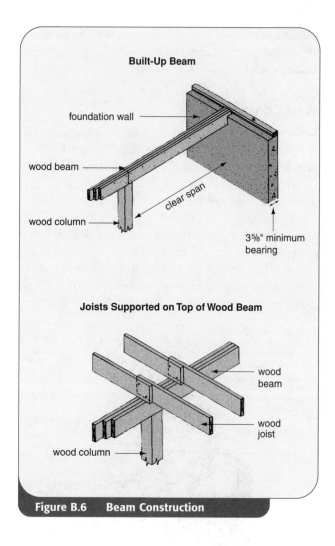

Built-Up Beam

foundation wall

wood beam

wood column

clear span

3⅝" minimum bearing

Joists Supported on Top of Wood Beam

wood beam

wood joist

wood column

Figure B.6   Beam Construction

BERM

Contoured landscaped areas, normally found on commercial or industrial properties that act as a buffer within the site plan for that particular enterprise. Berms often form part of a landscaping design for hotels, resorts, and restaurant facilities. Figure B.7 illustrates a typical berm situated on a commercial property.

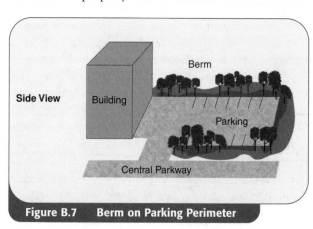

Side View   Building

Berm

Parking

Central Parkway

Figure B.7   Berm on Parking Perimeter

BID
(SEE ALSO AUCTIONEER)

A competitive system in which bidders submit sealed proposals to execute work for a specified monetary sum.

Application   The bidding process has migrated to real estate through the use of auctions. Commercial practitioners also refer to opening bids when discussing the initial offer made by a buyer/seller during negotiations.

BILL OF SALE

A written agreement/contract in which one person sells, assigns, or otherwise transfers right/title to chattels. A bill of sale is typically registered under the applicable provincial statute as evidence of a contract.

Application   For real estate purposes, a bill of sale could be used to record the transfer of personal property as itemized on the agreement/contract, e.g., the sale of appliances, furnishings, and other personal effects.

BINDER

A term indicating a preliminary agreement between parties evidencing a meeting of the minds and remaining in effect until the principal agreement can be executed.

Application   Binders are most frequently encountered in insurance-related discussions concerning immediate coverage granted by an insurance broker pending formal acknowledgement, i.e., an insurance policy from the insuring company. A binder is usually limited to a single page general description of coverage in anticipation of a fully detailed policy. The binder is subject to actual policy conditions and is signed by an authorized representative.

Example   *Binder*

Buyer Jones is arranging insurance coverage on his new commercial building and requires immediate confirmation regarding coverage for purposes of mortgaging the property. Accordingly, the insurance broker will issue a binder in the amount of $500,000 and provide a one-page letter detailing the name and address of the insured, the property being covered, the amount of coverage, and his (insurance broker) signature binding the property until the policy is issued.

BLANKET MORTGAGE

A single mortgage on two or more properties forming security for a loan. A blanket mortgage allows the lender, to gain recourse against *all* properties, upon default, and further protect his/her interest by not allowing the sale of any of the properties without specific permission.

Example   *Blanket Mortgage*

Owner Smith wants to renovate his cottage valued at $90,000 but is having difficulty securing a mortgage for $35,000 on the *recreational* property. His bank will, however, increase the existing first mortgage on his city home, valued at $185,000 from the current amount of $100,000 to $135,000, provided that the mortgage is registered against both properties.

Both parties achieve their objectives—Smith is able to secure the required funds and will probably receive a more favourable interest rate than normal for recreational property—the bank increased business with a client, maintained a conservative loan to value ratio ($135,000 ÷ 185,000 or .73) on the primary property, and obtained additional security (the cottage valued at $90,000).

A variation on blanket financing is found in large residential projects, particularly new home developments and condominium projects. A lender supplies a blanket mortgage over the entire condominium project for construction purposes and is fully secured by the developer's covenant during the construction stages. Upon completion, the condominium units are marketed and the lender is correctly positioned to provide financing for individual buyers. This is accomplished by *fracturing* the blanket mortgage. Once sold, the buyer must qualify for the unit and upon approval, a mortgage is created for that property to be registered at closing.

BLENDED PAYMENT

A method of loan repayment where periodic amounts of principal and interest are applied in a way that the payments remain constant in amount, although the portions attributed to principal and interest vary with each payment. This type of plan is sometimes referred to, erroneously, as an *amortized payment plan*. In reality, any payment plan through which principal amounts are spread over time to liquidation, regardless if the payments are equal or not, is an amortized payment plan. A true blended payment plan exists if, during the term of the mortgage, equal payments are made at regular intervals, and each payment is a blend of principal and interest.

Application   Blended payment plans have proven most popular with residential mortgage loans over the last several decades due undoubtedly to the fact that payments remain constant during the term of the loan and allow for better budgeting. Although any payment period can be agreed to by mortgagee and mortgagor, today's residential mortgage usually consists of monthly payments (although weekly, bi-weekly, and semi-monthly options are becoming more popular in a competitive mortgage market).

If a Canadian mortgage consisted of compound interest on a monthly basis (e.g., 8% per annum compounded monthly), the calculation of a blended payment would be a simple matter. Difficulty arises, however, since the *Interest Act* imposes a special restriction regarding disclosure of interest in blended payment plans. The *Interest Act* states:

> *Whenever any principal money or interest secured by a mortgage or real estate is, by the mortgage, made payable on the sinking fund plan, or on any plan under which the payments of principal money and interest are blended, or on any plan that involves an allowance of interest or stipulated repayments, no interest whatever shall be chargeable, payable or recoverable, on any part of the principal money advanced, unless the mortgage contains a statement showing the amount of such principal money and the rate of interest chargeable thereon, calculated yearly or half-yearly, not in advance.*

This Act applies only where principal and interest payments are blended. The reasoning is, since the interest amount is hidden in the blended payment, the borrower has no way of knowing just how much interest, or at what rate, the loan is being repaid.

The *Interest Act* does not attempt to control the rate of interest to be charged, it merely requires the effective rate of interest be quoted as: *calculated annually, not in advance;* or *calculated semi-annually, not in advance.*

The word *calculated* as used in the Act is synonymous with *compounded*. The more frequently interest is compounded, the greater the amount of interest charged. Obviously, the lender will select the calculation that produces the greatest return. In fact, interest is quoted as *calculated semi-annually, not in advance* in most blended payment mortgages in Canada. Lenders address the problem of compounding every six months, when the mortgage calls for monthly payments. Effectively, the lender builds in a rebate to the borrower to compensate for this factor. Advanced calculators and computer software programs easily handle mathematical complexities relating to Canadian blended payment mortgages.

Example   *Blended Payment*

Borrower Reed arranges a mortgage for $10,000 at an interest rate of 12% per annum with blended monthly payments. Interest must be calculated annually or semi-annually not in advance. As a result, lenders have established slightly reduced monthly interest factors to ensure that the compounding does not exceed *Interest Act* requirements.

The monthly interest factor used is .00975894. (Detailed tables are not provided.) By multiplying the factor by the principal owing during any period, the actual interest charged can be calculated. While this factor produces a true effective rate greater than 12% per annum (allowing for compounding), the result falls within federal guidelines.

BLENDED PAYMENT SCHEDULE
(SEE ALSO AMORTIZATION)

A schedule of payments typically prepared by a computer setting out the total payment under a blended payment plan, along with the interest and principal portions and the balance outstanding.

Calculating a Blended Payment Schedule

Interest factors are required to develop a schedule of payments for a blended payment plan in Canada. Although these schedules are normally prepared by a computer, an understanding of underlying calculations gives some insight into the concept of blended payments.

Example   *Blended Payment Schedule*

A mortgage of $50,000 has an interest rate of 14% per annum calculated semi-annually not in advance. Blended monthly payments, amortized over 25 years, are $586.94. Interest due at the end of the first month is:

.0113402605 x $50,000 = $567.01

The interest factor used (.0113402605) is derived from interest tables (not included in this text). Since the total payment is $586.94, if $567.01 of this covers interest, the remainder of $19.93 (586.94 − 567.01) can be used to reduce the principal to $49,980.07 (50,000 − 19.93).

The first line of the payment schedule would read:

PAYMENT #	TOTAL PAYMENT	INTEREST	PRINCIPAL	BALANCE
01	586.94	567.01	19.93	49,980.07
02	586.94	566.79	20.15	49,959.92
03	586.94	566.56	20.38	49,939.54

To generate the second line, retrace the same steps using a principal amount of $49,980.07, etc.

B

BLOCK LAYOUT

A systematic arrangement of real estate ownership interests, freehold or leasehold, as part of an overall strategy for land development, municipal planning, or similar purpose.

Example   *Block Layout*

Developer Reed has received draft plan approval for a new residential subdivision that contains building lots and street patterns setting out residential blocks within the plan. In addition, the layout includes a specific block of property set aside for parkland.

Application   The term *block layout* applies to a variety of circumstances. For commercial tenancies, the block layout is a preliminary sketch showing different rentable space on various floors of an existing or proposed building. The layout assists in evaluating the overall rental efficiency of the building and is a visual guide for property leasing and management. In the case of municipal planning, block layout refers to the arrangement of residential areas bounded by neighbouring and/or intersecting streets that identify specific geographic areas within the urban area. Block layout is also used in reference to the apportionment of specific areas of land (blocks) within a plan of sub-division. Plans of subdivision typically set out residential or com-

mercial building lots, street patterns, land for recreational facilities, park purposes (open space), and other reserved land (future use).

BOARD

(SEE REAL ESTATE BOARD)

BOARD OF UNDERWRITERS

An organization that establishes rates for fire insurance and other types of coverage. This type of organization normally maintains a laboratory that tests safety factors of materials, substances, electrical equipment, machinery, and other apparatus.

BOILER (HOT WATER SYSTEM)

A type of central heating system where heat is generated in one location and distributed via piping to various other locations. The term *boiler* is somewhat confusing in that hot water systems do not actually boil the water, but rather heat it to 160°F maximum.

Application   Hot water boilers consist of closed and open systems. Real estate practitioners will normally encounter only closed systems in which water in the boiler, piping, and heat source within individual rooms is under pressure. Pressure within the system is normally a few pounds higher than what is required to force water up to the highest level within the structure. Closed systems typically have a circulating pump to force the water through the system.

Open systems, common prior to the introduction of the closed system, utilizes an expansion tank located above the highest radiator in the structure. This tank provides for expansion when water is heated and comes equipped with an overflow pipe. Open systems do not utilize circulating pumps as gravity moves the water.

Boiler systems are most commonly associated with commercial properties, although hot water systems were popular in residential property during the early and mid portions of the twentieth century. All boiler systems, with the exception of electric boilers, have two major components: a heat exchanger and a burner. The heat exchanger contains the burning fuel on one side and the water to be heated on the other. The most common fuels are natural gas and oil. Burners on hot water systems are very similar to those on warm-air furnaces.

Figure B.8 illustrates simplified boiler systems and the flow of heated water. Convectors and radiant heating are viable alternatives to radiators. Hot water convectors are either cast iron or tubing (usually copper), with aluminum fins normally less than 12 inches high. Some hot water heating systems employ piping buried in the floor or ceiling that in turn radiates heat to the room.

BOMA STANDARD

A standard method of measuring office space developed by the Building Owners and Managers Association (BOMA) International, an organization of professionals in the office building industry.

Application   BOMA developed the *Standard Method of Floor Measurement for Office Buildings* to ensure consistency and promote an industry standard. The Standard has undergone successive revisions and the most recent is a building-wide method to ensure that measurement is applied on a consistent floor-by-floor basis and sets out procedures to measure the gross building area, common areas, as well as rentable and useable areas.The Standard is used extensively to measure space in both existing and new office buildings.

Reference   For detailed information, contact the Building Owners and Managers Institute of Canada, 415 Yonge Street, Suite 901, Toronto, ON M5B 2E7.

BOND, SURETY

A certificate under which a person, company, or government agrees to pay a specified amount at a pre-determined point. In insurance, a bond is a surety agreement that a specified amount of money will be paid in relation to the terms and conditions set out in that agreement.

Application   Real estate brokers handle trust funds that are received from the public, usually in the form of deposits with offers to purchase, or as rental receipts in the case of real estate brokers acting as property managers. Provincial real estate acts/regulations set out requirements concerning surety bonding for brokers, salespeople, and/or brokerages to provide a level of protection for consumers whose money is received and deposited in trust. The amount of bond required will vary across Canada, as will the range of consumer protection mandated by the applicable regulatory authority.

Provincial   See applicable reference materials.

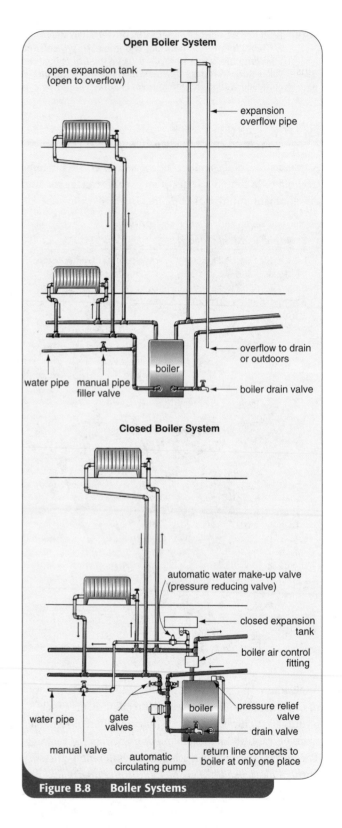

Figure B.8   Boiler Systems

BONUS

A term frequently identified with mortgages whereby funds are paid to the mortgagee by the mortgagor to increase the yield on the mortgage.

Application   Bonuses can be applied in two different ways essentially producing the same result. Example 1 illustrates a negotiated amount as an incentive to a mortgagee to permit a discharge (interest penalty). Such bonuses are less common given competitive mortgage markets in which lenders offer open provisions (no penalty), permitting partial prepayment or full discharge prior to the end of the mortgage term.

Example 1   *Bonus*

Seller Watson wants to discharge an amortized, blended payment mortgage with a four-year term during the second year. The lender does not provide for early discharge unless two months' interest penalty is paid. If the balance owing on this 7.75% mortgage is $100,000, the bonus is calculated by using an applicable two-month interest factor of .0127533647. The interest owing to discharge the mortgage early is $1,275.34 (.0127533647 x $100,000). (Detailed interest tables are not included in this texts.)

A bonus also refers to an extra obligation by a mortgagor at the point of arranging a mortgage to increase the mortgagee's yield. Example 2 details how mortgagee yield is increased by means of an initial bonus. While the discharge bonus increases yield at termination, the arranging bonus accomplishes a similar result at mortgage *inception*. The use of bonuses is particularly attractive to lenders during tight money situations, in high risk ventures, and in financing unique properties/enterprises.

Example 2   *Bonus*

Borrower McKay is having difficulty arranging financing for a speculative venture. Assume that a lender is prepared to advance $60,000 amortized over 20 years at an 8% interest rate and a bonus of $5,000. The mortgagor will only receive $55,000 with the face value on the mortgage showing $60,000. The net impact is an increased yield to the mortgagee. The yield amount will vary based on the term of the mortgage—the shorter the term (assuming the mortgage would not be renewed), the greater the yield.

Effective yield calculation based on an upfront bonus is complicated and practitioners use a rule-of-thumb for approximation purposes, but caution is always advised. The repayment of the $60,000 mortgage, according to mortgage payment factors, (see the **Appendix**) would produce a monthly payment of $497.01 [(8.283575 x 60(000)]. However, McKay only received $55,000. The salesperson would review monthly payment factors for successively higher rates to see what interest payment factor with a 20-year amortization and principal of $55,000 closely approximates the monthly payment of $497.01. A payment factor of 9.046598 (9.25%, 20-year amortization) produces a payment of $497.56. Without establishing the exact yield, the bonus has resulted in an increase of approximately 1.25% over the nominal 8% rate stated in the mortgage. The exact yield can be readily calculated using a financial calculator.

BONUS ACCRUALS

In corporate taxation, bonus accruals represent a method of reducing corporate income and thereby deferring tax until the next fiscal period.

Example   *Bonus Accruals*

ABC Realty Inc. has calculated the following net profit before taxes:

Gross Commission (to brokerage)	$500,000
All Expenses	−360,000
Net Profit Before Taxes	**$140,000**

The brokerage may decide to issue a bonus to the broker, manager, or other person within the brokerage. If the bonus were $50,000, profits would be $90,000 and corporate income tax would be payable on $90,000.

Gross Commission	$500,000	
All Expenses	−360,000	
Net Profit Before Taxes		140,000
Bonus Accruals		−50,000
Net Profit Before Taxes		**$90,000**

This, in effect, transfers tax payable on $50,000 from the brokerage to the recipient, and in certain cases has the net effect of deferring personal tax if the money is received immediately following the start of a new taxation year.

Such bonuses must be paid to the recipient within 180 days of the corporate year end. Bonus accruals appear most effective when the brokerage and broker/owner are moving from high to low income periods.

BOOKKEEPING

(SEE ALSO ACCOUNTING)

Bookkeeping consists of rules and procedures relating to the processing of financial data that ultimately leads to the preparation of financial statements.

Application   A bookkeeper normally prepares the day-to-day financial data for a real estate brokerage in a prescribed fashion usually outlined by the brokerage's accountant/financial advisor. Statutory requirements are set out in the applicable real estate act and regulations. Brokerages can elect to have the bookkeeping function performed by staff, an accounting firm, or a combination thereof.

Although the difference between accounting and bookkeeping can be somewhat vague, accounting generally relates to the transferral of information from various journals into the general ledger, with the subsequent production of financial statements for the brokerage. On the other hand,

B

bookkeeping focuses on the recording of entries into the journals, the maintenance of those journals, cheque issuance, and basic reporting usual to the day-to-day operation of the brokerage.

BOOKS OF RECORD

Books of record for a corporation are set out in applicable provincial legislation. Provincial requirements vary in regard to the type and scope of records to be maintained by a brokerage.

Example   *Books of Record*

The following is for illustration purposes only and is excerpted from *Business Corporations Act* for the Province of Ontario.

According to Part XI of the Business Corporations Act in the Province of Ontario, the following items are required for corporations (including real estate brokerages). The company must prepare and maintain:

- *Articles of incorporation and by-laws (along with any amendments);*
- *Minutes of meetings and resolutions;*
- *Register of Directors (including information concerning all people who are, or have been, Directors, along with pertinent details);*
- *Security register (including all people who have registered as shareholders, holders of debt obligations, and holders of warrants of the corporation for the past six-year period, along with pertinent details); and*
- *Transfers of securities (the securities register also must itemize all transfers of securities issued by the corporation). Records are to be kept in a bound or looseleaf book.*

The Act also provides for recording information by means of mechanical, electronic data processing, or other storage facilities.

In terms of financial records, an auditor is not required for corporations not publicly offering shares, when all the shareholders agree, company assets do not exceed $2,500,000, and revenues are less than $5,000,000.

Required financial statements are outlined in the Regulations and must include a minimum of: balance sheet, statement of retained earnings, profit and loss statement, and a statement of changes in financial position.

BORROWED LIGHT

A term, primarily used in commercial leasing, referring to a partition that contains glass or plastic panels and provides additional internal light (either by daylight or high intensity artificial light), to work areas within the building not immediately adjacent to external windows.

BOUNDARY LINE

The bounds or limits of a specific parcel of land. The term can also generally refer to a geographic area in the case of a neighbourhood or district.

Application   The resolution of problems concerning real estate boundary lines falls to provincial legislation. Procedures are established to verify the true location of the boundaries through a survey. Further, boundary issues are commonly associated with fences, disputes regarding such fences, and associated costs for repair, maintenance, and replacement. Legislation concerning line fences is either under a separate statute (e.g., *Line Fences Act*), or combined with the statute regarding boundaries (e.g., *Boundary Lines and Line Fences Act*). Provincial legislation will vary.

Provincial   See applicable reference materials.

BRANCH (BRANCH OFFICE)

Generally described as an office of a brokerage, other than the principal place of business, that is used on a regular basis by that brokerage as a location for providing real estate services and engaging in trades/transactions.

Application   Registration of a branch office is required, for example, in Ontario, Manitoba, Saskatchewan, and Nova Scotia. Legislation sets out requirements concerning the registration of the branch location, level of supervision (e.g., a broker (agent) or an individual authorized by the broker who meets certain criteria), and other requirements designed to ensure adequate supervision is afforded salespeople as well as sufficient protection for the public. The broker can impair his/her position from a legal and ethical perspective if proper leadership is not provided within the branch. Provincial registration procedures will vary as well as the scope of controls imposed on branch offices in their day-to-day operations from an administrative perspective.

Provincial   See applicable reference materials.

BRANCH MANAGEMENT

The ultimate responsibility of the broker (agent) is to ensure that branch activities conform to all legal, accounting, and procedural matters in day-to-day activities. Controls must be exercised over expenditures (or approval of them), while permitting adequate autonomy for the office manager. When operating a branch office, the broker should implement certain guidelines.

- Procedure for financial reporting, trade processing, and expense tracking.
- Separation of responsibilities.
- Control forms to provide weekly and monthly feedback on performance.
- Office inventory record (furniture, equipment, and supplies).
- Inspection procedures and maintenance requirements (office appearance, image compliance etc.).
- Listing and sale processing procedures.

Application   The allocation of responsibility and authority will vary by brokerage. Generally, procedures applied in the main office are mirrored throughout the branches which are typically viewed as individual profit centres with accounting functions centralized in the main office. All disbursements from the general and trust accounts are handled by head office in accordance with the applicable provincial real estate act/regulations and other requirements of the regulatory body.

A well-developed budget is essential, along with frequent reporting of sales performance and expenses (if controlled at the branch level). A profit and loss statement for each branch should be prepared monthly.

The branch manager is often permitted relative independence in day-to-day operations (depending on regulatory requirements coupled with prudence). Too much control discourages initiative. In some organizations, advertising allocation, personnel selection, and budgets are controlled directly by head office. On the converse, too little control impairs the ability to operate on an efficient, organized basis. The solution is at best a compromise based on individual circumstances, preferences, and regulatory considerations. The degree of autonomy is most evident in dealing with salespeople, decision-making regarding local expenditures, maintaining the office, and allocating advertising dollars (within limits), while informing the head office on a variety of matters.

The head office, through direct financial control and ultimate approval, becomes the monetary and procedural watchdog of the organization and maintains both the spirit and intent of the applicable provincial real estate act.

Example   *Branch Management*

Broker/Owner Johnson, of ABC Realty Inc., is hiring a new branch manager and wishes to effect control while providing flexibility for local management decisions. Ultimately, the following duties and functions will form part of the job description for the new manager.

- Make decisions concerning the allocation of advertising dollars within the local market area (to a specified limit).
- Conduct branch contests/awards (in addition to company programs).
- Select personnel for staff positions (with ultimate approval by head office).
- Recruit and hire salespeople (subject to head office approval).
- Make disbursements from petty cash (to a predetermined limit).
- Make recommendations for the purchase of all supplies, equipment, and furniture in the branch.
- Terminate unsatisfactory employees (subject to brokerage procedures and head office approval).
- Adhere to all policies, guidelines, and regulations set out in the policy manual.
- Adhere to brokerage responsibilities and authorities as per the agreements between commission salespeople, salaried staff, and the brokerage.
- Prepare budgets as required.
- Provide prudent and diligent administration.
- Maintain strict adherence to all by-laws, rules, regulations, laws, statutes, and other stipulations as required by federal, provincial, and municipal governments, the real estate board, and more specifically, the appropriate provincial real estate act/regulations regulating the profession.
- At all times be under the direct supervision of Broker/Owner Johnson.

BREACH OF CONTRACT
(SEE CONTRACT)

BREAKDOWN METHOD
(SEE ALSO OBSERVED CONDITION (BREAKDOWN) METHOD)

A method used in the appraisal of property to estimate accrued depreciation.

Application   In estimating accrued depreciation, this method is viewed as highly reliable as it *breaks down* the structure into its components and measures all physical, functional, and external causes of depreciation based on an observation of the actual physical and functional condition of the structure. The breakdown method includes three main categories of depreciation:

- Physical deterioration;
- Curable and incurable functional obsolescence; and
- External obsolescence.

BRICK MASONRY WALL

In residential construction, a solid brick wall is typically eight inches thick not including the interior wall finish. The inner wythe (layer) is most often brick, concrete block, or cinder block (stone, clay tile, or glass block can also be used). The outer wythe is usually weather-resistant brick or stone. Construction of brick masonry walls in commercial properties will vary based on the type of structure. See **Figure B.9**.

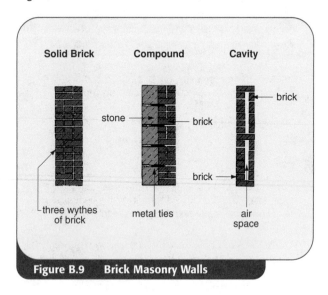

Figure B.9   Brick Masonry Walls

A wall is a load-bearing component of the building that transfers the weight of the roof and floors to the foundation. Brick masonry walls are identified by the header courses (brick rows turned endwise to tie the inner and outer wythes of the wall together), every five to seven courses (rows) up the wall. Occasionally every brick in the course is turned endwise, every other brick is turned, or the entire pattern is random. In most cases, however, there are at least some units that are turned every fifth, sixth, or seventh course.

If metal ties or specially sized bricks are used to join inner and outer wythes, then no header courses will be present. Masonry walls, with few exceptions, have not been used on single family homes since the early 1970s.

Application   Real estate practitioners should have a general awareness of potential problems associated with brick masonry walls.

Lean or Bow   Where the inner and outer wythes are not adequately secured together, the outer wythes can lean or bow outwards. This also occurs during foundation settlement or when the wall is too thin to carry its load. The ultimate danger is that it may fall, but the more immediate danger is that the rafters and joists resting on the wall can slip as the wall moves away from the building. If the ends of joists are resting on the wall by only an inch or two, a relatively small lean can create an unsafe situation. If floor or roof joists slip off their supports, the framing system will collapse.

Rafter Spread   Spreading roof rafters may push the top of the walls out, resulting in an unstable condition.

Out of Plumb   The wall may be built out of plumb, or be pushed out of plumb by mechanical forces (such as being struck by an automobile), or failure of another component in the building.

Wavy   A less than smooth appearance when looking up the wall with waves often having crests every five to seven courses. Wavy walls may be the result of building too quickly, as bricks are laid on top of mortar that has not had time to set and strengthen. This situation was particularly problematic with old lime mortars that took longer to set. Another theory to explain waviness is not placing a full bed of mortar between each course of brick. If ties or headers were used every five to seven courses, a full mortar bed would be used on these courses only. If the mason skimped on mortar, only the front edge of the brick would get mortar causing the back to come together and create a bulge at the front.

Deterioration   The structure of the wall can be compromised if the masonry units, or the mortar between them, deteriorate. Mortar strength should be similar to, but not stronger than, the brick.

On Side   Hollow bricks or concrete blocks are weak if laid on their sides and should not be expected to carry any type of load.

Cracks   Cracks should be used as clues, with their size, location, direction, and rate of growth as important indicators of problems. Generally, cracks through the mortar joints are less serious than cracks through the brick or block, but exceptions do exist.

When Correction Needed   A masonry wall may be unsound if bowed out of plumb by approximately one-sixth of its thickness (typically measured halfway up the wall). Joists may pull out of wall pockets before the wall actually falls, causing collapse of the framing system. A wall may also be unsound if leaning out of plumb by one-third of its thickness (measured from the top to bottom). In some cases, the brick wall can be tied back into the building using anchors and steel rods or cables. If the movement results from foundation difficulties, a rebuild of the wall may be required following the under-pinning of the foundation.

Establishing the appropriate action may require a structural engineer. Repairs should only be undertaken once the cause of the movement is fully understood.

BRICK VENEER WALL

A wood frame wall with an exterior single width of brick. The wood framing transmits the roof and floor loads down to the foundation and employs a structural wood frame inner wall, and a four-inch thick masonry outer section (veneer) which does not have any load bearing responsibility. Typically, metal ties are used to secure the brickwork to exterior sheathing and, consequently, no header courses are employed in the brickwork. This usually enables practi-tioners to visually differentiate between a brick masonry wall and a brick veneer wall.

Brick veneer walls have been used as long as builders have been building with brick and, in fact, are the only type of brick walls commonly found in single-family homes after about 1970. **Figure B.10** illustrates the construction of a typical brick veneer wall.

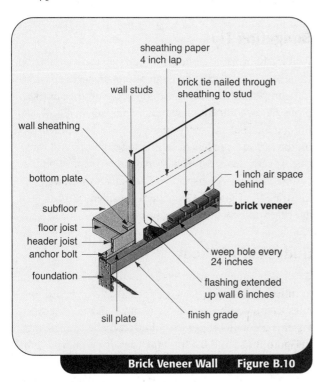

sheathing paper
4 inch lap

wall studs

brick tie nailed through
sheathing to stud

wall sheathing

bottom plate

1 inch air space
behind

subfloor

brick veneer

floor joist

header joist

anchor bolt

weep hole every
24 inches

foundation

flashing extended
up wall 6 inches

sill plate

finish grade

Brick Veneer Wall   Figure B.10

BRIDGE LOAN

An interim form of financing used in a variety of residential and commercial transactions.

Application   In residential sales, bridging may occur when a buyer is committed to completing the purchase of a property on a specific date, but will not have sufficient funds until a later time. This frequently arises when the buyer's property has sold with a late closing date, or the property remains unsold. Lending institutions may be prepared to advance funds under a bridge loan based on the borrower's personal covenant, verification of relevant documentation, and a direction for the payment of funds on completion of a sale, or when a mortgage is placed on the unsold property.

The bridge loan is also found in new construction. Bridge loans can assist a developer between scheduled advances (normally received through either an interim or permanent lender). The bridge loan is intended to provide cash to pay immediate expenses while awaiting the next formal advance and is said to bridge the distance between advances.

Example   *Bridge Loan*

Seller Smith's current home has a scheduled closing date of May 31, 20xx. Smith will net approximately $90,000 from the sale. However, his new home purchase with a negotiated selling price of $250,000 closes on April 30th. Smith requires a $100,000 downpayment in addition to the new first mortgage of $150,000. The downpayment will come from savings and equity in his current property. He has $20,000 and requires $80,000 to complete the sale. The bank arranging the first mortgage agrees to advance the additional $80,000 by way of a bridge loan until the prior property closes. Smith retains $10,000 of the $90,000 from the sale of his current home for moving and miscellaneous costs, with the balance being applied to the bridge loan.

BRIDGING/BLOCKING

A building component that restrains the joists from twisting and helps transmit loads from one joist to adjacent joists, thereby reducing the springiness in the floor. See **Figure B.11**.

Application   Diagonal bridging is most commonly found in residential construction where two-inch by two-inch pieces of wood are used to restrain the floor joists from springing. An alternative, referred to as *solid blocking*, uses wood with the same dimensions as the floor joists, excepting length. Traditionally, one set of diagonal bridging or solid blocking is provided for each joist span. Depending on the configuration and building code requirements, more or less may be required.

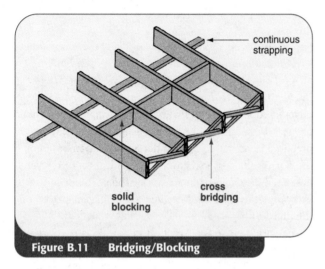

Figure B.11   Bridging/Blocking

BROKER (AGENT)

The precise definition and role of a broker (agent) will differ by provincial jurisdiction. The following is provided for descriptive purposes only.

> *A broker (agent) can be generally described as a person who, for another or others, for compensation, gain or reward or hope or promise thereof, either alone or through one or more officials or salespeople is licensed by the provincial regulatory body to trade in real estate.*

Application   The brokerage, as a partnership or corporation, is typically registered as a broker in addition to one or more individuals owning controlling interest in the real estate brokerage. Restrictions concerning non-broker ownership of brokerage offices will vary by provincial jurisdiction.

The broker/salesperson relationship is normally fully described by provincial legislation. In most instances, a salesperson is someone who is registered by the provincial regulatory body to trade in real estate and who is employed/contracted/appointed by a broker.

Since the broker is defined, in essence, as a person who legally represents another, it is obvious the broker is the agent in a real estate transaction. Unfortunately, it has become common place for both the public and media to refer to real estate salespeople as *agents*. Under the law, salespeople cannot be agents as this implies a degree of authority and independence of action that does not statutorily exist.

A salesperson is the broker's employee or appointee, authorized by the broker to trade in real estate for that broker. Legislation regulating the industry establishes a very definite relationship between broker and salesperson. Everything is done in the broker's name with the salesperson carrying out the broker's instructions and policies. Further, no salesperson is permitted to accept any commission or other remuneration from any person except the broker.

Provincial   See applicable reference materials.

BUDGETING

The orderly process of organizing data to be analyzed in a meaningful way to see trends and variances within the operation of the organization. Generally, budgeting is synonymous with planning for profits. The most accurate budgets are developed using several years of historical data.

Budgeting Tips

Real estate brokerage budgeting can represent significant challenges. The high mobility of sales staff, aggressive commission plans, fluctuating economic conditions, marketplace trends, competition within the market area, and other unique internal and external influences all take their toll on the rational process of estimating expenses and forecasting cash flows. A tip sheet may prove helpful to put various matters in perspective. The budget tip sheet, illustrated in **Figure B.12** includes considerations for existing and new brokerages.

Budget Worksheet

A range of budget worksheets are used by brokerages owing to differing internal practices, particularly in regard to salesperson compensation plans and allocation/recovery systems involving expenses. A budget format is provided in **Figure B.13a** and **B.13b** as the basis for establishing the chart of accounts. With minimal revision, this worksheet (also referred to as a *financial worksheet*), can accommodate

BUDGET TIPS

- Include a delay factor between sales production and the ultimate receipt of commission.
- Avoid being too optimistic in the number of salespeople that can be hired.
- Carefully assess the debt load that will be carried for losses during the first few months (or longer).
- Estimate additional cash requirements to handle expenses incurred by salespeople that will be subsequently recovered when commissions are received.
- Analyze market trends to establish realistic production goals for individual months in the budget.
- Include sufficient allowance for unusual expenses incurred at start up.
- Avoid starting out with too many full-time employees.
- Exercise care by not allocating too many dollars in start up costs without leaving sufficient money for slow periods.
- Avoid setting the budget solely on strong market conditions without regard for weaker markets.
- Put rules and procedures in place for collecting recoverable expenses, desk fees, and levies (depending on the compensation packages being offered).

- Ensure that the brokerage payout from commissions covers all reasonable expenses while returning a profit to the brokerage.
- Retain sufficient funds to carry on the operation for a realistic period of time if revenue was drastically cut.
- Develop contingency plans in the event that actual results differ substantially from forecast figures.
- Address the merits of leasing as opposed to acquisition in order to retain sufficient capital, should a downturn occur.
- Establish specific goals regarding recruiting and sales production.
- Ensure that performance goals are realistic given normal trends in the marketplace. Don't forget typical seasonal variations that traditionally arise in brokerage activity.
- Allocate all expenses as fixed or variable, and establish the minimum income required per month to address the expenses for which the brokerage is responsible.
- Carefully assess all incidental costs in opening an office, e.g., supplies, forms, and special printing requirements (cheques, business cards, and letterhead).
- Don't underestimate expenses. Include an allocation for legal, accounting, and other professional fees, dues, memberships, business taxes, special levies, and permits.

Budget Tips   Figure B.12

a variety of commission plans and expense recovery systems. This budget worksheet is customized for the Province of Ontario. Certain budget lines, e.g., Employer Health Tax, may require revisions to align with provincial variations.

Managers are concerned primarily with monthly cash flows and expenses as opposed to balance sheet items. The profit and loss statement usually takes priority in terms of internal analysis and decision-making. The worksheet is a form of profit and loss statement containing the most commonly used accounts from a brokerage chart of accounts.

The budget worksheet can assist in analyzing income and expense activities at the main or branch office. It forms the basis for brokerage bookkeeping and office budgeting, and can be expanded or altered to meet specific requirements.

In a cash accounting system, the worksheet organizes the brokerage in terms of cash received and disbursed. From an accrual basis, it can be used to forecast anticipated revenues and expenses for budgeting purposes.

Income Analysis

Commission Income   Can be divided into residential, commercial, or other categories as required. A similar change should then be made in the Commission Expense category to mirror this alteration: i.e., Commission to Salespeople (Res.), Commission to Salespeople (Com.).

Referral Income   Income received from outgoing referrals. Minimal expense is incurred to generate this revenue, so it is an interesting category to assist with bottom line results.

Contribution of Owner   Isolating the owner's income and expenses provides a more complete picture of the brokerage's financial strength. Further, this figure is typically removed for purposes of override payments to a manager. The worksheet provides a corresponding category isolating the owner's payout under commission expense so that brokerage performance can be analyzed separately.

Other Income   Refers to property management, appraisal, and other incidental income. It provides an account for miscellaneous revenue sources so that pure commission income is accurately isolated for analysis and tracking purposes. A more detailed set of accounts is required with brokerages having specific departments. Other Income can also include penalties and interest charges on overdue salesperson accounts.

Desk Fee Income   All income from desk fee arrangements is entered on this line. This would apply to total desk fee offices as well as offices providing variable plans that have one or more persons on a desk fee.

THE BUDGET WORKSHEET

PREPARED FOR	PERIOD

INCOME ANALYSIS

ADJUSTED GROSS INCOME	TOTAL
Commission Income	
+ Referral Income	
+ Contribution of Owner	
+ Other Income (Appraisal, Rentals, etc.)	
+ Desk Fee Income (If Applicable)	
= Gross Income	
– Commission (Other Brokers)	
– Referral Commission (Other Brokers)	
= ADJUSTED GROSS INCOME	

EXPENSE ANALYSIS

COMMISSION EXPENSE	FIXED	VARIABLE
Commission to Salespeople		
+ Commission to Owner		
= Total Commission Expense		

ADVERTISING EXPENSE		
Newspaper—Classified		
+ Newspaper—Institutional		
+ Sign Installations		
+ Radio		
+ Television		
+		
= Total Advertising Expense		

PERSONNEL EXPENSE		
Salaries—Full-Time		
+ Salaries—Other		
+ Management Override (If Applicable)		
+ Management Salary		
+ EI/CCP Contributions		
+ Employer Health Tax		
+ Benefits (Specify)		
+		
= Total Personnel Expense		

COMMUNICATION EXPENSE		
Telephone—Equipment/Misc.		
+ Telephone—Long Distance		
+ Cellular Telephone		
+ Fax/Courier		
+ Pager System		
+		
= Total Communication Expense		

Figure B.13a   Budget Worksheet, Page 1

EXPENSE ANALYSIS (cont'd)		
	FIXED	VARIABLE

OCCUPANCY EXPENSE

	FIXED	VARIABLE
Rent/Lease		
+ Utilities		
+ Janitorial Service/Maintenance		
+		
= **Total Occupancy Expense**		

OPERATING EXPENSE

	FIXED	VARIABLE
MLS Transaction Fees		
+ MLS Other Charges		
+ MLS Membership Dues		
+ MLS Supplies		
+ Photography		
+ Printing/Postage		
+ Office/Photocopy Supplies		
+ Insurance (E & O)		
+ Miscellaneous Operating Expenses		
+		
= **Total Operating Expense**		

GENERAL EXPENSE

	FIXED	VARIABLE
Membership Dues		
+ Professional Fees		
+ Licences		
+ Lease(s) (Specify)		
+ Automobile Expenses		
+ Business Taxes		
+ Business Promotion & Donations		
+ Sales Awards		
+ Travel & Conventions		
+ Professional Development		
+ Bank Charges		
+ Depreciation		
+		
= **Total General Expense**		

EXPENSE ANALYSIS SUMMARY

	FIXED	VARIABLE	TOTAL
Total Commission Expense			
+ Total Advertising Expense			
+ Total Personnel Expense			
+ Total Communication Expense			
+ Total Occupancy Expense			
+ Total Operating Expense			
+ Total General Expense			
= **TOTAL EXPENSES**			

NET INCOME BEFORE TAXES	
	TOTAL

	TOTAL
ADJUSTED GROSS INCOME (from Income Analysis)	
– TOTAL EXPENSES (from Expense Analysis)	
= **NET INCOME BEFORE TAXES**	

Commission (Other Brokers)   This payout factor is an important aspect of management analysis. Higher payouts can be a signal of weakened market position.

Referral Commission (Other Brokers)   This referral payout references monies received to which referral cheques must be issued to other brokers. The total income received is not specifically isolated: it is included in Gross Commission Income. However, it is possible to estimate total income generated from such referrals by merely *grossing up* the figure. For example: Referral Commission to Other Brokers: $4,500, Usual Split: .25 of Gross; therefore, estimate of gross income generated by incoming referrals: $4,500 ÷ .25 = $18,000.

Adjusted Gross Income   This is the basis for comparison of expenses to gross income. The adjusted gross is used as it is a *pure* figure of income to the brokerage, no other brokerage dollars are involved.

Expense Analysis

The accounts have been organized for ease of use in establishing percentages for month-to-month comparisons. The brokerage may organize these accounts to meet specific needs. The main expense divisions follow.

Commission Expense   This figure is a reflection of the commission and bonus plans in place. Comparisons using this category are important for internal purposes. However, analysis between companies is difficult. Ranges of commission payout will vary considerably based upon internal arrangements: i.e., salesperson's participation in various expenses, payment of desk fees etc.

Advertising Expense   The categories provided cover most advertising media usual to a real estate brokerage. Other classifications should be added as required. Detailed analysis, by individual newspaper for example, may unnecessarily complicate the worksheet.

Personnel Expense   Ensure that all EI and CPP expenses are included as well as Employer Health Tax. Owner's salary should be isolated and full and part-time staff should be separated to better analyze costs.

Occupancy Expense   If owner-occupied, the rent should be the economic rent for the premises. Additional categories may have to be added in relation to upkeep and repair.

Communication Expense   Telephone expense is broken into two parts for recovery of toll charges from salespeople. Additional blank expense classifications are provided to be used as required.

Operating and General Expenses

Confusion exists over the division of expenses beyond the main categories of commission, advertising, communication, and occupancy expense. Brokerage accounts will include such categories as: Selling Expense, Sales and Promotion, Administration Expense, Sales and Marketing Expense, etc. This causes confusion and compounds the process of analysis. In the recommended financial worksheet, only two general categories exist.

Operating Expenses   Operating expenses vary with the sales production of the brokerage. These variable expenses may or may not be recovered from salespeople, depending on the specific compensation plans being utilized. The budget worksheet lists nine different categories. Items should be added or deleted as required. Franchise fees are included in this category as most are calculated on a *production* or *per person* basis. Errors and Omissions insurance relates specifically to salespeople and is included. All production related charges from the real estate board are included with the exception of brokerage membership dues.

General Expenses   General expenses vary only slightly with the production of the brokerage. They tend to be fixed and somewhat predictable on a year-to-year basis. Normally, most owner-related expenses would appear in this category. The worksheet provides twelve different items. Professional fees relate to accounting and legal costs. Licences refer to operating licences for the brokerage only. Automobile expenses relate to brokerage vehicles and associated costs. Bank charges involve penalties, charges, and related costs owed lending institutions. Depreciation is included for all owned equipment. The general expenses are viewed as overhead and are either paid through the broker's portion of income or offset by appropriate desk fees.

To illustrate, consider the following examples:

Example 1   *General and Operating Expenses*

The photocopier lease is $233 per month and the current supplies used are $197. The lease is a general expense for the company; the supplies are an operating expense as they vary from month to month. Supplies, along with the lease cost, may be recovered through copy charges to salespeople. Alternately, the lease can be absorbed either as part of office expense and built into the overall commission split, or covered through a desk fee.

Example 2   *General and Operating Expenses*

Owner's car lease is $583 and gasoline for the car is $139. Both are charged to general expenses as these costs are part of the overhead of the brokerage.

Real estate board invoice is $955 ($300 for office membership; $100 each for 5 salespeople; and $155 for board supplies). The $300 is a general expense, the dues of $500 for salespeople is a variable expense that may be ultimately recovered, and supplies of $155 is also variable as it relates to sales production.

Net Income Analysis

Technically, the worksheet is designed to analyze cash flow based on trade closed dollars and actual expenses incurred. Many times, managers may use the same worksheet and budget future profits based on projected sales volume and average expenses. As such the worksheet becomes a type of budget format.

Financing Charges

The topic of financing charges requires special consideration. Traditionally, some brokerages deducted interest expense *following* the calculation of net income before interest and taxes (as illustrated below), instead of including it under a specific expense category. This has the net effect of highlighting such costs, distorts the true net income, and may impair meaningful comparisons. (Students may find this approach in some dated real estate publications.) The variation as discussed normally appears as follows:

```
      Net Income Before Interest and Taxes
        Less: Interest and Finance Charges
        Less: Income Taxes
    = Net Income
```

As an alternative, financing charges can appear either under operating or general expense. The exact allocation depends on the reason for acquiring the funds. If the bank charges and interest relate to an operating loan to offset negative cash flow then the amount should appear under operating expense. If the loan is of a fixed nature and relates to capital investment then it would fall under general expense. As with most unusual accounting issues, trained accounting professionals should be consulted relating to individual circumstances.

Cash Flow Analysis

The budget provides an overall estimate of financial performance that must be converted into cash flow projections. This task, broadly described as cash flow analysis, is normally completed based on historical operating data from the brokerage. In such instances, the exercise becomes largely one of refining prior year budget estimates in light of actuals and forecasted performance levels. In the case of income projections, if year-to-year comparisons are

unavailable (e.g., a new brokerage), previous MLS statistics provide a starting point, assuming that 80–90% of all transactions occur on MLS. Unfortunately, trend analysis for commercial brokerages is more difficult as MLS transactions may not constitute a large portion of market information.

Cash flow analysis begins with estimating a gross commission income for the upcoming year and then slotting this income in relation to typical MLS activity.

Example 1 Budgeting–Cash Flow Analysis

Summary cash flows for ABC Realty Inc. are illustrated including the broker's estimate of market activity within each particular month, the estimated sales income, and lastly the estimated monthly cash flow, based on a 90-day delay between the point of sale and receipt of the commission.

MONTH	AVERAGE MLS VOLUME (EXPRESSED IN 000'S)	% OF TOTAL
January	$22,550	5%
February	31,570	7%
March	45,100	10%
April	67,650	15%
May	72,160	16%
June	45,100	10%
July	22,550	5%
August	18,040	4%
September	49,610	11%
October	40,590	9%
November	22,550	5%
December	13,530	3%

MONTH	% OF TOTAL	ESTIMATED SALES INCOME	ESTIMATED CASH FLOW
October	9%	$225,000	90-day adjustment
November	5%	125,000	
December	3%	75,000	
January	5%	125,000	$225,000
February	7%	175,000	125,000
March	10%	250,000	75,000
April	15%	375,000	125,000
May	16%	400,000	175,000
June	10%	250,000	250,000
July	5%	125,000	375,000
August	4%	100,000	400,000
September	11%	275,000	250,000
October	9%	225,000	125,000
November	5%	125,000	100,000
December	3%	75,000	275,000

Expense calculations are also based on historical data. Selected organizations and larger brokerages provide guidelines for predetermined expense categories. Expense categories and selected budget amounts are for illustration only. Wide variations exist based on accounting systems used by individual brokerages, compensation plans for salespeople, and specific brokerage circumstances, e.g., a new brokerage would undoubtedly budget more dollars on premises, advertising, and communication than a well-established operation.

Example 2 *Budgeting—Cash Flow Analysis*

EXPENSE CATEGORY	% OF ADJUSTED GROSS INCOME*	% FOR BUDGET PURPOSES**
Commission Expense	65.32%	62.00%
Advertising Expense	6.42	9.00
Personnel Expense	5.74	6.00
Communication Expense	2.03	3.00
Occupancy Expense	2.76	5.00
Operating Expense	2.67	4.00
General Expense	3.00	3.00
	87.94	92.00

* Based on prevailing trends and historical data
** Adjustments based on judgement

Income Projections

Income projections are developed, where possible, based on historical brokerage information. MLS information may prove useful when allocating budgeted sales volume into workable monthly projections.

The broker must categorize monthly cash flow projections to align with financial statements. A range of income categories exist in the marketplace, particularly given differing methods of compensating salespeople. For illustration purposes, a four-month cash flow projection is included (**Figure B.14**) based on gross income (projections using MLS statistics), together with other sources of income, e.g., referrals, owner contribution, and desk fees. From that total, payouts to other brokerages are deducted to arrive at adjusted gross income. The analysis assumes a traditional office in which salespeople are paid a split of total commission and the brokerage is responsible for most expenses. The method by which salespeople are compensated can dramatically affect the budgeting process and organization of cash flow projections.

Expense Projections

Based on budget estimates, the broker is now able to complete the expense portion of the cash flow analysis.

The detailed four-month analysis is provided including adjusted gross income, total expenses, and estimated net profit before taxes (see **Figure B.14**).

Fixed, Semi-Variable, and Variable Expenses

Expense budgeting has been refined through the use of fixed, semi-variable, and variable expenses. Traditionally, only fixed and variable expenses were analyzed in the budgeting process. Fixed costs remain relatively constant despite increases and decreases in production. Variable expenses change with the amount of business transacted. Recently, budgeting theory has expanded to include semi-variable expenses. These items, although relatively constant, are subject to periodic increases as production rises and are most frequently encountered with equipment purchases. Normally, equipment costs remain static for a considerable period of time and then rise to a new plateau owing to growth requirements. See **Figure B.15**.

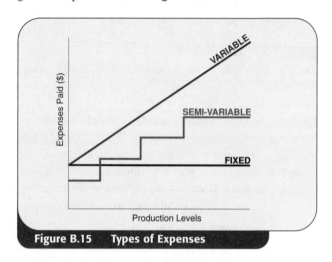

Figure B.15   Types of Expenses

New Brokerage Budgeting

The new brokerage (or branch office within a brokerage), seeks to gain market share while minimizing negative cash outlays in growth stages. During the first year of operation, most new offices are faced with high fixed expenses, delayed cash flows, and substantial start up expenses. Cash reserves become a critical consideration as fixed and variable expenses often exceed gross income. The prudent broker should plan for income delays due to (a) time lags between deals written and deals closed that can often exceed sixty days, and (b) time lags in sales production from hiring to actual production and receipt of commission income from new salespeople.

Revenue Units

Often referred to simply as *ends* (that is, each transaction has two ends, one listing and one selling; a transaction involving one salesperson with both listing and selling portion is referred to as *getting both ends* or *double ending*), revenue units are utilized by some brokerages to accompany budget figures and gain a more meaningful sales perform-

Cash Flow Projection—Income & Expenses

	JANUARY	FEBRUARY	MARCH	APRIL
Adjusted Gross Income				
Commission Income	$225,000	$125,000	$75,000	$125,000
Referral Income	3,100	1,700	1,000	1,700
Contribution Owner	7,500	4,200	2,500	4,200
Other Income	700	400	200	400
Desk Fee Income	0	0	0	0
Total Gross Income	236,300	131,300	78,700	131,300
Less: O.B. Payout	−58,300	−32,800	−19,700	−32,800
Less: O.B. Ref. Payout	−11,600	−6,600	−3,900	−6,600
Adjusted Gross Income	**166,400**	**91,900**	**55,100**	**91,900**
Expenses				
Commission Exp. (62%)	$103,200	$57,000	$34,200	$57,000
Advertising Exp. (9.0%)	15,000	8,300	5,000	8,300
Personnel Exp. (6.0%)	10,000	5,500	3,300	5,500
Communication Exp. (3.0%)	5,000	2,800	1,700	2,800
Occupancy Exp. (5.0%)	8,300	4,600	2,800	4,600
Operating Exp. (4.0%)	6,700	3,700	2,200	3,700
General Exp. (3.0%)	5,000	2,800	1,700	2,800
Total Expenses	**153,200**	**84,700**	**50,900**	**84,700**
Net Profit (Before Taxes)	**$13,200**	**$7,200**	**$4,200**	**$7,200**

Cash Flow Projection   Figure B.14

ance overview. They can also be effective in evaluating overall salesperson activity. Revenue units are normally tallied as follows:

EVENT	REVENUE UNITS
Single Listing Sold	1
Single Sale	1
Double End Sale (Listing and Sale)	2

Revenue units have proven very effective in evaluating activity compared with traditional methods that rely on sales volume. Sales volume comparisons are somewhat awkward as there is no universally accepted method of calculation and rapidly increasing prices can distort the true position, e.g., increased volumes are not due to market penetration but merely the sale of expensive properties. Market share can actually be shrinking while sales volume is increasing. By tallying units, brokerages can gather valuable year-on-year information concerning amount of activity generated and not just dollar volume.

The revenue unit is preferred to calculations based on total number of transactions as this approach ignores the importance of in-house (double end) sales.

Break-Even

There are four steps in determining break-even using revenue units. The broker must first estimate an adjusted gross income along with anticipated number of units to generate that income. Break-even relies on the traditional division of fixed and variable expenses. The example in **Figure B.16** illustrates a summary of a budget worksheet and is based on a brokerage generating 536 units of production during the year in question.

In this instance, the broker requires 327 *ends* in order to meet fixed expenses based on a forecasted, adjusted income of $1,093,740. Assuming that 10 salespersons are expected to equally contribute in sales activity, the minimum performance level is approximately 33 ends (327 ÷ 10) for the budget period. The broker can then establish goals with individual salespeople with the knowledge of minimum break-even performance levels and be in a better position to effectively manage the brokerage.

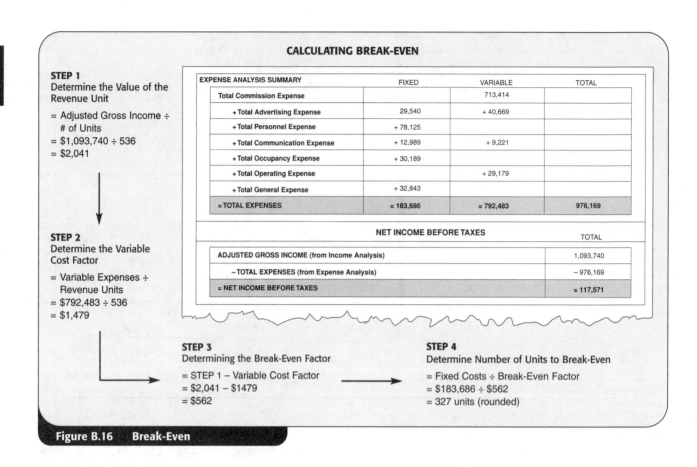

CALCULATING BREAK-EVEN

STEP 1
Determine the Value of the Revenue Unit

= Adjusted Gross Income ÷ # of Units
= $1,093,740 ÷ 536
= $2,041

STEP 2
Determine the Variable Cost Factor

= Variable Expenses ÷ Revenue Units
= $792,483 ÷ 536
= $1,479

EXPENSE ANALYSIS SUMMARY	FIXED	VARIABLE	TOTAL
Total Commission Expense		713,414	
+ Total Advertising Expense	29,540	+ 40,669	
+ Total Personnel Expense	+ 78,125		
+ Total Communication Expense	+ 12,989	+ 9,221	
+ Total Occupancy Expense	+ 30,189		
+ Total Operating Expense		+ 29,179	
+ Total General Expense	+ 32,843		
= TOTAL EXPENSES	= 183,686	= 792,483	976,169

NET INCOME BEFORE TAXES	TOTAL
ADJUSTED GROSS INCOME (from Income Analysis)	1,093,740
− TOTAL EXPENSES (from Expense Analysis)	− 976,169
= NET INCOME BEFORE TAXES	= 117,571

STEP 3
Determining the Break-Even Factor

= STEP 1 − Variable Cost Factor
= $2,041 − $1479
= $562

STEP 4
Determine Number of Units to Break-Even

= Fixed Costs ÷ Break-Even Factor
= $183,686 ÷ $562
= 327 units (rounded)

Figure B.16   Break-Even

BUFFER ZONE

An area of land specifically set aside, or otherwise identified, that separates two distinct land uses and commonly identified as areas of vacant land that separate different land uses, e.g., residential and commercial, and often zoned as open space.

Buffer zones are typically found within site plan agreements. These areas are not zoned as such, but are identified as landscaped areas including berms that *buffer* the use in relation to adjacent property. Practitioners refer to buffer zones in relation to actual uses, e.g., a heavy area of multi-residential buildings are viewed as a buffer between commercial property on an arterial road and single-family residential housing.

BUILD TO SUIT
(SEE ALSO DESIGN BUILD)

An agreement, typically between a landlord and a new tenant, whereby the landlord assumes the obligation of *fitting up* the demised space to tenant specifications within established building standards. The tenant takes possession when the space is completed.

Example   *Build to Suit*

Acme Manufacturing Inc. is seeking an industrial site in Anycity. Anycity Developments Inc. owns suitable property currently zoned for industrial use. Acme provides the specifications for the new building to a tenant representative (salesperson) employed by ABC Realty Inc. The salesperson negotiates with Anycity and develops a lease agreement that is subsequently signed by the parties. Anycity as the landlord, proceeds to build a structure to suit the tenant's specifications.

The example provided is not intended to narrowly focus build to suit arrangements within lease situations. Build to suit can involve combinations including owned or leased property as well as sale/leaseback arrangements. During the past decade, the term *design build* has gradually replaced *build to suit* when referencing such arrangements.

BUILDER'S/CONTRACTOR'S LIEN

A claim against a property that is filed by a person or corporation in the provincial land registry or land titles office for labour, services, or materials supplied in the performance of contractual work.

Provincial   See applicable reference materials.

BUILDING CODE

Regulations established by the federal, provincial, and local governments detailing minimum acceptable standards for building construction.

Application   Real estate practitioners may encounter building code requirements and minimum construction standards in both the residential and commercial fields. Building codes are based to a large extent on provisions of the National Building Code of Canada (NBC) and are statutorily established through an applicable provincial act, e.g., *Building Code Act*. The codes do not function as authoritative textbooks on building design, but rather set out requirements in regard to safety, fire protection, and structural sufficiency. Codes generally address:

- Specific uses and related occupancy requirements including acceptable fire and safety standards, means of exit, accessibility, service facilities, and loads.
- Structural loads, foundations, and design requirements for structural materials.
- Wind, water, and vapour protection including vapour barriers, air barriers, control of groundwater and rain penetration, and material specifications.
- Heating, ventilating, and air-conditioning including air duct systems, heating appliances, piping, refrigeration systems, and chimneys/venting equipment.
- Plumbing including materials, equipment, and specific requirements concerning piping, drainage, and venting, along with stipulations regarding the use of potable and non-potable water systems.
- Requirements for housing and small buildings.
- Change of use requirements and renovations.

Provincial   See applicable reference materials.

BUILDING CORE

The central or arterial part of a multi-storey building that integrates functions and service needs for occupant, e.g., tenants. Such areas are normally composed of toilet facilities, elevator banks, janitors' closets, utilities, smoke shafts, mechanical facilities, and stairwells.

Application   Practitioners will encounter both side-core or centre-core plans. Centre-core floor designs are better suited for multiple tenancies while side-core provides a larger open space on individual floors for larger tenants. The building core is most frequently near the centre of the building, particularly for multi-tenant occupancies. The popularity of central core construction derives from

its overall design efficiency. The central core building is commonly associated with full floor tenants who prefer perimeter window areas relegated to middle management and executive offices with internal areas used for other staff levels, reception areas, aisles, and hallways. High-rise office towers in downtown locations are predominantly centre core plans. See **Figure B.17**.

Off-centre building cores are frequently found where extensive numbers of people perform similar functions with no requirement for executive offices or preferential locations near windows. Off-centre cores have become increasingly popular with the advent of high-tech call centres and large centralized customer service organizations.

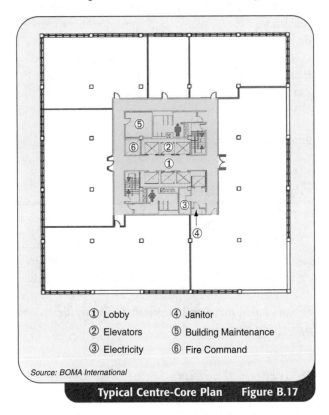

① Lobby	④ Janitor
② Elevators	⑤ Building Maintenance
③ Electricity	⑥ Fire Command

Source: BOMA International

Typical Centre-Core Plan   Figure B.17

BUILDING LINE
(SEE ALSO SET BACK)

A line fixed at a certain distance from the front and/or sides of a lot, beyond which no building can project.

BUILDING LOCATION SURVEY

A generic term describing a legal document prepared by a surveyor that shows the exact dimensions and positions of the land and buildings for a particular property, including any encroachments onto or from adjoining properties.

Terminology, procedures, and requirements concerning the use of building location surveys can vary by provincial jurisdiction, e.g., Surveyor's Building Location Certificate and Surveyor's Real Property Report.

Application   Building location surveys are important to both owners and real estate practitioners in setting out the physical extent of ownership, the correctness of address in relation to legal description, encroachments from adjoining property that may restrict the full use and enjoyment of a property, and easements that can also restrict the property's use. Building location surveys are normally required to obtain financing and provide municipal officials with the ability to see if the property conforms to applicable zoning restrictions as to location of buildings and other structures on the property.

Caution is advised concerning reliance on dated building location surveys as recent changes affecting the property can substantially impact the extent of ownership and use of the property.

Provincial   See applicable reference materials.

BUILDING MODULE

A unit of length and width by which the plan of a commercial building can be standardized to facilitate the design and layout of office space. The module places constraints on the configuration and size of various elements in the physical structure. In contrast, buildings of a non-modular design present many problems both for initial design and subsequent alterations.

BUILDING PERMIT

A document issued by the municipal authority certifying the blueprints for construction and authorizing work to commence.

Application   The building permit is one element in an overall regulatory plan concerning types and quality of construction that occur within municipal boundaries. Sellers and buyers considering any type of construction on a specific property are well advised to seek assistance from the local building department and/or building inspector prior to the start of any construction. If a permit is required, the building department requires an application outlining the planned work including plans, building sketches, and related documents.

Municipal staff will review the application to ensure that the planned construction meets with the applicable

building codes, local zoning by-laws for the area in which the construction is taking place, and other relevant regulations, e.g., special requirements for properties located in or near flood prone areas of a community.

Requirements for new construction, additions, alterations, renovations, relocations, and repairs or rehabilitation of a building or structure will vary. Building permits are typically required for a variety of projects.

- Finishing previously unfinished spaces such as family rooms, recreation rooms, or attics.
- Repair and underpinning of foundations.
- Installation of pools.
- Construction of decks in excess of a specific height above the ground.
- Construction of accessory buildings in excess of a specified square footage.
- Construction of attached and detached garages.

BUILDING OWNERS AND MANAGERS ASSOCIATION (BOMA)
(SEE BOMA STANDARD)

BUILDING RESIDUAL TECHNIQUE
(SEE CAPITALIZATION)

BUILDING RESTRICTIONS
(SEE ALSO ZONING)

Restrictions concerning the construction and location of buildings and services registered against the land or otherwise required through municipal restrictions in the form of zoning and land use control.

Application   In the case of general zoning provisions, practitioners will encounter a wide range of building restrictions that either directly reference the structure (e.g., minimum gross floor area, height of structure, type of structure based on use, and construction of accessory buildings), or indirectly limit it (e.g., various setback requirements dictating overall building size and shape). Residential zoning requirements typically set out restrictions relating to front, rear, and side yards, maximum lot coverage, minimum landscaped open space, parking needs, and various requirements concerning buildings located on the same lot. Commercial properties may also be restricted in terms of minimum setback requirements relating to lands abutting major highways, railway lines, and residential areas; specifics regarding storage areas, store size limitations within regional shopping malls and power centres; and limitations on gross floor area in neighbourhood, community, sub-regional, and regional shopping centres.

Restrictions can also arise by way of specific requirements applicable to a particular development or defined area, over and above those stated in general zoning by-laws, e.g., a larger minimum size of building or site. Such restrictions typically arise by agreement with the municipality at the time of development. Restrictions may also be imposed by the seller as part of an overall design strategy relating to development lands owned by that individual, e.g., architectural standards established for all residential units within a specific housing development.

BUILDING SHELL

A term commonly used in relation to commercial property referring to the building skeleton upon which the exterior and interior finishes are applied. The shell includes the building foundation, the building skin refers to materials covering the building shell.

BUILDING STANDARD

The specific construction standards established by the owner and architect to achieve a uniform element of design throughout the building and to establish a cost basis for fitting up charges and/or allowances.

Normally, such items are altered only with the approval of the building owner or the managing representative of a commercial property.

Provincial   See applicable reference materials concerning municipal building standards.

BUILT-INS

Appliances (e.g., a built-in dishwasher), furniture (e.g., a built-in shelving unit), or other equipment and items normally considered part of the real property.

Application   Practitioners must continuously address the issue of whether an item is included or excluded in the sale of property. While fixtures (affixed and immovable), are normally included and chattels (moveable, personal property), are not, the lines often become blurred. Such is the case when considering certain built-in items within both residential and commercial property. While a built-in may fulfill the legal requirements of a fixture, the seller may be under the impression that certain items will be

removed at closing due to an emotional attachment (e.g., a gift from someone), or simply by assuming that such is the case (e.g., a personally crafted, but attached, book shelf). Prudent practitioners routinely review all items within the listed property where confusion might exist and clearly identify those items that are included or excluded from the sale.

BUILT-UP ROOF

A multi-ply roofing system, commonly referred to as a *tar and gravel roof*, that is particularly popular in industrial buildings. The roof usually consists of two to five plies of roofing felts with a mopping of asphalt between layers. A flood coat of asphalt is then applied over the top and covered with gravel to reflect ultraviolet light and protect the roof from damage. Some roofers use roll roofing rather than gravel to protect and hold down the membrane.

BULK BASIS–SITE VALUATION

A basis of site valuation in which a price per lot is established when all lots in the particular development are approximately the same size and where minor changes in size may not affect market value. Caution is advised in bulk price comparisons as these lack the precision of other units of comparison such as price per front foot/metre or price per square foot/metre. Bulk basis is often viewed as a *rule of thumb* method as opposed to a precise method of site valuation.

Example   *Bulk Basis–Site Valuation*
Developer Reed is attempting to value a potential development site. According to the preliminary plan, 15 more or less equal lots can be created and no significant differences in value can be attributed. All lots are relatively level with no distinguishing characteristics, views, or special value attributed to abutting lands, e.g., parkland. Based on research in the immediate area, lots are being sold for $34,000 each. Therefore, based on a bulk basis valuation, Reed estimates that the potential lots are worth approximately: 15 x $34,000 = $510,000

BULK SALES ACT

Legislation typically designed to protect the creditors in the event of a sale of a business and/or sale of stock in bulk. The existence and scope of such legislation will vary by province.

Provincial   See applicable reference materials.

B

BUNDLE OF RIGHTS

Rights associated with the ownership of real property. The theory underlying the *bundle of rights* holds that the ownership of real property can be compared to a bundle of sticks, with each stick representing a distinct and separate right or privilege of ownership. These rights are inherent in ownership of real property and are guaranteed by law including: the right to use real property, to sell it, to lease it, to enter it, to give it away, and finally the right to refuse to exercise any of these rights. The highest level of ownership rights is fee simple.

Government Limitations

The legal definition of land implies complete ownership of the land and everything attached to it, under it, or over it. However, legal title to land does not imply unrestricted exercise of the bundle of rights. Such rights and privileges are limited by the following four government powers.

Police Power   The right of government to regulate property for promotion of public safety, health, morals, and general welfare. Zoning by-laws, building codes, traffic regulations, and sanitary regulations are also based on police power.

Power of Expropriation   A right reserved by the government to take private property for public benefit provided that *just* compensation is paid. This right has been extended to quasi-public bodies such as housing authorities and public utilities.

Power of Taxation   Right of all levels of government to generate revenue through the taxation of land. The most common and direct form being property taxation at the municipal level.

Escheat   Right to have ownership of the property return to the state if the owner dies having no will and no known or ascertainable heirs.

Government limitations on the bundle of rights can be far-reaching. For example, the *Criminal Code* permits law enforcement officers to enter one's lands if a crime is committed. An owner cannot create a nuisance in law, e.g., bring dangerous chattels such as dynamite onto the land. Although owners may excavate, lateral support to the neighbour's land must be retained. Riparian rights affect an owner's ability to interfere with the quality or quantity of water and taking action that might have a detrimental effect on other property owners sharing the waterway.

Private restrictions can limit the use, manner of development, or even the ownership that may be conveyed concerning real property. Encumbrances may require that the buyer be obligated to use the property subject to restrictions, e.g., deed restrictions, easements, rights of way, party wall agreements, and mortgages.

Various bundling of rights can produce a wide range of ownership options, as well as offering flexibility of use. While most immediately think of leasehold interests, real property has many ownership dimensions, e.g., life estates, sub-leasehold estates, and partial and fractional interests. In fact, fractional interests can be a significant value in an increasingly complex society, e.g., real property can be divided into different planes: subsurface rights, surface rights, and air rights.

Example   *Bundle of Rights*

An owner can sell or lease mineral rights while retaining the rights to use the surface area of his/her property. An absentee owner can rent the surface rights to one party and lease the subsurface rights to another. the remaining rights in the bundle can be sold, leased, transferred, or otherwise disposed of. In establishing a property's value, the rights remaining with the property and the effect of the loss of any of these private rights on its value must be taken into consideration.

BUSINESS

Any undertaking for the purpose of profit, including any interest in any such undertaking.

Business Brokerage

A registered real estate broker (agent) may be entitled to sell businesses under the provisions of the applicable provincial real estate act/regulations. The general definition of real estate typically includes:

> *...a business with premises, with or without fixtures, stock-in-trade, goods or chattels or any interest therein, in connection with the operation of the business.*

No mandatory listing forms or standard wordings exist for the listing authority. Real estate boards throughout Canada utilize a range of business-related forms in the Multiple Listing Services (MLS®), as do brokers when marketing businesses on an exclusive basis. The basic formats for the listing authority and data input forms do not differ substantially, but reflect local preferences. Businesses are typically divided into *types* for listing purposes, e.g., manufacturing, retail, service, wholesale.

The nature of the sale can involve the sale of assets only or shares. If only the assets of the business are to be sold, the seller normally assumes responsibility for any existing debt, but also receives the value of all accounts receivable. If shares are to be sold, the buyer assumes all assets and accepts all liabilities. The buyer also typically acquires the right to use the company name, copyrights, leases, real estate, and other assets unless otherwise negotiated. Typically, businesses are offered as *business only* and, to a lesser extent, *business including real estate*.

Factors Affecting Business Valuation

Business valuation can be complex given the range of potential factors and the variety of operating businesses. Prudent buyers and commercial practitioners must delve into situations beyond a thorough analysis of financial records and supporting documentation.

Eight important factors are detailed as a guide for practitioners in the valuation of businesses.

Location   As with all real estate, location plays a vital role in determining value. Value can be substantially enhanced by business location on a primary, arterial thoroughfare (as opposed to a secondary street), location on the arterial road, and availability of parking. Traffic and pedestrian counts are also important elements, plus proximity to other retailers with high customer appeal.

Appearance   Attractive, inviting appearance, high level of cleanliness and neatness, and well-stocked premises contribute to business appeal and can materially increase sales. Selected types of discount stores can be an exception as they deliberately use industrial racking, basic store fixtures, and heavy window display advertising to promote the image of minimum operating costs and consequent consumer bargains.

Span of Operation/Image   A long history of satisfied and repeat customers produces greater value for a business operation, as compared to a new venture that lacks a track record or reputation. An exception is the new franchise outlet that, while possessing no local track record, acquires a sense of longevity through an acquired, known image.

Competition   Generally, the less competition facing any particular business, the greater the chance of that business having higher sales and potential profit. This statement assumes, of course, a demand for the particular services and/or products being offered. High sales performance

normally translates into heightened value if operating costs fall within acceptable limits.

Demand   Certain businesses have high consumer demand and, sometimes, a perception of glamour in the eyes of the public. This preferred type of business will not only command a high price, but will also be easier to sell. For example, certain fast food and automotive franchises fall within the high demand category, while selected clothing and home fashion outlets attain glamour status.

Turnover   The number of times that stock is sold and replaced in a given year. The number of turns achieved varies by type of business. For example, four to five turns are normal for a department store, as compared to 30 to 35 for a supermarket. A major financial advantage exists concerning start-up costs for high turnover businesses. Most merchandise can be sold before payment is required, thereby freeing up lines of credit and capital for other purposes, e.g., leasehold improvements and advertising. On the converse, a major disadvantage of the high turnover enterprise lies in the commensurately increased levels of employed staff required to operate the enterprise and manage stock-related issues.

Service Quality   As a general statement regarding the service industry, the sales volume and ultimately the value of the enterprise is directly related to the quality of service provided to the customer. Further, a direct relationship has traditionally existed between the number of well-trained, adequately-compensated staff and the achievement of sales goals. Given the preponderance of low pay-scales for retail employees, service quality is a continuing problem for many employers. Successful entrepreneurs have overcome this through better compensation packages including the use of sales bonuses and the introduction of share participation programs. This enlightened philosophy normally translates into increased customer traffic and ultimately higher returns.

Ownership vs. Lease   Security of tenure and continued operation is of paramount importance to the typical business. An overriding priority for businesses in leased premises, is long term possession. When real estate is owned, this concern is eliminated or at least significantly minimized. However, such a statement requires qualification. Many commercial practitioners point to the benefits of leasing, despite uncertainties, as a rental arrangement permits the use of available capital more productively in the expansion of the business enterprise. Further, short term leasing may be ideal for a rapidly expanding business not wanting to be hampered by inadequate facilities during the growth pattern.

B

The listed criteria are provided for general guidance. Any business must be critically scrutinized including a thorough examination of financial records. Selected factors can be improved by a new owner (e.g., service quality), while other elements (e.g., location), are usually fixed. All of the above contribute to the present and future value of any business under review, however, their relative impact will vary by type of business.

BUSINESS CYCLE
(SEE ALSO REAL ESTATE CYCLE)

A series of events within the business environment that take place in roughly the same order and at the same approximate intervals. A business cycle is concluded when this series of periodically recurring events brings circumstances back more or less to overall conditions that existed when the cycle began.

Application   The concept of cyclical trends in business has remained a popular theoretical basis for analyzing, explaining, and forecasting long term economic trends. Cycles are particularly evident in real estate and are a consequence of supply and demand factors combined with a host of intrusive elements from both private and public sectors. No two cycles display the same time interval or intensity. The business cycle is typically associated with three phases as outlined in Figure B.18:

- Prosperity (high employment, consumer confidence and intense market activity);
- Recession (rising unemployment, waning consumer confidence, and no real growth); and
- Recovery (economic corrections and improvement in key growth indicators).

Economic recovery leads to prosperity and the cycle begins once more.

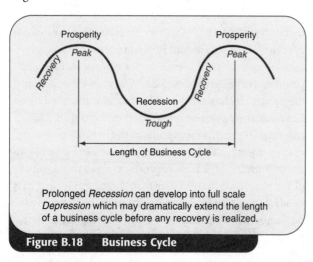

Prolonged *Recession* can develop into full scale *Depression* which may dramatically extend the length of a business cycle before any recovery is realized.

Figure B.18   Business Cycle

BUSINESS, LISTING OF

A registered real estate broker (agent), *if entitled to list and sell businesses under the provisions of the applicable real estate act*, typically treats this type of sale similarly to the sale of real estate. The regulatory definition of real estate, in such instances, normally includes real property, leasehold interests, and the business whether with or without premises, fixtures, stock-in-trade, goods, or chattels in connection with the operation of the business.

Application   As with any specialty area, real estate practitioners must understand unique requirements regarding the type of property being marketed. With businesses, various documents and special considerations also arise. The sum of all documents available to a potential buyer is normally referred to as the *documentation package.*

Business Shares or Assets   A vital factor in listing a business is establishing whether the shares of the business, or its assets, are to be sold. If shares in a corporation are being sold, the buyer assumes all assets and liabilities. He/she will have the use and benefit of such items as the company name, copyrights, leases, and real estate, unless otherwise agreed. If only assets are being sold, the seller normally assumes responsibility for any existing debt, e.g., accounts payable, but retains all accounts receivables. The buyer acquires the remaining assets, such as equipment, inventory, and goodwill. Tax implications arise from either approach and the tax position of seller and buyer can be complex. The listing salesperson is strongly advised to confirm that the buyer and seller have consulted accountants regarding such matters.

Financial Statements   The balance sheet (statement of assets and liabilities), as of the last day of the fiscal year of the business should be obtained for at least three (and preferably five or more), years of operation. Ideally, balance sheets are obtained from the seller's accountant and will be prepared for small businesses as unaudited statements used in the preparation of income tax returns.

The profit or loss statements (statement of revenue and expenses), should also be obtained for the same period, or as many years as available. The extent of historical financial documentation often translates directly into more accurate analysis of business trends and a more saleable listing.

Provincial requirements concerning the sale of a business may vary. In Ontario, for example, the *Real Estate and Business Brokers Act (REBBA)* requires that financial statements be delivered to the buyer or that the buyer waive compliance with this requirement. Standard forms have been developed for use by brokerages.

Fixtures and Chattels   Detailed lists of fixtures and chattels are needed:

- A list of items included in the sale; and
- A list of items not included in the sale.

The *Real Estate and Business Brokers Act (REBBA)* does not specifically require a list of *included* fixtures and chattels, but only those items *excluded*. If various fixtures and chattels are not excluded, REBBA states that all such items are deemed to be included. As a point of prudence, conscientious salespeople obtain both lists to avoid any confusion. REBBA wording is specific regarding the scope of the list: '...*a list of all fixtures, goods, chattels, rights and other assets...*' Make certain that lists are complete.

Lease   If the business premise is leased and not owned by the seller, a copy of the lease is required. The contents of the lease can directly affect both the value of the business and its marketability. Buyers will be particularly concerned with:

- Whether the lease can be assigned;
- Under what conditions the assignment can occur;
- The remaining term of the lease including any provisions for renewal; and
- The terms, benefits, and restrictions contained in the lease.

Where a relatively short possession period remains, the buyer may require assurances that a satisfactory extension of the lease agreement can be arranged and require a condition to that effect in the agreement.

Franchise Agreements   If the business operates under a franchise arrangement, a copy of relevant agreement(s) must be included in the documentation package. Conditions can exist within such documents that affect, or possibly nullify, the sale. For example, the franchisor normally charges an ongoing royalty fee for benefits accruing from the franchise affiliation. In most retail franchises, an advertising fee is also levied for regional and/or national promotional programs. The franchisor may further require approval of any new franchisee along with an appropriate condition inserted in any offer. The franchisor may also require that a new owner undertake specific product training.

Licences   Details of any operating licence(s) must be obtained from the seller and inserted in the documentation package. Depending on circumstances, information about how the buyer should obtain or have the licence(s) transferred is also necessary. A prime example would involve a licensed restaurant under the Liquor Licencing Board of Ontario. The licence is awarded to the owner (as an individual), who operates the restaurant and not to the premises. Any transfer of business ownership must be accompanied by the transfer of that liquor licence, subject to approval, to the new proprietor.

Financing Options   Buyers rarely pay all cash for a business and, consequently, seller financing is commonly encountered as well as additional outside financing. In either or both instances, details should be clearly set out concerning the range of financing options available, as these can translate directly into an improved marketing position. For example, the buyer may have a 30% downpayment based on the purchase price, but unable to secure funds elsewhere. The balance of the purchase price can then be financed by a *seller take back* mortgage with the assets of the business as security.

An *earnout* can be used to pay off the mortgage. The terms of the earnout are established to suit the parties. The buyer is able to pay the balance of the purchase price from cash flow, while the seller concludes a sale by offering a favourable and manageable financing option. The buyer may also ask the seller to remain as a consultant for a predetermined salary or fee. The buyer benefits from the seller's experience and knowledge, while the seller can ensure the continued success of the business and the payment of the outstanding balance.

Additional Documents   The range of documents is dictated by the type of sale (assets vs. shares), the specific business involved, and the creativity of the salesperson in providing a detailed offering to the marketplace. As with all commercial offerings, the better the documentation package, the more effective the overall marketing program, the better the prospects of a sale. Additional documents might include:

- Details of any equipment leases along with relevant terms and conditions;
- Copies of any notes, business contracts, or unique agreements that affect the business and will be assigned to the buyer, e.g., franchise agreements, employment contracts, licensing agreements, and client contracts;
- Demographic, economic, or other statistical information in support of the business, e.g., trends in retailing and traffic counts;
- Photographs of the business (both exterior and interior), including trade fixtures;
- Copies of any appraisals completed on chattels and fixtures included in the sale; and
- Selected tax return information relating to the business.

Provincial   See applicable reference materials.

BUSINESS PLANNING
(SEE CORPORATE STRATEGY)

BUSINESS PRACTICES LEGISLATION

The codification of specific business practices as unlawful and the right of government ministries/departments to investigate such practices. In some provinces, e.g., Ontario and Manitoba, provincial statutes codify specific business practices as unlawful regarding consumer representations respecting the offering of goods and services.

Application   Real estate practitioners fall within the general definition of a supplier concerning the offering of such services. With the increase of co-regulation and self-regulation within the industry, provincial statutes have generally addressed unfair business practices relating specifically to conduct, and/or the trading of real estate.

Provincial   See applicable reference materials.

BUSINESS, SALE OF

Requires specialized knowledge particularly concerning provincial legislative requirements that may impact the sale, including the use of specific forms.

Application   Prospects must be properly qualified concerning financial matters, particularly given the challenges of securing business financing.

- Establish precisely how much actual cash or liquid assets can be applied to the purchase price.
- Ascertain whether the buyer intends to work on a full-time basis in the business being acquired, or simply purchase the enterprise as an investment as this will have considerable bearing on selecting the appropriate type of business.
- Determine if the buyer has any practical skills in the business under consideration. Experience is frequently a determining factor in whether a seller will accept or reject an offer, particularly when providing financing.
- Obtain permission to conduct a credit check.
- A buyer's net worth statement can be advantageous in assisting the seller in making a decision about a particular offer.
- Since many businesses involve seller financing, the buyer's willingness to enter into a personal guarantee should be established at the outset.

- Lastly, evaluate the buyer's attitudes, temperament, experience, and aspirations. Often, businesses look attractive from an investment perspective but are not suited to a particular buyer, e.g., amount of manual labour needed, number of hours required; range of hours demanded (e.g., early or late), and necessity of specific skills.

By narrowing the field, both buyer and salesperson can work more productively in finding the right *fit*.

Provincial   See applicable reference materials.

BUSINESS TAXES

Taxes levied and due to the appropriate municipality for the operation of a business as defined by, and located within, that municipality. In commercial tenancies, business taxes of the tenant are normally paid by the tenant and include: licence/registration fees and other charges for the equipment and facilities of the tenant; the improvements within the leased space for the tenant; and the business carried on by the tenant (or subtenants).

Application   Business taxes are addressed differently within provincial jurisdictions. In Ontario, for example, business taxes were abolished during the 1998 taxation year, given a major overhaul of property taxation within the province.

Provincial   See applicable reference materials.

BUSINESS VALUATION
(SEE ALSO INVESTMENT ANALYSIS, CASH FLOW MODEL, AND DISCOUNTED CASH FLOW)

Three primary methods of valuation exist, although there are numerous variations based on the type of business under consideration. Summary descriptions are provided, however practitioners must be prepared to address unique complexities in the marketplace.

Direct Capitalization   Income generated by the business is capitalized based on market research involving analysis of comparable sale prices.

Discounted Cash Flows   Projected cash flows derived from both operations and ultimate sale of the property are discounted based on an acceptable discount rate to arrive at value. Appraisers reference this process as yield capitalization.

Adjusted Book Value/Asset Valuation These are normally used when assets are broken into components, valued, and summed to arrive at a selling price. Component valuation typically involves the sale of assets only without consideration of the operating business. In instances where the business is included, financial performance may have little or no impact on final value as acquisition risks (e.g., assuming leasehold interests), can equal or even exceed any value in retained earnings. Adjusted book value or asset valuation techniques vary significantly in the marketplace.

Application In practice, precise theoretical lines to valuation approaches are frequently blurred as buyers and sellers negotiate. Negotiating parties typically wrestle with value from personal perspectives, giving consideration to historical income performance and present circumstances, no matter whether they are bargaining based on the complete business or simply its assets. With assets, valuation can prove particularly complex, e.g., inventory for a retail sales operation (often referred to as a *distributive operation*), is treated much differently than a manufacturer's inventory consisting of raw materials, work-in-progress, and finished goods inventories.

While direct capitalization can be relatively straightforward for many commercial properties, the sale of a business introduces special considerations. For example, net operating income is often affected by the extent of owner contribution, the seller's unique skills in relation to a specific business, and a host of other judgemental factors. To further compound matters, unique combinations can arise in negotiating positions. Buyers and sellers utilize capitalization for certain items (e.g., determination of goodwill based on excess profits derived from average earnings), while calculating depreciated cost (book value) on other items such as equipment and stock, and applying wholesale values to still others.

Regardless of valuation procedures used, practitioners are advised to remember certain basic rules about businesses.

- Clearly identify the components of the business being sold.
- Establish an effective date for the valuation.
- Determine if market value or other type of value, e.g., book value, is required.
- Gather all pertinent documentation relating to identified components.
- Provide an estimate only after careful evaluation of all the facts.

Valuation by Direct Capitalization

Access to profit or loss statements is required in order to capitalize earnings. These statements will show the *gross income* from the business, *cost of merchandise*, and the resulting *gross margin* (gross operating income). Expenses relating to the operation are deducted from gross operating income to produce *net operating income (NOI)*. As with other types of commercial properties, the expense statement should be reconstructed based on acceptable appraisal procedures before calculating NOI. When establishing a capitalization rate, investor expectation is much higher than for other income-producing real estate and typically fluctuates between 15% and 50%. The value of a business often ranges between two and five times net operating income.

Certain qualifications apply when using capitalization rates for valuation purposes:

Capitalization Direct capitalization relies on the availability of comparable sold businesses and related financial information. Often net operating income is difficult to establish for comparable sales. This type of information is rarely available or withheld by the seller for a variety of reasons. Always establish the basis on which comparisons are made, understand the limitations, and inform the client accordingly.

Net Operating Income vs. Cash Flow Before Taxes (CFBT) Some specialists argue that net operating income is not sufficiently precise, and insist that cash flow before taxes (net operating income less annual debt service), produces a more accurate rate. Accordingly, an equity capitalization rate is used as opposed to an overall capitalization rate. However, two difficulties arise regarding CFBT analysis:

- Attempting to get accurate information on comparable sales; and
- Locating comparable sales with more or less equivalent debt service profiles.

Gross Income Multiplier (GIM) In selected instances, little more than gross income is available for comparable sales. Consequently, capitalization based on net operating income is not possible. An income multiplier is often used as an alternative. For example, the purchase price of a business may reflect three years of gross income, producing a GIM of three (based on gross income). Typically, the gross operating income (potential income *less* vacancy/credit losses *plus* other income), is used. Practitioners derive the GIM from sales of comparable businesses.

Terminology Retailers traditionally think in terms of margins and profits. Consequently, these terms have understandably migrated into real estate lingo, for example, the common reference to *gross margin* as opposed to *gross income*. Regardless, the overall process is similar to all real estate investment analysis and valuation. The best starting point is a reconstructed operating statement leading to net operating income (NOI). Practitioners should be cautioned that terminology such as *profit, income,* or *cash flow* may inadvertently be used interchangeably in the marketplace. Fortunately, increasing standardization has occurred as real estate investment analysis becomes firmly entrenched in the sale of business specialty field.

Working with Income Variances

If a significant variance in income has occurred in the past few years, it is advisable to use a weighted average for financial results to proportionately account for these variances. If a business demonstrates consistent earnings over several years, but exceptions exist in one or two years, attempt to analyze underlying reasons, e.g., major road repairs near business, recessionary period, high interest rates, or adjacent competition. Get all the facts.

Example   *Working with Income Variances*

Anycity Cleaners Inc. has experienced significant fluctuations in net operating income during the past four years. The weighted average can assist in smoothing out such fluctuations when analyzing income for valuation or related purposes.

	NET OPERATING INCOME			WEIGHTED AMOUNT
Year Four	$ 89,300	x 4 =		$357,200
Year Three	38,600	x 3 =		115,800
Year Two	71,800	x 2 =		143,600
Year One	46,500	x 1 =		46,500
Total	**$246,200**			**$663,100**

Average ($246,200 ÷ 4)	$61,550
Weighted Average ($663,100 ÷ 10)	$66,310

The weighted average is greater than the simple average reflecting the fact that Anycity Cleaners Inc. has enjoyed higher net operating incomes during its third and fourth years of operation. A real estate practitioner would take this into account when estimating value, as the business has grown over the four-year period and would undoubtedly be attractive to potential buyers.

Selecting the Capitalization Rate

Establish the capitalization rate through market-extracted data based on sales involving comparable businesses. Empirical research is the best avenue in deciphering investor expectations, however, data may be difficult to obtain for specialized businesses particularly in smaller urban centres. Remember, most buyers expect to recover their investment within two to five years when purchasing smaller businesses.

Example   *Selecting the Capitalization Rate*

Investor Mitchell is considering a small business in Anycity. The profit and loss statements over the past five years show increasing profits each year. Comparable sales indicate an overall capitalization rate of 35%. The reconstructed operating statement reveals a forecasted net operating income of $30,000.

Value = Net Operating Income ÷ Capitalization Rate
= $30,000 ÷ .35
= $85,714.29 (rounded to $86,000)

Discounted Cash Flow

The discounted cash flow method is most appropriate if both the business and real estate are being sold as a package, however, it can also apply in other situations. In a sale of real estate *and* business, the buyer can establish value by discounting cash flows on the business enterprise as well as the sale of real estate.

To make meaningful comparisons with other business ventures, practitioners must analyze the operating statements of the business in terms of projected income over a specific holding period along with the anticipated sale of the property at a future date. Forecasted cash flows can lead to either an estimate of market value (value to a typical buyer), or investment value (value to a specific investor). The conclusion reached is largely a matter of perspective and associated assumptions. Present value calculations, associated with discounted cash flows, provide a basis for comparison with other offerings. The internal rate of return calculation, also derived from discounted cash flows, can provide a benchmark to assess expected yield in relation to investor requirements.

Adjusted Book Value/Asset Valuation

Valuation techniques normally associated with the sale of a business and determined through analyzing component parts of that enterprise. The exact combination of components and their relative importance is often determined by the negotiating stance of the parties and the type of business involved.

While no hard and fast rule exists, typically, emphasis is placed on actual values of equipment, fixtures, inventory, and other assets. Value associated with the business may or may not be included. Adjusted book value or asset valuation techniques are frequently used to evaluate a business, particularly when a low or even negative return (profit) exists. Two approaches are discussed, although many others exist.

Adjusted Book Value

This approach may apply when a business has marginal earning potential but notable retained earnings. Retained earnings represent value received in the purchase of the business and may be included as part of overall adjusted book value. The book value or fair value (or combination thereof), of asset components is summed to arrive at a final estimate. *Fair value* (the amount at which an asset could be bought or sold between willing parties), is referenced given its frequent use by accountants when assets are fairly valued for purposes of financial reporting. Without delving too far into semantics, fair value in the accounting profession and market value in real estate brokerage can be viewed as roughly equivalent, while acknowledging subtle differences in the formal definitions.

Method of Calculation   Tangible net worth (retained earnings), is obtained from the latest statement of assets and liabilities. This amount is used as a component in arriving at a final value. Additional asset values would then be analyzed either at book value or an adjusted value that more adequately reflects fair or market value.

- Inventory at cost or fair value (as determined by the parties).
- Equipment/fixtures at cost or fair value (as determined by the parties).
- Leasehold improvements at cost or fair value (as determined by the parties).

The total value includes retained earnings plus adjusted book values.

Example   *Adjusted Book Value*

Investor Whelan is prepared to pay the seller an amount equal to the retained earnings for the immediately preceding year, as well as *book value* for inventory and *fair value* for equipment. While the entire business is being acquired, the buyer's review of financial performance indicates that little value exists beyond retained earnings and basic assets. Whelan will not consider direct capitalization of income or discounted cash flow analysis given the poor, often erratic, performance of the enterprise over the past five years. Whelan will be assuming certain risks and potential liabilities that, in his opinion, rule out serious consideration of financial performance beyond retained earnings. Accordingly, he values the business as follows:

Retained Earnings	$ 9,750
Inventory (Book Value)	+23,760
Fair Value of Equipment	+17,000
Total Estimate of Value	$50,510

In the example, fair value of equipment was included. The adjusted book value need not equal fair value and in fact a smaller value might have been negotiated, e.g., value under forced sale conditions.

Asset Valuation

Often businesses are valued simply based on saleable assets without regard to financial performance. Inventory, equipment, fixtures, and supplies are analyzed separately with no consideration given to the operating business as it is normally excluded from the sale. Obviously, the seller will want the highest figure and the buyer the lowest. The amount paid for assets largely depends on the negotiating strategies of the parties. As with adjusted book value, bargaining typically ranges between book value and fair value for assets. Asset valuation is a popular technique as the individual is not acquiring the business, only its assets. Accordingly, any potential liabilities are not being assumed.

A wide range of calculation methods are found in the marketplace given unique businesses and negotiating strategies. To complicate matters, clear-cut lines between asset valuation, adjusted book value, and other valuation techniques can become blurred. For example, goodwill can arise in negotiations despite financial performance of the business. This non-tangible asset may nevertheless have value, e.g., the longstanding reputation of the business, the capabilities of management and staff, and product reputation. Goodwill is typically quantified by analyzing above average return on investment (attributable to goodwill), however, this is not to say that goodwill cannot exist even with marginal earnings. Again, buyer and seller perspectives frequently drive negotiations. In such instances, goodwill is regarded like any other asset such as equipment, inventory, or other tangible items.

Asset valuation can also expand to other values, for example, leasehold interests. Assume a business leases 2,000 square feet with a particularly favourable rate, e.g., $7.00 per square foot for four years and current market rent is $15.00. If the current rate remains at $15.00, the leasehold benefit is:

2,000 square feet x $8.00 x 4 years = $64,000

Using the discounted cash flow and an appropriate rate, the present value of this economic benefit can be established and included in the value of the business.

NOTE   Adjusted book value or asset valuation can be useful as a secondary valuation technique to confirm or dispute capitalization or discounted cash flow approaches. Two alternate business valuation methods, the *liquidation method* and the *formula method*, are not detailed as they involve extensive judgemental factors by the valuator.

BUYER AGENCY

(SEE AGENCY)

BUYER REPRESENTATION PROPOSAL

The buyer representation proposal is rapidly becoming an essential part of buyer agency documentation involving commercial properties. Exact formats will differ among brokerages but the scope of such proposals can be generally grouped under five categories. The following guideline contains summary points only.

Objectives and Scope of Work

What goals must be achieved and what tasks are required?
This segment details goals concerning the search for qualified property. Customarily, this section includes a timetable leading to point of anticipated sale, along with a general description of sequential tasks involved.

Search Criteria

What location, features, and economic objectives must be addressed?
This stage is similar to a technical review found in the marketing proposal for a seller. The search criteria sets out requirements for an acceptable property:

Location	Geographic parameters and specific needs, e.g., general location, amenities, demographics, adjacent services, and proximity to transportation routes.
Site	Items such as soil conditions, zoning, access/egress, land size, and environmental conditions.
Building	Items such as size, ceiling heights, office finishes, utilities, sprinkler systems, HVAC, loading docks, security, and building construction.
Economic/Financial	Issues such as financing, taxes, and investor financial objectives.

Search/Analysis Process

What properties are best suited to the client?
Review all listed properties based on search criteria, including solicitation of leasing proposals (e.g., office space), or design build proposals (e.g., an industrial site), and also analysis of properties not currently listed for sale. Summarize all relevant properties on a comparative basis to determine best options for client including valuation of those options. This section can involve extensive analysis using accepted methods of investment analysis and valuation, e.g., cash on cash, direct capitalization, yield capitalization (discounted cash flows), present values, and internal rates of return.

Negotiations and Drafting the Agreement

How will negotiations be conducted and offers drafted?
For proposal purposes, practitioners normally detail the types of services commonly provided to clients during negotiations and drafting agreements.

Closing the Transaction

What follow-up processes and after sale services are provided?
Commercial brokerages have moved toward, and placed emphasis on, providing services after the signing of an agreement to the point of, and well beyond, closing. The sale or lease of a particular property opens other opportunities upon which resourceful companies have capitalized. The concluding segment of the proposal details after sale resources along with a detailed resume of both salesperson and brokerage.

◆

C

C

National Info Links

Construction (Home Building)
Canadian Home Builders' Association
Web Site   www.chba.ca

Construction (Home Inspection)
Canadian Association of Home Inspectors
P. O. Box 507
Brighton, ON K0K 1H0

Telephone   (613) 475 5699
Web Site   www.cahi.ca

Canadian Real Estate
The Canadian Real Estate Association
344 Slater Street, Suite 1600
Canada Building
Ottawa, ON K1R 7Y3

Telephone   (613) 237 7111
Web Site   www.crea.ca
www.mls.ca

CMHC
Canada Mortgage and Housing Corporation
700 Montreal Road
Ottawa, ON K1A 0P7

Telephone   (613) 748 2000
Web Site   www.cmhc-schl.gc.ca

Competition Policies/Practices
Industry Canada
Competition Bureau
50 Victoria Street
Hull, PQ K1A 0C9

Telephone   (819) 977 4282
(800) 642 3844
Web Site   strategis.ic.gc.ca

CANADA MORTGAGE AND HOUSING CORPORATION

(SEE ALSO NATIONAL HOUSING ACT)

Acronym: CMHC   As the housing agency for the Government of Canada, CMHC has a mandate to encourage:

- Construction of new houses;
- Repair and modernization of existing houses; and
- Improvement of living conditions and housing for Canadians throughout the country.

CMHC provides a range of publications and acts as a resource centre for both private and public organizations related to the housing industry. CMHC advises the government on housing matters and designs, as well as overseeing various federal housing programs. Real estate practitioners are most likely to encounter CMHC regarding mortgage financing alternatives and, in particular, insured high ratio loans offered through approved lenders.

Published Reports

CMHC is a primary source of housing market information and statistical reports. Selected reports may be of interest to real estate practitioners within their local market areas and they should contact their local CMHC office for market analysis information and other publications.

The availability of CMHC reports varies by province, territory, and/or region within Canada. The following reports were available for major Ontario marketplaces at time of printing, but are subject to change. Reports are designed to assist various professionals involved in the housing industry.

Local Housing Market Report   Addresses monthly or quarterly statistics on housing activity by local area. The publication includes information on housing starts, new home sales, economic indicators, and resale activity. Supplements are provided concerning important trends identified within a provincial marketplace.

Rental Market Report   Focuses on vacancy rates, rental housing demand, and summary tables for various occupancy types, e.g., private apartments, three units and over, row, etc. The report is based on a survey of both privately and publicly initiated apartment and row structures of three or more units offered for rent.

Real Estate Forecast   Designed to assist in assessing local market conditions through a review of key indicators affecting the housing market. The report reviews interest rates, sales, price fluctuations, and listing inventory.

Builders' Forecast   Focuses on the new housing market with particular attention paid to economic trends, affordability, housing starts, consumer patterns in new home purchases, and issues affecting builders within local market areas. The report contains a forecast summary with detailed estimates concerning total housing starts, existing housing market activity, rental market vacancy rates, and forecasting assumptions, e.g., mortgage rates, employment, and the number of household formations.

Retirement Home Survey   Summarizes the state of the retirement home market within the Toronto Branch territory. The Report contains information regarding vacancy rates in private retirement homes, per diem rates for private room retirement facilities, distribution of retirement home beds, and overall demographic trends affecting the retirement market.

Condominium Study   Acts as a supplement to the **Rental Market Report**. Produced annually, this publication provides an analysis of the condominium rental market, vacancy rates, occupancy distribution within condominiums, and new condominium construction.

Reference   For general enquiries regarding subscriptions or report information, contact the Canadian Housing Information Centre, CMHC, 700 Montreal Road, Ottawa, ON K1A 0P7.

Mortgage Loan Insurance Program

Canada Mortgage and Housing Corporation, through provision of mortgage loan insured products, is instrumental in increasing access to the housing market, financing rental accommodation construction, assisting in social housing projects, and generally furthering access of Canadians to a wide range of housing choices.

Mortgage loan insurance guarantees that the lender will be repaid if the homeowner fails to keep up the payments. In return for that guarantee, lenders will provide mortgages on housing purchases with a 5% downpayment, compared with 25% normally required for conventional mortgages. Basically, two types of programs exist: regular owner insurance and first home loan insurance.

The *National Housing Act (NHA)* and the *National Housing Loan Regulations* set out CMHC underwriting procedures and operating guidelines. Part I of the Regulations detail guidelines for processing and approving residential mortgages and defines the maximum loans permissible as well as term and amortization periods. Details about construction loans, inspections, progress advances, and holdbacks are outlined. The Regulations address procedures regarding GDS and TDS ratios. Part I provides extensive documentation on internal procedures, overall loan administration and claims procedures for lenders using CMHC mortgage facilities.

Lending Policies

The CMHC Mortgage Loan Insurance Program is designed to ensure that approved home buyers have an acceptable credit history, equity from personal resources, an ability to cover closing costs, and the income necessary to manage the mortgage payments.

Buyer Eligibility

CMHC has adopted various standards in underwriting loans and provides advisory materials to assist lenders when reviewing borrowers for mortgages insured by CMHC. The underwriting process involves three aspects: a review of the market, assessment of the borrower, and a review of the property.

In assessing the borrower, the following is required:

• Verification of employment and income;

• Verification of the source and amount of equity;

• Credit report; and

• An underwriter's analysis and rationale for decision.

The extent of information required may vary depending on the borrower and the individual lender's analysis. In terms of income, CMHC provides guidelines regarding overtime/secondary employment, commission income, bonuses, tips, self-employed earnings, rental and investment income, and alimony/child support.

GDS and TDS Ratios

Lenders use two basic measurements to determine if a borrower can afford to carry mortgage payments. The gross debt service (GDS) ratio compares the borrower's gross income to the expenses of carrying mortgage payments, including costs such as heat. The total debt service ratio (TDS) considers all loan payments of the borrower, not just those related to the house. As a guideline, a ratio of up to 30% is permitted under GDS (32% if heating is included), and 40% for TDS. In a condominium, a further 50% of common expenses is included. CMHC also requires a credit report that provides current file information concerning the borrower, specifically regarding credit received and outstanding balances.

Equity

CMHC supports the general notion that the greater the equity invested from a borrower's resources, the less likelihood of default. As with income, CMHC advances various guidelines to assist underwriters on such issues as gifts, use of applicant's savings, and borrowing against assets. As a general rule, first-time buyers must have at least 5% of the purchase price to qualify, with other homeowners requiring 10%. All or part of these amounts can come from an immediate family member, provided that the amount can genuinely be classified as a non-repayable gift.

Mortgage Terms

CMHC requires that first-time buyers qualify for an initial mortgage term of at least three years with amortization of no more than 25 years. Otherwise, the minimum term is six months. CMHC limits the mortgage amount and may have other restrictions specific to a particular jurisdiction. Contact the local CMHC office for conditions and requirements.

Fees and Premiums

Fees vary based on whether the property is an existing or new house. Insurance premiums are based on the loan to value ratio and whether one or more advances are required (e.g., sequential advances in the case of new home construction).

Mortgage Amount

The maximum mortgage loan is 95%, therefore minimum borrower equity is 5% of property value. The minimum term is six months with amortization up to 40 years. GDS is based on 32% (principal + interest + taxes + heat), and 50% of condo fees if applicable.

For existing housing, the lender must supply CMHC with the listing or recent photo of the property, copy of the agreement/contract, underwriting fee, appropriate CMHC form (i.e., Form 530, *Request—Certificate of Insurance*, premium (as mortgage funds are advanced), appraisal (optional), and if applicable, a list of intended property improvements.

With new homes, the lender must supply copies of architect's plans, underwriting fee, appropriate CMHC form (i.e., Form 530), premium (as mortgage funds are advanced), cost estimates/builder's quotes, list of changes, agreement/contract, and sales brochure of subject property or equivalent. A photograph or real estate listing is adequate for completed houses.

Reference   Requirements may change in regard to underwriting policies and terms/conditions concerning loan approval. Consult the local Canada Mortgage and Housing Corporation office for details.

Automated Approval System (EMILI)

In the past decade, advances in technology, demographic shifts, economic, and work/family balance have had a dramatic impact on customer demands and organizational response. CMHC's clients have indicated that their primary concerns for future delivery of mortgage insurance products focus on customer service, process efficiencies, and minimizing risk.

Two innovative business processes introduced by CMHC in the early 1990s enhance the Approved Lenders business operations. Direct Deposit Option (DDO) provides for the electronic transfer of funds between Lender clients and CMHC. The Accelerated Claims Payment Process (ACPP) improves the lender's ability to process mortgage insurance claims.

In September 1996, CMHC introduced an online service known as *EMILI* to receive and complete risk analysis on applications for mortgage loan insurance on existing housing. EMILI is designed for the receipt, interpretation, validation, approval/referral, and database update of electronically transmitted mortgage insurance requests for properties from approved lenders. Two-way communication lines provide direct electronic messaging between CMHC and its approved lenders. EMILI provides nearly instantaneous response to applications submitted to Canada Mortgage and Housing Corporation.

Within the EMILI umbrella, a self-approval option (delegated authority) is available to qualified approved lenders. Through the automated approval component, EMILI allows for instantaneous client service while improving the quality of the portfolio and reducing operating costs. EMILI has built-in pre-approval and post-approval quality control monitoring and reporting elements to ensure that quality business is being put on the books.

The approved lender electronically submits the data required by CMHC to assess the mortgage risk using this model system. Those applications where risk is acceptable to CMHC are automatically approved. CMHC underwriters will intervene when risk results from the models do not meet CMHC minimum limits. While EMILI initially focused on mainframe computer links, where required, a personal computer (PC) based facility is available for the approved lender to have real time access to EMILI for review and approval of loans. Technical requirements and procedures go beyond the normal scope of activity for real estate practitioners.

CANADA PENSION PLAN (CPP)
(SEE SOURCE DEDUCTIONS)

CANADIAN CONDOMINIUM INSTITUTE

The Canadian Condominium Institute (CCI) is an independent, non-profit organization formed in 1982 with chapters throughout Canada. CCI awards the ACCI designation (Professional Associate of the Canadian Condominium Institute), to those who meet experience requirements and successfully pass an examination. This organization is the only national Canadian association dealing exclusively with condominium issues affecting participants in the condominium community.

Reference   The national office of the Canadian Condominium Institute is located at Suite 310, 2175 Sheppard Avenue East, North York, ON M2J 1W8.

CANADIAN-CONTROLLED PRIVATE CORPORATIONS
(SEE ALSO SMALL BUSINESS DEDUCTION)

A Canadian controlled private corporation is a Canadian resident company that is not controlled directly or indirectly in any manner whatever by one or more non-resident persons and whose shares are neither publicly traded nor controlled by a company whose shares are traded (or any combination thereof). The type and status of a corporation has a bearing on how income is taxed. Many real estate brokerages fall within the definition of a Canadian controlled private corporation as contained in the *Income Tax Act*.

CANADIAN ENVIRONMENTAL PROTECTION ACT

Acronym: CEPA   The *Canadian Environmental Protection Act*, administered by Environment Canada, concerns various regulatory matters involving environmental issues in Canada. The CEPA is referred to as *enabling legislation* in that rules and regulations can be enacted through authority granted under this statute. The Act, enacted in 1988, was designed to provide a legislative framework for increasing standards, to assure citizens of certain rights concerning the environment, and to set out minimum standards for provincial environmental initiatives. The Act consolidates various pieces of federal legislation while addressing a broad range of environmental viewpoints involving most toxic substances used in the marketplace and their control throughout specific life cycles, whether in water, on land, or in the air.

In addition to Environment Canada, other federal agencies are involved in the environmental process through selected statutes, e.g., *Transportation of Dangerous Goods Act*, and the *Clean Air Act*. The federal government is also involved in environmental concerns through the *Fisheries Act*. However, most federal legislation falls under the CEPA.

Application Real estate practitioners have little involvement with federal agencies as most environmental land use regulations and activities concerning hazardous materials are provincially oriented. One notable exception involves waterfront property fronting on canals administered by Parks Canada (with input from the appropriate provincial authority responsible for fish habitat matters and shoreline regulations).

Example *Canadian Environmental Protection Act*

One of the roles of the federal government in environmental control is evidenced by action taken under the *Fisheries Act*. A Québec chemical producer was fined $1,000,000 and ordered to complete $3,000,000 in conservation work on fish habitats after pleading guilty to violating the Act. This manufacturer of titanium dioxide pigment had dumped millions of tons of chemicals in the St. Lawrence River since 1962.

Source: *Globe and Mail*, June 1993

Reference Copies of the *Canadian Environmental Protection Act* can be purchased through Renouf Publishing Company, 61 Sparks Street, Ottawa, ON K1P 5R1.

CANADIAN INSTITUTE OF CHARTERED BUSINESS VALUATORS

Acronym: CICBV   The Canadian Institute of Chartered Business Valuators trains and certifies individuals in business valuation and grants two professional designations, namely the CBV and EEE.

Reference See **Chartered Business Valuator** for additional description concerning the institute and associated designations.

CANADIAN REAL ESTATE ASSOCIATION

Acronym: CREA   The Canadian Real Estate Association (CREA) is the national organization for REALTORS throughout Canada, with offices located in Ottawa. CREA focuses on national and international representation of the profession (a growing function that will prove invaluable as the scope of organized real estate expands in both

size and complexity), with liaison to such organizations as the Appraisal Institute of Canada, the National Association of REALTORS, the Canadian Construction Association, the Urban Development Institute, and Canada Mortgage and Housing Corporation. CREA is the owner of the trademarks REALTOR and MLS in Canada.

Historical Sketch

Founded in 1943, CREA has become a major player in the daily activities of organized real estate. The association was born during the postwar period from the desire to have a national voice for all real estate practitioners in the legislative process. From that purpose, it has grown and prospered into a full-fledged national organization impacting daily on the activities of the members.

The first CAREB (Canadian Association of Real Estate Boards) meeting took place in Niagara Falls in 1944. At that time all members adopted the term REALTOR. Until 1964, this fledgling organization shared space and staff with the Toronto Real Estate Board. From 1964 to 1981, the Ontario and Canadian associations shared common space, at which time they divided responsibilities and engaged separate executive secretaries.

Growth within The Canadian Real Estate Association has been dramatic given its short history. In 1951, there were 1,852 members. Only ten years later, the number had increased to 12,000 and by the spring of 1968, the total membership stood at 21,000. In 1985, 57,700 names filled the roster of CREA and in 1999, membership grew to approximately 66,000.

From very modest beginnings in the 1940s, CREA has moved from shared quarters and no staff to a fully-staffed separate organization located in the nation's capital. CREA, in addition to being a major lobbyist, is now involved in a host of activities related to organized real estate across the country. The Canadian Real Estate Association was instrumental in the development of the Real Estate Institute of Canada.

CREA also provides information and publications including research reports, membership directories, and a broad range of member-related services.

Membership

Membership in CREA is dictated by Rule 5 of the *Rules and Regulations* published by The Canadian Real Estate Association. Rule 5 sets out requirements for local boards and the classes of membership within those boards, e.g., a board, individual, institute, affiliate, and honorary member.

CREA also has a membership category for provincial associations and maintains the Association Executives Council (AEC) and the National Commercial Council.

Trademarks

Members in good standing in real estate boards and associations are licensed/registered to use certification and design marks owned by CREA that include the following:

Trade Marks
- REALTOR, REALTORS, and REALTOR logo.

Certification Marks
- MLS®, Multiple Listing Service, and MLS® logos;
- Service inter-agencies, S.I.A. and S.I.A. logos;
- Service d'inscriptions multiples and SIM;
- Market Value Appraiser-Residential, MVA-Residential, Evaluateur de valeur marchande-Residentiel, and EVM-residentiel, with Associated Design logo; and
- CREA (used only when referring to The Canadian Real Estate Association or in connection with activities, initiatives, products, publications and services).

Administration

The Canadian Real Estate Association is administered by a board of directors that is composed of regional directors, directors-at-large, and the following appointments:

- MLS & Technology Council;
- National Commercial Council Director;
- Association Executives Council representative; and
- National Association of REALTORS representative.

The responsibility of the board of directors is to ensure that the aims and objectives of CREA are actively pursued. An executive committee, reporting to the board of directors, is empowered to convene meetings and generally conduct the affairs of the association. The board of directors reports to the members through the general assembly which constitutes the voting members of the association and is the governing body of the association.

Responsibilities

The Canadian Real Estate Association has responsibility for national/international representation of the real estate industry, the CREA Code of Ethics and Standards of Business Practice, the newly-created national Privacy Code, the maintenance, protection, licensing, and associated standards relating to various certification marks, e.g., MLS and REALTOR, assistance to real estate boards and associations, and arbitration between provincial associations and between members from different provinces.

Councils

Association Executives Council

The Association Executives Council (AEC), a council of The Canadian Real Estate Association, is an organization of real estate association and real estate board administrators designed to enhance the professional development of its members by providing and/or identifying education, networking, administrative and technical resources.

MLS & Technology Council

The MLS & Technology Council of The Canadian Real Estate Association prepares and recommends strategic plans, policies, and budgets to the CREA Board of Directors relating to the advancement of national technological services and standards. The MLS & Technology Council is directly involved in technology-based initiatives such as mls.ca, IXN, and REALTORLink.

National Commercial Council

The National Commercial Council (NCC), comprised of commercial real estate specialists from boards and associations across Canada, provides an interactive network for practitioners specializing in industrial, commercial, and investment real estate. The Council fosters co-operation in the exchange of information among its members and provides strategic leadership for the delivery of commercial services by local real estate boards to their respective membership and professional expertise through educational activities and programs.

Technology

cls.ca

A real estate public site (www.cls.ca) operated by CREA for the advertisement of commercial properties. Presently, only members of the National Commercial Council can advertise commercial properties on cls.ca. Property categories include industrial, investment, vacant land, and commercial.

iMIS

The Association Management System of The Canadian Real Estate Association contains member information and is the foundation for national authentification (i.e., the process of validating individual member right of access to information and web sites, including secure access to sites such as REALTORLink).

IXN (Information Exchange Network)

The Information Exchange Network, an extension of the national web site (www.mls.ca), permits the sharing of confidential information (e.g., legal description, municipal identification, and commission arrangements), between members of The Canadian Real Estate Association. IXN facilitates the uploading of data by boards in a similar manner to the MLS national web site.

mls.ca

The national gateway of organized real estate operated by CREA to put consumers in touch with REALTORS regarding MLS property advertisements. This web site (www.mls.ca) provides access to 99.9 percent of all MLS property advertisements across Canada.

REALTORLink

A secure password-protected web site for use by members of The Canadian Real Estate Association. The web site (www.realtorlink.org) provides up-to-date information of interest to REALTORS in today's marketplace, e.g., industry news, market reports/statistics, and marketing/promotion ideas.

Reference The above information has been summarized from CREA descriptive and promotional materials. For up-to-date information, contact CREA at (613) 237 7111 or access the web site: www.crea.ca.

CANADIAN REHABILITATION COUNCIL FOR THE DISABLED

Acronym: CRCD The CRCD has established a code for residential listings in co-operation with organized real estate to assist brokers and salespeople to identify accessible housing that is suitable for wheelchair-bound buyers and has potential for accommodating the needs of people with other forms of physical disabilities.

Application Accommodation suitable for the disabled is divided into wheelchair, mobility (e.g., ground level access, wide doorways, etc.), and convertible housing (may be converted at a reasonable cost). Practitioners require greater sensitivities to accessible housing given the aging Canadian population and the needs of physically challenged people.

CRCD Coding on Listings

Many provincial associations and boards have agreed to co-operate with the Canadian Rehabilitation Council for the Disabled (CRCD) in establishing a code for residential listings to assist brokers and salespeople in identifying housing that is suitable for wheelchair-bound buyers and has potential for accommodating the needs of persons with other forms of physical disability. The coding, if done diligently by listing salespeople, will save time searching

for suitable properties and assist in reducing the effort required to view properties for buyers with limited mobility.

The CRCD estimates that the percentage of disabled individuals in our communities ranges from 8 to 12 percent of the total population. A market need exists for this information; therefore, the objective is to assist members in quickly locating housing that will meet certain basic criteria of accessibility.

Steps are one of the most obvious problems, especially for people who are wheelchair-bound, and for those with conditions such as arthritis, cerebral palsy, or partial paralysis, who are not necessarily confined to wheelchairs but, who do have mobility difficulty and for whom steps are hazardous. Stairs are also detrimental for persons with invisible disabilities such as heart conditions and respiratory ailments.

Difficulties associated with space (extra large rooms, long narrow hallways), can be an issue. For people with arthritis and other degenerative conditions (e.g., multiple sclerosis), distance is associated with fatigue and possibly pain. Conversely, for a wheelchair-bound person, space can be advantageous to manoeuvre a wheelchair.

A house with a simple layout and few changes of level would be practical for blind or partially-sighted persons.

Wheelchair Housing

The primary housing problems faced by a person in a wheelchair are inaccessible entrances, access to upper and lower levels, unuseable washrooms, and the overall lack of space, particularly in hallways and bedrooms. In high rise developments, access to elevators may not be available. Although completely accessible conditions are rarely available in existing housing inventory, a house would qualify as acceptable if it conformed as closely as possible to the criteria outlined below.

Basic Criteria

- One level housing or a condominium apartment with ground level entrance, no steps, ramped entrance, and thresholds not exceeding 0.013 m (½").
- Minimum width of 0.864 m (2'10") for entry doors.
- Vestibules should lead directly to the interior of the house without the need for sharp turns. A vestibule (depth of 1.9 m (6' 2¾")) permits operation of one door at a time. Shallow vestibules prohibit or restrict wheelchair maneuverability.
- Toilets should have space, 0.762 m (2'6") to allow for the lateral transfer of a person from a wheelchair. An accessible area of approximately 0.762 m x 1.22 m (2'6" x 4') beside the bath is also desirable.

Mobility Housing

Housing built to normal space standards may encompass some the following accessible features.

- Ground level access (in condominium apartments). This is not intended to infer that apartments must be on the main floor only.
- In high rise apartments, elevators large enough to accommodate wheelchairs, with elevator buttons at an accessible level.
- Wide doorways.
- Extra large bathrooms to accommodate a person with some lack of mobility, for example a person with multiple sclerosis, who may be able to get out of the wheelchair for short periods.
- In high rise buildings, barrier-free balconies at least 1.83 m (6') deep.

Convertible Housing

Involves structures that can be renovated at a reasonable cost and may include condominium apartments, bungalows, and houses with ground-level entrances that have one or two steps but a large enough frontage that could be ramped. Main floor provisions for washroom and laundry facilities should exist.

Additional Features

- Walkways that are firm, smooth, constructed of concrete or asphalt, and at least 1.521 m (5') wide.
- Parking width 3.66 m (12'), preferably a garage with adequate allowance for wheelchair transfer, direct access to the house, and protection from weather.
- Outside approach to the main entrance of the house that is protected from the elements by means of an enclosed porch or canopy.
- Non-slip flooring.
- Houses without basements.

Housing that appears to fall into one or more of the three preceding categories and includes most of all of the additional features, should be indicated with a *Y* (for yes) in the CRCD category box on a listing data form.

Barrier-Free Housing

This is an area of growing concern that relates directly to real estate practitioners. What type of home best suits someone who is blind or has a visual impairment? How much space is required to manoeuvre a wheelchair through doorways, hallways, and around sharp corners? What kinds of difficulty do steps or slight inclines pose to someone with reduced mobility?

Most people don't give these concerns much thought until dealing with them personally. It is estimated that between 8 and 12 percent of the total population have some form of disability, with others, such as seniors, having special needs. To better serve these clients and customers, real estate practitioners are making themselves conscious of potential barriers that many homes may contain. The presence of stairs are often taken for granted, and the CRCD points out that, for people in wheelchairs or those with conditions such as arthritis, cerebral palsy, or partial paralysis, they are an obvious problem. Steps can also pose problems for parents with small children and temporarily disabled people. Steep stairways with little headroom can pose problems for extremely tall people and can also be taxing for others with health concerns, e.g., heart and respiratory conditions.

When selling an existing home, various items may require modification for a disabled individual.

- Light switches, fuse panels, and electrical outlets can be lowered to the reach of someone in a wheelchair.
- The fuse panel should be on the main floor.
- Kitchen/bathroom lower cupboards can be removed to allow access to counter space for wheelchair users.
- Closets can be retrofitted with wider doors and adjustable rods to make access easier.
- Electricity and plumbing modifications can be made to accommodate main floor laundry facilities.
- Existing decks and porches can be fitted or replaced with ramps for more accessibility.

For visually impaired buyers, the following should be considered:

- Different types of flooring can be installed to help people determine which rooms they are entering.
- Colour on corners and edges can be helpful.
- Many devices that produce sound or talk to homeowners (such as security alarms), can be installed in existing or new homes.

For clients who are deaf or hearing impaired, the following should be considered:

- Telephones and doorbells can be hooked up to light systems that flash to let people know when someone is at the door or on the phone.
- Special smoke detectors can also be connected to vibrating bed pads to wake people up in case of fire.

There are also a growing number of people with environmental sensitivities who may be concerned about the presence of certain types of substances in a home.

Reference The CRCD has recently adopted a new national name and is now known as the Easter Seals/March of Dimes National Council. Provincial affiliate names vary. The term CRCD is still widely used.

CANADIAN RESIDENTIAL APPRAISER
(SEE ALSO APPRAISAL INSTITUTE OF CANADA)

Acronym: CRA The Appraisal Institute of Canada (AIC) awards the Canadian Residential Appraiser (CRA) designation. The CRA denotes members who are qualified in the appraisal and valuation of individual, undeveloped residential dwelling sites and housing containing not more than four self-contained units.

The Institute grants the use of the CRA designation upon successful completion of the following:

- Course Series 1000;
- Appraisal Standards Seminar;
- Demonstration Appraisal Report formatted on a single-family dwelling; and
- Three years' relevant experience or article and attain one year (200 days) of appraisal experience in the residential category.

Upon application for designated membership, the National/Provincial Admissions Committee will request samples of current work product for review and an oral interview will be scheduled.

Reference The National Office of the Appraisal Institute of Canada is located at 1111 Portage Avenue, Winnipeg, MN R3G 0S8.

The above information was summarized from detailed materials provided by the Institute with no representation concerning its accuracy or completeness. Contact AIC for current requirements.

CANCELLATION CLAUSE

A provision in an agreement/contract that confers upon one or both of the parties the right to terminate the agreement/contract upon the occurrence of the condition or contingency set forth in the said clause.

Application Cancellation provisions are commonly found in commercial leases and provide the right to terminate upon a specified occurrence.

If 50% or more of all rented and rentable floor area in the Shopping Centre is at any time destroyed or damaged by any cause whatsoever or by demolition caused or necessitated thereby, notwithstanding that the Premises may be unaffected by such occurrence, then and so often as such event occurs, the Landlord may, at its option, to be exercised by notice in writing to Tenant within 90 days next following such occurrence, elect to cancel and terminate this Lease, provided that Landlord has terminated 50% or more (by number or by square feet) of the leases of tenants in the building in which the Premises are located. In the case of such election, the Term of this Lease and the tenancy hereby created shall expire by lapse of time upon the 30th day after such notice is given; the rent and other payments shall be adjusted as of the date of such occurrence and Tenant shall, within such 30 day period, vacate the Premises and surrender the same to Landlord with Landlord having the right to re-enter and repossess the Premises discharged of this Lease and to remove all persons therefrom.

CAPACITY (HEAT)

Refers to the amount of heat that a system can generate. The output rating is a percentage of the input rating and will depend on whether it is a conventional, mid-efficiency, or high-efficiency system. Ratings are given as BTUs per hour. A BTU is a *British Thermal Unit* representing the amount of heat required to raise the temperature of one pound of water, one Fahrenheit degree. Electric heaters are rated in kilowatts.

CAPACITY (OF THE PARTIES)
(SEE ALSO CONTRACT)

A contract requires that the parties entering into the agreement be legally competent to do so. Certain individuals are considered not to always have the capacity to make a contract and are protected by law so that others will not take advantage of them. Included in this group are infants or minors, mentally incapacitated persons, and intoxicated persons.

CAPITAL BUDGETING
(SEE ALSO CASH FLOW MODEL)

Capital budgeting is broadly defined as the process of selecting capital assets based on the allocation of limited resources with the anticipation of returns over an extended period. Today's capital budgeting involves management personnel identifying specific projects for possible acquisition that align with pre-determined investment goals and objectives. The most important criterion is expected return. Comparative analysis of forecasted returns permits investors to evaluate the merits of one project over another and cash flows generated from a capital project are fundamental in determining these returns. Consequently, considerable effort is expended in evaluating both cash flow before tax and cash flow after tax using a variety of investment tools such as payback period, discounted cash flows, present value, net present value, and internal rate of return.

Application   Modern capital budgeting theory has gradually migrated from financial markets into the real estate field, but not without modifications. The theory of capital budgeting rests on a fundamental premise that the value of a project depends on cost in relation to future incomes. The issue of financing does not factor into the equation in pure capital budgeting models developed by financial analysts. In fact, asset managers prefer the screening and selection of projects without regard to financing. Texts sometimes reference this technique as the *whole cost* approach which facilitates simplified decision-making based on the merits of particular projects followed by the acquisition of the best available financing to effect the capital acquisition(s).

The lack of consideration for financing was also prevalent in the appraisal field. Appraisers traditionally followed a *holistic* approach by concentrating on income analysis by way of a static snapshot of the property (capitalizing stabilized net operating income), or at minimum, analyzing property in terms of land and building components. Since the 1960s however, appraisers have paid closer attention to the division of equity and debt components in real estate investments. Direct and yield capitalization approaches now provide methods for detailed equity analysis (as separate from financing issues), either through income rates (direct capitalization), or yield rates (yield capitalization).

Real estate theorists are also departing from traditional capital budgeting processes given the unique qualities of real estate investment. While the impact of financing arrangements may be minimized in non-real estate capital assets (although the debate continues based on specific circumstances), real estate projects are typically linked directly to financing alternatives. The success or failure of a venture often hinges on favourable debt servicing terms. In fact, leverage is a focal point of conversation in most real estate acquisitions and contributes directly to the yield realized on the equity investment in real estate capital projects. As a result, modern comparative tools understandably favour the separation of equity and debt components. Further, real estate analysts show a distinct pref-

erence for after tax perspectives given inherent tax sheltering mechanisms built into real estate investments.

Capital budgeting methodologies, for real estate purposes, are focused on the discounted cash flow analysis model or simply the *cash flow model*. This model recognizes the inherent contribution of financing and leverage within decision-making strategies and proponents point to the advantage of including timely real estate debt costs in the proper evaluation of any project. The fact that capital budgeting techniques differ between real estate and other disciplines should not be overly emphasized. The difference of opinion merely reflects the unique qualities of income property ownership. Real estate investment analysis is acquiring a distinct status in the realm of capital budgeting.

CAPITAL COST ALLOWANCE

Acronym: CCA   Capital assets, though durable, have a limited lifetime and at some point will be replaced. Generally, the capital cost of a property is what the buyer pays for that property. Capital cost includes items such as delivery charges, GST, and PST. The *Income Tax Act* permits a deduction of part of the capital cost of the asset against the income from the business. Capital cost allowance (CCA) is the maximum rate set under the *Income Tax Act* that the taxpayer can claim for depreciation. CCA is not a cash flow issue but rather a matter of taxation and tax deductible expenses. CCA acknowledges the existence of depreciation that is the result of wear and tear over the life of an asset and the ability to offset income in relation to the cost of that asset.

Adjusted Cost Base

The adjusted cost base represents the acquisition price of a property with adjustments as prescribed by the *Income Tax Act* (S. 53, although other provisions apply).

The Act provides for various adjustments; selected examples are included for illustration purposes only as calculations can be complex.

- Mandatory capitalization of certain expenses (e.g., interest expense for vacant land or soft costs relating specifically to the construction, alteration, or renovation of a rental building).
- Adjustments allowed by the Act due to replacement property acquisitions.
- Selling costs for the disposition of capital property (e.g., legal/accounting fees).
- Reductions that arise through the receipt and use of public assistance funding.
- Reductions due to partial disposition of the capital property.

• Adjustments relating to various elections by corporations at time of acquisition or wind up.

Determination of the adjusted capital cost base can be complex. Real estate practitioners should seek expert tax advice on such matters.

Soft Costs

The calculation of soft costs can be a significant issue regarding the adjusted cost base. The Act does not define the term *soft costs*, but is understood to include, but not limited to, construction-related inspection fees, utility hookup charges, engineering fees, municipal fees, legal/accounting fees, and mortgage fees. Capitalization of soft costs is generally limited to the *construction* phase. Pre- and post-construction costs, subject to qualifications, may be deductible if incurred for the production of income. The Act also permits the amortization of selected expenses depending on their contribution to the long term earning capacity of the property and the ability to expense certain items regardless of whether they occur during, before, or after the construction period, e.g., costs associated with landscaping.

CCA as a Permissive Deduction

The rate of CCA applied to each class is specified as a maximum rate. A taxpayer may therefore claim any CCA amount up to the maximum by multiplying the CCA rate by the balance in the class at the end of the taxation year. Only the amount of CCA actually claimed is deducted from the balance of the class and the remaining balance is carried forward and available for future CCA claims.

CCA Classes

The *Income Tax Act* and Regulations detail various *classes* for purposes of CCA calculation.

Real estate brokerages are normally concerned with selected categories such as Classes 8, 10, 10.1 (more expensive automobiles), 12, 13, and 14. The table in **Figure C.1** shows selected CCA classes that might be used particularly by a commercial specialist.

CCA Restrictions—Rental Property

Before 1972, no restrictions existed regarding rental properties. A paper loss could be incurred if CCA deductions exceeded net operating income, resulting in tax savings from other income received by the taxpayer. Regulation 1100, subsections (11) to (14.2), now restricts CCA on rental properties owned by individuals, partnerships, and certain types of corporations. Life insurance companies

CLASS	TYPE OF ASSETS	HALF-YEAR RULE	RATE & METHOD*
1	Buildings after 1987 and excess renovations to Class 3 Buildings	Yes	4% DB
3	Buildings before 1988 and renovations after 1988	Yes	5% DB
6	Farm buildings, fences, and oil and water storage tanks	Yes	10% DB
8	Miscellaneous capital property not included in other classes, e.g., office equipment and furniture	Yes	20% DB
10	Automobiles or trucks used for business purposes; computers and system software	Yes	30% DB
12	Computer application software, tools, utensils, uniforms	Some Exceptions	100% DB
13	Leasehold interest and leasehold improvements paid for by tenant	Special Rules	SL
14	Patent, franchise of limited life, licence	No	Variable
17	Roads, sidewalks, parking areas or storage areas	Yes	8% DB

* Maximum CCA rate based on undepreciated capital cost (UCC). DB–Declining Balance, SL–Straight Line

Figure C.1   CCA Classes

and *principal business* corporations (or a partnership thereof), are excluded. A *principal business* corporation is defined as an entity whose principal business involves the leasing, rental, development, or sale of owned real property. Multiple-unit residential properties (MURBs) were, at one time, another important exception. Tax reforms during 1988 removed most advantages relating to this investment vehicle. As a result of Regulation 1100, the maximum allowable capital cost allowance is now limited to the total amount of taxable income before CCA. This requirement effectively eliminates the possibility of paper losses from CCA deductions.

Declining Balance Method

The most frequently used method to calculate depreciation. Declining balance involves the reduction of the capital cost by a percentage as set out for a particular class of property with subsequent reductions always applied to the declining balance (undepreciated capital cost), within that class.

Example 1   *Capital Cost Allowance–*
Declining Balance Method–
Existing Brokerage

ABC Realty Inc. begins the year with undepreciated capital cost in a specific class of $50,000 with purchases and dispositions made during that year. The CCA for the applicable year and the UCC for the beginning of the following year are calculated below.

UCC of class at beginning of year		$50,000
Add: Purchases during year		+5,000
Less: Less of Dispositions during year:		
Capital cost, or	$3,000	
Proceeds at disposition	$3,500	
		−3,000
UCC before adjustment		52,000
Less: 1/2 net amount (5,000 − 3,000 ÷ 2)		−1,000
(see Half-Year Rule)		
UCC before CCA		51,000
Less: CCA for class for the year		−5,100
Add: 1/2 net amount (see above)		+1,000
UCC of the class at beginning of the next year		$46,900

Half-Year Rule and Available for Use

The half-year rule (often referred to as the 50% Rule), was implemented to correct the fact that assets purchased at the end of a taxation year would otherwise provide an amount in a class eligible for the maximum capital cost allowance in that year. This rule provides that 50% of purchases during the year, minus the lesser of capital cost and proceeds of disposition of assets in the class during the year, is deducted before the CCA for the year is calculated. By effectively reducing the CCA on purchases (in excess of dispositions), made during the year, the tax advantage of a late purchase is reduced.

The Regulations limit the amount of capital cost available for newly acquired assets to one-half of the normal amount of CCA for the year of acquisition (1981 revision). For newly acquired properties, the Regulations were further amended for all taxation years following 1989. The half-year rule now applies only to properties that are *available for use*, otherwise, capital cost allowance is deferred to the following taxation year. Previously, CCA could be taken for properties under construction and not technically being used for income purposes. Now, the property must be *used* for generating income and the Regulations set out requirements in that regard.

CCA may be deducted in the year that the property was first used for generating income or 358 days following the taxation year in which the property was acquired. Regarding the issue of *available for use* –special rules, elections by

taxpayers, and relieving rules relating to the term *available for use* go beyond the scope of this publication. Expert advice is required.

Example 2   *Capital Cost Allowance–*
Declining Balance Method–
New Brokerage

On October 1, 2000, ABC Realty Inc. began operations and purchased office furniture at a cost of $8,700. In the following year, additional office furniture costing $15,000 was purchased. The maximum CCA that can be claimed for both years along with the UCC is calculated below.

Working Notes
Office furniture is Class 8–20% CCA rate, declining balance method. The 50% Rule applies in both years due to the additions. Since no dispositions occurred in either year, the net amount of additions only is used for calculations. As ABC Realty Inc. started operations on October 1, 2000 (a leap year), the ratio for pro-rating is 92/366.

2000	Additions	$8,700	
	UCC, December 31, 1999		$8,700
	Less: (50% Rule) 1/2 net amount		−4,350
	UCC before CCA		4,350
	CCA at 20% prorated (4,350 x .20 x 92 ÷ 366)		−219
	Add: 1/2 net amount		+4,350
	UCC at January 1, 2001		$8,481
2001	Additions	$15,000	
	UCC, December 31, 2001		$23,481
	Less: 1/2 net amount (15,000 x .50)		−7,500
	UCC before CCA		15,981
	CCA at 20%		−3,196
	Add: 1/2 net amount		+7,500
	UCC at January 1, 2002		$20,285

If there are no additions or dispositions in 2002, the CCA is: $20,285 x .20 = $4,057

Land and Building Allocation

As the cost of improvements to property will normally be categorized under the capital cost allowance provisions, allocating the purchase price between land and improvements is necessary. As a rule, such allocations must be fair, reasonable, and defensible. Expert advice is required. Seller and buyer perspectives on how this allocation occurs are usually different, owing to tax implications arising from the determination.

The allocation of purchase price between land and building is a key negotiating point in many commercial transactions. The buyer seeks to maximize building allocation (plus chattels associated with the sale), to establish a high capital cost for future CCA calculations—the seller wants to minimize the allocation to avoid recapture. Generally, a reasonable, mutually accepted allocation, if defensible, would undoubtedly be sufficient in the agreement/contract . Occasionally, commercial practitioners use municipal tax assessment ratios as a benchmark for the allocation. Alternatively, an appraiser may be retained to value the property and provide a supportable allocation between land and improvements.

If property is sold and improvements have no economic value, the seller may be able to allocate the full sale price to the land. The term *no economic value* generally means that the cost of demolition exceeds the building(s) value. From a taxation perspective, the position taken must be defensible. As a caution, the fact that the buyer sees no value in such buildings, owing to a different planned use for the property, does not in itself create *no economic value.*

Recaptured Capital Cost Allowance

At the time of property disposition, the *Income Tax Act* requires the recapture of capital cost allowances if the value of the improvements has been maintained or increased since originally acquired. The recapture cannot exceed the capital cost deductions allowed. As a rule, if the undepreciated capital cost (UCC) has a positive balance and no assets remain, terminal loss can be claimed. If a negative UCC balance occurs due to asset disposition, recapture (referred to as *income inclusion*) occurs, even if assets remain in that particular class. Recapture must be declared as income. Deferral of recapture is possible in some instances, e.g., a replacement property is acquired within a specified time limit. In this instance, an amount equal to the recapture is applied against the UCC for new property.

Recapture can occur either when analyzing taxable income from operations cash flows or sale proceeds at the point of disposition. An example is provided relating to the sale of property. As recaptured CCA will affect sale proceeds and consequently cash flows after tax, practitioners must be aware of basic procedures used in establishing whether a recapture is being realized. Further, accurate forecasting of sale proceeds after tax is necessary when calculating an after tax internal rate of return (IRR).

Example *Capital Cost Allowance– Recaptured Capital Cost Allowance*

Recaptured capital cost allowance for purposes of a sale involving a typical investment-grade property is calculated by establishing the lesser of **Improvement Allocations at Purchase** or **Improvement Allocations on Sale** and deducting *Undepreciated Capital Cost Improvement Allocations on Sale.*

Continued…

Acquisition Price	$1,000,000
Less: Total Soft Costs	–0
Less: Original Land Allocation	–300,000
Improvement Allocation at Purchase	$700,000
Improvement Allocation on Sale (established at the point of sale)	$930,000
Improvement Allocation (lesser of the two allocations)	$700,000
Plus: Capital Improvements	+0
Less: CCA Taken	–77,836
Undepreciated Improvements at Sale	$622,164
Recaptured Capital Cost Allowance	**$77,836**

Straight Line Method

Under the straight line approach, the useful life of the depreciable assets must be estimated according to the Regulations. The annual capital cost allowance taken represents a pro-rated amount based on the estimate.

The calculation of CCA for Class 13 (leasehold improvements paid by the tenant), uses a straight line as opposed to declining balance method. An example is provided regarding entries over a two-year period for an item with a useful life of ten years.

Example *Capital Cost Allowance– Straight Line Method*

Assume that the capital cost allowance for an item is ten years, with a pro-rated straight line calculation of depreciation. Following are the entries for the first two-year period:

Capital Cost	$10,000
First Year Depreciation ($1/10 \times 10,000$)	–1,000
Remaining Capital Cost (UCC)	9,000
Second Year Depreciation ($1/10 \times 10,000$)	–1,000
Remaining Capital Cost (UCC)	**$8,000**

Taxation Year Less Than 12 Months

In the first or last years of the operation of a business, or in a year in which there has been a change in the fiscal year, it is possible to have a taxation year of less than 12 full months. In such cases, CCA must be prorated by the proportion that the number of days in the taxation year is to 365 (or 366 in a leap year).

Undepreciated Capital Cost (UCC)

Undepreciated capital cost is the capital cost associated with a specific improvement under a particular class, less any capital cost allowance already taken and less previous disposals in the same class.

Example — Capital Cost Allowance–Undepreciated Capital Cost (UCC)

Assume that the capital cost allowance for an item is ten years, with a prorated straight line calculation of depreciation. Following are the entries for the first two-year period:

Capital Cost	$20,000
First Year Depreciation ($1/_{10}$ x 20,000)	−2,000
Remaining Capital Cost (UCC)	**18,000**
Second Year Depreciation ($1/_{10}$ x 20,000)	−2,000
Remaining Capital Cost (UCC)	**$16,000**

CAPITAL GAIN

(SEE ALSO CAPITAL COST ALLOWANCE)

The gain from the disposition of capital property, a percentage of which must be added to taxable income on disposition of the asset. This section of the *Income Tax Act* was introduced on December 31, 1971, commonly referred to as valuation day. Capital property is depreciable and generally includes any item in which a capital gain or loss would be realized, e.g., buildings, land, mortgages, share capital, artwork, and partnership interest.

Capital Gain Calculations

A capital gain is a gain on the sale or exchange of capital assets that meets the criteria for a capital gain as set out in the *Income Tax Act*. Two real estate examples are provided. The first details a gain by a corporation (including calculation of taxable gain based on an assumed taxation level), and the second provides the calculation for a gain realized by an individual. Calculations can vary based on the type of property and the circumstances surrounding the investor/owner. Both examples assume that the gain realized meets the criteria for a capital gain.

Example 1 — Capital Gain Calculations

Anycity Investments Inc. acquired a commercial building several years ago and has recently sold the property for $1,329,684. The adjusted cost base was determined to be 1,000,000. The president of the company is estimating both the capital gain and taxable capital gain as following:

Sale Price	$1,329,684
Adjusted Cost Base	−1,000,000
Cost of Sale	−59,832
Capital Gain Exemption	−0
Capital Gain	$269,852
Taxable Capital Gain (50%)	**$134,926**

Example 2 — Capital Gain Calculations

In 1969, Mrs. Jones purchased a rental property containing four units at a cost of $38,000. On December 31, 1971, the value was established at $40,000. Throughout the ensuing years, the property was well maintained and produced above average rental income. Before selling it in 20xx, a new furnace was installed at a cost of $7,000. Later in the same year, the property was sold at market value for $500,000. Real estate commissions and other allowable selling expenses amounted to $30,000 with legal fees totalling $2,800. The capital gain calculation is:

Sale Price	$500,000
Adjusted Cost Base (40,000 + 7,000)	−47,000
Cost of Sale	−32,800
Capital Gain Exemption	−0
Capital Gain	**$420,200**

The $134,926 taxable capital gain in *Example 1* does not constitute tax liability at the point of sale. Consideration must also be given to any recaptured capital cost allowance and unamortized expenses to arrive at a taxable income on sale. The applicable tax rate for the taxpayer is then applied to taxable income to arrive at the tax liability.

Capital Gain *vs.* Taxable Income

The *Income Tax Act* does not specifically set out whether or not a gain or loss is capital in nature. The taxpayer is responsible for reporting the gain as income or capital gain. This report may then be challenged by the Canada Customs and Revenue Agency with the onus of proof on the taxpayer.

Over the years, the determination has been made based on a number of factors such as the intention of the taxpayer, relationship to the taxpayer's business, frequency of transactions, length of time held, nature of the transaction, and objects of the corporation. Should a debate proceed to the Tax Court of Canada, the Court will consider relevant factors concerning taxpayer conduct before, during, and after the period under appeal. Certain factors carry more weight in the process.

Intention

What was the taxpayer's intention at the time the property was purchased?

When a property is bought for investment, any resale profit could still be considered taxable as ordinary income if the apparent intent was to resell for a profit at a future date. The Tax Court will consider such things as reasons for the sale, compelling necessity, change in circumstance, and external factors.

C

Relationship to the Taxpayer's Business

The Tax Court will undoubtedly classify profits as taxable under ordinary business income when a taxpayer uses expertise acquired in regular business activity to generate a profit on the purchase/sale of similar or related commodities. The Court also looks at the time and attention the taxpayer spent on the transaction. Real estate transactions of contractors, renovators, brokers (agents), salespeople, and appraisers have typically fallen under close scrutiny.

Frequency of Transactions

Revenue Canada will assess how often the taxpayer engages in the sale of capital property. Usually, frequency of such occurrences suggests the carrying on of a business for profit. Assessment as ordinary business income will be the result. However, even an isolated transaction can be so judged, given the right set of circumstances.

Nature of Transaction and Assets

Taxability as income may be indicated if the asset cannot normally be used either personally or for investment purposes. Mortgages are often judged under this test. If a mortgage is purchased at a substantial discount or has a short maturity date, the mortgagee may be viewed as being in a business that realizes profit from the transaction, thus invoking business income as opposed to capital gain.

Objects of the Corporation

The Tax Court will look at the articles of incorporation to determine if a transaction falls under the objects of the corporation, and if it is part of usual business. However, the absence of this provision may not be deemed conclusive by the Court. Proving that a specific sale fell beyond the normal course of affairs of the company is difficult and once again the burden of proof rests with the taxpayer.

Special Note: Real Estate Transactions

Profits would likely be taxed as regular business income if a taxpayer buys and sells real estate on a regular basis. However, if the taxpayer can prove that these dispositions were a planned and necessary part of a total investment program, then there may be a case for capital gains treatment of the profit. In the case of farmlands, if the taxpayer purchased or inherited the land and lived on it for a period of time, a disposition of the property will most likely be regarded as a capital gain.

Further, if a sale of real estate is not planned, that is brokers are not employed, the property is not advertised, no sign or other visible evidence of active marketing is present, then the profit may be, but not always, treated as a capital gain. In some cases the profit from an eventual sale of the property might be deemed as a capital gain where the taxpayer purchased real estate for a third party to whom he/she expected to transfer it without profit, and was then left with the property when the third party backed out of the transaction.

Exemptions

Exemptions to the payment of capital gains have varied throughout the past decades. A capital gain exemption for individuals (not corporations) can apply to certain sales of real property. The Federal Budget (February 1992) dramatically affected the exemption by eliminating it for almost all property; however, capital gains accruing prior to March 1992 on qualifying small business corporation shares may still be eligible for the exemption. Such issues go beyond the scope of this publication and expert advice should be obtained.

The major exemption for real estate practitioners to consider involves a principal residence. A principal residence is defined as a house, apartment in a duplex, apartment building or condominium, cottage, houseboat, trailer or mobile home, or a share in a co-operative housing corporation.

To qualify as a principal residence, certain criteria must be met:

- The taxpayer must own the housing unit, either jointly or solely;
- A family unit may only have one principal residence;
- The land upon which the housing unit sits cannot exceed one acre and any excess is not considered part of the principal residence unless the taxpayer can prove it is necessary for personal use and enjoyment;
- The unit must be ordinarily inhabited in the year (*ordinarily inhabited* is not defined in the *Income Tax Act*); and
- The unit must be designated as the taxpayer's principal residence for the year.

Appropriate expert advice should be sought in regard to capital gains issues and exemptions.

CAPITAL LOSS

The loss which is incurred from the disposition of capital property. Provisions in the *Income Tax Act* provide for the deduction of capital losses for both individuals and corporations.

Example   *Capital Loss*

In 1993, Mrs. Williams purchased a rental property containing four units at a cost of $488,000 and a few years later sold the property for $500,000. During the time of ownership, she made no significant improvements to the property. Real estate commissions and other allowable expenses amounted to $30,000 with legal fees totalling $2,800.

The capital loss calculation is as follows:

Sale Price	$500,000
Adjusted Cost Base	−488,000
Costs of Sale	−32,800
Capital Gain/Loss	**$(20,800)**

CAPITAL MARKET

A supply and demand market in which individuals trade long-term monetary instruments. In Canada, long-term instruments such as bonds, stocks, and mortgages should be differentiated from short-term instruments such as T-bills (treasury bills) and guaranteed investment certificates commonly associated with money markets.

CAPITALIZATION

(SEE ALSO TERMINAL CAPITALIZATION RATE)

Capitalization is the process of converting the income of a property into a capital value and, more specifically, the estimating of the present worth of a series of anticipated future periodic cash flows through the application of an appropriate rate or factor, referred to as a capitalization rate. More than one rate may be embodied in the factor:

- A rate providing for interest on the investment, (referred to as the discount rate).
- A rate providing for the recapture of capital (the recapture rate).

Two methods are used to arrive at value through capitalization: the *direct method* and the *yield method*. Capitalization, using either method, is most commonly associated with the income approach to value, one of three approaches used in the appraisal field (the others being the direct comparison approach and the cost approach). Capitalization, and more specifically the yield method, is increasingly associated with the field of real estate investment analysis.

Capitalization Rates

The ratios expressing a relationship between annual net operating income and present worth (value) or sales price.

Simply put, the capitalization rate expresses the mathematical relationship between the net operating income that a property produces and its capital value. Because income generated by income-producing property can take different forms and may be measured at differing levels of *net-ness*, different capitalization rates are applicable to various components of net income.

Capitalization rates are broadly grouped under income rates and yield rates. Income rates generally involve ratios derived from marketplace activity and are not necessarily tied to expected returns. Yield rates are derived from investor expectations concerning anticipated returns on property with regard to current market conditions. Income rates are associated with direct capitalization and yield rates are applied in the case of yield capitalization.

Direct Capitalization

Two methods are used to arrive at a capitalization rate:

- The *direct capitalization method*; and
- The *yield capitalization method*.

The direct method is most frequently associated with small income investment properties. The yield capitalization method applies more commonly to larger investment-grade commercial projects and properties.

Building Capitalization Rate

A rate that includes return *on* and return *of* capital invested in improvements, separate and apart from capital invested in the under-lying land. The building capitalization rate is used in residual techniques which separate property income into components attributable to land and improvements. Land exists in perpetuity and is not a wasting asset. The valuation of land does not require a factor for recapture of the investment. Buildings have a terminal life and must be addressed differently.

Equity Capitalization Rate

The equity capitalization rate expresses the relationship between cash flow before taxes and the equity invested in a comparable property.

Cash Flow Before Taxes
= Net Operating Income – Annual Debt Service

Equity = Value of Property – Mortgage Value

If the amount of mortgage financing on the subject property is known, the value of the property can be calculated using the equity capitalization rate.

Value of Property = Mortgage Value + Equity

Example *Capitalization–*
Equity Capitalization Rate

The subject property has a present mortgage of $225,000, and a cash flow of $4,124. A comparable property is found that provides the following:

Sale Particulars

Sale Price	$350,000
Equity	125,000

Financial Details

Net Operating Income	28,000
Annual Debt Service	−21,125
Cash Flow Before Taxes	6,875

Equity Capitalization Rate Calculation
$$= \text{Cash Flow} \div \text{Equity}$$
$$= \$6,875 \div 125,000$$
$$= 5.5\% \ (.055)$$

Subject Property—Estimate of Value
- Comparable property demonstrates that typical buyers will accept a 5.5% return on equity invested.(Appraisers would normally analyze three or more comparable properties to arrive at this rate.)
- Cash Flow Before Taxes is capitalized and added to the existing mortgage to arrive at value.

Estimate of Value
$$= \text{Mortgage Value} + \text{Equity (Cash Flow} \div \text{Equity Cap Rate)}$$
$$= 225,000 + (4,124 \div .055)$$
$$= 225,000 + 74,982$$
$$= 299,982 \ (\text{rounded to } \$300,000)$$

Mortgage Capitalization Rate

Expresses the relationship between the annual debt service and the mortgage value (remaining principal amount). If the equity for the subject property is known, the value of the property can be calculated by using the mortgage capitalization rate (frequently referred to as the *mortgage constant*), which requires various assumptions in order to arrive at value.

Overall Capitalization Rate

The overall capitalization rate is made up of two rates:
- The rate of return on the investment (discount rate).
- The rate of return of the investment (recapture rate).

Every investor is entitled to a return *on* and *of* invested capital. When a capitalization rate for an improved property is 10% or 12%, the rate is said to be blended:
- The rate of return on the money invested in both the land and the building (discount rate); and
- A rate of return of the money invested in the building which is a wasting asset (recapture rate).

The blended rate is known as an overall rate which:
- Expresses the relationship between the current year's income and value; and
- Represents a blend of rate of return *on* the investment and rate *of* return of the investment.

Value of Property = Net Operating Income ÷ Overall Capitalization Rate

$$V = I \div R$$

Example *Capitalization–*
Overall Capitalization Rate

The subject property has a net operating income of $16,400. The following comparable properties are found:

	SALE PRICE	NOI	CAP RATE
Sale #1	$187,500	$15,500	.0827
Sale #2	190,700	16,250	.0852
Sale #3	185,600	15,850	.0854
Sale #4	189,500	16,300	.0860

Assuming that Sales 2 and 3 are most current and also highly comparable, the appraiser reconciles the findings to arrive at a capitalization rate of .0850.

Value of Property = NOI ÷ Overall Capitalization Rate
$$= \$16,400 \div .0850$$
$$= \$192,941.18 \ (\text{rounded to } \$193,000)$$

Two methods are used to determine the overall capitalization rate.

Sale of Comparable Properties Net operating incomes of comparable properties are compared with their respective sale prices. Properties must be highly comparable, e.g., income/expense profile, financing, age, and type.

NOTE Practitioners must research sufficient comparables to ensure accuracy in the estimating process.

Band of Investment Method Equity and mortgage cap rates can be used to arrive at an overall capitalization rate based on the relative contribution of equity and mortgage components in the marketplace.

R = (Mortgage Ratio x Mortgage Capitalization Rate) + (Equity Ratio x Equity Capitalization Rate)

A slightly altered version of this formula is also found in appraisal textbooks that produces the same result.

R = (Mortgage Ratio x Mortgage Capitalization Rate) + Equity Capitalization Rate x (1 – Mortgage Ratio)

Example *Capitalization–*
Overall Capitalization Rate–
Band of Investment

The subject property has net operating income of $34,850 and financing can be obtained at 75% of appraised value. Research indicates that a mortgage to equity financing ratio of 75/25 is consistent with comparable properties in the marketplace. Based on further analysis, a mortgage rate of 13.5% (or mortgage capitalization rate of 13.656%) and an equity capitalization rate of 5.5% are determined.

Calculation of Overall Capitalization Rate (R)

R = (Mortgage Ratio x Mortgage Capitalization Rate)
    + (Equity Ratio x Equity Capitalization Rate)
  = (.75 x .136560) + (.25 x .055)
  = .102420 + .013750
  = .116170 or 11.617%

Estimate of Value

V = I ÷ R
  = 34,850 ÷ .116170
  = 299,991 (rounded to $300,000)

Residual Techniques

Income properties can be divided into analytic components for valuation purposes. Traditionally, residual techniques applied to land and building (improvement) components, but can be used with other components, e.g., equity and mortgage. Residual techniques consist of four steps.

1. The value of the known component is capitalized by the appropriate capitalization rate.

2. Annual income needed to support the known component is deducted from total net operating income to derive the residual income applicable to the unknown component.

3. The residual income is capitalized at an appropriate rate to derive the present value of the component.

4. Add the value of the residual component and the known component to arrive at an estimate of value.

The general term *appropriate capitalization rate* requires emphasis as the discount rate applies in calculating residual values.

Land Residual Technique   This technique is used when the building value is known and the value of the land is unknown. This method separates an improved property (existing or projected), into its physical components. The income necessary to provide for a competitive return *on* and an appropriate recovery *of* the building is deducted from net operating income to arrive at a residual. This residual income, available to provide a return on the capital invested in land, is then capitalized at the appropriate rate (discount rate) to arrive at an estimate of value for the land.

Example *Capitalization–*
Overall Capitalization Rate
Land Residual Technique

Assume a building value of $120,000 a net operating income of $18,000, a discount rate of 10% (.10), and remaining economic life of the building at 40 years (to establish the building portion cap rate: 100 ÷ 40 = .025).

Net Operating Income	$18,000
Income Earned by Building ($120,000 x (.10 +.025))	–15,000
Residual net operating income to land	3,000

Value of Land (3,000 ÷ .10) = $30,000

Therefore, the value of the property is:
$120,000 + 30,000 = $150,000

Building Residual Technique   This technique is used when the land value is known and the value of the building is unknown. This method separates an improved property (existing or projected) into its physical components. When the value of the land can be reliably estimated independently, the residual income (after allowing an appropriate return on the capital invested in the land), is capitalized at the appropriate capitalization rate (building cap rate), and added to the land value to arrive at a total estimate of value.

Example *Capitalization*
Overall Capitalization Rate
Building Residual Technique

Assume a land value of $30,000, a discount rate of 10% (.10), and a remaining economic life of building at 40 years.

Net Operating Income	$18,000
Income earned by land ($30,000 x .10)	–3,000
Residual net operating income to building	15,000

Value of Building ($15,000 ÷ (.10 + .025) = $120,000

Therefore, the value of the property is:
$30,000 + 120,000 = $150,000

Gross Income Multiplier (GIM)

The gross income multiplier expresses the relationship between the effective gross income (alternatively referred to as *gross operating income* in commercial reference materials) and the value. The GIM, while occasionally discussed under the general topic of capitalization rates, is technically a multiplier (the reciprocal of a capitalization rate), and is detailed separately. However, from an overall perspective, value is derived from similar facts concerning the subject and comparable properties.

Example *Capitalization*
Gross Income Multiplier (GIM)

Assume that the subject property has an effective gross income of $52,850 and a highly comparable property sold for $392,000 with an effective gross income of $56,000. The GIM is $392,000 ÷ 56,000 = 7. This multiplier is then applied to the subject property:

Estimate of Value = 7 x $52,850
= $369,950 (rounded to $370,000)

Yield Capitalization

Converts future benefits into present value by discounting all future benefits by an appropriate yield rate where the process of converting such benefits is referred to as discounting and the yield rate is commonly referred to as the discount rate.

Reference For further encyclopedia references regarding yield capitalization see: Yield Capitalization, Yield Rate, Cash Flow Model, Discount Rate, Discounted Cash Flow, Mortgage Yield Rate, and Equity Yield Rate.

CARE HOME

A *care home* (also referred to as a *home for special care* or *personal care home)*, is broadly described for legislative purposes as accommodation in which residents receive some form of care services. Care services include health care, rehabilitative or therapeutic, or services that provide assistance with the activities of daily living.

Application Legislation regarding care homes falls to provincial statutes and is typically grouped under tenancy. Considerable interest is focused on this topic given the aging Canadian population.

Provincial See applicable reference materials.

CASEMENT WINDOW

A casement window is hinged at the side and can open either inward or outward. A handle is located on the side of the window opposite the hinge along with a crank, and in some cases, a guide bar along the bottom of the window. An operating crank is often included at the bottom of modern casement windows. Glazing may be single, double, or triple. Manufacturing materials can include wood, metal, vinyl, or a combination thereof. Muntins may be used to separate the glass into smaller panes and is usually done on older, traditional style homes. Casement windows are popular as replacement windows owing to proper ventilation and degree of air tightness. Larger casement windows require quality hardware to ensure smooth operation. See **Figure C.2**.

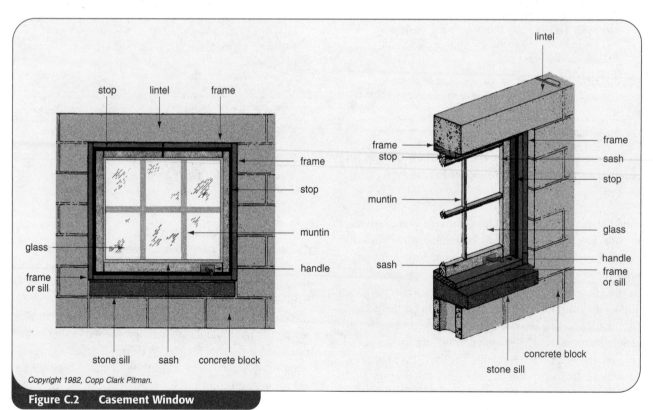

Copyright 1982, Copp Clark Pitman.

Figure C.2   Casement Window

CASH ACCOUNTING

(SEE ALSO ACCRUAL ACCOUNTING)

A single entry system with profit based on cash received less money expended in the same period. The *Income Tax Act* permits cash accounting in the case of farmers, fishermen, and commission salespeople. A real estate brokerage must use accrual accounting, also referred to as double entry or accounts payable/accounts receivable system.

CASH FLOW

A relatively generic term that has traditionally eluded precise definition. From an historical perspective, cash flow referred to the profit arising from a business and provided an indication of internal funds available for capital acquisitions and payment of dividends. In real estate, the buying and selling public typically view cash flow as any income generated by an investment. Differing terminologies have often made comparisons difficult. Consumers and practitioners often reference gross operating, gross rental, effective gross, and adjusted gross incomes to mention a few. To compound matters in real estate, no standard cash flow reporting formats are universally used in the real estate profession.

Application   Commercial practitioners and appraisers have sought to more accurately define cash flow as the net operating income generated by an investment property less debt service (more technically called *cash flow before taxes* (CFBT) or, *before tax cash flow*). During the past three decades, more precise terminology concerning cash flow has entered the marketplace. This is due, in no small way, to recent attention given real estate by financial analysts. Precision was inevitable as the convergence of commercial real estate with other capital markets occurred. Now, properties are screened, valued, and selected with tools commonly associated with the bond and equity financial markets. Institutional investors, familiar with capital budgeting and asset selection techniques, now routinely dissect real estate cash flows in their search to maximize returns.

The more or less widely accepted categorization of cash flow involves two parts: operations cash flow and sale proceeds cash flow.

Operations Cash Flow

The ongoing activities of an investment and the positive or negative cash generated. Appraisers and real estate practitioners calculate a single year's cash flow based on income and expense analysis to arrive at net operating income (NOI). Annual debt service is then deducted from NOI to arrive at cash flow before taxes (CFBT). Cash flow can be further analyzed from an after tax perspective. Cash flow before taxes is frequently used in market value estimates, while cash flow after taxes is applied with investment value estimates, although this distinction should not be overemphasized as the lines are often blurred. In reality, practitioners work in two worlds:

- The objective development and analysis of reconstructed operating statements and cash flows based on appraisal criteria to arrive at market value; and
- The more subjective, individual, investor-oriented forecasting of cash flows based on specific investor goals leading to investment value.

Sale Proceeds Cash Flow

Capital budgeting techniques have introduced a differing perspective on revenue generated at the point of sale. As with operations cash flow, sale proceeds can be viewed under sale proceeds before tax or sale proceeds after tax.

Asset managers typically review operations cash flow and reversionary funds (sale proceeds) within the overall analysis of any capital project. Consequently, real estate followed suit. This perspective on cash flow is particularly important when applying discounted cash flow (DCF) techniques in the analysis and valuation of investment-grade properties. DCF takes into account the initial equity, a specified holding period, the operations cash flow over a specified period, and the proceeds at the point of sale (reversion). The discount rate relates to individual investor expectations and/or marketplace trends relating to either before tax or after tax analysis.

Practitioners widely accept the DCF method as a valuable measure in accurately assessing the future benefits (cash flow) of a real estate investment. Appraisers group the DCF technique under yield capitalization, one of two methods used under the income approach to value.

CASH FLOW AFTER TAXES

Acronym: CFAT   Cash flow (periodic dollar amounts), relating to the operation of an investment property after all expenses are deducted including annual debt service and tax liability. CFAT refers to operations cash flow only and should not be confused with sale proceeds after tax. The latter involves cash flow resulting from disposition (reversion) of the property. The terms *after tax cash flow* and *cash flow after taxes* are synonymous for purposes of real estate investment analysis.

Application   CFAT is one component within the overall cash flow model in providing real estate valuation and investment comparisons. In particular, CFAT is most commonly associated with the analysis of real estate investments and the establishment of investment value (value to a specific investor), using the discounted cash flow model. The cash flow model provides a template for the analysis of CFAT derived from both operations and sale proceeds over a specified holding period.

Example	Cash Flow After Taxes	
Potential Rental Income	$200,000	
Vacancy and Credit Losses	−15,000	
Effective Rental Income		185,000
Other Income		+5,000
Gross Operating Income		190,000
Operating Expenses		−100,000
Net Operating Income		90,000
Annual Debt Service		−60,000
Cash Flow Before Taxes		30,000
Tax Liability		-8,000
Cash Flow After Taxes		**$22,000**

CASH FLOW BEFORE TAXES

Acronym: **CFBT**   Cash flow (periodic dollar amounts), received from the operation of an investment property after all expenses are deducted excluding a deduction for any tax liability. Operations CFBT is calculated by subtracting annual debt service from net operating income.

Application   CFBT is most commonly associated with the analysis of real estate investments based on the discounted cash flow model. The cash flow model provides a template for the analysis of cash flows before tax derived from both operations and sale proceeds over a specified holding period. CFBT is frequently used by appraisers in establishing market value based on discounted cash flows; however, its role

Example	Cash Flow Before Taxes	
Potential Rental Income	$200,000	
Vacancy and Credit Losses	−15,000	
Effective Rental Income		185,000
Other Income		+5,000
Gross Operating Income		190,000
Operating Expenses		−100,000
Net Operating Income		90,000
Annual Debt Service		−60,000
Cash Flow Before Taxes		**30,000**

extends to investment analysis and estimating of investment value depending on assumptions made in the analysis process.

CASH FLOW MODEL

A term used in commercial real estate denoting an analytical structure for estimating cash flows derived both from the operations of investment property (operations cash flow), and the cash flow arising from the sale proceeds of property (sale proceeds cash flow).

Application   Real estate practitioners can provide investment comparisons and estimate either market values or investment values through detailed analysis of operations and sale proceeds cash flows, either before or after taxes. The model contains four elements:

Initial Investment   Amount invested by the investor not including borrowed funds. Consequently, other non-investor capital would also be excluded, e.g., equity participation and joint venture capital from others.

Estimated Investment Holding Period   A forecasted time for both operations and sale proceeds cash flows, often for a period of three to five years. Cash flows within periods may vary and also be positive or negative.

Periodic Cash Flows   Cash flows must be consistent; that is, either before tax or after tax dollars and typically end of year (EOY). Periodic cash flows are referred to as *operations* cash flows.

Sale Proceeds Cash Flow   Cash flow realized from the reversion (sale) of property, expressed as *sale proceeds before taxes* or *sale proceeds after taxes*.

Consistent cash flows are required in investment analysis. If periodic cash flows are after tax, sale proceeds must also be after tax. The cash flow model applies to either before or after tax cash flow basis to arrive at investment analyses and value estimates. Commercial practitioners typically forecast cash flows after tax, to reflect a truer, more accurate measure of yield from an individual investor's perspective. Market value estimates are commonly associated with before tax perspectives.

CASH ON CASH

A rule of thumb measurement used for analyzing return on an investment property and calculated by dividing *cash flow before taxes* by the initial investment.

Application   Cash on cash calculations based on before tax cash flows are most commonly found in the Canadian marketplace, although some real estate brokerages prefer *after tax cash on cash*. The decision rests with individual preferences, the range of available data, and the needs of individual investors in specific marketplaces. Regardless, documented disclosure of procedures and terminology should accompany all calculations to ensure client understanding of the method being used.

Cash on cash should be viewed as a general comparison tool only as it does not take into consideration the present value of cash flow, any taxes payable on cash flow, or any appreciation/depreciation in the value of the property (which occurs when calculating the internal rate of return). However, cash on cash does take into account gross operating income, operating expenses, and annual debt service.

Example   Cash on Cash

Cash on Cash = Cash Flow Before Taxes ÷ Initial Equity Investment

Property A has a cash flow before taxes of $47,300 and the investor has made an initial investment of $235,000.

Cash on Cash = $47,300 ÷ $235,000
= 0.20 or 20%

The 20% reflects the cash flow in relation to the equity invested. The investor can compare cash on cash rates for various properties in the decision-making process.

CASH ON CASH (MODIFIED)

Modified versions of cash on cash calculations have recently appeared in the marketplace. Selected brokerages have adapted the cash on cash formula to include debt reduction (principal payments made due to mortgage amortization). The addition is referred to as *equity buildup*. The modified formula is frequently described as a *broker's rate of return*. The net result is typically a more favourable rate of return given the equity component. The modified version also uses cash flow after tax but, as referenced earlier, no universal pattern exists.

Occasionally, salespeople and brokers (agents) may also include an estimate of capital appreciation for the period under analysis. Obviously, if capital appreciation is included, an even more favourable rate would be obtained. Proponents point out that the amount should be net of all disposition costs. Opponents argue that this modification detracts from the original purpose of cash on cash as a measure of *cash flow* in relation to initial investment.

Neither equity buildup nor capital appreciation represent cash flow, but are simply assumptions that future cash flow will occur.

Example   Cash on Cash (Modified)

Cash on Cash (Modified) =

$$\frac{\text{(Cash Flow After Taxes + Equity Buildup (Debt Reduction))}}{\text{Initial Investment}}$$

Property A has a cash flow after tax of $36,923, a debt reduction due to principal payments on the mortgage amounting to $892, and an initial investment of $173,961.

Modified Cash on Cash = ($36,923 + 892) ÷ 173,961
= .2174 or 21.74%

CASH RECEIPTS/DISBURSEMENTS JOURNALS
(SEE ALSO ACCOUNTING)

Journals required for the recording of cash receipts and disbursements in an accounting system. The cash receipts journal is used to record cheques or cash received and deposited to the bank, while the cash disbursements journal records all payments made by the business.

Provincial   See applicable reference materials.

CASH TO MORTGAGE

A generic term used by many practitioners referring to funds required to pay the purchase price in a real estate transaction when the buyer is assuming an existing mortgage on the property.

Application   *Cash to mortgage* is often informally referred to by practitioners when providing buyers with a rough estimate of funds required to purchase a property, but does not represent an exact assessment of cash required in order to close the transaction. An accurate estimate requires, among other things, detailed analysis of adjustments at the point of closing.

Example   Cash to Mortgage

Investor McKay is considering a residential property in Anycity that is currently listed at $255,000 and has an assumable mortgage of $150,000. The cash to mortgage amount is $105,000. This amount does not include closing adjustments and is only a rough estimate of actual cash required to close a sale.

CAVEAT

A notice given to a legal authority not to do something until the person giving notice can be heard. The word *caveat* is derived from the Latin verb *caveo* meaning *to beware.*

Application In regard to the registration of real estate interests, a caveat is a statutory notice of a claim to an interest in a parcel of land or to a mortgage, encumbrance, or lease that affects the land. A caveat is a warning to the individual investigating the title that someone other than the owner is claiming an interest in that parcel of land. Any person dealing with the land after the registration of a caveat is subject to the interest being claimed, which may or may not be valid. However, if its validity is disputed by the owner, but upheld by the courts, any person dealing with the land after registration of the caveat is subject to the interest claimed.

The effect of a caveat on the market value of a property will depend on the interest that forms the basis of the caveat. Usually, a caveat will not directly affect market value. It may, however, affect the marketability of a property, that is, the ability of the owner to sell it.

Example *Caveat*

Examples of interests that might be registered by caveat include: a tenant's leasehold interest, unpaid liens, option to purchase, agreement for sale, assignment of a lease as security, easement, right-of-way, party wall agreement, shared wall agreement, development agreement, encroachment agreement, unregistered mortgage, building restrictions, restrictive covenants, or a zoning agreement.

Terminology concerning caveats and the type of forms used in the registration of such interests will vary by provincial jurisdiction.

CAVEAT EMPTOR (LET THE BUYER BEWARE)

A long-standing legal principle (Latin for *let the buyer beware*), based on the concept that the buyer is buying at his/her own risk and, consequently, places a responsibility on that buyer to inspect and establish the terms for what is being purchased. The seller cannot be held responsible for the quality of a product unless express warranties have been given. Courts, however, are reticent to allow sellers the benefit of *caveat emptor* in the case of non-disclosure of a material fact that is not readily apparent in a normal viewing by a buyer.

Application Caveat emptor is a continuing source of debate in listing and selling property. Recently, disclosure statements have gained popularity among practitioners and consumers to identify significant issues regarding listed properties, e.g., legal, structural, and environmental matters. A buyer should request a disclosure statement from the seller to protect himself/herself in a real estate transaction. If a serious problem then occurs with the property that was not disclosed in the disclosure statement and not readily evident to the buyer when he/she viewed the property, the seller may not rely on *caveat emptor* in a possible lawsuit. Obviously, the decision by a court will rest on individual circumstances and the overall merits of a particular case.

Example *Caveat Emptor*

A buyer elects to purchase a home directly from the seller without the use of either an agent or legal counsel. The seller clearly states that the property is being sold *as is,* and that the seller is not providing any warranties or representations concerning the condition of the property. The buyer is purchasing under the principle of *caveat emptor.* However, the buyer may have some protection in this case since the courts may not allow the seller to avoid disclosing a material fact to the buyer that the seller knows about, but which is latent, or undetectable, on close examination by the buyer.

Caveat emptor is most frequently in evidence relating a real estate auction, disposition by power of sale, or municipal sale for unpaid taxes.

Provincial See applicable reference materials. The content and format of disclosure statements vary by province. In selected areas of Canada, disclosure statements are mandated, but no uniform policy exists.

CEILING PLENUM

A totally enclosed area above the ceiling used for the handling of air.

CERAMIC/QUARRY TILE

A type of floor finish generally considered high quality and consisting of ceramic or quarry tiles that are hard-fired clay products that may be glazed or unglazed. A conventional wood flooring system generally has too much flex to permit this type of flooring, but this situation may be resolved through subfloor reinforcement and the use of modern epoxy glues.

CERTIFICATE OF INSURANCE

A certificate issued by an insurance company or its agent verifying that a specific insurance policy is in effect for stated amounts and coverage, and sets out the names of those insured.

CERTIFICATE OF PENDING LITIGATION

A legal document, referred to in some provincial jurisdictions by another title, e.g., *Notice of Pending Litigation*, giving notice to other parties that an action or proceeding is pending in the courts and affects the title to a property (formerly known as lis pendens).

Application   Both buyer and a seller, when entering a binding agreement/contract, have liens on the property. The seller has a lien for the sale price (amount to be paid by the buyer), and the buyer has a lien for the deposit and any funds advanced prior to the closing.

The liens are effectively removed (vacated) once the sale is concluded or a mutual release occurs. If the seller refuses to close, the buyer can register a certificate of pending litigation on title to protect his/her interest. This certificate gives notice that the title to the property is affected by pending litigation and effectively limits the seller's ability to resell and close the sale without addressing the certificate.

Example   *Certificate of Pending Litigation*

Buyer Jones forwards an initial deposit of $10,000 and a subsequent amount of $20,000 pursuant to a binding agreement of purchase and sale with Seller Smith. The purchase price of the property is $250,000, Seller Smith refuses to close without any prior notice and for no apparent reason. Conversations between the lawyers fail to resolve the matter and no mutual release is signed. Buyer Jones has already sold his prior home and must find alternate accommodation. Jones' lawyer files a certificate of pending litigation on Smith's property.

CERTIFICATE OF POWER OF SALE

(SEE ALSO POWER OF SALE)

Provincial   See applicable reference materials.

CERTIFICATE OF TITLE

A legal document identifying the registered owner of real property, particulars regarding the legal description, and the form of ownership under which the property is held.

Provincial   See applicable reference materials for various terminologies and forms used in provincial jurisdictions regarding certification of ownership in land registry or land titles offices.

CERTIFICATION

To attest to something as being certain, the truth, or fact.

Application   In an appraisal, a signed and dated certification may state that the appraiser has made a personal inspection, reviewed relevant factors, and has no interest, present or contemplated, in the property. The certification may also state that facts being used are believed to be true and factual and have been verified where possible; that the findings are subject only to assumptions and limiting conditions stated in the report; and that the valuation is not in any way contingent on the compensation received. **Figure C.3** is provided for general information purposes only. Significant wording variations are found in the marketplace.

CERTIFIED COMMERCIAL INVESTMENT MEMBER

(SEE ALSO COMMERCIAL INVESTMENT REAL ESTATE INSTITUTE

Acronym: CCIM   The Certified Commercial Investment Member is recognized for expertise in the discipline of commercial/investment real estate. The Commercial Investment Real Estate Institute (CIREI), an affiliate of the National Association of REALTORS, awards the CCIM designation to individuals who complete a series of graduate level courses in advanced concepts and techniques in commercial real estate. CIREI has three Canadian chapters: National Capital Region Chapter, Central Canada Chapter, and Canada West Chapter. CCIM education credits can be obtained through either an eighteen (18) credit program (three core courses plus nine electives), or a fifteen (15) credit program. Other requirements include, but are not limited to, the submission of a resume of qualifying experience and a comprehensive examination.

Reference   For details regarding the CCIM program, contact the Commercial Investment Real Estate Institute, 430 North Michigan Avenue, Chicago, IL 60611-4092.

The above information was summarized from detailed materials provided by CIREI and its Canadian Chapters with no representation concerning its accuracy or completeness. Contact CIREI for current requirements.

CERTIFICATION OF APPRAISER

I, Anne Appraiser, hereby certify that, to the best of my knowledge and belief:

- The statements of fact contained in this report are true and correct;

- The analysis, opinions, and conclusions are limited only by the reported assumptions and limiting conditions, and are my personal unbiased professional analysis, opinions and conclusions;

- I have no present or prospective interest in the property that is the subject of this report, and I have no personal interest or bias with respect to the parties involved;

- My compensation is not contingent upon the reporting of a predetermined value or direction in value that favours the cause of the client, the amount of the value estimate, the attainment of a stipulated result, or the occurrence of a subsequent event;

- I have made a personal inspection of the property that is the subject of this report;

- No one provided significant professional assistance to the person signing this report.

The subject property was inspected as of November 28th, 20xx. Having regard to all of the information contained in this appraisal, it is my professional and considered opinion that the market value as of November 29th, 20xx was:

Two Hundred and Forty Thousand Dollars ($240,000.00)

Signature: _____
Anne Appraiser

Date: November 30th, 20xx

Figure C.3   Certification of Appraiser

CERTIFIED LEASING OFFICER
(SEE ALSO REAL ESTATE INSTITUTE OF CANADA)

Acronym: CLO   The CLO designation is awarded by the Real Estate Institute of Canada (REIC) and is focused on individuals who negotiate leases or are involved in space planning, lease administration, or the acquisition/disposal of space by lease.

Before an individual can earn the CLO designation, he/she must achieve candidacy status by fulfilling the following:

- Be active in commercial leasing;

- Have at least one year of creditable experience, as defined by REIC;

- Be a high school graduate or equivalent;

- Complete the candidacy application form and forward to REIC with the appropriate application fee; and

- Be endorsed by the local REIC chapter.

Once accepted as a candidate, the individual must remain a candidate for a minimum of one year and a maximum of five years to meet the membership requirements. As a CLO candidate, the individual is required to complete a series of core and specialty courses.

To achieve CLO membership, the individual must:

- Successfully complete the CLO core courses;

- Successfully complete the CLO specialty courses;

- Have three years of creditable experience, as defined by REIC;

- Abide by the REIC Code of Professional Standards;

- Have been a candidate for a minimum of one year; and

- Be affiliated with and endorsed by the local REIC chapter.

Reference   For complete details regarding the CLO program, contact the Real Estate Institute of Canada, 5407 Eglinton Avenue West, Suite 208, Etobicoke, ON M9C 5K6.

The above information was summarized from detailed materials provided by REIC with no representation concerning its accuracy or completeness. Contact REIC for current requirements.

CERTIFIED PROPERTY MANAGER
(SEE ALSO REAL ESTATE INSTITUTE OF CANADA)

Acronym: CPM   The CPM designation is awarded by the Real Estate Institute of Canada (REIC) to individuals involved in the management of residential, commercial, or industrial properties.

An individual seeking this designation must first become a candidate and:

- Be currently working in the field of real estate management;

- Have a minimum of twelve months of qualifying experience;

- Be of legal age;

- Be a high school graduate or equivalent;

- Complete the candidacy application form and send it to REIC with the application fee; and

- Be endorsed by the local REIC chapter.

The individual must remain as a candidate for a minimum of one year. He/she has a maximum of ten years to meet requirements for CPM membership.

To achieve the CPM designation, candidates must:

- Have at least five years of qualifying experience, as defined by REIC;
- Successfully complete a 300-series course;
- Successfully complete REIC 260: Real Estate Investment Analysis and REIC 350: Finance in the Real Estate Context;
- Attend Course 500: Problem-Solving and Decision-Making for Property Managers;
- Complete a comprehensive management plan on an existing property;
- Successfully complete REIC 600: Ethics and Business Practice and view the Course 800 ethics video;
- Earn the requisite elective points by meeting further educational or experience criteria;
- Have been a candidate for at least one year;
- Reaffirm a commitment to the CPM Code of Professional Ethics; and
- Be affiliated with and endorsed by the local REIC chapter.

Reference   For details regarding the CPM program, contact the Real Estate Institute of Canada, 5407 Eglinton Avenue West, Suite 208, Etobicoke, ON M9C 5K6.

The above information was summarized from detailed materials provided by REIC with no representation concerning its accuracy or completeness. Contact REIC directly for current requirements.

CERTIFIED REAL ESTATE BROKERAGE MANAGER

Acronym: **CRB**   The CRB is awarded by the Real Estate Brokers Managers Council of the National Association of REALTORS (NAR) in the United States. The Council is recognized as the professional peer organization for brokerage owners and managers and is dedicated to providing quality education, value-added programs, products and services, and an array of membership benefits.

The CRB Management Certification Program is designed for those who want to earn the Certified Real Estate Brokerage Manager (CRB) designation. Enrollment qualifications include membership in NAR and real estate brokerage experience. Applicants must complete the enrollment application along with a letter verifying membership in a local real estate board and a management resume outlining past and/or present management position(s). The designation is awarded based on CRB credits which can be earned in three ways:

- Completion of CRB courses;
- Number of consecutive years' experience in real estate brokerage management; or
- Completion of management programs offered by approved companies under the CRB Accreditation Program.

Reference   For details regarding the CRB program, contact the Real Estate Brokerage Managers Council at 430 North Michigan Avenue, Chicago, Il 60611-4092.

The above information was summarized from detailed materials provided by the Council with no representation concerning its accuracy or completeness. Contact NAR for current requirements.

CERTIFIED IN REAL ESTATE FINANCE
(SEE ALSO REAL ESTATE INSTITUTE OF CANADA)

Acronym: **CRF**   The Real Estate Institute of Canada (REIC) awards the CRF designation to individuals involved in financial and investment analysis, loan underwriting, loan and risk evaluation, mortgage lending, and administration.

Prior to earning the CRF designation, an individual must achieve candidate status by fulfilling the following:

- Be currently active in the field of real estate finance and related financial analysis;
- Have the administration, underwriting and/or investment analysis experience, as defined by REIC;
- Be a high school graduate, or equivalent;
- Be of legal age;
- Complete the candidacy application form and submit it to the Real Estate Institute of Canada with the application fee; and
- Be endorsed by the local chapter of the Real Estate Institute of Canada.

When an individual becomes a candidate, he/she has a maximum of five years to fulfill the requirements for CRF membership. As well, he/she must:

- Successfully complete CRF core courses;
- Successfully complete CRF speciality courses;
- Have five years of creditable experience, as defined by the Real Estate Institute of Canada;
- Abide by the Real Estate Institute of Canada Code of Professional Standards;
- Have been a candidate for a least one year; and
- Be affiliated with and endorsed by the local REIC chapter.

Reference For details regarding the CRF program, contact the Real Estate Institute of Canada, 5407 Eglinton Avenue West, Suite 208, Etobicoke, ON M9C 5K6.

The above information was summarized from detailed materials provided by REIC with no representation concerning its accuracy or completeness. Contact REIC for current requirements.

CERTIFIED REAL ESTATE SPECIALIST
(SEE ALSO REAL ESTATE INSTITUTE OF CANADA)

Acronym: CRES The CRES designation is awarded by the Real Estate Institute of Canada to persons involved in the sale of residential real estate.

To become a CRES, the individual must:

- Complete the CRES application form and submit it to REIC with the application fee;
- Be of legal age;
- Be a high school graduate or equivalent;
- Successfully complete the CRES education requirements;
- Be a licensed/registered and active real estate sales practitioner with at least two years of experience; and
- Be endorsed by the local REIC chapter.

Educational requirements include the completion of an REIC ethics course or equivalent (REIC 250: Ethical Principles and Professional Standards Course is minimum), and adhere to the REIC Code of Professional Standards. CRES applicants are also required to complete a series of specialized training courses consisting of real estate valuation, finance, law, and other specialty courses. Various programs offered by provincial associations and regulatory bodies may fulfill many CRES requirements.

Reference For details regarding the CRES program, contact the Real Estate Institute of Canada, 5407 Eglinton Avenue West, Suite 208, Etobicoke, ON M9C 5K6.

The above information was summarized from detailed materials provided by REIC with no representation concerning its accuracy or completeness. Contact REIC for current requirements.

CERTIFIED RESIDENTIAL SPECIALIST

Acronym: CRS The CRS is awarded by the Residential Sales Council of the National Association of REALTORS (NAR) in the United States. The Council is a not-for-profit affiliate of NAR and works to increase knowledge and professionalism of residential real estate salespeople. REALTORS who earn the CRS Designation complete a specialized course of study and meet required transaction levels. The Residential Sales Council offers several programs, each requiring current membership in NAR. Under the General Program, the member must:

- Hold the GRI designation;
- Successfully complete three Residential Sales Courses, choosing from RS 200 to 207;
- Document either 50 closed transactions or $3 million in residential real estate with a minimum of 25 transactions; and
- Complete 15 elective credits.

Under the Pro Program, a member with five to nine years of experience must:

- Hold the GRI designation;
- Successfully complete any two Residential Sales Courses, choosing from RS 200 to 207;
- Document either 75 closed transactions or average $1 million in volume per year of experience with a minimum of 40 transactions;
- Verify number of years that the individual has held an active real estate licence/registration by submitting a letter from the local real estate board, state association, or state commission; and
- Complete these requirements within two years of application into the program.

Additional options are provided for members with ten years or more experience.

Reference The Residential Sales Council can be contacted at the National Association of REALTORS, 430 North Michigan Avenue, Chicago, IL 60611-4092.

The above information was summarized from detailed materials provided by the Council with no representation concerning its accuracy or completeness. Contact NAR for current requirements.

CHAIN OF TITLE

The sequence of conveyances and encumbrances affecting a title pursuant to the applicable property legislation within provincial jurisdictions. The term *chain of title* is most commonly associated with land registry. Practitioners may refer to the history of a property for a 40-year period (the typical statutory requirement), but chain of title actually extends to the Crown Patent.

Provincial See applicable reference materials.

CHANGE ORDER

Any written order setting out changes in regard to an original contract or purchase order.

Application   An order issued any time that there is a change in the specifications, price, or time set forth in the building contract as authorized by the owner, architect, and/or engineer. Change orders are most commonly associated with office, retail, and industrial projects. Such matters normally fall to the owner and general contractor.

CHANGE, PRINCIPLE OF

(SEE PRINCIPLES (APPRAISAL))

CHANNELLING

Cutting, chipping, or routing a prescribed area in a linear pattern on any surface, usually in concrete or plaster.

Usually found in poured concrete front or side driveway areas. Channels are cut at pre-determined distances thereby weakening the structural mass of the concrete at the channelling lines. Cracks due to settling or frost are most likely to occur within the channel as opposed to random occurrences throughout the finished surface.

CHARGE

(SEE ALSO MORTGAGE)

An encumbrance on land by way of a mortgage which has been registered in the land titles system. A mortgage is a charge on land created for securing a debt (existing, future, or contingent), or a loan and includes a hypothecation or pledge as security for the debt. The term *charge* originated as a result of land titles registration, while the term *mortgage* represents terminology relating to a real estate loan. The term *mortgage* is used throughout the encyclopedia to signify a charge or a mortgage.

Provincial   See applicable reference materials.

CHARGEE

The one to whom property is pledged as security for the payment of a charge; the lender or creditor. Commonly referred to as a mortgagee.

Provincial   See applicable reference materials.

CHARGOR

The one who gives the charge; the borrower or debtor. Commonly referred to as a mortgagor.

Provincial   See applicable reference materials.

CHART OF ACCOUNTS

A listing of all accounts that comprise the accounting system for a brokerage and are used to organize financial transactions. In fact, this chart includes all accounts making up the two major financial statements:

- Profit and Loss Statement; and
- Balance Sheet.

Individual accounts are grouped under various categories and the words *parent*, *child*, and *grandchild*. are often used to describe these groupings. **Figure C.4** illustrates the initial account groupings which make up the financial statements.

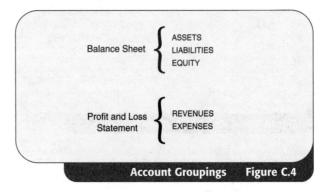

Account Groupings   Figure C.4

Application   Brokerages vary in terms of the number and variety of accounts required for an accounting system. The chart of accounts falls into five distinct categories. From these basic categories, a profit and loss statement and a balance sheet are developed. **Figure C.5** illustrates a type of account grouping (chart of accounts), that a typical brokerage might use in an accounting system.

Account Groupings

Classified Advertising   An expense account on the profit and loss statement. In the case of classified advertising, the initial grouping is *Expense* (parent), then subsequently differentiated from other expenses under the category *Advertising* (child), and lastly by its designated account name *Classified Advertising* (grandchild). See **Figure C.6** for an illustration of a *nested* expense account grouping relating to advertising.

C

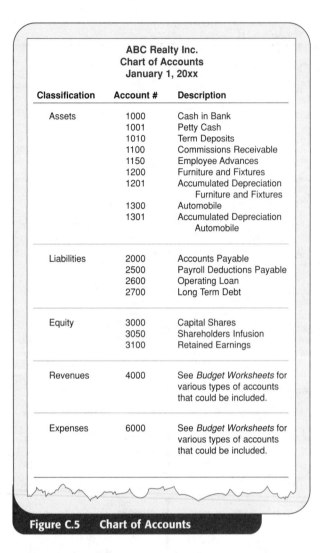

ABC Realty Inc.
Chart of Accounts
January 1, 20xx

Classification	Account #	Description
Assets	1000	Cash in Bank
	1001	Petty Cash
	1010	Term Deposits
	1100	Commissions Receivable
	1150	Employee Advances
	1200	Furniture and Fixtures
	1201	Accumulated Depreciation Furniture and Fixtures
	1300	Automobile
	1301	Accumulated Depreciation Automobile
Liabilities	2000	Accounts Payable
	2500	Payroll Deductions Payable
	2600	Operating Loan
	2700	Long Term Debt
Equity	3000	Capital Shares
	3050	Shareholders Infusion
	3100	Retained Earnings
Revenues	4000	See *Budget Worksheets* for various types of accounts that could be included.
Expenses	6000	See *Budget Worksheets* for various types of accounts that could be included.

Figure C.5   Chart of Accounts

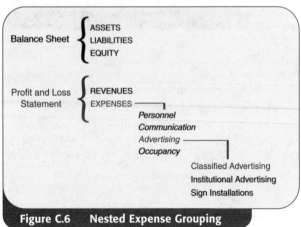

Figure C.6   Nested Expense Grouping

Bank–General Account   An asset account on the balance sheet. All assets are divided into either current or fixed categories. Therefore, it is initially defined as an asset account (parent), more specifically as a current asset (child), and lastly by its designated account name *Bank–-General Account* (grandchild). Figure C.7 illustrates this *nesting* effect as it relates to asset accounts.

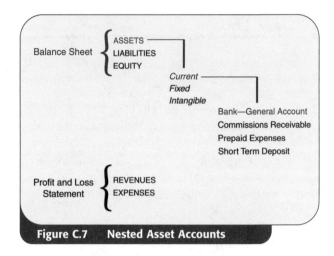

Figure C.7   Nested Asset Accounts

The chart of accounts is also grouped in terms of whether the account is normally a debit or credit account. The word *normally* is used as most entries appearing in that account will be predominately debits or credits. This debit/credit arrangement becomes very important in the posting procedure.

See Figure C.8 for the usual application of debit or credit in relation to financial statements.

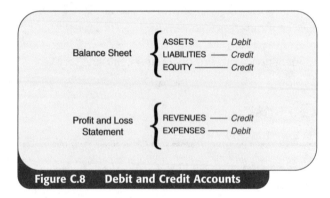

Figure C.8   Debit and Credit Accounts

Numbering and Expansion

No fixed rules exist for assigning account numbers but assets always appear first, followed by liabilities, equity, revenues, and finally expenses.

The accounts can be expanded at any time. If a certain area of expense is to be tracked, then appropriate account numbers are assigned along with account names. This information is then added to the chart of accounts and new ledger sheets are inserted in the general ledger.

Most computerized accounting packages use a suggested chart of accounts that requires modification to accommodate individual business needs. The following examples illustrate two different scenarios where account expansion would be useful in a real estate brokerage for more detailed tracking of expenses.

Example 1 *Chart of Accounts Numbering and Expansion*

Broker/Owner Johnson, of ABC Realty Inc., concentrates his advertising strategy on two newspapers. Originally two accounts were provided in the chart of accounts, namely Acct. #6050–Newspaper, Classified and Acct. #6100–Newspaper, Institutional. However, an increase in accounts appears wise to provide a more accurate delineation of expenditures:

Acct. #6060   Newspaper, Westside Classified

Acct. #6070   Newspaper, Westside Institutional

Acct. #6110   Newspaper, Gazette Classified

Acct. #6120   Newspaper, Gazette Institutional

Example 2 *Chart of Accounts Numbering and Expansion*

A chart of accounts should provide flexibility for future expansion of the business. This can be accomplished by providing sufficient numerical space between initial accounts to allow for new accounts (e.g., 6050, 6100, 6150, 6200, etc.). Further, a suffix can be added to the base number to identify departments or branches. Broker/Owner Johnson is opening a new branch in Westside and wants various expenses allocated between the main and branch offices. He establishes the following:

Acct. #6200.001   Rent, Lease Head Office

Acct. #6200.002   Rent Expense, West Side Branch

Acct. #6200.003   Rent Expense, East Side Branch

Acct. #6200.004   Rent Expense, North Side Branch

CHARTERED BUSINESS VALUATOR

Acronym: CBV   The Canadian Institute of Chartered Business Valuators (CICBV) is the largest professional business valuation organization in Canada. It is a non-profit institute, established in 1971, to promote high standards in business and securities valuations.

The CICBV trains and certifies individuals and grants the professional designation CBV or EEE (expert en evaluation d'enterprises) to those who have met the Institute's educational and experience credits.

Members and students are drawn from industry, accounting firms, independent valuation firms, investment dealers, and government regulatory agencies. Members determine the current worth of any business or its components and appear as independent experts on valuation matters before courts and regulatory bodies.

Reference   For details regarding the CBV program contact The Canadian Institute of Chartered Business Valuators, 277 Wellington Street West, Toronto, ON M5V 3H2.

The above information was summarized from detailed materials provided by CICBV with no representation concerning its accuracy or completeness. Contact CICBV for current requirements.

CHATTEL

(SEE ALSO FIXTURES)

Moveable possessions and personal property (usually items that may be removed without injury to the freehold estate).

Application   Practitioners should be aware that the legal nature of a chattel changes when it becomes fixed to the real property. Whether a chattel becomes a fixture depends largely on circumstances. No set rule exists, but the deciding factor tends to be degree and object of annexation.

Example *Chattel*

Thomson is selling his recreational property and advises Salesperson Lee that various items are not included in the sale. While understanding that chattels are moveable and fixtures are fixed to the property and improvements thereon, Lee must ensure that there is no confusion in relation to these items with either Thomson or a potential buyer. He prepares and attaches a schedule to the listing itemizing all excluded chattels. This list includes a 14 foot aluminum fishing boat, two outboard motors (5 HP and 10 HP), fishing tackle boxes, assorted rods/reels, two space heaters in the guest cabin, various lawn ornaments, and outside furniture.

CHATTEL MORTGAGE

A mortgage given on moveable possessions (e.g.,vehicles, boats, and trailers), or personal property (e.g., appliances, televisions, and stereos), that may be removed without injury to the freehold estate. The chattel mortgage is one of three common methods of taking security on moveable possessions, the other two being a conditional sales contract or a lease with an option to purchase (e.g., photocopiers and computers).

Provincial legislation addresses the registration of chattel mortgages. In Ontario and Manitoba, for example, the *Personal Property Security Act* governs methods of taking security and establishes priority by means of a system of registration of security interests. Applicable legislation varies throughout Canada.

Provincial   See applicable reference materials.

CHIMNEYS

A structure, typically vertical, that contains one or more flues for the discharge of smoke and/or gases from a fire or furnace. A flue is a separate and distinct channel or duct for such discharges. The most common materials used in chimney construction are masonry and steel. Masonry chimneys can be brick, block, or stone, and are sometimes stuccoed or parged. Each appliance within the house, with few exceptions, must have a separate flue. Two gas furnaces on the same floor within a house can share a common flue, as can a gas furnace and a gas hot water heater on the same level. Some fire codes allow wood stoves to share flues with gas or oil furnaces, while others allow wood stoves to share flues with gas or oil furnaces, if at the same floor level. Provincial fire and building codes or related legislation should be accessed for complete details.

Chimney Cap

Prevents water from penetrating the top of a masonry chimney. This cap should not be confused with rain caps that sometimes cover the tops of chimney flues to prevent the entry of rain water. A chimney cap is usually constructed of concrete, however, some are made from stone or metal. A good quality cap normally overhangs the sides of the chimney at least one inch to provide some protection for the chimney from rainwater dripping off the cap.

Flue Liners

Unlined flues, with masonry exposed on the inside are most common in pre World War II houses and have performed reasonably well for fireplaces and oil-fired furnaces. Gas-fired furnaces, on the other hand, usually require a liner. Flues may be lined with one of several materials: clay tile, metal, or asbestos cement pipe.

Removal

Many chimneys that are no longer required are removed to a point below roof level during re-roofing. This eliminates the need to maintain the upper section and reduces the risk of water leakage through the chimney flashing, a common source of problems. This is appropriate provided nothing is connected to the chimney that might be used inadvertently. Occasionally, abandoned chimneys are knocked down part way, but still protrude above the roof line. In some cases, the flue is sealed with concrete.

Practitioners should be aware that chimney deterioration is a common problem in both residential and commercial structures. Most often, water is the culprit. Metal chimneys corrode and masonry chimneys can suffer deterioration to the mortar, brick, and stucco. The source of the water can sometimes be wind driven rain, but often results from condensation within the chimney. One of the by-products of burning fossil fuels is water vapour. Exhaust gases, travelling up the chimney, cool and sometimes reach the dew point, thereby forming condensation. The water droplets are absorbed into masonry chimneys or sit on the interior of metal chimneys. These droplets are somewhat acidic due to their formation from combustible products and can cause corrosion in metal flues and deterioration within masonry flues.

The problem is compounded in masonry chimneys by use of cyclical heating. Chimneys are forever heating up and cooling down as furnaces, boilers, hot water heaters, and fireplaces are only operated intermittently. The moisture that has been absorbed into masonry chimneys freezes as the temperature drops, causing mortar to deteriorate, bricks to spall, and parging or stucco to loosen. This is a natural phenomenon with all chimneys and deterioration should be anticipated.

Certain masonry chimneys are lined with clay tile. The top flue tile should protrude at least two inches beyond the top of the chimney. If the top section of clay tile was too short to protrude, some brick masons simply raised the top tile, leaving a gap between the top two tiles in the flue. A ring of more rapid deterioration normally shows up on the exterior of the chimney, corresponding to the gap in the clay tile liner. The amount of deterioration dictates whether chimneys require repair or rebuilding. On tall chimneys or chimneys situated on steeply pitched roofs, building scaffolding is often required to facilitate repairs adding to the cost of repair.

CHLORINATION

The disinfecting of water through the use of chlorine. Chlorine is a greenish-yellow, incombustible, water soluble poisonous gas.

Application   Chlorination procedures for disinfecting water are set out by the appropriate provincial ministry/department and/or local public health unit. Procedures will vary by provincial jurisdiction regarding the proper use of chlorine (liquid, tablets, or powder), for well water disinfecting. Chemical disinfecting or chlorination is essential for new or reworked wells (dug or drilled), cisterns, springs, pumps, and pipes. Disinfecting the water by chlorination extends to electrical cables, ropes, pipes, well, well cap, and plumbing lines and fixtures in the house presently drawing water from the well. Bacteria may get into the water supply during construction or repair.

Disinfecting is the final step after all defects in location and construction have been corrected and before samples are collected for bacterial examination. Typically, a predetermined amount of chlorinated household bleach is poured into the well based on water depth, then all taps are opened until a chlorine odour is detected. The water in the pipes is then left to stand for a minimum of six hours and subsequently flushed. It is recommended that residents store enough clean water for three days for drinking, washing, and watering plants before well disinfecting. Another option is to boil all water used from the source. A bacteriological retesting of the water follows after several days. Meanwhile, all water used from that source must be boiled.

Reference   Contact the relevant provincial ministry/department responsible (environment or health), for a copy of the guidelines for disinfecting water wells by chlorination.

Provincial   See applicable reference materials.

CHLORINATION INJECTOR UNIT

A water treatment device used primarily in recreational property that feeds a weak solution of chlorine into the water distribution system immediately after it comes from the well. The water must then be pumped into a pressure or storage tank that is large enough to ensure that the water will be stored for a specified period of time to effectively destroy any bacteria. An alternative treatment device called a super chlorination unit is installed either before or immediately after the pump. As the water pump is activated, the unit feeds a strong solution of chlorine into the water. The water is then passed through an activated carbon filter to dechlorinate the treated water.

CHRONOLOGICAL AGE
(SEE ACTUAL AGE)

CLAUSES

Wordings inserted in agreements/contracts to accurately reflect the wishes of the parties. Many provincial associations have developed standard clauses for use by members in drafting agreements/contracts. Such clauses are provided solely for guidance purposes and do not in any way constitute required wordings.

Provincial   See applicable reference materials.

CLAY SHINGLES/TILES
(SEE ALSO SHINGLES)

Frequently used in turn of the century housing, e.g., on gable roofs. The life span is approximately 100 years, however, the shingles are brittle, subject to mechanical damage, and failure of fastenings (nails).

CLEAR SPAN
(SEE ALSO BAY AND BAY DEPTH)

The amount of floor area that is clear of interference from columns and support walls.

CLIENT DUTIES
(SEE FIDUCIARY RESPONSIBILITIES)

CLOSED MORTGAGE

A mortgage that does not provide for any prepayment of principal during the term.

Application   Considerable confusion exists concerning the topic of a mortgagor's ability to make prepayments on a mortgage. When a mortgagor signs a mortgage document, he/she has essentially entered into a contract with the mortgagee. Unless the mortgage terms or related documentation provides otherwise, the mortgagor has agreed to make payments according to a specified schedule and the contract is written to run for a stated period. During the term of such contracts, the mortgagor who decides to make extra payments, or discharge the loan in its entirety before the end of the term is in effect asking for an amendment to the agreement. Such amendment is possible, but only by mutual consent. The mortgagee is entitled to demand costs for giving consent or to refuse the consent entirely.

The *Interest Act*, a federal statute, is very specific regarding the closed period of a mortgage. If no prepayment privilege is stated in the mortgage document itself, then the borrower can only repay a conventional closed mortgage loan in certain situations.

- With special permission of the mortgagee and subject to conditions imposed by the mortgagee.
- A loan to an individual can, by law, be repaid after five years, subject to payment of three months interest penalty (bonus).
- A loan to a corporate borrower cannot be prepaid without the permission of the lender.

An open mortgage usually allows the borrower to make prepayments at any time in any amount during the term of the contract and in some cases, a penalty charge will be attached to such prepayments. Traditionally, a higher interest rate is charged for an open mortgage.

Consumers often use the phrase *open mortgage* or *closed mortgage*, when in fact only the *term* is open or closed. A *closed* term means that the mortgage cannot be paid fully or partially before the term expires. From the lenders point of view, the mortgagor has agreed to borrow the money for a specified period at a specific interest rate. Repaying the loan before it is due breaks the contract. If the borrower wishes to prepay the loan, all interest owing until expiry of the term must be paid.

An open mortgage provides for the prepayment of the principal, however, the amount and terms of prepayment will vary. Sometimes, mortgages will be described as fully open (payment of the amount owing), or partially open (specified times and amounts permitted). The issue of prepayment privileges and associated penalties requires clarification. Most lenders usually charge three months' interest or an interest differential, if the current rate is higher, whichever is greater. As a rule, payout penalties are calculated in simple interest. Due to the short time period (usually three months), the simple interest calculation will be greater than the compounded amount.

A range of prepayment options, with and without penalties, can be found in the marketplace. In Nova Scotia, for example, a statutory provision provides that if a mortgage executed after June 30, 1985 is silent with respect to prepayment, it can be prepaid without penalty at any time. Various requirements may be stipulated in provincial legislation.

Provincial   See applicable reference materials.

CLOSING COSTS
(SEE ALSO ADJUSTMENTS)

The total cost of buying a home involves not only the purchase price of the property, but also other costs that arise on closing the transaction. These expenses, incurred by the buyer, are necessary to complete the purchase but are outside of the purchase price for the property. Fees, types of services provided, and procedures required in the closing process will vary by provincial jurisdiction. The following list is provided for illustration purposes and is not exhaustive in nature.

- Adjustments for realty taxes and fuel.
- Legal expenses and disbursements, lawyers' services and expenses (items paid on behalf of the buyer).

- Mortgage expenses including interest on assumed mortgages (calculated as part of the adjustments), any arranging costs, and registration of a new mortgage in the land registry or land titles office.
- House insurance for fire and other hazards, typically including liability coverage.
- Title search and registration of appropriate documents in the land registry or land titles office.
- Cost of survey, zoning memorandum, tax certificate, and other related matters based on provincial requirements.
- GST: Most purchases of new housing require the payment of GST on the purchase price, although a partial rebate is available. Most purchases of resale homes do not require the payment of GST, however, confirmation of this fact should be obtained. As a guideline, GST is payable on properties other than resale residential property, subject to certain exceptions. GST is also payable on lawyer's fees and most disbursements.
- Land transfer tax.
- Personal expenses, e.g., moving costs and purchase of household goods.

Once a total is calculated, the closing cost can be substantially higher than the buyer anticipated. All buyers should be aware of these extra costs before finding themselves legally bound to an agreement/contract and possibly unable to fulfill the financial terms. Various costs apply when selling a home, however, the seller has the proceeds of the sale from which to pay them.

Practitioners are reminded that members of organized real estate are bound by the Code of Ethics of The Canadian Real Estate Association and are required to fully inform each party regarding the nature of expenses for which they may be normally liable. Article 7 states:

> *The REALTOR shall, prior to the signing of any agreement, fully inform the signing party regarding the type of expenses for which he/she may be normally liable.*

Additional requirements may be specified by the appropriate provincial regulatory body.

Provincial   See applicable reference materials.

CLOSING DATE
(SEE COMPLETION DATE)

CLOSING PROCEDURES

Provincial   See applicable reference materials.

CLOSING STATEMENT

A document itemizing the complete financial history of a real estate transaction including the deposit, downpayment, adjustments, balance due on closing, and mortgage amount.

Provincial   See applicable reference materials.

CLOUD ON TITLE

Any encumbrance or claim that affects title to real property.

CODE OF ETHICS (CREA)

The Canadian Real Estate Association (CREA) Code of Ethics is an overall statement of ethical goals and provides moral guidelines for members. Members pledge to maintain, and continually strive for improvements in their profession.

The Code is owned by CREA and all interpretations concerning its content, along with any modifications, are under its direct control. Local real estate boards and provincial associations throughout Canada have accepted and adopted the Code. Consequently, all individual members of boards are bound by the Code under the terms of their local membership as well as their automatic membership in CREA.

The Code of Ethics consists of three interrelated parts (see **Figure C.9**). First, the *Code of Ethics* is a general statement of ethical goals. Second, the *Standards of Business Practice* are more explicit rules of behaviour set out in articles. These constitute acceptable behaviour in day-to-day dealings with other members and the public. At present, there are 29 articles that define proper conduct for a multitude of circumstances encountered by sales representatives and brokers in the marketplace. Lastly, the *Interpretations of the Standards of Business Practice* provide additional guidance and clarification concerning individual articles.

The terms *professional standards* and *ethics* are used interchangeably and in fact, both are difficult to precisely define. Ethics refers to a voluntary set of rules or maxims that an individual adopts, often in concert with other persons in a professional organization, to elevate personal conduct beyond the minimum requirements as set out by law. The actual content of these rules of behaviour have

become known as *professional standards* within the real estate brokerage business. These standards more clearly and precisely articulate overall guiding principles.

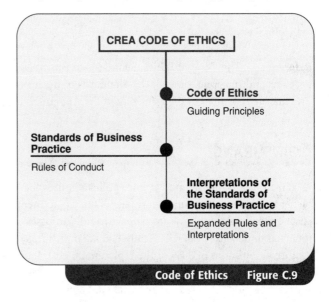

Code of Ethics   Figure C.9

Real Estate Boards

The Code of Ethics binds members of individual real estate boards through the members' affiliation with CREA. Further, based on by-laws, the board empowers specific committees to oversee the activities of its members, using the Code as a benchmark for deliberations. MLS® rules and regulations of a local board often flow directly from the Standards of Business Practice. The Code specifically requires that the REALTOR shall observe the by-laws, rules, and regulations established by the REALTOR's real estate board and/or association.

The REALTOR shall observe the By-Laws, Rules and Regulations established by the REALTOR's Real Estate Board and/or Association, in addition to the regulations, terms and conditions associated with any designation that the REALTOR may hold through membership in The Canadian Real Estate Association.

Provincial Real Estate Act/Regulations

The applicable provincial real estate act establishes general trading regulations and licensing requirements for brokers and salespeople. Further, regulatory bodies have developed trade practice guidelines and, in some instances, ethical requirements. The CREA Code of Ethics reinforces these legislative initiatives through a direct reference in the Standard of Business Practice Article 21:

Reference The Code of Ethics, Standards of Business Practice, and Interpretations of the Standards of Business Practice are reprinted in their entirety in the Appendix.

COINSURANCE

A coinsurance clause in an insurance policy requires the owner to insure a minimum percentage of the replacement cost of the property in order to be paid in full for losses incurred under that policy. Typically, Canadian insurers require a minimum of 80% of the replacement cost. If an amount less than 80% is covered, then the owner of the property becomes a co-insurer and bears the proportionate share of any losses incurred.

Example *Coinsurance*

Seller Smith has a fire insurance policy with Anycity Insurance Company Ltd. that requires a minimum of 80% coinsurance, subject to any deductibles stated in the policy. The replacement value of the property is $220,000 and Smith insures the property for $210,000 or 95.45% of replacement value. Therefore, Smith falls within the coinsurance guidelines and any loss would be paid in full (subject of course to any other provisions in the policy that might affect loss payment).

COLLAR TIE

Collar ties are laterally-placed, wood members installed between opposing rafters approximately halfway up the attic space. These ties are designed to prevent rafters from sagging inward and provide the same job as knee walls. Collar ties, two-by-fours or two-by-sixes, are installed horizontally halfway up the attic space, connected at either end to opposing rafters, and act as stiffeners to prevent the rafters from sagging in the middle. One collar tie should be placed for each pair of opposing rafters. If more than eight feet long, a rat-tail or other sort of bracing should be attached to the midpoint of the collar ties to prevent them from buckling in the middle. See Figure C.10 for placement of collar ties in relation to other roof and ceiling components.

Application Practitioners require awareness of certain problems that can arise regarding collar ties.

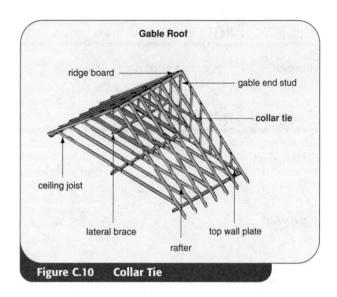

Figure C.10   Collar Tie

Buckling Collar ties are susceptible to buckling and discovering that the use of an inappropriate lumber size has been used is not uncommon. For example, a two-by-four makes an adequate collar tie, but a one-by-eight does not. Because of its very thin one-inch dimension, pushing on either end of a one-by-eight, which is what rafters do, will likely cause bending in the middle. Bending a two-by-four by pushing from either end is much more difficult.

Missing Securing collar ties on every third rafter was very common on older houses. However, such arrangements have proven inadequate particularly with the added weight of multiple layers of roof shingles. Collar ties should be provided for each rafter and can be readily added.

Bracing Collar ties more than eight feet may buckle if lateral bracing has been omitted. It can be easily installed.

Wrong Location Often collar ties are either too high or too low. Ideally, their placement should be near the midpoint of the rafter span.

Low Slope Roof Collar ties are only effective when the roof slope is *four in twelve* inches or greater. Larger rafters, or knee walls, are typically used on lower slopes on a retrofit basis to strengthen a roof. (See Roof.)

COLLATERAL MORTGAGE

A loan backed by a promissory note and then further secured by means of a mortgage on real property.

Application Money borrowed by a collateral mortgage is normally used for purposes other than acquiring the property being secured, e.g., a business venture, purchase of vacation property, home improvements, or vehicle purchase. If the borrower defaults, the lender has the right of recourse on both the loan note and the mortgage.

A collateral mortgage can be required by lenders as security for things other than promissory notes, such as a guarantee. Collateral loans are generally easy to arrange but are rarely assumed by subsequent buyers. They are similar to any other mortgage document and registered in the land registry or land titles office.

A collateral mortgage can also be used on leasehold premises provided that the leasehold interest is clearly identified on a schedule to the mortgage and that the leasehold interest has been registered on the property.

Example   *Collateral Mortgage*

Owner Smith is contemplating a new business venture and requires working capital. A lender is prepared to advance $30,000 and the parties have agreed that Smith will sign a promissory note for that amount along with a collateral mortgage on his residence. Essentially, Smith has agreed that the collateral mortgage (having the same date, terms, and conditions as the promissory note), will provide additional security. Both parties acknowledge that any payment under the promissory note is also a payment against the collateral mortgage.

COLLATERAL SECURITY

An additional form of security pledged to reduce the risk to a mortgagee that can be used to recover all or part of the debt.

Example   *Collateral Security*

Investor Thompson is considering a mortgage on property owned by Smith. Thompson has reservations about advancing mortgage funds owing to the risky nature of Smith's business. In addition to the covenant provided in the mortgage, Thompson demands additional security by means of collateral security covering various items owned by Smith including business equipment, vehicles, and the assignment of accounts receivable.

COMMERCIAL (ICI) BROKERAGE

A real estate brokerage specializing in the fields of industrial, retail, office, and/or other forms of investment real estate. A more precise definition is impossible given the diversity of sub-specialties making up the commercial marketplace. Increasingly, brokerages dealing with these properties are described as *commercial brokerages*. The term *ICI* (Industrial, Commercial, and Investment), is gradually losing stature.

Application   The exact delineation of specialty fields within commercial brokerage can prove troublesome. Commercial markets may be viewed in terms of types of activities performed, classification by property type, or categorization by specialty and sub-markets, geographic location, and trading areas etc. Commercial brokerage can also be viewed in terms of the particular clients being served. The most common differentiation is based on type and includes office, retail, industrial, business, multi-residential, and vacant land. Multiple listing services typically group listings under these categories, but no universal classifications exist.

Increasingly, commercial publications reference *user* and *investor* groups in detailing the activities of commercial brokerages. However, the lines between the two groups are not always clear. For example, a user may display various investor tendencies when selecting property. Conversely, the investor may introduce personal preferences and goals in otherwise rational decision-making driven by capital resources and forecasted cash flows. Regardless, the user/investor dichotomy provides a useful differentiation for descriptive purposes.

User

A buyer or lessee of retail, office, or industrial real estate who is attempting to satisfy individual needs in the acquisition of suitable property. The commercial brokerage must be adept in identifying needs of such users to satisfy specific requirements and by seeking appropriate property.

Investor

The *investor* is seeking property for neither individual use, nor the intent of occupying a selected site and/or structure, but rather for the return on the investment.

Satisfying the needs of the *investor* group can be complex and warrants detailed discussion. Investment buyers want to fulfill various investment objectives when entering the marketplace. They are most notably concerned with the current or planned use for the property when occupied by rent-paying users. Consequently, the property's value relates directly to that current or planned use and the commercial brokerage, dealing with investors, must be fully aware of pertinent principles, procedures, and investment calculations.

Investors normally seek a positive income stream for property. The commercial brokerage must determine the strength of the income stream with due consideration for expenses usual to the particular class or type of property being selected. Often, analysis includes the impact of taxation on income received by the investor. Taxation, for this purpose, is viewed in its widest possible definition, e.g., federal, provincial, and municipal taxes that impact various types of commercial property, the tax treatment of interest paid regarding debt service, the determination of capital cost allowances, and tax credits furnished as an incentive for certain types of investment.

Investors frequently seek the highest returns through leverage and the use of borrowed funds. Links between income stream, value, and financing are well established. Consequently, the commercial brokerage must be proficient in various mortgage calculations as well as assessing the relative benefits of financial packages.

Lastly, investors normally seek liquidity. The ease by which an investment is converted into cash can be a prime determinant when selecting property. As a result, the commercial brokerage must be sensitive to the marketability of an investment property. Its desirability can ultimately translate into a higher selling price and a quicker sale.

COMMERCIAL INVESTMENT REAL ESTATE INSTITUTE

(SEE ALSO CERTIFIED COMMERCIAL INVESTMENT MEMBER)

Acronym: CIREI   The Commercial Investment Real Estate Institute (CIREI) is an affiliate of the National Association of REALTORS in the United States. Having approximately 9,000 members CIREI provides education programs and services for professionals in commercial and investment real estate as well as allied industries. CIREI awards the CCIM designation to individuals completing a series of graduate level courses in advanced concepts and techniques in commercial real estate.

CIREI's vision statement is to be the leading edge professional association to the commercial real estate industry and the mission statement specifically identifies:

- Creating business and member services to foster individual and organizational success;
- Conferring the CCIM designation to qualified practitioners;
- Informing the public of the integrity, competence, and professionalism of designees; and
- Maintaining the highest quality real estate education.

Reference   For details regarding the CCIM designation, contact the Commercial Investment Real Estate Institute, 430 North Michigan Avenue, Chicago, Il 60611–4092.

Three Canadian Chapters of CIREI have been formed, namely, Central Canada Chapter, Canada West Chapter, and National Capital Region Chapter. Various boards across Canada offer credit courses toward the CCIM designation. Contact the ICI Council of The Canadian Real Estate Association for current information.

COMMERCIAL LEASE

(SEE ALSO BASE LEASE)

Commercial leases can be broadly grouped by three basic types: retail, office, and industrial. These lease agreements share basic similarities, but differ in structure and content based on uses and needs of the parties. A number of specialized leases are also found in the marketplace, e.g., the land lease and sale/leaseback. Commercial practitioners also encounter residential leases, but the format is often significantly different owing to legislative requirements affecting landlord/tenant relationships in selected provincial jurisdictions.

Provincial   See applicable reference materials.

COMMERCIAL LOAN

(SEE ALSO MORTGAGE DOCUMENTATION PACKAGE)

The sale of large income-producing structures and major commercial operations is complex and requires special expertise. Similarly, commercial loan arrangements concerning such properties are equally complicated.

Commercial loan underwriters normally concentrate on the ability of the property to generate sufficient cash flow for the mortgage debt. The term *commercial* applies to a range of property types. Consequently, lender application forms used for commercial loans vary considerably. As an overview, commercial projects are heavily reliant upon management ability and the assurance of a continued low vacancy factor. Information regarding the borrower and the income stream is closely analyzed.

COMMERCIAL PROPERTY

Real property used for the conduct of retail or service businesses, inviting public patronage by display of signs, merchandise, advertising, and other stimulants for public participation.

COMMERCIAL SALES

The sale of retail, office, industrial, multi-residential, and similar types of properties. Traditionally, the term *ICI* (Industrial, Commercial, and Investment), referred to the sale of such properties, however the generic term *commercial* is now frequently used. Practitioners will encounter both terminologies in the marketplace.

Professional Organizations

Various organizations offer programs and designations relating to commercial sales. Two long-standing international organizations bear special mention.

- The Commercial Investment Real Estate Institute (CIREI) holds institute status with the National Association of REALTORS. It offers programs leading to the CCIM (Certified Commercial Investment Member) designation in the United States and Canada. The program is recognized as a practical, highly technical series of courses.

- The Society of Industrial and Office REALTORS (SIOR) is recognized by many as the leading international industrial real estate network. A structured education program and other qualifying criteria lead to the SIOR designation.

Specialty Fields

While commercial fields tend toward specialties, the degree of specialization is largely reflected in the extent of urbanization within the local marketplace. In smaller centres, it is usual for residential real estate brokerages to have one or two individuals focused on commercial activities. In larger urban centres, the business is more specialized, with brokerages focusing on selected areas.

Three major divisions stand out in what is now broadly referred to as the commercial field:

Industrial Real Estate   Primarily involves the sale or lease of warehousing and manufacturing space to users. Industrial property and associated structures are generally categorized under three main types: general purpose, special purpose, and single purpose.

Retail/Office Real Estate   The sale or leasing of all forms of retail or office facilities. Sales of businesses, with or without ownership of land, are typically included under this category.

Investment Real Estate   The sale of industrial, office/retail, or residential income producing real estate to institutional or private investors (including syndicates), domestic or overseas. Investors are essentially buying an income stream rather than land and building. Investors, although concerned about the condition of physical property (as it will affect the stability and longevity of the income stream), are more focused on long-term, income-producing potential.

In practice, these three broad divisions consist of many sub-specialty sales fields as the Canadian commercial market expands and matures.

Industrial Land	Sale of industrial-zoned land to users, builders, or investors.
Retail/Office Land	Sale of appropriately zoned building lots to users, builders, and investors.
Residential Land	Sale of residential subdivision land to developers or builders.
Design Build	Retail, office, or industrial users requiring custom facilities.
Office Leasing	Leasing of medium and major office projects.
Residential Investment	Sale of apartment projects to investors.
Retail/Office Investment	Sale of retail plazas or office projects to investors.
Business Brokerage	The sale of ongoing businesses with or without real estate assets.

Property and Asset Management

Career Considerations

While many commercial specialists enter the profession with no background in residential real estate, a significant number have commenced their real estate careers in residential sales and then gravitated to commercial sales. In either case, practitioners agree that a knowledge of such matters as real property law, land description, economics, and contracts is essential. Since commercial practitioners deal with business people, work hours are normally matched to theirs. However, this does not preclude some degree of evening or weekend work.

Part of the commercial lure is the prestige and opportunities offered for involvement with high-profile projects along with correspondingly high commissions. While these opportunities exist, transactions take longer to develop, are subject to extensive research, negotiation, and satisfaction of conditions, and require lengthy periods to point of closing compared with most residential transactions. The rewards, although larger, are less frequent. Loss of an individual transaction is far more damaging both mentally and financially.

What is it that draws someone into the commercial field? Certainly potential monetary rewards are always a driving force, but most successful industrial, commercial, and investment practitioners suggest they derive their motivation from the excitement and gratification that come from involvement in large and important projects.

Practitioners are typically individuals who thrive on challenge and demands for ever more knowledge, skill, and specialized education.

COMMISSION

Remuneration paid to a brokerage on the sale or lease of property, usually as a percentage of the sale amount.

Application   The typical distribution usually involves two brokerages with commission being divided between the listing brokerage (listing commission) and the co-operating brokerage (selling commission). The distribution arrangement between brokerages can vary and is determined by the brokerages and their respective policies. The subsequent distribution to salespeople is completed in accordance with respective brokerage policies and the salesperson's contractual arrangements.

Example   *Commission*

Scenario 1

Sale Price	$200,000	
Commission Rate	5.0%	
Listing Broker	ABC Realty Inc.	
Selling Broker	ABC Realty Inc.	

	Listing	Selling
Brokerage Name	ABC	ABC
Commission Distribution	5% (100% of 5%)	
Gross to Brokerage	10,000	
Salesperson Names	Miller	Lane
Salesperson Commission Split	60/40	60/40
Salesperson Share	3,000	3,000
Net to Brokerage	2,000	2,000

Scenario 2

Sale Price	$200,000	
Commission Rate	5.0%	
Listing Broker	ABC Realty Inc.	
Selling Broker	XYZ Real Estate Ltd.	

	Listing	Selling
Brokerage Name	ABC	XYZ
Commission Distribution	2.5% (50% of 5%)	2.5% (50% of 5%)
Gross to Brokerage	5,000	5,000
Salesperson Names	Miller	Warden
Salesperson Commission Split	60/40	60/40
Salesperson Share	3,000	3,000
Net to Brokerage	2,000	2,000

In the example, the first scenario represents an in-house transaction in which the commission is divided into listing and selling portions respectively and then distributed to the appropriate salespeople. This example sets out a conventional split of commission in which the brokerage pays for various salesperson expenses and commission income is split on a pre-determined basis (i.e., a 60/40 split, but there are many variations on this). In a desk fee plan, the salesperson pays a pre-determined amount to the brokerage and is responsible for most expenses incurred in the selling process. As a result, the commission split might be 95/5. The last scenario of the example represents a transaction with two different brokerages involved. The commission is first distributed between listing and selling brokerages and paid to the respective salespeople.

COMMISSION PLANS

A term commonly referring to commission arrangements and associated policies established for salespeople within a brokerage. Commission plans are typically described in policy manuals and/or attached to employment contracts for salespeople.

A variety of commission plans are available in the marketplace but most are derived from two general categories:

- Conventional commission plans (referred to as *split plans*); and
- Desk fee plans (payment of a monthly fee by salesperson normally combined with a higher commission split than the conventional plan).

Conventional Plan

Commission is paid to the salesperson based on gross commission income received less payment to other brokerages, and fees and expenses paid by the brokerage, e.g., advertising, occupancy, communication etc.

Historically such plans offered a 50/50 or 60/40 salesperson/brokerage split with accrued bonuses paid at the end of the year or progressive splits based on sales volume paid during the year. Intense market rivalry has produced variations on this basic concept, as salespeople sought increased split participation and more involvement in selling expenses incurred in the sale process.

The selection of a salesperson compensation package will depend largely on competitive forces within the market, expenses paid and services provided by the brokerage, and the sales force size. In determining an appropriate plan, several factors must be analyzed, e.g., average production level of salespeople, range of estimated sales production for individual salespeople, net cash received by the brokerage, brokerage expenses, and distribution of cash flow throughout the fiscal and calendar years.

Desk Fee Plan

This plan has gained prominence in many parts of Canada as it attracts salespeople through high potential commission earnings. However, from the brokerage's perspective, such plans obliterate any real possibility for dramatic rises in income as a result of upward market swings and increased production of salespeople (except for increasing the number of salespeople). Profit objectives are commonly realized through aggressive recruiting strategies and efficient brokerage management.

Example	Commission Plans— Desk Fee Plan

ABC Realty Inc. operates a desk fee plan and both listing and selling salespeople are independent contractors, each paying $925 per month in desk fees. The total commission on a specific property is 5%. Based on a $200,000 selling price and assuming a 95/5 split between the brokerage and each salesperson and listing and selling portions being split equally, the following commission calculation would apply:

	Listing	Selling
Brokerage Name	ABC	ABC
Commission Distribution	5% (100% of 5%)	
Gross to Brokerage	10,000	
Salesperson Names	Miller	Lane
Salesperson Commission Split	95/5	95/5
Salesperson Share	4,750	4,750
Net to Brokerage	250	250

In a slightly different scenario with the same commission and sale price assume that:

• ABC Realty Inc. is the listing brokerage and XYZ Real Estate Ltd. is the selling brokerage;

• ABC Realty inc. has a 95/5 desk fee plan and XYZ Real Estate Ltd. has a conventional plan (60/40 split) and pays most expenses of the salespeople; and

• The commission allocation between listing and selling brokerages is 50/50.

	Listing	Selling
Brokerage Name	ABC	XYZ
Commission Distribution	2.5% (50% of 5%)	2.5% (50% of 5%)
Gross to Brokerage	5,000	5,000
Salesperson Names	Miller	Warden
Salesperson Commission Split	95/5	60/40
Salesperson Share	4,750	3,000
Net to Brokerage	250	2,000

NOTE	The selling salesperson receives less commission as various expenses are paid by the brokerage. Commission distribution arrangements can vary significantly in the marketplace.

Monthly brokerage income is directly tied to the number of salespeople remitting fees plus any minor participation in brokerage gross commission income. Typically, 95% of the commission is paid to salespeople with 5% flowing to the brokerage, but many variations exist.

COMMISSION—STATUTORY REQUIREMENTS

Provincial   See applicable reference materials.

COMMISSION TRUST ACCOUNT

A trust account, separate from all other accounts, in which funds for the payment of commission are held. This method of accounting protects commissions payable by a brokerage in the event of a business failure. A commission trust account is distinct from a real estate trust account that is mandated by provincial legislation.

Provincial   See applicable reference materials.

COMMITMENT

A pledge, promise, or affirmation of agreement which is binding in law. A commitment is most commonly associated with mortgaging in which a lender provides a commitment to advance funds on specific terms and conditions.

COMMITTEE OF ADJUSTMENT

A committee empowered to grant minor variances from the provisions of zoning by-laws, control alterations to uses that do not conform to the existing zoning by-laws, and grant consents to sever within certain defined parameters.

Provincial   See applicable reference materials.

COMMON AREA

The area used by two or more tenants and/or third parties, and not under the control of any one tenant, e.g., lobbies, corridors, and stairways, in either a residential or commercial building. Commercial floor plate diagrams typically show exclusive areas occupied by tenants and associated common areas in the building's centre-core, e.g., elevators, washrooms, and common lobby area. Common area should be clearly distinguished from common elements relating to condominiums.

COMMON AREA MAINTENANCE

Acronym: CAM In commercial real estate, CAM refers to landlord's costs attributable to the common areas involving the repair, maintenance, operation, supervision, and administration of such areas. CAM charges are usually prorated among the building tenants.

Application The lease provision, often referred to as the CAM clause, outlines the common area maintenance charges for the complex and the tenant's responsibility in that regard. A typical wording is provided for a tenant in an office complex.

> *It is the intent of the parties hereto that the rents reserved pursuant to this lease shall be absolutely net to the landlord free and clear of all payments, charges or obligations whatsoever excepting only taxes personal to landlord including income tax on the income of the landlord and landlord's financing costs and that all costs, expenses or outlays of any kind related to the premises shall be borne by the tenant and that the tenant shall, by payment of the tenant's proportionate share of the landlord's occupancy costs, share in the burden of all costs, expenses and outlays of any kind related to the common areas except as aforesaid.*

COMMON ELEMENTS

Property areas in a condominium, except the units, that can be used by all unit owners. Examples include lobbies, parking areas, recreational facilities, elevators, roofs, exterior walls, and any other physical aspects not described as a unit. The declaration of a condominium corporation may specify exclusive-use areas within common elements such as parking spaces, lockers, balconies, landscaped areas, or others that are to be used exclusively by a particular unit although the expenses will be shared by all. Common elements are subject to the by-laws and rules of the corporation.

To accurately delineate units as opposed to common areas, the boundary of a unit is normally described as the outside edge of the interior wall or door, so that the unit owner can control his/her wallboard or interior door. However, the exterior brick or door identifies the commencement of the common element to be regulated and controlled by the board of directors of the condominium corporation or its authorized manager/management team, e.g., painting, air-conditioning, and maintenance.

Unit owners share the cost of expenses relating to the common elements including such things as bulk-metered utilities, repairs, maintenance, and capital expenditures as required. Payment can be enforced by a lien against the defaulting owner's unit. Condominiums, best described legally as *creatures of statute*, fall within provincial regulatory control.

Provincial See applicable reference materials.

COMMON EXPENSES

A term most commonly associated with the cost of operating, managing, maintaining, and repairing the common elements of a condominium including the administration.

Provincial See applicable reference materials.

COMMON LAW

That part of the law that is formulated, developed, and administered by the common law courts, mostly unwritten and founded originally on common customs. Common law is based on principles more so than specific rules and has developed over the centuries using legal precedents as opposed to statutory provisions set out by parliamentary decree.

COMPARATIVE SALES METHOD– SITE VALUATION
(SEE ALSO DIRECT COMPARISON APPROACH)

A method of estimating value based on a comparison of the site being appraised, with the most recent sales data available on similar sites, preferably in the same neighbourhood. The assumption is made that, if the subject site had been vacant and offered for sale, it would have competed with the comparable sales and appealed to the same type of buyer. Six elements of adjustments are considered when comparing sites to the subject property:

- Rights conveyed by the transaction;
- Financing terms;
- Motivation of the parties;
- Market conditions (time);
- Location; and
- Physical characteristics.

The most common adjustments relate to the final three items. **Figure C.11** outlines adjustments to six properties. The two main methods of showing adjustments are dollar amounts (the most common) and percentages.

C

Scenario

Salesperson Lee is estimating the market value of a residential lot based on frontage values (per front metre), along with appropriate time, physical, and location adjustments.

Tabular Analysis of Comparative Sales

Sale No.	1	2	3	4	5	6
Front Metre	18	15	15	17	15	18
Sale Price	$30,000.00	$28,000.00	$27,000.00	$29,000.00	$29,500.00	$33,720.00
Price Per Front Metre (pfm)	1,666.67	1,866.67	1,800.00	1,705.88	1,967.00	1,873.33
Time Adjustment	+ 83.33	+ 0.00	+ 180.00	+ 85.30	+ 0.00	+ 0.00
Time Adjusted Total (pfm)	= 1,750.00	= 1,866.67	= 1,980.00	1,791.18	1,967.00	1,873.33
Physical Adjustment	− 140.00	+ 186.66	+ 99.00	+ 0.00	− 98.33	− 187.33
Location Adjustment	+ 350.00	− 93.33	− 99.00	+ 125.82	+ 98.33	+ 281.00
Total Net Adjustments	= + 210.00	= + 93.33	= 0.00	= + 125.82	= 0.00	= + 93.67
Adjusted Price PFM (rounded)	**$1,960.00**	**$1,960.00**	**$1,980.00**	**$1,917.00**	**$1,967.00**	**$1,967.00**

Reconciliation

A value range for the subject site has emerged from the analysis with a low of $1,917 to a high of $1,980 per front metre. Within this range, sales 2, 5, and 6 require only two adjustments, with no time adjustment. Most weight has, however, been given to sale 5 since it required the least overall percentage of adjustments.

Therefore, applying the adjusted front-metre price of sale 5 and the 15 metre frontage of the subject, market value can be calculated as:

$1,967 x 15 = $29,505 (rounded to $29,500)

Accordingly, the market value of the subject site, as of the effective date of appraisal is $29,500.

Comparative Sales Method–Site Valuation   Figure C.11

The process of making adjustments under the comparative sales method is essentially the same as used in the direct comparison approach.

- Select a sufficient number of good comparable sites that have recently sold in the area.
- Gather all necessary data on these sites to make a proper comparison.
- Compare each of the sales with the subject for differences that may exist.
- Make the necessary adjustments to the sale price of each comparable based on those differences.
- Reconcile the adjusted sale price of the comparables into an indication of value of the subject property.

COMPARATIVE SQUARE METRE/FOOT METHOD

A method that involves calculating the known cost per square metre (or its imperial equivalent), of a newly-constructed building similar to the subject, and then multi-plying this unit cost by the number of square metres in the subject structure. The accuracy of this method depends on the refinements made by the appraiser to cover the differences between the properties from which the unit cost is derived and the property being appraised.

It would be incorrect to ascertain the square metre cost of a two-storey house and apply this unit cost as a basis for estimating the cost of a bungalow. It would also be incorrect to apply the square metre cost of an odd shaped one-storey house to estimate the cost of a more conventional structure. To prevent this kind of inaccuracy, the appraiser ensures that the properties from which a cost estimate is derived are truly comparable to the property being appraised and that all cost estimates are current and apply as of the effective date of the appraisal.

This method is practical, particularly with new construction, provided that site values (that must be deducted from the sale price of the property), can be accurately estimated. An illustration is provided as **Figure C.12** in which the comparative square metre method is used for the analysis of the reproduction cost of a building.

Tabular Analysis—Comparative Square Metre

Sale No.	1	2	3
Sale Price of Property	$200,000	$218,000	$208,000
Site Value	−90,000	−96,000	−90,000
Value of Outside Improvements	−4,000	−6,000	−3,000
Building Cost	106,000	116,000	115,000
Building Time Adjustment	+ 4,000	+ 0	+ 0
Time Adjusted Building Cost	110,000	116,000	115,000
Bathroom Adjustment	−3,000	−3,000	−3,000
Quality of Materials Adjustment	−3,000	+ 0	+ 0
Recreation Room Adjustment	+ 0	−5,000	+ 0
Total Net Adjustment	−6,000	−8,000	−3,000
Fully Adjusted Building Cost	**104,000**	**108,000**	**112,000**
Size (m²)	208 m²	215 m²	225 m²
Indicated Cost per Square Metre	**$500.00**	**$502.33**	**$497.78**

Reconciliation

A value range of between $497.78/m² and $502.33/m² has emerged from this analysis. Within this range, most weight has been given to sale 3, since it requires the fewest adjustments and is a recent sale with no time adjustment. Accordingly, the estimated reproduction cost new of the subject building (with an area of 210 m²), as of the effective date of the appraisal, is calculated as follows:

$$\$497.78 \times 210 = \$104,533$$

Figure C.12   Comparative Square Metre Method

COMPARISON YEAR

(SEE ALSO BASE YEAR)

For purposes of commercial real estate, any year that is compared with a base year for establishing a rise or fall in operating costs is referred to as the *comparison year* in relation to leases that contain an escalator clause.

COMPENSATION

(SEE ALSO COMMISSION AND COMMISSION PLANS)

Payment or reward for performance of service. In real estate brokerages, compensation is typically paid by way of commission to salespeople.

COMPETITION ACT

The *Competition Act* (formerly the *Combines Investigation Act*) is a federal statute addressing many forms of competition. The Act is intended to promote fair competition and efficiency in the Canadian marketplace. The legislation provides a framework for selected basic principles involving the conduct of businesses throughout Canada and applies, with few exceptions, to all business enterprises. The Act covers criminal as well as civil law matters. Criminal offences relate to price-fixing, bid-rigging, and misleading advertising. Civil law issues include mergers, abuse of dominant position (activities to substantially lessen competition in the marketplace), exclusive dealing (hindering or preventing consumers from dealing with other suppliers), and refusal to deal (obstructing adequate supply of products to persons carrying on a business).

The Director of Investigation and Research, head of the Competition Bureau, is responsible for administration and enforcement of the Act. The Bureau falls under the responsibility of Industry Canada.

Prohibition Order/Compliance Guideline

During 1988, the *Competition Act* gained prominence in organized real estate relating to the operation of real estate boards and associations. Upon the application of the Attorney General of Canada, an Order of Prohibition relating to the *Competition Act* was issued on December 20, 1988. The Order was issued between the Federal Court and ten real estate boards named as respondents. The Canadian Real Estate Association (CREA), wishing to enter into the Prohibition Order, signed agreements with provincial associations and local boards in advance of the Order being issued. All members of CREA were required to undertake certain activities such as:

C

> **Pledge of Competition**
>
> Member Boards and Associations of The Canadian Real Estate Association support free and open competition. We believe in the principles embodied in the Competition Act of Canada. Therefore, we adhere to Principles of Competition which include the following:
>
> - Commission rates or fees members charge for services offered to the public, and the division of those fees among co-operating members, are solely the choice of those providing the services.
> - A brokerage may offer any variety of services, e.g., exclusive, MLS listings, etc. Boards and real estate associations accept MLS listings regardless of the price, commission rates or fees, or the division thereof.
> - Advertising by members and non-members is subject to the discretion of the individual, as long as it is honest and lawful. We encourage creative, competitive choice in the services advertised to the public.
> - The business relationship between broker members, their salespersons and non-members is theirs to determine. With regard to board and association membership, members may choose for themselves to work full or part time, as long as they remain available to serve the public on a regular basis and provided provincial enabling legislation does not otherwise authorize a limitation of such choice.
> - All members are required to meet uniform and reasonable financial and educational standards. They are required to demonstrate integrity and character necessary to protect the public.
>
> By using the MLS and REALTOR trademarks, all member boards and associations of The Canadian Real Estate Association proclaim adherence to these principles, designed to preserve free and open competition.
>
> (Source: The Canadian Real Estate Association, Dispatch 99-42, November 2, 1999)

Pledge of Competition   Figure C.13

- Provide new members until 1995 with a copy of the compliance guideline;
- Comply with the *Competition Act* and specific paragraphs;
- Publish a copy of the Order in or with the MLS listings once a year (local Board or Association); and
- Provide to CREA the names of any members whose membership in a board or association is terminated or refused, along with particulars.

A Compliance Guideline was developed by CREA to assist real estate boards and their members in recognizing competition problems that can result in serious criminal and civil penalties.

Bill C-20

In March 1999, Bill C-20 was proclaimed into law. This bill represented a significant overhaul of the *Competition Act* with amendments concerning deceptive telemarketing, disclosure by telemarketers, Competition Bureau interception of private communication in serious situations with judicial authority, and protection of individual identities for persons reporting offences. In addition, Bill C-20 provided a maximum statutory limit of ten years for prohibition orders issued after proclamation of the bill. The Federal Court subsequently ruled that the Prohibition Order involving real estate ended on March 18, 1999, the day amendments to the *Competition Act* were proclaimed.

Principles of Competition

The General Assembly of The Canadian Real Estate Association adopted a *Principles of Competition* document to ensure that the overall message of competition law remains in the forefront of real estate board decision-making. The document, according to CREA Dispatch 99-42 (November 2, 1999) is designed as both a compliance and an education vehicle. The *Principles of Competition* are designed to assist boards and do not apply to individual practitioners as members of real estate boards. By-law and rule amendments were required for individual boards to adopt these principles.

The Board of Directors of The Canadian Real Estate Association also approved a second associated document titled the *Pledge of Competition*. This pledge broadly encompasses the scope of principles and interpretations and is reprinted as **Figure C.13**.

Reference   The Competition Bureau provides information concerning the *Competition Act* through the Public Education Initiative. Contact Complaints and Public Enquiries Centre, Competition Bureau, Industry Canada, 50 Victoria Street, Hull, PQ K1A 0C9 or call toll-free 1-800-348-5358.

COMPETITION, PRINCIPLE OF

(SEE PRINCIPLES (APPRAISAL))

COMPETITIVE MARKET ANALYSIS

Acronym: CMA   An analysis used by real estate practitioners to assist the seller in comparing his/her property with others in the marketplace in order to establish a listing price. The competitive market analysis is not designed to establish market value.

Application   The CMA form typically includes homes that are currently for sale, have recently sold, or on which listings have expired or did not sell in a defined time period. This information provides the seller with an indication as to what buyers are prepared to pay, given current market conditions. The CMA is a valuable tool for salespeople when properly informing sellers regarding market conditions and obtaining saleable listings. No standard format for the CMA in Canada exists and content varies among brokerages, regions, and provinces.

Provincial   See applicable reference materials.

COMPILED PLAN

Associated with registry systems and was used in Ontario land registry offices as a method to clarify written metes and bounds descriptions. Such plans were designed to simplify the often complex process of searching registry information. For the most part, they do not constitute plans of survey, but certain exceptions exist.

Provincial   See applicable reference materials.

COMPLETION DATE

The date when title to real property transfers to the new owner at the land registry or land titles office, frequently referred to as the *closing date*. The transaction is normally viewed as complete when the respective solicitors meet at the land registry or land titles office and exchange the necessary completed documentation. When the deed or transfer is accepted for registration, the transaction is complete, and money and keys are exchanged.

Provincial   See applicable reference materials.

COMPOUND INTEREST

Interest charged on the initial principal for the current period for monies borrowed, and also on interest amounts accrued from previous periods. With compound interest, interest is charged at specified intervals (e.g., monthly, daily, quarterly).

When expressed as a formula, the calculation for *simple interest* is as follows:

Principal	x	Interest Rate	x	Time Period	=	Interest
P	x	i	x	n	=	I

Example 1   *Compound Interest (Simple)*

If a loan of $10,000 was for exactly one year at an annual interest rate of 12% per annum, the simple interest is:

P	x	i	x	n	=	I
10,000	x	0.12	x	1	=	1,200

If the same loan was taken for a period of 100 days then interest would be calculated as follows:

P	x	i	x	n	=	I
10,000	x	0.12	x	100 ÷ 365	=	328.77

In the case of *compound interest*, interest is charged at a specified time interval (e.g., monthly, daily, quarterly) with the result that:

- Each time period, the original sum is reinvested and continues to earn interest.
- The interest earned during each period is reinvested and also continues to earn interest.

Example 2   *Compound Interest*

The same $10,000 amount is used by a borrower but in this case, the interest rate is 1% per month instead of 12% per annum.

Principal Amount—1st month	$10,000
Interest Charged	+100
Amount Owing	**$10,100**

Principal Amount—2nd month	$10,100
Interest Charged	+101
Amount Owing	**$10,201**

Example 3   *Compound Interest*

Using the details from Example 2, the formula for *one month* compound interest calculation is as follows:

(Principal + Interest) x Interest Rate = Compound Amount
        (P + I)   x   i   =   A

When the remaining months in this year are calculated, the following results are obtained:

Third month: $10,303.01   Eighth month: $10,828.56
Fourth month: 10,406.04   Ninth month: 10,936.85
Fifth month: 10,510.10   Tenth month: 11,046.22
Sixth month: 10,615.20   Eleventh month: 11,156.68
Seventh month: 10,721.35   Twelfth month: 11,268.25

The actual return to the lender in this case is 12.68% (1,268.25 ÷ 10,000) as opposed to 12% return in the simple interest scenario.

The equation to determine the compound amount (principal and compound interest), at a particular time is:

$$A = P(1+ i)^n$$

where
A   Compound Amount
P   Principal Amount
1   Represents a unit of value
i   Interest Rate per compounding period
n   Number of time periods (e.g., squared, cubed, etc.—expressed as a power)

Example 4   *Compound Interest*

Lender Inc. is calculating the compound interest on a personal loan to Smith for $10,000. The monthly interest rate is 1% and is compounded over the period of one year. The total amount due including principal and interest at the end of 12 month period is:

$A = \$10,000.00 (1 + .01)^{12}$
$A = \$10,000.00 (1.01)^{12}$
$A = \$10,000.00 (1.126825)$
$A = \$11,268.25$

COMPOUNDING
(SEE ALSO COMPOUND INTEREST)

The amount by which an investment will grow over a given number of time periods including the accumulation of interest. Compounding is less frequently used than discounting in investment analysis. Discounting and compounding represent the basic methods to determine the *time value of money*.

Application   Compounding involves three different types of calculations; discounting involves another three. In combination, they are referred to as the *six functions of a dollar*. Compounding can involve:

- Compounding a single amount into the future, e.g., interest on a loan that compounds monthly but is not due until the end of the term;
- Compounding a stream of equal payments, e.g., investment of equal amounts over a specified period of time at a given rate of interest; and
- Compounding of a stream of equal payments to create a future amount (e.g., payments necessary to produce a given future value). This form of compounding is often referred to by financial institutions as a *sinking fund*.

Compounding is most frequently encountered from a lender's perspective when calculating yield in relation to loans advanced to borrowers, determining the value of an annuity, or establishing the periodic payments required to produce a specified annuity.

COMPUTER SOFTWARE

Many suppliers offer word processing, accounting, database, and publishing software that can be used in the real estate industry. Generally, provincial real estate associations and boards are not involved in the provision of computer software with the exception of software relating to MLS Systems. In some instances, these organizations establish special arrangements with specific suppliers for the benefit of their memberships.

Board MLS Systems

Software and hardware requirements for access to local real estate board MLS systems vary considerably. As a general guideline, most systems require a combination of the following:

- Computer terminal;
- External or internal modem with communications software;
- Telephone line; and
- Printer.

CONCRETE AND CLAY TILES

High quality roofing systems with life expectancies ranging from 50 to 100 years. Like slate, these roofs are heavy and can weigh four to five times as much as asphalt shingles, thus modifications to the roof structure are often required.

CONCRETE BLOCKS

(SEE ALSO BASEMENT)

The use of concrete blocks as upper exterior wall coverings for residential construction is rare in Canada, although the practice is widespread in southern US locations, e.g., Florida. Concrete blocks function well in northern climates as an exterior wall surface and are frequently used in industrial and commercial structures. Concrete block basements were extensively used in residential structures, but their popularity diminished in favour of poured concrete walls that now predominate in most urban residential construction. Concrete blocks are relatively porous and can allow water penetration, however, paint reduces this penetration significantly. As with all unit masonry construction, mortar deterioration is a common problem. **Figure C.14** illustrates the components of a wall using concrete blocks.

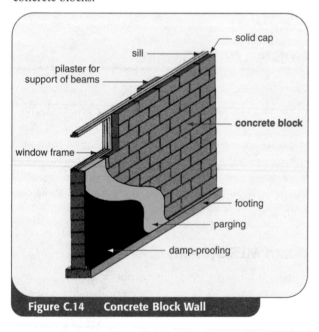

Figure C.14   Concrete Block Wall

CONCRETE FLOOR

In residential construction, these floors are usually not structural but rather rest on the ground. Modern building practices use three-inch thick slabs, although older ones can be as thin as two inches. Building codes set out requirements concerning *slabs-on-ground* in regard to the amount of granular fill required, sloping of floor surface to accommodate floor drains, thickness, and compression strength. Floor systems used for structural purposes, e.g., multi-level concrete building, fall under building code design requirements that detail sufficient structural capacity and integrity to effectively and safely carry specified dead and live loads. See **Figure C.15**.

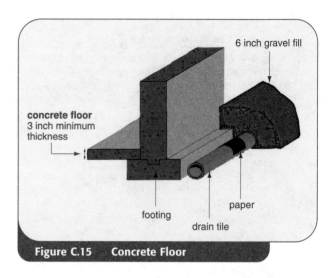

Figure C.15   Concrete Floor

CONCURRENT OWNERSHIP

(SEE ALSO JOINT TENANCY AND TENANTS IN COMMON)

Concurrent ownership arises when two or more persons have a right of ownership at the same time. Concurrent interests normally fall into two primary categories:

- Tenancy in common; and
- Joint tenancy.

Concurrent ownership can be disposed of by agreement of the owners. If concurrent owners cannot agree as to the disposition of the property, an application can be made to the court that then leads to the forced sale of the property and distribution of proceeds.

Example   *Concurrent Ownership*

The buyers, James Jones and Judy Jones, purchase a home as joint tenants and draft the offer in both names. Accordingly, the deed is prepared showing both parties as owners in joint tenancy. As such, Mr. and Mrs. Jones have concurrent ownership of the property.

CONDEMNATION

(SEE ALSO EMINENT DOMAIN)

The legal act of taking private property for public use under the right of eminent domain with adequate compensation to the owner. Condemnation is normally referred to, for real estate purposes, as *expropriation*. Provincial legislation typically sets out procedures for expropriation including the provision of notices, the scheduling of hearings, allowance for appeals, and compensation where appropriate.

Provincial   See applicable reference materials.

CONDITION

Broadly defined as a stipulation in a contract/agreement that provides for a consequent result on either the occurrence or non-occurrence of a specified event.

Application   For real estate practitioners, one of the most complex offer-writing situations involves the drafting of properly worded conditions. Generally, these conditions are inserted at the request of, and for the protection of, the buyer although this does not preclude a situation wherein a condition would be included for the protection of the seller.

Condition Precedent

A stipulation, the satisfaction of which must occur, before the contract can come into existence and, if satisfied gives rise to a legally binding contract. Typical examples include offers that are conditional on the sale of a buyer's home or the arranging of a mortgage.

Where a condition precedent exists, even upon acceptance of the offer, a fully binding contract is not created until the condition is met. If the condition is fulfilled as set out in the agreement/contract, a binding contract is formed. If the condition is not fulfilled as set out in the agreement/contract and if it is not waived (assuming that a waiver provision is included in the agreement/contract), no contract has ever been formed.

Two important effects of a condition precedent should be emphasized.

- The condition precedent makes the creation of a contract/agreement subject to the prior fulfillment of that condition.
- The insertion of a condition precedent will have the effect of relieving both the buyer and the seller of their respective obligations under the agreement/contract if that condition cannot be fulfilled, unless it is stated that the condition precedent is for the benefit of and may be waived by one of them (often referred to as a *waiver provision*).

When a condition precedent has been fulfilled, or waived by the buyer, and the selling party notified, the contract is capable of completion upon the balance of the terms and conditions contained in the offer and a binding contract is formed. Written confirmation of the fulfillment or waiver of the condition, must be delivered to the seller as soon as possible and within time constraints contained in the condition precedent.

If a condition precedent is not fulfilled, no contractual arrangement will have arisen between the seller and the buyer, the agreement will be null and void, and neither the buyer nor the seller will be required to satisfy respective obligations that would have risen had the condition been satisfied. Notice of non-fulfillment of any condition must be delivered to the seller and consent obtained from the seller for the return of the deposit to the buyer.

Most conditions precedent follow the same pattern:

- What is to be done (with specific definable details);
- Who is to do it;
- Who is to pay for it;
- Within what time limit;
- What is to happen in the event that it is not done; and
- That it may be waived.

Example   *Condition Precedent*

The following condition precedent is included for illustration purposes only. Phraseology and applicable forms will vary by provincial jurisdiction.

This Offer is conditional upon the Buyer arranging, at the Buyer's own expense, a new first mortgage for not less than Fifty Thousand Dollars ($50,000.00), bearing interest at the rate of not more than 14% per annum, calculated semi-annually not in advance and repayable in blended monthly payments of about Five Hundred and Eighty-Six Dollars and Ninety-Four Cents ($586.94), including both principal and interest and to run for a term of not less than five years from the date of completion of this transaction. Unless the Buyer gives notice in writing delivered to the Seller that the preceding condition is fulfilled on or before 11:59 p.m. on the 1st day of March, 20xx, this Offer shall be null and void and the deposit shall be returned to the Buyer in full without deduction. This condition is included for the sole benefit of the Buyer and may be waived at the Buyer's option by notice in writing to the Seller within the time period stated herein.

Waiver of Condition Precedent

Over the years, courts have established that, unless otherwise specified in an agreement, a condition precedent can be used by either party to the transaction and neither party has the right to simply waive the condition—it can either be performed or not performed. The inclusion of a waiver provision giving a specific right to waive the condition allows the party for whose protection the condition was included to remove it entirely, rendering the agreement/contract firm and binding.

While the majority of conditions include a waiver provision, it must be recognized that occasionally a true condition precedent will be encountered that cannot be waived. For example, an offer conditional on approval to assume an existing mortgage, or conditional on obtaining a consent to sever the property being sold from a larger parcel of land would be drafted as a condition precedent with no waiver. The completion of the agreement/contract as contemplated would depend on the fulfillment of the condition. It follows that a condition subsequent would not be suitable for such situations, since it is waived by lapse of time as stipulated in the condition.

Notice to Remove Condition

A notice relating to the satisfaction (fulfillment) or non-satisfaction (non-fulfillment) of a condition precedent. Such notices, including terminology and forms used will vary by provincial jurisdiction.

Condition Subsequent

This condition has divergent meanings and usages in real estate depending on provincial jurisdiction. The following description applies to practitioners within the Province of Ontario. For an alternate description, see: **Condition Subsequent: Province of Manitoba.**

Condition subsequent is formally defined as a condition in a contract referring to a future event upon the happening of which the agreement/contract becomes no longer binding on the parties. The term *condition subsequent* is a misnomer in that the clause provides an option allowing the termination of a contract under certain defined circumstances. Since the condition subsequent is an option to terminate, no waiver is necessary in order to have a firm and binding agreement.

Condition subsequent normally starts with the words:

> *The buyer may terminate this Agreement in the event that…*

Many of the same details usual to the condition precedent are found:

- What is to be done;
- Who is to do it;
- Who is to pay for it;
- What may happen in the event that it is not done: i.e., the agreement/contract can be terminated; and
- Within what time limit.

| **Example** | ***Condition Subsequent*** |

> *The Buyer may terminate this Agreement in the event that a new first mortgage for not less than Fifty Thousand Dollars ($50,000.00), bearing interest at a rate of not more than 14% per annum calculated semi-annually not in advance and repayable in blended monthly payments of about Five Hundred and Eighty-Six Dollars and Ninety-Four Cents ($586.94), including both principal and interest and to run for a term of not less than five years from the date of completion of this transaction, cannot be arranged by the Buyer at the Buyer's expense. The Buyer may notify the Seller in writing by 11:59 p.m. on the 1st day of March, 20xx of the inability to arrange such mortgage, thus rendering this Agreement null and void and the deposit shall be returned to the Buyer in full without deduction. If no such notification is received, this term of contract shall be deemed to be waived by the Buyer and the Agreement shall remain valid and binding whether or not such mortgage has been in fact arranged.*

Condition Subsequent: Province of Manitoba

A condition the satisfaction of which is to occur after closing and does not affect the validity of the contract.

A condition subsequent is an uncertain event that brings a promisor's liability to an end if it happens. Many of the details usual to the condition precedent are found:

- What is to be done.
- Who is to do it.
- Who is to pay for it.
- Within what time limit.

| **Example** | ***Condition Subsequent: Province of Manitoba*** |

If a buyer purchases a new home with a closing date in the winter, he/she might insert a condition subsequent in the offer to purchase stating that the offer is conditional upon the builder laying sod in the spring when weather permits. If the builder accepts this offer, thereby promising to perform the condition subsequent, the contract is binding upon both parties (assuming that any other conditions are satisfied), and the transaction will close as usual. However, legal liability under the contract will arise if the builder does not do as agreed to do by accepting the offer with the condition subsequent in it. Thus, if the builder does not lay the sod as promised, the buyer can sue the builder for damages under the contract, but he/she cannot rescind the transaction as the contract remains valid even if the builder does not do as promised.

A possible wording for the condition subsequent in the offer to purchase follows:

This offer is conditional upon Builder Anderson promising to lay sod in the front and back yards of 123 Main Street by May 15, 20xx, at his own expense.

Escape Clause

Certain obstacles can emerge with conditional offers, particularly for the seller. For example, in the sale of property, the seller, when agreeing to a condition may have to place the property back on the market if the condition is not fulfilled or waived by the buyer. For some conditions, this problem is not a major factor. It is unlikely that a competent salesperson would negotiate an offer conditional upon arranging a first mortgage unless:

- There was reasonable assurance that a lender would consider the buyer's mortgage application; and
- The time limit involved to secure the approval did not involve a lengthy period.

With respect to the sale of the buyer's property, the condition is usually for a longer period. Further, the decision to sell the property rests with that buyer during the conditional period. In most instances, an escape clause (also referred to as a *time clause*), usually improves the acceptability of such conditions by the seller. The following clause requires that the buyer remove all conditions within a stipulated time period, failing which his/her offer is null and void.

Example   *Condition–Escape Clause*

Provided further that the Vendor may continue to offer the property for sale and, in the event the Vendor received another Offer satisfactory to the Vendor, the Vendor may so notify the Purchaser in writing by delivery to the Purchaser or to the Purchaser's address hereinafter indicated. The Purchaser shall have __ hours from the giving of such notice to waive all conditions by notice in writing delivered to the Vendor, failing which this Offer shall be null and void and the deposit shall be returned to the Purchaser in full without deduction.

Provincial   See applicable reference materials.

CONDITIONAL SALES CONTRACT

Usually involves the sale of goods, in which the property remains in the seller's name until all installments set out in the contract have been paid by the buyer. This type of contract should be differentiated from a chattel loan in which the person acquiring the chattel conveys legal title to the creditor as security for repayment. Legislation sets out the procedures for registration of conditional sales contracts and other forms of security involving chattels.

Example   *Conditional Sales Contract*

Buyer Jones acquires a residential property with a swimming pool and decides to have a pool heater installed. The contractor agrees to furnish the heater at a price of $2,200 plus tax and accepts a $500 deposit with the balance payable in equal monthly installments of $100 plus interest at 9% per annum compounded monthly.

The contractor prepares a conditional sales contract stating the particulars of the agreement (also referred to as a *security agreement* or *conditional sales lien*), and registers the document under the applicable provincial personal property registry system. When all installments and interest are paid, ownership will transfer to Jones.

Provincial   See applicable reference materials.

CONDITIONAL SALES LIEN

A lien registered by a supplier of goods who retains the right to products installed at the premises, until full payment has been received. Statutory rights regarding conditional sales liens will vary by provincial jurisdiction.

CONDOMINIUM

Refers to a system of land ownership where each individual owner holds title to a specific unit as well as owning a share of common property (typically referred to as *common elements*). Many types of condominium units are found in the marketplace: an apartment suite in a high rise complex, one of a row of townhouses, a detached or semi-detached house, or even a vacant lot. Leasehold, as well as freehold, condominiums can also be found in selected provinces.

The characteristic that has bound all these diverse forms of ownership is that, in each, the owners of the condominium units also own an undivided interest in the common elements. Such elements might include hallways, elevators, parking structures or lots, landscaped areas, recreational facilities, roadways, and any other property owned in common by all unit owners within a specific condominium project.

Interestingly, even that fundamental distinction is now disappearing with the introduction of common element condominiums in which projects have no units but only common property (e.g., golf course). The term *unit* under such legislation refers to the common interest held by an

C

individual and not a specific unit beyond the common elements. The proportionate share of ownership is typically registered to property beyond the condominium project.

Provincial   See applicable reference materials. Condominium ownership in British Columbia is commonly referred to as a *strata* ownership.

CONFIDENTIALITY AGREEMENT

An agreement in which one party is entrusted with secret or private matters by another. In real estate negotiations, commercial brokerages and their salespeople may become involved in confidentiality agreements relating to the listing and selling of property. For example, a listing salesperson may have to inspect books of account or other documentation concerning a commercial enterprise as part of agency duties. Conversely, a company considering relocation may provide a buyer representative with confidential, proprietary information, and/or trade secrets in trust and confidence.

Wordings of confidentiality agreements vary considerably as most are drafted to address specific purposes, however, most follow a similar structure:

Parties   The agreement sets out the parties to the agreement, e.g., the corporation and the commercial brokerage including applicable salesperson(s).

Purpose   The reason that confidential information is provided, e.g., to search for and negotiate a site for an industrial facility. The information referenced is typically included by way of an attached list. The agreement may also allow the commercial brokerage to inspect the premises and talk with suppliers, employees, or other representatives of the company.

Provisions
- Hold all information confidential and to use such information solely for the intended purpose.
- Return all documentation at the conclusion of negotiations (or on demand).
- Make no copies or retain any information what-so-ever.
- Not disclose information to any other parties (unless the agreement also binds such parties).

In the event of a breach, confidentiality agreements commonly include reference to the rights of the injured party to seek relief through legal proceedings. Most agreements provide that any information known by the commercial brokerage or salesperson(s) before the agreement or *generally known* within the marketplace do not fall within the scope of such agreements.

CONFORMITY, PRINCIPLE OF
(SEE PRINCIPLES (APPRAISAL))

CONSERVATION AUTHORITY

An organization created by provincial statute in Ontario to oversee conservation matters. Individual provinces have established specific legislation to provide for the conservation, control, and prudent use of natural resources and consequently may affect the rights of property owners adjacent to such areas.

Laws were enacted to exercise authority over regulated areas such as rivers, forests, and other natural resources in order to protect and preserve through prudent management. Regulated areas typically include lands adjacent to watercourses that require special consideration because of potential for flood, land erosion, and pollution problems.

Provincial   See applicable reference materials.

CONSIDERATION
(SEE ALSO CONTRACT)

Something of value given or promised to make an agreement legally binding. The law will not enforce a purely gratuitous promise. To enforce a claim regarding a promise, the plaintiff must satisfy the court either that the promise was contained in a document under seal, or that it was supported by consideration. One commonly accepted definition of consideration is something of value given by a promisee to a promisor to make the promise binding. Consideration is therefore what a person receives or is to receive for what that person does or agrees to do. Whatever is given is referred to as *valuable consideration* in that value can be attached and may be:

- An act in return for an act;
- A promise in return for a promise; or
- An act in return for a promise.

Where a promise is made under seal, no consideration is required since the law presumes that the solemn act of sealing replaces consideration. Form and conduct indicate that the person signing the document gave careful thought to the nature of the transaction.

Following are selected rules relating to consideration.

- If a promise is not made under seal, consideration is necessary to make it binding.
- Must be of some value, but need not be equal to what is received in return. It has been held that a pepper-

corn is valuable consideration as long as the promisor accepts it as such.

- Must move from the promisee to the promisor. However, many ask what does the buyer (as promisee) receive as consideration for a promise not to revoke the offer? The answer in most instances is nothing, but the promise is usually made under seal.
- Must be lawful.
- The promisee cannot rely on past conduct or promises as consideration. It must be present or future consideration to be effective.

CONSISTENT USE, PRINCIPLE OF

(SEE PRINCIPLES (APPRAISAL))

CONSTRUCTION ALLOWANCE

Refers to a landlord's contribution to the cost of construction and/or alteration necessary to prepare space for a tenant's occupancy.

CONSTRUCTION AND COST ESTIMATE

A figure submitted in advance of construction, not binding unless submitted as a bid that is used to help decide the feasibility of a proposed project.

CONSTRUCTION AND UPGRADE COSTS

Various organizations (e.g., companies involved with cost estimating, home inspectors, lenders, and appraisers), provide or work with summary information concerning estimates for repairs and/or improvements by property type. Costs will differ by region and/or province and can vary widely from actual contractor quotations, given local market conditions and unique circumstances surrounding individual properties.

Provincial   See applicable reference materials.

CONSTRUCTION AREA

A term used in office building measurement regarding the total area of each floor in relation to the outside surface of exterior (outside) building walls. The construction area also includes all basement areas and other floors used for mechanical purposes. The construction area relates to the determination of building costs and should be clearly differentiated from useable and rentable areas commonly referenced in the leasing of office space.

CONSTRUCTION LIEN

A claim against a property that is filed by a person or corporation in the land registry or land titles office for labour, services, or materials supplied. Terminology will vary by province, e.g., builder's lien, construction lien, and mechanic's lien.

Provincial   See applicable reference materials.

CONSTRUCTIVE NOTICE

A legal term referring to something that is not actual but is accepted in law as a substitute for the real event, e.g., notice given by the recording of documents with a public official. All persons are charged with knowledge of such documents and their contents, whether or not they have actually examined them.

Example   *Constructive Notice*

Smith registers a mortgage on title. Members of the public have actual notice of the document and thereafter are deemed to have constructive notice of the terms of the mortgage whether or not they have actually examined the document.

CONSUMER

Generally defined as an individual that participates or may participate in a transaction involving goods or services. Provincial legislation typically provides a more precise definition for statutory purposes. For example, the definition of a consumer in Ontario in the *Consumer Reporting Act* (Province of Ontario) includes a person engaging in any transaction other than in the course of carrying on a business, trade, or profession.

Provincial   See applicable reference materials.

CONSUMER PRICE INDEX

Acronym: CPI   An indicator of consumer price fluctuations over a period of time. The CPI is based on a *basket* of goods and services and associated prices that Canadians must pay for these goods and services. The basket consis-

C

tently reflects equivalent quantity and quality and, as a result, the CPI measures true price movements. The CPI is generally regarded as a reliable measure of purchasing power, i.e., inflation (when the purchasing power of the dollar decreases) or deflation (when the purchasing power of the dollar increases).

Application   Practitioners commonly encounter the CPI in relation to commercial tenancy agreements in which rents are geared to CPI fluctuations over part or all of the lease term. However, the index has far-reaching applications for Canadian society involving such items as spousal and child support payments, Old Age Security pensions, Canada Pension Plan payments, and cost-of-living increases for labour contracts, often referred to as COLA (cost-of-living adjustment) clauses.

Components/Weightings

Canadians are most familiar with the *all-items* CPI that is regularly published in the media. This index is based on selected components and each component has a relative weighting of importance in making up the index.

- Household operations and furnishings 10.0%
- Shelter 27.9%
- Food 18.0%
- Alcoholic beverages and tobacco products 4.5%
- Recreation, education, and reading 10.4%
- Health and personal care 4.3%
- Transportation 18.3%
- Clothing and footwear 6.6%

Six hundred goods and services are tracked within these overall components. Each item is weighted based on its relative importance. The weighting used reflects the impact that a price fluctuation in a particular item would have upon the average consumer budget. For example, an increase in gasoline prices would have greater impact than a corresponding rise in tea prices, as most families are impacted more by the former than the latter. The combined weighting of all goods and services within a component is totalled for the overall weighting of that component. The current set of weightings represent household expenditures for 1992.

Scope of Indexes

The primary *all items* CPI is complemented by a range of sub-indexes. For example, each component has a corresponding index, e.g., transportation, shelter, and clothing. These in turn are broken into small *groups* made up of selected, similar products or services within the overall component, e.g., grouping of dairy products, childrens' footwear, and

specific tobacco products. In fact, the entire range of 600 goods and services is grouped under an elaborate classification system with the lowest level having 182 basic classes (products or services that have common end-uses or are viewed as substitutes for one another) and progressively consolidating to the eight major component classes.

Time Base

The current CPIs are time-based using the year 1986. In other words, the CPI for 1986 is 100 and all subsequent years are compared with that base year. If, for example, the current *all-items* CPI is 131.5, this means that consumer prices are 31.5% higher than in 1986. The time base is updated periodically by Statistics Canada.

Publication

The CPI is normally published by Statistics Canada in the third week of the following month. As already referenced, a wide array of sub-indexes are provided including major components right through to specific goods and services in basic classes. The CPIs are published for Canada, the ten provinces, the territories, and 16 major centres across the country.

CONSUMER PROTECTION

Generally refers to legislation regarding the protection of consumer rights in business transactions. Consumer reporting involves procedures concerning the type of information that may be maintained, the reporting methods relating to such information, and to whom and under what circumstances selected information may be reported. Business practices legislation normally focuses on the prohibition of unfair practices and misleading statements in making consumer representations respecting the offering of goods and services in the marketplace. Consumer protection, consumer reporting, and business practices legislation vary by provincial legislation.

Provincial   See applicable reference materials.

CONSUMER REPORTING

Provincial   See applicable reference materials.

CONTAMINATION–AIR QUALITY
(SEE INDOOR AIR QUALITY AND OUTDOOR AIR QUALITY)

CONTAMINATION–GROUND WATER/LAND
(SEE GROUND WATER CONTAMINATION AND LAND CONTAMINATION)

CONTEST
(SEE ALSO ADVERTISING GUIDELINES)

A competition for a prize sometimes used in the context of promotion of real property by developers, builders, or real estate brokerages and practitioners. The *Competition Act*, a federal statute, addresses promotions and guidelines for the introduction of contests or similar offerings to the public. Section 59 sets out certain procedures such as accurate and fair disclosure of the number and approximate value of prizes, material facts that affect the chance of winning, non-delay of prize distribution, and acceptable procedures for participant selection and distribution of prizes. Real estate practitioners contemplating this type of activity should carefully read relevant materials in the legislation.

CONTINGENCY (RESERVE) FUND
(SEE ALSO RESERVE FUND)

Money or securities set aside to cover unexpected costs or circumstances arising out of business operations. Reserve funds, for real estate purposes, are most commonly associated with condominiums.

Provincial   See applicable reference materials.

CONTRACT

A legally binding agreement between two or more capable persons for consideration or value, to do or not to do some lawful and genuinely intended act. A contract can contain any number of promises or terms to be performed by either party. The underlying intention of any contract is that it shall be binding on the parties.

Essential Elements

Certain elements must be present to make the contract enforceable.

- The parties entering into a contract must be legally competent to contract (*capacity of the parties*).
- The contractual arrangement must be lawful (*lawful object* or *legality of object*).
- Each party must receive something (*consideration*).
- There must be offer and acceptance (*mutual agreement*).
- Both parties must consent to the terms of the contract (*genuine intention*).
- The agreement must be certain (*definite and clear*).

A contract, not fulfilling all requirements, may be either void or voidable:

- Void (*never came into existence*);
- Voidable (*originally valid but capable of being rejected by the offended parties at a later time*); or
- Illegal (*not enforceable by the courts*).

Capacity of the Parties

Parties to a contract must, at the time when the contract is made, have the legal capacity to make the contract.

Persons   While contractual promises are enforceable against anyone having legal capacity, some persons are deemed by law as either incapable of contracting or having only limited capacity to contract. In cases involving limited capacity, the contract is usually considered voidable; that is, the contract is valid until the individual goes to court to void it. As long as the person of limited capacity allows the contract to exist, it may not be voided. Some examples of those with limited capacity to enter a contract include:

- Minors (those under the age of majority),
- Mentally incompetent persons,
- Intoxicated persons or persons incapable of understanding the nature of a contract by virtue of excessive use of drugs or chemicals, and
- Illiterates.

In the case of minors, each province has legislation concerning the age at which a person is considered an adult. For example, in Ontario, Manitoba, and Saskatchewan, the age is 18. In Nova Scotia, persons under 19 are considered minors or infants.

The capacity of parties extends beyond persons and requirements may vary by province. The following is provided for descriptive purposes only.

Corporation   Usually has the rights, powers, and privileges to enter into contracts concerning the purchase and sale of real property unless specific restrictions are located in the articles of incorporation or the corporation has not enacted empowering provisions in its by-laws. Two important cautions are required concerning corporations involved in acquisition or disposition of real estate. First, does the corporation exist and secondly, does it have the right to enter into such contracts?

Partnership   Normally provides under provincial legislation that any partner may bind the other partners in a transaction during the ordinary course of business.

Condominiums/Co-operatives   Permitted to enter into contracts for the purchase and sale of real property in line with incorporation documents or statutory regulations limiting the scope of such organizations.

Non-Profit Organizations   Have the rights, powers, and privileges to enter into contracts for the purchase and sale of real property. For example, incorporation documents of a real estate board often specifically mention the right to acquire and dispose of real estate.

Reference   For further encyclopedia references concerning the capacity of parties see: Executor/Executrix, Illiterate, Mental Incompetence, Intoxicated Persons, Minor, and **Partnership**.

Lawful Object

If the object of the contract is illegal by statute or common law, the contract will be void and unenforceable in the courts. For example, a contract would not be considered lawful if the acquisition involved criminal activity or was a direct violation of competition policy (*Competition Act*) or deliberate evasion of taxes (*Income Tax Act*). In such instances, the contract would be totally void. Examples of illegality or no lawful object would include contracts:

- Contrary to public policy or good morals;
- Injurious or prejudicial to the safety of the state or to the public service;
- Tending to pervert justice or abuse the legal process;
- In restraint of trade such as price fixing;
- In restraint of personal liberty or marriage; and
- For the commission of a criminal offence or civil wrong or relating to gambling or wagering (unless authorized by means of provincial statutes).

Often, buyers and sellers believe that a sale made on a Sunday is illegal and void. The Supreme Court of Canada held that the particular section of the *Lord's Day Act* relating to this issue was unconstitutional in view of the *Canadian Charter of Rights and Freedoms*.

Reference   Selected provinces have statutes making contracts illegal for specific days. In Nova Scotia, for example, business cannot be legally conducted on Remembrance Day. A similar statute exists in Manitoba.

Consideration

What each party receives or is to receive in exchange for promises to act in a certain manner and is something that is given by a promisee to a promisor to make the promise binding. The essence of a valid, binding contract is the idea of a *bargain* between the parties. The bargain is the consideration of a contract and may consist of an act in return for an act, a promise in return for a promise, or an act in return for a promise. As a result, each side receives something from the other. In real estate transactions, consideration usually takes the form of a promise from the seller to sell in return for a sum of money to be received from the buyer. Consideration is best viewed in terms of the following four headings.

Value   What either party receives must have some value. Interestingly, the court does not assess the adequacy of this value, but only its existence. Sometimes, practitioners misunderstand the concept of valuable consideration. This does not mean that the consideration given has some extraordinary worth associated with it. The courts are only interested that it exists. Of course, if the consideration was so minimal as to make the contract one-sided, the courts might act based on the unconscionability of the agreement. Further, the court might review the adequacy of the consideration if undue influence, fraud, duress, or misrepresentation exists.

Lawful   The best explanation is by example. If the buyer and seller knowingly agree to transact business based on stolen money or goods, the contract does not have lawful consideration.

Past Consideration   To quote an old phrase: *Old consideration is no consideration.* For example, the buyer of a cottage enters into an agreement to purchase a cottage for $85,000. Subsequent to that agreement, the seller mentions that he will include the boat. No documentation is prepared and no consideration is given. At closing, the boat has been removed by the seller. As consideration does not exist and past consideration ($85,000) did not include the boat, the buyer does not have an enforceable contract concerning the boat.

Seal   A contract can be made binding without consideration if a seal is used. Where a promise is made under seal, no consideration is required since the law presumes the act of sealing replaces consideration. Therefore, in the case of an agreement/contract, if legal seals are affixed at the time of signing, no consideration is required. This is only valid if the parties are clearly aware of the legal effect that a seal has on the contract.

The ancient method of sealing by wax and swearing a solemn oath has been replaced in modern legal practice by a variety of methods to indicate that the document has been signed under seal. Generally, the courts will now accept anything from red wafers to preprinted or hand written seals as long as it is clear the parties signing knew, or were directed to the fact, that they were signing under seal. Also, the legal seal of a corporation does not perform the same function, valuable consideration is still required, unless legal seals are also present.

While, in many instances, the corporate seal is unnecessary for signing documents, any document signed on behalf of a company under its corporate seal and indicating the authority of the person signing by inserting that person's position above the signature would be good business practice. If a corporate seal is not used, the following words should be used:

I have the authority to bind the corporation.

The act of placing a mark or symbol on a document is evidence and assurance of the intent to carry out promises contained therein. A sealed document provides added confirmation of intent of the parties to perform an agreement/contract. Under old conveyancing law, an official seal was often used as a substitute for consideration. Where a promise is made under seal, no consideration is required since the law presumes that the solemn act of sealing replaces consideration.

Provincial   See applicable reference materials.

Offer and Acceptance (Mutual Agreement)

A contract is formed when the offer (made by the offeror), is accepted by the other party (the offeree). The following items are general rules concerning basic requirements for an offer. The offer:

- Must be complete and definite in its terms.
- Must be made to one or more persons or corporations, or to the public at large.
- Must remain open for acceptance for a reasonable period of time.
- May be revoked or withdrawn prior to acceptance, subject to certain limitations.
- Must be communicated to the offeree.

The acceptance of the offer is based on four requirements. The acceptance must be:

- Unconditional.
- Communicated to the offeror.
- Made in the manner required by the offeror.
- Made within the time required by the offeror.

Where the communication of acceptance is permitted by mail, telegram, or fax, such acceptance is deemed to be completed upon the letter having been mailed, the telegram sent, or the fax transmitted. The contract is binding even if the letter, telegram, or fax is not received. Further, if an offer is made in the form of a promise upon the performance of a future act, the process of carrying out that act can constitute acceptance.

Genuine Intention

The agreement must be genuine and give more than the outward appearance of a contract. In other words, one of the parties may have been induced to enter into the agreement by improper means and the document does not express what was intended.

Inducements by improper means are caused by four different circumstances.

Mistakes   The term *mistake* is narrowly defined for contract purposes. The courts will not declare a contract void simply because of a mistake of the parties. Three types of mistakes are normally considered:

- A common mistake in which both parties make the same mistake: that is, each is mistaken about some underlying fundamental fact;
- A mutual mistake in which the parties misunderstand each other and are at cross purposes; and
- A unilateral mistake in which one of the parties is mistaken concerning a fundamental character of the contract.

Misrepresentation   A false statement or assertion made by one party to the other, before or at the time of contracting, with regard to some existing fact, matter, or circumstance affecting the contract. Misrepresentations are viewed as innocent, fraudulent, or negligent.

Duress or Undue Influence   Duress occurs when a person does not act with his/her free will, but instead through fear of personal suffering. Undue influence is the improper use of one person's power over another to induce that person into a contract. Following are selected examples that might fall under *undue influence.*

- One party is knowledgeable and experienced while the other is ill-informed and inexperienced.

- A gift is made by a child to an adult, guardian, or ward; a beneficiary to a trustee; a patient to a doctor; a person to a spiritual advisor; or, a client to a solicitor.
- A real estate salesperson purchases property from his/her client.

The person appearing to have exerted undue influence must prove that the transaction was reasonable and fair and that no advantage was gained due to his/her position. The fact that the person claiming undue influence received independent legal advice or valuation of a property is valid to establish that a reasonable transaction occurred.

Failure to Disclose   The non-disclosure of latent defects might invalidate a contract. A latent defect is generally described as a defect that is unknown to the buyer but is material to the enjoyment of the property. The buyer might not have entered into the contract had he/she been aware of the defect. An example could be the presence of ground contamination because of a prior owner's use and spillage/seepage of hazardous product. See also **Latent Defect, Mistake**, and **Misrepresentation.**

Definite and Clear

The terms of an agreement must be definite and clear and if the essential terms have not been agreed upon, a binding contact does not exist. However, this does not mean that the terms have to be decided. A term of a contract can be established through arbitration by a third party.

Some terms of a contract will, if necessary, be implied by law. A contract in which no date was specified for possession might be held to be invalid for lack of certainty, particularly if the phrase *time is of the essence* is contained in the agreement. If the terms, conditions, and other provisions of the agreement establish with reasonable certainty that the parties intended possession to occur within reasonable time limits, then the court might interpret the contract so as to give effect to the intent of the parties as determined from the additional circumstances.

A frequent cause of uncertainty is the agreement to negotiate some time in the future. A sale at a price to be fixed by arbitration through a third party is one thing, but a sale at a price to be fixed by subsequent negotiations between seller and buyer is not a concluded contract until these negotiations have resulted in an agreed price. This problem frequently arises with a right to renew a lease, or with a right given to a tenant to purchase property during or at the end of a lease. If the rent or price is simply left to be agreed upon, no agreement exists.

In summary, if a vital and material condition of the contract is undetermined, no contract exists, but merely an undertaking to seek a contract at a future time.

Contract Documents

Typically refer to the preprinted agreement/contract forms along with necessary schedules and addenda relating to that specific agreement.

Contract documents apply to the agreement of purchase and sale as well as leases. In residential real estate, contract documents for the purchase of a new home might include drawings, specifications, plans, schedules, descriptions, and warranties, that substantiate the terms of the contract. In commercial real estate, contract documents normally consist of the agreement/contract along with drawings, specifications, survey, buyer and seller covenants, conditions, additional contract terms, and assumption of mortgage. In the case of a lease, the documents would include the preprinted offer to lease together with the layout of the demised premises, landlord's and tenant's work, conditions, and additional lease details.

Contract documents also include any modifications following agreement of the parties. Modifications are generally documented by way of amendments. Formats will vary by provincial jurisdiction. The following are typical documents which may be attached to an agreement/contract to purchase a newly constructed home.

Example   *Contract–Contract Documents*
ABC Realty Inc. is selling new homes currently under construction. To provide a complete package for the buyer, the brokerage is including the following documents and schedules.

Agreement/Contract
Schedule A: New Home Warranty Plan
  (dependent on the provincial jurisdiction)
Schedule B: New Home Warranty Program
Schedule C: Construction Specifications
Schedule D: Upgrades and Alterations
Schedule E: Other Terms and Conditions

Provincial   See applicable reference materials.

Interpretation

When a dispute arises as to a contract's meaning or the rights under it, the courts apply varied legal rules of evidence and interpretation to discover what the parties to the contract intended. One important rule is the *parol evidence rule* which provides that a completed written contract may not be altered, varied, or amended except in writing and may not be explained or added to by verbal agreement or evidence as to the intention of the parties. Exceptions exist, but the general rule must be considered significant in the drafting of agreements so that every term, warranty, condition, or representation on which one or other of the parties relies will be incorporated into the written document.

Privity

The general rule is that only parties to the contract can enforce it or be bound by it. If A employs B to do work on C's house in return for payment, A and B have certain rights against each other that can be enforced at law, but C has no legal rights against B for non-performance of the work because he/she is not a party to or *privy* to the contract between A and B. (C does have legal rights against A for non-performance of the work because of the contract between C and A.)

Similarly, a broker (or salesperson) is only a witness to the signing of a contract for a property sale. Therefore, if a breach of the contract occurs, the seller can only sue the buyer and vice versa. The brokerage, acting on the seller's behalf, cannot be sued by either of the contracting parties under the terms of the contract since he/she is not privy to the contract. However, the brokerage may be sued independent of the contract if he/she encouraged the seller or the buyer to enter into the contract by the provision of misleading information or as a consequence of negligence or error. Only the brokerage, not the salesperson, can sue the seller for a real estate commission as the salesperson is not a party to the contract—he/she is only representing the brokerage.

An assumed but invalid exception is the case of a contract entered into by a broker who makes it known to the other party that he/she was in fact acting on behalf of an undisclosed principal. The principal can step in and enforce the contract since, according to the law of agency, he/she was really a party to the contract and the broker (or agent) was a mere extension of the principal.

Breach

Failure to fulfill an obligation under a contract. Breach, of a contract by one of the parties, results in the imposition of a new obligation in place of the broken one by conferring a right of legal action on the party injured by the breach. A breach may discharge the injured party from further obligations to perform his/her side of the bargain. Breach may occur through an express refusal to perform the contract, making it impossible to perform through one's own act, or through the failure to perform.

If a breach goes to the root of a contract, the injured party has the option to either accept the breach and treat himself/herself as relieved or discharged from performance, or to treat the contract as subsisting and, if available, seek other remedies such as specific performance. If the breach does not go to the root of the contract, it will give rise only to a right of the other party to sue for damages, not to an option to discharge the contract.

If there are several promises, only some of which are broken, or if there is only a partial failure to perform or complete the contract, a question may arise as to whether the other party can put an end to the contract or sue for damages. The answer will depend on the expressed or implied intention of the parties, and whether the breach was substantial enough to go to the root of the contract.

> **Example   Contract–Breach**
>
> Despite warnings from his real estate brokerage and lawyer, Buyer Jones insisted that the salesperson present an unconditional offer on a large home owned by Smith. Jones was confident that his present home would sell before the July closing of the new residence. By July, Jones was unable to sell his home and was declined interim financing to close the purchase. Smith sued for breach of contract and received damages to compensate for losses incurred in placing the property back on the market to secure another buyer.

Remedies

Five remedies are available in relation to a breach of contract involving real property.

Rescission

Set aside the contract, e.g., buyer requests the court to set aside a contract because the builder has encountered financial difficulties, has only begun renovation work, and is apparently unable to complete the job.

Damages

Compensation for losses incurred. The most common remedy is monetary damages awarded by a court to recompense an injured party for a loss suffered by reason of a breach. Every breach gives rise to a right to this remedy and the measure of damages recoverable is the amount that may fairly and reasonably be considered either:

- Arising naturally, (i.e., according to the usual course of events occurring from such breach of contract itself); or
- As may reasonably be supposed to have been in the contemplation of the parties at the time the contract was made.

Damages are given as financial compensation and not as a punishment for the breach or for the motive or manner of the breach, and so the plaintiff in a damage action must prove the actual amount of the damages. The plaintiff also has a duty to mitigate those damages by taking any reasonable steps available following the breach in order to reduce the extent of the loss.

C

> **Example   Contract–Remedies–Damages**
>
> Seller Smith sells his property unconditionally and Buyer Jones refuses to close due to insufficient funds. Smith places the property back on the market to find a new buyer. The damages normally sought would include the cost of re-marketing and disposing of the property, incidental costs incurred by the seller (e.g., cost of borrowing funds if a subsequent purchase was affected), any loss incurred if the property sold at a lesser price than originally agreed to with Jones, and a sum of money for inconvenience and related matters.

Quantum Meruit

A determination by the courts of a reasonable sum of money for work or services performed. If a contract has been discharged by breach after the injured party has done part but not all of what was promised under the contract, that person is entitled to the reasonable value (quantum meruit) of what was done from the party who committed the breach.

> **Example   Contract–Remedies–Quantum Meruit**
>
> ABC Realty Inc. enters into an exclusive two-year agreement to manage a building with a contract where compensation is received semi-annually for units rented during the preceding six-month period. Owner Smith breaches the contract eight months into the contract period and refuses to pay for ten units rented during the first six-month period. ABC Realty Inc. is entitled to compensation for the work performed.

Specific Performance

Takes the form of a decree or order of the court that the party in breach must do the specific thing that was promised. This is a discretionary remedy and not an absolute right. It will be awarded only where damages are not an adequate remedy, the contract is fair and just, and the injured party acts promptly and fairly in claiming a right to specific performance.

> **Example   Contract–Remedies–Specific Performance**
>
> Buyer Jones has a binding contract to purchase adjacent lands to his property for the purpose of expanding his business enterprise. The acquisition of this property is vital to meet local zoning regulations and environmental requirements. Prior to closing, Jones has already started expansion/renovation work in anticipation of the closing. The owner of the land refuses to close and lacks any substantive reason for doing so. Jones sues for specific performance.

An agreement to sell land is an example of the sort of contract that may be specifically enforceable, given the character of the particular land, or its importance to the buyer. It may be that damages would be insufficient compensation.

Injunction

Where the broken promise was to refrain from doing something, the court may award an injunction to restrain the offending party from doing that act. More simply put, an injunction is a court order stopping a party from continuing a breach.

The court will not compel the performance of a contract for personal service or employment, but may award an injunction to prevent the offending party from serving or performing elsewhere. The granting of an injunction, also a discretionary remedy, will be subject to the same conditions as in the case of specific performance.

A common case involves the breach of a covenant not to use the premises in a particular manner. A case might involve the tenant in a shopping plaza who agrees under the lease not to offer a specific service within the plaza and then proceeds to breach the agreement by offering that service.

Another instance might involve a tenant in a large industrial building who has specifically agreed not to store, process, or otherwise handle certain hazardous waste products on the premises and then breaches that agreement following occupancy.

In discussing remedies for breach of contract, the issues of costs and interest frequently arise. The successful litigant may be awarded interest on the amounts given. That interest may be calculated from the date of the breach and can vary depending on the prime rate. The court can also award costs that normally involve all disbursements paid to court officials and others involved in the litigation, and a proportion of the costs that are payable to the litigant's own lawyer. The award will vary with the amount of the claim and the particular court jurisdiction. In rare situations, the judge can order full compensation of all costs.

Termination/Discharge

There are five common methods to terminate a contract involving real property.

By Mutual Agreement   A contract may be discharged by mutual agreement of the parties that it shall no longer bind them, or that it shall be replaced by another contract in altered terms, which are substituted for discharge within itself.

By Performance   A contract may be discharged by performance or tender of performance of the contract, in which case the obligations of the performing party are fulfilled and the rights of the other party are satisfied.

By Impossibility of Performance   A contract may be discharged because of the impossibility of performance, or frustration, whereby supervening and unanticipated circumstances arising after the making of the contract are held to absolve the parties from their obligations.

By Operation of Law   A contract may be discharged by operation of law, e.g., discharge from bankruptcy, alteration by one party without consent of the other.

By Breach   Breach or the breaking of the contract by one of the parties, results in the imposition of a new obligation by conferring a right of legal action on the party injured by the breach.

Reference   See also Impossibility Of Performance, Mutual Agreement, and Operation Of Law.

CONTRACT/AGREEMENT/OFFER
(SEE AGREEMENT/CONTRACT/OFFER)

CONTRACTOR

An individual or firm used in performing work on construction projects. Different classes of contractors are found in the marketplace. Most often, persons referred to as contractors are in fact sub-contractors working on a project under a general contractor. The sub-contractor performs a particular task under the direction and co-ordination of the general contractor who, in turn, takes responsibility for managing the project according to the construction documents. The general contractor is normally selected through bidding procedures and is totally responsible for the satisfactory completion of the project.

CONTRACTOR'S AFFIDAVIT

A written statement, by a contractor, made under oath before a notary public, stating facts regarding the contract, sub-contracts, material suppliers, and labour, and setting forth amounts paid/unpaid and balance of payments due.

CONTRIBUTION, PRINCIPLE OF
(SEE PRINCIPLES (APPRAISAL))

CONVECTION SYSTEM
(SEE ALSO BOILERS (HOT WATER SYSTEMS))

A system in which heat is transferred through circulatory motion of a liquid or gas that occurs when the temperature varies due to the difference in density and action of gravity.

CONVECTOR

A heating unit in which air, warmed by contact with a heating device in a casing, is circulated by convection. A convector also refers to the liquid or gas that is transferring heat by convection.

A hot water convector, constructed from cast iron or tubing with aluminum fins, is an alternative to a radiator. Convectors normally take up less space than radiators in terms of height but must be longer in length to produce the same heat. Convectors tend to heat up and cool down faster than radiators, resulting in uneven heating.

CONVENTIONAL MORTGAGE

A first mortgage granted by an institutional lender such as a bank, loan, or trust company in which the amount does not exceed 75% of the appraised lending value of the property. This type of mortgage is not normally insured or guaranteed by any government or private agency, e.g., Canada Mortgage and Housing Corporation (CMHC) or GE Capital Mortgage Insurance Canada.

Example   *Conventional Mortgage*

Buyer Jones has just purchased a home for $200,000 and has a $60,000 downpayment. In arranging a mortgage (assuming that the property appraises for $200,000), the lender may approve a conventional mortgage as the loan to value ratio is as follows:

$140,000 ÷ $200,000 = 70%

If Jones' downpayment had been $40,000 then the loan to value ratio would have been:

$160,000 ÷ $200,000 = 80%

In the second instance, the loan (if approved by the lender), would have to be insured as it exceeds the maximum limit of 75% for conventional loans.

CONVERSION FACTOR
(SEE ALSO RENTABLE/USEABLE (R/U) FACTOR)

A factor used in the measurement of commercial office space to convert useable area to rentable area.

CONVEYANCE

The transfer of an interest in property from one party to another; the means or medium by which legal title to property is transferred. A conveyance is recorded by a transfer form that is registered in the registry or land titles office. Procedures and forms will vary by provincial jurisdiction.

Provincial   See applicable reference materials.

CO-OPERATIVE

As a general description, the underlying premise of a co-operative is open, voluntary membership where members accept responsibilities of membership in return for services provided by the co-operative.

Co-operatives are free to define their own membership conditions as well as member rights and responsibilities provided that they comply with provincial legislation (if applicable). Co-operatives include a wide variety of uses. Worker co-ops are businesses owned and operated by the employees as members. Co-ops are also frequently formed to provide business and consumer services to members. Childcare co-operatives provide a vehicle for parents as members to have some degree of control in the administration of the child care facility.

Application   For real estate purposes, the co-operative can provide affordable housing while permitting resident members the opportunity to have a say in the upkeep and management of their residence. As a general description, a housing co-operative is a corporation that owns real estate, usually a multi-family dwelling, including the building and land on which it is built. Shareholders do not own their units but have the right to live in them. The main purpose and general activities of such a co-operative housing corporation are to provide living accommodation to its shareholders along with a legal mechanism for joint ownership.

Under a co-operative, a corporation is formed to own the real property. The shareholders of the company each own a share of the company and do not own their units, but are given occupancy rights by the corporation under tenancy agreements. Corporate law, the shareholders' agreement, provincial tenancy legislation, and the occupancy arrangements determine the rights of the parties. Co-operatives are subject to provincial legislation.

Provincial   See applicable reference materials.

COPPER EAVESTROUGH

A high quality drainage system for roofs having a life span of 50 to 100 years and, while expensive, is considered the best type of eavestrough.

CORE
(SEE BUILDING CORE)

CORING

A mechanical system of removing a cylindrical section of concrete from the existing floor to gain access to the duct system. Coring is also used to determine earth strata by analysis of core samples.

CORPORATE CULTURE

A concept flowing from a popular modern leadership philosophy in which a company is viewed as a human institution, a place where individuals can freely operate, express opinions, and share values and beliefs. A dynamic leader ensures that a clear and definitive culture exists within that environment.

A strong culture is manifested through a shared belief in the purpose and values of the company. It is embedded in the mission statement, clarified in the objectives, and reinforced through core values underlying all decisions. **Figure C.16** illustrates the corporate values, mission statement, and specific objectives for ABC Realty Inc.

ABC REALTY INC.

Corporate Values

Quality Service
Specialized Marketing Service
Professional Advice & Assistance
Knowledgeable Salespeople
Well Known, Established Company
Modern & Innovative

Mission Statement

ABC Realty Inc. is committed to top quality service throughout the community by specializing in residential income properties. Procedures used will be professional, innovative, and ensure that the brokerage maintains a leadership position in the marketplace.

Specific Objectives

- To maintain 20% share of the local residential market.
- To provide detailed market analysis on all listings and update on a regular basis.
- To complete and sign a letter of guarantee of services for all clients agreeing to market their properties through the brokerage.
- To hire three new salespeople from industries affiliated with the residential rental market.
- To promote the image of the brokerage as a well established, locally owned organization.

Figure C.16   Corporate Culture

CORPORATE STRATEGY

Strategy and a well-designed business plan are key to a successful brokerage. The effective leader can then direct and control growth while maximizing market opportunities. Three primary growth options should be considered in any overall strategy: *service development, market development,* and *diversification.* In each, options exist for assessing both existing and new market areas, therefore the brokerage has six alternative strategies to consider.

Growth within this context is not specifically limited to an increase in sales force, but refers to a host of alternatives by which a brokerage can improve image, accomplish market penetration, diversify cash flow, maximize specialities, or consolidate competitive position, to mention a few. **Figure C.17** sets out growth options.

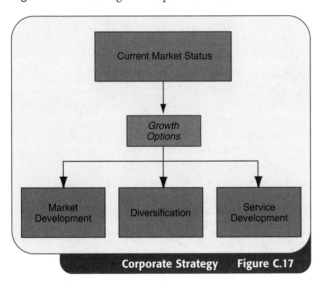

Corporate Strategy **Figure C.17**

CORPORATION

A form of business organization created by statute law that is legally considered as a separate entity.

Application   The corporation, unlike the sole proprietor and partnership, provides a distinction between the business operation and its owner(s). As a legal entity, the corporation is capable of merging, creating subsidiary companies, and generally operates distinct and separate from its owners.

Signing On Behalf of the Corporation

In terms of signing authority, under both provincial and federal legislation, the company seal is not necessary on documents except those that, if made between persons, would require a seal. The seal is not essential but the problem of authority of the person signing on behalf of the company would still exist.

No company will be liable as the principal on a contract unless it expressly, or by necessary implication, authorized the contract. Obtaining the corporate seal should be difficult for an unauthorized person, and still more difficult for that person to obtain a certified copy of the resolution of the company authorizing the transaction. Some solicitors insist on a corporate seal and even a certified copy of the resolution, knowing that thereafter, it would be more difficult for the signing officer's authority to be disputed. Prudent practice suggests that any document be signed on behalf of a company under its corporate seal, with the authority of the person signing indicated by noting the position held within the company, e.g., ABC Development Limited per John Jones, President. If a corporate seal is not used, the following words should be added:

I have the authority to bind the corporation.

Corporations operating as real estate brokerages fall under applicable real estate legislation, e.g., procedures for the selection of names, registration procedures, books of record, and share requirements.

Example   *Corporation*

John Doe is registered as a sole proprietor under the applicable provincial real estate act as John B. Doe, Real Estate Broker. As broker and sole proprietor, John owns all assets and is responsible for all debts, is entitled to the profits, and is accountable for any losses.

In the case of a corporation, as John Doe Real Estate Limited, John Doe (the president) is generally *not* responsible for the debts of the corporation unless he has signed documents to the contrary, e.g., a personal covenant with a lending institution. John Doe can incur debts without facing the same exposure as in a sole proprietorship.

Continuity of the brokerage is assured if John dies, provided that a licensed/registered broker wishes to continue the brokerage business. Tax advantages may exist for both the corporation and John personally. John will incur incorporation fees, name search fees, and the expense of filing the corporate documents. Further professional fees for the ongoing maintenance of legal and financial records for the corporation will be an added expense.

Generally, John Doe Real Estate Limited is a more structured operation than John B. Doe, Real Estate Broker, consequently more paperwork results.

Provincial   See applicable reference materials.

CORRUGATED PLASTIC TILE

A single-ply, translucent roof surface generally used over patios and light structures. Such roofing is considered low quality, subject to fading/discolouring, and leakage at the joints. Corrugated plastic tile is most commonly associated with accessory buildings and structures.

> **Example**   *Corrugated Plastic Tile*
>
> Buyer Jones, lacking sufficient funds to install a fully winterized addition to the lakeside portion of the cottage, elects to build a wooden deck with an overhanging roof attached to the main roof. To minimize weight on the structure, Jones uses a wooden grid arrangement for the roofed area and installs corrugated plastic tile. This material provides additional light (opposed to a solid roof), protection from rain, and is relatively inexpensive until a more substantial addition can be built.

COST APPROACH

An approach used in the appraisal of real property based on the concept of objective value. Objective value affirms that the *cost to create* is the main criterion in estimating value and guided by the principle of substitution, which maintains that a prudent buyer will pay no more for a property than the cost of producing or creating an equally desirable property, providing no delay occurs in making the substitution. In other words, at any point in time, building values cannot rise above their reproduction cost.

Application   Basic steps in applying the cost approach are itemized in four stages.

- Estimate the value of the site.
- Estimate the reproduction cost as if new on the effective date of the appraisal. Replacement cost may be used depending on the circumstances.
- Estimate the accrued depreciation suffered by the improvements from all causes.
- Subtract the accrued depreciation from the reproduction cost new (or replacement cost, if applicable), of the improvements.
- Add the value of the site to arrive at an estimate of the market value of the property.

The cost approach is particularly applicable when the property involves relatively new improvements that represent the highest and best use of the land, or when the site possesses unique or specialized improvements, for which there are no comparable properties on the market. **Figure C.18** illustrates the cost approach leading to an estimated value of an industrial site and associated improvements.

COST ESTIMATING

A process (in the construction industry), involving an estimate based on a quantity survey that includes the cost of all materials, labour, and other essentials. In appraising, it is a process of estimating the reproduction or replace-ment cost of an improvement by one of several methods, including: comparative square metre method, cost services method, quantity survey method, and unit-in-place method.

Cost estimates from a real estate perspective typically involve hard (direct) costs and soft (indirect) costs. For example, in a residential development, the estimate would include curbs, sidewalks, paved roads, street lighting, and water/sewer services (hard costs), and professional fees such as surveying, engineering, and legal (soft costs).

COST SERVICES METHOD

A method of estimating reproduction cost under the cost approach in an appraisal, in which dollar costs are provided by cost service manuals. Following, is an abbreviated list of companies that provide costing manuals.

Marshall & Swift Valuation Service
Marshall & Swift Publication Company
Los Angeles, California

Boeckh Valuation and Cost Systems
General Appraisal Corporation
Toronto, Ontario

Yardsticks for Costing
Southam Business Publications Ltd.
Toronto, Ontario

Dodge Building Cost Calculator & Cost Guide
McGraw-Hill Information Systems Company
New York, New York

The Walke Building Estimator's Reference Book
Frank R. Walke company
Chicago, Illinois

Lansdowne's Construct Cost Handbook
David K. Lansdowne and Partners Limited
London, Ontario

Application   Costing manuals provide basic unit costs for a range of building structures of differing qualities. Also included are costs of physical considerations, e.g., fireplace, finished basement, and cost differences based on the size and the shape of building. This information is provided in the form of photographs, charts, and tables with supplements provided on a periodic basis. These supplements furnish the necessary time and geographic location adjustments, by way of multipliers, which are then applied to the basic costing manual.

The appraiser's job is to select a structure within the chosen manual that is most similar to the subject property. Differences between the subject and the manual's benchmark structure must be adjusted based on amounts obtained from the manual. The costing of a building by the cost services method may appear to be replacement cost rather than reproduction cost because some of the subject property's obsolete features can be replaced in the costing

Scenario

An industrial site is being valued. Improvements include a small main building and attached storage area. Three comparable sites have been found. Prices for properties have been increasing at an even rate of 0.4% per month. For depreciation purposes, both structures have an effective age of ten years and a remaining economic life of 30 years. The square footage for each site is: Sale 1–8,312 square feet; Sale 2–7,770 square feet; and Sale 3–7,976 square feet. The subject site has 8,000 square feet.

Site Valuation	Sale 1	Sale 2	Sale 3	
Sale Date	6 months ago	2 months ago	1 month ago	
Sale Price	103,900	101,750	103,275	
Time Adjustment	2.4%	0.8%	0.4%	
Time Adjustment Calculation	0.024 x 103,900	.008 x 101,750	.004 x 103,275	
Adjusted Sale Price	106,394	102,564	103,688	
Adjusted Sale Price psf	12.80	13.20	13.00	
			Site Valuation	**$104,000**

(based on comparables and the appraiser's judgement of $13.00 psf)

Reproduction Cost New Estimation	Main Building	Storage		
Measurement	30 x 66	18 x 32		
Total Square Footage	1,980	576		
Reproduction Cost	34.50	21.00		
Reproduction Cost New	68,310	12,096		
			Total Reproduction Cost New	**$80,406**

Accrued Depreciation Estimation	Main Building	Storage		
Effective Age ÷ Economic Life	10 ÷ 40	10 ÷ 40		
Reproduction Cost New	68,310	12,096		
Depreciation	17,078	3,024		
			Total Accrued Depreciation	**$20,102**

Depreciated Cost of Improvements		
Total Reproduction Cost New	$80,406
Accrued Depreciation	−20,102
Depreciated Cost of Improvements	**$60,304**

Indication of Value		
Site Value	$104,000
Depreciated Cost of Improvements	+60,304
Indication of Value	**$164,304**
(rounded to $164,300)	

Cost Approach   Figure C.18

approach by their modern counterparts. For example, the current base cost per square foot shown in the manual for a standard building will likely include factory-made kitchen cupboards, as opposed to carpenter-made cupboards in the subject building. Any loss in value resulting from a lack of modernization in the subject building will be considered by the appraiser and accounted for as an item of curable functional obsolescence in the depreciation schedule.

The cost services method can be an effective method of estimating building costs provided that the appraiser selects the most comparable building and appropriate adjustments are made. No two buildings are identical therefore, adjustments are likely required and the accuracy of the cost services method depends on the appraiser's choices. **Figure C.19** illustrates an estimate using cost services information from the Marshall & Swift Valuation Service.

COTTAGE
(SEE RURAL, RECREATIONAL, AND AGRICULTURAL SALES)

COUNTER OFFER

The rejection of an offer by a buyer or seller (offeree) with a simultaneous offer made back to the offeror. In the typical offer presentation process involving a listed property, sellers are often willing to counter offer or sign back the original offer, rather than rejecting it outright. In this instance, the counter offer is nothing more than an offer to sell the property, open for acceptance for a specified period of time, and offered to a particular buyer. A binding agreement/contract exists if the counter offer is accepted

COST SERVICES METHOD

Purpose	To estimate the reproduction cost new of the subject structure as at Oct. 21st, 20xx (using Marshall Valuation Service).
Subject Property	One storey, detached residence of average quality and rectangular shape.
Area	Ground floor: 77.66 square metres Perimeter: 35.62 metres (building).
Construction	Average quality with solid brick exterior walls.
Extras	Finished basement with forced air heating; fireplace; garage containing 18.56 square metres.
Deductions	Lacks a two-piece washroom in basement.
Location	Toronto, Ontario

Cost Estimate Calculation

(Class—C; Quality—Average; Shape—Rectangular)

CALCULATION	COST ESTIMATE	
1. Ground Floor Living Area	77.66 m^2 x $462.85 per m^2	35,944.93
ADJUSTED BASE COST (Area x Area-Shape Multiplier)	$35,944.93 x 1.063	38,209.46
2. Add: Basement area (Unfinished/Unheated)	54.06 m^2 x $107.10 per m^2	+ $5,789.83
3. Add: Basement area (Finished/Unheated)	23.60 m^2 x $192.68 per m^2	+ $4,547.25
4. Add: Basement forced air heating (Moderate Climate)	77.66 m^2 x $20.45 per m^2	+ $1,588.15
5. Add: Fireplace (One storey average)		+ $1,775.00
6 Deduct: Lack of ½ Bathroom in finished basement area	Two fixtures at $425.00 each	− $850.00
7. Add: Garage (Class D; Type—Low Cost)	18.56 m^2 x $159.85 per m^2	+ $2,966.82
TOTAL REPRODUCTION COST NEW OF IMPROVEMENT		= $54,026.51

Local Multiplier for Toronto is 1.43
Cost Multiplier (Time) as at October, 20xx is 0.9865

REPRODUCTION COST NEW	**$54,026.51 x 1.43 x 0.9865**	**$76,214.93**

In conclusion, based on the above, the current reproduction cost new of the subject property, including finished basement and garage, as at date of appraisal is $76,214.93 (rounded to $76,215.00).

Figure C.19   Cost Services Method

by the buyers within the time limit provided and communication of this acceptance takes place.

Risks

The person making the counter offer must understand certain legalities in the process. For example, assume that a seller has rejected an offer by the buyer and prepared a counter offer. Once the counter offer is conveyed, the original offer as it was presented has been rejected and, therefore, ceases to exist. A degree of risk is inherent when preparing a counter offer since it releases the buyers from any obligation with respect to the original offer—they may have changed their minds or have seen another property they wish to purchase.

The seller should also be counselled regarding the irrevocable date on the counter offer since it is an offer to sell and can be accepted by the buyers, the property is effectively removed from the market for the period that the counter offer is open for acceptance. If another offer is presented during that interval, the seller is unable to accept it unconditionally until the fate of the counter offer is determined. Accepting the second offer could result in agreeing to sell the property to two buyers simultaneously. This situation can be prevented by advising the seller to accept a second offer on the condition that the counter offer is rejected or, is terminated by way of a mutual release.

Advantages

Several distinct sales advantages are inherent in the counter offer when compared with an outright rejection. Even if the counter offer is at full price, the buyers will have an indication of the terms upon which the sellers will agree to sell the property. *Keep in mind that a listing does not force the seller to sell under any circumstances.* If the counter offer is for a reduced price, or some other concessions have been granted to find common ground between the sellers and buyers, then such action does indicate a desire to negotiate seriously on the part of the sellers and keeps the transaction progressing.

Methods

Two methods of counter offering are found in the marketplace. However, caution is advised as the following represents a general description only. Procedures and policies regarding counter offers and the use of one or both methods can vary between provincial jurisdictions.

Amended Offer

A common method of preparing a counter offer is simply to make alterations to the original offer. This approach has proven expedient as the person making the offer is already familiar with the terms of the document, and the salesperson is free to deal strictly with amendments or changes to those terms. In addition, acceptance of the counter offer requires only a matching of initials with the changes and a fresh signing procedure is not required. This method should be used if changes are minor. If changes are numerous and/or extensive, a *counter offer form* should be used.

To prepare the counter offer, the sales representative should effect all the necessary changes on every copy of the offer, and then have the appropriate party(ies) initial all changes. Assume that the seller is making the counter offer, ensure that every change is initialled by the seller. Essentially, he/she must understand exactly what changes are being made in the counter offer to which each set of initials applies. Once all of the changes have been made and initialled, the seller would also sign and date his/her signature, indicating agreement with the terms of the counter offer. If the buyer is willing to accept the terms of the counter offer, he/she simply matches initials with those of the sellers' on each copy of the agreement/contract and completes any additional documentation as required in the appropriate provincial jurisdiction.

Counter Offer Form

The counter offer form is completed with a list of amendments to the buyer's original offer. Enough copies of the counter offer form are prepared to match the copies of the buyer's original offer. Once the counter offer forms are prepared, the seller (assuming a seller counter offer), is requested to sign them and a copy of the form is attached to each copy of the buyer's offer. If the buyer also signs acceptance of the counter offer and this is communicated back to the seller, then a bona fide agreement/contract exists.

The sellers' signatures will never appear on the original offer. Although this procedure is clean and professional,

negotiations can be complicated by a lack of familiarity with a new document and a different signing procedure.

As a general guideline, a counter of the counter offer is not normally made if an amended offer or a counter offer is being used. Instead, a new offer is prepared; but, provincial practices may differ on this point.

Provincial See applicable reference materials.

COVENANT

An agreement between two or more parties that creates a legal obligation whereby either of the parties pledges himself/herself to the other that something is or will be done. Covenants may be positive such as stipulating the performance of some act, or negative as in forbidding the commission of some act.

Mortgage documents contain covenants affecting both the mortgagee and mortgagor. For example, a mortgage contains a mortgagor personal covenant and covenants to pay taxes and maintain the property.

The following is a typical wording concerning covenants of the mortgagor with regard to payments:

That the mortgagor, his heirs, executors, administrators and successors or some or one of them shall pay or cause to be paid to the mortgagee, its successors or assigns without deduction or abatement the principal money secured by the mortgage with interest as set out in the mortgage at the times and in the manner therein limited for payment thereof, and shall do, observe, perform, fulfill and keep all the provisions, covenants, agreements and stipulations particularly set forth in the mortgage and without limitation, shall pay any taxes, rates, levies, charges or assessments upon the mortgaged premises or in respect thereof, no matter by whom or by what authority imposed, which the mortgagee has paid or have been rendered liable to pay and shall also pay all other sums as the mortgagee may be entitled to under this mortgage.

COVENANT, IMPLIED

A covenant that is not expressly set out in writing or stated, but still creates a positive or negative obligation.

Mortgages registered in a land registry or land titles office can involve implied covenants on the part of the mortgagor. In Ontario, for example, if a mortgage does not reference a set of standard charge terms within the document, three statutory implied covenants attach themselves. The first implied covenant is often referred to as the *usual covenants*, e.g., make mortgage payments, pay

C

taxes, insure building, and grant of quiet possession when not in default. The second implied covenant provides that the mortgagor covenants that the land held in fee simple is owned with good title. The third covenant relates to leasehold property wherein the mortgagor covenants that the lease is valid and up-to-date, and further that reimbursement will be made by the mortgagor for non-payment or non-performance of other covenants under the lease.

In Manitoba, the *Real Property Act* states that unless otherwise expressed, the transferee of a parcel of land covenants to pay the principal money and interest owing under a mortgage registered thereon and will be bound by every other covenant, term, or condition in the mortgage. In other words, when a buyer buys a property and has it transferred to his/her name, the covenants and promises contained in any previously registered mortgage being assumed will be deemed to have been accepted by the buyer as if he/she had executed the actual mortgage document itself.

Implied covenants can also apply to deeds. As with mortgages, the covenants are dictated by statute and not included with the registered document.

Provincial   See applicable reference materials.

COVERAGE RATIO

The ratio of the coverage of a building in relation to its land size.

Application   Coverage ratios and related restrictions on the total square footage of a building footprint on a site are usually contained within zoning by-laws by type of properties. Coverage ratios are intended to complement front, rear, and side yard requirements, height limitations, and floor space ratios, to ensure that sufficient open space is maintained around the building for parking, landscaping, buffer zones, and generally to achieve a more desirable setting for the building.

Example   *Coverage Ratio*

A building with 25,000 square feet footprint being placed on land amounting to 50,000 square feet is said to have a coverage ratio of .50 or 50%.

CRANE

A device used for lifting and moving heavy items.

Application   Cranes are generally classified in one of three categories for industrial purposes.

Bridge Crane   Operates on a system of horizontal rails and requires column-free areas within the structure. Bridge cranes (often several operating in sequential order), can work on a series of related tasks by moving the product along the work floor.

Gantry Crane   Best described as a portable bridge crane operating on wheels, can be moved about the work floor area or in outside yard areas. The word *gantry* refers to the framework making up the crane.

Jib Crane   Has an arm attached at an angle to a rotating mast that permits 360° swivelling around that mast. In many instances, the jib crane is attached to a structural column in the building that restricts the swivel to a half-circle.

CRCD
(SEE CANADIAN REHABILITATION COUNCIL FOR THE DISABLED)

CREDIT
(SEE ALSO DEBITS AND CREDITS)

A term commonly referenced in regard to the ability or right to buy or borrow in return for a promise to pay later. For accounting purposes, credit refers to an entry on the right-hand side of an account. A credit records increases in *liabilities, shareholder's (owner's) equity, revenues*, and *gains*, and decreases in *assets* and *expenses*.

CREDIT BUREAU

A central clearing house, also referred to as a *credit investigating agency*, for all types of credit related information. Essentially, companies involved in lending money provide the bureau with customer information and, in return, have access to the files established for each consumer. Credit reports are provided on request. The credit bureau receives information not only from lenders (credit grantors), but also from public record sources (judgments, bankruptcies). Most companies using credit cards within Canada, such as financial institutions, oil companies, and department stores, use the service. Selected banks input information and the major Canadian-based automobile financing companies are also part of the system.

Application   The credit bureau provides information that is usually updated on a 60-day basis. This varies depending on how information is transmitted between individual lenders and the bureau. Often, information is sent electronically which has improved both the accuracy and timeliness. Of course, the consumer has the ability not only to verify information being held on file but also to dispute or alter incorrect data.

Credit bureaus only compile information relating to credit. No data is collected relating to personal habits, affiliations, political, or social connections. Further, not all credit information about an individual will be found in the records. The completeness of data is limited by the number of lenders that participate as members with the bureau in any particular locale. The report on an individual may be limited but still a useful indicator of the positive and negative aspects of a personal credit history.

Credit bureaus in Canada produce reports using a common or standardized language to ensure that reporting is consistent and that all credit grantors use the same terms to describe specific types of pay habits. The common language is broken into three parts:

Kind of Business   In most instances, the first letter of the business is shown on the report, e.g., automotive is A, banks are B, clothing is C, etc. The business classification is combined with the member number. The two in concert make up the trade source information, e.g., A-1111 refers to Automotive member number 1111.

Usual Manner of Payment   Payment history is detailed on a sliding scale of 0–9, where 0 indicates too new to rate; 1 pays within 30 days of billing/pays account as agreed; and 9 indicates bad debt, placed for collection.

Terms of Sale   Reference to the type of account: **O** is an open account that is normally expected to be paid in full within 30 to 90 days with no interest or service charge; **R** is a revolving account with regular monthly payments for a balance due; and **I** refers to an installment account with a fixed number of payments that are specifically itemized.

Provincial   See applicable reference materials.

CREDIT REPORT

A report on the credit position of a borrower that is in conformity with applicable provincial legislation relating to the gathering and reporting of credit information.

Provincial   See applicable reference materials.

CREDITOR

A person to whom a debt is owed by another person termed the debtor.

> **Example   Creditor**
>
> Buyer Jones, when acquiring a new home, decides to purchase various items of furniture under a *no interest* plan for one year. The furniture company (or finance company underwriting the no interest plan, if applicable), is the creditor and Jones is the debtor.

CROWN LANDS
(SEE ALSO NATIVE LANDS)

Property vested in the Crown and administered under provincial legislation and procedures. For example, in Ontario, all crown land falls under public land as defined in the *Public Lands Act*. Indian lands are an exception as they originate with the federal government and the Crown in Right of Canada. Accordingly, all registration documents are filed federally.

Application   Practitioners frequently encounter crown lands in two ways: title matters associated with the crown patent and disposition of crown lands.

Crown Patent

A crown patent is an original title deeded by the government and generally accepted as the root of all title. Most property in Canada commences the legal chain of title from the Crown Patent. The passing of title from the Crown is typically accompanied by certain reservations, e.g., save and except for mineral rights and/or trees. Further, a portion of land may be reserved for the purpose of future road construction. The extent of such reservations are set out in the original patents for such lands and can vary based on when the patent was issued. Practitioners, particularly those dealing with rural and recreational properties, should be aware of such limitations as property value can be directly impacted. Salespeople are not expected to decipher all the intricacies of crown patents and should seek legal advice.

Disposition of Crown Land

The method by which Crown lands are patented and sold will vary by province pursuant to applicable legislation, procedures of the administrative body handling these lands, and requirements of the land registration system. Patents are typically processed following research involving the appropriate government agency and subsequent issues of a patent that is registered in the appropriate land registry office. Practitioners most commonly encounter disposition of crown lands relating to cottage lots in remote locations.

CURABLE DEPRECIATION

One component in estimating depreciation by means of the observed condition (breakdown) method. This type of deterioration refers to those items that are economically feasible to cure and therefore customarily repaired or replaced by a prudent property owner.

The term *curable* is used because it would be economically sound for an owner to correct the physical situation based on the value of these repairs in light of depreciation incurred by the current state of the property. Curable depreciation can arise either through physical deterioration or functional obsolescence.

Example   Curable Depreciation

The cost to repaint the property interior is $1,900 and the actual depreciation in value due to the current state of painting is $2,500. The curing of this deterioration makes economic sense. This situation should be contrasted with incurable depreciation that applies to items that are not economically sound to cure at the time, since the cost of correcting the condition is greater than the anticipated increase in value.

CURRENT (ELECTRICAL)

Current, measured in amps, is the flow of electricity that results when a voltage is applied across a given resistance.

Application   Voltage is the potential energy of the electrical system. A large electrical voltage means that a significant potential electric force is available. Most houses are equipped with a 240-volt system that provides 240 or 120 volts.

The resistance of any given material of the movement of electricity through it, is measured in ohms. When there is no electrical flow, the resistance is considered to be infinitely large and is referred to as an *open circuit*. When effectively no resistance exists, the current load is very large and is referred to as a *short circuit*. This is usually unsafe and will blow a fuse.

The current flowing through the electrical system is what electrocutes individuals. Generally, a current of less than one amp is capable of killing someone. A 60-watt light bulb normally draws about 0.5 amps, however, the amount of current depends on resistance. Water in close proximity to a live electrical wire is extremely dangerous and must be avoided.

Example   Current (Electrical)

When an appliance is turned on, the flow of electricity generates heat—the more amps flowing through a circuit, the hotter the wire becomes. Since the voltage is fixed at roughly 120 volts, the amount of current that flows will be the result of the resistance in the circuit. If an appliance malfunctions or too many appliances are plugged in, the amount of electric current flowing through the wire will be more than can be safely handled and will begin to overheat. The purpose of a fuse or circuit breaker is to shut off the electricity at the point when overheating may occur.

CURRENT RATIO
(SEE ALSO ACCRUAL ACCOUNTING)

A ratio of current assets in relation to current liabilities that determines whether a business can meet short-term obligations. This ratio is derived from information contained in the balance sheet. The formula is expressed as follows:

Current Ratio = Current Assets ÷ Current Liabilities

Example   Current Ratio

ABC Realty Inc. has current assets amounting to $450,000 and current liabilities of $350,000. The current ratio is:

Current Ratio = Current Assets ÷ Current Liabilities
= $450,000 ÷ $350,000 = 1.29

For each dollar of current liabilities, there is $1.29 in current assets. If all current assets were converted to cash, the sum of current debt could be retired with funds still available to the business. A business should maintain an average current ratio between 1.0 and 2.0. A very high current ratio is indicative of idle assets, while a low ratio, places the company in a financially precarious position when meeting current obligations.

Caution   The current ratio calculation must be interpreted with care. Due to the nature of real estate transactions, closings can be scheduled into the future. This information is not normally provided on a brokerage balance sheet, given the prevailing method of accruing income derived from real estate trades. In fact, commission receivables can be somewhat misleading.

Acid-Test Ratio (Quick Ratio)

This is a variation of the current ratio that indicates the firm's ability to meet short-term debt. The formula is:

Quick Ratio = Cash and Marketable Securities and Receivables ÷ Current Liabilities

This calculation produces a ratio that addresses only the most liquid assets of the company.

D

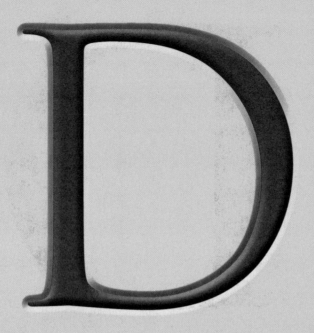

D

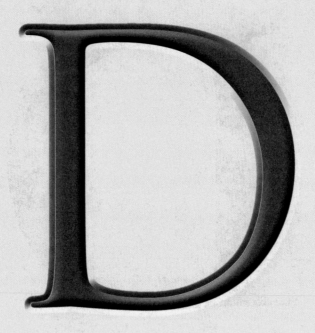

National Info Links

Deemed Disposition (Property)

For all matters concerning the *Income Tax Act*, contact:

> Canada Customs and Revenue Agency
> Web Site   www.ccra-adrc.gc.ca

See the local telephone directory for addresses and telephone numbers of Tax Services Offices and Tax Centres.

Demographics/Population

> Statistics Canada
>
> Telephone   (800) 263 1163
> Web Site   www.statcan.ca

For a directory of regional Statistics Canada reference centres visit www.statcan.ca/english/reference/refcentre.html.

Depreciation (CCA Allowances)

For all matters concerning the Income Tax Act, contact:

> Canada Customs and Revenue Agency
> Web Site   www.ccra-adrc.gc.ca

See the local telephone directory for addresses and telephone numbers of Tax Services Offices and Tax Centres.

Disability

> Easter Seals/March of Dimes National Council
> 90 Eglinton Avenue East
> Suite 511
> Toronto, ON M4P 2Y3
>
> Telephone   (416) 932 8382
> Web Site   www.esmodnc.org

Promotes national programs regarding physical disabilities. Recently renamed from the Canadian Rehabilitation Council for the Disabled (CRCD). The term CRCD may still be found provincially, e.g., MLS listings.

ABC Realty

DAMAGES
(SEE ALSO CONTRACT AND TORT)

Compensation or indemnity for loss owing to breach of contract, or a tort (civil wrong).

Example 1   *Damages–Leases*

If Landlord Smith breaches any covenants, Tenant Jones may sue for provable loss resulting from the breach. In rare circumstances, a breach by a landlord will give the tenant rights other than to damages.

If Tenant Jones vacates possession, the rent must still be paid until proper termination of the lease occurs. The tenant agreed to pay a rental amount and is liable for that amount. The landlord can sue for damages for any loss resulting from the tenant's failure to pay rent as agreed. That loss may include the unpaid rent, any deficiency in monies received from a new tenant, and the cost of re-renting, including legal fees and leasing agent commission.

Example 2   *Damages–Agency Agreement*

ABC Realty Inc. may be liable to Seller Smith for damages involving negligence or breach of duty (e.g., incompetence). Seller Smith would have a claim against the brokerage who committed the wrongful act that caused damage to the principal. Since a loss can involve a reduction in property value, carrying costs, legal fees and interest, the amount can be substantial.

Example 3   *Damages–Contract*

Seller Smith refuses to close a sale after a binding agreement was entered into with Buyer Jones. Assuming this situation proceeds to litigation, the court will probably assess the measure of damages as the amount that may fairly and reasonably be considered either arising naturally (according to the usual course of things) from the breach, or such as may be reasonably supposed to have been contemplated by the parties at the time they made the contract.

In other words, Jones may incur direct damages for expenses related to finding other accommodation. However, Jones may also have had unique plans for the property: e.g., partial use for a new business enterprise. His inability to establish the business, as a consequence of the breach, may factor into a final assessment of damages. As with all court cases, the awarding of damages or the extent of an award varies on the merits of the case.

DAMPER

A valve or plate operated mechanically or manually to regulate air flow to or from any prescribed point.

Application   Dampers are commonly found in wall and ceiling diffusers to regulate the air flow from duct work to rooms being heated or cooled. A damper consists of several metal veins that move from open to closed by using a simple mechanical device. In gravity furnaces, dampers were commonly installed to restrict the general flow of air within the duct system, thereby controlling the amount of heat to all or selected parts of the structure.

DAMP-PROOFING
(SEE ALSO BASEMENT)

Materials used in construction to make various components of structures resistant to dampness and moisture.

Application   Damp-proofing exterior walls in a residential property normally requires coating with a waterproof bituminous material and parging with a one-quarter inch layer of mortar, which ideally extends down to the footing. The foundation/footing joint is also covered to improve the seal and direct water into the drainage tile. Tar is applied from grade level to the footing for protection against moisture.

Experts may recommend exterior basement insulation. Rigid glass fibre insulation board designed for use below grade provides good insulation and helps keep the basement dry. Water, entering the insulation, flows down to the drainage tile.

Reference   See Figure C.14 under Concrete Blocks.

DEALING IN REAL ESTATE

A term commonly used in the real estate profession referring to the sale, purchase, lease, or other acquisition or disposition of real estate by persons licensed/registered as salespersons and brokers. Provincial regulatory bodies establish specific procedures to allow practitioners to acquire and dispose of real estate, most notably the requirement of full disclosure.

Provincial   See applicable reference materials.

DEALS WRITTEN/DEALS CLOSED
(SEE ALSO ACCRUAL ACCOUNTING)

In applying accrual accounting, two methods of recording income are used: date trade is written; and date trade closes. The latter is more popular but both are acceptable.

Debenture

A document evidencing a promise to pay by a corporation, sometimes including a mortgage over real property of the corporation as security for the performance of that promise.

Application A debenture may affect specific real property as well as chattels by way of a fixed and itemized mortgage on specified property and assets, or it may be more general and contain a floating mortgage on property and assets that are not subject to a fixed mortgage. A debenture with respect to a fixed mortgage on specific real property is usually registered against the land. A debenture can be registered as an instrument on its own, similar to a mortgage, or it can be registered by caveat (caution). Registration procedures will vary by provincial jurisdiction.

Debits and Credits

In accrual accounting, a double set of entries is required. For every *single* transaction, *two* accounting entries are made: a debit and a credit. In its simplest form, an account has only three elements:

- A title, consisting of the name of the particular asset, liability, shareholder's (owner's) equity, revenue, or expense;
- A left side, which is called the debit side; and
- A right side, which is called the credit side.

This form of account is called a T-account given its resemblance to the letter **T**, see **Figure D.1**. T-accounts are used to explain, in simple terms, the recording of entries in various accounts.

An amount recorded on the left or debit side of an account is called a *debit*, or a *debit entry*. An amount on the right or credit side is called a *credit*, or a *credit entry*. The act of recording a debit in an account involves debiting the account; the recording of a credit involves crediting the account. A debit to an account is also sometimes referred to as a charge to the account. An account is there-

fore debited or charged when an amount is entered on the left side of the account.

Often, people have erroneous notions about the meaning of the terms *debit* and *credit*. For example, the word *credit* may carry a favourable connotation and the word *debit* may be associated with debt. Such connotations have no validity in the accounting profession.

The dollar difference between total debits and total credits in an account is the balance. If the debits exceed the credits, the account has a debit balance; if the credits exceed the debits, the account has a credit balance.

Asset, Liability, and Equity Accounts

In an asset account such as cash, increases are recorded on the left or debit side of the account and decreases are recorded on the right or credit side. This custom reflects the fact that a common format for a balance sheet shows assets on the left side of the balance sheet. All asset accounts normally have debit balances; that is, increases are greater than decreases. It is hard to imagine an account for an asset such as land having a credit balance, as this would indicate that the business had disposed of more land than it had acquired and had reached the impossible position of having a negative amount of land.

Increases in liability and owners' equity accounts are recorded by credit entries with decreases recorded by debits. The relationship between entries and their position on the balance sheet may be summed up as follows:

- Liability and owners' equity accounts normally have credit (right-hand) balances.
- An increase in a liability or shareholder's (owner's) equity account is recorded on the right (credit) side of the account.

Revenue and Expense Accounts

Since revenues increase and expenses decrease the owner's equity, the rules of debit and credit for recording revenue and expenses logically follow this relationship. Applying this rule to revenue and expenses, the following results are obtained:

- Revenue increases owner's equity; therefore, revenue is recorded by a credit.
- Expenses decrease owner's equity; therefore, expenses are recorded by debits.

Double-Entry Accounting

Every business transaction affects two or more accounts. The double-entry system takes its name from the fact that equal debit and credit entries are made for every transaction. If only two accounts are affected, as in the purchase

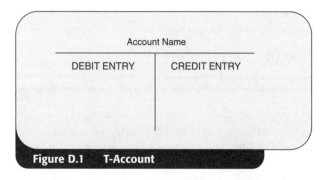

Account Name	
DEBIT ENTRY	CREDIT ENTRY

Figure D.1   T-Account

of a computer for cash, the asset account called **COMPUTER** is debited and another asset account **CASH** is credited for the same amount. If more than two entries are affected by a transaction, the sum of the debit entries must be equal to the sum of the credit entries. Recording equal amounts of debits and credits for each transaction ensures that the balance sheet equation of *Assets = Liabilities + Owner's Equity* will always be in balance.

The double entry system is based on the principle of exchange, i.e., every business transaction involves two considerations: value received and value given. For simplicity, in the case of an asset, value received is a debit (DR) and value given is a credit (CR). Therefore, if a desk is purchased for $500 cash, two things occur:

• A desk worth $500 represents a debit.

• $500 paid for the desk represents a credit.

Example **Debits and Credits**
Double Entry Accounting

The following depicts typical ledger entries illustrating the use of debits and credits.

Date	Account	DR	CR
Feb. 2	Office Equipment (Desk)	$500.00	
	Cash		$500.00
	Paid for purchase of salesperson modular desk unit.		
Feb. 3	Cash	$2,250.00	
	Commission Income		$2,250.00
	Earned and collected a commission for selling a home.		
Feb. 5	Advertising Expense	$270.00	
	Accounts Payable		$270.00
	Newspaper advertising ordered, payment to be made in 30 days.		
Feb. 7	Accounts Receivable	$3,390.00	
	Commission Income		$3,390.00
	Commission for sale of home, to be paid in 60 days.		
Mar. 6	Accounts Payable	$270.00	
	Cash		$270.00
	Payment for advertising ordered on Feb. 5.		
Apr. 8	Cash	$3,390.00	
	Accounts Receivable		$3,390.00
	Commission collected for sale on Feb. 7		

Thus, all transactions are expressed by means of a debit and a credit and, at all times, the total of debits and the total of credits are equal. Before financial statements are prepared, a trial balance is completed to ensure the equality of debit and credit entries, i.e., that the total of all accounts with debit balances is equal to the total of all accounts with credit balances.

The T-account is convenient for illustrative purposes as it provides a conceptual picture of the elements of a business transaction. In formal accounting records, more information is needed, e.g., the date and explanation of the transaction. The T-account is replaced by the traditional ledger account.

Example **Debits and Credits**
Double Entry Accounting
Salesperson Expense Account

Assume that ABC Realty Inc. maintains an expense account for each of its salespeople. Salesperson Lee's account for the month of May might look like the following in which expenses were incurred on May 5, 9, 12, and 13. On May 30th, ABC Inc. Realty received a cheque from Salesperson Lee to pay down his account.

Salesperson: Salesperson Lee Accounts Receivable
Code: 0001

DATE	PARTICULARS	DR	CR	BAL
May 5	Advertising	100.00		100.00
May 9	MLS Listing Fees	45.00		145.00
May 12	Board Fees	50.00		195.00
May 13	Advertising	50.93		245.93
May 30	Rec'd from Lee		200.93	45.00

DEBT COVERAGE RATIO

Acronym: DCR   The debt coverage ratio expresses the relationship between net operating income and debt service, e.g., principal and interest payments, for an income-producing property.

Application   Lenders use this ratio to assess the ability of net operating income derived from an investment property to meet the debt service for that property. The debt coverage ratio is frequently applied when lenders are analyzing investment property for mortgage loan purposes.

Debt Coverage Ratio =
Net Operating Income ÷ Annual Debt Service

This ratio is viewed as a measure of risk associated with mortgage applications involving commercial properties. Generally, when the DCR moves above 1, lender risk decreases and as it sinks below 1, risk increases.

Example   *Debt Coverage Ratio*

Investor McKay is attempting to secure a mortgage for a commercial building that realizes a net operating income of $43,292. The annual debt service (principal and interest payments), for the mortgage is $38,792. Lender Inc. requires a debt coverage ratio not less than 1.10.

Debt Coverage Ratio = $43,292 ÷ $38,792
= 1.1160 or 1.12 (rounded)

Therefore, McKay's application meets the lender's criteria.

DEBT RATIO

One of several commonly used financial ratios based on data found on the balance sheet, profit and loss statement, or a combination of the two. The simplest example is the ratio of total liabilities to total assets that measures the proportion of assets financed by borrowings.

Example   *Debt Ratio*

If total liabilities for ABC Realty Inc. are $238,540 and total assets are $717,440, the debt ratio is:

Debt Ratio = Total Liabilities ÷ Total Assets
= $238,540 ÷ 717,440
= 0.33

When the debt ratio is 0.50 (50%) or higher, creditors have a larger investment in the firm than the owners. The debt ratio may range in value from 0 for a company with no debt to 1.0 for a firm financed entirely by debt. Creditors typically prefer a lower debt ratio, given the cushion of safety provided by the owner's investment.

Debt to Net Worth Ratio

A modified measure that determines average debt to worth and can be an indication of excessive debt. The debt to net worth ratio formula is:

$$\frac{\text{(Total Debt - Commissions Payable)}}{\text{Tangible Net Worth}}$$

This ratio is probably better suited to real estate brokerage analysis given the significant role that commissions payable to salespeople plays in financial matters.

Example   *Debt Ratio–*
Debt to Net Worth Ratio

Assume that ABC Realty Inc. has a tangible net worth (profit) according to the balance sheet as of December, 31, 20xx of $137,000 with total debt (less commissions payable) of $104,000.

Debt to Net Worth Ratio = $104,000.00 ÷ $137,000.00
= 0.76

Presumably, ABC Realty Inc. would have no trouble paying its creditors if required. In this calculation, commissions payable is deducted, since it is a contracted debt. If a transaction fails to close and commission is not received, then no commission is payable.

DECLARATION

The constitution of a condominium corporation that creates the condominium and defines the responsibilities of the owners and the corporation.

Provincial   See applicable reference materials.

DEED/TRANSFER

A legal document, duly executed and delivered, that conveys title or an interest in real property. A deed is most commonly associated with registry, while the term *transfer* typically applies to land titles.

Provincial   See applicable reference materials.

DEED OF TRUST

A transfer of the title to a trustee (neutral party) by the trustor (borrower) as security for the performance of specified obligations.

Application   The use of a deed of trust instead of a mortgage is found in selected North American jurisdictions. In California a mortgage instrument involving a mortgagee and mortgagor is not used (as in Canada). Instead, the borrower (referred to as a *trustor*) gives the legal title to a neutral third party (the *trustee*) to be held on behalf of the lender (beneficiary). When the loan is repaid, the trustee reconveys the title back to the trustor. If a default occurs, the trustee can proceed to foreclose on behalf of the beneficiary. Proponents of the deed of trust cite shorter time limits for foreclosure as opposed to traditional procedures under a mortgage.

Example   Deed of Trust

Buyer Jones, through ABC Realty Inc., wishes to purchase an office tower but is unable to find one lender who will advance the mortgage monies necessary to close the transaction. He does, however, have several interested lenders who will take a portion of the loan. Jones gives a deed of trust (sometimes referred to as a *bond mortgage*), to a trustee who holds the title to the office tower in trust for the various lenders participating in the mortgage.

If Buyer Jones defaults on payments, the trustee is in a position to take possession of the property and operate it for the lenders or sell the complex and disperse the proceeds among those lenders. When Jones pays off the total loan plus interest, the trustee conveys title of the property to Buyer Jones.

DEED RESTRICTION

(SEE ALSO RESTRICTIVE COVENANT)

An imposed restriction in a deed to limit the use of the land.

DEEMED DISPOSITION

Income Property

The term *deemed* refers to tax considerations under the *Income Tax Act* regarding the disposition of income-producing property.

Application   Upon occasion, a taxpayer may change an income property into a principal residence. In such an instance, a sale has not been effected but a deemed disposition (change in use), has occurred. Provisions under the *Income Tax Act* give a taxpayer the right to elect that no change in use has taken place and the unit may qualify as an income property for that particular taxation year. Such a provision is subject to various qualifications. If no election is made, the owner has re-acquired the property personally with potential capital gains tax and also tax for recaptured capital cost allowance.

Principal Residence

The term *deemed* refers to tax considerations under the *Income Tax Act* regarding the disposition of real property designated as a principal residence.

Application   On occasion, a taxpayer may vacate a principal residence and then rent the property. In such an instance, a sale has not been effected but a deemed

disposition (change in use), has occurred. Provisions under the *Income Tax Act* provide that a taxpayer may elect that no change in use has taken place and the unit may qualify as a principal residence for that particular taxation year.

Reference   Deemed dispositions are subject to various qualifications. Professional advice should be obtained.

DEFAULT

Failure to fulfill a promise or obligation.

Application   Default is most frequently referenced in relation to mortgages and the failure to fulfill obligations under a mortgage. A mortgagor would be in default if he/she failed to satisfy any of the covenants, but most defaults specifically arise from failure to make the mortgage payments. When default does occur, it is uncommon for the mortgagee to seek legal action immediately. The mortgagee will normally weigh practical considerations and attempt to remedy the situation through personal contact with the mortgagor. Normally, once these personal negotiations have broken down, the mortgagee will seek legal action.

If the default situation has become untenable and all practical alternatives have been explored, a mortgagee will normally seek professional counselling, as a variety of possible remedies are available to him or her. Some remedies require court action while others are authorized by the mortgage agreement. Default procedures are subject to provincial legislation.

Example   Default

Buyer Jones acquires a home at 123 Main Street for $200,000 with a $150,000 first mortgage and monthly payments of $1,423 PIT. Within three months of buying the property, his employment is terminated and he is unable to maintain the payments. The first payment missed was the May 1st remittance, only five months following closing. At that point, Buyer Jones is legally in default.

DEFAULT REMEDIES

Default is a failure to fulfill obligations under the terms of an agreement. In mortgages, default is not specific only to payments, but can relate to other obligations such as taxes, requirement to pay common expenses in a condominium, or to keep property in a good state of repair.

If a default occurs, legal action can be commenced in line with appropriate remedies. Remedies are available assuming that the mortgagee has direct control over the loan and can act at will to enforce the document. If Canada Mortgage and Housing Corporation (CMHC) insures the loan, procedures must be in accordance with that organization.

Application   When default occurs, it is uncommon for the mortgagee to immediately seek legal recourse for practical reasons. The lender is not normally in the real estate business and does not want to dedicate personnel to manage property. Further, legal disputes can be costly.

Payment problems may reflect financial management difficulties that are best corrected in a positive fashion, e.g., reorganizing debt load and restructuring payments. Most lending institutions have policies concerning delinquency. Regardless, mortgage documents and provincial legislation set out legal remedies that can be pursued by the mortgagor including power of sale and foreclosure. While the mortgagor may seek to resolve default issues through non-legal means, legal remedies may be taken immediately.

Example   *Default Remedies*
Typical Procedure on Default

The following is provided for illustration purposes:

- 5–10 days following default: form letter requesting payment within five days.
- 20 days following default: second letter or call to request payment and/or interview regarding status of account.
- 35–45 days following default: registered letter concerning pending legal action.
- 50–55 days following default: documents forwarded for legal action.

Time frames and procedures vary, based on market conditions, history of the mortgagor, and condition of the property. Further, various non-legal actions may be taken to remedy the default at the point of an interview between customer and lender. This could involve a payment grace period, a re-negotiation of the loan amount, or the consolidation/re-amortization of debt.

Provincial   See applicable reference materials.

DEFEASANCE

A clause in a mortgage that negates an obligation upon the performance of certain acts or conditions within the agreement. The defeasance clause provides that the mortgagor has the right to redeem the property by the payment of the full amount owing. Upon full payment the mortgagor can obtain a release (discharge) from the mortgagee.

Example   *Defeasance*

Owner Smith currently has a mortgage with Lending Inc. The defeasance clause within that document reads as follows:

Provided that this mortgage shall be void upon the mortgagor, his heirs, executors, administrators, successors or assigns or any of them paying or causing to be paid to the mortgagee, its successors or assigns the principal sum set forth in the mortgage and interest thereon as well after as before maturity and default and judgment at the rate set forth in the mortgage at the days and times and in the manner set forth in the mortgage and all other amounts payable by the mortgagor hereunder and paying any taxes, rates, levies, charges or assessments upon the mortgaged premises no matter by whom or what authority imposed and observing and performing all covenants, provisos and conditions herein contained.

DEFERRED MAINTENANCE
(SEE ALSO DEPRECIATION)

Ordinary maintenance that is not performed and negatively affects a property's use and value.

Example   *Deferred Maintenance*

Seller Smith has owned his present home for ten years and is now offering it for sale through a local brokerage. The roof on the home is approximately 25 years old and is in need of replacement. Smith, despite its unsightly appearance and potential for leakage, elects not to replace the roof in hopes that the property will sell. While he may be avoiding an immediate cash outlay, the market value of the home is probably affected by his decision. Ironically, the ultimate selling price of the home may be less than if he replaced the roof and added this cost to his asking price. The obvious poor state of the roof may limit the number of buyers seriously considering the property. Buyers may fear that other items have also not been maintained on the property.

DEFERRED PAYMENT
(SEE ALSO GRADUATED PAYMENT MORTGAGE)

Payment obligations that are delayed until some future date. The graduated payment mortgage provides for deferred payments through lower initial principal and interest payments during the first years with successively higher payments to compensate during latter years.

DEFICIENCY DISCOUNT

A reduction in rent to induce a tenant to accept a sub-standard apartment. Substandard in this context does not refer to violations of any statutory requirements affecting tenancies, but rather the general condition of the apartment regarding such things as decorating, overall appearance, and the lack of a promised amenity, e.g., pool. Provincial tenancy legislation may limit or otherwise impact the use of deficiency discounts.

Example *Deficiency Discount*

Landlord Smith is having difficulty renting a two-bedroom unit in his multiple-unit building. He is renting it in an *as is* condition with no decorating or other changes following the last tenant's departure. The asking price is $1,400 per month but few prospective tenants have shown any interest. Those who did secured accommodation elsewhere given the condition of this particular unit.

Renter Jones approaches Smith with a suggestion. He will rent the apartment for $1,250 per month for two years and complete all decorating to the landlord's specifications, during the first six months of occupancy. Smith agrees to a deficiency discount of $150 per month for the two-year tenancy period.

Provincial   See applicable reference materials.

DELEGATION OF DUTIES

(SEE ALSO AGENCY)

The authorization given by one party to another to carry out specific responsibilities.

Application   The most common form of delegation, for real estate practitioners, involves agency. An agent has undertaken to perform all duties personally when the principal has given sole agency to the brokerage. Circumstances exist where an agent can use others to provide assistance in fulfilling obligations. For example, statutory delegation to an employed salesperson is typically found in a provincial real estate act.

DELINQUENCY RATE

For real estate purposes, the number of mortgages that are in arrears expressed in relation to a total mortgage portfolio. The delinquency rate can be expressed either as the number of delinquent mortgages in relation to the total number, or as the dollar volume of such mortgages in relation to total dollar value of the portfolio.

Example *Delinquency Rate*

Lender Inc. has a mortgage portfolio totalling 375 mortgages of which 23 are delinquent. The delinquency rate is:

$$23 \div 375 = .0613 \text{ or } 6.13\%$$

However, in terms of dollar volume, the mortgages in arrears represent a more significant portion of the total portfolio. The 23 delinquent mortgages amount to $7,398,982 with the current total mortgage portfolio as $50,812,500. The dollar volume delinquency rate is:

$$\$7,398,982 \div \$50,812,500 = .1456 \text{ or } 14.56\%$$

DEMAND FACTORS

Factors affecting real estate demand include:

Demographics   Population changes, size, family formation rates, household growth, and migration.

Consumer Financial Status   Employment trends, income levels, amount of disposable income, number of wage earners, and personal savings rates.

Mortgage Financing   Maximum loan amounts, lending ratios, interest rates, qualifying levels, and lending policies.

Consumer Attitudes   General marketplace confidence.

DEMAND LOAN

An arrangement typically between a business customer and a financial institution permitting loans to a maximum amount of credit allowed for that business. An initial credit level is established, based on the credit worthiness and cash flow abilities of the business. The line is renewed, usually annually, upon presentation of financial statements and the stated interest rate generally fluctuates with the prime rate. As a rule, brokerages should not rely upon a line of credit for asset acquisition, but rather only to meet short term operating requirements.

Example *Demand Loan*

ABC Realty Inc. requires financing for expansion. To satisfy the lender that the brokerage is capable of making the payments and to confirm cash flow, a commission receivable aging report for a five-month period is provided. This assists the lender in assessing the quality of the receivables, which are normally the largest liquid asset within a brokerage. Financial statements will be provided on an annual basis as support of the line of credit/demand loan.

DEMISED PREMISES

A portion of real property in which an interest or estate has been transferred temporarily, such as an interest conveyed in a lease. The demising clause (example follows) in a lease sets out the specific property being leased between landlord (lessor) and tenant (lessee). The word *demise* is synonymous with *lease* or *let*.

> *Premises*
>
> *The Landlord hereby leases to Tenant the premises being that portion of the Shopping Centre described as Unit _____ shown as the area outlined in red on the site plan annexed hereto as Schedule "A" which premises (herein referred to as "Premises") contain an area of approximately _____ square metres (_____ square feet). All measurements of the Premises made in relation to this Lease shall be made in accordance with the provisions set out in Schedule _____.*

DEMOLITION

The tearing down or destruction of a building. A demolition permit must be obtained from the local building department. In granting the right to demolish, additional requirements may be imposed that necessitate the hiring of a professional engineer to co-ordinate and oversee the demolition process. In some instances, a permit may not be available, or special requirements may apply, e.g., structures intended for or formally designated as heritage buildings. Practitioners also encounter the issue of demolition in regard to mortgages.

> **Example   *Demolition–Mortgaged Property***
>
> Developer Reed wishes to purchase property with the intent of removing existing improvements to make way for a new structure. Since the property is financed with a seller-take-back mortgage, a clause is inserted within the agreement/contract stating that the mortgagor has the right to alter or demolish any or all of the existing buildings without such activity constituting waste under the terms of the mortgage, provided that such demolition is conducted pursuant to applicable by-laws, appropriate permits.

DENSITY

For real estate purposes, the maximum allowable usage for a given parcel of land, e.g., number of people, amount of residential units, or total square footage.

> **Example   *Density***
>
> A specific district might be identified for single-family and two-family dwellings and certain other specified uses such as schools, parks, churches, and facilities normally associated with residential areas. Residential requirements could include minimum site areas from 5,000 to 6,000 square feet with minimum lot widths ranging from 40 to 60 feet. As a result, density varies from 5.5 dwelling units per acre in areas developed solely with single-family dwellings to approximately 11 dwellings per acre in areas with two-family dwellings.
>
> The following might be found in an official plan concerning low density requirements in a residential area:

> *Low Density Residential*
> 4.2.2 In low density residential designations the following dwelling types may be permitted subject to the provisions of the zoning code:
>
> a) detached, semi-detached, duplex and other attached grade-related dwellings;
>
> b) lodging houses; and
>
> c) group homes.
>
> *Density and Height*
> 4.2.3 Development in low density residential designations shall not exceed a net density of 35 units per hectare and a height of three storeys. The maximum density and height permitted on any site shall be further specified in the zoning code.
>
> *Existing Buildings Exceeding Density*
> 4.2.4 Existing triplex, fourplex and low rise apartment buildings in Low Density Residential designations are permitted uses even if they exceed the maximum net density of 35 units per hectare or the maximum height of three storeys. They may be rehabilitated or replaced in accordance with appropriate zoning standards for parking and open space.

DEPOSIT

Payment of money or other valuable consideration as a pledge for fulfillment of a contract. If failure of performance occurs, the deposit is usually forfeited. If performance is undertaken, the deposit usually acts as a part payment toward the purchase price.

Application   The deposit in real estate transactions, which may be paid by cheque, certified cheque, or cash, forms two functions. First, it is a sign of good faith and sincerity by the person making the deposit; secondly, it represents part of the purchase price. Five to ten percent of the offered price appears sufficient to illustrate good faith in the transaction.

Provincial   See applicable reference materials.

DEPOSIT OF TITLE DEED

One of three common forms of equitable mortgage, the other two are *Vendor's Lien* and *Mortgage of the Equity of Redemption*. An equitable mortgage does not involve the conveyance of title. In a *Deposit of Title Deed*, an equitable mortgage exists if the borrower gives the lender the deed as a security for a loan, or shows a written intention that the real property is to be charged as security for a loan. Even if a formal mortgage is not given, it is still an equitable mortgage and the lender can deposit notice of it on the title to the land. An equitable mortgage is used by some banks to better secure a personal loan.

DEPRECIATION

A loss in value due to any cause. Depreciation also arises in the estimating of values in the appraisal process.

Accounting

Fixed assets such as office furniture, office equipment, and automobiles can be kept intact and in useable condition for several years but eventually must be replaced. An asset, as an economic resource, is an item that has the ability or potential to provide future benefits to the business, e.g., cash used to purchase inventory or equipment.

Depreciation accounting is a procedure in which the cost or other recorded value of a fixed asset less its estimated residual value (if any) is distributed over the estimated useful life of the asset in a systematic and rational manner. As such, depreciation accounting is a process of cost allocation, not of valuation. Separate *accumulated depreciation* accounts are maintained for each group of depreciable assets. The entry to record depreciation is a debit to *depreciation expense,* which appears on the profit and loss statement, and a credit to *accumulated depreciation,* which appears on the balance sheet. This entry has no effect on *current* assets or liabilities as it does not require any sort of payment.

The *Accumulated Depreciation* account reflects the total depreciation charged on an asset since acquisition. The book (carrying) value of an asset is the initial cost of the asset less the accumulated depreciation. When computing income for income tax purposes, the *Income Tax Act* permits a deduction similar to depreciation, known as capital cost allowance.

Investment Analysis and Taxation

Investment analysis requires the calculation of operations and sale proceeds cash flows to arrive at cash flows after taxes. An important calculation involves the loss of value associated with tangible assets and their treatment under the *Income Tax Act,* which establishes limits concerning allowable deductions for loss of value against the capital cost of specific capital items.

Application   The allowable deductions, referred to as *capital cost allowances,* can be applied against income generated within each tax year. Capital cost allowance (CCA) deduction levels are delineated by means of *classes.* Classes of property are set out in the regulations under the *Income Tax Act.* Commonly used classes for commercial properties include:

CLASS	METHOD RATE	DESCRIPTION
1	DB, 4%	Most investment buildings acquired after Dec. 31, 1987 1988. The construction materials used and date of acquisition will dictate the use of other classes, e.g., Class 3, Class 6, Class 31 and Class 32 that use different rates. Note: Classes 31 and 32 apply to Multiple Unit Residential Buildings (MURBs).
8	DB, 20%	General equipment, furniture, appliances, and other chattels.
17	DB, 8%	Paving, parking lot lighting.
13	SL	Leasehold improvements.

DB–Declining Balance   SL–Straight Line

Capital cost allowances are calculated based on a percentage allocation in relation to the acquisition cost (*adjusted cost base*). While most are declining balance calculations, CCA for selected items is determined through amortization of the acquisition cost (the useful life established under guidelines provided in the Regulations), using the straight line method, i.e., leasehold improvements under Class 13. For real property, the purchase price must be allocated between depreciable (building and equipment), and non-depreciable (land), portions to establish the basis for CCA calculations. The depreciable portions are then subject to capital cost allowances. The CCA can be deducted from income derived and, as a result, becomes an important tax shelter vehicle.

Deductions for capital cost allowances are accounting entries and do not affect day-to-day cash flows, but do influence taxable income and therefore impact both *cash flow after taxes* (operations cash flow), and *sale proceeds after taxes* (reversion or disposition cash flow).

Consequently, the determination of capital cost allowances, along with related tax calculations is very important in analyzing the merits of any investment property from a specific investor's point of view.

Appraisal

In real estate appraisal, depreciation refers to any decline in the value of a physical asset resulting from physical deterioration (ordinary wear and tear), and functional/external obsolescence. Appraisers rely on two perspectives regarding depreciation. In the cost approach to value, accrued depreciation is calculated, while in the income approach to value, accruals for depreciation are used. For a detailed analysis of depreciation relating to deterioration and obsolescence, see **Accrued Depreciation**.

DESCRIPTION, LEGAL
(SEE LEGAL DESCRIPTION)

DESIGN BUILD

An arrangement typically involving an owner of land agreeing to build a structure of a size, quality of construction, and overall appearance in accordance with requirements of a specific tenant. The owner, as landlord, then leases the completed structure to that tenant. In today's marketplace, design build activities have expanded and include numerous arrangements and variations.

Application   Most design build activities begin with a detailed analysis of the user's needs, building and site criteria, and a detailed costing. Commercial brokerages have extensive information concerning hard and soft costs and a range of typical land values to help in cost estimating. Hard costs include all structural, mechanical and electrical components, site preparation (e.g., excavation, fill, landscaping, asphalt, and curbs), and contractor overhead and profit. Soft costs normally include project management, engineering, legal and consulting fees, financing charges, and connection fees.

Brokerage involvement in a design build strategy can also include analysis of *lease* versus *own* options. Clients may then evaluate various possibilities including: ownership by acquiring suitable land and constructing a building, leasing of a completed building based on pre-determined building/site criteria, or acquisition of suitable land followed by a sale/leaseback arrangement where a new owner (the developer), constructs the building and enters a long term lease with the former owner (the client), as a tenant.

Design build arrangements are commonly associated with a seller's market when demand for land is high and existing space is limited. Ease of financing at attractive rates is also an important element in the growth of design build activity. Conversely, such activity is dramatically reduced in markets where ample lease space exists at very competitive rates and buildings are available for sale below replacement cost.

Design build scenarios can be complex given the particular needs of users. Commercial brokerage activities will often include not only detailed costing estimates, e.g., land and building costs as well as interim and permanent loan costs, real estate commissions, closing expenses, and contingencies, but also detailed pro forma statements outlining all cash flow projections, present value estimates, and internal rates of return. A rent quotation is established for the tenant following cost estimates and development of a pro forma statement.

From a real estate perspective, the typical design build involving a tenant progresses through six stages:

Tenant Qualification
Establish financial capabilities and specific needs/criteria for the site and building.

Preliminary Proposal
Evaluate options/strategies for the tenant and develops initial proposal for presentation to a selected developer.

Developer Meeting
Discuss and evaluate preliminary proposal from the developer's perspective.

Detailed Proposal
Practitioner, with developer and other expertise (e.g., architect and lender), develop a detailed proposal along with a rent quotation.

Presentation/Acceptance
Prepare detailed proposal and rental quotation submitted for acceptance.

Follow Up
Provide follow-up and assistance as required leading to project completion.

DESIGN DEVELOPMENT/COST

Budgeted costs relating to a specific design (normally an industrial, commercial, or investment structure), based on agreed parameters, e.g., diagrams, specifications, and plans, where specific units or parts have been identified and separately costed in relation to the overall project.

The design development stage involves the process by which, upon approval of the schematic design, the architect proceeds with development of the plans and elevations of the building. Drawings establish all major elements and outline specifications. A revised estimate of construction costs is usually made at that time.

DESIGNATED APPRAISER COMMERCIAL

Acronym: DAC   The DAC designation is awarded by the Canadian National Association of Real Estate Appraisers (CNAREA) to members qualified to perform appraisal assignments on all types of real property. To attain this designation, an individual must have the DAR designation, five years full time appraisal experience, and complete the CNAREA education program or its equivalent.

Reference   See Designated Appraiser Residential.

DESIGNATED APPRAISER COMMERCIAL (AGRICULTURE SPECIALTY)

Acronym: DACA   The DACA designation is awarded by the Canadian National Association of Real Estate Appraisers (CNAREA) to members qualified to perform appraisal assignments on all types of real property with a specialty in agriculture. Requirements include the DAC designation and completion of the CNAREA education program or its equivalent.

Reference   See Designated Appraiser Residential.

DESIGNATED APPRAISER RESIDENTIAL

Acronym: DAR   The DAR designation is awarded by the Canadian National Association of Real Estate Appraisers (CNAREA) to members qualified to perform appraisal assignments of residential-type properties consisting of no more than four housing units. Requirements include 2,000 hours of full-time appraisal experience over a minimum two-year period and the successful completion of the CNAREA education program or its equivalent.

Reference   For details, contact the Canadian National Association of Real Estate Appraisers, 59 Wallingford Drive, Toronto, ON M3A 2V2. Information has been summarized from materials provided by CNAREA with no representation concerning its accuracy or completeness.

DESIGNATIONS

A range of real estate designations is offered to brokers and salespeople by institutes and organizations. A *limited* listing is provided as **Figure D.2** for designations included in the encyclopedia. For detailed information, see under appropriate designation.

DESK COST

The financial cost associated with the employment of salespeople by a brokerage. Desk cost is used as a method to determine and assess the optimum sales force for a particular office and expected minimum production of that sales force to meet office expenses. Desk cost can be calculated in two ways as illustrated in **Figure D.3**.

Calculation Using Total Expenses
- Determine the number of persons that can operate within the office, given the size of the premises, equipment, salaried staff, and related considerations.
- Summarize all fixed, semi-variable, and variable expenses using a budget worksheet.
- Divide the operating expenses by the number of people to obtain the annual desk cost.
- Divide the result by 12 to determine the monthly desk cost.

This method provides a rough indication of costs involved in maintaining a sales representative and forms the basis in setting performance objectives.

Calculation Excluding Commission Expense
Commission paid to salespeople is not included as only operating costs owed to third parties by the brokerage are used. The basis for this calculation is limited to expenses payable on behalf of salespeople and the office in general.

The method has become popular as it reflects the true expenses of the brokerage when dealing with desk fee arrangements and commission plans that rely heavily on salesperson contribution to variable and fixed expenses.

Future Considerations
The desk cost concept must be expanded in today's marketplace to take into consideration savings through the use of virtual offices and salespersons operating primarily from their homes.

The term *desk cost* should not be confused with desk fee plan and associated costs. Desk fee plans refer to a commission distribution options offered to salespersons.

DESIGNATION		AWARDING INSTITUTE/ASSOCIATION
AACI	Accredited Appraiser Canadian Institute	Appraisal Institute of Canada
ACCI	Associate of Canadian Condominium Institute	Canadian Condominium Institute Toronto and Area Chapter
AFM	Accredited Farm Manager	American Society of Farm Managers & Rural Appraisers
ALC	Accredited Land Consultant	REALTORS Land Institute
ALO	Accredited Leasing Officer	Real Estate Institute of Canada
AMO	Accredited Management Organization	Institute of Real Estate Management
ARA	Accredited Rural Appraiser	American Society of Farm Managers and Rural Appraisers
ARM	Accredited Resident Manager	Institute of Real Estate Management
CBV	Chartered Business Valuator	Canadian Institute of Chartered Business Valuators
CCIM	Certified Commercial Investment Member	Commercial Investment Real Estate Institute
CLO	Certified Leasing Officer	Real Estate Institute of Canada
CPM	Certified Property Manager	Real Estate Institute of Canada
CRA	Canadian Residential Appraiser	Appraisal Institute of Canada
CRB	Certified Real Estate Brokerage Manager	Real Estate Brokerage Managers Council – NAR
CRES	Certified Real Estate Specialist	Real Estate Institute of Canada
CRF	Certified in Real Estate Finance	Real Estate Institute of Canada
CRS	Certified Residential Specialist	Residential Sales Council – NAR
DAC	Designated Appraiser Commercial	Canadian National Association of Real Estate Appraisers Inc.
DACA	Designated Appraiser Commercial Agriculture	Canadian National Association of Real Estate Appraisers Inc.
DAR	Designated Appraiser Residential	Canadian National Association of Real Estate Appraisers Inc.
EEE	d'Expert en Evaluation d'Enterprises	Canadian Institute of Chartered Business Valuators
FRI	Fellow of the Real Estate Institute	Real Estate Institute of Canada
FRI(A)	Fellow of the Real Estate Institute Appraisal Specialist	Real Estate Institute of Canada
FRI(E)	Executive Fellow of the Real Estate Institute of Canada	Real Estate Institute of Canada
MIMA	Member of the Institute of Municipal Assessors	Institute of Municipal Assessors of Ontario
MVA	Market Value Appraiser—Residential	Canadian Real Estate Association. Administered in Ontario by the Ontario Real Estate Association.
RGA	Registered General Appraiser	International Institute of Public Appraisers Ltd.
RPA	Registered Public Appraiser	International Institute of Public Appraisers
RPA	Real Property Administrator	Building Owners and Managers Association
SIOR	Member Society of Industrial and Office REALTORS	Canadian Real Estate Association

Figure D.2   Real Estate Designations

D

TWO APPROACHES FOR CALCULATING DESK COST

OPTION 1
Desk Cost Calculation Using Total Expenses

STEP 1   Determine Optimum Sales Staff for Office

Estimated to be 25 persons based on the available number of desks and general space within the office.

STEP 2   Establish Total Expense for Office

Total fixed costs are $183,686 and variable are $792,483, therefore the total expenses for the brokerage are $976,169.

STEP 3   Determine Annual Desk Cost

= Total Expenses ÷ Sales Staff
= $976,169 ÷ 25
= $39,047

STEP 4   Calculate Monthly Desk Cost

= Annual Desk Cost ÷ 12
= $39,047. ÷ 12
= $3,254

According to the figures provided, each salesperson must produce approximately $3,254 per month for the brokerage in *adjusted gross income*. (See **Budgeting** for an example of a complete budget worksheet including adjusted gross income.)

OPTION 2
Desk Cost Calculation Excluding Commission Expense

STEP 1   Determine Total Expenses (Excluding Commissions)

= Total Expenses − Total Comm. Expense
= $976,169 − $713,414
= $262,755

STEP 2   Determine Annual Desk Cost

= Total Expenses ÷ Sales Staff
= $262,755 ÷ 25
= $10,510

STEP 3   Calculate Monthly Desk Cost

= Annual Desk Cost ÷ 12
= $10,510. ÷ 12
= $876

In this example the monthly desk cost is $876. Each salesperson must generate this level (following commission expense) to meet brokerage expenses.

BUDGET WORKSHEET EXCERPT

EXPENSE ANALYSIS SUMMARY	FIXED	VARIABLE	TOTAL
Total Commission Expense	0	713,414	713,414
+ Total Advertising Expense	+ 29,540	+ 40,669	+ 70,209
+ Total Personnel Expense	+ 78,125	+ 0	+ 78,125
+ Total Communication Expense	+ 30,189	+ 0	+ 30,189
+ Total Occupancy Expense	+ 12,989	+ 9,221	+ 22,210
+ Total Operating Expense	+ 0	+ 29,179	+ 29,179
+ Total General Expense	+ 32,843	+ 0	+ 32,843
= TOTAL EXPENSES	= 183,686	= 792,483	= 976,169

DETERIORATION

(SEE ALSO PHYSICAL DETERIORATION)

An impairment of condition. Deterioration is a cause of depreciation as it reflects the loss in value caused by wear and tear, disintegration, use in service, and action of the elements. Deterioration is synonymous with physical depreciation, which may be further classified as curable or incurable depreciation.

Example   *Deterioration*

Developer Reed recently purchased an older building and is considering the cost of remodelling to attract potential tenants. Given that components of a building are classified as curable and incurable, he starts to make a list under each category. The list would vary substantially, based on a variety of factors relating to the building, cost of improvements, and overall market conditions.

Curable items are those which the typical buyer would repair or replace immediately on taking possession, where the cost of repair or replacement is offset by the increased utility, and where it is economically sound to repair or replace. The developer immediately puts the carpeting, decoration in common hallways, bathroom facilities, and the main lobby area on his list.

Incurable items are components which are old or outdated, but which most buyers would not repair or replace because the cost to cure would outweigh benefits. Under this list, the developer itemizes the exterior windows, existing elevator facilities, and other major structural components of the building.

DEVELOPER

An individual or other legal entity that engages in the subdivision and improvement of land. Improvements typically include the provision of municipal services and roads and may extend to the full development of the property including all structures and other improvements.

Example   *Developer*

J. Jones, the owner of a development company, has just purchased a piece of land and intends to obtain zoning for the construction of single-family homes in a registered plan of subdivision. His function, as a developer, is one of converting the land from vacant agricultural zoning to a plan of subdivision. Jones' function is typically distinct from other persons who may play a role in the development: e.g., the home builder who acquires individual lots from the developer and builds new homes. However, in some instances, the developer may be involved in all phases of the project.

DEVELOPMENT LOANS

A development loan (sometimes referred to as *construction loan*), is advanced by a lender to a company for the specific purpose of servicing and improving land to the point of building construction. The term of the loan is normally one to three years. The payout of the loan occurs when the serviced land is sold to builders or to a general developer for the construction of new homes, a plaza, or a rental project. Normally this type of loan is not amortized over a specific period of time, but takes the form of a collateral loan with specific guarantees, and interest only payments throughout the mortgage term.

Example   *Development Loans*

Developer Reed is considering the purchase of a five-acre tract of land for residential development. The asking price is $499,000. Reed estimates that servicing of the property, associated costs for rezoning of the lands, and other development costs will amount to $285,000 excluding Reed's own time and interest on monies invested. The final development will contain 30 residential lots with an estimated value of $1,350,000.

A lender is interested in a development loan for $600,000 to be paid in successive stages starting at the point of purchase and being fully advanced on completion of servicing. No principal payments are required, the term is for two years, and interest must be paid monthly based on amounts advanced. Reed is also required to make partial discharges ($20,000 per lot), for lots sold during the two-year period.

DIFFUSER

A device for reducing the velocity of air flow from a mechanical duct system supplying air within a commercial structure. Usually circular or square, the diffuser is set in the ceiling at pre-determined locations to diffuse air within a defined space. Diffusers, in residential property, are the small rectangular grates normally located at floor level.

DIKES

Embankments for controlling or holding back rivers or the sea. Provincial regulations set out flood control measures including the use of dikes in flood-prone areas. Matters concerning floods, floodways, diking systems, flood control restrictions on buildings, and related topics fall primarily to provincial jurisdictions.

Provincial   See applicable reference materials.

DIMENSIONS

(SEE LOT SIZE)

DIRECT CAPITALIZATION

One of two methods used to establish the present value of a future income stream for purposes of estimating value and also providing a basis for comparison of investment-grade properties. Direct capitalization is clearly distinguished from yield capitalization as it involves a single year's projected income and expenses in arriving at value. This method involves the straightforward division of net operating income by an appropriate capitalization rate. The more complex yield capitalization requires forecasted income and expenses over a projected investment period and is based on four steps:

- Determination of a specified holding period;
- Projected income and expenses over that period;
- Selection of an appropriate discount rate, and
- Estimating present value based on that discount rate.

Direct capitalization is used for estimating market value and is generally preferred by appraisers (assuming sufficient market data to establish a capitalization rate), as it is market-driven and has limited assumptions. Yield capitalization involving discounted cash flows is more complex, but favoured by commercial practitioners in addressing individual investor goals and objectives.

DIRECT COMPARISON APPROACH

An approach in appraisal analysis based on the proposition that an informed buyer will pay no more for a property than the cost of acquiring an existing property with the same utility.

Steps Required

- Locate and select all available comparable sales and listings. Look for four primary qualities in selecting a good comparable sale:
  - Within the local market area;
  - At or near the date of the appraisal;
  - Truly comparable in that it will appeal to the same type of buyer who would consider buying the subject property being appraised, e.g., if the appraisal is for a single-family home, then a duplex would not normally be a good comparable; and
  - A bona fide arm's length transaction.

Based on the selections made, the appraiser would:

- Collect pertinent information on each comparable to make meaningful adjustments and gain a true understanding of the comparable properties. Direct inspection of comparables is an advantage in that regard.
- Analyze all relevant data, including differences that exist between the comparable and subject, e.g., time of sale and features.
- Compare each property with the subject property, making the necessary adjustments. Adjustments can be either dollar amounts or percentages. Real estate practitioners typically use dollar adjustments.
- Reconcile the data and arrive at a reasonable value estimate.

Sources of Information

A variety of sources exist for sales data to use in the direct comparison approach. The best resources are the brokerage's files and the real estate board MLS system. Selected data can also be obtained from registry or land titles offices. Banks, lending institutions, and insurance companies may supply information regarding mortgage financing and details of mortgaged property. Other sources of information are newspapers as well as legal and other professional publications.

Residential Property Comparisons

The most acceptable method of comparison in residential properties is a physical one. Consideration is given to various characteristics such as number of rooms, physical condition of the building, number of garages, bathrooms and fireplaces, and a finished or semi-finished basement. If these and many other factors are taken into consideration separately and a dollar factor allocated to each, then a proper comparison can be made.

Various factors must be considered in making comparisons of residential property.

Comparability

The single most important factor is the selection of truly comparable properties.

One-storey houses cannot be compared with one and one-half storey or two-storey ones, new houses cannot be compared with old houses, 50-acre fruit farms cannot be compared with 100-acre vegetable or dairy farms, and large lots to small ones. The best test of comparability lies in the size of the individual adjustments that are necessary. Big adjustments indicate poor comparability. Small adjustments indicate proper selection of comparable properties.

D

Time

The time element is all important in comparative analysis. The general economic conditions that existed at the time of sale of the comparable property may be quite different from those existing at the time or date of the appraisal. The appraiser must understand and recognize the significance of changing conditions and make appropriate adjustments.

Significant Characteristics

Adjustments should be made for significant and pertinent characteristics only. Each lump sum adjustment should be defensible by market data. For example, the market may indicate that the difference in price paid for a house with an attached garage as compared with one without a garage is $20,000, notwithstanding that the cost of adding the garage may be greater than that amount.

Value Not Cost

Adjustments are made on the basis of value, not cost. The cost of the garage is not the issue; its value is. The assumption made is that the presence or absence of factors being considered will make a difference to the price paid for a property. Therefore, any adjustment has to be made in consideration of a typical buyer's actions.

Sum Versus Parts

A buyer purchasing a residence acquires an entire package that includes land and improvements at a given price. If the house was separated into parts such as the garage, recreation room, or extra washroom and a cost assigned to each, a higher value would probably be derived than what a typical buyer would pay. As a parallel, consider assembling an automobile using individual parts bought at retail prices from a dealership. The cost of the finished product would be prohibitive compared to that of a new car off the assembly line. While not a perfect analogy, the appraiser must always remember that adjusted amounts must reflect the contribution of the parts to the whole.

Preparing Adjustments

Adjustments are required to effectively make comparable properties similar to the subject property, so that a valid comparison can be made.

If a feature in the comparable is better than the subject property, a minus adjustment is made to the sale price of that comparable. For example, if the comparable has two baths and the subject has one, the comparable is better in this respect and a minus (negative) adjustment is required. If the feature in the comparable is poorer or less desirable than the subject, a plus adjustment is required to the sale price of that comparable, e.g., the comparable has an old

kitchen and the subject a modern one. The comparable is inferior, consequently a plus or positive adjustment is required.

While percentage adjustments are possible, dollar amounts are preferred because the direct comparison approach is market oriented. This approach reflects the reaction of a typical buyer who, in comparing property with another, consciously or subconsciously adds or subtracts sums for differences in properties. Under each heading in an adjustment chart, plus and minus amounts appear reflecting what a typical buyer would allow.

Practitioners are reminded that an appraisal is only an opinion of value and cannot be accurate within a few hundred dollars, usually the final estimate is rounded to the nearest five hundred dollars. In some cases, a value range might be quoted as opposed to a single figure.

Figure D.4 illustrates three comparable properties being adjusted to arrive at an adjusted sale price for use in establishing an estimate of value of a subject property under the direct comparison approach.

Reconciliation

A logical reasoning process used to narrow down the value range to a final estimate of value. When all adjustments have been made, each comparable sale will provide a different adjusted sale price (original sale price plus or minus total adjustments). If three comparable properties are used, the adjustment process will likely result in three different figures. The process of reducing this range of adjusted sale prices to a final estimate of value is referred to as a *reconciliation.*

The appraiser must examine all information used in arriving at the reconciliation. A properly completed reconciliation will include the final estimate, along with written justification. No two appraisers will necessarily approach the reconciliation in precisely the same manner. The overall objective is to give the most weight to the best evidence, least weight to the poorest evidence, and look for any overall trends that indicate the value of the subject property.

In preparing a reconciliation, the appraiser should:

- Check all calculations;
- Review the comparability of each sale;
- Give less weight to sales requiring extreme adjustments;
- Give more weight to sales with the highest degree of comparability; and
- Make final value estimate.

Summary: Strengths/Weaknesses

The direct comparison approach is applicable when an active market provides sufficient quantities of reliable data that can be verified from authoritative sources. While being the most popular approach, particularly in residential markets, it can be somewhat unreliable in an inactive market or in estimating the value of properties for which no real comparable sales data is available.

This approach also falls under close scrutiny when sales data cannot be accurately verified with parties to the trans-action. For example, the sale price may not be at arm's length, but rather a disposition involving family members. Fortunately for real estate practitioners, the abundance of real estate data provided through MLS systems proves invaluable in obtaining comparable properties for appraisal purposes. Despite any shortcomings, the direct comparison approach remains the most popular appraisal method.

D

MARKET DATA ANALYSIS

Subject Address: 31 Hazel Lane

	Comparable 1	Comparable 2	Comparable 3
Address	42 Centre St.	200 Avenue Rd.	77 Walton Blvd.
Distance from Subject	1 Block	1/2 Block	2 Blocks
Date Sold	Oct. 18, 20x1	Dec. 10, 20x1	Nov. 15, 20x1
Sale Price	$191,000	$207,000	$208,000

Direct Comparison Approach

	Subject Description	Comparable 1 Description	Adj.	Comparable 2 Description	Adj.	Comparable 3 Description	Adj.
Time	Dec. 31, 20x1	Inferior Market	+ 5,000	Similar	0	Inferior market	+ 2,000
Location	Quiet Side Street	Similar	0	Similar	0	Similar	0
Lot Dimensions	30 x 150	31 x 150	0	29 x 148	0	31 x 155	0
Age of House	45 Years	42 Years	0	45 Years	0	43 Years	0
House Style	Detached Bungalow	Detached Bungalow	0	Detached Bungalow	0	Detached Bungalow	0
Total Square Footage	1000 sq. ft	992 sq. ft.	0	988 sq. ft.	0	1004 sq. ft.	0
Bedrooms	2 + 1	2 + 1	0	2 + 1	0	2 + 1	0
Bathrooms (pieces)	1 1/2	1	+ 2,000	2	– 2,000	2	– 2,000
Sep. Dining Room	Yes	Yes	0	Yes	0	Yes	0
Family Room	No	No	0	No	0	No	0
Recreation Room	Yes	Yes	0	Yes	0	Yes	0
Garage	No	Single	– 3,000	No	0	Single	– 3,000
Construction Quality	Above Average	Above Average	0	Above Average	0	Above Average	0
Fireplace(s)	One	One	0	One	0	None	+ 2,000
Central Air	Yes	No	+ 2,000	Yes	0	Yes	0
Condition	Modernized Very Good	Well Maintained Good	+ 5,000	Modernized Very Good	0	Modernized Very Good	0
Total Adjustments			+ 11,000		– 2,000		– 1,000
Adjusted Sale Price			$202,000		$205,000		$207,000

Value by Direct Comparison Approach $205,000

Comments & Explanations: The adjusted sale prices range from a low of $202,000 to a high of $207,000. The most weight was given to Comparable #2, as it had the least amount of adjustments when reviewing all other comparables. Therefore the value assigned to the subject property by the Direct Comparison Approach as of the date of this Appraisal is estimated at:

Two Hundred and Five Thousand Dollars $205,000.00

Direct Comparison Approach   Figure D.4

DISBURSEMENTS
(SEE CLOSING COSTS AND ADJUSTMENTS)

DISCHARGE OF MORTGAGE

A discharge of a mortgage is provided by the mortgagee and registered in the land registry or land titles office once a mortgage has been paid in full, or if it no longer stands as security.

Provincial   See applicable reference materials.

DISCIPLINE COMMITTEE

A committee established by a local real estate board to oversee disciplinary matters concerning the conduct of its members through the use of hearing committees . The discipline committee represents one component in an overall structure to enforce standards of conduct as established by The Canadian Real Estate Association (CREA). The CREA Code of Ethics and Standards of Business Practice must be adhered to by all members.

Application   The discipline committee is charged with responsibilities that must be administered in a fair, unbiased manner. The exact structure and procedures underlying this committee vary according to the nature of individual real estate board by-laws. Generally, the discipline committee is empowered to undertake hearings referred by the professional standards committee.

Provincial   See applicable reference materials.

DISCLAIMER

The repudiation or denial of a claim. Disclaimers can be found in listing agreements or data input forms relating to the accuracy of property details.

Application   For real estate purposes, the Marketing Practices Division of the Bureau of Competition Policy (Industry Canada) provides selected guidelines concerning the use of disclaimers. Under normal circumstances, a disclaimer in an advertisement is permitted but it must not in any way mislead the reader by the overall impression given. The disclaimer must only include reasonable limitations placed upon an offering, e.g., market evaluations provided within a certain defined territory and relating to specific types of property.

As a general test, any advertisement should be capable of standing on its own merit without regard to the disclaimer. The disclaimer should provide a logical extension of the offering and reasonable limitations associated thereto.

Example   *Disclaimer*

The most common disclaimer used in real estate brokerage concerns promotional flyers, letters, coupons, and other documents being forwarded to consumers by real estate brokerages and salespeople. Wordings vary greatly, but the general intent is as follows:

This is not intended to solicit property currently listed for sale by other real estate brokerages.

This disclaimer arises primarily from an ethical obligation under the CREA Code of Ethics and Standards of Business Practice not to interfere with contractual undertakings or other agreements between brokers and clients while promoting individual or company services. Provincial regulatory requirements may also apply.

Provincial   See applicable reference materials.

DISCLOSURE
(SEE ALSO AGENCY AND FIDUCIARY RESPONSIBILITIES)

The open and forthright discussion of relevant matters by an agent to his/her principal.

Legal Responsibility

The agent, under common law, is required to place the interests of the principal above all else except the law. Disclosure forms part of that duty. For example, where the agent has any personal interest, direct or indirect, in a transaction, the agent has a strict duty to make full disclosure to the principal. Further, all pertinent facts that could affect the principal's judgement when considering an offer must be disclosed.

Ethical Duty

Individuals who are members of organized real estate must adhere to the Code of Ethics and Standards of Business Practice of The Canadian Real Estate Association (CREA) (reprinted in the **Appendix**). The Code has several requirements most notably focused on disclosure when acquiring or selling property and disclosure procedures relating to an agency relationship.

Provincial   See applicable reference materials.

D

Statutory Requirements

Provincial regulatory requirements typically address selected disclosure procedures for persons registered under the applicable real estate act, e.g., when buying and/or selling property and disclosures relating to agency relationships.

Provincial   See applicable reference materials.

DISCOUNT RATE
(SEE ALSO OPPORTUNITY COST)

A discount rate, for purposes of real estate investment analysis, is best described as the cost of lost opportunity. In other words, an investor invests in one property at the expense of not having invested in another. If prevailing investments with similar risk provide a 9.5% rate of return, then the opportunity cost of that money is 9.5% when pursuing an alternate investment.

Components

The discount rate takes into account the opportunity cost (often referred to as the *hurdle* rate), and is, in effect, a predetermined benchmark rate of return. The discount rate need not always align with the opportunity cost. Often the rate based on lost opportunity merely represents a minimum cost. The investor may perceive an additional risk for a given investment option and add a *risk premium* to that rate.

The discount rate is used in determining the present value of future cash flows and is an integral aspect of capital budgeting and asset selection criteria. For real estate capital assets, the discount rate is applied to operations and sale proceeds cash flows over a specified holding period. The resulting discounted cash flows can lead to investment comparisons and/or estimates of value. Commercial practitioners most commonly discount cash flow after tax to arrive at investment value based on the goals and objectives of a specific investor.

In real estate, investors and practitioners typically work with a hurdle rate that represents both opportunity cost and risk. The opportunity cost is usually derived from the marketplace by weighing out differing investment vehicles that possess similar risks, capital requirements, and holding periods. The resulting discount rate provides the basis to analyze cash flows and arrive at present values.

Summation Method

The discount rate represents the return that could be realized on the next best investment alternative(s), i.e., the cost of lost opportunity. However, when lacking comparable properties, the investor may attempt to construct a discount rate (Example 1) based on summing the *safe rate* of return with allowances (risk premiums), for various factors or influences affecting real estate.

Example 1   *Discount Rate–Summation Method*

The summation method provides a theoretical framework to establish the discount rate in the absence of comparable circumstances. First, a base *safe* rate is selected typically a risk-free rate taken from the marketplace. e.g., the treasury bill rate might be used because it promises liquidity and practically no default risk. To this amount, a risk premium factor is added (risk associated with property and marketplace), along with factors of illiquidity (difficulty of quickly selling real estate assets), and the burden of management (necessity for varying degrees of real estate management).

Safe Rate	4.5%
Risk	3.0%
Illiquidity	1.5%
Management	1.0%
Discount Rate	10.0%

Sometimes, the discount rate is simply the safe rate (risk-free), plus a risk premium deemed to include such factors as illiquidity and management requirements.

Risk-Adjusted Cost of Capital

Corporations often establish a discount rate through the risk-adjusted cost of capital, (Example 2). The rate reflects *at minimum* the costs associated with obtaining capital from various classes of investors. A weighted cost is established based on prorating in relation to those sources. Corporations typically raise capital through three avenues: mortgage debt, preferred shares, and common shares. The proportionate contribution of each (based on an after tax perspective), is used in arriving at the final cost.

Example 2   *Discount Rate*
             Risk-Adjusted Cost of Capital

Corporation A obtains 60% of capital from debt financing with an after tax cost of 8.75%, 20% from preferred stock at 12.50%, and common stock for the remainder at 11.50%.

Weighted Cost of Capital
   = (.60 x 8.75) + (.20 x 12.50) + (.20 x 11.50)
   = (5.25 + 2.5 + 2.3)
   = 10.05%

The corporation would then add a risk component to arrive at the final opportunity cost of capital.

DISCOUNTED CASH FLOW
(SEE ALSO CASH FLOW MODEL)

A method used to assess the relative merits of real estate investments based on present value comparisons of future cash flows. Discounted cash flow (DCF) involves the analysis of operations and sale proceeds (reversionary) cash flow. DCF analysis can be before tax or after tax depending on circumstances surrounding the analysis.

Application   This method provides a dynamic portrayal of cash flows, as opposed to a static one-year projection used in direct capitalization. After tax analysis of cash flows is commonly associated with investment value estimates, however, DCFs have relevance to both before and after tax perspectives.

The deciding factor is often the purpose of the analysis and availability of relevant information. Regardless, investors can make informed decisions based on the systematic presentation of forecasts involving diverse properties under consideration.

Discounted cash flow is a relative newcomer to the field of real estate investment analysis. In the appraisal field, appraisers now use both discounted cash flows and direct capitalization. The discounted cash flow technique is grouped under the broader category of yield capitalization. Yield and direct capitalization make up the two approaches used under the income approach to value.

DISCOUNTING
(SEE ALSO COMPOUNDING)

The process of converting future sums into present value. Discounting is one of two common techniques used by practitioners to analyze yield realized on a real estate investment. The other measure is compounding. In concert, these represent the foundation for assessing the *time value of money*. In real estate most emphasis is placed on discounting given the frequent need to compare and/or value investment properties based on forecasted cash flows.

Application   As most real estate investment decisions centre on the anticipation of future benefits (cash flows), today's value of those future benefits is crucial to value estimates, property comparisons, and rational decision-making. Most investments involve the payment of an initial cash outlay with the anticipation of future periodic payments (e.g., operations cash flow through the collection of rent and payment of expenses), followed by the disposition of the property (sale proceeds). Real estate investment analysis involves both forms of cash flow. For example, a practitioner can calculate yield if the present value of an investment is known and the net operating income for successive months/years is forecasted along with the ultimate proceeds from disposition (reversion). Alternatively, if an investor requires a specific rate of return, future cash flows can be discounted at that rate to provide indications of present value.

Discounting involves three different types of calculations with compounding adding a further three. In combination, these calculations are referred to as the *six functions of a dollar*. Discounting calculations are:

- Present value of a future amount (e.g., the present value of $1,000 received two years from now).
- Present value of a series of future equal payments (e.g., the present value of 12 payments of $100.00 received over 12 months).
- Payment required to amortize an amount (e.g., the payment required to repay a loan of $1,000 borrowed at 8% in four equal monthly payments).

Fortunately, with the arrival of calculators and computer software programs, traditional tables setting out discounting values for these three functions are virtually obsolete.

DISCOUNTING (MORTGAGES)

The process of purchasing the face or remaining value of a mortgage at a lower cost to increase yield.

Application   Discounting frequently occurs when a mortgagee wishes to sell a mortgage in the secondary mortgage market. By using discount tables, both the buyer and seller of a mortgage can establish the relative mortgage value in relation to various yield levels.

Example   *Discounting (Mortgages)*

Seller Smith is taking back a second mortgage for $30,000 at 14.5% with a term of four years and amortized over 25 years. An investor wishes a yield of 16%. Based on the discount table, the factor to be paid per $1,000 is 958, therefore, the present value to produce that yield is:

$30(000) x 958 = $28,740

Discounted Mortgage Evaluation
Per $1,000 Outstanding Principal

ANNUAL RATE   **14.5%**
AMORTIZATION   **25 Years**

YIELD RATE	REMAINING TERM (YEARS)			
	1	2	3	4
8.00	1059	1114	1164	1210
8.50	1054	1104	1150	1192
9.00	1049	1095	1136	1174
9.50	1045	1086	1123	1157
10.00	1040	1077	1110	1139
10.25	1038	1072	1103	1131
10.50	1035	1068	1097	1123
10.75	1033	1063	1090	1114
11.00	1031	1059	1084	1106
11.25	1029	1054	1077	1098
11.50	1026	1050	1071	1090
11.75	1024	1046	1065	1082
12.00	1022	1041	1059	1074
12.25	1019	1037	1053	1066
12.50	1017	1033	1047	1059
12.75	1015	1029	1041	1051
13.00	1013	1024	1035	1043
13.25	1011	1020	1029	1036
13.50	1008	1016	1023	1029
13.75	1006	1012	1017	1021
14.00	1004	1008	1011	1014
14.25	1002	1004	1005	1007
14.50	1000	1000	1000	1000
14.75	997	995	994	992
15.00	995	991	988	985
15.25	993	987	983	978
15.50	991	983	977	972
15.75	989	979	972	965
16.00	987	975	966	958 ←
16.25	984	972	961	951
16.50	982	968	955	945
16.75	980	964	950	938

Reference   Discounting tables have been largely replaced by financial calculators and software programs. Advanced courses concerning investment property address both compounding and discounting calculations.

DISCRIMINATION

The act of making a distinction, either favourable or unfavourable, regarding an individual or a thing based on group, class, or other category to which that individual or thing belongs.

Provincial   See applicable reference materials.

DISPOSAL SYSTEMS

Provincial   See applicable reference materials.

DISTRAIN (DISTRESS)

Right of the mortgagee or landlord to seize and auction chattels, after due notice of a public auction, in settlement of the mortgagor's or tenant's debt.

Example   *Distrain (Distress)*

Smith is negotiating a lease with Jones for a commercial retail store. The wording concerning distrain follows:

If the tenant is in default as defined in the lease, the landlord, in addition to any other right or remedy it may have, will have the right of immediate re-entry and may remove any person or property from the premises. The property may be stored in a public warehouse or elsewhere at the cost of and the account of the tenant, all without service of notice or resort to legal process and without the landlord or its agents being considered guilty of trespass or becoming liable for loss or damage occasioned thereby. Any of the property of the tenant, namely goods and chattels on the premises, when seized will be sold and applied to the indebtedness owed by the tenant to the landlord.

DISTRESS SALE

A sale in which the owner is in a state of anxiety (usually finance related), and frequently requiring disposition of property for an amount less than true market value.

D

DISTRESSED PROPERTY

A property under foreclosure or other legal remedy, or such action is imminent due to default concerning financial obligations relating to that property.

Provincial   See applicable reference materials regarding foreclosure and other legal remedies for default.

DISTRIBUTION PANEL

An electrical panel providing the interface between the service entrance wires to a structure and the wires for dispersing power throughout that structure.

Application   Real estate practitioners require a basic knowledge of components making up electrical systems. The distribution panel, as an interface, is connected by service wires from the main disconnect. The black and red wires are each connected to a live busbar (a current carrying metal bar with several connection points), and the white wire is connected to the neutral busbar. Each household circuit fuse (or breaker) is directly connected to either the red or black busbar.

The distribution panel typically has several 120-volt circuits (10 are required for most homes), and one or more 240-volt circuits for large electric appliances. Many codes now require a panel with room for 24 120-volt circuits. Real estate practitioners may also encounter auxiliary panels which do not bring additional power into the house, but simply allow for more branch circuits to carry electricity to various areas of the home. Figure D.5 illustrates several types of distribution panels that are typically encountered in residential structures.

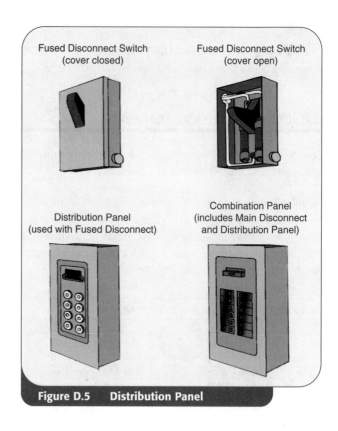

Figure D.5   Distribution Panel

DOCKS

Waterfront structures that are normally floating (see Figure D.6), cantilevered, or post-supported, usually built of wood, and used for recreational purposes.

Application   The construction of docks normally requires municipal approval as well as approval from the appropriate provincial ministries/departments, and Parks Canada in the case of federal canal systems.

Approvals are normally granted with various conditions such as: all in-water work to be completed between Labour Day and March of the following year; turbidity to be kept to a minimum; dredged materials to be stabilized to prevent erosion; wood treatment chemicals (such as creosote preservative) not be used; and all associated permits as required from regional and municipal authorities. Generally, if docks are permitted, such structures must take into account sensitive habitat areas and allow for the free movement of water and fish.

Minimum disturbance to bottom cover is normally achieved by using posts rather than cribs. Environmentally friendly alternatives such as floating and cantilever docks, marine railways, and boat slips are often preferred as they minimize shoreline alteration. Care should be taken in selecting the type of dock or wharfing system given wave action, strength and direction of current, prevailing winds, and winter ice conditions.

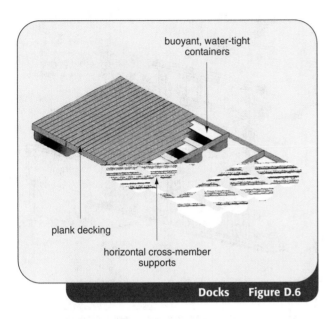

buoyant, water-tight containers

plank decking

horizontal cross-member supports

Docks   Figure D.6

Figure D.7 illustrates a right-of-way over Lot 2 (the servient tenement) as an interest attached to Lot 1 regarding access to the lake.

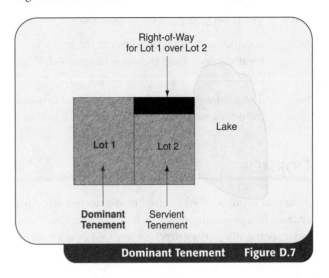

Right-of-Way for Lot 1 over Lot 2

Lot 1

Lot 2

Lake

Dominant Tenement

Servient Tenement

Dominant Tenement   Figure D.7

D

DOMINANT PORTION

(SEE ALSO BOMA STANDARD)

A term used in the measurement of commercial space for leasing purposes. The dominant portion of the outside wall of an office is relevant when calculating both the rentable and useable areas of a commercial property.

Application   The dominant portion of the outside wall, according to the BOMA standard, is that portion accounting for more than 50% of the vertical floor-to-ceiling dimension of the inside finished surface of the permanent outer building wall. For example, if the outside wall consists of more than 50% glass, then the measurement would be taken from the inside surface of the glass. In the case of a non-vertical (angular) permanent outer building wall, the point of measurement would be the inside finished surface of the wall where that wall intersects with the finished floor. Given the variety of outer wall configurations, practitioners are advised to obtain detailed standards concerning both the measurement of rentable and useable areas, as well as the determination of the dominant portion of outside walls.

DOMINANT TENEMENT

The estate or interest in land that derives benefit from an easement over a servient tenement, as in a right-of-way.

An easement must confer a benefit on the dominant tenement. As long as the easement properly serves the dominant tenement, the dominant and servient tenements need not be adjoining. The owner of the dominant tenement has no right to enlarge the use for which the easement was granted.

DOOR/DOOR FRAME

A solid barrier for opening or closing an entrance-way including associated framing materials. Solid wood doors have been the traditional exterior door as wood has certain natural insulating properties, although weather tightness is always enhanced with the addition of a storm door. However, the heaviest wood door does not provide as much insulation value as a poorly insulated wall.

Application   Practitioners should be familiar with basic facts regarding doors. Solid wood doors provide reasonable security depending on the amount of glass area, the hardware used, and the quality of installation. Hollow wood doors are generally not for exterior use and are inferior to solid wood doors regarding insulation, security, and durability. Deterioration of the wood veneer on the surface exposed to the exterior is a common problem.

Metal doors, often having decorative plastic mouldings on the surface, are commonly used as exterior doors in modern construction and typically have a metal exterior skin together with internal insulating material (usually polystyrene or polyurethane). Magnetic weatherstripping can be used to create a proper air seal. Problems have occurred when a storm door is added to an insulated metal door. The space between the doors may become overheated, the plastic mouldings can be affected, and in some instances, the metal door panel may even buckle. Many manufacturers do not recommend the use of storm doors for this type of metal door.

The framework, upon which a door is hung, is made of wood or hollow metal and includes the following:

Head	The horizontal top portion of the door frame;
Jamb	Either the left or right vertical portion of the frame;
Sill	The bottom of the door at floor level;
Stop	A continuous projection around the frame to resist the door from travelling beyond a closing point; and
Buck	The sub-frame of wood or pressed metal to which the door case is fixed.

DORMER

A vertical window, often referred to as a dormer window, encased in a projecting structure from a sloping roof and most commonly associated with Cape Cod or colonial architectural designs.

DOUBLE-GLAZING
(SEE GLAZING)

DOUBLE-HUNG WINDOW

A window constructed with two moving parts: an outer part in the top half of the opening and an inner part on the bottom half of the opening Both halves can be moved up and down in their guides. See Figure D.8.

Early versions of double-hung windows were held open by using a counterweight system. Some modern double-hung windows use a spring loaded mechanism concealed in the side of the sash. Certain high quality versions are pivoted so that the external glass area can be swung inside for cleaning. Double-hung windows can be wood, metal, vinyl, or a combination thereof.

DOWER

A future interest in property by a spouse. The concept of dower arose to provide a widow with a life interest in one-third of her husband's real estate. To convey clear title, a wife would have to release her interest (bar her dower rights), if the husband was an owner and wished to sell or mortgage the property. However, this concept fell into disrepute as a result of technical legal devices designed specifically to circumvent this type of interest.

Provincial   See applicable reference materials. Dower has been abolished in most provincial jurisdictions.

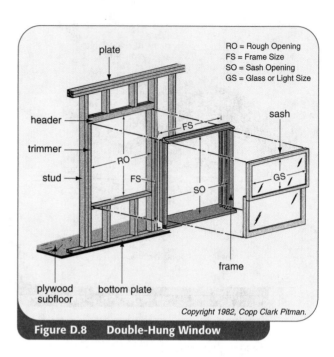

RO = Rough Opening
FS = Frame Size
SO = Sash Opening
GS = Glass or Light Size

Copyright 1982, Copp Clark Pitman.

Figure D.8   Double-Hung Window

DOWN ZONING

A change of zoning to a less intensive land use such as an amendment from commercial to residential purposes.

Example   *Down Zoning*

Buyer Jones is acquiring an older commercial establishment in the downtown area and plans to fully convert the property into a triplex. Jones makes application for a down zoning of the property and receives appropriate approvals. With the down zoning, he is now able to secure a building permit to make the necessary alterations to the structure.

DRAFT PLAN

A preliminary plan of subdivision prepared by a developer to be circulated to various ministries/departments for approval.

Provincial   See applicable reference materials. The term *draft plan* is unique to specific provinces.

DRAINAGE

A system of drains, either artificial or natural, used for the removal of liquid. Drainage is most commonly associated with a system of piping, conduits, ditches, or similar drainage devices for the run off of water on land and/or near building structures on surface or sub-surface levels.

Application   Provincial building codes establish drainage requirements including tile pipe standards as well as minimum size requirements related thereto.

Figure D.9 illustrates the components of a typical drainage system at the footing level of a residential structure.

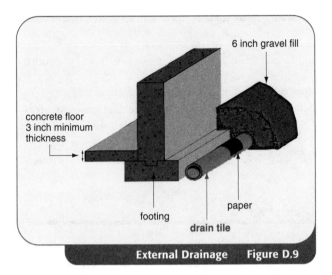

External Drainage   Figure D.9

External

Practitioners most commonly encounter drainage requirements in relation to foundations. Building codes set out sub-surface specifications concerning the type of granular materials needed to drain the bottom of the foundation, and the location of drainage disposal piping including drainage tile, sump pits, and dry wells.

Surface drainage requirements typically necessitate site grading to prevent the accumulation of water at or near the building. Such drainage must also ensure that adjacent properties are not adversely affected. Requirements also apply to wells and septic disposal beds, the use of catch basins where required for runoff water, and the proper installation of downspouts.

Internal

Internal systems are often installed by property owners to remedy dampness or the influx of ground water into a basement. Drainage is accomplished by installing tile inside the footings below basement floor level leading to a sump pump or waste sewage system. This approach is less desirable than the external approach, since water has no natural inclination to find this drainage tile.

Water may accumulate on the outside of the foundation for some time and could leak through the exterior walls before it is carried away by the drainage system on the inside. The water must pass through the foundation or footing system, or go under the footing to reach this tile. Also, with no exterior excavation, damp proofing or

waterproofing the outside of the foundation wall is not possible. Occasionally, holes are drilled through the foundation wall just above the footing to allow water to drain into the internal tile system.

Dredging

Dredging in or near watercourses requires approval by municipal, regional, and other governmental ministries/departments. Figure D.10 illustrates a typical shoreline dredging plan. Dredging generally falls under guidelines concerning shoreline conservation. Most guidelines are designed to help conserve fish habitat and natural areas within watercourses. Dredging projects are normally reviewed on an individual basis.

Provincial   See applicable reference materials.

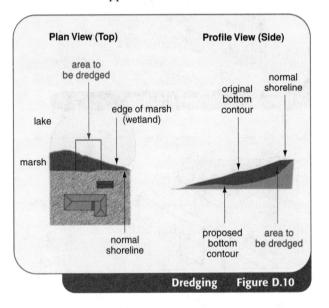

Dredging   Figure D.10

Dry and Wet Bulb Thermometer

An instrument, also known as an *hygrometer*, for measuring relative humidity through the use of two thermometers.

Drywall

Drywall and plaster are basically the same material (usually gypsum) except that drywall is pre-manufactured while plaster is mixed and applied by trowel on site. Occasionally, aggregate or fibres are added to the gypsum as stabilizers and strengtheners. Drywall now dominates the residential marketplace in the finishing of interior areas. Figures D.11 and D.12 are provided relating to installation and finishing processes.

D

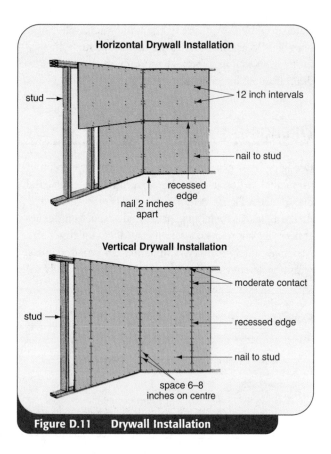

Figure D.11   Drywall Installation

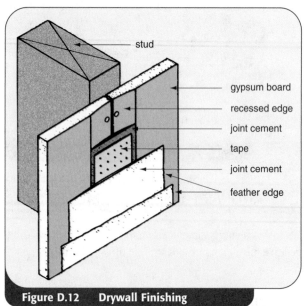

Figure D.12   Drywall Finishing

DUAL AGENCY
(SEE ALSO AGENCY)

Representation of two principals (usually seller and buyer), by the same agent in the same transaction. Real estate practitioners should exercise caution concerning such relationships and only undertake dual agency relationships

using recommended disclosure procedures. Provincial regulatory bodies may establish exact procedures to follow. Practices vary by provincial jurisdiction.

DUCT

A pipe, tube, channel, or other unit necessary for conveying gases, liquids, or solid units from one point to another.

Application   Ducts are usually identified with air-conditioning/heating systems where the transfer of air is necessary. This is accomplished through sheet metal ducts. The term also applies to underfloor duct systems for conveyance of telephone lines and other electrical conductors.

DUPLEX

A two-family dwelling or house having two self-contained residential units normally held under one title of ownership. Duplexes most commonly have an upper/lower configuration. Terminology may vary by provincial jurisdiction.

DURESS
(SEE ALSO VOID AND VOIDABLE)

The threat of violence, force, or undue pressure to coerce a person into an action against his/her will.

In real estate agreements, where duress or undue influence can be established, the contract can be voidable, but not void. A void contract is a nullity at law and does not legally exist.

Example   *Duress*

Smith is attempting to sell his vacant property to Jones, an adjacent neighbour. While the discussion has centred on verbal promises, Smith is getting anxious and wants to put the agreement on paper, but Jones is hesitant. Smith, in a bout of anger, tells Jones that if the sale doesn't go through, he will contaminate the property and ultimately affect Jones' water supply. While uncertain whether or not Smith's threat is real, Jones elects to sign an agreement for fear that Smith's actions will affect his land value and ability to use the property. Smith is exerting duress on Jones and the contract may be voidable.

DYKES
(SEE DIKES)

E

National Info Links

Economic Indicators

Statistics Canada

Telephone (800) 263 1163
Web Site www.statcan.ca

For a directory of regional Statistics Canada reference centres visit www.statcan.ca/english/reference/refcentre.html.

Environment

For national environmental initiatives, contact:

Environment Canada
Inquiry Centre 351 St. Joseph Boulevard
Hull, Québec K1A 0H3

Telephone (819) 997 2800
(800) 668 6767
Web Site www.ec.gc.ca

For provincial environmental legislation contact the appropriate provincial ministry/department.

Employment-National Benefits Programs

Human Resources Development Canada

Web Site www.hrdc-drhc.gc.ca

See local telephone directory for addresses and telephone numbers for Human Resources Centres. For provincial employment legislation contact the appropriate provincial ministry/department.

EARN OUT

A method of financing the sale of a business predicated on actual performance. By first deducting the downpayment, the balance of the purchase price of the business, suitably secured, can be based on the actual performance (productivity) of the business after the date of closing.

Application   Using earnout as the basis for debt payment can often solve the inevitable difference between what the seller wants and what the buyer is willing to pay. A buyer may be unwilling to meet a seller's price, even though the past performance of the business would indicate that the price is reasonable. In reality, this is often a sign that the buyer is concerned about the future potential of the business for any number of reasons. The balance of the payment can, therefore, be spread over a specific period of time, with the amount of each payment based on the earnings of the business.

Three basic types of earnout are found in the marketplace although a wide range of possibilities are possible based on specifics of the business under consideration.

Base Period Earn Out

Additional payments in excess of the balance due on the purchase of a business are paid as a proportion of the increase in profits produced from the operation, over and above those profits derived in a particular base year.

The base year is frequently the fiscal year immediately before the year the sale was consummated. If the prior three to five years fluctuated noticeably, a weighted average would probably be taken to arrive at the necessary base amount. Increases achieved above the base are then capitalized at an agreed upon factor, established before closing, to arrive at the actual dollar value of the year-to-year earn out payment. This capitalization rate is frequently the same rate employed at the outset to establish the value of the business. The seller would normally require full audit and inspection control capabilities.

Incremental Earn Out

This approach is similar to the base period earn out except that additional payments over fixed debt are calculated on a proportion of the year-to-year increase, capitalized at the agreed rate. In other words, the profits must increase each year, relative to the previous year, for a payment to become due. This type of earnout favours the buyer. However, the seller can counterbalance this by demanding a lower capitalization rate and, therefore, a larger payment than might be considered reasonable under the base period approach.

Cumulative Earn Out

The cumulative earn out calculation is based on the total increase in earnings over the base year for the number of years contracted. This amount is then paid to the seller at the expiration of the term of the agreement, with or without interest, as the case may be.

The disadvantage to the seller is that funds are not received until the end of the term and the payment could be received in depreciated dollars. Alternatively, if the owner remains as manager or consultant and is thus able to generate and verify increased profits, higher profits could be achieved over and above original anticipated levels.

A variation to this approach is possible where a predetermined additional consideration exists for each year of the term as a fixed prepayment, subject to adjustments based on operating results. The seller's advantage, if he/she continues to be engaged in the business as a manager/consultant, is increased profits and thereby an increase in the end value of the business. Alternatively, the seller could negotiate fixed additional compensation for each successive year of payout of the earnout, subject to the final adjustment of actual results achieved at the end of the agreed upon term.

Example   *Earn Out–Cumulative*

Buyer Jones wishes to acquire the business operated by Smith. Jones has $200,000 as a downpayment with Smith taking back a mortgage for the $300,000 balance. The parties agree that Jones will repay the loan over a 36-month period, using a base period earn out arrangement.

To make this approach effective, Smith agrees to stay on as a manager at an agreed level of compensation for the first 18 months to oversee the business without interference from Jones. Jones assumes the role of an investor, but will also work along with Smith to learn the day-to-day operation. By this arrangement, Jones has the benefit of knowledgeable management and the expectations of reasonable profits to repay the debt, while Smith is reasonably assured of receiving payments as agreed under the sale agreement.

EASEMENT

A right enjoyed by one tenement over another tenement, for example, one land owner with a right over another land owner, usually granted for a special purpose rather than for the general use and occupation of the land. An easement is an interest that runs with the land.

Once granted, an easement attaches to the land and binds subsequent owners. An easement must have both a dominant tenement (land that benefits from the easement), and a servient tenement (land that serves or is subject to the easement). Separate ownership of the dominant and servient tenements must exist and the right must confer a benefit on the dominant tenement. The two tenements need not be adjoining.

Application   Agreements relating to easements are usually registered against titles to both properties. However, such is not always the case, for example, when statutory easements are involved (see subsequent details). The title to an adjacent property may have to be searched before determining if a particular property benefits from a registered easement over another's land. These agreements may be registered as instruments on their own and appear on the title under that particular name, or they may be registered by way of a caveat (a warning or notice on title), in some provincial jurisdictions.

Typical Easements

Real estate practitioners encounter a wide range of easements including a party wall agreement such as in a duplex or semi-detached home, an encroachment agreement, e.g., when one owner has inadvertently built a fence over the adjoining owner's land, a right-of-way for pedestrians or vehicles, or a utility agreement granting a utility company the right to place and maintain utility lines, pipes, or equipment.

Party wall agreements and rights-of-way warrant further discussion. Registered owners of adjoining parcels of land, e.g., semi-detached houses in which each side has a separate title, may enter into a party wall agreement. The agreement will declare the dividing wall between the dwelling units a party wall and set out the rights, privileges, easements, and covenants that exist in respect of the party wall. These will usually be the same for both parties. Therefore, a party wall agreement is similar to a mutual easement. Legal descriptions and characteristics of party walls varies by provincial jurisdiction.

The right-of-way is also a frequently encountered form of easement, e.g., the right to pass over the land of another or make use of a designated strip of land. While a right-of-way is seemingly distinct from an easement, in reality, it is only a matter of terminology as both possess the same legal characteristics. A right-of-way is an easement that includes the right to enter upon the lands of the servient tenement, as illustrated in **Figure E.1**, for the purpose of maintaining the easement and making repairs as in cases involving public utilities such as telephone, railway, telegraph, gas, and oil rights. Often such rights-of-way are referred to as statutory easements if the right is created by the authority of a statute, e.g., a public utilities act, pipeline act, or power corporation act.

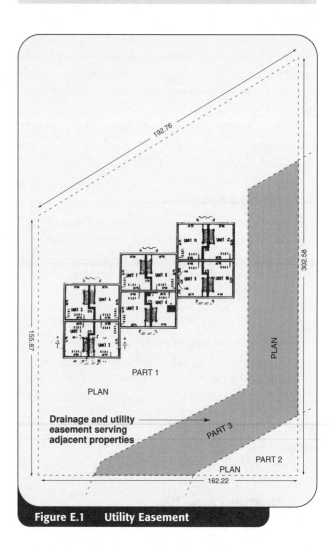

Figure E.1   Utility Easement

Creation

Easements can be created by express grant, prescription, implication, or statute.

Express Grant   The easement can be created whenever an owner decides to grant a privilege, (a right-of-way or easement), in favour of the adjoining owner.

Prescription   An individual can obtain a right-of-way or easement by adverse possession, also known as *by prescription* or *squatters' rights*, in certain circumstances if the usage of the right-of-way was open and continuous for a specified period of time.

Implication   Best described by using an example. Assume that a sale of land adjoining the seller's land causes a parcel of land to be landlocked, the law implies that a purchaser would have an easement over the seller's remaining land by way of necessity. Another example would involve mutual support. A shared docking area by two cottagers would naturally preclude the ability of one party to destroy his/her portion of the docking facility to the detriment of the other's structure.

Statute   Easements created by statute involve groups such as public utilities and telephone companies who gain the right to string wires, install equipment, and maintain services by virtue of various provincial statutes. A statutory easement is created by the authority of the statute and does not require a dominant tenement.

Termination

Merge
An easement is extinguished if the ownership of both dominant and servient tenements merge.

> **Example**   *Easement–Termination–Merge*
>
> Seller Smith, a cottage owner, has an easement over his neighbour's vacant piece of land for purposes of accessing a road, without which Smith could only get to his property by boat. Uncomfortable with this situation, Smith approaches the neighbour offering to buy the property to make one large cottage lot. Upon closing the sale, Smith's original easement is extinguished as the properties merge into one parcel of land.

Release
The person entitled to the benefit of an easement may release it to the servient tenement by removing the easement from the title.

> **Example**   *Easement–Termination–Release*
>
> Seller Smith has a precisely described easement across a neighbour's property for purposes of accessing a rear lane. With the passage of time, the lane has become unuseable and Smith no longer requires access. Further, neighbour Jones wishes to build a garage on the rear of his property that would obstruct the easement. The neighbours agree to extinguish the easement by signing and registering appropriate documents.

Ceasing of Purpose
If the purpose of the easement disappears, so does the easement.

> **Example**   *Easement–Termination*
>   *Ceasing of Purpose*
>
> Seller Smith owns a right-of-way to a cottage. The right-of-way subsequently becomes a public thoroughfare and the easement ceases to exist given this change. The easement would also disappear if it is abandoned by an actual intention to abandon (not merely by non-use).

Provincial   See applicable reference materials. Legal terminology and procedures concerning the creation of easements vary by provincial jurisdiction.

EAVESTROUGH/DOWNSPOUTS

Building components that have two major functions in residential and commercial structures:

- Protect against wall damage and localized ground level erosion caused by roof runoff.
- Assist in keeping basement areas dry by directing water away from the foundation.

Regardless of the type of foundation wall, the possibility of water penetration always exists. The less water in the soil near the foundation wall, the less likelihood of water penetration into the basement. Eavestroughs should collect all water runoff, and downspouts should discharge the water into proper drains or onto the ground a safe distance away from foundation walls.

The two most common sizes of eavestrough are four and five inch widths and are normally either attached to the fascia board or form an integral part of the eaves. Four inch is acceptable for small roof areas, while five inch is usual on larger, as well as steeply pitched roofs owing to greater capacity.

Application   The most common types of eavestrough are aluminum, galvanized steel, plastic, and copper. Aluminum does not rust, but dents easily. The number of joints required is less than other systems as it is often fabricated on the site. Aluminum is pre-finished thereby offering low maintenance and a life expectancy of 20 to 25 years. Galvanized eavestrough requires periodic painting and has a life expectancy of 20 to 25 years. Plastic is generally designed for do-it-yourself activities, with limited colour selection. Copper eavestrough is very expensive but considered the best, with a life expectancy of between 50 and 100 years.

Common Problems

Figure E.2 illustrates various problems that can occur with eavestrough.

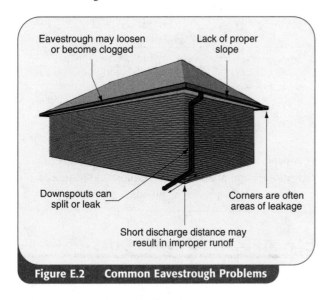

Figure E.2   Common Eavestrough Problems

Leakage   The most common problem is that galvanized eavestrough rusts and holes can develop in copper eavestrough as well. All types are prone to leakage at the joints. Missing end caps are another source of leakage.

Loose   This type of problem is normally due to improper fastening during original installation or damage caused by ice during winter months.

Damage   Ladders and tree limbs frequently cause mechanical damage.

Slope   Lacking proper slope, eavestrough will collect and hold water resulting in accelerated deterioration.

Debris   Screens can be installed to prevent clogging from twigs and leaves, however, they often come loose, fall out, and can make proper cleaning difficult.

Malfunctioning eavestroughs can result in serious problems. The water leaking out of the troughs usually ends up in the structure, causing rot and other damage.

Downspout Discharge

Downspouts take the water from the eavestrough and discharge it into drains or onto the ground. Underground drains (usually made of clay tile, cast iron or plastic), can plug or break. Often, this problem cannot be determined from a visual inspection. If an underground drain malfunctions, localized water problems will likely develop in the basement in the area adjacent to the downspout. If this

occurs, two options exist: exterior digging and repair, or disconnect the downspout and redirect the discharge away from the house.

All downspouts that discharge onto the ground should be directed a good distance from the house: six feet or more, if possible. The slope of the ground in this area should direct water away from the basement. On pre-1950 homes, downspout drains are often connected to floor drains in the basement. A significant amount of debris in the discharge from the downspouts can plug the basement floor drains and cause backup.

ECONOMIC AGE-LIFE DEPRECIATION METHOD

A measure of depreciation of a property based on the anticipated life of a structure.

Application   In the economic age-life method, (traditionally referred to as the age-life method), an estimate is made of both the effective age of a building and its remaining economic life. The effective age and remaining economic life together comprise the economic life of the building. The ratio of the effective age to the economic life multiplied by the reproduction cost of the structure is a measure of the accrued depreciation. The economic age-life method takes physical deterioration into account but does not measure loss in value due to functional and/or external causes. Accordingly, this approach is often viewed solely as a rule of thumb or cross check for more complex methods.

Example   *Economic Age-life Depreciation Method*

Assume that a building has an actual age of 15 years, an estimated effective age of ten years, a remaining economic life of 40 years, and a reproduction cost on the date of the appraisal of $71,150. The accrued depreciation estimated by the age-life method would be as follows:

Effective Age ÷ Economic Life = 10 ÷ **50**
= 20% or .20

Accrued Depreciation = .20 x $71,150
= **$14,230**

ECONOMIC AGE-LIFE DEPRECIATION METHOD (MODIFIED)

A modified measure of depreciation of a property based on the anticipated life of a structure using the economic age-life method.

Application This modified approach breaks down and measures the depreciation of the physical components of the building structure based on two categories:

- Physical Deterioration—Curable; and
- Physical Deterioration—Incurable: Short-Lived and Long-Lived.

However, as with economic age-life depreciation, the modified method does not take into account either functional and/or external obsolescence. Consequently, appraisers normally use this approach only when it is apparent that the property being appraised is not affected by such factors; or when this method is combined with other techniques that do account for functional and/or external obsolescence.

Example *Economic Age-life Depreciation Method (Modified)*

Salesperson Miller has been asked to estimate the value of a property based on the cost approach. As no functional or external obsolescence has occurred, Miller selects the modified economic age-life method for purposes of calculating depreciation and completes the analysis based on curable and incurable physical deterioration.

See **Accrued Depreciation, Figure A.13** for a detailed example.

ECONOMIC LIFE

The period over which improvements to real estate contribute to the value of the property. See **Figure E.3**.

Application Economic life is used to establish the capital recovery period for improvements in the residual technique of income capitalization. It is also used in the estimation of accrued depreciation (diminished utility) in the cost approach when establishing a value estimate.

Example *Economic Life and Depreciation*

Salesperson Lee is attempting to establish the value of a property by the cost approach. The economic life of the structure, a 20-year old brick veneer bungalow, is estimated to be 35 years. In other words, 35 years represents the life span of the bungalow in terms of viable economic contribution to the overall value of the property. Upon inspection, the structure reveals an effective age of 15 years. Accordingly, Lee will apply a depreciation rate of:

(15 years (effective age) ÷ 35 years (economic life)) x 100

= .4286 or 42.86%

Figure E.3 visually demonstrates economic life in relation to effective and actual ages.

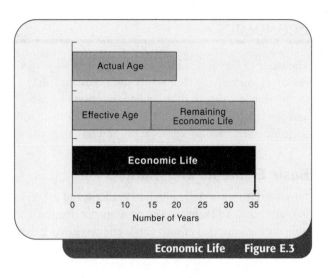

Economic Life   **Figure E.3**

ECONOMIC OBSOLESCENCE

(SEE ALSO LOCATIONAL OBSOLESCENCE)

Impairment of desirability or useful life or loss in the use and value of property arising from economic forces outside the building or property. Economic obsolescence can result from changes in optimum land use, altered economic circumstances within the community, e.g., loss of a major employer, legislative enactments that restrict or impair property rights, or other changes affecting supply/demand relationships.

Economic obsolescence should be distinguished from locational obsolescence which refers to localized factors adjacent to the property that impact that property. Economic obsolescence involves broader economic issues within the overall area that affect properties. These forms of obsolescence are grouped by appraisers under the general category of external obsolescence.

Example *Economic Obsolescence*

When Seller Smith originally built his ranch style bungalow in the east end of Anycity approximately 30 years ago, Eastern Heights was very popular with young families. However, in the past several years, the neighbourhood has been changing. Recent plant closings have affected economic prospects for the community, various homes on neighbouring streets currently sit vacant, and generally, the entire area is in a state of decline. While redevelopment will undoubtedly occur in the future, immediate prospects are anything but encouraging. From an appraisal perspective, Smith's property is being negatively affected by economic obsolescence.

ECONOMIC RENT

(SEE MARKET RENT)

ECONOMICS

The study of how individuals and society allocate scarce resources in satisfying their wants and needs, including the production, distribution, and consumption of goods and services to meet the needs of various economic units (e.g., individual, family, corporation, and government).

Basic Elements and Markets

People utilize resources, capital, technology, and expertise to create goods and services. The creation, distribution, and ultimate consumption of such goods and services is largely dictated by the forces of supply and demand. Further, the amount of production and its ultimate use by consumers, determines the standard of living enjoyed within a particular society.

Embodied within the national economy are thousands of individual markets, in which buyers and sellers meet to bargain and exchange desired commodities and services. Economics seeks to apply certain theoretical principles and axioms to explain the shifts, trends, and fluctuations within these interwoven markets.

All economies require four basic elements in order to produce goods and services:

- Land;
- Labour;
- Capital; and
- Entrepreneurial skills.

Collectively, these are referred to as the *factors of production.* The overall effectiveness of the economy is dictated by its basic philosophic orientation. A capitalistic economy operates on individual decisions in an open marketplace. Command systems, usual to socialist countries, are based on government bureaucratic decisions in both the selection of priorities, and the means of distribution of goods and services to the society.

Figure E.4 summarizes the interplay of consumers and businesses in the production and consumption of products and services, recognizing that government plays an integral role in the process.

The Canadian Economy

Canada's economy, best described as *mixed*, entails the interplay of individuals and government in the direction of economic activity and production of goods and services. This situation frequently pits opposing forces on the same economic battlefield, resulting in a complicated structure full of intermingling philosophies, factions, and activities, fluctuating in perpetual push/pull motions.

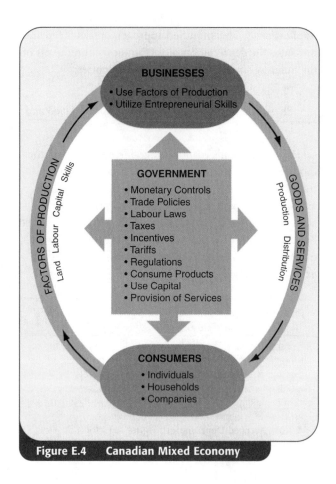

Figure E.4   Canadian Mixed Economy

The entire process underlying the Canadian mixed economy can be depicted as a cyclical mechanism commencing with consumers (individuals, families, households, and companies), leading to the factors of production in the resource market, the creation of goods and services by businesses utilizing entrepreneurial skills, and finally returning full circle to the consumer. The government, situated at the hub, affects the flow variously as a user, regulator, and producer of many goods and services.

Money is exchanged in countless transactions each and every day throughout the country, in accordance with the economic current and moves from consumer demand, through the factors of production and, finally, to the final purchase of goods and services. The payment of money circulates in a counter-clockwise direction to the flow on the chart. Because most transactions involve the payment of money in return for goods and services, the Canadian economy is considered to be a *price* system as opposed to a barter/exchange system.

Market Indicators

Today's economist faces the complicated, if not impossible, task of weighing the relative impact of subtle natural market forces against a myriad of vested interests intruding on the perfect equilibrium envisaged in supply/demand economics. As a result, specialists have increasingly relied on business statistics to provide insight and illuminate important trends within our complex economy. The real estate practitioner, although not requiring extensive knowledge of such information, should be aware of *key indicators* having a direct bearing on real estate, as well as many other interlocking markets in the overall economy.

Inevitably, nearly all indicators utilized by economists relate directly back to factors in the cyclical flow of the national economy. These are:

- *Resource Markets*
  (land, labour, capital, entrepreneurial skills),
- *Businesses* (supply), and
- *Consumers* (demand).

Unfortunately, statistical information often mirrors the disturbing complexities found in the marketplace. However, certain key indicators (as follows), demonstrate a high degree of reliability in predicting market swings.

Resource Markets

Labour   Possesses an understandable priority with most economists. The national unemployment rate is the most widely publicized, but other, more finely tuned indices measure such things as job creation and job vacancy statistics. This information, broken down by regions throughout the country, is very meaningful when analyzing local markets. Labour indicators not only measure the strength of the economy, but also the efficiency with which manpower is being utilized in addressing consumer demand.

Capital   Statistics Canada provides worthwhile information not only on existing capital investment from private and public sectors but also on anticipated allocations of capital dollars by large and small companies. The availability of capital and attractiveness of interest rates charged are directly tied to economic expansion.

Businesses

National Production   The supply of services and goods in the marketplace is a critical measure of the economic output. Economists have focused on two major indices prepared by the federal government:

- **Gross National Product (GNP)**   The most widely known indicator is the Gross National Product (GNP). This indicator measures total production in the economy, and consequently is considered statistically representative of overall prosperity within the country. The GNP measures production by Canadian residents, corporations and individuals, both within and beyond Canada.

- **Gross Domestic Product (GDP)**   This indicator gauges production located solely within the country, and is a complementary indicator for the GNP.

Manufacturing Activity   Statistics Canada also produces information concerning manufacturer's new orders, shipments, and inventories. This information is necessary when assessing overall demand through the depletion and replenishment of goods.

Utilization Rates   Although no key indicator exists assessing the effective use of production facilities within the country, economists do rely upon various topical reports from Statistics Canada. These attempt to illustrate whether the economy is operating at its full potential, utilizing the available production factors.

Consumers

Retail Sales—Selected Retailers   Statistics Canada tracks information concerning retail sales volume. These statistics are normally viewed as a lead indicator foreshadowing overall trends in the economy. Swings in retail sales will usually be reflected in the GNP.

Consumer Confidence and Spending   The Conference Board of Canada produces a quarterly report on consumer attitudes that has proven to be a fairly reliable indicator of future economic trends. If attitudes are positive and consumers are aggressive in the marketplace, increased expenditures on goods and services will normally result.

Consumer Disposable Income/Debt   The ability of consumers to expend dollars in the marketplace relates to both the amount of disposable income (used for acquisition of goods and services), and overall household debt load (ability to pay for acquisitions). A rise in disposable income, coupled with high consumer expectations and lowering debt loads, normally result in economic growth.

The Consumer Price Index (CPI)   The CPI is a combined measure of both the forces of *supply* and *demand* in the marketplace. The CPI, often incorrectly labeled as the cost of living index, measures the price of goods and services relating to 600 items which are commonly purchased by an average family living in a metropolitan area. The CPI contains a price index for new houses (labour and material prices only; land value is not included), as well as a rental index. The Consumer Price Index and related sub-indices are valuable indicators as they:

- Quantify family expenditures;
- Provide input on price trends; and
- Reflect current inflationary trends.

Indicators and Statistical Analysis

Real estate practitioners require an awareness of statistical techniques used in economic analysis. Unfortunately, data can be manipulated to accentuate certain facts or provide credence to a specific point of view. Conversely, certain worthwhile measures genuinely assist the reader in analyzing data and identifying trends.

Indexes   Economists frequently utilize indices to show the change of a particular indicator over time. A base year is selected, and all subsequent years are compared as a percentage of the base. A hypothetical housing index for Anycity is illustrated in Figure E.5.

ANYCITY HOUSING INDEX

BASE YEAR: 1980

YEAR	HOUSE PRICES	% CHANGE
1985	$100,000	0%
1990	$115,000	15%
1995	$130,000	30%
2000	$145,000	45%

This example is called a simple index, however, not every index is derived in this basic manner. Complicated mathematical calculations utilizing weighted means, standard deviations, and moving averages may be required.

Figure E.5   Anycity Housing Index

Seasonally Adjusted   Occasionally economists want to take the peaks and valleys out of data (i.e., seasonal variations in production or employment due to time of year). By averaging seasonal fluctuations, it is possible to reveal underlying trends. Seasonally adjusted figures are normally used when comparing data within one year. Unadjusted figures are more commonplace in year-to-year analysis.

Three Month Moving Average   In order to minimize monthly fluctuations some statistical reports provide a three month moving average, which is normally calculated as follows:

REPORTING MONTH	MONTHS INVOLVED AND HOUSING UNITS SOLD	3 MONTH MOVING AVG.
March	Jan. 200; Feb. 300; Mar. 400	300
April	Feb. 300; Mar. 400; Apr. 500	400
May	Mar. 400; Apr. 500: May 600	500

A moving average should not be confused with a quarter to quarter change (one three-month period compared to another).

Weighted Average   Occasionally economists will work with weighted, as opposed to simple, averages.

Example   Economics–Market Indicators Weighted Average

Two-storey homes command $180,000, split levels $150,000, and bungalows $120,000. Therefore, the simple average of house sale prices is $150,000. However, further investigation reveals that these figures were derived from 100 sales (40 bungalows, 40 split levels, and 20 two-storeys). The true average price should reflect the higher activity in the lower price ranges. Therefore, the weighted factors are:

Bungalows	.40 (40 out of 100) x $120,000 =	$48,000
Split Levels	.40 (40 out of 100) x $150,000 =	$60,000
Two-Storeys	.20 (20 out of 100) x $180,000 =	$36,000
Combined Weighted Average		$144,000

Graphs/Charts   Lastly, caution is advised when reading business statistics and studying graphs and charts—appearances can be deceiving. Two charts portraying the same information can appear dramatically different if the incremental values on the vertical axis are altered as illustrated in Figure E.6.

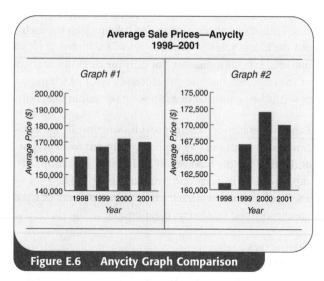

Figure E.6   Anycity Graph Comparison

Market Dynamics

Supply/Demand Forces

The dynamics of the marketplace determine price through the interaction of supply and demand. In a perfect world, the forces of supply and demand dictate the most favourable price, as buyers and sellers negotiate freely in the marketplace. Markets in this perfect world would be completely unfettered from intrusion, permitting exchange based solely on universal supply/demand principles. The

Canadian economy is far removed from such an unencumbered structure. Real estate is but one of numerous interconnected markets comprising the overall economy, others include the stock market, the commodities market, the capital market, and the labour market.

Demand is demonstrated in markets throughout the country by the quantity of goods or services that buyers are capable of acquiring at various prices. Supply, representing the opposing force, embodies the quantity of goods or services that sellers are capable and willing to produce at various prices.

Under perfect market conditions, when the price of a product falls, the demand for that item will increase and, conversely, as the price rises, the demand is progressively weakened. This interplay of price and quantity sold is diagrammatically represented by supply and demand curves as illustrated in Figure E.7. The optimum point at which supply and demand curves intersect is said to be *market equilibrium*. A shift in either supply or demand will alter the equilibrium and, therefore, affect what is referred to as the *balanced price*.

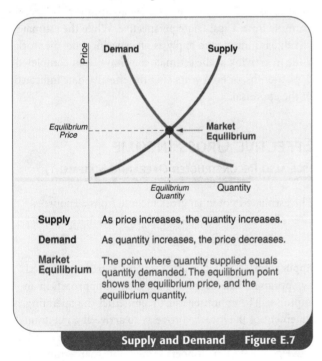

Supply	As price increases, the quantity increases.
Demand	As quantity increases, the price decreases.
Market Equilibrium	The point where quantity supplied equals quantity demanded. The equilibrium point shows the equilibrium price, and the equilibrium quantity.

Supply and Demand   **Figure E.7**

Market Equilibrium

Economists have traditionally explained the operation of the economy in terms of market supply/demand curves and creation of a perfect equilibrium, where prices paid and value received reflected a true exchange. An underlying assumption exists that market forces constantly seek absolute parity between production (supply), and utilization of services and goods (demand). Traditional economic theory held that a natural tendency existed for market

mechanisms to operate efficiently, ensuring optimum balance, and producing the fairest market prices. Consequently, the system would function to the best advantage of society as a whole. This philosophic perspective has changed substantially during the twentieth century.

The modern economy is a more complex picture of competing forces, which defy simple interpretation through equilibrium doctrine. In fact, contemporary industrial economies, including Canada, wrestle with instabilities as opposed to balance in the marketplace. This is due, in no small part, to the intrusion of competing factions nurturing pre-determined concepts of what constitutes a *just* economic system. Most notably, disputes arise over the allocation of rewards to meet certain political, social, or economic aspirations. As a consequence, simple concepts of supply, demand, and equilibrium become entwined with the potential for almost unlimited obstructions to the free flow and pricing of goods and services.

Government Intervention

The government represents a primary interruption to the natural forces of supply and demand. Interference from federal, provincial, and municipal levels of authority is visible from several perspectives.

Spending Policies   Governments can directly impact the market through its acquisition of goods and services, thus directly affecting the natural forces of demand as follows:

- By the issuance of government contracts to purchase supplies;
- By intrusion in the capital markets to support federal or provincial expansion programs;
- By the establishment of lending policies and related monetary policies.

Similarly, in the case of supply, marketing boards may withhold product to artificially *peg* the balanced equilibrium and dictate market prices. Further, government departments may control the use of specific raw resources or limit exploration for these substances.

Crown Corporations   The mere existence of government owned companies influences the natural supply and demand equation in the economy. Government economic objectives and social policies are often inextricably tied to decision-making processes. For example, the decision for a crown-owned airline to service certain remote areas may be based on political/social objectives, as opposed to economic reality. Therefore, the allocation of resources is directed in a manner which would not have otherwise occurred under the auspices of pure economic principles. Governments have undertaken the privatization of selected Crown corporations.

Taxation The government allocates economic benefit through its taxation policies. Certain groups within society will pay proportionately more taxes to support social policies, which they may neither want nor expect to utilize. Conversely, the government may introduce incentives to promote the production or acquisition of goods and services, to the detriment of other social goals.

Statutes/Regulations Governmental policies affect practically every aspect of Canadian life. Regulations and statutory laws monitor, direct, and control countless transactions in Canada on a daily basis through such things as production specifications, environmental requirements, duty and export directives, and price controls, to mention a few.

EDUCATION

Provincial See applicable reference materials for education requirements leading to licensing/registration under the appropriate provincial act.

EFFECTIVE AGE

The estimated age in years as indicated by the condition and utility of a structure based on the age of structures of equivalent utility, condition, and remaining life expectancy, as distinct from chronological age. See **Figure E.8.**

If a building has had better than average maintenance, its effective age may be less than its actual age. If there has been inadequate maintenance, it may be greater. A 40-year-old building may have an effective age of 20 years due to rehabilitation or modernization. The effective age is an important consideration in appraisal as it affects the amount of depreciation deducted when estimating value by the cost approach.

Example *Effective Age*

Buyer Jones is acquiring Smith's home, built 20 years ago. The appraiser is attempting to establish the value of the property for lending purposes and is preparing a form report. Based on the condition of the property, the appraiser estimates that Smith's home has an effective age of only 15 years. The lower effective age is due to various improvements that Smith has put in the property: e.g., new kitchen cupboards, addition of a second full bathroom, new carpeting, and updated decor in most principal rooms.

Figure E.8 visually demonstrates effective age in relation to economic life and actual age.

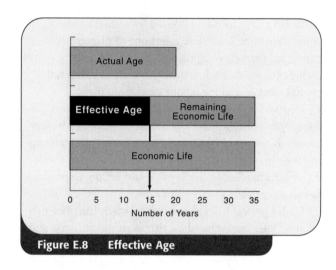

Figure E.8   Effective Age

EFFECTIVE DATE

The day or date upon which something occurs or ceases to occur.

Application The effective date of an appraisal is a good example from a real estate perspective. While the estimate of value is indicated to apply as of a specific date, the work done in arriving at the estimate may have been completed days, months, or even years after the effective date indicated in the appraisal.

EFFECTIVE GROSS INCOME
(SEE ALSO RECONSTRUCTED OPERATING STATEMENT)

The estimated potential gross income from all sources after allowance to cover losses due to vacancies and bad debt.

Application Effective gross income is frequently used by appraisers when applying the income approach in an appraisal. The appraiser must reconstruct the operating statement of the income property to arrive at a net annual operating income that is then capitalized to arrive at value (see **Figure E.9**). Practitioners should note that terminology concerning calculation of income and expenses is not standardized. For example, individuals involved with real estate investment analysis frequently use the term *gross operating income* as opposed to *effective gross income*.

EFFECTIVE INTEREST RATE
(SEE ALSO MORTGAGE MATHEMATICS)

The true rate of interest charged on a loan.

```
Appraiser's Reconstructed Statement
(Partial—Income Portion Only)


Rent Collections
18 1-bedroom units x $600/month x 12      129,600
78 2-bedroom units x $750/month x 12     +702,000
                                          831,600

Add: Ancillary Income
Parking—96 spaces x $40/month x 12         46,080
Laundry—96 x $20/month x 12                23,040
Total                                     +69,120

Gross Income                              900,720

Less: Vacancy and Credit Losses           −27,000

Effective Gross Income                   $873,720
```

Effective Gross Income Calculation   Figure E.9

Example   *Effective Interest Rate*

Buyer Jones is seeking a personal loan that a private lender is prepared to advance if the rate of interest (nominal rate) is 10% per annum. However, the lender wants the loan interest compounded semi-annually. In fact, the rate is 5% for each of the two periods. Using the compounding formula, Jones discovers the difference between nominal (stated) and true (effective rates).

A = Compounded Amount
P = Principal
N = Number of Periods Expressed as a Power
1 = A Unit of Value
I = Interest Rate per Compounding Period.

Therefore:
$$A = P(1+I)^N$$
$$= P(1 + .050)^2$$
$$= \$10,000 \ (1.05)^2$$
$$= \$10,000(1.1025)$$
$$= \$11,025.00$$

The interest received by the lender due to the two compounding periods was $1,025. Therefore, the effective rate of interest on the $10,000 borrowed was 10.25%.

Application   The stated or nominal interest rate is most commonly discussed in the marketplace and normally refers to the interest rate charged on a loan without consideration for any compounding that occurs during the time period. If no compounding takes place, the stated (or actual) and effective rates would be the same. The effective rate takes into consideration the impact of compounding and consequently produces a higher, true rate of interest.

Effective rates are particularly important in relation to mortgages. For real estate practitioners, most discussions with consumers concerning mortgages centre on the nominal or stated rate. As with all loans in which compounding occurs, the effective rate is higher than the stated rate. However, the *Interest Act* sets out specific requirements concerning how the effective rate is calculated on mortgages involving blended monthly payments. The federal statute dictates that if a mortgage has blended principal and interest payments, the interest must be *calculated annually* or *semi-annually, not in advance*. The net effect of this requirement is to reduce the effective rate through no more than two compounding periods per year and such compounding cannot be calculated in advance.

Without delving into the complexities of calculating semi-annual not in advance payments, a simple example using a personal loan will illustrate the difference between nominal and effective rates. If an amount is compounded on an annual basis, the nominal and effective rates are the same. However, when compounding occurs more frequently, the effective rate rises above the nominal. In the example, the difference is 0.25%.

EFFECTIVE RENT

Most commonly used with commercial leasing and the comparison of true costs associated with different leased premises. As a generally accepted definition, effective rent (based on the tenant's perspective), includes the contracted base rent plus all additional costs, less any concessions and allowances. Effective rent is typically calculated based on the annual, as opposed to the monthly rent. Effective rent can also be expressed as a rate, e.g., annual rate per square foot. The calculation of either effective rent or rate is most commonly associated with tenant cash flows. However, effective rental calculations can also be developed from the landlord's perspective.

Effective rents can also be calculated from either before tax or after tax perspectives. The effective rate is usually calculated based on rentable area as opposed to useable area, but advanced packages provide comparisons using both approaches.

Application   When representing tenants, commercial practitioners develop detailed cash flow estimates and effective rents for selected properties to generate accurate comparisons involving various offerings. Understandably, given the wide variety of lease arrangements, each calculation of effective rent has its own distinct considerations. Historically, effective rent simply referred to rental amounts (contracted base rent *plus* all additional rents *less* any concessions and allowances). Detailed comparisons are now possible given the proliferation of software packages, advanced financial calculations, and the ability to manipulate variables and develop alternate scenarios. The following items are considered when developing effective rents.

Tenant Costs   Tenant costs include all tenant-paid improvements, moving costs, buy out from a previous lease, and operating costs including provisions for escalations based on the CPI or other formulae. Normally, out-of-pocket expenses by the tenant that would apply to *any* new location would not be included in the calculation, but no rigid rule exists regarding this issue.

Landlord Costs   Concessions and allowances by the landlord are included, e.g., free rent, improvement allowances, moving allowances, and any other concessions provided to the tenant. Concessions and allowances can either be shown in the calculations or netted against tenant costs.

Cash Flow Before Tax   Detailed cash flow estimates are typically included. The sum of contracted rent, plus all tenant costs, less landlord costs produces a cash flow analysis (before tax occupancy cost), for successive years in the lease term.

Total and Annual Effective Rents

Both annual and total effective rents are usually provided. The total effective rent refers to the sum of all expenditures over the lease period, while the annual effective rent involves expenditures for one specific year.

Discounted Effective Rents

Effective rents can be discounted based on a market-extracted discount rate. Advanced programs include this ability as it ensures accurate comparisons of various leasing arrangements by accounting for the timing of cash flows throughout the lease term. The calculation typically acknowledges the timing of lease payments including the allocation of various costs and concessions/allowances depending on the particular year and month in which they occur. When calculating the discounted effective rent, most costs are typically entered on a cash accounting basis with no consideration for the amortization of such costs. In selected instances, tenant improvements may be amortized over the lease period.

Cautions

Two important cautions are necessary regarding effective rent calculations:

- Effective rent for the tenant (user) will often vary from effective rent for the landlord (investor). For example, various costs identified may not be paid to the landlord, but relate solely to the tenant, e.g., moving

expenses in the relocation process. In this instance, the effective rent for the tenant would be higher than the effective rent for the landlord (assuming the landlord had no offsetting concession or allowance). Practitioners must clearly identify whether the tenant's or landlord's perspective is being examined, as well as detailing relevant factors under consideration. Generally, most references to effective rent relate to the user (tenant) and not the investor (landlord) unless otherwise noted.

- Divergent terminologies and procedures exist within the marketplace. For example, commercial landlords frequently calculate the net effective rent over the term of the lease when comparing competing lease proposals. Leasing expenses, concessions, and allowances are prorated over the term of the lease and the net effective rent to the owner (excluding additional rent) is calculated on an annual square foot/metre basis. Any calculation of effective rent should clearly detail any definitions, assumptions, and calculations used. At all times, the commercial practitioner must ensure consistency when calculating effective rent to ensure accurate comparisons.

EFFICIENCY APARTMENT

A small apartment without a separate bedroom usually with less than a standard-sized kitchen.

EFFICIENCY FURNACE
(SEE FURNACE)

EFFICIENCY RATIO

A *rule of thumb ratio* commonly associated with commercial property and more specifically, the leasing of office space. The efficiency ratio refers to the percentage of total building square footage in relation to its net leaseable area. Net leaseable area is broadly defined as all areas of the building excluding elevators, common washrooms, hallways, maintenance closets, building management offices, facilities for heating and cooling, and other areas not specifically included within tenant-leased areas.

Practitioners are cautioned as no standard procedures exist in regard to the calculation of efficiency ratios. Further, methods used to measure net leasable area can vary as well as associated terminology. For further discussion, see **Rentable Area, Rentable/Useable Factor**, and **Useable Area**.

Example   *Efficiency Ratio*

Developer McKay is constructing an office building consisting of 50,000 square feet on five floors. The net leaseable area for each floor (excluding hallways, common washrooms, elevators, and other support/service areas), is 8,300. The efficiency ratio for this building is:

$$(5 \times 8,300) \div 50,000 = .83 \text{ or } 83\%$$

EFFLORESCENCE

A whitish mineral deposit sometimes seen on the interior of foundation walls.

Application   The presence of efflorescence suggests moisture penetration, although its existence does not tell a great deal about severity or whether the problem is active. Water passing from the outside through the wall dissolves salts in the masonry, concrete or mortar, and arrives on the inner surface with various minerals. A crystalline salt deposit is left as water evaporates from the surface of the wall. Efflorescence can pose certain problems for real estate practitioners both in listing and selling property.

Example 1   *Efflorescence–Listing Property*

Salesperson Lee is completing an exclusive listing agreement on Smith's property. Accompanied by the seller, Lee enters the basement to take various measurements of the improved areas, namely a family room and a finished three-piece bath. In one corner of the basement, a whitish substance is evident on an exterior block wall next to the gas furnace.

The salesperson makes a point of discussing the potential moisture problem with Smith, however, the seller is concerned that this information will affect the home's saleability and wants the situation ignored. Lee explains that water leakage is a significant fact and that both he and the seller could be liable if this information was not shared with prospective buyers. Smith, now with a better understanding of the situation, agrees to remedy the problem before marketing his property.

Example 2   *Efflorescence–Purchasing Property Subject to Home Inspection*

Buyer Jones completed an inspection of a residential property at 110 Main Street. While seriously interested, he noticed efflorescence in the corner of the basement. The salesperson, noting this concern, suggested that a home inspector view the property. Accordingly, the following clause was inserted in the agreement/contract.

Continued…

This offer is conditional upon the inspection of the subject property by a qualified home inspector and the obtaining of a report satisfactory to the buyer at the buyer's own expense. Unless the buyer gives notice in writing delivered to the seller by 12:00 P.M. on the 1st day of May, 20xx that this condition is fulfilled, this offer shall be null and void and the deposit shall be returned to the buyer in full without deduction. The seller agrees to co-operate in providing access to the structure for the purpose of this inspection. This condition is included for the sole benefit of the buyer and may be waived at the buyer's option by notice in writing to the seller within the time period stated herein.

EGRESS

A means of exiting a building or property.

Application   Provisions regarding egress from residential units are detailed in provincial building codes. Particular emphasis is placed on upper and lower storey egress within smaller residential property. In commercial, multi-residential, and other investment grade properties, detailed regulations concerning egress are normally grouped under exit requirements such as exterior doorways, passageways, ramps, stairways, and fire escapes.

Egress also relates to the attractiveness of specific tracts of land. The value of many commercial properties is directly related to visibility and accessibility. Easy, clearly-marked entrances and exits provide for better traffic flow and typically translate into improved business potential. Difficult entrances, median obstructions, one-way streets, or limited access near major intersections can pose significant problems for retailing operations.

ELECTRIC FURNACE
(SEE FURNACE)

ELECTRICAL DISTRIBUTION PANEL
(SEE DISTRIBUTION PANEL)

ELECTRICAL INSPECTION

An inspection of the electrical system in either residential or commercial properties that is normally conducted by representatives of the appropriate local power utility or an electrician who reports to that local utility. Procedures vary by province including whether a charge is levied, the amount of that charge, and specific services offered.

ELECTRICAL MAIN DISCONNECT

A disconnect switch used to provide or shut off all power in a structure. Switch handles are located on the outside and main fuses or breakers are inside. Hydro authorities often seal the cover on the main disconnect.

Application   The main disconnect is frequently incorporated into the distribution panel. In some structures, the main disconnect is simply a box that stands alone. In either case, the rating on the main disconnect box itself must be at least as large as the service entrance cables and fuses inside. For example, if a house has a 100-amp service, a main disconnect box rated for only 60 amps is not acceptable. More than 60 amps passing through this main disconnect may lead to overheating.

ELECTRICAL SERVICE ENTRANCE CABLE

Electrical service provided by overhead or underground wires from the street supply to the structure.

Application   A typical house has 240 volts brought in through overhead or underground wires from the street supply. A normal system is composed of three wires. The black and red wires are live, and the white wire is neutral. The potential between the black and white wire is 120 volts, as well as between the red and white wires, however, between the black and red, the potential is 240 volts. Incidentally, the red wire often has black sheathing.

The size of the service entrance cable determines how much electricity is available. Either copper or aluminum cable may be used. Aluminum connections should be coated with an anti-oxidant, grease-like material, to prevent rusting.

ELECTRICAL SERVICE (RURAL)

Electrical services in rural areas are impacted by unique circumstances owing to geographic distances and isolated locations. Consequently, certain additional costing factors must be considered.

Application   Provincial utilities, in servicing rural areas, will install primary lines along dedicated/accepted road allowances for properties such as seasonal cottages up to a

pre-determined distance. Any additional costs are normally borne by the customer. The utility company also typically provides secondary lines on the customer's property for a pre-determined distance (referred to as free wire), with additional costs borne by the customer.

Certain costs may be reduced if electrical and telephone services are installed at the same time. For marine cables, the user must obtain a separate quotation. However, the use of marine cables has been dramatically curtailed owing to environmental considerations.

Reference   Questions concerning procedures and quotations for the provision of electrical services in rural areas should be directed to the appropriate utilities office.

ELECTRICAL SERVICE SIZE

The size of the electrical service (amps) provided from the primary line to the building. As the power enters the house, it travels into a main disconnect with two fuses or two circuit breakers, sometimes connected together to look like one big breaker. One fuse is for the black wire and one fuse is for the red. No fuse is necessary for the neutral wire. The fuse is rated by the amperage that the wire can safely carry (60 amps, 100 amps, etc.).

Application   Service entrance cable size will determine service size, however, the two fuse ratings on the main panel are normally reliable in determining that size. Two 100 amp fuses in that main disconnect, for example, would normally indicate a 100 amp service—the two fuses are NOT added together. However, certain exceptions apply and caution is recommended. Real estate practitioners can also encounter 60 amp services in older residences. While this service size is adequate for normal household lighting and small appliances, heavy appliances in conjunction with the operation of normal appliances can exceed the maximum load. Many institutional lenders are unwilling to finance a home with 60 amp service, unless the electrical service is upgraded.

Again, it is important to emphasize that one cannot add the two fuse ratings together to get the house service. Increasing the service size means replacing the wires coming from the street to the house, and providing a new main disconnect. If the wires run overhead, the conversion is not normally a major undertaking. However, if the wires are underground, a problem may present itself if the conduit through which the wires are passed is not large enough to hold a larger set of wires. This would mean excavation and replacement of the conduit. The appropriate utilities office should be contacted.

ELECTRIFIED FLOOR

For real estate purposes, commercial practitioners use this term when referring to a floor containing ducts that house telephone and power lines, and emerge from the floor at frequent intervals for easy installation of telephones and power equipment.

ELECTROMAGNETIC FIELDS

Acronym: EMF   Over the years, many studies on electric and magnetic fields and their effect on humans have been completed worldwide. Some studies have shown certain biological responses. Some have indicated a possible association between electric and magnetic fields and human health effects while others have not. The world-wide scientific community has not reached a definitive conclusion on this topic.

While power utilities are sensitive to public concerns regarding possible health effects from electric and mag-netic fields, at present, no conclusive scientific evidence exists to justify modification of existing practices or facil-ities for the generation, transmission, and distribution of electricity. At the same time, exposure remains an issue.

Recommended exposure limits to prevent acute health effects have been put forth by an international committee of experts. The recommended exposure limit is 5 kV/m and 1 Gauss for 24-hour exposure of the general public.

Reference   Contact the local power utility and public health authority for additional information regarding current research studies.

Nature of Electric and Magnetic Fields

Fields found near any device that transmits, distributes, or uses electricity are often referred to as *extremely low frequencies (ELFs)*. ELF fields are at the low frequency end of the electromagnetic spectrum. Electric fields are measured in units of kilovolts per metre (kV/m) and are related to the voltage on the conductor, whereas magnetic fields, measured in milliGauss (mG) or microTesla (uT) are pro-duced by the flow of current in the conductor.

Electric fields may be produced by an appliance that is plugged into an electrical outlet regardless of whether or not the appliance is operating. Magnetic fields are produced only when the appliance is operating, that is, when current is flowing. Electric fields do not easily penetrate most materials and are usually shielded or reduced by buildings and other obstacles. Magnetic fields, however, penetrate most materials quite readily. Both electric and magnetic fields decrease in strength very rapidly as distance from the source increases.

Power Delivery Systems

To understand electromagnetic fields, practitioners must appreciate the process by which electricity is delivered to a home. The objective of an electrical power delivery system is to provide an uninterrupted supply of electricity to the consumer in a safe and cost-effective manner.

For real estate practitioners, the entire power delivery system is best visualized through three major elements: generation, transport, and end use.

Generation   The process by which raw energy is harnessed and converted to electricity.

Transport   The process of transporting electricity from the point of generation to the ultimate point of delivery occurs in two basic steps: transmission and distribution. Electric transmission lines, which carry large blocks of electrical energy from the generating station are familiar sights, and are often distinguished by towers that support the lines. A transmission line's route ends at a substation, where the energy is parcelled out into smaller blocks, and routed into neighbourhoods along distribution lines. The electricity carried on transmission lines is characterized in terms of voltage and current. The flow of electricity on a transmission or distribution line can be compared to the flow of water through a pipe. The pressure driving the water is the counterpart to the voltage on the electrical line, and the water's rate of flow in the pipe is the counter-part to the electric current on the line. Transmission and distribution lines operate at constant voltages and the currents on these lines fluctuate according to load demands.

End Use   Electricity used by consumers at home, school, or work constitutes the last stage of the energy's journey from its point of generation. At every stage in that journey, the transportation and use of electricity produces electric and magnetic fields. These fields result from the voltages and currents applied to our power delivery systems, as well as from all end uses of electricity, including lights, kitchen appliances, electric blankets, power tools, television sets, and computers.

ELEVATION

The exterior of a structure, usually viewed from the front or as otherwise identified, e.g., side or rear elevation.

E

EMINENT DOMAIN

The right of a government or municipal quasi-public body to acquire private property for public use. Eminent domain is acquired through a legal action called condemnation or expropriation in which the appropriate body determines the use is a public use and decides the price or compensation to be paid to the owner.

The expropriating authority is the Crown or any other agency empowered by provincial legislation, namely an expropriation act. Legislation typically sets out procedures for application to expropriate, appropriate hearings, and methods of compensation.

Example   *Eminent Domain*

Smith's property is situated directly in the path of a new transportation route that will include highway and rail facilities, along with open space buffer zones, given rapid population expansion within the immediate area. The provincial government is acquiring property for this public use.

Accordingly, Smith's property falls under eminent domain and through condemnation is taken over by the government body. Smith is compensated based on prevailing market values within the immediate area.

Provincial   See applicable reference materials for provincial procedures relating to expropriation and condemnation.

EMPLOYER HEALTH TAX

Acronym: EHT   A tax overseen by the Ministry of Revenue in the Province of Ontario relating to provision of provincial health services. Funding for such services will vary by provincial jurisdiction.

Provincial   See applicable reference materials.

EMPLOYMENT

Issues concerning employment typically fall to provincial jurisdictions. General information is provided concerning employment applications, contracts, and overall parameters of employment legislation. Detailed information is included under *Brokerage Management*.

Applications for Employment

Organized real estate does not provide a standardized *Application for Employment* form. Guidance can be obtained from Human Resources Development Canada or the local employment services office.

If brokerages use customized application forms, such forms must comply with guidelines set out in applicable provincial employment legislation and related statutes, particularly in regard to the type of information requested of prospective employees.

Employment Contracts

In a real estate brokerage, a contract is often established between a salesperson and an employing brokerage setting out the terms of employment.

Provincial associations may provide standard employment contracts for both employees and independent contractors acting in the capacity of sales representatives for brokerages. Brokerages often customize portions of these agreements to meet individual circumstances. Terms of employment are subject to federal and provincial legislation and any changes must comply with such provisions. While commission salespeople are usually hired either as employees or independent contractors, the reader is cautioned that for purposes of most provincial real estate acts, salespeople are employees and duly authorized representatives of the brokerage.

Schedules attached to employment agreements can address a wide range of information. The following represent topics frequently found in such schedules:

- Designated office for salesperson and related matters;
- Anniversary date for commission calculation and contract renewal;
- Commission split arrangements;
- Desk fees; and
- Fixed or variable expenses paid by salesperson.

Provincial   See applicable reference materials for further details on the use of salesperson employment contracts, brokerage policies, and employment-related provincial legislation.

Interviewing

The employment interview for a sales position is designed to accomplish several objectives. First, the interviewer must determine the applicant's sales abilities and compatibility with staff, existing sales force, and overall corporate goals. Second, the interviewer should portray a favourable image of the brokerage to the interviewee. Third, the interviewer must clearly inform the candidate of specific duties and responsibilities of the job and brokerage policies.

Initial interviews should be scheduled for a time when the interviewer can have an uninterrupted private session with the applicant. The professional manager realizes that this is an ideal opportunity to get important facts and should carefully plan what to do and what not to do. See Figure E.10.

Qualities to Assess Assessing potential applicants for a sales career is a difficult task. Following are some generally accepted positive factors that can provide guidance.

- Knowledge of the market area;
- Good communication skills;
- Previous sales experience;
- Knowledge of real estate;
- Average to above average educational background;
- Persistence and ability to deal with rejection;
- Self motivation;
- Empathy;
- Ego drive and the need to achieve;
- Personal organization and clearly defined goals;
- Self determination; and
- Personal and financial security.

The *Do's*	The *Don'ts*
Provide proper surroundings and ensure privacy.	Don't rush or hurry the applicant or the interview.
Listen carefully and watch for positive and negative answers given.	Don't allow interruptions or outside disturbances.
Keep on track and watch for positive and negative qualities.	Don't repeat any questions. Have a prepared list.
Stay alert and watch for body language.	Don't force the speed of the interview.
Obtain exact dates and information about the applicant and check inconsistencies.	Don't avoid the truth. Tell the applicant of expectations (hours, dress code, etc.).
Provide a clear and concise picture of the brokerage and the expectations of management.	Don't oversell the job or its opportunities.
Probe into past employment history to understand the applicant's true patterns of behaviour.	Don't make the decision on the initial interview.

Interviewing Do's and Don'ts   Figure E.10

Temporary Employment

Brokerages will occasionally use temporary help during peak periods and summer vacation months. A statement concerning this status is provided as **Figure E.11** to ensure that no confusion exists relating to the temporary nature of the employment. Specific forms or procedures concerning temporary employment may be required by provincial legislation.

When hiring minors, certain rules apply. Further, most provinces have passed legislation to ensure that persons between the ages of 6 and 16 years must attend school during prescribed daytime hours. Even beyond the normal school day, provinces have regulations concerning the employment of such persons.

Provincial   See applicable reference materials.

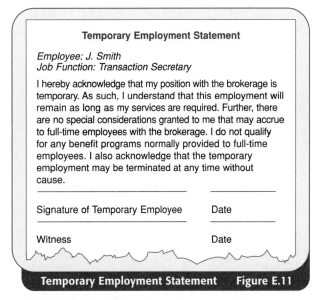

Temporary Employment Statement

Employee: J. Smith
Job Function: Transaction Secretary

I hereby acknowledge that my position with the brokerage is temporary. As such, I understand that this employment will remain as long as my services are required. Further, there are no special considerations granted to me that may accrue to full-time employees with the brokerage. I do not qualify for any benefit programs normally provided to full-time employees. I also acknowledge that the temporary employment may be terminated at any time without cause.

Signature of Temporary Employee   Date

Witness   Date

Temporary Employment Statement   Figure E.11

Termination

Brokers and managers are strongly advised to seek legal counsel concerning correct procedures for terminating employees, licensed/registered or otherwise. Further, employment agreements currently used should be reviewed to ensure adequate remedies for the employer, along with proper provisions for termination.

Provincial   See applicable reference materials.

EMPLOYMENT INSURANCE
(SEE ALSO SOURCE DEDUCTIONS)

Acronym: EI   Effective January 1, 1996, *Employment Insurance* replaced UI (Unemployment Insurance). The new system provides Canadians with basic income protection, plus a range of new re-employment benefits to help unemployed workers get jobs.

Reference   Contact the nearest office of Human Resources Development Canada—Human Resource Centre for additional details.

ENCROACHMENT

The unauthorized intrusion onto the lands and property of another.

Application   The right to an encroachment by one land-owner over an adjoining owner's property is sometimes granted by express written agreement, e.g., when a window sill, eave, deck, porch, or chimney extends over a side yard area. This is particularly common in older urban areas where side yards can be particularly narrow. When the overhang is no longer present, the encroachment ceases to exist. No right to substitute an encroachment exists if one is lost, except by further agreement.

E

Example   *Encroachment*

Salesperson Lee, when listing Smith's property, is reviewing various documents and notes an apparent encroachment involving one of the accessory buildings. Smith acknowledges that the garage encroaches a few feet on a public right-of-way. However, he adds that the municipal by-law enforcement officer has acknowledged the fact and felt that the municipality would not require its relocation. In any event, a local contractor would do the job for approximately $1,000 if it was necessary.

After some discussion, Lee insisted that a reference to the encroachment be included in the listing. The *Remarks* section read as follows:

Beautifully maintained and upgraded home only 10 minutes drive from Southville. Note: Single-car garage encroaches on right-of-way. Estimated cost to move: $1,000. Call listing salesperson for further information.

ENCROACHMENT AGREEMENT

An agreement permitting the encroachment of an improvement onto an adjoining parcel of land that may be registered against the title of both properties affected by the encroachment.

Application   Under an encroachment agreement, the owner whose land has been encroached upon by the improvement essentially forebears from exercising his/her legal right to require the improvement be removed from the land. Encroachment agreements are often encountered where one owner has inadvertently built a building, fence, or driveway over adjoining land.

An encroachment agreement may contain provisions that call for the removal of the offending improvement upon the happening of a future event, e.g., destruction by fire or wind, or by a specific time. The market value of the property may be adversely affected to the extent that a risk exists and/or that the offending improvement might have to be removed at a certain time or in the event of partial or full destruction by fire or other cause.

ENCUMBRANCE

Outstanding claim or lien recorded against property or any legal right to the use of the property by another person who is not the owner.

Application   Encumbrances are frequently referred to in relation to mortgages registered against the title to a property. However, the term has a much broader scope including anything that places a burden on property title including a lien, mortgage, or other registered interest (e.g., rights-of-way, restrictions, and covenants). Preprinted agreements/contracts contain standard wordings (as illustrated), concerning the acquisition of property free of encumbrances except minor encumbrances or those specifically referenced. Exact wordings vary by provincial jurisdiction.

TITLE: Provided that the title to the property is good and free from all registered restrictions, mortgages, liens, and encumbrances except as otherwise specifically provided in this agreement…

Provincial   See applicable reference materials.

ENERGY CODE
(SEE NATIONAL ENERGY CODE)

ENERGY CONSERVATION
(SEE ALSO NATIONAL ENERGY CODE)

Any program established for reducing energy waste and promoting sound conservation policies.

Application   Energy conservation relating to residential and commercial structures involves various provincial and federal energy ministries/departments. The reduction of energy consumed reduces environmental impact associated with both energy production and consumption. National energy codes have been developed by the *Canadian Commission on Building and Fire Codes* and published by the *National Research Council of Canada* as models setting out minimum standards for houses and buildings. These detailed models are designed as guidelines for new construction. Under the *Constitution Act*, regulations concerning buildings are provincial and territorial responsibilities. The models are designed to assist the provinces and territories in performing their mandates while promoting consistent approaches to energy conservation.

ENGINEERING BREAKDOWN METHOD

A method of estimating accrued depreciation under which separate estimates are made for individual components of a structure and then totalled. This method is more commonly referred to as the **Observed Condition (Breakdown) Method**.

ENVIRONMENT
(SEE ALSO CANADIAN ENVIRONMENTAL PROTECTION ACT)

Environmental issues increasingly impact real estate practitioners. Provincial ministries/departments provide excellent resource pamphlets and publications as background information for real estate practitioners.

Assessment

An environmental assessment is broadly defined as a systematic and comprehensive process involving the identification, analysis, and evaluation of the environmental effects of proposed projects. Provincial ministries/departments typically work in concert with professional organizations and suppliers of environmental services to develop common assessment procedures. The overall goal is to establish and ensure effective, rational, and compatible processes for assessment throughout a given jurisdictional area.

Audit

Buyers may require an environmental audit to assess overall environmental condition prior to purchase, as hazards and contamination can represent a significant risk. Lenders contemplating financing of such acquisitions will also normally seek similar assurances. While audits are typically associated with industrial and commercial lands, their use can be relevant to a wide range of property types and related circumstances. Environmental audits are broadly grouped under three levels of analysis, referred to as *phases*. A brief overview of each is provided.

Phase 1   Visual inspection combined with a review of owner documents, registry information, ministry/department records and certificates, and other relevant environmental records. A Phase 1 audit determines if reasons exist to believe that a property may have some form of environmental contamination.

Phase 2   More costly investigation involving various tests, hazardous waste assessment/analysis, and soil/water sampling. A Phase 2 audit determines the scope of environmental problems along with recommendations for remedial action.

Phase 3   The final phase involves detailed remedial steps and costs associated with circumstances identified in Phase 2.

Provincial   See applicable reference materials.

Checklists

Environmental concerns affect every transaction, beginning with listing property through to negotiating and closing. Provincial associations and regulatory bodies have established checklists or other guidelines in relation to provincial environmental legislation to assist practitioners in identifying potential problem areas.

Clauses

No single wording in an agreement/contract can address all environmental situations. However, seven considerations are primary when drafting such clauses:

- Compliance with appropriate laws, regulations, and other related requirements;
- No hazardous conditions or substances exist;
- No limitations or restrictions exist affecting the use of the property;
- No pending litigation, outstanding department/ministry orders, investigations, charges ,or prosecutions;
- No prior use as waste disposal site;
- All applicable licences in force; and
- Documents, records, and reports will be provided on request.

Example   *Environment—Clauses*

Salesperson Martin, a buyer representative, is inspecting a 5-acre tract of land with a potential buyer. While prior owners/occupants are not referenced on the listing, the condition of the property suggests previous industrial uses even though the land is currently used to store intermodal shipping containers.

The salesperson expresses concerns after noting the lower portion of the land is strewn with debris and an abandoned block structure is located near the gated entrance. Accordingly, when drafting an offer, a condition precedent is inserted, along with an appropriate waiver provision, allowing the client 90 days to verify that:

Continued…

This offer is conditional upon the Buyer determining, at the Buyer's expense that: All environmental laws and regulations have been complied with, no hazardous conditions or substances exist on the land, no limitations or restrictions affecting the continued use of the property exist, other than those specifically provided for herein, no pending litigation respecting environmental matters, no outstanding orders, investigations, charges or prosecutions by the [insert name of provincial ministry/department] *respecting environmental matters exist, there has been no prior use as a waste disposal site, and all applicable licences are in effect. The vendor agrees to provide to the purchaser on request all documents, records, and reports relating to environmental matters in possession of the vendor. The vendor further authorizes the* [insert name of provincial ministry/department] *to release to the purchaser, his agent or solicitor, any and all information that may be on record in the ministry office with respect to the property.*

Provincial   See applicable reference materials.

Federal/Provincial Responsibilities

Federal and provincial governments share the legislative responsibility for protecting the environment. Each has developed environmental management legislation and administrative processes to fulfill respective mandates. Since this can result in overlap and duplication, the two governments often agree to co-ordinate their efforts and as such the Canadian Council of Ministers of the Environment was established to further this inter-jurisdictional co-operation. In 1990, the Council adopted a statement that called for a commitment by each government to act while respecting the jurisdiction of other governments, recognize each other's strengths and capabilities, co-operate in a spirit of partnership, and provide timely notification and appropriate consultation where one jurisdiction's legislation, policies, or programs affect those of another jurisdiction.

Hazards

Environmental issues, and more specifically environmental hazards, are significant factors in real estate transactions. Practitioners must ensure accurate information is provided and due care is taken in directing consumers to seek expert advice. Fortunately, specialists are available to assist, e.g., environmental auditors and environmental lawyers.

No easy method exists to categorize significant hazards. In some instances, hazardous conditions have not gained widespread public awareness or condemnation, conse-

quently, real estate salespeople are challenged with everyday marketplace negotiations compounded by vagueness and ambiguity.

Environmental hazards are not restricted to commercial and industrial users. Various hazardous products are usual to the average household and caution is advised. Hazardous waste depots are provided in most urban areas for dropping off such items as automotive spray paints, glues, cement, paint strippers, enamel or oil-based paints, latex and water-based paints, stains, finishes, insecticides, herbicides, rat and mouse poisons, thinners, turpentine, unused medicines, nail polish remover, wood preservatives, and rust removers. Hazardous products should not be disposed of as ordinary garbage or poured down drains. Considerable literature is available at the federal, provincial, and municipal levels to provide guidance on such matters.

Reference   Significant environmental hazards impacting real estate practitioners are listed under appropriate headings, e.g., Asbestos, Lead, Radon, Electromagnetic Fields, Urea Formaldehyde Foam Insulation, and Polychlorinated Biphenyls (PCBs).

Legislation

Environmental legislation involves both federal and provincial statutes and has become an increasingly important component when listing and selling real estate. Most land use regulations involving environmental matters fall to the provinces. The goal of provincial legislation can be broadly described as preventing environment damage and ensuring that the environment is protected for future generations. This goal is attained through various measures including public participation in environmental decision-making, procedures to assess impact of developments on the environment, and controls/regulatory requirements concerning such developments. Ministries/departments operating under provincial acts are generally mandated to further sound environmental planning and investigate matters concerning pollution, waste management, and waste disposal.

Provincial   See applicable reference materials.

Risks in Listing/Selling

Duties and responsibilities of real estate professionals do not normally extend into the complex world of environmental legislation, or an understanding of the intricacies of environmental laws and technical complexities of environmental problems. At the same time, an awareness of potential hazards and a general knowledge of key environmental provisions legislated to combat them is beneficial in everyday real estate negotiations with consumers.

Four recommended steps are outlined to minimize risk concerning environmental issues:

- Be well informed (keep updated, learn about the issues, and watch for environmental matters affecting the local market area);
- Ensure honesty/fairness in negotiations (inquire, investigate, verify, and disclose);
- Draft accurate agreements/contracts; and
- Seek expert advice when necessary.

Testing

Provincial jurisdictions have various organizations and procedural systems for the testing of such items as water quality, air quality, and hazardous waste assessment/analysis. Both public and private sector organizations can be involved in meeting the needs of business, industry, government and the general public.

Provincial   See applicable reference materials.

EQUITABLE MORTGAGE

The most common form of equitable mortgage from a real estate perspective is a mortgage of the equity of redemption. If an owner mortgages a property, he/she retains the right to the equity of redemption. This right, as an *interest* or *estate*, can be dealt with as any other interest. More importantly, this interest can be transferred to a mortgagee in return for funds. The subsequent mortgage gives way to a further equity of redemption that can again be mortgaged, and so on.

Application   Legally, numerous successive equitable mortgages can exist on the same property with the owner retaining a final equity of redemption to the last mortgage given. From a practical perspective, the giving of equitable mortgages will ultimately be limited by the amount of equity available to mortgage.

If the first mortgage is a legal mortgage, the second is against the equity. The second mortgagee, therefore, has a desire to see his/her interest protected. Two rights are associated with this subsequent mortgage holder:

- The right to ensure that no default occurs in the first mortgage.
  If the mortgagor fails to make payments on time, pay taxes, or insurance, the second mortgagee may pay these to stave off action by the first mortgagee. He/she will then add these amounts to the debt of the respective mortgage. Action could be taken on the initial amount plus all other overdue payments and expenses.

- The right to be notified.
  If a mortgagee takes foreclosure action, he/she must sue not just the mortgagor, but all subsequent encumbrancers to successfully foreclose all equities. The subsequent encumbrancers are notified and can take steps to protect their interests. If the mortgagee proposes to sell under power of sale, he/she must similarly notify all subsequent encumbrancers.

Provincial   See applicable reference materials.

EQUITY

Ownership interest in the assets of an entity after deducting its liabilities. The balance sheet contains an owner's equity or shareholder's equity section that includes, in the case of the latter, types of share capital, contributed surplus, and retained earnings.

Application   For real estate purposes, equity typically refers to the difference between the market value of the property and the mortgages, and liens, against the property.

Example   *Equity*

Buyer Jones has just completed an appraisal on his home purchased approximately four years ago for $225,000 with a first mortgage of $150,000. Assuming that Jones paid fair market value for the property, his equity was:

$225,000 – $150,000 = $75,000

The recent appraisal has now placed the value of his property at $241,000, owing primarily to improvements made to the home since the purchase. Further, the balance owing on the first mortgage now stands at $147,500. Jones' equity in the property has increased from $75,000 to $93,500:

$241,000 – $147,500 = $93,500

EQUITY CAPITALIZATION RATE
(SEE ALSO CAPITALIZATION)

A capitalization rate expressing the relationship between cash flow and the equity invested in a property, that is usually obtained from research involving the sale of comparable properties.

EQUITY FINANCING

Mortgages given based primarily on the equity of the property with secondary consideration for the covenant of the borrower.

E

Example   *Equity Financing*

Buyer Jones is acquiring a fully occupied 96-unit apartment complex that provided the previous owner a consistent net annual operating income (before debt service), of $350,000 over each of the past seven years. Jones, having a substantial downpayment, requires a first mortgage of $2,000,000. The purchase price is $4,900,000.

The lender is prepared to advance funds by way of a first mortgage at 8% amortized over 20 years and due in five years. The annual mortgage payments are $198,805.80. The debt service represents approximately 57% of anticipated net annual operating income. Given the sizeable downpayment and the past financial performance of the building, the lender is not focused on Jones' personal covenant, but rather on the significant equity position in the property and the resulting high cash flows to address annual debt service.

EQUITY LOAN

(SEE EQUITABLE MORTGAGE)

EQUITY OF REDEMPTION

The right of the mortgagor to reclaim clear title to the property upon full repayment of the debt. This right is granted to mortgagors but is extinguishable under foreclosure.

Example   *Equity of Redemption*

Buyer Jones acquires a property at a purchase price of $150,000. For ten years, he makes regular payments of $1,206.41, principal and interest, on an 8% mortgage in the amount of $100,000 amortized over ten years. Upon completion of 120 payments, Jones has retired the debt. A discharge of the mortgage is prepared and registered on the title to the property and Jones, as mortgagor, exercises his equity of redemption and reclaims clear title to the property.

EQUITY TAKEOUT LOAN

A term generally referring to the mortgaging of equity in property for a variety of reasons. Individuals may borrow money from their equity through arranging new financing or renegotiating existing mortgage(s).

Application   Equity takeout loans rely more on the equity position of the owner and the actual security, with GDS and TDS considerations often taking a more secondary position in the qualifying process. A basic guideline for lenders is maximum equity takeout of 70% (loan to value ratio) for any property under consideration.

Property Value	$150,000
Equity	−100,000
Existing First Mortgage	$ 50,000
Maximum Equity Loan (70%) (.70 x 150,000)	**$105,000**

Example   *Equity Takeout Loan*

Owner Smith has a mortgage-free cottage and wishes to purchase a home near his work. Smith's credit rating is very good but, given only minimal downpayment, he is seeking an equity takeout loan on the recreational property. Smith is self-employed and operates as an independent trucker with his own rig. After all expenses, Smith's yearly income has varied between $76,000 and $80,000 over the past four years.

Cottage Value	$80,000
Equity Takeout	−40,000
Downpayment for House	$40,000
PIT Monthly Payment on Cottage Equity Loan	$ 413.76
PIT Monthly Payment on House Mortgage	+937.37
Total Monthly Payments	$1,351.13
Total Annual Payments ($1,351.13 x 12)	$16,213.56
Income Required to Qualify **($16,213.56 ÷ 30 x 100)**	**$54,045.20**

Smith used his equity takeout to secure a downpayment, acquire the city house, retain the cottage and property, and qualify under the lender's 30% GDS ratio for both loans.

EQUITY YIELD RATE

An appraisal term relating to the rate of return applicable on the equity portion of a real estate investment over a specified holding period.

Application   For real estate investment analysis, the equity portion refers to the capital provided by an investor in acquiring property, as distinct from the debt component. The *equity yield rate* is a measure of return based on initial capital invested in relation to projected operations and sale proceeds cash flow over a specified holding period. The *mortgage yield rate* is the comparable rate of return for the debt portion of the investment.

Equity yield rates are typically calculated on a before tax basis, but nothing prevents analysis based on cash flow after tax. Most appraisal activity involves the former, with commercial practitioners often comparing after tax positions for specific clients (referred to as *after tax* equity yield). Equity yield rate should be clearly distinguished from the equity capitalization rate which expresses the relationship between a single year's operating income and expenses and capital invested. Similarly, the mortgage yield rate (interest rate on the mortgage), should be differentiated from the mortgage capitalization rate.

EQUIVALENT UTILITY

The concept of equivalent utility is applied in most buyer decisions and is found in the principle of substitution within the appraisal field. A buyer of real property will normally compare properties offered for sale that provide equivalent utility and will acquire the one that can be purchased at the lowest price. The principle of substitution states:

> *When a property is replaceable, its value tends to be set by the cost of acquiring a similar and equally desirable property, provided there is no delay in making the acquisition.*

The buyer is not only comparing specific features, but also the equivalent utility of these attributes, with cost being the underlying factor.

Example   *Equivalent Utility*

Buyer Jones is comparing two different properties. Home A has approximately 2,600 square feet on the main and upper levels with an asking price of $248,000. Home B is approximately 300 square feet smaller and lacks a main level family room. However, it has a beautiful, spacious recreation room on the lower floor and Jones, with a growing family, is primarily interested in space. Best of all, Home B is priced at $220,000.

Applying the concept of equivalent utility, Jones is primarily concerned with finished area in the home as opposed to location of the family room. Accordingly, cost becomes the major factor and Home B is selected.

ERRORS AND OMISSIONS INSURANCE
(E & O INSURANCE)

Insurance coverage relating to professional liability arising from the activities of professionals such as architects, engineers, lawyers, real estate practitioners, accountants, and insurance brokers. Insurance plans designed for real estate practitioners typically cover financial loss due to errors, omissions, or negligent acts occurring in the course of duties as brokers and salespersons. Mandatory E & O insurance is a growing trend within provincial jurisdictions. Terms and conditions, extent of coverage, exclusions, and claim reporting procedures will vary.

Provincial   See applicable reference materials.

ESCALATION CLAUSE

A clause in a contract providing for increases or decreases in rent payments in accordance with fluctuations of certain direct costs or expenses of the landlord (e.g., property taxes) or determined using an appropriate economic indicator or index.

In leases, provisions may exist for the rent payment to be increased during the term, or at renewal of the contract. A lessee may be required to pay a gross rent, as well as any additional increase in the real property taxes attributable to that portion of the property occupied by the tenant. This increase normally applies to additional taxes over a stated year, commonly referred to as the base year. Alternatively, a lease may contain provisions for increases tied to the Consumer Price Index (CPI) or various sub-indices published by Statistics Canada.

ESCHEAT

The reversion of property to the state or some agency of the state in the event that the owner dies leaving no will and having no legally qualified heir to whom the property may pass by lawful descent.

Escheat remains as one of few examples in existence today of the old tenurial relationship. The owner, as tenant to the Crown who retains paramount claim to all land within the realm, is not able to fulfill the services required during tenure. Therefore, the land escheats to the lord and original grantor.

Provincial   See applicable reference materials.

ESCROW

A written agreement between two or more parties providing that certain instruments relating to property be placed with a third party to be delivered to a designated person upon fulfillment or performance of some act or condition.

Application   The escrow process, particularly popular in the United States, varies based on state laws. For example, in some jurisdictions, escrow can only be handled through an attorney. In others, the process of escrow can be administered by a title insurance company representative.

The escrow agent handles matters concerning the purchase of the property including deposit monies, the agreement, and all paperwork relating to the transaction. Once requirements are fulfilled, the escrow agent closes the transaction and the property is transferred.

> **Example** *Escrow*
>
> Buyer Jones, a Canadian, has purchased a property in Florida, where an escrow officer can be used to close the sale. The officer is an employee of the title insurance company issuing the title policy on Jones' new property and the escrow officer will receive all documents and monies for the transaction. At close of escrow, the escrow officer provides a buyer's closing statement plus the deed to the buyer and the seller's closing statement plus funds received by the seller.

ESTATE
(SEE ALSO OWNERSHIP)

An interest in land or more specifically the degree, quantity, nature, and extent of interest that a person has in real property. The historical background of an estate lies in the development of British law. The status of the person holding a land interest (a tenant), for a lord of the land (a landlord), became known as an estate in the land.

When disputes arose involving interest in property, traditionally, they were brought before the royal courts and decisions ultimately formed part of common law. Property disputes specifically became known as real actions involving real estates. In modern language, the term *estate* is now used to define concepts of interests in, or rights to deal with, land and its components. Estates can be classified under several general headings.

Estate to Uses

The estate to uses concept was at one time a method of holding ownership. Normally, such ownership was obtained by deed, will, or possession. Estate to uses flowed from trust ownership in which title was in the name of a registered owner who may have held title as a trustee for the real or beneficial owner.

This concept gave rise to *estate to uses* where ownership was held for a future buyer and was often used to avoid a dower right. Dower right has been largely replaced by provincial legislation concerning spousal rights in regard to land ownership and, consequently, estate to uses has fallen into disuse.

Fee Simple

The highest estate or absolute right in real property. The holder of such an estate has the most rights and fewest limitations and can use, sell, lease, enter, or give away the property, or refrain from any of these rights. This bundle of rights, known as ownership, is subject to restrictions imposed by laws of governing authorities.

Fee Simple With Conditions

Fee simple can be created so that it terminates under certain conditions. A determinable fee simple is one that automatically terminates on the occurrence of some event, which may never happen. While prevalent historically, such arrangements are infrequently found and may be considered contrary to law and public policy.

For example, a tract of land might be dedicated for educational purposes and would revert back if such use was ever terminated. Another example of fee simple with conditions would be a grant from the grantor to Smith and his heirs so long as the property is used as a farm. The fee simple interest will cease and the land will revert to the grantor or the heirs if the land ceases to be used as a farm.

> **Example** *Estate–Condition Contrary to Public Policy*
>
> Fee simple may be granted subject to a condition, and if the condition is breached then the grantor can put an end to the estate. Assume that the deed provided a tract of land to Jones and his heirs on condition that Jones does not marry Smith, then on Jones' marriage to Smith the grantor could re-enter the property. However, as earlier referenced, many such historical restrictions would now be in contravention of public policy and/or law.

Fee Tail

An historical fee that restricted the inheritability of land to a limited class of heirs, such as the eldest male. Such provisions, often found in old deeds/wills, are no longer valid.

Future Estate

Future estates normally arise with life estates. Since a life estate is not everlasting, a large portion of the fee simple remains when the life estate ends. This remaining portion is called a reversion when the grantor of the life estate reserves the balance for himself. If, however, the grantor gives the balance to a third party, the remaining portion is called a remainder.

The life estate and the estate in remainder co-exist. The life tenant and the person entitled to the remainder both have an interest in the property from the beginning of the life estate. The difference is that the person with the remainder cannot use the property so long as the life estate exists, while the life tenant is restricted in what he/she can do with the property. In a general sense, the life tenant is responsible for current obligations and has the benefit of current assets while the ultimate owner has the capital benefits and obligations. If, however, the life tenant and the person with the remainder are in agreement, the property may be dealt with in any manner they choose, e.g., sell the property, tear down buildings, or dig up the land, because their combined interests form the entire fee simple.

Leasehold Estate

A leasehold estate is an interest in land for a definite period of time—a week, a month, a year, 99 years, or any other specific period of time. The estate cannot, however, be longer than the estate from which it was granted. In a leasehold estate, the person to whom the interest is granted is called the lessee or tenant, and the grantor of the interest is called the lessor or landlord. These individuals are governed partly by old established rules of common law and partly by provincial tenancy legislation.

Life Estate

A grantor in a deed or will may grant an interest in the lands to someone for a lifetime period. That interest will cease on the death of the named individual: for example *to Jones for his life*. The grantor may specify rights and obligations that affect the life tenancy, e.g., use of the land, limitations on alterations/improvements, and payment of usual expenses such as taxes and maintenance. This type of estate often arises under the terms of a will.

Example   *Estate–Life Estate*

Seller Smith wishes to provide a life estate but wants to codify various rights and obligations that affect the life tenancy. Jones, the life tenant, has exclusive right of possession, use, profits, enjoyment, and rents derived from the land. The land can be leased, but the lease will terminate upon the life tenant's death, as a higher ownership interest than that which is enjoyed cannot be granted.

Jones cannot commit waste and, therefore, cannot cut down trees, except for incidental general maintenance. He cannot cut down the apple tree in the back yard, but he can enjoy the apples. If valuable minerals exist below the surface, Jones could not mine on that property. If Jones elected to plant a crop, he could reap that crop including the last crop by his heirs upon his death. Jones cannot remove fixtures but is required to pay realty taxes and all maintenance.

Smith will pay capital expenses such as fire insurance and the principal amount of any mortgage against the property. Jones pays the mortgage interest. In a general sense, the life tenant is responsible for current obligations and has the benefit of current assets, while Smith as the ultimate owner has the capital benefits and obligations.

ESTOPPEL

A bar to alleging or denying a fact because of one's own previous actions or words to the contrary.

Application   The concept of estoppel comes into play with agency relationships. Such a relationship can arise when a person's conduct is such that another person acts upon a reasonable inference that the relationship exists.

The person is then estopped from denying the relationship. The relationship cannot be denied if it was the person's own conduct that led to a reasonable, but inaccurate conclusion. For example, a principal may be estopped because the principal's conduct of allowing that person to be his agent prevents the principal from denying that he/she gave the authority. Estoppel may also arise:

- When no actual authority was given to an agent;
- When only a limited authority was given; or
- Where the authority has been terminated but the circumstances lead others to believe that the agent has full authority.

This gives the agent an apparent or ostensible authority to act. The principal will be bound by contracts made with third parties who acted in good faith.

The apparent authority that an agent may have in a specific instance will depend on the nature of the business involved, local laws, and trade customs. For example, a mercantile agent who has possession of goods may have authority to pledge them for credit. A stock broker may be able to borrow against bearer certificates in his/her possession. A real estate broker, in some jurisdictions, may be able to sign an agreement/contract on behalf of the seller, however, a real estate broker is usually empowered to trade in real estate by assisting in the formation of contractual relationships between a seller and buyer. This apparent authority is not as extensive as that of other types of agents.

ETHICS
(SEE ALSO CODE OF ETHICS (CREA))

Rules of behaviour established, periodically modified, and accepted by business to provide fair, honest, proper and moral practice.

Provincial   See applicable reference materials.

EVICTION

The forced removal, by legal means, of a tenant from the leased premises.

Provincial   See applicable reference materials.

EXCESS LAND

A site that is larger than standard where the additional size does not provide proportional utility or proportional increase in value.

Example   *Excess Land*

As a basic illustration of the concept, consider two lots zoned for single-detached homes both with 40' frontages. Lot A, which is 120 feet deep, is usual to the area and lot B is 145 feet deep. The two properties sell for $45,000 and $47,800 respectively as the additional depth does not proportionately add to value and is therefore viewed as excess land from a valuation point of view. To more accurately quantify the excess nature of this land, consider the square footage of both lots in relation to their value. Lot A has a total of 4,800 square feet, while Lot B is approximately 21% larger with a square footage of 5,800. However, the price for Lot B is approximately 6% higher.

EXCHANGE

A real estate transaction in which one property is traded for another but the transaction may or may not require additional consideration.

Application   In practice, finding two properties that are identical in terms of equal utility is difficult. Therefore, most exchanges involve the payment of consideration by one of the parties to compensate for such difference. While exchanges are not common in the Canadian marketplace, traditionally, listing agreements have provided for such an eventuality, e.g.,

> *I* [name of seller] *hereby give you the exclusive and irrevocable right to act as my agent to lease, sell* **or exchange** *[bold inserted] the said property…*

Wordings for listing authorities vary by real estate board as well as provincial jurisdiction.

Provincial   See applicable reference materials.

EXCLUSIVE AGENT

(SEE ALSO AGENCY)

Generally defined as one who has the exclusive rights to sell, lease, or exchange the property owned by another for a fixed period. The exclusive authority is granted to the real estate brokerage named in the listing agreement.

An MLS exclusive listing agreement has a similar wording but provides an additional authority for the brokerage to co-operate with other brokerages who are members of that real estate board, or as otherwise defined, to assist in the marketing of the property.

Application   The authority, along with other preprinted clauses within the listing agreement, normally provides that all marketing of the property, negotiations with the seller, and other matters relating to the marketing process be conducted through the exclusive agent until expiry of the listing. An exclusive authority is contrasted with a non-exclusive or open listing in which any number of brokers might be involved in marketing the property with a commission paid to the successful brokerage upon an agreement being signed and the completion of that sale.

Example   *Exclusive Agent*

Salesperson Lee has completed an exclusive listing agreement with Seller Smith. The authority granted by the listing is exclusive. Following is an excerpt from the preprinted listing form:

> *In consideration of your listing my property known as 123 Main Street in the City of Anycity, I hereby give you the exclusive and irrevocable right to act as my agent to lease or sell the property until 11:59 p.m. on the 23 day of May, 20xx…*

The increased use of buyer agency representation in a real estate transaction has given rise to exclusive agency relationships with the buyer. Wordings for both listings and buyer representation agreements vary by real estate board as well as provincial jurisdiction.

Provincial   See applicable reference materials.

EXCLUSIVE LISTING

An exclusive listing involves the giving of the sole right to sell the described property according to the terms of the agency agreement.

Application   Under an exclusive listing, one brokerage is authorized by the seller to sell the property during a specific time. If the property is sold during that time, the brokerage receives a commission. With this form of listing, only the brokerage with whom the agreement is signed may sell the property and receive the commission, however, the brokerage has the option of co-operating with other brokerages.

Provincial legislation typically sets out requirements for a listing, signatures related thereto, and delivery of copies. An MLS listing is a special form of exclusive listing where co-operation with other brokers is specifically addressed.

Provincial   See applicable reference materials.

EXECUTIVE PROPERTY MANAGER

A person directly responsible for all management policies, procedures, and employees in a property management firm.

EXECUTOR/EXECUTRIX

A person appointed by the testator to carry out the provisions of the testator's will. While Executor/Executrix are familiar to most people, the term *estate trustee* is now commonly used in most provincial jurisdictions.

Application While legal issues concerning executors go beyond normal real estate practice, certain guidelines should be followed. In dealing with executors of an estate, practitioners must be sure that all executors of the estate sign the agreement/contract. Should only one of two (or more) do so and even though such person may purport to have the authority to do so, a valid and enforceable contract may not exist.

To ensure validity, an agent should insist that all executors sign and should seek a notarized copy of probate documents to ensure that all have signed. As well, the trustees must have a power to sell under the will, since in certain circumstances the beneficiaries under the will may have to sign as well. Whenever doubt exists, the salesperson should request the solicitor for the estate to confirm who the representatives of the deceased are, and who is empowered to sign all contracts, including listings and agreements.

If a person dies leaving no executor, the court will make an appointment. When a death occurs and no will exists (dying intestate), the court will confirm arrangements by appropriate documentation. If a valid will exists but an executor was not named, the court will address this situation. The distribution of the deceased's assets can then proceed subject to various statutory regulations and provisions.

The reader is reminded that legal terminologies and procedures differ by provincial jurisdiction. Legal advice is strongly recommended on all matters concerning executors.

EXPANSION JOINT

An opening designed for expansion that is located between independent segments of a structure, e.g., in walls, floors, and/or roofs. Exact locations and distances between expansion joints will vary, based on the type of structure and the location, e.g., more frequently in vertical walls than roof areas. **Figure E.12** provides a cross-section of a foundation wall including an expansion joint.

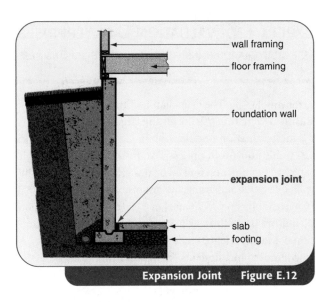

Expansion Joint   Figure E.12

EXPENSE RATIO
(SEE ALSO FINANCIAL RATIOS)

A ratio reflecting the mathematical relationship between expenses and income.

EXPENSE STOP

The point at which a landlord *stops* paying selected operating expenses in a commercial lease and the tenant assumes payment of those expenses.

Application The expense stop is one of several factors to consider in analyzing a tenant's cash flow when negotiating a lease. Dependent on market conditions, the landlord may offer various incentives (concessions and allowances), that improve tenant cash flow, normally for a pre-determined portion of the lease period. The expense stop sets out the maximum landlord contribution concerning any or all of the concessions.

Example   *Expense Stop*

Salesperson Ward is representing a commercial tenant and is comparing various offerings in Anycity. In one of the properties under consideration, Landlord Wilson agreed to pay for HVAC (heating, ventilation, and air-conditioning), to a maximum of $2,000 yearly and, above that amount, the tenant would be responsible.

In the yearly cash flow analysis, Ward must allow for this expense stop and estimate the tenant's HVAC expense for each year of the lease to arrive at an accurate analysis. Salesperson Ward is then in a position to compare this offering with others in the marketplace.

EXPERT EN EVALUATION D'ENTERPRISES
(SEE ALSO CANADIAN INSTITUTE OF CHARTERED BUSINESS EVALUATORS)

Acronym: EEE   The Canadian Institute of Chartered Business Valuators (CICBV) is the largest professional business valuation organization in Canada. Established in 1971, this non-profit professional Institute promotes high standards in business and securities valuations. The CICBV trains, certifies, and grants the professional designation CBV (Chartered Business Valuator) or EEE (expert en evaluation d'enterprises) to those who have met the Institute's educational and experience credits.

Members and students are drawn from industry, accounting firms, independent valuation firms, investment dealers, and government regulatory agencies. Members determine the current worth, or its components, of any type of business.

Reference   For details regarding the CBV program, contact the Canadian Institute of Chartered Business Valuators, 277 Wellington Street West, Toronto, ON M5V 3H2.

The above information was summarized from detailed materials provided by CICBV with no representation concerning its accuracy or completeness. Contact CICBV for current requirements.

EXPIRED LISTING

A signed authority that has expired either as an exclusive or an MLS listing.

Application   An expired listing is frequently referred to as an unsold expired listing. Provincial legislation does not normally address record keeping methods or other requirements concerning the storage of expired listings, however, real estate brokerages typically have established guidelines regarding such matters.

EXPRESS AUTHORITY

A precise instruction, either in writing or orally, in which an authority is granted.

Application   In real estate terms, express authorities normally apply to listing situations. An authority delegated by the principal clearly sets forth in exact, plain, direct, and well-defined limits those acts and duties that the agent is empowered to perform on behalf of the principal. If there is a definite understanding between the principal and agent, then the agency relationship has been established by express agreement. This may be oral, in writing, or in writing under seal. An exclusive listing agreement between an owner of real estate and a real estate brokerage is an obvious example of written express authority.

Provincial   See applicable reference materials.

EXPROPRIATION

Provincial   See applicable reference materials.

EXTERNAL OBSOLESCENCE

A loss of value arising from external factors that influence the property either by affecting the marketability of the property and/or its utility. External obsolescence is commonly grouped under two types: *locational obsolescence* relating generally to factors in close proximity to the subject property and *economic obsolescence* regarding more generalized conditions in the community that affect the property.

EXTERNALITIES, PRINCIPLE OF
(SEE PRINCIPLES (APPRAISAL))

EXTRAPOLATION

The projection of certain statistical trends beyond the known based upon selected variables and the assumption that such variables will continue into the future.

Example   *Extrapolation—Average Price*

Broker/Owner Johnson is reviewing average prices for single-family residential homes in Anycity.

Year	Average Price	% Change
1997	173,000	
1998	179,920	+ 4.0%
1999	187,117	+ 4.0%
2000	193,666	+ 3.5%

Johnson assumes that future market conditions are similar but places most emphasis on year 2000. Accordingly, he extrapolates based on a projected rate of 3.5%.

2001	200,444	+ 3.5%
2002	207,460	+ 3.5%
2003	214,721	+ 3.5%

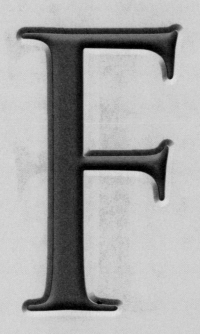

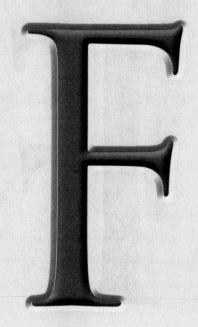

F

National Info Links

Farm

For national agricultural/farming initiatives and programs, contact:

> Agriculture and Agri-Food Canada
> Web Site   www.agr.ca

For provincial agricultural and farming legislative matters contact the appropriate provincial ministry/department.

Farm and Agricultural Financing

> Farm Credit Corporation
> 1800 Hamilton St. P.O. Box 4320
> Regina, SK S4P 4L3
>
> Telephone   (306) 780 8100
>   (877) 332-3301
> Web Site   www.fcc-sca.ca

Farm credit corporation offices are located in various areas across Canada. Contact the corporate head office or web site for addresses and telephone numbers.

Fire

For national fire research and related codes, contact:

> The Institute for Research in Construction (IRC)
> Web Site   www.nrc.ca

For provincial fire protection/prevention regulations, see applicable provincial reference materials.

Flood Damage/Control

For national flood damage initiatives, contact:

> Environment Canada
> Web Site   www.ec.gc.ca

For province-specific information, contact the appropriate provincial ministry/department or local conservation authority (if applicable).

FACTORS OF PRODUCTION

(SEE ALSO ECONOMICS)

Components, also referred to as *agents of production* and *factors in production*, used in the production of wealth, income, or services that can be sold for money. Factors of production include labour (natural resources), management (co-ordination), capital, and land.

Labour has the first claim on the gross income from any enterprise. The costs of *labour* include wages, salaries, and benefits, such as health insurance and employment insurance. Costs of *co-ordination* follow labour and involve entrepreneurial incentive together with those services necessary to co-ordinate the other three factors and weld them into a productive unit. The cost of *capital* refers to payments for the use of capital, and interest on and

amortization of investment concerning buildings, equipment, and furnishings, but not land. Lastly, a claim for *land* is made against the residual portion of the gross income.

Application In appraisals, factors of production are used where applying the principle of surplus productivity. This principle states that when the net income remaining after all expenses necessary to the operation have been paid and the capital invested in improvements has been satisfied, the remainder is imputable to the land and tends to fix its value. The land is valuable according to the surplus productivity imputable to it. More simply put, the land is only as valuable as the income that can be attributed to it after all expenses have been addressed.

Figure F.1 illustrates the successive levels in which gross income is applied. The last of which is land.

F

Example *Factors Of Production*

Buyer Jones constructs an income-producing building on land that he owns and invests $1,200,000 of his own capital. In operating this business, Jones anticipates an annual effective gross income of approximately $400,000 based on prevailing vacancy and bad debt factors. From this income, three levels of return are addressed (labour, coordination, and capital), and a fourth (land) commands any residual following payment to the other factors.

Labour Jones must pay wages for property management which include remittances for such items as CPP and EI, where applicable.

Coordination Jones must make payments for various services necessary to operate the property, for example, public utilities, real estate taxes, insurance, supplies, and repairs.

Capital Jones must address an interest factor on capital invested in the improvements along with a return of that capital over a stated period of time.

Land Last in order is the return on the land. Jones cannot attribute any net income to the land unless all other factors have been met; hence the term *residual* applies to this factor.

Following is Jones' income property along with a calculated value of the land based on the factors of production discussed and the principle of surplus productivity.

In this example, Jones' capital investment for the building and improvements is $1,200,000, labour costs are $40,000; coordinating costs amount to $180,000; capital requirements for the improvements are 10% (interest factor) and 2.5% (recapture of capital over 40 years), making a total of 12.5%; and, the residual to land is $30,000. For purposes of this example, the capitalization rate is .10 when estimating the land value.

Gross Annual Income	$400,000
Labour	−40,000
Coordination	−180,000
Capital (12.5% x $1,200,000)	−150,000
Residual/Surplus Attributable to Land	$ 30,000
Value of Land (30,000 ÷ .10)	**$300,000**

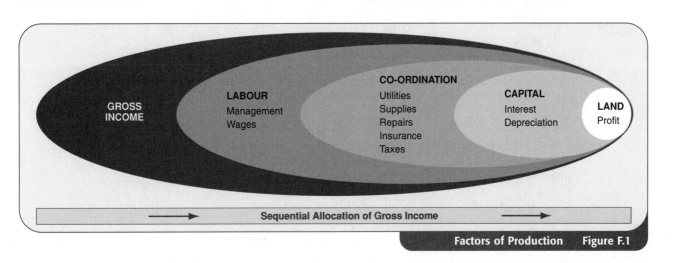

Factors of Production   Figure F.1

FAIR HOUSING PRACTICES

Provincial   See applicable reference materials.

FAIR MARKET VALUE
(SEE MARKET VALUE)

FALSE AND MISLEADING ADVERTISING
(SEE ALSO ADVERTISING)

Statutory regulations and common law address a host of consumer-driven concerns about advertising practices. Professional organizations have also developed codes of conduct to set higher standards in this regard.

Application   The Canadian Real Estate Association (CREA) *Code of Ethics and Standards of Business Practice* addresses false and misleading advertising. This code is adopted by all members of organized real estate as a requirement of membership in CREA, provincial real estate associations, and local real estate boards.

Article 18 of the Code of Ethics, along with associated interpretations is reproduced as Figure F.2 and provides guidelines on the matter.

Example   *False and Misleading Advertising*

Salesperson Lee has just completed a brief course in effective advertising and wants to empower his classified ads. Beginning with a powerful lead line is bound to attract attention. He quickly jots down several:

- *Fabulous Investment;*
- *Profit Guaranteed;* and
- *My Promise—You Can Live Rent Free.*

The ethical issue with all three headings is centred on true presentation. A real estate practitioner must ensure accuracy in all ads. Who knows whether the investment will be fabulous? To quote an old phrase: Hindsight is the best judge of any transaction. If Salesperson Lee uses *Profit Guaranteed*, he is entering the murky world of potential false representation. Who is prepared to guarantee profit from any venture? What about catastrophic events, sudden increases in mortgage rates, environmental hazards discovered on the property with remedial action required, etc.? Lastly, living rent free is a great idea; the personal promise is not.

Provincial   See applicable reference materials.

**The Canadian Real Estate Association
Code of Ethics and Standards of Business Practice**

ARTICLE 18

REALTORS shall ensure a true presentation in all advertising. Properties and services shall not be advertised without identifying the firm or, where applicable, the individual practitioner, in accordance with provincial licensing legislation.

Interpretations

18-1   The contents of a REALTOR's advertising, in any form, should accurately reflect the property or services being advertised. (Also applies to Article 25.)

18-2   A REALTOR should not advertise property in any form or in any medium in a manner that is contrary to the requirements of provincial legislation. (Also applies to Article 25.)

18-3   No REALTOR should advertise any property owned by himself or herself or by another person without identifying the REALTOR as a real estate practitioner, and such identification should be in the manner that may be required by the applicable regulatory legislation.

18-4   Interpretation 22-3 also applies to Article 18.

18-5   A REALTOR shall not use as search engine keywords for his/her Internet web sites, the trade names or trade marks of any firm, franchise, board or organization other than those with which the REALTOR is affiliated or otherwise authorized in writing to use.

Figure F.2   Code of Ethics–Article 18

FALSE REPRESENTATION

(SEE ALSO MISREPRESENTATION)

A false statement or assertion made by one party to the other, before or at the time of contracting, regarding some existing fact, matter, or circumstance affecting the contract. Misrepresentation is a false statement of fact.

Sometimes, it is difficult to distinguish between a representation and a mere exaggeration or statement of intention or opinion. The statement:

This is the best deal in town!

might be treated as a mere exaggeration, not giving rise to legal rights, although the *Competition Act* could render this statement a federal offense.

A representation is a specific statement made about a property, for example, an assertion that a property can be put to a certain type of use. If it proves to be false, it is a misrepresentation and is normally categorized as either innocent, fraudulent, or negligent. False representations may also be addressed in the applicable provincial real estate act/regulations.

FARM DEBT MEDIATION ACT

The *Farm Debt Mediation Act* is a federal statute enacted in 1998 that amends the *Agriculture and Agri-Food Administrative Monetary Penalties Act* and repeals the *Farm Debt Review Act.* The Act is designed to assist farmers who are, for any reason, unable to meet financial obligations as they become due, who have ceased paying current obligations in the ordinary course of business, or whose property is not, at fair valuation, sufficient to address payment of all obligations (due and accruing due), through a fairly conducted sale under legal process.

Application   Agriculture and Agri-Food Canada (AAFC) provides farm debt mediation services to insolvent farmers and their creditors pursuant to the *Farm Debt Mediation Act.* The Act sets out mediation and appeal procedures that promote resolution of insolvency issues without resorting to court proceedings, although parties retain recourse to the court should matters not be successfully resolved.

FARM DEBT REVIEW ACT

(SEE FARM DEBT MEDIATION ACT)

FARM LAND LEASING ARRANGEMENTS

Three common land leasing arrangements apply to crop land.

- Crop share lease;
- Cash rent lease; and
- Flexible cash lease.

In all three types, the landlord normally supplies the land, the grain storage, and pays the property taxes. The tenant pays the operating expenses and supplies the labour and machinery to farm the land.

The division of income varies with the type of leasing arrangement. In the case of a crop share lease, the most common division is one-third share of all crop sales to the landlord and two-thirds share to the tenant. The income is often divided as the crop is sold. In the cash rent lease, the tenant receives the income from the crop sales but pays the landlord a fixed amount each year as rent. Normally, the rent is paid in advance or by one-half payment in the spring before seeding and the balance in the fall after harvest of the crop. With a flexible cash lease, the tenant receives all the income from crop sales, but the dollar amount paid to the landlord varies with either the price of grain, the yield of grain, or both. This type of lease arrangement, which combines some of the features of the other two lease arrangements, provides some flexibility in rental rates and is important when sharp swings in grain prices occur within the marketplace.

Application   In farm leases, many issues arise that are particular to farm situations and not incurred in any other commercial lease. The following is provided for illustration purposes only and is not exhaustive in nature.

- Possible restrictions on the crops to be grown.
- Possible restrictions on chemicals to be applied to the soil.
- How the land is to be left at the end of the lease, e.g., fall tillage.
- How the drainage ditches or natural water courses are to be maintained.
- What erosion control practices must be used.
- Use of any of the buildings on the land, e.g., for grain storage.
- Adherence to weed control legislation provisions.
- Whether an incoming tenant can plow the land in the fall after harvest.
- Whether the tenant can remove the crop off the land the following spring after the termination of the lease.

F

In a crop share lease agreement, additional matters should be considered.

- Who will make the cropping decisions?
- Who will determine the amount of crop inputs to apply and how these costs shall be shared?
- The extent of crop insurance.
- Who will receive any government payments or subsidies?
- Who is responsible for the sale of the grain?

FARM LAND TAXATION

For income tax purposes, farm land is treated no differently than any other type of improved real property. On sale, any capital gain is subject to a tax on a percentage of the capital gain included in the seller's income. Further, if any depreciable property is sold as part of the real property, then any capital cost allowance previously claimed may be recaptured if the sale price exceeds the undepreciated capital cost.

However, two provisions in the *Income Tax Act* allow for income tax-free sales of farm property. The first is a sale by an individual to that individual's child, so long as the property involved is qualifying farm property. The second is a $500,000 capital gains exemption available to defer any capital gain realized on farm property regardless of whom the buyer is. This exemption also applies to shares of family farm corporations and interests in family farm partnerships. Treatment of farm property varies, depending on when the property was acquired. A test for how long the property must have been used in farming is different for property owned prior to June 18, 1987 than for property acquired after June 17, 1987.

Provincial   See applicable reference materials regarding property taxation.

FARM OFFER/AGREEMENT

Provincial   See applicable reference materials.

FARM OPERATING AGREEMENTS

An agreement in which individuals pool assets, labour, and management for the purpose of earning a profit, but assets are normally owned individually. Each operator in the agreement shares in the income and operating expenses of the joint operation in proportion to the assets, labour, and management contributed.

FARM QUOTA/SPECIAL CROP CONTRACT

Regulatory or other restrictions concerning the production and distribution of farm products. Many products are subject to regulated marketing through marketing boards or in some way controlled pursuant to production contracts with processors.

Application   Practitioners encounter farm quotas and special crop contracts in establishing value when listing and marketing farms. The value of a farm can be significantly affected in relation to whether or not an assignment of a quota or a production contract can be obtained. For example, a dairy farm without a milk quota is of little value, even if it has first-class milk production facilities. Practitioners should include, in any agreement of purchase and sale for a farm, specific conditions providing for successful transfer or assignment from seller to buyer of any quota, entitlement, or contract that the buyer requires to market the product for which the farm is organized. Marketing boards have their own transfer/assignment procedures and should be contacted directly for guidance.

FARMER

Any individual, corporation, co-operative, partnership, or other association of persons that is engaged in farming for commercial purposes. Source: *Farm Debt Mediation Act*, Consolidated Statutes of Canada, F 2.27, 1997, c.21.

FARMING

No universal definition exists for activities falling within the term *farming*. The *Farm Debt Mediation Act*, a federal statute, defines farming as follows:

- The production of field-grown crops, cultivated and uncultivated, and horticultural crops;
- The raising of livestock, poultry, and fur-bearing animals;
- The production of eggs, milk, honey, maple syrup, tobacco, fibre, wood from wood lots, and fodder crops; and
- The production or raising of any other prescribed thing or animal.

Definitions within provincial jurisdictions will vary. Source: *Farm Debt Mediation Act*, Consolidated Statutes of Canada, F 2.27, 1997, c.21.

FARMING (PROSPECTING)

A systematic method of prospecting used by real estate salespeople with the objective of developing an ongoing, long-term referral network of customers and clients.

Application Farming involves the selection of a specific territory (geographic or otherwise, e.g., social), and the development of that territory by the sales representative. The farm territory need not be large. A salesperson can develop a rewarding career in residential real estate sales with a base of as few as 200 to 300 homes. Most practitioners select a territory that they already know and enjoy working in. Obviously, an additional advantage is being known to at least some persons within the farming area. Regardless, the practitioner must become aware of, and totally familiar with, all the political, social, physical, and economic features of the entire territory.

The overall objective of *farming* is to become acquainted with everyone who resides within the area, make a good impression, and become indelibly established in their minds as the person who offers real estate services. The accomplishment of this goal means regular communication through an organized, logical system. Mailings, novelties, and institutional advertising are tools that can assist in this regard, but are only aids in the overall campaign. No substitutes exist for personal and friendly contact.

Having the correct name of each owner in the district is critical for mailing lists and personal contact. The local taxation office is an excellent source of information. Mailers are frequently designed to pave the way for personal contact. When follow-up is done, having the mailer to refer to, and confirm that the owners did receive it, is advantageous.

The objective of general contact is to keep owners aware of what is happening in the local market, e.g., recent activity, price levels, and market conditions. All homeowners are interested in the value of their home. Through personal informative meetings, a regular program of contact can be maintained with all owners in the farm territory. This is essential, not only for direct listings, but also for referrals and repeat business.

FEASIBILITY ANALYSIS
(SEE ALSO INVESTMENT ANALYSIS)

The examination of costs and benefits arising from a contemplated economic endeavour.

Application Feasibility analysis is most commonly associated with comparison of commercial properties in line with specific investor objectives. Feasibility studies include both objective analysis of income streams typically combined with subjective interpretations based on the needs, wants, and objectives of individual investors.

FEE AGREEMENT
(SEE LISTING AGREEMENT)

FEE APPRAISAL
(SEE APPRAISAL)

FEE SIMPLE
(SEE ALSO ESTATE)

The highest estate or absolute right in real property. Fee simple provides the most rights with the fewest limitations and is generally considered absolute ownership. However, this bundle of rights (the right to use, sell, lease, enter, give away, or refrain from any of these rights in regard to property), is subject to various restrictions imposed by laws of governing bodies.

> **Example** *Fee Simple*
>
> Mr. and Mrs. Jones acquired a property in fee simple and are now convinced that as owners they are free to do whatever they want on the property. The lawyer points out that fee simple is subject to important restrictions. For example, the Criminal Code of Canada permits peace officers to enter Mr. and Mrs. Jones' lands if a crime is committed. Further, as owners, they cannot alter lands, (e.g., drainage) to adversely affect a neighbouring property; the Crown may have reserved various mineral and timber rights with the original Crown grant; municipal regulations may set out minimum construction standards and the right of inspection; and the owner cannot create a nuisance in law by bringing dangerous chattels (dynamite, wild animals, etc.) or obnoxious uses (smelter, glue processing, etc.) onto the property. Such uses might be permitted, depending upon local municipal requirements and provided that various governmental regulations and procedures are followed.

FEE TAIL
(SEE ALSO ESTATE)

The establishment of a fixed line of inheritance through lineal descent. If the succession is dictated as through males only, the fee tail is referred to as a *fee tail male* and, if through female descent, a *fee tail female*. Such provisions are no longer valid.

Fellow of the Real Estate Institute

(SEE ALSO REAL ESTATE INSTITUTE OF CANADA)

Acronym: FRI   The FRI designation is awarded to licensed/registered individuals who have completed the Real Estate Institute of Canada (REIC) education program and who have demonstrated throughout the course of their careers, their dedication and determination to provide only the highest degree of real estate service and to adhere to FRI standards of practice. Before an individual can earn the FRI designation, he/she must first become a candidate;

- Be licensed/registered and active in the practice of real estate;
- Have a minimum of 12 months of creditable experience as defined by REIC;
- Be a high school graduate or equivalent;
- Be of legal age;
- Complete the candidacy application form and send it to REIC with the application fees; and
- Be endorsed by the local REIC Chapter.

To achieve the FRI designation, candidates must:

- Successfully complete specified FRI Core Courses;
- Successfully complete specified FRI Specialty Courses;
- Have five years of creditable experience as defined by REIC;
- Abide by the REIC Code of Professional Standards;
- Have been a candidate for a minimum of one year;
- Be affiliated with and endorsed by an REIC chapter; and
- Be a member in good standing with The Canadian Real Estate Association or local real estate board.

Reference   For details regarding the FRI program, contact the Real Estate Institute of Canada, 5407 Eglinton Avenue West, Suite 208, Etobicoke, ON M9C 5K6.

The above information was summarized from detailed materials provided by REIC with no representation concerning its accuracy or completeness. Contact REIC for current requirements.

Fellow of the Real Estate Institute
(Appraisal Specialist)

(SEE ALSO REAL ESTATE INSTITUTE OF CANADA)

Acronym: FRI(A)   FRI members, who specialize in residential appraisals, further their professional recognition with this accreditation. The FRI(A) denotes the Appraisal Specialist who has met the stringent and internationally accepted benchmark for the performance of residential appraisals and valuations of dwellings including a triplex and undeveloped building sites. FRI members, having a minimum of five years residential appraisal experience, may achieve the FRI(A) by completing advanced studies in economics, title searching, and building construction.

Reference   For details regarding the FRI(A) program, contact the Real Estate Institute of Canada, 5407 Eglinton Avenue West, Suite 208, Etobicoke, ON M9C 5K6.

The above information was summarized from detailed materials provided by REIC with no representation concerning its accuracy or completeness. Contact REIC for current requirements.

Fellow of the Real Estate Institute
(Executive)

(SEE ALSO REAL ESTATE INSTITUTE OF CANADA)

Acronym: FRI(E)   Unlicensed/unregistered management professionals, who are not involved in residential or commercial sales, confirm their industry expertise with this designation. The FRI(E) verifies leadership skills, competence, and ensures knowledge of current marketplace trends and issues. Persons may qualify upon completion of the FRI education program, five years of real estate experience, and other FRI designation requirements.

Reference   For details regarding the FRI(E) program, contact the Real Estate Institute of Canada, 5407 Eglinton Avenue West, Suite 208, Etobicoke, ON M9C 5K6.

The above information was summarized from detailed materials provided by REIC with no representation concerning its accuracy or completeness. Contact REIC for current requirements.

Fence

A structure typically built to enclose real property for purposes of confining, preventing entrance, or marking of boundaries.

Application   Practitioners most commonly encounter fence issues in relation to requirements concerning the construction, location, and purposes that are typically detailed in municipal zoning by-laws, e.g., fence height and type of construction, requirements for properties zoned as commercial or industrial adjacent to residential areas, and special requirements relating to such areas as parking lots, corner lots, pedestrian walkways, open space zones, public parks, and recreational facilities. Provincial legislation sets out regulatory requirements concerning the construction and maintenance of fences that mark boundaries of a property and methods to resolve fencing disputes arising between owners of abutting properties.

Provincial   See applicable reference materials.

FIDUCIARY RELATIONSHIP

A person to whom power or property is entrusted for the benefit of another.

Application   The relationship between a principal and his/her agent is deemed to be a fiduciary relationship. Many types of fiduciary relationships exist in the market, such as a lawyer working on behalf of a client, a trustee acting on behalf of an estate, and a real estate broker working as agent for a seller or buyer.

Fiduciary responsibilities are usually discussed based on six primary areas: *accountability, confidentiality, competence, good faith/full disclosure, loyalty,* and *obedience.*

Example   *Fiduciary Relationship*

Seller Smith is affixing his signature on an exclusive listing authority. Pausing briefly, he asks the salesperson exactly what relationship he is establishing in the marketing of his home. Salesperson Lee explains that Smith, upon signing the agreement, is creating an agency relationship in which Lee, his broker, and all other salespeople within the brokerage office owe their primary duty to protect and promote his interests as a client. In practical terms, this means that the brokerage will attempt to get the best possible price for the home, work aggressively to sell the property, show the property to prospective customers, and work with Smith in ultimately disposing of his home.

FIDUCIARY RESPONSIBILITIES

An agent owes his/her principal various fiduciary duties including: accountability, confidentiality, competence, good faith/full disclosure, loyalty, and obedience.

Accountability

This requirement, often referred to as *full and complete accounting*, is owed by an agent to his/her principal in a real estate transaction. The agent, upon request, must provide details of all funds held in trust and all monies handled on behalf of a principal. Brokerages must maintain accuracy in record keeping to ensure that all transactions comply with the provincial regulatory requirements and generally accepted methods of accounting.

**Example   *Fiduciary Responsibilities–
            Accountability***

ABC Realty Inc. offers property management services. In accordance with the duty as an agent to provide full and complete accounting, the brokerage establishes a record for each property being managed that confirms particulars and details of the agreement. For accounting purposes, a ledger card for each property is prepared and includes all revenues and expenses along with a monthly reconciliation.

Confidentiality

An agent must not use information acquired as the principal's agent for any purpose likely to cause the principal harm or to interfere with the principal's business.

The duty of confidentiality should not be confused with a real estate professional's responsibility to disclose any known material facts about the property to non-principals. This obligation to disclose material facts, including defects, is based on the professional's duty to treat all persons honestly. The duty of honesty does not depend on the existence of an agency relationship.

**Example   *Fiduciary Responsibilities–
            Confidentiality***

Seller Smith is facing financial hardships in his newly-acquired business and informs Salesperson Lee of his predicament. To meet immediate financial obligations, he must sell a rental property in Anycity and wants to list with ABC Realty Inc. While anxious for an offer on the property, Smith is emphatic that information concerning his financial problems be held in strictest confidence. Lee agrees as such information, if known, might impair Smith's negotiating position with the property as well as his business endeavour.

Competence

An agent must have sufficient knowledge and skill to carry out required duties. In representing a principal, the agent must exercise a degree of care and skill that might be expected from an average person in that trade or profession.

The *Code of Ethics and Standards of Business Practice* of The Canadian Real Estate Association addresses competency in Articles 4 and 17. Article 4 sets out the need to discover facts relating to every property to avoid error, misrepresentation, or concealment of pertinent facts. Article 17 imposes on the member the obligation of rendering a skilled and conscientious service.

Provincial regulatory bodies may also detail specific requirements concerning competency as well as other fiduciary responsibilities.

> **Example** *Fiduciary Responsibilities–*
> *Competence*
>
> Salesperson Lee has just listed a property for sale in the city's midtown. The property has a *mutual* side drive. The seller asked Lee to inspect the home, prepare the listing, and then drop around his place of business for a signature. The seller, upon Lee's arrival at his store, is preoccupied with customers and quickly signs the document. The listing clearly states that there is a *private* side drive, an assumption made by Lee.
>
> A buyer, the client of another brokerage, ultimately acquires the property under that same assumption. While the results of legal action will depend on a variety of circumstances surrounding this situation, the issue of Lee's competency will be a focal point in the deliberations.

> With pleading eyes, the seller looks in Lee's direction seeking some magical answer to his obvious dilemma about price. On the down side, this is the first offer on the property in more than 90 days; on the up side, three showings have occurred during the past 24 hours. In fact, one salesperson called just before Lee left the office and said that another offer might be coming in.
>
> While nothing is certain, the duty of good faith is uppermost. Salesperson Lee must protect and promote the interests of his client. Carefully, Lee explains to the seller everything within his knowledge that would assist with the deliberations. After weighing out the options, the seller decides to wait until 8:00 p.m. that evening and then sign this agreement if nothing else is forthcoming from the other showings.

Good Faith/Full Disclosure

The requirement for good faith/full disclosure is an important duty owed by an agent to his/her principal in a real estate transaction. Good faith can best be described as honesty of intention and abstention from taking advantage of another.

The duty of good faith encompasses a wide range of responsibilities. For example, should the agent have any interest in a transaction, this fact must be fully disclosed to the principal. Also, the law does not allow an agent, trustee, or other person in a position of confidence or trust to let personal interests conflict with duty. It does not matter if the interest is direct or indirect, or that no loss was sustained by the principal. The agent's duty also includes the requirement to act in good faith by not making any secret profit from the transaction.

The agent must also disclose any information to the principal that is relevant to the transaction. An agent must tell the principal of all known relevant and material information that pertains to the scope of the agency. This duty to disclose includes any facts affecting the value or desirability of the property. If there is any doubt whether the information is important to the principal, the agent must disclose it and let the principal decide.

> **Example** *Fiduciary Responsibilities–*
> *Good Faith/Full Disclosure*
>
> A challenging market is facing most buyers and sellers in Westside. Homes are not selling well and the average time on the market now exceeds 80 days. The seller, Salesperson Lee's client, is seriously studying the first offer received since the property was listed more than three months ago. There is no question the offered price is low, but the time has come for a decision.
>
> Continued…

Loyalty

Loyalty is typically viewed as the most important duty owed to a principal. The agent must place the interests of the principal above all else except the law. The duty of loyalty obligates the agent to act at all times solely in the best interests of the principal, excluding all other interests, including that of the agent.

Agents must disclose information that would reveal a conflict, actual or potential, between the interests of the agent and those of the principal. The agent must not act for more than one principal to the transaction except with the informed, written consent of all principals after receiving full information from the agent.

> **Example** *Fiduciary Responsibilities–*
> *Loyalty*
>
> Salesperson Lee, following a telephone conversation with Seller Smith, met with Smith to discuss the listing of a property located at 123 Main Street in Anycity. Upon arriving at the address, Lee realized that this property was immediately adjacent to a retail building owned by a client, Investor McKay. McKay had expressed interest in acquiring additional property, particularly any land abutting or adjacent to his retail establishment, and had signed an exclusive buyer agreement with Lee several weeks ago. Lee's loyalty is owed to McKay. Lee's loyalty is owed to McKay and he must remain faithful to commitments made pursuant to that agreement. Lee informs Smith that he will not list the property as a conflict of interest would arise.

Obedience

Real estate brokers, as agents, are under a duty to follow the principal's lawful instructions whether the agent agrees with them or not. It is immaterial whether the agent uses reasonable judgement while actually ignoring the principal's specific orders. An example might involve a principal's stockbroker being instructed to sell shares when the price reaches $10 and the broker does not do so owing to a professional opinion that the values will increase. If the share value falls below $10, the stockbroker could be responsible due to the failure to follow lawful instructions.

Example *Fiduciary Responsibilities–Obedience*

Salesperson Lee made a listing presentation to Smith, the owner of a residential property. Lee explained the benefits of listing with ABC Realty Inc. as well as details regarding MLS. Smith was particularly interested in the Multiple Listing Service given added exposure provided for the home and the involvement of other brokerages in the marketing process.

Shortly after the property was listed, another salesperson with ABC Realty Inc. obtained an offer, acceptable to Smith, conditional on the sale of the purchaser's property. An escape clause was inserted allowing Smith to continue to offer the home for sale. The owner was concerned that marketing efforts would diminish during the conditional period. Lee gave assurances that such would not happen.

A salesperson with a co-operating brokerage called during the 30-day period and wanted to show the property. Lee, confident that the condition would be removed, advised the caller that Smith's home was sold and no further showings were being arranged. In actual fact, the condition was never removed and the seller's home remained unsold throughout the listing period. Salesperson Lee demonstrated a lack of obedience in carrying out his fiduciary responsibilities.

FIELD (ON-SITE) OBSERVATION

For real estate purposes, the direct inspection of a property and/or improvements located thereon.

Application   In conducting an appraisal, an appraiser would undertake a detailed on-site observation of the lands and all improvements along with appropriate working notes. These observations would form the basis of a subsequent formalized appraisal report. In the case of new construction, an architect would use field observation to ensure successful completion of the project.

Real estate practitioners most commonly use field (on-site) observations in the listing process to confirm various details concerning the property and also when showing properties to prospective buyers.

Example   *Field (On-Site) Observation*

Anne Appraiser is inspecting a single-family residence at 110 Main Street and making various field notes regarding the functional utility of the house. A poorly planned house in terms of overall design, layout, and livability can directly affect value. Anne has a list of items to consider in making her field inspection. The list is provided for illustration purposes only and is not exhaustive in nature.

Continued…

Hallway Configuration   Overall efficient use of hallway space, length, width, and accessibility to various rooms.

Room Sizes/Shapes   Functional use of rooms, including adequate sizing.

Layout   Traffic patterns and proximity of appropriate rooms.

Privacy   Access to bedrooms and bathrooms.

Laundry Facilities   Location, size, and size of storage areas.

Floor Levels   Overall floor layouts.

Ventilation   Adequacy of windows, obstructions, and existence of outside air exchanger.

Plumbing/Water/Sewage   Adequacy in relation to house size, convenience, and adequacy of systems.

Mechanical   Type and adequacy of heating/air-conditioning system, electrical system capacity, convenience and adequacy of switches, outlets, and fixtures.

Garage   Access to house, size, location, lighting, and special features, e.g., workshop and electric door openers.

FINAL ESTIMATE OF VALUE

An estimate of value made in the appraisal process following the selection of the most appropriate approach to value for the property being appraised and the completion of the reconciliation.

Application   The final estimate can be given as a single point estimate or range of value. Usually, clients will ask for a single point estimate. However, if a range is requested, it should be realistic as a wide range will not be of practical use. The final estimate of value should be given in rounded, as opposed to exact terms, since the appraisal process uses judgement and experience, and the value given is an estimate only.

Example   *Final Estimate of Value*

Anne Appraiser is providing an appraisal report on 213 Main Street for ABC Lender Inc.

Mr. and Mrs. Jones, the buyers, wish to secure a high ratio mortgage on the property. Following a property inspection and data collection, Anne prepares the appraisal report, specified by ABC Lender Inc., and arrives at a final estimate of value. The following summary highlights the appraiser's reconciliation process leading to a final estimate of value.

In the report, Anne Appraiser provides general property details (e.g., property address, legal description, zoning, and taxes), along with a description of the neighbourhood, site, and improvements. An estimate of value by the cost approach is then completed.

Continued…

Land Value		$135,000
Add: Reproduction Cost	+80,000	
Less: Depreciation	−14,000	
Estimate of Value		$201,000

An estimate of value by the direct comparison approach is completed using three comparable properties that sold recently for $191,500, $206,000 and $207,500. Adjustments are made in line with that approach to arrive at adjusted sale prices of $202,000, $205,000 and $207,000 respectively. In the report, she mentions that few adjustments were required as all three properties were in the same general locale, sold within the past 30 days, and, like the subject property, were bungalows. In estimating the value, Anne Appraiser places most emphasis on the second sale of $205,000 as it required the least adjustments.

In the reconciliation and final estimate of value, she indicates that the cost approach was limited by the difficulty of accurately estimating reproduction cost and depreciation. The greatest weight was given to the indication of value by the direct comparison approach because of the quality of the data on which it was based and the narrow range obtained after adjusting the comparable properties. Based on all data and analysis, an estimate of market value of the subject property, as of the effective date of the appraisal, was $205,000.

FINAL ORDER OF FORECLOSURE

Judgment taken against a mortgagor, extinguishing the equity of redemption.

Provincial   See applicable reference materials.

FINANCIAL MANAGEMENT RATE OF RETURN

(SEE ALSO INTERNAL RATE OF RETURN)

Acronym: FMRR   A method of analyzing discounted cash flows in investment properties to arrive at a rate of return. The FMRR was developed (as was the modified internal rate of return), in response to limitations involving the internal rate of return (IRR) calculation.

Application   The IRR (while mathematically sound), can lead to ambiguities if successive positive and negative cash flows occur within the investment period. Also, the IRR, while effective in analyzing individual properties based on investor expectations, lacks the facility to analyze alternate properties based on a pre-determined lump sum available for investment as these properties may have differing

initial investments and lengths of holding periods. The FMRR was developed as a method to effectively make such comparisons and eliminate sign change problems (+ and −). The approach involves four steps:

Adjustments	Adjust future negative cash flows against prior positive cash flows with appropriate discounting as required.
Negative Cash Flows	Discount remaining negative cash flows back to Year 0 using an appropriate *safe* rate.
Positive Cash Flows	Compound remaining positive cash flows forward at an appropriate *reinvestment* rate.
Investment Disparities	Adjust for initial investment and timing disparities.

The FMRR applies the principle of reinvestment and, therefore, considers external factors in the analysis process. To fully understand the use of FMRR, the reader is directed to other references concerning the internal rate of return (IRR) and the modified internal rate of return (MIRR). Considerable debate is associated with MIRR and FMRR approaches. Critics are quick to point out that the IRR is strictly an *internal* rate of return and performs that function correctly. Both the MIRR and FMRR, they assert, introduce external factors and more importantly inject the profitability of those external investments into the asset being analyzed. The introduction of reinvestment and safe rates, according to some, does little more than contaminate a less than perfect, but nevertheless valid, IRR measure of return.

FINANCIAL RATIOS

(SEE ALSO CURRENT RATIO, DEBT RATIO, AND PROFIT RATIO)

Financial ratios are grouped using four classifications.

Liquidity	Includes Current Ratio and Quick Ratio.
Debt	Includes Debt Ratio and Debt to Net Worth Ratio.
Profitability	Includes Gross Profit Margin and Net Profit Margin Ratios.
Coverage	See Debt Coverage Ratio.

Application   The first three are most applicable to real estate brokerage operations and the appropriate formulae are provided. The coverage ratio applies to investment property analysis. Current debt and profit ratios are calculated from data found on the balance sheet, profit and loss statement, or a combination of the two. Figure F.3 illustrates the formulas for commonly used financial ratios.

Liquidity	
Current Ratio =	$\dfrac{\text{Current Assets}}{\text{Current Liabilities}}$
Quick Ratio =	$\dfrac{\text{Cash/Marketable Securities \& Receivables}}{\text{Current Liabilities}}$
Debt to Net Worth	
Debt to Net Worth =	$\dfrac{\text{Total Debt} - \text{Commissions Payable}}{\text{Tangible Net Worth}}$
Profitability	
Gross Profit Margin =	$\dfrac{\text{Commission Income} - \text{Commission Expense}}{\text{Commission Income}}$
Net Profit Margin =	$\dfrac{\text{Net Profit}}{\text{Commission Income}}$

Financial Ratio Formulas   Figure F.3

FINANCIAL RISK

(SEE RISK)

FINANCIAL STATEMENTS

Timely financial data is essential to decision-making. Without proper tracking systems, brokerages are unable to accurately monitor sales performance, branch office profit levels, and true production expenses, to mention a few. A basic understanding of accounting is required so that proper forecasting and tracking systems can be developed and implemented.

Balance Sheet

The balance sheet lists in order all assets, liabilities, and equity of a business as of a specific point in time. As such, this financial statement provides a snapshot portrayal of a particular business operation. Within each major classification, subheadings appear and under these subheadings, the individual accounts. In examining a balance sheet, the following equation applies:

Total Assets = Total Liabilities + Shareholders' Equity

This relationship exists because all debits must equal all credits in the accounting system.

Figure F.4 illustrates the balance sheet of a typical real estate brokerage. Descriptions for each category are provided for guidance only and expert advice is strongly recommended.

ABC Realty Inc.
Balance Sheet
As at December 31, 20xx

Assets

Current Assets		
Cash	$71,500	
Commissions Receivable	41,328	
Prepaid Expenses	3,785	
Short Term Deposit	15,000	
Total Current Assets		$131,613
Fixed Assets		
Office Building	270,000	
Computer Equipment	18,500	
Office Equipment	25,000	
Less Accumulated Amortization	(37,100)	
Total Fixed Assets		276,400
TOTAL ASSETS		**$408,013**

Liabilities and Equity

Current Liabilities		
Expenses Payable	2,200	
Commissions Due	31,234	
Accounts Payable	21,242	
Taxes Payable (Fed. and Prov.)	432	
Total Current Liabilities		55,108
Long Term Liabilities		
Mortgage	106,500	
Notes Payable	10,000	
Total Long Term Liabilities		116,500
Equity		
Retained Earnings		236,405
TOTAL LIABILITIES AND EQUITY		**$408,013**

Balance Sheet   Figure F.4

Assets

Items used in the business, including anything of future use to that enterprise, the beneficial interest of which is part of that business. They may be monetary or non-monetary, tangible or intangible, and either current or non-current.

Current Assets

Includes cash and other assets (that will most likely be converted to cash within the operating cycle of the business), usually one year from the date of the balance sheet. Real estate trust account funds, if shown on the balance sheet, are *not* current assets and will have an offsetting equal amount in a trust liability account.

Cash   Money or deposits in the real estate general account.

Commissions Receivable   Amounts due to the brokerage for deals that have not yet closed (if recording deals written), or amounts due to the brokerage on deals closed but money not yet received (applicable if recording deals closed or deals written).

Advances   Monies advanced that should be repaid from future commissions in the case of salespeople.

Prepaid Expenses   Infrequent expenses, usually substantial amounts, that do not relate to a specific month, for example, insurance premiums.

Within the classification of current assets in a manufacturing or wholesale operation, inventory would also be listed, e.g., raw materials, work in progress, and finished goods. In a real estate brokerage, inventory might consist of houses or land owned by the brokerage that is available for sale, or large stocks of supplies or promotional items being depleted by the brokerage over time.

Fixed Assets (Non-Current)   Assets used in the business not intended for resale, such as furniture and fixtures, leasehold improvements, computers, and vehicles.

If the brokerage owns land and a building used as office premises, then these assets are also classified as fixed assets.

Accumulated Depreciation   Reduction in the value of the assets over their lifetime. All fixed assets except land are depreciated.

Other Assets   Assets that do not fit into the listed categories, e.g., deposits made against future expenses such as a hydro deposit, the final month's rent on a lease, and incorporation costs. Other non-current assets are long term investments, goodwill (intangible asset), franchise initial fees, patents, and trademarks.

Assets are typically recorded at the lower of cost or market value. This supports the accounting doctrine of conservatism, but presents a problem where land and buildings are carried on the balance sheet. A balance sheet may show a value for land and building purchased several years ago when, in fact, the real value of the property is significantly greater than declared.

Liabilities

Claims against a business payable on a fixed or determinable future date. Liabilities, like assets, are generally current or non-current.

Current Liabilities

Those claims that will be paid from items listed as current assets; claims due usually within one year from the date of the balance sheet.

Accounts Payable   Amounts due to suppliers for goods and services received.

Commissions Payable   Amounts due to sales representatives and other brokerages for deals not yet paid.

Deductions Payable   Statutory deductions from payroll such as CPP, EI, income taxes, and any other deductions, including the employer's portion where required.

Bank Loan Payable   If indebtedness to the bank appears in the current liabilities section this entry usually denotes a demand loan or the current portion of a term loan.

Corporate Income Tax   Corporate income tax is viewed as a current liability, as taxes are due within six months of corporate year end.

Non-Current Liabilities

Long-Term Loan Payable   Indebtedness that is due later than one year from the date of the balance sheet. The terms of long term indebtedness are usually disclosed as a footnote to the balance sheet.

Accrued Liabilities   Liabilities that will appear at some future date, the exact amount of which is unknown, e.g., audit and legal fees.

Shareholder's (Owner's) Equity

Capital Stock

Different classes of shares in the corporation that can be issued.

Common Shares   The voting shares of the company. Common shareholders are at the greatest risk, but also stand to gain the most if stock value increases. Common shareholders are entitled to dividends only after preferred shareholders, if any, are paid in full. However, no limit is put on dividends that can be paid to them.

Preferred Shares   Senior to common shares. Preferred shareholders have a claim on the assets of the company subordinate to that of debt holders but have preference over common shareholders in dividend rights and liquidation.

A company might issue preferred shares as 10% cumulative, $100 par value. Shareholders are entitled to a 10% dividend per year, which must be paid before any dividend distribution to the common shareholders. If no dividends are declared and paid in a particular year, they accumulate in favour of the preferred shareholders and must be paid before any dividend distribution to common shareholders is made.

Retained Earnings

The accumulated net income of a corporation since the inception less any distribution of dividends. If the company is in a loss position, it is termed a deficit. Year end financial statements will include a statement of retained earnings, either as a separate financial statement or combined with the profit and loss statement.

Profit and Loss Statement

A detail of all the income and expenses of the brokerage over an accounting period (also referred to as an *income statement*). The actual title and format for this report will vary but the basic heading for the statement is:

> **ABC Realty Inc.**
> *(Legal Name of the Business)*
> **Profit And Loss Statement**
> *(Title of the Statement)*
> **For the year ended December 31, 20xx**
> *(Time Frame)*

Figure F.5 illustrates a typical profit and loss statement for a real estate brokerage.

Statement of Changes in Financial Position

The analysis of net increase or decrease in working capital. The change in financial position discloses the net change in each element of working capital. This statement provides the brokerage with valuable information as it shows the source of cash used to effect changes to the balance sheet accounts, such as purchasing new assets and retiring long-term commitments. Figure F.6 depicts typical calculations reflecting changes in financial position.

ABC Realty Inc.
Profit and Loss Statement
For Month Ended January 31, 20xx

Revenue

Commission Income	$102,000	
Total Revenue		$102,000

Expenses

Commission Expenses	61,600
Advertising	10,000
Bank Charges & Interest	700
Rent	4,200
Insurance & Taxes	800
Office Salaries & Benefits	11,000
Office Supplies & Expenses	1,600
Utilities	3,200
Telephone	2,400
Accounting & Legal	1,000
Depreciation Expense	1,400
Total Expenses	97,900
NET PROFIT	**$ 4,100**

Profit and Loss Statement   Figure F.5

ABC Realty Inc.
Statement of Changes in Financial Position
For the Year Ended December 31, 20xx

Source of Funds

From Operation

Net Income	$110,000	
Add: Depreciation	7,000	
Total Funds from Operations		$117,000
From Sale of Equipment		1,000
From Issuance of Common Stock		6,000
TOTAL FUNDS FROM SOURCES		124,000

Use of Funds

Retirement of Long-term Debt	20,000	
Purchase of Computer Equipment	45,000	
TOTAL USE OF FUNDS		65,000
NET INCREASE IN WORKING CAPITAL		**$ 59,000**

Statement of Changes in Financial Position   Figure F.6

FINANCIAL WORKSHEET

(SEE ALSO BUDGETING)

The financial worksheet, also referred to as a *budget worksheet*, can assist in analyzing income and expense activities at the main or branch office of a real estate brokerage. The worksheets are used for budgeting and forecasting purposes. These recommended worksheets are structured using a chart of accounts that would apply to a traditional real estate brokerage operation. Brokers must modify income and expense categories based on individual needs and recommendations from appropriate accounting experts.

FINDER'S FEE

A fee paid to a person or other entity for information that initiates a business transaction. Various types of finders' fees or referral fees can be generated from real estate transactions, the most common involving listing or selling properties (e.g., client referrals) and arranging financing. The Code of Ethics of The Canadian Real Estate Association sets out guidelines concerning disclosure of such fees or other money received, other than from the client. Provincial regulatory requirements may also apply.

Provincial   See applicable reference materials.

FIRE

Classes

A classification system used as the basis for determining appropriate fire extinguishing equipment required in a fire plan.

Class A Fires   Start in ordinary materials which burn easily, such as paper, wood, cloth, rubber, and many plastics. Such fires can usually be extinguished with water.

Class B Fires   Involve grease or flammable liquids that burn rapidly, such as gasoline, oil, lacquers, paints, mineral spirits, alcohol, fats, and greases. A smothering or blanketing effect is needed to stop them.

Class C Fires   Start in energized electrical equipment, such as air-conditioning compressors, motors, transformers, generators, and electrical wiring. The use of water or a chemical that carries an electrical charge may result in death or injury for the person trying to stop such a fire and should therefore not be used.

Class D Fires   Start in combustible metals such as aluminum, magnesium, titanium, zirconium, sodium, and potassium.

Definitions

Real estate practitioners encounter various terminologies relating to the practical application of provincial fire codes in regard to residential occupancies.

Following are a few, frequently encountered definitions included for illustration purposes only.

Access to Exit   That part of a means of egress within a floor area that provides access to an exit serving the floor area.

Alarm Signal   An audible signal transmitted throughout a zone or zones or throughout a building to advise occupants that a fire emergency exists.

Closure   A device or assembly for closing an opening through a fire separation such as a door, shutter, wired glass or glass block assembly, and includes all components, such as hardware, closing devices, frames, and anchors.

Dwelling Unit   A room or suite of rooms operated as a housekeeping unit used or intended to be used as a domicile by one or more persons and that may contain cooking, eating, living, sleeping, and sanitary facilities.

Exit   That part of a means of egress that leads from the floor area it serves and includes any doorway leading directly from a floor area to a public thoroughfare or to an approved open space.

Fire-Protection Rating   The time in hours, or fraction thereof, that a closure, window assembly, or glass block assembly will withstand the passage of flame when exposed to fire under specified conditions of test and performance criteria, or as otherwise prescribed in a provincial building code.

Fire-Resistance Rating   The time in hours, or fraction thereof, that a material or assembly of materials will withstand the passage of flame and the transmission of heat when exposed to fire under specified conditions of test and performance criteria, or as determined by extension or interpretations of information derived therefrom as prescribed in a provincial building code.

The actual rating assigned to a material, assembly of materials, or structural members of a building, is based on test results conducted according to the *Standard Methods of Fire Endurance Tests of Building Construction and Materials.* Fire resistance ratings provide the basis for assessing types of material and establishing required minimums for their use in exterior walls, supporting construction, floor, ceiling and roof assemblies, fire separations, firewalls, exit corridors, and partition walls.

Fire Separation   A construction assembly that acts as a barrier against the spread of fire and may or may not have a fire-resistance rating or a fire-protection rating.

Firewall   A fire separation of noncombustible construction that subdivides a building or separates adjoining buildings to resist the spread of fire that has a fire-resistance rating as prescribed in a provincial building code and the structural stability to remain intact under fire conditions for the required fire-rated time.

Floor Area   The space on any storey of a building between exterior walls and required firewalls and includes the space occupied by interior walls and partitions, but does not include exits and vertical service spaces that pierce the storey.

Means of Egress   A continuous path of travel provided by a doorway, hallway, corridor, exterior passageway, balcony, lobby, stair, ramp, or other egress facility or combination thereof, for the escape of persons from any point in a building, floor area, room or contained open space to a public thoroughfare, or other approved open space and includes exits and access to exits.

Smoke Alarm   A combined smoke detector and audible device designed to sound an alarm, within the room or suite in which it is found, when smoke is detected.

Figure F.7 illustrates acceptable and not acceptable locations for smoke alarms in residential structures. Provincial fire codes set out detailed requirements regarding inspection, testing, and maintenance of smoke alarms.

Fire Code

The *National Fire Code of Canada* (NFC) establishes levels of fire safety for both new and existing buildings related to both occupants and emergency responders. The national fire code is published by the Institute for Research in Construction (IRC), an organization within the National Research Council. The NFC complements the *National Building Code* in the construction, renovation, or maintenance of buildings. Provinces also have fire codes establishing specific requirements that apply within provincial jurisdictions. Fire codes are continuously evolving, particularly in the areas of fire prevention, fire protection, and public safety.

Provincial   See applicable reference materials.

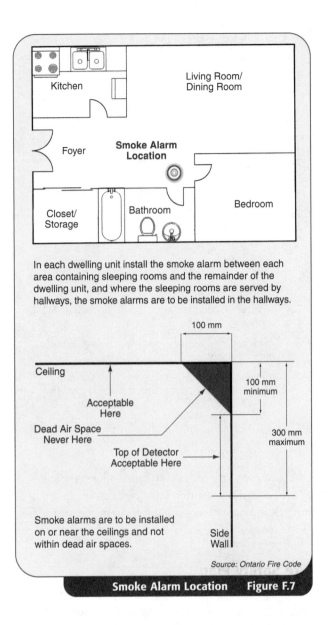

In each dwelling unit install the smoke alarm between each area containing sleeping rooms and the remainder of the dwelling unit, and where the sleeping rooms are served by hallways, the smoke alarms are to be installed in the hallways.

Smoke alarms are to be installed on or near the ceilings and not within dead air spaces.

Source: Ontario Fire Code

Smoke Alarm Location   Figure F.7

Fire Fighting Extinguishers

Fire extinguishers are classified according to their extinguishing capacity and class of fire.

Water Type   A pressurized cartridge consisting of soda acid to be used only for Class A fires.

Foam   Releases a mass of carbon dioxide bubbles that smother a fire and are good for Class B fires. In an emergency they can be used for Class A fires.

Conventional Dry Chemical   Releases a bicarbonate of soda that smothers fire. Work well on Class B and C electrical fires, but are not recommended for Class A fires.

Multi-Purpose Dry Chemical   Releases a stream of ammonium phosphate, smothering the fire and may be used on all classes of fire.

Many different types of portable fire extinguishers are used. The following is provided for illustration purposes only and is not exhaustive in nature.

TYPE OF EXTINGUISHER	TYPE OF FIRE
Pump Tank Water Extinguishers (hand-carried pump tanks, or backpack pump tanks commonly used to fight wildland fires)	Class A
Stored Pressure Water Extinguishers	Class A
Aqueous Film Forming Foam (AFFF) Extinguishers	Class A and B
Halon 1211 Extinguishers	Class B and C
Halon 1301 Extinguishers	Class B and C
Carbon Dioxide Extinguishers	Class B and C
Dry Chemical Extinguishers—Ordinary Base	Class B and C
Dry Chemical Extinguishers—Multi-Purpose Agent	Class A, B, and C
Dry Powder	Class D

Various requirements apply concerning the placement of fire extinguishers within buildings. Persons installing fire fighting equipment should refer to the provincial fire code for specifics.

Fire Safety Plan

While the establishment of some emergency procedures is simply good practice, a fire safety plan for most buildings is typically required under provincial fire codes. Exact procedures will vary, but generally the plan sets out emergency procedures to be used in the case of fire including the appointment and organization of designated staff, preparation of diagrams depicting type, location, and operation of building fire emergency systems, the holding of fire drills, actual procedures to be followed in the case of a fire, the control of fire hazards in the building, and the inspection and maintenance of building facilities for the safety of occupants.

Provincial   See applicable reference materials.

Commercial Property

Real estate practitioners are not expected to be experts in fire safety issues. However, commercial specialists should be aware of unique circumstances that can affect retail office and other commercial properties. The following is for illustration purposes and does not represent a complete discussion of relevant matters. Practitioners should access provincial fire code and building code legislation and regulations for detailed information.

Fire Department Access Route   The site, as well as building design, of new commercial construction must take into account such issues as fire access routes based on the type of fire fighting equipment being used within the local area.

Sprinkler System Design   Additional sprinkler design criteria are normally required in structures that have high fire loads; in other words, structures such as warehouses with high storage facilities or those buildings involved in the use, storage, and/or manufacture of highly flammable materials. Considerations include the amount, location, and direction of sprinklers. Special requirements can also apply to parking areas.

Building Height   The *chimney effect* and movement of smoke through successive floors by means of elevator, stairs, or other vertical service shafts pose special challenges for fire protection systems. Requirements can be found in appropriate fire and building codes.

Corridors/Obstructions/Special Requirements   Various regulations affect unique issues such as kiosks in retail malls, minimum doorway widths in exit corridors, properly-sized landings in egress stairways, special provisions for the disabled including temporary refuge, fire fighter elevator requirements (e.g., to fit stretchers), elevator recall systems, and special requirements concerning non-ambulatory patients in nursing homes.

Sprinkler Systems

Five types of sprinkler systems are found in the marketplace.

Wet Pipe   Filled with water under pressure. A plug will melt at high temperatures and release water immediately.

Dry Pipe   Contains compressed air extending from a sprinkler head to a dry pipe valve. When the plug melts, the air pressure drops and water flows through the sprinkler head.

Pre-Action   Contains air that may or may not be under pressure. The water is held back by the automatic valve operated by a heat-activated device and is generally more sensitive than a normal automatic sprinkler.

Deluge   Used where unusual fire hazards exist and large quantities of water are needed quickly over large areas.

Valves can be coordinated to open either manually or automatically by heat-activated devices.

Combined Dry Pipe and Pre-Action   Employs automatic sprinklers attached to a piping system containing air under pressure.

Nearly all automatic sprinkler alarm systems include a trigger operated by a flow of water that sets off a water or electric alarm. Both systems can be connected to a local fire alarm. The release of carbon dioxide, a colourless, odourless, heavier-than-air chemical, has been a valuable system for extinguishing fires in electrical equipment, gasoline, oil, grease and paints. Since carbon dioxide leaves no residue, the area can be entered immediately.

FIRE INSURANCE

Provincial   Issues relating to fire insurance are typically addressed in provincial standard forms. See applicable provincial reference materials.

FIREPLACE

Generally viewed as recreational, as opposed to functional, in that most take more heat away from a structure than they generate. Fireplaces provide radiant heat into a room but use the warmed house air for combustion. The air that goes up the chimney typically represents more heat loss than the radiant heat gained from the flames. A roaring fire can draw three to four hundred cubic feet of air out of a structure every minute. Heatilators, glass doors, and outside combustion air intakes help reduce heat loss.

Figure F.8 illustrates a traditional fireplace. Provincial building codes set out detailed specifications for fireplace inserts and hearth mounted stoves.

Example   *Fireplace*

Owner Smith is contemplating the construction of a traditional fireplace with the following specifications.

- A footing and foundation system (usually of the same material as the house foundation).
- A hearth (floor of the fireplace), constructed of poured concrete and one inch of slate, firebrick, stone, or tile, and extends at least sixteen inches beyond the front of the fireplace and at least eight inches beyond either side.
- Firebox walls (usually brick, stone, or concrete), with a firebrick liner giving a total wall thickness of eight inches.

Continued…

- A mantel lever or inside firebox control damper to be installed. The damper should be firebox width, at least six inches above the fireplace opening, and closer to the front than the back.
- A smoke shelf behind the damper that provides for deflection of downdrafts and rain/snow.
- A smoke chamber located above the damper and below the chimney, typically brick, stone, or concrete block, and is often specially parged for smoothness to allow better smoke movement.
- A chimney made of the same masonry as the fireplace with clay liners, approximately ⅝ inch thick, mortared together.
- Fire mantle having no combustible materials within six inches of the fireplace opening.

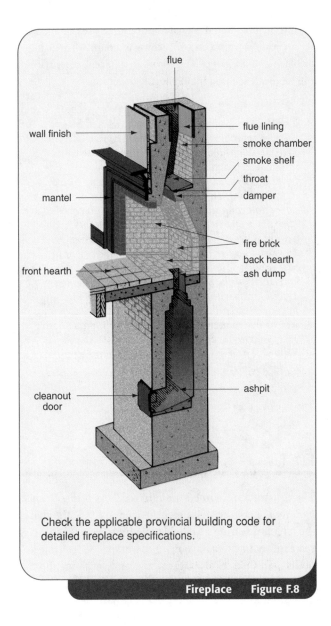

Check the applicable provincial building code for detailed fireplace specifications.

Fireplace   Figure F.8

FIREPLACE, ZERO CLEARANCE

Insulated metal units that are light in comparison to masonry fireplaces. Such fireplaces are typically connected to metal chimneys specially designed for this use. Zero clearance fireplaces usually have no smoke shelf and many include a built-in heatilator system.

FIRST RIGHT OF REFUSAL

An agreement between the owner and a prospective buyer allowing that buyer to make an offer to purchase prior to the real property being sold to another potential buyer. In commercial leasing, the term is used frequently to denote a concession giving a tenant the first right, within a limited period of time, to a designated additional area or space.

A clause is provided concerning a tenant who wishes to place a first right of refusal on an adjacent suite with the landlord seeking financial consideration.

The Landlord agrees that Tenant Jones will have the first right of refusal on the suite known as Suite 1701 at 195 Main Street being approximately 3,000 square feet, if and when the space becomes available for rent during 20xx. Such right will extend for 30 days from written notice provided to Jones on such terms and conditions as the Landlord is prepared to offer the property to other prospective tenants. Tenant Jones agrees to pay the Landlord a sum of $500 as a non-refundable deposit for such right of first refusal. If Jones does not enter into a written agreement with the landlord for said premises on agreed terms within the 30-day period, Tenant Jones will forfeit the deposit of $500 and the Landlord will be free to accept another tenancy. If Jones does enter into an acceptable tenancy agreement, the $500 will be applied against the last month's rent under such tenancy agreement.

FIT UP

The construction, sometimes referred to as *fitting up* or *build-outs*, necessary within enclosing walls (i.e., the space the tenant is leasing), to divide and improve a tenant's space into a functional layout, e.g., partitions, doors, electrical outlets, finished surfaces, paint, tile, and carpeting, up to the point of furnishing with personal property. The degree of fit up is largely determined by negotiations between landlord and tenant as are the costs associated with such improvements.

Example   *Fit Up*

Tenant Jones is responsible for fit up in his unit. When inquiring what items are supplied by the landlord, the following brief summary was provided. The landlord:

- Is responsible for building the demising walls and common corridor if needed, e.g., more than one tenant on a particular floor;
- Ensures that light fixtures and ceiling tiles are installed as per engineering drawings;
- Supplies hot and cold potable water to space if required, e.g., kitchen and washrooms;
- Balances existing HVAC and ensures operational order; and
- Supplies required power to the suite to integrate with tenant's improvements.

All other improvements are the responsibility of the tenant, e.g., interior doors, partitions, decorating, blinds, carpeting, electrical, plumbing, kitchen facilities, etc.

FIXED ASSETS

Assets, frequently referred to as *capital assets*, that add value to a business and are used in the operation of the enterprise. Such assets are not held by the company for the intention of resale. While this does not preclude the right to sell such items at some future time, it was not a prime motive during initial acquisition. Fixed assets include: automobiles, computer hardware, purchased telephone systems, neon signs, and buildings and land provided that they are used as office premises and are not part of a property inventory for resale.

Example   *Fixed Assets*

Broker/Owner Johnson, of ABC Realty Inc., acquires new computer hardware consisting of two CPUs, 19" colour monitors, accessories, and a laser printer for use within the office. The cost of these items is $8,497.70 (including PST). Accordingly, the value of capital assets increases by that amount.

FIXED EXPENSES

Charges that do not vary with occupancy, e.g., ad valorem taxes and fire insurance, and are paid whether the property is occupied or vacant. Such expenses are not necessarily fixed in amount, but tend to be semi-variable and fluctuate from year to year and are contrasted with variable expenses that fluctuate with volume of business. Variable expenses usually include advertising, signs, long distance, MLS listing fees, etc. and normally increase with heightened activity and diminish when activity slows.

Example *Fixed Expenses*

Broker/Owner Johnson, of ABC Realty Inc., is developing a budget worksheet for the brokerage, based on the prior year's actual expenses. To assist in the process, Johnson has assigned each income and expense category as fixed (F) or variable (V). An excerpt from the worksheet relating to advertising is illustrated.

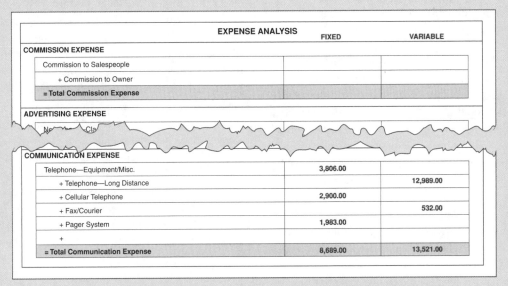

EXPENSE ANALYSIS	FIXED	VARIABLE
COMMISSION EXPENSE		
Commission to Salespeople		
+ Commission to Owner		
= Total Commission Expense		
ADVERTISING EXPENSE		
COMMUNICATION EXPENSE		
Telephone—Equipment/Misc.	3,806.00	
+ Telephone—Long Distance		12,989.00
+ Cellular Telephone	2,900.00	
+ Fax/Courier		532.00
+ Pager System	1,983.00	
+		
= Total Communication Expense	8,689.00	13,521.00

FIXED PRINCIPAL PAYMENT LOAN

Regular principal payments along with interest outstanding often referred to as a *straight line reduction loan*. The borrower is normally asked to pay interest in conjunction with the principal payments. Interest is payable only on the outstanding balance of the loan during any given interval. Therefore, while principal payments are constant, interest payments are gradually reduced. The advantage of this plan is that payments are extremely easy to calculate and consequently a popular arrangement with private investors.

Example *Fixed Principal Payment Loan*

Buyer Jones requires a first mortgage of $50,000 and has negotiated the loan based on an annual interest rate of 10%, a five-year term, and yearly principal reduction payments of $10,000. In this example, the loan is paid off at the end of the fifth year.

While not all principal reduction loans are structured to fully repay the principal at the end of the term, the overall structure of payments is the same. The only difference is a balloon payment at the conclusion of the mortgage term.

TIME PERIOD	TOTAL PAYMENT	INTEREST	PRINCIPAL	PRINCIPAL BALANCE
Year 1	15,000	5,000	10,000	40,000
Year 2	14,000	4,000	10,000	30,000
Year 3	13,000	3,000	10,000	20,000
Year 4	12,000	2,000	10,000	10,000
Year 5	11,000	1,000	10,000	0

FIXED-DOLLAR RENTAL

A set rental amount for a retail store where no adjustment is made based on volume of business.

Example *Fixed-Dollar Rental*

Smith is leasing 3,200 square feet of retail store space in a local mall on a fixed-dollar rental. The price per square foot is $18. The appropriate section of his lease reads as follows:

Rent Payable: Tenant shall pay to Landlord throughout the term as rental for the premises, without any set-off or deduction whatsoever, the following rentals: an annual rental of $57,600 (based $18 per square foot per annum).

This type of lease should be distinguished from a percentage lease. If an additional rent were due for upward or downward adjustment of business volume, the fixed dollar amount would become the minimum rent due under the lease and a subsequent clause such as the following is added:

…a percentage rental equal to _____ % of Gross Sales in excess of $_____ during each rental year; provided however that the gross sales to which the percentage rental applies shall be adjusted proportionately (on a per diem basis), for any rental year which is less than 12 calendar months.

Fixtures

(see also Chattels)

An improvement or item of personal property on the real property becomes a fixture when it is so attached to the real property or building that it becomes part of it.

Application Whether a chattel becomes a fixture depends largely on the circumstances, with particular emphasis placed on the method of how the item is affixed, the intent of the party(ies), and degree of importance to the property. A chattel designed for temporary use or convenience could remain as a moveable item. However, if its purpose was to enhance the property and is affixed thereto, it might well become a fixture. As with chattels, practitioners must clearly identify in any agreement/contract what *is* and *is not* included. The general rule is that fixtures are part of the real property and go with the sale unless specifically excluded.

Rented items must also be listed and acknowledged by the buyer as excluded from the purchase price. In commercial tenancies, the tenant can remove trade fixtures at the end of the lease term, repairing any damage caused by their removal.

Example 1 *Excluding Fixtures*

Seller Smith wants to retain the dining room chandelier that is now permanently affixed to the ceiling and the decorator rods in the living room. Salesperson Lee informs Smith that both fixtures should be clearly excluded in the listing as well as in the agreement/contract.

Example 2 *Chattels vs. Fixtures*

In a simpler time, real estate practitioners confidently separated chattels from fixtures; the former were always detached and movable, while the latter remained affixed as improvements. While common sense should prevail in such matters, doubt can arise.

- A 500 lb. Grecian urn adorning the patio, is it movable or not?

- An intricate interlocking paved drive; looks permanent, but is it attached?

- The pool equipment, some are attached and some are not. Which are chattels and which are fixtures?

The list goes on and on: indoor vacuum cleaning attachments, wall-to-wall carpeting (fitted but not stapled), and satellite dishes.

Many real estate salespeople have wisely abandoned old legal concepts in favour of practical solutions. For example, in cottage property, the use of detailed lists of included/ excluded items is quite common. While chattel/fixture differentiation has merit, a detailed listing avoids confusion. The feature sheet also reinforces the list approach by highlighting all significant items that could cause confusion for either the buyer or the seller. Feature sheets are typically kept on file with the listing documentation and copied for circulation to interested parties.

The traditional division of chattels and fixtures by degree of attachment is still relevant, but it is only a starting point. Make certain the listing is complete. Don't assume anything, especially the obvious. Ask about the attractive ceiling fans, the large area carpet, the built-in bookshelf, the garage workbench, the satellite dish, the television antennae, the ornate poolside sculpture, and the solar pool cover. A few minutes wisely devoted to identifying chattel/fixtures can avoid potential embarrassment, confusion, and disgruntled consumers. Remember, chattels and fixtures are largely in the eyes of the beholder. The best protection is a detailed list acknowledged by the parties to the transaction.

Flashing

Sheet metal or other material used in roof and wall construction to shed water. Flashings, typically made of metal, are used wherever the roof changes direction or meets an obstruction such as a chimney. If the flashings rust, a section of the roof may have to be removed to install new ones.

Flat Payment

A payment structure in which the borrower is not required to repay any of the principal until the maturity date. During the term of a mortgage, the borrower is usually required to pay interest at regular intervals.

Example *Flat Payment*

Buyer Jones requires a first mortgage of $50,000 and has negotiated the loan based on an annual interest rate of 10%, a five-year term, with no principal reduction payments. The balloon payment at the end of Year 5 is $50,000.

TIME PERIOD	TOTAL PAYMENT	INTEREST	PRINCIPAL	PRINCIPAL BALANCE
Year 1	5,000	5,000	0	50,000
Year 2	5,000	5,000	0	50,000
Year 3	5,000	5,000	0	50,000
Year 4	5,000	5,000	0	50,000
Year 5	5,000	5,000	0	50,000

FLOOD

A temporary rise in the water level resulting in the inundation of areas adjacent to a watercourse not ordinarily covered by water.

Application   Flood control, including the administration of flood plain lands, generally falls to provincial jurisdictions and typically involves more than one authority, e.g., conservation authorities, municipalities, and/or environmental departments/ministries. Flood control measures are frequently intertwined with other responsibilities involving the conservation and wise management of water resources through proper planning principals and the administration of flood plain or flood prone areas. The Government of Canada, while not directly involved in flood matters, enacted the *Flood Damage Reduction Program (FDRP)* in 1975 under the *Canada Water Act* in the interest of provincial co-ordination. In addition to other initiatives, the FDRP is involved in the establishment of flood forecasting and warning systems. Reduction programs are joint responsibilities resulting from agreements between individual provinces and the federal government.

Provincial   See applicable reference materials.

FLOOR DUTY

Floor duty or opportunity time is assigned to salespersons for servicing phone calls and walk-in trade pertinent to enquiries about, and listing of, properties. Usually, the requirement for floor duty and related procedures such as handling of prospects and showings is not specified in the salesperson's employment agreement, but is included in the office policy manual.

Floor duty is typically found in brokerages that employ salespeople under a standard employee-employer arrangement. This requirement normally does not apply to those salespeople working on an independent contractor basis with the brokerage.

Example   *Floor Duty*

Maria Garcia is a new salesperson employed by ABC Realty Inc. No independent contractors work with the brokerage. Accordingly, the brokerage can set out various specific duties for individual employees. As a new licensee/registrant, the broker wants Maria to gain experience with customers and clients immediately. For the next four weeks, Maria's floor schedule is set as follows:

Continued…

Weekdays: Monday, Wednesday, Friday
9:00 – 11:00 a.m. and 7:00 – 9:00 p.m.
Weekends: Saturday
9:00 – 11:00 a.m.

This schedule allows adequate time for other activities, (e.g., canvassing, listing presentations, showings, and open houses), while providing 14 duty hours to increase contacts with potential buyers and sellers.

FLOOR LOAD

The ability of a floor to support a live load. A live load generally consists of three components:

- The weight arising from the assembly of persons;
- The weight of the accumulation of equipment and furnishings; and
- The weight of stored materials.

Live load should be clearly differentiated from a dead load. Dead load refers to the weight of the structural member itself, e.g., the materials incorporated in the structural member and permanent equipment.

Application   Provincial building codes set out live load requirements according to use and occupancy that are normally expressed in terms of pounds per square foot (or the metric equivalent), for various types of uses. The minimum specifications are typically stated as a uniformly distributed live load on an area of floor in relation to its particular use. The building code will set out differing minimum specifications for equipment, service, assembly, office, garage, factory, and corridor areas. Live load requirements apply to both residential and commercial structures. Load requirements also apply to other building components such as roofs, balconies, elevated walkways, and footbridges.

FLOOR SPACE RATIO

The ratio of total floor area of a building to the total land area on which the building is located. The floor space ratio is often quoted in zoning by-laws and deed restrictions in subdivisions. This ratio is frequently detailed within the broader confines and restrictions referenced under site coverage.

The definition of what constitutes total floor area will vary based on definitions included within applicable municipal regulations. Practitioners should consult the local zoning by-laws.

Example *Floor Space Ratio*

Seller Smith owns a six-storey commercial building consisting of 10,000 square feet on each floor located on a 15,000 square foot site. The floor space ratio is determined by taking the total floor space of 60,000 square feet (10,000 x 6 floors) expressed as a ratio of 15,000 square feet 60,000:15,000 or 4:1. If Smith's property were 7,500 square feet on a single floor, the floor space ratio would normally be expressed not as a ratio but as a factor or a percentage, for example:

7,500 ÷ 15,000 = .50 or 50%

Foot Candles Maintained	
Private Offices (Preparation of offers, use of computers, reading, handwriting)	70
General Offices (Typing, computer use, reading handwriting, and filing)	70
Entrance Lobby and Hallways	50
Conference Rooms	30
Washrooms	30
Corridors and Stairs	20

FLOOR SYSTEMS

(SEE BEAM, BRIDGING/BLOCKING, JOIST, POST/COLUMN, SILL, AND SUBFLOOR)

FLUE

(SEE ALSO FIREPLACE AND CHIMNEYS)

A separate and distinct channel for the discharge of smoke on the inside of the chimney. Each appliance, requiring a flue, must have a separate flue with certain exceptions, for example, a gas furnace and a gas hot water heater on the same level may share one flue. Some flues are unlined, i.e., exposed masonry on the inside of the flue. This type of flue is commonly found in pre-Second World War houses constructed for fireplaces and oil-fired furnaces. Some building codes may allow wood stoves to share flues with gas or oil furnaces, if at the same floor level. Detailed requirements concerning flues can be found in the applicable provincial building code.

FOOT CANDLE

A measurement of light level equivalent to the light intensity made by one candle at a distance of one foot.

Example *Foot Candle*

Broker/Owner Johnson, of ABC Realty Inc., has completed construction of his new office and wants to ensure sufficient lighting in shared work areas and private offices, conference rooms, lobby and hallways, and washrooms. Johnson conducts a lighting survey following completion of all fluorescent ceiling fixtures to ensure that recommended lighting levels are achieved. He uses illumination levels recommended by the *Illuminating Engineering Society of North America* (IESNA) expressed as foot candles maintained with appropriate modifications suiting a real estate brokerage office.

Continued…

The *Illuminating Engineering Society of North America* (IESNA) is a society that provides recommendations and disseminates information concerning lighting including measurement and testing procedures. Recommended levels are based on foot candles maintained.

FOOT CANDLES MAINTAINED

The level of light that will be maintained after the initial drop off of foot candles following installation, usually measured after the first 100 hours of burning.

Example *Foot Candles Maintained*

Broker/Owner Johnson, of ABC Realty Inc., in conducting a lighting survey, uses a light meter to determine whether sufficient lighting is present within the brokerage office. Originally, he contemplated having various illumination levels as set out by the *Illuminating Engineering Society of North America*. While establishing the initial floor layout, however, Johnson realized that maximum work station flexibility was essential given his growth plans for the next three to five years. Accordingly, he opted for a uniform grid pattern in the suspended ceiling permitting 100 foot candles maintained for all areas within the sales and general office areas. Reduced illumination levels were confined to washrooms and corridors. The front lobby contained special ceiling lighting to complement the decor.

FOOTING

The widened section, usually concrete, at the base or bottom of a foundation wall, pier, or column.

The footing transmits the weight of the structure to the soil, without allowing the structure to sink. Footings are typically 16 to 24 inches wide and 6 to 16 inches thick.

Generally, the heavier the building and the weaker the soil, the larger the footing required.

Application   When the footings fail, the entire structure moves causing a situation that can be expensive and sometimes impossible to correct. Since the footings are located below grade and under the basement floor, the cause of the failure is often difficult to ascertain. The failure may be restricted to a single area and not be uniform below the entire structure. Consequently, the building may not sink straight down but rather lean to one side or another. Frequently, one part of the structure will pull away from the rest, leading to cracking of interior and exterior wall surfaces.

Figure F.9 demonstrates the distribution of load from beams and joists down to wall and column footings.

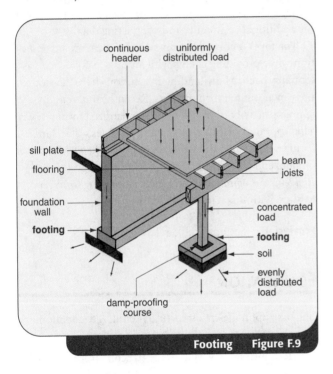

Footing   Figure F.9

FOR SALE SIGN

The *for sale* sign has traditionally been viewed as the most effective and efficient method of marketing property. This marketing device, frequently referred to as *the silent salesperson*, is on duty 24 hours a day.

Application   Both ethical and legal requirements exist concerning *for sale* signs. The Canadian Real Estate Association (CREA) and real estate boards set out rules for members of organized real estate, while provincial real estate acts also address the topic of signs.

CREA Ethical Requirements

Interference With Sign   A portion of Article 25 of The Canadian Real Estate Association Code of Ethics is quoted, subject to specific qualifications contained in the Interpretations (see the **Appendix**):

> ...REALTORS shall not interfere with another real estate broker's sign.

Signage By More Than One Member   A portion of Article 25 of the CREA Code of Ethics states:

> Signs in respect of the sale, rent, lease, development or exchange should not be placed on any property by more than one REALTOR unless authorized by the seller/landlord ...

Municipal Requirements

Municipalities set out various sign requirements in by-laws. By-laws typically address two issues: the placement of signs on property (e.g., size and number of signs), and the use of directional signs (e.g., open house directions), on public thoroughfares, particularly at or near intersections. Most real estate board requirements also generally reference such requirements within the *MLS rules and regulations*. A sample wording follows:

> Signs giving notice of sale, rent, lease, development, exchange, or open house shall only be placed and maintained at a location in a manner that complies with all relevant municipal by-laws, provincial requirements, and other relevant government regulations.

Real Estate Board Requirements

Real estate boards also require that a sign placed on a property listed through the MLS system have a form of MLS identification (e.g., MLS sticker) as authorized by the board. This requirement is normally set out in the local MLS rules and regulations.

Provincial   See applicable reference materials for regulatory controls affecting *for sale* signs and other types of advertising.

F

FORCE MAJEURE

A term commonly associated with commercial leases. A force majeure denotes a significant event that could affect either the landlord or the tenant in carrying out duties or responsibilities under the terms of the lease.

Application   Actual wording varies but essentially either party is excused for the period of a force majeure, however, such excusing can specifically exclude the payment of rent. A force majeure is broadly defined to include a strike, act of God, insurrection, war, power failure, and rebellion.

Example   *Force Majeure*

Tenant Jones recently occupied a 3,200 square foot suite in a Class A building. Under the lease agreement, the landlord is responsible for all maintenance and cleaning of the suite as well as all common areas. A strike involving all cleaning and maintenance staff has forced the tenant to maintain his own premises. Jones is seeking a rebate on rent given the lack of promised services. The landlord refuses based on the following clause within the lease:

If the Landlord or the tenant is, in good faith, prevented from carrying out any duties or obligations required under this lease because of a force majeure including but not limited to an act of God, a strike, civil insurrection, riot, war, or rebellion, then despite anything to the contrary, the affected party will do what was prevented after the force majeure, but this does not excuse either party from other obligations and payments of amounts that are required at the times specified in the lease.

FORECLOSURE

The termination of the mortgagor's right to property by the mortgagee resulting from the breach of a covenant by the mortgagor, e.g., the non-payment of moneys due. The foreclosure action deprives the mortgagor of his/her right to redeem the property (*equity of redemption*), subject to statutory provisions that exist in individual provincial jurisdictions.

Provincial   See applicable reference materials.

FOREIGN LANDS

Provincial real estate acts/regulations may include specific provisions concerning the advertising, selling, or leasing of subdivided property situated outside the province when marketed within that province. A prospectus concerning such properties must be filed with the appropriate regulatory body and a certificate of acceptance granted. Historically, such lands have been referred to as *foreign lands* as control falls beyond provincial jurisdiction.

Provincial   See applicable reference materials.

FORM REPORT (APPRAISAL)

A type of appraisal form used frequently by appraisers when providing appraisal reports for financial institutions, relocation companies, and government agencies. This type of report consists mainly of preprinted information that must be checked off where relevant. Space is also available for additional comments and supporting details.

The form report allows for a brief, systematic presentation while providing clients with an easy-to-follow consistent approach. Many lending institutions have developed their own unique form reports. Recently, the trend in appraisal activity is toward more standardized form reports. The Appraisal Institute of Canada provides a standard form report called the *Uniform Appraisal Report Form*. Organized real estate in Canada has developed the *MVA–Residential Program* with provinces developing form reports to align with this national initiative.

Provincial   See applicable reference materials.

FOUNDATION

The base upon which a structure is built. A foundation has three basic functions.

- To transmit the weight of the structure from the above-grade walls and floors down to the footings.
- To resist the lateral pressure of the soil on the outside of the basement and act as a retaining wall.
- To carry the weight of the structure below the frost line to prevent frost heaving.

Typical materials include stone, brick, poured concrete, concrete block, cinder block, clay tile, and wood. Most of these materials behave in similar fashion, with wood foundations being the exception. **Figure F.10** illustrates the components of a typical foundation.

Application   Practitioners should be aware of certain problems that can arise with foundations. Foundations that do not provide enough lateral support will deflect inwards. This can be a result of:

- Mechanical forces exerted during backfilling;
- Backfilling with frozen soil;
- Unusual frost development in the soil immediately outside the building;
- Foundation walls that are too thin or do not have adequate reinforcement; or
- The floor system does not provide adequate bracing for the top of the foundation wall.

This last problem is common on the high side wall on a sloping lot. Both unit masonry walls and poured concrete walls can fail if not properly built.

Foundation walls that move inward can be repaired by tying them back from the outside, using ties and anchors common in conventional retaining wall construction. Alternatively, buttresses can be provided on the interior that often consist of concrete or concrete block structures built against basement walls. A third choice is to build a new foundation wall inside the old. Occasionally, replacing the foundation is necessary.

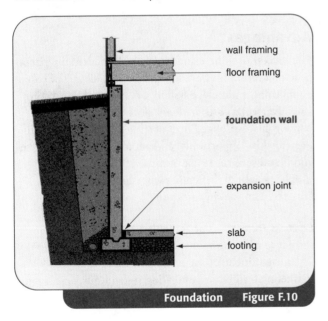

wall framing
floor framing

foundation wall

expansion joint

slab
footing

Foundation Figure F.10

Wood Foundations

Introduced in the early 1960s the life expectancies of below grade wood foundations are estimated in the 50 to 100-year range, considerably less than many traditional building foundation materials. Some manufacturers offer 60-year limited warranties. The wood is chemically treated to retard rot. Chemical treatment for wood used in foundations is more intensive than that typically used in wood for decks, and fencing. Wood foundations may rest on concrete. Special care must be taken to ensure that the foundation can perform its retaining wall function (adequately resisting

lateral forces) as it is not known whether rot and termites will become a major problem. If this were to occur, masonry or poured concrete foundations could be retrofitted.

FOURPLEX

A residential structure consisting of four self-contained residential units.

FRACTIONAL (PARTIAL) INTEREST

An interest in real estate that represents only a part of the total bundle of rights found in fee simple ownership.

Application The correct identification of interests in property is vital in determining the rights associated with that interest as well as estimating its value. Many distinct fractional interests can be created within one specific property, e.g., leased fee, leasehold, and sub-leasehold interests can be created through leases. Property can also be divided in terms of vertical interests, e.g., sub-surface rights, ground level rights, and air rights. Easements are also regarded as fractional interests established by legal documents in which one owner of land may enjoy specific rights over the land of another owner. Condominium, co-operative, and time-share ownerships can also be viewed as fractional interests that are established by statutory requirements to address special needs in the marketplace. During recent decades, the securitization of real estate has added a further dimension in which interests in real estate are held within a corporation and partial interests are marketed to investors as shares. The growth of real estate investment trusts is testimony to the growing interest in this form of partial interest.

FRAMING

The rough timber works of a structure, including studs, plates, lintels, and rafters.

Application Two types of framing predominate in Canada. Balloon framing was common in the late 19th and early 20th centuries. This wood frame construction technique used conventional wood studs and floor joists. The principal difference was that the wall studs were built before the floor systems, and the wall studs were continuous from the foundation up to the roof line. In modern day platform framing, a different approach is taken. A wood floor joist and subfloor system is provided on top of the foundation and studs are erected over this system, that are one-storey high. If the house is two-storeys, a second floor platform is assembled on top of the studs and then a second set of studs is put on top of this platform.

Figure F.11 illustrates typical framing components in a two-storey structure.

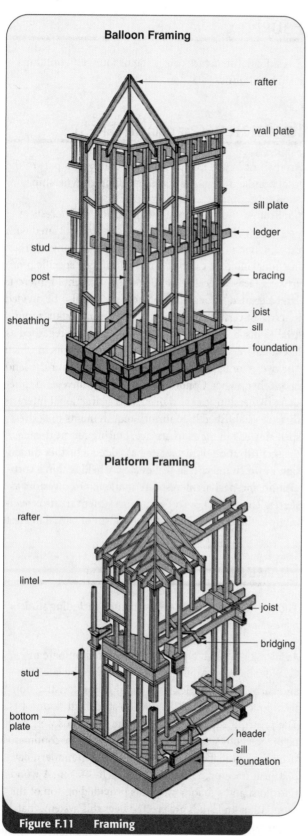

Figure F.11   Framing

FRANCHISE

A style of business entrepreneurship, under which the franchisor, for a fee or other remuneration, grants to the franchisee, for a term, the right to sell goods or services perfected by the franchisor, according to a plan, utilizing the franchisor's name, logo, and methods of expertise.

Franchising provides the small business person with a ready-made image, start-up and operating support mechanisms, and technical expertise in marketing. The extent of franchisor involvement varies in the marketplace depending on the specific service or product offered. The fastest growing franchises are those that offer a comprehensive business format, including training and ongoing management support. Participation in a franchised system gives the buyer insider knowledge of the industry, expert assistance in site location, and fully-developed operating and marketing techniques. Franchising succeeds for many reasons including co-operative advertising, collective buying power, rapid market penetration, and widespread visibility.

Advantages

The success of franchising is usually dependent on market penetration to ensure maximum image building. The cost of establishing a franchise system is substantial. Marketing and advertising costs are high, since franchisors must develop a two-pronged market strategy: one for marketing the franchise opportunity, and another for promoting the goods and services to the end-user.

The benefit of franchise ownership can be roughly grouped using seven categories.

Business Format   The franchisor provides a complete format to assist both in startup and ongoing operations. The format includes such things as trade mark and logo, marketing techniques, operating systems, physical layout, personnel structure, and product selection.

Franchise Expansion   The rapid growth of the franchisor increases the likelihood of success for the franchisee. A degree of flexibility and security are afforded both franchisor and franchisee that is not possible under other marketing systems and, therefore, a greater probability of success. Both parties benefit from the synergistic effect of expansion.

Image   The franchisor typically has an established image in the marketplace that provides the franchisee with *brand name* identification to attract consumers.

Training   Franchises offer training for new franchise owners regarding operating systems. Training often extends to employees as well, and may include additional topics such as general business techniques, marketing strategies, and financial record-keeping.

Operating Assistance   Most franchise agreements provide that the franchisor takes an active role in launching and supporting the new franchise unit. A franchisor typically assists with site selection, lease negotiation, decorating, obtaining equipment/products, and recruiting personnel.

Group Purchasing   As the franchise grows, significant cost savings can be accomplished by co-ordinating the purchase of products and services for franchise units.

Business Value Appreciation   As the successful franchise grows, the franchise fee for new entrants generally increases, thereby translating into added market value for existing franchisees.

Categories

Business format franchises generally fall into three categories:

Retail   Fast food chains, specialty food shops, automobile products and services, convenience stores, and other retail products including electronics, pet products, home improvements/hardware, photo finishing, books, clothing, and record stores.

Business/Personal Services   In-house cleaning services, security systems, car/truck rental and leasing services, tax returns, real estate brokerage, employment services, quick printing, education, exercise training, and computer training.

Travel and Leisure   Travel agencies, tanning parlours, hotel chains, and campgrounds.

Disadvantages

Cost   Initial cost for established franchise operations can be quite high.

Ongoing Costs/Fees   Fees for ongoing operations can add up to significant amounts, e.g., up to 10% of sales revenue.

Loss of Business Freedom   Franchisor standards must be met and often stringent operating procedures must be closely followed.

Purchase of Franchisor Products   Franchises involving the sale of products normally require that all products be acquired from the franchisor (often including a markup).

Remote Head Office   If the franchisor's head office is located in another country, redress may be difficult if the franchisor fails to live up to promises and obligations.

Listing/Selling

Franchise operations are listed and sold like any other business. Normally, most franchisors have a unique marketing plan for selling franchises. Some franchisors may, however, enlist the aid of a real estate brokerage, particularly concerning site selection, arranging a lease, or sometimes finding franchisees. Real estate brokerages can also be involved in the resale of a business for the franchisee. The franchise fee paid by the franchisee must be taken into consideration when evaluating the business to arrive at a listing price. The buyer must also agree to abide by the terms of the franchise agreement.

In any resale, practitioners should read franchise documentation carefully. Many franchisors will want to maintain control over a particularly valuable location, by taking a head lease on the site and subleasing it to the franchisee. Accordingly, the franchisor will have considerable control including insistence on a standard form sublease. Some franchise agreements provide that the franchise is strictly personal to the franchisee and is not assignable to others without the franchisor's prior approval. Practitioners must be diligent in their review of all franchise documentation to ensure that marketing efforts can result in a successful sale.

Real Estate Brokerage

As a strategic alternative, the real estate franchise offers an attractive package for independent brokerages whose success will vary depending on a number of issues. Financial stability upon joining the franchise, proper use of marketing tools provided, market conditions, and acceptance by the sales staff can all play a part in the success or failure of the venture.

The selection of a franchise should be made in relation to the overall goals of the brokerage. Too often, this growth option is picked for the wrong reasons. The competitive position of the brokerage and management commitment are important considerations. Ultimately, any selection should be based on two fundamental questions:

- How can this affiliation help the brokerage to grow, offer better services, and actively compete now and in the future?
- Are the initial and ongoing costs warranted and justified in relation to anticipated benefits?

Simple answers do not exist and strengths and weaknesses must be assessed. An undeniable synergistic effect can evolve from image compliance of the members. The public becomes aware of the network through signage, advertising, and promotional programs. The network may also give the brokerage opportunities to compete for corporate relocation business. Professional advertising is

F

normally available on a cost-effective basis, along with a full range of marketing and sales tools, given the purchasing power of the organization.

National and international referral networks can prove worthwhile for additional revenue and client/customer convenience. The franchise affiliation also allows for sharing of ideas through brokerage meetings and informal member gatherings. Also, organized training programs can be both cost effective and key to the development of sales staff.

On the converse, the franchise option is limited by certain bottom line considerations.

- Fees paid should be offset with corresponding gains through increased market share;
- Supply costs should be greatly reduced;
- Larger referral volume should be realized; and
- Sales personnel should be more effective.

The franchise association may severely overshadow any independent image that was once enjoyed by the brokerage. Paper work, reporting forms, and revisions to procedural/accounting systems may be time consuming for office personnel. Other considerations relate to conversion costs, e.g., changing signs, stationery and supplies, and office modifications.

The decision requires careful consideration, as corporate records must be altered, multi-year contracts signed, and up front dollars required. Real estate franchising has made substantial inroads in the brokerage business beginning in the early 1970s. Currently, a wide range of franchisors exist in the Canadian marketplace with differing fee structures, territorial arrangements, and degrees of exclusivity.

Provincial statutes may govern the selling of franchises including the provision of a disclosure statement and rights to rescind a franchise agreement if disclosure materials are not provided within a required time period.

Scenario

Broker/Owner Johnson, of ABC Realty Inc., is seriously considering a franchise to improve his market position in the West End. An acquaintance in a neighbouring community has recently decided to join that particular franchise. Johnson calls the acquaintance to get some advice and is provided with eleven guidelines that he used to make his decision:

- Carefully assess the financial stability of the franchisor and, if possible, request financial statements as the franchisor may be undercapitalized for the size of the market being sought, or the goals of the organization may be too expansive, given financial resources.
- Obtain all information about the geographic base of the franchisor, the market share in various areas of the country, the types of member brokers and their track record in terms of growth, market share, and rate of attrition.
- Analyze the exclusivity arrangements regarding territories.
- Carefully read the franchise agreement with particular attention to:
  - the initial term and procedures for the renewal of the agreement;
  - rights of the franchisor to inspect books of account and other items in the brokerage;
  - allotment of territories and rights concerning adjacent areas;
  - provisions for termination by either party;
  - requirements for a deposit and terms concerning its return should the agreement not be completed; and
  - conditions requiring direct purchases (supplies, forms, etc.) from the franchise company.

- Ensure the franchise organization has received approval to operate within the province and that signage has been reviewed under applicable guidelines and/or requirements set out in the real estate act/regulations.
- Assess the extent of assistance to be supplied by the franchisor in the area of education, management, and general support ensuring such representations are included in any agreement. As well, assess the depth of expertise within the franchise organization.
- Request a copy of the trademark registration of the franchisor to ensure that the investment in an image is properly protected under trademark law.
- Have a lawyer carefully review all contractual material to be signed.
- Consult an accountant regarding conversion expenses, purchase of rights, and deductibility.
- Carefully review the range of services offered and ensure that the franchisor is actively pursuing research and development of new products and services. Remember, one of the main reasons for joining an organization is not just to be competitive today, but also tomorrow.
- Have a complete understanding of fee calculations, provisions for increases in fees, how funds are remitted, reporting systems, the existence of any special assessments, and added costs at point of renewal such as a renewal fee and repeat registration of any trademark rights.

Figure F.12   Acquiring a Brokerage Franchise

FRAUD

The intentional use of deception in which the victim suffers some loss or injury.

Application   The *Criminal Code of Canada* distinguishes between fraudulent concealment (a person for a fraudulent purpose takes, obtains, removes, or conceals anything), and fraud that affects the public market (any one who by deceit, falsehood, or other fraudulent means, whether it is a false pretense within the meaning of this Act, defrauds the public or any person whether ascertained or not, of any property, money, or valuable security). Source: *Criminal Code of Canada (s. 341 and s. 380).*

Fraud affecting public markets also extends to fraudulent activities involving stocks, shares, merchandise, or anything offered to the public, the falsification of records and documents, and fraud under the *Bank Act.*

The *Criminal Code of Canada* (s. 386) references fraudulent registration of title relating to real property, e.g., a material false statement or concealment of material documents and/or facts. Real estate acts/regulations in specific provinces may also address fraudulent misrepresentation, promises or representations not made in good faith, the failure to account for funds received, and such conduct or activity that has the intent to deceive the public.

Provincial   See applicable reference materials.

FREEHOLD

(SEE ALSO ESTATE)

An interest in real estate for an infinite period of time (e.g., fee simple) or a defined time (e.g., life estate).

FRONT FOOT

A traditional method of expressing value based on the linear distance of a lot along a public road or public waterway, assuming generally uniform sized lots within the general area under investigation.

Example 1   *Front Foot–Urban Residential*

Salesperson Lee, of ABC Realty Inc., plans to market vacant lots in Anycity Heights to prospective builders. Lee's client, Developer Reed, requires that all lot prices be based on $1,200 per front foot. Accordingly, Lee has listed the adjacent lots of generally uniform size as follows:

Continued…

LOT	FRONTAGE	PRICE PER FRONT FOOT	LISTING PRICE
Lot 1	50.0	1200	60,000
Lot 2	47.5	1200	57,000
Lot 3	52.0	1200	62,400

Example 2   *Front Foot–Waterfront Recreational*

Salesperson Martin, of XYZ Real Estate Ltd., is listing a waterfront building lot on East Lake. Recent sales of comparable properties indicates a value of $980 per front foot. The subject property has a lake frontage of 74.5 feet. The indicated value of the subject property based on comparables is:

74.5 x $980 = $73,010 (rounded to $73,000)

FRONTAGE

The extent of a building or of land measured in linear distance along a public road. In recreation waterfront property, frontage may refer to the lot dimension abutting the waterway.

Example   *Frontage*

Salesperson Lane, of ABC Realty Inc. has just listed a property at 123 Main Street, Anycity, with a frontage of 75 feet (22.86 metres) on Main Street and a depth of 100 feet (30.48 metres).

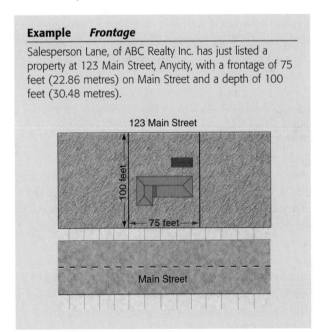

FRUCTUS INDUSTRIALES

Annual crops resulting from manual labour that are sown and harvested in the same year, such as potatoes, wheat, sugar beets, flax, and oats.

Application Such crops are not deemed to be part of the land and do not pass in title to a buyer when the farm is sold. Persons whose interests in land are limited in duration, that is to say, people leasing the land or only holding the land for the duration of their life, are empowered directly or through their personal representatives to enter upon the land after their interest in the land has expired to harvest the fructus industriales.

FRUCTUS NATURALES

Perennial crops such as apple trees, strawberry patches, rhubarb plants, shrubs, rose bushes, and lawn grass that are broadly categorized as growing naturally. Such crops are deemed to be part of the land and *do* pass in title to a buyer when the farm or property is sold.

FRUSTRATION, DOCTRINE OF

A legal concept involving the nullifying or thwarting of one's efforts. A primary consideration in law is that contracts in general should be binding on the parties involved. However, something may occur after the agreement is made that is unforeseen and beyond the control of either party which makes it impossible to perform the contract, e.g., the structure is destroyed by fire or the property is expropriated. The law recognizes that, in such cases, the contract is discharged by frustration. In other words, the contract is incapable of performance because circumstances have changed so drastically that the thing that was contracted for is different from what would now occur if the contract was to be performed.

Application Frustration can be encountered in a real estate transaction. A decision that a contract has been discharged by frustration is a practical and reasonable solution to a situation that was unforeseen and beyond the power of the parties to prevent. In such cases, both parties are released from their duty of further performance and returned to the situation they were in prior to the agreement, and the deposit (if applicable) returned to the buyer. Many agreements/contracts address the unforeseen situation of the subject matter being destroyed. The buyer has the option to avoid the contract or have the property returned to its original condition.

The doctrine of frustration is somewhat complex and it should not be assumed that a contract can be cancelled without close examination of the relevant facts. A lawyer should always be consulted before attempting to avoid a contract on this basis.

FUNCTIONAL OBSOLESCENCE

The impairment of functional capacity or efficiency and reflects the loss in value brought about by such factors as overcapacity, inadequacy, and changes in technology that affect the property item itself or its relation with other items comprising a larger property. A structure is said to be functionally obsolete when it cannot adequately perform the function for which it is currently employed. The method used to estimate loss of value varies based on the form of functional obsolescence.

Curable

Described as loss of value due to deficiencies or superadequacies, that the prudent owner or buyer would be justified in replacing, adding, or removing because the cost of effecting a cure would be at least offset by the anticipated increase in utility, and ultimately in market value.

Deficiency refers to an inability to perform to today's standards owing to some missing item (requiring an addition), e.g., installation of smart building technology for energy conservation including software, hardware, and communication links, or inadequacy regarding the improvements (requiring a substitution or updating/modernization), e.g., a 100 amp electrical service that can be easily converted to 200 amp for a cost that is less than the value that would accrue to the property by its addition. A superadequacy might involve high ceilings in a structure that affect both overall appearance and heating costs. The lowering of the ceilings not only reduces energy costs, but also improves overall appearance resulting in an increase in market value exceeding the cost.

Example	***Functional Obsolescence Curable–Deficiency (Modernization)***

Practitioners commonly encounter functional obsolescence resulting from lack of modernization. The cost to cure from an appraiser's perspective is the cost of the new item, plus its installation, less the present value of the old item currently in the building. Assume that the subject building has older-style kitchen cupboards that were no longer popular and buyers would, on moving in, replace them with modern cabinets as the value would be increased by the cost of the cupboards.

Incurable

Loss in value due to deficiencies or superadequacies that the prudent buyer or owner would not be justified in replacing, adding, or removing because the cost of effecting a cure would be greater than the anticipated increase in utility or market value resulting from the replacement, addition, or removal.

While the correction of the problem may be physically or technically possible, such a change is termed incurable because the typical buyer would not make the correction because the cost would be greater than the anticipated increase in value. In other words, it would not make economic sense to correct the obsolescence and most buyers would not do so.

Two types of incurable functional obsolescence exist: deficiency and superadequacy. A deficiency might relate to the lack of internal air-conditioning and associated ductwork with no cost effective method to remedy. Superadequacy might involve an over improvement that does not realize any economic benefit, e.g., excess number of parking spaces.

Example **_Functional Obsolescence Incurable–Deficiency_**

Anne Appraiser is attempting to measure the estimated or actual rental loss from an income property arising out of incurable functional obsolescence and more particularly, deficiencies within that rental property. The subject property has a poor floor plan and insufficient closet space. As a result of this deficiency, the building would rent for less than a similar rental property that did not suffer from this problem and, accordingly, a loss in value is attributable arising from functional obsolescence.

FUNCTIONAL UTILITY

The sum of the attractiveness and usefulness of the property including its ability to perform the function for which it was intended, in terms of current market tastes and standards. Elements of functional utility in a residential structure include architecture, design and layout, traffic patterns, sizes and types of rooms, and performance standards.

Example **_Functional Utility_**

Anne Appraiser is determining the functional utility and consequently the amount of depreciation to apply in arriving at the value of a property by means of the cost approach. Upon inspecting the home, she discovers that room layout is poor, bedroom sizes are unusually small compared with comparable properties, and the general architecture significantly dates the property.

As a result, the attractiveness and marketability of the property are affected. When arriving at a value, she will allow for these factors when determining the amount of depreciation to deduct under the cost approach. The deduction is required due to the lack of functional utility in the property under consideration.

FURNACE

A central heating system in which heat is generated in one location and then distributed through the structure, typically through sheetmetal ductwork. With the exception of electric furnaces, all furnaces have three major components: heat exchanger, burner, and blower.

Electric Furnace

An electric furnace has no actual combustion and consequently no need for a heat exchanger, burner, or a chimney. These components are replaced by electric heating elements sitting directly in the air stream. The blower simply forces air across the heating elements and the warmed air returned to the rooms via ductwork.

Figure F.13 illustrates the movement of air from point of entry through to the exit.

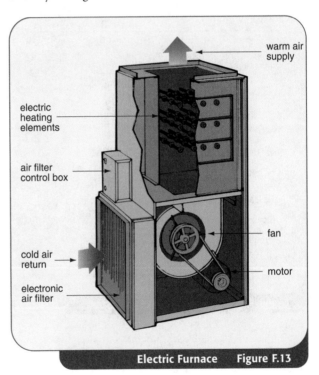

electric heating elements

air filter control box

cold air return

electronic air filter

warm air supply

fan

motor

Electric Furnace   Figure F.13

Gas Furnace

Gas furnaces can generally be divided into four levels for purposes of residential and commercial usage in the Canadian marketplace:

- Conventional;
- Mid-efficiency;
- High efficiency; and
- High efficiency pulse.

Efficiency

Furnaces and boilers are classified by their efficiency. Most systems, until the mid-1970s, had an operating (steady state) efficiency of approximately 80%. However, this rating only applies to continuous operation. Given losses, particularly when the unit is starting up and shutting down, the actual efficiency is about 55 to 65%.

Mid-efficiency furnaces using devices such as vent dampers (to prevent heat from escaping up the chimney when the unit is shut down), and the replacement of continuously operating pilot lights by spark ignited pilots, now provide a seasonal efficiency in the eighty percent range. High efficiency furnaces and boilers go a step further as mid-efficiency furnaces are limited due to condensation. High efficiency systems (also known as condensing units), are designed to withstand corrosive condensation and have a drainage system to get rid of the condensate. Also, such units have more than one heat exchanger, some having three. A conventional gas furnace is shown in **Figure F.14**.

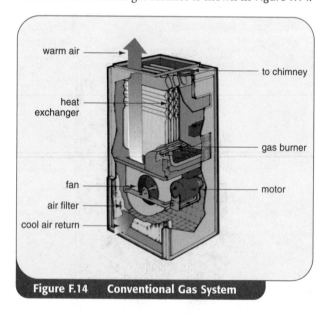

Figure F.14   Conventional Gas System

Some manufacturers also employ a pulse process for improved combustion. This system relies on pressure waves to force products of combustion out of the combustion chamber, the pressure wave is then reflected back and ignites the next gas/air mixture to continue the pulse process that becomes self perpetuating. The hot gases, forced out of the combustion chamber, pass across a heat exchanger where the heat is transferred (see **Figure F.15**). These systems tend to be noisier than most high efficiency systems. High efficiency furnaces incorporate features (as do mid-efficiency systems), to limit off-cycle losses. High efficiency furnaces have a seasonal efficiency in the mid to high 90 percent range.

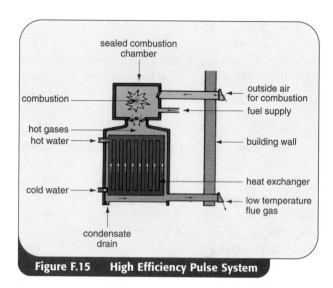

Figure F.15   High Efficiency Pulse System

Gravity Furnace

The gravity furnace, often referred to as the *octopus furnace*, operates similarly to a conventional furnace except that no fan exists to draw house air to the furnace, blow it through the furnace, and push it out of the air registers. Instead, the system works on gravity (convection), relying on warm air to rise through the supply ducts and cool air to settle back through the return ducts to the furnace. Gravity furnaces are now viewed as obsolete due primarily to their inefficiency. **Figure F.16** illustrates a typical gravity furnace with a large return air inlet to accommodate convection and an outlet at floor level for warm air leading from the furnace.

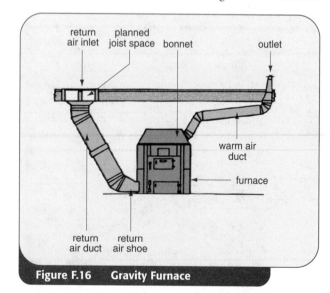

Figure F.16   Gravity Furnace

FUTURE ESTATE
(SEE ESTATE)

G TO H

G to H

National Info Links

Goods and Services Tax/Harmonized Sales Tax

Canada Customs and Revenue Agency
Web Site   www.ccra-adrc.gc.ca

Health/Toxic Substances

Joint federal responsibility involving Environment Canada and Health Canada.

Environment Canada
Web Site   www.ec.gc.ca

Health Canada
Web Site   www.hc-sc.gc.ca

Historic/Heritage Sites—National

Parks Canada National Office
25 Eddy Street
Hull, PQ K1A 0M5

Web Site   www.parkscanada.gc.ca

Home Building

Canadian Home Builders' Association
Web Site   www.chba.ca

Housing Statistics

Canada Mortgage and Housing Corporation
700 Montreal Road
Ottawa, ON K1A 0P7

Telephone   (613) 748 2000
Web Site   www.cmhc-schl.gc.ca

Human Rights

For national perspectives on human rights, contact:

Canadian Heritage
15 Eddy Street
Hull, PQ K1A 0M5

Telephone   (819) 997 0055
Web Site   www.pch.gc.ca

For wording of *Canadian Human Rights Act* (The Department of Justice Canada), see:
http://laws.justice.gc.ca/en/h-6/index.html

For provincial *Human Rights Code* information refer to the applicable provincial reference materials.

G

GABION

A metal enclosure made of mesh or chain link normally filled with stone designed to act as a retaining wall.

Gabions are often used to reduce erosion caused by the water movement at or near the shoreline and are normally discouraged if they affect the natural water flow or fish habitat. Installation of gabions are subject to local and provincial ministry/department approval. Figure G.1 illustrates a cross-section of a typical gabion installation.

Provincial   See applicable reference materials.

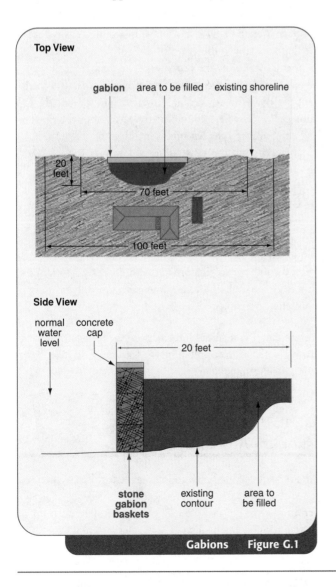

Gabions   Figure G.1

GABLE

An inverted *V* or triangular shaped portion of a wall, extending to the roof line, above the first floor level and may contain a window or a decorative structure.

Application   Historically, a gable-end house referred to a structure where at least the front, and sometimes rear elevations contained gables. However, modern usage refers to gables anywhere on the structure. For example, rural and recreational practitioners frequently refer to bungalows as a gable or cottage roof style. The gable-end structure has two inverted V shaped gables typically on the side elevations. The cottage end structure has sloped roof lines at both ends instead of gables.

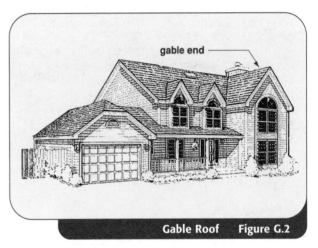

Gable Roof   Figure G.2

GAIN
(SEE ALSO CAPITAL GAIN)

Increases in the owner's equity caused by a transaction that is not part of the typical, day-to-day operations and not part of an owner's investments or withdrawals. Gains (and losses) generally apply to non-operating, incidental, peripheral, or non-routine transactions, e.g., the gain on the sale of land in contrast to gross profit on the sale of inventory.

GAP LOAN

An interim financing vehicle that provides funding between construction advances and the placement of permanent financing.

Application   While no standard scenario exists, a gap loan is normally associated with the following circumstance.

A large construction project has an interim lender that advances funds based on projected costs. A permanent lender advances funds at project completion and the assurance of an income stream on the property. In some cases, the project is completed and final draws have been taken under interim financing, but the permanent lender has only advanced part of the take-out funds, due to the borrowers failure to secure full rental of all space as required in the mortgage commitment, e.g., the permanent lender advances 75% of the total commitment because 25% of the floor space remains unrented. The gap loan is used to augment permanent financing advanced until full rental is achieved.

Example   *Gap Loan*

Developer Reed is constructing an office building for $10,000,000 with an agreed take-out loan from a permanent lender for $7,500,000 based on 90% occupancy of the completed structure. The interim lender has agreed to provide three consecutive draws of $2,000,000 based on predetermined stages of construction completion. The interim lender provides all draws as agreed totalling $6,000,000. The permanent lender subsequently advances $6,000,000 to repay the interim lender, but withholds $1,500,000 awaiting required occupancy levels. The developer, lacking sufficient funds to complete final construction secures a gap loan from a different lender for $1,500,000 until all funds from the permanent lender are advanced.

GARDEN APARTMENT

A low-rise building designed for multi-family living, usually located in a suburban area. This terminology is most frequently associated with the United States and should not be confused with garden suites commonly referenced in the Canadian marketplace.

GARDEN SUITES

Separate, self-contained residential structures that contain one occupancy unit and usually designed for portability. Garden suites (granny flats) are generally in the side or rear yard of an existing house and are typically regulated by local municipal zoning by-laws.

GARNISHMENT

A proceeding whereby property, money, or credit of a debtor, in the possession of another (the garnishee), are applied to the payment of debts by means of process involving the debtor and the garnishee.

Example   *Garnishment*

Broker/Owner Johnson, of ABC Realty Inc., received a court order that a garnishment is to be placed against the earnings of an employed salesperson. The garnishment concerns failure to make child support payments pursuant to a separation agreement. The notification requires ABC Realty Inc., to withhold an amount equal to 20% of all income before taxes and remit to the appropriate agency.

GE CAPITAL MORTGAGE INSURANCE CANADA

A private mortgage default insurer and the only *private* supplier of mortgage default insurance in Canada, the other supplier being Canada Mortgage and Housing Corporation (CMHC). GE Capital provides a wide range of flexible products for the purchase, renovation, or financing of homes.

During 1995, GE CAPITAL acquired the residential lending insurance portfolio previously owned by the Mortgage Insurance Company of Canada (MICC). MICC was originally created to provide mortgage insurance that reduced the lender's risk in the event of default. The insurance fee is normally paid by the borrower. The majority of loans insured are high ratio mortgages, however, insurance can be provided on conventional financing. To qualify, the mortgagor must meet requirements as set out by the insuring company and the lending institution. In addition, the financial organization providing the monies must adhere to specific lending policies as set out by that insuring organization.

GE Capital Mortgage Insurance now offers a fully automated delivery and decision system called GE Excel that electronically receives customer applications, processes requests, and approves applications within minutes. GE Excel combines a scoring process with property information and underwriting guidelines to ensure not only fast, but consistent decisions.

Reference   The above information has been summarized from information supplied by GE Capital Mortgage Insurance Canada.

GENERAL ACCOUNT— REAL ESTATE BROKERAGE

An account established by a brokerage for the payment of general office expenses. Shares of commission or other remuneration are also paid into the general account for distribution to the brokerage's salespersons and other employees. However, exceptions do apply, i.e., monies owed to salespersons are sometimes placed in a separate account maintained by the brokerage, called a *commission trust account*, for distribution.

Typically, certain minimum books and records are required in regard to the general account.

- Duplicate deposit book (or slips).
- Cheque books with stubs attached or duplicated cheques in an automated system.
- Monthly bank statements with cancelled cheques.
- Cash receipt and disbursement journal.
- Monthly bank reconciliation.

Application Provincial regulatory acts generally describe the function and operation of general accounts, but devote most emphasis to transfers from trust to general account. While requirements differ, every withdrawal from a brokerage's trust account (including transfers to the brokerage's general account of trust money once that money has been earned and is no longer required to be held in trust), must be made by cheque or other acceptable transfer and must refer to the appropriate transaction.

A commission cheque received from another brokerage, after completion of the sale, may be deposited directly into a general account or other account maintained by the brokerage for purposes of paying commissions to licensed/registered salespeople and others as dictated by the appropriate real estate act.

Example *General Account—Real Estate Brokerage*

Broker/Owner Johnson, of ABC Realty Inc., wants to ensure accuracy in the control of records concerning his general account and follow both the letter and intent of the provincial real estate act.

As a broker, he knows the importance of accurate and timely financial information including detailed cross-referencing for a proper paper trail. He insists that all accounting entries relating to commission income be clearly identified with the address and source of funds. While trade numbers may be adequate for record keeping purposes, he feels the added information can improve overall accuracy and make error searches easier. Various instructions have been given to the staff.

Postings

All postings must be weekly and whenever possible, even more frequently.

Reconciliations

Written monthly bank reconciliations are required for approval by the broker in conformance with the provincial real estate act.

Continued...

Journal Entries

All entries in journals and supporting records must be fully identified for cross-referencing purposes (trade number when commission payments or related transfer of funds is made); all entries recorded on deposit books, cheques, and stubs are fully identified (including trade numbers when transactions are involved).

Deposit Book Entries

Johnson insists that deposits to the general account clearly show source, trade number, and address of the property as this can substantially reduce error tracking time.

Cheques and Stubs

All cheques and stubs involving commission should clearly reference pertinent details from the transaction. Therefore, each cheque should show the address and trade number along with seller or buyer name.

Payroll Journal

A ledger sheet for each salesperson and salaried staff member showing all payroll entries, trade/address identification (as required), and deductions. This format will better organize payroll records and improve overall accuracy.

General Ledger

While cash receipts and disbursement journals are adequate, Johnson also sets up a general ledger that provides a complete summary of all accounts. Without a general ledger, neither a balance sheet nor an income statement can be generated. If the brokerage firm is not using a computerized accounting system, a loose leaf binder should be used for this ledger to allow for expansion as new accounts are added.

Provincial See applicable reference materials for accounting requirements concerning general and trust accounts.

GENERAL CONTRACTOR

A contractor in a construction project, normally selected through bidding procedures, who is responsible for completion of the project in a skillful manner acceptable to both architect and owner.

The general contractor may be contracted to handle all work within a particular project, as in the case of a multi-storey office building where the same contractor is used for all tenant space construction. The contractor could also contract on a time-and-material basis.

The general contractor who deals directly with the owner is not to be confused with a subcontractor who provides specific services to the general contractor.

Example *General Contractor*

ABC Realty Inc. has acquired a small retail site with the intent of occupying approximately 20% of the planned structure and leasing the balance to other tenants. Following acquisition of the lands, ABC Realty Inc. hires an architect to co-ordinate overall design, layout, and specifications. The agreed upon structure is then put out to bid. Contractor B is selected as the general contractor and negotiates a price to construct the building according to the specifications. Contractor B then hires subcontractors to perform various aspects of the work.

GENERAL PARTNER

(SEE ALSO LIMITED PARTNERSHIP)

The participant in a limited partnership who manages the operation and is liable for all debts. The general partner, in the case of real estate, is usually a developer who allows other individuals (limited partners) to participate in a project to raise necessary funding.

Application   The general partner will probably prepare projections indicating the viability of the project and consequential benefits to be obtained by the limited partners. The general partner may also incorporate a *shell* corporation, the assets of which are limited to those sums contributed by the limited partners. Under such an arrangement, if the project was unsuccessful, the limited partners would have no recourse or power to force the general partner to fulfill obligations. Therefore, limited partners may look beyond the terms of the partnership agreement to ensure that the general partner supplies sufficient additional guarantees to secure the limited partners' positions.

Example *General Partner*

Developer Reed wishes to undertake a residential development involving a 40-acre tract of land. To fund the project, the developer will invest $1,500,000. He also prepares detailed plans and financial projections concerning the project and its overall feasibility, and incorporates a corporation for the sole purpose of completing this project.

Based on presentations to investors, he is able to secure sufficient commitments ($300,000 per investor) to raise the necessary equity of $3,000,000 required by the lender who is contemplating financing the project. Reed becomes the general partner, with the individual investors taking on limited partner status in the land development.

GENERAL PURPOSE INDUSTRIAL BUILDING

(SEE INDUSTRIAL BUILDING CATEGORIES)

GENUINE INTENTION

(SEE ALSO CONTRACT)

An authentic desire to follow through on an agreement. An essential element in a contract is the mutual consent or meeting of the minds of the parties. Instances may arise where all the other elements of a valid contract (such as lawful object and consideration), are in place, but the promise of one or both of the parties has been given based on, or affected by, some misunderstanding, false inducement, force, or the like so that the offended party may avoid the contract and even have the right to redress. In other words, a valid intent was not present given no meeting of the minds. Generally, such actions fall into one of the following categories: duress, undue influence, mistake, or misrepresentation (innocent, fraudulent, or negligent).

Example *Genuine Intention*

Buyer Jones is inspecting the premises and briefly encounters the seller on a rear patio area. Jones strikes up a short conversation and inquires directly of seller Smith as to the exact location of the rear survey pins. Jones wants to install a pool and a surrounding deck area. Smith casually points in a generally northward direction and identifies a small stone pile in the rear yard that is the location of the north west pin. He assures Jones that the other survey pin is directly across from that point near the woods. Unfortunately, Jones is looking at a different pile of stones that is a much further (approximately 40 feet), than the one identified by the seller.

In accordance with the agreement, a new survey is completed but Jones, relying on Smiths representation, does not examine it closely. On closing date, Jones finally realizes the misunderstanding and refuses to close arguing that the yard is too small for the planned pool/deck improvements. He argues that there was never a meeting of the minds and therefore no genuine intention.

GLAZIER

A person responsible for handling and installing glass.

GLAZING

The act of furnishing and/or fitting panes or sheets of glass as in the case of windows and doors.

Application   Prior to 1950, all windows were single-glazed (one pane of glass). The insulation value of a single conventional pane of glass is approximately R-1. Double-glazing is either factory sealed or vented. The factory sealed, double-glazing is designed to have no air infiltration or exfiltration between the two panes. Vented double glazing allows for outside air movement to the space between the two panes of glass.

Optimum air space between the panes is widely debated but is usually considered to be roughly ⅝ to ¾ inch. Typical double-glazed windows have an approximate R-value of 2. The triple-glazed window provides for two air spaces between three panes of glass with an R-3 or slightly higher insulating value.

Example *Glazing*

Buyer Jones is concerned about energy loss from windows. The commercial property under consideration lacks factory sealed, double-glazed windows. Admittedly, the two front windows are factory sealed with double-glazing, but all remaining windows consist of a primary (inner) window and a separate storm (outer) window. Jones calls in an energy expert to review the situation.

The expert explains that the value of a primary plus a storm window is not significantly more than a primary window. Therefore, the single pane of glass on all but the front windows translates into roughly R-1 whereas double-glazing produces R-2 and triple, R-3. The expert explains that energy costs relate not only to the R-value, but also the amount of air leaks given the primary/storm arrangement. In summary, Jones must address two issues: first, the loss of energy by heat conduction owing to a low R-value in the primary/storm window combinations, and second, outside air infiltration due to leakage in and around the frames of those windows.

GOING CONCERN VALUE
(SEE ALSO BUSINESS VALUATION)

The value attributable to the ongoing operation of a proven business venture. Going concern value includes both the tangible aspects of the real property such as buildings and other improvements as well as the intangible aspects of the business owing to its economic viability.

GOING-IN CAPITALIZATION RATE
(SEE ALSO TERMINAL CAPITALIZATION RATE)

A rate used to convert the income of a property into a capital value. The going-in rate applies to a current time period as distinguished from a terminal capitalization rate that is applied to a forecasted income at anticipated point of disposition. Both going-in and terminal capitalization rates are usually overall capitalization rates that consist of two components: rate of return *on* the investment and rate *of* return of the investment. Going-in rates are based on current research in the marketplace, while terminal cap rates are forecasted using a number of assumptions, one of which is the element of future risk.

GOOD FAITH
(SEE ALSO FIDUCIARY RESPONSIBILITIES)

Honesty of intention, abstention from taking unconscionable advantage of another including appropriate disclosures as required, and freedom from knowledge of circumstances that ought to cause a reasonable person to investigate.

Good faith is one of several fiduciary duties owed by an agent to his/her principal. Other duties include accountability, confidentiality, competence, loyalty, and obedience.

GOODS AND SERVICES TAX

G to H

Acronym: GST GST is a form of value-added tax, similar to that used currently by members of the European Union. A business registered for the GST collects the 7% tax on the sale of applicable goods or services. Registered businesses are entitled to claim a refund or an input tax credit for GST paid on goods and services purchased for use in taxable activities. Nova Scotia, New Brunswick, and Newfoundland combined provincial sales tax with GST to create the harmonized sales tax (HST). HST applies to the same base of goods and services as GST, but at the rate of 15%, consisting of 7% federal and 8% provincial.

Calculations

Basic Calculations

Tax remitted to the government in a given period equals the gross amount of tax collected minus the total of input tax credits for that period. Where the input tax credits exceed the tax collected on sales for a particular period, a business receives a refund.

Example	GST–Calculations– Basic Calculations					

The following example illustrates the basic mechanics on how the GST flows through to the final consumer.

	SP	GST	PP	ITC	NT
Paper mill sells paper to wholesaler	100	7	0	0	7
Wholesaler sells paper to advertiser	200	14	(100)	(7)	7
Advertiser provides services to brokerage	600	42	(200)	(14)	28
Brokerage provides services to client	1,000	70	(600)	(42)	28
Total Tax					**70**

SP–Sales Price
PP–Purchase Price
GST–Goods and Services Tax on Sales
ITC–Input Tax Credit
NT–Net Tax

The total tax of $70 can also be calculated by multiplying the final retail price of $1,000 by the 7% tax rate. In this regard, the GST is similar to a retail sales tax. However, the mechanics of applying the GST, whereby tax is collected and remitted on the value-added at each stage, is the key difference between the two systems.

Calculations Concerning Real Estate Brokerage

The GST applies to most businesses operating in Canada. Special rules apply to some specific types of businesses. Real estate firms are required to collect and remit GST on fees earned by them in respect of the sale or lease of real property. GST is payable by the buyer of goods and services.

Businesses are required to collect tax from their customers as agents of the government. See **Figure G.3** for a simplified example of GST computation for a real estate brokerage. Figures are expressed in thousands.

ABC Realty Inc.
Goods and Services Tax Calculation

	SP	GST	TOTAL	REM	NET
Revenue					
Real estate services	2,800	196	2,996	196	2,800
Appraisal fees	200	14	214	14	200
	3,000	210	3,210	210	3,000
Expenditures					
Payments to firms/ independent agents	1,000	70	1,070	(70)	1,000
Employee comm.[1]	1,400		1,400		1,400
Computer system[2]	150	10.5	160.5	(10.5)	150
Professional services	5	.35	5.35	(.35)	5
Postage	1	.07	1.07	(.07)	1
Depreciation[2]	10		10		10
Interest[1]	75		75		75
Rent	100	7	107	(7)	100
Office Supplies	5	.35	5.35	(.35)	5
	2,746	88.27	2,834.27	(88.27)	2,746
Net Amount	**254**	**121.73**	**375.73**	**121.73**	**254**

SP–Amount Before GST
TOTAL–Total (SP + GST)
NET–Net Amount
GST–Goods and Services Tax on Sales
REM–Amounts Remitted or (Refunded)

Amounts are expressed in thousands (000's).

[1] These items are not subject to GST.

[2] A full input tax credit is available for capital purchases at the time of the purchase: hence, there is no credit allowed for depreciation.

Figure G.3 GST Calculations

Simplified Accounting Method

Small firms and independent contractors with annual revenues of $200,000 or less (including GST) are able to use a simplified method called the *Quick Method* to complete their GST return. Qualifying service businesses, including real estate firms, may use a rate of 5% of their gross revenues (including GST) to calculate their net GST remittance. This simplified approach does not mean that small firms can charge 5% on their real estate or commission fees. They must still collect 7% on commissions and pay 7% on their taxable purchases.

The benefit of the *Quick Method* is that a qualifying small brokerage may calculate the remittance to the government based on a simple formula. The business is not required to separately identify the GST collected on revenues and then deduct the amount of GST paid on purchases that are eligible for an input tax credit. However, under this method, brokerages are allowed to claim an input tax credit on capital purchases.

The firm may revoke this election, but the revocation must be a minimum of one year after the original election to use the Quick Method.

Example   GST–Calculations–Quick Method

Assume that a brokerage has annual real estate commissions of $150,000 plus $10,500 GST and purchases a computer for $8,650 (including GST) during the year. Simplified calculation:

Gross Commissions	$150,000
GST @ 7%	+10,500
Total	$160,500
GST Liability (5% (prescribed rate) x 160,500)	$8,025
Input Credit Available (7 ÷ 107 x $8,650)	−566
Net GST Remittance	**$7,459**

The *Quick Method* may not be beneficial to independent contractors or brokerages who conduct a significant amount of split-commission work. The flat rate of 5% must be calculated on gross commissions in which case the remittances will be considerably higher than under normal rules of GST.

Example   GST–Calculations–Normal Method

Assume an independent contractor receives 100% of his/her commissions but is obliged to pay 40% to a firm for administrative services. The independent contractor earns gross commissions of $100,000 for the year. Under the normal rules and *Quick Method* this individual could calculate his/her GST remittance as follows:

Normal Method	AMOUNT	GST
Gross Commissions	$100,000	$7,000
Administrative Expenses	−40,000	−2,800
Net Income and GST	$ 60,000	$4,200

Quick Method		
Gross Commission		$100,000
GST @ 7%		+7,000
Total		$107,000
Prescribed Rate	5 %	
Net GST ($107,000 x 0.05)	$5,350	

Extra Cost of Using Quick Method
($5,350 − $4,200) = $1,150

In this example there is an extra cost of approximately $1,150 in using the *Quick Method*.

Small real estate firms and independent contractors must carefully consider the advisability of using the *Quick Method*. Although it may reduce the costs of accounting and filing GST returns, it may noticeably increase GST costs where there are significant expenses subject to GST.

Taxable and Non-Taxable Items

The GST replaced the Federal Sales Tax on January 1, 1991. However, unlike the Federal Sales Tax, which applied almost exclusively to manufactured goods, the GST applies to a much broader range of goods as well as to most services. In general, all goods and services are subject to GST unless they are specifically designated as non-taxable. Non-taxable goods and services fall into two categories: zero-rated and tax-exempt. The difference between a zero-rated sale and a tax-exempt sale is that a supplier making a zero-rated sale is entitled to a refund of input tax credits, but a supplier making tax-exempt sales is not so entitled. Effectively, a zero-rated supply bears no GST at all. A list of goods and services that are zero-rated is provided.

- Basic groceries.
- Prescription drugs.
- Certain medical devices.
- Exports of goods and services.
- Certain agricultural and fishing activities.

Businesses do not charge GST on the tax-exempt sales of goods and services and they are not able to claim an input tax credit for the GST paid on the purchase of goods and services related to those tax-exempt sales. As a result, all tax-exempt goods and services have some tax content that business buyers are not able to recover as part of the input tax credit mechanism. Certain charities and non-profit organizations can recover a portion of the GST that they pay on their purchases regardless of whether they are registered for GST.

As an example, residential rents are tax-exempt, and the costs incurred by the landlord, such as repairs, are GST taxable to the landlord. Since the landlord is not eligible for input tax credits, GST is effectively reflected in the landlord's rent structure. A list of tax-exempt goods and services is provided.

- Sales of existing residential properties.
- Residential rents on residential property including parking spaces.
- Most health care and dental services.
- Daycare services.
- Legal aid services.
- Many educational services (however, many business courses which are not required to obtain or maintain accreditation will be taxable).

- Financial services, including interest, dividends, insurance and mortgage brokerage services.
- Most sales and long-term leases of real property by non-profit organizations.
- Supplies by many public sector organizations including certain types of charitable and non-profit organizations.
- Certain supplies of goods or services provided to the federal or provincial government.

Real estate brokerage fees or commissions relating to real property situated in Canada are subject to tax at the rate of 7%. Real estate firms are required to collect tax on their real estate commission revenues but are also entitled to recover tax paid on their purchases of goods and services by way of input tax credits. Although licensed/registered practitioners may be providing services in respect of the tax-exempt sale of existing residences, their services are subject to GST.

Mortgage brokers are included in the financial services sector and so their fees and commissions are exempt from GST. Mortgage brokers are, therefore, not required to charge GST on such fees but are unable to claim input tax credits for GST paid on purchases connected with that business.

Commissions and Fees

Bad Debts

In some instances, a brokerage is unable to collect a commission that is due and payable and the brokerage has already filed the GST return. The commission will normally be written off in the brokerage's books of accounts as a bad debt. Where a bad debt is realized on an arm's length account receivable that included GST, an input tax credit equal to the portion of the total GST that related to the uncollectible accounts receivable can be claimed.

Effectively the GST component of any bad debt is eligible for a credit where GST has been remitted. The allowances for bad debts or provisions for doubtful accounts will not trigger the credit. Only the actual write-off of a bad debt will qualify for this credit.

In some cases, a seller is prepared to pay the commission but refuses to pay the GST on the commission. Where the amount of the GST is considered to be a bad debt, however, only the portion of the total GST that related to the uncollectible amount can be claimed as a credit. Although the bad debt may have been related to the GST portion, the government considers that each $1.07 collected has seven cents of GST included.

The credit may be claimed in the same reporting period in which GST is remitted on the debt. Where a debt is written off in the same reporting period as the GST is remitted, the brokerage is required to report the GST for that reporting period and claim an offsetting credit. GST must be remitted equal to the amount of input tax credit that had been claimed as part of a bad debt that related to any part of that bad debt subsequently recovered.

Commissions Earned by Employed Salespeople

Real estate salespeople classed as employees (as opposed to independent contractors), need not register for GST purposes and are not required to charge their employers GST on commissions or fees earned by them. Employed salespeople may, however, be entitled to claim rebates on certain expenses incurred by them in the course of their employment. (See the section entitled *Expenses*.)

Commissions Earned by Independent Contractors

Many real estate salespeople are, for income tax purposes, considered independent contractors and not employees. A discussion of the rules governing how independent contractor status is attained is beyond the scope of this guide. The Canada Customs and Revenue Agency (CCRA) has confirmed that if a salesperson has independent contractor status under the *Income Tax Act*, the same status will be granted for GST purposes.

Example	GST—Commissions and Fees— Commissions Earned by Independent Contractors

Assume that an independent contractor is entitled to a commission of $1,000. Under his arrangement with his brokerage, 40% of the commission is payable to the brokerage for administrative fees.

	AMOUNT	GST REC'D	GST PAID	TOTAL
Gross Commission	$1,000	$70		$1,070
Administrative Fee	400		28	428

If this were the independent contractor's only transaction in the period, the GST return would reflect the following:

GST Collected	$70
Input Tax Credit	−28
Net Remittance	$42

Independent contractors are required to register for GST purposes if their annual gross revenues exceed $30,000. They are required to charge GST on their gross commissions or fees earned and are entitled to claim credits for the GST paid on expenses related to these taxable activities. Independent contractors who are entitled to the full amount of the commissions through a brokerage will be required to collect GST on the full commission. Where the independent contractor pays a percentage or fixed amount to the brokerage for administrative and operating costs, the independent contractor will be charged GST on those amounts and is entitled to recover the GST paid as an input credit on filing their GST return.

Commissions/Fees Subject to GST

All commissions and fees earned by salespeople and brokers with respect to the sale or lease of real property situated in Canada are subject to tax. Real estate fees are taxable even if the sale of the real property is exempt. For example, GST does not normally apply to sales of used housing, however, real estate fees earned on the sale of used housing are taxable.

It should be noted that income paid to employed real estate salespeople, including commissions, is not subject to GST since payments to employees are exempt from GST. Commissions and other amounts paid to independent contractors are subject to GST.

Other revenues earned by salespeople or brokers such as appraisal, referral, and consulting fees, except for mortgage brokerage fees, are also subject to tax. Referral fees or other fees in relation to real estate outside Canada are not subject to GST and are considered as zero-rated fees.

Mortgage brokerage fees are, however, treated as exempt because these fees are considered as a *financial service* for GST purposes.

Practitioners may, in isolated instances, provide listings and negotiate sales for members of their families. These are considered as transactions with related parties. Upon completion of a sale in such circumstances, a commission is often not charged on the basis that the work done is regarded as a *gift*. The salesperson or broker should be aware that provisions exist in the *Excise Tax Act* that require the GST to be paid on the fair market value of the commission foregone. It is reasonable to anticipate that the CCRA will not use these provisions to require tax to be paid when the facts of a particular situation clearly indicate that the work performed was a gift. However, where commissions are routinely foregone and input tax credits continue to be claimed on expenses incurred or the transaction involves a split commission, the Canada Customs and Revenue Agency has the ability to assess tax owing even though no commission has been charged.

Commissions Payable to Co-operating Brokerages

Commissions payable to co-operating brokerages are subject to GST. The listing brokerage is required to collect tax on the total commission payable by the seller of the property. The selling brokerage invoices the listing brokerage for its share of the total commission and is required to collect GST on that share. The listing brokerage may claim an input tax credit for the GST charged by the selling brokerage. The input tax credit is available to the listing brokerage when the GST is paid or becomes payable to the selling brokerage.

In many cases the fee that the co-operating brokerage receives is contingent on the commission paid by the seller of the property. Although a co-operating brokerage may issue a notice to the listing brokerage which appears to be an invoice requesting payment, the notice is not regarded as an invoice which triggers an obligation to remit GST. The notice is not regarded as notification of an obligation to pay the amount as long as the fee to the co-operating brokerage is contingent on the listing brokerage being paid. Similarly, the listing brokerage would not be able to claim any input tax credit on basis of such notice issued before the closing date of the sale where the fee is contingent on the listing brokerage being paid.

Where the listing brokerage is paid a commission pursuant to its agreement with the seller, the entire amount of that commission must be included in the brokerage's revenue to compute revenues for GST purposes. As previously mentioned, however, the listing brokerage is entitled to an input tax credit for any tax paid on the commission to a co-operating brokerage.

Small Brokerages and Independent Contractors

Brokerages with annual revenues of $30,000 or less are not required to register and collect GST although they may elect to do so. Those who choose not to register do not collect tax on their fees and commissions, nor are they able to claim input tax credits on their business expenses, including commissions paid to co-operating brokers.

Independent contractors or brokerages with annual revenues of $200,000 or less may elect to use a simplified accounting method to compute their GST liability. Under this method, instead of remitting the difference between 7% of revenues and actual tax paid on expenses during the period, an independent contractor or a brokerage may simply remit 5% of total revenues for the period except for capital purchases, and forego claiming actual input tax credits. This method would only be advantageous if actual tax paid on non-capital expenses did not significantly exceed 2% of gross revenues. See previous topic entitled *Simplified Accounting Method*.

Taxable vs. Tax Exempt

Referral and other fees relating to real estate situated outside of Canada are zero-rated. See **Figure G.4**.

Tax Extra vs. Tax-Included Real Estate Fees

Under the GST, brokerages have the option of pricing their products or services by:

- Showing the GST as a separate amount payable on invoices or in written agreements; or
- Including the GST in the final price of a product or service.

In real estate terms, this would translate as follows:

• Commission or fee realized from the sale of a property plus 7% (GST) on the commission or fee; or

• Commission or fee with 7% GST already included into the total owed to the firm by the seller.

The first option made the GST clearly visible to consumers of housing and easier to identify as the government's tax, not something that is being charged by real estate practitioners for their services.

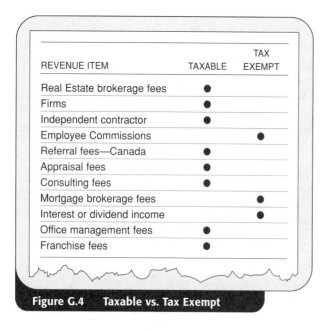

REVENUE ITEM	TAXABLE	TAX EXEMPT
Real Estate brokerage fees	●	
Firms	●	
Independent contractor	●	
Employee Commissions		●
Referral fees—Canada	●	
Appraisal fees	●	
Consulting fees	●	
Mortgage brokerage fees		●
Interest or dividend income		●
Office management fees	●	
Franchise fees	●	

Figure G.4   Taxable vs. Tax Exempt

When Tax on Commission is Payable

The GST legislation provides that the tax normally becomes payable on the earliest of the following events.

• Date payment is made by the customer/client

• Date of issuance of an invoice to the customer/client

• Date shown on the invoice

• Due date for payment stipulated in a written agreement with the client/customer.

In the case of real estate listing agreements where the brokerage's right to the commission is contingent on the amount at the time the sale is closed, the CCRA has confirmed that GST is payable on the date of completion. For other agreements where the commission is not contingent on closing, the timing of the liability will depend upon the terms of the listing contract. Unless these agreements are amended to expressly provide for the payment of the commission on completion of the transaction, GST may be payable at an earlier date (e.g., date of execution of the agreement/contract).

Some brokerages may, in advance of the closing date, issue various reminder notices to the seller of the property (or to the seller's lawyer), of the expected commission that may become due and payable on the date of closing. In addition, the seller may prepare a notice to the lawyer advising the lawyer to pay the commission to the real estate brokerage upon closing.

The Canada Customs and Revenue Agency has accepted that the issuance of a reminder notice in a situation where the listing agreement provides that the commission is contingent (i.e., payable only if the transaction closes), will not trigger the liability to remit GST before the closing. Therefore if a commission is due and payable under a written agreement when a transaction is complete (i.e., the closing date) then GST is payable on the closing date and the issuance of a reminder notice prior to closing does not cause the GST on the commission to become due.

Where a listing agreement is not contingent but provides that the commission be paid on the closing of the sale of a certain property, the brokerage must be careful in issuing a reminder notice. If the reminder notice is considered to be an invoice requesting payment on the closing, the GST will become payable on issuance. However, the CCRA accepts that a reminder notice, which does not request payment but rather reiterates the provisions of the listing agreement, will not trigger the GST liability.

A direction issued by the seller authorizing the seller's lawyer to pay the brokerage the amount of the commission on closing will not trigger the GST liability. A direction is not an invoice for GST purposes since it is a communication between the seller and his/her solicitor.

Expenses

Input Tax Credits—General Rules

A basic principle of GST is that a registered brokerage or individual is normally entitled to receive credit for the tax paid on purchases used in connection with the business. This recoverable tax is referred to as an *input tax credit*. Generally, input tax credits are allowed for the full amount of the GST paid or payable on purchases of all property and services (including capital property or fixed assets), used in connection with a taxable or zero-rated activity. An input tax credit can be claimed as soon as the invoice is received even though payment may not be made until a subsequent period.

In other words, there is generally no *matching principle* in GST. Similarly, input tax credits can normally be claimed on the full amount of any capital purchases. No requirement is provided to spread the input tax credit over the life of the capital asset.

Figure G.5 describes the application of tax to certain types of expenses incurred by a real estate brokerage and indicates which expenses are subject to GST (this chart assumes that the expenditure is incurred in Canada).

EXPENDITURE ITEM	GST PAYABLE	GST NOT PAYABLE
Commercial rent	●	
Property taxes		●
Business taxes		●
Office equipment	●	
Office supplies	●	
Telephone and fax charges	●	
Photocopier charges	●	
Payments to other brokerages	●	
Insurance		●
Interest expense		●
Bank charges		●
Meals and entertainment	●	
Travelling expenses	●	
Hotel accommodation	●	
Automobile purchase	●	
Automobile expenses	●	
Advertising	●	
Legal and accounting fees	●	
Promotional expenditures	●	
Salaries/payments to employees		●
Pension plan payments		●
CPP and EI payments		●
Employee life insurance, medical and disability plan payments		●
Postage	●	
Gifts	●	

GST Applications   Figure G.5

To the extent that expenditures are incurred in activities which are related to taxable or zero-rated revenues, any GST paid may be recovered as an input tax credit. This is normally the case except where a brokerage earns significant mortgage brokerage fees or investment income. Nevertheless there are situations where input tax credits are restricted. In instances where brokerages earn both exempt mortgage broker fees and taxable commissions, input tax credits can be partially claimed to the extent that expenses can be related to taxable activities. Where a particular expense can be directly related to a taxable activity, input tax credits can be fully claimed. However, expenses such as general overhead must be allocated between taxable and exempt activities on some reasonable basis.

The CCRA will not prescribe or impose such methods of allocation on registrants. Brokerages may wish to consider allocations based on time spent in each activity on a daily basis. If the effort required to earn each type of revenue is approximately the same, an allocation based on revenue could be used, however, revenue allocation is not always appropriate. Situations also exist where input tax credits are restricted. These are discussed in other sections under the general topic of *Expenses*.

Reimbursement of Employee Expenses

There are times when employed salespeople may be reimbursed by an employer for expenses incurred on the employer's behalf. Any GST associated with such expenses is considered to have been paid by the employer. The employer should retain invoices or receipts for these expenses, showing the amount of GST paid, in order to claim input tax credits in the normal manner.

In some cases it may be difficult to comply with the documentation requirements for employee expense accounts. As a result, the government will allow a factor of $6/106$ths to be applied to expenses plus GST reimbursed to employees. This amount will then be eligible for input tax credits subject to the restriction for meals and entertainment discussed below. Brokerages may choose the type of expense reimbursements in which to apply the factor method. Nevertheless, brokerages will have to apply it consistently to all employees.

Brokerages are also entitled to claim input credits for reasonable per diem allowances paid to employees to cover meals, auto expenses and incidental costs incurred during business trips in Canada. The amount of the input tax credit is $7/107$ths of the allowance paid. This is referred to as a *notional input tax*.

A fixed monthly allowance paid by a brokerage to an employee to cover the costs of operating a vehicle will not be considered to be a reasonable allowance for GST purposes. As such, the brokerage is not eligible for a notional input tax credit with respect to the fixed car allowance. On the other hand, reimbursement of car expenses based on kilometres driven will be eligible for a notional input tax credit where the rate of reimbursement is reasonable.

Meals and Entertainment

GST paid by brokerages and independent contractors on the cost of business meals and entertainment receives the same treatment accorded these expenses for income tax purposes, that is, 50% is recoverable for expenses incurred. For easier accounting, the government allows a business to claim the full GST for meals and entertainment when filing returns through the year. At the fiscal year end, however, 50% of the input tax credits claimed for meal and entertainment expenses incurred will have to be repaid.

Automobile and Other Travel

GST is payable on accommodation in Canada and on air fares to destinations in Canada, the continental U.S.A. and the islands of St. Pierre and Miquelon. Other international travel fares are not taxed. Any GST paid on travel expenses is fully recoverable if the expense is for business purposes.

Input tax credits on the purchase or lease of an automobile are restricted. Where the vehicle is used exclusively (more than 90%) for personal purposes, no input tax credit will be allowed. Where the automobile is used for business purposes, input tax credits will only be allowed on the first $24,000 of a car purchase or $650 per month of a car lease. These same thresholds are used to restrict claims for income tax purposes and are determined before any GST or provincial retail sales tax has been included.

The rules for claiming input tax credits on automobiles differ, depending on whether the automobile is owned by the brokerage and is provided to an employee or whether the automobile is owned personally by an independent contractor who is an individual GST registrant.

Where the automobile is owned by a brokerage and is provided to an employee, the extent to which an input tax credit may be claimed depends upon the extent of personal and commercial use of the automobile. For most individuals who only carry on taxable activities this total will be 100%. However, where a vehicle is used exclusively (more than 90%) for personal purposes by the employee, the employer will not be able to claim an input tax credit. Therefore, unless the vehicle is used more than 90% personally, a practitioner should be able to claim an input tax credit subject to the restrictions discussed above. However, the employer is required to assess a taxable benefit to the employee for the amount including the GST. This amount is to be included in the amount of the taxable benefit reported to the employee on the T4 slip.

Where the automobile is used by an individual GST registrant partly for business purposes and partly for personal use, a full input tax credit is not available on the purchase. Instead the individual must claim the GST portion (7/107ths) of any tax depreciation claimed on his annual tax return. Input tax credits on car leases can be claimed only to the extent the vehicle is used for business purposes.

Expenses Incurred by Employed Commission Salespersons

Commission salespeople defined as employees under the *Income Tax Act* are not required to register and collect the GST. However, to the extent they incur expenses which are deductible by them for income tax purposes, employed salespeople are able to claim a rebate, on an annual basis, for the GST paid on qualifying expenses, including automobile and other travel as discussed above. Rebate claims will be filed along with their income tax returns for the relevant year using the *Employee and Partner GST Rebate Form*.

When an employed real estate salesperson purchases capital items such as pagers, computer terminals, and cellular telephones for business use, income tax deductions for financing costs and appropriate capital cost allowance are not permitted. The same holds true for claiming rebates under the GST. Only self-employed commission salespeople (independent contractors) may claim GST rebates on the purchase of these items. However income tax deductions and rebates may be claimed by employed salespeople where the capital equipment is leased, but only on the amount that reasonably relates to earning commission income.

Real Estate Board Fees

Most boards and associations have taxable membership fees. Where membership and other fees are subject to the GST, the members (brokers, salespeople, and brokerages), are normally entitled to claim input tax credits or rebates for GST paid on these fees.

Personal Expenses

GST input tax credits/rebates are available only for business-related purchases and not for personal and living expenses.

Mortgage Brokerage Fees

Commissions or fees earned for arranging mortgage financing are exempt from GST if those commissions are charged separately from any taxable real estate commissions charged. Brokers who earn both real estate commissions and mortgage brokerage fees are required to prorate (i.e., apportion) the tax paid on certain purchases to determine the input tax credits they may claim.

The Canada Customs and Revenue Agency has declined to provide guidance on how to apportion GST paid between taxable and exempt activities except to suggest a percentage be applied to the input tax credits in determining taxable activities versus exempt activities. The amount of input tax credits attributed to the exempt activities are not refundable. The method used should be applied on a consistent and reasonable basis.

Real Estate

Basic Rules and Exemptions

The GST applies to all sales or rentals of real estate unless the sale or rental fits one of the following exemptions:

- Residential rents.
- Sales of used residential housing other than substantially renovated property; (a substantially renovated building is one in which all or substantially all of the building other than the foundation, exterior walls,

interior supporting walls, floors, roof and staircases, has been removed or replaced).

- Sales of personal use land by an individual or a trust.
- Certain sales of farmland to related individuals where the farmland is for personal use.
- Most sales and rentals of real property by charities, non-profit organizations and selected public service organizations.

In all other cases, the tax applies to the sale or rental of real property. Businesses involved in such activity claim input credits on relevant purchases in the normal manner. The exemption for small traders does not apply to sales of real property. Real property sales are taxable even if they fall below the $30,000 small traders' threshold.

Sellers do not have to collect tax on the sale of real estate in the following circumstances:

- All sales by non-resident to residents.
- All sales of non-residential property to persons registered for GST purposes.
- Sales of residential property to companies registered for GST purposes, other than individuals.

Where tax is not collected by the seller, the buyer will have to self-assess the tax. The buyer is required to remit the tax directly to the government, using a special GST return, which is due at the same time as the return in which the input tax credit is claimed. As a result the GST liability and the input tax credit may be offset against each other when the returns are filed together.

Residential Rents

The following residential rentals and associated services are tax exempt:

- Rentals of one month or more by an individual on a continuous basis.
- Short-term accommodations where the rental charge does not exceed $20/day or $140/week by an individual on a continuous basis.
- Residential rents which include incidental services such as cleaning, heating, electricity, and parking.
- Rentals of one month or more on a continuous basis of land on which a residential unit is located.
- Charges for parking spaces related to the residential unit throughout the period of at least one month.

Landlords of tax-exempt residential rental properties described above are not entitled to recover any tax paid on the purchase, repair, or improvement of these residential complexes. All room rentals in a hotel or motel are normally taxable.

Commercial Rents

Commercial rents are subject to the GST. GST paid on related expenditures is recoverable under the normal input tax credit rules. In commercial situations, additional rent is commonly charged that includes adjustments for heating, electricity, maintenance, property taxes, etc. Notwithstanding that additional rent may relate to items that are GST exempt, the entire additional rent is subject to GST at 7%.

Commercial lease agreements typically involve a base rent as well as additional rents (e.g., common area expenses, property taxes, insurance, and water charges). Where payment under a lease includes amounts for additional rents, the landlord must collect the GST on the total value of the lease (even if additional items are itemized separately). If, for example, the landlord requires the payment of property taxes then GST must be included. However, if the tenant is directly responsible for the payment of property taxes to the municipality, GST will not apply. As a general statement, tenants who are GST registrants are eligible to recover all or a portion of the tax on additional rents as input tax credits.

Resale Housing

The sale of used residential property (e.g., house, condominium, summer cottage or apartment building), is generally GST exempt. The sale of newly constructed or substantially renovated residential property is taxable. Thus it becomes very important to determine when a property is *used*. As a general rule, a residential property is considered to be used when it is substantially complete and has been sold (single unit) or when any unit has been occupied as a residence (multiple unit). For example, if a new house is purchased and resold before being occupied by an individual who has purchased the residence with intention of resale, GST applies on the sale. On the other hand, if an individual is required to sell a new house before it has been occupied because his employer moves him, the resale is not subject to GST. However, if a partially completed house is purchased by a builder, its subsequent resale after completion is taxable.

The GST rules for the vast majority of resale housing are simple and straight forward: GST is not chargeable. However, in a small but significant, minority of transactions, there will be problems. Great care should be taken when approaching a transaction that is 'out of the ordinary' in any way. The buyer and seller are responsible, not the brokerage, to ensure that the GST is correctly applied.

New Housing

The *Excise Tax Act* provides for a new housing rebate. The application for this rebate is to be filed within four years after the date that ownership was transferred on all transactions prior to July 1, 1996. The filing date for transactions after June 30, 1996, is within two years of the date that ownership was transferred. The rules on filing for this rebate are more complex for owner built and substantially renovated houses.

The new housing rebate is equal to the lesser of $8,750 and 36% of the total GST paid where the property has a fair market value up to $350,000. Where the fair market value of the property is over $350,000 but less than $450,000, the calculation of the rebate involves the following two steps:

Step One
Determine the lesser of:
- 36% of tax paid, and
- $8,750

Step Two
Multiply the amount determined under Step One by:
($450,000 – Fair Market Value) ÷ $100,000

Where the property has a fair market value in excess of $450,000, there will be no rebate. The purpose of knowing the fair market value of the property is to determine whether the owner will receive a full rebate, partial rebate, or no rebate.

Renovated Housing

The sale of a used home is normally exempt from GST. However, there are situations where a renovation may be substantial enough that the home is deemed *new* and is therefore subject to tax. The following details the GST rules for substantial and other renovations.

Substantial Renovations   The sale of a substantially renovated residential dwelling in the course of business is taxable. The sale of the substantially renovated dwelling is treated in the same manner as the sale of a new home and it may qualify for a new housing rebate. A residential dwelling is considered to be substantially renovated if it incorporates less than 10% of the original building other than the supporting walls, roof, floors, staircases, foundation and other minor ancillary parts. A registrant in the substantial renovation business claims input tax credits on all taxable purchases relating to a substantial renovation. However, no input tax credit is available in respect of the purchase price of the used home since it presumably will have been exempt.

Since the substantial renovation test is based on structural changes to the dwelling, renovators may attempt to plan renovations so that they do not qualify as substantial. In this case, the resale of the renovated dwelling may be exempt. If not, it is noted that the GST will apply to the full value of the renovated dwelling, including the value

of the land (subject to any new housing rebate available). These rules apply to a person in the business of buying and substantially renovating a residential dwelling. The rules do not apply to a homeowner who undertakes a substantial renovation for his own use.

Other Renovations   Different rules apply where, in the course of a business involving sales of real property, a person purchases and renovates a home, but not to the degree that it qualifies as a substantial renovation. In this situation, a *self supply* rule applies to tax the value added by the renovator. The renovator is required to pay tax on those costs that would be capitalized for income tax purposes if the property were capital property. In essence, this rule requires the renovator to pay an additional tax based on the labour component of the renovation only. Once again this self-supply rule only applies to someone in the business of buying, renovating and selling residential property. It does not normally apply to a homeowner who contracts for or makes renovations to his/her home.

Vacant Land and Other Personal Use Real Estate

The sale of vacant land by an individual is one of the most confusing areas of the GST. The same parcel of land may be taxable or exempt, or the seller may have a choice depending upon the circumstances. For example, an individual who is in the business of buying and selling land will have a taxable sale. On the other hand, an individual who sells a vacant lot that was to be used for a future cottage, will not be required to charge tax.

In most cases, individuals selling country property, non-commercial hobby farms and other personal-use real estate do not have to collect tax on the sale. However, where an individual sells land that was used primarily in a business, or sold in the course of a business, tax applies. The sale of subdivided or severed land is subject to GST unless the land had been subdivided into only two parts and there was no previous subdivision or severance or the land was transferred to a related individual for their personal use or enjoyment.

Some individuals may not actually carry on a business of buying and selling land, but may speculate in raw land. Such an individual would normally be required to treat the gain as fully taxable for income tax purposes since the sale would be considered an adventure or concern in the nature of trade. In this situation, the individual can treat the sale as being taxable for GST purposes.

Why would an individual choose to treat the sale as being taxable? The buyer will not mind if the sale is taxable if any GST on the purchase is recovered as an input tax credit. The individual seller will be able to recover any tax paid on the purchase or other expenses by electing to treat the sale as taxable. In many cases the election will be beneficial.

It should be noted that the special rules discussed above apply only to individuals or a trust, all of the beneficiaries of which are individuals. Corporations or partnerships that sell vacant land are required to treat the transaction as being taxable.

Commercial Sales

All sales of commercial real property are subject to tax. However, on the sale of a commercial property to another registrant, the seller of the property is not required to collect GST. In this situation the registered buyer is responsible for the GST and is required to account to the government. The buyer is required to file a special GST return which is due at the same time as the regular GST return for the reporting period. Filing the returns together allows the buyer to offset the GST liability on the special return against the available input tax credit on the regular GST return. This results in no cash flow requirement to fund the GST for a registrant who purchases commercial property to be used exclusively in taxable activities.

As of January 1, 1997, where a registered buyer purchases commercial real estate, the buyer will not have to file a special GST return provided the property has been purchased for use primarily in the buyer's business. In this case, the GST will be reported on the buyer's regular GST return and the GST will be paid no later than the due date of that particular return. In any other case, the requirement for a special return will remain and the GST will be required to be paid and the special return filed no later than one month following the calendar month that the GST became payable.

Certificate on Exempt Sale

Persons purchasing exempt real property should obtain a statement or certificate from the seller that the property is exempt from GST. Since the determination of the tax status may depend on the use of the property by the seller, the buyer may not always properly determine its status. If the buyer obtains a certificate and has no reason or basis to doubt its accuracy, it is the seller who is liable for the GST. Buyers of real estate that is exempt from GST should obtain a certificate or written statement that the property meets the exempt requirements in order to protect themselves from GST liability in the event that the seller's representations prove to be incorrect.

It will not always be clear whether the sale of vacant land by an individual will be exempt under this rule. A long line of court decisions under the *Income Tax Act* deal with sales of land and whether the sale qualifies for capital gains treatment or income treatment. Due to the confusion that often exists concerning the GST status of vacant land sales by individuals, it would be prudent for the buyer to obtain a certificate from the seller.

The certificate is not a prescribed form nor is it mandatory. The CCRA has indicated that this position will not change despite numerous requests for guidelines as to acceptable wording of the certificate. Brokerages should be aware that their duty to their client would normally end with the provision of advice as to the use of a certificate. The wording of the certificate should be left to legal counsel.

Farmland

The sale of a farm may be treated in different ways under the GST. If the farm was (and will be) used as an operating farm, it is normally subject to GST when sold. The portion of the farm used as a residence (on which no input credit has been claimed for GST previously paid), is GST exempt.

On the other hand, if the farm has not been used for commercial farming or any other business but was for personal use and enjoyment, it may be exempt from the GST. Certain sales of farmland between family members and related parties may also be exempt, provided the farmland is subsequently used by the buyer for personal use and enjoyment (i.e., non-farming uses). The taxation of farm sales under the GST is a complex area and professional advice should be sought.

Condominium Fees

Upkeep and maintenance services provided by a condominium corporation or a co-operative housing corporation to the owner of a residential unit in that corporation or to any tenant of the owner, are GST exempt. Condominium corporations and co-operative housing corporations are not able to recover any GST paid on their purchases of services such as snow removal or landscaping. In this respect, these residential corporations are treated in the same manner as residential landlords.

Self-Supply

A special self-supply rule normally applies where a landlord constructs an apartment building or other residential structure which subsequently is to be rented. The landlord is able to claim input tax credits in the normal manner on purchases related to the construction of the residential complex.

However, at the time the completed dwelling is put into rental use, the landlord is required to pay GST on the fair market value of the land and buildings. The complex thereafter qualifies as a used residential dwelling and any subsequent resale is exempt. The reason for this rule is to treat the landlord in the same way as any other landlord who would be required to pay GST on the purchase of a new building for rental purposes. This avoids any advantage for landlords who construct their own residential units over landlords who purchase completed residential units for rental purposes.

Example   *GST—Expenses—*
Self-Supply

Assume a landlord incurs costs of $10,000,000 in constructing a new residential complex on which GST of $700,000 has been paid. During the construction phase, the landlord will be entitled to recover this $700,000 in GST through the input tax credit mechanism. At the time the building is first put to rental use its fair market value is (say) $15,000,000. The landlord will be liable for GST at that time in the amount of:

$$(\$15,000,000 \times 7\%) = \$1,050,000$$

No further input tax credits may be claimed by the landlord while the building is being rented. Upon resale of the building no GST will normally apply as it will qualify as a used residential complex.

Input Tax Credit at Time of Purchase

Input tax credits at the time of purchase are generally allowed to the extent that the real property is for use in a taxable activity.

Example   *GST—Expenses—*
Input Tax Credit at Time of Purchase

If a new ten-storey apartment building is purchased and the bottom floor has commercial stores and the other nine floors are residential units, any input tax credit must be apportioned between the commercial activities (which are taxable), and the residential activities which are exempt. If the commercial area was 10% of the building, then input tax credits might be 10% of the GST paid on the purchase. Two exceptions to this general rule are outlined:

No input tax credit is allowed for the commercial use of any real property acquired by an individual where it is primarily for the owner's personal use. Accordingly, no input tax credit is allowed for an office in a house where the house is primarily used as the individual's place of residence.

For real property acquired by a charity, nonprofit organization, government or other public sector organization, a full input tax credit is allowed if the real property is acquired primarily (more than 50%) for use in a taxable activity. Otherwise, no input tax credit can be claimed.

Change of Use

Where the use of commercial real property, that is, capital property, changes significantly, change-of-use rules apply. If the commercial usage increases, the registrant is entitled to an input tax credit to the extent of the increased use. The credit is normally based on the lesser of the GST paid on acquisition of the property and the tax that would be payable on the fair market value of the property at the time the use changed. Conversely, where the commercial use decreases, a GST liability arises on the increased non-commercial use. No input tax credit is allowed for real property on which the owner has never paid GST, even where the commercial use increases.

Example   *GST—Expenses—*
Change of Use

Assume an individual acquires, in 1996, a new ten-storey apartment building for $600,000 plus GST of $42,000. In 1997, the owner decides to convert the bottom floor to commercial rental. At this time, the fair market value of the apartment building is $800,000. The individual will be entitled to an input tax credit as follows:

Lesser of 10% of

- GST paid on original purchase   **42,000**
- 7% of fair market value (i.e., 7% of $800,000)   56,000

that is, $42,000.

Input Tax Credit at Time of Sale

In some cases, a registrant is required to collect tax on the sale of real property for which no input tax credit, or only a partial input tax credit, has been claimed. For example, a medical practitioner who owns the commercial building, in which he/she practises, may also rent out part of the space commercially. Because the medical services will be exempt, the practitioner is able to claim only a partial input tax credit at the time of purchase, but the building is fully taxable on resale. In this case, the seller is able to recover any previously unclaimed input tax credits at the time of sale.

The input tax credit at the time of sale is the lesser of:

- The unclaimed portion of the GST actually paid by the registrant on the original acquisition of and subsequent improvements to the building; and
- The proportion of the tax on the fair market value of the building at the time it is sold representing the extent it was used outside the commercial activity.

The effect of this rule is that on sale all the remaining tax is removed from the building provided the building has not decreased in value.

Homes on Leased Land

The GST rebate applies to new residential units purchased by individuals where the homebuyer acquires a leasehold interest rather than the *normal* freehold interest in the land. The homebuyer must have an option to purchase the land or the lease must be for a period of 20 years or longer.

The rebate will be calculated at 2.34% of the price for the residential unit. Where the fair market value of the unit (including land) is between $350,000 and $450,000, the rebate is phased-out such that no rebate is available on units worth more than $450,000. In addition, the builder is considered to have sold both the land and the building and is required to remit GST on the fair market value. If the land and building are subsequently sold, the general rules will normally apply to exempt this sale. Therefore, the objective is to treat the purchase of a long-term leasehold interest in a new home as the purchase of a new home. This requires the assessment of GST on the full value of the home and also allows a GST New Home Rebate to be claimed.

Residential and Non-Residential Portion

Where the sale of real property with both a residential portion and a non-residential portion occurs, each portion is to be treated as a separate sale for GST purposes. A residential complex includes land, a building or part of a building, and a residential trailer park.

Registration and Filing Requirements

GST Registration

All businesses with annual taxable and/or zero-rated gross revenues in excess of $30,000 must register with the CCRA to collect and remit GST. Note that salespersons who are employees cannot register. Special rules apply to them as discussed below. Registration is optional for businesses with annual gross revenues of $30,000 and below.

Registration is accomplished by submitting a single business number registration form (Form RC1). The CCRA will issue a single business number with an *RT* suffix. The form must include an original signature of an authorized person. The form should be submitted to the local CCRA Taxation Service Centre.

A quarterly filing frequency based on the year end indicated on the registration application will automatically be assigned. If an applicant qualifies to file annually, and wishes to do so, or if an applicant wishes to file monthly, a separate election form must be completed and filed with the Canada Customs and Revenue Agency.

Filing Requirements

Businesses registered for the GST are required periodically to remit the net tax due after input credits or claim a refund on a GST return. Filing requirements vary by the size of business according to dollar volume. Reporting periods are at regular intervals throughout its fiscal year for income tax purposes or if a company elects, throughout the calendar year. Filing periods are as follows:

Taxable and Zero-Rated Gross Revenues	GST Return Required
$500,000 or less	Quarterly, but can elect to to file annually with quarterly installments
$500,001–$6,000,000	Quarterly
$6,000,001 and over	Monthly

NOTE Businesses in the first two categories may elect to file more frequently, which makes good business sense when there is a refund to be claimed.

Gross commission revenues should be used in calculating the business volume, which determines the frequency of filing GST returns. Business volume should not be considered as net fees after payments to co-operating brokers.

Returns filed quarterly and monthly are due within one month after the end of the reporting period; those filed annually, within three months after the year end. Tax due must be remitted with the return. Penalty and interest will be charged from the due date on any unpaid tax.

GST refund claims are also made in the registrant's periodic return. Outstanding refund claims will be credited with interest beginning 21 days after the return is received by the CCRA. Registrants with annual reporting periods are required to pay four equal quarterly installments within one month after the end of the quarter.

Supporting Records and Documentation

The GST is based on invoices. Certain information must be recorded separately on each sale or purchase invoice issued to a registered business to enable registrants to claim input credits where appropriate.

Supporting records can include invoices, cash register receipts, formal written contracts (including contracts for periodic lease payments), credit card receipts or any valid documents issued or signed by a registrant concerning a transaction on which GST is paid or payable.

Information required for each invoice depends on the value of the purchase.

	PURCHASE AMOUNT		
	<$30	$30–$150	>$150
Seller's name (trading name)	●	●	●
Date	●	●	●
Total consideration paid or payable	●	●	●
Total amount of GST, charged on the supply or service or, alternatively, statement that price includes GST		●	●
Tax status of each item where the invoice or receipt covers both taxable supplies or services and supplies or services that are zero-rated or tax-exempt		●	●
Seller's GST registration number		●	●
Buyer's name (trading name)			●
Terms of sale (cash, discount, etc.)			●
Description of the supply or service			●

● = Required

Registrants are not required to obtain supporting documentation for tax credit claims in certain circumstances such as purchases from coin-operated machines, reasonable allowances paid to employees and other special cases.

Registered sellers are required to issue appropriate documentation to another registrant who purchases taxable goods or services from that seller.

The retention period for supporting records for GST is the same as under the *Income Tax Act*, namely, six years.

The CCRA has indicated that where payment of a commission is contingent upon a sale and is paid or payable based on a percentage of that sale, in addition to the required information previously listed, sufficient documentary evidence must also be maintained to establish:

- That the sale has been made;
- The amount of the sale; and
- The time of the sale.

The Canada Customs and Revenue Agency is looking for a *package* of information that will provide the documentation they require to verify the transaction and the CCRA has indicated that such a package can vary depending upon the particular transaction.

In instances where a registrant is paying a commission to a listing brokerage, offers of sale or purchase and reminder notices will not usually constitute sufficient documentation. A listing agreement and a completed sales agreement which together contain all required information would usually provide the input tax credit documentary requirements for a registrant acquiring a brokerage's services, to recover the tax paid.

Where listing brokerages are paying commissions to selling brokerages, for the listing brokerage to claim an input tax credit, the reminder notice from the selling brokerage does not constitute sufficient evidence. The CCRA has suggested the only satisfactory evidence that tax on the inter-firm commission is paid or payable by the listing to the selling brokerage is a form of receipt containing required information and issued at the time the sale is completed. This receipt could be a Notification of Completion or similar document.

GST Planning and Administration

Registration and Compliance

Self-employed brokers and independent contractors with annual taxable and/or zero-rated gross revenues in excess of $30,000 must register with the CCRA to collect and remit GST. These individuals must register in order to claim input tax credits on business purchases.

With the advent of GST, real estate brokerages have a greater need to keep proper books and records. Adequate documentation is required to support the remittance which accompanies the periodic GST return.

The primary document used in the administration of GST is the invoice. Invoices must contain the appropriate prescribed information, otherwise the CCRA could disallow a claim for an input tax credit.

It is important to meet filing and remittance deadlines. A missed deadline could result in an assessment from the CCRA of interest charged at a high daily rate, which changes quarterly, plus a penalty.

Cash Flow

Brokerages may experience a cash flow benefit from GST if the tax is collected from the client before it must be remitted to the government. This will occur, for example, when the liability for the tax arises and the client pays the balance on the closing of the sale. Monthly and quarterly filers will not have to remit the tax until the end of the month following the period in which the GST liability was incurred. This results in a minimum of a 30-day period where the brokerage may hold the amount of the GST.

A negative cash flow will result in situations where the brokerage must remit the GST before collecting it from the client. This would occur where GST is triggered prior to the end of a monthly or quarterly GST return, but the GST is not collected before the end of the month following the period end.

Brokerages with gross revenues of $500,000 or less may elect to file annually with quarterly installments. Depending on the year end of the business and the annual business cycle, the brokerage who files annual returns may experience positive or negative cash flows. For example, a small brokerage may experience a surge in sales and thus commissions in the period of March 1 to May 31 of each year. By structuring the fiscal year end to be February 28 or earlier, the brokerage will benefit from the collection of GST on March 1 to May 31 revenues which can be retained and remitted in even quarterly installments based on the expected annual revenues. This scenario cannot be used when a business is changing its year end to December 31st as a result of the income tax requirements for sole proprietorships and certain partnerships. In this situation the GST reporting requirements will be changed as well to December 31st. For businesses that elect to use off-calendar year ends, the GST reporting requirements will not change. New businesses which start up may want to review the advantages and disadvantages using an off calendar year end with their advisors.

Careful planning is required to ensure that the registrant is maximizing the cash flow effects of the GST. Some or all of the following steps might improve the cash flow of the business and minimize the need to finance GST remittances.

- Do not issue an invoice for services rendered until the earliest of the closing of the sale, the date of payment for the services or the date specified in a contract for payment of the services. Consider the issuance of reminder notices rather than invoices in order to avoid triggering the GST liability prior to the closing date.
- Ensure that there is no delay between the date of the invoice and the date it is sent to the client.
- Implement a payables system to record purchase invoices as soon as they are received. This will permit a timely claim for input tax credits.
- Delay the payment of purchases on account. (This will counteract the seller's attempts to collect the account quickly so that the seller does not have to finance the remittance of the GST.)
- Make large capital purchases (such as computer systems and automobiles that are used exclusively for business purposes), at the end of a reporting period.

GST collected with revenues is to be held in trust for the government. Although the brokerage may take advantage of cash flow planning opportunities, it must budget for the GST remittances as failure to remit on the deadlines could result in penalties and interest assessments.

Quarterly and annual filers will have the option of electing a more frequent reporting period. A cash flow analysis that takes into account the cyclical nature of your business should be conducted before deciding on the preferred reporting period for the business.

Client Education

The *Excise Tax Act* requires that brokerages collect 7% GST on real estate commissions. Brokerages should ensure that clients are aware of the obligation to collect GST on the commission to minimize clients' reluctance to pay the tax and avoid any expectation that the brokerage will absorb it.

The client must pay the tax in addition to the brokerage's commission and salespeople should advise all clients of this situation. Standard agreements should contain a clause that makes it clear regarding the client responsibility concerning GST. Any time nonstandard contracts are used, the salesperson should review the contract to ensure that a proper GST clause is included. In cases of doubt, professional advice should be obtained.

Accounting Systems

Accounting systems and records must provide an audit trail which may be subject to periodic review by the Canada Customs and Revenue Agency.

In the revenue system, information must support the correct remittance of GST. In the expenditure system, the amount of GST paid or payable on purchases must be tracked to support the periodic input tax credit claims.

For financial statement presentation, the GST collected should not be included with revenues. Similarly, GST incurred on expenditures should not be included in expenses or capital if it is eligible for a refund as an input tax credit or rebate. This rule will have to be modified if the quick or simplified method for GST is being used.

Accounting systems require, as a minimum, a GST liability account to record the GST collected or collectible on revenues and a GST receivable account to record GST incurred on expenditures. More complex systems will be required where the revenue system is computerized and performs functions such as invoice-generation and automatic posting to the accounts.

Staff who work with the accounting systems must be knowledgeable about the proper treatment of GST on revenues and expenditures to ensure that the business is not missing opportunities to claim input credits nor exposing itself to the risk of being assessed by the CCRA.

Rebates for Employed Salespeople

Individuals who are commissioned employees of real estate brokerages are not required to register with the CCRA for the GST. They are not required to charge GST on their commissions or file a GST return. The commissions earned by their employer are taxable; however, it is the employer and not the employee who must collect and administer the GST.

Employed salespeople may claim a rebate of the GST paid on certain business expenses. The most common expenditures on which GST will be recoverable are automobile, advertising, membership dues, and promotional expenses. As long as the expenditure is deductible for income tax purposes, the rebate may be claimed on the annual income tax return (may be claimed within four years after the year in which the expenditure was made), with proper GST receipts/invoices to support the claim.

The purchase of capital equipment such as cellular phones, computers, and fax machines is not deductible or depreciable for income tax purposes by an employed salesperson. The GST rebate is therefore not available on these purchases. It might be better to lease these items in order to qualify for the income tax deduction and the GST rebate.

GST claims on business expenses are restricted in a manner similar to restrictions under the *Income Tax Act*. The GST rebate on an automobile used for business purposes is calculated as 7/107ths of the capital cost allowance deducted for income tax purposes. The GST rebate on meals and entertainment expenses is restricted to 50% of the tax paid. Membership fees in a club, the main purpose of which is to provide dining, recreational or sporting facilities, are not income tax deductible and do not generate a GST rebate.

Reference Direct all enquiries to the Canada Customs and Revenue Agency.

GOODWILL
(SEE ALSO BUSINESS VALUATION)

An intangible business asset that arises from the expectation of continued business activity accruing from the reputation of a business.

Application   Goodwill can be a saleable asset of a corporation and as such may be included in the balance sheet. Goodwill is best viewed as the value placed on intangible benefits over and above the strict valuation of tangible assets less liabilities in an operating business.

Real estate brokerages, as with all successful businesses, can enhance value through goodwill. While in theory, the sale of a real estate brokerage includes value for goodwill, normally reputation is more precisely quantified under such things as right to operate using the corporate name and value attributable to a franchise grid or marketing rights associated with a specific trademark.

Consequently, a general reference to goodwill is rarely found, although it is undoubtedly factored into the amount paid. To retain value associated with a brokerage's reputation, the buyer is more likely to contract with the existing brokerage for a specified period to permit the smooth transition to the new owner. Value associated with goodwill may be reflected in the prior owner's contract during the transition period.

Example   *Goodwill*

Salesperson Lee, a salesperson with a local real estate brokerage, has the opportunity to purchase an existing franchise operation in the same general vicinity. Lee has met all regulatory requirements to be a broker.

The agreed purchase price is $140,000 that includes all chattels and fixtures in the leased office premises, assignment of existing independent contractor agreements (if agreed by individual salespeople), prior owner participation for a six-month period, acquisition of the corporate name, and the franchise grid. No specific reference to goodwill is included in the agreement.

GOVERNMENT REGULATIONS

Federal legislation and related topics having national scope and applicable to real estate activities in all provinces are included under the appropriate heading, e.g., **Bankruptcy, Goods and Services Tax,** and **Capital Cost Allowance.** Provincial legislation and related topics are included in the applicable provincial reference materials.

GRADE
(SEE ALSO LOT GRADING)

The surface slope and more particularly, for real estate purposes, the ground surface around a foundation wall.

Application   Real estate practitioners most commonly encounter the term *grade* in relation to rough and finished grades regarding the development of residential and commercial properties. Rough grade refers to the incomplete stage of grading when an approximate grade level is established typically through the levelling of backfill in preparation for finished grade. Finished grade normally refers to the final grade level including any necessary slope for the property when top soil has been added and levelled.

GRADUATED LEASE

A lease that provides for increases or decreases in rent at definite times during the term of that lease.

Example   *Graduated Lease*

Tenant Jones has negotiated a graduated five-year lease for a small office suite of 1,520 square feet of rentable area. The negotiations apply only to the base rent and not to any additional rents charged each year by the landlord.

Year One $380 per month based on $3.00 per square foot of the rentable area.

Year Two $443.33 per month based on $3.50 per square foot of the rentable area.

Year Three $506.67 per month based on $4.00 per square foot of the rentable area.

Year Four $570 per month based on $4.50 per square foot of rentable area.

Year Five $633.33 per month, based on $5.00 per square foot of the rentable area.

GRADUATED PAYMENT

A payment plan with regular, specified increases of individual payments to a pre-determined level.

GRADUATED PAYMENT MORTGAGE

Acronym: GPM   A mortgage payment plan designed to reduce monthly payments during initial years, ultimately leading to constant monthly payments during the latter years. The amounts and timing of the increments in the payments are established by a pre-determined formula.

Normally, the payment increments of about 5% per year form part of the mortgage contract.

The initial years (usually the first ten), show an increase in the actual principal sum owing, as principal and interest payments are not sufficient to address cumulative interest accruing on the loan. Following the initial ten years, the payment is gradually increased to a level that not only addresses outstanding interest but is also sufficient to commence a steady reduction in principal. This flat monthly payment, as shown in the illustration, remains the same for the duration of the loan.

This type of blended repayment plan gained some popularity during the 1970s, but has not enjoyed any wide acceptance with lenders and consumers in the current Canadian mortgage market.

Figure G.6 demonstrates the difference between a normal blended payment and the GPM program for a $35,000 mortgage at 10.25% with a 25-year amortization.

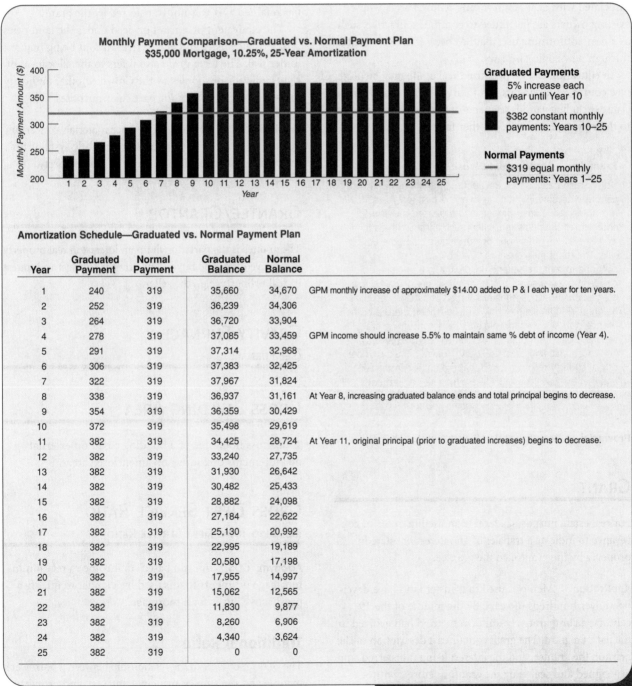

Monthly Payment Comparison—Graduated vs. Normal Payment Plan
$35,000 Mortgage, 10.25%, 25-Year Amortization

Graduated Payments
- 5% increase each year until Year 10
- $382 constant monthly payments: Years 10–25

Normal Payments
- $319 equal monthly payments: Years 1–25

Amortization Schedule—Graduated vs. Normal Payment Plan

Year	Graduated Payment	Normal Payment	Graduated Balance	Normal Balance	
1	240	319	35,660	34,670	GPM monthly increase of approximately $14.00 added to P & I each year for ten years.
2	252	319	36,239	34,306	
3	264	319	36,720	33,904	
4	278	319	37,085	33,459	GPM income should increase 5.5% to maintain same % debt of income (Year 4).
5	291	319	37,314	32,968	
6	306	319	37,383	32,425	
7	322	319	37,967	31,824	
8	338	319	36,937	31,161	At Year 8, increasing graduated balance ends and total principal begins to decrease.
9	354	319	36,359	30,429	
10	372	319	35,498	29,619	
11	382	319	34,425	28,724	At Year 11, original principal (prior to graduated increases) begins to decrease.
12	382	319	33,240	27,735	
13	382	319	31,930	26,642	
14	382	319	30,482	25,433	
15	382	319	28,882	24,098	
16	382	319	27,184	22,622	
17	382	319	25,130	20,992	
18	382	319	22,995	19,189	
19	382	319	20,580	17,198	
20	382	319	17,955	14,997	
21	382	319	15,062	12,565	
22	382	319	11,830	9,877	
23	382	319	8,260	6,906	
24	382	319	4,340	3,624	
25	382	319	0	0	

Graduated Payment Mortgage   Figure G.6

GRADUATED RENT
(SEE GRADUATED LEASE)

GRANDPARENT CLAUSE

A colloquial expression, historically referred to as a *grand-father clause*, pertaining to a rule or regulation placed in force, but exempting various persons or situations owing to pre-existing conditions. The term *grandparenting* is often associated with changes in zoning requirements where existing owners are permitted to continue a practice, such as a non-conforming use, that has been effectively ended through new zoning by-laws.

In education circles, organized real estate may institute new course requirements, but then provide a grandparent clause excluding various segments of the membership owing to their experience levels or other factors.

Example *Grandparent Clause*

Seller Smith has a basement apartment that has been continuously occupied by tenants over the past ten years. With recent legislative amendments and increased municipal approval requirements concerning such units, Smith enquires as to the status of this unit before putting his home up for sale. The municipality verifies that the new owner may continue to rent the second unit owing to a grandparent clause in the municipal zoning by-laws. This clause permits the continuance of existing rental units (built and occupied before 1990), in single-family areas provided there is compliance with all applicable fire standards concerning fire separation for each unit, smoke alarms, escape (egress) from each unit, and electrical safety. However, the municipal official strongly recommended that the unit be inspected and that the buyer contact the appropriate department directly as other regulations could impact its continued use.

Provincial   See applicable reference materials.

GRANT

For real estate purposes, a legal term used in deeds of conveyance to indicate a transfer of an interest or estate in real property by the grantor to the grantee.

Application   Methods used to transfer land have developed over hundreds of years. By the middle of the 19th century, a comparatively uniform method had evolved in the use of a grant. The grant contained a description of the grantor, the grantee, and the interest being transferred, and was signed and sealed by the grantor before a witness. Since the document was under seal, it was often called a *deed of conveyance*, frequently shortened to deed.

The most common way of disposing of interests in land is by transfers between living persons, such as the voluntary grant in the performance of a contract for the sale of land. Another way includes the compulsory transfer of land known as expropriation. A transfer of an interest in land can have two results. If the transfer is of the whole interest, then the interest remains unaltered but it is in the hands of another person. If the transfer is of only part of the interest, the interest is divided into two parts with two holders—the grantee with the interest he/she has obtained under the grant, and the grantor with the interest he/she has retained as it was not transferred by the grant.

The equivalent of a grant or deed under the land titles system is a transfer and is effective without being made under seal. The term *grant* also refers to the allocation of rights, powers, or monies by the Crown or other authority to particular persons or for particular purposes.

Provincial   See applicable reference materials concerning documents used in registry and/or land title systems for the transfer of an estate or interest in real property.

GRANTEE/GRANTOR

The grantee is the party to whom an interest in real property is conveyed, e.g., the buyer. The grantor conveys an interest in real property, e.g., the seller.

GRAVITY FURNACE
(SEE FURNACE)

GROSS BUILDING AREA

Total gross floor area of a building based on external measurements excluding any unenclosed areas.

GROSS DEBT SERVICE RATIO
(SEE ALSO TOTAL DEBT SERVICE RATIO)

Acronym: GDS   A ratio based on income in relation to mortgage payments that is used by a lender to qualify a prospective buyer for a mortgage.

Traditional Ratio

The GDS ratio refers to the relationship between a borrower's income and the sum of principal, interest, and property tax payments during the year. Normally, the acceptable ratio is between 27% and 30% depending on the lender. In other words, a borrower would be allowed between 27% and 30% of gross income to satisfy mortgage principal, interest, and tax payments during any particular year.

GDS = (Principal & Interest + Taxes) ÷ Gross Income

Example *Gross Debt Service Ratio*

Buyer Jones has a gross income of $58,000, $50,000 for a downpayment, and is considering a $170,000 purchase. Taxes on this type of property are $4,120. Jones would like a $120,000 conventional mortgage, amortized over 25 years, with a five-year term. Current rates are 7.5% and the monthly payment factor per $1,000 outstanding is 7.315549.

Monthly Mortgage Payment
$120(000) x 7.315549 = $877.87

Annual Mortgage Payment
$877.87 x 12 = $10,534.44

Annual Mortgage Payment and Taxes
$10,534.44 + $4,120.00 = $14,654.44

Jones' GDS ratio is calculated as follows:

GDS = (Principal & Interest + Taxes) ÷ Gross Income
    = $14,654.44 ÷ $58,000 = 25.27%

As Jones falls below the 30% level for this lending institution, he will probably qualify for the mortgage.

Refined GDS Ratio Including Energy Cost

Recently, some lenders began relying on a refinement in this measurement that includes the heating cost (energy factor) of the residence. Normally, an additional 2% is added to the ratio to account for energy expense, thereby effectively raising the limits to between 29% and 32%.

Refined GDS Formula:

(Principal & Interest + Taxes + Energy) ÷ Gross Income

Let's reconsider Jones' situation assuming a 32% GDS (including estimated heating costs), based on the same circumstances, i.e., a gross income of $58,000 with a $50,000 downpayment and a $170,000 purchase.

Example *Gross Debt Service Ratio– Refined Formula Including Energy*

Monthly Mortgage Payment
$120,000 ÷ $1,000 x 7.315549 = $877.87

Annual Mortgage Payment
$877.87 x 12 = $10,534.44

Annual Mortgage Payment, Taxes, and Heat
$10,534.44 + $4,120.00 + **$1,350.00** = $16,004.44

Continued…

Jones' GDS ratio is calculated as follows:

GDS = (Principal & Interest + Taxes + Energy) ÷ Gross Income
    = $16,004.44 ÷ $58,000 = 27.59%

As Jones falls below the 32% level for this lending institution, he will probably qualify for the mortgage.

GDS Ratio—Condominium

In condominium purchases, this ratio is altered to include a portion of the common expenses (normally 50% of those expenses). Again, consider Jones' situation:

Example *Gross Debt Service Ratio Formula–Condominium*

Buyer Jones has a gross income of $58,000, $50,000 for a downpayment, and is considering a $170,000 condominium purchase. Taxes are $4,120 and maintenance fees amount to $325 per month ($3,900 per year). Jones would like a $120,000 conventional mortgage, amortized over 25 years, with a five-year term. Current rates are 7.5% and the monthly payment factor per $1,000 outstanding is 7.315549.

Monthly Mortgage Payment
$120,000 ÷ $1,000 x 7.315549 = $877.87

Annual Mortgage Payment
$877.87 x 12 = $10,534.44

Annual mortgage payment, taxes, and maintenance fees
$10,534.44 + $4,120.00 +($3,900 x .5) = $16,604.44

Jones' GDS ratio is calculated as follows:

GDS = (Principal & Interest + Taxes + Maintenance (50%)) ÷ Gross Income
    = $16,604.44 ÷ $58,000 = 28.63%

As Jones falls below the 30% level for this lending

GROSS DOMESTIC PRODUCT
(SEE ALSO ECONOMICS)

Acronym: GDP   Personal consumption expenditures plus government purchases of goods and services, and gross domestic investment, and net exports of goods and services. GDP is the basic measure of aggregate economic activity and comprises the total value of goods and services produced in Canada, excluding double counting.

GROSS FLOOR AREA
(SEE ALSO GROSS LEASEABLE AREA)

The total floor area of an individual floor based on external measurements excluding any unenclosed areas.

TO G H

GROSS INCOME (BROKERAGE)

(SEE ALSO BUDGETING)

Income in a real estate brokerage refers to total income from all sources paid to the brokerage.

Application   In the traditional brokerage offering only commission splits with salespeople (that is, no desk fees), a typical list of accounts making up gross income might include commission income, referral income, contribution of commission income by owner, and other income. In a desk fee brokerage operation, a typical listing of accounts making up gross income would probably include commission income, desk fee income, general levies, special promotions, administration/processing fees, penalties/late charges, and other income.

GROSS INCOME MULTIPLIER

Acronym: GIM   The gross income multiplier represents the relationship (ratio) between sale price (value) and income. Traditionally referred to as the gross rental multiplier (GRM), the GIM was introduced to reflect the fact that gross income frequently involves more than rental revenues in commercial property. Further, gross rental multipliers typically involved unadjusted rental amounts, i.e., gross rental amounts only. Gross income multipliers now use gross income or adjusted income figures. The decision rests largely on the availability and scope of data on comparable sales. Practitioners will encounter differing methods of calculation in the marketplace.

For descriptive purposes, the GIM is discussed based on effective gross income. The term *effective gross income*, used primarily by appraisers, is not universally found in the marketplace. Often, commercial practitioners refer to *gross operating income*. Regardless, the calculation is the same: gross income less an allowance for vacancy and bad debt plus any other incidental income.

The formula commonly used to calculate the GIM is:

GIM = Sale Price ÷ Effective Gross Income

Application   The first step in calculating a GIM is to select a number of comparable properties from which sufficient information can be developed. Comparable properties should be similar in terms of size, price, location, financing, expense ratios, and rents. The appraiser should also look at the gross rents of the comparable properties to ensure that rents are collected on the same basis as the subject property. In other words, the practitioner should always seek a high degree of comparability to ensure accuracy in

using the gross income multiplier.

Example   *Gross Income Multiplier*

The subject property has an effective gross income of $50,000. A comparable sale with an effective gross income of $56,000 and a selling price of $392,000 is found (in actual practice, several comparables would be located and analyzed).

GIM = Sale Price ÷ Effective Gross Income
    = $392,000 ÷ 56,000
    = 7

The comparable sold for seven times its effective gross income. This multiplier can be used with the subject property to arrive at a capital value:

V = Gross Income Multiplier x Effective Gross Income
  = GIM x EGI
  = 7 x $50,000
  = $350,000

Typically, buyers of a relatively small investment property will arrive at values using the GIM, since it is easy to understand, calculate, and apply and relevant data is normally readily available. This procedure does not take into account variations in expenses and mortgage financing in properties being used for comparative purposes and consequently has significant limitations.

GROSS LEASE

(SEE ALSO NET LEASE)

An agreement in which the tenant pays a fixed rental and the owner pays all operating expenses such as insurance and taxes associated with the property. This type of arrangement has largely given way to various forms of net leases. Landlords prefer net lease arrangements as sudden increases in costs must be absorbed by the owner under a gross lease, but can be effectively passed through to the tenant under a net lease.

Example   *Gross Lease*

ABC Realty Inc. is establishing a new branch office. Available space in a local retail mall amounts to approximately 1,450 square feet. The landlord is not interested in a net lease with all the financial calculations and apportionment of expenses necessary in such an arrangement. He is prepared to lease the property based on a gross lease at $20 per square foot per year including all expenses over a two-year period. ABC Realty Inc. agrees and provides monthly cheques of $2,416.66:

$20 x 1,450 ÷ 12 = $2,416.67

GROSS LEASEABLE AREA
(SEE ALSO RENTABLE AREA AND USEABLE AREA)

Acronym: GLA   A measurement of the total floor area designed for the occupancy and exclusive use of tenants in a commercial enterprise such as a shopping centre or office complex. Methods used to calculate gross leaseable area may differ in various parts of the country. Standards established by the Building Owners and Managers Association (BOMA) are recommended.

GROSS LIVING AREA (RESIDENTIAL)

A measurement often used in residential property that represents the total above-grade space for a residential structure. Detailed measurement procedures are included in the **Appendix**.

GROSS NATIONAL PRODUCT
(SEE ALSO ECONOMICS)

Acronym: GNP   A widely known indicator concerning total production in the economy, and consequently considered statistically representative of overall prosperity within the country. The GNP measures production by Canadian residents (corporations and individuals) both within and beyond Canada. Gross national product is approximately equal to the total value of all goods and services produced by Canadian-owned factors of production, that is, land, labour, and capital. GNP is equal to the gross domestic product less the return to foreign capital in Canada, net of the return to Canadian-owned capital invested in other countries.

GROSS OPERATING INCOME
(SEE ALSO CASH FLOW)

For real estate investment purposes, the total income from an investment property based on 100% occupancy *less* vacancy and credit losses *plus* other income (e.g., laundry facilities, parking charges, and advertising billboards). The calculation of gross operating income is one of several procedures used in estimating operations cash flow and ultimately total cash flow forecasts for investment property.

Application   The term *gross operating income* is typically found in commercial courses as opposed to *effective gross income*, traditionally referenced in appraisal texts. While terminology and expense/income categories can differ

among various professions analyzing financial statements, underlying procedures for reconstructed operating statements and related forecasts are generally the same.

Example	*Gross Operating Income*	
COMMERCIAL VERSION		
(popularized by the Commercial Investment Real Estate Institute)		
Potential **Rental Income**	$200,000	
Vacancy and **Credit Losses**	−10,000	
Effective Rental Income		190,000
Other Income		+14,000
Gross Operating Income		$204,000
APPRAISAL VERSION *(popularized by The Appraisal Institute)*		
Potential **Gross Income**	$200,000	
Vacancy and **Bad Debt**	−10,000	
Total Gross Income		190,000
Other Income		+14,000
Effective Gross Income		$204,000

Limited uniformity on income/expense terminology exists in the marketplace. Practitioners may also encounter differing calculation procedures in arriving at gross operating income or effective gross income.

GROUND FAULT CIRCUIT INTERRUPTER

A device specifically designed to shut the power off to a circuit when as little as .005 amps are leaking. If there is a flaw in the system, some electricity may be flowing to a dangerous spot, but not enough to blow a fuse or trip a breaker. The ground fault circuit compares the electricity flowing from both the white wire and black wire. If the difference is more than .005, the system will be shut off.

Application   If a nail has inadvertently been driven through an electrical cable and is barely touching the black wire, there may be a small current of less than one amp flowing from the black wire into the nail. Under normal circumstances, this would not be detected and since the nail presents a high resistance (not connected to a good conductor), electricity leaking out of the system would probably not be noticed. However, this can become very dangerous if a person (particularly if not well insulated with rubber gloves or shoes or is perhaps wet), touches the nail. The resistance is lowered and a very large electrical current can flow through the person to the ground thus creating an electrical shock hazard. Ground fault circuit interrupters are normally used for bathroom circuits and exterior outlets, but could be utilized in various situations.

GROUND LEASE

A lease involving the rental of land only (also referred to as a *land lease*). In most instances involving non-agricultural or non-recreational lands such as commercial, industrial, or investment property, a ground lease is usually of long duration involving a tenant who covenants to build a structure on the said land. The building is security for rental payments and if the tenant defaults, the landlord may terminate the lease. The ground lease may prove attractive to owners of land in highly desirable areas. Further, the tenant can build a building while avoiding additional capital outlays for the property.

Application   Ground leases provide a method by which the tenant can leverage existing financial resources and potentially use land at a lower cost than if the property was purchased. However, difficulties can arise if expansion of the buildings is required or the tenant needs additional financing and the landlord obstructs these changes owing to his/her equitable position, as owner of the land and landlord under the lease, and refuses to subordinate those interests.

Example   *Ground Lease*

Owner Smith has a valuable piece of property at the intersection of Main and King Streets. Jones wants to operate a retail establishment from that location for 15 years. Smith will not sell, but agrees to a ground lease for ten years with a right of renewal for a further five years. While there is a structure on the property, it will require considerable renovation work. The parties agree to all the major items (lease term, rental amounts, etc.), but Smith is concerned about the condition of his property at the end of the term.

After considerable negotiations, the parties agree as follows:

Improvement to Land   Any building or improvement built by the tenant on the leased land (including building equipment and mechanical items as outlined in the proposed building design), and including any replacements, additions or changes/alterations thereto shall become the property of the landlord at the termination of the lease for whatever reason, e.g., failure to pay, or expiration of the term.

Equipment Usual to Tenant   Any equipment usual to the tenant's business operation not specifically referenced in the building design shall remain with the tenant upon termination of the lease subject to provisions, in the event of non-payment of rent.

Alterations During Lease Term   All replacements, additions, or changes are subject to the landlord's approval, not to be unreasonably withheld.

Continued…

Option to Purchase   If at any time during the term of the lease, the Landlord receives a bona fide offer from any party to purchase the land, the tenant shall have the right to purchase the lands within twenty-five (25) days on the same terms and conditions.

Jones and Smith agree in principle to the four items and then contact their respective lawyers to draft the detailed ground lease and sort out other issues concerning Jones' ability to mortgage the improvements and the landlord's position if and when the property is taken back at the termination of the lease.

GROUND WATER CONTAMINATION

Ground water/land contamination encompasses a broad range of issues concerning such things as prior use of land, seepage from industrial, commercial, residential and agricultural uses, and the presence of asbestos, lead, PCBs, and other environmental hazards.

Application   Real estate transactions are increasingly scrutinized regarding a wide range of hazardous substances along with associated liability and clean up costs. To compound matters, damage can extend well beyond the site to adjacent properties. In fact, some environmental problems start off-site and, through seepage, enter subject lands. Real estate practitioners need not be experts to exercise proper diligence in inspecting property for visual clues that might forewarn of problems and prompt the involvement of experts.

Detection

Land currently used for industrial/manufacturing purposes is an immediate red flag worthy of attention. Many more indications exist and require careful, methodical inspection, coupled with common sense.

Practitioners should exercise due care concerning:

- Gas stations, dry-cleaning facilities, automobile maintenance garages, rail yards, refinery areas, and similar operations;
- Residential properties near potential sources of contamination;
- Old landfill sites;
- Vacant land strewn with debris or abandoned structures;
- Vacant land with surface water that is odorous and/or discoloured;
- Property that has a lower grade level than an adjacent potential source of contamination;

- Evidence of metal bulk storage containers or barrels, including remnants thereof;
- Any indication of underground buried materials, e.g., surface vents and metal cover plates;
- Commercial buildings that have been altered and uses changed since original construction;
- Older buildings with few or no mechanical or structural upgrades, or in a general state of disrepair, including surrounding grounds; and
- Land planned for development, if there is any confusion at all about past uses of that land.

The real estate practitioner does not have to be an expert but, diligence in carrying out one's tasks appears as a primary issue in litigation concerning environmental problems. Practitioners should be familiar with the fundamentals of environmental regulations and attempt to provide *basic guidance only* on such matters, draft agreements to ensure honest, accurate, and fair provisions for the buyer, and use due care when answering questions.

Provincial   See applicable reference materials.

GROUNDED OUTLETS
(SEE ALSO OUTLETS (RECEPTACLES))

A type of electrical outlet found in most modern structures owing to increased government standards. Until 1950, all electrical outlets were ungrounded with only two slots, one connected to a black wire and one connected to a white. Some had two slots of different sizes (polarized receptacles), so that a polarized appliance could only be plugged into the receptacle in the proper orientation. The convention is that the smaller slot is for the black wire and the larger for the white.

Grounded outlets have a third *ground* wire that normally conducts no electricity, providing a safety escape route in case something goes wrong with the appliance or receptacle. Live electricity may be brought to a point where it could be touched by a person, leading to electric shock when an appliance malfunctions, a cord is damaged, or a receptacle is faulty. The purpose of the ground wire is to provide a path that the electricity will follow. It should be understood that grounded receptacles are only of value where appliances with ground plugs are used.

GST
(SEE GOODS AND SERVICES TAX)

GUARANTOR

Person providing a separate personal covenant over and above a named party in a contract regarding some obligation, such as a mortgage, personal loan or lease.

Application   In a mortgage, the guarantor normally agrees to do the following:

- Perform and carry out the covenants as outlined in the mortgage document; and
- Make such payments on dates set out in the mortgage document.

It being a condition of the making of the loan secured by this mortgage that the covenants hereinafter set forth should be entered into by the Party(ies) of the Third Part, NOW AND IN CONSIDERATION of the sum of TWO DOLLARS ($2.00) now paid by the Mortgagee to me/us (receipt of which is hereby acknowledged), I/We

for myself/ourselves, my/our heirs, executors, administrators, successors and assigns, in consideration of the making of said loan by the Mortgagee and the advance in whole or in part of the moneys hereby secured, do hereby covenant promise and agree (jointly and severally) as principal debtor(s) and not as surety(ies) that I/we shall and will well and truly pay or cause to be paid to the Mortgagee, the principal sum and all other moneys hereby secured together with interest on the same at the days and times and in the manner in this mortgage set forth and shall and will in all matters pertaining to this mortgage well and truly do, observe, fulfill and keep all and singular the covenants, provisos, conditions, agreements and stipulations in this mortgage made binding upon the Mortgagor(s) and do further agree that my/our covenant shall bind me/us notwithstanding the giving of the time for payment of the mortgage or the varying of the terms of payment thereof or the rate of interest thereon or by any other indulgence granted by the Mortgagee to the Mortgagor(s).

The guarantor does not normally receive a release until all covenants outlined in the mortgage document are satisfied. Further, the mortgagee does not have to exhaust all avenues against the original mortgagor before turning to the guarantor. The guarantor will not usually be notified that a default has occurred, and remedies that might be taken need not be the same as exercised against the mortgagor nor with the same degree of leniency.

A variety of clauses can be used for the purposes of adding a guarantor either within the mortgage document or as an attachment. One such clause is provided for illustration purposes. This clause, in essence, creates a separate personal covenant that can be acted upon by the mortgagee. The lender's position is further secured and risk reduced. Applicants who would otherwise not be able to qualify may find this an acceptable avenue, given the agreement of a third party to become involved in the mortgage transaction.

GUTTER
(SEE ALSO EAVESTROUGH)

An eavestrough used to convey rainwater from the roof to the downspout.

HABENDUM CLAUSE

A clause in older deeds under the registry system setting out the interest granted by that deed.

The habendum clause begins with the phrase *to have and to hold*, followed by a description of the interest being transferred and any qualifiers or limitations associated with that interest. A typical habendum clause would read:

> *TO HAVE AND TO HOLD unto the said grantee his heirs and assigns to and for his sole and only use forever.*
>
> *SUBJECT NEVERTHELESS to the reservations, limitations, provisos and conditions expressed in the original grant thereof from the Crown.*

Legislation concerning provincial registry systems has gradually led to standardization of forms. Various wordings such as the *habendum clause* traditionally found within deeds are now relegated to the status of implied covenants that need not be repeated in every deed.

Provincial   See applicable reference materials.

HARD COSTS/SOFT COSTS

Costs involving land development and/or building construction. While no clear distinction exists between hard costs and soft costs, most practitioners view hard costs as tangible items as opposed to soft costs that are intangible.

Application   Real estate salespersons typically discuss hard and soft costs in relation to development proposals and pro forma statements associated with potential developments. In land development, hard costs traditionally refer to sewers, curbs, roads, overall grading, street lighting, and the costs of constructing a building shell plus most of the cladding/covering materials. This is contrasted with soft costs such as architectural design expense, development planning, zoning, professional fees, levies, interest costs on borrowed capital to complete the project, legal costs in drafting agreements, and other matters of a non-structural nature that are nevertheless important to the overall enterprise.

Example   *Hard Costs/Soft Costs*

Developer Reed is reviewing plans for a new retail centre. While cost of land and all direct building, including site work costs, are readily identified as hard costs, Reed is having difficulty quantifying the soft costs and asks his accountant to prepare a detailed list for review. The accountant prepared the following:

Schedule of Soft Costs	
Landscape Architect Fees	$10,000
Survey Fees	8,000
Soil Testing Fees	5,000
Engineering Inspection Fees	12,000
Lot Levies ($10,000 per hectare)	60,000
Building Permit	20,000
Realty Taxes	30,000
Accounting Fees	12,000
Market Study Fee	12,000
Leasing Fees	371,000
Legal Fees	200,000
Land Interest	738,000
Building Interest	532,000
Soft Cost Interest	49,000
Operating Costs—Annual Realty Taxes	53,000
Annual Maintenance	67,000
Overhead	100,000
Total Soft Costs	**$2,279,000**

Additional Details

Survey Fees   Includes an elevation site survey, a survey of each finished store in the shopping centre, and an overall building survey on the lands.)

Leasing Fees   Brokerage awarded leasing contract on the entire centre based on $2.00 per square foot for major stores and $3.00 per square foot for smaller commercial retail units.

Legal Fees   Includes cost associated with formation of a new company, production of a standard lease, reviewing all leases, negotiations with major tenants relating to their lease forms, certifying title, site plan agreements, issuance of letters of credit, registration of notices of lease on title, contracts, and payment arrangements with contractors.)

Land Interest   One-year interim financing is required.

Building Interest   Estimate based on five months interim financing less monthly construction draws from a permanent lender.

Annual Maintenance   Centre is to be substantially completed 60 days before opening. Landlord to absorb realty taxes plus maintenance costs for that period until tenants are operating.

Overhead   Office staff, office equipment, and incidental items required for development including centre manager on staff one year prior to opening.

HARMONIZED SALES TAX
(SEE ALSO GOODS AND SERVICES TAX)

Acronym: **HST**   Three provinces (Nova Scotia, New Brunswick, and Newfoundland) combined provincial sales tax with GST to create the harmonized sales tax (HST). HST applies to the same base of goods and services as GST, but at the rate of 15%, consisting of 7% federal and 8% provincial. HST uses the same basic operating rules as GST, including input tax credits and registration/filing procedures.

HAZARDOUS MATERIALS

Hazardous materials and environmental issues impact all forms of real estate in terms of occupant safety, operational procedures, cost of remedy, and ultimately value of property. Hazardous materials are discussed under individual headings, e.g., **Asbestos, Lead, Polychlorinated Biphenyls, Radon,** and **Urea Formaldehyde Foam Insulation**.

Provincial   See applicable reference materials.

HEARING

A session or meeting conducted within a legislative framework or, often in the case of real estate, by a professional organization in which arguments are heard concerning some specific circumstance involving real estate practitioners and evidence is submitted for consideration in relation to established rules of procedure.

Application   In organized real estate, the term *hearing* is most commonly referenced in regard to professional standards (ethical conduct) and arbitration (disputes concerning commission). Hearing procedures differ within individual real estate board jurisdictions. Board by-laws establish both the composition of hearing panels and the responsibilities of such panels in determining ethical violations under the Code of Ethics of The Canadian Real Estate Association, or resolving financial disputes under established arbitration procedures.

Within a legislative context, provincial regulatory bodies may institute procedures for the enforcement of rules, regulations, procedures, and other matters including the use of hearings and hearing panels concerning practitioners and the trading of real estate.

Provincial   See applicable reference materials.

HEATED WATER LINES

Specially designed water pipes for recreational property to facilitate year round water supply. The lines normally consist of an automatic thermostatic control combined with a heating element that extends through the plastic water line. For temporary installations, these lines lay on the ground, however, the heating elements can also be installed in existing buried water lines.

HEATING SYSTEMS

Convection or radiant systems, or a combination of both used to heat structures. Hot air, hot water, and steam are the most common heating systems.

Warm Air   Heat is distributed to the various rooms of the house through metal *hot air* ducts with cool air returned through returning *cold air* ducts. The temperature is controlled by a thermostat. The air flow may be by gravity or forced by means of a blower fan that is placed at the entrance of the cool-air passage into the furnace. Forced air systems are the most common.

G to H

Steam Heating   Heat is distributed by means of steam from the boiler to cast iron radiators. Steam gives up its heat to the radiator, becomes cool, condenses into water, and returns by gravity to the boiler.

Hot Water Heating   This type of system can operate by gravity, or water may be forced through the system by motor-operated impellers or circulators. The system may have either a one-pipe or a two-pipe configuration. In the one-pipe system containing a single main, the hot water passes through each radiator, returns to the main, and mixes with the hot water travelling to the next radiator. The cooler water returning from the radiator reduces the temperature of the water in the main. The two-pipe system has a separate pipe for the return of the cooler water from the radiator to the boiler. Hot water heating, in addition to quiet operation, provides steady, even. Hot water heating systems are fairly common in older homes.

Radiant Heat   Most systems are not entirely radiant as convection is also used. In panel heating, for example, the direct heating units are sections of the floor, ceiling, or wall. Heat is obtained by circulating water through copper pipes embedded in the concrete floor of houses without basements.

Electric Heat   Two main types of electric heating systems are found in homes: baseboard resistance heater and radiant heating cables or coils that are placed in the ceiling or floor. Electric heat has several advantages such as quiet operation, cleanliness, elimination of chimneys, thermostatic control for each room, and cheaper installation cost.

HEATING, VENTILATING, AND AIR-CONDITIONING

Acronym: HVAC   The mechanical unit(s) regulating the even distribution of heating, cooling, and fresh air throughout a building. A broad range of HVAC systems are used in the marketplace. Commercial HVAC systems are commonly mounted above suspended ceilings with supply air diffusers strategically placed within that ceiling along with return air ducts. Following are selected components:

Air Handler   The blower or series of fans within an HVAC system used to move heated or conditioned air through the structure, normally by means of duct work.

Condensing Unit   Normally situated outside the structure, the condensing unit contains a compressor that *compresses* freon, thereby providing the cooling effect within an air-conditioning unit.

Ductwork   A series of ducts used for the distribution of warm or cool air throughout a structure to various rooms, offices, and work areas. The ducted system permits the return flow of air back from various portions of the structure to the HVAC unit.

Roof Top HVAC   A large HVAC unit mounted on the roof of a structure that provides cooling and heating for the structure.

Unit Heater   A large interior, roof-hung unit that heats open areas.

Application   A commercial lease will typically outline the landlord's duties regarding the air-conditioning, humidification, and heating throughout the leased premises and common areas. The lease will also detail tenant responsibilities concerning energy costs, upkeep, and associated matters. The range of landlord/tenant relationships can vary significantly. In some commercial developments, the tenant will be required to install and pay for the HVAC in accordance with landlord specifications. In others, the landlord will prefer to undertake the HVAC installation and charge back the cost to the tenants. The example (on the following page) provides that all costs associated with HVAC are paid by the tenant. **Figure H.1** illustrates an HVAC system and its components.

Example   *Heating, Ventilating, and Air-Conditioning*
R. Smith, President of Anycity Fasteners Inc., is currently negotiating a new lease for his company as the sole tenant in a building. The lease document references the HVAC system and Smith's responsibilities as follows:

Heating/Air-Conditioning

Throughout the term, the tenant will pay all costs of heating, ventilating, and air-conditioning the premises. This includes, without limitation, the costs of operating, repairing, maintaining, inspection and depreciation, plus interest at a rate equal to four percent in excess of the prime interest rate from time to time charged by chartered banks at the beginning of each fiscal period. The charge applies to the undepreciated capital cost (including personal property taxes if any) of the machinery, equipment, HVAC systems, and other facilities required for such heating, ventilating and air-conditioning plus 15% of the total thereof for administration.

Continued...

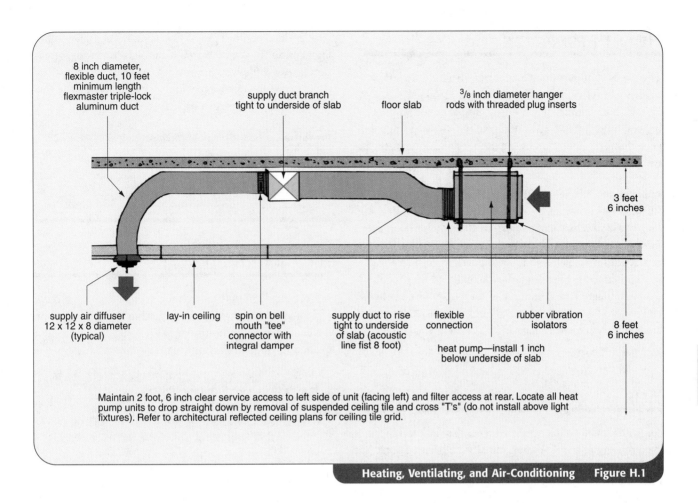

8 inch diameter, flexible duct, 10 feet minimum length flexmaster triple-lock aluminum duct

supply duct branch tight to underside of slab

floor slab

$^3/_8$ inch diameter hanger rods with threaded plug inserts

3 feet 6 inches

8 feet 6 inches

supply air diffuser 12 x 12 x 8 diameter (typical)

lay-in ceiling

spin on bell mouth "tee" connector with integral damper

supply duct to rise tight to underside of slab (acoustic line fist 8 foot)

flexible connection

heat pump—install 1 inch below underside of slab

rubber vibration isolators

Maintain 2 foot, 6 inch clear service access to left side of unit (facing left) and filter access at rear. Locate all heat pump units to drop straight down by removal of suspended ceiling tile and cross "T's" (do not install above light fixtures). Refer to architectural reflected ceiling plans for ceiling tile grid.

Heating, Ventilating, and Air-Conditioning   Figure H.1

The tenant will operate, maintain, and regulate all the HVAC systems installed in the premises in such a manner as to maintain comfortable conditions of temperature and humidity within the premises. The landlord may, from time to time, stipulate reasonable conditions of temperature and humidity to be maintained in the premises and the tenant will comply with such stipulations and with all reasonable regulations of the landlord pertaining to the maintenance and operation of such equipment.

HECTARE

A metric area measurement of 100 x 100 metres consisting of 10,000 square metres. The hectare is equivalent to 2.4711 acres. Figure H.2 illustrates a hectare in relation to an acre.

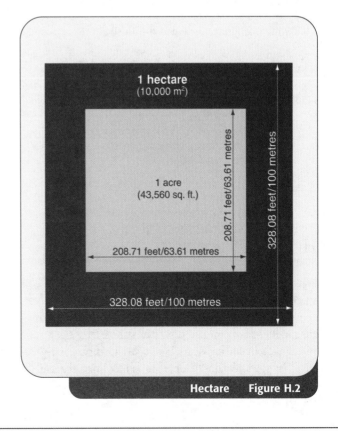

1 hectare (10,000 m²)

1 acre (43,560 sq. ft.)

208.71 feet/63.61 metres

328.08 feet/100 metres

208.71 feet/63.61 metres

328.08 feet/100 metres

Hectare   Figure H.2

HEIGHT RESTRICTION

The maximum permitted height of a structure normally set out as a restriction under municipal zoning by-laws. Usually the height restriction is expressed in feet and/or metres, however, in some municipalities, the wording provides for a limitation by the number of floors. In such instances, the height of a floor is also specified.

Application   Height restrictions are normally straight-forward. For example, a zoning by-law may state that the *height of a structure shall not exceed 10 metres as measured from grade.* For commercial and industrial sites, height restrictions may have an impact on design considerations as well as intended use. An industrial building may require a certain height to accommodate storage. In the commercial sector, the height will directly impact gross leaseable area and, consequently, the cash flow and ultimate return on the building.

HEIR

An individual who inherits or who has the right to inherit the property of another upon the death of that person.

Application   Agreements/contracts for real estate typically include a clause indicating that the agreement/contract shall be binding on all respective successors, heirs, assigns, administrators, and personal representatives.

Two wordings are provided for illustration purposes.

> • *The heirs, executors, administrators, successors and assigns of the undersigned are bound by the terms herein.*
> • *This agreement shall be binding upon and shall enure to the benefit of the Vendor and Purchaser and each of their respective successors, assigns, and personal representatives.*

HERITAGE PROPERTY

Land and structures identified as historically significant and worthy of protection for the inheritance of future generations. Provincial legislation typically sets out procedures for the identification and protection of *heritage significant* properties, including districts of special historic, architectural, or cultural value. Properties so identified are usually registered through local municipalities and/or provincial registry systems.

Identified heritage properties typically fall under guidelines concerning exterior modifications. Provincial legislation usually empowers appropriate government ministries/departments to acquire real and personal property in the preservation of heritage property.

Provincial   See applicable reference materials.

HIDDEN DEFECT
(SEE LATENT DEFECT)

HIGH RATIO MORTGAGE

A mortgage loan that exceeds the normal limit for a conventional first mortgage, with regard to the percentage of the loan amount to the property's lending value, and is insured through a mortgage insurance plan.

Example   *High Ratio Mortgage*

Buyer Jones requires a mortgage on a new house purchase of $150,000. Canada Mortgage and Housing Corporation is prepared to insure a high ratio mortgage on the property as follows:

Maximum Loan (90% of $150,000)	$135,000
Minimum Downpayment (150,000 – 135,000)	15,000
Total Price of House	**$150,000**

Jones will have to pay an insurance premium that can be either paid in cash or added to the mortgage amount. The rate of insurance is calculated based on the loan to lending value ratio.

Application   The phrase *high ratio* refers normally to mortgages arranged through a chartered lending institution where the loan amount exceeds 75% of the purchase price or appraised lending value, whichever is the lesser. Until 1970, major financial institutions in Canada were prohibited from making such loans. However, federal legislation covering banks, insurance companies, loan, and trust companies permitted loans higher than 75% if they were insured. Insurance is provided by Canada Mortgage and Housing Corporation and GE Capital Mortgage Insurance Canada.

HIGH RISE APARTMENT

Generally defined as a multi-family structure having ten or more storeys.

HIGHEST AND BEST USE
(SEE ALSO PRINCIPLES (APPRAISAL))

That use which, at the time of the appraisal, is most likely to produce the greatest net return in money or amenities to the land over a given period of time.

Application   Highest and best use is analyzed from two perspectives: the value of the land *as though vacant* or *as improved*. The *as though vacant* approach establishes how the land can best be utilized, not necessarily how it is currently used. The *as improved* approach provides an indication of value based on the current structure, but with regard to the highest and best use for that structure. Consequently, highest and best use analysis can arrive at differing values based on assumptions made.

Regardless of the approach, several criteria must be satisfied. The appraiser must give consideration to uses that are legally permissible with due consideration for zoning and other regulations. The scope of such regulations can be extensive including environmental factors, historic property designations, deed restrictions, and building codes. Appraisers must also give due consideration to the physical aspects of the property. Issues such as soil testing, road access, and availability/size of municipal servicing are included that go well beyond the mere consideration of size and shape.

Having satisfied these criteria, the appraiser must then assess whether the highest and best uses selected using the first two criteria are financially feasible. Financial feasibility is determined through investment analysis and projected cash flows. Commonly, the analysis includes both direct and yield capitalization techniques. The final step requires analysis of the most productive use from the perspective of land only. In other words, income attributable to improvements is deducted to arrive at residual income attributable to the land (referred to as the *residual land technique*, see **Capitalization**). The highest return to the land based on uses being analyzed represents the highest and best use.

Example   *Highest and Best Use*

Investor McKay is considering the acquisition of an existing commercial site in Anycity that presently contains an older three-bay auto repair garage and small restaurant. The property is zoned for general commercial purposes and McKay wants to know what the highest and best use is. Anne Appraiser analyzes the property based on highest and best use *as improved* and *as though vacant*. The property, as it exists, can be converted to a higher and better use as a video store or comparable retail outlet. Such a change is both legally and physically possible, however, returns are low based on comparable operations.

Continued…

From an *as vacant* perspective, the large 150 ft. x 300 ft. site will accommodate a small neighbourhood mall consisting of five retail stores and ten second floor professional offices. The proposed building maximizes current zoning provisions, meets all government requirements relating to the site, has proper road access, and can use existing services. Further, returns generated are higher than an alternate configuration involving four retail stores and 15 residential units.

HIGHWAY

Provincial   See applicable reference materials.

HISTORIC STRUCTURES
(SEE HERITAGE PROPERTY)

HOLDBACK
(SEE ALSO LENDER HOLDBACK)

A term relating to the withholding of a specified amount, typically a percentage of the total contract price, concerning contracted work in the erecting or repairing of a structure. Terminology and procedures will vary by provincial jurisdiction.

Provincial   See applicable reference materials.

HOLDING AREA

A space or room, usually in the freight-docking area, where deliveries to a tenant or building management may be held until deliverable to the recipient. A holding area is sometimes referred to as a *receiving area*.

HOLDING COMPANY

A corporation that owns or directly controls other corporations and thereby directs the activities of these entities owing to its position of controlling interest.

HOLDING OVER

The act of a tenant retaining possession of the premises longer than the term expressed in the lease; often referred to as *overholding*.

Application   In residential tenancies, provincial legislation normally sets out requirements concerning overholding. Typically, if the landlord continues to accept rent from the tenant, he/she thereby agrees to the tenant's continued occupancy as defined by provincial laws. Provincial legislation affecting residential tenancies varies significantly.

In commercial tenancies, leases may have a provision concerning overholding that involves an excess premium and is assessed on a monthly basis to the tenant. Many reasons may exist why a commercial lease might not be renewed within its proper time schedule, and overholding might occur, e.g., arbitration might be in effect between landlord and tenant, or the tenant may wish to remain in occupancy but has not finalized the necessary rent negotiations with the landlord. However, as the following example illustrates, a commercial tenant can pay a hefty premium for overholding.

Example   *Holding Over—Commercial Tenancy*

Tenant Jones is unhappy about a 15% rent increase planned by the Landlord and refuses to sign a new commercial lease pending the outcome of a dispute over the issue. In less than a week, the lease expires placing Jones in an overholding arrangement. Currently, his gross rent amounts to $3,200 per month. The Landlord, while sympathetic, claims that he has eager tenants waiting to occupy Jones' space and wants a decision. Casually, he reminds Jones to read the original lease carefully. The appropriate clause is reprinted.

Holding Over

If the tenant continues to occupy the premises after the expiration of the term, without any further written agreement, the tenant shall be a monthly tenant at a monthly gross rent equal to one-sixth of the highest annual gross rent that was payable by the tenant during any rental year of the term and otherwise on the terms and conditions herein set out with such changes as are appropriate to a monthly tenancy. This provision is not to affect the tenant's obligation to deliver up vacant possession at the expiration of the term.

Provincial   See applicable reference materials.

HOLDING PERIOD

The length of time that a property is held before disposition.

Application   Holding periods are frequently referenced in relation to the length of period that a property is held for tax purposes and resulting calculations leading to capital gains and related taxation. For commercial practitioners, a holding period is also associated with the projected length of time that a property is held for purposes of real estate investment analysis. The holding period provides the timing framework for analysis of projected operations and sale proceeds cash flow for purposes of valuing income property, screening investment options, and making appropriate investor-related decisions.

HOLDING TANK

Provincial   See applicable reference materials for matters concerning waste disposal, wastewater management systems, and sewage systems.

HOLDOVER PROVISION

A provision in an agreement/contract remaining from a former period.

Application   A holdover provision is found in practically all listing agreements used by real estate brokerages. Under this provision, while the listing brokerage's authority ends upon the expiry date, if the brokerage introduces a person to the property during the term of the listing who effects a private sale with the owner during a specified period after the expiry, the owner is liable for a commission payment to that broker.

**Example 1   *Holdover Provision—
Buyer Introduced During Listing Period***

Seller Smith signs a 90-day listing with ABC Realty Inc. that contains a holdover provision. Following expiration, a buyer originally introduced to the property by a salesperson in ABC Realty's employ returns to negotiate directly with Smith. The buyer clearly wants a lower price to gain the benefit from Smith not paying any commission. Smith, uncertain as to his position, takes the exclusive agreement to his lawyer. The lawyer confirms that if Smith sells the property to this buyer, then a commission is payable to ABC Realty Inc.

**Example 2   *Holdover Provision
Subsequent Listing and Holdover Clause***

Seller Smith was unhappy with Salesperson Lee because the property did not sell within the 60-day listing period despite several showings. While Lee insisted that a price reduction was necessary, Smith elected not to renew the listing but rather to select XYZ Real Estate Ltd.

Continued…

G TO H

Interestingly, within the first month of this new 120-day listing authority, Smith agreed to reduce the price. Two months later, it was sold unconditionally by a co-operating brokerage to a buyer who was introduced to the property when ABC Realty Inc. was the listing agent. Smith, alluding to the holdover clause, expressed concerns that he might have to pay two commissions. XYZ Real Estate Ltd. assured him that such was not the case as the original listing provided that the holdover did not apply if the property was subsequently listed and sold by another brokerage pursuant to a new listing agreement.

The exact wording and time limit of the holdover period in a listing agreement can vary. In some instances, the time period is not pre-printed but left blank for completion by the broker or salesperson.

HOME INSPECTION

The process by which a qualified person examines and evaluates various components of a residential building including but not limited to structural aspects, components, exterior coverings, roofing system, plumbing, electrical, heating, central air-conditioning, insulation, ventilation, and interior structure.

Application The home inspection is designed to provide a client with a thorough understanding of the condition of a property as of the date of inspection. The resulting report represents a written summary of the visual inspection of accessible features of the home. Home inspectors have not been traditionally licensed/registered or otherwise controlled by a specific statutory law relating to the field of home inspection.

Recently, Canadian organizations have been formed setting out qualifications for membership to enhance professional image (education, technical background, and experience), standardize methods of home inspection, and provide consumer protection. Members of the Canadian Association of Home Inspectors (CAHI) must adhere to the association's code of ethics that demands fairness and impartiality toward clients. In addition, to maintain membership, an inspector is required to meet annual continuing education requirements.

Provincial See applicable reference materials.

HOMESTEAD

Generally described as a property consisting of land and buildings occupied by the owner. Selected provinces have legislation relating to homesteads and the provision of rights of spouses concerning the disposition of such properties.

Provincial See applicable reference materials.

HORIZONTAL ANALYSIS

One of two simple methods used for analyzing financial statements, the other being vertical analysis.

Horizontal analysis involves the search for significant changes in trends comparing current year (or month) to previous periods in either the balance sheet or profit and loss statement. Each account is scrutinized to determine increases/decreases along with a general analysis of events, for example, did the money spent increase revenues?

Example *Horizontal Analysis*

ABC Realty Inc. is completing a horizontal analysis of the financial statements looking for significant year-to-year changes and trends. Following are examples under analysis including questions that ABC Realty Inc., is posing:

Profit and Loss Statement In 20xx, entertainment was $29,000 while in the prior year, it was $18,000. Did the $11,000 increase in spending generate more business? What special circumstances affected the totals in both years? Was it wisely spent? Is a more detailed analysis required?

Balance Sheet Cash in 20xx was down substantially to $15,000 from a previous year level of $32,000. However, on closer inspection, fixed assets increased from $32,000 to $45,000. All other things being equal, it would appear that most of the cash used (−$17,000), flowed to fixed assets (+ $13,000).

HOT WATER HEATER

A tank or reservoir used for heating water in commercial or residential structures.

Application Hot water heaters, regardless of heat source (gas, oil, or electricity), operate in essentially the same way. Cold water is pumped into the heater from a supply source and heated water is discharged from the other end of the tank. The temperature of the tank water is typically maintained at approximately 140°F. When hot water is removed by opening a faucet, cold water is introduced to the tank, triggering the thermostat. If enough hot water is removed from the tank, the tank will cool down. Therefore, the larger the holding tank (40 to 60 gallons), the greater the supply of hot water available. **Figure H.3** illustrates the components of a typical electric hot water heater.

The recovery rate is important, with oil having the fastest rate of recovery, followed by gas, and then electricity, depending on the size of the burner or element provided. The faster the recovery rate, the more water can be drawn off without depleting the hot water supply. Hot water tanks are now insulated to ensure higher energy efficiency. In many cases, hot water supply pipes are also insulated to minimize heat loss.

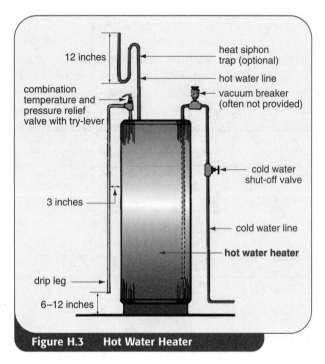

Figure H.3   Hot Water Heater

HOUSING ABSORPTIONS

A term generally referring to the taking in and utilization of new housing within the real estate market. Canada Mortgage and Housing Corporation (CMHC) provides a range of widely accepted definitions concerning the absorption of residential housing.

Absorption   Newly completed units sold or rented. Units sold or leased before construction are not considered as *absorbed* until the completion stage. Condominium units are absorbed when a firm sale has been reported, even though the unit may not be occupied.

Completed and Not Absorbed   Newly constructed, completed units that have never been sold or rented.

Completion   Completion of a single detached or semi-detached home occurs when 90% or more of a structure is complete. In row housing and apartments, completion occurs when 90% or more of the dwelling units within a structure are completed and ready for occupancy. Generally,

a structure may be considered complete and ready for occupancy when seasonal deficiencies and/or minor infractions of building codes remain.

HOUSING START

A term generally referring to the commencement of construction of a residential dwelling unit. Canada Mortgage and Housing Corporation (CMHC) provides a range of accepted definitions concerning residential housing starts.

Housing Start   A dwelling unit in which construction has advanced to a stage where full (100%) footings are in place. In the case of multiple unit structures, the definition of a start applies to the entire structure.

Pending Start   A dwelling unit where a building permit and/or *National Housing Act* (NHA) approval exists but construction has not started.

Total Supply   The total number of new units including pending starts, units under construction, and units completed but not absorbed.

Under Construction   The inventory of units currently being constructed.

HUMAN RIGHTS CODE

A set of standards typically embodied in legislation, e.g., the *Canadian Human Rights Act* based on the principle that all individuals have equal opportunity to pursue their needs without being hindered by discriminatory practices. Rights enjoyed by Canadians are also contained within the *Canadian Charter of Rights and Freedoms* and are generally grouped under fundamental freedoms such as freedom of conscience and religion, freedom of thought, belief, option, and expression, freedom of peaceful assembly, and freedom of association. The Charter also sets out democratic rights, mobility rights, legal rights, equality rights, official languages of Canada, and minority language education rights. Provinces also establish human rights codes consistent with, and complementary to federal legislation.

Provincial   See applicable reference materials.

HURDLE RATE
(SEE DISCOUNT RATE)

I TO K

I to K

National Info Links

Income Tax

For all matters concerning the *Income Tax Act*, contact:
Canada Customs and Revenue Agency

Web Site   www.ccra-adrc.gc.ca

See the local telephone directory for addresses and telephone numbers of Tax Services Offices and Tax Centres.

Interest/Bank Rates

For bank rates, exchange rates, and monetary policy, contact:

Bank of Canada
234 Wellington Street
Ottawa, ON K1A 0G9

Telephone   (613) 782 7713
(800) 303 1282
Web Site   www.bank-banque-canada.ca

Industry/Trade Development

Industry Canada Communications Branch
Attention: Enquiry Services 2nd Floor, West Tower
235 Queen Street
Ottawa, ON K1A 0H5

Web Site   www.ic.gc.ca

For provincial initiatives, contact the appropriate provincial ministry/department.

I

ILLEGAL RENT (RESIDENTIAL)

Provincial   See applicable reference materials.

ILLITERATE
(SEE ALSO NON EST FACTUM)

Unable to read or write. In terms of a contract, the question about an illiterate person and whether the contract is binding rests on whether the person knew what was being signed (a rule known as *non est factum*).

Example   *Illiterate*

Buyer Jones, having practically no knowledge of reading or writing, inspected a property on Main Street with his wife and daughter. The salesperson was unaware of the buyer's limitations as he was able to converse freely on a wide range of topics, particularly concerning house construction and design.

The salesperson drafted an agreement/contract based on instructions from the buyer and delivered it for signature. Once signed by Jones (he was capable of affixing his signature only), the agreement/contract was accepted by the sellers. However, only two days before closing, Jones refused to close, arguing that he was unable to read or write and, therefore, the contract was not binding.

While the ultimate decision by a court concerning Jones' illiteracy would depend on circumstances, several arguments can be put forth against his claim. Jones displayed a working knowledge of houses and was capable of carrying on a full and complete discussion with the salesperson. His family was present to assist (assuming they were literate), and lastly, he provided the salesperson with details of how the offer was to be drafted.

IMPERIAL MEASUREMENTS

Reference   See the **Appendix**.

IMPLIED

Created by the conduct or words of other parties, and not arising from explicit agreements.

Application   Implied situations arise in various real estate matters. Implied agency can develop when the agent by his/her actions or deeds with a buyer or seller gives the indication that a client relationship exists. In the case of an implied easement, the assumption is made that such right exists given the continuous use of the property, despite the lack of any formal agreement.

All brokers and salespersons should attempt to make express or implied agreements into written agreements that clearly delineate the responsibilities, expectations, and specific details of any contractual undertaking.

Example   *Implied*

Salesperson Lee is conducting a showing to a prospective buyer. While neither discussed the exact relationship being established, Lee frequently refers to the buyer as a client and states: *Don't worry, I will get you the right house, and at the best price!* The salesperson is creating an implied client relationship, regardless of whether any explicit, written agreement is made between the parties.

IMPLIED COVENANTS
(LAND REGISTRATION)

Covenants presumed to exist in a deed or a mortgage document registered under the appropriate provincial land registration system, regardless of whether they appear in such documents.

Provincial   See applicable reference materials.

IMPLIED (UNINTENDED) DUAL AGENCY

Implied dual agency arises when a brokerage inadvertently represents two parties or unwittingly is placed in the position of working for two principals, usually the buyer and seller, in a real estate transaction.

This situation is most likely to occur in a traditional agency relationship when the seller has listed with a brokerage. The brokerage, and all employed representatives, owe fiduciary duties to the seller through express agreement as set out in the listing agreement/contract. However, one of the salespeople could inadvertently assist the buyer through some form of counselling and advice.

Both the seller and buyer may be under incorrect assumptions. The seller may think that the brokerage works solely in his/her best interest. The buyer, upon receiving counselling, is led to believe that an implied agency relationship exists as the salesperson is working in his/her best interest. The result is implied (or unintended) dual agency.

Example *Implied (Unintended) Dual Agency*

Salesperson Lee completed a listing agreement/contract with Seller Smith. During the conversation, Lee was very explicit regarding his duties to Smith as a client and stated that all buyers would be treated as customers and owed honesty and fairness. Buyer Jones got an entirely different impression from Lee at an open house. Lee was forthright in providing information about Smith's circumstances concerning the sale and assured Jones that he could get the property for a low price.

While the listing authority created an express agreement with the seller, given Lee's actions, an implied dual agency relationship was established with both the buyer and seller.

IMPOSSIBILITY OF PERFORMANCE

A contract may be discharged because of the impossibility of performance, or frustration due to intervening and unanticipated circumstances. Such impossibility may occur in a relationship between an agent and principal.

Example *Impossibility of Performance*

The listing agreement/contract may involve something that no longer exists (e.g., a house was destroyed by fire), and consequently is terminated. It should be noted that, occasionally, the listing agreement/contract may contemplate this eventuality and provide for the sale of the land only.

IMPROVED LAND

Raw land including the installation of municipal services, roads, curbing, street lighting, and rough grading in preparation for development. The term is commonly associated with residential and commercial developments in which land is prepared for construction of buildings.

IMPROVEMENTS ON SITE

Also referred to as *improvements on land*. While no precise definition exists to differentiate *improvements on site* from *improvements to site*, improvements on site are generally limited to enclosed structures such as buildings, garages, and sheds, situated on a site so that the land can be used for a specific purpose.

Application In a residential appraisal, the improvements on site are normally restricted to the main building and any significant accessory buildings, such as a detached garage or permanent garden shed.

IMPROVEMENTS TO SITE

Also referred to as *improvements to land*. Improvements to site include items that either add to or detract from the outside enjoyment of the property. Examples include fencing, landscaping, paved driveway, patio, deck, outdoor swimming pool, parking areas, and exterior lighting. An outdoor pool is an improvement *to site*, an indoor pool within an enclosed structure is an improvement *on site*.

INCOME (APPRAISAL)
(SEE INCOME APPROACH)

INCOME (BROKERAGE)
(SEE ALSO ACCOUNTING SYSTEM AND BUDGETING)

Income for a brokerage typically includes commission income, referral income, and other sources such as appraisals, property management, or associated fees. Desk fee income is also included for organizations using desk fee plans. The chart of accounts varies considerably, based on the size of the brokerage and the types of commission arrangements within the organization.

INCOME APPROACH
(SEE ALSO CAPITALIZATION)

A procedure in appraisal analysis that converts anticipated benefits (dollar income) to be derived from the ownership of property into a value estimate.

Application The income approach is widely applied in the appraisal of income producing properties through the use of either yield or direct capitalization processes. This approach assumes that there is a relationship between the income that a property is capable of earning and its value at any given time and can be briefly summarized in five successive steps.

Step 1. Estimate the potential annual gross income minus the likely vacancies and bad debts.

Step 2. Estimate the total annual operating expenses.

Step 3. Calculate the net operating income.

Step 4. Select the appropriate capitalization rate.

Step 5. Estimate the value of the property based on the selected capitalization rate.

The appraiser estimates the potential annual gross income for the current year. A market-derived vacancy and bad debt loss allowance is subtracted from this to arrive at effective gross income. Operating expenses are deducted from the effective gross income, leaving net operating income. The appraiser selects and applies a rate and method of converting the net operating income into value by a mathematical process called capitalization.

The yield method of capitalization, while utilizing Steps 1, 2, and 3, requires alternate steps in the determination of operations cash flows (before or after tax), for a specified holding period including the reversionary value at point of sale (sale proceeds before or after tax). The result is discounted at an appropriate discount rate to arrive at present value.

INCOME CAPITALIZATION

(SEE CAPITALIZATION)

INCOME MULTIPLIERS

Numbers representing the relationship between the rent that can be obtained from a property and its selling price. Two income multipliers are commonly referred to in the marketplace: the monthly rental factor (MRF) and the gross rent multiplier (GRM). These multipliers are used in the valuation of either residential or income properties, when the rent from the property is known.

Application   The use of the MRF or GRM is generally grouped under the income approach to value. Care must be taken to ensure that the properties have similar characteristics before multipliers can be used. If the appraisal involves an apartment building, then comparable properties must be in the same price range and of similar size and location. If the subject property is an office building, then similar types of properties with comparable operating expense ratios and remaining economic lives must be used. The importance of using truly comparable properties is evident because multipliers are arrived at from actual income earned at the time of sale.

The advantage of such multipliers is their speed and ease of application. The disadvantages are that they do not provide for differences in properties, make no provision for variances in net incomes when gross incomes may be similar, and are only valid when sufficient comparable data is available. Practitioners should exercise prudence in applying multipliers and seek corroborating evidence through other techniques.

Monthly Rental Factor (MRF)

The MRF is the ratio of value to gross monthly rent. For example, if the value is $60,000 and the monthly rent is $600, then:

$$\text{MRF} = 60,000 \div 600 = 100$$

This calculation demonstrates that the property sold for 100 times its monthly rent. In calculating the MRF, the sales price of the property and the monthly rent are used without adjustments. This factor is applicable to the valuation of small income properties and single-family residences. The MRF is applicable if the monthly rent is known and an MRF can be determined from similar properties to the subject property.

Example   Income Multipliers— Monthly Rental Factor (MRF)

After gathering sales of similar properties and verifying their prices and monthly rents, Anne Appraiser calculates the following monthly rental factors.

SALE #	SALE PRICE	MONTHLY RENT	MRF
1	$92,500	$865	107
2	90,000	820	110
3	85,000	765	111
4	94,500	860	110
5	89,000	795	112
6	93,000	850	109

Anne selects a monthly rental factor of 110 based on multipliers derived from properties that are most similar to the subject property in terms of location, size, property features, and expense characteristics. The subject property rents for $850 per month. Using the MRF of 110, she estimates the value of the subject property as:

$$\$850 \times 110 = \$93,500$$

Gross Rent Multiplier (GRM)

The GRM represents the ratio of value to gross annual rent to estimate the value of income producing properties. In using this factor, as with the MRF, care must be taken to ensure that a high degree of comparability exists in comparable properties. If the buildings are not truly comparable, then, since the GRM is derived from actual gross figures without adjustment, a misleading valuation of the subject property can result.

Application   The term *gross rent multiplier* is gradually losing stature in favour of *gross income multiplier* as calculations involving commercial properties address all income and not just rent. Further, practitioners may seek increased accuracy by using adjusted rental figures (e.g., consideration for bad debt and credit losses and other income), if available for comparable properties.

Reference   See also **Gross Income Multiplier**.

INCOME PROPERTY

(SEE ALSO COMMERCIAL BROKERAGE)

A generic term referring to any type of real property that generates an income stream, e.g., multi-residential, office, industrial, and retail properties, as opposed to owner-occupied property or other properties that are not specifically used for generating revenue, e.g., parks. Investors typically assess income-producing property using existing and forecasted operations and sale proceeds cash flows.

The listing and marketing of income property are usually associated with commercial brokerages, although smaller investor-owned units are often serviced by residential brokerages.

INCOME RATE

A term, commonly associated with appraisers, that denotes the relationship between a single year's projected income and the value of the property. Income rates are not rates of return, but rather standard measures that are used for estimating values. The overall capitalization rate and the equity capitalization rates are examples of income rates. Income rates should be clearly differentiated from yield rates. Yield rates represent the return to an investor based on all future benefits arising out of ownership, e.g., cash flows from operations and sale proceeds. Yield rates are associated with yield capitalization techniques, while income rates relate to direct capitalization.

Example   *Income Rate*

Salesperson Warden establishes an overall cap rate of 9.2% based on market research for a specific type and class of property. This market-derived figure does not reflect an assumed rate of return, but a mathematical rate used strictly for calculation purposes. Assuming a projected single year's net operating income is $23,291, the estimate of value based on an overall cap rate of 9.2% is:

$$\$23,291 \div .092 = \$253,163$$

The capitalization rate is merely a numeric value reflecting income/sale price ratios found in the marketplace. The cap rate might be higher, lower, or identical to the true rate of return.

INCOME SOURCE VERIFICATION (LENDING)

Lenders vary in terms of the type of proof required to support an application for mortgage financing. A typical Income Verification Form is illustrated in **Figure I.1**. The form, completed by the applicant's employer, provides information concerning both the reliability and durability of the applicant's income stream. The questions are designed to demonstrate not only current income information, but also prospects for the future. Other proof may also be used but each has its limitations.

Income Tax—T4 Form

Useful but reflects only last year's income, does not show increases during the current period, and may not reveal certain passive income sources appearing on T5 forms. Lenders may request a Notice of Assessment that is provided to the taxpayer by the Canada Customs and Revenue Agency. This serves to confirm amounts stated by the borrower regarding income tax filings.

Letter from Employer Regarding Hourly Rate

Can be misleading as it does not reflect seasonal layoffs, hours per week, and overtime.

Pay Stub

Can be inaccurate as a weekly or monthly pay stub will not normally reflect variances in hours worked and overtime considerations.

Detailed Letter from Employer

A properly constructed letter from the employer providing current and anticipated income, length of employment, and future prospects, is often best as it closely approximates the items contained in the Income Verification Form.

Self-Employed or Commissioned Person

As much information as possible including copies of T4 forms and assessment notices as a well-documented record of earnings is required. All business records, properly organized, should be brought to the interview with the lender as proof of income.

The lender will also require the following in most transactions: copy of the agreement/contract, copy of the listing, payment of the application fee, and confirmation of downpayment.

VERIFICATION OF INCOME

Confidential: To be completed and signed by your Employer.

The following salary or wage verification is provided to _____
in strict confidence, as requested by the employee to support an application for a loan.

DATE

EMPLOYEE'S NAME	EMPLOYEE'S ADDRESS

NAME OF EMPLOYER

NO. OF YEARS EMPLOYED	PRESENT POSITION OR JOB CLASSIFICATION

GROSS EARNINGS FOR PREVIOUS YEAR	PRESENT REGULAR SALARY OR WAGE RATE	
$ _____	$ _____	☐ Per Hour ☐ Per Month ☐ Per Year

ADDITIONAL DETAILS
(earnings from overtime work, bonuses, commission, etc., that employee may receive during the year)

PROSPECTS OF CONTINUED EMPLOYMENT

OTHER REMARKS

_____
SIGNATURE (certified that the above information is true and correct)

_____
TITLE

Income Source Verification   Figure I.1

INCOME STATEMENT
(SEE ALSO FINANCIAL STATEMENTS)

An income statement, more commonly referred to as a *profit and loss statement* is used to evaluate the performance of a business by matching the revenue earned during a given time period with the expenses incurred in obtaining that revenue. The statement (see **Figure I.2**) reflects how much a business makes or loses during a given period of time and whether or not the business has been profitable during that time. Alternative titles for this statement are *Statement of Profit and Loss*, *Statement of Earnings*, or *Statement of Operations*.

The income statement shows all revenues (income) and all expenses of the firm for the period covered. By subtracting expenses from revenues, a net profit is obtained if revenues exceed expenses; if expenses exceed revenues, then a loss occurs.

INCOME STREAM
(SEE ALSO RECONSTRUCTED OPERATING STATEMENT)

For purposes of industrial, commercial and investment-grade properties, an income stream refers to the actual cash flow for a revenue producing property during a specified time period, usually expressed in annual terms.

Appraisers, commercial practitioners, and mortgage lenders generally approach the analysis of income property in a similar fashion by starting with actual and forecasted income streams.

ABC Realty Inc.
Income Statement
For Month Ended January 31, 20xx

Revenue		
Commission Income	$102,000	
Total Revenue		$102,000
Expenses		
Commission Expenses	64,000	
Advertising	10,000	
Bank Charges & Interest	700	
Rent	4,200	
Insurance & Taxes	800	
Office Salaries & Benefits	11,000	
Office Supplies & Expenses	1,600	
Utilities	3,200	
Telephone	2,400	
Accounting & Legal	1,000	
Depreciation Expense	1,400	
Total Expenses		97,900
NET PROFIT		$ 4,100

Figure I.2   Income Statement

INCOME STREAM VERIFICATION

Mortgage applications concerning investment properties will vary by lender, but most have similar requirements regarding income verification. Lenders seek assurances that debt service can be met, given revenues and expenses of the property under consideration.

Application   Verification items normally include:

• Terms of individual leases and monthly rents;
• Items included/not included in leases (heat, hydro, cable, etc.);
• Current status of any residential rent applications under applicable residential tenancy legislation;
• Renewal and cancellation provisions; and
• Special tenant privileges, options, and unusual arrangements.

This range of information is augmented by tenant credit reports, financial statements, and business history.

INCOME TAX ACT

The *Income Tax Act*, a complex legislative document, affects a wide range of personal and corporate activities. On a personal basis, the Act sets requirements regarding capital cost allowances, independent contractor activities, allowable travel expenses, personal expenses, and promotional activities, etc. Similarly, a host of corporate rules are in place concerning allowable corporate expenses, taxation of corporations and related matters.

In terms of real estate transactions, practitioners require selected knowledge of the Act concerning such items as capital gains on selected properties, capital gain versus business income, definition of principal residence, allowable rental expenses, capital cost allowance, and collection of taxes from nonresidents. The Canada Customs and Revenue Agency is responsible for the administration of this Act.

Reference   For additional information contact the local office of the Canada Customs and Revenue Agency. Taxation topics are addressed under the appropriate heading.

INCOME TAX DEDUCTIONS
(SEE SOURCE DEDUCTIONS)

INCREASING AND DECREASING RETURNS
(SEE PRINCIPLES (APPRAISAL))

INCURABLE DEPRECIATION
(SEE ALSO CURABLE DEPRECIATION)

A loss in value resulting from physical deterioration or functional obsolescence that either cannot be corrected, or can only be corrected at a cost greater than its contribution to the value of the property.

Application   Incurable depreciation applies to items in a structure that are not yet ready to be cured, that cannot be cured, or for which it is not economically sound to cure at this time since the cost of correcting the condition or effecting a cure is greater than the anticipated increase in value. While the correction of a condition may well be physically or technically possible, the criterion is whether or not it is economically sound to cure. Incurable depreciation is one dimension of estimating depreciation by means of the observed condition (breakdown) method, the other being curable depreciation.

I TO K

INCURABLE FUNCTIONAL OBSOLESCENCE

(SEE FUNCTIONAL OBSOLESCENCE)

INCURABLE PHYSICAL DETERIORATION

(SEE PHYSICAL DETERIORATION)

INDEMNIFY

To secure against hurt, loss, or damage; to provide compensation for incurred hurt, loss, or damage.

INDEMNITY

The obligation to indemnify, i.e., the assurance of one party to make financial compensation or repair and make good for any loss or damage that has been incurred or may be incurred on another party. Alternatively, the right of one party to claim damages against another.

The specifics of an indemnity are often detailed in an indemnification agreement between the parties or a clause set out within a contract between the parties.

Example   *Indemnity*

ABC Realty Inc. is contemplating a move to a larger office within a commercial office tower. The brokerage specializes in commercial and industrial property sales and leasing and the new location will be conveniently close to several important corporate customers.

The landlord of the property is concerned about the brokerage's overall financial strength and seeks some form of indemnification, failing which, lease negotiations will be at an end. Fortunately, Broker/Owner Johnson owns a successful development company with a proven ten-year financial track record.

The landlord insists on an indemnity agreement with Johnson's development company stating that, in the event of default by ABC Realty Inc., the company will:

• Pay all rent if the tenant, ABC Realty Inc., fails to do so.

• In the event of an early termination, be responsible and effectively become the landlord's tenant (at the landlord's option), in terms of obligations under early termination.

The landlord is not required to notify the indemnifier that the tenant has failed to fulfill any obligations under the lease. In the case of a default, the landlord may pursue the indemnifier directly. The indemnity agreement can only be altered by mutual agreement of landlord and indemnifier as it is absolute and unconditional.

Indemnity by a Principal

The principal must indemnify the authorized agent against losses, liabilities, and expenses incurred in the lawful performance of the undertaking. The agent must have acted within the authority granted. The principal has no duty to indemnify an agent who acts unlawfully or negligently, or is in breach of duty.

Example   *Indemnity by a Principal*

Salesperson Lee lists Seller Smith's house exclusively for $155,000 after carefully inspecting the property and preparing the listing agreement/contract.

At the point of signing and in the presence of another salesperson from the brokerage, Lee asks Smith specifically if he has had any problems with basement leakage. The question was posed because of a faint water stain on part of the downstairs panelling. Smith explained that he had inadvertently left an outside hose running for several hours. Satisfied with the answer from his client and seeing no further evidence, Lee highlighted the water stain on his notes but disregarded any reference to it in the listing.

Later, when a buyer acquired the property, the true extent of water damage and ongoing leakage was discovered. The buyer sued both seller and agent. The agent proceeded with a counterclaim against the principal arguing that he was operating under the authority granted, was misled by the principal, and was seeking indemnification for any damages successfully pursued by the buyer.

Indemnity by an Agent

The agent is liable to indemnify the principal for any acts undertaken personally or delegated to that agent's employees, salespeople, or sub-agents. The principal may be liable to third parties for acts carried out by the agent under the doctrine of vicarious responsibility. The principal will then claim indemnity from the agent, who will be responsible for all losses resulting from the breach of duty. The third party may claim compensation that includes legal costs. The principal may recover monies paid out, legal expenses, and interest on all such payments.

Real estate practitioners, in carrying out their function, encounter various situations that can give rise to litigation involving indemnity, e.g., representations made on behalf of a client (buyer or seller), failure to correctly carry out duties in listing and marketing a property, and matters involving the drafting and presentation of offers.

Example   *Indemnity by an Agent*

Salesperson Ward listed a property adjacent to a river. Seller Green advised Ward that the rear part of the property was within a flood risk area and subject to applicable provincial

Continued…

---

legislation. Several years ago, Green had been unable to put an addition on the property owing to restrictions relating to the flood risk area. Ward, while making a mental note of the situation, forgot to mention anything in the listing. Due to an unexpected interruption during the listing process, Green had to leave and agreed to meet again the following day. Salesperson Ward, unable to attend, sent another salesperson to complete the documentation. As an incentive, the salesperson would split any listing commission. No further mention of rear yard restrictions appeared on the listing.

The salesperson placed several ads about the property. The heading for one read: *Pool-Sized Yard*. A prospective buyer, seeing the panoramic view and wishing to fully landscape the rear yard, acquired the property only to discover that his plans for a deck, swimming pool, and other improvements were not possible owing to flood area restrictions.

The buyer sued the seller. The seller in turn sought indemnification from the agent and sued the brokerage, claiming that the agent was liable for misrepresentations made to the buyer.

INDENTURE

In real estate, a deed or agreement setting out specific objects executed by the parties to that agreement. Within the broader business context, an indenture refers to a written agreement outlining terms concerning the issuance of bonds or debentures.

Application   In a real estate context, an indenture typically involves the transfer of ownership between parties, but may also refer to an indenture of mortgage. The term *indenture* is gradually disappearing in regard to deeds and mortgages in provincial land registration systems.

Provincial   See applicable reference materials.

INDEPENDENT APPRAISAL

An appraisal establishing value conducted by an appraiser who is independent of the valuation. In other words, the appraiser has no real or contemplated interest in the property being valued and is at arm's length from the individual or company requesting the appraisal. Independent appraisals are differentiated from appraisals provided by an individual in some way affiliated with the client or the property, e.g., an employee of the lending institution requesting the appraisal, the owner of the property on his/her own behalf, or a property manager employed by the owner of the building being appraised.

INDEPENDENT CONTRACTOR
(SEE ALSO AGENT AND MASTER/SERVANT)

An individual who works according to his/her own methods and judgement. The independent contractor's work is self-directed and decisions concerning methods used for accomplishing contracted jobs are made without interference from others. The contractor could be, for example, a plumber, truck driver, doctor, or electrician. Independent contractor status has become particularly widespread with commissioned salespeople in the field of real estate brokerage. There are various common law tests applied by such organizations as the Canada Customs and Revenue Agency (CCRA) and the applicable provincial revenue ministries/departments to determine whether an individual is an independent contractor (contractor for service) or an employee (contract of service). The mere existence of a contract is not always the determining factor.

Application   Precise rules that a government ministry/department might apply in establishing employee versus independent contractor status will vary substantially based on individual circumstances. Essentially, most are built on four main tests found in common law.

Control

Is the employer able to control, or generally regulate through supervision, the activities of the individual? The relevant fact is not whether the control is exercised, but rather that it can be. As well, methods of termination are an important consideration. The more control, the more an individual is perceived as an employee.

Contract for Service

The contracting of an individual for a specific service and a specified result with supporting documentation is a strong indication of independent contractor status.

Integration

This common law test assesses whether the individual forms an integral part of the hiring organization's business or is an accessory to that business. Further, from the contracted person's perspective, integration refers to the extent that an individual operates his/her own business independent of the hiring organization.

Ownership/Economic Reality

An independent contractor owns his/her tools or other materials necessary to perform the contracted services.

Further, that ownership extends to various things usual to an independent business, e.g., the opportunity to profit, risk associated with a business venture, and investment in the business.

Within the real estate profession, this term refers to the status granted by the CCRA to those salespersons of a brokerage who meet specific taxation criteria. The taxation status must be confirmed by the CCRA after the salesperson has made application outlining the terms of employment. A ruling by the Canada Customs and Revenue Agency does not automatically mean that the applicable provincial ministry/department responsible for revenue matters will take the same position. Provisions typically included in independent contractor agreements for salespersons may vary by provincial jurisdiction based on tax interpretations as well as regulatory requirements set out in the applicable real estate act.

Provincial   See applicable reference materials.

INDEX

A statistical calculation that provides an indication of trends relating to an economic or financial circumstance in the marketplace. Major financial indexes for stock trading include the Toronto Stock Exchange (TSE), the Dow Jones, S & P 500, and NASDAQ.

Application   For real estate purposes, the Consumer Price Index (CPI) is commonly used as a price index. For example, office lease rates may be adjusted based on the CPI. Assume that the CPI index is 1.00 and the current rent is $24,000 per year with an escalator clause based on the CPI. If the index moved upwards to 1.05, then the rent for the subsequent year would be:

$$1.05 \times \$24,000 = \$25,200$$

Indexes are also used in mortgage financing. Adjustable rate mortgages are sometimes referenced as *fully indexed*. In other words, the mortgage rate will vary directly in proportion to an indexed base rate, e.g., the prime rate, T-bill rate, or another declared rate. The lender selects a base rate and then adds a margin to arrive at the mortgage rate, for example:

prime + .0250 (2.5%) (margin) = mortgage interest rate

The adjustable rate mortgage is then modified at predetermined intervals based on changes in the prime. As a qualifying note, adjustable rate mortgages for residential purposes are rarely fully indexed but rather are limited by *cap* provisions restricting:

- The maximum change in a mortgage interest rate during specified periods (e.g., adjustment not to exceed 1.5% in any year); and
- The maximum rate that can be charged.

INDEXED LEASE

A lease in which the lease amount payable is adjusted by means of an index; most commonly, the Consumer Price Index.

INDEXED MORTGAGE

A mortgage in which the interest payable is adjusted by means of an index; most commonly a widely accepted benchmark rate of interest.

INDIVIDUAL METER

A utility measuring device for each unit in a multi-unit building.

Application   Energy use is measured by kilowatt hours (kWh) and kilowatt consumption is measured by using a kilowatt hour meter. It operates by means of the magnetic field created when electricity moves through the meter. The meter disk rotates in proportion to the amount of magnetic force applied to the disk. The amount of force is directly proportionate to the consumption of electrical power within the unit.

Example   *Individual Meter*

Smith owns a large condominium townhouse that is one of thirty-six units in the development. Each townhouse is separately metered and bills are received by all homeowners directly from the utility company, as is the case with most detached and freehold properties. However, Smith also pays a monthly maintenance fee for all common areas that includes energy use for such items as the pool and tennis court lights, each of which is metered separately and billed to the condominium corporation.

INDOOR AIR QUALITY

Acronym: IAQ   The issue of indoor contaminants is becoming a major pollution concern owing to the extensive use of spray cleaners, pesticides, personal care products, and a host of other chemical products within both residential and commercial establishments. Further, the present emphasis on energy efficient structures has served to reduce free flowing air/ventilation and consequently such structures have the potential to contain more pollutants.

A new term called the *Sick Building Syndrome* has entered the marketplace. According to national standards established under the *Environmental Protection Act*, the *Sick Building Syndrome* occurs when 20% of the occupants complain of ailments relating to rashes, dizziness, breathing problems, fatigue, etc. Such problems ultimately lead to decreased worker efficiency.

Contracting firms now provide services ranging from HVAC inspection and maintenance to air quality testing and delivery system cleaning (duct cleaning). There are many causes and diligent effort is required to ensure that air quality is maintained. In addition to routine maintenance, air filters are being installed in buildings. These can range from disposable filters (common in residential air cleaning systems), that remove small objects in the air, referenced as particulate matter, to antimicrobial treated pleated filters that not only clean the air but destroy micro organisms on contact.

In residential property, the appropriate ministry/ department involved with environmental issues and the provincial home builder's association (if applicable) can provide guidelines on the reduction of indoor air pollution. Recommendations typically include the installation of an air exchanger, provision for outside air ventilation, and assurances that all paints, chemicals, and pesticides are completely sealed and stored in well ventilated areas.

Residential air filter system alternatives tend to mirror commercial grade products including both particulate filters and antimicrobial versions. Various efficiency levels are available in filters ranging from the filtering of pollen, plant spores, and human hair to smog, tobacco smoke, viruses, and lung damaging dust.

INDUCEMENTS

The act of persuading or in some way influencing the actions and/or attitudes of others by means of promises, representations, or the provision of some tangible benefit such as money.

Application   Provincial real estate acts typically set out requirements concerning representations and promises made by a licensed/registered person concerning the purchase, sale, or exchange of real estate. Members of organized real estate are also bound by requirements set out in the CREA Code of Ethics.

> **Example   *Inducements***
>
> Salesperson Lee has just heard that Seller Smith accepted an offer of $220,000 on his home that had been listed for $275,000. Immediately realizing that his buyer, who had inspected the property one month ago, would have paid $230,000 for the property (had he only known that Smith was that negotiable), Lee calls Smith and urges him to get out of the other deal, assuring the seller that a $230,000 offer is guaranteed. To sweeten the deal, he also agrees secretly to kick back part of his commission as a further incentive. Lee will undoubtedly be found guilty of inducement to break a contract under the applicable provincial regulatory act.

Provincial   See applicable reference materials.

INDUSTRIAL BUILDING CATEGORIES

Represent a classification system based on purpose. Most industrial specialists divide industrial properties into three main categories.

General Purpose   Buildings offering features and facilities for a wide range of alternate uses. General purpose buildings are understandably the most common type of structure as they have the widest appeal in the industrial market. Speculative construction is almost totally devoted to this category.

Special Purpose   Buildings offering selected features of particular interest to specialized industrial processes, e.g., distribution centres that have extensive loading dock facilities. Often such buildings have loading docks on both sides to facilitate cross-docking. Other types of specialized warehousing or manufacturing buildings may require reinforced floors for storage and heavy vehicular traffic. The special purpose building is not restricted to one particular user, but is best described as one that has narrower applicability than a general purpose structure.

Single Purpose   The single purpose building has little or no potential for conversion to uses other than those of the intended user, for example, an oil refinery or selected types of heavy industrial manufacturing plants. A single purpose building could be converted, but the cost of conversion would be significant and usually neither economically feasible nor practical.

Single purpose buildings have traditionally proven difficult to market given unique features constructed for a specific user. As well, such facilities can be challenging from an appraisal perspective owing to the usual lack of comparable properties.

INDUSTRIAL PARK

A controlled, park-like development designed and zoned to accommodate specific types of industry and to provide such things as public utilities, streets, railroad sidings, and water/sewage facilities. Industrial parks (sometimes referred to as *industrial park districts*), are intended to provide areas for industrial development that do not detract from adjacent residential areas or other uses. Regulations impacting industrial parks include compliance with performance standards relating to noise, vibration, odorous, toxic and noxious matter, radiation hazards, fire and explosive hazards, glare, and heat. An industrial park may serve as a buffer between heavy industrial activities and business or residential districts.

Application   An industrial park requires comprehensive planning to ensure adequate roads, proper land use and site coverage, lot sizes, and minimum acceptable architectural and landscaping requirements. Industrial parks frequently require detailed site plans for all construction and strictly enforce building requirements through deed restrictions.

A well-planned industrial park should properly integrate with the remainder of the community by using buffers and restrictions/requirements concerning the preservation of open lands. It should also ensure that consistency is maintained within the development in the interest of protecting the stakeholders, be they the developer and tenants or individual owners. Municipalities typically require site plan control agreements in relation to individual properties within an industrial park.

The *Society of Industrial and Office REALTORS* has identified various elements essential to a well-planned industrial park including: comprehensive planning, compatibility among industrial operations in the park, consistency between the industrial park and existing activities/character of the community, design controls, openness and park-like setting, harmonious integration into the neighbourhood, zoning to protect surrounding areas, and a continuing responsibility of park management to preserve compatibility.

INDUSTRIAL PLANT

A structure in which industrial activities such as the manufacturing, processing, storage, and distribution of tangible goods takes place. The industrial plant includes not only the portion of the building devoted to such activities but also all accessory buildings and other structures relating to the process located on the site.

INDUSTRIAL REAL ESTATE

Property used for the processing and manufacturing of goods. Industrial real estate includes all land and buildings either utilized or suited for industrial purposes.

Application   While most practitioners think of industrial property as specifically relating to manufacturing, the term has a much broader meaning that includes production, storage, and distribution of tangible goods (as opposed to intangible goods, e.g., professional services). Traditional uses normally centred on manufacturing, warehousing, or transportation. More recently, industrial areas now contain business enterprises including a wide diversity of activities such as data processing, advanced computer technologies, communications, publishing/printing, and a variety of support industries.

For zoning purposes, permitted uses will vary by municipality and commonly include manufacturing and warehousing, research/training facilities, transportation uses including truck and rail terminals, public works depots, contractor yards, service and repair operations, electric power facilities, and automotive service establishments. In recent years, industrial areas have become more varied in terms of land use with the appearance of large-scale entertainment centres, recreational facilities, fitness clubs, fraternal organizations, and large vertical market retailers. This wide diversity of uses has served to blur traditional lines separating retail/office and industrial markets.

As for actual placement within a community, industrial properties are ideally grouped in planned areas to minimize impact on adjacent uses. Buffer zones are frequently utilized. For example, a residential zone would buffer the agricultural zone from the commercial, which in turn buffers the residential zone from light industry, and light industry serves to separate the more severe impact of heavy industry. Light industry is normally classified as warehouses and non-offensive manufacturing operations. Heavy industry would cover such operations as machine works and automotive, steel, and chemical plants.

INFANT
(SEE ALSO MINOR)

A person who is a minor, under the age of legal competence (which varies by province), and thus incapable of the independent judgement necessary to undertake a legal obligation. Practitioners should be particularly sensitive to situations involving potential minors transacting real property.

I
TO
K

INFILL HOUSING
(SEE ALSO INTENSIFICATION)

Any project that creates new housing within an existing, established neighbourhood. Infill could include the demolition of one single-family home with its replacement being another single-family home or duplex, the construction of townhouses where one or more single-family homes previously existed, the building of additional housing units on existing vacant lands, or major additions and/or renovations to existing housing stock.

> **Example**   *Infill Housing*
>
> Seller Smith has a 100 x 160 foot lot together with a single-family home. The current zoning is R2, classified as a low density residential designation and permits detached, semi-detached, duplex or other attached dwelling, e.g., an accessory apartment. Smith wants to renovate the existing structure on the westerly portion into a duplex, while severing the remaining 50 x 160 foot lot for a single, detached home. The municipality agrees with the duplex conversion subject to compliance with all fire, building code, and municipal regulations. The severance application would also be viewed favourably as appropriate infill that is consistent with housing in the immediate area.

INFRASTRUCTURE

Facilities and support services within a community designed to serve the population on an ongoing basis including water, sewage, utilities, road, and bridge systems together with all supporting services for their ongoing operation, repair, and replacement.

INHERITANCE

For real estate purposes, property that passes to heirs after the death of the owner. When someone dies without a will, that person is said to die intestate. The estate passes to the legal heirs or other disposition as provided by law. If a will is executed, the terms of that will become effective to deal with the property of the deceased. In certain circumstances such as those involving infants or mentally incapacitated persons, approvals may be required from a court or appropriate government representative in the course of disposing of the deceased's property. The prudent real estate practitioner should seek legal advice when dealing with estates and issues surrounding inheritance and the disposition of property.

Provincial   See applicable reference materials.

IN-HOUSE MANAGEMENT
(SEE ALSO PROPERTY MANAGEMENT)

Management originating from within an organization; i.e., staff of the corporation owning the property, rather than expertise brought in from outside the organization.

Application   For real estate practitioners, this normally refers to property managers operating as employees of the landlord as opposed to contracted personnel providing services under a management agreement.

INJURIOUS AFFECTION

A term usually identified with the effect of expropriation, including related works concerning the expropriated land, on the residual land remaining. Claims by an owner of residual land relating to such action typically involve loss of access to other land, roads, or docks retained by the owner, loss of landscaping and parking areas, delaying of construction, denying of access to business premises, damage to crops, dirt and noise from construction, and relocation of a creek bed or erosion caused by alterations by the expropriating authority (less any added value contributed by those alterations).

Provincial   See applicable reference materials.

INSPECTION RIGHT (PRIOR TO PURCHASE)

Most agreements/contracts concerning the purchase of real estate contain a provision stating that the buyer, in making the offer, has had the opportunity to personally inspect the property prior to making such offer.

Provincial   See applicable reference materials.

INSPECTION RIGHT (RECORDS)

Authorized representatives of the regulatory body under the applicable real estate act/regulations are typically empowered to fully inspect records of real estate brokerages. In fact, the scrutinizing of brokerage operations is generally viewed as a routine procedure to ensure that all statutory requirements are being met. Such individuals may at any reasonable time enter upon the business premises of the brokerage to make an inspection and ensure compliance. No one may obstruct or otherwise hinder the investigation.

If authorized representatives wish to further investigate any particular situation, additional rights exist over and above access including the right to remove and copy documents. Remedies are also available if the appointed investigator is obstructed.

Provincial   See applicable reference materials.

INSTALLMENT CONTRACT
(SEE ALSO AGREEMENT FOR SALE)

Commonly referred to as a *conditional sales contract* that can involve either goods or property. In a real estate transaction, an installment contract for the sale of property requires that the purchase price be paid in installments over an extended period by the buyer, who is in possession of the real estate. Title is retained by the seller until the final payment is received from the buyer.

INSTITUTIONAL ADVERTISING
(SEE ADVERTISING)

INSTRUMENT

A form of written legal document. The term *instrument* has traditionally included legal documents whereby title to land in various provinces may be transferred, disposed of, mortgaged or otherwise encumbered, or affected in any way. The term *instrument*, generally associated with registry systems in the eastern parts of Canada, has largely fallen into disuse with the advent of standardized forms, form titles, and terminology.

Provincial   See applicable reference materials.

INSULATION (R-VALUE/RSI-VALUE)

Provincial building codes establish minimum requirements for new structures based on R-values. Most codes set out minimum thermal resistance of insulation to be installed in building elements exposed to exterior or unheated spaces, such as ceilings below attics, foundation walls, and floors.

Application   An *R-value* is a numerical representation of thermal resistance, the higher the number, the greater resistance to heat transfer. The *RSI-Value* is the metric equivalent of an R-value (divide the R-value by 5.6). Figure I.3 outlines the R-values which are currently recommended in many northern areas.

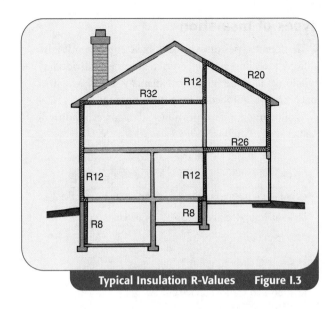

Typical Insulation R-Values   Figure I.3

Exterior Insulation

A beneficial modernization in older homes, provided that window and door modifications are made, along with care in installing new insulating materials. If not done properly, old uninsulated cavities may short circuit much of the effectiveness. Normally, external insulation is not cost-effective unless the exterior of the building, for example new siding, is also installed.

Interior Insulation

Insulation involves limiting the movement of air through techniques including air barriers, vapour barriers, caulking and weather stripping, and various types of batt or similar insulation. Insulation is rated based on its R-value. Figure I.4 is provided showing batt type wall insulation (viewed from above).

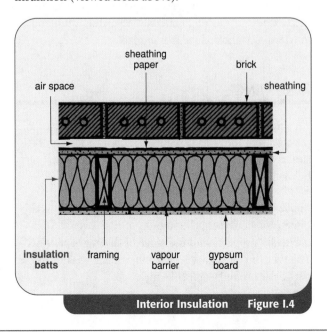

Interior Insulation   Figure I.4

Types of Insulation

Different types of insulation have correspondingly different R-values. In fact, even the form of individual types will affect R-value (glass fibre insulation in the form of batts has a higher value than if in loose form).

Following are six types along with corresponding R-values:

TYPE	R-VALUE
Glass Fibre Insulation	2.9–4.2 per inch
Mineral Wool/Rock Wool	3.0–3.2 per inch
Cellulose Fibre	3.4–3.6 per inch
Vermiculite	2.3 per inch
Wood Shavings (treated with fire retardant/moisture resistant materials)	2.4 per inch
Plastic Board	3.7–6.0 per inch

INSULBRICK

Insulbrick, a popular form of exterior siding particularly during the 1930s and 1940s, consists of fibre board coated with tar and sprinkled with granular material commonly embossed with a brick-like appearance.

Application   Practitioners should be aware that most lending institutions will not place mortgages on properties with insulbrick exteriors. Given that situation, combined with its low-quality construction standard and combustibility, this type of facing has gradually disappeared as better exterior finishing materials (e.g., aluminum and vinyl siding), entered the marketplace.

INSURANCE

An agreement in which one party (insurer) promises to pay a sum of money to another (insured) if the latter suffers a particular loss, in exchange for a premium paid by the insured.

Application   Insurance coverage for real property is two-dimensional: namely, the amount of risk covered for a particular property and the range of coverages provided. The type of coverage will vary substantially, based on the particular property and risks included.

Residential

Residential insurance coverage is generally grouped under owner and tenant policies. Both types are commonly *packaged*, that is, various coverages are included within a single policy. Most consist of four basic sections:

Property Insurance   What property is being insured against loss or damage, what is not insured, and the types of causes of such loss or damage that will be paid under the policy. The range of coverages will vary from basic perils to more comprehensive coverages. Typically, insurance policy wordings concentrate on coverages excluded rather than those included. A wide variety of coverage extensions are available through most insurers.

Liability Insurance   Specified limits for liability arising out of accidents or occurrences as detailed in the policy. Liability can extend to specific personal actions liability, premises liability, tenant legal liability, and selected medical payments. Once again, a wide variety of coverages are available through insurers.

Endorsements   Additional coverage that is added to the insurance policy, for example, coverages relating to valuable personal articles.

Policy Conditions   Various policy conditions relating to procedures concerning claims, general policy provisions, and matters addressed in applicable provincial insurance legislation.

Commercial Property

Commercial policies are structured to provide basic coverages for property insurance and liability coverages, with additional endorsements and other policies to meet the needs of specific business activities. Specialized policies are often required. Following are a few commonly encountered business insurance coverages.

Boiler and Machinery Coverage   Repairs and/or replacement of all major heating, ventilating and air-conditioning equipment. The premium will be directly related to the type of maintenance contract for the care of the particular item insured.

Errors and Omissions   Protection for the insured if some unforeseen occurrence develops from negligence in the operation of the business.

Fidelity Bond   Insures the employer against the acts of dishonest employees.

Loss of Income   Loss of income suffered by the insured in the event of damage to the building and resulting disruption of business as a result of that damage.

Multi-Peril Risk   Combination of fire and liability coverages that generally align with the basic structure of residential packaged policies. These package policies normally provide premium discounts for broader coverage features than would be the case with separate policies for fire, extended perils, and liability.

Condominium

Insurance requirements for condominiums consist of three separate groups.

- The condominium corporation requires insurance for the unit structures (excluding any improvements or betterments made by the owner), and common elements. In addition, the corporation is responsible for liability coverage, any bonding coverage required for employees and directors/officers, and director liability.
- The unit owner should insure any improvements (built-in items, carpeting, and personal belongings), and generally any risk not covered by the corporation (including the owner's liability).
- Renters should ensure that all personal belongings are insured and appropriate legal liability coverage is obtained.

Insurers typically provide owner policies for condominium owners structured on the same general basis as is the case for residential property. Tenant package policies are structured for both condominium tenancies as well as other rental accommodation. Real estate practitioners should note that the rental agreement for a condominium may specify that the tenant provides coverage for those items owned by the landlord on the premises, e.g., appliances and carpeting.

INSURANCE—ERRORS AND OMISSIONS

Acronym: E&O   Insurance coverage involving mistakes or omitted items and associated claims arising from the usual practice of real estate brokerage including listing, marketing, and selling residential and commercial properties. The scope of coverage varies in the marketplace. E & O insurance may be administered by the provincial regulatory body or offered through the provincial real estate association.

Provincial   See applicable reference materials.

INSURED, NAMED

The person(s) or company(ies) named in an insurance policy who are to be indemnified and receive the proceeds of insurance in the event of insurable loss or damage.

> **Example   *Named Insured***
>
> Broker/Owner Johnson, of ABC Realty Inc., is insuring his brokerage office for property damage, general liability, and various incidental endorsements. All insured items are owned by ABC Realty Inc., subject to a first mortgage on the land and buildings with ABC Trust Inc. Accordingly, the policy is issued with the named insured being ABC Realty Inc., subject to the mortgagee's interest in the property. In other words, the mortgagee would receive the proceeds of the insurance in the event of loss up to the amount owing by ABC Realty Inc. to that mortgagee. The balance would be paid to ABC Realty Inc.

INTANGIBLE ASSET

An asset that does not physically exist save and except for any written documentation or agreement between parties supporting its value.

Application   A mortgage can be considered as an intangible asset because only written documentation supports its value. Commonly, commercial practitioners selling businesses must address the value of goodwill or other intangibles making up value, frequently referred to as *going concern value*. Reputation of the business, trademarks associated with the business operation, consistent earnings over a lengthy period of time can all represent intangible assets that contribute to value.

INTENSIFICATION

Intensification, a term coined in urban planning and government circles, involves the expanded use of buildings and serviced land to provide additional housing stock and more effectively utilize existing municipal services, as opposed to the creation of new housing stock through outlying subdivision developments. Intensification has various dimensions including the increased use of existing housing stock through additional dwelling units.

Intensification is usually identified with additional second units (accessory apartments) in houses. However, the concept goes much further in the advocacy of creative housing options including mixed-use developments along arterial roads within urban areas and the redevelopment of existing industrial lands for residential purposes.

INTEREST

The ownership of a right in real property. For additional information on types of ownership interests, see Estate.

For mortgage purposes, interest is the price paid by a borrower to a lender for the use of the lender's money. For calculation methods involving mortgages, see Mortgage Mathematics.

INTEREST ACT

The *Interest Act (Canada)* specifically references interest on monies secured by a mortgage on real property. The *Interest Act* directly affects methods for calculating mortgage interest in Canada and also imposes certain limitations on the amount of interest that can be charged. Following is a brief summary of significant items impacting mortgages.

Section 2—No Restrictions

Essentially, no restrictions are made as to the rates charged between lender and borrower according to the Act. However, provincial consumer legislation typically provides recourse when interest rates or such other terms are inequitable and excessive, given risks involved and the availability of other suitable financing.

Section 3—Interest Rate Not Provided

The *Interest Act* states that where no interest rate appears in a document concerning debt, the interest rate is deemed to be 5% per annum.

Section 4— When Per Annum Rate Not Stipulated

If rates are stated but not the annual rate, then the rate will be deemed to be 5% per annum. Section 5 states that sums can be recoverable if paid in excess of stated limits when no annual rate was provided. Mortgages in real estate are an exception (should the per annum not be stated, it is assumed to appear).

Section 6— No Interest Recoverable in Certain Cases

If mortgages are repaid on a blended basis (principal and interest portions are not immediately discernable), then the interest will be calculated yearly or half-yearly, not in advance. The Act refers to such mortgages as a *sinking fund plan* or a *blended payment*. This section of the Act was introduced to protect borrowers who would not be able to calculate the true rate of interest being charged.

INTEREST ADJUSTMENT DATE

The date in a blended payment plan, prior to the commencement of the mortgage term, to which accrued interest computed on the various advances is calculated. A typical mortgage will provide for a specific interest adjustment date on which the interest calculation begins. For example, if the interest adjustment date is April 1, 20xx, payments of principal and interest will commence one month later on May 1, 20xx.

INTEREST BEARING ACCOUNT

Acronym: IBA   The use of interest bearing accounts in real estate brokerages focuses on interest collected on deposits held in trust. Provincial regulatory bodies establish procedures regarding the use of such accounts and, more generally, requirements regarding the depositing, reporting, and distributing of trust funds including interest collected.

Provincial   See applicable reference materials.

INTEREST EXPENSE

Interest costs associated with debt service for a specified period. In the case of real estate, interest costs are associated with real estate investment analysis and the computation of cash flows from the operation of an investment property. Commercial practitioners commonly use investment analysis worksheets to analyze forecasted cash flows (both before and after taxes), to arrive at valuations, to make investment comparisons, and to calculate internal rates of return.

INTEREST IN LAND
(SEE ESTATE)

INTEREST ONLY MORTGAGE

A mortgage on which interest only is paid with no reduction of principal during the term. Also referred to as a *flat payment mortgage*.

INTEREST RATE
(SEE ALSO MORTGAGE MATHEMATICS)

The percentage charged for the use of borrowed money. Real estate practitioners must distinguish between nominal rate (stated rate) and effective rate (actual interest rate charged based on compounding), in order to perform various mortgage calculations.

INTERIM FINANCING

Short-term or temporary financing to address immediate needs as distinguished from long-term debt structure.

Application   For real estate purposes, interim financing can involve any type of temporary arrangement until a *permanent* mortgage is put in place. Often, interim financing for new commercial projects involves temporary or gap funds to be used until scheduled advances are received in relation to the project.

INTERIOR (NON-STRUCTURAL) PARTITIONS

Interior non-load-bearing panels, dividers or walls that enclose or subdivide space typically made of steel, wood, glass, masonry, or combinations of these materials. Such partitions can be either movable or non-movable, prefabricated, or built on the job.

INTERNAL RATE OF RETURN

Acronym: IRR   The discount rate at which the present value of future cash flows is equal to the initial capital invested. Alternatively worded, the IRR is the discount rate at which the present value of cash flows equals zero. For real estate investment analysis, the internal rate of return represents the yield on invested capital in a property, most commonly stated as an annual rate as the vast majority of calculations involve forecasted yearly cash flows over holding periods typically ranging from five to ten years. The internal rate of return provides a comparative method for analysing different investment projects based on their internal operations and sale proceeds cash flows, and is widely accepted as a valid measure of internal investment return, particularly when used with present value calculations.

Guidelines

Several guidelines apply when using the IRR:

- If only the initial investment is returned by way of periodic cash flows during the investment period, the IRR will be 0.
- If the sum of future periodic cash flows is greater than the initial investment, the IRR will be greater than 0.
- If the sum of future periodic cash flows is less than the initial investment, the IRR will be less than 0. (Certain cautions apply in regard to a negative IRR).

The IRR is a valuable tool when:

- Comparing the relative merits of various real estate investments. Each property is considered as a separate investment option with the IRR providing a benchmark for screening purposes.
- Providing an indication of whether a specific property meets the financial objectives and minimum yield requirements of the investor.

The IRR is an *internal* rate of return as all calculations involving cash flows relate to the internal operation of the investment being analyzed. In other words, the IRR is concerned only with revenue and expenses within the project and nothing external to it.

While the IRR is a popular measure of yield, certain cautions must be noted. Over the years, opponents have levelled criticism against the internal rate of return. The most notable are described.

Ambiguous Results

Negative Cash Flows
The IRR can provide ambiguous results or no definitive answer in selected circumstances. The internal rate of return is particularly vulnerable to negative cash flows over the holding period that exceed initial investment. Practitioners should also be wary of investment properties that generate a negative present value (the IRR is of little practical use as it is designed as an indicator of positive return), have little or no equity (may cause extreme IRR swings based on minor fluctuations in initial investment), or otherwise result in a negative IRR.

Negative/Positive Sign Changes
The IRR is also vulnerable to more than one set of negative/positive sign changes in cash flows and can potentially provide ambiguous results or no definitive answer as a result. The modified internal rate of return (MIRR) addresses this issue, but the MIRR is often criticized due to its use of reinvestment rates.

Reinvestment
Criticism regarding reinvestment considerations have been frequently voiced in current investment publications and can be generally summarized as follows.

- With positive cash flows, distortions may occur because the IRR model assumes that surplus cash will be reinvested at the IRR rate. This rate can be much higher than the *reinvestment rates* (the rate, dictated by marketplace, at which excess funds can be invested in typical investments at after tax yields in excess of the safe rate).

- In the case of negative cash flows, distortions may also occur because the model assumes that funds set aside for negative cash flows are discounted at the IRR rate rather than a realistic *safe rate* (rate earned on funds until needed to cover negative cash flows).

Given these reinvestment factors, two options might produce similar IRRs, however, if negative and positive cash flows were considered based on actual safe and reinvestment rates, an altered picture could result. Obviously, if such rates are at or near the IRR rate, the distortions are minimal.

Property Comparisons

The IRR does not provide comparisons based on a lump sum available for investment. No adjustment is made for differing initial investments where Property A requires an equity investment of $100,000 and Property B requires an equity investment of $145,000. What happens to the $45,000 if Property A is selected? According to some experts, an accurate analysis should consider this disparity and make adjustments, i.e., a separate investment established for the excess $45,000. Similarly, two investments of differing duration must be adjusted. Property A has a holding period of three years, with Property B having four. Proceeds from Property A at end of year three (EOY3) must be reinvested to align with the longer investment period for Property B.

Internal vs. External Factors

IRR proponents, while acknowledging certain cautions regarding negative IRRs and multiple sign changes, largely disregard the remaining criticisms and point to the operative word *internal*. As an internal measure of return, the IRR is not intended to assess alternative investments based on a defined pool of funds, nor is it designed to consider external yield for outward flowing positive cash flows beyond the project or conversely, monies held in a savings account to offset future negative cash positions. The focus is strictly internal without regard to external influences or opportunities. For most applications, the IRR is reliable for general comparative work if its function and limitations are fully understood. IRR is best used in conjunction with net present value (NPV) when screening and ordering investment options. While these measures have slightly different perspectives, they generally corroborate each other. Obviously, contradictory results must be carefully analyzed.

Certain altered IRR formulae have been developed to address remaining criticisms. The modified internal rate of return (MIRR) eliminates sign change difficulties thereby eradicating the possibility of ambiguous results and introduce reinvestment and safe rates to quell criticism

regarding positive and negative cash flows. The financial management rate of return (FMRR) provides an even broader reinvestment model based on safe and reinvestment rates, with refinements to address differing initial equities and holding periods.

INTERPOLATION

The mathematical process of establishing a new or estimated figure between two existing payments, factors, or rates.

Example *Interpolation*

Salesperson Ward is discussing a *seller take back* (STB) mortgage with Owner Smith. The buyer asked for the seller take back mortgage in order to facilitate the sale. Ward feels that she can sell the $60,000 mortgage to an investment group for $55,000 and will seek written confirmation if Smith agrees in principle with the idea. The mortgage will have a 20-year amortization and term.

Ward needs to calculate the approximate return to the mortgage company as it must meet or exceed a minimum required return of 13.00%.

Ward takes the following steps:

- Consults her mortgage payment factors and determines that the monthly repayment for $60,000 is $648.58 (12%, 20-year term, 20-year amortization).

- Consults her mortgage payment factors once again to see what interest rate a $55,000 mortgage (that's the amount paid by the investors), most closely approximates the payment of $648.58.

- $640.39 will repay $55,000 @ 13.25%. $649.67 will repay $55,000 @ 13.50%. Ward now knows that the yield is somewhere between 13.25% and 13.50%.

- To gain a more precise calculation, Ward interpolates the two findings. The difference between the payments is:

  $649.67 − $640.39 = $9.28

  The difference between the actual payment and the lowest of these two is:

  $648.58 − $640.39 = $8.19

  Therefore, the desired figure is 0.88 of the distance between the two interest rates:

  $8.19 ÷ 9.28 = 0.88

- Consequently, Ward multiplies .88 by the difference between the two interest rates to arrive at 0.22:

  0.88 x (13.50 − 13.25) = 0.22

  The more precise yield rate is 13.47% (13.25 + 0.22).

The investors will probably accept this mortgage based on the yield of 13.47%.

INTESTATE

A person who dies without a will, or leaves a will that is defective in form, in which case his/her estate descends by operation of law to the heirs or next of kin. Procedures regarding the distribution of a person's estate when no will exists or a defective will has been drawn are set out by provincial statute.

Provincial   See applicable reference materials.

INTOXICATED PERSONS

Under contract law, two conditions must generally exist in order that a buyer or seller can avoid a contract based on the fact that he or she was intoxicated. First, the individual must have been so inebriated when the contract was signed that he or she did not understand what was taking place. Second, the condition of that party must be known to the other party to the contract. If these two conditions are satisfied, then such a contract would be considered to be voidable.

INVESTIGATIONS (BROKERAGE)

Provincial real estate acts and regulations set out investigative powers to appointed persons to inspect trust account records, transaction documentation, and other materials relating to the operation of real estate brokerages. The scope of such powers and range of inquiry vary by provincial jurisdiction.

Provincial   See applicable reference materials.

INVESTMENT ANALYSIS

Real estate investment analysis refers, in the broadest sense, to the relationship between the acquisition price of a property and the future benefits anticipated from that acquisition.

Static vs. Dynamic Indicators

The evaluation of real estate investment properties is undertaken to assess individual projects (properties), in relation to long-term investor objectives. For years, commercial practitioners relied on rudimentary investment rules of thumb together with valuation techniques centred on direct capitalization. In recent decades, capital asset selection and budgeting concepts slowly entered the real estate marketplace from investment management and financial markets. Consequently, real estate investment analysis has expanded beyond traditional (static), methods to more detailed (dynamic), capital budgeting techniques for the acquisition, operation, and disposition of real estate assets. *Static* in this context refers to comparisons based on a single snapshot portrayal of the property (e.g., one year's net operating income), as opposed to *dynamic* analysis involving forecasted cash flows over a specific holding period.

Expanded Investment Perspective

The increasing sophistication of real estate analysis is no accident. Large investors, investment trusts, and pension funds routinely acquire properties as part of strategic investment portfolio mixes. In fact, institutional investors have grown into a major force in the real estate marketplace. Portfolio managers routinely make acquisition decisions concerning long term, real estate capital assets (as opposed to short term capital assets, e.g., inventory), as they would with stocks or bonds. Discussions involving yields, cash flow analysis, before tax and after tax returns, present values, and internal rates of return now inundate the commercial marketplace. Understandably, real estate brokerages and their salespeople are steadily drawn into more complex investment methods to support the needs of clients.

Commercial practitioners increasingly operate in two worlds given this new emphasis on capital budgeting and investment analysis. At one time, most real estate comparisons beyond rules of thumb centred on real estate appraisal techniques. The emphasis was typically focused on market value and the probable selling price given reasonable exposure in the marketplace. Value was established using the income approach and, more specifically, direct (income) capitalization techniques. *Cap rates* were applied to a single year's stabilized net operating income to arrive at the estimate of value. While reliable, this time-tested approach came under increasing pressure with the growing interest in analyzing dynamic cash flows and yield calculations.

Investment Value vs. Market Value

Investment managers brought a different perspective to the marketplace. Real estate, as with any investment project, can be analyzed in terms of stated investment objectives. Emphasis is placed on the suitability of particular capital projects in line with those objectives. Consequently, the term *investment value* entered hallowed halls once reserved solely for *market value*. With investment value, the relative worth of specific properties was viewed through the eyes of individual investors and their respective goals and objectives. Therefore, any capital project (including real estate acquisitions), faced evaluation in terms of whether a specific project was worth the required investment. To decide, dynamic cash flow forecasts were required taking into account specific investment criteria and objectives of the investor.

Interestingly, the importance of analyzing projected cash flows did not go unnoticed in appraisal fields. From humble beginnings in the sixties that centred on forecasting regular income stream patterns (annuities) and present value calculations, appraisers now routinely use discounted cash flows and analyze irregular income and expense forecasts to arrive at estimates of value. Yield capitalization (the broader classification of appraisal techniques involving discounted cash flow analysis), is now given equal recognition with direct capitalization under the income approach to value.

Capital Budgeting Techniques

The capital budgeting process has also brought refinements to the real estate asset selection. Where once real estate acquisitions were viewed in relative isolation, portfolio managers introduced more rigid assessment systems to analyze, screen, and provide a preference order for available properties. Asset selection in the real estate market became increasingly formalized.

Analysts pose probing questions of real estate just as they would with other investment options:

- What types of capital activities (e.g., equity stocks, mortgages, real estate, etc.), fall within the investment strategy of the client?
- Is real estate worthwhile as a capital asset from the company's perspective?
- Assuming a positive response, what types of property enhance investment objectives and further investment goals and business strategy? In other words, what is the range of real estate opportunities available, e.g., multi-residential, retail, office, development land, and/or industrial?
- Given a specific type of real estate investment, what properties are the best investments within that particular type based on maximizing returns with tolerable levels of risk?
- Of those selected, in what preference order should they be placed and which ones should be acquired?

The capital budgeting and asset selection process brought with it various investment tools, techniques, and procedures to glean the best investments. Commercial practitioners now benefit from yield models that provide for the rational analysis of all investment property through detailed comparisons, cash flow before tax and cash flow after tax analysis, present value calculations, and internal rates of return.

INVESTMENT PROJECT

An investment opportunity available for review in the capital asset selection process.

Application   In the case of real estate, an investor normally assesses investment projects by type (e.g., retail, office, industrial, and vacant land), although this need not always be the case. The review of individual projects typically involves the evaluation of the cost of purchasing, operating, and ultimately disposing of the capital asset in relation to defined investor goals. Consequently, commercial practitioners routinely provide discounted cash flows, including operational and sale proceeds cash flows, to arrive at standard methods of comparison. This permits the investor to select the most favourable investment options based on limited resources available for such capital acquisitions.

INVESTMENT SCREENING

The analytic process of sorting capital asset opportunities that best satisfy investment goals with the ultimate objective of acquiring individual projects (specific properties in the case of real estate), that maximize returns in relation to such goals. In simple terms, investment screening establishes a *short list of investment possibilities*. From that short list, the investor must decide which of the acceptable projects (ranked in order from highest to lowest), is preferred given financial resources available to acquire and operate these projects.

Application   For screening purposes, capital projects can be examined based on three headings.

Mutually Exclusive

A mutually exclusive project or property is one that is being selected to perform a specific function. The screening activity results in the selection of one property from a group of possibilities. The selection of one will, by definition, dictate the rejection of all others. A good example involves a franchise organization that requires one site in a particular urban location. While the company will screen and rank many sites, the selection of one will automatically nullify all others in that general locale.

Mutually Inclusive

Mutually inclusive projects or properties are selected given their interrelated nature. The selection of one property requires that other mutually inclusive projects would also be included in the purchase decision. For example, an investor will only acquire the specific tract of land based on the assumption that other adjacent properties can also be acquired. If all properties cannot be purchased, then the investor's plan for development of the lands would be impractical and/or not economically justified. Land assembly schemes and large-scale developments are typically mutually inclusive projects.

Independent Projects

Unlike mutually inclusive projects, the purchase of an independent project has no direct bearing on the acquisition of other projects. For example, a builder may acquire individual building lots. The viability of each purchase is directly tied to terms concerning that specific purchase. The limiting factor is the amount of available resources to acquire properties, not the decision to acquire one property over another.

INVESTMENT TRUST

(SEE ALSO REAL ESTATE INVESTMENT TRUST)

A trust established to act as an investment conduit that enables investors to pool financial resources and participate in various forms of investment. The most commonly referenced trust from a real estate perspective is the real estate investment trust (REIT). This type of trust is specifically designed to acquire income producing properties as well as speculative real estate with the hopes of providing an ongoing return to participating investors.

INVESTMENT VALUE

Investment value is defined as the value of an investment property from the perspective of a specific investor. Investment value must be clearly differentiated from market value. Market value focuses on the most probable price that a property will sell for based on a typical buyer and seller. Many appraisers reference market value as *value in the marketplace*. Both market value and investment value flow from the present value of future anticipated benefits. However, differing assumptions and conditions can alter the perception of such benefits. Investment value is slanted to the individual's objectives and unique investor circumstances that can affect yield; for example, marginal tax

rate or distinct operating methods that may affect income and/or expense projections. Accordingly, forecasted cash flows will vary based on the extent and weighting of these factors and these, in turn, impact the valuation process.

Application   Many investor-oriented factors can intercede in arriving at investment value. Commercial practitioners, in providing estimates, must carefully review all income and expense forecasts in relation to the individual investor. For example, the net present value (NPV) of future cash flows is a direct consequence of the selected discount rate. The discount rate may be derived totally from the marketplace but ultimately be modified to reflect such factors as investor tolerance for risk and stated corporate policies regarding anticipated returns. Even minor alterations to a discount rate can significantly impact value. The investor's tax position will also affect cash flows after tax and directly impact both the screening and selection process.

Interestingly, commercial practitioners work in two worlds: market value estimates and investment value estimates. On the one hand, a salesperson may be required to estimate market value assuming no specific buyer when working with a seller client. Conversely, he/she may analyze prospective properties based on the needs and dictates of a specific buyer client and arrive at a unique investment value. The difference between these values is dependent on assumptions made. Market value and investment value can be the same theoretically, but rarely are in practice. Practitioners may prepare both market and investment value estimates, or even a range of values for each based on selected assumptions. The client is then furnished with parameters in which to select both an initial bid position as well as overall negotiating range.

INVESTOR UNIT FINANCING

Financing required for non owner-occupied single-family units purchased for investment purposes. Mortgage lenders have developed financing programs for investors involved with detached, semi-detached, row and apartment style accommodation. Persons qualifying for this type of financing are not full-time real estate specialists, but rather part-time investors.

Application   Lender interest in such investments varies based on real estate market conditions, the supply of mortgage funds, and competition within the mortgage market. Assuming favourable lending conditions, investor unit financing is provided based on the personal covenant of the buyer, GDS and TDS criteria, and additional considerations concerning the reliability and durability of rental income and cash flow following expenses and debt service.

IRREVOCABLE

Incapable of being recalled or revoked, unchangeable, or unalterable. Agreements/contracts for the purchase and sale of real estate typically provide for an irrevocable date by either the buyer or seller until a specific time on a specified date, after which time, if the offer is not accepted, it becomes null and void and the deposit is returned to the buyer in full without deduction. Irrevocable dates also apply in the case of counter offers.

In some instances, e.g., Province of Manitoba, the statutory offer to purchase form does not contain a clause pertaining to the irrevocability of the offer. However, it is fundamental to contract law that a person making an offer to purchase real estate may withdraw that offer at any time prior to the communication of acceptance of the offer back to the offeror (unless otherwise provided for in the agreement/contract). Therefore, once communication has taken place the offer becomes a legally binding contract and thus is irrevocable.

Application   A question always arises as to whether a prospective buyer is actually bound by the word *irrevocable,* as there is no contract until the seller accepts the offer and the buyers generally receive no consideration for their promise not to withdraw the offer. However a promise made under seal is generally binding on the person making the promise, even in the absence of consideration. This is one of the main reasons for having the seals on agreements/contracts.

However, no unanimous agreement exists among members of the legal profession as to the effectiveness of the seal in binding the buyers to the irrevocable date. Sales representatives must do everything possible to make sure the offers they present are free of legal loopholes. Prudent sales representatives should always have the offer signed under seal, and if a dispute arises, advise sellers to refer the matter to their solicitor.

The person making the offer has the right to specify the length of the irrevocable time. The irrevocable period is undoubtedly one of the most potent pressuring devices available in making an offer or a counter offer. Some buyers and sellers will attempt to keep the irrevocable time extremely short to swing negotiations in their favour. The prudent salesperson should negotiate a reasonable time period so that the parties can make an informed decision and complete the agreement/contract within the required time period.

Provincial   See applicable reference materials for clauses concerning irrevocability when completing agreements/contracts.

JOB DESCRIPTION

A document setting out tasks associated with a specific workplace function.

Salespersons

Currently, standardized job descriptions for salespersons do not exist, although extensive work has been carried out by the *Alliance for Canadian Real Estate Education (ACRE)*. ACRE has completed analysis and research reports relating to job skills analysis for brokers, managers, property managers, salespersons (residential, commercial, new home, and rural/recreational). These initiatives have led to advancements in standardized educational products while acknowledging specific requirements of provincial licensing/registration bodies. Research concerning skill sets and resulting curricula have also served to enhance licence/registration portability across Canada in line with federal government initiatives.

At present, salesperson job-related tasks are detailed in employment or independent contractor agreements and reinforced through brokerage policy manuals. While documentation varies significantly within brokerage companies, research and reports developed by ACRE will provide the backdrop for consistency in job descriptions and the development of more standardized employment-related forms.

Provincial   See applicable reference materials.

Administrative Staff

Administrative job descriptions will vary dramatically based on brokerage size, specific markets being served, and a host of local considerations. For a small residential brokerage office, the job description for an individual involved in administrative and secretarial duties might include the following:

- Processing of trade records, listings, and associated sale documents;
- Providing filing, typing, and clerical functions as required by management;
- Directing calls from customers and clients, and other enquiries from any source;

I TO K

- Operating all equipment including computers and software used by the brokerage;
- Maintaining good business relationships with other staff, commission salespeople, and the public;
- Providing management reports as requested in a timely fashion; and
- Performing other activities as called upon by management to ensure the productive and efficient operation of the brokerage.

This list is included for illustration purposes only. Job descriptions will vary substantially based on expected tasks within the office and the structure/size of the brokerage.

JOINT AND SEVERAL

A term commonly associated with loans and mortgages in which one or more parties are liable for the repayment of the debt. Each person can be pursued for the entire debt or any portion thereof and not simply his/her prorated amount of such debt. In other words, the parties are responsible individually as well as collectively.

Application   A partnership operating a brokerage office would have joint and several liability for obligations created within that partnership. Legislation concerning partnerships generally reaffirms that every partner in a firm is liable jointly with the other partners for all debts and obligations of the firm incurred while he/she is a partner. Specific wordings of relevant legislation vary by provincial jurisdiction.

Example   *Joint and Several*

Broker/Owner Johnson, of ABC Realty Inc., is leasing office space through his brokerage. Given the firm's brief corporate history, the landlord requires an indemnity agreement signed by Johnson and his wife personally. The indemnity agreement sets out various guarantees concerning the payment of rent, notices under these guarantees and generally the responsibilities of the indemnifiers. Johnson's wife takes particular note of one item and asks for further clarification from her lawyer. The clause reads as follows:

If two or more parties are named as indemnifier, each party is responsible for the obligations of the indemnifier both jointly and severally.

The lawyer explains that Johnson and his wife can be pursued individually or together with the other party (jointly and severally) for terms set out in the indemnity agreement.

Provincial   See applicable reference materials.

JOINT TENANCY

(SEE ALSO TENANTS IN COMMON)

Ownership of land by two or more persons whereby, on the death of one, the surviving tenant(s) acquire the whole interest in the property.

Creation

In joint tenancy, all the owners have the same size of interest, the same possession, and the same title to the land. Described alternatively, joint tenants between themselves have equal rights, but against everyone else they are in the position of a single owner. A joint tenancy arises only when expressly created in the grant of the estate or afterwards by an express agreement between the holders of the estate. For example, a will could state:

I leave my fee simple in 123 Main Street to my five nephews equally.

However, stating that the five nephews are to hold the interest in the property equally is not enough to create a joint tenancy. A presumption exists, typically spelled out in provincial legislation, that a grant of land to two or more people will be a tenancy in common unless clear intent is evident that it be a joint tenancy. Where co-owners exist on a deed, the assumption is that they are tenants in common unless the title specifies otherwise.

Four Unities

Even though a clear intention exists to create a joint tenancy, one will not be formed unless the *four unities* are satisfied. If these conditions are not satisfied, then a tenancy in common has been created.

Title

All joint tenants must derive their title from the same instrument, e.g., deed or will.

Example   *Joint Tenancy—Four Unities— Unity of Title*

Buyer James Jones acquires an interest in a home and subsequently transfers one-half interest in the property to his spouse, Judy. If the ownership is not obtained at the same time by the same document, Jones and his spouse will own the property as tenants in common.

However, James Jones can transfer the title of the property to "James Jones and Judy Jones as joint tenants and not as tenants in common."

Time

The interest of each joint tenant must begin at the same time.

> **Example**   *Joint Tenancy—Four Unities—*
> *Unity of Time*
>
> Buyer James Jones acquires one-half interest in the home on Monday and his wife Judy receives the remaining portion on Tuesday. In this case, James Jones and his wife will be tenants in common, not joint tenants, as their interests were not received at the same time.

Possession

Each joint tenant is entitled to undivided possession of the whole of the property and none holds any part separately to the exclusion of the others. Perhaps a clearer way to explain unity of possession is to say that it gives all joint tenants an interest in all of the property, but an exclusive interest in none of the property.

> **Example**   *Joint Tenancy—Four Unities—*
> *Unity of Possession*
>
> If Jones and Smith own two acres of land as joint tenants, they both own two acres—not one person one acre and the other person the other acre. In addition, neither has an exclusive right to any particular part of the land as they both together own the whole. Accordingly, one joint tenant cannot maintain an action in trespass against the other.

Interest

The interest of each joint tenant must be identical in nature, extent, and duration.

> **Example**   *Joint Tenancy—Four Unities—*
> *Unity of Interest*
>
> If three brothers hold the fee simple in a property as joint tenants, each has a one-third interest in the fee simple.

Additional Considerations

If any of the four unities are missing, or cease to exist during joint tenancy, then the owners will automatically become tenants in common. If these four unities are present and there is a clear intention that a joint tenancy should exist, then a joint tenancy will be created.

> **Example**   *Joint Tenancy—Four Unities—*
> *Additional Considerations*
>
> Buyer James Jones and Judy Jones purchase a duplex at the same time and by the same document. However, James insists that the lower unit be specifically owned by Judy
>
> Continued…

and that he will hold title to the upper unit. In this case, joint tenancy cannot apply as both parties must have an undivided interest in the property. Neither can specifically point to one portion of the lands and improvements and claim ownership to those specific areas.

> **Example**   *Joint Tenancy—Four Unities—*
> *Additional Considerations*
>
> Buyers James Jones and William Jones are purchasing an investment property and want to create ⅔ and ⅓ interest, as they are not contributing equally to the purchase. They also inform the lawyer that they would like to acquire title as joint tenants. The lawyer explains that joint tenancy is not possible in this situation as the same quantity of ownership would not be demonstrated.

Survivorship

The right of survivorship is an important aspect of joint tenancy in that the interest of the deceased tenant (owner) is automatically transferred to the surviving tenant (owner). This means that, if one joint tenant dies, his/her interest does not pass to his/her estate (such as a personal representative or to heirs), but passes directly to the surviving joint tenant or tenants.

Joint tenancy is often encountered when a husband and wife obtain title to the family home as joint tenants. In such cases, on the death of either spouse, the survivor is automatically entitled to immediately receive full title to the property. The joint tenancy is thus an advantage to the surviving spouse because the house does not form part of the deceased's estate where it could become entangled in problems of settling the estate.

A joint tenant cannot bequeath his or her interest by means of a will because the transfer to the other joint tenant is automatic at death. Effectively, the deceased joint tenant's interest ceases to exist.

> **Example**   *Joint Tenancy—*
> *Survivorship*
>
> If James and Judy Jones are joint tenants in fee simple, and Judy dies, James immediately becomes the owner of the whole interest. This is true even if Judy tries to dispose of it by will. The right of survivorship takes precedence.

Spousal Interest

The general rule concerning right of survivorship in a joint tenancy is subject to an important exception. Under applicable provincial legislation, if a married person dies owning an interest in a matrimonial home jointly with someone other than his/her surviving spouse, the joint tenancy is deemed to be severed immediately before the time of death. Consequently, the interest becomes a tenancy in common and thereby provides a basis for the appropriate spousal interest in the assets of the deceased spouse's estate. Provincial procedures and requirements will vary.

Provincial   See applicable reference materials.

Termination

If joint tenants sever their joint tenancy relationship, they automatically become tenants in common. Obviously, if both parties agree to sever voluntarily, then the parties become tenants in common as a result of that agreement.

A joint tenant may destroy the right of survivorship before his/her death without the consent of the other joint tenant(s). This process, called *severance*, turns the joint tenancy into a tenancy in common with the other tenant or tenants. Even after an act of severance, if there are two or more other tenants remaining, they still remain joint tenants with each other, but are tenants in common with the person who holds the severed interest. The most common method of severance is by a joint tenant granting his/her interest to a third party. The grant has the effect of turning the interest transferred into a tenancy in common with the remaining interests.

Other modes of severance exist, such as when all the joint tenants mutually agree to end the joint tenancy and instead hold their interests as tenants in common. For example, with a marriage separation, the joint tenancy termination can be mutually agreed upon as part of the separation agreement. A joint tenancy may also terminate by partition, i.e., splitting the land by means of an application to a court. If proper grounds exist, the court will order that the property be divided according to the joint tenancy. When it would be impractical to divide the property into different sections, as the case would be for a residential home, the court can order that the property be sold and the proceeds divided up.

The termination or severance of a joint tenancy has a significant impact on property ownership and must be done properly. A lawyer should always be consulted.

> **Example   Joint Tenancy– Termination**
>
> Jones, Smith, and Taylor are joint tenants. If Jones sells his share to Wilson, then Wilson becomes a tenant in common (one-third) with Smith and Taylor (two-thirds). Smith and Taylor remain as joint tenants. If Smith dies, Taylor will become the owner of the two-third interest and will hold it as a tenant in common with Wilson (two-third ownership by Taylor and one-third ownership by Wilson).

JOINT VENTURE

A real estate project undertaken by a group of investors in which the parties share in the project including any profits or losses.

Application   Joint ventures generally tend to be specific in nature with a defined time limit. The exact legal structure of a joint venture varies in the marketplace. It could, for example, take the form of a limited partnership, corporation, or syndication. Joint ventures are similar to a partnership in that two or more persons/corporations are pooling resources to purchase real estate or undertake some other project. The nature of the joint venture is usually an extension of the business of one or more of the participants.

The characteristics of a joint venture are:

Control   No venturer can unilaterally control the venture.

Project Life   The life of the joint venture is usually limited to a specific project.

Proportionate Interest   All of the income and expenses are assigned to the joint venturers, and in turn each member is assigned his/her share of the assets and liabilities.

Flexibility   Each participant of a joint venture calculates his/her income for tax purposes without regard to the other participants. This provides for discretionary decisions concerning personal tax positions.

Undivided Interest   As in partnerships, an undivided interest exists in the project. That means that no specific unit or part of a property is assigned to, or owned by, a single investor. This may pose a difficulty if an investor wishes to sell his/her interest, or use his/her equity as collateral for financing, since a lender would have difficulty registering an interest against a proportionate share of the joint venture.

Because joint ventures do not have formal status from the Canada Customs and Revenue Agency's perspective, no flexibility exists in creating a fiscal year end other than the calendar year. Since some joint ventures have several co-owners with different fiscal year ends, it can be a mathematical nightmare to attempt to determine a separate profit and loss statement for each co-owner's year end. For this practical reason, the tax department has accepted, in practice, a non calendar year end for joint ventures, provided that no undue taxable benefit or advantage is thus obtained. Practitioners are advised to seek appropriate accounting/legal advice on such matters.

Broker/Owner Johnson, of ABC Realty Inc., wants to expand his main office located in Anycity. To be cost effective and gain sufficient expansion area, Johnson wants to acquire an adjacent vacant commercial lot and create a retail plaza on the assembled parcel that will add approximately 10,000 square feet of retail space in addition to the new brokerage office.

Johnson approaches a builder for whom his brokerage has marketed new homes and recommends a joint venture. Johnson and the builder will participate jointly on a 50/50 basis through their respective companies, with Johnson's real estate office becoming a tenant in the new mall.

JOIST

One of a series of horizontal wood members, usually of 2-inch nominal thickness, used to support a floor, ceiling, or roof.

Application   Joists are laid on edge and derive their strength largely by their depth. The adding of a joist, by putting another of the same size beside it, will double its resistance to bending. Doubling the depth of a joist increases its deflection resistance eight times. Typical joist materials include wood, and more recently, metal, plywood, and wafer board. **Figure J.1** illustrates the components of a typical joist assembly.

The deflection of a floor and joist system in modern construction may be quite surprising. A typical code allows a floor to deflect 1/360th of its length under normal live loading, if there is a finished ceiling below. For example, the following situation is acceptable by current code: 2 x 10 inch floor joists spaced 16 inches on a centre span of 15 feet. When the room is empty, there should be no perceptible deflection. When the room is occupied with furniture and people, the centre part of the floor can be ½ inch lower than the floor edges. A ½ inch drop in the floor over a distance of 7½ feet is certainly noticeable. While this is permitted by modern codes, it may not be satisfactory to some home owners. It should be noted that codes are intended as minimum standards. Further, a very brittle floor finishing material such as ceramic tile, would not tolerate this degree of flex.

Example   *Joist*

Buyer Jones has viewed and is now seriously considering the purchase of an older resale property. Following the first visit, Jones has retained a home inspector to accompany him on a subsequent trip to the property. Jones notices that the

Continued…

living room floor has a springiness and asks the inspector to comment. The inspector explains the building code standards including permitted deflection on a floor in relation to span. However, he wants to personally inspect the floor joists, citing four significant problems that can arise.

- Floor joists that are over spanned (undersized) are prone to excessive sagging. The acceptable span is determined by load, species and grade of lumber used, and joist depth/spacing. Usually, over spanning can be readily corrected by adding joists or a beam below the joists.

- Mechanical damage to joists is also common. Joists are notched, drilled and even cut through to accommodate heating, plumbing, and electrical systems. Joists are sometimes notched at the end to rest on a beam or foundation wall. This can weaken the joist considerably. The joist usually cracks horizontally from the top of the notch toward the midpoint of the span.

- Joists may be prone to crushing at the ends and/or slipping off the beam or foundation where less than 1½ inch end bearing is provided,

- Joists below partitions are subject to concentrated loads and are more prone to sagging. Beams or walls, as opposed to joists, should not be used below load-bearing partitions.

One of the problems often unfairly blamed on joists is that of an offset bearing wall. In houses with a beam and post configuration or a bearing wall in the basement, there is usually a wood-frame bearing wall above. Ideally the wall above is directly over the beam or basement wall. In practice this is rarely the case. If the wall is offset enough (sometimes 12 inches is sufficient), the floor joists under the first floor wall will be deflected (see **Figure J.2**). This will lead to a low spot and a hump on the floor immediately above the basement beam or bearing wall. This can be arrested by running a second beam and post system or bearing wall in the basement under the offset wall.

JOURNALS (FINANCIAL)
(SEE ACCOUNTING SYSTEM)

JUDGMENT

The decision of a court having competent jurisdiction over a particular matter.

Application   A judgment is most commonly evidenced as a lien registered against land and is more fully described as a charge or lien upon the lands of a debtor. The court decree, which must be properly entered, declares that the debtor is indebted and fixes the amount of the indebtedness.

The judgment must only be placed against the debtor's property. Once a judgment lien is registered, any subsequent owner of the land is subject to it.

Example *Judgment*

Jones has a dispute with Smith over a business dealing and successfully gains a judgment from the court in the amount of $100,000 against Smith. Smith owns a property worth approximately $350,000 with an outstanding mortgage of $120,000. Jones' judgment attaches to the property but does not take priority over the outstanding mortgage owing to its prior registration.

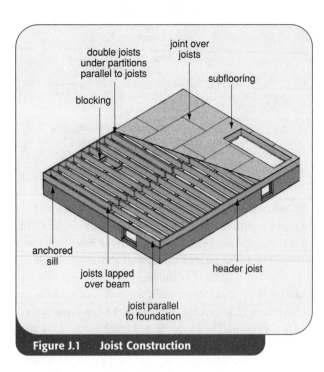

Figure J.1   Joist Construction

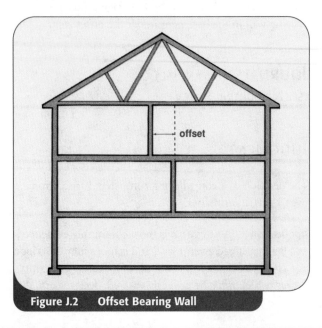

Figure J.2   Offset Bearing Wall

JUDICIAL SALE

The judicial sale is one type of remedy available to a mortgagee when a mortgage is in default. The mortgagee can sue for judicial sale, payment, and possession, as opposed to the more frequent option of foreclosure. The reader is cautioned as procedures will vary in individual provinces. The following is provided for general description only.

In the judicial sale, the mortgagee looks to the court to sell the property with the proceeds being applied against the mortgage debt. Any deficiency could be pursued under the mortgagor's personal covenant. If any excess funds arose from the judicial sale, the money would be returned to the mortgagor. The judicial sale is not as popular because the court would usually accomplish the disposition of the property by auction. This could potentially realize fewer dollars than a sale in the open market. Further, the mortgagor receives any excess funds as opposed to foreclosure where all proceeds are received by the mortgagee if the property is subsequently sold.

Provincial   See applicable reference materials.

JURISDICTION

For legal purposes, the authority of a person or organization to act within the defined limitations of that authority.

Application   In real estate, provincial legislation concerning trading in real estate sets out the jurisdictional control of registrants for specific provinces. The statute delineates the scope of power to license/register, investigate, and otherwise deal with real estate brokerages, brokers, and salespeople.

In organized real estate, the most common reference to jurisdiction and jurisdictional boundaries involves real estate boards. Each board defines a geographical territory described either within the by-laws or as a separate schedule to the by-laws.

K

KEY LOT

The term *key lot* originally referred to a long lot bounded on one (or both) side(s) by several adjoining lots facing another street as illustrated in **Figure K.1**. In the illustration, part of Lot 2 and all of Lots 3–5 abut the key lot. As a result, the key lot had less privacy and often more noise from neighbours and was consequently defined as an inferior lot.

Currently, the term often takes on a different meaning in reference to property development and, more specifically, land assembly. Often the key lot is a specific lot or parcel of land that is particularly important to an overall land assemblage to achieve the highest and best use. In other words, the lot is key to the assemblage. Given the diverse meanings, **Figure K.1** is provided depicting the original meaning along with the following descriptive example for the modern variation. For additional details see **Assemblage** and **Plottage**.

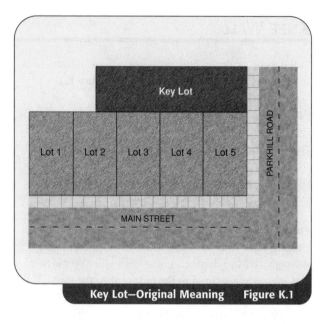
Key Lot—Original Meaning   Figure K.1

| **Example** | ***Key Lot—Assemblage*** |

Developer Reed requires a rezoning of certain residential lands through the municipal council. The official plan permits rezoning from residential to commercial uses, provided such uses are limited to professional and service-related offices, along with restricted neighbourhood retail uses.

To realistically obtain this change, Reed requires a minimum site of 50,000 square feet. While the buildings, landscaping, and parking areas do not demand this site size, rezoning of this nature is rarely approved without sufficient buffer zones in relation to adjacent neighbourhoods. The council is sensitive to adverse effects upon such areas, particularly given the density, traffic volumes, and other considerations relating to the proposal.

Reed approaches 12 property owners whose lands would cumulatively represent approximately 53,000 square feet. One particular property owned by Smith it vital to the project. His lot measures in excess of 8,000 square feet and is situated at the precise location identified by city planners for street access to and from the development. No other option exists, given precise guidelines concerning access in relation to the nearest intersection. Smith's property becomes the key lot in this assemblage and Reed is forced to negotiate with Smith.

KEYSTONE

A wedge-like stone normally in an archway or similar span that traditionally provided the central support for other dependent bricks or stonework. In modern commercial and residential construction, the keystone above entrance-ways and garages has taken on a decorative as opposed to functional role.

KICKER

A slang term referring to an essential part of an agreement or deal required by one party to the transaction over and above usual terms relating to a specific product or service.

Application   Kickers are most commonly associated with mortgage financing where a lender requires an additional payment over and above principal and interest in order to underwrite a loan, e.g., a percentage rent, additional up front fees, or other financial concessions by the borrower.

KIOSK

An open building traditionally referring to a pavilion, an ornamental summerhouse, a bandstand, or similar structure.

Application   A kiosk, for real estate purposes, refers to a small, often portable, retail stand typically situated within a common walkway area of a retail mall.

KNEE WALL

Small walls, typically built with wood two-by-four studs in the attic, that prevent rafter sag. See Figure K.2.

Application Knee walls in 1½ or 2½ storey houses sometimes form the walls of a room on the upper floor as they run from the attic floor up to the underside of the rafters near their midpoint. Upper rooms created by this approach often have partly sloped ceilings as a result. Certain problems can arise concerning knee walls.

Poorly Secured and Weak Floor As with any wood component, knee walls are subject to rot, termites, mechanical damage, and fire damage. These walls will also move if not adequately secured to the rafters or to the joists. If the floor joist system below is not strong enough, the knee wall can cause deflection in the ceiling below with resulting damage to the ceiling finish.

Location The knee wall may not be effective in preventing rafter sag if not located at the mid span of the rafters. Typically, where the roof line is fairly long, a knee wall is used on the lower end of the rafter to provide immediate support and a collar tie is used higher up. Where both a collar tie and a knee wall are used, their placement should provide for equally-sized rafter spans.

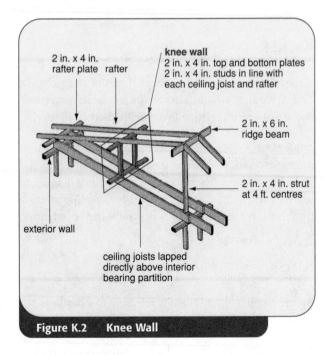

Figure K.2 Knee Wall

KNOB-AND-TUBE

Knob-and-tube wiring was used in residential construction during the early part of the last century (pre-1950). The wiring set derives its name from the ceramic knobs by which the wire is secured and the ceramic tubes used where it passes through wood-framing members such as joists. Insulation breakdown is the most frequent reason for replacement.

Application Real estate practitioners must be aware of recent concerns regarding knob-and-tube electrical systems. In particular, insurance companies are increasingly cautious both about 60-amp services and older buildings with knob-and-tube wiring. While some insurers will renew existing policies on such properties, a change of ownership and/or selection of a new insurer can lead to a refusal. Older systems may not be inherently dangerous, but problems can arise with overloading due to new appliances and other modernization within houses.

A fire inspection is recommended for older properties. Buyers and sellers should be aware that a fire inspection may result in expenditures on the electrical system. For example, knob-and-tube in the basement area (next to heat ducts and copper plumbing pipes), will probably have to be replaced.

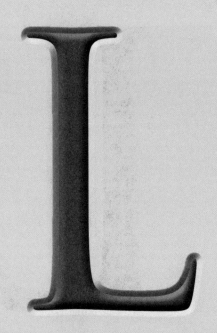

20,000 to 200,000 sq. ft.

AVAILABLE

5 - 10 Acres
- Land For Sale
- Land For Lease
- Build to Suit

New Home of
Anycity
Computer Services

NOW LEASING
PRIME BUSINESS SPACE

2000 FT. OFFICE

XYZ REAL ESTATE LTD.

22-0000
Since 1979

L

National Info Links

Lenders

For mortgage and related information for the five major Canadian lenders (banks), contact:

Canadian Imperial Bank of Commerce (CIBC)
Web Site www.cibc.com

Royal Bank of Canada
Web Site www.royalbank.com

Toronto-Dominion Bank
Web Site www.td.com

Bank of Nova Scotia
Web Site www.scotiabank.com

Bank of Montreal
Web Site www.bmo.com

Licence Law

For regulatory requirements for salespersons and brokers in various North American jurisdictions, contact:

The Association of Real Estate License Law Officials
Post Office Box 230159
Montgomery, Alabama USA
36123-0159

Telephone (334) 260 2902
Web Site www.arello.org

For provincial regulatory requirements contact the appropriate provincial ministry/department or regulatory agency. For a list of provincial regulatory agencies, see page **494**.

Living Area (Residential)

A standard measurement procedure for living area in residential property has not been adopted across Canada. Measurement guidelines have been provided by ACRE (see the **Appendix**). Contact:

Alliance for Canadian Real Estate Education
99 Duncan Mill Road
Don Mills, ON M3B 1Z2

Telephone **(416) 445-9910**

LAND

The surface of the earth, air space, and sub-surface area.

Application   Land is usually referred to by real estate practitioners as *raw acreage, raw land, vacant land,* or *unimproved land,* because no alteration for specific purposes has occurred. This is not to be confused with the term *site* that traditionally refers to a parcel of land that has been subdivided and often serviced, at least to some degree.

Land, for registration purposes, refers to the physical property, tenements, inherited property, appurtenances, and any estate or interest in them. The term *subject land* normally denotes a specific piece of property identified for purposes of an application (e.g., zoning) or an agreement/ contract (e.g., for sale or lease).

LAND BANK

Land acquired and held for some future purpose.

Application   Traditionally, the term broadly referred to the acquisition of land for a projected purpose involving private developers. Today, land banking is commonly associated with government acquisitions for future public use in line with established land use policies. Canadian public agencies have set aside land banks for various reasons, e.g., communication, transportation, and environmental considerations.

Proponents of land banking argue that the planned acquisition of property can aid in orderly development of services and infrastructure for growing communities, while permitting the acquisition of necessary property before any value escalation due to speculation and/or development. Public investment can also be averaged over an extended period and spread across numerous properties in a land banking scheme.

Land banking policies differ substantially, based on specific governments in power, e.g., funding, type of land (undeveloped, land for public services, waterfront, etc.), and whether the development of such lands is done in conjunction with private developers.

LAND/BUILDING RATIO

For real estate purposes, the land/building ratio (also frequently referred to as the *building/land ratio*), is based on the measurement of property, e.g., total land area in relation to gross building area (external measurements, excluding any unenclosed areas). The term *land/building ratio* is often used in the marketplace to refer to the pro-

portionate value of land in relation to the building. For example, the value allocation of land and building forms the basis for tax calculations involving the adjusted cost base, capital cost allowance, capital gain, and tax liability when investment property is transacted.

> **Example**   *Land/Building Ratio*
>
> Salesperson Lee, of ABC Realty Inc., is preparing a cash flow estimate and needs to estimate capital cost allowance for a specific investment property. The land is valued at $60,000 and the buildings at $140,000. Therefore, the land/building ratio is 30/70 or conversely, the building/land ratio is 70/30.

LAND CAPITALIZATION RATE
(SEE ALSO CAPITALIZATION)

A capitalization rate based on direct capitalization that converts the annual income stream from the rental of land to an estimate of value.

LAND CHARACTERISTICS

Real estate as a commodity, consists of raw land as nature provided it, and all man-made permanent improvements that affect the utility of a given parcel of land. Improvements made on the land which are intended to be permanently affixed to the property for the useful life of the improvements, such as a house built on land, convert the commodity of land into the commodity of real estate. The land itself remains basic and essentially unchanged.

Application   A practical definition of land for real estate practitioners includes not only the surface of the earth and the improvements *on* and *to* the land, but also the minerals and substances below the ground and the air rights to space above the ground. To understand the commodity of land and how it functions, it is necessary to first understand the characteristics of land.

Immobility

Land cannot be moved. Its physical immobility causes it to be classified as *real* estate, a term denoting an owner's right to land and its improvements and the physical permanency of that interest.

Durability

Land is physically indestructible and will remain forever. However, obsolescence of use may destroy the land's value or economic durability. In the case of an abandoned house or factory, for example, the economic value of the improvement or building may wholly disappear even though the land remains and may have economic value in itself.

Uniqueness

No two parcels of land are ever exactly alike. While a high degree of similarity may exist, all parcels differ even if the only variance is the geographic location.

Scarcity

Although the physical supply of land is fixed, no real shortage of land exists in terms of total supply. However, while the total supply is likely adequate to meet the foreseeable needs of humankind, certain types of land in given locations are in comparatively short supply. The scarcity of land is an economic factor rather than a physical factor. The value of land is directly related to its location. For example, a lake front lot is typically more valuable as a cottage lot than a rural property that is six miles from the lake and lacks waterfront amenities.

Rigidity

Once labour and capital expenditures have been committed for improvements on the land, the investment becomes fixed in place and, for all intents and purposes, permanent. Drainage, sewage, electricity, water, and gas facilities, or buildings cannot be economically dismantled and shifted to locations in which they would be in greater demand.

LAND CONTAMINATION
(SEE ALSO GROUND WATER CONTAMINATION)

The act of rendering land unsuitable for a specified use due to prior uses of the land involving pollutants or other contaminants that have impacted the property. Real estate is increasingly under close scrutiny by prospective buyers, particularly commercial and industrial sites, concerning evidence of land or ground water contamination. To compound matters, damage can extend beyond the immediate site to adjacent lands, or conversely, abutting lands can impact the subject property under consideration.

Application   Real estate practitioners are not deemed to be experts in such matters, but should exercise prudence in inspecting property for visual clues and be aware of general guidelines in the site restoration process. This process typically includes four steps:

- A site assessment is completed identifying actual or potential contamination.

- Samples and subsequent analyses are made to confirm the existence of contamination on the site.
- A remedial plan is developed that will restore the site to an appropriate condition as established by the ministry/department.
- The remedial plan is implemented, restorative actions taken, and completion is confirmed and recorded according to statutory requirements.

A site record is then prepared by the individual undertaking the restorative actions and filed for future reference. The scope of restorative work and associated expense can vary depending on the environmental sensitivity of the site, e.g., soil conditions and existence of wetlands on or adjacent to the property.

Example   *Land Contamination*

Salesperson Ward is meeting with a prospective buyer at an industrial site. Buyer Jones, prior to the appointment, had undertaken a preliminary investigation of previous uses and discovered that the property had been used for automobile repairs. The listing details referenced a site condition report that had been filed with the appropriate local environmental ministry/department attesting to restorative work.

Ward and Jones made a complete inspection of the property. Jones acknowledged, based on a previous inspection approximately one year ago, that debris and abandoned buildings had been removed and the entire site had been cleared. They then went to the local environmental office to review the site report prepared by a local engineering firm on behalf of the current owner. The report detailed the extent of work completed on the property including summary data of soil samples and related items as proof that the site met applicable environmental standards. The report also confirmed that the remedial work had eliminated contaminated materials that were discovered on the property as a result of a previous environmental assessment.

Provincial   See applicable reference materials.

LAND CONTRACT
(SEE ALSO AGREEMENT FOR SALE)

A contract for the purchase of real estate (land) on an installment basis. Upon payment of the last installment, the deed is delivered to the buyer.

LAND DESCRIPTION

A written description by which property is precisely identified, often referred to as a *legal description*. Methods of land description vary significantly by provincial jurisdiction owing to circumstances associated with prevailing methods of land registration at the point of original settlement, passage of various treaties, use of registry and/or land titles, and unique historical events associated with individual provinces entering confederation.

Provincial   See applicable reference materials.

LAND DESCRIPTION— METES AND BOUNDS
(SEE METES AND BOUNDS)

LAND DEVELOPMENT METHOD— SITE VALUATION

An appraisal method that is one of four techniques to arrive at the value of a parcel of land and is normally applied when comparable sales are not available to use the more popular direct comparison approach. The appraiser must construct a hypothetical plan of subdivision or a building design based on the highest and best use, determine the sale price of the eventual development, evaluate costs associated with time delays, e.g., debt service, servicing costs, and marketing costs, and arrive at a final estimate of the price that a developer would pay in light of such future anticipated gains. Given the wide range of assumptions, this approach has limited use, but may be the only method to arrive at a value or range of value for a specific property.

Other methods of site valuation include: **Abstraction Method–Site Valuation, Comparative Sales Method–Site Valuation,** and **Land Residual Method–Site Valuation.**

LAND IMPROVEMENTS

Expenditures incurred in the process of bringing land to a useable condition, e.g., clearing, landscaping, and servicing.

LAND LEASE
(SEE GROUND LEASE)

LAND RATIO
(SEE ALSO LAND/BUILDING RATIO)

The proportionate value of land in relation to the total property value. A term commonly associated with appraisers particularly in regard to band of investment and residual techniques used in the capitalization process.

LAND REGISTRATION SYSTEMS
(SEE ALSO LAND TITLES AND REGISTRY)

Two land registration systems are commonly used in Canada, both established and maintained through provincial legislation. Registry and land titles systems provide the administrative framework for registration of real property interests. The use of one or both systems is largely a matter of historical fact owing to unique circumstances surrounding the development of Canada as a nation and the formalizing of legal systems within individual provinces.

As a general statement, registry has been traditionally associated with eastern provinces and land titles with western provinces. Selected provinces operate both systems in coexistence. However, once again, the east/west trend is evident. Land titles is the only system used in the western provinces, i.e., Saskatchewan, Alberta, and British Columbia. Manitoba has approximately 90% of all land registration falling under land titles. Most of Ontario was originally under registry. However, given the outdated, and often cumbersome attributes of registry, the province is now undergoing a large-scale land titles conversion project. Registry remains the dominant form of land registration in the Maritime Provinces.

Provincial   See applicable reference materials.

LAND RESIDUAL METHOD— SITE VALUATION

Based on the principle of surplus productivity, the principle affirms that the net income remaining after satisfying the requirements of labour, coordinating services, and capital is attributed to land and sets its value through the capitalization process.

Application   The land residual technique is used to find a value estimate of a site that is readily adaptable for use as the location for an income producing property.

- A hypothetical building, that will develop the site to its highest and best use, is projected for the site and the cost of erecting the structure is calculated based on current building cost.
- Potential annual gross income is estimated based on current rental rates. From this, an allowance for vacancy and bad debts is subtracted to arrive at the effective gross income.
- Expenses to operate the building are then deducted, resulting in a net income attributable to the property. This net income figure already takes the

cost for labour and coordination into consideration, as they are part of the operating expenses of the building.

- To satisfy capital requirements, an amount equal to the building value, multiplied by the combination of the interest rate plus the recapture rate, is deducted from this net income.
- The resulting residual income is attributable to the land value as detailed in the principle of surplus productivity. The actual conversion of income into value is achieved by capitalizing this residual income by an appropriate rate.

Land Severance

A consent granted by an appropriate authority for the division of land, provided that certain conditions are met as dictated by the appropriate ministry/department pursuant to provincial planning legislation.

Provincial   See applicable reference materials.

Land Titles

A system of land registration, often referred to as the *Torrens System* (named after an officer in the Australian marine shipping registry), in which the government certifies the accuracy of title as shown on the record. Unlike cumbersome registry systems relying on an historical chain of conveyances to prove that a property has good and marketable title, the land titles system provides a current record of all land certified as correct and provides a guarantee of title. The registry system does not. Variations exist in provincial jurisdictions regarding procedures used in the recording and certification of title.

The land titles system is built on the three principles described.

The Mirror (or Indefeasibility) Principle

The register of title is a mirror that accurately and completely reflects the current facts that are material to a property. The register is conclusive evidence that the person named as holding an interest is in fact that person and that the holding is not subject to any condition or encumbrance other than those shown on the register (subject to certain statutory exceptions). The certified title given, at any particular time, is conclusive evidence of all interest relating to each parcel of land.

The Registration Requirement Principle

The land titles system requires that, before documents dealing with land can be operative, the documents must first be registered. Each registration is given priority over previously registered documents or instruments. When documentation is being registered, an examiner ensures that it is in registrable form and in compliance with all procedural requirements stipulated by applicable provincial statutes. If acceptable, the registration will be completed. If not, the document will be rejected until the defect is corrected.

The Compensation or Assurance Principle

As the land titles system provides conclusive proof of ownership, a compensation arrangement is necessary for any inadequacies of the system. For example, a property could be transferred to an innocent party and the title challenged by another due to an error in the registration system. Therefore, the system provides for compensation through an assurance fund to those who have lost an interest in land and cannot recover the interest in damages through a court action. The structure and limits of liability of such assurance funds will vary by provincial jurisdiction.

Provincial   See applicable reference materials.

Land Titles Assurance Fund

A fund established by provincial statute to provide financial compensation to a person who sustains loss or damage through certain omissions, mistakes, fraud, or wrongful acts, including but not limited to errors made by the land titles office. The fund is typically financed through a percentage of fees charged or similar arrangement. The scope of liability associated with an assurance fund and its operation varies by provincial jurisdiction.

Provincial   See applicable reference materials.

Land Transfer Tax

A tax imposed on real property typically calculated on the value of the property being registered in a land registration office. Land transfer tax may not be imposed in all provinces and the means of calculation will vary by provincial jurisdiction.

Provincial   See applicable reference materials.

LAND USE DESIGNATIONS

(SEE ALSO ZONING)

Intended uses for all lands within a prescribed area, normally a municipal jurisdiction (often referred to as *land use categories* or *land use zones*). Terminology used to designate specific areas varies, based on local needs. Two examples of land use designations are illustrated for a predominantly urban environment and a rural township containing recreational areas.

Individual land use designations are subsequently broken down into applicable regulations, e.g., specific types of uses, permitted structures, and detailed specifications.

Typical Land Use Designations—Urban

RR	Rural Residential
F	Flood Plain (F)
PR	Parks and Recreation (PR)
PR-L	Park – Landfill (PR-L)
C	Commercial (C)
OI	Office and Institutional Buildings (OI)
CR	Regional Shopping Centre (CR)
M	Industrial (M)
R1	Single Family Residential (R1)
R2	Two Family Residential (R2)
RM	Multiple Family Residential (RM)
MH-P	Mobile Home Park (MH-P)

Typical Land Use Designations—Rural/Recreational

EP	Environmental Protection
RU	Rural
RE	Recreational Open Space
HR	Hamlet Residential
RR	Rural Residential
ER	Estate Residential
SR1	Shoreline Residential Type One
SR2	Shoreline Residential Type Two
SR3	Shoreline Residential Type Three
RTP	Recreational Trailer Park
C	Commercial
M	Industrial
D	Development

LAND USE REGULATIONS

Regulations imposed by municipal authorities and provincial/federal governments relating to the use of land. Such regulations can involve a wide array of requirements and restrictions for such items as: flood management policies, grading and site requirements, zoning by-laws, and building code restrictions.

LAND USE STUDY

A detailed study normally produced for developers and investors setting out various development options based on the highest and best use for a particular parcel of land or the anticipated highest and best use based upon a change of use through re-zoning.

Land use studies, also referred to as *feasibility studies*, must be clearly defined to avoid misunderstandings as to the purpose and type of value estimate required. Land use studies may also be used in the planning process at a municipal level.

A common example of a land use study involves municipal planning and the designation of areas for specific usage under an official plan and corresponding controls (zoning by-laws). **Figure L.1** illustrates a typical strategy underlying a municipal land use study in which overall goals are established, land use designations are described, and location uses identified.

LAND (SITE) VALUATION

The process of estimating the value of land. Typically, valuation involves market value, that is the highest price in terms of money assuming a willing buyer and seller and a reasonable exposure in the marketplace.

The direct comparison approach is the most common of several methods of valuing land. This approach is highly dependent on careful selection of, and adjustments to, comparable land. Once adjusted prices are established, the use of various units of comparison as a standard for that comparison is customary. The most popular include price per front foot/metre, price per square foot/metre, price per lot, and price per acre/hectare.

Methods of land (site) valuation include: **Direct Comparison Approach, Abstraction Method—Site Valuation, Comparative Sales Method—Site Valuation, Land Development Method—Site Valuation,** and **Land Residual Method—Site Valuation.**

Goals

- To provide for the efficient use of land within the municipality.
- To avoid and/or reduce land use conflicts in the interest of sound overall planning.
- To provide a balanced response, based on various needs identified for selected sectors of the municipality.
- To provide a range of land uses (land use designations) to accommodate the long term needs of the municipality, its citizens, and businesses.

Land Use Designations

Identify the intended land use for all lands within the municipality through a system of land use designations. The following are permitted in all land use designations, subject to various provisions as set out in the official plan:

- Utilities and telecommunication works and transmission lines serving the immediate community.

- Schools and neighbourhood parks.
- Community and public facilities such as day care centres, libraries, recreational facilities, and community centres.
- Places of worship.
- Fire halls, police and ambulance stations, and post offices.

Locational Uses

In establishing criteria for designated areas and zoning by-laws and reviewing amendments thereto, the municipality will have regard for the following:

- Compatibility of the proposed use with surrounding land uses (including on-site buffers to minimize adverse impact).
- Size and shape of the site in relation to use.
- Traffic patterns.
- Need and demand for the facility.

Figure L.1   Strategy—Land Use Study

LANDLORD

A person or company who owns tenanted real property. The statutory definition for landlord will vary by provincial jurisdiction in accordance with applicable tenancy legislation. A typical wording is illustrated:

A person who is a lessor, owner, the person giving or permitting the occupation of the premises in question, and these persons' heirs, assigns, and legal representatives.

The duties of a landlord, set out statutorily and by common law, vary depending on both the type of property and the tenant. Basically, the landlord is required to guarantee possession to the tenant for the duration of the lease period. If this covenant is broken, the tenant may pursue legal damages. The landlord cannot use the premises retained in such a way that the tenant is unable to use his/her leased premises (derogation from the grant).

Landlord duties are often detailed in the lease document as the following example for a commercial property illustrates.

Example   Landlord

Salesperson Lee has just leased a 3,000 square foot office to a new real estate brokerage opening in the west end of the city. When asked about the landlord's obligations, the salesperson detailed a list of items taken from a standard lease used by the landlord.

The landlord will:

- Pay realty taxes;
- Provide heating, ventilating and cooling to the common elements and the leased premises;
- Maintain and repair the common elements;
- Provide janitorial service in keeping with standards appropriate to the building; and
- Control the management and operation of the building, including employing personnel, making changes or improvements, and such other acts as deemed prudent, using good business judgement.

Provincial   See applicable reference materials.

LANDLORD'S AND TENANT'S WORK
(SEE WORK LETTER)

LANDSCAPING

The planting of shrubs, grass, and trees including alterations to the contours of the property to improve the overall aesthetic appeal of the site. Landscaping often forms part of the requirements in site plan control agreements and zoning requirements, particularly in regard to buffer zones facing adjacent properties.

LAPSE OF CONSENT

A term used in selected provinces relating to the granting of a consent to sever or subdivide, the associated conditions to be fulfilled in relation to that severance or subdivision, and the lapsing of such consent if those conditions are not fulfilled within a stated period.

Example *Lapse of Consent*

Seller Smith made application to the appropriate body involved with land severances and received a consent, subject to the following conditions:

- A parkland dedication amounting to 5% of the property; or cash equivalent based on market value.
- A widening of the existing roadway to 66' to meet township standards.
- Entering into a site plan agreement concerning the development of the site.

   The severance approval issued by the appropriate body set out these conditions and advised that they must be completed within one year from the date of the written notice of the decision. Further, Smith must forward a letter to the approving body within the time limit acknowledging that all three conditions have been met, along with corroborating letters or approvals from appropriate agencies. If the conditions are not met within this one-year period, the application for consent, along with the conditional approval, will automatically be deemed to be null and void.

Provincial   See applicable reference materials.

LATENT DEFECT
(SEE ALSO PATENT DEFECT)

Frequently referred to as a *hidden defect*. A physical deficiency or construction defect not readily ascertained from a reasonable inspection of the property, such as a defective septic tank or underground sewage system, or improper plumbing or electrical lines. Conversely, a patent defect is readily discernable to the untrained eye.

Application   The latent defect presents one of the greatest hidden dangers to real estate practitioners. Salespeople find themselves increasingly watching for situations that may remain largely unnoticed by the buying and selling public. While no clear guidelines exist, the real estate practitioner is expected to be knowledgeable about certain circumstances that might not be readily apparent to the casual observer. Even if such defects cannot be directly seen, an awareness of their existence (actual or contemplated), may be required.

   Prudent salespersons are increasingly using seller disclosure forms when listing property. Notwithstanding the merits of such forms, four guidelines can assist.

Inquire   Take the time to ask specific questions of the seller concerning such items as roofs, water seepage, condition of mechanical equipment, and pools.

Investigate   Carefully analyze the condition of such items through direct personal inspection.

Verify   Point out any deficiencies to the seller, based on personal investigation, and request additional information and/or assurances concerning such matters. Inform the seller that items of a material nature must be disclosed to the buyer.

Disclose   Disclose the existence of any material matters concerning the property and allow the buyer sufficient time to investigate such items further.

Example *Latent Defect—Termites*

If termites are prevalent in a specific geographic locale, practitioners should pursue the topic with a seller, assuming a client relationship, to determine possible infestation of the listed property. Secondly, even if none are discovered or suspected, a further duty of care exists to inform the buyer of their potential existence, given widespread occurrences within that specific locality. The issue of termites has been a subject of Canadian litigation, but is far more common in the southern areas of the United States.

Example *Latent Defect—Condition of Pool*

If a property has a swimming pool, then the listing salesperson should make reasonable enquiries as to the pool's overall condition. That same practitioner should be forthright and honest in discussing the overall condition with a buyer/customer including the drafting of a condition, if warranted, to allow time for a full inspection.

Provincial   See applicable reference materials for any recommended or mandated seller property disclosure forms.

Lawful Object

Broadly defined as within the bounds of the law. The object in a real estate transaction is the transferral of ownership of the seller's property to a buyer. If this object is illegal according to a statutory provision or common law then the entire contract would be void and unenforceable.

Example   *Lawful Object*

The showing on Smith's property was proceeding smoothly. Salesperson Ward had just completed touring the upper floors with Buyer Jones and was currently viewing the main floor rooms. Smith, while patiently following the salesperson and buyer, was frequently excusing himself to answer incoming telephone calls on a cellular phone. When reaching the basement, the salesperson discovered a flurry of activity. Instead of the traditional family room, the area was buzzing with activity. A full off-track betting operation unfolded before his eyes. The seller, noticing the salesperson's look of amazement, simply turned to the buyer and said:

Don't worry, we've had this operation going for two years. If you want to make some big money, why not join in. We'll continue to rent the basement. Just get Ward to put in an appropriate clause in the agreement.

Ward is now contemplating an unlawful act that affects the lawful object of the contract.

Leaching Bed
(SEE ABSORPTION BED)

Lead

A bluish-grey metal contained in various products, e.g., lead pipe, lead-based paint, and grooved bars found in stained glass windows. Lead is listed as a designated hazardous substance under provincial legislation and may have implications when transacting property. Lead-based products were particularly prevalent prior to 1950 and, as a result, lead is found in varying degrees throughout most regions of the country.

Application   During the past 40 years, lead content has been dramatically diminished, if not completely removed, from a variety of products. However, lead is found practically everywhere in Canada in varying degrees of concentration. Scientists have known for a long time that prolonged exposure to substantial amounts of lead is a definite health risk. Recently, even low level exposure has been found to cause problems, particularly with the normal development of children, e.g., behavioural difficulties, ability to learn, and development of the nervous system.

Real estate practitioners should be particularly aware of the following.

Lead Paint   Frequently found in older properties. Problems are heightened as painted areas peel, crack, and generally deteriorate.

Lead Pipes   Old pipes/soldered pipes are a second source. Often, older pipes and joints contain lead, however, these often become coated with minerals through continued use.

Dust and Soil   Properties adjacent to industries using lead (e.g., battery recycling facilities and printing facilities), large metal structures painted with lead-based paint, and proximity to busy highways (lead-free gasoline has significantly improved this situation), may represent a problem.

Practitioners should be particularly aware of possible lead contamination in structures built before 1970, with the highest risk in pre-1950 structures. Lead dust from renovations in older homes can be a serious health danger and appropriate expert advice is required.

Reference   For detailed information, contact Health Canada, the provincial ministry/department responsible for environmental matters and/or the local public health unit/laboratory. Lead testing kits can be purchased at selected retail stores.

Lease

A contract between a landlord (lessor) and a tenant (lessee) for the occupation or use of the landlord's property by the tenant, for a specified time and for a specified consideration. Under the terms of a lease, the lawful owner of the property (the landlord) transfers the rights of use, possession, and enjoyment to another (the tenant) for a specified period of time, or at will for a consideration (rent). A lease may also be referred to as a tenancy agreement.

The purpose of a lease is to establish a written record of an agreement between the parties for a tenancy arrangement within a defined period. A lease can be verbal or written, express or implied. A lease document, whether residential, commercial, or industrial, is a detailed document setting out the responsibilities of the parties, rents payable, and obligations of both landlord and tenant, along with a wide range of provisions concerning notices, remedies, and termination.

Assignment

The assigning of rights, ownership, and interest in a lease whereby the assignor, or lessee, transfers the entire remainder of the term created by the lease.

The tenant, as assignor, may transfer all of his/her leasehold interests to a new tenant but, unless he/she is released by the landlord, the assignor remains liable for the lease obligations to the landlord. It should be noted that the assignor may not remain liable for performance under the lease if such is specifically set out in the terms of the lease pertaining to assignment. If the tenant transfers something less than an entire interest, he/she sublets it. This may be either the subletting of part of the term or part of the premises. Again, the tenant remains liable to the landlord, unless otherwise stipulated in the lease.

A tenant may assign or sublet at will without the approval of the landlord unless the lease stipulates otherwise or provincial legislation establishes certain requirements or procedures. In fact, most leases contain an express covenant that the tenant will not assign or sublet, or a qualified covenant that there will not be any assignment or subletting without the prior written consent of the landlord. This clause may be further qualified so that the landlord's consent will not be withheld arbitrarily. In these circumstances, the tenant can apply to a judge to obtain approval for an appropriate tenant who intends to use the premises in a reasonable manner. Usually both the tenant and the assignee or subtenant will sign a form agreeing to be bound by the main lease and the landlord will consent to this agreement. The parties will pay the landlord's reasonable costs in arranging for this consent and they will include any legal expenses. There may be other requirements concerning subtenants for residential tenancies in government-subsidized housing or government-owned projects.

Creation/Registration

A lease can be written or verbal, express or implied by a person's conduct. Its terms are found in common law, and in provincial statutes concerning commercial or residential tenancies. Normally, the parties will enter into a written signed lease or tenancy agreement in order to precisely describe their relationship. A wide range of lease forms and associated wordings are found in the marketplace.

When a property owner agrees to lease property, the tenant acquires an interest in that property and may register applicable documents in the land registration office giving notice of this interest. Methods will vary based on whether the property is registered under land titles or registry and upon specific registration requirements set out in individual provincial jurisdictions.

Elements

Lease forms differ substantially, but whether for residential, commercial, or industrial purposes, all must contain the following elements to make them legally enforceable:

- Statement of the correct names and signatures of legally competent parties.
- The full legal name, correctly spelled, of the individual(s) and/or corporation(s) that are party to the lease must appear.
- The person signing must be legally competent. This is particularly important in the management of retirement and nursing homes, and the signatures of spouses and guarantors are obtained, where applicable.
- Legal description of the leased premises should ideally be entered. However, as long as the description allows the space and specific property to be readily identifiable (including address, dimensions, and a floor plan), this requirement can be considered fulfilled.
- Consideration, that is, the exchange of something of value. In a lease, the amount of rent, method of payment, and to whom the payment is due are detailed.
- A lease must include a description of the legal purpose for which the premise is to be used. By virtue of this clause, for example, tenants can be controlled in the particular type of business being carried on, thereby permitting exclusive use within a retail complex and providing assurance that other tenants will not be in direct competition.
- Commencement and expiration dates must be included since, if these two dates were omitted, the lease would be so vague as to be unenforceable. Any renewal privileges should be spelled out in detail.
- Rules and regulations, policies, procedures, and generally what is expected of each party must be clearly delineated.

History

For centuries, the law recognized freehold estates as property interests, and permitted only a person who possessed a freehold estate to bring an action to protect his/her real estate. All other interests were less significant and considered personal in nature. The introduction of leasehold interests into law and the increasing use of this land holding method required a change in legal concept.

Leaseholds became known as estates that were less than freehold, but as estates nevertheless. One major distinction between freehold and leasehold estates is that, while both are a measurement of time, the freehold is for an uncertain time, whereas a leasehold is for a time that is certain or capable of being made certain.

In discussions of feudal doctrines and concepts, the relationship of landlord and tenant was of major significance. The courts were called upon to decide disputes between the two, and the results often favoured the landlord by strict interpretation of principles of land law. The land and its right of occupancy were the major assets of most aristocracy and land was prized for the wealth and power it bestowed.

In its simplest form, the lease is a grant of an interest in land. In practice, it is usually a grant by way of a contract whereby the owner, called the lessor or landlord:

- Transfers exclusive use and possession of real property to another person, called the lessee or tenant;
  - For a period of time, called the term; and
  - For valuable consideration, called the rent.

While there are various requirements in a lease, the most important aspect involves the granting of exclusive possession. If the parties contract for something less than that, the law might not recognize the arrangement as a lease, but as some other legal personal arrangement, such as a licence. The distinction has practical significance, in that a lessee may enforce entitlement to rights against a subsequent owner while a licensee may not be able to do so. Therefore, a contract that may not grant exclusive possession is not a lease and the occupant does not have the right to exclude all other persons from the premises.

Such contracts may involve mall kiosks or residential roomers/ boarders. The latter can be complex, since landlord and tenant law historically did not consider roomers to be tenants, whereas modern statutes, such as those of rent control, may consider them to be covered by specific legislative protections. In a leasehold arrangement, the landlord retains an interest called a reversion. The tenant's estate is a lesser one than that of the landlord. If it were otherwise, the arrangement would amount to a transfer of entire interests and constitute a sale.

Offer/Agreement to Lease

An offer setting out material terms regarding a proposed tenancy arrangement between landlord and tenant that, once agreed by the parties, becomes the reference document for drafting a lease.

In most lease transactions, the practitioner is involved in two steps:

- An offer to lease is signed, setting out the basic terms of the agreement between the parties.
- Terms in the offer to lease flow to a detailed lease agreement that must be signed by the parties.

Practitioners frequently attach a preprinted blank lease to the offer as an assurance that all parties are aware of terms set out in the agreement that will be subsequently completed and signed.

Provincial See applicable reference materials.

Sublet

Involves the leasing of premises to a third person by the lessee in which the lessee conveys the same interest for a shorter period of time, or a portion of the interest for the same or shorter period. Subletting typically occurs when a lessee wants to sublet the premises with the intention of moving back in prior to the expiration of the original lease with the landlord.

Practitioners should clearly differentiate subletting from the assignment of a lease. When an entire interest is transferred, it is said to be assigned. Thus, the tenant as assignor may transfer all of his/her interest to a new tenant, the assignee. The original tenant remains liable for the lease obligations to the landlord.

As a general statement, a tenant may assign or sublet at will without the approval of the landlord unless the lease stipulates otherwise or provincial legislation establishes certain requirements. In reality, most commercial leases contain an express covenant that the tenant will not assign or sublet or a qualified covenant that there will not be any assignment or subletting without the prior written consent of the landlord. This clause may be further qualified so that the landlord's consent will not be withheld arbitrarily. If this occurs, the tenant may be able to apply to a judge and obtain approval for an appropriate tenant.

Usually both the tenant and assignee or subtenant will sign a form agreeing to be bound by the main lease and the landlord will consent to this agreement/contract. The parties will pay the landlord's reasonable costs in arranging for this consent including the legal expenses, credit investigations and similar expenses.

Typically, matters concerning assignments and subletting of residential leases are addressed in provincial legislation. Specific procedures are set out concerning the rights of both landlords and tenants including required notices, content of such notices, and associated items.

Provincial See applicable reference materials.

LEASE BUYOUT

A cash payment or other settlement made by the tenant to the landlord to terminate a lease. Lease buyouts can also involve a cash payment or other settlement of the remaining portion of a tenant's lease by a landlord as an incentive for the tenant to move to a new location.

Example *Lease Buyout*

Owner Smith is reticent to release Tenant Jones from an existing lease agreement with a remaining term of two years. Jones' base rent on the commercial space is $750 per month and additional rent, while varying in the past three years, is approximately $1,500 per month. The actual revenue generated for the remaining term will be:

($750 + $1,500) x 24 months = $54,000

Smith has a 95% building occupancy rate and would probably lease the space within a three to four month period, or at worst, a year. Further, Smith could easily rent the space for a base rent of $1,200 per month plus the $1,500 in additional rent.

Jones suggests a lease buyout of $31,000 and a complete release of all covenants under the existing lease agreement. If Smith accepts this buyout, he will have no further recourse against Jones if the property is not rented. However, on the converse, Smith may realize significant profits if a tenant appears immediately.

Example *Leaseback Financing*

Seller Smith owns a large industrial parcel of land with a small industrial casting operation that comprises approximately 6,000 square feet. The property can accommodate a much larger facility. Smith wants to expand and capture part of the new international market for his product, but lacks sufficient capital to undertake such a project.

The land in question is valued at approximately $1,500,000 and a new structure would cost approximately $2,500,000. Accordingly, Smith approaches Investor Thompson with a sale/leaseback arrangement in which Thompson will purchase Smith's land and then provide a leasehold mortgage to permit Smith to build a structure on the property sufficient to meet expansion plans.

Smith, as a tenant, agrees to leaseback the property for a 40-year period. The leaseback furnishes Smith with much needed capital to update and build the larger facility, purchase equipment, and add marketing facilities. The investor secures a prime piece of industrial land, a good rate of return, and a 40-year lease agreement with a suitable and motivated long-term tenant.

LEASE OF NATIVE LANDS

(SEE NATIVE LANDS)

LEASEBACK FINANCING

A method of obtaining financing through the sale and leasing back of a property by the borrower. Many variations exist in the marketplace. The overall objective is to provide financing through the owner becoming a tenant and a leasehold mortgagor.

Application The owner can obtain nearly 100% financing for a project. Normally 100% of the land and 75% of the improvements are financed under the leasehold mortgage. The monies received by the original owner are dedicated to improvements, e.g., a shopping mall or a commercial/industrial facility. At lease termination, normally exceeding 25 years, the property reverts to the new owner who, in Figure L.2 is the investor/lender. In this illustration, the land owner sells the land to an investor but retains occupancy as a tenant while receiving leasehold financing from the new owner.

The leaseback was originally conceived to generate financing leverage for an owner. In recent years, it has become popular for owners to lease land due to tax considerations. Also, owners of prime property are often reluctant to relinquish ownership. Instead, they enter long-term leases with developers who concurrently secure leasehold mortgages to finance improvements on the land. The original owners thereby retain ultimate control of prime sites.

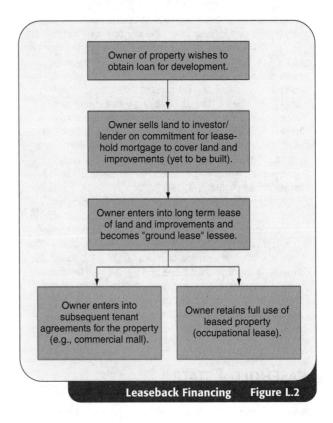

Leaseback Financing   Figure L.2

LEASED FEE ESTATE

The ownership interest or estate in a property when the right of occupancy has been granted by a landlord to a tenant by means of a lease.

LEASED FEE ESTATE VALUATION

The value of a landlord's interest in a property during the term of the lease.

Application   In return for permitting occupancy under a lease, the landlord is entitled to receive rental payments along with the right to repossess the property at lease termination. The value of these benefits is calculated by establishing the present value of all rental payments received under the lease agreement, plus the present value of the value of the property at point of reversion to the landlord. The discount rate selected for purposes of estimating the present value of the estate (interest in the property), can vary according to risk inherent in the leasing arrangement. Consequently, the discount rate may be more or less than a rate chosen when valuing the property had the leased fee estate not been created.

Example   *Leased Fee Estate Valuation*

An owner of a freestanding retail structure leases the property to a tenant for four years. The net operating income is $127,200 for each year. The estimated value of the property at the EOY4 (end-of-year four), is $1,375,500 following costs of sale deductions. The leased fee estate value is estimated by calculating the present value of the operations cash flow (Years 1 through 4), along with the reversion value. A discount rate of 11.20% was derived from the marketplace and reflects returns expected for this type of investment property, along with a risk premium associated with the lease and the creditworthiness of the tenant.

Calculation of present value (PV) reveals a leased fee estate present value of $1,292,535.

A higher discount rate (e.g., increased risk premium), results in a lower value. Assume that the risk associated with a particular tenant and lease is higher. The practitioner, in analyzing the situation, attributes a higher risk component of 0.50. The resulting discount rate of 11.70% would produce a lower present value of $1,272,389. The underlying assumption is that rent charged is consistent with market rents. If the contract rent falls below market rent, adjustments would be required and value is affected.

LEASEHOLD ESTATE

An interest in real estate for a definite period of time, e.g., an interest or estate held by a tenant in a property during the term of a lease.

LEASEHOLD ESTATE VALUATION

The value of a tenant's lease interest in a property during the term of the lease.

Application   While the lease in itself represents value through the right to occupy and use the property, *leasehold value* is used to describe the increased value that accrues to the tenant due to the difference between contract rent and market rent, as the tenant is deriving an economic benefit from that variance. The difference is often referred to as *differential cash flow*: the greater the differential cash flow, the longer the lease terms, the higher the leasehold value. A tenant can acquire leasehold value even if the property cannot be sublet under the lease agreement. Arguably, the tenant gains financial advantage from the arrangement although the interest is described as a non-marketable leasehold interest.

Differential cash flow, as with any cash flow, can be discounted to estimate present value. The value of the leasehold estate, as in the case of the landlord's leased fee estate, is determined by selecting an appropriate discount rate. The discount rate is dictated by market-extracted data as well as the risk associated with the leasehold interest.

Example   *Leasehold Estate Valuation*

Tenant Smith is currently occupying retail space consisting of 2,000 square feet with a contract rent of $18.00 per square foot per year with a remaining five-year lease period. The market rent for this space is currently $24.00 per square foot. The leasehold value is determined based on differential cash flow.

Contract Rent
For 1 year ($18.00 x 2,000)	$36,000
For 5 years ($36,000 x 5)	$180,000

Market Rent
For 1 year ($24.00 x 2,000)	$48,000
For 5 years ($48,000 x 5)	$240,000

Differential Cash Flow
$$\$240,000 - 180,000 = \$60,000$$

The economic advantage to the tenant is $60,000. An appropriate discount rate of 10.5% produces a leasehold present value of $44,914.

LEASEHOLD IMPROVEMENTS

Additions and improvements made by the tenant to the leased premises, most commonly associated with interior finishings and mechanical systems provided by a commercial tenant pursuant to a lease agreement.

LEASEHOLD INTEREST

(SEE ESTATE)

LEASING COST ANALYSIS
(SEE ALSO EFFECTIVE RENT)

The examination of costs incurred in a lease agreement, commonly associated with comparison of commercial lease alternatives for clients seeking rental premises.

Application A leasing cost analysis can be generated from either landlord or tenant perspectives. To properly compare costs, the full *cost of occupancy* must be established followed by an effective rent calculation. Analysts also provide discounted effective rent in which rental costs are discounted at an acceptable discount rate to arrive at a present value.

Most discussions of effective rent centre on tenant-related analysis given its prevalence in the marketplace. The cost of occupancy for the renter can include items not traditionally viewed as leasing costs, for example, moving expenses. In the simplest scenario, the cost of occupancy would be:

• The contracted rent for the period;
• PLUS any additional costs incurred (e.g., tenant improvements);
• LESS any allowances or concessions provided by the landlord.

With longer leases, the calculations become more complex. For example, various costs of the tenant can be allocated to successive time periods. Similarly, concessions provided by the landlord will be slotted into appropriate years of the lease. Practitioners then typically apply a discount rate to the cash flows (cost of occupancy), in recognition of the time value of money. Costs are typically analyzed on a cash accounting basis.

LEGAL DESCRIPTION

A written identification and formal depiction of land by which the property can be precisely located.

Application The legal description typically ensures that the property being purchased is, in fact, the same one being offered for sale. Further, this description is required when mortgages are being arranged. Primary documents containing the legal description include the deed and survey. Secondary documents such as assessment notices and municipal tax bills also include this information. Practitioners should always rely on primary source documents.

Provincial See applicable reference materials.

LEGAL (FIRST) MORTGAGE
(SEE ALSO MORTGAGE)

The legal mortgage in land registry transfers the estate or interest in land or other property for securing the repayment of debt. Since the legal title can only be transferred once by the current owner (mortgagor) to a mortgagee, it follows that only the first mortgage can hold this distinct status. A legal mortgage is therefore a document in which the direct conveyance of title is involved subject to the repayment of a debt.

LEGAL-GOVERNMENTAL FACTORS

One of several factors involved in analyzing a site for appraisal purposes, the others being physical, locational, and economic factors. Legal-governmental factors deal with the lawful and restrictive uses of the site.

Application Restrictive uses can be analyzed under several categories.

Deed Restrictions or Restrictive Covenants

Private restrictions generally contained in the deed have varying effects on value. Developers often include deed restrictions or restrictive covenants for the protection and interest of other owners. For example, developers may include restrictions on such things as colour of siding, types of fencing, and minimum size of dwelling.

Easements

Easements reduce rights of ownership. The impact of easements on value can be minimal or substantial. For example, a pipeline easement may have little effect on farm productivity, but in a residential area, the same easement could severely limit site utility.

Leases

Leasehold interests create split interests, dividing the value between the leaseholder and the freehold owner. A long-term lease may preclude a freehold owner from gaining maximum returns from a site for a specific future period. For example, a commercial lease may involve a parcel of land that is only partially improved. If the remaining land lease is for 15 years, the tenant could preclude the freehold owner from developing the excess land for that whole period. The tenant may be unwilling to develop the site because of inability to recover the cost during the tenancy. Consequently, future use is restricted.

Legal Description

The written description details the physical extent of ownership. Methods used for the development of legal descriptions will vary by provincial jurisdiction.

Taxes and Assessment

Taxes and assessments are normally levied on an equitable basis. Occasionally, a property is subject to some form of special assessment that reduces net returns and decreases its value.

Title Data

Essential facts include the name of the registered owner, legal description, registered mortgages and any subsequent discharges, liens, and consideration paid for the property.

Zoning

Zoning is a political force affecting value. The zoning by-law is the dominant legal document that sets out the minimum physical requirements of a site and specifies the various uses allowed. Unless there is reasonable probability that zoning could be changed within a reasonable time, the site must be valued according to its present legal use.

LEGAL NON-CONFORMING USE
(SEE NON-CONFORMING USE)

Provincial   See applicable reference materials.

LENDER

A person or organization providing temporary use of money through loans and/or mortgages for the acquisition of real property. Lending sources can be grouped under three categories: major direct lenders, agent sources (mortgage brokers), and private investors. The inclusion of various sources does not reflect current availability of funding in the marketplace.

Major Direct Lenders

Chartered Banks

Governed by the *Bank Act*, major banks in Canada such as the Bank of Montreal, Bank of Nova Scotia, Canadian Imperial Bank of Commerce, Royal Bank of Canada and the Toronto-Dominion Bank, offer a full range of mortgage facilities including special purpose financing.

Life Insurance Companies

Regulated under two separate federal statutes: The *Canadian and British Insurance Companies Act*, and the *Foreign Insurance Companies Act*, life insurance companies have traditionally been very strong in the field of residential and commercial mortgages. They have recently moved more in the direction of commercial and industrial property as well as activities involving pension funds and registered retirement savings plans. Various life insurance companies are expanding their base of financial services.

Trust Companies

Trust companies have entered domains once deemed exclusive territories of investment dealers, banks, and finance companies. Trust companies are a major force in the mortgage financing market. The expansionary role placed by trust companies in mortgage financing is controlled by the *Trust Companies Act*. Trust companies now provide financial services touching all aspects of residential financing and special purpose loans.

Loan Companies

Often affiliated with trust companies because the trust organizations are permitted a good deal of latitude in the investment of trust funds. Traditionally, two differences exist between the loan company and a trust organization. The loan company cannot act as an agent or trustee and must obtain funds through the use of debentures as opposed to short term certificates and savings deposits. The loan company can complement the operation of a trust company.

The *Trust and Loan Companies Act* is the governing federal legislation. Loan companies may be further controlled under applicable provincial legislation. Loan companies are not normally as visible as the chartered banks, trust companies, and life insurance companies.

Credit Unions

Regulated by the *Credit Unions and Caisses Populaires Act*, credit unions have become more competitive in the field of mortgage financing and have invested in resale residential, farm, and small income properties. As a co-operative organization, credit unions must deal solely with members in relation to real estate financing.

Finance Companies

Finance companies are not bound by the variety of legislation that applies to banks, trust companies, and most traditional lenders. They have the flexibility to customize financial packages for consumers to cover not only real estate security but also chattels. Finance companies also actively pursue the purchase of mortgages, subject to pre-defined yield requirements.

Provincial Credit Corporations

Provincially operated credit corporations may be established to provide funds under specific mandates, e.g., agricultural credit corporations for funding of farm operations or small business development corporations to assist in the financing of business ventures.

Agent Sources

Mortgage Brokers

Represent either the lender or the borrower and bring the two parties together in a lending transaction. Sometimes referred to as *mortgage dealers*, they are registered under provincial legislation. Real estate practitioners may be exempt under such legislation but, if so, the scope of the exemption will vary by provincial jurisdiction.

Private Investors

Lawyers are a reliable source, as they act on behalf of private investors and estates willing to place funds in the real estate market. These investors can range from local new home builders to sellers accepting a take back mortgage to facilitate a sale.

Salespeople should have private investor sources, as a backup to conventional lenders, who can assist in unique circumstances. Ensure that all parties seek legal counsel, the intent of the parties is clearly documented, and terms regarding any financing is carefully outlined in the agreement/contract. Buyers should be made aware of the lack of legislation imposed on such investors.

Provincial   See applicable reference materials.

LENDER HOLDBACK

Funds not advanced by a lender until specific requirements and/or conditions are met by the borrower.

Application   A lender may require a holdback of funds until certain work is completed or repairs are made to a property being considered for mortgage financing. This could apply, for example, when electrical service must be brought up to standard, the furnace replaced, siding installed, or structural changes made. Normally when a holdback is required, a specified time limit is set for completion of work along with a re-inspection of the property. Frequently such holdbacks pertain to household improvements of a relatively minor structural or cosmetic nature. If substantial alterations are undertaken (e.g., an addition), mortgage funds are normally advanced in progressive stages as construction proceeds.

Example   *Lender Holdback*

The cottage property meets all loan underwriting criteria of the lender with the exception of 60-amp wiring. A loan to value ratio of 75/25 is approved subject to the installation of a 100-amp service. The lender estimates the cost of this upgraded electrical service is approximately $850.

Appraised Value for Lending Purposes: $82,500

Amount of Approved Mortgage (.75 x $82,500)	$61,875
Amount of Holdback Pending Completion of 100 Amp Service	–850
Mortgage Advanced to Owner	$61,025

LENDING CRITERIA (PROPERTY)

Lending institutions establish lending criteria for the types of properties, conditions of those properties, and whether a first mortgage (legal) or second mortgage (equitable) etc. is being arranged. The lender may refuse to finance properties or seek an increased equity position by limiting the size of the mortgage, demanding a higher interest rate, requiring certain repairs including a holdback on funds until the repairs are completed, or any combination thereof.

Application   Various conditions can impact the approval of a mortgage, the interest rate charged, and whether specific holdbacks are required. A typical list of limiting conditions is provided.

Physical Detractions

- Certain types of siding (e.g., insulbrick).
- Lack of a central heating system and reliance on space heaters.
- Outdated wiring system, such as a 60-amp service.
- Low water gallonage per minute test, usually under 2 gallons per minute.
- Dug well.
- Partial basement and/or dirt floor.
- Major amenities in structural state of disrepair, e.g., a pool.

Legislative Inadequacies

- Failure to comply with local building codes.
- Noncompliance with local zoning by-laws.

Other Limiting Factors

- Non-conformance (other than zoning) with prevailing property types in the area.
- Interior and exterior design weaknesses.
- Deteriorating neighbourhood.

Example   Lending Criteria (Property)

ABC Lending Inc. is offering conventional mortgages in isolated areas of the province but emphasizes that amounts advanced and ultimate approval can be affected by certain factors set out in lending criteria policies.

Buyer Jones requires financing on his recent purchase of an older two-storey house located 15 miles north of the village of Smallville. The home cost $95,000 and Jones is seeking a mortgage of $60,000 at the prevailing interest rate (8%) with a 25-year amortization. Upon inspecting the property, the appraiser estimates the market value at $93,500, but identifies the following limiting factors:

- No central heating system–reliance on space heaters;
- Dug well; and
- Partial basement with dirt floor.

The lender, considering these factors, is prepared to lend $60,000, but requires an interest rate of 8.75% and a 20-year amortization. More important, the lender will not advance any funds without proof that a central heating system has been installed. Further, the lender will only advance $50,000 following the heating system installation. The balance of $10,000 will be advanced once a drilled well is completed and a concrete floor is poured in the partial basement to meet building code specifications.

LESSEE

A tenant under a lease who has an interest in a property as a consequence of that lease.

Provincial   See applicable reference materials.

LESSOR

A landlord granting use of property to a tenant pursuant to the terms of a lease.

Provincial   See applicable reference materials.

LETTER OF COMMITMENT

A written commitment by a lender confirming the terms under which a loan or mortgage will be granted to a borrower. The terms typically include a specific interest rate together with a time period that the lender is bound by the commitment.

Often referred to as a *mortgage loan commitment*, this document also details any special privileges (e.g., repayment privileges), fire insurance requirements, survey requirements, processing costs, and special conditions.

LETTER OF CREDIT
(SEE ALSO LINE OF CREDIT)

A letter or document issued by a lending institution on behalf of a customer authorizing the person named to withdraw a specified amount of money based on certain prearranged terms and conditions. Letters of credit are most commonly associated with commercial ventures.

LETTER OF GUARANTEE

Often used in development projects involving a municipal body. The letter of guarantee assures the existence of funds and provides a form of promise on the part of the lending institution to step in and complete the development using its own resources, if such is necessary. The lending institution provides this guarantee to assure municipal authorities of the developer's solvency, given that a lender is prepared to back the company and the project.

LETTER OF INTENT

A written, general understanding of the parties setting out various provisions, covenants, terms, and other matters that may ultimately lead to a detailed agreement between those parties. A letter of intent is viewed as a preliminary agreement between the parties and is not a formal contract.

Example   Letter of Intent

Owner Smith and Buyer Jones are attempting to negotiate a complex sale involving an industrial property, a wide range of fixtures and chattels, business contracts, and other assets of Smith's corporation. As a further complication, the sale will require certain zoning amendments, approvals by the applicable ministry/department, and a detailed accounting analysis to determine tax implications for both buyer and seller.

The parties have agreed to enter into a brief letter of intent (agreement) setting out the purchase price subject to modifications, anticipated closing date, and general conditions to be fulfilled. Most important, the entire agreement is subject to a more detailed contract being signed within a 60-day period. Essentially, the 60 days will afford both parties sufficient time to clear a number of potential hurdles prior to a formal agreement.

Application   The letter of intent can, for example, be used in real estate transactions to provide an overall framework between a developer and owner of the lands, or a commercial landlord and a potential tenant. Generally, a letter of intent is simply a statement of general understanding and does not constitute a formal contract, nor does it create any obligation or liability unless such terms are specifically detailed.

LETTER OF OPINION

A brief, unsubstantiated statement of an appraiser's opinion of value or value range that is not recommended as a method of appraisal reporting.

Application   Although only limited information is given in the letter of opinion, the individual providing such an opinion should understand that a complete appraisal process must still be conducted and all relevant data, analysis, and conclusions kept within the appraiser's files. Indeed, completion of a full appraisal report may be required at some future date to substantiate the opinion.

While clients may expect a large reduction in the fee charged (assuming that a letter of opinion is a timesaving method of appraisal), a form report can usually be completed more quickly and easily. Also, given the vagueness of the letter of opinion, it often tends to create confusion and problems between the client and appraiser, resulting in both parties being dissatisfied. Letters of opinion are usually not accepted by lending institutions.

LETTER OF TRANSMITTAL

A letter, prepared by an appraiser, that formally presents an attached, detailed appraisal report to the person for whom the appraisal was undertaken. The letter normally includes a brief synopsis of property particulars, purpose of the appraisal, effective date of the appraisal, and the estimate of value. Form and content will vary.

LEVEL ROOF HEIGHT

A term applying to industrial structures when height of office and factory building components are the same.

Application   Level roof height buildings allow flexibility in the allocation of office/factory space ratios as occupant needs change, however, they are generally more costly to construct. Often, users prefer the *box on box* arrangement in which the office component with a lower roof is attached to a larger factory structure with a higher roof. In both instances, the roof deck materials are similar, e.g., metal or gypsum deck, precast concrete planks/beams, or wood trusses with plywood sheathing.

LEVERAGE

The use of borrowed funds to make an investment in real property in the hope of realizing a profit in addition to monies necessary to pay for the borrowed funds.

Application   Most real estate transactions in the commercial field involve the use of borrowed funds as leverage, thereby reducing the owner's initial investment and permitting him/her to participate in various projects within defined financial capabilities. Leverage has the potential to increase the owner's return on any given investment, but risk is a consideration. Three types of leverage can occur.

Positive Leverage   A situation in which the yield to an investor exceeds the overall rate of return that would have been realized on a property had no financing been put in place.

Neutral Leverage   Occurs when no increase or decrease in yield occurs as a consequence of leverage.

Negative leverage   Exists when the use of borrowed funds results in a lower equity yield than the overall rate of return that could have been realized had no financing been put in place.

The amount of leverage within any particular project is expressed as a percentage or decimal factor using the loan amount as the numerator and the value of the project as the denominator. For example, if the loan amount is $800,000 and the value is set at $1,000,000, then the leverage ratio, frequently called the loan-to-value ratio, is .80 or 80%. Figure L.3 illustrates positive leverage occurring as a result of acquiring two properties with an anticipated return of 18% as opposed to 14% if all available resources were committed to one property.

LEVY

To impose or assess a tax on a person or property by means of a lawful process.

Application   The term *levy* for real estate purposes generally refers to the assessment process leading to tax calculations with the resultant levy being the amount of taxes to be imposed in a given locale for a given class (or other categorization) of property. Owners receive notices of assessment concerning property as a prelude to actual tax notices.

Provincial   See applicable reference materials.

Scenario

Jones is considering the purchase of a property. His first year projections are roughly as shown below:

Cost of Acquisition	$200,000
Amount of Mortgage	−100,000
Amount of Downpayment Required	$100,000
Projected Net Income	$24,000
Cost of Borrowed Money @ 10% (assuming interest only mortgage)	−10,000
Projected Return to Owner	$14,000

Percentage Return on Equity ($14,000 ÷ $100,000) = 14%

When reviewing these figures and discussing the matter with experts in the field, Jones realizes that he can increase his return by leverage while acquiring two buildings rather than one and dividing his downpayment between the two properties.

	Building A	Building B
Cost of Acquisition	$200,000	$200,000
Amount of Mortgage	150,000	150,000
Amount of Downpayment Required	$50,000	$50,000
Projected Net Income	$24,000	$24,000
Cost of Borrowed Money @ 10% (assuming interest only mortgage)	15,000	15,000
Projected Return to Owner	$9,000	$9,000
Percentage Return on Equity ($9,000 ÷ 50,000)	18%	18%

As a result of reducing the downpayment and assuming a *return to owner* in the range of $9,000 per building, Jones, by means of leverage using borrowed funds, can effectively increase his equity return by acquiring two properties.

Figure L.3   Leverage

L

LIABILITY

(SEE ALSO CONTRACT)

A debt or other obligation. In accounting, current liabilities relate to debts that are normally due in one year as opposed to long-term liabilities of greater duration. In legal terms, liability refers to the general responsibility for one's conduct such as one party being responsible for loss or damage to another party. Legal liability has many dimensions, e.g., contractual liability, strict liability, tort liability, and joint liability. Practitioners most commonly encounter contractual liability that arises as a result of a buyer or seller not performing a contract/agreement for the purchase or sale of real property and the resulting responsibility for loss or damage. Remedies for a breach of contract include rescission, damages, quantum meruit, specific performance, and injunction.

LICENCE

A right or permission given to a person that allows the individual to act in some specific manner that would otherwise not be legally permissible. Alternatively worded, for purposes of real estate activity, permission given by a licensing authority to an individual or corporation to engage with a defined capacity in the trading of real estate. Traditionally, practitioners as well as consumers think in terms of licences, such as a broker's licence or salesperson's licence. In reality, most provincial regulatory bodies do not *license* individuals or brokerages, but rather *register* them under the applicable provincial real estate act. Accordingly, such individuals or brokerages are referred to as *registrants*.

Provincial   See applicable reference materials.

LICENCE LAW

A general reference in real estate to the regulatory controls imposed on real estate practitioners by a governing body. Licence laws are generally put in place to regulate the activities of licensees/registrants, while pursuing adequate consumer protection, and maintaining defined standards in the leasing, sale, or exchange of real property. Provinces have differing real estate licence laws.

Application   The primary goals of most licence laws are:

- To provide educational requirements to ensure that registrants are competent to deal with the public;
- To screen applicants for registration by reasonable methods to ensure that they are suitable to deal with the public; and
- To monitor and investigate the actions of registrants to secure the public interest.

ARELLO Mission Statement

The primary purpose of the Association of Real Estate License Law Officials shall be better administration and enforcement of real estate licence/registration and regulatory laws in member jurisdictions. This distinctive task of the Association is to help equip its members to fulfill their roles as regulators. That role is to protect the public interest in real estate brokerage transactions. Protecting the public interest does not mean advocating an industry or a consumer position. Instead, it means assuring each individual's right to justice and equal opportunity under the law. Therefore, the public interest demands the regulator's best effort to achieve impartial administration of the law.

Statement of Purposes

ARELLO shall:

1. Provide opportunities for communication on licence/registration law matters;

2. Manage and research information on licence/registration law matters;

3. Provide educational development for personal and professional improvement;

4. Encourage and develop co-operation with other organizations of similar nature;

5. Share expertise, information, and networking techniques.

ARELLO Mission Statement   Figure L.4

On an international scale, the Association of Real Estate License Law Officials (ARELLO) was established as a federation of real estate licence law officials to assist each other in the administration and enforcement of licence/registration laws in the United States and Canada. Figure L.4 contains the Mission Statement and Statement of Purposes of ARELLO as excerpted from the *Digest of Real Estate License Laws, United States and Canada* (ARELLO, 1996).

LICENSEE

An individual or corporation who holds a licence, e.g., a licensee/registrant trading in real estate.

Provincial   See applicable reference materials.

LICENSING

Provincial   See applicable reference materials.

LIEN

A right of encumbrance affecting any property. Generally, a lien can be either in the form of an agreement between two parties, namely, the party owing the money (lienor) and the party to whom those funds are due (lienee), or by statutory provision as in the case of a tax lien imposed by the Canada Customs and Revenue Agency.

Application   In real estate, liens are most commonly associated with statutory provisions to protect and give priority to work performed and materials furnished in constructing, repairing, or modifying a structure. Terminology will vary by province, e.g., construction holdback, mechanic's lien, and builder's lien. Issues regarding purchaser's and vendor's liens in relation to agreements/contracts for real property go beyond the scope of this text.

LIEN HOLDBACK

Provincial   See applicable reference materials.

LIFE ESTATE
(SEE ALSO ESTATE)

An interest in property that continues for the life of an individual and terminates in favour of others in the event of his/her death.

LIFE SAFETY SYSTEM

A system installed within a building that provides for the life and safety of occupants and, more specifically, the integrity and operation of these systems during an emergency. The scope of life safety systems and associated regulations are typically governed by provincial fire codes.

Application   Practitioners normally encounter life safety systems in commercial structures. Such systems include the use of alarms, emergency communication systems, strategically placed firewalls, automatic door closures, emergency lighting, emergency ventilation, auxiliary power, and sprinkler systems. The life safety system will depend on the size of the structure, the particular uses of that structure, and regulatory controls imposed by statutes.

Example   *Life Safety System*

Buyer Jones is concerned about the life safety system in a high rise condominium unit that he is considering for his family. In reviewing the resident's manual provided to all unit owners and tenants, various documents from the property management office, and personal notes from an inspection of the premises, he has determined the following systems are in place:

Fire Hose Cabinets and Extinguishers   Fire hose cabinets equipped with individually pressurized water extinguishers are located on each floor. Each has a 100' hose and nozzle. Additional wet and dry fire extinguishers are located in the mechanical rooms, parking levels, maintenance areas, and common areas.

Fire Alarm Panel   The panel is located at the concierge desk in the main lobby.

In-Suite Smoke Alarms   The smoke detectors in each unit are not attached to the main alarm system and consequently do not activate the main system. Individuals must sound the main alarm system separately.

Emergency Generator   The generator, located in the lower parking area, provides emergency power to emergency lighting, fire alarm system, wet and dry sprinkler systems, stairwells, elevator fans, security card access system, garage doors, service elevator and one elevator at a time until all elevators are resting on the ground floor.

Air Circulation   All air systems in the building shut down when the fire alarm is sounded.

Elevators   One elevator is assigned as the fire service elevator for use by the fire department.

Voice Communication   All suites, stairwells, common areas, and floors are equipped with voice communication speakers.

LIFE SAFETY TESTING (BUILDINGS)

A test designed to prove that the intended level of performance of a building's life safety systems has been achieved and are operational in accordance with the requirements as set out in applicable codes, e.g., fire and building codes. Provincial and/or municipalities may require life safety testing on specific types of buildings, e.g., high-rise and special design buildings.

LIMITATION OF ACTIONS

Under common law and the law of contract, a promisee who has a right of action against a promisor who defaults on payment of a debt or who is in breach of contract must begin an action within a prescribed period or lose the right to sue.

Application   In the common law provinces, the remedy for breach of ordinary contracts is barred within a specified period as set out in an applicable limitation statute. A person must start court proceedings within the specified period or lose the right to take the matter to court. Such limitations on actions are justified as being in the public interest. The opportunity for court action should end after a certain period of time, first, because it is unfair for a person who neglects to take court action to leave the other person in a state of uncertainty, and second, because as time passes, it becomes more and more difficult to determine the facts of the case as memories fade, witnesses move or die, and documents are misplaced or otherwise lost. Length of limitation periods for specific actions will vary by provincial jurisdiction and expert legal advice is required on such matters.

Provincial   See applicable reference materials.

LIMITED LIABILITY
(SEE ALSO CORPORATION)

Limitation of an investor's obligations to a corporation of which he/she is a shareholder in the event of legal action. Liability is normally limited to the amount of money invested by that shareholder in the enterprise. Limited liability also applies to the corporation to the extent of the assets of that corporation, unless such things as personal guarantees are attached to the corporation.

Practitioners should be aware that personal liability may attach to directors and officers of a corporation as a consequence of provincial legislation.

LIMITING CONDITIONS

Example   *Limited Liability*

Johnson, a registered real estate broker, is establishing a new brokerage and debating the merits of sole proprietorship, partnership, or corporation. Limited liability is a significant consideration and, consequently, the broker selects a corporate structure, as shareholders are not generally responsible for the debts of the corporation beyond assets invested in that corporation, unless some form of personal guarantee is provided (e.g., in the case of securing necessary mortgage financing or operating loans). Assuming no personal guarantees are required, Johnson may negotiate lines of credit and incur debts without facing the same exposure as with a sole proprietor or partnership.

Johnson's lawyer, however, is quick to remind him that, as the sole shareholder and director of this new corporation, other factors must be considered. While business corporation legislation in his specific province does state that shareholders are not generally liable for any act, default, obligation or liability of the corporation, exceptions exist. For example, if funds owed Johnson by the corporation were reduced or extinguished to the detriment of a creditor, then Johnson can be ordered by a court to return the funds. Also, if the corporation were dissolved, Johnson, as the shareholder may remain subject to action for a civil, criminal, or administrative action or proceeding relating to that corporation for a period of time from point of dissolution.

Johnson's lawyer also reminds him that, as a director, he may be liable for unpaid wages that are owed to employees for certain deductions, GST, and specific unpaid taxes. In addition, certain actions and decisions can result in director liability (e.g., environmental issues). Other provisions may also affect the extent of limited liability.

LIMITED PARTNER

A participant in a limited partnership whose liability is confined to his/her investment and who does not have a voice in the management of the partnership and is viewed as a passive investor.

Example   *Limited Partner*

Investor McKay has been approached to invest $20,000 in a land development project in which he, as a limited partner, will receive a return based on his proportionate interest in the entire project. The developer, as a general partner, is prepared to invest $100,000 in the project together with five other limited partners (each contributing $20,000). The developer will oversee and manage the development through a corporation specifically formed for this project.

McKay will participate in all profits in proportion to his contribution. The partnership has $200,000 ($100,000 + 5 limited partners @ $20,000) therefore McKay's proportionate interest is:

$$\$20,000 \div \$200,000 = 10\%$$

LIMITED PARTNERSHIP

(SEE ALSO GENERAL PARTNER)

An investment arrangement that limits a partner's liability to the amount invested while also limiting the profit he/she can make. A limited partner is not permitted to have a voice in the management of the project.

Application   To understand limited partnerships, a brief discussion of partnerships is required. Generally, under common law, a partner is jointly and severally responsible for the debts of the partnership. In addition, a partner can bind his/her other partner on decisions made for the partnership. Since a partnership is not a limited company, the partner's liability extends, from time to time, beyond the capital specifically invested in the partnership. A limited partnership falls somewhere between a limited company and a partnership.

Limited partnerships must be registered and have at least one general partner, whose liability is not restricted. The limited partners enter into an agreement whereby their liability is restricted to individual capital investment. Limited partners must be passive investors and turn over the management and general operation of the project to the general partner.

Example   *Limited Partnership*

Developer Reed wishes to undertake a residential development involving a 30-acre tract of land. To fund the project, Reed will invest the sum of $1,000,000. He prepares detailed plans and financial projections concerning the project and its overall feasibility and incorporates a corporation for the sole purpose of acting as general partner for the project.

Based on presentations to investors, Reed is able to secure eight commitments ($250,000 per investor) to raise the necessary equity of $3,000,000 required by the lender considering the project. Developer Reed's new company becomes the general partner, with the individual investors taking on limited partner status in the development of the land. The limited partners each have a 8.33% interest in the venture.

LIMITING CONDITIONS

A series of qualifying statements and assumptions commonly associated with appraisal reports in which the appraiser sets out items that define, limit, and/or restrict the scope of the appraisal and inform the client accordingly. Limiting conditions are usually grouped under *Assumptions and Limiting Conditions* that may be included in a letter of transmittal, but more commonly at the end of the appraisal report.

L

Limiting conditions normally relate to such issues as legal title (no warranty by the appraiser concerning title validity), the appraiser's reliance on information furnished by others is deemed to be correct, the improvements on the property are assumed to be confined within the property boundaries, a disclaimer that the appraiser does not have expertise concerning the existence of hazardous materials or their impact on value, and other matters that the appraiser feels should be specifically highlighted to the person requesting the report.

Appraisers will vary the scope of assumptions and limiting conditions based on circumstance. Consequently, no standard can be identified in the marketplace. Professional appraisal organizations do publish typical wordings for the assistance of their respective memberships.

LINE OF CREDIT

A line of credit is a highly flexible form of interim financing based on past performance and strength of personal or corporate covenants. In real estate development, a line of credit is used either in lieu of mortgages and associated advances or in addition to them. Monies advanced are secured by demand notes up to a limit specified by the applicable lender.

Application   The line of credit, in effect, can provide interim financing or complement existing arrangements. The interest charged is normally higher than conventional mortgage rates. While it is common to see a line of credit rate one or two points above conventional mortgage rates, the rate charged depends on a host of circumstances surrounding the project, the borrower, and the lender.

The demand notes underlying a line of credit can be for a specified period. More commonly, a stated amount of credit is established and all notes are processed in line with that maximum. Typically, all such notes are on a demand basis, that is, the loan may be called at the lender's option. Normally, the financial status of the borrower is reviewed on an annual or semi-annual basis.

LINKS/LINKAGES

The terms *links* or *linkages* are related to site accessibility involving industrial, commercial, and investment real estate and is a major consideration in real estate analysis.

Application   Linkage analysis is made from two perspectives that take economic and time/cost elements into consideration.

Economic Incoming/Outgoing Links
A commercial practitioner, when assessing a site for a specific buyer, must take into consideration access to production inputs, e.g., labour, raw materials, and utilities, as well as accessibility to bring products and/or services to the larger marketplace, e.g., rail and highway links, availability of high speed data access lines, and location and ease of access to selected markets.

Spatial Time/Cost Links
While geographic locale dictates the availability of both incoming and outgoing economic linkages, time/cost considerations for receiving production inputs or delivering production outputs (goods and services), are also vital. Geographic distances may be small, but time and cost variables can be prohibitive. Alternatively some sites may involve large distances that can be addressed in a cost effective and timely fashion.

Interestingly, the relative weighting of these two dimensions of accessibility has undergone dramatic changes during the past few years. Retail outlets, including big box retail operations, seek ready access dictated by highway links, spatial location, and time/cost considerations. However, electronic innovations have affected location analysis for selected industries and services. For example, courier operations, internal banking facilities, security services, and computer support organizations are increasingly driven by time/cost considerations in their search for location. Consequently, the past decade has seen the relocation of call centres and operations headquarters to distant locales, given the availability of high speed data transmission facilities, lower development costs, lower operational costs, and the efficiencies of centralized control.

LINTEL

A horizontal structural member (beam) that supports the load over an opening, such as a door or window.

Application   A lintel performs the same function as an arch. Typically flat, it relies on the inherent strength of the material used to transmit the load, as opposed to the arch principle. The area that the lintel supports can safely be thought of as a triangle above the lintel. The height of the triangle is roughly half the width of the opening. Accordingly, a window with twenty stories of brick above requires the same lintel as a window with six feet of brick above. Lintels are typically constructed of steel, wood, stone, or concrete (see **Figure L.5**). Typical problems include undersizing in relation to load requirements, improper end bearings, and general deterioration.

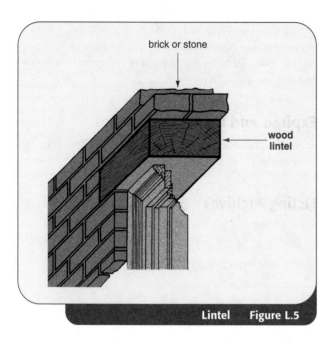

brick or stone

wood lintel

Lintel   Figure L.5

LIQUIDITY

The ease by which assets can be readily converted into cash. Funds held in chequing accounts, savings accounts, and short-term guaranteed investment certificates are generally viewed as highly liquid, as opposed to holdings in long term bonds, mortgages, and ownership of real estate. Liquidation is often referenced in relation to businesses and the ability to convert assets into cash, e.g., liquidation sale.

Application   For real estate purposes, liquidity in operations cash flows is particularly important to ensure the continuance of an investment. The investor must be able to meet the cash demands of the enterprise in terms of current and future operating expenses. Further, the marketability of the property plays into the equation. At some future point, the investor will seek to sell the investment. Sale proceeds cash flows can be a significant portion of overall return.

Practitioners concentrate on analyzing cash flows and discounted cash flows (present value of anticipated cash flows), to evaluate the attractiveness of one investment property over another. While the ownership of real estate is viewed as a non-liquid asset, care in the selection process and prudent forecasting of cash flows generated can address both liquidity and returns.

LIQUIDITY RATIO
(SEE CURRENT RATIO)

LIS PENDENS

Notice of the commencement of a court action recorded on the title of property in the land registration office.

Application   Lis Pendens is a Latin term meaning *litigation pending*. The term *lis pendens* is gradually disappearing from legal parlance and has been replaced by terms such as *Notice of Pending Litigation*, *Certificate of Pending Litigation* and *Pending Litigation Order*. Exact terminology will vary by province; some retain *lis pendens*. Basically, the registration of pending litigation on title makes it very difficult for a defendant to dispose of interests in the land until the court action is decided and the matter settled. Otherwise, the defendant, fearing a loss, could sell lands and dispose of the funds before the decision, thereby frustrating the plaintiff in collecting any monies as a result of the court decision.

> **Example   *Lis Pendens***
>
> Mr. and Mrs. Smith enter into an agreement/contract with Buyer Jones for the sale of their home. The closing date is scheduled six months following acceptance of the agreement/contract. Unknown to both parties, the city is planning a redevelopment scheme that positively affects the Smith property. Two weeks before closing, Smith realizes the potential for a windfall and refuses to close, wishing to resell the property at a much higher price.
>
> Jones, having complied with all conditions in the agreement/contract, has a firm contract and is intending to close on schedule. The dispute does not get resolved and the closing date passes. Jones tenders proof of his willingness to close and registers notice of pending litigation to warn other potential buyers of the circumstances.

LISTING AGREEMENT

An oral or written agreement under which the owner appoints a real estate brokerage for a designated period of time to sell, lease, or exchange a property based on the owner's stated terms, and under which the owner agrees to pay the brokerage a commission.

Application   The listing agreement performs several basic functions. As the basis for the agency relationship between the seller and real estate brokerage, the listing establishes well-defined limitations on the agent's authority and provides detailed information regarding the property for assistance when answering inquiries from prospects' buyers. This listing agreement also provides the foundation for offer negotiations, the drafting of an offer and, if necessary, a mortgage application.

L

Listing agreements will vary by provincial jurisdiction given differing regulatory requirements in the authority granted, commission agreements, and listing procedures. Further, standard agreements may be mandated, either provincially or within specific real estate board jurisdictions. Most listing agreements consist of two essential parts. The authority involves the appointment of the agent and includes the agreement to pay commission. The data input form provides detailed information on the property. A property disclosure statement may or may not be included. Accuracy and care in completing a listing agreement are crucial. The listing agreement is a legal document and must be completed with due regard and consideration for its completeness and accuracy.

Provincial   See applicable reference materials.

LISTING BROKERAGE

The real estate brokerage that lists a property and is granted the authority by the seller to market the property in accordance with terms and conditions set out in a listing agreement (also commonly referred to as the *listing brokerage*). For purposes of descriptive consistency and to avoid confusion in terminology, all sole proprietorships, partnerships, and companies registered as brokers are referred to as *brokerages*.

A listing brokerage should be clearly differentiated from a selling brokerage that is involved with a buyer who purchases the listed property. A listing brokerage may also perform the function of a selling brokerage subject to provincial statutory requirements and/or generally accepted disclosure procedures.

Example   *Listing Brokerage*

Salesperson Lee, a salesperson with ABC Realty Inc. has listed a residential property at 123 Main Street in Anycity. As an employee of ABC Realty Inc., Lee is authorized to act on behalf of the brokerage in securing and marketing listings. In this instance, Lee is typically referred to as the *listing salesperson* and ABC Realty Inc. as the *listing brokerage* or *listing broker*.

LISTING MANAGEMENT SYSTEM

Listing management procedures may be recommended in licensing education programs as part of an overall coordinated approach to listing and sales records. Provincial regulatory requirements do not typically address specifics of such systems, consequently significant variations can

be found. Descriptive materials are included as a general guide only. Listing management systems have improved significantly with the introduction of integrated brokerage administration software.

Expired and Cancelled Listings

Expired and cancelled listings are normally filed alphabetically by street address or seller's name.

Listing Archives

Expired and cancelled listings can be organized in file folders based on the following format.

- Listing checklist.
- True copy of listing.
- Correspondence with seller.
- Copies of materials provided by the seller.
- Copies of advertisements.

Listings converted to sale status are organized in one of two methods. Brokerages often file all transaction-related documentation (including listing documentation), in one file organized in numerical order, based on a recommended or required numbering system within a specific provincial jurisdiction. Alternatively, listing information is kept separate from trade particulars in a separate listing archive. Procedures in provincial jurisdictions will vary.

Listing Checklist

A listing checklist ensures that various procedures are followed in processing listings. The content will vary considerably, based on internal office procedures. See **Figure F.6** for a basic checklist that could be used with appropriate modifications in a residential brokerage.

NOTE   The section called *LISTING ON HOLD AWAITING* is specifically inserted as a quality control measure, if listings cannot be immediately processed due to incomplete or inaccurate information.

Listing Inventory

Two common methods for organizing listing records are:

- File by address; and
- File by name (sometimes used in smaller rural offices).

In either instance, a filing guide should be included in the policy manual, e.g., acceptable addresses, descriptions not permitted, record organization for large projects, and methods for correctly identifying rural property.

LISTING CHECKLIST

LISTING ON HOLD AWAITING _____

REC'D?	DATE	INITIALS	
❏	_____	_____	_____
❏	_____	_____	_____
❏	_____	_____	_____
❏	_____	_____	_____

PROCESSING OF LISTING

	DATE	INITIALS	
❏	_____	_____	Record in Listing Register
❏	_____	_____	Prepare Card for Cross Reference
❏	_____	_____	Thank you Letter to Customer
❏	_____	_____	Type Listing on Required Form
❏	_____	_____	Distribute Copies for sales staff
❏	_____	_____	Listing sent to Board (if MLS)
❏	_____	_____	Mortgage Verification (if applicable)
			Other Verification:
❏	_____	_____	_____
❏	_____	_____	_____
❏	_____	_____	_____
❏	_____	_____	Listing File Prepared

LISTING AMENDMENTS

	DATE	INITIALS	
			Amendment: _____
❏	_____	_____	Revised Listing Distributed to Salespeople
❏	_____	_____	Amendment to Board (if MLS)
❏	_____	_____	Listing Register Updated
❏	_____	_____	Reference Register Updated
			Amendment: _____
❏	_____	_____	Revised Listing Distributed to Salespeople
❏	_____	_____	Amendment to Board (if MLS)
❏	_____	_____	Listing Register Updated
❏	_____	_____	Reference Register Updated

Listing Checklist   Figure L.6

Listing Register

The listing register, often referred to as the *listing book*, is needed for assignment of listing numbers. A basic listing register provides for listing number, address of property, price, listing salesperson, listing date, expiry date, and disposition (see **Figure L.7**). Software programs for real estate brokerages typically provide automatic listing and transaction number assignment as well as detailed, cross-referenced listing/transaction directories.

LISTING REGISTER

Listing	Address of Property	Price	Listing Salesperson	Listing Date	Expiry Date	Disposition
A90098	123 Main Street East	$279,000	Jane Smith	09/01/xx	09/03/xx	Relist 09/03/xx MLS 11229 Sold 15/04/xx
A90099	3468 White Road	$309,000	Bill James	09/01/xx	31/05/xx	
A90100	9 Amberdale Street	$197,500	Grace Wong	15/01/xx	25/02/xx	Expired Relisted Excl. 01/06/xx See A90143

Listing Register   Figure L.7

LISTING/MARKETING
(RESIDENTIAL PROPERTY)

A variety of tips and guidelines are provided concerning the salesperson's role in the listing and marketing of residential real estate. The inclusion of various techniques is not an endorsement of such practices, but rather a summary of various suggestions commonly found in sales-oriented materials. Practitioners should seek assistance from their employing brokerage or sales technique experts in the marketplace. All sales techniques must be viewed within the context of regulatory requirements in individual provinces and policies established by employing brokerages.

Listing the Property
Characteristics of a Saleable Listing
Certain features and/or qualities are associated with saleable listings. These characteristics refer both to property issues and professional skills of the salesperson.

Exclusive　An exclusive listing indicates that the sales representative, on behalf of the brokerage, has obtained a measure of confidence from the seller and has obtained a degree of understanding with the seller as to marketing the property and services to be performed. The brokerage and salesperson have reasonable assurances of commission payment.

If an MLS listing (that is an exclusive listing with special features), the seller has the added advantage of other brokerages' services. Simply put, a written, signed and valid listing is fundamental to a saleable listing.

Reasonable Time Period　Listings require adequate exposure to the market. A reasonable time will vary based on market conditions prevalent at the time of marketing the property, typically available from real estate board reports. Most boards also have a minimum time period for placing a listing on the Multiple Listing Service.

Accurate Information　The listing is a contract and information must be complete and accurate. Ask the seller to produce documents concerning the property. Verify all information, including the mortgage (using a mortgage verification form). Inaccurate or incomplete information can have disastrous consequences.

Price　Have all the necessary information to establish price. The sellers must understand that the issue is not what they wish to get, but what a willing and informed buyer will likely pay. Experienced salespeople know that listing too high above the market value estimate will only frighten off genuine prospects who would have otherwise made reasonable offers. Generally, the greater the disparity between market value and listing price, the less chance of a sale within a reasonable period of time.

Confidence　The salesperson has the responsibility to instill confidence in the relationship with the seller. The best way to do that is by demonstrating knowledge, ability, resourcefulness, and a positive attitude. Fully discuss the marketing plan and develop a rapport with the seller early in the relationship.

Knowledge of the Property　A working knowledge of the property is essential. Simple procedures such as opening closet doors, checking the location of light switches, finding out about the neighbours, and discovering why the seller purchased the home in the first place, will pay dividends during subsequent showings to prospective buyers.

Counselling the Seller
Successful salespeople carefully plot their course of action when servicing and marketing listings. Open and candid discussion at the time of listing will give the seller a better understanding of what is involved and the actual procedures of showing and offer presentation. The seller can greatly assist in the marketing process by:

- Having the home ready for showings. Any necessary repairs, cleaning, or decorating should be discussed and agreed upon.
- Being flexible for showing appointments. Assure the owners that as much advance notice as possible will be given. Also discuss those times when short notice may be required and gain the sellers' agreement.
- Avoiding involvement in the showing process. Many representatives prefer that the owner not be present to enable more frank discussions with buyers who are viewing the property. If present, the owner should be advised to stay in the background and participate only if questions are asked of them by the sales representative.

- Allowing an open house. Discuss this option candidly, including the responsibilities of the seller and the brokerage, procedures, and benefits when inviting the public to inspect a home by open house.

- Referring direct contacts by buyers to the listing salesperson. Circumstances may occur when prospects and/or sales representatives will attempt to circumvent the courtesies of dealing through the listing representative and contact the sellers directly. The sellers should be instructed to call the listing salesperson immediately if such a contact takes place. An adequate supply of the listing salesperson's business cards should be left with the owner for this possibility.

- Dealing with offer presentations. The salesperson should clearly set out the various scenarios in which offers may be presented (e.g., working with co-operating brokerages as subagents and buyer brokerages, and the implications of dual agency, if a possibility), and explaining in detail the listing salesperson's role in the offer presentation.

Farming

The term *farming*, for real estate prospecting purposes, refers to the selection of a specific geographic territory, although it may be a social or economic sphere of influence.

Several basic guidelines can assist in effectively using this strategy.

- Start with a base of as few as 200 or 300 homes.
- Select a known territory, one in which you will enjoy working.
- Become totally familiar with the political, social, physical, and economic features of the territory.
- Establish a plan to become well known as the sales representative in the area.
- Make regular contact with people in the territory (mailings, personal contact, and newsletters).
- Develop accurate mailing lists and customer contact cards. Be a conscientious record keeper about all contacts with people in the territory.
- Maintain a regular program of contact with all owners in the territory.
- Maintain a consistent advertising program direct to all owners within the territory.

Listing Interview Preparation

Several successive steps are recommended before meeting with a potential seller.

- Get backup information from available sources, e.g., office files and MLS records.
- Make certain that the listing kit is complete, e.g., forms, presentation manual, listing book, and handouts.

- Be prepared to establish the most competitive listing price for the seller, i.e., develop a comparative market analysis detailing all available inventory, sold listings, and expired listings within the immediate area that are comparable to the seller's property.

- Be able to complete and fully discuss the comparative market analysis with the seller.

- Develop an overall strategy for establishing a listing price and marketing the property.

- Have a range of suggestions concerning how the seller will get the best price.

- Be prepared to answer the seller's concerns and demonstrate all marketing services.

- Bring supporting documentation, e.g., other listings, market trend information, and related analysis, to assist in the discussion.

A comparative market analysis (often referred to as a *Residential Market Comparison Guide*), is very effective for general discussion purposes, as no appraisal adjustment process is used. Owners are free to form conclusions as to the best listing price with the assistance of the salesperson as required. The salesperson should ensure that sellers receive all necessary information to make a well-informed decision.

Listing Sources

According to many sales representatives, successful listing practice is the key to a profitable career in real estate. Every real estate practitioner uses some method of promotion to win the attention of property owners who want to sell. Most employ a variety of available methods of obtaining listings. Many sources of residential listings exist, as well as a variety of reasons why people sell their properties. Often, the development of listing techniques is a matter of recognizing these reasons and developing a method of keeping in contact with owners who are contemplating a move and require real estate services. Some basic reasons to move include family, employment, financial status, neighbourhood, and prestige requirements.

Application Experienced salespeople report a wide range of popular listing sources.

- For sale by owner ads and signs.
- Former buyers.
- Neighbours of listings taken.
- Expired listings that did not sell.
- Direct mail to prime areas.
- Cold calling (telephone).
- Advertising for specific properties.
- Furniture for sale ads.
- Business transfer notices.

- Builders of custom homes.
- Social contacts and clubs.
- News items regarding marriages and business changes.
- Lawyers, estates, and foreclosures.
- Mortgage companies, insurance companies, and lenders.
- Legal notice column in the local newspaper.
- Personnel officers in key industries.

The above list is by no means complete. Salespeople should develop their own favourite forms of prospecting for listing leads and referrals.

Marketing the Property

Once a listing is obtained, a copy should be returned to the brokerage and copies distributed within the office, pursuant to brokerage policy. The salesperson is responsible for verification of any information not completed at time of listing. If the listing is MLS, as opposed to exclusive, a copy must be forwarded to the real estate board pursuant to appropriate rules and regulations.

A convenient time should be arranged for an initial inspection by the sales representatives working for the brokerage (and co-operating brokerages if an MLS listing). An inspection immediately acquaints a large group of salespeople with the property, assists in verifying the value of the property, creates a good impression on both the seller and the salespeople, and saves the owner from a host of individual inspections.

Floor Duty Time

Office time assigned to sales representatives for servicing phone calls and walk-in trade pertinent to inquiries on, and listing of, properties. The procedure for handling floor duty, assignment of times, and in fact the existence of such times vary greatly and are wholly dependent upon brokerage policy and employment contracts between salespeople and the employing brokerage.

If duty time is provided in the brokerage, certain tips and guidelines might help.

- The immediate impression of potential clients contacting the brokerage is often dictated by the floor duty person.
- Be well informed about all listed property, have ready access to needed books, and be aware of all advertised property. In particular, keep the most recent advertisements within easy reach for fast reference. Don't forget to have copies of good *backups* to the advertised property. Remember! The caller seldom buys the advertised property. It just caught their interest. It's up to you to find the right property.

- Be well organized. Don't shuffle needlessly to get such things as listing books, scratch paper, calculator, amortization book, area maps, and appointment books.

Some brokerages use a recording sheet completed by the sales representative to provide input about which properties are generating activity and which advertisements are effective. Often, the duty salesperson will provide assistance to other salespeople and co-operating brokerages. In small offices, this can include handling calls and taking messages for fellow sales representatives.

For Sale Sign

A sign is on duty 24-hours a day. The lack of a sign can seriously limit a high percentage of potential customers or clients as many prospective buyers often drive around areas looking for signs.

The *for sale* sign informs all the neighbours that the home is for sale. Neighbours are a good source of referrals for their friends and relatives. Some may even be potential buyers. Sellers may occasionally object, saying that they do not wish the neighbours to know. In reality, the neighbours will know given all the marketing activity planned and frequent visits by salespeople.

Many factors should be considered concerning the use of a *for sale* sign.

- In a high traffic area, the sheer volume of people walking or driving by the property is effective advertising for the listing.
- The sign allows the property to speak for itself.
- For the real estate salesperson and brokerage, the sign is a form of general advertising that enhances personal as well as brokerage image, and the sold sticker is an excellent success advertisement for the neighbourhood.
- The *for sale* sign is an inexpensive form of advertisement.
- Don't forget, a sign placed too long may become an advertisement of lack of action and other sellers may not use your services.
- Signs should be regularly inspected and maintained.
- Lack of attention to the sign can seriously affect the brokerage's relationship with the owner. Consider the impression left if the seller has to report that the sign has been down or damaged for the last few weeks.
- Most real estate boards have MLS rules and regulations concerning the placement of MLS stickers on signs.

Municipalities often control the size and placement of signs on properties. Certain areas require permission to erect a sign (e.g., adjacent to a public highway or thoroughfare), or areas where signs are not permitted (e.g., obstructing the view at an intersection).

Handling Calls

The two major objectives in handling a call are:

- Create a good first impression; and
- Arrange for a face-to-face appointment.

Use an incoming call form to:

- Serve as a reminder to get specific information regarding the caller; and
- Provide backup questions to gain needed information.

Develop good telephone etiquette: speak to prospects, not at them. Be forthcoming with information, involve the prospect, qualify as to needs, ask pertinent questions, and above all, be helpful. The telephone call paves the way for a successful face-to-face meeting.

Meeting the Prospect

People buy from people they like and trust. Keep in mind that buyers are forming a first impression and may have had unsatisfactory experiences in the past.

- Demonstrate genuine interest and sincerity. Pay special attention to the image projected, overall demeanour, and verbal and body language portrayed.
- Take the time to determine whether the prospects are genuinely interested as well as qualified buyers.
- Qualify the prospects specifically concerning their needs, desires and financial capabilities.
- Review agency with them and establish the ground rules.

Obtaining the Offer

So much has been written and so many opinions expressed about closing the sale that many believe it is a separate and distinct function that can only occur at a pre-determined point. Nothing is further from the truth. Closing begins at the point of listing the property. An old saying is worth repeating: *a well-listed property is half sold.* With a realistically priced, well described property, the process is already under way.

A point exists in every successful transaction when the sales representative must ask for the offer. However, nothing is worse than asking for an offer before someone is ready to buy.

- Closing is not a pressure technique, but a matter of providing assurance to buyers that what they have in mind emotionally also has merit from an objective viewpoint.
- Good salespeople listen and watch for signs of true interest, e.g., minor criticisms, phrases indicating acceptance, anticipated presence in the home (e.g.,

We could use this room as a den.), and confirmation of a certain preference (e.g., *That's a great location for the TV*).

Many closing techniques are advanced in sales training materials. Following are four popular approaches.

Comparison   Faced with two alternatives, the buyer can make exact comparisons of benefits and features. The process then becomes not one of *Should I buy?* but rather *Which one should I buy?*

Advantages vs. Disadvantages   This approach is often referred to as the *Benjamin Franklin technique.* Franklin would draw a line down the middle of a sheet of paper and list all positive arguments on one side and all negative arguments on the other. An affirmative decision would simply be based on positives outweighing negatives.

Minor Details   Often buyers can progress from minor details to major decisions. The preparation of an offer involves a number of more or less minor items, e.g., chattels, fixtures, and conditions. Start there and work toward the major decision.

Confirming Advantages   Ideal for buyers who have found the right property but are unsure about making a decision. By summarizing major advantages and directing their attention away from minor details, things fall into proper perspective. Don't forget to summarize the benefits of home ownership and not just the features of a specific home. Home ownership can provide security, a hedge against inflation, an attractive neighbourhood, and above all personal satisfaction.

Open House

The open house can be an effective marketing tool if used correctly. The three purposes for holding an open house are:

- To expose the listed property to available buyers;
- To build a portfolio of potential buyers; and
- To demonstrate to the sellers that the best efforts are being used to market and sell the property.

The overall success of an open house often hinges on seller as well as salesperson preparation. Discuss in detail the brokerage's policies concerning the holding of open houses. The protection of the sellers' personal property is particularly important. Valuables such as jewellery, knick knacks and fragile decorative items should be removed and stored away from view. Risk of theft or damage should be minimized.

A few extra tips might help:

- Brokerage policies should clearly set out seller and salesperson responsibilities when offering an open house.
- Have a marketing strategy to attract traffic, e.g., classified ads, flyers, advising neighbours, and calls/faxes to other brokerages.
- Don't forget directional signs on the day of the open house.
- Be prepared to be present throughout the time period, with provision for backup should an overflow of viewers occur or an individual visitor requires extra attention.
- Salespeople often provide feature sheets regarding the property. Make certain they are accurate and up-to-date.
- Have a registration system (name, address and telephone number), for all persons visiting the property.

Open house control is the salesperson's responsibility. If too large a crowd is causing a problem, admit new visitors only as others leave.

- When the open house is over, each room should be checked carefully and left in the same condition as before the event.
- Brokerages typically have specific policies concerning open houses and lock-up/closing procedures.
- Owners should be thanked and provided immediate feedback.

Thank You notes to guests and follow-up of leads obtained are essential.

Qualifying the Buyer

Qualifying is more an art than a science. One of the most effective methods is to be totally open with the buyers. Bring them to the realization that it is a waste of everyone's time to show them properties that they cannot afford to buy or those that do not satisfying their needs. Listen carefully and look beyond responses given to questions to determine basic needs as opposed to desires, as well as underlying motivating factors. During the qualifying process, it is not uncommon to probe several times in determining actual motivations. Two of the most effective phrases to accomplish this are simply: *Why do you feel that way?* and *Are there any other reasons?*

To properly qualify a buyer, the salesperson should delve into three areas.

- General background, such as employment information, details about existing home, amount of equity (if applicable), lifestyle information, amenities and features in present home, and goals.

- Physical and functional requirements such as number of bedrooms required, number of cars, preferred heating system, need for certain large rooms (e.g., dining room or family room), interests, hobbies, and *absolutely must have* versus *would be nice to have*.
- Financial capabilities including discussion of GDS and TDS ratios, type of information required, examples of common mortgage application forms used in the local area, and a general understanding of the price range of property to be inspected.
- The urgency of the buyer's desire to relocate will shed light on the primary motivation to seek a new home, e.g., a busy street could indicate a motivation to provide a better, safer environment for small children.
- Discussion of the buyer's experiences in the real estate market may indicate factors that the salesperson will have to overcome. For example, they may have already seen fifteen or twenty houses and have become confused or frustrated by the exercise.
- Determine whether the buyers are analytical or emotional about a purchase and respond accordingly.
- Determine whether someone else's approval will be required, for example, another family member.

The scope of qualifying will depend on the salesperson's role with the buyer, i.e., fiduciary (client) or non-fiduciary (customer).

Showing the Property

Proper qualification of buyers sets the groundwork for successful showings. The actual showing is a pivotal step. Be adequately prepared and sensitive to feedback during the showing. Various guidelines are provided to assist with more effective showings.

- When setting appointments, avoid meeting the buyers at the property. There are several reasons:
  - a loss of opportunity to show the neighbourhood;
  - they may not find the property;
  - the buyers may arrive early and attempt to contact the seller directly or take a dislike to the exterior and drive away, leaving behind a frustrated seller and salesperson; and
  - it is too convenient for the buyers to simply depart without any opportunity for post qualifying.
- Make sure that all appointments are confirmed on the day of showing, both with prospective buyers and with sellers.
- Always try to prepare the seller well in advance so that he/she can *spruce up* the property in addition to acting on any recommendations made at the time of listing the property.

- Try not to have the seller present unless situations arise where they are an essential source of information, or can in some way assist in the showing.

- When showing properties listed with other brokerages, make all arrangements through the listing brokerage. Circumstances may arise requiring the listing salesperson to be present during the showing of the property. However, procedures on such matters will vary.

- All properties should be thoroughly inspected ahead of showings to avoid unpleasant surprises. If the property has not been pre-inspected, the salesperson should openly disclose this to the buyer.

- Showing of several properties can cause confusion. Following each showing, the buyer should be re-qualified. This may, in turn, necessitate rearranging subsequent appointments.

- Some salespeople prefer to prepare information lists regarding each property being shown and briefly introduce the buyer to these lists before the showing process. In addition, many booklets are available that give buyers basic information about purchasing a property including a home evaluation checklist.

- If there are negative attributes about a property, disclose these before the showing. The buyer is then not surprised by the drawbacks and not so easily predisposed to a negative impression. Caution is advised, however, as people's tastes differ. What the sales representative views as a drawback may not in fact appear so to others.

- Some believe that an ideal sequence to the order of showing properties exist, but in reality many factors can vary the approach.

- According to experienced salespeople, the majority of buyers purchase the location first and then the specific features within a home second. Therefore, place emphasis on the neighbourhood, amenities and general locale of the house. Secondly, discuss the layout and specific features. Plan the route taken and make certain the drive is a safe one, in a clean car.

- During the drive, discuss the amenities offered in the locale and be sensitive to the buyer's reaction. You may have selected the wrong area.

- Be patient during the showing and allow the buyer adequate time to investigate the property.

- If an important feature has been overlooked, mention it. Otherwise, resist any attempt at ongoing conversation, except to expand on comments made. Effective listening is a vital aspect of any showing.

- Watch the actions and expressions of the buyer.

- Try to keep the showing positive from the start to the end, regardless of whether the buyers like the property. Remember, both positive comments and criticisms have value in narrowing the field.

- Empathize with the concerns raised. Tread carefully, be helpful and understanding. It's their decision, not yours.

- Do not be misled or dismayed by people who are critical. Often, people criticize what they like, and are merely setting the stage for negotiations. No objections can often mean no interest. Experience will inevitably show that someone who loves everything may have great difficulty in making a decision.

- Do not be afraid to leave people alone for a short period of time. Often they need that time to discuss key issues.

- People who bring an expert friend are often insecure about their own competence. Be prepared to treat such friends as true experts and sell to them as much as to the buyer.

- Following the showing and assuming that a particular property is not the house to buy, continue the qualifying process. There is no such thing as an unsuccessful showing. By constantly requalifying the buyers as to required features and benefits, the right property is moving one step closer.

LISTING PRESENTATION (MANUAL)

A structured, typically visual, presentation package used by various brokerages to present real estate marketing services. Most listing presentation manuals contain information about the brokerage, salespeople, and services provided to the buying and selling public. The manual is often customized to suit a salesperson's needs. The majority of listing presentation manuals focus on answering three fundamental questions.

- Why list through a brokerage?
- Why utilize this brokerage?
- Why utilize a specific salesperson?

A typical listing presentation manual might include:

- Brokerage history.
- Examples of advertising.
- Pictures of office and salespeople.
- Statement of brokerage expertise including specialities.
- Listing forms.
- Market comparison guide.
- Reference and 'Thank You' letters.
- Complimentary services to assist in marketing property.
- Success statistics/testimonials.

In addition, many manuals have flexibility to include personalized information to suit individual selling situations. The manual can be used to direct and guide conversation during the listing interview, to reinforce the sales representative's case for listing the property, and explain to the owner how the property would be marketed, if the owner decides to list with that brokerage.

LISTING PRESENTATION (PROCESS)

Most owners realize that selling a home is a complicated matter and seek professional, knowledgeable service. A salesperson should be prepared to demonstrate how he/she will provide such services and in doing so, should explain how many complications can be minimized through the use of a brokerage.

Application   Practitioners can be better prepared to answer questions and provide a well-researched presentation by recognizing the concerns of most owners. While every presentation is unique, the answers to various questions and tips for better presentations can assist in the process.

Questions to Consider

- Do I know the owner's motivation for selling?
- Do I know the neighbourhood and site?
- Do I know financing alternatives?
- Do I know when they purchased and for how much?
- Do I have comparable properties ready?
- Do I have ready, motivated prospects?
- Did I advise the owner to gather all legal documents?
- Will I require one or two appointments?
- Do I have my listing presentation planned?

Tips for a Better Listing Presentation

- Take the same amount of time in listing a property as you would if you were presenting an offer.
- Go to the sellers well prepared to make a proper listing presentation.
- Know all the recent comparable sales in the area.
- Know the financial status of the average buyer who will be looking for a home in that area.
- Study the mortgage business and be well enough informed to properly advise sellers wishing to participate in seller take back financing.
- Get accurate and complete information regarding the listing, e.g., lot size, taxes, and mortgages.

- Discuss with sellers the harm that is done by listing property too high and that in fact, overpriced listings help sell other houses.
- Explain to the sellers how they can easily lose the right buyer for their home. If they are thinking in terms of an asking price and a selling price, the difference must be very small or they may discourage genuine buyers.
- Show the seller the difference between sentimental value and real value.
- Be fair with sellers. Accentuate the selling features of the home and, at the same time, point out all the features that will impede the sale of the property.
- Point out to sellers what they should do to make their properties show better without additional costs, e.g., tidying up and general appearance.

LISTING PRICE

The price at which a property is offered for sale in the market, frequently referred to as the *asking price*. The listing price may equal market value depending on circumstances surrounding a particular property and seller. Listing price is usually established based on information concerning current sales, available inventory in the market of a comparable nature, and properties recently for sale that did not sell, and were removed from the market.

Application   Ideally, the listing price is established to attract informed buyers, while being competitive with other properties now on the market that offer similar features and/or benefits. Experience and judgement are required in establishing a realistic listing price that will attract willing buyers and result in the highest price assuming a reasonable exposure of the property to the market. A salesperson's ability to properly establish listing price, given market conditions and supply/demand forces, can directly impact the final selling price of a property.

LISTING TYPES

Three basic listing types are found in Canadian markets.

Open Listing

Generally described as relatively loose, verbal arrangements in which the owner gives one or more brokerages authority to find a buyer for the property. Occasionally the owner may even agree to the placing of the brokerages' signs on the property (more common with vacant land). The seller reserves the right to sell the property himself/herself and avoid any commission.

The terms of an open listing may be committed to written form, but in practice, most sellers who will not agree to an exclusive or MLS listing, will also typically refuse to sign a written open listing. Since most open listings are verbal, they are usually avoided, or at least very cautiously handled by most real estate brokerages.

Exclusive Listing

An exclusive listing gives one brokerage the authority to offer a property for sale, lease, or exchange, during a specified time period. The seller agrees to pay the listing brokerage a commission, even if he/she sells the property directly. A variety of listing agreements and data input forms (used for property particulars), exist in the marketplace.

MLS Listing

An MLS listing is an exclusive listing with an added marketing feature. Multiple Listing Services are operated by real estate boards. A signed multiple listing form contains an authority from the seller permitting the listing brokerage to employ the services of co-operating brokerages who are members of the real estate board. The responsibility regarding promotion, negotiations, and payment of commission to co-operating brokerages rests with the listing brokerage. An MLS listing is always in writing.

LIVE LOAD

The dynamic or moveable weight within a structure, for example, furniture, machinery, personnel, and inventory. Dead load refers to components making up the actual floor structure, e.g., floor weight and bearing partitions on the floor. Live load is measured in terms of number of pounds per square foot (psf) or its metric equivalent. Building codes are typically written based on distributed live loads.

Example	***Live Load Calculation***

An office has two chairs, a desk, a credenza, and three book shelves. The live load is calculated as follows:

	# OF POUNDS
Two Chairs (40 pounds each)	80
Desk	125
Credenza	100
Shelves (40 pounds each)	80
Books, Records, and Other Items	350
Personnel	200
Total Live Load	935

Continued...

If the office measures 12 feet x 15 feet, the total square footage is 180. If each pound of live load was evenly distributed over the floor area, the distributed live load would be 5.19 pounds per square foot (live load divided by area).

Selected live loads (metric and imperial), excerpted from a provincial building code, are provided in **Figure L.8** for illustration purposes only. Live load requirements depend on the intended use and occupancy of a particular structure. See the applicable provincial building code for detailed requirements.

Typical Specified Uniformly Distributed Live Loads

	kPa	psf
Office areas in office buildings (main floor)	4.8	100
Office areas in office buildings (above first floor)	2.4	50
Equipment areas and service rooms	3.6	75
Exits and Fire Escapes	4.8	100
Corridors, lobbies and aisles	4.8	100

Distributed Live Load   Figure L.8

LIVING AREA (RESIDENTIAL)

The Alliance for Canadian Real Estate Education (ACRE) provides guidelines concerning the measurement of houses and living areas. The premise of these guidelines is that the living area of a residential building is the total floor area of the building situated above grade level.

In the case of bi-level, split level and other multi-level buildings, the living area is the sum of the gross area of each floor included within the structure, situated at or above grade. Living area includes the square area of all utility rooms, storage areas and cupboards, located on the same level(s) as the main living areas(s).

The following should not be considered or included as part of the living area of residential buildings: porches, decks, patios (closed in, screened in, or not), garages, carports, recreational or cold rooms in basements, or other areas situated below grade that do not have (at minimum) crawlspace below. These areas, situated below grade, should be shown separately on the listing under property description.

In the case of a condominium, the living area is usually defined by the square area resulting from measurements taken from the centre line of the demising walls. In multi-level condominiums, the area of each floor would be added.

Reference   See the **Appendix** for measurement guidelines.

LOADING DOCK

An area found primarily in commercial and industrial structures designed for the on-loading and off-loading of products, usually at truck level height. Common dock features are itemized.

- Shelters are flexible, enclosed canopies designed to reduce wind drafts between trucks and interior areas.
- Levellers provide an adjustable platform between trucks and the permanent docking areas. Levellers are rated in terms of lift capacity and are normally driven by hydraulic motors.
- Wells service inclined dock areas for structures built at grade level. The inclined areas require storm drains and, therefore, are not as popular in modern buildings.
- Dock high loading offering direct loading, has become popular. The dock height will depend on the type of facility being serviced, e.g., a courier company will have lower dock levels to accommodate package vans, while a food distribution terminal will have higher docks for tractor-trailer units.
- Grade level loading for areas that are level with surrounding parking and related areas permitting direct access to and from the structure by forklifts and other vehicles. Various big-box retailers provide grade level loading areas for customer pickup, e.g., electronic, building materials, and furniture stores.

LOAN COMMITMENT
(SEE LETTER OF COMMITMENT)

LOAN CONSTANT
(SEE MORTGAGE CONSTANT)

LOAN-TO-VALUE (LEVERAGE) RATIO

The ratio of the principal amount of a loan or mortgage to the lending value of the property. This ratio is one of several measures used by lending institutions in determining whether to grant a loan or mortgage.

Example   *Loan-to-Value (Leverage) Ratio*

Jones wants to purchase a property for $200,000 and is seeking a $150,000 mortgage. The lender advises Jones that he can secure a conventional mortgage on the property provided that the loan ratio is .75 (75% of the appraised value of the property). If the value comes in less than that amount, a high ratio mortgage will have to be obtained. The lender sends its loan officer to inspect the premises and determine the market value. The appraisal report places the value at $205,000 or a loan-to-value ratio of .73 (73% of appraised value).

LOCATIONAL FACTORS

A term most commonly associated with the appraisal of real property. The location of a particular property must be viewed in terms of its relationship to surrounding facilities and conditions impacting the value of that property. The assessment of locational factors forms part of the overall process of site analysis when appraising property. Common locational factors include such things as patterns of land use within the immediate area, availability of utilities, access to transportation, stores, and recreation, general upkeep of the neighbourhood, hazards and nuisances, and traffic flows.

Example   *Locational Factors*

Seller Smith is having his residential property appraised for mortgage purposes. The appraiser is particularly interested in locational factors affecting value. Smith inquires about just what types of locational factors might impact his property. The appraiser provides the following explanation:

Location is always expressed in terms of the relationship of the site to surrounding and nearby facilities and nuisances. In looking at your property, I will probably consider the following four major factors.

1. Land Use Pattern in the Area
The location of various types of land uses within a city or neighbourhood is not determined at random. Uses come about in response to market demand and are effectively controlled by zoning by-laws. Your home is not adversely affected as most properties in the area are similar in size, structure, and overall condition.

Continued…

2. Access
Proximity to desired facilities such as schools, shopping centres, workplaces, recreational centres, and other civic facilities is a plus factor. While your home is located somewhat distant from the main shopping areas, a small shopping complex is only two blocks away. Public transportation facilities are just down the street, as is a small park. Overall, these locational factors are a positive force in establishing your value.

3. Corner Influence
The effect of a corner location on value depends on the type of land use. Commercial corners provide the site with additional access and exposure for advertising purposes. Corners for single-family residential properties may have an adverse effect on value. Residential corners often lack private rear yards, an amenity usually sought by the buyer. Corner properties may also cause the owner additional maintenance, e.g., snow removal and side yard upkeep. The fact that your home is located on a corner will have a negative impact on the value.

4. Hazards and Nuisances
The existence of nearby hazards and nuisances such as non-conforming land uses, noise, odour and traffic have a detrimental effect. There are no such deficiencies impacting your property or its value.

LOCATIONAL OBSOLESCENCE

The loss in value that a structure incurs as a result of negative environmental forces beyond the boundaries of the property. Locational obsolescence is one of two subcategories under the broader category of external obsolescence, the other being economic obsolescence.

Application   Depreciation due to locational obsolescence is normally calculated based on paired sales data or capitalization of income loss. With paired sales data, appraisers isolate the impact of locational obsolescence through analysis of comparable properties. The amount of depreciation may be attributable to the building and land, to the land only, or to the building only, depending on circumstances surrounding the subject property. With capitalization of rent loss, depreciation is determined by capitalizing the rent loss attributable to locational factors. The resulting capitalized value will represent the loss to both the land and building. The appraiser must make the determination of whether the loss in value is attributable to both land and building, or otherwise.

Example   *Locational Obsolescence–Building*

The subject property is located next to a gas station. As a result, the appraiser estimates that the rental loss will be $1,080 per year. Analysis of overall capitalization rates suggests a rate of 9%. For illustration purposes, the ratio of the value of land to buildings is 1 to 3 or 25% of value to land and 75% of value to building.

Depreciation = Annual Rental Loss ÷ Overall Cap Rate
= $1,080 ÷ .09 = $12,000

Ratio of Land to Building: 1:3
(or .25/.75 expressed as a decimal)

Building Depreciation = $12,000 x .75 = $9,000

LOFT (CONDOMINIUM)

A type of condominium usually created through the renovation of existing warehousing and factory buildings in downtown core areas of large urban centres. Loft condominium units are typically *open concept* in design while integrating structural components of the existing building. Facilities and amenities will vary based on the targeted clientele. Loft condominiums have become particularly popular with young urban professionals given the eclectic nature of many projects and the ease of access to downtown retail, business, and entertainment areas.

LONG-LIVED ITEMS

Basic structural components that, in the normal course of events, have economic lives that match or exceed the economic life of the entire structure.

Example   *Long-Lived Items*

Anne Appraiser is determining the value of an older property in the downtown area. For appraisal purposes, she places the total economic life of the improvements at 50 years and bases various calculations concerning depreciation on that figure. Two long-lived items meet or exceed that 50-year level. The exterior supporting walls have an economic life that matches that of the total structure. The property also has a copper roof that should function effectively for 80 to 100 hundred years. Both are considered long-lived items.

LONG-TERM LIABILITY
(SEE ALSO BALANCE SHEET)

For accounting purposes, financial obligations that are due beyond one year, such as a mortgage.

LOT GRADING

The preparation of rough and finished grades for a site, typically based on construction specifications set out in appropriate development plans.

Application   Proper lot grading is particularly important when dealing with wet basements. No foundation wall system is completely impervious to water. Therefore, the likelihood of water penetration into basements and crawl spaces is partially dependent upon the grading of the land adjacent to the foundation walls. If less water is present in the soil on the outside of the foundation wall, theoretically, less chance exists of water getting to the interior.

The majority of wet basement problems can be eliminated, or at least reduced to a tolerable level, by improvements to exterior grading and proper performance of eavestroughs and downspouts. The ground immediately adjacent to the foundation wall should slope away from the house at a rate of one inch per foot for at least the first six feet. This can usually be accomplished by adding topsoil (not sand or gravel).

Where the general topography of the lot and surrounding lots is such that water is directed toward the house, further measures are sometimes required. A swale (a shallow ditch with gently sloped sides) can be constructed to divert water run off around the house to areas that are lower-lying. If the general topography of the neighbourhood is such that the house lies in the lowest area, grading improvements may help the situation; however, further measures may be necessary.

LOT SIZE

For appraisal purposes, the dimensions of a site consist of the following:

- Frontage is that side of a site that abuts a public street or highway. Frontage is basic to value and is an important factor in determining accessibility and prominence.
- Depth is the distance between the front and rear lot lines.
- Width is the distance between the side lines of a lot. The depth and width of a lot may be consistent, or they may vary, depending upon its shape.
- Shape of a site is its form, determined by the frontage, depth, and width.
- Area is the size of the site, measured in square metres, square feet, hectares, and acres.

As a matter of consistency in real estate documents, when making reference to the frontage and depth of sites, the frontage measurement is always shown first.

In waterfront cottage properties, frontage commonly refers to the side that abuts the body of water given its inherent value. If applicable, practitioners should clearly set out lot size so that prospective buyers are not confused and the appropriate frontage is identified. Typically, a seller can provide an existing survey pending full investigation of the property by the buyer.

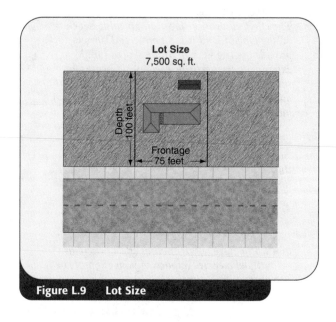

Figure L.9   Lot Size

National Info Links

Mapping

For national initiatives involving mapping and geospatial information, contact:

Natural Resources Canada
Canadian Geospatial Data Infrastructure
615 Booth Street
Ottawa, ON K1A 0E9

Telephone   (877) 221 6213
Web Site   www.cgdi.gc.ca

For provincial programs involving aerial mapping and related projects contact the appropriate provincial ministry/department.

Market Data

For national, provincial, and local housing statistics, contact:

Canada Mortgage and Housing Corporation
700 Montreal Road
Ottawa, ON K1A 0P7

Telephone   (613) 748 2000
Web Site   www.cmhc-schl.gc.ca

For national statistics on Canadian MLS activity, contact:

Canadian Real Estate Association
344 Slater Street, Suite 1600, Canada Building
Ottawa, ON K1R 7Y3

Telephone   (613) 237 7111
Web Site   crea.ca
            www.mls.ca

Multiple Listing Service

The Canadian Real Estate Association provides Internet access to most local real estate board MLS services.

Web Site   www.mls.ca

MAJOR TENANT
(SEE ANCHOR TENANT)

MAJOR VERTICAL PENETRATIONS

A term used in BOMA standard measurements for buildings—includes stairs, elevator shafts, flues, pipe shafts, vertical ducts and the like, including enclosing walls, which serve more than one floor of a building. These penetrations do not include stairs, dumbwaiters, lifts, etc., exclusively serving a tenant occupying offices on more than one floor.

Application   Major vertical penetrations impact the total rentable area in a commercial office building. The rentable area is used to set the tenant's pro rata share of the entire office floor on which the tenant is situated. The tenant's actual space is referred to as the *useable area*. The difference between rentable and useable areas is reflected in this pro rata share. When determining rentable area of an office floor, major vertical penetrations are excluded from the measurement process.

MAJORITY, AGE OF
(SEE ALSO MINOR)

The age at which an individual is legally entitled to certain rights of citizenship, e.g., voting and entering into contracts.

MALL

An area designated for pedestrian use commonly found in shopping centres or downtown areas in which parts or all of selected streets have been closed for pedestrian traffic. Also, the term *mall* is frequently used to reference a shopping centre, e.g., an outlet mall, a regional shopping mall, and a neighbourhood mall.

MANAGEMENT (REAL ESTATE BROKERAGE)

The achievement of pre-determined objectives and goals through the activities, efforts, and actions of others. In real estate brokerage, major management duties can be summarized under the following headings:

Legal   To ensure that salespeople conform with all legal responsibilities concerning real estate transaction.

Regulatory   To ensure that salespeople conform with all regulatory requirements pursuant to the provincial real estate act.

Ethical   To promote and maintain high ethical standards and professional conduct and enforce applicable codes of ethics.

Record Keeping   To provide a proper accounting, sales record, and trade processing system that ensures accuracy in all documentation and is in full compliance with regulatory directives and accepted industry practices.

Personnel   To administer the office and all personnel in a diligent and fair manner, in compliance with acceptable procedures and legal requirements.

Training   To offer educational programs that provide staff with skills development and up-to-date material relating to the marketplace.

Quality Control   To render competent advice and direction to salespeople in all matters relating to real estate transactions usual to a brokerage office.

Application   Real estate management is somewhat unique given the reality of overseeing commission salespeople. While typically the legal relationship under the applicable provincial real estate act is one of employee/employer, real estate salespeople operate much more independently than their counterparts in the corporate world.

- Rarely are salespeople asked to conform to a structured work schedule, or paid any form of salary. While acknowledging accountability to the brokerage, today's sophisticated salespeople perceive the brokerage portion of gross commission as a cost of doing business. This attitude, uncommon in the salary-driven corporate world, can be a challenge to management.

- The relationship between salespeople is also unique. Although they work together, the salespeople are usually in competition with each other. The manager must create a team feeling that complements individual, often conflicting, aspirations and career perspectives.

- High employee turnover and the nature of the working relationship are in contrast to the corporate world of pensions, seniority levels, and normal corporate stability. Success in real estate management is the ability to develop and maintain a productive, stable sales force, given such factors.

- External influences, including economic swings, government legislation, and local municipal decisions can cause sudden, sometimes dramatic, marketplace shifts. These can affect both personnel attitudes and confidence levels.

- Salespeople can often be prone to personal, financial, and domestic concerns, given the instability of the work. Self-discipline in salespeople and leadership in management are essential qualities.

Real estate management can be unique. The following example illustrates how a salesperson's skills may not always translate into management expertise.

Example   *Management (Real Estate Brokerage)*

B. Davis recently received a promotion to manager of the east branch of ABC Realty Inc. He had been a salesperson at the same location for the past two years. His efficiencies were noted by Broker/Owner Johnson. Davis always prided himself on his extensive client retention system and computer-driven, mail-merge program. Happily, he brought this talent to his new management role. Notice boards became crammed with management directives, training programs were compulsory, precise guidelines abounded for practically every situation: e.g., letter preparation, procedures for open houses, and required materials in listing presentations and, of course, his client retention system was mandatory.

Two top salespeople, slighted as they had not been seriously considered for the promotion, started an office undercurrent. Very quickly, *for Davis* and *against Davis* camps sprouted in the office. Three months later, both top people had left, the office structure and morale were in shambles, a number of salespeople were physically there but mentally gone, and the client retention system was gathering dust. To avoid further confrontation, Broker/ Owner Johnson took over the management reins and Davis' retreat back to selling was a foregone conclusion.

Davis was a victim of real estate management reality. New managers can rarely progress without respect, acceptance, and commitment by the sales force. The Davis' story might have been different had he taken the time to manage one-on-one. Proper techniques directed at individual salespeople might have blossomed over time into effective control. Perhaps, initially, a few could have tried his client system. Their successes might have provided the testimonies and building blocks in converting others. The mandatory meetings also caused problems—the term *compulsory* is often viewed by salespeople as offensive or threatening. Salespeople are justifiably preoccupied with their own needs. If the meeting is valued, it will be attended. B. Davis was entrenched in efficiency, but forgot to be effective.

MANAGEMENT AGREEMENT

A written agreement, typically involving a property owner who contracts the management of a property to an individual manager or firm. The agreement details the rights and obligations of both parties.

In a brokerage, a management agreement usually refers to an agreement between the broker/owner and real estate office manager concerning the administration of the head office or a branch office. Standard management agreements do not exist, but as the example illustrates, certain topics are typically addressed.

Example   *Management Agreement*

Broker/Owner Johnson, of ABC Realty Inc., is designing a management agreement for B. Gallo, the new office sales manager. The agreement consists of four parts along with attached schedules.

Management Agreement—ABC Realty Inc.

Part 1: Status of Parties and Terms of Engagement
- Contract to spell out requirements as set out in the applicable real estate act/regulations.
- Statement of general role of the manager and responsibilities to brokerage.
- Inclusion of probationary period.

Part 2: Responsibilities and Rights of the Broker
- Payments of compensation.
- Provisions of services, facilities, and management assistance as required.
- Reasons and procedures for immediate termination.
- Return of company materials and related matters upon termination.
- Monies due manager at time of termination.
- Non-disclosure of confidential information.

Part 3: Responsibilities and Rights of the Manager
- Payment of selected expenses by brokerage.
- Provision of any benefit plans.
- Duties and responsibilities.
- Compliance with applicable rules, regulations, board by-laws, and provincial statutory requirements.
- Procedures for negotiating disputes.

Part 4: General Provisions
- Inability to assign agreement.
- Delivery of notices.
- Partial invalidity and enforcement of remaining contractual terms.
- Contract represents the entire agreement.
- All remedies are cumulative in nature.
- Schedules attached to and forming part of agreement.

Attached Schedules
- Method of compensation, e.g., salary, override, and/or bonus.
- Method of computing overrides, if applicable.
- Definition of terms used in calculating compensation, e.g., gross commission income, adjusted gross income, and net profit.

M

MANAGEMENT DIARY

A brokerage diary, often referred to as the *deal diary*, that provides a convenient follow-up system for key dates involving the listing and selling of properties.

Application   The management diary is a central reference document for the manager and/or administrative staff to track such things as expiry dates on listings, supplementary trust deposits, conditions to be fulfilled, and closings. Some managers extend the diary's function to include expiry dates on salesperson registrations and brokerage related dates, e.g., expiry of insurance policies. Modern computer software packages for real estate brokerages are typically equipped with management features including listing and transaction tracking facilities together with integrated modules that link to the accounting system.

MANAGEMENT PRECEDENT FILE
(SEE ALSO POLICY MANUAL)

A recording system recommended for real estate brokerages in which all disputes, revisions, and other precedents relating to the brokerage policy manual are filed for future reference.

Application   This cumulative file is an important source document when amending policies, supporting decisions based on precedents, and providing proof that the office is consistent in making decisions regarding the policy manual should a legal dispute arise between the broker and employed salespeople. The file also serves as a reference point when the brokerage policy manual is periodically updated.

> **Example   *Management Precedent File***
>
> Broker/Owner Johnson, of ABC Realty Inc., has instituted a comprehensive brokerage policy manual based on procedures recommended by the provincial real estate association. At the same time, to ensure that policies and procedures unique to the office are properly documented, various appendices to the manual are provided.
>
> Following the announcement and distribution of the policy manual, Johnson receives and implements various recommendations from salespeople. These changes concerning dress codes, procedures for registering agreements with co-operating brokers, and mediation of internal disputes are documented and placed in the *Management Precedent File* for quick reference should appropriate situations arise. Johnson intends to update the policy manual on a semi-annual basis. The manual has already proven valuable as a handy reference for both administrative and sales staff.

MANAGER (REAL ESTATE)

Provincial   See applicable reference materials.

MANAGER, LICENSING OF

Provincial   See applicable reference materials.

MANDATORY REQUIREMENTS (EDUCATION/LICENSING)

Provincial   See applicable reference materials.

MAPS (GOVERNMENT)

Various mapping services are provided by provincial governments that can be of assistance to real estate practitioners, particularly those specializing in farm, recreational, and other rural properties. Typically, mapping services include:

- Aerial photographs, including air photo mosaics, flight index maps, and diapositive photos (positive transparency of the original negative).
- Topographical maps (availability and scope of mapping will vary by provincial jurisdiction).
- Various maps detailing highways, roads, railways, airports, ferry routes, parks, conservation areas, picnic parks, hospitals and first aid stations, car pool parking lots, service centres, tourist attractions, travel information centres, and enlargements of cities and towns (availability and scope of mapping will vary by provincial jurisdiction).

MARGINAL TAX RATE

A composite tax rate, including both provincial and federal taxes relating to real property income, applied to cash flows from investment property. The marginal tax rate normally refers to the next higher tax rate that a taxpayer would pay on additional income received, i.e., starting with the next dollar received.

In real estate investment analysis, the marginal tax rate is a forecasted rate, based on average tax rates, to provide the client with an estimate of after tax cash flows. The accuracy of the marginal tax rate depends on information provided by the client and his/her accountant, as well as the type of investment property that is under consideration.

The application of marginal tax rates is important in after tax calculations concerning real estate investment property. Estimates of after tax cash flows can be used for more accurate comparison and valuation of investment options for specific investors.

MARINE (SUBMERGED) CABLES

Cables, typically telephone and hydro, extending underwater to service locations.

Application   Traditionally, marine cables have been used in recreational areas to provide services to islands and distant cross-water locations that would otherwise not be economically viable to provide land or above-water connections. Provincial environmental requirements have curtailed the use of such cables and consequently new installations may be refused or encounter significant delays, additional requirements, and limiting conditions pending any final approval.

Reference   Contact the applicable department/ministry responsible for environmental legislation.

MARITAL HOME

Provincial   See applicable reference materials concerning spousal interests in real estate and applicable provincial legislation. Also referred to as a *matrimonial home.*

MARKET DATA APPROACH
(SEE DIRECT COMPARISON APPROACH)

MARKET-EXTRACTED DATA

A term commonly associated with appraisal techniques in which the basis for establishing estimates relies on sufficient availability of comparable sales data taken directly from the marketplace. Market-extracted data is then analyzed to estimate value or complete other calculations in the appraisal process, e.g., calculating depreciation.

MARKET GAP

A demand for real estate not currently serviced in the marketplace. Market gaps are most commonly associated with commercial properties but, in fact, apply to all types

of real estate. The size of the gap is proportionate to the opportunity for a supplier to satisfy that gap. The extent of the gap, the widening or narrowing of that gap, and the anticipated length of time that the gap will persist are determinative of the opportunity available.

Application   The assessment of market gaps can be particularly significant in commercial brokerage activity. Gap analysis is often included under the topic of *market analysis* in marketing proposals for sellers or representation proposals for buyers.

Example   *Market Gap*

Currently, 1,000,000 square feet of commercial office space is located in the downtown core of a large Canadian city. However, the anticipated demand (absorption) of commercial office space within the next year is forecasted to be 1,350,000 square feet. Assuming that no construction project will provide additional office space within the forecasted period, the market gap at the end of that year will be 350,000 square feet.

MARKET INDICATORS

In real estate brokerages, informed decisions concerning everything from budget projections to market share rely upon accurate market indicators. Given the computerization of MLS systems throughout Canada, brokerages and salespeople enjoy increasingly sophisticated measures of the market.

- Measures of the market typically include sale to list price ratio, number of days on the market, average and median price, inventory turnover ratios, and sales volume/sales unit production figures.

Brokerages have developed a wide range of complementary indicators to assess competitive stance and public awareness. The scope of indicators will vary for residential and commercial brokerages.

- Measures of the competition include MLS market share and sales force production statistics.
- Public awareness measurements have not been widely used in real estate brokerage, but can include results from customer satisfaction cards, informal data gathering, and local market surveys.

A detailed example is provided outlining typical market indicators used by residential brokerages and real estate boards. Commercial brokerages typically utilize more in-depth analysis of specific property types including factors such as vacancy and absorption rates, as well as detailed research on available inventory.

M

Example *Market Indicators (Residential)*

Broker/Owner Johnson, of ABC Realty Inc., is creating a newsletter to keep the sales force informed concerning market conditions. While still in the design stage, Johnson pinpointed certain market indicators for residential tracking purposes.

Sale to List Price Ratio This ratio measures market spread between listing and selling prices within the area serviced by ABC Realty Inc. A widening spread could be symptomatic of various factors, e.g., dropping prices, fewer buyers, and/or seller resistance to lower markets. Johnson recognizes that this measure has little relevance in isolation, but gains strength when combined with other indicators. This ratio varies only slightly over an extended period unless dramatic market shifts occur. It is therefore, of limited immediate practical value.

Number of Days on the Market This indicator reflects market strength, or more simply put, the willingness of buyers and sellers to reach agreeable terms. Salespeople need this measure not only to assess market strength, but also to illustrate the need for specific listing periods to sell reasonably priced properties.

Average Price Johnson wants to include average price, often referred to as a measure of central tendency. While of little value in any single month, average price trends can provide important insight when combined with median price over an extended period of time.

Median Price The midpoint price of all properties sold has relevance over an extended period of time. The distribution of sales within various price ranges in combination with average and median price trends can reveal a great deal about the marketplace, ranging from the types of buyers participating, amount of trade-up activity, and general trends in prices.

Turnover Provides an indication for listing/selling potential for realistically priced properties. Higher turnover translates into increased unit sales for brokerages within a particular market area. Two turnover ratios are frequently used:

Sale to Listing Ratio This ratio measures the number of sales to total inventory. Historically, a ratio of 30% has been viewed as a stable marketplace, e.g., neither buyer nor seller dominate the market. Ratios lower than 30% indicate movement toward a buyer's market with rates above 30% toward a seller's market.

Sale to New Listing Ratio This ratio measures the number of sales in relation to incoming marketplace inventory. The *Sale to New Listing Ratio* is best viewed as the replenishing factor and can be more volatile than the sale to listing ratio. Ratios approaching 1.00 (1 for 1 ratio) indicate a seller's market in which for every property listed, a property is being sold in the marketplace. Ratios above 1.00 normally appear with depleting inventory generated through a strong seller's market.

Johnson also wants to track his competition. MLS statistics in the ABC Realty Inc.'s board jurisdiction provide details of listing and selling brokers for all transactions recorded through the Multiple Listing Service. Following is an excerpt from Johnson's custom report for May involving the top four brokerages in the immediate trading area based on the *Sale to New Listing Ratio*.

Sale to New Listing Ratio for May Trading Area W07

BROKERAGE	LISTINGS	NEW LISTINGS	SALES	RATIO
LMN Realty Inc.	645	200	170	.85 to 1
XYZ Real Estate Ltd..	62	37	29	.78 to 1
ABC Realty Inc.	41	26	18	.69 to 1
EFG Realty Inc.	34	16	10	.63 to 1

MARKET POSITION

Based on the concept that market niches exist within the overall marketplace. These niches present an opportunity to provide a specific service, offer a unique product, or generally promote a distinctive image to the public.

Market positioning is likened to a horse race. In theory, consumers gain familiarity with a limited number of contenders within a specific product or service range. In simple terms, the leaders occupy a win, place, or show position. Smaller, less visible competitors are often referred to as *also rans*. The concept of market position has been particularly popular with automobile rental companies, fast-food chains, and large retail operations that require high visibility in the public's mind. This is not to say that only major players can occupy niches and that brand names always dominate. On the contrary, entrepreneurs may find specific market niches by specializing, geographically limiting their area, or identifying a unique stance that is readily understood by the buying and selling public.

Market positions must be carefully analyzed. Brokerages, for example, acquire franchise rights to assure exclusivity and promote national or international image awareness within specific territories, others promote independent status and reputation, still others concentrate on specialty markets, such as condominiums and new houses. In determining a position, it is vital to assess the competition carefully and determine what market niches are currently available and what brokerages are vulnerable to additional competition.

Example 1 *Market Position—*
Expanding Market Scope

Broker/Owner Johnson, of ABC Realty Inc., is redefining his market position. To this point, the brokerage's advertising has emphasized the long-standing leadership position in residential single-family home sales. However, the trading area is changing with more upscale condominium projects, higher density residential developments, and increased retail developments. Johnson is contemplating a more full service position to handle these opportunities.

In deciding whether or not to alter current image and promotional strategies, Johnson assesses the following items regarding market position:

Competition   What are the competitors doing? Are they increasing market share in condo and other forms of co-ownership? Have their new thrusts produced meaningful results? What types of obstacles and opportunities have confronted them?

Consistency   If the brokerage's market position changed, would the new move into alternative residential types be consistent with the image built over many years? Would the new approach be compatible with brokerage values and goals? Can the salespeople make the transition?

Financial Strength   Is there sufficient capital? Must new salespeople be recruited? What about retraining costs for existing staff? How costly is a complete image change? What are the cash requirements, if market activity diminishes during the changeover period?

Uniqueness   After the change, will the company have a unique position as a full service real estate brokerage? Will the move set the brokerage apart from the competition? Is there a better approach?

Public Acceptance   Johnson must retain existing clientele, while promoting new services. What will the public think of a new image? What are the down sides? Could the brokerage lose in the long haul if the conversion to full service does not reap immediate benefits? Will a new image be accepted?

Example 2 *Market Position—*
Expanding Market Area

Broker/Owner Johnson, of ABC Realty Inc., is considering a new branch office within a highly competitive trading area. MLS statistics indicate a steady growth in inventory and sales activity, as the area is undergoing dramatic expansion. Johnson relies heavily on market positioning theory.

Here are the questions he has developed:

- What are the unique services provided by our brokerage and how do they compare with the competition?

- Will the new location complement the broker-age's existing image and are the surrounding residential areas consistent with types of property usually marketed by ABC Realty Inc.?

Continued…

- Do the west-end residents know our image and if not, what will it cost to gain market awareness?

- Are there new marketing opportunities, that is a specific niche not occupied by the competition that might provide market share within the area?

- What types of services are offered by the competition and how will they impact our planned marketing strategy?

- Have there been brokerage failures or significant losses in market share by other new companies entering the market?

- Can ABC Realty Inc. bring a unique approach to marketing real estate that is not already being done in that particular area?

MARKET PRICE

The amount paid, or to be paid, for a property in a particular transaction. Market price is an accomplished or historic fact, as opposed to market value that remains an estimate until proven otherwise. Market price involves no assumption of prudent conduct by the buyer and/or seller and does not assume the absence of undue stimuli, reasonable exposure to the marketplace, or any other condition basic to the market value concept. Under an efficient market system, where property is openly offered and promoted to well-informed, capable buyers, market price and market value closely approximate each other.

Example *Market Price*

Seller Smith decides to offer his property for sale, but does not want to involve a real estate brokerage. Based on his cursory review of the market, Smith determines that his home is worth approximately $140,000.

A neighbour, during casual conversation, mentions that friends of his, Mr. and Mrs. Jones, would probably be interested. Smith agrees to show them the property, but is adamant about the price. Mr. and Mrs. Jones purchase the property for $135,000 with a condition on financing. The appraiser, based on recent comparable sales in the immediate area, estimates the value of the property at $148,000. Accordingly, the lender approves the mortgage.

The buyers paid the market price; the appraiser estimated the market value.

MARKET RENT

The rental income that a property would most probably command on the open market, as indicated by current rentals being paid for comparable space as of the effective date of the analysis. The term *market rent* is synonymous with *economic rent* in appraisal terminology.

M

Example — *Market Rent*

Broker/Owner Johnson, of ABC Realty Inc., is attempting to determine the market rent for office space in a high rise *Class A* office complex. While competitive space in adjacent buildings is offered with a number of incentives such as rent free periods and other landlord concessions, Johnson has adjusted the base rents of five comparable office leases that contain approximately the same square footage as the subject property. All five leases were drafted within the past four-month period and involved *Class A* or *Class B* buildings.

For purposes of illustration, assume that all additional rents payable are approximately the same. Based on this information and other factors concerning these leases, Johnson determines that the market rent (base rent) is $6.40. Therefore, the subject property, consisting of 1,740 square feet of rentable area would probably have a base rent of approximately $11,100 (rounded):

1,740 sq. ft. x $6.40 = $11,136.

LEASE	DATE	RENTABLE AREA	CLASS	BASE RENT PSF
Lease #1	Jan. 20xx	1650	A	$6.40
Lease #2	Jan. 20xx	1950	A	$6.25
Lease #3	Feb. 20xx	1750	B	$5.35
Lease #4	Mar. 20xx	1850	A	$6.15
Lease #5	Apr. 20xx	1700	B	$5.55

MARKET SURVEYS

For business purposes, a survey (either formal or informal), designed to gather opinions typically for the purposes of better understanding customer needs and wants, assessing the impact of a specific product or service in the market-place, and/or evaluating company performance in providing products or services.

Application Few brokerages currently undertake extensive market surveys. Informal studies, while not statistically significant, can assist in gaining a limited impression of public awareness of services, perception of the brokerage, satisfaction with services, and market position. **Figure M.1** illustrates a typical survey that is brief, easy to administer, and can produce interesting results.

Brokerages may discover that significant advertising dollars may have little impact, that people misunderstand the brokerage's specific services, or that customers select the brokerage for entirely different reasons than anticipated. The survey can be carried out with minimal cost. Simply ensure that the sample is sufficiently broad. Professional interviewers can be used, however, assuming limited budgets and informal results, alternate approaches may be best (e.g., use of students).

If the desired results require statistical significance and proper random sampling, get ready for a more substantial cash outlay. Keep the questionnaire short and to the point. Four or five questions will usually suffice. If productive information is received, plan a more aggressive survey strategy the next time.

MARKET SURVEY

1. Overall, how would you rate ABC Realty Inc.?
   ❏ Excellent   ❏ Good   ❏ Fair   ❏ Poor

2. Please rate the sales representative involved in your particular transaction: (check appropriate column)

	Excellent	Good	Fair	Poor
Technical Knowledge	❏	❏	❏	❏
Keeping You Informed	❏	❏	❏	❏
Overall Attitude	❏	❏	❏	❏

3. Would you recommend ABC Realty Inc. to others?
   ❏ Yes   ❏ No

   Would you recommend the sales representative to others?
   ❏ Yes   ❏ No

4. What originally prompted you to contact our brokerage? (check any or all)
   ❏ An advertisement in the newspaper
   ❏ A lawn sign on a property
   ❏ Referred by a friend/acquaintance/relative
   ❏ Dealt with ABC Realty Inc. in the past
   ❏ Personally knew a salesperson with ABC Realty Inc.
   ❏ Other_____

Sample Market Survey   Figure M.1

MARKET VALUE

The highest price in terms of money, that the property will bring to a willing seller if exposed for sale on the open market; allowing a reasonable time to find a willing buyer, buying with the knowledge of all the uses to which it is adapted and for which it can be legally used, and with neither buyer or seller acting under necessity, compulsion nor peculiar and special circumstances.

Application Market value is not to be confused with market price, i.e., the amount paid, or to be paid, for a property in a particular transaction. Market price is an accomplished or historic fact. Market price tends to closely align with market value in an efficient market system involving willing, informed buyers and sellers acting rationally and prudently, given reasonable periods of time with no undue influences. Successive market prices in the sale of comparable homes form the basis of estimating the market value of a particular property.

Market value should not be confused with cost. Expending $150,000 in constructing a new home plus $80,000 for the purchase of the land in no way ensures a market value of $230,000. However, assuming a reasonably efficient market, the difference between actual cost and market value may be negligible unless obsolescence was built into the property or intervening factors affect the marketplace, such as lack of housing supply, dynamic growth in a particular market, or extremely depressed market conditions.

Example   *Market Value*

Anne Appraiser is attempting to arrive at the market value of a property using the direct comparison approach. In completing a detailed form report, Anne has selected three comparable properties that sold within the immediate area for sale prices (market prices) of $179,000, $193,000, and $188,000. All three properties are similar to the subject property, were sold within the past four weeks, and were arm's length transactions. Anne made various adjustments to the comparable properties and arrived at the following adjusted sale prices.

PROPERTY	SALE PRICE MARKET VALUE	TOTAL ADJUSTMENTS	ADJUSTED SALE PRICE
123 Main	$179,000	+$4,500	$183,500
123 Centre	$193,000	−$8,500	$184,500
141 Main	$188,000	−$2,000	$186,000

Based on these adjusted sale prices and other factors, Anne estimates that the market value of the home using the direct comparison approach is $185,000.

MARKET VALUE APPRAISER

Acronym: MVA   A professional designation for REALTORS who have met prescribed standards and experience requirements. Courses leading to the MVA—Residential designation are offered through provincial associations.

Basic Program Structure

The Alliance for Canadian Real Estate Education (ACRE) is the grantor of the *MVA–Residential* designation. The MVA–Residential Committee at the provincial association level is charged by ACRE with the responsibility of maintaining this program. The *MVA—Residential* designation is granted for one year only, with annual renewal upon submission of documentation.

Professional Requirements

- Proof of completion for required courses;
- Proof of five years current and active experience;
- Submission of a demonstration form appraisal report;
- A proven understanding and application of the direct comparison and cost approaches;
- Proof of errors and omissions insurance;
- Certification of board/association membership; and
- Adherence to the Code of Ethics and Standards of Business Practice of The Canadian Real Estate Association.

Renewals

MVA—Residential Designees: Annual renewal entails submission of the following items:

- Renewal certificate form;
- Renewal application fee; and
- Proof of errors & omissions insurance.

Reference   Complete program details and current requirements can be obtained by contacting the appropriate provincial real estate association. Applications should be directed to the Director of Education .

The above information was summarized from detailed materials provided by ACRE with no representation concerning its accuracy or completeness.

MARKETABLE TITLE

A title that a court of equity considers to be so free from defect that it will legally force its acceptance by a buyer. Marketable title does not assume the absolute absence of defect, but rather a title that a prudent, informed buyer in the reasonable course of business would accept. For real estate practitioners, the most complete reference to title issues is found in the preprinted wording contained within an agreement/contract.

Provincial   See applicable reference materials.

MARKETING PERIOD

The length of time taken to market real property. For real estate brokerage purposes, the marketing period begins with the listing of a property to the point of sale. The average lengths of marketing periods for various types of property are an important indication of overall market conditions and are commonly tracked by real estate broker-ages and Multiple Listing Services.

MARKETING PLAN
(SEE ALSO MARKETING PROPOSAL)

A detailed description of a marketing strategy including a plan of action for the promotion of a specific property by a salesperson and real estate brokerage.

Application   A marketing plan normally includes an out-line of promotional materials to be used, intended target markets, signage, types of media selected, schedule of contacts with identified target markets, salesperson and brokerage promotional activities, and any special publicity or advertising associated with an individual project. Associated costs may be detailed and tracked, particularly if both the brokerage and the client are participating in related expenses.

Marketing plans are an essential component of any presentation to a client. In the case of residential real estate, plans are normally outlined at the point of listing presentation. With commercial specialists, both the amount of advance preparation and scope of presentation are far more extensive. The commercial marketing plan is usually contained within a broader research framework included in a *Marketing Proposal*.

MARKETING PROPOSAL

A proposal made to a seller that sets out objectives, strategy, and scope of activities for the marketing of a property. While detailed marketing proposals can be developed for residential real estate, most are associated with commercial properties.

Application   The commercial marketing proposal is typically an essential component in the listing of com-mercial properties, and actual formats will differ in the marketplace. A general layout is described.

Proposal Objectives and Scope of Work

This segment details goals concerning the marketing of the property and the tasks/responsibilities for both the client and the commercial brokerage. In other words, the *who, what, when, and at what cost* details. Customarily, a timetable is included to point of anticipated sale or lease; costing considerations (e.g., survey, engineering services, legal/accounting, environmental assessment, mortgage

cancellation fees, and marketing costs); and a detailed roll-out or schedule of activities. The proposal normally details expenses, as applicable, borne by the client and brokerage respectively.

Site, Building, and Market Analysis

Often referred to as the *technical review*, this segment out-lines several levels of analysis starting with the site (e.g., soil conditions, zoning, access/egress, land size, and environ-mental conditions), the building (e.g., size, ceiling heights, office finishes, utilities, HVAC, sprinkler systems, loading docks, security, and building construction), related matters affecting both site and building, (e.g., taxes and financing), and lastly, market analysis including community profile information, demographics, and supply/demand analysis.

The location of market analysis data within a marketing proposal is a matter of individual preference. Sometimes, statistical information is included within *Marketing Plan Development*.

Marketing Plan Development

In most proposals, this segment is best described as a pre-liminary discussion only. Having set out market indicators, the proposal identifies the selected target market along with a description of planned marketing devices (e.g., brochures, flyers, and target mailing lists). The degree of detail varies from practitioner to practitioner. At minimum, the plan should set out activities including brokerage co-operation, signage, marketing items, promotional material frequently referred to as the *offering statement*, and targeted mailing lists.

Property Valuation

Commercial practitioners rely on all three approaches to value: cost, direct comparison, and income. Normally, the proposal details the strengths/weaknesses underlying each approach, market or other information (e.g., costing con-siderations), in support of the approach(es) taken, and indicated values using each approach. At proposal stage, a range of values is customarily indicated under each approach, together with a recommendation concerning the possible range of offered price.

Listing Process and Marketing Plan Implementation

This segment details the listing process and schedule for marketing implementation. The amount of detail will vary based on individual brokerages. Brokerages may provide summary details at proposal stage, while others furnish the client with marketing prototypes and plan specifics. Given the introduction of user-friendly databases, Internet links, and desktop publishing facilities in recent years, many brokerages have pre-designed templates (referred to as *boilerplate*), for such items as marketing brochures, target letters, primary/secondary market analysis, and local statistical reports.

Negotiations and Drafting the Agreement

For proposal purposes, practitioners usually detail the types of services commonly provided to clients during negotiations and drafting agreements e.g., drafting offers to meet the specific needs of the client, presenting offers, preparation and submission of counter offers, creation of amending and condition removal forms, and such other activities as appropriate to the furtherance of the real estate transaction.

Closing the Transaction

Commercial brokerages have increasingly perceived the value of providing services to point of, and beyond, closing. The sale or lease of a property opens other opportunities that aggressive organizations have capitalized on in building market share. The concluding segment of the proposal also provides an opportunity to include a detailed resume for both salesperson and brokerage.

MASTER LEASE

A term commonly associated with leasehold interests in commercial property. The master lease is a controlling lease for the demised premises as opposed to a sublease.

MASTER/SERVANT

A master directly controls and supervises the work of the servant, who is bound to comply with all of the master's reasonable orders. The master is responsible to third parties for the servant's actions in the performance of that work. Although this relationship may have originated with the ancient doctrines of servitude, the concept persists today in relationships involving most employees in the typical business situation, including a registered real estate salesperson employed by a broker.

This employment relationship is often contrasted with an agency relationship created between principal and agent. The degree of control and direction by an employer is greater than in the relationship between principal and agent. The contrast is even greater with the independent contractor relationship, which will only be recognized when little or no direct control is exercised over the ongoing activities of the employee.

> **Example   *Master/Servant***
>
> Broker/Owner Brown, of XYZ Real Estate Ltd., is expanding her brokerage. She wants to hire approximately eight salespeople particularly to service the new house market. The salespeople will be registered under the applicable regulatory act as employees. However, each new licensee/registrant will work as an independent contractor. Accordingly, Brown is creating employee status in line with provincial statutory requirements, but each salesperson will have considerable independence in their day-to-day activities.

Provincial   See applicable reference materials.

MATRIMONIAL HOME

Broadly described as any property in which a person has an interest as a spouse, and including a property that is or was at the date of separation occupied by the person and the spouse as their family residence. Condominiums, co-operatives, and leasehold interests can be matrimonial homes from a legislative perspective. Caution is advised as terminologies, scope of property deemed to be matrimonial, and procedures concerning such properties differ by province.

Provincial   See applicable reference materials.

MATURITY (BALANCE DUE) DATE

The final day in the term of an agreement most frequently used in real estate with respect to mortgages in which any amount owing is due and payable.

MAXIMUM RENT

A term commonly associated with rent control provisions established by some provinces under residential tenancy legislation. Maximum rent normally refers to the highest rent that can be charged for a rental unit. The landlord can charge less than that amount, but not more. The maximum rent is typically based on the rent charged when the unit became a rental, plus any guideline increases permitted or other increases above the guideline allowed by previous or current legislation. Guidelines are usually revised annually.

Provincial   See applicable reference materials.

Example   *Maximum Rent*

Owner Smith owns two rental units that fall under statutory requirements because the province in which the units are located has rent control legislation. During 20xx, the maximum monthly rent was established at $975 and $925 and the one-year lease renewals are now being negotiated.

In accordance with provincial legislation, Smith is permitted a maximum statutory rent increase of 2.8%. Therefore, the maximum rents that can be charged for the following year are $1,002.30 for the main floor unit and $950.90 for the upper unit.

MEAN

The sum of a group of numbers divided by the number of values within that group. For real estate purposes, the most common measure of market activity involves the mean or average price for specific types of property. Real estate boards commonly track average prices as one of several indicators of market conditions. Average price, as a measure of central tendency, has limited value when considered in isolation and should be analyzed in conjunction with other market indicators.

Example   *Mean*

Salesperson Lee, of ABC Realty Inc., is attempting to find the average price of comparable homes recently sold on Oak Street in Anycity. Following are recently reported sales.

SALE	ADDRESS	SALE PRICE
Sale #1	38 Oak Street	$149,900
Sale #2	44 Oak Street	139,750
Sale #3	139 Oak Street	144,900
Sale #4	293 Oak Street	152,700
Sale #5	412 Oak Street	146,500

The average price is:

($149,900 + 139,750 + 144,900 + 152,700 + 146,500) ÷ 5 = $146,750

MEASUREMENTS
(METRIC/IMPERIAL EQUIVALENCES)

Reference   See the Appendix.

MEASUREMENTS (RESIDENTIAL)

Guidelines for calculating the area of residential buildings is provided by the Alliance for Canadian Real Estate Education and includes:

- One-storey, one and one-half, with and without dormers.
- Basic two-storey.
- Two-storey with a built-in garage.
- Two-storey with a bay window, 2nd floor overhang and side addition on main floor.
- Two and one-half-storey.
- Bi-levels.
- Split level.
- Three level split, with and without a built-in garage.

Reference   See the Appendix.

MECHANIC'S LIEN

A statutory provision designed to protect and give priority to work performed and materials furnished in constructing, repairing, or modifying a structure. Terminology will vary by province, e.g., construction lien, construction holdback, mechanics' lien, and builder's lien.

Provincial   See applicable reference materials.

MEDIAN

The midpoint in an array of sequentially ordered numbers. Real estate boards commonly track the median, a measure of central tendency, as one of several indicators of market conditions. Median and average prices are commonly reported in market reports. As with other market indicators, the median has limited value when considered in isolation and should be analyzed in conjunction with other market indicators.

Example   *Median*

Salesperson Lee of ABC Realty Inc. is attempting to find the median price of comparable homes recently sold on Oak Street in Anycity. Following are the most recent reported sales taken from information provided by the Anycity Real Estate Board for the past three-month period.

SALE	ADDRESS	SALE PRICE
Sale #1	38 Oak Street	$149,900
Sale #2	44 Oak Street	139,750
Sale #3	139 Oak Street	144,900
Sale #4	293 Oak Street	152,700
Sale #5	412 Oak Street	146,500

Continued…

The median price is determined by reorganizing the sales in ascending sale price order as follows:

SALE	ADDRESS	SALE PRICE
Sale #2	44 Oak Street	$139,750
Sale #3	139 Oak Street	144,900
Sale #5	412 Oak Street	146,500
Sale #1	38 Oak Street	149,900
Sale #4	293 Oak Street	152,700

The median price is $146,500. If an even number of values make up the range, then the average of the two sales at the midpoint position is taken. Assume that Salesperson Lee finds another comparable sale (Sale #6) at 397 Oak Street for $145,500. The amended order is as follows:

SALE	ADDRESS	SALE PRICE
Sale #2	44 Oak Street	$139,750
Sale #3	139 Oak Street	144,900
Sale #6	397 Oak Street	145,500
Sale #5	412 Oak Street	146,500
Sale #1	38 Oak Street	149,900
Sale #4	293 Oak Street	152,700

The median is:

$$(\$145,500 + 146,500) \div 2 = 146,000$$

MEETING OF THE MINDS

(SEE ALSO CONTRACT)

Mutual agreement concerning the significant elements and overall substance of a contract. A meeting of the minds is said to occur when all parties agree to enter into a contract and when complete and exact terms have been agreed upon.

Example   Meeting of the Minds

Seller Smith and Buyer Jones have finally agreed upon all the details after considerable negotiations relating to Smith's property located in the west end of Anycity. The salesperson involved, following several countersigns, has an agreement/contract for the sale of 123 Main Street at a price of $238,000, a closing date of June 30th, and an initial deposit of $20,000.

The agreement/contract is subject to Jones arranging a new first mortgage of not less than $140,000 within 16 days of the acceptance of the offer. Both Smith and Jones have signed the agreement/contract, copies have been distributed, and the salesperson is merely waiting for confirmation that the mortgage financing has been arranged. In a legal sense, Smith and Jones have a meeting of the minds.

MEMBER OF THE INSTITUTE OF MUNICIPAL ASSESSORS

Acronym: MIMA   The MIMA designation is offered by the Institute of Municipal Assessors. The objects of the Institute are to promote the interests, education, and professional efficiency of persons engaged in valuation of real property for the purposes of municipal assessment and taxation.

The first courses available in Canada for assessors were developed by the Institute and offered through the Extension Department of Queen's University in 1954. Today, the Institute sponsors and maintains continuing education programs for its members and for persons new to the assessment field.

Like other professionals, assessors require special study, knowledge, and skill. Because the fair and equitable assessment of property for taxation purposes requires a high level of professional ability, the Institute of Municipal Assessors initiated a professional designation program designed to raise the professional competence of assessing personnel through education.

The MIMA designation is the Institute's highest standing and anyone attaining this designation is classified as an Accredited Member. The AIMA designation (Associate Member of the Institute of Municipal Assessors) must be attained before an individual can be considered for the MIMA designation.

Reference   The Institute of Municipal Assessors can be contacted at Suite 303, 190 Railside Road, North York, ON M3A 1B2. Details are summarized using information supplied by the Institute, with no representation concerning its accuracy or completeness. Contact the organization directly for current requirements.

MENTAL INCOMPETENCE

(SEE ALSO CONTRACT)

In relation to parties to a contract, any person declared to be mentally incompetent is incapable of contracting. Any listing or agreement entered into by such a person for the purchase, sale, exchange, or other disposition of property is voidable. If a person does not declare his/her mental incompetency and the other party knows of this mental incompetency, then the contract may be voidable by the undeclared mentally incompetent person.

Provincial legislation normally sets out requirements relating to individuals of diminished mental capacity entering into contracts including the sale of real property. Expert advice is required on such matters.

MERIDIAN LINES

One component of a system of latitude and longitude lines to precisely identify geographic location.

Lines of latitude run parallel to the equator and are evenly spaced. Lines of longitude, or meridians, run north and south and are drawn, due to the curvature of the earth, so that they converge at the north and south poles. Lines of longitude and latitude are indicated in degrees, as are meridian lines. The meridian that passes through Greenwich, near London, England, is labelled 0 degrees. Meridian lines to the east of this line are labelled in degrees east longitude up to 180 degrees; meridian lines to the west are also labelled up to 180 degrees but are in degrees west longitude.

Application The First Meridian in the western provinces is at 97 degrees 27' 28.4" west longitude, approximately 14 miles west of Winnipeg, and has been identified with an official marker (or cairn) placed on the north side of the TransCanada Highway near Headingley, Manitoba. It was called the First or Prime Meridian because it was the start line for the new method of land survey in Canada and also marked the western limit of settlement up to that date. Five other meridians were located to the west of the Prime Meridian at approximately every 4 degrees longitude. As shown in **Figure M.2**, the Second Meridian is at 102 degrees west and forms part of the boundary between Manitoba and Saskatchewan. All grid system land in Manitoba is either east or west of the Prime Meridian and is often abbreviated as EPM or WPM.

Provincial See applicable reference materials. Relevant only for Western Canadian provinces.

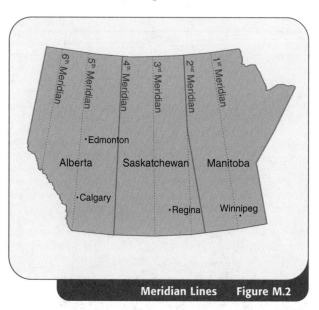

Meridian Lines   Figure M.2

METES AND BOUNDS

A system of written land description whereby all boundary lines are set forth by use of terminal points and angles; metes referring to a limit or limiting mark (i.e., distance) and bounds referring to boundary lines (i.e., directions). All descriptive text and illustrations are based on metes and bounds descriptions as recorded in land registry.

Provincial See applicable reference materials regarding land descriptions and surveying methods.

Analyzing a Metes and Bounds Description

A typical metes and bounds description is provided in **Figure M.3** along with a diagrammatical sketch. Initially, the wording makes little sense, but the application of certain key concepts will assist.

- The reference to degrees, minutes, and seconds represents very accurate compass directions. The division of degrees into 60 parts called minutes, and minutes into a further 60 parts called seconds, enables the draftsman to be very accurate in describing the angle. One can imagine that the less accurate the initial compass direction is at its starting point, the greater the error along its line of extension.

- With respect to distances, notice that even where the description is so accurate that the measurements are given in hundredths of a foot, the expression more or less is still used. Some measurements are said to be more or less to allow for minor error. The reason is that the description must completely enclose the parcel of land. There can be no gaps.

- The line running from West to East along the South of the parcel must get to a point in the Westerly limit of the road allowance. Similarly, when the description proceeds Northerly along the road, the measurement is not as important as the fact that the line must reach the place of commencement.

- The description establishes the location of the property in general terms. The third paragraph establishes a point of commencement, and the description proceeds to indicate the perimeter of the parcel by setting out directions and distances.

- The bearings are compass directions. The first direction is always true north or south. A survey will always indicate the compass direction in relation to north. This is followed by instructions to swing away a certain number of degrees (minutes and seconds) in an easterly or westerly direction.

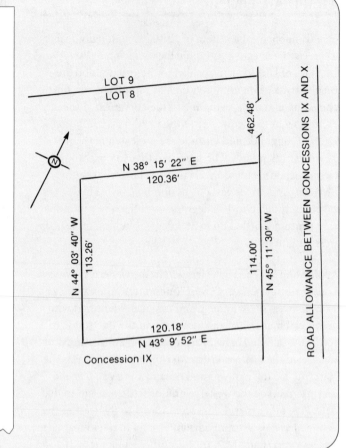

ALL AND SINGULAR that certain parcel of land and premises situate lying and being in the Township of Anytownship, in the County of Anycounty and being composed of part of Lot 8, Concession IX in said Township, more particularly described as follows:

Premising that the Westerly limit of the road allowance between Concessions IX and X has a bearing of North 45 degrees 11 minutes, 30 seconds West and relating all bearings herein thereto;

COMMENCING at a point in the westerly limit of said road allowance distant 462.48 feet measured on a bearing of South 45 degrees 11 minutes 30 seconds East along the Westerly limit of said road allowance from the Northeast angle of said lot 8;

THENCE South 38 degrees 15 minutes 22 seconds West a distance of 120.36 feet to a point;

THENCE South 44 degrees 03 minutes 40 seconds East a distance of 113.26 feet to a point;

THENCE North 43 degrees 09 minutes 52 seconds East a distance of 120.18 feet, more or less, to a point in the said Westerly limit of the road allowance;

THENCE North 45 degrees 11 minutes 30 seconds West along said Westerly limit of road allowance a distance of 114 feet, more or less, to the point of commencement.

Figure M.3   Metes and Bounds

M

To clarify the directions indicated, follow these steps to create the diagram as illustrated in Figure M.4.

1. Draw a circle.
2. Draw a line from top to bottom and mark the top north and the bottom south.
3. Draw a horizontal line intersecting the first line at the centre of the circle.
4. Mark the right end of the line where it cuts the circle east and the other end west.
5. Draw a line from the centre of the circumference halfway between north and east: i.e., dividing this quarter of the circle in two. A circle contains 360 degrees, each degree contains 60 minutes, each minute contains 60 seconds; between north and east is a quarter of a circle or 90 degrees. By dividing this quarter in two, a line is created that is described as north 45 degrees east.
6. Extend this line to a point on the circle halfway between south and west. This is known as the back or reverse bearing, or south 45 degrees west.

One line has two descriptions, one of which indicates one direction and the other the exact opposite. Therefore, in reading a description, one can tell which direction on the straight line is being followed.

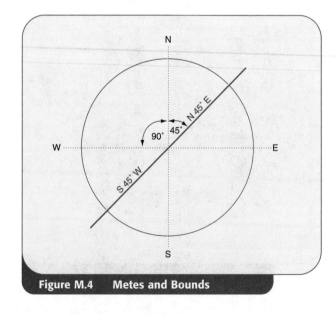

Figure M.4   Metes and Bounds

Current Requirements

Metes and bounds requirements are set out in applicable provincial legislation relating to surveys, plans, and descriptions of land. The vast majority of new severances of land created are described by reference to numbered or named units of land illustrated on a plan. Therefore, very few new written metes and bounds descriptions of land are now being prepared. Also, a land registrar may rule that an existing description is vague or complex and require that the land be described in accordance with a reference plan.

Historical Descriptions and Variations

Metes and bounds descriptions arose from a necessity to sever land originally described by means of township surveys that were generally patented as whole lots or fractional parts of lots. As demand increased for smaller lots, severances were required. Until recently, new severances that did not form part of a plan of subdivision were generally described by means of a metes and bounds description. Often land descriptions were provided by the seller or buyer without benefit of a survey.

Example   Early Form of Metes and Bounds Description

ALL AND SINGULAR that certain parcel or tract of land and premises situate, lying and being in the Township of Anytownship in the County of Anycounty and being composed of part of Lot 4, Concession III in the said Township and being more particularly described as follows:

COMMENCING at a point in the northern limit of the road allowance between concessions II and III distant 198 feet measured westerly there along from the south east corner of said Lot 4;

THENCE westerly continuing along the northern limit of said road allowance a distance of 330 feet;

THENCE northerly parallel to the eastern limit of Lot 4 a distance of 264 feet;

THENCE easterly parallel to the northern limit of the said road allowance a distance of 330 feet;

THENCE southerly parallel to the eastern limit of Lot 4 a distance of 264 feet more or less to the place of commencement.

Many variations of metes and bounds descriptions are found given the lack of rigid rules in historical land description and registration. Two of many examples are provided for illustration purposes.

Example 1   Metes and Bounds— Historical Descriptions and Variations

Land has been described as that part of a lot lying to one side of a described line (preamble omitted).

That part of Lot 3 lying South of a straight line drawn from a point in the Western limit of the lot, distant 950 feet measured northerly there along from the South West corner of the said lot, to a point in the Eastern limit of the said lot, distant 1,200 feet measured northerly therealong from the South East corner of the said lot.

Example 2   Metes and Bounds— Historical Descriptions and Variations

Land has also been described by reference to the perpendicular width of a rectangular part of a rectangular lot (preamble omitted).

That part of Lot 5 which lies North of a line parallel to and perpendicularly distant 69 feet, measured southerly, from the Northern limit of said lot.

Refined Historical Descriptions Based on Surveys

In circumstances previously outlined, a real possibility existed that the location of the property as described in the deed might not agree with the actual position of the property on the ground. In older crown patents and many earlier deeds, the dimensions were given in chains, links, rods, perches, or poles and the areas were occasionally provided in square chains.

In the example, the directions are given in quadrantal bearings. Quadrantal bearings are a method of expressing the direction of a line in terms of the acute angle it makes with the north-south line chosen as the reference line for that particular survey. For example, the lines having bearings of North 20 degrees 49 minutes 30 seconds West and South 20 degrees 49 minutes 30 seconds East both form angles of 20 degrees 49 minutes 30 seconds with the north-south line used for this description.

In older surveys, the north-south direction may have been determined either by astronomic observations, by using magnetic north as shown on a compass, or merely by arbitrarily assuming a direction to be North. Today's surveys must comply with rigid legislative and professional surveyor requirements.

M

For example, the *Registry Act* and the Standards for Surveys of the Association of Ontario Land Surveyors require the bearings to be determined by astronomic observation or derived from a line of known astronomic bearing.

Example   ***Metes and Bounds—***
Refined Form of Metes and Bounds
Descriptions Based on Surveys

During the past few decades, increasingly precise metes and bounds descriptions have been derived directly from surveys. A typical wording follows.

ALL AND SINGULAR that certain parcel or tract of land and premises situate, lying and being in the Township of Anytownship in the County of Anycounty and being composed of that part of Lot 7, Concession IV, described as follows:

PREMISING that the northern limit of the road allowance between Concessions III and IV as shown on Plan 899 registered in the Land Registry Office for the Registry Division of Anycounty has a bearing of North 69 degrees 10 minutes 30 seconds East and relating all bearings herein thereto;

COMMENCING at a point in the northern limit of the said road allowance distant South 69 degrees 10 minutes 30 seconds West, 369.72 feet measured therealong from the South East corner of the said Lot 7;

THENCE North 20 degrees 49 minutes 30 seconds West, a distance of 300.00 feet to a point;

THENCE South 69 degrees 10 minutes 30 seconds West, a distance of 200.00 feet to a point;

THENCE South 20 degrees 49 minutes 30 seconds East, a distance of 300.00 feet more or less to a point in the Northern limit of said road allowance;

THENCE North 69 degrees 10 minutes 30 seconds East, a distance of 200.00 feet more or less to the point of commencement.

METRIC MEASUREMENTS

Reference   See the Appendix.

MEZZANINE

A floor, consisting of a smaller square footage than other floors in a structure, that typically forms part of an overall main entrance design along with the main floor area in office buildings, hotels, theatres, and retail establishments including malls.

Mezzanine levels may also have a higher or lower floor to ceiling measurement than other regular floors in the structure. The lowest balcony in a theatre is also referred to as a *mezzanine*.

MILL

A monetary unit consisting of one-tenth of one cent, a measure used to indicate the property tax rate, e.g., a tax rate of one mill per dollar is the same as .001 of the assessed value.

Application   The mill rate, is calculated by dividing the projected annual operating budget of a municipality by the tax base. Assume that the total assessment (tax base) for a municipality is $20,000,000 and the estimated expenditures (budget) for the coming year are $1,000,000; $1,000,000 divided by $20,000,000 equals $0.05. If the municipality charges five cents for each dollar of assessment, it will gain the necessary revenue to meet budgeted expenses.

Tax rates, in some provincial jurisdictions, are quoted, not in dollars or cents, but in mills. Based on the calculation provided, the published mill rate would be (.05 x 1,000) 50 mills. Mill rates are set once each year based on projected operating budgets. To calculate the tax on an individual property, the mill rate is multiplied by the assessment of the property. Since the assessment is in dollars and cents and the mill rate in thousandths of a dollar, moving the decimal point three places to the left in the resulting calculation is necessary.

Example   ***Mill***

A salesperson is listing a residential lot assessed at $46,000. The mill rate in the municipality is 34.6129: 34.6129 x 46,000 = 1592193.400. Moving the decimal three places to the left and rounding off produces a tax amount of $1,592.19. Moving the decimal three places to the left is equivalent to dividing by 1,000.

Mill rates are largely being replaced by a more straightforward tax rate expressing the proportion of assessment being taxed. In the example, the tax rate is 3.46129% or a factor of .0346129.

Provincial   See applicable reference materials.

MINERAL RIGHTS

The owner of land may or may not have title to the mines and minerals on or under the land. The rights of ownership to minerals may be severed from the title to the surface rights and separate titles can be created. The rights of ownership to mines and minerals can be transferred in much the same manner as the land itself.

Provincial   See applicable reference materials.

MINI-WAREHOUSE

A storage facility housing small cubicles ranging in size from 50 to 250 square feet. Most are constructed of concrete blocks with a garage-style entrance door for ease of loading/off loading items and can be heated or unheated. Mini-warehousing has experienced significant growth particularly in the last two decades.

MINIMUM LOT SIZE/AREA

A minimum lot size, normally set out in square feet/metres or acres/hectares upon which a building may be built, is found in municipal zoning by-laws. Regulations concerning the construction of a dwelling detail various requirements such as minimum lot size/area, frontage, coverage permitted, front, side and rear yards, and minimum floor area on the main floor of the structure.

Example   *Minimum Lot Size/Area*

Buyer Jones recently acquired a recreational lot zoned *Rural/ Residential* on which he intends to build a winterized cottage. Ultimately, he hopes to retire to the property. The local township office advised Jones that he could build a structure, but only in accordance with the following provisions. The regulations vary, based on whether or not the property is serviced with municipal water and sanitary sewers.

	NEITHER	WATER ONLY	WATER AND SEWER
Minimum Lot Size (sq. m.)	1850	700	510
Minimum Lot Frontage (m.)	30	23	18
Maximum Lot Coverage	12%	30%	35%
Minimum Front Yard* (m.)	7.5	7.5	7.5
Minimum Side Yard* (m.)	1.5	1.5	1.5
Minimum Rear Yard* (m.)	10.5	10.5	10.5

*Subject to various additional requirements and provisions.

MINIMUM WAGE

Provincial employment legislation addresses minimum wages for employees. Exemptions may apply in specific provinces concerning registered real estate salespeople

licensed/registered under the applicable real estate act. Minimum wage may also vary between students and other classifications of employed individuals.

Provincial   See applicable reference materials.

MINING LEASES

Provincial   See applicable reference materials.

MINOR

A person who is under the age of legal competence. Simply put, all contracts with infants for the sale or purchase of land are generally voidable, sometimes void, and not usually considered valid and binding on the minor.

Application   In the case of a voidable contract, the minor would be entitled to avoid the contract at any time until a reasonable time after age of majority. However, if the contract is ratified after majority, the right to avoid it generally disappears. Avoidance is the privilege of the minor and the other side is bound until the minor repudiates the contract.

The age of legal competence (age of majority) was traditionally 21 years of age, but provinces have established differing ages, typically either 18 or 19 years of age. In Ontario and Manitoba, for example, the age of majority is 18 years while in Nova Scotia it is 19 years.

Example   *Minor*

Broker/Owner Johnson, of ABC Realty Inc., is conducting a brief review session for salespeople on the fundamentals of contract law concerning agreements/contracts and, in particular, legal issues surrounding persons under the age of majority.

Apparently, one of the condominium site salespeople encountered an unusual situation at an open house. A young couple wanted to submit an offer on a one bedroom unit. The salesperson, on discovering that one of the two individuals was a minor, called Johnson for guidance. A brief conversation with the potential buyers confirmed the salesperson's suspicion. The offer was drafted in the non-minor's name (following confirmation of age), and the seller/ developer was informed about the situation.

Following is a brief synopsis of Johnson's notes for the sales meeting regarding the status of a minor involved in the agreement/contract for real property:

Continued…

- All contracts of minors for the purchase or sale of land are voidable by the minor. It is immaterial whether or not the minor has purported to be over the age of majority. In rare circumstances the court could hold that a reasonable purchase of a home was a necessity and a contract for such was binding on the minor.

- A minor may avoid a contract made during the age of minority for a reasonable time after majority, providing that nothing occurs after majority that might be deemed to be ratification of the contract, such as making an additional deposit or payment.

- The contract is binding upon the other party until avoided by the minor, but it is doubtful if the minor can obtain specific performance unless the other party has received all the benefits given under the contract.

- Should the minor avoid the contract, any benefits obtained must be returned, but it is not clear whether this must be done at the time of avoidance.

- The minor, in the absence of any fraud by the other side, cannot recover any payment made upon the contract.

- If the contract contains a penalty or is otherwise to the disadvantage of the minor, it is probably void. In that case, the minor can always recover payments that have been made, at least if no consideration has been received under the contract.

MINOR VARIANCE

A term normally associated with zoning when a property has a minor deviation from zoning regulations. The owner may seek remedy by approaching the applicable municipal authority to seek acknowledgement and approval for such variances.

Provincial   See applicable reference materials.

MISLEADING ADVERTISING
(SEE FALSE AND MISLEADING ADVERTISING)

MISREPRESENTATION

A representation may be defined as a statement or assertion made by one party to the other, before or at the time of contracting, regarding some existing fact, matter, or circumstance affecting the contract or its object. Simply put, misrepresentation is a false statement of fact.

Distinguishing between a representation and a mere exaggeration or statement of intention or opinion can be difficult. The statement *'This is the best deal in town.'* may be treated as an exaggeration, not giving rise to legal rights, although it might be false or misleading pursuant to the *Competition Act*. If, however, a specific statement is made to the effect that a property can be put to a certain type of use, this statement is a representation. If proven false, a misrepresentation has been made.

Misrepresentation is a complicated area of law that is usually categorized as innocent, fraudulent, or negligent. The following is provided as a general guideline only.

Innocent Misrepresentation

A statement by one party of a material fact that is untrue, but is honestly believed to be true. If the victim of misrepresentation is induced into a contract based on such a statement, he/she may refuse to complete the contract, attempt to have it set aside, and attempt to recover anything paid or delivered under it. He/she can also defend any action brought against him/her under the contract, but as a general rule cannot recover damages if the misrepresentation was innocent.

Example 1	*Misrepresentation–* *Innocent Misrepresentation*

Seller Smith is offering his home for sale through the local real estate board's MLS service. A buyer, upon inspecting the property, asks if the nearby school offers grades K–8. The seller, unable to reach the school, calls a neighbour and confirms that fact. The buyer relies upon this statement and purchases the property only to discover that both his children could not attend this school, but would have to travel five miles by bus. The school now provides only junior grades K–4. He refuses to close the transaction arguing that a misrepresentation, no matter how innocent, has occurred.

Example 2	*Misrepresentation–* *Innocent Misrepresentation*

Salesperson Lee, when asked if the basement had any leakage, informed the buyer that the seller had clearly stated to him at the time of listing that there were no leakage problems whatsoever in the basement area. The salesperson did, however, suggest to the buyer that he could place a condition in the offer or require a warranty from the seller regarding his concern. The buyer elected to place a warranty in the agreement. Following closing, water seepage occurred in the property. Salesperson Lee had innocently misrepresented this situation, based on what he believed were sincere, honest representations made by the seller.

Fraudulent Misrepresentation

A fraudulent misrepresentation has three elements:

- The misrepresentation must be made with the knowledge of its falsity or with reckless disregard for its truth on the part of the person making it.
- The purpose must have been to induce the other party to enter a contract.
- The misrepresentation must have been acted on to the other party's prejudice.

Where such fraud exists, the party deceived may resist enforcement of the contract, and that party has the right to recover damages for deceit.

**Example 1   *Misrepresentation—*
*Fraudulent Misrepresentation***

Salesperson Lee is listing Seller Smith's property. During casual conversation, Smith admits to a problem of basement leakage, but emphasizes that this only occurs in a heavy downpour. Smith insists that Lee not mention this fact and Lee agrees.

Buyer Jones purchases the property following assurances from Lee that no dampness problem exists in the basement. Jones closes the sale and discovers the leakage problem. A law suit ensues to recover damages on the basis of fraudulent misrepresentation.

A principal is liable for misrepresentations made by his agent, if made with express or implied authority. Authority will be implied where the misrepresentation is made in the course of, and within the scope of, duties of the agent, e.g., when showing the property.

The owner may be liable for representations about the property made by the broker or sales representative. With fraudulent misrepresentation made by an agent, both the person making it and the principal will be liable for damages. Salesperson Lee, in the preceding example, agrees with the seller and fails to disclose pertinent information about the leakage. Consequently, both the selling brokerage and sales representative could be liable for damages.

**Example 2   *Misrepresentation—*
*Fraudulent Misrepresentation***

Salesperson Ward, when asked if the well provided an adequate water supply, told the buyer that there was more than ample water to meet all usual household requirements. The salesperson had already been told by the seller that gallonage tests performed last summer revealed less than two gallons per minute, although the flow revived somewhat during spring and fall periods. However, the seller asked that this information not be disclosed to any potential buyer. Salesperson Ward has made a fraudulent misrepresentation.

Negligent Misrepresentation

If there is a special relationship between the parties and a misrepresentation is made negligently, then the person who is misled will have an action for damages. When it is clear that the statement was made with intention that it be relied on, and that the person did rely on it, then a claim for damages may arise. This could occur in situations where the buyer has relied on a real estate salesperson, who is agent for the seller, for example, the agent misrepresented the financial statements of the seller's business.

An agent has also been held liable for negligent misrepresentation as to the quantity of property included in a transaction; and for failing to confirm information in a listing and making wrongful representations of the property carrying costs, knowing that the buyer was relying on his/her expertise and advice. It is negligent to misrepresent that the property may be used for a specific purpose if, in fact, that use may be illegal under the zoning by-laws of that municipality. Appraisers have been held responsible for inaccuracies in their reports that were relied upon by lenders. In all these situations an assumption is made that care, as well as honesty, is demanded.

**Example 1   *Misrepresentation—*
*Negligent Misrepresentation***

A mortgagee employed an appraiser to appraise a property for mortgage loan purposes. The appraiser relied on statements of the mortgagor and gave a high value based on the property having been approved for a subdivision. Such approval had not been given. A mortgage was subsequently registered, a default occurred, and a deficiency also arose on a subsequent sale. The court held that the appraiser was liable to the mortgagee for the deficiency for failing to make enquiries that a reasonable, careful, and prudent appraiser would have made.

**Example 2   *Misrepresentation—*
*Negligent Misrepresentation***

Salesperson Lee listed a two-storey home backing onto a new housing development. When securing the listing, the seller admitted that he could not locate the rear boundary of the property. To complicate matters, no recent survey existed. Lee showed the property to a prospective buyer. When asked about the size of the property, Lee confidently pointed to two iron bars at the extreme rear left and right corners of the lot, then paced off the distance and informed the buyer that the depth was around 250 feet.

Based on this representation, the buyer bought the property, only to discover that the two survey pins related to the development area and not to the property. In fact, the lot had a depth of 150 feet. The buyer sued the brokerage and the seller for negligent misrepresentation arguing that the salesperson owed a duty of care in providing information that misled and injured the buyer.

MISSION STATEMENT

A concise, written declaration of an organization's overall purpose and direction. The mission statement should embody and promote the corporate values of the organization, while, at the same time, provide a central reference point for the development of specific operating objectives and action plans.

Application   Mission statements arise from a well-defined corporate culture. A strong culture is identified by consistency and common awareness within an organization. The outward expression of culture can be found in how consumers view a particular company.

For real estate, a consumer view or outward expression of culture might be:

> *ABC Realty Inc. specializes in new home sales and provides the best service in the west end.*

or

> *Give ABC Realty Inc. a call. They really know the condominium market in this town.*

Culture can also be found within the working ranks of a corporation, e.g., consistent expression of key values, the types of decisions made, and various rewards for specific activities. These basic beliefs and values are then transferred into a mission statement.

Example   *Mission Statement–Brokerage*

Broker/Owner Johnson, of ABC Realty Inc., is attempting to build a more powerful corporate culture. The values Johnson wishes to instill are:

- Quality Service
- Specialized Marketing Services
- Professional Advice and Assistance to Consumers
- Knowledgeable, Capable Salespeople
- Well Known, Established Brokerage (Yet Viewed as Modern and Innovative).

Given these key values, Johnson develops a mission statement for prominent display in the reception area of the brokerage office. It reads as follows:

> *ABC Realty Inc. is committed to top quality service, professional innovative marketing programs and the newest technology to ensure the company's established leadership in the field of residential real estate brokerage.*

Example   *Mission Statement–Real Estate Boards*

Real estate boards and associations often develop mission statements to clearly identify underlying goals and values to the membership at large. Following are four of many variations found in the marketplace.

> *The* [name of real estate board] *is an association of co-operating REALTORS that provides services and advances professional standards for members. The Board preserves and promotes the Multiple Listing Service to benefit buyers and sellers of real property.*

> *The* [name of real estate board] *is an association of REALTORS that provides services, education, professional standards for business practice and information to its members. The Board liaises with governments and related organizations on behalf of its members.*

> *Promoting and fostering a professional environment to enable the Members to carry out their practice of real estate, keeping the public interest and a favourable image in the forefront.*

> *Pursuing excellence and professionalism in real estate through commitment and service.*

MISTAKE

The word mistake, in legal terms as it applies to real estate contracts, has a narrow meaning. Not every mistake or simple error affects a contract and is considered a legal mistake of fact. The law does not simply declare a contract void simply because one or other of the parties makes a mistake. Only certain types of mistakes give rise to a remedy. Obviously, the determination of a mistake and its impact on a contract is a legal issue and appropriate advice should be obtained.

Application   As a guideline for real estate practitioners, mistakes can be grouped under three common headings.

Common Mistake

Both parties to the contract know the intention of the other, accept it, but are somehow mistaken concerning some underlying material or fundamental fact. As an example, both seller and buyer believe that the property includes a right-of-way to the beach, but in fact nothing supports this belief. The buyer and seller enter into an agreement/contract that, among other terms, describes a specific right-or-way along with appropriate measurements. The error does not in fact create an easement or any beneficial interest and is viewed only as a common mistake between the parties.

Mutual Mistake

The parties misunderstand each other and are at cross purposes. For example, the seller owns two lots on opposite sides of a lake. The buyer believes he/she is buying the south shore property, while the seller believes the north shore property is being sold. The parties would be agreeing based on a mutual mistake regarding location.

Unilateral Mistake

One party is mistaken and the other party knows of this mistake concerning a fundamental aspect of a contract. As an example, the buyer believes that the lot is approximately one acre in size, and the seller is clearly aware of this mistaken belief and does not make the buyer aware of the situation. The buyer then proceeds with the purchase based on the mistaken fact.

MISTAKENLY SIGNED DOCUMENT
(SEE ALSO NON EST FACTUM)

The signing of a document that is fundamentally different from that which was contemplated.

Application   As a general guideline for real estate practitioners, where a person is induced by the fraud of another to sign a written document, such as a listing agreement, agreement/contract, amendment, or notice, that is materially or fundamentally different from that which was expected, the person signing may successfully plead that the document is not valid. This is known as the doctrine of *non est factum*. Basically, the person never intended to sign the document and therefore in the eyes of the law never did sign the document. As with any mistake in legal documents and contracts, the exact circumstances are subject to close scrutiny and legal advice is recommended.

> **Example**   *Mistakenly Signed Document*
>
> Seller Smith is marketing a large tract of industrial land. All the signage, supporting documents, and verbal information provided to Buyer Jones and his buyer representative indicate that the property has an area of approximately 90,000 square feet. This figure is also clearly stated in the agreement/contract and an old, barely readable, survey is provided to Jones at the time of signing.
>
> At the point of closing, Jones refuses to complete the sale, as the property only contains about 60,000 square feet. Smith argues that the old survey in Jones' possession has the correct square footage and, therefore, he must close. Jones argues that the document is not valid and had he known the material difference in size, he would never have signed the agreement/contract.

MIXED USE PROJECT

A planned structure that provides at least two types of uses, such as retail/office or office/residential within a single project. The phrase *mixed use* can also refer to a subdivision plan that includes various uses within the overall design.

MLS
(SEE MULTIPLE LISTING SERVICE (MLS))

MOBILE HOME

A commonly accepted definition does not exist as most provinces, for the purposes of real estate transactions, define *mobile home* within applicable provincial statutes and/or through municipal zoning descriptions. Occupancy of mobile homes typically falls under residential tenancy legislation but may vary by province.

A mobile home can be broadly defined as a portable dwelling unit that is transported on its own chassis and running gear by towing or other means and is designated to be used as living quarters or for travel, recreation, or vacation purposes. Provincial tenancy legislation normally is directed solely to mobile homes used for living quarters.

Provincial   See applicable reference materials.

MOBILE HOME PARK

A commonly accepted definition does not exist as most provinces, for the purposes of real estate transactions, define *mobile home park* within applicable provincial statutes and/or through municipal zoning descriptions.

Typically, a definition references a residential complex where two or more mobile homes are located for a specific period and includes the land, structures, and services/facilities provided by the landlord for the common use and enjoyment of the tenants. Most mobile homes are on leased land.

Provincial   See applicable reference materials.

MODERNIZATION

The process of bringing a property into conformity with current standards of style and utility, by making interior or exterior corrections or additions. Modernization normally involves replacing parts of the structure or mechanical equipment with modern ones.

> **Example   *Modernization***
>
> Owner Smith is debating the merits of selling or renovating his home. While the house is mechanically and structurally sound, modernization is required, particularly in the kitchen and bathrooms. The contractor's quote of $68,000 includes the installation of kitchen cupboards, all built-in appliances, and an extended eat-in area with extensive glass to a patio area. The quotation also includes the modernization of two large baths, including all fixtures, cabinets, tiling, skylights, and decorating. Smith estimates the cost of moving to a newer property with such amenities is approximately $80,000. The move would require having a smaller lot size in a newer subdivision. Smith elects to proceed with the modernization.

MODIFIED ECONOMIC AGE-LIFE DEPRECIATION METHOD
(SEE ECONOMIC AGE-LIFE DEPRECIATION METHOD (MODIFIED))

MODIFIED INTERNAL RATE OF RETURN
(SEE ALSO FINANCIAL MANAGEMENT RATE OF RETURN AND INTERNAL RATE OF RETURN)

Acronym: MIRR   A modified method of calculating an internal rate of return (IRR) that considers the impact of multiple positive and negative cash flows. The MIRR is used when more than one negative to positive cash flow change occurs, as the IRR may produce ambiguous results. Effectively, the MIRR sums all positive and negative cash flows and produces two amounts (one plus and one minus). As such, the MIRR equates the present value (PV) of the negative cash flows and the initial investment to the future value (FV) of positive cash flows when calculating an internal rate of return.

In the case of negative cash flows, the amount is discounted to PV using a *safe rate* and added to the initial investment. The amount is set aside today to cover future negative cash flows. The MIRR is usually less than IRR, as negative cash flows are at a lower assumed rate than market rates. For positive cash flows, the amounts are compounded to future value (FV) at the end of the holding period based on the reinvestment rate.

Application   The MIRR calculation involves three steps:

Step 1   Calculate PV of Negative Cash Flows
Step 2   Calculate FV of Positive Cash Flows
Step 3   Calculate IRR Based on One Positive and One Negative Cash Flow

The MIRR, while referred to as an *internal measure of return*, is actually built on the concept of reinvestment using external interest rates for positive and negative cash flows. Critics level the same criticism against this measure as they do with the FMRR. The introduction of external factors, they argue, contaminates results with variables beyond immediate internal cash flows. The MIRR, as with the IRR, is not designed to evaluate the performance of a specified capital sum given various investment opportunities having different equity requirements and holding periods.

Detailed IRR, MIRR, and FMRR calculations are not included given inherent complexities, but addressed in appropriate commercial specialty courses.

MODULAR/MANUFACTURED HOME

A home initially constructed within a factory, then partially or fully disassembled for the purpose of transportation. Once delivered to a site, the pieces are reassembled.

MOLD

A growth of minute fungi traditionally associated with decaying vegetable or animal matter that has taken on increasing prominence in real estate. Ironically, modern construction techniques may be a significant contributing factor as building envelopes become increasingly airtight. Furnace and air-conditioning systems may only compound the matter by recirculating contaminated air. A wide range of molds can flourish in damp areas within buildings and research has linked various health problems to these growths including sinus infections, asthma, and certain respiratory infections.

Stachybotrys atra is a particularly dangerous mold that has been associated with severe breathing difficulties, dizziness, memory loss, and bleeding in the lungs. This mold produces mycotoxins and prolonged exposure to these airborne toxins can prove harmful. Fortunately, most household molds are mild in comparison to stachybotrys atra and other related molds (e.g., memnoniella), but nevertheless research has linked various molds to chronic sinus infections, asthma, and other ailments.

Application   Molds require water to grow and damp areas in buildings are often the culprits. Homeowners, or others responsible for building management, should watch for discolouration in building finishes and carefully inspect areas in which dampness might collect, e.g., basement storage areas and kitchen cupboards. Further, air-conditioning units and furnaces (including ducts) should be cleaned regularly and any stagnant water, e.g., in drainage pans, should be eliminated. Finished basement recreation rooms can be particularly susceptible as interior building materials may hide dampness problems entering through exterior walls. Above all, take note of any changes in personal health that may signal mold-related problems, e.g., respiratory ailments, breathing difficulties, recurring dizziness, severe headaches and/or loss of balance, and extreme fatigue.

MONEY LAUNDERING

The *Proceeds of Crime (Money Laundering) Act*, which became law on June 29, 2000, is a federal statute designed to detect and deter money laundering and facilitate investigations and prosecutions of money laundering offences. Money laundering, as defined by the United Nations, refers to *any act or attempted act to disguise the source of money or assets derived from criminal activity.* The Financial Transactions and Reports Analysis Centre of Canada (FINTRAC) is the federal agency responsible for the collection, analysis, and disclosure of information to assist in the detection, prevention, and deterrence of money laundering in Canada and abroad.

Regulations under the Act are divided into two parts:

* *Suspicious transaction reporting* is effective as of November 8, 2001.
* Regulations regarding *large cash transactions over $10,000* are currently at draft stage with an anticipated effective date in 2002.

Suspicious Transaction

A suspicious transaction is a financial transaction for which there are *reasonable grounds to suspect* that it is related to the commission of a money laundering offence. Such an offence involves concealing or converting property or the proceeds of property (e.g. money), knowing or believing that these were derived from the commission of an offence referred to in Section 462.31 of the *Criminal Code.* A money laundering offence may also extend to property or proceeds derived from illegal activities that took place outside Canada.

Reporting Requirements

The Act requires reporting of suspicious transactions by various persons and entities including real estate brokers and salespersons. Real estate brokers and salespersons are subject to reporting requirements when engaged in any of the following activities on behalf of any person or entity in the course of a real estate transaction:

* Receiving or paying funds (e.g., cash, currency, securities, and negotiable instruments);
* Depositing or withdrawing funds; and
* Transferring funds by any means.

Guideline

A suspicious transaction can involve several factors that may seem individually insignificant, but together may raise suspicion that the transaction is related to the commission of a money laundering offence. A transaction may be connected to money laundering when a broker or salesperson thinks that it (or a group of transactions) raises questions or gives rise to discomfort, apprehension, or mistrust. Transactions may give rise to reasonable grounds to suspect that they are related to money laundering regardless of the sum of money involved. No minimum dollar value applies to a suspicious transaction.

Specific Indicators for Real Estate Salespersons and Brokers

FINTRAC has developed both general and specific indicators of suspicious transactions to assist persons and entities affected by the Act. Taken together, the general and industry-specific indicators may point to a suspicious transaction. The following specific indicators relate to real estate brokers and salespersons, as guidance when carrying out defined activities on behalf of clients.

* Client arrives at a real estate closing with a significant amount of cash.
* Client purchases property in the name of a nominee such as an associate or a relative (other than a spouse).
* Client does not want to put his or her name on any document that would connect him or her with the property or uses different names on offers to purchase, closing documents, and deposit receipts.
* Client inadequately explains the last minute substitution of the purchasing party's name.

- Client negotiates a purchase for market value or above asking price, but records a lower value on documents, paying the difference under the table.
- Client sells property below market value with an additional under the table payment.
- Client pays initial deposit with a cheque from a third party, other than a spouse or a parent.
- Client pays substantial down payment in cash and balance is financed by an unusual source or offshore bank.
- Client purchases personal use property under a corporate veil when this type of transaction is inconsistent with the ordinary business practice of the client.
- Client purchases property without inspecting it.
- Client purchases multiple properties in a short time period, and seems to have few concerns about the location, condition, and anticipated repair costs, etc. of each property.
- Client pays rent or the amount of a lease in advance using a large amount of cash.
- Client is known to have paid large remodelling or home improvement invoices with cash, on a property for which property management services are provided.

These industry-specific indicators may point to a suspicious transaction. Practitioners are reminded that behaviour is suspicious, not people. The consideration of many factors—not just any one factor—can lead to a conclusion that reasonable grounds exist to suspect that a transaction is related to the commission of a money laundering offence.

Compliance Regime

The legislation requires persons or entities to implement a compliance regime regarding obligations that include reporting, recordkeeping, and client identification.

Guideline 4: Implementing of a Compliance Regime sets out various requirements including:

- The appointment of an individual responsible for the implementation of the regime.
- The development and application of compliance policies and procedures.
- The review of policies and procedures, as often as necessary.
- Where the person or entity has employees, an ongoing employee compliance training program.

Filing a Report

A suspicious transaction report must be filed with FINTRAC when reasonable grounds exist to suspect a transaction is related to the commission of a money laundering offence.

Time Limit

The report must be filed within 30 days and the time limit begins at the time when a fact about a specific transaction constitutes reasonable grounds that this transaction is related to the commission of a money laundering offence. For example:

- If the fact were detected at point of completing an agreement, the 30-day time period would start at that point.
- If the fact were detected at point of a review of a transaction file by a broker at closing, then this event would trigger the 30-day time period.

Submission

Reports can be submitted electronically via the FINTRAC web site (www.fintrac.gc.ca) or by paper copy. Paper copies can be printed from the web site, or requested by phone (800) 346-8722 and then faxed (866) 226-2346 or forwarded by mail to: Financial Transactions and Reports Analysis Centre of Canada, Section A, Ottawa, ON K1P 1H7.

With web-based communication, an electronic acknowledgment is sent by FINTRAC. A paper copy is sent if the report is received by fax or mail. A sample of the *Suspicious Transaction Report* is also provided on the web site.

Penalties

Failure to report a suspicious transaction can result in a $5 million fine and/or five years in jail.

Reference   The FINTRAC web site (www.fintrac.gc.ca) provides detailed background information, program descriptions, and procedures. Practitioners are strongly encouraged to access the site for complete details.

MONEY MARKET

A supply and demand market in which individuals trade short-term monetary instruments. Short-term instruments in Canada such as T-bills (treasury bills) and short-term guaranteed investment certificates (GICs) should be differentiated from longer term market instruments such as bonds, stocks, and mortgages associated with capital markets.

MONEY SUPPLY
(SEE ALSO ECONOMICS)

The supply of money is a key ingredient in the real estate market. Two basic control mechanisms are associated with money supply and are subsequently described.

Regulatory Activities (Bank of Canada)

The Bank of Canada performs a major role in money supply through the purchase and sale of federal bonds that ultimately affect the amount of money circulating within the economy. For example, if the bank wishes to restrict the money supply, it sells bonds on the open market thereby drawing funds from the market.

The Bank of Canada also announces prime bank rate changes weekly on loans made to the chartered banks. These weekly variations act as a signal to lending institutions, which normally follow suit for lending rates charged in the consumer marketplace and further impact the flow of money. Prime rate changes can also significantly impact economic activity

Voluntary Controls

Financial institutions underwrite loan portfolios based on sound lending policies. Accordingly, various restrictions are a natural consequence of good business practices in establishing credit limits, interest rates charged, and overall borrower ability to repay debt. As such, lenders, in varying their policies indirectly affect money supply. In difficult economic times, lenders may be more restrictive than in periods of prosperity thereby limiting the flow of money.

MONTH-TO-MONTH TENANCY
(SEE ALSO TENANCY (TYPES))

A form of periodic tenancy arrangement, not uncommon in residential tenancies, created when no definite lease term is specified by the parties, or a written rental agreement expires, the tenant remains in the property, and the rent is payable monthly. A month-to-month tenancy may be written or oral, and typically can be terminated at the end of any month with at least 60 days prior notice by either party. Otherwise, it continues automatically from month-to-month on the same terms. The notice period, termination provisions, and other tenancy matters will vary by provincial jurisdiction.

Example	*Month-to-Month Tenancy*

Smith owns a triplex and is renting all three units on a month-to-month basis. The rents are $750, $725, and $700 respectively. Initially, all tenants had leases for the first year, but following the end of the lease term, Smith didn't bother having the leases renewed. Consequently, the three tenancies continue on a month-to-month basis until a notice is provided pursuant to applicable legislation.

Provincial   See applicable reference materials.

MONTHLY RENTAL FACTOR
(SEE INCOME MULTIPLIERS)

MONUMENTATION

A method of identifying corner points in a survey through the use of standard bars. The types of standard bars used are described on the legend included with a plan or survey, e.g., standard bar (1" x 48") and short standard bar (1" x 24").

A survey contains four components:

- Research;
- Measurement;
- Monumentation; and
- Plan and/or report.

Monumentation refers to the marking of the property as set out in the applicable provincial legislation. The most common form of monumentation is the standard iron bar. Historically, other types of monumentation have been used such as posts, stakes, pegs, mounds, pits or other marks to denote boundary corners. Provincial legislation relating to surveys will detail acceptable methods and means concerning monumentation.

Provincial   See applicable reference materials.

MORATORIUM

A legal authorization relating to mortgages to delay payment of money due, owing to a specific circumstance, thus delaying the mortgagor's obligations as stipulated in the mortgage document. The term is also used in reference to the actual time period for that delay.

Example	*Moratorium*

Smith is currently in arrears on mortgage payments for the family farm. The lending institution, while acknowledging Smith's financial difficulties, starts foreclosure proceedings during the spring. Smith argues that he will be able to pay all arrears, but requires sufficient time to harvest the crops and seeks court action to stop the foreclosure proceedings. The judge, hearing Smith's plea, decides in his favour and places a moratorium on any further foreclosure action until December of that same year. This period of time should provide sufficient delay for Smith to harvest and sell crops and repay the debt.

MORE OR LESS

A term often found in a property description, intended to cover slight, unimportant, or unsubstantial inaccuracies of which both parties are willing to assume the risk.

MORTGAGE

A charge on land as security for the payment of a debt with certain remedies for nonpayment. A mortgage is a claim or encumbrance upon the real property given by the owner of the property to the lender as security for money borrowed and typically registered in the applicable provincial land registration system.

The two parties to a mortgage transaction are referred to as the *mortgagor* (borrower) and the *mortgagee* (lender). The lender *gives* or lends the money and registers the mortgage against the property. In return, the borrower gives the mortgage as security for the loan, receives the funds, makes the required payments, and maintains possession of the property. The borrower has a right to have the mortgage discharged from the title once the debt is paid off.

Assignment

The assigning of a mortgagee's rights, ownership and interest in a mortgage to a new mortgagee. The mortgage is an interest in land and can be sold, transferred, or assigned without the consent of the mortgagor. The mortgagor is given notice in writing of the assignment and thereafter makes his/her payments to the assignee. The assignee acquires all the rights of the mortgagee and can exercise these against the mortgagor. This individual acquires only the rights that the mortgagee had and no agreement between the mortgagee and the assignee changes any rights that the mortgagor already has, nor can it impose any additional burden on the mortgagor.

The assignee takes the mortgage subject to the state of accounts between the mortgagee and mortgagor. If, for example, due to a prepayment privilege, the mortgagor had made an additional payment off the principal of which the assignee was not aware, the assignee would have no claim on the mortgagor. After the mortgagor is expressly notified of the assignment and if he or she continues to make payments to the original mortgagee, the assignee can take legal action against the mortgagor to collect the money.

Example *Mortgage—Assignment*

Investor Thompson holds a mortgage on property owned by Smith. Thompson assigns the mortgage as of February 1, 20xx to ABC Investments Ltd. and formally notifies Smith. The mortgage amount is $24,512 as at February 1, 20xx and the mortgage payment date is the fifteenth of each month. Thompson's interest of $24,512 is transferred to ABC Investments Ltd. Smith's February payment is apportioned using the February 1, 20xx date. All future payments should be made to ABC Investments Ltd. Smith is liable to ABC following that date even if he inadvertently keeps forwarding payments to Thompson. As a protection, the new assignee may require a guarantee of the mortgage by the original mortgagee and an indemnification agreement to further support his/her position in the event that the original mortgagor defaults.

Provincial   See applicable reference materials. The ability to assign or transfer a mortgage along with appropriate procedures is regulated by provincial statutory provisions.

Assumption

Existing mortgage financing may be assumed by the buyer provided that the mortgagee agrees and, in most instances, the buyer qualifies by being eligible to obtain a loan of this nature from the lender, just as the original mortgagor did. When a buyer assumes the mortgage, he/she takes over the mortgage balance and becomes responsible for the payments, terms, and all monies owed. By assuming an existing mortgage, the buyer may save appraisal fees, some legal costs, and survey costs. The advantage to the seller may be a savings of any payout penalty or interest differential that may apply.

Provincial   See applicable reference materials. Mortgage covenants of the original mortgagor can still apply. Legislation may vary by provincial jurisdiction.

Categories

While a wide array of mortgages is possible, most fall under one of the following categories or classes:

Conventional Mortgages

In accordance with federal and provincial legislation, chartered lending institutions entrusted with public funds are not permitted to arrange first mortgages in excess of 75% of the appraised value of the property. Loans above this amount must be insured.

Privately Insured or High Ratio Mortgages (Conventional Insured Mortgages)

Mortgages up to 95% of lending value may be insured by private mortgage companies (subject to rules, regulations, and changes within the financial markets). Currently, GE Capital Mortgage Insurance Canada provides this service.

CMHC Insured (NHA Loans)

Mortgages up to 95% of lending value are insured by the government through the *National Housing Act*. See **Canada Mortgage and Housing Corporation**.

Default/Legal Action

Mortgagees are provided certain statutory rights when the mortgagor is in default on a mortgage. Such rights and procedures are detailed under provincial legislation.

Six commonly used avenues for the collection of monies or legal remedies under a mortgage include:

- Quit claim deed (release of the equity of redemption).
- Sue for possession.
- Sue for payment.
- Sue for foreclosure.
- Judicial sale.
- Power of sale.

Legislation Affecting Mortgages

Various acts, both federal and provincial, affect mortgages. A brief description follows.

Federal

Interest Act   The *Interest Act* imposes requirements on how interest is described and calculated in loan and mortgage documents. The parties to a mortgage are free to agree on any rate of interest they choose. However, where the mortgage is retired by payments that combine principal and interest, the mortgage must contain either a mechanism by which the borrower may determine the amount of interest he/she is paying or express the interest at a rate compounded half-yearly, or yearly, not in advance. The *Interest Act* also gives the mortgagor the right to repay the mortgage in full with a bonus of three months' interest prior to maturity if the mortgage is for a term of more than five years, unless the mortgagor is a corporation.

Criminal Code   The *Criminal Code* makes it a criminal offence to charge a rate of interest in excess of 60% per annum. In this legislation, the term *interest* is broadly defined to include the aggregate of all charges and expenses, whether in the form of a fee, fine, penalty, commission or other charge or expense paid for the advancing of credit.

Loan Companies Act   The *Loan Companies Act* outlines conditions under which funds held with a loan company can be loaned to borrowers and provides limitations as to the scope of their lending practices.

Provincial

Provincial legislation relating to mortgages is typically outlined under four categories.

Mortgage Registration   Provincial legislation provides a mechanism for the registration of mortgages and the establishment of priority for purposes of mortgagor and mortgagee rights with land titles or registry.

Marital (Matrimonial) Property   Legislation addresses the rights of spouses in regard to matrimonial property and the consent of a spouse to either sell or mortgage such property.

Rights/Powers   Provincial legislation details the rights and requirements of mortgagee and mortgagor and statutory powers (particularly regarding power of sale).

Mortgage Brokers and Mortgage Dealers   Legislation addresses the licensing and associated rules/regulations governing mortgage brokers and/or dealers (terminology will vary by province).

Other Legislation Other provincial legislation affecting mortgages can include statutory requirements concerning credit unions, and specialized legislation such as unconscionable transactions.

Mortgage Insurance

The mortgage balance must be insured, at a cost to the borrower, in all cases where a borrower uses high-ratio financing, i.e., the loan to value ratio is greater than 75%, and for all NHA loans. This form of insurance is not for the protection of the borrower, but rather for the lender. Should the borrower default on payment, the loan will be repaid by the insuring company who then assumes the title to the property and disposes of it to settle as much of the debt as possible. Do not confuse this form of insurance with the life insurance offered by many lenders that repays the loan in the event that the borrower dies.

The mortgage insurance premium, payable by the borrower, is based on the loan amount. Insurance premiums vary with market conditions and the rates are determined by the insuring company. The premium may be paid by the mortgagor either in one lump sum in advance or added to the loan amount and amortized over the life of the mortgage. Currently, Canada Mortgage and Housing Corporation and GE Capital Mortgage Insurance Canada, insure mortgages.

Priority of Mortgages

Mortgages are described according to priority as registered against title in the provincial land registration system. The earliest mortgage registered against the title is referred to as the first mortgage (also frequently referred to as the *senior* mortgage). Subsequent mortgages, such as second and third mortgages, are sequentially registered against the property based on time of registration. There are no restrictions as to the number of mortgages which can be registered against a title.

Mortgages registered after the first are often referred to as *secondary mortgages* (also called *junior* mortgages). Secondary mortgages are important where:

- A borrower requires additional funding but does not wish to disturb, or cannot prepay, an existing mortgage;
- Additional funding is required, but the conventional mortgage limits have been reached; or
- The primary lender does not want increased exposure due to condition, location, or type of property. However, a secondary lender will assume the risk in consideration of a higher rate of return.

Provinces using the registry system have traditionally referred to first mortgages as *legal* mortgages and secondary

mortgages as *equitable* mortgages. The legal mortgage transfers the estate or interest in the property as security for the debt. Since the legal title can only be transferred once, all subsequent mortgages rely on equity as security for the debt, hence the term *equity* or *equitable* mortgage. Under land titles, mortgages are registered as charges against the property and no actual conveyance of title occurs. Priority is only distinguished by date of registration.

Priority of Other Encumbrancers

Different parties can have claims of various types against the same property at the same time by registering their interest on title. Certain unregistered documents or claims can have priority despite registered encumbrances and their apparent priority. However, the priority of registration will prevail unless actual notice is provided regarding these specific unregistered interests, but exceptions do exist.

Descriptions are provided for illustration purposes only subject to a variety of exceptions and related provisions in provincial legislation.

Municipal Taxes

Municipal taxes in arrears have priority over mortgages. Consequently, most sets of standard charge terms specifically outline precise methods for payment of taxes and provisions for maintaining these payments, even when the loan is in default. Mortgagees often insist on paying the taxes themselves to protect their security in case of non-payment of taxes by the mortgagor. Typically, mortgagors' payments include principal, interest, and taxes (PIT). If taxes are not part of the monthly payment, the mortgagee will require proof each year that taxes have been paid in full.

Condominium Maintenance Fees (Common Expenses)

Provincial condominium legislation typically provides that common expenses in condominiums have priority over everything except taxes. Therefore, many mortgagees collect these fees along with monthly payments of principal, interest, and taxes in order to protect their security.

Registration

Priority of a mortgage over any other claim is only by registration on title, and the date and time of that registration.

Liens

Lien claims registered on title prior to a mortgage have priority over the mortgage.

Judgments

Judgments against the owner of the land are encumbrances on the land, as the land can always be sold for the judgment.

Judgment executions against the mortgagor that arise after registration of the mortgage do not have priority over the mortgage. Judgment executions registered before the mortgage do have priority over the mortgage.

Leases

Leases made prior to the granting of a mortgage have priority over the mortgage. Even when the mortgagor defaults, the mortgagee cannot get vacant possession until the expiration of the lease. The mortgagee can, however, give proper notification of foreclosure or possession and the lessee must then pay rent to the mortgagee. Provincial legislation may impact the relationship of tenant and mortgagor.

Privileges

Various common privileges are associated with mortgages. The following is provided as a general description only. Provincial legislative requirements and procedures may differ.

Prepayment Privilege

The concept of prepayment is not a right under the mortgage document, but a privilege. Unless otherwise specified, the mortgagor has agreed to make payments according to a specified schedule and the contract is written to run for a specified period.

Renewal Privilege

Some mortgages have a built-in renewal privilege. However, this is an exception to the general rule. Most Canadian mortgages do not specifically spell out the opportunity to renew, and consequently, this opportunity does not exist. Normally, lenders prefer to reserve the right to renew based on financial circumstances of the borrower at the end of the mortgage term.

Transfer Privilege

The ability to transfer a mortgage again depends on the wording of the mortgage document. Generally, three different approaches exist in the Canadian mortgage marketplace. First, the mortgagor may be able to transfer without the consent of the mortgagee, but he/she may remain liable through the personal covenant. Second, lenders may now insert sale/approval clauses requiring approval of any person who will be assuming the mortgage at the point of property sale. Third, certain lenders insist on non-transferability, e.g., in the instance where a borrower has mortgaged his/her property with a lender as security for business loans, or in the case of a credit union who mortgaged a member's property and does not wish to continue financing the property after the member sells.

Postponement Privilege

An existing mortgagee, if provided with a reasonable degree of security, may agree to postpone the priority of his/her mortgage in favour of a prior mortgage being replaced or another mortgage being created.

Purpose/Function of a Mortgage

When one party lends money to another, he/she may lend the money without taking back any security for the loan. If the borrower defaults in repaying the loan, the person lending the money may sue the borrower, but the lender's claim will rank with any other debts owed by the borrower. However, the lender may choose to take security for the loan that provides a claim upon the security and takes precedence over other creditors in relation to that security. Accordingly, the main function of a mortgage is to provide security and that security may be any type of property.

Personal property is often mortgaged in the form of a chattel mortgage. For example, security is usually required when a bank lends money for the purchase of a car. If the borrower defaults on the loan, the lender repossesses the automobile.

The most common way of creating a mortgage is by registering the mortgage document in the provincial land registration office (registry or land titles). The mortgage document declares that the mortgagor is the owner of a piece of property and the mortgagee has agreed to loan money on the security of the property. The document contains covenants, or promises, on the part of the mortgagor to the mortgagee in return for the advancement of funds by the mortgagee. Many standard form mortgage documents exist, but most contain basically the same covenants. Examples of such covenants are:

- The covenant to pay principal and interest to the mortgagee;
- The covenant to pay all taxes when due;
- The covenant to insure the property against fire and damage; and
- The covenant to keep the property in good repair.

Registration

Registration procedures and information required in a mortgage document being registered in the registry or land titles systems will vary by provincial jurisdiction. All documents, including mortgages, registered against a title are a matter of public record. A search of either system will reveal ownership and other interests including mortgages.

Provincial   See applicable reference materials for details concerning registration systems.

Renewal

A provision set out in a mortgage document whereby the lender may extend the term of the mortgage usually subject to revised arrangements, e.g., amount of principal repayment, and interest rate amendment.

In drafting a renewal privilege, practitioners must clearly delineate the terms and conditions for the further renewal period. For example, a renewal clause might permit the mortgagor to renew the mortgage when not in default, on the same terms and conditions save and except for a further renewal. A more restrictive renewal clause might include a requirement that the interest rate be set 30 days prior to the expiration, based on a pre-determined formula, and the term be specifically identified, e.g., one, two, or three years, and that such renewal be subject to the continued credit worthiness of the mortgagor.

> **Example** *Mortgage–Renewal*
>
> Owner Smith has agreed to a seller take-back mortgage to facilitate a sale to buyer Jones. Jones is uncertain whether he will require the mortgage for one year, or at most, two years. He has other property that may be sold and these funds would be used to discharge the mortgage completely. Accordingly, the following clause is inserted in the agreement:
>
> *This mortgage shall contain a clause permitting the mortgagor, when not in default, the privilege of renewing this mortgage on its maturity for a further term of one year on the same terms and conditions save and except for the right to any further renewal and at a rate of interest which is to be mutually agreed upon.*

Specialty Financing

Various types of specialty mortgage financing are available to serve specific purposes. Selected types are identified along with encyclopedia references for additional information.

Blanket Mortgage   A mortgage covering two or more specific parcels of real property or two or more mortgages. See **Blanket Mortgage**.

Chattel Mortgage   A mortgage on personal property. See **Chattel Mortgage**.

Collateral Mortgage   A collateral mortgage is a loan backed by a promissory note and then further secured by means of a mortgage on real property. See **Collateral Mortgage**.

Equitable Mortgage   A mortgage subsequent to the first (legal) mortgage. See **Equitable Mortgage**.

Special Purpose Financing   A range of special purpose packages have arisen to meet specific needs. Information concerning these packages can be found under the appropriate heading. See **Bridge Loan, Gap Loan, Letter Of Guarantee, Line Of Credit, New Home Construction Loan,** and **Stand-by Loan.**

Seller Take-Back Mortgage   A mortgage loan where the seller carries the mortgage (becomes the lender), for the buyer. This allows the buyer to negotiate mortgage terms and avoid some of the paperwork/regulations imposed by conventional lenders. See **Seller Take-Back Mortgage**.

Standard Charge Terms

Sets of standard charge terms are registered in a registry or land titles registration system. Such terms can then be referred to in individual mortgage documents and do not need to be filed with each mortgage. This practice results in a significant reduction in the number of pages that would otherwise be processed when registering a mortgage.

Provincial   See applicable reference materials. Specific provincial jurisdictions may provide *plain language standard charge terms* for purposes of registration.

Terms
Fixed Rate

A mortgage having a fixed interest rate for a predetermined term, usually between six months and 25 years, and cannot be renegotiated except upon payment of a prepayment penalty or related costs.

Variable Rate (or Floating Rate)

A mortgage in which payments are fixed for a period of one to two years, although interest rates may fluctuate from month to month depending upon market conditions. If interest rates go down, more of the payment is applied to the principal. If rates go up, a larger portion of the monthly payment goes toward interest.

Open Mortgage

A mortgage that can be prepaid at any time prior to maturity, without a prepayment penalty.

Closed Mortgage

A mortgage that cannot be prepaid, renegotiated, or refinanced prior to the expiry of the term, except with an interest penalty or other cost.

MORTGAGE BACKED SECURITIES
(SEE ALSO SECURITIZATION)

Securities packaged and secured by pools of mortgages originated in the primary mortgage market. The process, commonly referred to as *securitization*, allows mortgages to be converted into bond-like securities of relatively small denominations, thereby opening up financial markets, long associated with institutional lenders, to small investors.

MORTGAGE BANKING

A term frequently used to describe activity in the secondary mortgage market in which investor groups, finance companies, and a host of private lenders participate in the buying and selling of mortgage paper.

In fact, large institutions may purchase entire portfolios of mortgage investments. The concept of mortgage bankers has become a major part of the US financial scene. These bankers develop portfolios of mortgages and then sell them to investors. Often, the sale to an investor includes a long-term management agreement with the mortgage banker to service and generally administer the portfolio.

Application The concept of mortgage banking has not gained the same prominence in Canada, undoubtedly because of the more centralized structure of the Canadian banking system, the limited size of the secondary mortgage market, and the concentration of banking activities among a few large lenders.

During the mid-1980s, the Canadian government introduced a mortgage-backed securities (MBS) system that parallels in many respects financial products in the United States. Under this arrangement, mortgages originating with institutional lenders are pooled for investment purposes through an issuer. Predetermined criteria (one of which is CMHC mortgage insurance), determine which mortgages are selected for these mortgage pools. The mortgages are then sold to investors in block amounts, e.g., $5,000 minimum investment. The investor is protected by CMHC, who guarantees the mortgages in the event of default.

A considerable amount of interest and activity is now centred on the development of both mortgage and equity investment portfolios. The growth of mortgage banking is an integral aspect of that development.

MORTGAGE BROKER (DEALER)

A person or other legal entity who carries on the business of lending money on the security of real estate. A mortgage broker (dealer) is normally regulated by applicable provincial legislation.

Provincial See applicable reference materials.

MORTGAGE CAPITALIZATION
(SEE ALSO MORTGAGE CONSTANT)

One of several capitalization methods used in the income approach when appraising property. The rate expresses the relationship between the annual debt service and the mortgage value (principal amount), at a particular point in time. The formula to calculate this rate is:

Mortgage Capitalization Rate
= Annual Debt Service ÷ Mortgage Value

The mortgage capitalization rate, when combined with the equity capitalization rate, is used in the band of investment method for calculating an overall capitalization rate. The mortgage capitalization rate is calculated with the same formula as the mortgage constant but is used for valuation, as opposed to cash flow analysis.

Example	*Mortgage Capitalization (Appraisal)*

The subject property has a new first mortgage of $225,000, at an interest rate of 13.5% repayable at $2,560.50 monthly (principal and interest, amortized over 25 years). From this, the applicable mortgage capitalization rate is calculated as:

Mortgage Capitalization Rate
= Annual Debt Service ÷ Mortgage Value
= ($2,560.50 x 12) ÷ $225,000 = .13656 or 13.7%

MORTGAGE COMMITMENT

A written confirmation or other formal indication by a lending institution that it will grant a mortgage and advance funds, based on certain conditions and/or limitations. See **Figure M.5**.

Application The mortgage commitment sets out details of the property, type of mortgage, amount, and terms. While forms vary, most contain processing costs, repayment privileges, tax payments, fire insurance coverage, and special conditions. The commitment also sets a future date until which time funds are available, at which time the commitment may be amended or withdrawn at the lender's option.

Limiting Conditions

Normally, limiting conditions include verification that the taxes are not in arrears, proof of insurance, satisfactory

M

MORTGAGE LOAN COMMITMENT

Loan No. A10461

To

Mr. Anthony Smith
R.R. #1, Anycity

Loan Amount

Basic Loan	$152,000
Mortgage Insurance Premium	0
Total Loan	$152,000

Property

Civic Address	42 Leafy Drive, Anycity
Legal Description	Lot 23, Plan 99M–1631

Terms

Interest Rate	8.25%
Term	5 Years
Amortization	25 Years
I.A.D.	September 1, 20xx
First Payment Date	October 1, 20xx

Type of Mortgage

Conventional

Repayment   Repayable in blended monthly installments of $1,184.43 plus an amount which in our opinion is sufficient to enable us to pay the property taxes on your behalf by the first due date of the tax bill each year, currently estimated at $196.64. It is understood that repayment will be by preauthorized cheque drawn on your bank.

Taxes   In order to satisfy the foregoing tax requirement, we shall withhold funds from our mortgage advance to accumulate sufficient credit in your tax account. The amount of $1,245.00 will be deducted for this purpose.

Fire Insurance   We shall require evidence of fire insurance coverage in the amount of not less than $140,000 taken with an insurer acceptable to us. Such policy must contain the standard Insurance Bureau of Canada mortgage clause and must indicate our interest as first mortgagee.

Survey Requirement   An acceptable survey prepared by a duly certified Land Surveyor is to be furnished to our Solicitor prior to the disbursement of funds.

Solicitor   B. Watson be appointed to act on our behalf in this transaction. All documentation including but not limited to survey, title and insurance must be acceptable to us prior to the advance of funds.

Costs   A processing fee amounting to $50.00 will be deducted from our advance of funds. Should the loan not be proceeded with, this fee will still be payable in any event. You are to pay all legal and survey costs incurred in this transaction.

General Conditions
   (i)   This approval is based upon and subject to the accuracy of information furnished in connection with your application.
   (ii) In cases where there is a construction loan, advances will be made at the discretion of the lender, who will always retain sufficient funds to complete construction.
   (iii) Funds are available under this mortgage until October 1, 20xx at which time, this commitment may be amended or withdrawn at our option.

Privileges   There is a 10% prepayment privilege. See Attached. This mortgage is open for full discharge with 3 months bonus. See attached. Mortgagor is responsible for total 20xx taxes.

Special Conditions   If this mortgage loan covers a newly constructed house or house being constructed for sale, our Solicitor will be required to obtain a certified copy of the New Home Enrollment form, endorsed by ONHWP before making any mortgages advances.

Acceptance of Offer   This offer of mortgage loan is open for acceptance by you until the close of business on August 7, 20xx by which time, the enclosed copy of this letter, duly executed, plus a deposit of $NIL being a Standby Fee shall be in our hands. The aforementioned deposit without interest will be refunded to you upon the disbursement of mortgage funds, but will be retained by us if this commitment is cancelled by you after acceptance as liquidated damages and not as a penalty.

This commitment is not transferable and the benefit may not be assigned. If the above conditions are satisfactory to you, please indicate your acceptance by signing and returning the enclosed copy to us, at the above address.

Accepted as above, this _____ day of _____ , 20xx

_____
Applicant's Signature

Figure M.5   Mortgage Loan Commitment

evidence of title to the property being mortgaged, and the provision of a survey acceptable to the mortgagee. The application fee paid for the processing of the loan may not be refunded if any or all of the preceding conditions are not fulfilled and/or the loan is not advanced.

Payment of Taxes

The lender normally specifies a method by which taxes are paid. The commitment may contain a provision whereby an amount, (usually between ¼ and ½ of the estimated annual taxes), is withheld for payment of taxes so that such payments are always current. Lenders usually adjust the monthly amount to gradually build a tax reserve.

Fire Insurance

Usually cancelled by the seller and rewritten by the buyer, prior to the closing date. The mortgage document (and often the mortgage commitment), outlines the precise coverages required. Full replacement value coverage ensures the mortgagee that the total risk is insured against loss. Limited insurance to cover only the mortgage amount would unnecessarily expose the mortgagee in case of a partial loss. Sufficient funds may not be available to fully correct the damage.

Example   *Mortgage Commitment–Fire Insurance*

A house is valued at $150,000 for replacement cost and currently has a $50,000 mortgage. The mortgagee requires the face amount of the mortgage to be insured. The mortgagor experiences partial loss of the building and the insurer only pays a part of the $50,000 because only a part of the total property ($50,000/$150,000) was insured with that company. Therefore, the loss payment is $16,667.

Survey Requirement

The statement typically specifies that the survey must be acceptable to the mortgagee's solicitor. Costs relating to the survey are normally paid by the buyer.

Acceptance/Guarantee of Terms

The commitment will contain a time limit for acceptance. Normally, quoted interest rates are fixed for a specified period (usually 60–90 days from date of commitment).

MORTGAGE CONSTANT

The percentage of a loan that must be paid periodically to pay off the debt. The mortgage constant is typically

expressed as a yearly percentage. The constant for fully amortized loans is calculated by dividing yearly principal and interest payments by the amount of the mortgage.

Application   The calculation of a mortgage constant can apply to any point during the duration of a mortgage, based on the balance outstanding in relation to annual debt service. The mortgage constant is an income rate and should be differentiated from a mortgage yield rate (i.e., interest rate charged).

Mortgage Constant = Annual Debt Service ÷ Mortgage Amount

**Example 1   *Mortgage Constant–
Based on Amortized Payment***

Investor McKay has secured a new mortgage of $300,000 @ 8% calculated semi-annually not in advance amortized over 25 years. The mortgage constant is calculated as:

Monthly Mortgage Payment $2,289.64
(7.632135 (monthly payment factor per $1,000) x 300(000)

Annual Debt Service $27,475.69

Mortgage Constant   .0916 or 9.16%
($27,475.69 ÷ 300,000)

The mortgage constant for a blended mortgage includes both principal and interest payments. The mortgage constant in an interest-only mortgage is equal to the interest rate. In the example provided, the debt service represents 9.16% of the face amount of the mortgage. This constant would then be used by investors to analyze the impact of financing on cash flows before taxes (leverage) and ultimately the effect on yield.

As with most financial measurements and rules of thumb, prudence is required. Mortgage constants can assist in assessing the merits of financing packages, however, all investment decisions are best viewed within the context of investor objectives. Leverage is only one of several criteria applied in most buying strategies. **Figure M.6** illustrates the impact of debt service on cash flow.

MORTGAGE DOCUMENTATION PACKAGE

Applicable to both residential and commercial marketplaces, these packages (sometimes referred to as *mortgage request packages*), are most commonly associated with industrial, office/retail, and investment properties. The submission contains information relevant to the lender in making a mortgage financing decision involving a specific property or project.

Mortgage Constant—Cash Flow Before Taxes

Consider the impact of various mortgage terms on cash flow before taxes. (Cash flow before taxes (CFBT) is determined by subtracting annual debt service from net operating income (NOI).)

AMOUNT	RATE	AMORTIZATION	ANNUAL DEBT SERVICE	NOI	CFBT	CONSTANT
$100,000	9%	25	$ 9,935.73	$20,000	$10,064.27	9.94% (.0994)
100,000	10%	25	10,733.85	20,000	9,266.15	10.73% (.1073)
100,000	10%	15	12,747.24	20,000	7,252.76	12.75% (.1275)
100,000	9%	10	15,094.63	20,000	4,905.37	15.09% (.1509)

The combination of interest rate and amortization can significantly impact cash flow before taxes and the return on invested dollars (return on equity). In the following example, the overall return remains constant at 10% (NOI ÷ Total Investment) as debt financing is not factored into the calculation. However, the impact of financing is readily seen when comparing the mortgage constant with return on equity (CFBT ÷ Equity). As the mortgage constant rises, the cash flow falls resulting in lower equity yields. Option 1 produces positive leverage, while Options 2, 3 and 4 generate negative leverage (return on equity is less than overall return).

TOTAL	MORTGAGE	EQUITY	CASH FLOW	OVERALL RETURN	RETURN ON EQUITY	MORTGAGE CONSTANT
$200,000	$100,000	$100,000	$10,064.28	10%	10.06%	9.94% (.0994)
200,000	100,000	100,000	9,266.15	10%	9.27%	10.73% (.1073)
200,000	100,000	100,000	7,252.76	10%	7.25%	12.75% (.1275)
200,000	100,000	100,000	4,905.37	10%	4.9%	15.09% (.1509)

Overall Return = NOI ÷ Total
Return on Equity = CFBT ÷ Equity

Mortgages may initially appear appealing, but prove otherwise—at least from a strict cash flow perspective. The 9% mortgage over 25 years provides much better cash flow than both the 10% mortgage amortized over the same period and the 9% mortgage amortized over ten years. However, the latter will be paid off sooner, thereby increasing investor yield at the point of disposition.

Figure M.6   Mortgage Constant Calculations

M

Application   The range of materials varies significantly by property type, project scope, lender requirements, and the specific investor.

- Site and property information along with relevant statistics, sketches, valuation estimates, and associated supporting documentation.
- Fully completed mortgage application, appraisal, verification of income/salaries, credit check, verification of resources and other financial commitments, and the agreement of purchase and sale.
- In the case of resale properties, the lender will usually insist on financial statements for at least the past three to five years, along with a review of existing leases on the property.
- For new construction, pro forma income statements, letters of commitment from prospective tenants (or suitable analysis identifying potential for lessees), details concerning principals involved in the project, feasibility studies, and applicable construction information (if relevant), are normally requested.

The overall structure of a typical documentation package is illustrated, but scope and format varies.

PART 1	Summary Statement of Objectives
PART 2	Site Description (general description, site data, relevant statistics)
PART 3	Improvements (detailed description of existing or planned improvements)
PART 4	Financial Profile (personal and/or corporate)
PART 5	Mortgage Financing Request (amount, terms, and special requirements)
APPENDIX	Supporting documentation (fully completed mortgage application, credit references, financial information)

Practitioners are well advised to seek additional information from lending institutions regarding typical practices within the local market.

MORTGAGE FINANCING

Basics of Mortgage Financing (Residential)

Application

Most applications are designed to elicit information about three items: the property, the applicants, and financial status. The lending institution may ask for a standby or processing fee. Standby fees are commonly related to non-residential transactions and represent a payment to guarantee a specified set of mortgage terms (e.g., the interest rate), for a defined period. Application fees are more commonly found in residential mortgages. Whether or not the fee is refundable and under what circumstances a refund would be made will vary by individual lender.

Once the offer is accepted, the application is forwarded to the lender. Make certain it is complete, accurate, factual, and precise. A covering letter is sometimes used by salespeople to point out any personal observations or relevant comments that will assist the lender. Several items normally accompany the application: namely, proof of income, a copy of the agreement/contract, copy of the listing, payment for processing costs (administration fee), confirmation of downpayment, and any other documentation that will support information included on the mortgage application.

Appraisal and Credit Check

The lender reviews the application, applies GDS and TDS ratios, and considers the stability and future prospects regarding the income stream as well as personal/financial information of the applicant. An appraiser or bank representative will inspect the property to ensure that it meets lender criteria and determine the lending value of the property. Residential appraisal reports normally include both direct comparison and cost approaches, and are prepared on standard formats approved by the lender.

A credit check is usually performed to verify financial stability of the applicant. Persons (institutional or private lenders), completing a credit check, must comply with the provincial statutory provisions regarding such matters.

Commitment

The mortgage commitment is usually a letter from the lender agreeing to make the loan subject to satisfactory title and other conditions that the commitment may specify. See **Mortgage Commitment** for limiting conditions and other requirements.

Unfortunately, instances have occurred where individuals have mistakenly believed that a letter from a lender simply quoting the loan amount they would consider, if a property was purchased, was a commitment. This is not so, as most institutions currently financing a property would require a formal signed application, approval of the sale price, and approval of the buyer before issuing any commitment. Such letter is merely a letter of intent and has little, if any, legal stature and should never form the basis for removal of a mortgage condition in an agreement/contract, or be the basis for a buyer not requiring an appropriate condition when an offer is drafted.

Lender Selection

Once information regarding the property to be financed has been obtained, the practitioner is involved in several steps. Assuming that no pre-approval has occurred and that all relevant buyer information has been collected, the salesperson may assist the buyer in deciding where to obtain the loan, e.g., a bank, trust company, private lender, life insurance company, or credit union.

- Develop a short list of the most likely lenders for preliminary contact. (Many brokerages have various local lender application forms on file with which that brokerage frequently does business.)
- Salespeople occasionally assist the buyers in completing the application form. Often, lenders require a meeting with the applicant at their own office to complete such forms.

Listing, Offer, and Acceptance

While financing methods on a sale will vary from one brokerage to another, certain common patterns emerge in most transactions subject to particular variances at a local level.

- At the point of listing, the maximum amount, interest rate, and even the source of funds for any new mortgage will be partially dictated by the type, location, and value of the property.
- The financial circumstances of the buyer must be assessed. The downpayment provides an indication of probable financing requirements, and information as to the buyer's income, obligations, stability, and future prospects of income stream will assist in determining the payments that the buyer can afford. Many sales representatives have the buyer complete mortgage application forms before viewing property, to determine the amount of financing required.
- Prior to preparing any offer, the buyer should have received pre-approval, or the salesperson should:
    - Qualify the buyer financially;
    - Pre-determine the type and amount of new mortgage necessary;
    - Pre-determine the probable interest rate, payments, term, and special privileges for the mortgage;
    - Pre-determine the lender who will be approached;

- Pre-determine the amount of time that will probably be involved to arrange a mortgage;
- Pre-determine the expenses involved in arranging a mortgage; and
- Pre-determine the probability that the mortgage will be arranged.

A detailed knowledge of the buyer's ability to arrange financing is vital for protection of the seller, who, in accepting an offer, will effectively take the property off the market on the risk that this mortgage can be arranged for the buyer within the specified time limit.

Pre-Approved Buyer

The buyer usually visits his/her lending institution and, after discussion/disclosure of financial position, receives a pre-approval certificate, outlining the maximum amount that can be borrowed, the interest rate to be charged, and the monthly payments. The approval is subject to a satisfactory appraisal of any house being purchased and confirmation of taxes. The interest rate is normally guaranteed for a 60–90 day period and the monthly payment is based on an estimate of taxes. In condominiums, common expenses are also estimated. The offer should be conditional on the lender approving the property, arranging a satisfactory appraisal, and any other conditions spelled out in the pre-approval document.

The terms *pre-approved* and *pre-qualified* may not have the same meaning from the lender's perspective. Take the time to read the exact terms of the certificate carefully.

Commercial Requirements

The sale of large income-producing properties and major commercial operations requires special expertise. A salesperson could become involved in assisting a buyer in arranging financing for a project. Most lenders require:

Feasibility Report   This can range from a brief letter to a fully detailed report on the economic, market, and physical characteristics of the venture.

Construction and Site Analysis   Complete documentation regarding the property, architectural drawings, detailed construction plans, utilities, landscaping, parking, buffer zones, adjacent zoning, and zoning amendments required.

Borrower Information   Past projects with addresses, financial statements for the past two to three years, credit check and background of the company/individual with supporting documents.

Estimated Income/Operating Expenses   Full details of estimated gross income, vacancy rates expected, expenses (excluding debt service), and net operating income.

As a rule, more information is better than less. The lender must be comfortable with both borrower and project as project financing can represent a significant commitment by a lender.

Historical Development

While the basic concept underlying mortgages has remained the same throughout history, certain evolutionary steps should be highlighted. As early as 1886, the *Dominion Insurance Act* provided for mortgage investment, but set no limitations as to ratio of *loan to lending value*. It was not until 1910 that the *Insurance Act* set conventional mortgage maximums at 60% of the value of the property. The introduction of the *Dominion Housing Act* during 1935 was a milestone in mortgage financing. This first major piece of housing legislation was designed to stimulate housing construction throughout the country.

The *Dominion Housing Act* had no reference to an *insurable* mortgage. Instead, the Act provided government funds for new home building based on a *joint loans system*. The conventional lender would advance a loan up to 60% of the value of the property. The balance (to a total loan maximum of 80%) was accessed from federal funds. The *Dominion Housing Act* also extended mortgage terms from 5 to 10 years along with corresponding amortization periods.

In 1938, the *National Housing Act* was introduced to replace the *Dominion Housing Act*. This new Act was designed to accomplish three objectives:

- Reduce the amount of unemployment within the housing industry,
- Improve general housing conditions throughout Canada, and
- Encourage the development of individual home ownership through better financial programs.

The year 1954 brought major changes that are with us today. During that year, chartered banks were approved as lenders under the *National Housing Act (NHA)* to meet the high demand for mortgage funding within residential markets. At the same time, an insurance fund was set up to change the NHA scheme from one of joint lending policy to that of insured loans. This major change saw Central Mortgage and Housing Corporation (CMHC) limit activity as a direct lender of mortgage funds and switch to providing the insurance for approved lending institutions. The name was subsequently changed to Canada Mortgage and Housing Corporation.

Major changes took place in 1970. The *Canadian and British Insurance Companies Act* was amended to permit institutional lenders to become involved in *high ratio* financing. This allowed mortgage investment above the 75% level provided that such loans were insured by private mortgage insurance firms. Prior to this time, investors had been able to participate in high ratio financing solely through the *National Housing Act*. With this amendment, high ratio financing found its way into nearly every sector in the housing market through combinations of government approved facilities and private market institutions.

Owner-Occupied Income Property

While larger rental units are financed based on income stream, small owner-occupied properties normally represent a composite of both personal covenant and income stream. Consequently, with an owner-occupied duplex, for example, while the actual value is normally determined using comparable sales, the qualifying GDS ratio will typically include consideration for rental income from the second unit.

In larger owner-occupied rental property the same general principle applies. Lenders will often include a percentage of gross rents in applying the GDS ratio to the borrower's income. The mixture of personal covenant and income stream normally involves six units or less. Above that size, the primary determinant is income stream but practices and underwriting procedures will vary by lender.

Example **Mortgage Financing—**
Owner-Occupied Income Property

Buyer Jones wishes to purchase a duplex and is seeking mortgage financing. The lender's qualifying criteria states that a maximum of 32% of gross family income can be devoted to PIT payments and energy costs, with a maximum loan to value ratio of 75%. The lender also includes one half of the revenue derived from the unit in the calculation of gross family income. Taxes are estimated at $3,600. Heating costs are $2,400 per year and the current mortgage rates are 9%. Jones wants to apply for maximum financing but is concerned about the income level required.

Value of Duplex	$240,000
Maximum Loan	$180,000

Monthly P & I	1,490.35
Monthly Tax Payment	+300.00
Monthly Energy Costs	+200.00
Total PIT + Energy	1,990.35

Qualifying Income Required:
$1,990.35 x 12 ÷ .32 = 74,638.13

Income Derived from Rental Unit:
$8,400 ÷ 2 = 4,200

Therefore, the owner's income must be no less than:
$74,638.13 − 4,200 = **$70,438.13**

Sources of Financing

Lending sources for real estate professionals are grouped into three main categories:

- Major Direct Lending Sources: Chartered Banks, Life Insurance Companies, Trust Companies, Loan Companies, Credit Unions, and Finance Companies.
- Agent Sources: Mortgage Brokers/Dealers.
- Private Investor Sources.

MORTGAGE FINANCING—SPECIALTY FIELD

Historically, the lending business was relatively limited and rigidly structured. Banks, trust companies, insurance companies, and credit unions each controlled their own segments of the mortgage market, with a limited variety of financing alternatives. Times have changed. Alternative lenders have entered the marketplace and competition has increased. Each institution is now offering a wide range of alternatives. The fixed-term five-year mortgage, with payments amortized over 25 years, which was the mainstay of residential financing, is no longer the norm.

Given the wide variety of alternatives, and the fact that financing tends to be a technically demanding part of a real estate purchase for most consumers, a great need for mortgage financing expertise exists. Unquestionably, every real estate salesperson must understand the basic legal, conceptual, and mathematical information related to mortgage financing, even if he/she will not be arranging a mortgage as part of the sale.

In any sales field, one of the basic procedures before attempting a sale is to qualify buyers as to their needs and capabilities. Part of this process involves qualifying the buyer financially in terms of downpayment and debt service. Financing capabilities are limited, not only by what the buyers personally think they can afford, but also by policies and guidelines that lenders apply to safeguard themselves. Only through continuous updating and familiarity with the policies and procedures of lenders, along with financing alternatives, can a real estate salesperson begin to qualify buyers properly and establish the range of properties to be viewed.

Financing is also important when drafting agreements/contracts that involve the assumption or discharge of existing financing, arranging new financing, or seller participation by way of a take back mortgage.

Aside from arranging financing as a normal function of real estate sales, specializing in mortgage financing as a full-time profession is possible, whether as a representative of a lending institution, or as a mortgage broker (dealer) or representative of a mortgage broker. Persons acting as mortgage brokers are usually registered under a provincial statute. Some specialize in arranging interim financing for large projects, industrial or commercial lending, the sale of mortgages as investment vehicles, and the placement of mortgages for the residential market.

Mortgage brokers (dealers) fulfill several functions by:

- Providing up-to-date information on policies and requirements of lending institutions and private lenders;
- Assisting borrowers by arranging financing to suit specific needs;
- Completing documentation as required to assist both borrower and lender in the financing process;
- Negotiating directly with parties in setting up specific financial packages; and
- Providing appraisal referrals and assistance for lenders as may be required.

The mortgage broker (dealer), as an advisor, becomes involved in packaging financial arrangements, obtaining approvals, ensuring that the funds are available for closing and that instructions are carried through. Due to the integration of mortgage financing and real estate sales, a great deal of information regarding financing is provided in real estate licensing/registration courses.

Provincial   See applicable reference materials.

MORTGAGE INFORMATION STATEMENTS

(SEE ALSO MORTGAGE VERIFICATION)

Mortgage balance information must be accurate as it affects the mortgagor, mortgagee, and any potential buyer. The best and only true reliable source of mortgage information is the lender or mortgagee. However, the term *mortgage balance* means different things to a lender, depending on the use of the balance figure. Several types of information statements are available in the marketplace. Terminology used, the availability, and the scope of such reports can vary by provincial jurisdiction.

Mortgage Statement (Annual)

A statement sent to the mortgagor by the mortgagee each year. Basically, this statement contains the following information:

Mortgagor Information   Name(s) and address.

Mortgage Information   Mortgage number, mortgage type (fixed or variable rate), maturity date, interest rate, mortgage description (i.e., conventional, high ratio, etc.), amortization remaining in months, payment frequency

(weekly, bi-weekly, monthly etc.), and principal/interest payment (and property taxes and insurance if applicable).

Principal   Opening balance, amount of regular and any lump sum payments, charges or adjustments, and closing principal balance.

Interest   Interest paid and accrued.

Property Taxes   Opening balance of tax account, tax payments received, taxes paid on behalf of mortgagor, adjustments (amount of any tax rebates or tax refunds), interest earned or paid by mortgagor depending upon the balance in the tax account, and closing balance of tax account.

Liquidation Statement

This statement represents the NET amount to be paid by the mortgagor to obtain a discharge of the mortgage and includes:

- Principal balance;
- Interest from last payment date to anticipated payoff date;
- Tax account/reserve balance (plus or minus);
- Prepayment penalty, if any; and
- Service or discharge fee.

Assumption Statement

This statement represents the amount of the mortgage loan that is outstanding and would be assumed by a buyer. The statement includes:

- Principal balance as at the due date of the last payment to be paid by the seller;
- Interest from the date of the last payment by the seller to the assumption date; and
- Tax account balance (plus or minus).

Unpaid Principal Balance Statement

This statement generally provides only the outstanding principal balance. Interest and tax account balances may or may not be included.

Information Statement for Listing Purposes

When requesting a mortgage information statement from a lender for listing purposes, ask for the following in writing:

- Principal balance;
- Tax account balance if any (plus or minus);
- Interest rate;

- Remaining portion of term;
- Remaining portion of amortization;
- Monthly payments;
- Name and address of mortgagee;
- If the mortgage is open or closed. If open, what penalty, if any, applies;
- If the mortgage can be assumed by a subsequent buyer with or without the lender's approval, with or without qualification; and
- If there are any arrears and if so, have foreclosure proceedings commenced.

Provincial   See applicable reference materials.

MORTGAGE MARKET

Mortgage activity both in the primary market, i.e., the origination of mortgages through various lenders in Canada and in the resale of such mortgages and related securities in the secondary market. Canada Mortgage and Housing Corporation and GE Capital Mortgage Insurance Canada play major roles in the mortgage market through the insuring of loans and promote activity both in primary and secondary markets.

MORTGAGE MATHEMATICS

Amortization

An amortized mortgage refers to the gradual retirement of a mortgage debt by means of partial payments of principal at regular intervals. Amortization is the time period required to completely retire the mortgage debt through scheduled payments of principal and interest.

Mortgage payment factors are provided for weekly, bi-weekly, semi-monthly, and monthly payment periods, with amortization covering 5, 10, 15, 20, and 25-year periods. See the **Appendix**.

Averaging

A process of determining the average interest paid on two or more mortgages, ideally having the same term and amortization. By averaging the interest rates, better comparisons of financing alternatives is possible.

Practitioners, when applying mortgage averaging, must be aware of limitations. Basing a decision solely on the *averaged* interest rate, without considering other variables, could be quite misleading for several reasons:

- The term of each mortgage may be different, with no means of accurately determining the rate of interest that may be applied when one has to be renewed.
- Mortgages may not have the same amortization periods and could utilize different payment plans.
- Special privileges can affect the true rate of interest, e.g., bonus payments, prepayment penalties.
- The actual cost of arranging mortgages may differ substantially, thereby nullifying or reversing advantages seen through the averaging formula.

Example   ***Mortgage Mathematics– Averaging: New Financing***

Buyer Jones requires $100,000 in financing and is considering two options:

- Mortgage 1 (M1): Seller discharges existing financing and Jones arranges a new first mortgage for $100,000 at 8.5%.
- Mortgage 2 (M2): Buyer assumes existing first mortgage of $55,000 at 7.0% and arranges a new second mortgage for $45,000 at 9.50%, with the same term and amortization.

The mortgage averaging formula is:

(Amount M1 x Interest Rate) + (Amount M2 x Interest Rate)
Total Amount Being Financed

= (($55,000 x 7.0%) + ($45,000 x 9.5%)) ÷ $100,000
= (3,850 + 4,275) ÷ 100,000
= .08125 or 8.1% rounded

The first/second mortgage combination appears to have the lower overall rate. However, the comparative cost of arranging either option could be a major consideration. It should be noted that this mortgage averaging concept can be used for any number of mortgages.

Calculating Nominal and Effective Rates

Most discussions of mortgage interest rates centre on the nominal rate. For example, a first mortgage will be stated as having an interest rate of 10% and is commonly referred to as the *face*, *stated*, or *named* rate. The effective rate is the true rate of interest, given any compounding factor within the mortgage.

Statutory requirements in Canada dictate that blended payment mortgages must be calculated either annually or semi-annually, not in advance. The semi-annual effective rate is slightly higher than the nominal annual rate, owing to the twice-yearly compounding factor. If no compounding factor was present, the nominal and effective rates would be the same. For additional information regarding the calculation of mortgages involving blended payments, see **Interest Act**.

Calculating Outstanding Mortgage Balances

The most accurate method of determining an outstanding balance involves a custom computer printout for a specific mortgage. Selected software packages provide this feature. Financial calculators can also determine mortgage balance for Canadian mortgages. A rough estimate can be determined by using traditional charts that indicate the dollar balance remaining per $1,000 loan. These tables are based on the original interest rate, amortization, and elapsed time (stated in years) on the mortgage.

Loan progress charts have not been included in this text, given the prevalence of software packages and calculator programs capable of providing such calculations.

Discounting and Yield Calculations

These calculations have traditionally been determined through the use of monthly yield/discount tables. Most tables provide detailed discount and yield factors, calculated using the remaining years of a mortgage and the nominal interest rate stated on the mortgage. Discounts are expressed in terms of per $1,000 outstanding principal. Through the use of these discount tables, the relative value of a mortgage in relation to certain yield levels can be established. The amount of discount increases as anticipated yield rises. Further, the amount of discount is directly tied to the length of the mortgage term. The effect of a discount combined with a prepayment privilege is, if anything, a potential bonus for the investor since the rate of return will increase should the mortgage be paid off in advance of the stated term. However, the investor must reinvest in the marketplace earlier than originally anticipated.

Discount/yield factors are not published in this text, given the proliferation of software packages and calculators capable of providing such calculations.

Fully Amortized Loan

A mortgage loan wherein the stipulated payments repay the loan in full by its maturity date. Amortization periods for most residential mortgages range between 15 and 25 years. If, for example, a mortgage of $100,000 has a 25-year amortization at 8.5%, all principal and interest would be paid after 300 (25 x 12) monthly payments of $795.36.

While practitioners commonly think in terms of monthly mortgage payments, fully amortized loans are frequently written on a weekly, bi-weekly, or semi-monthly basis. The **Mortgage Payment Factors** in the **Appendix** include various factors relating to amortization periods of five to 25 years.

Example   *Mortgage Mathematics—Fully Amortized Loan*

Seller Smith is renovating his home. There is no mortgage on the property and Smith requires approximately $40,000 to complete renovations. The lender and Smith agree to the following terms:

Principal Amount:	$40,000
Interest Rate	8%
Amortization Period	10 years

Using the mortgage payment factors (monthly), Smith will make a monthly payment of:

Monthly Payment Factor (per $1,000 at 8% for 10 years)	12.064090
Monthly P&I Payment (12.064090 x 40(000))	$482.56

Over the duration of 10 years (120 payments), Smith will completely retire the debt.

Mortgage Interest Factor

To understand the importance of monthly interest factors, a brief review of the *Interest Act* is required. The *Interest Act*, a federal statute, provides that in those cases where the principal and interest payments are blended, the mortgagee cannot recover any interest at all unless the mortgage document contains a statement showing the amount of such principal and the interest rate charged on it calculated yearly or half yearly, not in advance.

The phrase *calculated not in advance* simply means that the interest is calculated as due at the end of each compounding period and principal payments must be credited against the amount owing when they are made. The provisions of this Act apply only where principal and interest payments are blended. The reasoning appears to be that since the interest amount is hidden in the blended payment, the borrower has no way of knowing just how much interest, or at what rate he/she is paying. The *Interest Act* does not attempt to control the rate of interest being charged, but requires that the effective rate of interest be quoted.

The word *calculated*, as used in the Act, is synonymous with *compounded*. The more frequently interest is compounded, the greater the return. Given the two choices of yearly or half yearly, lenders invariably select calculated semi-annually not in advance. This requirement creates a problem. How does the lender reconcile the fact that the *Interest Act* permits the compounding of interest every six months, yet the mortgage calls for monthly payments of principal and interest? To accommodate this, the lender builds into the monthly interest charge a rebate to the borrower to compensate for the more frequent payments and thereby comply with the Act.

Example *Mortgage Mathematics— Mortgage Interest Factor*

If a borrower arranged a mortgage of $10,000 at an interest rate of 6% per annum compounded semi-annually, then (assuming no interest payments in the interim), at the end of six months, he/she would be charged interest of $300 and owe the lender $10,300. However, if the lender compounded monthly instead of semi-annually (that is, charge ½ of 1% or .005 per month), the interest would total approximately $303.77.

On a blended payment mortgage, the lender would be prohibited from charging $303.77, and of course there is the added complication of monthly payments of principal and interest. The lender therefore charges a monthly interest rate somewhat less than .005. In this instance, the monthly interest factor is .0049386024. This is the interest factor for the calculation of interest for 1 month at 6% per annum compounded semi-annually.

While monthly interest factors set out in tables can be used to manually determine the interest payable in any particular month, the most effective method to calculate mortgage interest is through a computer service, a financial software package, or selected financial calculators. Computing service companies, for a nominal fee, will provide a detailed *loan amortization schedule* on any mortgage arrangement. The schedule is produced, based on a selected amortization and term and shows the interest and principal portions of each payment along with the balance of the loan after each successive payment.

Mortgage Payments/Amortization

Amortization of a mortgage involves the repaying of the principal over a period of time in a series of regular payments. To simplify the calculation required to amortize a mortgage loan, lenders traditionally used some form of amortization table. Detailed payment/amortization tables are available, i.e., *Financial Payment Tables for Canadian Mortgages*, however, most practitioners now use either mortgage payment factors (factors per $1,000), or rely on financial calculator programs.

Reference   For the calculation of mortgage payments involving an amortized mortgage, see the Appendix. Factors quoted are per $1,000 of loan amount.

Simple and Compound Interest

Interest is the amount paid by a borrower to a lender for the use of that lender's money. Interest rate is the rate charged for each time period for the use of that money. The time element is vital. For example, the interest rate on a mortgage can be quoted as 12% per year, while the

interest rate on a charge account can be quoted as 1.5% per month. All the interest rate does then, is distinguish the time period over which the interest is being calculated.

There are two types of interest: simple interest and compound interest.

- Simple interest is interest on the principal only and is calculated using the following formula:

  Interest = Principal x Rate Of Interest x Time

  For example, the interest on $1,000 at 12% for one year is:
  = 1,000 x .12 x 1
  = $120

  If the term is only four months, the interest is:
  = 1,000 x .12 x 4 ÷ 12
  = $40

  If the term is 50 days, the interest is:
  = 1,000 x .12 x 50 ÷ 365
  = $16.44

  With simple interest, a loan is taken out for a short period and the principal is paid in full along with the accrued interest.

- Compound interest is interest on both the original principal and on the interest accrued. The formula for calculating compound interest is more complicated since it involves calculating interest not only on the principal, as in the case of simple interest, but also on the accruing interest. Compound interest is the type of interest used most frequently in residential mortgages. In the case of compound interest, interest is charged at a specified interval, e.g., monthly, daily, quarterly, and annually. Since, the arithmetic involved in producing compound interest is quite complex, most financial institutions use tables of monthly interest factors.

MORTGAGE PAYMENT FACTORS

Mortgage payment factors per $1,000 of mortgage amount are provided for selected interest rates and amortization periods based on weekly, bi-weekly, semi-monthly, and monthly payments. See the Appendix.

MORTGAGE PAYMENT PLANS

Over the years, a number of payment plans have been developed to suit the needs of both borrowers and lenders in mortgage transactions. Four commonly used plans are briefly detailed but such arrangements can vary significantly with the creativity of lenders in a competitive market.

Flat Payment Plan

Sometimes referred to as an *unamortized loan* or *straight loan*, this payment plan does not require the borrower to repay any of the principal until the maturity date. During the term of the mortgage, the borrower is usually asked to pay interest at regular, specified intervals.

Fixed Payment Plan

This plan is sometimes referred to as a *straight principal reduction plan*. The borrower agrees to repay a *fixed* amount of principal at specified intervals during the term of the loan. At regular intervals, the borrower is also asked to pay interest which is payable only on the outstanding balance of the loan during any given interval.

Blended Payment Plan

This plan provides for equal payments that are made at regular intervals during the term of the mortgage. Each payment is a blend of part principal and part interest.

Variable Rate/Term

The variable rate mortgage involves a mortgage where the interest rate fluctuates according to the market rate.

MORTGAGE POOL

A collection of mortgages originated in the primary mortgage market that is subsequently sold as a group or portfolio. This packaged grouping is then used as security for the issuance of mortgage-backed securities in the capital market. Mortgage-backed securities in smaller denominations are then sold to investors.

Example   *Mortgage Pool*

Lender Inc. has assembled a collection of first mortgages insured by Canada Mortgage and Housing Corporation. The mortgages represent an overall portfolio value of $40,000,000 that is subsequently packaged in the capital market as mortgage-backed securities. The offering is marketed to individual investors based on individual bond-like securities of $10,000 each.

MORTGAGE, SUBSIDIZED/ASSISTED

Mortgages in which the mortgagor receives some form of assistance, typically in regard to the interest rate charged, when borrowing for the purchase of a home.

Application   Two types of assisted programs involving government and private sources are briefly described.

Government

In recent years, both federal and provincial governments have been involved in subsidy programs such as: a direct grant (non-repayable); interest-free loans usually secured by way of a second mortgage; or interest rate buy-down programs to lower the effective rate of interest on loans. Selected programs may rely on the third option that effectively lowers qualification criteria, permitting persons normally unable to acquire property to do so and be qualified through conventional lenders.

The example illustrates a subsidy by way of direct payment. This approach is one of several variations that exist and does not imply such an assistance plan is available. Subsidized/assisted financing can take on many variations given prevailing social/political forces at work.

Example   *Mortgage, Subsidized/Assisted– Government*

The following is a hypothetical subsidy plan in which the buyer receives a direct subsidy payment thereby reducing the gross debt service ratio required by the lender.

Loan Amount	$100,000	
Interest Rate	8.5%	
Monthly P & I		$795.37
Estimated Taxes (Monthly)		$120.00
Total PIT		$915.37

Required Income (assuming a single wage and 30% GDS):

$$\$915.37 \times 12 \div .30 = \$36,614.80$$

If the subsidy is applied:

a. 10% Subsidy

Subsidy ($915.37 x .10)	$91.54 per month
Annual Payment ($915.37 − $91.54 x 12)	$9,885.96
Required Income ($9,885.96 ÷ .30)	$32,953.20

b. 20% Subsidy

Subsidy($915.37 x .20)	$183.07
Annual Payment ($915.37 - $183.07 x 12)	$8,787.60
Required Income ($8,787.60 ÷ .30)	$29,292.00

Corporate

Corporate relocation programs are another potential source of lower rates or subsidized loans for company transfers. Programs can be designed to offset pricing discrepancies between similar housing in the origination and destination locations for a transferred employee, and/or provide some form of interest rate relief to offset existing mortgage rates and new rates encountered in the acquisition of a property.

MORTGAGE VERIFICATION

As part of the listing procedure, real estate practitioners often examine mortgage documents that the owners have in their possession and question the owners as to their knowledge of the present status of existing financing.

Application   The type of information gathered in this fashion, and noted on the listing document, would include:

Full Name of Mortgagee   Often including the address of the mortgagee.

Type and Balance   Specify whether the mortgage is a first mortgage, second mortgage, etc. and what the principal balance outstanding is at the time of listing.

Interest   Give the rate of interest and frequency of compounding (if required to clarify calculation method).

Repayment   Specify the type of payment (e.g., flat, fixed, or blended) and, if blended, record the constant amount for principal and interest payment. Also include details of any taxes or condominium maintenance fees that may or may not be collected with the mortgage payments.

Expiry   The phrases *expiry date*, *due date*, and *maturity date* are interchangeable and indicate the end of the term. Both sellers and buyers often confuse the term of a mortgage with the amortization period, sometimes with disastrous results. The concept of amortization is used strictly to establish a payment plan and has no place in the legal description of a mortgage.

Special Privileges   Any special privileges should be described in detail. The existence, or non-existence, of such privileges as prepayment, non-transferability, or demolition may prove vital to the eventual sale. Many variations of mortgage privileges exist. The exact wording of such privileges should be included in the listing. If a mortgage is to be assumed as part of a sale, the exact wording will be needed when the offer is being drafted. It is also vital to be aware of whether the ability to assume the mortgage is subject to prior approval of the mortgagee.

Obviously, very few owners would have all information available. Practitioners often make use of a mortgage verification form. Typically, the top of the form sets out the authority given to the agent to secure details about the mortgage and the lower portion, completed by the mortgagee, provides important information concerning the actual mortgage such as the principal balance outstanding as of a specific date, interest rate, monthly payment, amortization period, maturity date, special payment privileges, any pay-out penalty, whether or not the mortgage is assumable, and whether or not the mortgage is in good standing. By having the form completed by the mortgagee, it is usually possible to avoid the potentially disastrous results of inaccurate information regarding existing financing.

In conjunction with the use of a mortgage verification form, it is wise for the listing sales representative to contact the existing mortgagee, not only concerning the possibility of assumption of the mortgage, but also to explore whether the mortgagee would be amenable to refinancing the property for a new buyer if necessary, and if so, what terms would likely be quoted.

The importance of this initial contact with an existing mortgagee cannot be overemphasized. This contact provides the listing sales representative with a better knowledge of the flexibility of available financing and also keeps the mortgagee aware of what is happening with respect to the property, avoids unpleasant surprises, and establishes a rapport that could be essential to refinancing at point of sale.

Provincial   See applicable reference materials.

MORTGAGEE

The one to whom property is conveyed or pledged as security for the payment of a debt; the lender or creditor.

Application   Rights of a mortgage can be generally grouped under two headings.

Right to Assign the Mortgage

The mortgage, as an interest in land, can be sold, transferred, or assigned without the consent of the mortgagor. The mortgagor must be notified of the assignment. The assignee acquires the rights of the mortgagee. This individual acquires only the rights that the mortgagee had and no agreement between the mortgagee and the assignee changes any right that the mortgagor already has, or imposes any additional burden on the mortgagor. In some instances, the new assignee may require an indemnification agreement from the mortgagee in the event that the mortgagor defaults.

The assignee takes the mortgage subject to the state of accounts between the mortgagee and mortgagor. If an additional payment off the principal had been made, of which the assignee was unaware, the assignee would have no claim against the mortgagor. If after notification, the mortgagor continues to pay the original mortgagee, the assignee can take legal action against the mortgagor to collect the money.

Right to be Paid

The mortgagee has the right to be paid the principal sum advanced and interest thereon based on arrangements spelled out in the mortgage document. Failure on the part of the mortgagor to pay on those terms, to fulfill covenants, or to observe the provisions of the mortgage will give rise to a number of remedies that can be exercised by the mortgagee including power of sale and foreclosure. If all covenants are fulfilled, a discharge is provided to the mortgagor.

MORTGAGOR

The one who gives the mortgage; the borrower or debtor. Mortgagor rights are grouped under three headings.

Right to Quiet Possession

The mortgagor has the right to quiet uninterrupted possession when not in default. He/she has the right to use the property and is not responsible to the mortgagee for ordinary wear and tear on the structures, but must exercise reasonable care and maintain the property.

Right to Redeem the Property Free of the Mortgage

The mortgagor retains the right to sell or mortgage his/her interest, and to deal with it in the same manner as any interest in property. This right is extremely important. Any provision inserted in the mortgage document that attempts to prevent the mortgagor from exercising this right will be struck down as invalid. For example, if a mortgage contained a provision that the mortgagee had an option to purchase the property, it would be invalidated, as the mortgagor must never be prevented from redeeming the property free of the debt.

Right to Discharge the Mortgage

When the loan is paid off, the mortgagor obtains a discharge signed by the mortgagee. The discharge fee is normally paid by the mortgagor. If a discharge cannot be obtained, the provincial statute relating to mortgages typically provides for the mortgagor to make application through the courts to obtain a court order based on supporting evidence.

MOULD
(SEE MOLD)

MULTIPLE LISTING

An arrangement among brokerages who are real estate board members, whereby each brokerage shares information regarding listings with the other members, who may negotiate transactions involving these listings.

MULTIPLE LISTING SERVICE (MLS)
(SEE ALSO REAL ESTATE BOARD)

The trademarks known as MLS, Multiple Listing Service and the MLS design marks are certification marks registered and owned by The Canadian Real Estate Association (CREA). These marks are protected throughout Canada for the exclusive use of members of CREA in connection with services defined as listing to effect the purchase and sale of real estate. The certification marks may only be used in association with listing services performed as part of a plural system arrangement and are performed by members in good standing of The Canadian Real Estate Association.

MULTIPLIER
(SEE INCOME MULTIPLIERS)

MUTUAL AGREEMENT

One of several essential elements of a contract. Mutual agreement is created by an offer, the acceptance of the offer, and communication of the acceptance back to the offeror. Mutual agreement is the basis for a meeting of the minds between the contracting parties.

A contract may also be discharged by the mutual agreement of the parties so that it will no longer bind them, or that it will be replaced by another contract in altered terms substituted for discharge within itself. This would apply in circumstances such as the nonfulfillment of a certain condition or the exercise of a cancellation option.

In a real estate transaction, a mutual release is normally signed to provide written confirmation that the parties have mutually agreed that an agreement/contract no longer binds them.

MUTUAL (SHARED) DRIVE

A strip of land shared by adjoining neighbours used as a joint driveway by both parties, created by an easement on each property.

Application   Mutual drives are a potential source of confusion, or worse, litigation. As a listing salesperson, the best approach involves a clear understanding of the exact location of the mutual drive, any obstructions related thereto, and careful inquiry if there have been any difficulties or disputes with the drive. Analysis of errors and omissions claims show that many problems start with simple confusion of material facts and later become major obstacles.

MUTUAL RELEASE

A term commonly referring to a mutual release form signed by the appropriate parties acknowledging that an agreement no longer binds them. Form titles, e.g., Notice of Conditions Not Satisfied, and wordings will vary by provincial jurisdiction.

The preprinted wording for a mutual release published as a standard form by the Ontario Real Estate Association is included as an example in **Figure M.7**. The form provides for a full release of all liabilities, covenants, obligations, claims and sums of money arising from an agreement/contract. This form also releases both parties from any claim from the agent involved in the transaction except as otherwise provided for.

Provincial   See applicable reference materials.

Ontario Real Estate Association
MUTUAL RELEASE

REALTOR®

BETWEEN:

PURCHASER: ....

AND

VENDOR ....

AGENT ....

(Listing Broker)   (Co-operating Broker)

RE: Agreement of Purchase and Sale between the Vendor and Purchaser, accepted the ....day of........................,

20 ...., concerning the property known as: ....

....

as more particularly described in the aforementioned Agreement of Purchase and Sale.

We, the Purchasers and the Vendors in the above noted transaction, hereby release each other and the Agent in the proposed transaction, from all liabilities, covenants, obligations, claims and sums of money arising out of the above Agreement of Purchase and Sale, together with any rights and causes of action that each party may have had against the other and/or the Agent, and we direct the deposit holder to disburse the deposit of:

.... Canadian Dollars ($Can........................)

as follows: ....

....

....

The Agent hereby releases both parties from any claim that he may have had for commission or other remuneration in the above transaction, except as may be here in before specifically provided.

This release shall be binding upon the heirs, executors, administrators and assigns of all the parties executing same.

DATED at.. this ....day of.., 20............
SIGNED, SEALED AND DELIVERED in the presence of: IN WITNESS whereof I have hereunto set my hand and seal:

⬤ DATE........................
(Witness) ....   (Purchaser) ....   (Seal)

⬤ DATE........................
(Witness) ....   (Purchaser) ....   (Seal)

DATED at.. this ....day of.., 20............
SIGNED, SEALED AND DELIVERED in the presence of: IN WITNESS whereof I have hereunto set my hand and seal:

⬤ DATE........................
(Witness) ....   (Vendor) ....   (Seal)

⬤ DATE........................
(Witness) ....   (Vendor) ....   (Seal)

SIGNED, SEALED AND DELIVERED in the presence of: IN WITNESS whereof I have hereunto set my hand and seal:

⬤ DATE........................
(Witness) ....   (Listing Broker/Manager) ....   (Seal)

⬤ DATE........................
(Witness) ....   (Co-operating Broker/Manager) ....   (Seal)

OREA Standard Form: Do not alter when printing or reproducing the standard pre-set portion.   Form No. 114   01/00

Figure M.7   Mutual Release

N TO O

N TO O

National Info Links

Native Lands

Indian and Northern Affairs Canada Terrasses de la Chaudière
10 Wellington, North Tower
Hull, PQ   Postal Address:
Ottawa, ON K1A 0H4

Telephone   (819) 997 0380
  Web Site   www.inac.gc.ca

Natural Resources

Natural Resources Canada

Telephone   (613) 995 0947 (general enquiries).
  Web Site   www.nrcan.gc.ca

For provincial activities contact the appropriate
provincial ministry/department.

New Homes

A national new home warranty program does not exist.
For provincial warranty information please contact the
appropriate provincial office.

Building codes and related regulations are administered
provincially. Contact the appropriate provincial
ministry/department for information.

NOTICE
HUNTING PROHIBITED
THIS IS AN INDIAN RESERVE

NARRATIVE REPORT

(SEE ALSO APPRAISAL REPORT)

A real estate appraisal report, that is the most comprehensive of three appraisal methods. The other two are the form report and letter of opinion. The narrative report provides full details of all eight steps in the appraisal report and is, in itself, the final step of the appraisal reporting process.

Application A narrative report can vary substantially in size based on the type of property and purpose of the appraisal. This type of report provides a logical and systematic presentation of pertinent facts, theoretical premises, and explanations leading to a final opinion of value. Narrative reports tend to be lengthy, fully documented, and time consuming to prepare. A residential appraisal may consume between 50 and 100 pages and provide a full description of the appraisal process so that the reader can follow the logic leading to a final estimate of value.

Example *Narrative Report*

Anne Appraiser is preparing a detailed narrative report on a residential property owned by Smith. Smith requires the appraisal for pending expropriation plans concerning new highway construction. Anne carefully details the main topic areas within the planned narrative report.

- Appraisal Summary
  (important facts and conclusions).
- Letter of Transmittal
  (summary letter to the client).
- Title Page.
- Table of Contents.
- Taxes and Assessment
  (specific information regarding taxes on the property, taxation trends, and impact on value).
- Area and Neighbourhood Analysis
  (description of external factors impacting value).
- Site and Improvement Analysis
  (exterior and interior description of the property).
- Approaches to Value
  (application of the market data, cost, and income approaches to value).
- Reconciliation
  (details how the value estimate was determined).

Continued…

- Limiting Conditions
  (information to client concerning assumptions and conditions underlying the report).
- Exhibits
  (documentary evidence including such things as maps, diagrams of the property, and floor plans).

NATIONAL CODE OF REAL ESTATE EDUCATION

(SEE ALLIANCE FOR CANADIAN REAL ESTATE EDUCATION)

NATIONAL ENERGY CODE

The National Energy Code consists of two components:

- National Energy Code for Houses (NECH); and
- National Energy Code for Buildings (NECB).

These models are intended to operate in concert with other Canadian standards and regulations, e.g., National Building Code, and also with provincial building codes. They provide an integrated standards reference system to assist the construction industry, manufacturers of materials and equipment, and promote standardized, energy-efficient construction practices.

The NECH, the first code developed by the Canadian Commission on Building and Fire Codes, is a code of minimum standards used for construction of small residential buildings. The code takes into account various factors, for example, climate, fuel types and costs, and construction costs, to arrive at minimum standards depending on the specific locale. The long-term objective is to ensure that new home construction provides energy-efficient structures.

The National Energy Code for Houses is focused on the design, construction, and occupancy of new buildings of three stories or less in building height, with a building area not exceeding 600 square meters, and containing dwelling units (including ancillary service rooms, shared means of egress or garages serving the units, and additions to existing buildings). The code addresses such issues as the building envelope, lighting, heating, ventilating and air-conditioning systems, service water heating systems, electrical power, and building energy performance compliance.

The National Energy Code for Buildings (NECB) applies to all other types of buildings and generally follows the overall structure of its predecessor, the NECH.

The NECB and NECH are not mandatory models that must be adopted by provinces. The *Constitution Act* does not provide any mandate for the federal government to impose such standards. Under the Act, provincial and territorial governments have the responsibility for regulations of buildings. Neither code is law until adopted within a particular provincial jurisdiction.

Reference Energy Efficiency Branch, Natural Resources Canada, 580 Booth Street, 18th Floor, Ottawa, ON K1A 0E9.

NATIONAL HOUSING ACT
(SEE ALSO CANADA MORTGAGE AND HOUSING CORPORATION)

The *National Housing Act (1954)* revised and superseded previous housing and mortgage policies and facilitated the insuring of *National Housing Act (NHA)* loans made by approved lenders, as well as direct mortgage lending under a variety of programs by Canada Mortgage and Housing Corporation (CMHC).

Application The National Housing Loan Regulations set out procedures under which CMHC operates when lending mortgage funds. The Regulations do not establish exact costs such as processing fees, but delineate overall requirements. **Figure N.1** provides a summary of Parts in the Regulations.

These Regulations are an outcropping of the more all-encompassing *National Housing Act* and provide guidelines for processing and approving residential mortgages. Part I, the most extensive portion of the Regulations, defines maximum loans permissible, terms, and amortization periods. Construction loans are detailed, along with requirements for monitoring structure construction and stages at which inspections must be completed. Progress advances and mortgage fees charged are also discussed. Under NHA, a maximum of four advances is allowed and a 15% holdback applies to all residential construction loans. Gross debt service and total debt service ratios are outlined, however, specific percentages are not included, nor are costs, fees, and related items. These figures are contained in operating procedure manuals used at local offices of CMHC. Part I devotes considerable documentation to lender reporting procedures, submission of claims, and general loan administration.

**National Housing Act
Regulations**

Part I   Insured Lending, New and Existing Housing Guidelines.
          Procedures for the processing, insuring, buyer qualifying, and general administration of residential loans.

Part II   Housing for Rental Purposes, Assisted Rental Program.
          Procedures concerning contributions and supplemental assistance for low income families.

Part III Land Acquisition and Leasing.
          Leasing of land to a non-profit corporation.

Part IV   Home Improvement Loans.
          Regulations relating to repairs, alterations, and additions of a permanent nature to a residential unit(s), housing project or business premises with family housing units.

Part V   Rehabilitation and Conversion of Existing Residential Buildings.
          Amount of loan to be forgiven and limits on loans for rehabilitation/conversion.

Part VI.1 Loans to Facilitate Home Ownership.
          Outlines limits of annual contributions and amount of interest rate reductions for specific types of loans made under the *National Housing Act.*

Part VI.2 Interest Deferment Plan.
          Procedures for maximum guarantee and contribution for eligible home owners.

Part VII Public Housing.
          Loans for public housing and rental contributions.

Part VIII Loans for Student Housing Projects.
          Applications and required standards.

Part IX   Water and Sewage Projects.

Part X   General.

Figure N.1   National Housing Act Regulations

NATIVE LANDS

Reserved lands held by the Crown for the use and benefit of native people. Fundamentally, the *Indian Act* states that reserve lands are held by the Crown for the use and benefit of native peoples. To convey such property to other persons, the land must be surrendered to the federal government. The government then, in turn, may convey titles by way of sale, or grant leases on the surrendered land.

Application   Real estate practitioners marketing this type of property require an understanding of methods by which such lands are controlled, registered, and developed. Certain complexities exist in negotiations concerning native lands.

Methods associated with the surrender and management of lands by the federal government have caused much debate. The *Indian Act* and various amendments dating from the mid-1800s have failed to adequately address various difficulties. Historically, all lands surrendered ceased to be viewed as lands for the use and benefit of native people. Control of such properties was vested in the Federal government once any surrender was undertaken. However, Subsection 38(2) of the *Indian Act (1951 Revision)* clearly states that a surrender may be absolute or qualified, conditional or unconditional. In light of this, much debate has centred on the more recent idea of conditional surrender. Various court decisions have found that conditional surrender, such as a lease, does not eradicate the basic premise that these lands are still reserved for native people.

The fundamental benefit of conditionally surrendered land lies in the native people being able to develop the property through leases to outside interests, while retaining underlying ownership. However, to effect meaningful ownership of the lands, native bands require control over the property for purposes of regulation, servicing, taxation, and a host of other responsibilities usual to a municipal government.

Unfortunately little guidance can be found in the *Indian Act*. As a result, individuals other than native people on leased property find themselves caught between an outdated federal act, band councils that regulate affairs within the native lands (including the surrendered area), and provincial governments/local municipalities that seek to tax and otherwise control the endeavours of such persons and enforce land planning requirements.

The real estate practitioner is cautioned as expert advice is essential, together with direct band council contact and proper guidance and documentation from Indian and Northern Affairs Canada. The government ministry has also maintained a national Indian lands registry since 1968. In essence, the system parallels provincial registry procedures and is generally modelled on the land titles system (although no guarantee of title is attached to ownership). The land registrar is required to maintain both a reserve land register and a surrendered land register.

NAVIGABILITY

(SEE ALSO SHORELINE/SHORELAND OWNERSHIP)

Navigability is an important matter when establishing the ownership of shoreline property and associated rights. Provincial acts do not define navigability, as such issues have been left to the discretion of the courts. Generally, a body of water is said to be navigable if it can be traversed by small and/or large craft for recreational or commercial use. This status is not altered by seasonal fluctuations, interruptions to navigation (dams, canals, etc.), and periods when no navigation occurs.

Application Following are general guidelines for information purposes only. Practitioners are strongly encouraged to leave such issues to legal counsel.

> Navigable Waterway—Low Water Mark Ownership
>> If the body of water is navigable, then the extent of ownership is the lower water mark.
>
> Non-Navigable Waterway—Middle Ownership
>> If the body of water is non-navigable, then the extent of ownership goes to the centre of the body of water.
>
> Exception
>> If an express grant from the Crown includes land under a navigable waterway, then such lands will be conveyed as part of the deed or title in future transactions.

NEGATIVE AMORTIZATION

Amortization of a loan in which the principal amount outstanding increases as a result of insufficient payments to offset interest charged. Negative amortization can occur when a principal and interest payment remains constant but the mortgage is subject to interest changes during the term. An increase in interest rate results in high interest being charged, but constant payments are not large enough to address the additional interest. Such interest is then added to the outstanding balance. See Graduated Payment Mortgage for an example of negative amortization in the initial years of a mortgage.

NEGATIVE CASH FLOW

An income property, for purposes of real estate investment analysis, with operating expenses and debt service exceeding gross operating income. For additional details on methods used by commercial practitioners in estimating cash flows, see Cash Flow Model.

Example   *Negative Cash Flow*

Investor McKay is analyzing one of several investment properties. The following summary, prepared by Salesperson Jamieson, represents estimated cash flow before taxes for the upcoming year. The property has a negative cash flow before taxes of $2,000. Jamieson will use this analysis as the basis for a detailed five-year forecast using the cash flow model.

Potential Rental Income	$200,000	
Vacancy and Credit Losses	−15,000	
Effective Rental Income	185,000	
Other Income	+5,000	
Gross Operating Income	190,000	
Operating Expenses	−100,000	
Net Operating Income	90,000	
Annual Debt Service	−92,000	
Cash Flow Before Taxes	**−$2,000**	

NEGATIVE LEVERAGE
(SEE LEVERAGE)

NEGLIGENCE
(SEE ALSO MISREPRESENTATION)

For purposes of real estate, the failure of a real estate practitioner to exercise a degree of care that is reasonable in relation to a commonly expected standard (usually established by the courts), and is prudent based on the specific circumstances.

NEIGHBOURHOOD

A portion of a larger community, or an entire community, in which there is a homogeneous grouping of inhabitants, buildings, or business enterprises. Inhabitants of a neighbourhood usually have a more than casual community of interest and a similarity of economic level or cultural background. Neighbourhood boundaries may consist of well-defined natural or man-made barriers, or may be more or less well defined by a distinct change in land use or in the character of the inhabitants.

Age (Life) Cycle
The economic lifespan of a highly similar grouping of structures within a naturally defined or man-made area known as a neighbourhood. The age cycle of any neighbourhood is composed of three distinct phases:

Growth	The neighbourhood is under development and is gaining consumer acceptance and public awareness.
Stability	The area becomes built up and prices stabilize.
Decline	Buildings pass their prime economic life and start to decline.

Various programs and initiatives may tend to extend cycles, particularly during the decline stage. Renewed interest in declining neighbourhoods can give way to new forms of growth and promotion of higher and better use of the land, such as larger houses following demolition of original homes within specific areas, and demolition of older residential property in favour of new office and retail complexes.

Example   *Neighbourhood Age (Life) Cycle*

Salesperson Lee has been asked to establish fair market value for a home at 13 Main Street. The subject property is approximately 40 years old and has been extremely well maintained. However, the general vicinity, while once primarily single-family housing, has changed particularly during the past five-year period. While the property being reviewed would be worth approximately $160,000 in a more stable neighbourhood, the broker must make adjustments for the deteriorating neighbourhood. In particular, adjacent houses on the street are in a poor state of repair. Lee identifies the neighbourhood as declining, makes a note in his appraisal report and, after detailed research, establishes a fair market value of $146,000.

Analysis

One of several steps involved in the process of data collection and analysis for purposes of an appraisal. For additional information regarding steps in the appraisal process, see **Appraisal**.

In viewing a neighbourhood, the appraiser will assess its age cycle in terms of growth, stability or decline, boundaries, and any factors or forces affecting that neighbourhood. A neighbourhood analysis requires reliable and accurate data. Appraisers are normally reasonably familiar with the neighbourhood and consequently, their own files provide much of the required information. Understandably, the exact approach will vary, based on the type of use, e.g., low density, apartments, industrial, commercial or rural. Examples are provided illustrating differing appraisal perspectives on neighbourhood factors concerning four different types of property.

Example   *Analysis—Single-Family*

Salesperson Ward has been asked to provide an appraisal for a single-family home in a low density neighbourhood. Ward describes the neighbourhood in terms of four factors:

Physical   First and foremost, Ward will assess the property's location. Poor location can offset many other factors that would otherwise enhance its value. Besides location, Salesperson Ward will consider proximity of public transportation, parks, schools, churches, retail and service outlets, topography, landscape, and availability/quality of utilities. Her checklist also includes nuisances or hazards such as smoke, noise, pollution, and heavy traffic.

Economic   Ward will also give regard to stability of uses, property values, vacancies, new construction, personal and family income levels, degree of maintenance (pride of ownership), stage in the neighbourhood age (life) cycle, amount of undeveloped land available, mortgage lending policies, interest rates, sale price trends, and rate of turnover.

Political or Governmental   Ward must be aware of legal factors affecting low density residential values, such as zoning regulations, building codes, property taxes, local improvement taxes, official plans, site plan control agreements, and deed restrictions.

Social   Significant social factors include population trends with respect to growth or decline, trends to larger or smaller family sizes, harmony or lack of harmony of ethnic or economic groupings, educational attitudes, level of prestige, crime rates, age groupings, and population densities.

Example   *Analysis—Multi-Residential*

Anne Appraiser has been asked to establish the fair market value of an apartment building. Skilled in this type of appraisal work, Anne will consider various factors that impact on the estimate of value.

Transportation   Located near public transportation.

Major Thoroughfares   Close to major traffic arteries so that apartment tenants need not pass through residential areas to access these arteries.

Services   Proximity to shopping, schools, churches, and other services.

Amenities/Recreational Facilities (Physical)
Proximity to parks, playgrounds, or other related features adds to desirability and reduces the effects of possible future competition.

Vacancies   Assessment of short-term apartment vacancies, resulting from boom construction, in conjunction with the possible future market for apartment units in the neighbourhood, i.e., concern with possible long-term vacancies throughout the economic life of the building.

Boundaries

The bounds or limits of a grouping of inhabitants, buildings, or business enterprises. Several characteristics set a specific neighbourhood apart from surrounding areas and make boundaries easier to delineate:

Natural	e.g., rivers, lakes, hills, mountains, and ravines.
Political	e.g., municipal boundaries or city limits, land use or zoning change, and school areas.
Man-Made	e.g., railroad tracks, major highways or roads, and rights-of-way for public utilities.

Factors

Significant items that impact the nature, design, composition and overall make-up of a neighbourhood. Appraisers view most neighbourhoods in terms of four characteristics:

Physical   Location in relation to services and amenities.

Economic   Stability of uses, property values, vacancies, and sale price trends.

Political   Legislative impact such as taxation, local improvements, and official plan restrictions.

Social   Population growth/decline, crime rates, and age groupings.

In apartment neighbourhoods, important factors tend to centre on transportation, major thoroughfares, social and recreational facilities, services, and vacancy rates. Retail neighbourhoods are usually analyzed in terms of access, parking facilities, compatibility of uses, growth trends, vacancy factors, and competitive position (in relation to other retail areas). Industrial sites, in addition to selected factors referred to above, must consider specific services required (rail, utilities, etc.), labour pool, and access to raw materials. Farm appraisers analyze distance to market, soil types, types of crops/yields, typical size of farm units, and services.

NEIGHBOURHOOD SHOPPING CENTRE

A relatively small retail district (approximately 25,000 to 75,000 square feet), designed to provide convenience shopping for day-to-day consumer needs within a more or less defined neighbourhood.

NET INCOME
(SEE ALSO CAPITALIZATION)

Income remaining following the deduction of expenses from revenue.

Application   Net income as such, can apply to analysis of real estate brokerages, but is not commonly used in real estate investment analysis. Instead real estate practitioners typically work with profit and loss statements to reconstruct (stabilize) revenue and expenses to arrive at the financial performance of a typical building for valuation and/or comparison purposes. Further, revenue and expenses can be forecasted to project cash flows both before and after taxes which can lead to valuation and/or comparison. See **Cash Flow**.

NET LEASE

A lease in which the tenant pays a portion of expenses associated with the leased premises.

Three categories of net leases are referred to by practitioners:

> **Net (Single-Net) Lease**
> An agreement in which the tenant pays the rent and certain expenses connected with the leased premises.
>
> **Net/Net Lease**
> An agreement in which the tenant pays all maintenance and operating expenses, plus property taxes.
>
> **Net/Net/Net (Triple-Net) Lease**
> An agreement in which the tenant pays maintenance and operating expenses, property taxes, and insurance.

Application The division of net leases into net, net/net, and net/net/net has caused confusion in the marketplace, particularly given a host of leasing arrangements devised by enterprising commercial tenants and landlords. Generally, most practitioners now analyze rental options in terms of a base rent plus additional rent. Base rent represents the basic obligation of the tenant, normally calculated on a cost per square foot per year for more or less fixed costs of occupancy. Additional rent is defined in the tenancy agreement setting out landlord/tenant responsibilities concerning *who is to pay what* regarding operating costs. A rental arrangement in which the landlord pays all expenses and the tenant submits an agreed upon amount for the leased premises which is referred to as a *gross lease*.

Example   *Net Lease*

Broker/Owner Johnson, of ABC Realty Inc., is opening a small branch in a neighbourhood mall. The landlord wants a triple net lease which requires a minimum rent plus costs relating to maintenance, operating expenses, property taxes, and insurance. The demised premise contains 1,520 square feet.

Johnson suggests a lease agreement using base/additional rent terminology to ensure no misunderstanding. The base rent is payable according to the rentable square foot area of the demised premise. The wording of the lease concerning the base rent reads as follows:

> *The tenant will throughout the term pay to the landlord at its head office, or any other place designated by the landlord, in Canadian funds, without demand and without deduction, abatement, set-off, or compensation, as Base Rent, the annual sum of $4,560 payable in equal consecutive monthly installments of $380 each in advance on the first day of each calendar month. The Base Rent is based on an annual rate of $3.00 per square foot of the rentable area of the premises.*

The lease also provides a method for computing the additional rent. Johnson's space has 1,520 square feet and the total rentable area of the building is 155,102 square feet. Consequently, the tenant's proportionate share is:

$$1,520 \div 155,102 = .0098 \text{ or } .98\%$$

If the estimated total operating expenses and taxes for the year are $1,368,000, the tenant's share would be:

$$\$1,368,000 \times .0098 = \$13,406.40$$
$$\text{or } \$8.82 \text{ per square foot } (\$13,406.40 \div 1,520)$$

The monthly additional rent would be $1,117.20 ($13,406.40 ÷ 12), assuming that property taxes were equally distributed throughout the twelve-month period. In practice, landlords may collect the entire year's taxes during the first six-month period. Further, if the actual building expenses exceeded the estimated amount by $36,000, the landlord would provide a statement of actual amounts payable and request the following amount:

$$\$36,000 \times .0098 \text{ (tenant's proportionate share)} = \$352.80$$

NET LEASEABLE AREA
(SEE ALSO GROSS LEASEABLE AREA)

Floor space in a rental property that is available for rent to tenants. Net leaseable area normally excludes such areas as corridors, equipment rooms, and other common areas and should be clearly differentiated from gross leaseable area that represents the total floor space.

NET OPERATING INCOME
(SEE ALSO RECONSTRUCTED OPERATING STATEMENT)

Acronym: NOI   Income derived from a real estate investment after deducting all fixed and variable expenses from gross operating income (commonly referred to by appraisers as *effective gross income*), but before deducting annual debt service and tax liability.

Application Net operating income is normally analyzed on an annual basis for real estate investment and valuation purposes, but can in fact apply to any specified period. Net operating income, for purposes of market valuation, is obtained through a reconstructed operating statement. The appraiser must follow specific rules and procedures in developing this statement so that it reflects a typical example for a specific type of property under analysis. The reconstructed operating statement is built on historic information for the property in question, along with consideration of performance trends for similar properties. First, potential rental income is estimated less an allowance for vacancy

N
TO
O

and credit losses. Next, other incidental income is added to arrive at the gross operating income. Total expenses (both fixed and variable), are deducted from gross operating income to determine net operating income. Various procedures must be followed in establishing expenses for the reconstructed operating statement.

Net operating income derived from a reconstructed operating statement for a single year's operation can be capitalized under the direct capitalization method to arrive at market value. Capitalization refers to the conversion of future income into a single capital value. The capitalization rate selected is usually derived from net operating income/ sale price ratios established through market research. The reconstructed operating statement is also frequently used as the basis for forecasting future cash flows within a specified holding period through yield capitalization. Forecasted cash flows are then analyzed using discounted cash flow techniques leading to net present values and/or internal rates of return, or alternatively value estimates (market value or investment value dependent on assumptions made in developing the forecasted cash flows). Both direct and yield capitalization are acceptable approaches to valuation under the income approach to value.

NET PRESENT VALUE

Acronym: NPV   The sum of present (discounted) values of future cash flows netted against the initial investment.

Application   The net present value calculation provides a method of ranking investment options by applying a discount rate to future cash flows. A positive NPV indicates surplus above the discount rate. A negative NPV indicates a negative dollar amount that is, in effect, a penalty or loss, in relation to the discount rate. The NPV is not intended as a comparative measure, but rather as a technique to analyze individual properties based on absolute dollars received in relation to specific investor objectives. A degree of comparative analysis is possible if properties are highly comparable, equity invested is the same, and the identical discount rate is applied.

As a profitability measure, the NPV is frequently used in conjunction with internal rate of return (IRR) and is generally judged more reliable given certain ambiguities that can arise with IRR involving multiple sign changes in cash flows, as well as negative and minimal cash flows in relation to invested capital. Investment analysts often plot NPVs of alternate investments or develop NPV profiles for specific investment options based on a range of discount rates.

For additional details, see **Discounting** and **Investment Analysis.**

Example   *Net Present Value (NPV)*

J. Savard is considering an investment that requires an initial infusion of $20,000 with an asking price of $185,000. Salesperson Lee, of ABC Realty Inc., completes a detailed cash flow forecast for the property and arrives at the present value of $22,938.50 for future cash flow based on a discount rate of 7.8%. Lee selected this discount rate based on research in the marketplace. The NPV is:

$$\$22,938.50 - \$20,000$$
$$= \$2,938.50$$

In other words, this investment would provide a return of 7.8% on the money investment plus an additional return of $2,938.50.

Assume that another comparable property under analysis generated a present value of $24,928.13 (same discount rate), and required an initial investment of $20,000, the net present value would be:

$$\text{Net Present Value} = \$24,928.13 - \$20,000$$
$$= \$4,928.13$$

In this instance, the investment would provide a return of 7.8% plus an additional return of $4,928.13. Assuming that both properties are comparable, Savard would select the latter property given the higher net present value.

NET WORTH

Total assets less total liabilities. Net worth, for real estate purposes, represents total current value of property less all outstanding liabilities. For example, Investor McKay has total assets in real property amounting to $1,750,000 less outstanding liabilities of $642,500 representing mortgages on those properties. McKay's net worth is $1,107,500.

NEW BROKERAGE OFFICE

The layout of a brokerage office requires careful consideration. The space must provide adequate room for employees, while ensuring sufficient privacy, acceptable levels of security, and cost efficiencies.

Application   Office layouts and physical needs of brokerages can vary considerably given the advent of modern communication systems, home offices, virtual real estate brokerages, and the overall increased mobility of salespeople. Three example layouts are provided.

Layout 1: Single Aisle

A single aisle plan, as illustrated in **Figure N.2** on the left side of the diagram, offers important advantages to small and medium sized offices:

- Fits easily into a single store front, e.g., mall location;
- Provides space for a manager's private office and two closing/conference rooms;
- Includes separate administration/accounting office;
- Permits individual work stations or private offices, or combinations thereof; and
- Accommodates single, double, or quad offices.

Layout #2: Single Floor in Multi-Level Building

Figure N.2 (right side of diagram), provides a design for a multi-level office tower accommodating a sales staff of 66, along with general administration offices, three conference rooms, a broker's office, and a manager's office. The kitchen

facilities are adjacent to a general meeting room that is ideally suited to boardroom purposes. Accounting and administrative functions are centralized.

Layout #3: Double Aisle

Often referred to as the *closed square design*, the double aisle configuration is common in brokerages above 3,000 square feet (see Figure N.3). The plan illustrated would accommodate approximately 70 salespeople. The layout is extremely flexible. By simply converting two or three offices on the left aisle, additional room for other management personnel (e.g., administrator and bookkeeper) is possible. In some instances, brokerages complete a portion of both aisles leaving the balance of rent space unfinished until needed.

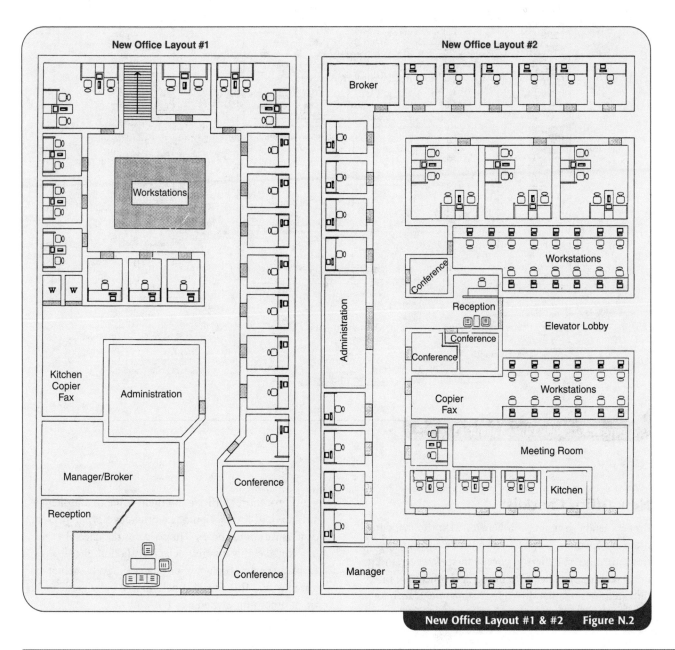

New Office Layout #1 & #2   Figure N.2

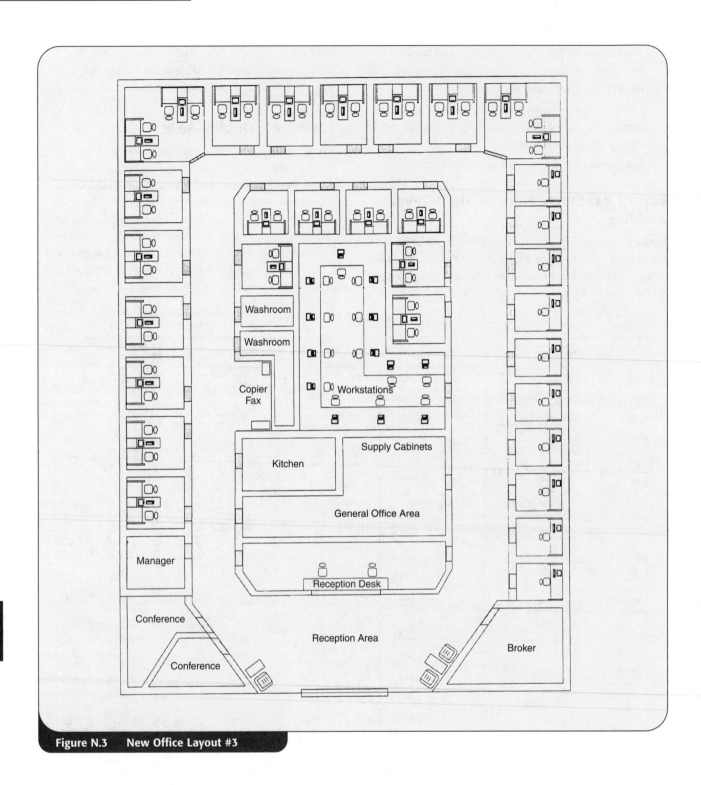

Figure N.3   New Office Layout #3

New Office Checklist

Brokers establishing new brokerages, as with most entrepreneurs opening new facilities, must deal with everyone from furniture suppliers to contractors. However, unique items relating specifically to brokerages offices are rarely fully itemized in a handy reference document, such as requirements of the provincial real estate act, real estate board procedures, office equipment usual to a brokerage, and standard forms. **Figure N.4** provides a brief checklist for illustration purposes. The scope of the checklist will vary considerably by provincial jurisdiction. Brokers contemplating a new brokerage or establishing a branch operation may find this checklist helpful as a basic guideline to which other unique items can be added.

NEW OFFICE CHECKLIST

Provincial Regulatory Requirements

❑ Proper notification and completion of necessary forms
❑ Salespersons' registrations to be transferred (if applicable)
❑ Transfer of other registrations as required

Real Estate Board

❑ Submission of necessary forms for approval
❑ Payment of Fees
❑ Connection to MLS computer service
❑ Purchase of MLS listings forms, approved stickers, and general supplies

Office Equipment (Major Items Only)

❑ Telephone equipment (purchase/lease)
❑ Availability of lines and number assignment
❑ Deadline for new telephone directory (e.g., advertising and white page listing)
❑ Photocopier (lease/purchase) and features needed
❑ Facsimile (lease/purchase) and features needed
❑ Forms software
❑ Computer (lease/purchase) and features needed
❑ Computer facilities for MLS service
❑ Wiring for networking capabilities (if applicable)
❑ Salesperson computers (if applicable)
❑ Pager systems

Office and General Administration Forms

❑ Standard forms such as agreements/contracts, listing agreements, amendments, notices, and waivers
❑ General and trust account materials
❑ Journals as required under the provincial real estate act.
❑ Trust ledgers
❑ Bank reconciliation forms
❑ Contact printing firms specializing in real estate forms for other forms required
❑ Brokerage policy manual
❑ Employee contracts (salaried and commission sales, both employee and independent contractor)
❑ Management forms such as:
  • Reference Register
  • Listing Register and Checklist
  • Sale Register
  • Transaction Report
  • Trade Processing Checklist
  • Employee Profile
  • Office Performance
  • Financial Worksheet
  • Budget - Fixed/Variable Expenses

  • Monthly Cash Flow Estimate
  • Employee Application Forms
  • Checklist—New Salesperson Orientation
  or suitable software packages.

Office Premises

(list will vary greatly depending upon the size and type of premises and whether the property is owned or leased)

❑ Alterations to outside appearance
❑ Outside sign arrangement (lease/own)
❑ Interior office layout
❑ Available space for future expansion
❑ Location of kitchen, general service areas, sales area, computer, facsimile, and photocopier
❑ Acoustics (management offices, conference rooms, and individual sales offices)
❑ Mechanical/wiring/plumbing coordinated with office layout and adequate for reasonable period in future
❑ General storage areas and accessibility/security
❑ Reception area configuration (accessibility/security/proximity to general account/administration areas)
❑ Meeting room: special heating, ventilation, and equipment considerations
❑ Waste disposal, snow clearing, and general maintenance
❑ Parking (with consideration for future expansion)
❑ Present zoning, restrictions, and changes if necessary
❑ Appropriate building permits
❑ Special considerations such as custom wiring requirements, modems, network facilities, links between management, and administration areas

Permits/Approvals

❑ Check with building or by-law officer for permits required
❑ Sprinkler alarm systems
❑ Fire and exit door requirements
❑ Notification to the Canada Customs and Revenue Agency and other ministries/departments as required
❑ Remittance forms for EI, CPP, and Income Tax
❑ GST Registration Number(s)

Reference Centre

A reference centre is advisable given the increasing complexities of operating a real estate brokerage. The *Real Estate Encyclopedia* is an excellent starting point. However, brokerages are well advised to expand the basic library to include: provincial statutes affecting real estate, provincial reference material provided by provincial real estate associations, regulatory bodies, and CREA, and other materials based on specialty fields.

NEW HOME CONSTRUCTION LOAN

A mortgage typically involving sequential advances by the lender to the borrower during pre-determined stages of construction.

Application   The timing and amounts of mortgage advances for new home construction will vary depending upon the lender's policies. A five-stage schedule is illustrated, but many variations exist in the marketplace.

First Draw (15%)	Primary excavation, lot grading, and construction of foundation.
Second Draw (20%)	Concrete block wall complete, trusses placed, and roof sheathed.
Third Draw (20%)	Rough plumbing, electrical and mechanical, and installation of windows and doors.
Fourth Draw (25%)	Drywall, trim, and painting completed.
Fifth Draw (20%)	Installation of all equipment, landscaping, utility connections, and appropriate occupancy permits.

Some lenders operate with as few as three draws (advances). Inspections are normally necessary at each draw and holdbacks are usually required.

Example   *New Home Construction Loan*

Smith is building a new home on his existing lot and has arranged a $100,000 conventional mortgage with a local lender. The lender requires that advances be made at three points during construction. The first draw (33.333%) can be taken when the primary excavation and full basement are completed, the trusses placed, and the roof sheathed. The next 33.333% draw occurs when all rough plumbing, electrical and mechanical items are installed, doors and windows are in place, and drywall and trim completed. The final draw of 33.333% occurs upon completion of the house and receipt of appropriate municipal approvals and occupancy permit. With each draw, an amount equal to 15% of the draw is withheld in recognition of the applicable provincial construction (lien) act. This holdback is released following the expiration of rights for claims under that act. Therefore, Smith will receive the following amounts during construction:

Total Amount of Mortgage	$100,000
First Advance (33.3% of $85,000)	−28,333
Second Advance (33.3% of $85,000)	−28,333
Third Advance (33.3% of $85,000)	−28,334
Total Holdback (15%)	$15,000

NEW HOME SALES

Activities of a new home sales specialist differ markedly from resale activities. Also, under selected provincial real estate acts, builders or developers may employ their own sales staff without enlisting the assistance of a real estate brokerage. Procedures regarding employed sales staff will vary by province. For example, in some provinces builders are permitted to employ sales staff and not be registered under the Act. In others, the builder must be registered. In either instance, such sales staff normally have to limit themselves to selling only the properties owned by their employer, and would be in violation of the law if they handled any other sales or accepted any form of compensation related to sales of other properties. This is noteworthy, since many buyers of new homes already possess properties that must be sold to facilitate the new home purchase.

Application   Unlike resale homes, salespeople have little direct involvement with the listing function, or in the offer presentation. The function resembles a retailing situation involving qualifying the buyers and closing the sale. Typically, fixed hours of floor duty time are established during which a salesperson will be on site in a model home, or other site office. Showing may consist of furnishing information, demonstrating diagrams and plans (if no models are yet constructed), providing specifics, and answering buyers' questions.

Salespeople qualify buyers both financially and in terms of needs and desires. Prepackaged financing is usually available. Ultimately, counselling and discussions centre on the preparation of an agreement/contract. Details of possession date, financial terms, conditions, and such matters as colours and upgrades of materials have to be determined.

At present, no universally accepted standard agreements/contracts exist for new homes, either under construction or fully completed. Practitioners sometimes use standard agreements/contracts designed for resale homes, however, substantial amendments and additional schedules are required, as several issues unique to new home construction must be addressed.

Provincial   See applicable reference materials.

NEW HOME WARRANTY PROGRAM

A form of insurance plan, typically operated by a government agency or self-regulated body, for new homes that involves warranties for specified defects over a prescribed period of time.

Provincial   See applicable reference materials.

NOMINAL INTEREST RATE
(SEE MORTGAGE MATHEMATICS)

NON-CONFORMING STRUCTURE
(SEE ALSO NON-CONFORMING USE)

A structure that was lawfully existing prior to the effective date of a zoning by-law and does not comply with one or more of the applicable regulations on the effective date of the by-law or amendment thereto.

Application   Generally, a non-conforming structure may be enlarged or extended provided that the use of the structure conforms with the regulations of the applicable zoning district and the enlargement or extension does not create a new non-conformity or increase the degree of non-conformity. The addition or enlargement must therefore conform to all of the applicable zoning district regulations in which the non-conforming structure is located. Typically, repairs or incidental alterations may be made to a non-conforming structure. Exact provisions will vary by municipality.

The right to maintain a non-conforming structure usually terminates when the structure is substantially damaged, deteriorated, or abandoned. Exact provisions and the definition of substantial damage falls to local zoning by-laws. Requirements concerning non-conforming structures, if located in applicable zoning by-laws, are typically grouped with non-conforming uses.

NON-CONFORMING USE

The use or existence of a structure that does not comply with, nor conform to, the present zoning status for its location as well as the use of land prohibited by the terms of the current approved zoning by-law. This circumstance frequently occurs as the result of a change in zoning. Existing uses are normally allowed to continue regardless of the change in zoning.

Application   Real estate practitioners frequently encounter the term *legal non-conforming use* that identifies a use, although non-conforming, which was in existence before the passage of the by-law, and therefore is permitted to continue. A legal non-conforming use cannot be enlarged or substantially altered without approval from the municipality.

Zoning provisions generally permit interior alterations, restoration of the property to a safe condition, and reconstruction of damaged existing buildings in the case of

lawful non-conforming uses. However, zoning regulations should be consulted as they vary considerably between municipalities on this issue.

> **Example   *Non-Conforming Use***
>
> Seller Smith has owned and operated a small repair garage within the community for the past forty years. Recently, an official plan was adopted, along with corresponding by-laws. Henceforth, Smith's property and the immediately surrounding area is zoned single-family residential. Concerned that he may be forced out of business, Smith makes a direct inquiry at the municipal offices. The planning department points out an important statement under the general zoning provisions that reads as follows:
>
> *The provisions of this zoning by-law shall not apply to prevent the use of any lot, building, or structure for any purpose prohibited by this by-law if such lot, building, or structure was lawfully used for such purpose on the date of passing of the by-law, so long as it continues to be used for that purpose.*
>
> Smith is also concerned if the building was somehow damaged. Would he be allowed to repair the structure? This eventuality was also covered in the by-law:
>
> *Nothing is this by-law shall apply to prevent the reconstruction of any lawful non-conforming building or structure, existing as of the date of passing of this by-law which is damaged by causes beyond the control of the owner, provided that such reconstruction is proceeded with as expeditiously as possible.*

NON EST FACTUM

Literally translated as *it is not his deed*. This terminology relates to the legal rule that a person who was induced innocently or fraudulently by another to sign a written document, which is fundamentally different from that which he/she contemplated, is not bound by that document. The document is invalid on the grounds that the mind of the signer did not accompany the signature. He/she never intended to sign and, therefore, in contemplation of the law, the individual never did sign the document to which his/her name is appended.

Non est factum cannot be pleaded where a person misunderstands something that he/she intended to sign. If a person believes that the contract says one thing, but does not read it and then finds out that the contract says something else, he/she has no defence. In this situation, the person has simply been negligent in not reading the contract. Similarly, a blind or illiterate person, who knows the general nature and effect of the contract, would be bound by it unless the contract was falsely read to the individual or it was not read when he/she requested that it be.

Pleading of non est factum in regards to a contract is not a simple matter and expert legal advice should be obtained.

Example   *Non Est Factum*

Buyer Jones signed an agreement to buy a lot on Main Street, owned by Smith, and intended to build a new home. At time of inspection and signing of the agreement, Smith was not involved, but rather another person representing Smith.

Smith ultimately confirmed that the individual representing his interests had done so fraudulently and without proper authority. As a result, Smith argued successfully that the agreement was non est factum and he was not bound in any way by that agreement.

NON-MONETARY BENEFITS

A financial advantage, gained by an individual or other legal entity, other than money that may be viewed as a financial gain from the perspective of taxation.

Application   Most discussions of non-monetary benefits centre on taxation and benefits received by individuals either as a shareholder, owner, or employee. A non-monetary benefit might include selling a company-owned vehicle to a shareholder at a price lower than its value. The difference between the fair market value and the actual selling price could be viewed as a taxable benefit for purposes of federal taxation.

Example   *Non-Monetary Benefits*

Broker/Owner Johnson leased a new automobile for a two-year period. The original purchase price was $33,500 with an optional 62% buyback of $20,770 at the end of the lease period. Johnson decided to exercise the buyback, as it reflected fair market value.

Johnson then purchased the vehicle from his company for $15,000. The accountant, upon reviewing the situation, advised Johnson that the difference between the fair market value of $20,770 and the actual selling price of $15,000 would be viewed as a taxable benefit.

NON-OWNER SPOUSE

Provincial   See applicable reference materials.

NON-PROFIT (NOT-FOR-PROFIT) HOUSING CO-OPERATIVE

A non-profit housing co-operative in Canada can be broadly described as a co-operative without share capital having the primary object of providing housing to its members without the purpose of gain for those members. At the point of dissolution, the co-operative would typically distribute any remaining property, after payment of debts and liabilities, among one or more non-profit housing co-operatives or charitable organizations. The exact structure and operation of non-profit housing co-operatives will vary by provincial legislation.

Provincial   See applicable reference materials.

NON-REALTY INTERESTS

Interests in a property other than the land and improvements that are taken into consideration in the valuation process.

Application   Real estate practitioners most commonly encounter non-realty interests in the sale of an operating business. The business may have rights associated with trade marks, licences, and copyright materials. The enterprise may also operate under a franchise agreement that accrues various benefits, e.g., an exclusive territory for the franchisee and the use of franchisor trademarks. Specific client contracts that transfer with the sale could also impact the value of the business.

NON-RESIDENT OWNERSHIP

Provincial   See applicable reference materials.

NORMAL WEAR AND TEAR (TENANCY)

A term, for purposes of tenancies, referring to the tenant's ability to use the rented premises and return them in good condition to the landlord, subject to normal wear and tear. The tenant is not responsible for loss in value that occurs, without negligence, from such normal wear and tear.

Residential tenancy legislation normally sets out the tenant's responsibility for ordinary cleanliness of the rented premises and the duty to repair damage caused by the wilful or negligent conduct of the tenant or of persons who are permitted on the premises by the tenant.

N TO O

Example *Normal Wear and Tear (Tenancy)*

Smith has owned a ten-unit rental property for the past two years. Since purchasing this investment property, he has just received notice of the first vacancy. Anxious to see the condition of the apartment, he asks permission of the tenant to inspect the unit to determine if anything is needed before renting the apartment. During his visit, everything appears in good order, except various scuff marks on painted walls and baseboards. Further, the appliances are showing signs of deterioration, given their age.

These details are considered normal wear and tear. Consequently, before accepting a new tenancy, Smith has all the walls, ceilings and trim painted, cleans all carpets, and replaces the dishwasher and stove. The remaining appliances, while in good working order, may require replacement within the next several years.

NOTARY PUBLIC

An officer appointed by the Province with authority to take the acknowledgement of persons executing documents and to witness the signature(s) and affix a notarial seal.

NOTE

(SEE ALSO MORTGAGE)

A financial instrument that provides legal acknowledgement of a debt owed. The term *note* is most commonly associated with promissory notes, but can be broadly interpreted to include any written promise to pay. For real estate purposes, the mortgage is the most commonly encountered acknowledgement of debt in the normal course of business activity.

NOTICE

Information about, or warning of, something. Notice may be by personal observation or by written or oral message from another person.

Application   Legally, various types of notice exist, including notice by publication (e.g., publishing a notice in the newspaper to bring a lawsuit, estate probate, or bankruptcy to the attention of the public), and a constructive notice (notice presumed to have been received, e.g., as in the mailing of a notice in lieu of delivery). The most frequent form of notice for real estate purposes is a personal notice that represents direct written or oral communication with the parties to a transaction. Real estate practitioners encounter notices most frequently concerning conditions

being fulfilled in the agreement/contract, e.g., conditional upon financing and sale of the buyer's home and the associated notice removing the condition.

Example   *Notice—*
Notice Concerning Change of
Ownership

Salesperson Garcia has just sold a rental property with 12 units. Both the current owner and the new buyer want to ensure a smooth transition. One issue involves personal notice to the tenants concerning the change of ownership and related matters. Garcia, in addition to various other clauses in the agreement, inserts the following:

> *Upon completion of this sale, the seller shall provide the buyer confirmation of a notice to all tenants advising them of the new owner and requiring all future rents to be paid as the buyer directs. The seller will pay to the buyer any rent paid to the seller in error or in violation of the direction for a period of six months following completion, after which the seller may refuse to accept rent from tenants or return it to them.*

Example—*Notice Concerning Condition*

Salesperson Ward is drafting an agreement/contract that includes a condition concerning financing. She wants to ensure that all financial arrangements are concluded within fifteen days and that proper notice is given when the arrangements are concluded.

> *This offer is conditional upon the buyer arranging, at the buyer's own expense, a new first mortgage for not less than Eighty Thousand Dollars ($80,000.00), bearing interest at a rate of not more than 7.5% per annum, calculated semi-annually not in advance, repayable in blended monthly payments of about Five Hundred and Eighty-five Dollars and Twenty-five Cents ($585.25) including both principal and interest, and to run for a term of not less than 5 years. Unless the buyer gives notice in writing delivered to the seller by 5 p.m. on the 25th day of February, 20xx that this condition is fulfilled, this offer shall be null and void and the deposit shall be returned to the buyer in full without deduction. This condition is included for the benefit of the buyer and may be waived at the buyer's sole option by notice in writing to the seller within the time period stated herein.*

NOTICE (AGREEMENTS/CONTRACTS)

Forms and wordings of notices vary by provincial jurisdiction. Typical notices include the removal of conditions, waiver of conditions, and extensions regarding such conditions. Special notices may also apply concerning power of sale proceedings and the listing of associated property.

Provincial   See applicable reference materials.

NOTICE (REAL ESTATE BROKERAGE)

Certain notices must be completed by registrants under the provincial real estate act and/or mandated by the appropriate regulatory body. Notices include such items as address changes and changes of officers or directors of a corporation registered under the Act.

Provincial   See applicable reference materials.

NOTICE OF PENDING LITIGATION
(SEE ALSO LIS PENDENS)

A certificate issued by the court and registered in the provincial land registration office giving notice that litigation is pending, or in progress, in which some interest in land is called into question. A person claiming an interest or estate in a parcel of land, or in a mortgage or encumbrance registered against a parcel of land, can commence a court action to enforce his/her claim and register such a notice. Title/contents of notice forms will vary by province.

Application   A copy of the statement of claim should be obtained from the court to determine the details of the litigation. The notice acts as a caution, similar in many respects to a caveat. Its effect on market value will depend on its nature but will undoubtedly affect marketability of title until the dispute is resolved or the notice is removed. Most prospective buyers will want to avoid buying in the midst of a litigious matter.

NOTICE OF TAX SALE

A notice registered against the title to land after municipal property taxes are in arrears for a specified period of time. Title and form contents will vary by province.

Provincial statutes give a municipality the right to sell land for arrears of taxes. The municipality must follow statutory procedures to sell the land by public auction to recover the taxes and the municipality itself usually has the right to bid at the auction. The owner of the land sold for taxes may redeem the land before it is sold by paying the amount outstanding together with any penalties. The person will then be entitled to register the appropriate notice of redemption at the land registration office. Alternatively, a tax certificate is issued by the municipality to the person who purchases the land at the tax sale. This certificate is the basis upon which the buyer becomes the registered owner of the land in question.

NOTICE OF TERMINATION (TENANCY)

A notice given by a landlord or a tenant to the other, either during or at the end of the tenancy period according to provisions set out in the applicable provincial tenancy statute. Procedures, timing of notices, and reasons for notices during and at the end of the tenancy period vary by province.

Provincial   See applicable reference materials.

NOTICE TO VACATE (TENANCY)

A legal notice (title will vary by province), requiring tenants to remove their possessions from the premises within a stated period or upon a specified date and to deliver vacant possession of the premises to the owner, agent, or designated successor.

Provincial   See applicable reference materials.

NPV
(SEE NET PRESENT VALUE)

NUISANCE

An act that affects the enjoyment and/or use of a person's property. For example, an individual may introduce some form of contamination that is injurious to a neighbour and/or his/her property. The neighbour could bring an action for damages. This type of nuisance is frequently referred to as a *private nuisance*, as opposed to a *public nuisance* that affects the overall community.

Application   The issue of nuisances is often identified with adjacent properties. Given the close proximity of urban residential housing, noise and other disturbances can give rise to disputes between neighbours. Municipalities enact by-laws to resolve such issues.

On an environmental level, real estate practitioners should look beyond the listed property for nuisances either of a private or public nature, especially environmental contamination. While expert knowledge is needed to determine the existence or extent of contamination in an adjacent property, prudent real estate professionals require an awareness of certain circumstances in adjacent property that could signify potential problems.

- Commercial/industrial sites (particularly those on a higher grade level than the subject property).
- Vacant land with a history of commercial/industrial uses.
- Old garbage or dump sites.
- Proximity to an old septic tank near the lot line.

NULL AND VOID

Having no legal force or effect.

Application　This term is commonly found in an agreement/contract for the sale of real property that involves a condition and related waiver. A typical wording for the waiver follows:

> *Unless the buyer gives notice in writing delivered to the seller by _____ p.m. on the _____ day of _____, 20xx, that this condition is fulfilled, this Offer shall be null and void and the deposit shall be returned to the buyer in full without deduction. This condition is included for the benefit of the buyer and may be waived at the buyer's sole option by notice in writing to the seller within the time period stated herein.*

Example　*Null and Void*

Seller Smith entered into an agreement with Buyer Jones for the sale of his home at 123 Main Street. The offer was conditional upon Jones securing a new first mortgage for not less than $140,000, with an interest rate of 7.5%, and payments of about One Thousand and Twenty-four Dollars and Eighteen Cents ($1,024.18). Jones was unable to qualify, based on the lender's 32% GDS ratio. The offer had stated that if a notice confirming that the mortgage has been arranged was not provided by the time specified, then the agreement/contract would be null and void. Jones provided notice to Smith of his inability to secure mortgage financing within the stated time limit. The contract became null and void and the brokerage issued a cheque to Jones for the amount of the deposit after both parties signed a mutual release.

OBJECTIVE VALUE
(SEE ALSO SUBJECTIVE VALUE)

The value of a property based on the analysis of costs associated with the reproduction of that property (an exact replica), or one of equal utility, (a replacement). Replacement cost is most commonly used given the ease of obtaining accurate information.

Application　Objective value plays a significant role in determining value by means of the cost approach. Essentially two schools of thought have arisen over the concept of value. One school emphasizes the objective nature of value as it relates to the actual production cost of creating a property (the cost approach). The other, representing advocates of subjective value, believes that value exists only in the mind of potential buyers, sellers, owners, and users of real estate (the direct comparison approach).

In the residential appraisal process, both methods of valuation are used reflecting these schools of thought, but the direct comparison approach is more heavily relied upon.

Five steps make up the cost approach.

Step 1.	Estimate the value of the site.
Step 2.	Estimate the cost of reproducing or replacing the existing improvements as though they were new on the effective date of the appraisal.
Step 3.	Estimate the amount of accrued depreciation in the improvements suffered because of physical deterioration, functional obsolescence, and external (economic or locational) obsolescence.
Step 4.	Subtract the total accrued depreciation from the replacement or reproduction cost new of the improvements to arrive at the depreciated cost of improvements.
Step 5.	Add the depreciated cost of the improvements to the estimated value of the site to arrive at an estimated market value of the whole property.

Example *Objective Value*

Salesperson Lee is preparing an appraisal form report including both the direct comparison approach and the cost approach for a lender. Before completing the final report, Lee summarized his calculations concerning the cost approach as follows:

Estimated Value of Site	$ 77,000
Estimated Reproduction Cost New	117,550
Estimated Amount of Accrued Depreciation:	
Physical Deterioration	21,200
Functional Obsolescence	8,350
Economic Obsolescence	3,600
Total Depreciation—All Sources	−33,150
Depreciated Value of Improvements	+84,400
Market Value (Site + Depreciated Value)	**$161,400**

OBSERVED CONDITION (BREAKDOWN) METHOD

A method of estimating accrued depreciation that separately considers and estimates the deductions for physical deterioration, functional obsolescence and economic obsolescence. These estimates are then added to provide a lump sum deduction from reproduction cost new.

Under this method, accrued depreciation is broken down and measured under the following classifications:

- Physical deterioration—curable;
- Physical deterioration (short lived and long lived)—incurable;
- Functional obsolescence—curable;
- Functional obsolescence—incurable; and
- External (economic or locational) obsolescence.

See **Figure A.13 – Accrued Depreciation** for a detailed example.

OBSOLESCENCE

One of the causes of depreciation involving the impairment of desirability and usefulness caused by new inventions, changes in design, improved processes for production, or by external influencing factors. Obsolescence makes a property less desirable and less valuable for continued use in the marketplace.

Application Obsolescence is generally discussed under two categories:

- Functional obsolescence (curable or incurable); and
- External (economic or locational obsolescence).

Obsolescence is an integral part of five basic steps to establish value by the cost approach:

Step 1.	Estimate the value of the site.
Step 2.	Estimate the cost of reproducing or replacing the existing improvements as though they were new on the effective date of the appraisal.
Step 3.	Estimate the amount of accrued depreciation in the improvements suffered because of physical deterioration, functional obsolescence, and external (economic or locational) obsolescence.
Step 4.	Subtract the total accrued depreciation from the replacement or reproduction cost new of the improvements to arrive at the depreciated cost of improvements.
Step 5.	Add the depreciated cost of the improvements to the estimated value of the site to arrive at an estimated market value of the whole property.

Example *Obsolescence*

Salesperson Ward is preparing an appraisal for a single-family detached home at 19 Main Street. She has already established the value of the site, reproduction cost of the improvements, and the amount of physical deterioration. The next step involves determining functional and locational obsolescence.

Following are her observations:

Curable Functional Obsolescence:	
Modernization of Cupboards	$7,300
Depreciated Value of Existing Cupboards	−700
Curable Functional Obsolescence	6,600
Incurable Functional Obsolescence:	
Deficiency ($50 x 90)	4,500
(Monthly Rent Loss x Monthly Rental Factor)	
External (Locational) Obsolescence (Building):	
Monthly Rent Loss x Monthly Rental Factor $2,250 ($25 x 90)	
Ratio of Land to Building: 1:3 or .25/.75	
Therefore: .75 of $2,250	1,687.50
Total Obsolescence	**$12,787.50**
($6,600 + $4,500 + $1,687.50)	

OCCUPANCY PERMIT

A permit issued by a municipality allowing the premises to be occupied for the uses intended. Occupancy permits are most frequently encountered by real estate practitioners in new construction, where the property must meet all municipal guidelines and building standards before the issuance of a permit.

OFF-SITE MANAGEMENT
(SEE ALSO PROPERTY MANAGEMENT)

Management of a property by persons not residing or maintaining regular office hours at the subject property.

OFFER AND ACCEPTANCE
(SEE ALSO CONTRACT)

A proposal by one party, called the offeror, to another party, called the offeree, to accept the basic terms of the agreement and the offeree's subsequent acceptance of that agreement. Once the acceptance has been communicated to the offeror, the contract will bind both parties to its terms.

OFFER PREPARATION/PRESENTATION

The preparation and presentation of an offer cannot be a hit and miss affair. The following guidelines assume a relationship in which the listing brokerage and salespeople are working for the seller in a seller agency relationship and the selling brokerage and salespeople are working for the buyer in a buyer agency relationship. Descriptions are based on the listing salesperson's perspective when providing guidance to the seller and are designed for general information purposes only. Local and/or provincial practices concerning offer presentations and specific circumstances surrounding a particular transaction will dictate what topics are discussed with the seller and when. Descriptive text is limited to a typical residential transaction.

Initial Preparation

Once an offer has been signed by the buyers and is ready for presentation in accordance with local and/or provincial practice, the listing salesperson requires certain information to assist the seller in making an informed decision. Buyer representatives may also contemplate selected items discussed below in preparing for their role in the presentation process.

Review the Listing File   Any offer should be examined in light of the terms under which the sellers agreed to market the property. Circumstances may have changed since the property was originally listed.

Review Marketing Activity   Summarize information such as frequency of advertising, responses, number of showings, previous offers, and open houses conducted. Relevant comments from buyers can be helpful.

Review Comparables   Prepare or update a market analysis showing recent sales or properties that remain unsold.

Review Buyer Information   Information, if provided by the selling brokerage concerning the buyer, can provide important background details that will assist the seller in making a decision.

Prepare Seller's Net   Advance preparation of financial information can assist the seller regarding approximate selling costs and net proceeds if the offer is accepted.

Review of Terms

In addition to price, any offer to purchase contains a variety of terms, each of which can have an impact on the seller's decision. The offer should also be reviewed in light of the seller's circumstances in contemplation of a broad range of questions that might arise during the presentation. Various key issues are detailed.

Deposit
- Is the deposit sufficient and, if by cheque, has its validity been verified?
- The larger the deposit, the greater the degree of practical security for the seller.
- A substantial deposit adds credibility and integrity to the buyer's offer.
- A substantial deposit is a strong plus in any offer presentation.
- A small deposit can show lack of commitment.

Closing/Completion Date
- Non-alignment of buyer's completion date with that of the seller's will usually become a major item of discussion.
- The question of interim financing can loom if the seller must complete his/her new purchase prior to closing of the currently-owned property now under negotiations.
- In the opposite situation, the seller may be asked to vacate the premises prior to a new property being ready for occupancy. This will initiate questions concerning such items as interim accommodations, costs, and storage of furniture.

- Preparation of facts and costs concerning such matters will make the presentation more effective.

Chattels Included/Fixtures Excluded

- Often the terms of the buyer's offer do not exactly match the seller's plans regarding chattels and fixtures as indicated on the listing. Such discrepancies can detract from the offered price.
- Excluded items may hold emotional value to the seller and as such are non-negotiable.

Financing

- If a mortgage is being taken back by the seller, then a *seller take back (STB)* presentation should be anticipated to enable the seller access to complete information when making a decision.
- In some instances, the seller contemplating an STB may require cash for a subsequent transaction. Consideration must be given to the possible sale of the mortgage, associated costs and procedures, and final net to the seller.
- Sometimes a seller is required to discharge an existing mortgage as part of the transaction. The salesperson should be aware of discharge costs and advise the client accordingly.
- The salesperson may wish to develop alternate scenarios to show the seller what he/she would net from other hypothetical offers including different forms of financing.

Price

- Sellers tend to look at the price on an offer and react emotionally to it without examining the other terms and how they impact the overall price. Obviously price is important, but other factors such as closing date, terms of financing, and items included or excluded can directly affect bottom line considerations for the seller.

Other Issues

Various other questions are often worthy of exploring prior to any presentation.

- How does this offer compare with the salesperson's original advice provided to the sellers as to what they could expect? Is this a reasonable offer?
- How does the offer compare to others that the seller has rejected? How much activity has there been since listing?
- The salesperson should ask himself/herself: *If I were the seller would I accept this offer?*
- Is it, in all honesty, the best possible offer that can be obtained from this buyer?

- Are there any other serious prospects who might be prepared to make a better offer?
- What is likely to happen if the seller rejects or counters this offer?

Making the Appointment

Since every offer sets a time limit for acceptance, and the offer may no longer be accepted upon the expiration of the set time, the buyer who executes such an offer has a right to expect that real estate salespersons involved will present it at the earliest possible time. Also, an offer may be subject to revocation prior to acceptance (some variance exists on this issue in provincial preprinted wordings within offers). It is obviously in the salesperson's own interests to present the offer for acceptance as promptly as possible and to expediently communicate acceptance, if given, back to the buyer.

The listing salesperson may have his/her broker or another salesperson in the listing brokerage office make the appointment. The salesperson is not put in the awkward position of having to discuss the details of the offer over the telephone. Most real estate board jurisdictions have precise rules when presenting offers involving listing and selling brokerages.

Naturally, the offer should be presented in writing to the sellers as soon as possible after the salesperson has prepared all of the information. The presentation should take place when sufficient time is available to deal with the offer in a relaxed atmosphere and where all of the parties who are involved in the decision-making process can be present. Notwithstanding that statement, time is of the essence in all offer presentations.

When the offer is presented to the seller, the salesperson should provide explanations of fundamental terms. Failure to make these explanations might be considered negligence that could result in a lawsuit, the loss of the real estate commission, or both.

Right to Legal Advice

Sellers and buyers must be protected from accepting terms in an offer that they are not able to perform, or terms over which they have no control. A lawyer is in the best position to advise a seller whether he/she can freely accept an offer and is in a position to fulfill terms stipulated in the offer.

The CREA Code of Ethics in Article 11 states:

> *The REALTOR shall not discourage parties to a transaction from seeking legal counsel.*

Such legal counsel should be independent representation. Several points concerning legal advice follow.

- The seller and buyer have an absolute right to independent legal advice and salespersons must in no way attempt to deprive them of such advice.

- In certain instances, in fact, the salesperson should insist that the client obtain legal advice, e.g., complex transactions involving environmental issues.

- A salesperson should not hesitate to advise the seller of a concern about a condition or other matter that is not completely understood and suggest that the seller consult his/her solicitor.

- The seller has the right to full disclosure of any and all information known by the seller's agent that could affect the decision regarding acceptance of the offer.

- While a salesperson may act in an advisory capacity to the extent of his/her abilities and suggest alternatives, no salesperson has the right to deprive sellers of their prerogative to make their own decision.

Upon occasion, inexperienced salespeople have difficulty dealing with a request by the seller or buyer to see a lawyer. Usually, concerns are more imagined than real. First, agree with the wisdom of seeking legal counsel at the outset of the transaction. Second, ask to be present to answer any questions that might concern their solicitor. Offer to drive the individual to the solicitor's office or fax a copy of the agreement with a follow-up telephone call. Third, during the conversation or direct meeting, do not attempt to argue points of law. Remember that the individual is the solicitor's client and the solicitor has a duty to advise the client as to whether or not the offer properly sets out his/her intentions. However, when it comes to matters within the salesperson's expertise, such as price negotiations and financing, the knowledgeable salesperson should have no trouble in assisting both solicitor and buyer or seller.

In short, salespeople who have confidence in their own knowledge, ability, and integrity, and who are prepared for such a meeting or telephone conversation will welcome a lawyer's scrutiny without concern. However, do make both the lawyer and the client aware of practical limitations and time concerns.

Counter Offers

If terms of an offer are not acceptable, the seller may either reject the offer or make a counter offer. A counter offer reverses the roles of the parties, as the seller now becomes the offeror. Since any counter offer is an offer to sell upon conditions set out, it becomes, in fact, a new offer. A seller, who wishes to make a counter offer, may select a new

irrevocable period. Methods and forms used in counter offers will vary by provincial jurisdiction.

Acceptance

A sufficient number of copies must be signed in accordance with the provincial regulatory act. At minimum, one copy is provided to each of the parties to the transaction as well as to the listing brokerage and the selling brokerage.

- If the property is owned jointly by husband and wife, then both names appear as sellers and both sign all copies.

- If the property is not jointly owned by the husband and wife, but could be considered as a marital (matrimonial) home under the provisions of the applicable provincial act, then the salesperson must ensure that the non-owning spouse grants consent to the transaction by signing in the space provided on the offer at the time the offer is accepted.

- Each party should acknowledge receipt of his/her copy, which can be done on the back of the agreement retained by the brokerage.

Copies for Solicitors

No law requires a real estate practitioner to provide a copy, signed or otherwise, for the solicitors of the parties involved, however, it has become an accepted business practice to do so. Sellers and buyers may procrastinate regarding choosing solicitors and forwarding them copies of documentation. This delay can be disastrous, particularly for the buyer's solicitor, who has a limited time period to search title. Emphasize the importance of getting copies of the agreement/contract into the hands of the solicitors as soon as possible. If a lawyer has not been selected, make the urgency of doing so, obvious.

Occasionally the buyer and seller will ask a salesperson to suggest a good lawyer. This represents a potential conflict of interest and should be avoided. Most practitioners placed in this position follow the practice of suggesting several names, allowing the party concerned to make the final selection.

Provincial   See applicable reference materials.

OFFER PROCESS

A process that begins with initial discussions and the drafting of an offer to purchase real property. An offer to purchase (or other similar form) is used that, when signed, becomes an agreement/contract by which one party agrees to purchase and another agrees to sell. Title passes upon the payment of an agreed purchase price and the registration of a transfer for the title of that property.

Specific processes and requirements regarding offers to purchase are governed by provincial regulatory requirements. Standard preprinted forms may be commonly used in provincial jurisdictions. The following information, provided for illustration purposes, relates only to a typical residential transaction.

Offer Negotiations

When homeowners decide to list their property, their primary contact is with the listing salesperson. This individual, representing the listing brokerage, completes the listing agreement and decides, with the seller, whether other co-operating brokerages will be used. The selling salesperson, whether employed by the listing brokerage or a co-operating brokerage, rarely deals directly with the seller, as he/she is typically representing the buyer in the real estate transaction. When the selling salesperson finds a prospective buyer, he/she contacts the listing salesperson, not the seller, to present the offer.

Throughout offer negotiations, the communication process remains constant. The seller contacts the listing salesperson who then contacts the selling salesperson and so on. It is possible of course for the listing salesperson and the selling salesperson to be the same person.

An offer, when completed by a buyer, is an indication of a willingness to contract, but not a contract in itself. An offer only becomes a contract when it has been unconditionally accepted by the seller and communication of acceptance back to the buyer has occurred.

Once a prospective buyer makes a written offer, the offer must be presented to the seller without delay. This is true regardless of what type of listing is in force, whether it is an exclusive, multiple, or open listing. By delaying presentation of an offer, all parties involved will be affected. If the salesperson delays presenting the offer to the seller, an opportunity occurs for the prospective buyer to rescind the offer (based on the wording of the preprinted offer), or the time period for its acceptance may expire. It is imperative to present the offer as soon as possible to avoid complications and properly perform the function of a diligent practitioner.

Once the offer is presented to the seller, he/she has three options. If the terms and conditions are satisfactory, the seller can accept the offer. Communication of acceptance to the offeror or buyer then makes the offer a legally binding contract on both parties. If the terms of the offer are not acceptable to the seller, the seller can either reject the offer or make a counter offer.

Essential Elements

All offers must comply with the following six elements of contract law in order to ultimately lead to a contract:

- The parties to the contract must, at the time when the contract is made, have the legal capacity to make the contract.
- The parties must intend to effect their legal relationship with one another.
- The parties must be in agreement.
- The terms of the agreement must be definite and clear.
- Unless the contract is made under seal, there must be consideration received in return for the promises made by each party.
- The contract must not be illegal.

Contracts for the sale of land must be in writing. The essential elements of an offer are generally similar in provincial jurisdictions although the exact content and format of preprinted forms will differ. In some provinces, the provincial real estate act sets out specific requirements concerning the essential elements of an offer and/or requires a mandatory form be used. In others, standard preprinted forms have evolved due to the efforts of local boards and/or provincial real estate associations. Regardless, certain key elements appear in offers, the most notable of which are itemized.

- The date on which the offer is made.
- The names and addresses of the offeror and offeree.
- The address and legal description of the real estate.
- The price offered by the offeror and the terms and conditions of the purchase.
- The amount of deposit, if any, made by the offeror at the time of the offer and whether or not the deposit is to form part of the purchase price.
- A brief description and list of any chattels that are to be included in the sale price (and fixtures excluded).
- The date of possession by the offeror and whether possession shall be vacant or otherwise.
- The time within which the offer must be accepted.

Provincial   See applicable reference materials.

Negotiations

Prospective buyers who have confidence in the salesperson naturally seek his/her advice as to price and other terms that should be offered. Methods used are largely dictated by the agency relationship with that buyer.

If the real estate brokerage is acting for the seller and treating the buyer as a customer, then the listing clearly sets out the manner in which the property is to be offered for sale. Without the authority of the seller, no salesperson working on behalf of that owner has the right to ask for or suggest a lower price or terms other than those contained in the listing contract. However, notwithstanding this fact, the salesperson has the very practical task of negotiating the terms of the prospective buyer's offer while ultimately serving the interest of the client or seller to sell his/her home. One way to handle this situation is to question the prospect as to what he/she is prepared to offer. If the suggestion as to price and terms appears ridiculous, the salesperson clearly has a duty to discuss the implications of such an offer. While the salesperson's wish is to obtain an acceptable price for the seller, this cannot cloud the duty to be fair and reasonable with the buyer. The salesperson's duty is to persuade, not dictate.

In a buyer agency relationship, the salesperson owes a fiduciary duty to the buyer to represent his/her best interests. The concern rests with protecting that interest and gaining the best possible price for the buyer. However, at the same time, the terms of the offer should ultimately be decided by the buyer. Too low a price could start the negotiating process on the wrong foot and permanently impair negotiations with the seller. Too high a price can adversely affect the buyer's position. And, of course, the possibility of competing offers always exists.

Acceptance

The basic premise of any contract is a proposal by one party (the offeror, usually the buyer), to another party (the offeree, usually the seller), to accept the basic terms of the offer. If the offeree indicates assent to the proposal, there is an acceptance and, once this acceptance is communicated to the offeror, the contract will bind both parties to its terms. Certain basic elements must be present in order for there to be acceptance:

Unconditional   A conditional assent to the offer does not constitute acceptance. For example, the seller cannot vary the terms of the offer and then accept it. Should the offeree (or seller), change any of the terms of the offer, a counter offer has been made. The counter offer has the effect of negating the original offer, and reversing the roles of the parties, as the seller becomes the offeror in this instance.

Communicated to the Offeror   No agreement/contract exists until acceptance is communicated back to the offeror, or buyer in most cases. Communication of acceptance of the offer must be done in the manner set out in the offer.

Made in the Manner Required by the Offeror   If the offer stipulates a time during which it is open, then acceptance must be made within that time. If no time is stipulated, the offer must be accepted within a reasonable time depending on the circumstances. Preprinted offers used by practitioners include a clause relating to the time period and provide for the insertion of a date and time by the salesperson. The acceptance by the seller and the communication back to the buyer must be completed prior to the specified date and time or the offer expires.

Time is of the Essence   Acceptance of the offer must be made within the time required by the offeror. In addition, all the dates and time frames stipulated in the offer must be strictly adhered to.

Provincial   See applicable reference materials for any statutory requirements.

Amendments, Conditions, and Clauses

Any amendments made to an offer must be initialled by the party making the change. No amendments/changes may be made after the agreement/contract has come into existence unless by mutual consent of both parties.

Provincial regulatory bodies or real estate organizations may provide standard clauses for the drafting of commercial and/or residential offers.

Provincial   See applicable reference materials.

Delivery of Copies

When an offer has been accepted, all parties to the transaction receive a copy along with one copy for the listing brokerage and one copy for the selling brokerage. Copies should be provided with minimum delay. Customarily, the listing broker keeps the original of the accepted offer. A common business practice is to send a copy of the accepted offer to the buyer's and seller's solicitors.

OFFER/AGREEMENT TO LEASE
(SEE ALSO LEASE)

An offer to lease, when accepted, represents an agreement between parties to enter into a lease. The offer to lease sets forth the basic terms such as the date of the lease, the full names of the landlord and tenant, address of the property, term of the lease, rental payment particulars, landlord and tenant covenants, and material facts agreed by the parties.

N
TO
O

OFFER/AGREEMENT/CONTRACT TO LEASE
(COMMERCIAL OR RESIDENTIAL)

Provincial   See applicable reference materials.

OFFER/AGREEMENT/CONTRACT TO PURCHASE

Provincial regulatory bodies (or provincial real estate associations in selected instances), commonly provide preprinted offer forms for various types of properties, e.g., condominium, farm, commercial, and residential.

Provincial   See applicable reference materials.

OFFICE POLICIES
(SEE POLICY MANUAL)

OPEN HOUSE

The practice of licensed salespersons and brokers demonstrating listed property by inviting other brokerages or the public to inspect properties within selected hours on specific days.

Application   Most sellers working with real estate brokerages experience two types of open houses. The first, a salespersons' open house, is normally provided to all salespeople within the brokerage and co-operating brokerages in the case of MLS listings. Inspection tours for salespeople can be organized on specific days of the week and/or by geographic area. The second type of open house is an open invitation to the public to inspect the listed property at a specified date and time. In recent years, variations on the open house concept have appeared, particularly in the area of upper-range residential property, in which open houses may be offered by invitation only.

OPEN LISTING
(SEE ALSO LISTING)

A listing given to any number of brokerages without liability to compensate any, except the one that first acquires a buyer ready, willing, and able to meet the terms of the seller, or secures the acceptance by the seller of a satisfactory offer. Considerable variation exists both in form and meaning associated with open listings. In practice, an open

listing can be in writing and involve two or more brokerages on a non-exclusive basis, a simple letter of introduction providing assurances that the brokerage will be paid if the named buyer acquired the property within a specified period, or simply a verbal instruction by the seller accompanied by basic property details.

Example   *Open Listing*

Builder Anderson has constructed homes for many years in Anycity. Currently, he has 20 homes for sale in Westside and has been working with two different brokerages. Each brokerage has given him excellent service in the past. Rather than signing an exclusive authority, he wants to allow both brokerages the right to market all his homes, but must come to an amicable arrangement.

After discussing the situation, Anderson and the two brokers arrive at a solution. The builder will sign an open listing with both organizations for all properties with the following provision written into the two listing agreements:

This listing agreement is a non-exclusive open listing agreement with both ABC Realty Inc. and XYZ Real Estate Ltd. In the event that either brokerage brings a valid offer to purchase on any or all properties as detailed in this listing authority, I agree to pay a commission of 3.5% of the sale price of the property or properties only to that brokerage.

OPEN MORTGAGE
(SEE ALSO MORTGAGE)

A mortgage containing some form of prepayment privilege for the partial or total reduction of principal with or without penalty. Caution is advised as the term *open* is often subject to certain qualifications and restrictions. Original source documents should always be consulted.

OPEN SPACE

A descriptive term generally used by real estate practitioners to describe portions of a property or properties preserved in their natural state. The actual purpose of such open space will vary dramatically depending on the type of property. In the case of condominiums, open space can refer to landscaped areas for the common benefit of all unit owners. In larger tracts of land (e.g., recreational/rural), open space more often refers to lands kept in their natural state for the benefit of all.

The concept of open space is also used in official plans for municipalities to designate lands intended for recreational purposes. The designation also applies to land which is either unuseable for development purposes or in some way possesses significant natural or environmentally sensitive elements. While permitted uses within open space areas vary by municipality, the following permitted uses are commonly addressed in zoning by-laws.

- Public parkland;
- Recreational facilities such as arenas, golf courses, community centres, and baseball fields;
- Private open space;
- Transmission corridors used for public utilities; and
- Marinas and yacht clubs.

OPERATION OF LAW

One of five generally recognized methods by which a contract may be discharged. For example, a contract may be discharged by operation of law if the party goes bankrupt. Also, rights and obligations under a contract may merge into a subsequent higher contract, e.g., a warranty concerning some aspect of the property may merge or terminate at the closing unless there is some specific wording within the agreement/contract that clearly states that such warranty shall survive the closing. A contract may also be discharged by operation of law when one party alters the contract without the consent of the other.

The remaining four methods by which a contract may be discharged are mutual agreement, performance, impossibility of performance, and breach of contract. See Contract.

OPPORTUNITY COST
(SEE ALSO DISCOUNT RATE)

A term used in capital budgeting, appraisal, and real estate investment analysis, based on the concept of *lost opportunity*. Any decision to make an investment has an associated cost, i.e., the opportunity lost in another comparable investment. Just as a lender applies an interest rate to principal so that he/she is assured that an initial investment grows to a larger amount, an investor must apply an opportunity cost to any investment decision.

Application   Typically, opportunity cost is determined by assessing other investments that would realize an equally acceptable return. When lacking reliable market information, investors often rely on mortgage and bond markets to establish the base opportunity cost or *risk-free* rate.

This base cost summed with a risk premium, given the investor's perception of risk, is applied to the property under consideration.

Example   *Opportunity Cost/Risk*

Investor Smith has $100,000 to invest. He estimates that, with prudent investing in stocks and bonds, this money should return 11% during the period of a year based on periodic interest payments. Periodic payments are assured, however, an element of risk exists (e.g., downturn in stock prices). At the same time, an attractive real estate investment with a potential return of 16–18% in one year has been presented for his consideration. In weighing the options, the 11% return becomes the *opportunity cost*.

If Smith seriously contemplated the real estate investment, he must factor in the cost of lost opportunity. The decision centres on whether the additional return is sufficient given risks associated with the stocks as opposed to the real estate. Basically, the real estate investment appears attractive from a pure opportunity cost perspective, but a more detailed analysis is required concerning risk.

OPTION

A continuing offer of contract by which the owner of real property, for a consideration, agrees to permit another to buy or lease the real property at a fixed price within a specified period.

OPTION COMMISSION AGREEMENT

An agreement used in conjunction with an option to buy/purchase concerning the payment of commission in the event that an option is exercised or not exercised. The agreement also typically covers the situation in which the option is not exercised, but a lease is entered into between the parties relating to that property. A commission agreement typically forms part of a preprinted option to buy/purchase form. See Figure O.1 as an example.

Provincial   See applicable reference materials.

OPTION TO BUY/PURCHASE

A right given by the owner of property to another (for valuable consideration), to buy certain property within a limited time at an agreed price.

Application   An option to buy, referred to in some jurisdictions as an *offer to purchase*, allows a seller and buyer to enter into an option that gives the buyer the right to

Ontario Real Estate Association
OPTION COMMISSION AGREEMENT
(TO BE USED IN CONJUNCTION WITH OREA FORM 104)

IF OPTION EXERCISED

In consideration of the services of ....

(herein called Agent) in obtaining the Option attached hereto, I agree to pay the Agent a commission of.......................................
in the event the said Option is exercised.

I shall pay the Agent the said commission if within........................ days after the expiration or other termination of the Option or the sale contemplated therein I sell or exchange the property to or with the same Optionee or his Assigns.

It is understood and agreed that upon the exercise of the said Option the Agent shall become entitled to deduct the amount of the commission due to him out of the deposit at the time of the completion of the sale. In the event that the monies paid by the Optionee by way of deposit shall not be sufficient to pay the amount of the commission herein, then I hereby authorize and irrevocably instruct my solicitor to pay any unpaid balance of the commission out of the proceeds of the sale if and when the proceeds of the sale come into my solicitor's hands.

IF OPTION NOT EXERCISED

In the event that the Optionee does not exercise the said Option, I agree that the Agent herein shall be entitled to receive one half of the consideration herein or the amount of his above noted commission whichever shall be the less amount and the Agent shall be entitled to deduct this amount from the

consideration and credit it to his own account and pay over the balance to me or...

....

IF LEASED

In the event the Optionee does not exercise the said Option but at any time within............................days after the date provided for exercise of the said

Option enters into a leasing agreement for the property I agree to pay the Agent a commission of.......................................% of the first year's rental

and.............................% of the rental of any one renewal of the lease. Said commission being due and payable on the earlier of the signing of the lease or taking of possession by the Optionee/Lessee.

It is further understood and agreed that in the event the Lessee purchases the property within the term of the lease or within ....years from

the date the Optionee does not exercise the said Option (whichever occurs first), I agree to pay to the Agent a commission..............................

representing.............................% of the agreed upon sale price reduced by the amount already received by the Agent as a result of any lease agreement between the Optionee and me.

Wherever the terms of this Agreement conflict with any Listing Agreement between the Optionor and the Agent the terms of this Agreement shall prevail.

DATED at .... this................................ day of .... 20...................
SIGNED, SEALED AND DELIVERED in the presence of: IN WITNESS whereof I have hereunto set my hand and seal:

....   ⬤ DATE...............................
(Witness)   (Optionor)   (Seal)

....   ⬤ DATE...............................
(Witness)   (Optionor)   (Seal)

OREA Standard Form: Do not alter when printing or reproducing the standard pre-set portion

Form No. 105   **01/00**

Figure O.1   Option Commission Agreement

buy the seller's property at an agreed price at some future date. An option to buy is not normally used in residential transactions, but would have application in transactions dealing with industrial, commercial and investment properties, e.g., a developer wishes to option certain lands for a period of time to obtain development approvals and/or adjoining lands.

An option to buy is distinct from an agreement/contract in that the latter creates immediate mutual rights and obligations on both seller and buyer. The option to buy only gives the buyer a right to purchase the property within a specified period without imposing any obligation to purchase. An option is not to be confused with a conditional contract, i.e., one that depends on the occurrence of some specified event. When a condition is inserted in an agreement, the courts have determined that an obligation exists for the party to make a reasonable effort to satisfy the condition. The option to purchase gives the buyer the right to purchase but does not impose any obligation to do so. If the option is not exercised, the contract will be at an end.

If the option is exercised by the buyer, then a binding agreement/contract will result. The seller must understand that, while the option period is in existence, he/she cannot sell the property to a third party. All terms of the option to purchase must be completed in the same detail as one would with any agreement/contract.

Provincial   See applicable reference materials.

ORDER OF POSSESSION

A court order that enables the applicant to occupy vacated premises. Typically, an order of possession is obtained by a mortgagee to take possession of the mortgaged premises when in default or by an owner who seeks to have occupants who illegally occupy premises removed from the premises. In the case of residential tenancies, special provisions commonly apply to terminations and orders of possession. Terminology concerning such orders varies by provincial jurisdiction.

Provincial   See applicable reference materials.

ORGANIZED REAL ESTATE

The term *organized real estate* has traditionally referred to the voluntary association of licensed real estate practitioners as members of real estate boards, provincial real estate associations, and The Canadian Real Estate Association. Organized real estate is most commonly identified with the exclusive use of REALTOR by members, the Multiple

Listing Service offered through real estate boards, and the adoption of a Code of Ethics and Standards of Business Practice by all members.

Roles and responsibilities of respective groups within organized real estate vary.

Real Estate Boards

- Primary responsibility is contact with individual members of their board.
- Membership processing, recording, and dues collection.
- Forward provincial and CREA dues to respective associations.
- Arbitration between brokerage firms.
- Multiple Listing Service.
- MLS (rules and regulations compatible with provincial association guidelines).
- Operations, facilities, promotion, and statistics.
- Trademark compliance assistance, jointly with provinces and CREA.
- Establish board corporate jurisdictions, jointly with provinces and CREA.
- Enforcement of the CREA Code of Ethics.
- Industry representation on local government relations.
- Delivery of continuing education and new member orientation.
- Member products and services best delivered by the local board.
- Social and community service programs.

Provincial Associations

- Ultimate contact is the member, primarily through the boards in their province.
- Where provincial associations' by-laws provide for individual members, the provincial association will process, record, collect and remit such dues to CREA.
- Includes direct membership processing in non-board areas, recording, and dues collection.
- Advice and support to boards and members on ethics enforcement, media relations, governance and other issues, and act as a conciliator between boards.
- Arbitration between members from different boards in the same province.
- Research and develop seminar materials and instructor cadre for continuing education delivery by boards, in a manner complementary to the boards as required.
- Standard forms including research and development of new forms to be used by boards for members.

- Multiple Listing Service.
- Establish board corporate jurisdiction, jointly with boards and CREA.
- Trademark compliance assistance, jointly with boards and CREA.
- Develop operational MLS (Rules and Regulations).
- Develop or facilitate interboard agreements, access agreements, subscription agreements, regionalization or provincial MLS.
- Industry representation on provincial relations to public and private bodies.
- Member products and services best coordinated from the provincial association.
- Involvement in licensing standards and licensing education requirements. Extent of involvement in licensing education varies significantly by province.

Canadian Real Estate Association

- Ultimate contact is the member, primarily through local boards and provincial associations.
- Advice and support to provincial associations, local boards, and members.
- Maintain role as a facilitator in the provision of services to boards and provincial associations as requested.
- Maintenance, protection, licensing, and standards for MLS (certification, including MLS rules and regulations).
- Arbitration between provincial associations and for brokerages from different provinces.
- Develop and monitor national Code of Ethics and Standards of Business Practice.
- Industry representation on national and international relations to public and private bodies.
- Member products and services best co-ordinated from the national association.
- Co-ordinate national internet web site and MLS.
- Establish board corporate jurisdiction, jointly with board and provinces.
- Trademark compliance assistance, jointly with boards and provinces.
- MLS (research and development).

CREA Directory

The Canadian Real Estate Association publishes a CREA Directory that provides addresses and telephone numbers for all provincial real estate associations, real estate boards, and broker members within those boards throughout Canada. This publication also details councils of CREA, e.g., the Association Executives Council.

ORIGINATION FEE

A term, traditionally encountered in the United States, referring to a fee charged by a lender to process a mortgage application, prepare necessary documents, and record those documents on title. The origination fee is normally a percentage of the mortgage amount. In Canada, most lenders charge an application or processing fee to cover the initial costs regarding conventional, residential mortgages. If the loan is high ratio, a fee to GE Capital Mortgage Insurance Company or Canada Mortgage and Housing Corporation would apply. However, such charges are not generally viewed as synonymous with the term *origination fee*.

A closer Canadian parallel involves large commercial loans. Canadian banks charge a setup fee typically based on a percentage of the loan amount. Mortgage brokers (dealers) are also involved in origination fees pursuant to various regulations as set out in provincial statutes, e.g., requirements concerning disclosure statements and collection of fees.

Example   *Origination Fee*

Seller Smith is attempting to secure mortgage financing on a downtown commercial building. A lender has agreed to provide $2,500,000 as a first mortgage at 9.25% with an amortization of 30 years and a 5-year term. However, a setup fee amounting to 0.05% of the mortgage must be paid to the lender in consideration of costs associated with processing, drafting of appropriate agreements, and generally negotiating various matters concerning the loan. The setup fee is an origination fee.

OUTDOOR AIR QUALITY

Highways and roads, sewage treatment plants, industrial operations, waste management facilities, and livestock operations that are near residential properties increasingly fall under public scrutiny. The appropriate provincial ministry/department involved with environmental matters usually assesses the impact of these major facilities on surrounding air quality. While separation distances can be set in new developments, problems may arise with existing uses. In rural areas, for example, the appropriate ministry involved with agriculture and food normally provides guidelines concerning proximity of new developments to livestock operations. Ministries responsible will vary by provincial jurisdiction.

Application   For most residential real estate transactions, the best rule of thumb is to develop a sensitivity to matters that go beyond the lot lines of a property. If nearby commercial, industrial, or public waste operations pose a threat to air quality, then the matter should be openly discussed with all parties to a transaction. Odours and emissions impact air quality and consequently can affect value. While government agencies monitor such pollutants, established standards may not align with individual preferences when purchasing property.

As with most environment issues, proper disclosure of pertinent facts is always the best avenue. Exercise due diligence in identifying potential air quality problems near property that will be marketed and shown to prospective buyers. Honesty and fairness is always appreciated. Direct any specific questions to appropriate authorities.

OUTLETS (RECEPTACLES)

A receptacle into which electric appliances can be plugged. Prior to 1950 all electrical appliances were ungrounded, with two slots, or two slots of different sizes (polarized) so that only polarized appliances could be installed in the proper orientation. Grounding of electrical outlines became popular after 1960, as the third ground wire affords additional protection

Figure O.2 illustrates three types of typical outlets found in residential properties.

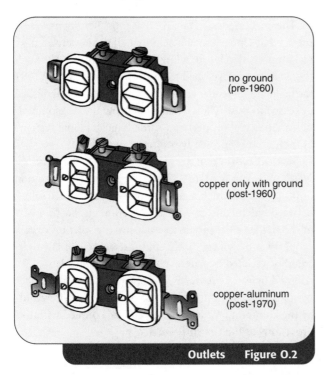

no ground (pre-1960)

copper only with ground (post-1960)

copper-aluminum (post-1970)

Outlets   Figure O.2

OVER IMPROVEMENTS

The placement of improvements on a property that are excessive and consequently inconsistent with the overall size, quality, or appearance of other improvements within the general vicinity. An example would be the construction of a large expensive home within a neighbourhood consisting almost exclusively of small, detached, older bungalows. The cost of the over improved property may not be reflected in market value as determined by an average buyer ready, willing, and able to acquire the property.

For appraisal purposes, the appraiser would typically calculate a loss in value (depreciation), owing to locational obsolescence, i.e., loss in value due to negative external influences in the immediate area.

The following example illustrates the extent to which value is affected when over improvements are involved in renovations to a structure.

Example   *Over Improvements*

Salesperson Lee is attempting to explain the concept of over improvement to a potential seller/client. The owner, Mr. Wilson, recently renovated his home, not realizing that a corporate transfer was in the future. Wilson's home was originally an 1,100 square foot bungalow with a garage. Most of the properties in the area are roughly the same size and general range of value. Wilson just completed a sizeable addition, costing approximately $55,000, on the rear of the house. The addition added a main level family room, laundry room, and a three-piece bath.

Lee demonstrated with a comparative market analysis that most homes in the immediate area sell for between $160,000 and $175,000. However, two properties in the neighbourhood had also undergone significant additions and both recently sold for less than $200,000. Lee, while sympathetic to Wilson's significant cash outlay, estimated that the property would probably realize approximately $200,000. Had the home been left in its original condition, the market value would have been around $170,000. Effectively, Wilson's investment of $55,000 has a market value of approximately $30,000.

OVERHOLDING
(SEE HOLDING OVER)

OWNERSHIP (REAL PROPERTY)
(SEE ESTATE)

OWNERSHIP HISTORY

In the history of Canada, two doctrines of law relating to land ownership have arisen: the original doctrine of tenure, and the subsequent doctrine of estate. For the majority of provinces, the present-day system of land holding has its roots in English medieval law.

The Feudal System of Tenure

After the fall of the Saxon empire in 1066 to King William of Normandy, a military regime was imposed on the entire English countryside. Under this regime, a land-holding system was instituted known as *feudalism*. Through this system, King William appointed approximately 1,500 tenants-in-chief who became the King's principal tenants of all England, thus becoming in turn the lords of the land (or landlords) of the entire domain. The tenants-in-chief, who were the principal lords of the realm, did not own the land, but were merely tenants of their king. Payment by services of different kinds was demanded by the sovereign for allowing the lords to occupy these large tracts of land. The lords, in their turn, were allowed to sublet.

A system of parcelling land was established that allowed the respective tenants to pay with goods and services. This system was one of tenure, or the holding of land subject to some superior right rather than ownership. The type of tenure held was related to the duties owed to the landlord, the payment exacted became traditional with each type of tenure so that if one knew the nature of services due, one could identify the type of tenancy held.

Doctrine of Estates

The earliest use of the word *estate* is found in the medieval *Year Book*, where lawyers of the time were found to use this term in their reports to describe the interest that a tenant held in his land. *Estate*, connected with the Latin word *status*, was used to convey the legal position. The recognition of estates in land law arose through legal action that brought disputes over ownership before the royal courts. Before the Norman conquest of 1066, the jurisdiction of the royal courts was rather narrow, since the administration of local justice was left to the lords of the realm who made it a very profitable business. After 1066, King William saw fit to intervene frequently between the tenants-in-chief and their subtenants, thereby establishing a more or less uniform system of rights, which is said to have led to the establishment of the principle of common law.

Modern law was developed as a result of the many disputes brought before the royal courts. These actions, where interests in the property were recognized, became known as real estates, thus leading to the phrase *real estate* in modern usage to define interest in, or rights to, land.

Development of Canadian Law

At one time, every part of Canada was a colony under English law. The method of establishing English law depended entirely on how those lands became colonized. If a territory became a colony because of direct British settlement, English statute and common law was established immediately as a general rule, unless local conditions made this impossible. Following the establishment of a local legislature, power was granted to enact laws of a local nature under some form of control by Britain.

If a colony was acquired by conquest or cession, laws in force at the time were generally adopted until altered or modified. With cession, these alterations or modifications were subject to treaty. The various colonies that now comprise Canada were acquired in all three ways. Ontario was mainly a settlement, but at one time it belonged to Québec, which in turn, according to one's view of history, was acquired either by cession or conquest.

In 1774, the *Québec Act* greatly enlarged the boundaries of the province, including what was to become Upper Canada (now Ontario). One part of the Act provided that the then laws of Canada (i.e., French law) applied to civil rights and matters of property. At the separation of Canada in 1791 into Upper and Lower Canada under the *Constitutional Act*, French law with some minor exceptions still took precedence. Since the great majority of Upper Canada was settled by the British, steps were taken to alter this situation. The new legislature of Upper Canada enacted *The Property and Civil Rights Act* of 1792, and noted that the province had been principally settled by British settlers unaccustomed to French law. Among other things, the Act repealed that particular provision of the *Québec Act*.

The enactment of *The Property and Civil Rights Act* meant that Upper Canada acquired all the laws related to real property developed in England over centuries. Although these laws had developed from the feudal system, by 1792 the incidence of feudal tenure had long since been abolished or ceased to exist. Thus, while influencing the development of Canada's real property laws, the English feudal system as such has never directly been part of them.

By the *Constitution Act* of 1867 (formerly the *British North American Act 1867*), Canada became a confederation of provinces in which legislative power was divided between federal and provincial governments. Section 92 of the Act gave the provinces exclusive jurisdiction over property and civil rights, except those aspects of law that could be enacted by federal parliament. English law, adopted by most provinces, has obviously been modified by statutes passed into law by provincial legislatures, and by the common law decisions of courts, coupled with the provisions of the *Constitution Act*.

OWNERSHIP LIMITATIONS

Provincial   See applicable reference materials.

P TO Q

P TO Q

National Info Links

Parks Canada

For federal programs concerning national historic sites, federal heritage buildings, national conservation areas and heritage rivers, contact:

Parks Canada National Office
25 Eddy Street
Hull, PQ K1A OM5

Web Site   www.parkscanada.gc.ca

Parks Canada has service centres throughout Canada. Contact information for regional centres is available on the Parks Canada web site.

Privacy (Public and Private Sectors)

The Privacy Commissioner of Canada
112 Kent Street
Ottawa, ON K1A 1H3

Telephone   (613) 995 2410
(800) 267 0441 (National Capital Region)
Web Site   www.privcom.gc.ca

Professional Conduct

For national ethical requirements involving members of organized real estate, contact:

The Canadian Real Estate Association
344 Slater Street, Suite 1600, Canada Building
Ottawa, ON K1R 7Y3

Telephone   (613) 237 7111
Web Site   www.crea.ca
www.mls.ca

For provincial ethical requirements involving licensees/registrants, contact the appropriate regulatory agency (see page 494) or provincial real estate association (see Provincial/Territorial Real Estate Associations).

P

PAPER TRAILS

A series of documents in support of and in evidence of past conduct. A well-documented paper trail is critical should past events come under scrutiny. Poorly documented files are a source of risk for real estate practitioners.

Research indicates that the weakest link in a paper trail may attract liability. Injured parties, be they customers or clients, frequently undertake a careful examination of all documentation prepared by salespeople and brokers seeking evidence for legal action.

Application　Real estate practitioners should maintain a personal filing system, the extent of which will depend on individual needs and preferences, as well as the contractual relationship with the brokerage. Salespeople can retain copies (not originals), of key documents concerning transactions in which they are involved. Ensure that all items entering the filing system are date stamped and file short notes concerning circumstances affecting specific transactions. These notes can prove invaluable should issues arise. Invest in a proper paper-based or electronic planner system as detailed notes regarding appointments and events are important when personally reconstructing the past. A duplicate message log at home is advised as many key messages are received during evenings and weekends. A paper log of e-mail correspondence is also prudent.

PARENTAL LEAVE

A provision allowing for parental leave of absence from work in addition to maternity leave as set out in provincial employment legislation. The existence of such a provision and its legislative scope in relation to employees falling under legislation will vary by province.

Provincial　See applicable reference materials.

PARTIAL DISCHARGE

A portion of an interest, right, or obligation that is released, most frequently in relation to mortgages.

Application　Two types of discharge, either *partial* or *full*, are commonly discussed. A *full* discharge removes a registration completely from all affected land. A *partial* discharge releases a registration *in part*, i.e., a portion of the affected land, and the rest of the land remains subject to that registration.

If a registration is made against more than one title, then a partial discharge may remove that registration from some of the titles and not others. If a registration is registered against one title, then a partial discharge may remove that registration from part of the land in that title and leave it on the rest. A partial discharge must be carefully reviewed to determine what part exactly is being discharged.

> **Example**　*Partial Discharge*
>
> Developer Reed has recently developed a small condominium project involving 14 units in Anycity. Financing was provided by the Canadian National Bank. At point of registration, the bank agreed to partial discharges for those units transferred to their respective owners from the development company. At present, nine units have been transferred to their owners and the remaining five units have been sold but are not scheduled to close for several weeks. A partial discharge can be registered now for the nine units. When the last unit has been transferred to its respective owner, Reed will have fully discharged the first mortgage held by the Canadian National Bank.

PARTICIPATION FINANCING

Special purpose financing involving the lender in direct participation with the borrower in some profit or ownership position for a particular venture.

Application　A variety of participation financing arrangements are possible. However, most can be generally grouped under two major categories.

Income Participation　The lender's involvement in the cash flow, net income, and/or potential income of the enterprise.

Equity Participation　The lender's participation in proceeds of the disposition of the property and/or business enterprise.

Typically, participation mortgages are used in tight money situations and times of high interest rates. For example, the lender may grant a participation mortgage on the basis of reducing the effective interest rate charged, increasing the mortgage amount to the borrower, and/or extending the term. The lender, in return, receives a percentage of equity or a share of income received. Alternatively, the lender may seek a percentage participation in gross sales activity.

Example *Participation Financing*

Developer Reed is attempting to secure $3,500,000 in financing for a neighbourhood shopping complex. A lender will provide the funds provided that a 3% of gross income participation factor is included in the package. In return, the lender will advance funds at 1% less than comparable lenders for five years. To facilitate this arrangement, the lender has certain requirements.

- Reed must report gross sales activity from all tenants within the project during the term of the mortgage.

- All tenants must be on a percentage lease arrangement, with the participation portion being no less than 3% of the amount exceeding base sales for the minimum rents as established and agreed between the lender and Reed.

- Reed will report all gross sales activity within 30 days of receiving reports of gross sales from tenants. The tenants must provide such reports no later than the tenth day after the last day of each calendar month of the term, including the calendar month in which the first day of the term occurs. The lender will require an original written statement from each tenant or by an authorized officer or independent auditor of the tenant, showing the gross sales for the preceding calendar month.

- Reed will remit payments directly to the lender in accordance with statements provided by the tenants.

- If Reed fails to deliver the statements within the stipulated time, the lender, in addition to any rights in the mortgage document, may employ an independent chartered accountant qualified to practice in the provincial jurisdiction in which the property is situated, to examine the books and records of Reed and report upon and certify the amount of gross sales due to the lender.

PARTIES TO A CONTRACT

In a real estate transaction, those individuals or corporations directly involved in, and having a vested interest in, an agreement/contract as sellers or buyers, or as duly authorized representatives of the seller or buyer. The parties to a contract must be clearly identifiable.

The capacity of parties to a contract is further discussed under **Executor/Executrix, Illiterate, Intoxicated Persons, Minor, Partnership,** and **Corporations.**

PARTNERSHIP (BROKERAGE)

When two or more individuals or entities pool their personal and financial resources in a joint effort. Partnerships involving real estate brokers are regulated under the applicable provincial real estate act.

Application A partnership is created by the prospective partners entering into a partnership agreement that can be oral or in writing. Certain advantages as well as disadvantages are identified with partnerships. Increased capital resources and improved borrowing power can result when two or more persons form a partnership. A partnership also permits partners to specialize, e.g., one in residential real estate and the other in commercial real estate. Partnerships also tend to have low start-up costs and are easy to form. The primary disadvantages are individual liability for all debts of the partnership incurred during the term of the partnership and the binding authority of one partner over all other partners. When terminating, unless the partners can agree as to who is the remaining partner, the partnership commonly ceases to exist through notification under the appropriate provincial legislation.

Provincial See applicable reference materials.

PARTNERSHIP (REAL ESTATE)
(SEE ALSO JOINT VENTURE)

A joint effort involving the ownership of real property by two or more individuals or entities that should be clearly differentiated from a joint venture. A partnership is not specifically defined in the *Income Tax Act*, but relies on common law concerning whether a partnership does exist in any given situation. Individual provinces typically have legislation concerning the structuring and registration of partnerships.

Application From a tax perspective, the distinction between holding property under joint venture or partnership is critical. In a partnership, the income of a partner for tax purposes is calculated at the partnership level. An unincorporated partnership is not a limited company and therefore each partner must report his/her share of profits/losses without regard to drawings that may have been received. Consequently, the partnership does not provide as much tax planning flexibility as a joint venture. Further, the transfer of assets to and from a partnership can be complicated with inherent tax pitfalls.

Partnerships may select a year end other than the calendar year and the income/loss will be allocated to the individual partner in the year that the partnership year end is established. This provides for a certain amount of tax planning for a new partnership. The advice of a chartered accountant is highly recommended.

PATENT DEFECT

(SEE ALSO LATENT DEFECT)

A fault, failing, imperfection or weakness that is readily observable to the untrained eye.

PAYBACK PERIOD

A traditional rule of thumb used to assess the potential of a particular investment property to return the initial capital invested through cash flows. Payback period is often viewed as a rough measure of risk associated with a particular investment property. Although no formal, standard formula exists, payback generally refers to the length of time required for an industrial, commercial, or investment property to return the initial investment by way of projected cash flows (before deduction of taxes), based on a one-year forecast.

While the one-year forecast period is popular as the basis of analysis, it fails to acknowledge the common problem of fluctuating cash flows during subsequent years. Consequently, practitioners seeking more accurate payback calculations may estimate individual yearly cash flows before taxes for a projected holding period, e.g., five-year to ten-year period. However, this approach is also limited as future cash flows are not discounted to accurately reflect cash flows in terms of today's dollars. During the past few years, discounted cash flow analysis has become popular given such limitations.

Example 1   *Payback Period—*
**   *Payback Based on a One-Year Forecast***

Jones is contemplating the purchase of a small commercial property in the town of Anytown. The initial investment in the project amounts to $200,000. Based on a rough estimate of rents generated from three commercial tenants in the building, Jones forecasts that the property will generate a
Continued…

cash flow before taxes of approximately $25,000 for Year 1. While, as a prudent buyer, Jones will want to fully investigate the property, he has traditionally operated on the premise that a payback period of ten years or less is worthy of further consideration. This property reveals a payback period of eight years ($200,000 ÷ $25,000) based on the projected cash flow for a one-year period.

Example 2 *Payback Period—*
**   *Payback Based on a Seven-Year Forecast***

Jones, seeking increased accuracy, estimates cash flow before taxes at the end of each year (EOY) during a seven-year period. Following a detailed review of revenue potential and anticipated expenses, he arrives at the following:

YEAR	CASH FLOW BEFORE TAXES	CUMULATIVE TOTAL	INITIAL INVESTMENT
			$200,000
EOY1	$25,000	$25,000	
EOY2	32,000	57,000	
EOY3	31,000	88,000	
EOY4	28,000	116,000	
EOY5	34,000	150,000	
EOY6	36,000	186,000	
EOY7	40,000	226,000	

Jones' analysis reveals that his initial forecast for Year 1 (see example 1), while valid for the first year of operation, failed to address potential rent increases as well as expense savings that might be realized by more efficient operation of the building. The combination of these two factors produced higher cash flows before taxes and an improved payback period that now occurs in subsequent years.

PERCENTAGE LEASE

A lease, found primarily in the retail sector, under which the tenant pays a fixed minimum monthly rent plus a percentage of gross monthly income in excess of base sales calculated using the minimum rent.

Application   In a lease document, both minimum rent and percentage rent based on that minimum are clearly outlined. In most percentage leases, the wording normally requires the following:

- Reporting of monthly sales figures to enable the landlord to receive monthly interim cheques for any percentage rent due, rather than having to wait until the end of the year.
- A continuous reporting of sales levels of tenants that allows the landlord to determine accurate percentage rents as well as monitor tenant success levels and probability of failures. Sales charts of all tenants are

455

normally kept by landlords for week-to-week, month-to-month, and year-to-year comparisons. Regular sales reporting also allows the landlord and tenants to evaluate the effectiveness of advertising and special promotions.

Differing rates apply to various types of businesses operating in a shopping centre. Traditionally, supermarkets pay the lowest rates, usually 1.25% to 1.50%. In the case of a supermarket with 3,000 square metres and paying $120 per square metre per annum, the sales volume above which percentage rent would be payable is set high, e.g., $360,000 ÷ .015 = $24,000,000. The varying rates of percentage rent applied to selected tenants reflect markup levels of goods sold or services offered, the typical turnover or sales volume, and the profitability of the operation. Certain types of tenants, such as drugstores, supermarkets, and department stores, exclude from the gross sales reports certain low profit margin items, such as tobacco products.

Reference   Professional shopping mall publications detail typical percentage rental rates and average minimum rentals for small, medium, and large shopping centres.

Example   *Percentage Lease*

Smith owns a retail commercial property and Jones is interested in leasing space within the complex. Other tenants are currently under percentage leases ranging from 1.5% to 10% of gross sales. Tenants are required to pay such amounts to Smith annually after deducting the amount paid as minimum rent. Jones is planning to occupy 150 square metres and his minimum rent is $200 per square metre per annum. Total minimum rent equals $30,000 per annum. The agreed upon percentage is 6%. Jones is anticipating first year sales volume totalling $420,000. Jones' obligation would be calculated as follows:

= $420,000 x .06
= $25,200 – $30,000
= –$4,800

Since a negative amount is calculated, no percentage rent is due. Jones' estimate of second year sales volumes could well reach $520,000. The calculation is:

= $520,000 x .06
= $31,200 – $30,000
= $1,200

In the second year, Jones would be required to pay $1,200 in addition to the minimum rent. Jones wants to know at what precise point that the percentage rent is payable. Smith provides a base sales calculation obtained by dividing the annual minimum rent by the particular percentage, e.g., $30,000 ÷ .06 = $500,000. Jones would have to exceed $500,000 in gross sales before any percentage rent was paid. This base sales calculation is normally stated in the lease.

PERSONAL CARE HOME

A *personal care home* (sometimes referred to as a *home for special care* or *care home*), is broadly described as accommodation in which residents receive some form of care services. Care services typically include health care services, rehabilitative or therapeutic services, or services that provide assistance with the activities of daily living.

Application   Legislation regarding care homes falls to provincial statutes and is typically grouped with other tenancy arrangements.

Provincial   See applicable reference materials.

PERSONAL INFORMATION

Provincial   See applicable reference materials.

PERSONAL PROPERTY

All property, except land and the improvements thereon.

Application   For real estate practitioners, personal property normally includes various chattels on the property that are referred to as *consumer goods*, e.g., refrigerators, stoves, drapes, house maintenance equipment, clothing, toys, books, and furniture.

Example   *Personal Property*

Salesperson Lee has just listed a cottage owned by Mr. and Mrs. Smith who have no further plans to vacation in the area. Consequently, a wide range of personal items is being offered as part of the purchase price. These are outlined on a schedule to the listing agreement/contract as included items. Salesperson Lee has also completed a list of excluded items to avoid any confusion.

Registration

A method of recording and storing information concerning personal property registered as security for a loan, a chattel mortgage, or collateral mortgage within individual provinces. Both consumers and lenders can check for indebtedness or liens against personal property before buying such items or accepting them as collateral. Creditors register their financial interest by means of a provincially-administered registration system.

Provincial   See applicable reference materials.

PERSONAL SAFETY

The issue of individual safety has become an increasingly important consideration for real estate salespeople. Brokerages should include personal safety information in policy manuals and review this material in sales meetings. Because of the nature of the profession, safety for a real estate salesperson goes beyond the confines of the office.

Application   Commission salespeople are, by necessity, involved in various activities that extend beyond the normal eight-to-five workday. Following are some suggestions regarding personal safety.

The following tips have been compiled from a variety of sources and are by no means exhaustive.

Personal Safety Tips

- *All salespeople should use reason and common sense to avoid a harmful encounter. Personal safety should be a primary consideration at all times.*
- *When leaving the office, let someone know where you will be and how you can be contacted. If the circumstances merit, call the office upon arrival and arrange for call-backs on an agreed time interval.*
- *Never meet a stranger at a property for a showing as it heightens the chance of being a victim.*
- *When showing property, always make careful note of exits. You may have to use them unexpectedly.*
- *Carry a whistle or similar alarm device.*
- *Carry a minimum of banking materials and, while showing property, do not leave a lady's handbag or other valuables unattended. A good place for such valuables is the trunk of your car, but don't forget to carry the car keys.*
- *Always drive your own car and ensure it is locked during showings. Keep the keys with you at all times. Carry a duplicate car door key, separate from your other car keys, to avoid locking yourself out of the car.*
- *Be alert to the people around you. Be suspicious of unusual circumstances, odd suggestions, and illogical requests.*
- *Get to know your prospects right at the start: names, addresses, and telephone numbers. If necessary, get verification by means of credentials, licences, etc.*
- *Develop a buddy system. Don't go to unfamiliar locations without being accompanied by another salesperson. A buddy system can work well both in prospecting for, listing, and showing properties.*

PHYSICAL DETERIORATION

A reduction in utility and consequently a loss in value resulting from an impairment of physical condition.

The amount of physical deterioration ultimately translates into depreciation (the cost to cure), resulting from the actual breakdown of structures and their components.

Application   For purposes of appraisal, physical deterioration is most commonly categorized as curable and incurable, i.e., *physical deterioration–curable* and *physical deterioration–incurable*.

Physical Deterioration—Curable

Curable deterioration refers to the physical breakdown of structures and their components that the prudent owner would anticipate correcting immediately. The cost of effecting the correction or cure is typically less than the anticipated addition to utility, and hence, ultimately, to value associated with the cure. Curable physical deterioration is frequently referred to as *deferred maintenance* or *rehabilitation*, because these terms reflect the type of activity typically associated with correcting the condition.

Physical Deterioration—Incurable

Involves the physical breakdown of structures and their components that are not feasible to correct, based on market conditions as of the date of the appraisal. The cost of correcting the condition or effecting a cure is estimated to be greater than the anticipated increase in utility and hence, ultimately, in value of the property that will result from correcting or curing the condition. The correction of the condition may be physically or technically possible; however, the criterion is whether it is economically sound to cure. All components of the structure not accounted for, or measured for depreciation under physical deterioration–curable, must be measured under physical deterioration–incurable.

For purposes of appraisal analysis, incurable physical deterioration may be divided into short-lived and long-lived elements.

Short-Lived Items   Those components that are not yet ready to be replaced but that will require replacement sometime before the end of the remaining economic life of the structure. In other words, their life expectancy is less than the remaining economic life of the building. The depreciation is measured by taking the ratio of the effective age (by observation), of the component to its life expectancy, and applying it to the reproduction cost of the item. Actual age in lieu of effective age could be used for certain components whose ages are more readily discernible than effective age.

Long-Lived Items   Components that have suffered some physical deterioration but will not require replacement during the economic life of the structure. Depreciation is measured by taking the ratio of the effective age of the structure as a whole to its economic life, and applying it to the balance of the reproduction cost; i.e., the total reproduction cost less the reproduction cost of the items considered under curable physical deterioration and incurable physical deterioration short-lived.

Reference   See Accrued Depreciation for detailed calculations involved in the appraisal process.

PHYSICAL FACTORS (SITE ANALYSIS)
(SEE ALSO APPRAISAL)

That portion of a site analysis within the appraisal process where the appraiser evaluates the site in terms of such things as overall dimensions, soils, topography, services and utilities, landscaping, easements, and encroachments.

PIERS

Individual columns or piers used to support a building where continuous foundations are not provided. The piers should rest on a footing below the frost line and, typically, the pier supports a beam. The beam, in turn, supports the floor, wall, and roof loads.

Application   Piers are commonly found in houses with partial basements. A crawl space at the rear of the house often has a pier system supporting the structure above. Porches are also commonly supported by piers. Typical materials include stone, brick, concrete block, cinder block, and wood. Most of these materials behave in a similar fashion. Wood, of course, is the most vulnerable to moisture and insect damage. As a rule, wood/soil contact is best avoided.

Pier problems are often the result of inadequate footings resulting in the settlement of the pier and the building above. If the pier base is not below the frost line, frost heaving can also be a problem. In both these cases, the piers usually have to be rebuilt. If the piers have too large a span between them, the beams may sag or the concentrated loads may cause the piers to sink. Additional piers are the obvious solution.

Where piers are used in lieu of a continuous foundation, the space between the piers usually has to be filled to prevent soil from falling into the basement or crawl space. In above-grade situations, skirting keeps out animals and, to some extent, rain, snow, and cold. Skirting may be wood, masonry, or poured concrete. Since skirting is not structural, repairs are rarely a priority. Wood skirting often deteriorates where it contacts the soil.

PLACEMENT FEE
(SEE ALSO ORIGINATION FEE)

A fee, also frequently referred to as a *setup* or *origination fee*, charged by a lender or mortgage broker for securing a mortgage on a specific property.

PLAN OF SUBDIVISION

A plan prepared by a land surveyor showing lots, blocks, or parcels of land intended to be dealt with separately, as such separation has been fully approved by the planning authorities, registered in the land registration office, and complies with provincial planning legislation.

Application   Plans of subdivision arose from the need for smaller units of land, in addition to severances from township lots by means of written descriptions. At point of registration, each plan is assigned a number.

Subdivision plans divide land into numbered or named units such as lots, blocks, streets, and roads. Plans of subdivision, upon registration, create a new geographic identity. The land is no longer referred to as part of the township lot but rather by the subdivision plan and numbered or named units. See **Figure P.1** as an example.

Provincial   See applicable reference materials.

PLAN OF SURVEY

Provincial   See applicable reference materials.

PLANNING ACT

Planning legislation for the control and regulation of land use governed by provincial legislation and, by delegated authority, to municipalities within the individual province.

Provincial   See applicable reference materials.

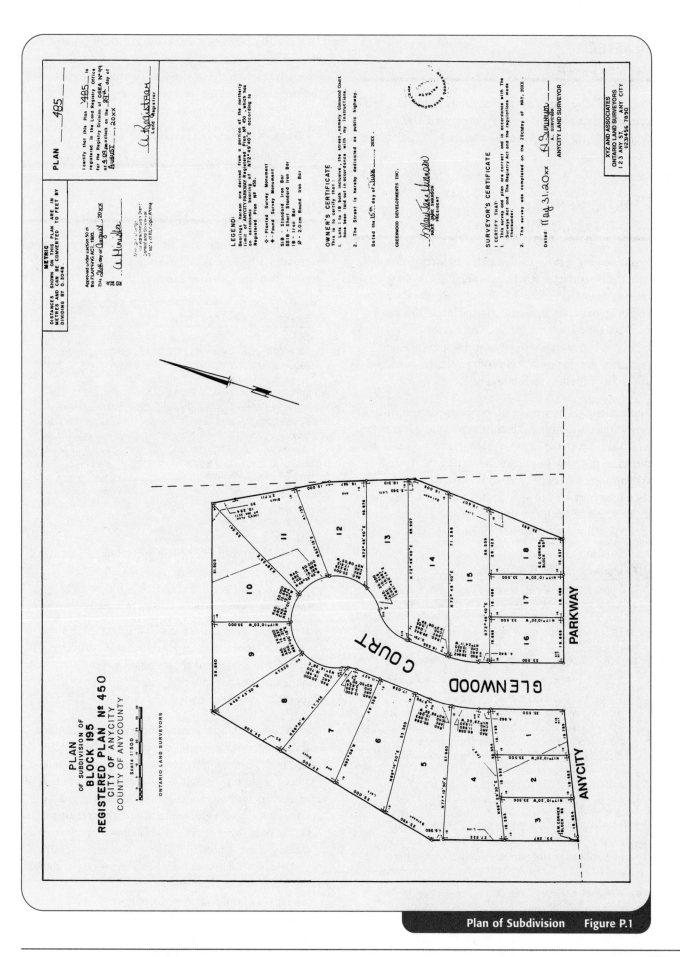

Plan of Subdivision   Figure P.1

PLASTER
(SEE ALSO DRYWALL)

Wall and ceiling components in residential and commercial construction, made largely of gypsum, used for interior finishes. Plaster is mixed on the site, while drywall is pre-fabricated wallboard.

PLASTIC VENTING
(MID-EFFICIENCY FURNACES)

Plastic venting systems used in mid-efficiency gas furnaces have the potential for failure, according to various government releases. If a furnace has one of these venting systems and the pipes crack or separate at the joints, flue gases that contain carbon monoxide may be released into the home. Carbon monoxide is an odourless and colourless poisonous gas. Exposure can result in nausea, headaches, and under extreme conditions, death.

Application   The venting system in question consists of plastic pipes with fittings (three or four inches in diameter), which are connected to the furnace. These pipes take the flue gases from the furnace outdoors. Plastic venting systems were sold under various trademarks and an expert should be contacted to assist in identifying a furnace with defective plastic venting systems. Homeowners can contact their gas utility for additional information.

> **Example   *Plastic Venting***
>
> Salesperson Ward, before showing a property to Buyer Jones, discovers through the listing salesperson that the mid-efficiency furnace once had plastic venting. While the seller had replaced the plastic venting, Jones wants additional proof that the current system is safe. Accordingly, Salesperson Ward drafts the following condition for inclusion in the offer:
>
> > *This offer is conditional upon the buyer receiving from the seller a formal acknowledgement by the gas company that the mid-efficiency furnace on the subject property meets the requirements of the gas company. Unless the seller delivers this acknowledgement to the buyer or the buyer's address by 12 p.m. on the 1st day of May, 20xx, this offer shall become null and void and the deposit shall be returned in full without deduction. This condition is included for the sole benefit of the buyer and may be waived at the buyer's option by notice in writing to the seller within the time period stated herein.*

A condition of this nature should include a waiver (as illustrated), because it is dependent upon an action by the seller who may be able to avoid the agreement/contract by choosing not to deliver the notice.

PLATFORM CONSTRUCTION
(SEE FRAMING)

PLOTTAGE

A value increment resulting from the assembly of two or more sites, when the combined utility is proportionately greater than the sum of the individual utilities.

> **Example   *Plottage***
>
> Seller Smith currently has a vacant residential lot measuring 50' x 160' in an area zoned for single and multiple family residential. As a lot for a single-detached home, the property is estimated to be worth about $90,000. Under current zoning by-laws, multiple units are not considered by the municipal council unless the total ground area exceeds 10,000 square feet. Recently, an adjacent vacant piece of property came on the market at $95,000. This property is also limited under the current by-law to single-family usage, owing to its 51' x 160' size. Smith is considering the purchase of the adjacent lot, as that acquisition could potentially increase the value of the combined properties well beyond the sum of the two values ($90,000 + $92,000), if rezoning is granted and a building permit issued for a multi-unit structure.

PLUMBING

A system of piping and associated fittings designed for two basic purposes: the supply of water for drinking, washing, and cooking to appropriate areas of a structure, and the disposal of water and waste from that structure. Figure P.2 illustrates a typical plumbing system.

Application   Standards concerning water distribution and drainage systems are set out in provincial building codes. In the case of water distribution, copper piping has been traditionally used in residential and commercial construction for both underground and above ground applications, subject to detailed permitted use requirements. Recently, polyethylene, PVC, CPVC, and polybutylene pipes and fillings have appeared. Building codes set out certification standards concerning piping and cement types allowed for hot and/or cold water systems.

In regard to drainage systems, copper plumbing was used commonly after World War II until the mid 1960s for drain lines, main stacks, and vent piping but has become rare in single-family residential homes, as plastic plumbing is much less expensive. In multi-family construction, copper waste plumbing is used where authorities will not allow plastic piping.

Galvanized steel plumbing is used only for purposes of venting. Cast iron (for main stack venting), and lead pipes were both prevalent in the 1950s, but have fallen largely into disuse. ABS plastic piping has become practically the exclusive waste plumbing material. Its only noticeable disadvantage is the noise factor when water is passing through it. Efforts to control the noise include wrapping the pipes with fibre glass insulation.

In order for water to drain freely out of a house waste system, adequate venting must be provided. Venting performs three functions.

- Allows air in front of the water rushing through the waste pipe to be pushed out of the way.

- Allows air to be re-introduced to the piping after the water has passed. If a system is not properly vented, the water passing through the drain line will siphon the water from the various fixture traps. The trap at each plumbing fixture provides a water seal that prevents sewer odours from entering the house.

- Allows sewer gases to escape outside through a vent stack.

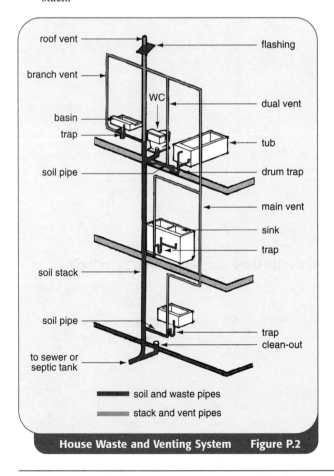

House Waste and Venting System   **Figure P.2**

POINT OF COMMENCEMENT

A known point in a land description used as a reference to precisely delineate real estate by means of a metes and bounds description.

Application   In order for metes and bounds to be complete, it must have a known point of commencement and completely enclose the subject property. An excerpt from a description details how the point of commencement is referenced both at the beginning and the end of the description (see bolded blue text in the illustration provided). The following wording is taken from a metes and bounds description in the Province of Ontario.

> *ALL AND SINGULAR that certain parcel of land and premises situate lying and being in the Township of Anytownship, in the County of Anycounty and being composed of part of Lot 8, Concession IX in said Township, more particularly described as follows:*
>
> *Premising that the Westerly limit of the road allowance between Concessions IX and X has a bearing of North 45 degrees 11 minutes, 30 seconds West and relating all bearings herein thereto;*
>
> **COMMENCING at a point** *in the westerly limit of said road allowance distant 462.48 feet measured on a bearing of South 45 degrees 11 minutes 30 seconds East along the Westerly limit of said road allowance from the Northeast angle of said lot 8;*
>
> *THENCE South 38 degrees 15 minutes 22 seconds West a distance of 120.36 feet to a point;*
>
> *THENCE South 44 degrees 03 minutes 40 seconds East a distance of 113.26 feet to a point;*
>
> *THENCE North 43 degrees 09 minutes 52 seconds East a distance of 120.18 feet, more or less, to a point in the said Westerly limit of the road allowance;*
>
> *THENCE North 45 degrees 11 minutes 30 seconds West along said Westerly limit of road allowance a distance of 114 feet, more or less,* **to the point of commencement.**

POINTS

A term used in mortgage lending referring to the amount of money either paid to the lender by the borrower or deducted from the mortgage monies advanced. Each point represents 1% of the face amount of the mortgage. Increases in points required will translate into higher yields for the mortgagee.

Application   The use of points, commonly found in US jurisdictions, has not gained the same degree of popularity in Canadian residential markets. However, points are becoming more commonplace in relation to commercial loans and secondary financing for residential property. Points are most commonly discussed in relation to their impact on investor yields and true loan costs from a borrower's perspective.

Example   *Points*

Seller Smith wants to arrange a new first mortgage for his industrial building in the amount of $200,000. Anycity Mortgage Services Inc. will provide the mortgage provided that Smith agrees to two points being deducted from the mortgage advance. The amount to be deducted will be 2% of $200,000 or $4,000. Effectively, Smith will only receive $196,000, thereby affecting the true rate of interest charged, as a smaller principal amount is received, but the interest is calculated on the original $200,000.

POLICY MANUAL

A manual setting out detailed procedures and practices. No standard policy manual exists for real estate brokerages, owing in large part to divergent operating methods both within and between provinces. Provincial associations and regulatory groups may provide additional input and content for policy manuals. Selected information is provided for illustration purposes only.

Checklist (Administrative/Secretarial)

An administrative procedure manual is recommended for front desk staff and other administrative employees. A guideline should be available for handy reference as it can provide uniformity if part-time staff is used frequently and can be particularly valuable given staff turnover.

The following are general guidelines only.

- Procedures on processing trades and related documentation.
- Procedures concerning processing listings.
- Steps required in closing a transaction and distribution of commission.
- Handling incoming calls.
- Form completion, e.g., employee records, source deduction forms, and real estate act requirements.
- Office opening and lock-up procedures.
- Preparing financial/accounting forms.
- Procedures for handling front desk customer and client enquiries.

- Miscellaneous procedures (awards systems and bonuses, sales volume calculations, duty schedules, MLS rules and regulations, special administration/fees charges, unique franchise forms, referrals, advertising guidelines, and lock box system).

Checklist

A checklist is provided in **Figure P.3** outlining items that a broker might consider in establishing a brokerage policy manual. The list is illustrative only and by no means exhaustive in nature. Practitioners should consult with the appropriate provincial regulatory body for specific legislative requirements impacting any topics identified in the checklist.

Expansion

A policy manual, whether as a loose collection of memos or a typeset publication, has tremendous value to management and/or owners. Besides items identified in the policy manual checklist, special attention should be directed to a variety of issues, such as:

- Interface of policy manual and employee/independent contractor agreements;
- Clear delineation of methods used for employing salespeople;
- Need for a consistent method of updating and inserting revisions;
- Precise wording and enforcement procedures when setting office standards;
- Full details concerning alternate commission plan payments;
- Advertising (requirements, ethical standards, recovery systems, and responsibilities);
- Methods of providing/controlling advances for salespeople;
- Brokerage policies concerning agency relationships (particularly dual agency); and
- Personal safety.

Orientation (Administrative/Secretarial)

The range of duties within administrative/secretarial functions will vary considerably by size of brokerage. Various items are included that might apply to general front office duties in a relatively small brokerage office (employing 10–15 salespersons) in which personnel handle general record-keeping, processing of transaction documents, and inquiries from the public. The checklist provided as **Figure P.4** is illustrative only, by no means exhaustive in nature, and does not address provincial regulatory requirements.

POLICY MANUAL CHECKLIST

Remuneration

- ❏ Payment of commission
- ❏ Policy for splitting commission
- ❏ Commission disputes and arbitration
- ❏ Co-op, MLS sale with another brokerage
- ❏ Commission payment and legal disputes
- ❏ Deductions of CPP, EI, or other statutorily required amounts
- ❏ Income tax provisions and deduction from commission
- ❏ Draws against commission
- ❏ Contributions toward health or related plans
- ❏ Payment (deduction) for membership dues (e.g., real estate board)

Office Organization

- ❏ Sales meeting attendance
- ❏ Tour attendance (exclusive and MLS)
- ❏ Appointment procedures
- ❏ Maintenance of records
- ❏ Inspection tour policies
- ❏ Checkout and lockup procedures
- ❏ Duties of secretaries/administration
- ❏ Telephone procedures
- ❏ Submission of offers and listings
- ❏ Key policy

Office Co-Operation (Internal and Between Brokerages)

- ❏ Procedures on MLS listings
- ❏ Procedures for co-op listings and sales

- ❏ Documentation required
- ❏ Internal co-operation between salespeople
- ❏ Ethical conduct

Personal Standards

- ❏ Dress and appearance
- ❏ Minimum income level
- ❏ Minimum listing inventory
- ❏ Loyalty to the brokerage
- ❏ Purchase and sale of property in own name
- ❏ Organizational memberships
- ❏ Other office requirements

Operating Standards and Policies

- ❏ Policy regarding MLS membership
- ❏ Approval of letters and other document preparation by salespeople
- ❏ Allocation of advertising expense
- ❏ Desk space
- ❏ Expenditure of brokerage funds
- ❏ Legal expenses
- ❏ Termination
- ❏ Credit reports
- ❏ Maintenance of registrations
- ❏ Liability insurance and related policies
- ❏ Commission controversies
- ❏ Advertising procedures
- ❏ Automobile insurance and bonding procedures.

Policy Manual Checklist   Figure P.3

POLYCHLORINATED BIPHENYLS

Acronym: PCBs   Synthetic organic chemicals, typically referred to as PCBs, that are no longer manufactured but remain a health hazard as polychlorinated biphenyls demonstrate a high resistance to degradation and can remain in the environment for decades. PCBs were banned in Canada during the late 1970s, after studies demonstrated a potential link to cancer and other health problems. PCBs are associated with cancer in laboratory animals, as well as causing problems with the skin, liver, nervous system, and reproduction in humans.

Application   From a real estate perspective, the PCB issue focuses primarily on industrial storage and landfill sites and assurances that no contamination of the food chain occurs. Real estate practitioners should be sensitive to the possibility of PCB contamination when marketing properties near such locations.

PCBs were used as a coolant in ballasts and other electrical equipment, e.g., capacitors and electrical transformers. At issue, besides large electrical equipment, are the millions of older ballasts in fluorescent lights that have accumulated. Each ballast may contain about 20 grams of high strength PCB liquid. These types of fixtures, phased out after 1980, ultimately found their way into municipal landfill sites. Practitioners should seek expert guidance on such matters particularly in relation to the listing and selling of older industrial facilities.

Reference   Contact the applicable provincial ministry/department responsible for environmental matters.

P
TO
Q

ADMINISTRATION-ORIENTATION CHECKLIST

❑ Supply key to office and assign parking location (if applicable).

❑ Fill out necessary government forms and open employee file.

❑ Explain the *check in and out* system for salespeople.

❑ Introduce staff with follow up for persons not currently available.

❑ Explain how listings are processed and provide a procedure sheet to be included in the front desk manual.

❑ Review functions and operation of all equipment.

❑ Illustrate a complete real estate transaction in terms of processing and closing.

❑ Review all files to which access is permitted and review filing procedures.

Discuss procedure for handling customers:

   ❑ Walk-in procedures

   ❑ Duty call priority

   ❑ Directing of calls to salespeople

   ❑ Messages/commitments

   ❑ Showing appointments

   ❑ Information to be provided

   ❑ Confidential information

Cover any of the following items that may be part of the function:

   ❑ Performance reports on salespeople

   ❑ Awards systems and bonuses

   ❑ Volume calculations

   ❑ Floor duty schedules

   ❑ MLS regulations/board forms

   ❑ Special fee/administration charges

   ❑ Unique franchise forms

   ❑ Referral procedures

   ❑ Advertising procedures

   ❑ Keys/lock boxes

Review all forms related to the job function:

   ❑ Listing forms and amendments

   ❑ Agreements of purchase and sale

   ❑ Location of supplies/forms

   ❑ Standard letter formats

   ❑ Filing requirements/checklists

   ❑ Brokerage brochures

   ❑ After sale procedures

Figure P.4   Administration Orientation Checklist

POSSESSION

Right of an owner to occupy property. When the property is occupied by a tenant, possession is transferred to the tenant by the landlord, however, the landlord has constructive possession by right of title and may re-occupy the property at termination of the tenancy period.

POSSESSION DATE

Possession date refers to the date upon which the buyer or tenant obtains possession of the property. Unless otherwise agreed, the term *possession date* in an agreement/contract involving real property refers to the date upon which vacant possession shall be given. Preprinted wordings for agreements/contracts rarely refer to a possession date but rather identify the completion or closing date, i.e., the day that title passes to a new owner. Vacant possession may or may not occur coincident with closing depending on the type of property, e.g., a rental property.

Provincial   See applicable reference materials.

POST/COLUMN

A structural component to carry the load of a beam vertically down to the footings. Occasionally, a post or column is introduced to carry a concentrated load (a large piano, for example), straight down to the footings without benefit of a beam. Typical materials include brick, concrete block, poured concrete, wood, or steel. Every post or column should have a footing, typically concrete. The illustration in **Figure P.5** has been provided to demonstrate the components in a column and associated footing.

Application   Practitioners should be aware of various problems that can arise in the use of posts/columns.

Moisture   Masonry posts may deteriorate due to moisture or poor mortar. Rising dampness, a common problem with brick columns, is characterized by deteriorated mortar and efflorescence (white salty deposits), on the bottom of the post.

Out of Plumb   Posts that are built (or have been pushed) out of plumb lose their strength. Generally, if the amount by which the column or post is out of plumb approaches

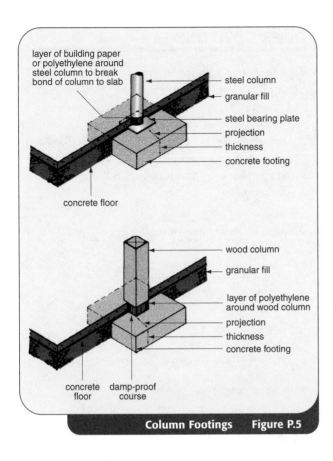

layer of building paper
or polyethylene around
steel column to break
bond of column to slab

steel column
granular fill

steel bearing plate
projection
thickness
concrete footing

concrete floor

wood column
granular fill

layer of polyethylene
around wood column
projection
thickness
concrete footing

concrete floor   damp-proof course

Column Footings   Figure P.5

one-third of the thickness of the column, structural integrity may be a concern.

Rust   A serious problem, often found in a chronically flooding basement, that will quickly reduce the load-carrying capacity of a steel post.

Footing   A sinking post is usually the result of an absent or inadequately-sized footing.

Undersized   Column collapse is unusual, but is normally the result of an undersized column or one that has suffered mechanical damage. A brick column should be at least 12 inches by 12 inches or 10 inches by 15 inches. Rectangular concrete columns should be at least 8 inches by 8 inches. Circular concrete columns should be no less than 9 inches in diameter. Steel posts are 3 inches in diameter under normal circumstances. A top and bottom plate at least 4 inches square is required if the beam is wood. With a steel beam, the four-inch plate is not needed, as long as the post is secured to the beam. Consult building codes for provincial specifics.

Secured to Beam   A post that is not well secured to the beam above can allow the structure to shift during wind uplift forces. The beam should also be supported laterally to prevent it from moving sideways.

Fire   Fire will damage wood and steel posts. A steel post will fail much earlier than a solid wood post, although it will not burn.

POSTDATED CHEQUES (TENANCY)

Provincial residential tenancy legislation may provide that the landlord in a residential tenancy cannot require the delivery of postdated cheques for the payment of rent. However, the tenant and landlord may mutually agree upon this payment arrangement. Provincial legislation will vary. It should be noted that normally no such statutory provision applies to commercial tenancies and, in fact, the requirement for postdated cheques is often included in commercial lease documents.

Provincial   See applicable reference materials.

POSTPONEMENT

A term commonly associated with mortgages whereby the mortgagee agrees to maintain a position of subsequent priority in the event of re-arrangement and re-registration of a prior mortgage.

Application   A mortgage may contain a postponement clause by which a mortgagee agrees to maintain a position of subsequent priority and permit the mortgagor to renew or replace an existing mortgage that falls due before the maturity date of the later registered mortgage. A properly drafted postponement clause should also provide that any increase in the principal amount of the renewed or replaced mortgage shall be paid in reduction of principal owing under the later registered mortgage.

Example   *Postponement*

Salesperson Ward is showing a property to Buyer Jones. The listing agreement states that an existing first mortgage can be assumed at an attractive rate of interest, with a remaining four-year term. Jones lacks enough money to offer cash to mortgage, but informs Ward that he has an uncle with private funds, however, the uncle would prefer a five-year commitment on the second mortgage. Accordingly, Ward drafts an agreement/contract based on assuming the first mortgage and conditional upon securing the second mortgage from the uncle. Given that the first mortgage would come due prior to the second, Garcia includes the following clause in the agreement/contract:

Continued…

P TO Q

> *This second mortgage shall contain a clause permitting the renewal or replacement of the existing first mortgage at any time, provided that any increase in the principal amount of the new first mortgage over the amount of principal owing under the first mortgage at the time of renewal or replacement shall be applied in reduction of the principal amount of this mortgage; and the mortgagee hereunder shall execute and deliver to the mortgagor such postponement agreement, mortgage statement, or other documents as the first mortgagee may reasonably require, forthwith upon request.*

POTENTIAL GROSS (RENTAL) INCOME

The income that a property will produce with 100% occupancy at market rent, assuming typically competent and prudent management (frequently referred to as *potential rental income*). This income is generally derived by multiplying the rental value per unit by the number of units in the building. Potential gross (rental) income should be clearly differentiated from effective gross income (frequently referred to as *gross operating income*). The latter represents all amounts under potential gross income, LESS allowances for vacancy and bad debts and PLUS other income such as parking and laundry fees.

Example   *Potential Gross (Rental) Income*

Anne Appraiser is reconstructing the owner's operating statement for a 96-unit apartment building to arrive at fair market value by the income approach. In doing so, she includes all apartment rentals at 100% occupancy, using current market rent. Following are the calculations.

Potential Gross (Rental) Income

18 1-bedroom units x 800 per month x 12	$172,800
78 2-bedroom units x 1,175 per month x 12	+1,099,800
	1,272,600
Vacancy and Credit Losses	−63,630
	1,208,970
Other Income	
Parking—96 spaces x $20 x 12	+23,040
Laundry—96 x $10 x 12	+11,520
Effective Gross Income	$1,243,530

(Gross Operating Income)

POWER OF ATTORNEY

Delegated written authority to a person to act legally, including the signing of documents, on behalf of another.

A power of attorney must be executed and witnessed. A power of attorney may involve a very general power to act on behalf of another or it can be precisely described and limited in scope. Procedures for the registration of powers of attorney in land registration offices will vary by provincial jurisdiction.

Example   *Power of Attorney*

Seller Smith will be out of the country for several months while his property is being offered for sale. To avoid various problems if an offer were presented, Smith signs a power of attorney with his lawyer. The power of attorney addresses various issues that must be attended to in his absence. The specific reference to the marketing of his home provides that the lawyer shall sign on Smith's behalf any offer that meets or exceeds the minimum acceptable price of $190,000. The power of attorney also states that the lawyer shall have full power to negotiate other terms and conditions leading to the sale of the property.

Provincial   See applicable reference materials.

POWER OF SALE

The right of a mortgagee to force the sale of a property, without judicial proceedings, should default occur. The term *power of sale* indicates a sale under the power contained in the mortgage document and/or pursuant to appropriate provincial legislation. Procedures concerning power of sale will vary by province.

Provincial   See applicable reference materials.

PRE-APPROVED BUYER

Approval of a buyer by a lender for mortgage purposes subject to specific conditions. Pre-approved mortgage financing has become increasingly popular as it adds negotiating strength in the marketplace. The buyer becomes virtually a cash buyer, *subject to the conditions of the pre-approval*. Although no standard pre-approval form exists, most consist of a confirmation document setting out the maximum amount that can be borrowed, the interest rate to be charged (guaranteed for a fixed period), and the monthly payments. The confirmation is subject to an appraisal of the property being mortgaged.

Example   Pre-Approved Buyer

James and Judy Jones are contemplating a home purchase and have gone to the Canadian National Bank for a pre-approved mortgage. They received a pre-approved mortgage certificate concerning the maximum approved mortgage. Now the Joneses can negotiate with confidence, knowing just how much Canadian National Bank will lend them and how much they are able to spend for their home subject to specified conditions, e.g., an appraisal.

The Canadian National Bank
Pre-Approved Mortgage Certificate

Date: January 15, 20xx

Name: James and Judy Jones

Address: 123 Main Street
            Anycity, [Province], Canada

This is to certify that the above person(s) named has/have qualified for the following mortgage, subject to a satisfactory appraisal of the property and a credit review by the Bank at the time of actual mortgage application.

Amount: $105,000

Interest Rate: 7.5%

Monthly Payment: $768.13
(based on a 25-year amortization)

The mortgage amount is based on details supplied at the time of application for a certificate. The interest rate is guaranteed for 60 days from the date stated above provided that the mortgage is fully advanced within a 60-day period. The pre-approval is for a five-year term mortgage, but a shorter term may be selected, the interest rate will either be the rate in effect as of the date of this certificate, or at the time at which the selection is made, whichever is less.

The monthly payment of $768.13 includes principal and interest repayment only. Based on our estimate, the taxes would be approximately $2,800 per annum and the heating costs would be approximately $840.00 per annum. Based on the mortgage amount on this Pre-approved Mortgage Certificate and the downpayment stated in your application, you should consider purchasing a home in the range of $130,000 to $140,000.

The Canadian National Bank
Branch Manager/Lending Officer
Tel: (800) 555-1212

PREGNANCY LEAVE

A provision allowing for pregnancy leave of absence from work as set out in provincial employment legislation. Procedures and particulars of this provision will vary by province as employment-related matters are governed by provincial employment statutes.

Provincial   See applicable reference materials.

PRELIMINARY INSPECTION AND PLANNING THE WORK
(SEE ALSO APPRAISAL)

The second formal step in the appraisal process representing field work that involves an overall inspection of the neighbourhood in which the subject property is located. The preliminary inspection provides the appraiser with general information to determine six main factors when planning the work.

- Preliminary estimate of highest and best use.
- Determine type of data needed and sources.
- Determine the approaches to value to be used.
- Design research program.
- Outline the appraisal report.
- Set out the work schedule.

PREMISES

A term broadly referring to a building, surrounding land (if applicable), and other appurtenances associated with the building. In real estate, the term is commonly used in relation to commercial lease documents and may in this instance be referring to a part of a building. The demised (leased) premises refers to the physical space leased and occupied by the tenant and described by a site plan or similar schedule attached to the lease document.

Example *Premises*

Jones has just completed negotiations for retail space in a midtown retail office complex. The leased premises are described as follows:

> *Suite No. 903, being part of the 9th floor of the Building Described in Paragraph 7 of the Lease as shown crosshatched on Schedule "A" (the floor plan) attached consisting of 4,230 square feet useable area and 4,632 rentable area.*

PREPAYMENT

Full or partial payment of all or part of the principal, separate and apart from payments called for under a mortgage agreement.

Example *Prepayment*

Owner Smith currently has a mortgage balance of $98,328.23 as of the next regularly scheduled payment date of May 1, 20xx, which also represents the first year anniversary date of the mortgage. The mortgage is open and can be repaid in part or in total provided that the payment is made on the anniversary date in any particular year during the five-year term. Smith makes a lump sum payment of $20,000 (over and above his principal and interest payment for that particular month), thereby reducing the balance outstanding as of that date to $78,328.23, less $97.21 of principal included in the regular payment.

PREPAYMENT CLAUSE

A clause inserted in a mortgage giving the mortgagor the privilege of paying the mortgage debt in advance of the maturity date based on stipulated terms.

Application Real estate practitioners encounter a number of possibilities concerning prepayment privileges. For example, a fully open privilege permits the mortgagor, when not in default, to prepay the whole or any part of the principal sum outstanding at any time or times without notice or bonus. From a practical perspective, this type of arrangement would undoubtedly cause difficulties as any

combination of amounts and times is possible. More frequently, prepayment privileges are precisely defined for purposes of the mortgage document.

Example *Prepayment Clause*

Broker/Owner Johnson, of ABC Realty Inc., is providing a brief training session for two salespeople concerning prepayment privileges in mortgages. Apparently, both practitioners had used the following clause in drafting agreements involving seller take back mortgages:

> *This mortgage shall contain a clause permitting the mortgagor, when not in default, the privilege of prepaying the whole or any part of the principal sum outstanding on any payment date or dates without notice or bonus.*

This wording would cause difficulties in a blended payment mortgage as the subsequent monthly payment schedule would be altered each time a partial payment was received that didn't exactly match the principal portion of the monthly payment required under the mortgage. Johnson felt that this fully open clause is best reserved solely for mortgages that do not have blended payments and asked both salespeople to use the following wording:

> *This mortgage shall contain a clause permitting the mortgagor, when not in default, the privilege of prepaying all or part of the principal sum on any payment date or dates without notice or bonus, provided that any partial prepayment shall equal the sum of the principal amounts of the payments next falling due under the mortgage.*

Alternatively, he suggested that they might consider anniversary-only open privileges to simplify the process:

> *This mortgage shall contain a clause permitting the mortgagor, when not in default, the privilege of prepaying on each anniversary date a sum not to exceed _____ % of the original principal amount, without notice or bonus.*

PRESENT VALUE

The total of all values (benefits) accruing to an investor discounted by an appropriate discount rate, or alternatively worded, the present worth (today's dollars) of a future income stream (tomorrow's dollars).

Application Present value (PV) is commonly used in estimates involving yield capitalization techniques under the income approach to value. Traditionally, PV tables were used to estimate the present value of variable income streams (e.g., successive cash flows from an investment property), or level income streams (e.g., successive equal lease and mortgage payments received). Various refinements, including complex formulae to address straight-line (constant amount) or exponential-curve (constant ratio) changes in income were subsequently introduced. However, PV estimates of future cash flows remain a complex mathematical exercise not easily reduced to financial tables.

The use of financial calculators has effectively eliminated the need for tables and complicated calculations concerning the discounting process. Cash flows, regardless of whether they are variable, level, or changing in fixed amounts can easily be converted to present value. As well, reversionary values (sale proceeds) are routinely computed with operations cash flows to arrive at summary present values that would have otherwise been computed separately and summed by the appraiser.

Present value must be distinguished from net present value (NPV). NPV is a measure of profitability in which a discount rate is applied to all cash flows with the initial investment deducted to arrive at a net amount. NPV, expressed as a positive or negative amount, reflects the surplus or loss in comparison with investor expectation.

PRESENTATION (OFFERS)

Procedures regarding presentation of offers are normally set out in MLS rules and regulations for individual real estate boards and/or detailed with other trading practices as established by provincial regulatory bodies. Article 15 of The Canadian Real Estate Association Code of Ethics also details ethical requirements regarding the presentation of all written offers and counter offers as soon as possible after receipt.

Provincial See applicable reference materials.

PRESSURE TANK (PLUMBING SYSTEM)

Maintains water pressure within a plumbing system so that the pump is not activated each time water is drawn from the system. Air is pressurized within the tank as required to compensate for dispensing water. With water depletion, air pressure drops and the pressure pump is activated. A high limited switch controls maximum pressure. Typical settings are between 25 and 50 psi.

PREVENTIVE MAINTENANCE

A program of regular inspection and care that allows potential problems to be prevented or at least detected and solved before major repairs are needed.

> **Example** *Preventive Maintenance*
>
> A property manager oversees a 400-suite condominium project in a metropolitan centre. Every four years, the condominium corporation undertakes a reserve fund study to ensure that adequate monies are available to maintain the common elements, including the repair and replacement of components. The reserve fund study provides the basis for a logical, orderly preventive maintenance program.

PRICE

A term used in various situations concerning the listing and selling of real estate. In the listing process, real estate practitioners refer to the *asking, listing,* or *offered price* of a property, as opposed to the market price. Market price, refers to the purchase price agreed to by the parties. Market price should not be confused with market value as it is an accomplished or historic fact, whereas market value is and remains an estimate until proven. Market price involves no assumption of prudent conduct by the parties, or absence of undue stimuli, or of any other condition basic to the market value concept.

> **Example** *Price*
>
> Smith decides to list his property with Salesperson Lee and will offer the property at the asking price (offered listing price) of $249,000. Lee, advises Smith that based on comparable sales in the area, he feels the value (market value) of the property is $240,000. The property is offered for sale and ultimately sold for $238,000 (market price).

PRICE MAINTENANCE
(SEE ALSO COMPETITION ACT)

A violation of the *Competition Act* involving an activity by which a person engaged in a business attempts to influence the price at which another person supplies, offers to supply, or advertises a product of service. The relevant section of the Act is reprinted in Figure P.6.

It is a federal criminal offence to influence or attempt to influence upwards the price or fees other parties charge for products and services, or to reduce such fees, including the offering of discounts.

Competition Act, Sec. 61(1)

No person who is engaged in the business of producing or supplying a product, who extends credit by way of credit cards or is otherwise engaged in a business that relates to credit cards, or who has the exclusive rights and privileges conferred by a patent, trade-mark, copyright, registered industrial design, or registered integrated circuit topography, shall, directly or indirectly, (a) by agreement, threat, promise or any like means, attempt to influence upward, or to discourage the reduction of, the price at which any other person engaged in business in Canada supplies or offers to supply or advertises a product within Canada; or (b) refuse to supply a product to or otherwise discriminate against any other person engaged in business in Canada because of the low pricing policy of that person.

Figure P.6   Price Maintenance

Example   *Price Maintenance*

Salesperson Lee, a specialist in recreational properties, is making a listing presentation to Seller Smith regarding his northern retreat property. During the presentation, Smith asks what commission rate is charged for recreational property. Lee responds that his commission rate is 7% due to the distance involved to market the property and an aggressive advertising strategy. Smith tells Lee he will get back to him, and Lee, suspecting that Smith will call his friend and closest competitor, calls the friend in advance. Apparently, the friend owes Lee a favour and Lee tells the friend to quote a commission to Smith higher than 7%.

At worst, Lee advises his friend, *you've repaid a favour, and at best, you get the listing at a higher commission rate.* Salesperson Lee has attempted to influence what another party will charge for services.

PRIME TENANT
(SEE ALSO ANCHOR TENANT)

A tenant, often referred to as an *anchor tenant*, who occupies a significant part of the space available within a given building.

PRINCIPAL

Usually thought of as an individual instructing and controlling an agent to act on his/her behalf. However, several common uses of the term *principal* are found in real estate.

- The person or company who authorizes the real estate brokerage to act in a seller agency capacity to lease, sell, or exchange the property under an agency agreement or a person or company who authorizes a real estate brokerage to act in a buyer agency capacity to represent his/her interests in a real estate acquisition.
- The original sum invested in the acquisition of real estate, as distinguished from income or profits derived therefrom.
- The amount borrowed on a mortgage (principal) as well as the amount due and payable (principal owing) as of a specified date (as distinct from interest paid and/or owing).

PRINCIPAL (AGENCY)
(SEE ALSO FIDUCIARY RELATIONSHIP)

For agency purposes, an individual who authorizes the agent (real estate brokerage) to act on his/her behalf in an agency (principal/agent) relationship.

Principal/Agent Relationship

The relationship created by express or implied agreement or by law, whereby one party delegates the transaction of some lawful business, with more or less discretionary power, to another who undertakes to manage the affair and render an account thereof.

Example   *Principal (Agency)— Principal/Agent Relationship*

Salesperson Ward has just completed a listing agreement with Owner Jones. This exclusive authority to sell Jones' home is for a period of 90 days at a listing price of $149,000. As such, Jones and XYZ Real Estate Ltd., have entered into a principal/agent relationship. The creation of this relationship is best described in the wording of the listing:

I hereby give you the exclusive and irrevocable right to act as my agent to lease or sell the property until 11:59 p.m. on the 1st day of May, 20xx for the price of One Hundred and Forty-Nine Thousand Dollars ($149,000), and upon the terms particularly set out herein, or at such other price or terms acceptable to me. It is understood that the price set out above is at my personal request, after full discussion with your representative regarding potential market value of the property.

Duties

The primary duties owed to an agent by a principal are remuneration and indemnification. In terms of remuneration, the principal is obligated to pay the agreed upon amount. Where no specific agreement exists, the agent is entitled to a reasonable sum, based on compensation for similar services within that particular locale. The principal must also provide indemnification in respect of all acts undertaken or liabilities incurred by the agent, provided that the agent has acted competently and within the lawful instructions of that principal.

See **Agency** regarding responsibilities and duties owed to a principal by an agent.

Example	*Principal (Agency)— Duties*

A salesperson obtained a listing agreement for the sale of two adjacent properties. Negotiations commenced immediately on the smaller property, following the buyer's introduction to both parcels. An agreement was ultimately entered into between the buyer and seller. At a later date, the buyer proceeded to enter into another agreement with the seller for the second property through a corporation owned by the buyer (without involving the real estate brokerage). The brokerage sued, arguing that the seller knowingly and deliberately evaded the contractual understanding between the seller and the named brokerage. The Judge agreed.

The court agreed that a contractual understanding did occur that involved both properties. The brokerage was awarded a commission based on the prevailing rate for the area.

Remedies

Remedies available to a principal in the event that an agent does not carry out his/her duties include dismissal, damages for breach of contract, action to recover property in the agent's possession, action for an accounting of all that has been received on the principal's behalf, action to resist payment (i.e., refuse to pay the commission), prosecution, and indemnity.

The final remedy bears special mention. The agent can be liable to indemnify the principal for any acts undertaken personally or delegated to employees or sub-agents when that agent does not carry out his/her duties. While the principal may in fact be liable to third parties for such acts (doctrine of vicarious responsibility), the principal will then claim indemnity from the agent for all losses flowing from the breach of duty. As the example shows, the principal may successfully pursue remedies, regardless of whether the agency relationship was formally agreed and documented between the parties.

Example	*Principal (Agency)— Remedies*

The salesperson was approached by an individual wishing to invest personal funds in the mortgage market. The approach was made based on the salesperson's apparent knowledge of mortgage investments in that particular suburban marketplace. Sometime following this discussion, the same salesperson sold a property conditional upon the sale of the buyer's property. As events unfolded, however, the closing date of the new property was fast approaching with no sale of the prior home. As a result, the salesperson contacted the investor referenced earlier and recommended that his investment funds be placed by way of a second mortgage on the new property. The investor, trusting the salesperson, delivered the funds as promised and the transaction closed. As an aside, the salesperson also committed funds to assist in the closing. In fact, according to the full text of the judgment, the first and second mortgages exceeded the purchase price.

Ultimately a default occurred and the investor sued the mortgagors (buyers), the real estate brokerage, and the salesperson. Without delving into all aspects of this case, one focal point is relevant to all real estate practitioners. The Judge, while conceding that the courts have had difficulty defining fiduciary duty, found that the investor relied upon the professionalism of the salesperson and that the investor was dependent upon that individual. While acknowledging that a customer/brokerage relationship need not be a fiduciary one, this circumstance did fall within accepted definitions of fiduciary duties. Because a fiduciary duty did exist, the salesperson failed to provide full disclosure regarding various matters, including but not limited to the merits of investing monies in the property; and the salesperson's undisclosed role in contributing funds to facilitate the closing. The Judge ordered that the defendant (salesperson) be responsible for the return of the plaintiff's (investor's) money.

PRINCIPLES (APPRAISAL)
(SEE ALSO FACTORS OF PRODUCTION)

The appraisal of real estate involves various principles that are either fundamental to understanding value or explain how various components of real estate contribute to value. These principles are isolated for discussion purposes but, in fact, are interrelated in the marketplace.

Anticipation

A principle affirming that value is created by the anticipation of benefits, that is money or amenities, to be derived in the future. Value may be defined as the present worth of all rights of future benefits. When buying a home, buyers anticipate that certain benefits will accrue in future years, and the purchase price is based on the present worth of those anticipated future benefits.

Example *Principles (Appraisal)—Anticipation*

Buyer Jones is attempting to decide whether he will purchase Smith's home for approximately $180,000 or another property listed at $169,900. Jones evaluates the listing information from both properties. While they are identical in many ways, the Smith property contains a family room fireplace and patio doors leading to an oversized deck. The competing property, while containing a cozy family room, lacks the sunlight that flows through the sliding doors. Further, Jones can already visualize his family sitting by a blazing fire on the cold winter nights ahead. Jones, unwittingly, is applying the principle of anticipation. He is mentally deciding whether the future benefits of Smith's property justify the additional asking price.

Balance

A principle holding that value is created and maintained in proportion to the equilibrium attained in the amount and location of essential uses of real estate. The degree of value of a property is governed by the balance of apportionment of the *factors in production*. Loss in value will result if there are less services and agencies than a neighbourhood needs or more services than a neighbourhood can support. For example, where there are too many drugstores in a community, either some will be successful at the expense of the others or none will yield an adequate return on the investment they represent.

With an individual property, the agents or factors in production (labour, coordination, capital, and land), must be in proper balance in order to maintain maximum value. Too much or too little of any one of the factors, in proportion to the services rendered by the others, tends to reduce value, for example, having two building custodians where only one is needed will result in less net income, which in turn translates into less value when income is capitalized in the appraisal process.

Example *Principles (Appraisal)—Balance*

A commercial building derives its value from various component parts such as parking facilities. Inadequate parking (an imbalance in apportionment), could negatively impact the value of the property as essential uses and appeal of the real estate to commercial tenants are affected, owing to this deficiency. A similar situation might arise in a downtown residential condominium project. Given limited space, too few parking spaces might be available to unit owners, along with little or no guest parking facilities. This could negatively impact the value of the property as consumer appeal is affected by the deficiency. Obviously, this is not a simple cause/effect relationship. Other factors would come into play, such as adjacent parking lots, convenience/availability of public transit services, owner demographics, and size of units.

Change

A principle stating that economic and social forces are constantly at work and that changes caused by these forces affect real property. Accordingly, the appraiser views real property and its environment as in transition, observing evidence of trends that may affect the property in the future. The principle of change is fundamentally the law of cause and effect. The principle of change illustrates the fact that a value estimate provided by an appraiser is only valid as of a specific time. This principle is a constant consideration when estimating value and the effective date of an appraisal is always clearly identified in the report.

Example *Principles (Appraisal)—Change*

Anne Appraiser is hired to estimate the value of a property at 123 Main Street. This two-storey residence occupied by the Smith family is zoned single-family residential. Mr. Smith requires the appraisal as he is placing a first mortgage on the property with a new lending institution. Anne completes the lender's standard form report and states in writing that the property is worth $240,000 as of November 30th, 20xx. One week following the appraisal and before the bank issued a commitment letter on the mortgage, the major employer in the community, in a totally unexpected move, files for bankruptcy leaving more than two thousand workers, one-fifth of the total work force in the town, unemployed. Real estate inventory swells immediately with supply far outpacing demand. Within sixty days, a noticeable downturn in prices occurs. The lender, now more cautious, calls for a second opinion from another appraiser. The second appraisal, impacted by economic factors not present earlier, is $195,000.

Competition

A principle, in terms of appraisal theory, stating that excessive profits will tend to breed competition that, in turn, has a negative impact on profits; or as often heard and simply put: *excess profit breeds ruinous competition.*

Example *Principles (Appraisal)—Competition*

Smith anticipates and initially receives high returns from a *You Store It (Anycity) Inc.* facility on the east side of the city. His forecasted demand proves correct and, although lacking any market data to suggest a larger facility, he confidently starts a second phase, effectively doubling the number of storage units. However, various large tracts of land are zoned for similar facilities and within months, three competing firms have increased the supply of units by 500%. Smith, as well as the competitors, are subsequently drawn into a price war to capture the finite market for this type of service. The value of the real estate is affected given lower levels of income.

Conformity

An appraisal principle stating that land must be utilized to reasonably conform with the existing standards of the area in order to maintain maximum value. The word *reasonable* denotes the degree of conformity. Too much conformity results in monotony that could be as detrimental to value as not having conformity at all. In residential areas, variety in building styles of the same quality presents a more pleasing appearance than rows of identical houses. Zoning regulations protect a neighbourhood from conversion to or intrusion of inharmonious uses and generally support the principle of conformity. This principle is useful in detailing a neighbourhood analysis.

Consistent Use

A principle stating that when improved land is in transition to another highest and best use, it cannot be appraised with one use allocated to the land and another to the building or other improvements. If an appraiser is estimating the market value of a parcel of land improved with an old house, and estimates that the highest and best use is for an office building development, then the appraisal should not accord any value to the house over that of the land. Adding value for the old house would be inconsistent as its worth in the market is overshadowed by the commercial value of the land and cannot be additive to it. In dealing with compensation for expropriated property, this theory is referred to as *double recovery*.

Contribution

A valuation principle stating that the value of any component of a property is measured by how much it adds to the net income (or market value, i.e., the subject property is non-income producing, such as a residential house), by reason of its presence, or detracts from the net income (or market value) by reason of its absence. Therefore, the value of any factor in production depends upon its contribution to net income or value and not upon its cost. The principle of contribution is sometimes known as the *principle of marginal productivity*.

Example   *Principles (Appraisal)—Contribution*

Buyer Jones is attempting to justify the cost of new bathroom installation amounting to $18,000 in a townhouse valued at $169,000. While the true cost is $18,000, the market value may only be increased by $5,500. Based on the principal of contribution, the new bathroom is said to have a contributory value of $5,500. The addition of this bathroom would constitute an over improvement (superadequacy), and would not normally be justified.

External Factors

A principle (sometimes referred to as *externalities* by appraisers), involving a broad array of situations that can impact the value of property. External factors can include circumstances or situations near the property or more distant influences that nevertheless impact value. In the case of adjacent factors, value may be enhanced by the existence and proximity of services provided to the property. On a more general perspective, overall economic conditions within the immediate area, the region as a whole, or for that matter, the country can impact the value of real estate. Real estate is vulnerable to economic prosperity as well as economic slowdowns. Real estate can also be impacted by government regulations and requirements that affect the marketability of real estate.

Example   *Principles (Appraisal)—External Factors*

Buyer Smith acquired a residential bungalow in East Ridge, a suburb of Anycity, approximately two years ago. At the time of acquisition, the property was valued at $159,000. Since that time, Anycity has lost three major employers resulting in double-digit unemployment figures. To compound matters, significant improvements to various municipal services have resulted in a dramatic increase in property tax. These two external factors have affected property values. Local real estate brokerages report that residential properties are being sold for approximately 10% less than two years ago. Smith has had his property appraised and the market value is currently estimated at $143,000.

Highest and Best Use

That use which, at the time of the appraisal, is most likely to produce the greatest net return in money or amenities to the land over a given period. Net return may be monetary as with an income producing property or may, in the case of a single-family dwelling, take the form of amenities such as pride of ownership, comfort, and convenience. In cases where a site has existing improvements, the present use may fail to meet the criteria of this definition. The highest and best use may very well be determined to be different from the existing use. The present use will typically continue, however, unless and until land value in its highest and best use meets or exceeds the total value of the property in its existing use.

The appraiser, in estimating market value, must consider not only the current use, but also the likely uses to which it is adapted and is capable of being used in the reasonably foreseeable future. Purely speculative future uses may not be considered.

Since owners have a natural tendency to utilize their property as advantageously as possible, and since economic pressures usually dictate the optimum or most profitable use, the highest and best use of a property will most often be its present use. However, this is not always the case. Instances exist where owners, for various reasons, do not use their property at its highest and best use, at least as the term is used in the appraisal sense. This is especially true along major new highways and rapidly expanding areas where relatively sudden changes in demand occur and appropriate uses are necessitated. Also, the passage of time typically causes radical changes in optimum land usage.

Example 1   *Principles (Appraisal)–*
                     Highest and Best Use

Seller Smith owns a detached, but rundown, bungalow in a rapidly expanding commercial area of Anycity. The property was appraised two years ago at a value of $140,000 for the 40 year-old house and 90' x 100' lot fronting on Main Street, based on residential single-family occupancy. However, just two years later, developers are now prepared to pay approximately $2,200 per front foot for land in the area. The city has assured potential buyers that any property fronting on Main Street within the general vicinity of Smith's property can be rezoned to C4 (retail shopping centre other than regional shopping centres). Based on this information, Smith's lot alone appears to be worth 90 x $2,200 or $198,000. The highest and best use has shifted from single family to retail commercial, given rapidly changing optimum use patterns.

Example 2   *Principles (Appraisal)–*
                     Highest and Best Use

Seller Jones owns a farm that now falls within the expanded municipal boundaries of Anycity. As Anycity expands, the farm acreage will undoubtedly become more valuable as a residential subdivision site than as a farm. Anne Appraiser has been retained to appraise the property and concludes that the highest and best use of the farm property would be a site for a subdivision. Accordingly, she prepares the appraisal for purposes of a potential subdivision site rather than as a farm. However, before basing a value estimate on a use other than its existing farm use, she must be convinced of three things:

- The property is physically adaptable to the other use.

- Actual demand exists for the other use sufficient to enhance market value.

- The property is available for such other use and would not violate existing zoning by-laws or private deed restrictions.

The third point should be emphasized. Anne Appraiser may consider a use that is presently prohibited by the zoning by-laws if good reason and evidence exists to believe that a change to permit this particular use is probable and not simply possible, and that the change is imminent.

Increasing and Decreasing Returns

A valuation principle stating that when successive increments of one or more factors of production are added to fixed amounts of the other factors, an initial enhancement of income in dollars, benefits, or amenities occurs, to a point of maximum return (the point of diminishing returns), followed by a relative decrease in incremental value in relation to the value of the added factor(s). This principle is also referred to as the *principle of diminishing returns* or the *principle of variable proportions*.

Example 1   *Principles (Appraisal)–*
                     Increasing and Decreasing Returns

Builder Anderson discovers an amazing fact about house construction in Anycity. While a 1,200 square foot bungalow with a single garage commands $125,000, the same bungalow with a double garage (costing $15,000 more), adds $25,000, bringing the value to $150,000. Several sales at this level confirm his theory. Anderson then concludes that the addition of a third garage (at a cost of $15,000), will produce a similar increase raising the market value to $175,000. However, after constructing a bungalow with the triple car garage, the property remained unsold for six months and ultimately sold for $157,500. Anderson has experienced the law of increasing and decreasing returns. While the two-car garage added value beyond its cost, the successive addition of more garages does not incrementally increase market value.

Example 2   *Principles (Appraisal)–*
                     Increasing and Decreasing Returns

Owner Smith is constructing a 98-suite condominium project. Currently, comparable condominiums are selling in the range of $135–obstructed view to $150–unobstructed view per square foot within the immediate area. Smith has a combination of 1,000, 1,500, and 2,000 square foot units and wonders how much higher than $150 per foot he can receive for additional upgrades within the units. As a rule of thumb, Smith wants to increase the final selling price by $2.00 for every $1.00 invested in the unit. Various selling prices of one bedroom units with unobstructed views are listed below along with upgrades invested.

UNIT #	SALE PRICE	UPGRADES
606	$150,000	0
608	$153,000	$1,500
704	$154,000	$2,000
708	$155,000	$3,000
802	$156,000	$4,000
804	$158,000	$5,500
806	$160,000	$7,000
808	$161,000	$9,000

Continued...

P TO Q

The principle of diminishing returns is at work in this condominium development. Smith achieved his objective of a $2.00 increase for every $1.00 invested beyond the base price of $150,000 in the case of Units 608 and 704. However, by increasing the value of upgrades, he did not realize a proportionate increase in price with other units. In Unit 808, for example, for every $1.00 invested, the return in terms of selling price was only $1.22:

$$(\$161,000 - \$150,000) \div \$9,000 = \$1.22$$

Example 3   Principles (Appraisal)– Increasing and Decreasing Returns

Smith operates a manufacturing plant that produces electrical appliances. Owing to an increased administrative workload, he is unable to effectively manage the 20 employees on a daily basis. Consequently, worker efficiency and production quality have suffered. Smith, based on the advice of a consultant, hires a full-time manager to oversee the day-to-day operation. As a result, overall efficiency leaped 15 percent with customer returns of defective equipment dropping by 50 percent over three months. Corporate profits rose by 10% after paying the manager's salary.

Seeing the impressive results, Smith reasoned that two managers could achieve even better results and hires a second person. In the next three months, no appreciable difference was evident and, in fact, profits dipped slightly. Smith experienced the principle of increasing and decreasing returns. The addition of management expertise is only effective to a point after which the incremental value of that additional factor of production (in this case, labour) becomes proportionately less and less effective.

Progression

A principle, as an extension of the principle of conformity, stating that in the case of properties that are dissimilar, the value of the poorer property will be affected positively by the presence of the property of higher value. The principle of conformity outlines that to maintain maximum value, land must be utilized to reasonably conform with the existing standards of the area.

Example   Principles (Appraisal)–Progression

Buyer Jones has often heard the old adage about buying the worst house on the street. However, he is now experiencing the reality of the statement. Jones is looking for a three-bedroom home with a single-car garage while seeking the advantage of the principle of progression. Through a buyer representative, he has located three properties that are roughly comparable in terms of size, condition, and overall appearance:

Continued…

	ADDRESS	LISTED PRICE
Property 1	42 Main Street	$168,500
Property 2	233 West Street	$172,000
Property 3	136 The Ridge	$215,000

Properties 1 and 2 are located in single-family residential areas where the majority of homes are priced between $155,000 and $175,000. Property 3, however, is the smallest home on The Ridge. Homes adjacent to the property and in the immediate area sell between $240,000 and $350,000. Jones is particularly attracted to Property 3, but doesn't want to pay the higher price. The salesperson, sympathizing with his client's position, is realistic. Value accrues to the third property owing to its proximity to higher priced homes. The principle of progression is at work.

Regression

An extension of the principle of conformity which states that to maintain maximum value, land must be utilized to reasonably conform with the existing standards of the area. The principle of regression extends that concept by stating that between dissimilar properties, the value of the better property will be affected adversely by the presence of the property of lesser value.

Example   Principles (Appraisal)–Regression

Buyer Jones understands the advantages of acquiring the worst home on the street and benefiting from the principle of progression, i.e., the value of the lower priced property will be positively impacted by the presence of properties of greater value. However, he is about to experience the opposite effect, known as the principle of regression.

Jones acquired an attractive bungalow with a single-car garage without regard to adjacent older properties. The home is obviously the best property in the general area. When Jones listed the property, many buyers were impressed, but no offer was forthcoming. The listing salesperson provided three comparable sales that were almost identical to Jones' property in terms of size, condition, and overall appearance, but located in better neighbourhoods:

	ADDRESS	SALE PRICE
Property 1	402 Main Street	$214,500
Property 2	321 West Street	$205,000
Property 3	136 The Ridge	$215,000

Despite the listing salesperson's recommendation to market the property at $195,900, Jones could see no appreciable differences (except for the neighbourhood), and listed at $215,900. After two months with no offers, he reduced the price to $199,900 and the property sold for $194,500. As the listing salesperson explained, the value of Jones' property was directly impacted by lower priced properties in the immediate area.

Substitution

A principle stating that a prudent buyer would pay no more for real property than the cost of acquiring an equally desirable substitute in the marketplace. This principle presumes that buyers will consider the alternatives available to them, that they will act rationally and prudently on the basis of information about those alternatives, and that time is not a significant factor, i.e., the substitute property can be acquired without unreasonable delay.

Example   *Principles (Appraisal)–Substitution*

Buyer Jones is seriously considering two properties: a one-year-old, resale bungalow offered at $179,900 and a new unoccupied bungalow built by the same builder on an adjacent street priced at $179,500 (including GST). After inspecting both properties, Jones discovered the following differences. The resale property, while showing minor wear and tear, was fully decorated. In addition, all landscaping was completed and the driveway was paved.

Jones, in making his ultimate decision, is unwittingly using the principle of substitution. He is carefully weighing out alternatives in terms of desirability and cost. His ultimate conclusion will be rationally based on differences noted between the two properties assuming that both can be acquired for approximately the same price.

Supply and Demand

A valuation principle stating that market value is determined by the interaction of the forces of supply and demand as of the date of the appraisal. According to this principle, if the supply increases but the demand remains constant, the price will decrease. If the demand increases but the supply remains constant, the price will increase. If both supply and demand increase or decrease proportionately, price will remain relatively stable. The value of real estate tends to be set by the relationship between supply and demand at the time of valuation. See also Economics for a general discussion of market dynamics and the interplay of supply and demand in the establishment of prices within Canadian markets.

**Example   *Principles (Appraisal)–*
Supply and Demand

The importance of this principle is obvious. Consider the effect on house prices if a large corporation moves its head office and employees from City 'A' to City 'B'. In City 'A,' prices will fall because of oversupply, while in City 'B' prices will rise due to increased demand (assuming that supply and demand were previously equal in both cities).

As another example, if construction of new homes exceeds demand, the resulting over-supply will ultimately impact prices.

Surplus Productivity

A principle relating to the net income remaining after all expenses necessary to the operation have been paid and the capital invested in improvements has been satisfied. This remaining net income is imputable to the land and tends to fix the value of the property. As a result, the land is valuable according to the surplus productivity imputable to it.

In the operation of an income producing property, three levels of return are necessary, while the fourth (the land) can command only the residual income with no fixed or necessary rate of return. These four levels are called the factors in production and must be satisfied in order of labour, coordination, capital, and land. Surplus attributable to land largely determines its value and with well-developed real estate, the land should yield a reasonable return, based on its current realistic value.

**Example   *Principles (Appraisal)–*
Surplus Productivity

Salesperson Jamieson is applying the principle of surplus productivity to arrive at the value of land. The improvements on the subject property have an estimated value of $150,000 and a forecasted net operating income of $27,000. Market research indicates that a discount (return) rate of 10% applies and that the remaining economic life of the building is 40 years. The income is capitalized based on the return rate (10%) plus the recapture rate of 2.5% (100 ÷ 40 or 2.5% per year).

Net Operating Income	$27,000
Income Earned by the Building (150,000 x (.10 + .025)	18,750
Residual (Surplus) Income Attributable to the land	8,250
Value of the Land ($8,250 ÷ .10)	82,500

PRIOR ACTS INSURANCE

Insurance designed to assist salespersons who have transferred from a brokerage that has cancelled its errors and omissions insurance or has ceased to operate. The need for prior acts insurance will vary depending on errors and omissions insurance arrangements in individual provinces. Errors and omissions insurance is provided either under the authority of the regulatory body or furnished by private insurers in the marketplace.

Provincial   See applicable reference materials.

PRIVACY CODE

Privacy and the collection, use, and disclosure of personal information is a federal government priority. Current privacy legislation under consideration will directly impact real estate practitioners. Recent initiatives to protect the dissemination of personal information is due in no small part to the flourishing electronic marketplace unfolding in Canada. Presently, most provincial governments have statutory requirements concerning the government use of personal information, but such procedures do not typically extend to the private sector.

The *Personal Information Protection and Electronic Documents Act* (PIPEDA), effective January 1, 2001, provides that personal information cannot be collected, used, or disclosed in Canadian commercial activities without the informed consent of individuals providing such information. The real estate profession, a frequent user of personal information during the listing and selling process (e.g., mailing lists, information concerning buyers and sellers, and dissemination of listing information), is directly impacted. This legislation will apply to the real estate profession effective January 1, 2004 or upon passage of similar provincial legislation, whichever comes first.

In anticipation of such requirements, The Canadian Real Estate Association formed a Privacy Task Force in 2000 to examine the impact of federal legislation on practitioners and to develop practical privacy tools. For example, CREA has introduced various clauses to be inserted into selected documents, e.g., listing agreements, buyer agency agreements, and agreements/contracts/offers used in provincial jurisdictions.

On October 27, 2001, the CREA General Assembly submitted a proposed privacy code for consideration by delegates at the national conference. The provision that every real estate board must enforce the code throughout Canada met with resistance. An amendment, initiated by the Ontario Real Estate Association (OREA), was successful in altering the mandatory requirement. The amended motion subsequently passed to adopt the *Privacy Code of The Canadian Real Estate Association*. As a result, real estate boards have the option of choosing to enforce the code or not, as they see fit. The OREA concern centred on the fact that the Ontario government plans to introduce provincial privacy legislation that will supplant the *Personal Information Protection and Electronic Documents Act*. Enforcing a privacy code based on federal legislation could result in significant conflicts, once new provincial legislation is passed.

The *Privacy Code of The Canadian Real Estate Association*, consisting of ten principles regarding the collection, management, and use of personal information, is reprinted in its entirety in the **Appendix**.

PRIVATE ACCESS

A right of entry most commonly associated with private roads leading to cottage and other types of rural properties. Salespeople should be particularly wary of private rights-of-way or other access arrangements.

Difficulties arise because of vague or non-existent descriptions concerning the extent of such private accesses. Ambiguous, obscure wordings are of particular concern. Further, buyers may be unaware that maintenance and repair obligations normally rest with the user of the private access. Lastly, in some instances, the actual access road may take a different route than that which is described in legal documents. Corrective action may prove costly.

Application   A brief overview of easements is necessary to better understand private access. An easement must consist of a dominant and servient tenement, with the former enjoying some benefit over the latter. The tenements must be:

- Contiguous (adjoining or in close proximity);
- Held by different persons; and
- Reasonably definite in description.

Easements can be created through several legal circumstances.

Express Grant

Clearly defined in registered documents of the dominant and servient tenement.

Implied Grant

Two types of implied grants exist: a right of mutual support and a right-of-way by necessity. As the name suggests, implied is a naturally inferred right due to some related circumstance. With mutual support, a shared docking area with access rights by both owners would naturally preclude the ability of one party to destroy his/her portion of the docking facility to the detriment of the other's structure. In an urban setting, this would also apply in semi-detached units. The second form of implied grant relates to access and rights-of-way that are necessary for the reasonable enjoyment of a property. The essential elements of an implied grant involving access are three-fold:

- The owner used the right-of-way as though it was appurtenant to the property.
- The use was both apparent and continuous.
- The right-of-way was necessary for the reasonable and convenient use of the property.

By Prescription

This right arises through the undisputed use of a right-of-way for a requisite period of time, with the informed knowledge of both parties. The onus of proof is always on the person claiming the right and various legal complexities arise concerning easement by prescription. Suffice it to say that expert legal advice is required.

Example *Private Access—By Prescription*

Salesperson Martin is concerned that the buyer fully understands the implications of using an unregistered easement for purposes of accessing a listed cottage. The seller has already stated that his family has used the access for the past 40 years with no problems whatsoever. He cannot recall whether or not the easement was registered on title.

The salesperson inserts the following clause in the agreement:

> *The buyer acknowledges that the road to the said property may be an unregistered easement. The seller shall provide to the buyer, on or before completion, a statutory declaration or declarations establishing that the existing road has been used by the seller to gain access to the said property on an uninterrupted basis for the last 40 years.*

PRIVATE NUISANCE

(SEE ALSO PUBLIC NUISANCE)

The use of land by one occupier in such a way as to interfere unreasonably with the way in which the neighbouring land occupiers can use their land. This legal concept is based on the premise that an occupier has a right to normal use and enjoyment of his/her land, free from such interferences as noxious fumes, soot, contaminating liquids, noises, and vibrations. The term *occupier* includes not only the owner of land but tenants as well. Since most members of the public qualify as owners or tenants of their homes, they may legally complain of private nuisances. A person who acquires land knowing that it is already exposed to a nuisance may nevertheless have a right to sue the offending party. Provincial legislation may limit such rights, e.g., normal farming practices near residential developments.

Application Does the law give an occupier a right to absolute freedom from these various annoyances? The answer is a relative one, weighing competing interests in society. Two main issues at stake:

- The degree of interference with the occupier's use and enjoyment of his/her land.
- The economic importance of the offending activity.

The level of interference that a community as a whole already tolerates, and hence that individual members of it must tolerate as reasonable use (i.e., justified use which is not considered tortious), varies according to local conditions. The standard of reasonable use of adjoining lands in an industrial area might be quite unreasonable and amount to tortious use in a resort area.

Even when an activity clearly amounts to a nuisance and seriously affects a plaintiff's use of his/her land, the question arises whether it would be too high a price to pay to grant that individual an injunction forcing the offending user to cease business. In theory, the court has two options. It may grant an injunction, or it may only award the plaintiff damages without restraining the defendant's continued activity. Where the nuisance is so severe as to make the land unuseable, the second decision amounts virtually to an expropriation in return for the damage award. In almost every action by an individual against a large industrial enterprise, greater public issues loom concerning the economic viability of the industry should it be excessively restricted, versus the dangers presented, e.g., unabated pollution.

PRIVITY OF CONTRACT

(SEE ALSO CONTRACT)

A basic principle of contract law, stating that, with few exceptions, only the parties to a contract can enforce or be bound by that contract.

PRO FORMA STATEMENT

(SEE ALSO CASH FLOW MODEL)

Literally translated from Latin as *according to form*. The term generally refers to financial statements showing the projected costs and income of an existing or new project.

Application For real estate brokerage purposes, the term has taken on a slightly different meaning. A pro forma statement prepared by a real estate salesperson usually concentrates solely on cash flow. The pro forma statement can be built using a simplified summary of projected income and expenses leading to cash flows, either before taxes or after taxes, for a specified period of time. More comprehensive pro forma statements include a detailed financial forecast involving a rigorous analysis of development costs, income/expense projections, financing estimates, and return on investment.

Increasingly, commercial practitioners rely on a standardized analytical structure for the analysis of income property that is referred to as a *cash flow model*. This model provides a framework to analyze investment property based on operations cash flow and sale proceeds cash flow within a defined investment (holding) period. Salespeople are then able to provide investment comparisons to clients using discounted cash flow techniques to arrive at net present values and internal rates of return.

PROBABILITY

(SEE ALSO RISK ANALYSIS)

The likelihood or chance that an occurrence will take place. Probabilities are usually expressed as a percentage in which 1 represents a certainty that an occurrence *will occur* and 0 represents a certainty that it *will not*. A coin flip provides the simplest scenario. If a two-sided coin is flipped, the probability of either heads or tails is 50% (.50), and the certainty is .50 + .50 = 1.00. The two probabilities can be added together provided that each is mutually exclusive. One of the two events can and must occur.

Probabilities assigned to events can either be objective or subjective. An assignment based on empirical research and rigorous verification is viewed as an objective assignment. If, for example, a coin was flipped 100,000 times and heads appeared 50,448 times, a degree of accuracy and certainty can be attached to probability. In real estate, the assignment of probabilities relies heavily on the subjective element as the practitioner's viewpoint or judgement is often involved. However, modern probability techniques and the ever expanding range of empirical data will ultimately give way to more objective analysis.

Application   Probability theory is proving increasingly valuable in real estate when assessing relative risk associated with investment decisions. Investors traditionally seek methods to minimize risk while maximizing return. Often the result is a delicate mixture of individual risk tolerance and the desire for anticipated returns. The stock market investor seeks high returns but insists on a diversified portfolio or the gambler seeks the big payoff while attempting to limit odds through alternate bets. The real estate investor has also developed various risk reduction techniques, e.g., prudent property selection, portfolio diversification, and risk shifts (e.g., acquisition of insurance, limited liability agreements, transferring risk to tenants,

and requiring guarantees from lessees). However, many factors lie beyond his/her immediate control as the marketplace is vulnerable to a host of positive and negative forces.

Probability techniques and statistical analysis can, however, assist in transforming certain uncertainties into quantified risk allocations. Unfortunately, while past market data can be carefully analyzed from an objective stance, most real estate probability analysis retains a subjective element given the complex interplay of forces at work. Nevertheless, estimates based on probability concerning economic conditions and factors relating to the property often provide a range of possible outcomes to frame the investment decision-making process. A basic example is illustrated as the scope of real estate probability analysis, while increasingly relevant, remains a complex issue.

The example provided is for illustration purposes only. The impact of varying market conditions on net operating income will fluctuate by property and individual circumstances. In this scenario, probabilities are assigned to various market conditions leading to a prudent offering price. Probability analysis is only one dimension in an overall investment strategy.

Example   *Probability*

Investor McKay is concerned about the impact of differing economic conditions on cash flow. Salesperson Lane initially develops a forecasted operating statement for the following year and arrives at a net operating income of $100,000. Research indicates that the overall capitalization rate for this type of property is .095, and market value is estimated at $1,052,632 (rounded to $1,053,000). However, Lane acknowledges that market conditions could affect this estimate. McKay wants the salesperson to quantify the risk more accurately. Accordingly, Lane analyzes net operating income based on probabilities and develops a weighted average. The assigned probabilities are derived from market trends over the preceding five years in conjunction with personal judgement. The salesperson details the following:

TYPE OF MARKET	PROBABILITY	NOI ($'s)
Very Weak Market	.10	75,000
Less Than Average Market	.20	85,000
Average Market	.50	100,000
Above Average Market	.15	107,000
Very Strong Market	.05	112,000

The salesperson then applies a weighted average to re-estimate the net operating income given these probabilities.

Continued…

TO **P** **Q**

TYPE OF MARKET	PROB.	NOI	WEIGHTED AVG.
Very Weak Market	.10	75,000	$ 7,500
Less Than Average Market	.20	85,000	17,000
Average Market	.50	100,000	50,000
Above Average Market	.15	107,000	16,050
Very Strong Market	.05	112,000	5,600
			$96,150

Accordingly, based on probabilities, McKay would reduce risk by negotiating a lower sale price. In this instance, the lower value indicated is:

$$\$96,150 \div .095 = \$1,012,105 \text{ (rounded to \$1,012,000)}$$

The reader should also note that risk remains a factor, e.g., the appearance of a *Very Weak Market* would suggest a value of:

$$\$75,000 \div .095 = \$789,474$$

The weighted average has merely shifted value slightly based on a subjective range of probabilities.

PROFESSIONAL CONDUCT

Ethical behaviour in keeping with high standards and skillful work relating to a particular profession. Ethics involves morals, treating moral questions, and rules of conduct and is derived from the Greek word *ethikos* that means customs, usage, or character. Ethics is a branch of philosophy dealing with the art of right living and also relates to the whole field of moral science, such as right and wrong, morality and immorality, conduct, and relationships with others. To a great extent, ethics finds its origins in religious and moral teachings. As an example, there is probably no safer guide to what is proper conduct than the Golden Rule: *Do unto others as you would have them do unto you.*

Ethical Principles

Ethics must be expressed as a set of principles or values to be useful and effective. The individual is then able to guide his/her own conduct and judge that of others by means of a standard of conduct. Too frequently, ethics is confused with law. They are related and some overlap exists, but they are not identical. While the system of laws under which we live provides a substantial basis for ethical conduct, ethics is much more comprehensive than laws or regulations. Law deals with people as they are, setting a minimum standard of conduct. Ethics seeks to lead people to what they ought to be and do and, consequently, establishes a higher standard.

Law is designed to keep us from doing wrong while ethics encourages us to do that which is right and good. Law is thus negative while ethics is positive. The law is not concerned with a person's motives or reasons for obeying its demands and avoiding wrongful acts, but is satisfied by compliance and obedience, whatever the reason. Not so with ethics. The reason or motive for one's actions as they affect others becomes important. Ethics is an attempt to change, to improve, and to elevate people's motives, as well as actions.

The means of enforcement is also different. Law is enforced through the police and courts or administrative tribunals, such as tribunals formed under provincial real estate acts. Ethics is generally enforced by the governing bodies of a profession. Law and ethics do overlap, but ethics is more extensive, continuing on where the law leaves off. Thus, while all that is ethical is also lawful, the reverse is not always true.

Professional Conduct and the CREA Code of Ethics

While the legal regulation of the real estate industry provides a basis for ethical conduct, ethics is more comprehensive than the law. The study of ethics provides the standards or criteria that can be used to decide the rightness or wrongness of alternative courses of action. The Canadian Real Estate Association (CREA) has developed a *Code of Ethics* to supplement the law and safeguard public trust in the real estate practitioner. The Code ensures that members of organized real estate act professionally by outlining expected ethical conduct and providing a mechanism for disciplining those who violate that standard of conduct.

All real estate boards and associations in Canada have adopted CREA's *Code of Ethics and Standards of Business Practice*. The CREA Code does not have any enforcement provisions contained within it. Its enforcement is left up to the individual local boards, or in certain circumstances, provincial associations. It is very important to be aware of the provisions enacted by the local boards and provincial associations to enforce the Code in order to fully understand what rights a member has if he/she is required to appear before a disciplinary hearing.

Before the Code is enforceable by any real estate organization, it must be ascertained whether or not the real estate practitioner who is to be investigated has agreed to be bound by the Code. A person who voluntarily becomes a member of a provincial association or one of the local real estate boards in a province agrees to adhere to the Code as a condition of membership. Once it has been established that the real estate practitioner falls within the provisions of the Code, the individual board or association actually enforces the duties under the Code. If a dispute is between two members of the same board, then that local board has jurisdiction to hold a hearing according to its own procedures. A dispute that arises between members of different boards, however, is investigated and heard by the provincial association. The mechanics for providing a fair hearing for a member alleged to be in breach of the Code and the sanctions which can be imposed are contained within the constitutions and by-laws of the applicable real estate boards and the provincial associations.

Provincial variations can exist concerning disputes, particularly those between a member of the public and a member of the board. Complaints often involve both regulatory as well as ethical issues and procedures are established at a provincial level to address such issues.

Provincial   See applicable reference materials.

Professional Conduct and the Law

The system of common law, used in all of Canada with the exception of Québec, embodies principles that have evolved by judgments over the centuries on a case-by-case basis. Little of this law has been embodied in any definitive document or statute and, therefore, must be drawn or deduced from reported cases. The common law system uses principles established in previous cases to decide present conflicts. This is referred to as *stare decisis*. This feature of common law ensures a sense of fairness in that similar cases are decided in a similar manner. The law of agency and law of contract are two areas of the common law system that directly impact the real estate practitioner.

Statutes passed by parliament and by provincial legislatures supplement the common law. The provisions of provincial regulatory acts relating to real estate govern the conduct of real estate brokers and salespeople in individual provinces. Such acts are generally designed to:

- Protect the public from improper practices by registrants;
- Ensure that brokers and salespeople are reasonably qualified; and
- Standardize certain aspects of practice within the provincial real estate industry.

Real estate acts serve primarily to codify the common law and do, to varying extents, supplement common law by providing express guidelines that must be followed by registrants. Typically, real estate acts are administered and enforced by a provincial regulatory bodies. The powers granted to these organizations to investigate complaints are extensive and far-reaching and generally encompass those activities deemed necessary for the protection of the public and the administration of provincial real estate acts.

While common law and statutory law seem distinct, some interplay exists between them. For example, as the courts interpret the provisions of provincial real estate acts, they are guided by cases previously decided in the particular area, i.e., by the common law. At the same time, in handing down their decision, the courts are adding to the core of principles of common law which will then be used as a guide in future interpretations of applicable provincial acts.

Real Estate Professionalism

In real estate, issues of ethical conduct are very real, everyday concerns. Real estate practitioners help people make important decisions about the largest asset most will ever own. When buying or selling real estate, people are trading much of the financial worth that they have accumulated over many years. Often, an emotional investment exists in addition to the large financial one. Most sellers are owner/occupants and have lived in, and often improved, the property that is being sold and naturally develop a strong emotional attachment to the property. With such large amounts of money and emotion involved, the stakes are high. Any misconduct or unethical behaviour can be damaging to the seller, the buyer, the public, the real estate broker and salesperson, and to the real estate profession as a whole.

When completing a transaction, various parties to the transaction put the real estate salesperson in a position of trust. They rely on his/her professional expertise, skills, knowledge, competence, and integrity. Thousands of real estate practitioners base their business on such trust and the reputation for honesty, integrity, and reliability. When a real estate practitioner acts unethically, public confidence is undermined, not just in the person involved, but in the whole industry.

All real estate practitioners are required to abide by the provisions of applicable provincial real estate acts and to adhere to the requirements of agency law and contract law. Enforcement of these legal obligations is exercised by the courts and the appropriate regulatory body.

Registrants who become members of organized real estate have the additional obligation to act in accordance with the *Code of Ethics and Standards of Business Practice* of *The Canadian Real Estate Association*. This Code and accompanying standards outline accepted levels of conduct for all real estate practitioners in Canada who are members of a real estate board and/or a provincial association. CREA members are charged with the obligation of promoting a code of ethical conduct and abiding by the provisions of that code and any sanctions imposed for a breach thereof. By enforcing a code of professional conduct, real estate boards and associations are helping to protect the reputation of the total industry and the livelihoods of their members. Non-members fall under requirements of provincial legislation. Historically, such statutes initially provided limited mechanisms for monitoring behaviour and sanctioning any breaches of proper conduct. However, with the continuous expansion and refinement of provincial real estate acts, more and more activities relating to all registrants come under the close scrutiny of provincial regulatory bodies.

Standards of Conduct

Until relatively recent times, many people in business took such a limited view of ethics that they used bare legality as the sole standard for their conduct in business affairs. The 19th century business person took the attitude that *the public be damned* and the public did not seem to care. If it did, the public lacked the means to protect or correct the situation, for at that time it was generally felt that government should not control or regulate business conduct.

Around the turn of the century, the business community concluded that there was a right and wrong way of doing things, not only in private life but also in dealings with customers, employees, and competitors as well. For example, many real estate boards across Canada were established during the early decades of the twentieth century and required members to be bound by a code of professional conduct.

Over the years, business has attempted to improve both image and motives. This transition has occurred in part because of government intervention. The development of laws and regulations have been in response to the public demand to be protected from the uncontrolled use of economic power along with the disregard of public interest. This change has also come about because of a change in attitude within the business community itself. Business leaders, for the most part, now recognize that:

- The purpose and function of any business is to serve the public, not just to satisfy the personal ambitions of those who own or run the business;
- Ethical conduct and financial success do go hand-in-hand;
- Business has a responsibility to the community which supports it; and
- A failure to recognize and exercise such responsibility could lead to greater governmental intervention and control.

For the most part, business has steered away from the term *ethics*, preferring to use terms such as *good business practices*, *principles of professional conduct*, or *standards of business practice* as in the case of real estate practitioners.

As a matter of note, provincial regulatory bodies have displayed an interest in ethical requirements as well as statutory procedures. In Ontario, for example, the regulatory council has established a code of ethics for all licensed practitioners in addition to any professional standards relating to organized real estate, e.g., the Code of Ethics of The Canadian Real Estate Association.

PROFESSIONAL STANDARDS COMMITTEE

A committee duly appointed by a local real estate board to oversee the voluntarily accepted level of behaviour set out in the *Code of Ethics and Standards of Business Practice* of The Canadian Real Estate Association. The creation and maintenance of professional standards and discipline committees are required to enforce the Code and provide an alternate means (other than the law and regulatory provisions set out in provincial real estate acts), to resolve disputes. Professional standards and discipline committees are guided by two overriding goals:

- To protect board and membership integrity; and
- To educate members about the Code and its application.

Differences exist concerning procedures for the operation of a professional standards committee owing to different by-laws in real estate board jurisdictions. Contact the appropriate board and/or association regarding specific procedures. For additional information regarding boards, including ethics enforcement, see **Real Estate Board**.

Provincial   See applicable reference materials.

PROFIT A PRENDRE

The right to enter upon a property based on a written agreement and take something from it, such as crops, minerals, or timber. This right can, in some instances, pass with title upon the sale of the property.

Example   *Profit A Prendre*

Owner Smith has entered into a lease arrangement with Jones for 200 acres of farmland that is currently being used for the production of corn. Originally, Smith had planned to harvest the crop, but instead has decided not to pursue farming and returned to his city employment. Jones, already possessing the necessary harvesting equipment, leases the property as of the July 20xx for five years. The lease specifically provides that Jones, for an agreed annual rental sum, shall remove the existing crop during the current year and thereafter harvest crops for the remaining four-year period.

PROFIT AND LOSS STATEMENT
(SEE FINANCIAL STATEMENTS)

PROFIT RATIO

A business ratio derived from information included on the profit and loss statement. Such ratios provide a proportional relationship between either gross or net profit and commission income generated.

Gross Profit Margin

This ratio determines the profit of the brokerage after the salespeople and others brokers have been paid.

Gross Profit Margin

= (Commission Income – Commission Expense) ÷ Commission Income

Gross profit margins have limited applicability in real estate given the range of commission splits and methods of allocating and recovering salesperson expenses. This situation is further complicated by a lack of industry-wide data upon which to make meaningful comparisons. This ratio might be used when comparing a particular period with a prior corresponding period to identify significant changes in gross profit. Large brokerages and franchises may provide information for the establishment of ratios to assist in budgeting and performance comparisons.

Gross commission income figures can be misleading. This revenue category can represent all dollars collected by the brokerage, including amounts due co-operating brokerages, thereby blurring the true financial picture. The ratio is more accurate if an adjusted gross income is used that excludes co-operating brokerage payouts.

Example   *Profit Ratio–Gross Profit Margin*

ABC Realty Inc. generated a total commission income of $1,450,000 less commission expense of $1,005,000 in the prior year and produced a gross profit margin of:

($1,450,000 – $1,005,000) ÷ $1,450,000 = 30.7%

At the end of the current year, the ratio dropped significantly given a commission income decrease of $240,000 with only marginally less commission expense ($980,000). The resulting ratio was:

($1,210,000 – $980,000) ÷ $1,210,000 = 19.0%

Net Profit Margin

This ratio determines the net profit before taxes after payment of all expenses. Limitations detailed under *Gross Profit Margin* should also be reviewed regarding this ratio.

Net Profit Margin

= Net Profit ÷ Commission Income

Example   *Profit Ratio (Brokerage)– Net Profit Margin*

ABC Realty Inc. has a gross income of $1,450,000 with a net profit of $40,000. The net profit margin is:

$40,000 ÷ $1,450,000 = 2.8% (rounded)

PROGRESS ADVANCES
(SEE ALSO NEW HOME CONSTRUCTION LOAN)

Loan advances made on a property during sequential stages of construction whereby the lender makes such advances while retaining a sufficient amount of the loan to complete the building should the borrower be unable to do so.

Progress advances are most commonly associated with residential construction but actually are used in all forms of new construction. Typically, advances are made in three to five sequential stages during construction.

PROGRESSION, PRINCIPLE OF
(SEE PRINCIPLES (APPRAISAL))

PROMISE

A declaration or other indication, either written or verbal, that something either will or will not be done. Provincial regulations may set out requirements for registrants concerning specific types of promises made in the furthering of a real estate transaction.

Provincial   See applicable reference materials.

PROPERTY
(SEE ALSO PERSONAL PROPERTY AND REAL PROPERTY)

Property is either real or personal. The distinguishing factor is mobility, with personal property being movable. Real property is the freehold ownership of land, including the tangible elements (physical elements) and the intangible elements (rights that accrue from the ownership of the physical real estate). Real estate usually refers to the physical tangible property, while real property is the more all encompassing term that includes both real estate and rights of ownership.

Salesperson Martin is trying to understand the difference between real and personal property. The broker provides a straightforward example. When a property is listed, the land, house and all improvements (e.g., garages, decks, and accessory buildings), represent the real estate, but are also viewed as the tangible items of real property. The rights associated with the land, (e.g., the right to occupy, mortgage or sell the property), are the intangible items. In combination, the tangible and intangible items make up what is referred to as real property. All the chattels or moveable possessions of the seller are personal property (e.g., furniture, automobile).

PROPERTY ANALYSIS WORKSHEET

The *Property Analysis Worksheet* provides a standard format for commercial practitioners to analyze cash flows. The worksheet offers the flexibility to properly serve the needs of both buyer and seller clients. Further, information developed can lead to investment analysis or valuation. This form, having three primary functions, is illustrated in **Figure P.7** along with typical comments and calculations that might be found on an actual worksheet.

Actuals   Analysis of actual financial reports for a specific property to assist the seller in assessing alternatives including marketing the property, making adjustments in selected income/expense categories, and acquiring or renegotiating debt service. The worksheet provides a basis for testing scenarios and arriving at a range of net operating incomes and/or cash flows before taxes.

Reconstructed   Preparation of a reconstructed (stabilized) version of the owner's statement to be used with the direct (income) capitalization approach in establishing value. This statement is also normally the first stage in preparing reconstructed income/expense projections for a defined holding period and establishing market value by means of yield capitalization.

Forecast   Preparation of a forecast for a defined holding period that typically leads to cash flow after tax analysis and determination of investment value in conjunction with *Operations Cash Flow Worksheet* and *Sale Proceeds Cash Flow Worksheet*.

Reference   For detailed information regarding reconstructed statements, see **Reconstructed Operating Statement**. Calculations involving the property analysis worksheet and other related worksheets are covered in commercial courses.

PROPERTY CONDITION DISCLOSURE STATEMENT

A disclosure statement, designed for sellers when offering property for sale, that sets out particulars concerning the offered property. Topics addressed typically include items that would be of interest to a prospective buyer regarding the overall condition of the improvements, any relevant legal matters affecting the property, environmental problems, structural deficiencies, and condition of water and waste systems.

Application   Regulatory bodies and real estate boards throughout North America have introduced property condition disclosure statements with a resulting wide variance of questions and formats found in the marketplace. Questions posed on any property condition disclosure statement, or similar document, should be carefully reviewed with the seller, completed, and signed by the seller and a copy given to a prospective buyer. The completion of this form by the seller does not relieve the brokerages from those obligations that would otherwise be present with respect to ascertaining the condition of the property. The information contained on the form should be used to assist in meeting those obligations.

Disclosure statements are gaining popularity in the marketplace. Such statements provide a written record of representations and furnish buyers with information about the property that might not be readily discernible through a casual inspection. Disclosure statements contain a list of points or questions that are designed to uncover various problems that may or may not be present in the property.

Following are key points to consider about the use of such forms:

- Assists in protecting real estate practitioners and the seller from possible legal action.
- Provides the opportunity to obtain information in an orderly and consistent manner.
- Furnishes a supporting document to buyers, i.e., should be given to a prospective buyer even if not requested by the buyer.
- Reduces the risk of non-disclosure of pertinent facts about the property.
- Diminishes the chance of serious problems that can delay closing and/or lead to litigation.

Practitioners should be aware that misrepresentations regarding physical attributes of property are a common source of litigation.

Provincial   See applicable reference materials.

PROPERTY ANALYSIS WORKSHEET

CLIENT NAME	FUNCTION	
W. Warren, Landsite Investigations (Anycity) Inc.	☐ Owner's Actuals	☐ Seller's Position
PROPERTY LOCATION	☒ Broker's Reconstructed	☐ Buyer's Position
1342 Gateway Drive, Southgate	☐ Forecast	
PROPERTY TYPE		
Multi-Residential		

INCOME

LINE		YEAR ___20xx___	COMMENTS/CALCULATIONS
1	Potential Rental Income	311,534	302,460 + (302,460 x .03), Previous Year Plus 3%
2	− Vacancy & Credit Losses	− 7,788	2.5% of Potential Rental Income (As Per Research)
3	= Effective Rental Income	= 303,746	
4	+ Other Income	+ 0	
5	**= Gross Operating Income**	**= 303,746**	

OPERATING EXPENSES

6	Real Estate Taxes	29,561	Taxes as Previous Year Plus 2%
7	+ Property Insurance	+ 10,517	Package Policy
8	+ Property Management	+ 13,669	On-Site, Part-Time Manager
9	+ Payroll: Onsite Personnel	+ 11,160	Part-Time (1 Person)
10	+ Expenses/Employee Benefits	+ 1,953	Includes EI/CPP
11	+ Repairs and Maintenance	+ 23,540	Includes Selected Amortized Expenses
	Utilities:		
12	+ Utilities	+ 42,524	As Per Previous Year Plus 3.5%
13	+		
14	+		
15	+ Accounting and Legal	+ 2,760	Based on Previous Year
16	+ Real Estate Leasing Commissions	+ 4,150	As Per Forecasted Activity Report
17	+ Advertising/Licences/Permits	+ 2,040	Based on Previous Year
18	+ Supplies	+ 2,640	Based on Previous Year
19	+ Miscellaneous		
	Contract Services:		
20	+ Lawn Care Services	+ 1,950	Based on Previous Year
21	+ Solid Waste Disposal	+ 7,101	Based on Previous Year
22	+		
23	**= Total Operating Expenses**	**= 153,565**	

CASH FLOW ANALYSIS

24	Gross Operating Income (Line 5)	303,746	
25	− Total Operating Expenses (Line 23)	− 153,565	
26	**= Net Operating Income**	**= 150,181**	
27	− Annual Debt Service	N/A	
28	**= Cash Flow Before Taxes**	**N/A**	

TO **P Q**

Broker's Reconstructed Property Analysis Worksheet   Figure P.7

PROPERTY MANAGEMENT

Property management represents an important specialty field in real estate. Real estate brokerages usually become involved in property management as a result of rental activity. Selected topics relating to property management are included as a brief overview.

Budgeting

Budgeting procedures can vary considerably in the property management field. Generally, there are five commonly used methods.

- Annual net operating income projection.
- Monthly net operating income projection.
- Annual cash flow budget.
- Monthly cash flow budget.
- Capital reserve budget.

Insurance

Various insurance coverages are necessary to adequately protect both the building structure and activities surrounding the general management of that building.

Following is a list of typical coverages to consider.

- Fire and extended coverage.
- Comprehensive general liability and property damage.
- Multi-peril risk policy (combination policy) providing a pre-packaged group of coverages.
- Errors and omissions (relating to the managing agent).
- Catastrophe (damage to adjacent buildings due to negligence).
- Rental income (loss of rental income due to building damage).
- Boiler and machinery coverage.
- Money and securities.
- Employee benefits.
- Additional hazards (elevators, swimming pools, motor vehicles, etc.).

Expert advice is advised on all insurance matters. Insurance brokers have the skills to package insurance coverages to meet specific property and property management needs.

Leases

Three types of leases are commonly encountered by property managers, but a wide range of variations exist in the marketplace.

Gross Lease   The tenant pays a fixed rental and the owner pays all the expenses associated with the operating of the property. Normally, the responsibility for utility costs and extraordinary repairs are subject to negotiations between the parties.

Net Lease   This lease provides that the tenant not only pays the rent but also assumes responsibility for certain expenses connected with the leased premises. There are three subtypes normally associated with the net lease: single-net lease, net-net lease, and triple-net lease. Increasingly, net leases are discussed in terms of base and additional rents rather than the traditional net, net/net, and net/net/net (triple-net) terminology.

Percentage Lease   The rent is normally based on a percentage of gross sales or net income earned on the premises, or a minimum fixed rent, whichever is greater. It is important to note that numerous combinations and variations are found in the Canadian marketplace.

Maintenance Plan

Provides for the orderly upkeep of the managed property. There are four steps involved in developing a plan.

- Assessing the property's needs.
- Identifying the capabilities of on-site staff and equipment.
- Estimating the time each job will take.
- Rearranging the maintenance tasks according to personnel.

Management Agreement

A management agreement sets out the roles and responsibilities of all parties to that agreement and contains certain key elements.

- Parties to the agreement.
- Property description.
- Term of the property management contract.
- Powers and duties granted within the agreement, for example, collection of rent and other income due, execution of leases and other documents, maintenance of the property, advertising, employees, indemnification, insurance, bank account clause, accounting and reporting, and a cancellation or termination clause.
- Property management fees.
- Other fees such as lease commission, repairs and alterations, additional accounting, conducting special reports and appraisals, tax appeal services, and other consultation services.

Property Management Bookkeeping

Bookkeeping systems for property managers take on various forms and procedures. As with overall bookkeeping, the tracking of receipts and disbursements is subject to a wide diversity within property management operations across Canada. Provincial regulatory bodies may set out recommended or required methods.

Provincial   See applicable reference materials.

Security

Property managers should clearly understand the need to provide more than just superficial security procedures. Judges and courts are enforcing the premise that tenants are entitled to expect management to take reasonable care to protect them. The components of a security system include consideration of hardware, design, people, and management elements. A well-designed plan must include all four dimensions.

In addition to adherence to legislative requirements and security arrangements, the property manager can improve relationships between owner and tenant in various ways. The interaction between the property manager, tenants, and building staff is crucial to a successful operation. The establishment of clear and precise guidelines is vital and can be accomplished in several ways.

Following are selected guidelines:

- Develop a comprehensive procedural manual. Begin with all procedures and policies and commit this information to an organized manual.
- Document key personnel policies.
- Establish tenant policies, for example, rent collection, property damage, tenant complaints, and moving procedures.
- Create a tenant guidebook for the property.
- Develop rules and procedures for building amenities, e.g., recreation facilities, laundry, and parking areas.

PROPERTY MANAGEMENT SPECIALTY

Property management offers great opportunities for real estate practitioners. The total value of buildings in Canada is probably the greatest single form of invested capital. Each year rent collected from these buildings represents a substantial portion of the national income. Thousands of people derive employment from the maintenance and servicing of these buildings, and governments derive significant tax payments from these properties. Yet few people realize the need for efficient and organized management of this vast investment.

Application   Property management is often mistakenly confused with the activities of rental agencies or even building superintendents. Under property management, the manager not only acts as administrator for the owner, but typically assumes all executive functions necessary to carry out agreed objectives, thus relieving the owner of the burdens normally associated with the operation of an income-producing property. Responsibilities and activities may vary, from contracting for labour and services necessary for property upkeep, to matters as extensive as major renovations or redevelopment projects and initial renting related thereto.

The duties of a property manager basically fall into four areas.

- Keeping the property leased;
- Collecting property income;
- Paying the property expenses; and
- Maintaining the physical integrity or soundness of the property.

Although many property managers or property management companies still manage all types of properties, in this age of specialization, an increasing number of specialists manage only specific kinds of properties.

Residential	Apartment buildings, condominiums, co-operatives, and public housing.
Office	Office buildings and medical buildings.
Retail	Strip retail malls and shopping centres.
Industrial	Factories and warehouses.
Mixed Use Complexes	Office/retail and retail/residential.

Property management is a people business and requires better than average people skills. Property managers are frequently required to communicate at widely differing levels. Personnel management and the settling of disputes is a commonplace activity, as is the negotiation of contracts. With respect to residential properties, statutory requirements govern many aspects of landlord/tenant rights and the regulation of rents.

Property management has developed into a highly specialized branch of the real estate profession. As an organized profession, property management is of relatively recent origin, dating back to 1933 when the Institute of Real Estate Management was founded under the auspices of the National Association of REALTORS in Chicago. In Canada, Certified Property Managers (CPM) are certified through the Real Estate Institute of Canada.

Provincial   See applicable reference materials for any property management licensing provisions.

PROPERTY MANAGEMENT TRUST ACCOUNT

An account, separate and apart from one's personal monies, typically regulated by applicable provincial real estate legislation relating to property management activities.

Provincial   See applicable reference materials.

PROPERTY OWNERSHIP

Provincial   See applicable reference materials.

PROPORTIONATE SHARE
(SEE ALSO RENTABLE/USEABLE FACTOR)

A term most commonly associated with office and retail leasing in which a percentage set out in the lease document provides the basis for determining the payment of additional rent (e.g., operating costs) by the tenant over and above the base rent. Usually, this proportionate share is established as a fraction with the numerator being the rentable area of the leased property and the denominator being the rentable area of the building.

Example   *Proportionate Share*

A tenant has a rentable area of 760 square feet and is paying a base rent of Three Hundred and Eighty Dollars ($380.00) per month based on an annual rate of Six Dollars ($6.00) per square foot for the rentable area as described in the lease. The total building rentable area is 155,102 square feet.

Consequently, the tenant's proportionate share is:

760 ÷ 155,102 = 0.0049 or 0.49%

Assume for the moment that estimated total operating expenses and taxes for the year are $1,368,000. The tenant's annual proportionate share would be:

$1,368,000 x .0049 = $6,703.20

The monthly additional rent would be ($6,703.20 ÷ 12) or $558.60, assuming that property taxes were equally distributed throughout the twelve-month period. In practice, landlords may collect the entire year's taxes during the first six-month period. Further, if the actual building expenses exceeded the estimated amount by $18,000, the landlord would provide a statement of actual amounts payable and request the following amount:

$18,000 x 0.0049 = $88.20

PROSPECTS

A term frequently used by real estate practitioners to refer to potential buyers of property. Traditionally, under seller agency, the vast majority of residential buyers were viewed as customers. These individuals were owed honesty and fairness in real estate negotiations. Real estate brokerages represented sellers and owed fiduciary duties to those clients. Over the years, the terms *customer* and *prospect* became almost synonymous.

The rapid growth of buyer agency beginning in the 1990s heralded a new era in Canadian real estate brokerage. Now, the predominant agency relationship involves either a selling brokerage representing the seller (seller agency) or a buyer brokerage representing the buyer (buyer agency). If one brokerage represents both buyer and seller, the relationship is broadly referred to as *dual agency*. Given this fundamental change, the term *prospect* lacks the specificity required in today's agency relationships and the need for full and complete disclosure of agency responsibilities to buyer and seller. Practitioners normally refer to buyers or sellers as *clients* if a fiduciary relationship exists to ensure that no confusion arises when dealing with consumers.

PROVINCIAL/TERRITORIAL REAL ESTATE ASSOCIATIONS

In organized real estate, a provincial/territorial association is defined as any duly incorporated provincial association or territorial association that is a member of The Canadian Real Estate Association (CREA) as set out in CREA By-law No. 1, Appendix A Rules and Regulations.

Currently, the list of provincial associations and territorial associations includes those in British Columbia, Alberta, Saskatchewan, Manitoba, Ontario, Québec, New Brunswick, Nova Scotia, Prince Edward Island, Newfoundland, and Yukon Territory.

The term *provincial* is used throughout this text in the interest of readership when referring to provinces and territories.

Application   These real estate associations perform valuable services to members. Objects set forth in the Letters Patent for these associations vary. Typical areas of service are itemized for illustration purposes only. Also, Figure P.8 lists addresses and related information regarding provincial/territorial associations. Contact the appropriate organization for full details concerning services offered, benefits of membership, and overall structure.

- To promote and maintain a high standard of conduct in the transaction of all real estate business by its members in their dealings with one another and with the public.

- To unite and represent those people engaged in the real estate industry within the province for the purpose of exerting a combined and beneficial influence upon matters affecting real estate.

- To assist, generally, in the development of the province to promote the well being and prosperity of its people.

- To increase public confidence in and respect for those engaged in the real estate industry.

- To advocate and promote the enactment of just, fair, and desirable legislation affecting real estate within the province.

- To promote and increase the knowledge, skill, and proficiency of its members in all matters relating to the real estate industry.

- To make available to its members educational courses of the highest practical standards.

- To encourage and promote the right to private ownership of real property

- To promote and advance self regulation of the real estate industry.

The British Columbia Real Estate Association
309 – 1155 West Pender Street
Vancouver, BC V6E 2P4

Telephone (604) 683-7702
Fax (604) 683-8601
Web Site www.bcrea.bc.ca

The Alberta Real Estate Association
Suite 310 – 2424 – 4th Street SW
Calgary, AB T2S 2T4

Telephone (403) 228-6845 or 1-800-661-0231
Fax (403) 228-4360
Web Site www.abrea.ab.ca

The Saskatchewan Real Estate Association
231 Robin Crescent
Saskatoon, SK S7L 6M8

Telephone (306) 373-3350
Fax (306) 373-5377
Web Site www.saskatchewanrealestate.com

The Manitoba Real Estate Association
2nd Floor – 1240 Portage Avenue
Winnipeg, MB R3G 0T6

Telephone (204) 772-0405
Fax (204) 775-3781
Web Site www.realestatemanitoba.com

Ontario Real Estate Association
99 Duncan Mill Road
Don Mills, ON M3B 1Z2

Telephone (416) 445-0910
Fax (416) 445-2644
Web Site www.orea.com

Québec Real Estate Association
(Federation des Chambres Immobilieres Du Québec)
600 chemin du Golf
Ile-des-Soeurs, PQ H3E 1A8

Telephone (514) 762-0212
Fax (514) 762-0365
E-Mail fciq@cigm.qc.ca

The New Brunswick Real Estate Association Inc.
Suite 301, 358 King Street
Fredericton, NB E3B 1E3

Telephone (506) 459-8055
Fax (506) 459-8057
E-Mail nbrea@nbnet.nb.ca

Nova Scotia Association of REALTORS
7 Scarfe Court
Dartmouth, NS B3B 1W4

Telephone (902) 468-2515
Fax (902) 468-2533
Web Site www.nsar.ns.ca

Prince Edward Island Real Estate Association
75 St. Peter's Road
Charlottetown, PEI C1A 5N7

Telephone (902) 368-8451
Fax (902) 894-9487
E-Mail office@peirea.com

Newfoundland Real Estate Association
251 Empire Avenue
St. John's, NF A1C 3H9

Telephone (709) 726-5110
Fax (709) 726-4221

Yukon Real Estate Association
P.O. Box 5292
Whitehorse, YK Y1A 4Z2

Telephone (867) 668-2070
Fax (867) 668-2070
Web Site www.yrea.yk.ca

Provincial/Territorial Real Estate Associations   **Figure P.8**

PUBLIC AREA

A space in a property for public use that is typically not restricted by any lease or other agreements, for example, a lobby, corridor, or courtyard. A public area should be differentiated from a public corridor that refers to a space leading to different tenants' demised premises from a central building core.

PUBLIC NUISANCE

(SEE ALSO PRIVATE NUISANCE)

A small group of public offences known as public nuisances include blocking public roads, interfering with other public amenities such as parks, and emitting dangerous substances in public places. Actions against the wrongdoer may ordinarily be brought only by some level of government on behalf of the public as a whole.

PUMP

A device used to move water from source to destination within a structure. Piston type (reciprocating) pumps are most frequently found in older buildings, while centrifugal pumps are found in more modern installations. Shallow wells may use reciprocating or centrifugal pumps, while deep well pumps are predominantly centrifugal (jet type or submersible). Figure P.9 illustrates two types of pumps commonly found in rural and recreational properties.

PUNCH LIST

Most commonly associated with a construction checklist, however, exact usage will vary in the marketplace. The typical punch list is prepared by the architect, designer, and owner following inspection of completed construction. This document is formally submitted to the contractor to note any deficiencies and provide assurances that such work has been, or will be, completed in a good and workman-like manner in compliance with the contract documents.

Application   An alternate form of punch list is found in the marketing of commercial property. Practitioners offering tenant representation services may refer to a punch list in relation to the needs and wants of a specific client. For example, the *tenant needs punch list* will itemize and prioritize various requirements for new space and provide a standard template to compare properties at point of inspection. The punch list typically includes such items as

building amenities (e.g., type, number of floors, parking, services, and management), space requirements (e.g., rentable/useable areas, office configuration, and load factor), improvements (e.g., lighting, washroom facilities, interior finishes, HVAC, and entry/interior doors), and financial considerations (e.g., lease term, escalations, occupancy date, and special lease privileges). The punch list provides the basis for functional comparison of various buildings and may be used in conjunction with effective rent calculations to provide an overall perspective when representing a tenant.

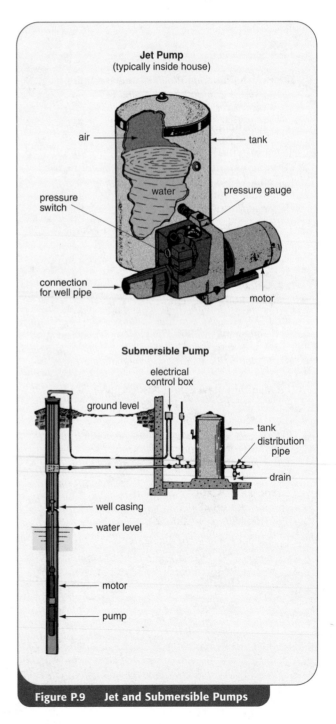

Figure P.9   Jet and Submersible Pumps

PURCHASER

The buyer of a property. Traditionally, the term *purchaser* was and is still widely used in Eastern Canada. The term *buyer* is more commonly associated with Western Canada. During the past few years, published materials are gradually migrating to *buyer* and *seller* in the interest of national consistency.

Application   In an agreement/contract, the full legal name of the proposed buyer should be spelled correctly. If there is more than one buyer, then each full name should be shown as:

> *James Paul Jones and Judy Wilma Jones.*

Special circumstances may involve the description of the buyer as a trustee or agent. Words should be used such as:

> *James Paul Jones as trustee only on behalf of a company to be incorporated.*

The buyer may authorize the title to be prepared in favour of other parties. This may occur when one spouse signs the offer, but then determines that title should be taken in the name of the other spouse or by them as joint tenants, or otherwise. This is accomplished by the buyer named in the offer signing a direction to the seller authorizing this change. Nevertheless, the buyer is still responsible for the contract and may be required to guarantee any mortgages being assumed or given to the seller under the agreement. Procedures may vary by provincial jurisdiction.

PURCHASER (BUYER) AGENCY
(SEE AGENCY)

A fiduciary relationship in which the buyer is treated as a client.

PURCHASER (BUYER) AGENCY AGREEMENT

Provincial   See applicable reference materials.

PURCHASING PROPERTY, REGISTRANTS

Provincial real estate acts typically set out requirements for registered salespersons and brokers acquiring property as a principal.

Provincial   See applicable reference materials.

PV
(SEE PRESENT VALUE)

QUANTITY SURVEY METHOD
(SEE ALSO UNIT-IN-PLACE METHOD)

A method of construction cost or reproduction cost estimating.

Application   In its strictest application, this method is a repetition of the contractor's original procedure used in the structures when estimating labour hours required and applying costs to material and labour quantities, with additional allowance for indirect costs such as overhead, labour, insurance, and contractor's profit.

The quantity survey, although still an estimate, is the most accurate and provable method. However, this approach is time consuming to prepare, and its general use is confined to contractors and to the valuation of public utility and special purpose properties. The unit-in-place method, often referred to as the *modified quantity survey approach*, is more frequently used in appraisal calculations.

QUANTUM MERUIT

The amount that should be paid as merited by the extent and quality of the original service performed in a contract.

If the contract has been discharged by breach after the injured party has done part, but not all, of what was promised under it, that person is entitled to the reasonable value of what was done, from the party who committed the breach. Quantum merit is one of several remedies for a breach of a contract, the others being damages, specific performance, and injunction.

Example *Quantum Meruit*

Property Manager Williams agreed to manage a 30-unit rental property owned by Smith through a contract with Williams' company. An agreement was signed in which Williams would receive a flat fee of $2,500 per month for management services, including maintenance of rental records, handling of tenant inquiries/complaints, negotiating agreements with contractors for upkeep of the property, and disbursing funds as required and agreed upon by Smith.

After six months, Smith failed to pay the agreed upon amount. Smith claimed that Williams had not completed his tasks as required. Williams terminated the relationship in writing and demanded payment for services rendered. As part of the pleadings, Williams, as the plaintiff, produced various documents to prove that he had fulfilled his obligations under the contract and that the money was owed as merited by the extent and quality of that work. As an aside, Williams may have been justified in suing for damages for breach of contract in addition to quantum meruit.

QUARTER SECTION

A quarter section of land contains 160 acres with a measurement of 2,640 feet by 2,640 feet. Figure Q.1 illustrates a quarter section.

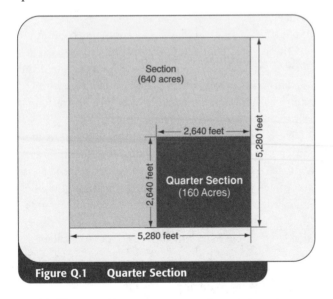

Figure Q.1   Quarter Section

QUIET ENJOYMENT

A covenant, usually inserted into a lease or conveyance on the part of the grantor, promising that the tenant or grantee

shall enjoy possession of the premises in peace and without disturbance. In mortgages (often referred to as *quiet possession*), the term refers to the mortgagor's right to uninterrupted use of the property when not in default.

QUIT CLAIM DEED

A general release of all claims or rights to a parcel of land pursuant to requirements as set out in provincial land registration procedures.

Provincial   See applicable reference materials.

QUORUM

The minimum number of persons that must be present at a duly constituted meeting of an organization to transact business on behalf of that organization.

Example *Quorum*

Broker/Owner Johnson of ABC Realty Inc., a firm member of the local real estate board, is planning to attend a special meeting for the purpose of deciding on new computer equipment for the board office. Johnson strongly supports the plan and wants to ensure that a quorum is achieved and hopefully the motion passed. In this board jurisdiction, at least 10% of all firm members who are entitled to vote must be present either in person, by their voting representative, or forward a proxy to establish a quorum. No business can be conducted at the meeting unless the required quorum is present at the beginning of and throughout the meeting. In concluding the meeting, only if there is a quorum, the chairperson of the meeting may, with the agreement of a majority of the firm members in person, by their voting representatives, or by proxy, declare the meeting adjourned. If there is no quorum, the chairperson of a meeting must declare the meeting adjourned.

While Johnson expended a great deal of effort, only 50 firm members appeared. The quorum needed for that particular real estate board was 62 firm members. As a result, the chairperson discussed the situation with those in attendance and the chairperson declared the meeting adjourned. Fortunately, a subsequent meeting was held. Johnson took extra care to ensure that all members understood both the purpose of the meeting and the financial implications that could arise. On the second attempt, the quorum was achieved and appropriate decisions were made concerning the new computer equipment that truly reflected the needs of firm members.

R

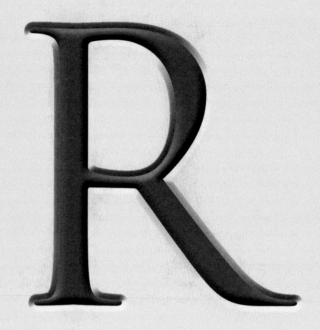

R

National Info Links

Real Estate Associations (Provincial/Territorial)
See Figure P.8, for a list of Provincial/Territorial Real Estate Associations with addresses, contact numbers and/or web sites.

Real Estate Boards
See The Canadian Real Estate Association web site for addresses and telephone numbers:

Web Site   www.crea.ca

Regulatory Agency/Organization
No national regulatory agency exists regarding real estate practitioners. Contact the appropriate provincial regulatory agency:

Real Estate Council of British Columbia
Web Site   www.realestatecouncil.bc.ca

Real Estate Council of Alberta
Web Site   www.reca.ab.ca

Saskatchewan Real Estate Commission
Web Site   www.srec.sk.ca

The Manitoba Securities Commission
Web Site   www.msc.gov.mb.ca

The Real Estate Council of Ontario
Web Site   www.reco.on.ca

Association des courtiers et agents immobiliers du Québec
Web Site   www.acaiq.com

New Brunswick Real Estate Association
E-Mail   nbrea@nbnet.nb.ca

Nova Scotia Real Estate Commission
Web Site   www.nsrec.ns.ca

P.E.I.: Consumer, Corporate and Insurance Division
Web Site   www.gov.pe.ca/oag/ccaid-info/index.php3

Government of Newfoundland and Labrador
Trade Practices and Licensing Division
Web Site   www.gov.nf.ca/gsl

Yukon Justice, Consumer & Commercial Services
Web Site   www.gov.yk.ca

Revenue Canada
Changed to Canada Customs and Revenue Agency

Web Site   www.ccra-adrc.gc.ca

See the local telephone directory for addresses and telephone numbers of Tax Services Offices and Tax Centres.

RADON

An invisible, odourless, tasteless gas produced by the decay of uranium that occurs naturally in the earth's crust. The gas itself is not dangerous, but becomes hazardous when it breaks down into progeny that cling to dust and soil particles. These radioactive particles also attach themselves to lung tissue when the radon gas is inhaled. Outdoors, radon is diluted, however, indoor levels of concentration can reach hazardous levels.

Application   Measurement is the only way to determine the existence and extent of radon. Radon gas is measured by picoCuries (peek-o-kur-eez), per litre (pCi/L), and radon progeny, which emit alpha, beta, and gamma radiation, is measured in working levels (WL). The federal government considers any level above 0.1 or approximately 20 picoCuries of radon gas per litre to be unacceptable.

Radon escapes naturally into the air from sub-surface minerals and is not a problem at these low levels of concentration as it disperses quickly. When radon enters buildings through cracks in basement floors and walls, openings around pipes and wires, through water supplies, basement floor drains, and porous building materials, the gas can build up to dangerous levels. The highest radon readings are generally found in the lowest levels of a building in winter months when doors and windows are kept closed. A significant decrease in radon typically occurs in higher levels of a building.

Indoor radon levels depend on many factors: the concentration of radon in the underlying soil, the ease with which it moves through the soil, and the construction of the dwelling, which determines how the radon enters and becomes trapped within the structure. The amount of radon will vary by location across Canada.

The consensus of experts is the greater the exposure to radon, the greater the risk of developing lung cancer. Radon levels within structures can vary significantly, based on the season, spaces, construction materials between rooms and levels, condition of basement (e.g., cracks and openings around pipes), and basement structure (e.g., number of vent pipes through walls and the sump pump pit). Radon is typically detected using two testing devices.

Charcoal Canisters   Activated charcoal in a canister that absorbs radon is placed in a home for two days and then returned to a measuring company for analysis. Although generally reliable, the canister method is susceptible to decay factors and the breaking down of radon, leading to reduced accuracy of measurement.

Alpha Track Detector   The alpha track detector uses a plastic sheet that is sensitive to radon. Decaying radon gas

in the form of radioactive emissions of alpha particles strike and damage the plastic. The measuring company counts the number of strikes (marks) on the plastic to determine the level of radon. A minimum of three months is suggested for a proper reading as opposed to the short period for charcoal canisters, hence the popularity of the charcoal method.

Health Canada estimates that less than 1 percent of Canadian homes have indoor radon levels exceeding the 20 PCi/L levels identified by the government as unacceptable. If a homeowner discovers levels between 2 PCi/L and 20 PCi/L, subsequent testing should be undertaken to accurately verify levels and take appropriate action if necessary. If the level is above 20 PCi/L, subsequent testing should still be done, along with remedial work.

Remedial action includes sealing cracks and openings within basement areas, sealing sump pump holes and service related entrance points, and covering any exposed earth such as in crawl space areas. Ventilation of basement areas and crawl space areas is also an effective means of reducing radon. Air filtering and cleaning, and increased ventilation of floor/wall cavities is also important.

Reference   Real estate practitioners should be prepared to provide general information concerning radon and refer queries to expert advice. Additional information can be obtained by contacting the Canadian Institute for Radiation Safety, Toronto, Ontario. Firms specializing in radon testing equipment are normally located under environmental categories in the telephone directory.

RAFTER

A roof component commonly associated with sloped roofs, whereas a similar member under a flat roof is referred to as a *roof joist*. The rafter supports the roof sheathing and transmits the roof loads to bearing walls and beams below. See **Figure R.1**. Some rafters support finished ceilings such as cathedral ceilings. In this case, insulation is often fitted between the rafters.

Application   Real estate practitioners should be aware of certain problems that can occur with rafters.

Over Spanned   Wood rafters are susceptible to rot, termite, and fire damage. Further, the roof will sag if rafters are over spanned or spaced too far apart.

Rafter Spread   Rafters may spread if not adequately secured to the walls at the bottom edge. This is a common problem on older houses, particularly those with gable roofs. Rafter spread is often noted at the soffits, as they will

R

pull away from the wall when the spreading occurs. In other cases, the rafters may push the top of the wall outward, causing serious problems.

Condensation   Attics with good insulation but poor ventilation may be susceptible to condensation problems. Condensation will attack roof sheathing and rafters. Left unchecked, this problem can lead to structural failure. Corrective action includes improved ventilation and replacing damaged wood.

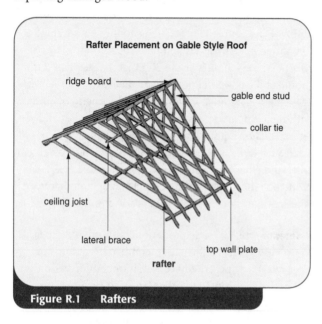

Rafter Placement on Gable Style Roof

ridge board

gable end stud

collar tie

ceiling joist

lateral brace

top wall plate

rafter

Figure R.1   Rafters

RAIN SCREEN PRINCIPLE

A construction principle involving the dispersal of rain relating to brick veneer wall. Since approximately 1970, brick veneer walls provide a rain screen for the dispersing of rain through air space and weep holes. **Figure R.2** illustrates wall components including weep holes every 24 inches. The underlying principle acknowledges that a wind driven rain will pass through the brick wall. A one inch air space is left behind the brick, between the inner face of the brick and the sheathing on the wood studs. Water is allowed to pass through the wall and run down the inner face of the brick, or the outer surface of the sheathing paper, and through the weep holes.

RANGE LINES

(SEE ALSO MERIDIAN LINE)

Longitudinal lines within a grid system of survey most commonly associated with the Western Provinces. This system provides a simplified method for describing and

locating parcels of unsubdivided land through the use of latitude and longitude lines to specifically identify location. Lines of longitude, or meridians, run north and south and are drawn, due to the curvature of the earth, so that they converge at the north and south poles. Meridian lines, however, are too far apart to precisely locate and describe parcels of land. Range lines are vertical lines running north and south between the meridians to overcome this problem.

Application   Range lines are approximately six miles apart and are numbered consecutively moving westward from each meridian. For example, if a parcel of land is described as being in Range 6, West of the First Meridian, the property would be approximately 36 miles (6 miles x 6 range lines) west of the Prime Meridian. In order to more precisely locate this parcel of land, the practitioner must also know the township in which the property is located and the appropriate township line. Township lines run east and west and are approximately six miles apart and are numbered consecutively (e.g., 1, 2 , 3, etc.) toward the north.

Provincial   See applicable reference materials. Range lines are only relevant to land descriptions in Western Canada.

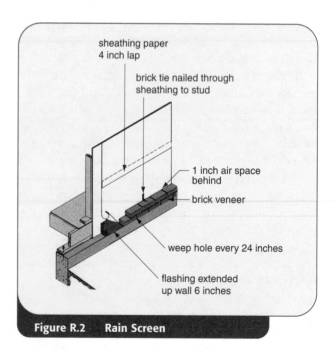

sheathing paper
4 inch lap

brick tie nailed through
sheathing to stud

1 inch air space
behind

brick veneer

weep hole every 24 inches

flashing extended
up wall 6 inches

Figure R.2   Rain Screen

RATIFICATION

A process in which a person may initially purport to act for someone as his/her agent knowing that authority to do so has not been granted, or that the limits of authority have been exceeded. The subsequent adoption of the agent's acts by the principal is called *ratification*. This affirmation of the conduct of the agent after the fact is usually considered to put the parties in the same legal position as if the agent always had authority to represent the principal.

Application Certain conditions must exist before this doctrine applies. The principal must have been in existence and capable of adopting a legal contract. The principal must have been in the contemplation of the agent, and the relationship must have been disclosed to the third party. The principal must be aware of the acts of the agent and adopt them unconditionally.

Although these rules generally apply, exceptions may exist at the provincial level. For example, at common law, a limited company does not normally become a legal person until it is incorporated. It, therefore, cannot ratify an act purportedly made on its behalf before it was created unless statutory law provides for this eventuality. In Ontario, this situation has been altered by statute so that a company can adopt a pre-incorporation contract made on its behalf. The words used in a typical agreement/contract are:

> *X, as trustee only, on behalf of a company to be incorporated.*

The efficiency and speed with which an Ontario numbered company can now be created, sometimes in one day, has also largely eliminated certain underlying concerns.

RAW LAND

A term commonly used in the real estate development field to denote lands that exist in an unused manner (and not necessarily in a natural state), before the construction of services, e.g., water and sewers, and the addition of structural improvements.

Example   *Raw Land*

Developer Reed has purchased vacant land on the outskirts of Anycity that had been used solely for outside storage of construction equipment approximately ten years ago. No services or improvements had ever been undertaken on the property other than limited clearing of vegetation and levelling/grading of areas for storage purposes. At time of acquisition, the property had been unused for several years and would be generally viewed as raw land.

REAL ESTATE

The land and any improvements found on it. Real estate as a commodity consists of raw land, as nature provided it, and all man-made permanent or fixed improvements to the land, which affect the utility of a given parcel of land. The term *real estate* includes any improvements made on the land which are intended to be permanently affixed to the land for the useful life of the improvements such as a house built on land. For an historical perspective, see **Ownership History**. For a discussion of related legal rights, see **Estate** and **Property**.

Provincial   See applicable reference materials.

REAL ESTATE ACT

Provincial   See applicable reference materials.

REAL ESTATE BOARD

A non-profit corporation operating in a town, city, township, administration district, county or any combination of such for the benefit of its members as set out in the objects of the corporation.

Board By-Laws

The objectives or goals of a real estate board are set out in the by-laws. More precisely, they usually make up the preamble within the by-laws. While exact wordings will vary, most have a more or less standard structure. A typical example is provided as **Figure R.3**.

Using these purposes as a starting point, the board then operates in terms of the board by-law, along with rules and regulations. The board by-law typically addresses, but is not limited to, selected categories:

- Corporate structure and definitions.
- Classes of membership.
- Rights of membership.
- Fees.
- Meetings.
- Board of directors.
- Committees.
- Arbitration and appeal procedures.
- Professional standards and discipline committees.
- Use of symbols.
- Order of procedure at meetings.

R

- Membership in CREA and applicable provincial real estate association.
- By-law amendments.
- Dissolution.

This by-law forms the basis for all activities and actions undertaken by the board. MLS procedures are normally found under MLS rules and regulations.

Preamble—Purposes Underlying a Real Estate Board

- To improve relations with the public and promote interest in real estate.
- To increase public confidence in all persons involved in the real estate profession.
- To promote and protect the use of *REALTOR*.
- To encourage the study of real estate.
- To render a better service through the promotion and management of listing systems.
- To promote better systems for the benefit of the membership.
- To establish and maintain funds for charitable or benevolent purposes.
- To make grants and donations from excess of receipts over disbursements.
- To hold interest in land and buildings.
- To promote the ownership of real property.
- To generally assist in the development of the local community.

Figure R.3   Board By-Laws

Board Formation and the Growth of MLS

New members of a real estate board are introduced to various rules, regulations, and by-laws that are unique to specific locales. However, individual boards basically conform in general makeup with other such organizations scattered across the country.

The first real estate board on record was established in 1880 in the United States. The first Canadian board appeared in Victoria in 1888. The Toronto Real Estate Board was formed in 1920, even before the creation of the Ontario Association of Real Estate Boards (now known as the Ontario Real Estate Association). However, Winnipeg receives the honour of being the longest continuously operating board in Canada from its inception in 1903. The Victoria board would have received this honour had it not faltered during the First World War and then re-established itself in 1919.

Currently, over 100 real estate boards operate across Canada. The need for shared information on properties in no small way contributed to the growth of real estate boards. However, at the same time, members realized the definite need for rules and regulations to govern the operation of the system and also ensure proper co-operation between brokers.

The first marketing systems called the CO-OP or PHOTO CO-OP appeared in Canada in 1951. From that beginning, the modern MLS system evolved. The MLS was a major factor in the growth of real estate boards during the 1950–1987 period. The first CO-OP sales statistics on record indicated that 31 real estate boards reported a total volume of $166 million. During the next three decades that figure grew to $17.1 billion in 1984. (PHOTO CO-OP changed to MLS in 1962.) Volume figures for selected years are provided:

1960	$445 million
1667	$1.2 billion
1970	$1.7 billion
1974	$4.6 billion
1980	$14.4 billion
1985	$23.8 billion
1990	$35.8 billion
1995	$37.9 billion
2000	$54.8 billion

The rapid rise in volume has brought the MLS system and real estate boards in general under closer scrutiny by both the government and the press. Further, real estate boards have not traditionally been concerned with membership drives. The popularity of the MLS service combined with generally active real estate markets has assured a steady influx of salespeople.

Classes of Membership

Real estate boards when enrolled with The Canadian Real Estate Association must maintain, as a minimum, the following classes of membership:

Licensed Member   Broker or salesperson member.

Institute Member   Specific provisions concerning persons holding the FRI designation.

Affiliate Member   Persons, firms, or corporations who are active in some related branch of real estate, but are not licensed.

Honorary Member   Granted for meritorious achievement.

Individual boards may use differing terminologies provided that the four major categories are included.

Governance Structure

The real estate board operates in similar fashion to most non-profit organizations in terms of overall governance. Figure R.4 depicts the connections between membership, staff, the board of directors, and operating committees. Significant variations can be found in real estate boards.

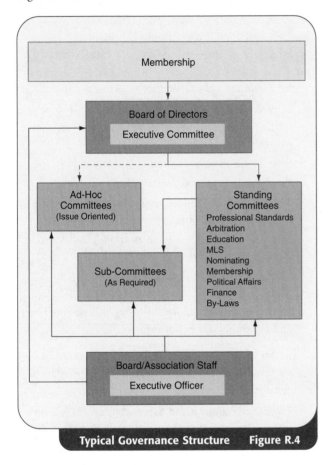

Typical Governance Structure   Figure R.4

Jurisdictional Area

The most common jurisdictional area referred to in relation to boards is the corporate jurisdiction. This is the geographic area shown in the by-laws of the board and specifically describes the geographic perimeters of the corporation. The second jurisdictional area involves the membership jurisdiction representing the area from which applications for membership with that board may be accepted. The membership jurisdiction is, at a minimum, the geographical jurisdiction.

MLS Rules and Regulations

Board by-laws require that members comply with the by-laws, MLS rules and regulations, and the Code of Ethics and Standards of Business Practice. In fact, all three are interwoven and cross referenced. The MLS rules and

regulations can be very detailed, depending upon the size and scope of board operations.

No standard set of by-laws exists for real estate boards. Practitioners will encounter many variations, but most typically include procedures relating to:

- General rules;
- Agency disclosure;
- Listing agreements;
- Advertising and appointments;
- Commissions and deposits;
- Open houses;
- Submission of offers;
- Reporting of sales; and
- Computer services.

In addition, real estate boards typically set out policies (approved by the board of directors as is the case with the rules and regulations), that provide detailed information on the operational aspects of the MLS system, e.g., instructions concerning the listing form, MLS data information sheets, sale and price information, and use of photographs.

MLS Service

Real estate boards enrolled with CREA are authorized to use certain certification marks relating to the operation of a real estate data base service, namely, MLS, Multiple Listing Service, and MLS logos.

Individual real estate boards must maintain by-laws and rules/regulations pertaining to the operation of the MLS service that give effect to a number of CREA requirements. Specifically, CREA sets out requirements for the operation of the real estate data base service, e.g., access to the listing service is normally limited to licensed real estate brokers and salespersons who are members; all listing contracts must be signed by the registered owner and submitted to the board; limited access to non-members (other than listing access); the general scope of listing information to be circulated; and notification of sales and other related information. Individual real estate boards may permit access to non-licensed affiliate members by way of specific contracts.

Organized Real Estate

Within the framework of organized real estate, real estate boards represent one dimension in a three-way relationship involving The Canadian Real Estate Association (CREA) and provincial associations. (All references to provincial associations are deemed to include territorial associations in the interest of readership.) To be a part of organized real estate, real estate boards must be enrolled with CREA.

R

Conditions of enrollment include:

- Only one board may operate within each defined jurisdiction.
- Provide names of all members and forward dues.
- Furnish membership list to CREA prior to March 31st of each year.
- Create and maintain membership categories as stipulated by CREA.
- Hold membership in the appropriate provincial or territorial association.
- Applicants for membership in board must agree to abide with by-laws, rules and regulations for board, provincial association, and CREA.
- Applicants are entitled to use CREA certification marks provided that terms and conditions are complied with.

Many real estate practitioners, as members of a local real estate board, fail to understand the true scope of their membership and the interplay between board activities and the rest of organized real estate. The three-way agreement sets out the relationship between the three levels of organizations.

The underlying benefit of this agreement is to ensure that individual membership in the board provides automatic membership to both a provincial association and CREA, and also that members derive certain benefits from this association, namely:

- All the benefits of CREA and provincial association membership are extended to boards;
- Symbols such as MLS and REALTOR can be used by members; and
- Membership in the board signifies membership in all three and members agree to pay appropriate fees.

Real Estate Boards, Provincial Associations, and CREA

The three-way relationship between real estate boards, provincial associations, and The Canadian Real Estate Association is generally described based on four roles involving MLS, Code of Ethics and Standards of Business Practice, Use of *REALTOR*, and Education/Special Services.

MLS

The MLS logo and Multiple Listing Service are owned by The Canadian Real Estate Association and through licence are provided to real estate boards for their use. The first real estate boards were real estate exchanges where individual members would gather on a specific day of the week to exchange information about properties offered and to trade real estate on behalf of principals.

The concept of sharing information is still continued today in many small boards where listings are reviewed on an appointed day of the week. The term *multiple listing* was in use in the United States at the turn of the 20th century. As previously referenced, the term *Co-operative Listing Service* was initially used in Canada. The *Co-op* began in 1950, with pictures added the following year. The *Photo Co-op* arrangement persisted until difficulties across provincial lines made it impractical to continue. As a result of certain legislative impasses, organized real estate moved toward the use of MLS.

The advantages of MLS are noteworthy:

- Buyers and sellers receive the benefit of wider exposure in the marketplace, as opposed to limited, individual broker promotion.
- Sellers gain greater marketing access.
- Buyers enjoy expanded market selection.
- The needs of both buyer and seller are more easily addressed through the larger marketing system.
- Procedures are subject to rules and regulations as established by the boards.
- Communities have a central source for inventory, trends, and general market information.
- Centralized information ensures that clients, members, and the public are better informed.

The Multiple Listing Service can be described as a system for the orderly co-ordination and dissemination of listing information to members. MLS operates as follows:

- The board regulates the day-to-day activities of the MLS service through rules and regulations that are incorporated by reference into the board by-law.
- The Canadian Real Estate Association oversees the use of the logo and protects its position as owner of the trademark.
- The provincial association promotes the effective use of the service in keeping with the Code of Ethics and Standards of Business Practice.

The function of the provincial association is perhaps the least precise of all three and, in fact, is a gradually evolving function. Provincial associations typically provide advice and clarification on issues and recommendations concerning MLS rules and regulations. This role involves the associations in a variety of situations that are difficult to accurately quantify. For example, a provincial association may become involved in various legal aspects of the rules and regulations imposed by boards within their local jurisdictions. Further, an association may offer assistance in the face of legislation affecting the MLS service from a provincial perspective and assist in establishing specific rules concerning co-operation between boards.

R

Code of Ethics and Standards of Business Practice

As a member of a local real estate board, real estate practitioners agree to abide by the *Code of Ethics and Standards of Business Practice* that are under the direct control of The Canadian Real Estate Association. Each board agrees to abide by these rules. In fact, the standards of business practice are the basis upon which actions of members are assessed, should ethical disputes arise in day-to-day activities.

These standards are also the focal point in hearings initiated under powers granted the professional standards committee. Further, the standards represent a basic reference point when rules and regulations are enacted at the local board level that impact the public and the membership at large.

Use of REALTOR

The term *REALTOR* and associated logos are controlled by The Canadian Real Estate Association. Traditionally, the term *REALTOR* within Canada referred to a level of service offered to the public. At the national convention held in October 1987, this description was amended. Now, the term *REALTOR* refers to a person who is a member of CREA and is consistent with procedures currently in place in the United States, as the logo now used in Canada conforms with its US counterpart.

Education/Special Services

Provincial associations provide voluntary educational programs to the membership at large. At the same time, some boards are also involved to varying degrees in offering such programs locally. In selected provinces, the provincial association may also be the nominee of the government (or the appropriate provincial regulatory body), in administering licensing education programs for both salespeople and brokers in the province.

Boards and associations may also be involved in specialized services including mandatory continuing education based on local needs and regulatory structure.

REAL ESTATE BROKER
(SEE BROKER (AGENT))

REAL ESTATE BROKERS ACT

Provincial   See applicable reference materials.

REAL ESTATE CYCLE
(SEE ALSO REAL ESTATE MARKET)

The real estate market generally moves through phases similar to general business cycles. However, real estate may demonstrate more pronounced peaks and valleys. Prosperity can occasionally linger in the marketplace, buoyed by fervently optimistic consumers and speculators. Conversely, recessions deepen unnecessarily as developers flood an overheated market with new structures, only to see consumer demand vanish before their completion. On a more optimistic note, real estate markets have traditionally tended to be on the leading edge of the recovery cycles as improved economic conditions emerge.

Application   Economists have long debated the existence of both long- and short-term cycles operating in the real estate market. However, to date, both defy the regularity and consistency necessary to permit accurate predictions. Many believe that the long cycle is driven by demographics (e.g., age composition, marriage patterns, population changes, and migration), transportation patterns, macro economic growth cycles, and long-term government policies. The shorter cycle appears affected predominately by interest rates, consumer confidence, and general economic conditions, particularly within the local area or region.

Some argue that the current, long-term cycle originated in the mid-forties with the appearance of baby boomers, post Second World War consumer confidence, substantial immigration to Canada, favourable government regulations, and an expanding easy money policy in both public and private lending institutions. The 1945–2000 period appears as an extended recovery/prosperity curve in a long-term cycle, following the disastrous impact of the depression years. Others dispute the long cycle theory but point to the sustained attractiveness of real estate holdings. Despite various fluctuations, the size and strength of real estate markets have moved in progressively upward trends.

Other industry observers contend that the real estate market has demonstrated consistent short cycles. The duration seems to be approximately every six to ten years. However, it is important to emphasize that the length and intensity of the prosperity, recession, and recovery stages may vary considerably by geographic locale. As with extended cycles, conflicting opinions must be noted. Some assert that the existence of short cycles is largely illusory and too simplistic to address economic complexities in the real world. These individuals insist that unique events in the marketplace (e.g., credit restrictions, short-term housing scarcity, government policies, and employment trends), randomly impact the housing market, thereby creating unusual, often erratic activity that defies accurate

R

cyclical prediction. Such movements may not be recession/recovery cycles but merely statistical evidence of the constant imbalance of supply and demand. Based on this explanation, economists may be force-fitting market blips into neatly packaged cycles where none really exist. Obviously, the entire topic is one of ongoing investigation. **Figure R.5** illustrates variances in a real estate cycle compared to a business cycle.

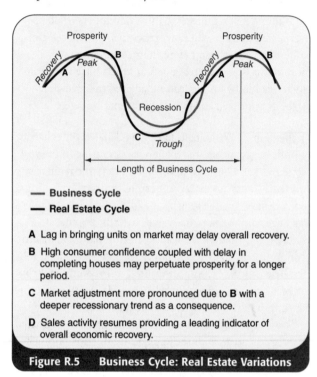

Prosperity

Prosperity

Recovery

Peak

B

A

Recovery

Peak

B

A

D

Recession

C

Trough

Length of Business Cycle

— **Business Cycle**

— **Real Estate Cycle**

A Lag in bringing units on market may delay overall recovery.

B High consumer confidence coupled with delay in completing houses may perpetuate prosperity for a longer period.

C Market adjustment more pronounced due to **B** with a deeper recessionary trend as a consequence.

D Sales activity resumes providing a leading indicator of overall economic recovery.

Figure R.5   Business Cycle: Real Estate Variations

REAL ESTATE INSTITUTE OF CANADA

Acronym: REIC   In 1955, the Canadian Association of Real Estate Boards formed the Canadian Institute of REALTORS to carry out its aims in the field of education. A three-year university course was prepared in co-operation with the University of Toronto. Successful students received a designation in real estate from the Institute.

In 1971, when CREA was organized, the Canadian Institute of REALTORS became a division of CREA. The name was subsequently changed to the Real Estate Institute of Canada. Terry Barber, FRI, AACI, of Winnipeg was the first governor of the new Institute. The primary purpose of REIC was to act as the educational arm of CREA and to co-ordinate education courses on a national basis.

From seminars, to intense professional education, to the leading professional designations, all of REIC's programs serve its mission: establishing, maintaining, promoting, and advancing professional standards of practice among those occupations concerned with real estate. REIC offers courses leading to the various designations including:

ARM	Accredited Residential Manager
CLO	Certified Leasing Officer
CLP	Certified in Land Planning & Development
CMR	Certified in the Marketing of Real Estate
CPM	Certified Property Manager
CRES	Certified Real Estate Specialist
CRF	Certified in Real Estate Finance
CRU	Certified Residential Underwriter
FRI	Fellow of the Real Estate Institute
FRI(A)	Appraisal Specialist
FRI(E)	Executive

All REIC members must fulfill ongoing professional development requirements.

Reference   The Real Estate Institute of Canada is located at 5407 Eglinton Avenue West, Suite 208, Etobicoke, ON M9C 5K6. REIC has chapters across Canada that administer education and member services.

For further information concerning designations offered, see under appropriate heading, e.g., **Fellow of the Real Estate Institute.**

REAL ESTATE INVESTMENT TRUST

Acronym: REIT   A form of trust ownership that combines capital from various investors in the acquisition or financing of various types of real estate. REITs, focused on property ownership, are referred to as *equity REITs*; those specializing in mortgage financing are called *mortgage REITs*. A REIT offering a combination of both is known as a *hybrid REIT*. Presently, most real estate investment trusts are equity REITs. Several sub-classifications also exist. For example, an equity REIT in Canada might specialize in acquiring shopping centres, office buildings, and warehouses, while another focuses on health facilities and residential apartments.

Application   REITs are playing an increasingly important role in real estate investment strategies. The REIT concept, while only recently introduced in Canada during 1993, has a much longer history dating back approximately 40 years in the United States. In fact, over three hundred REITs are publicly traded on US stock exchanges. In Canada, a much smaller number of REITs can be found; the majority of which are located on the Toronto Stock Exchange. The REIT concept was originally designed to provide small investors with the opportunity to invest in the ownership and financing of large real estate projects. REITs are

R

usually managed by appropriate professionals under the scrutiny of a board of directors.

Taxation guidelines are clearly set out for real estate investment trusts in the United States. However, the tax status of the REIT in Canada is not as clear due to the lack of specific REIT guidelines (as of the writing of this publication). Further, no standard accounting practices presently exist in the marketplace regarding the distribution of REIT income. The development of statutorily sanctioned REITs in Canada will undoubtedly appear as this investment vehicle grows in popularity. Anyone considering this type of investment vehicle should obtain expert advice.

REAL ESTATE MARKET

Characteristics

The real estate market is somewhat unique as it lacks various characteristics of the typical sales market. For example, no physical marketplace exists where sellers display goods and buyers come to shop. Other distinctive qualities are grouped under six main headings.

No Standard Product

No two houses are ever exactly the same. Even in new subdivisions where builders erect numerous houses with virtually the same plan, each property is ultimately adapted to the needs of the owner.

Although a number of homes may be physically different, they may be *exchangeable* in a monetary sense due to their utility. For example, six homes, all different in appearance, shape, and geographical site, may fall into the same price range because all are six-room bungalows in the same general area, roughly the same size in square footage, having three bedrooms, and built to the same set of building regulations. The usefulness of all six homes would be approximately the same, but subtle price variations arise due to age, upkeep, special features and amenities, and geographic location.

Local Real Estate Market

Interprovincial and international real estate transactions do occur. Nevertheless, the real estate market remains largely local in character because the commodity cannot be moved. Ownership may change hands outside the community, but it is generally what happens within the community that determines supply and demand and thus price or value. Consequently, real estate salespeople in one Canadian city are primarily concerned with, and must have knowledge of, market conditions in that community, as opposed to other locations across the country.

Fixed Location

Real estate is one commodity that cannot be taken to the consumer. The consumer must come to the property. The marketplace is the property site and negotiations may take place in an office, but the real sale is made at the location.

Market Not Standardized

Although the Multiple Listing Service, offered by various real estate boards, provides a degree of orderly process in marketing properties, any attempt at large-scale organization or a central control system for the real estate market beyond the local level faces significant challenges given the fixed location and lack of a standard commodity. Even though MLS listings may be viewed on the Internet, marketing still remains local in nature.

Slow Supply/Demand Adjustment

With an oversupply of most consumer goods, production can usually be slowed or halted quickly. Existing supply is typically used up and the market seeks balance between supply and demand. This is seldom true of real estate. When demand is high, numerous building projects are often commenced. If the market changes and demand drops, the projects are completed anyway, adding to the oversupply. Because of the durability of real estate, the supply remains. On the other hand, when a sudden surge in demand occurs, no quick solution is available given the time required to plan, finance, develop, and build.

Private Transactions

Generally, the purchase of real estate is a private transaction between buyer and seller, the results of which are not published for the public at large. Information regarding ownership is, however, available through documents registered at provincial land registry offices.

Function

A market of any kind usually functions to facilitate the exchange of goods and services. Under normal circumstances, a market is a centre of distribution, a pricing system, and a control centre of operations, e.g., locally, regionally, and nationally.

In a money economy, goods are exchanged for money and money for goods. The result of these exchanges is a redistribution of goods and money. In the real estate market, the process of exchange results in the production and allocation of properties according to the preferences of users in the marketplace and their financial capabilities. Thus, the real estate market functions to redistribute existing properties, cause an increase in the supply of new properties, determine the use of such properties, and establish the value of those properties.

Influencing Forces

The real estate market is sensitive to changes in the balance of economic, political, and social forces influencing the supply and demand for real estate. The following are among the most important influences.

Changes in Family Composition

The family is the primary housing consumer unit. For example, when a young man leaves his family to marry a girl from another family, their marriage sets up a third family. Normally the new couple establish an independent household and thereby absorb a unit of housing. This is known as the *family formation rate*.

Employment Conditions and Wage Levels

In periods of prosperity and increased employment, a strong demand for housing exists. For example, new home-owners enter the market by buying their first home and existing homeowners move up by acquiring a larger homes. The converse is also true. High unemployment over a period of time will adversely affect the real estate market, although employment insurance programs have cushioned, to some degree, the shock of layoffs. Also, pensions and other social security programs, coupled with an increase in life expectancy, have enabled seniors to continue as home-owners after retirement, although perhaps they may buy a smaller home or condominium.

Mortgage Volume

Loans are based on the lender's confidence in the borrower and the security that the borrower offers. Loans made on the security of real estate are no exception. Loans are only made when lenders feel that real estate is sound, will retain its value, and the borrower will earn sufficient sums to provide for repayment of the loan.

Mortgage Interest Rates

If interest rates are high, the real estate market is usually adversely affected as people tend to *stay put* in their exist-ing housing accommodations. As debt is frequently a major component in a house purchase, any significant interest increase directly impacts the market. If interest rates are low, then mortgages become more affordable and consum-ers react accordingly.

Building Activity

Substantial building activity may depress real estate values by introducing new supply in excess of demand. Unless the increase in supply is coupled with a corresponding increase in consumer demand, real estate prices can exper-ience a downward trend. Conversely, sudden increasing demand can place upward pressure given the time frame to build additional inventory.

Types

Seller's Market

In a seller's market, the number of buyers wanting homes exceeds the supply of homes. This type of market is char-acterized by homes that sell quickly, rising prices, many buyers looking for homes, and a minimal inventory of homes available for sale. These characteristics have impli-cations for the buyer, who has to make decisions quickly, must pay more, and frequently has conditional offers rejected.

Buyer's Market

In a buyer's market, the supply of homes on the market exceeds the demand for homes. Characteristics of this market include longer selling periods for homes on the market, fewer buyers compared to homes available, higher inventory of homes, and stabilized or declining prices. The implications for the buyers in this type of market are more favourable negotiating leverage, more homes from which to choose, and more time to search for a home.

Balanced Market

In a balanced market, the number of homes on the market equals the demand. The characteristics of this market include houses selling within a reasonable period of time, demand equalling supply, sellers accepting reasonable offers, and prices generally stabilized. The atmosphere is usually more relaxed.

REAL ESTATE OPTION
(SEE OPTION TO BUY/PURCHASE)

Provincial   See applicable reference materials.

REAL ESTATE SALESPERSON

Provincial   See applicable reference materials.

REAL ESTATE TRUST ACCOUNT

Provincial   See applicable reference materials.

REAL PROPERTY
(SEE ALSO PERSONAL PROPERTY AND REAL ESTATE)

The combination of the tangible and intangible attributes of land and improvements.

REAL PROPERTY ADMINISTRATOR

Acronym: RPA   The RPA designation is awarded by the Building Owners and Managers Institute of Canada (BOMI). The institute is affiliated with the Building Owners and Managers Association (BOMA). The RPA designation is designed for property managers. Other designations awarded are: FMA–Facilities Management Administrator, SMT–Systems Maintenance Technician and SMA–Systems Maintenance Administrator.

The requirements to complete the RPA include:

- Completion of the RPA curriculum including five required courses plus the *Ethics is a Good Business* seminar, and two other courses from five electives;
- Having a minimum of three years verifiable experience as a property manager. The experience must be gained in 15 of 24 categories set out by the Institute and must be performed on a portfolio or building of 40,000 square feet or larger; and
- Abiding by the *Code of Professional Ethics and Conduct*.

Reference   The Building Owners and Managers Institute of Canada can be contacted at Suite 106, 885 Don Mills Road, Don Mills, Ontario M3C 1V9.

The above information was summarized from detailed materials provided by the Institute with no representation concerning its accuracy or completeness. Contact BOMI for current requirements.

REAL PROPERTY REPORT (SURVEY)

Provincial   See applicable reference materials.

REALTOR

The term *REALTOR* refers to real estate professionals in Canada who are members of The Canadian Real Estate Association (CREA) and to members of the National Association of REALTORS (NAR) in the United States. Members subscribe to a high standard of professional service and to a strict code of ethics. Members in Canada are licensed by CREA to use the REALTOR marks in connection with or in reference to themselves and their real estate businesses.

CREA is responsible for maintaining authorized and proper use of the trademarks REALTOR, REALTORS, and the REALTOR logo in Canada. CREA has an agreement referred to as the *Trademark License and International Affiliate Agreement* with NAR (being renegotiated at time of printing) concerning the REALTOR trademarks.

Application   Only individuals who are members of CREA by virtue of holding membership in a member board or association, are licensed to use one or more of the REALTOR marks in connection with or in reference to themselves as individuals and for their real estate business, but not as part of their corporate name or business name. The marks may be used by brokers or salespeople as marks that identify membership in CREA and not as synonyms for broker or salesperson or any other real estate professional calling.

The criteria for membership in a local board are determined by that board. A member board may not confer membership that entails use of the REALTOR marks on individuals engaged in activities not currently recognized in the definition of real estate business as set out in the CREA publication titled *Real Estate Trademarks Manual.*

An individual's licence to use the REALTOR marks terminates automatically in the event such individual ceases to be a member in good standing of a member board, for failure to pay dues, or any other reason, or in the event such individual ceases for any reason to be a member in good standing of The Canadian Real Estate Association. A non-member is never authorized to use the REALTOR term or logo in connection with his/her name or business.

What the term *REALTOR* does not identify is the occupation of its user. In fact, REALTORS may be engaged in many occupations that form part of the real estate business, e.g., real estate brokerage, property management, mortgage financing, appraising, real estate counselling, real estate syndication, land development, and building.

Trademarks are nothing more than unique terms, symbols, or combinations of terms and/or symbols that communicate some specific message to the public. Over time, marks become associated with standards of quality or care and the public looks upon such marks as guarantees of repeated quality of care.

Trademarks not properly protected are soon lost. Preservation of trademarks requires that they be used only in their trademark sense, that they be distinguished from words of ordinary use by the use of capital letters, and that the rules governing use of the marks be adhered to in accordance with certain standards of services or qualifications of their user.

Selected Rules–REALTOR Logo

The Canadian Real Estate Association has established various rules regarding REALTOR:

- The REALTOR logo consists of a futura typeface R on a sharply contrasting background to form a block R, under which is centred the term *REALTOR*. This typeface was chosen for its clear, clean graphic character and should not be replaced by any other typestyle.

- Guidelines and policies dealing with such issues as spacing, size, colour contrast, and positioning of the REALTOR logo are designed to ensure that, through uniform and consistent use, the public will continue to recognize the REALTOR logo as a distinctive trademark and not simply some decorative symbol.

- The colour identity between the term *REALTOR* and the rectangle must be observed, as must the colour identity between the R and the understock paper. To ensure proper use, the following three rules must be adhered to:

  - Any two colour combinations may be used but the colours must be sharply contrasting.

  - The block surrounding the R and the REALTOR term must be the same colour; i.e., if the block surrounding the R is black, then the REALTOR term must also be black.

  - The R and the paper colour around the logo must be the same. For example, it is not proper to print a red R on a white paper background. Similarly, if grey paper is used, then the R must also be grey.

- Use of decorative script typefaces of copy adjacent to the REALTOR logo should be avoided because it tends to detract from the distinctive design features of the logo. In particular, futura typeface, which is used for the stylized R in the logo, should never be used in adjacent copy.

- The REALTOR term should never be used to create a new term or phrase such as *REALTORific*. Modification of the term, in any manner, tends to weaken the distinctiveness of the mark and undermine its identifying functions.

- The REALTOR logo should never be superimposed over any graphic pattern or design, as such use detracts from the distinctive design of the mark.

- Do not use the term *REALTOR* to mean real estate broker, agent, or salesperson as in *Anycity's leading REALTOR*. The term is used only to identify members of CREA.

- The block R of the logo should never be used as part of a brokerage or individual name, or as the first letter of any words beginning with R, particularly words like *Real Estate*, *Realty*, or the term *REALTOR*.

- Never replace the term *REALTOR* with another identifier, such as *Realty* or *Real Estate*. The logo consists of three major elements: the block, the stylized R, and the identifying term REALTOR. All three must be present.

- It is improper use of the trademark to refer to an individual or brokerage that is not a member of CREA as a *non-REALTOR*.

- Do not use the word REALTOR in connection with the name of a firm. It is not permissible for a member to incorporate under a name that includes the term *REALTOR* or to register or use a name that includes the term. If the term is used in connection with a member firm's name, then punctuation must be used to separate the term from the business name such as *ABC Ltd., REALTORS. ABC REALTORS Ltd.* is not permissible.

- Regardless of local dialect and custom, the trademark REALTOR has only one pronunciation: REAL'TOR and not REAL-A-TOR.

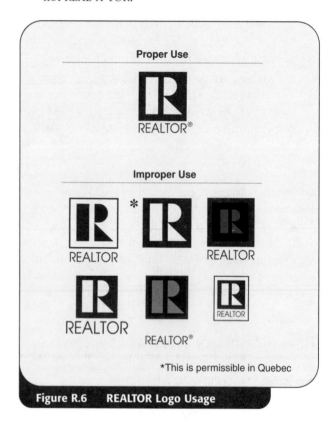

Figure R.6   REALTOR Logo Usage

Selected information has been cited directly from the *Real Estate Trademarks Manual* of The Canadian Real Estate Association to ensure descriptive consistency.

REALTY WATCH

A roving crime watch system, similar to *Neighbourhood Watch*, first introduced in Canada by the Vancouver Island Real Estate Board, and now implemented as a community service project by many real estate boards across Canada. Real estate practitioners are in the unique position to observe crime about to happen or already in progress. The real estate profession requires travel through residential and commercial areas, giving board members the opportunity to assist the police.

Realty Watch is a co-operative effort between police and the real estate industry to stop crime before it happens, a pro-active instead of a re-active method of policing that enhances *Neighbourhood Watch* and *Block Parent* programs.

Most property crimes are committed during the weekday daylight hours between 10:00 a.m. and 3:00 p.m., a time when many homeowners are at work or shopping. This is the same time when real estate practitioners are travelling the community streets, showing potential buyers various neighbourhoods, holding open houses, and attending open houses.

The objectives of the Realty Watch program are as follows:

- Reporting, by real estate board members, of criminal or suspicious incidents.
- Promoting crime prevention.
- Promoting the crime prevention unit of the local police force and enhancing the efforts of other crime prevention organizations such as *Neighbourhood Watch* and *Block Parents*.
- Enhancing the image of the real estate industry in the community.

Application   The Realty Watch program, as it relates to real estate practitioners, works as follows:

- Local crime prevention police officers conduct Crime Awareness Training Sessions in either members' offices or at the board office. During a session, a participant learns how to detect suspicious activity; how to spot and describe a potential criminal; how to report a (suspected) crime; and what NOT to do when witnessing a crime.
- Trained real estate practitioners watch and listen for suspicious activity wherever they go.
- Once spotted, suspicious activity is reported to the local police for investigation.

Practitioners use the following reporting procedure when a crime is suspected:

- Call the police;
- Identify himself/herself as a member of Realty Watch;
- Give name and address;
- Describe what happened, where, and when;
- Describe any injuries;
- Describe suspect vehicle(s) and direction of travel;
- Describe suspect person and direction of travel; and
- Remain in contact with the police dispatcher.

At no time whatsoever is a Realty Watch participant to become physically involved. The job is to report a suspected crime and the police will take over from that point.

Reference   Various real estate boards across Canada have implemented the Realty Watch program. Contact the local board for additional details.

RECAPTURE
(SEE ALSO CAPITAL COST ALLOWANCE)

The excess of value over depreciated value allowed by the Canada Customs and Revenue Agency in relation to the sale of a capital asset.

Application   The *Income Tax Act* permits a deduction of part of the capital cost against the income of the business. The sale or other disposition of capital assets for value exceeding the depreciated value of such capital assets will usually represent a recapture that must be declared as income during the year of the sale.

Example   *Recapture*

Broker/Owner Johnson, of ABC Realty Inc., purchased a car for business purposes through the brokerage. After three years, the depreciated value of the automobile was $16,575 on the corporation books. However, its fair market value was estimated to be $20,000. Johnson was able to sell the car privately for $19,750. Therefore, in the disposition of this capital asset, the sale exceeded depreciated value by $3,175, which amount represents recapture and must be claimed as income.

RECONCILIATION
(SEE ALSO APPRAISAL)

The process by which the appraiser evaluates and selects from two or more alternative conclusions or indications, to reach a single-value estimate. It is important, during reconciliation, to review and check all calculations and the reliability and relevance of the data, analysis, and conclusions used to reach the required estimate.

Reconciliation is required in a variety of situations throughout the appraisal process, for example, the reconciliation of capitalization rates obtained from the market or the reconciliation of comparables in the direct comparison approach. The final reconciliation represents the seventh step in the appraisal process. See **Appraisal** for details regarding all eight steps in the process.

The following is a hypothetical final estimate of value for a single-family residential property. Two value estimates were derived from the appraiser's research and subsequently reconciled to the final estimate of value.

Example **Final Reconciliation (Excerpt from Appraisal Report)**

Value indicated by Cost Approach	$185,000
Value indicated by Direct Comparison Approach	$180,000

The cost approach required three separate value estimates (i.e. site value, current building and site improvement costs, and depreciation), and as a result required a significant number of adjustments. In addition, estimating the current reproduction costs and accrued depreciation of a 25-year old building, such as the subject, was found difficult to measure and support. Apart from these difficulties, a typical buyer would likely find it hard to think of a 25-year old building in terms of reproduction cost new less accrued depreciation. As a result, less weight has been given to this approach, although its use tends to support the value indicated by the direct comparison approach.

The direct comparison approach was found to reflect market behaviour, and is most widely used and understood by a typical buyer for the subject property. Furthermore, this approach required far fewer adjustments with the comparables being relatively recent sales. In addition, the quality of the data left no doubts as to its reliability. Accordingly, bearing in mind the purpose of this appraisal and the type of value required, most weight was given to this approach.

Final Estimate of Value

Therefore, the market value of the subject property as of (the effective date of appraisal), is estimated to be:

ONE HUNDRED AND EIGHTY THOUSAND DOLLARS

$180,000.00

ADVANTAGES	DISADVANTAGES
The Cost Approach	
• People understand it. • Often the only method to use in the appraisal of special-purpose properties. • Relatively easy to make a cost calculation.	• Difficult to estimate depreciation, particularly in older buildings. • While the cost of construction appears relatively easy to estimate, no exact cost figure can be given as several methods yield varying costs. • Construction costs are constantly changing.
The Income Approach	
• Applicable in estimating the value of investment properties by means of cash flow analysis.	• Difficulty in selecting an appropriate capitalization for direct capitalization (or a discount rate in the case of yield capitalization). • Estimating income and operating expenses can some times prove difficult, and a slight error in either estimate is magnified on capitalization. • Of limited use in the appraisal of owner-occupied and/or special-purpose properties.
The Direct Comparison Approach	
• Consumers generally understand and use it. • Avoids various problems associated with estimating and forecasting, e.g., building costs, depreciation, revenues, expenses, and cash flows. • Generally accepted by courts and the general public.	• Sometimes difficult to obtain good comparable sales. • Making adjustments for differences in properties requires careful judgement and experience. In some instances, such adjustments are often difficult to support and explain satisfactorily. • Difficult to obtain relevant information relating to each sale, particularly with reference to seller or buyer motivation. • The data is historical in nature.

Figure R.7   Approaches to Value: Advantages/Disadvantages

R

Application   Reconciliation requires careful analysis and judgement and the appraiser should not substitute this for a mathematical or mechanical process such as averaging or calculating the median. Generally, two approaches to value are used in an appraisal. In the majority of cases, each approach will result in a slightly different value estimate of the subject. The object of the final reconciliation is to arrive at a single point of value that is defensible and convincing.

In considering which of the approaches to value should be given the most weight, the final reconciliation process will include identifying the strengths and weaknesses of each approach.

Figure R.7 illustrates the advantages and disadvantages of the three common approaches to value. Direct comparison is the most widely used approach.

RECONCILIATION (TRUST ACCOUNT)

Provincial   See applicable reference materials.

RECONSTRUCTED OPERATING STATEMENT

Function

Appraisal

The reconstructed operating statement is most commonly associated with appraisers. This statement, typically representing a one-year analysis of income and expenses, is derived from an owner's statement for an investment property with adjustments to properly reflect typical revenues and expenses. Adjustments are made based on research involving comparable properties. The reconstructed operating statement can also provide the basis of extended cash flow forecasts typically for a five-year to ten-year period. One-year reconstructed statements lead to estimates of value based on direct capitalization. Longer cash flow forecasts are applied when estimating value by means of yield capitalization.

The reconstructed operating statement consists of two primary sections: income and expenses. The appraiser must reconstruct actual operating statements by first adjusting income to reflect market rental rates (subject to vacancy and collection losses), and then reconstruct expenses in relation to reasonable ranges found in the marketplace. This activity will include stabilizing certain fluctuating expense items, properly amortizing selected costs, and making adjustments for other items based on prevailing ranges within comparable properties.

Real Estate Investment Analysis

Practitioners involved with industrial, commercial, and investment properties are frequently involved in both real estate valuation and real estate investment analysis. As with appraisals, both one-year reconstructed statements and longer term cash flow forecasts are analyzed. However, the distinct needs of salespeople in servicing the interests of investment clients has led to modified applications.

Over the past few decades, custom worksheets have evolved within real estate brokerages for the reconstruction of operating statements as well as the forecasting of future cash flows. Terminologies and formats vary from those used by appraisers. Further, practitioners may approach the analysis differently depending on circumstances. For example, he/she may wish to reconstruct statements (as an appraiser would), leading to an estimate of market value, or take into consideration the unique goals of specific investors, forecast cash flows in relation to such needs and investment objectives, and analyze the result from before and/or after tax positions. To arrive at detailed forecasts, cash flows are analyzed in terms of two components: operations and sale proceeds cash flows.

Practitioners frequently work with three worksheets. The first generally resembles the appraiser's reconstructed operating statement, but can perform three functions including reconstructing, forecasting, and/or analyzing actual financial performance. The remaining two are designed to analyze sequential cash flows on either a before tax or after tax basis over a forecasted holding period leading to detailed investment analysis and value estimates.

Property Analysis Worksheet   One-year analysis of revenue and expenses based on actual statements, reconstructed amounts, or forecasted amounts. When used as a reconstructed statement, this worksheet is often simply referred to as a *reconstructed worksheet.*

Operations Cash Flow Worksheet   Multiple-year forecast of before or after tax cash flows using either reconstructed amounts for a typical building, or forecasted amounts specific to an individual investor.

Sale Proceeds Cash Flow Worksheet   Analysis of sale proceeds, either before tax or after tax, at the end of the forecasted period.

Reference   The use of reconstructed statements by real estate practitioners is a complex topic given the diversity of needs in serving investment clients. For additional information, see **Cash Flow, Cash Flow Model, Investment Analysis,** and **Property Analysis Worksheet.**

OWNER'S THREE-YEAR OPERATING STATEMENT

	3 yrs ago	2 yrs ago	1 yr ago	Ref.
REVENUE				
Rent Collections	$372,761	$379,964	$385,630	1
Parking/Laundry Income	33,975	35,375	35,450	2
Total Revenue	406,736	415,339	421,080	4
EXPENSES				
Realty Taxes	50,940	52,375	53,642	5
Superintendent—salary, etc.	9,500	10,500	11,500	6
Janitor—salary, etc.	4,800	5,280	5,808	7
Water	8,450	8,720	8,950	8
Electricity	974	1,135	1,217	9
Fuel	3,700	5,150	7,200	10
Insurance	2,000	2,000	2,000	11
Maintenance and repairs	5,800	6,800	4,000	12
Painting and decorating	16,400	10,500	18,400	13
Supplies	850	1,020	1,224	14
Legal and Audit	1,000	1,650	1,250	15
Elevator Maintenance	1,200	1,200	1,200	16
Depreciation	42,000	57,000	54,150	17
Mortgage Payments	206,750	206,750	206,750	18
Total Expenses	358,364	368,080	375,291	
NET INCOME	$48,372	$47,259	$45,789	

APPRAISER'S RECONSTRUCTED STATEMENT

		Ref.
POTENTIAL GROSS INCOME		
Rent Collections:		
18 1-bedroom units x $300/month x 12	$ 64,800	
78 2-bedroom units x $375/month x 12	351,000	
	415,800	1
ADDITIONAL INCOME		
Parking—96 spaces x $20 x 12	23,040	
Laundry—96 x $10 x 12	11,520	
	34,560	2
Total Gross Income Potential	450,360	
Less Vacancy and Credit Losses (5%)	−22,518	3
Effective Gross Income	427,842	4
OPERATING EXPENSES		
Realty taxes	$ 54,100	5
Superintendent	17,000	6
Janitor	9,989	7
Water	9,216	8
Electricity	1,320	9
Fuel	9,000	10
Insurance	2,700	11
Maintenance & repairs	4,000	12
Painting & decorating	18,000	13
Supplies	1,469	14
Legal and audit	1,300	15
Elevator maintenance	1,500	16
Management (3%)	12,835	19
Total Operating Expenses	142,429	
NET ANNUAL OPERATING INCOME	$285,413	

EXPLANATION

1. The potential annual gross income from rental collections is based on the market rent for each apartment with all suites fully rented. This amount would include the rental income collected for the suites presently occupied as well as those suites provided rent free for the superintendent and janitor.

2. In addition to normal rent, each tenant must pay $20 per month for parking and $10 per month for laundry facilities.

3. A vacancy allowance of 5% of both rental and ancillary income is based on current competitive conditions as indicated by a survey of comparable properties in the area.

4. The effective gross income represents the total potential gross income less an allowance for vacancy and bad debts.

5. The current year's taxes as shown in the reconstructed operating statement were derived by multiplying the present assessment by this year's tax rate.

6. The superintendent's salary was adjusted upwards from last year's at the same rate of increase as previous years. Allowance of the free two-bedroom suite is also added.

7. The janitor's salary was adjusted upwards at the same rate as previous years. The allowance of a free one-bedroom suite occupied by the janitor was also added.

8. Water costs based on present consumption worked out to an average of $8.00 per suite per month. This checked out very closely to published figures for water consumption costs in this general area.

9. Electricity expenses pertain only to the public areas and to the equipment. The average current cost is estimated at $110 per month. Tenants are responsible for their own consumption, individually metered to each suite.

Figure R.8a   Owner's and Appraiser's Statements

R

EXPLANATION (Continued)

10. Fuel costs have been rising rapidly over the last three years. The estimate for the current year is based on the average consumption for the last three years at a rate quoted by the gas company for this year's heating season.

11. The annual insurance premium has now increased from $2,000 to a new rate for the current year of $2,700.

12. As a result of the property rehabilitation program undertaken almost two years ago, it is expected that expenses for maintenance and repairs will remain the same as last year's expense for at least the next two or three years.

13. The current year's painting and decorating expense is based on the cost of $500 per suite once every three years, and a total cost of $10,000 to paint the public areas and exterior trim once every five years.

14. Expenses for supplies have been increasing steadily by 20% per year. The current year's expenses are projected on this basis.

15. Legal and audit expenses for the current year are an average of the last three years.

16. Elevator maintenance expenses are based on a new three-year contract for $1,500 per year.

17. Depreciation is not a deductible expense for the purpose of deriving net operating income for appraisal purposes.

18. Mortgage payments of principal and/or interest are not a deductible expense in arriving at net operating income.

19. No management costs were reported in the owner's statements. The typical management cost for this type of property and operation in this area is 3% of the effective gross income.

Owner's and Appraiser's Statements (Continued)   Figure R.8b

Detailed Analysis

A step-by-step example of an appraiser's reconstructed operating statement is illustrated in **Figure R.8** including:

- The owner's three-year operating statement;
- The appraiser's reconstructed statement; and
- An explanation of each adjustment in the reconstructed statement.

Estimating Operating Expenses

The process of estimating operating expenses within a reconstructed operating statement can be complex, particularly in the case of larger, multi-residential properties and commercial enterprises.

In establishing an estimate of total expenses, the appraiser must:

- Include only the expenses that are necessary to maintain the flow of rental income estimated as of the date of appraisal;
- Base the nature and level of expenses on typical management and should be consistent with market expenses; and
- Stabilize or smooth out expenses on an annual basis, since some expenses are concentrated in a particular year and not in others. For example, if a building is painted every five years at a cost of $10,000, then the expenses for painting should be shown as $2,000 per year. If this is not done, a buyer/investor might be lulled into paying more for the property during a year when the painting expense was not shown.

The appraiser will reconstruct the operating expenses to fairly reflect reasonable expenses for the subject property based on:

- The prior operating experience of the subject property over the past three or more years;
- Market data available on comparable properties; and
- Published studies or reports concerning expenses of comparable properties.

In reconstructing the operating statement, appraisers will exclude certain items that might otherwise be included when preparing an operating statement for income tax purposes. The appraiser focuses on those expenses that directly relate to the property and not the owner. Excluded items usually include business tax, depreciation or capital cost allowance, interest on mortgage or loan, and capital improvements.

The only time the appraiser may be justified in including a reserve for replacement of such short-life components in the operating expense statement is when the market indicates that this is normal practice adopted by property owners in the area and when the overall capitalization rate used by the appraiser in capitalizing the resulting net income has been extracted from comparable properties treated in the same way; i.e., provision was also made for reserves for replacement in arriving at their net operating income.

As a further description, an example is provided in which various operating expenses are detailed as well as items that would not be included, e.g., business tax and interest on a mortgage.

R

Example   Reconstructed Operating Statement—Estimating Operating Expenses

Anne Appraiser is analyzing the operating statements of a rental property and is attempting to reconstruct the statement. As a preliminary step, she has isolated selected expense categories for in-depth analysis in the reconstruction process.

Taxes   The annual realty taxes are calculated by multiplying the total assessed value of the property, land, and buildings, by the current tax rate. Local improvement charges would be included in the operating statement.

Insurance   Insurance normally includes fire and extended coverage, landlord's liability, boiler coverage, and plate glass insurance. Only premiums relating to the functioning of the property should be included, not the cost of the owner's business insurance.

Management   The fee is usually calculated as a percentage of the effective gross income. A charge must be inserted in the statement if the owner is the manager and has not charged a fee.

Utilities   Usually includes heating, electricity, gas, and water if paid by the owner.

Superintendent/Janitor   If a free suite is provided, then market rent must be included in gross income and then deducted as an operating expense. Wages are included along with employer's portion of CPP and EI.

Supplies   Annual amount sufficient to pay for consumable supplies such as light bulbs and cleaning items.

Repairs/Maintenance   Those repairs that are consistent with typically competent management; e.g., exterior/interior painting, caulking, and repairs to mechanical and electrical systems.

Site Maintenance   Expenses usual to exterior maintenance such as gardening and snow removal.

Professional Fees   Legal, accounting, and leasing services.

Certain expenses appearing in an owner's statement would be excluded:

Business Tax   This tax applies to the business and not the real property.

Depreciation or Capital Cost Allowance   Depreciation is omitted in a reconstructed statement, but normally appears in an owner's statement. The capitalization rate chosen to determine value by direct capitalization (one of two methods under the income approach), allows for the recapture of capital invested. Consequently, if depreciation were included, it would amount to a double entry.

Interest on Mortgage   Not a direct cost of calculating net operating income.

Capital Improvements   These expenditures, which enhance the property's value, are really designed to increase its income potential. Consequently, they are not operating expenses necessary to maintain the potential gross income. If items such as alterations, mechanical equipment, and chattels, cannot be legitimately charged as expenses for repairs or maintenance, then the full amount of these capital cost expenditures must be added to the remaining capital cost of the structure, and not included as an operating expense.

RECORD OF EMPLOYMENT

Acronym: ROE   A form each employer must complete for every employee who stops working in insurable employment. Generally, an ROE must be issued within five calendar days, subject to selected exceptions, after the later of the interruption of earnings itself or the date the employer becomes aware of the interruption, in accordance with information published by Human Resources Development Canada.

Employment information contained on the ROE is used to decide if a person qualifies for employment insurance benefits, the benefit rate, and length of eligibility.

Application   Human Resources Development Canada provides an excellent employer guide titled *Employment Insurance–The New Employment Insurance System and Employers*. The Guide offers general information and step-by-step instructions for completion of the ROE and contains five parts:

- The record of employment (general description);
- How to complete the record of employment;
- Instructions for special groups of workers;
- Information on insurability; and
- General information on record of employment related investigation programs.

The guide, along with blank copies of the Record of Employment, can be obtained from a local Canada Employment Centre.

RECORDS (REAL ESTATE BROKERAGE)

Procedures concerning the maintenance and organization of general office records in real estate brokerages vary across Canada. Provincial regulatory bodies are understandably focused on the handling of trust funds and related consumer protection issues. More specifically, legislation is directed to procedures concerning financial records, e.g., trust account(s), general account(s), basic financial records, and trade records. However, certain requirements may be outlined in regard to general office records, e.g., listings, correspondence, and overall organization of filing systems.

Application　　Records of a real estate brokerage understandably revolve around real estate transactions. Most brokerages establish a co-ordinated system, either manual or automated, that involves integrated cross-referencing between listings and sales. This method of record keeping is complemented by quality control and performance tracking mechanisms. Advanced computer systems normally address both financial and general office records through integrated modules that typically include front office operations, accounting records, form preparation, general management reports, and add-on packages specifically designed for salesperson activities.

Provincial　　See applicable reference materials.

RECORDS (TITLE)

Provincial　　See applicable reference materials.

RECOVERABLE EXPENSES

Function and Purpose

Real estate brokerages have a wide range of compensation packages and consequent variations concerning salesperson participation in expenses. In some instances, the brokerage pays selected expenses on behalf of the salesperson and then recovers these amounts through separate billings. The brokerage will track total expenses by category, recovered amounts, and any net or residual amounts, within the financial reporting system.

Application　　When using recovery accounts, expense categories are divided into two major columns. The first column contains total expenses and recovered expenses, while the second column provides cumulative figures for each account, showing the net expense to the brokerage.

The recovery account system has proven attractive to brokers, given its accuracy in tracking gross expense, recoverable dollars, and net brokerage expenditures on various items. Further, this arrangement provides a mean-

ingful grouping by expense category within the profit and loss statement. Otherwise, monies collected from salespeople would be lumped together and recorded as other income with no adjustment made to appropriate expense categories. This approach would produce a very distorted picture of revenue.

Categories

While most operating expense categories are generally viewed as *recoverable*, some are determined by exact usage (e.g., long distance telephone calls, classified advertisements), while others are pro-rated (e.g., portion of applicable insurance and meeting costs).

Further, the allocation of common and recoverable expenses will vary from one brokerage to another based on specific contractual arrangements with salespeople.

In theory, brokerage recoverable accounts would be at 0 if all funds expended are retrieved from the salespeople. Recovery accounts are usually set up to show:

(a) Total paid by Brokerage
(b) Total Recovered from Salespeople
(c) Net Paid by Brokerage (if any).

A residual amount in (c) could be recovered by a desk fee, retrieved through a general levy or treated as a brokerage expense offset by brokerage revenues.

Example　　*Recoverable Expenses—Categories*		
Selected expense categories are illustrated.		
Newspaper—Classified	$7,239.49	
Newspaper—Classified (Recovered)	−5,329.92	
Net Newspaper—Classified		$1,909.57
Sign Installations	$659.50	
Sign Installations (Recovered)	−175.50	
Net Sign Installations		$484.00
Telephone—Long Distance	$739.45	
Telephone—Long Distance (Recovered)	−321.00	
Net Telephone—Long Distance		$418.45

Shadow Expense Accounts

The shadow expense account system provides a device to track non-recovered expenses incurred by the brokerage. The chart of accounts separates expenses in terms of general ledger accounts, e.g., classified advertising, institutional advertising, and signage. Recovery accounts more clearly delineate expenses for any particular category, as well as showing the amount recovered from the salesperson along with the resulting net owed by the brokerage.

R

The shadow expense concept is used by brokerages to to track and allocate expenses to individual salespeople even though no attempt is made to collect these amounts. The system can more accurately portray salesperson activity in relation to costs of having that person working for the brokerage. The term *shadow* refers to the fact that the tracking of these items shadows and is separate from the formal bookkeeping system within the brokerage. However, it is possible to merge this information when reviewing individual salesperson production in relation to that individual's costs.

**Example   Recoverable Expenses–
Shadow Expense Accounts**

Branch Manager Gallo sets up a detailed chart of accounts including recovery accounts for a branch office. Following is an example using three operating expense categories (totals for all salespeople):

Advertising/Classified	$4,421.00	
Advertising/Classified (Recovered)	–3,627.45	
Net Advertising/Classified		$793.55
Photocopier		$148.00
Board Fees	$1,728.00	
Board Fees (Recovered)	–1,470.00	
Net Board Fees		$258.00

The manager, in developing these accounts can precisely track both *Advertising/Classified* and *Board Fees*, but not individual usage associated with the photocopier. While it is possible to introduce a card access system for the copier and precisely charge for copies, the manager wants to track this type of expense outside of the bookkeeping system, but not charge the salespeople. In other words, she wants a *shadow system* that is not part of the formal bookkeeping system. In theory, any number of office expenses can be allocated as either recoverable or shadow items. The salesperson's account can be simple or complex at the discretion of the brokerage.

Salesperson Lee, according to photocopy records, used 346 copies during the month of May. His statement of account will not reflect the shadow expense of (346 x .10) $34.60. However, the manager's version will show the full statement reflecting both recoverable items and the photocopy allocation.

Once shadow expense accounts are developed, an additional subsection is required in a detailed statement of account. In **Figure R.9** Salesperson Lee would receive a statement showing Section A (monthly invoice). The manager would receive Sections A (recovered amounts), Section B (commission income retained by the brokerage generated by the salesperson), and Section C (costs attributed to, but not recovered from the salesperson).

Variations are often found in the marketplace based on specific commission plans and unique requirements within brokerage offices. For example, in a desk fee

operation, the desk fee payable would also be included in Section B to fairly reflect salesperson contribution to the overall brokerage operation.

Figure R.9 illustrates a detailed salesperson account along with explanatory notes regarding the statement of account, salesperson income, and shadow expenses.

RECREATIONAL PROPERTY LISTING

Provincial   See applicable reference materials.

RECREATIONAL SALES
(SEE RURAL, RECREATIONAL, AND AGRICULTURAL SALES)

REDEMPTION
(SEE EQUITY OF REDEMPTION)

REFERENCE PLAN

A term used in relation to the registry system of land registration. A reference plan is a plan of survey meeting requirements as set out in applicable provincial legislation relating to surveys. Reference plans provide a graphic illustration of otherwise complex metes and bounds descriptions.

Provincial   See applicable reference materials.

REFERENCE REGISTER

A card index system for brokerages to cross-reference pending, completed, or cancelled sales. The reference register is helpful in retrieving sale information, as brokerages may file transactions by trade number. Procedures will vary based on brokerage office and any applicable provincial requirements associated with record keeping.

Application   Reference card systems were historically popular for front desk administration purposes, directing of calls, and quick access to listing/sale information, but have been largely replaced by electronic versions in brokerage offices. The card index system normally includes the property address, seller name, listing number (and MLS number, if applicable), name of listing salesperson, trade number and details of disposition. The reference register is now typically one component within an integrated computer software program that typically tracks all brokerage records.

DETAILED SALESPERSON STATEMENT

Salesperson: Salesperson Lee
Code: 0001   Month: May, 20xx

Section A: Statement of Account

DATE	PARTICULARS	DR	CR	BAL
May 5	Advertising	100.00		100.00
May 9	MLS Listing Fees	45.00		145.00
May 12	Board Fees	50.00		195.00
May 13	Advertising	50.93		245.93
May 30	Rec'd from Lee		200.93	45.00
May 31	Service Charge	20.00		65.00

Section B: Salesperson Income

May 31	Commission Income for May (Brokerage portion only)	$2,953.00

Section C: Shadow Expenses

May 14	Membership Dues	$250.00
May 19	Telephone	150.00
May 31	Occupancy	650.00
May 31	Signs	75.00
May 31	Photocopier	34.60
Total Shadow Expenses		$1,159.60

EXPLANATORY NOTES

Section A

- The number of entries in the salesperson's statement will depend upon actual expenses recovered from salespeople. In desk fee systems and high payout commission plans, most expenses will be included as recoverable items.
- Statements are usually prepared on a monthly basis illustrating a balance forward, charges levied and payments received. Every attempt should be made to include a reasonable explanation of charges and credits to avoid confusion with the sales staff.

Section B

- Income is normally taken from trades. Detailed analysis of the income should be contained in ledger sheets for individual salespeople on either a deals written or deals closed basis.
- More detailed reports can be provided (i.e., year to date or anniversary period to date earning figures), to give management a better perspective of long range earning history.

Section C

- Shadow expenses can, as in the case of recoverable items, apply to virtually any expense category within the financial worksheet.
- As the sample statement shows, it is possible to assess an office rental cost and show that within the shadow expenses. Brokers arrive at this figure by dividing the total occupancy cost for the premises by the number of offices within the premises (or by the size of each office as a percentage of the total area).
- The sample statement illustrates only a few shadow expenses. Many fixed expenses can be allocated as well as variable expenses to provide a more complete picture of the true profit received from sales staff within the office.

Detailed Salesperson Statement   Figure R.9

Brokerage software packages provide integrated management/accounting systems that offer sophisticated cross-referencing capabilities and have largely replaced the need for a paper-based reference card index system. **Figure R.10**, provided for a manual record keeping system, indicates the type of information typically included in such systems.

REFERRAL

A term commonly used in real estate brokerage referring to the act of a salesperson or broker recommending or otherwise directing a prospective buyer or seller to another salesperson or broker operating within or beyond the referring salesperson's registration jurisdiction, geographic area, or specific field of professional expertise.

Application   Some form of referral agreement is normally used when relaying information concerning a seller or buyer from a referring brokerage to a receiving brokerage. This form should also set out any commission arrangements between the brokerages. Practitioners should also be aware of ethical standards and statutory requirements concerning referrals and the collecting and payment of fees in relation to such referrals.

Example   *Referral*

Salesperson Lee has just listed a property owned by the Smith family which is moving from Ontario to British Columbia as a result of Mr. Smith's employment relocation. Mr. Smith inquires of Lee if he is aware of any knowledgeable brokers/salespeople who could assist at their new location. Lee advises Smith of successful dealings with a particular brokerage and will call them to get the process under way. Lee also informs Smith that it is customary for the salesperson referring a customer to collect a referral fee from the other brokerage, if a sale is completed.

Provincial   See applicable reference materials.

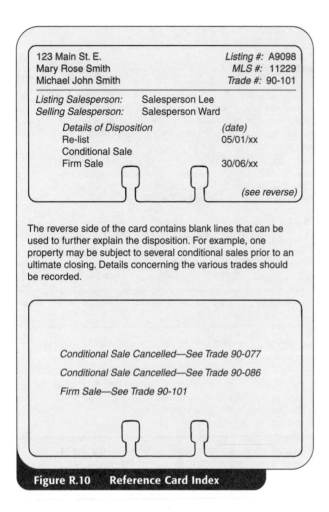

```
123 Main St. E.                    Listing #:  A9098
Mary Rose Smith                       MLS #:   11229
Michael John Smith                  Trade #:  90-101

Listing Salesperson:    Salesperson Lee
Selling Salesperson:    Salesperson Ward
    Details of Disposition      (date)
    Re-list                     05/01/xx
    Conditional Sale
    Firm Sale                   30/06/xx

                                (see reverse)
```

The reverse side of the card contains blank lines that can be used to further explain the disposition. For example, one property may be subject to several conditional sales prior to an ultimate closing. Details concerning the various trades should be recorded.

Conditional Sale Cancelled—See Trade 90-077

Conditional Sale Cancelled—See Trade 90-086

Firm Sale—See Trade 90-101

Figure R.10   Reference Card Index

REGIONAL SHOPPING CENTRE

A large retail district, usually involving from 300,000 to 1,000,000 square feet, that offers a wide selection of merchandise and serves a large residential market.

Example   *Regional Shopping Centre*

Developer Reed is a limited partner in a local shopping centre with significant plans to elevate the centre into a regional shopping complex. Forty-five to fifty new outlets are scheduled in a three level 350,000 sq. ft. expansion underway at Metro Centre on West Road. The expansion will increase the centre's leaseable area to 600,000 sq. ft. A 740-car parking lot connected to the shopping centre by a glass walkway will also be needed. The 14 year-old mall serves an immediate population of 120,000 and a secondary population of 180,000.

REGISTERED GENERAL APPRAISER

Acronym: RGA   The RGA designation is awarded by the International Institute of Public Appraisers Ltd. to candidates who have completed basic courses in appraisal or

assessment and have acquired credit for two years experience in real estate sales, assessment, appraisal review, appraisal, or property management. The RGA classification applies to the appraisal of any type of property, e.g., residential, commercial, to a value of $500,000.

All Registered General Appraisers are bound by the *Competency Provision* of the College of Registered Public Appraisers and the *Uniform Standards of Professional Appraisal Practice* of the Appraisal Foundation and have acquired credit for a narrative demonstration appraisal report on a residential property or credit for work samples completed by the candidate. Proof of errors and omissions insurance coverage is also required.

Reference   Information provided has been summarized from details supplied by the International Institute of Public Appraisers Ltd., P. O. Box 3132 B, Fredericton, NB E3A 5G9 with no representation concerning its accuracy or completeness.

REGISTERED PLAN OF SUBDIVISION

A plan prepared by a surveyor that has received approvals pursuant to provincial planning legislation, setting out lots, blocks, or parcels of land for registration in the applicable provincial land registry system and subsequently dealt with as separate and distinct lots, blocks, or parcels of land.

Provincial   See applicable reference materials.

REGISTERED PUBLIC APPRAISER

Acronym: RPA   The RPA designation is awarded to real estate appraisers who have satisfied the requirements of the International Institute of Public Appraisers Ltd. with respect to technical education, creditable experience, and ethical conduct. Appraisers must complete the Institute's comprehensive examination. Following registration, individuals may be required to meet continuing education requirements.

Education requirements include 165 classroom hours in courses specified in the detailed requirements. Applicants must have five years of acceptable appraisal experience. Continuing education includes ten classroom hours in courses or seminars for each year. Applicants must also have acquired credit for a comprehensive narrative demonstration appraisal report on a residential property and an investment property or acceptable alternatives as set out in the requirements. Proof of errors and omissions insurance coverage is required.

R

Reference   Information provided has been summarized from details provided by the International Institute of Public Appraisers Ltd., P. O. Box 3132 B, Fredericton, NB E3A 5G9 with no representation concerning its accuracy or completeness.

REGISTRANT

Provincial   See applicable reference materials.

REGISTRAR (REAL ESTATE)

An official recorder, overseer, and administrator of a provincial regulatory act who is granted certain specified powers concerning persons registered under that act.

Provincial   See applicable reference materials.

REGISTRATION

Provincial   See applicable reference materials.

REGISTRY SYSTEM

A system of land registration providing for the registration of instruments affecting real property and regulated by provincial statute. Registry is one of two systems prevalent in Canada, the other being land titles.

Provincial   See applicable reference materials.

REGRESSION, PRINCIPLE OF
(SEE PRINCIPLES (APPRAISAL))

REGULATED AREAS

A defined territory under the control of an agency responsible for flood plain management and legislative protection of lands, such as a conservation authority. Regulated areas are normally adjacent to watercourses and as such require special consideration because of the potential for flood or erosion damage and pollution problems. Such areas require the need for an overall administrative scheme to preserve natural habitat and protect the environment.

Provincial   See applicable reference materials.

REHABILITATION

The process of lengthening a building's economic life within its present design by restoring it to a well-maintained condition.

Application   Practitioners may encounter rehabilitation regarding the restoration to good condition of deteriorated structures, neighbourhoods, and public facilities. Neighbourhood rehabilitation encompasses structural changes, and may extend to street improvements and the provision of such amenities as parks and playgrounds.

Rehabilitation, on a much smaller scale, may involve the restoration of a single building. Restoration and the consequent extending of economic life of a building must be taken into consideration in the valuation process as depreciation (in the cost approach) is based in part on the remaining economic life of the building.

Example   *Rehabilitation*

Owner Smith's income property was built in 1960, with a total economic life of fifty years. Assuming that the date of appraisal is May 2000, the actual age of the property is 40 years, and the remaining economic life is 10 years. However, over the last five-year period, Smith has spent money rehabilitating the property. In addition to changes to meet amendments to the Fire Code, Smith has also upgraded all kitchens, bathrooms, and common areas. He also invested heavily in new insulation, upgraded windows, and has installed high quality roof shingles. In doing so, Smith has effectively extended the remaining economic life from 10 years to 25 years. Therefore, although the actual age is 40 years, the effective age is much less due to the improvements.

REINVESTMENT RATE

Commonly used in calculating rate of return. The reinvestment rate is an interest rate, dictated by the marketplace, at which excess funds can be invested in typical investments at after tax yields in excess of the safe rate. Funds invested at the reinvestment rate are presently surplus and are not needed to meet immediate cash requirements.

Application   The reinvestment rate is used by commercial practitioners when calculating the modified internal rate of return (MIRR) or financial management rate of return (FMRR). Use of a reinvestment rate overcomes selected shortcomings associated with internal rate of return (IRR), but also introduces external elements to an otherwise internal perspective on rate of return and consequently, has been criticized accordingly. See **Safe Rate, Internal Rate Of Return, Modified Internal Rate Of Return,** and **Financial Management Rate Of Return.**

R

RELEASE

A discharge by an act and/or a written document in which some claim, right, or interest in a property is relinquished.

Provincial   See applicable reference materials.

REMAINDER

A legal term used in reference to that part of an interest (estate) in land that remains upon the cessation of a prior interest in the land, such as a life estate. A *remainder* should not be confused with a reversion in which an interest reverts back to the original person who granted the estate.

Example   *Remainder*

Owner Smith established a future estate for his wife on the family homestead, with the understanding that Smith's son would ultimately inherit the entire property upon the death of his mother and father. In this scenario, Smith's son will inherit the remainder of the estate, following the life estate of his mother.

REMAINING ECONOMIC LIFE
(SEE ALSO ECONOMIC LIFE)

The estimated number of years remaining in the economic life of the structure or structural component, as of the date of the appraisal.

Example   *Remaining Economic Life*

Owner Smith's home was built in 1980, with a total economic life of 40 years. Assume that the date of appraisal is July, 2000, the actual age of the property is 20 years and the remaining economic life is 20 years. If Smith improved the property by replacing various components in the house, the remaining economic life could be extended.

REMUNERATION

One of two duties owed an agent by his/her principal, the other being indemnification.

Application   An agent is entitled to payment for services rendered as agreed between the parties. In a real estate transaction, this normally takes the form of an agreement, such as an exclusive listing agreement or a buyer agency agreement. If no agreement exists, but the agent acts on behalf of the client and fulfills a duty that is ratified, the agent will be entitled to remuneration, subject to compliance with the applicable provincial real estate act.

Example   *Remuneration*

Owner Smith wants to sell his property and has agreed to a five percent commission on any sale effected by ABC Realty Inc. during the currency of an exclusive listing. The list price was $159,900 and the property sold for $155,000. Accordingly, Smith as the principal, owes ABC Realty Inc., the agent, the sum of $7,750 (0.05 x $155,000). If a real estate brokerage other than ABC Realty Inc. sells Smith's property, ABC Realty Inc. would forward the selling portion of the commission to the selling brokerage pursuant to local real estate board procedures in the case of an MLS listing, or as agreed between the brokerages.

RENT

Compensation paid for the temporary use and/or occupation of real estate by a tenant. Compensation is typically in the form of periodic payments of money, but may be otherwise, e.g., labour.

Example   *Rent*

Landlord Smith and Tenant Jones are attempting to arrive at the base rent payable by Jones under a *commercial* tenancy agreement (often referred to as net/net/net rent or alternatively a triple net lease). They are creating a lease with an amount payable based on the rentable square foot/ square metre area of the demised premises. The following is the agreed upon wording:

The tenant will, throughout the term, pay to the landlord at its head office, or at any other place designated by the landlord, in Canadian funds, without demand and without deduction, abatement, set-off, or compensation, as base rent, the annual sum of $48,000 payable in equal consecutive monthly installments of $4,000 each in advance on the first day of each calendar month. The base rent is based on an annual rate of $4.00 per square foot of the rentable area of the premises.

As well, Smith and Jones inserted clauses in the lease to set out provisions for the payment of percentage rent, the payment of expenses, prorating of any partial month, the provision of postdated cheques for each consecutive year within the lease term, and a penalty for any cheques that are not honoured when presented.

Provincial   See applicable reference materials.

R

RENT CONTROL

A term commonly referring to government controls imposed on residential rental properties to regulate rent and rental increases.

Provincial   See applicable reference materials.

RENT FREE PERIOD

A period of time granted to a tenant to occupy premises at no cost as an incentive to signing a lease, usually applying to commercial properties.

Application   The phrases, *rent free* and *at no cost,* require qualification. Generally, the rent-free concept applies only to *base* and not *additional rents* and practitioners must ensure a clear understanding of exactly what is meant. Rent-free periods are normally found in new commercial buildings where the landlord is seeking to *rent-up* (fully occupy) the building. Such periods are also common in the re-lease market when excess square footage exists within a defined market area. Rent-free periods are popular as the landlord can maintain a desired *per square foot* rate on leases while offering a tangible incentive to tenants. On the other hand, tenants can use rent savings to offset relocation expenses.

In most instances, rent free periods occur in advance of the commencement date of the lease.

> **Example**   *Rent Free Period*
>
> Tenant Smith is interested in 2,150 square feet of space in the new Anycity Executive Complex. Less than 30% of the tower is occupied and the landlord is seeking to rent-up the building. In return for signing a four-year lease with a base rent of $9.50 per square foot, Smith will receive three months rent-free occupancy (base rent only) prior to the start of the lease. The value of the rent free period is:
>
> (2,150 x $9.50) ÷ 12 x 3   = $5,106.25

RENT REGULATIONS

Provincial   See applicable reference materials.

RENT ROLL

A term used by commercial practitioners when referring to a detailed listing of tenancies within an industrial, office/retail, or investment property.

Application   Presently, no widely accepted set of criteria exists as to the type of information required in a rent roll. This circumstance is further complicated by the diversity of properties and range of relevant information relating to those types of property. For example, a rent roll detailing tenancies in a multi-unit residential property will usually differ from a similar role for an industrial complex. The former might include: suite number, full tenant name, annual rent, other payments (e.g., utilities and cable), last rent increase (assuming rent legislation requirements apply to the building and/or units), lease expiration, and any additional details. The latter might include the unit number, total rentable area, annual base rent, base rent per square foot, additional rents, options, and lease expiration. The rent roll is often attached as a summary schedule to the agreement/contract. The actual leases making up the rent roll are normally requested by the buyer's solicitor as part of the closing documentation.

RENTABLE AREA
(SEE ALSO RENTABLE/USEABLE FACTOR)

Most commonly associated with the measurement of office buildings and more specifically individual tenanted areas. The rentable area is best described as the useable area of the tenanted space plus an allocation of floor common areas (e.g., lobby, janitorial areas, washrooms, and electrical room). For example, a leased space for a tenant on a multi-tenant floor may have a useable area of 2,795 square feet with a rentable area of 3,035 square feet. The additional 240 square feet represents the proportionate allocation of common areas on that particular floor. The rentable area is normally used as the basis for determining base and additional rents. In the above instance, if the base rent is $7.50 per square foot, then the base annual rent would be $22,762.50 ($7.50 x 3,035 square feet).

Application   In the United States and Canada, three methods of measuring rentable area in office buildings are generally used:

1) Association of Building Owners and Managers (BOMA) International;
2) General Services Administration; and
3) The New York Method.

The BOMA standard is most frequently found in the Canadian marketplace. BOMA describes the total rentable area of a commercial office floor as the gross floor area, less any columns or projections necessary to the building. Such items on an upper floor of a modern office building would include the elevator shafts, stairways, and

R

ventilation shafts. The relationship between rentable and useable areas on a particular floor is often referred to as the *R\U Ratio*.

Example   *Rentable Area*

Owner Smith has calculated that Tenant Jones' rentable space within the complex is 4,335 square feet with a useable space is 4,024 square feet. Jones enquires how these measurements are determined. Smith explains that the rentable area includes a proportionate allocation of all common areas on the floor that Jones is located. To clarify the point, he refers to the following definition in the lease:

Rentable area is computed by multiplying the useable area by a fraction, the numerator being the aggregate floor area of the floor on which the leased premises is located (calculated from the inside surface of the exterior glass, including washrooms, telephone, electrical, and janitorial closets, columns, projections, and elevator lobbies, but excluding any elevation shafts, stairs, flues, stacks, pipe shafts, and vertical ducts with their own enclosing walls used in common), and the denominator being the aggregate useable area of all leaseable premises on such floor, all according to established measurement in use for the building. The rentable area of the building shall be equal to the aggregate of the rentable area of all leaseable premises in the building calculated on the foregoing basis.

RENTABLE/USEABLE FACTOR

Acronym: R/U Factor   The mathematical relationship between rentable and useable areas in commercial real estate often referred to as an *efficiency factor*. The R/U factor can be expressed as a decimal or a percentage and, in some areas, real estate practitioners refer to this as the *conversion* or *add-on* factor.

Application   If the rentable area of a leased office is 1,650 square feet and its useable area is 1,450 square feet, the efficiency or R/U factor is $1,650 \div 1,450 = 1.1379$. Consequently, to determine the amount of rentable space when the useable space is known, the useable space is multiplied by the R/U factor. In some instances, the R/U factor is merely expressed as an additive figure, in other words 0.1379 or 13.79% as opposed to the true R/U factor that is 1.1379. In multi-level buildings with multiple tenants on each floor, the landlord normally computes R/U factors and exact useable and rentable areas of all suites for the information of prospective tenants.

As a matter of practical importance, not all rental buildings are accurately measured for useable and rentable areas. In fact, the factor referenced by the landlord may not precisely reflect rentable/useable areas, but merely represent an approximation. Depending on the strength of the local market, the add-on could be smaller or larger than a true measurement would reveal.

R/U Factor Formulae

Rentable Area	÷	Useable Area	=	R/U Factor
Rentable Area	÷	R/U Factor	=	Useable Area
Useable Area	x	R/U Factor	=	Rentable Area

RENTAL AGREEMENTS/CONTRACTS

Provincial   See applicable reference materials.

REPLACEMENT COST
(SEE ALSO REPRODUCTION COST)

The cost of construction, at current prices, of a building having utility equivalent to the building being appraised, but built with modern materials and according to current standards, design, and layout.

REPRESENTATIONS/WARRANTIES

A statement made by one party to another either before or coincident with the entering into an agreement involving another party for the sale, lease, exchange or other trading of real property. The representation typically involves some fact regarding the property that is of importance in the negotiations. A warranty is an assurance by one party, typically but not necessarily reduced to writing within an agreement/contract, that verifies, confirms, or otherwise attests to a specific circumstance and that the party receiving such warranty may rely upon such warranty and not investigate the issue further.

Application   Real estate practitioners encounter situations where buyers wish to have certain matters confirmed regarding the property and improvements related thereto. For example, the buyer may express concern about the condition of the swimming pool and the salesperson may be required to insert a clause to cover potential problems. While many variations exist, one particular wording is provided for illustration purposes.

R

The seller represents and warrants to the best of the seller's knowledge and belief that the swimming pool and equipment are now, and on the completion date shall be, in good working order. The parties agree that this representation and warranty shall survive and not merge on completion of this transaction, but apply only to the state of the property existing at completion of this transaction.

The seller represents and warrants, to the best of the seller's knowledge and belief, that all sewage systems serving the property are wholly within the limits of the said property, and have been constructed according to the proper regulations and have received all required certificates of installation and approval pursuant to the [appropriate environmental legislation].

In specialized areas of real estate, such warranties and representations can be very detailed. For example, in the case of a dock, boathouse, or pier involving a recreational property, the seller may have to represent and warrant to the best of his/her knowledge that the dock has received all necessary approvals and permits from the appropriate municipal, provincial, and/or federal departments/ministries as well as other required authorities.

Recommended warranty clauses usually state *the party* (buyer or seller) *represents and warrants.* These two terms should be clearly differentiated. A representation is a statement made by one party to the other, before or at the time of contracting, regarding some existing fact or to some past event, which is one of the causes that induces a contract and therefore could be the basis for rescinding the agreement. A warranty is a statement or covenant that is subsidiary or collateral to the contract. Breach of warranty entitles the buyer to damages only and does not permit the buyer to rescind the contract.

These terms, in turn, should be differentiated from a condition. Whether or not a specific statement is a warranty or a condition is a question of contract and precise wording. The decision to use a condition, warranty or other representation will depend largely on circumstances. Following are two warranty clauses that might be found in an agreement/contract to address specific situations, e.g., well and sewage systems. These clauses are inserted for information purposes only as wordings will vary by provincial jurisdiction.

The seller represents and warrants, to the best of the seller's knowledge and belief, that during the seller's occupancy of the property, the pump and all related equipment serving the said property have performed adequately, and that the well is capable of supplying adequate water volume of not less than ____ gallons per minute at standing level and that the water is potable. The parties agree that this representation and warranty shall survive and not merge on completion of this transaction, but apply only to the state of the property at completion of this transaction.

To illustrate the difference between a warranty and a condition, the first clause has been worded as a condition precedent and includes a time limit for the performance of the condition and also a waiver provision.

This offer is conditional upon the buyer determining at the buyer's own expense that:

1. The pump and all related equipment serving the property are in proper operating condition.

2. There is an adequate supply of water of not less than ____ gallons per minute at standing level and that the water is potable.

Unless the buyer gives notice in writing delivered to the seller by 12 p.m. on the 1st day of May, 20xx, that these conditions have been fulfilled, this offer shall become null and void and the deposit shall be returned to the buyer in full without deduction. These conditions are included for the sole benefit of the buyer and may be waived at the buyer's option by notice in writing to the seller within the time period stated herein.

Example   *Representations/Warranties*

Owner Smith has provided various representations and warranties about the property to Buyer Jones. In particular, two representations concern any problems with electrical, plumbing and heating systems, and structural aspects of the building. Jones and Smith have agreed that the warranties shall survive and not merge on completion of the transaction, but apply only to the state of the property at the point of completion. Following is the clause drafted by the selling salesperson that follows various warranties set out in the agreement/contract.

The parties agree that the representations and warranties stated herein shall survive and not merge on completion, but shall expire at 12 p.m. on the 1st day of May, 20xx, and be of no further force and effect unless the buyer, prior to such expiry has given written notice of a claim under the warranties to the seller.

R

REPRODUCTION COST

The cost of construction, at current prices, of an exact duplicate or replica, using the same materials, construction standards, design, layout, and quality of workmanship, while embodying all the deficiencies, superadequacies, and obsolescence of the subject building.

Application Appraisers use reproduction cost since it involves a costing of the actual building to be appraised. Replacement cost may be selected, for example, in an older building where the materials used are no longer available and/or when the building suffers from severe forms of obsolescence, such as excessive foundation walls or ceiling heights. In this instance, replacement cost would more easily handle the difficulty of estimating the current costs of materials no longer available and would eliminate the need for estimating the obsolescence due to the super-adequacy.

In reality, the decision to use reproduction or replacement cost is the appraiser's responsibility. However, keep in mind that:

- The older the building, the more effective the replacement cost estimate.
- The newer the building, the more effective the reproduction cost estimate.

Reproduction cost is estimated using several alternative methods:

- Comparative Square Metre Method;
- Quantity Survey Method;
- Unit-In-Place Method; and
- Cost Services Method.

For a detailed example, see **Cost Services Method.**

RESERVE (TAXATION)

A reserve, provided under the *Income Tax Act*, when all or a portion of the disposition of capital property is not received by the investor by the end of the current taxation year. The reserve, in effect, provides for a tax deferral. The amount and extent of the deferral will vary based on individual circumstances regarding the sale, determination of capital gains, and the amount of money not yet received at the end of the taxation year. The following example is provided for illustration purposes using the general rule: Reserve = (Gain ÷ Sale Price) x Amount Owing at End of Year. Caution is advised and expert advice is required as the application of the reserve provisions of

the *Income Tax Act* involve complexities, e.g., time limits, definition as inventory or capital property, and status of the taxpayer.

Example *Reserve (Taxation)*

Investor McKay sells an industrial property for $1,000,000 with a downpayment of $300,000, a new first mortgage for $500,000 and a seller take back second mortgage for $200,000 (payable interest only), due and payable in the following year. Assume that the adjusted cost base at sale is $700,000 and the capital gain after allowable cost of sale disbursements is $250,000.

Reserve = ($250,000 ÷ $1,000,000) x $200,000
= $50,000 (taxable income deferred)

RESERVE FUND

A special fund established for the purpose of some contemplated future event.

Application Practitioners most commonly encounter reserve funds in condominiums as legislation normally sets out requirements regarding such funds. The fund is set up by the corporation by way of a special account for major repairs and replacement of common elements and assets of the corporation. The reserve fund is typically used for repair and replacement of such items as roofs, exterior finishes, roads, sidewalks, recreational facilities, parking facilities, sewer, heating, electrical, and plumbing systems.

Example *Reserve Fund*

Buyer Jones is considering the purchase of a two-bedroom unit in a condominium high-rise with 250 condominium units in total. Jones is concerned, however, about the size of reserve fund for this building. According to the buyer representative involved with Jones, the average reserve fund per unit for this type of property, in this community is $1,450 and the average contribution of reserve fund dollars, as a percentage of total common area expenses, is 17%. Upon reading the condominium documentation, Jones discovers that:

- The common expenses for the last fiscal year were $732,600.
- The allocation for reserve fund for that fiscal period was $80,586 (11% of common expenses).
- Total reserve fund (including $80,586 from prior fiscal year), was $870,987.

Based on these figures, the building has a reserve fund per unit of $3,483.95, ($870,987 reserve fund divided by 250 units).

Legislation concerning minimums required in condominium reserve funds and the method of calculating such minimums will vary by province.

Provincial   See applicable reference materials.

RESIDENTIAL DWELLING UNIT

A reference to residential occupancy commonly found in provincial legislation and/or municipal regulations. For example, the term *residential dwelling unit*, *residential unit*, or simply *dwelling unit* is formally defined in zoning by-laws and official plans. Dwelling units are usually divided into dwelling types, e.g., detached, semi-detached, and duplex; multiple dwelling units, e.g., townhouses or other forms of horizontal multiple housing; and high density multiple unit buildings, e.g., high-rise apartment.

Example   *Residential Dwelling Unit*

The following definition was taken from a provincial statute and provided for illustration purposes only, as numerous variations can be found in the marketplace.

A residential dwelling unit:

- *Must consist of a self-contained set of rooms in a building or structure;*
- *Must be used (or intended for use), as residential premises, and contain kitchen and bathroom facilities that are for the use of that unit; and*
- *Must also have a means of egress to the outside of the building but it may be through another residential unit.*

RESIDENTIAL MARKET COMPARISON GUIDE

A form designed to show the owner of a property how his/her property ranks in competition with others that are now, or have been, on the market. Often referred to as a CMA (Comparative Market Analysis) in various jurisdictions in Canada, this guide is used to determine the probable asking price of the property. The form also contains additional lines to detail anticipated selling price, selling costs, and ultimately estimated net proceeds to the seller.

Application   A typical *Residential Market Comparison Guide* is provided as **Figure R.11** detailing various comparables to arrive at a recommended listing price.

Form Preparation

The form has space for a description of comparable properties for sale now, comparable properties sold within the past 12 months, and comparable properties that expired during that same period. The form and its preparation parallel in certain limited ways the direct comparison approach used in appraisals. However, this form is intended only as a general guide for the competitive pricing of property with no exact adjustments, as would be the case in an appraisal report.

Certain basic guidelines are provided to assist in the form completion.

Comparables for Sale Now   The competitive position of the seller's house is extremely important. The selection of properties should be made with careful consideration to overall comparability with the subject property. Under *Features/Comments*, highlight significant differences and/or similarities. The *available for sale* market provides the seller with an overall perspective in assessing his/her likelihood of selling and in what general price range. Properties should be listed in order of highest comparability based on type, location, and features.

Comparables Sold Past 12 Months   This category represents what the buyers paid. The more recent the comparables, the more relevant the information, assuming that most properties selected are more or less comparable with the seller's house. The order should start with the most comparable and proceed sequentially.

Comparables Expired Past 12 Months   This category outlines properties that did not sell. While the precise reasons for a *no sale* situation will vary, this information provides valuable insight concerning the *top of the market* for a particular type of property. Again, list as much detail as possible.

Presenting the Residential Market Comparison Guide

Supporting information is always helpful when reviewing details from the guide with the seller.

- Provide detailed information concerning comparables used, particularly the top two or three in each category.
- Be prepared to discuss major market trends occurring within the immediate neighbourhood and surrounding community.
- Have historical information concerning the average length of time properties are on the market until sold,

R

RESIDENTIAL
MARKET COMPARISON GUIDE

Subject Property:	123 Main Street, Anycity
Prepared for:	John and Mary Smith
Prepared by:	Salesperson Lee, ABC Realty Inc.

Date: January 13, 20x2

COMPARABLES FOR SALE NOW:

ADDRESS	PRICE	FEATURES/COMMENTS
16 Maple Street	$269,000	Many upgrades
19 Main Street	242,500	Similar home
205 Riverdale Ave.	265,000	Homes more expensive in this location
45 Cedar Ave.	249,000	Larger lot, on corner
67 Elm Street	247,700	Poor condition, needs redecorating

(Use back of form for additional features/comments if required)

COMPARABLES SOLD PAST 12 MONTHS:

ADDRESS	PRICE	FEATURES/COMMENTS
13 Oak Street	$240,000	Similar home, sold in November, 20x1
136 Main Street	235,000	Required redecorating, sold in December, 20x1
96 Main Street	242,500	Exceptional landscaping, sold in October, 20x1
118 Riverdale Ave.	239,000	Sold this month

(Use back of form for additional features/comments if required)

COMPARABLES EXPIRED PAST 12 MONTHS:

ADDRESS	PRICE	FEATURES/COMMENTS
88 Pine Street	$269,000	Inground pool
93 Main Street	242,500	Rented, $1,500 per month
401 Riverdale Ave.	265,000	Corner lot
29 Frank Street	249,000	

(Use back of form for additional features/comments if required)

ESTIMATED SELLING COSTS

Brokerage Fee	$14,400.00
Mortgage Payout Penalty	
Mortgage Discount	
Approximate Legal Costs	2,600.00
Miscellaneous	
Total	$17,000.00

Recommendations: as of January 13, 20x2

I recommend a maximum list price of:	$	$245,500
With estimated selling price of:	$	240,000
With estimated outstanding mortgage balance of:	$	81,000
With estimated selling costs of:	$	17,000
Anticipated net proceeds would be:	$	142,000

Signature *Salesperson Lee*

N.B.: The above information is NOT an appraisal and is to be used for marketing purposes only.

R

Figure R.11   Residential Market Comparison Guide

turnover of property in the immediate area, listing to sale price ratios, and other relevant indicators.

- Establish objectively the strengths and weaknesses of the seller's home in relation to comparables in the guide, e.g., location, extras, buyer appeal, special neighbourhood amenities, site features, functional room layout, and attractive financing.
- Discuss the problem of overpricing a property, e.g., difficulty in getting other salespeople and brokers enthused about the property; may remain unsold and become market stale, can appear in the wrong price category and thereby restrict the number of qualified buyers who might otherwise have looked at it, and may be shown only for comparison purposes to sell other well-priced property.

The sample form provides space for recommendations concerning both maximum list price and probable selling price and expenses leading to an estimate of net proceeds. Completion of any/all of these, including the salesperson's signature, is optional. Often salespeople complete information on comparables only, and then use this form as a guide for general discussions with the seller.

If the net proceeds portion is completed, practitioners must ensure that details regarding mortgage balance and selling costs are accurate.

Provincial   See applicable reference materials.

RESIDENTIAL RESALES

The residential resale specialty involves extensive work with consumers and their changing needs and wants in the marketplace. Typical clients are sellers who are selling the family home due to employment, monetary, or family changes. Typical prospects are buyers relocating due to the same motivating factors as those of sellers. In both cases, emotional issues are involved and people skills become paramount.

Residential resale work also calls for irregular hours, since most activities are dictated by the availability of both sellers and buyers. Open houses are routinely scheduled on weekends to maximize market exposure. Offer presentations and showings often involve very late hours. Phone calls at home at all hours are the norm for residential salespersons and very seldom is it possible to totally get away from the job.

Application   To appreciate the type of work involved, the progress of a typical residential transaction (if in fact any transaction can be classified as *typical*) is detailed.

The Listing

The listing agreement is entered into between seller and real estate brokerage, authorizing the brokerage to act as the seller's agent in offering the property for sale. A large portion of residential resale activity involves developing leads and converting them into saleable listings to provide the brokerage with goods on the shelf. Skill is uppermost as listings that are not at or close to market value or in which the confidence and co-operation of the seller has not been obtained usually result in lost effort, money, and image.

The Agency Obligation

Once a saleable listing has been obtained, the brokerage is the official agent for the seller, and in that capacity has duties as outlined in the listing agreement. The brokerage is also obligated to duties and limitations imposed by provincial real estate legislation, common law (agency and contract law), and by the standards accepted by the profession if the brokerage is a member of organized real estate (*Code of Ethics and Standards of Business Practice*). Since a real estate salesperson generally carries out the duties imposed on the brokerage by acting as the employee or authorized representative of the brokerage, each salesperson must fully understand these obligations.

Prospecting

Involves the search for qualified buyers for listed property. The public probably has the impression that this means placing an ad in the paper and a sign on the property. Although these activities are examples of prospecting, experienced residential salespersons use other methods of active prospecting that may be far more effective than classified advertising.

There is an old saying in the real estate profession that the property will qualify the buyer. In other words, the property, in terms of type, location, and price range will provide an experienced salesperson with a profile of a typical buyer and will target the marketing activities and efforts. Real estate sales challenges the initiative, imagination, and dedication of residential practitioners.

Qualifying and Showing

Qualifying involves determining the buyer's needs, wants, and financial capabilities. This means getting to know the potential buyer, assisting that individual in sorting out priorities, establishing preferences, and determining available cash and amount of loan that can be carried. The exact role assumed by the practitioner in relation to a potential buyer depends on whether the buyer is a *client* (buyer agency) or a *customer* (seller agency while owing honesty and fairness to the buyer). The agency role is vital to the relationship and must be fully disclosed.

Qualifying is followed by the selection of a limited number of properties to be shown. One of the purposes of qualifying is to narrow the field to avoid confusion and wasted time and effort. Following the appropriate selection, the process of showing and providing accurate and complete information follows.

Obtaining the Offer

Closing is the process of asking for and obtaining the offer. People skills are paramount as there is no point in asking for the offer unless the property is the right one for the buyer. Experienced salespeople know the signs to look and listen for and also recognize that timing and positive reinforcement are important. Make no mistake, sales practitioners must typically ask for the offer.

The offer itself is a complex document, involving a great deal of detail with numerous decisions to be made by the buyer. In preparing an offer, the salesperson accepts a very serious responsibility to ensure that the offer contains all of the terms and conditions required by the buyer, and that all of the elements necessary to create a binding agreement, according to the common law of contract, are present.

Presentation, Acceptance, and Delivery

Presentation of the buyer's offer to the seller involves an analysis of the document itself and discussion of such matters as market conditions and the buyer's circumstances. The precise roles played by salespersons involved in the presentation will depend upon their agency relationships with the buyer and seller.

The seller may accept, reject, or counter (sign back) the buyer's offer. Countering the offer means that the seller signs an offer to sell the property to the buyer under terms differing from the buyer's offer to purchase. This would then require an offer presentation to the buyer. When involved in this type of cycle (i.e., offer, counter-offer, etc.), it is not uncommon for salespeople to bounce back and forth between seller and buyer several times before the parties agree on the final terms.

If an offer is ultimately accepted, copies are delivered to all parties and their respective solicitors. Since the transaction takes place under the supervision of, and in the name of, the brokerage, a copy of the accepted agreement, together with a detailed trade record sheet and record of deposit (which is placed in a special real estate trust account), are maintained in the brokerage's office. Exact procedures will vary by provincial jurisdiction.

The previous information provides a thumbnail sketch of typical activities of a residential resale salesperson. In making a career choice, another factor to be considered is that most residential salespersons typically work entirely on a commission basis. While this involves tremendous potential, a considerable amount of risk is also created. Lack of listings and available prospects, clients, or customers, translates into no income. Further, even for the best salespeople, the volume of listing and sales activity is dramatically affected by market conditions. Self-discipline and good work habits are essential. Real estate is not a structured work environment wherein activities and objectives are provided and assignments are given and directly supervised on a regular basis. A good broker or manager will provide both initial orientation and ongoing training and assistance, but the salesperson must organize systems for generating leads and contacts and then spend time productively and effectively.

RESIDENTIAL TENANCY

Provincial   See applicable reference materials.

RESTRICTIVE COVENANT

A limitation placed on the use of property contained in the title for that property. More specifically, a restrictive covenant is a contract between two land owners, by which the person obtaining the promise (the covenantee) acquires the right to restrain the covenantor from putting the land to certain specific uses. Such contracts between landowners run with the land and can involve a wide array of limiting conditions regarding a property.

Restrictive covenants have certain characteristics:

- A dominant tenement (benefited land) and a servient tenement (burdened land) must exist.

- The covenant must be negative in nature and represent a burden on the covenantor's land. No positive or affirmative covenant can be imposed on the land, unless by statute.

- The covenant must directly benefit or enhance the value of the covenantee's land.

- Both the covenantee's and covenantor's land must be clearly defined, the agreement between the owners should state that a covenant is being imposed, and titles to both benefited and burdened lands must be registered (unless provided otherwise by statute).

- The covenant must be reasonable in nature and not arbitrary or contrary to the public interest.

Application   Historically, restrictive covenants were widely used in residential areas to regulate the uses to which land could be put. Typical restrictive covenants prohibited the use of land for other than residential purposes, limited building on the land to one-family dwellings, and required minimum frontage per house.

A prudent buyer who intends to use the lands for a specific purpose would be wise to do some preliminary title investigations and zoning enquiries before completing his/her offer to purchase. This research is particularly important because, if the restriction is being complied with at the time of purchase, it cannot be used as an objection to title unless appropriate provisos are added to the agreement to protect the buyer. Exact wordings in pre-printed agreements/contracts concerning restrictive covenants will vary by province.

Restrictive covenants are usually created by express promises contained in the grant of the property to the buyer who has previously agreed to accept title subject to these covenants. Restrictive covenants are often found in sub-divisions, where all the owners are obliged to conform to various stipulations. These served as the forerunners of municipal by-laws. Real estate practitioners should be aware of all restrictions that affect any subdivision in which they are marketing homes so that they can provide accurate information to buyers.

Example   *Restrictive Covenant*

Buyer Jones is considering a resale property owned by Seller Smith. Various restrictive covenants were imposed on buyers within this subdivision when the new homes were first marketed. These restrictive covenants run with the land and must be assumed by Jones. The following is a brief list for example purposes:

- Six foot maximum height for fences and only permitted in side and rear yard subject to front yard setback requirements.
- Prohibited use of television antennas.
- All fuel to be supplied by pipeline as opposed to individual fuel tanks.
- No unauthorized removal of trees or other significant vegetation, or alterations to drainage.
- Prohibition of clothes lines.
- Property restricted to single-family residence.
- Prohibition against the storage of motor homes, except in enclosed areas.
- No alteration to front elevations of houses or exterior colours on houses, without approval.
- In the case of alterations to vegetation, house elevations, and exterior colours on house, such plans must be first approved by the developer or his nominee; such approval not to be unreasonably withheld.

REVENUE UNIT

A measure developed by organized real estate to assist in the budgeting process. Traditionally, brokerages relied on sales volume calculations to determine market position and percentage market share. Sales volume, however, has certain deficiencies, particularly in terms of actual activity generated by the brokerage. Such volumes are subject to upward and downward price movements and commission rates charged can raise or lower sales volumes. Revenue units represent a simple tally system regardless of underlying forces at work in the marketplace.

Application   Revenue units are tallied quite simply:

EVENT	REVENUE UNITS
Single Listing Sold	1
Single Sale	1
Double End Sale (Listing and Sale)	2

The revenue unit is preferable over total number of transactions in the office. The counting of transactions ignores the importance of in-house (double end) as opposed to external (single) sales. This is an important factor in viewing both the profitability and market position of a brokerage.

Example   *Revenue Unit*

Broker/Owner Johnson, of ABC Realty Inc., is estimating how many revenue units are required each month for budgeting purposes. Last year, the brokerage generated $2,500,000 gross commission income, with a total of 860 units. He knows approximately how much volume of business is traditionally written by the salespeople during each month and expects that sales volumes for the upcoming year will be approximately equal to the prior year.

MONTH	PERCENT OF TOTAL	BUDGETED GROSS INCOME	REV. UNITS REQUIRED
January	5%	$125,000	43
February	7%	175,000	60
March	10%	250,000	86
April	15%	375,000	129
May	16%	400,000	138
June	10%	250,000	86
July	5%	125,000	43
August	4%	100,000	34
September	11%	275,000	95
October	9%	225,000	77
November	5%	125,000	43
December	3%	75,000	26

R

REVERSE MORTGAGE

A term used to describe a variety of home equity conversion products. A reverse mortgage is a variation on the traditional mortgage concept that allows a homeowner to convert some of the equity (net value accumulated in the home), into cash or a stream of income payments, while retaining ownership and possession of the home. No repayment of the reverse mortgage or interest takes place until a specified time in the future: when the homeowner sells, when the homeowner moves permanently, when a preset period (perhaps five or ten years), ends, or when the homeowner dies.

Reverse mortgages also differ from traditional mortgages in other ways. Since the homeowner receives payments or equity advances rather than making monthly repayments, the balance owing on a reverse mortgage increases over time, while the homeowner's share of the equity in the home decreases. While semi-annual compounding is common in reverse mortgages, the frequency of compounding in these mortgages currently has no legal limit.

Application   The homeowner's income is not a factor in qualifying for a reverse mortgage; even a homeowner without any income can arrange a reverse mortgage. Qualification for reverse mortgages is based on the appraised value of the property and the age and sex of the homeowner(s). Reverse mortgages are designed for older homeowners. Lender's payments to the homeowner are based on projections of the homeowner's life expectancy, which differ for each sex. Therefore, the older the homeowner, the greater the reverse mortgage payments possible from the lender.

A reverse mortgage should only be selected when it is clearly the best choice, from all perspectives, for home equity management and helping the homeowner stay in the home. Variations are based on fixed-tenure and lifetime payment arrangements and the four basic types of reverse mortgages.

Simple Reverse Mortgages

The lender and the borrower (homeowner) agree on the principal (amount of the reverse mortgage), which can be paid to the borrower in a lump sum payment, several installments or a combination of these arrangements.

Reverse Annuity Mortgages (RAMs)

A reverse mortgage is registered against a property to release the funds necessary to purchase an income-generating annuity. An annuity is a contract in which a buyer (either homeowner or lender), gives an insurance company a lump sum of money in return for receiving regular payments for an agreed period extending into the future. In some RAMs, all the equity released may not be used to purchase the annuity. The homeowner may elect to take some in cash and/or the lender may hold back a portion to cover administration fees.

Reverse Mortgage Line of Credit

The lender approves the full amount of the reverse mortgage and the homeowner then has ready access to this preset amount of equity. Homeowners can withdraw cash at their own discretion and make repayments if they wish to control the growth of the debt.

Shared Appreciation Reverse Mortgages

Shared appreciation, a variation developed in the United States, is a provision in a reverse mortgage contract that reduces the risk for the lender and, therefore, increases equity advance payments and eventual costs for the homeowner. This provision stipulates that the lender receive a share, or percentage, of any increase in property value (the appreciation), which may occur during the reverse mortgage. In exchange for a share of the appreciation, the lender may offer larger equity advances or a reduced interest rate.

Although home equity conversion, the common term for using equity while retaining ownership, is not a new idea, the Canadian reverse mortgage marketplace is still in its infancy. Since the mid-1970s, a great deal has been written and said about home equity conversion options, especially reverse mortgages, but only a few pioneering lenders have emerged. When consumer demand intensifies and more lenders enter the market, homeowners will enjoy the full advantage of shopping in a competitive home equity conversion market, especially in rural areas.

Figure R.12 and the following example illustrate basic considerations relating to reverse mortgage benefits and costs.

Example   *Reverse Mortgage*

Seller Smith is contemplating a reverse mortgage to convert the equity in his home so that he can continue his retirement travel plans and renovate his home. He approaches a lender enquiring as to the best available reverse mortgage product. The lender explains that reverse mortgage features should correspond to the homeowner's individual requirements for income, security, and estate planning, with particular regard to costs incurred by the homeowner. Seller Smith's research has shown that product comparisons should centre on three basic questions:

Continued…

What do I get?
Equity Advances   The amount of equity released to the homeowner(s) through the reverse mortgage, while ownership and possession are retained by the homeowner(s); and any other amount paid to the homeowner by the lender.

What will it cost?
Loan costs   The expenses, including interest, incurred by the home owner(s) in arranging a reverse mortgage; and, the amount the lender collects as interest and fees to cover profit and costs for providing the homeowner's reverse mortgage.

What will be left?
Residual Equity   The amount of equity remaining for the homeowner after the equity advances and the loan costs, including interest, have been withdrawn; and, the agreed amount of equity that is not part of the reverse mortgage and is, therefore, not available to the lender.

There may not be any residual equity left by the time the reverse mortgage terminates. Recovery of the reverse mortgage debt by the lender is usually limited to the value of the home by a provision in the reverse mortgage contract.

Reference   Information on reverse mortgages was adapted, with permission, from P. J. Wade, *Have Your Home and Money Too*, John Wiley & Sons, Rexdale, 1999.

Practitioners are strongly advised to seek expert advice on the topic of reverse mortgages.

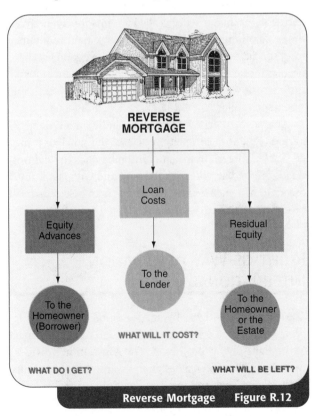

Reverse Mortgage   Figure R.12

REVERSE OSMOSIS

A procedure involving the removal of dissolved solids and minerals (e.g., chloride and sulphate), from a water supply that is frequently used in recreational properties. Reverse osmosis entails forcing water through a semi-permeable membrane. The membrane passes fresh water leaving behind minerals and other solid content. Such units have limited gallonage-per-day capacities.

Example   *Reverse Osmosis*

Buyer Jones is concerned about the quality of water in his new home and purchases a reverse osmosis drinking water system that will reduce the total dissolved solids by up to 95%. The system, located below the kitchen sink, is fully automatic, the storage compartment holds approximately 2.0 gallons of water and the unit operates with a pre-filter (large sediment) and a carbon filter for tastes and odours. The actual reverse osmosis is handled by a membrane (thin film polyamide), through which water passes and dissolved solids are left behind and flushed away by the system. The water production rate of the unit is estimated at 18 gallons per day. The entire unit is only 22 inches high, within an overall width of 12 inches.

REVERSION (SALE OF INVESTMENT PROPERTY)

The term *reversion*, for purposes of commercial brokerage, refers to the cash proceeds (cash flow) received from the sale of an investment property. Reversionary value can either be viewed on a *before tax* or *after tax* basis. Forecasted cash proceeds, after deducting estimates of cost of sale items, outstanding mortgages, and tax liability (in the case of after tax analysis), is used in analyzing real estate investments. The cash flow from sale proceeds together with the operations cash flows arising during the forecasted holding period can be used to establish both an internal rate of return and present value of the property.

REVERSION/REVERSIONARY INTEREST
(SEE ALSO ESTATE)

The return of an estate and the right to the future enjoyment of the property that is presently in the possession of, or is occupied by, another. The term *reversion* or *reversionary interest* is most commonly used in relation to the landlord's retention of an interest in the property in which the tenant's estate is a lesser estate and the property reverts to the landlord upon the termination of the tenancy agreement. However, other situations can arise that involve a reversionary interest, e.g., a life estate.

RIDER

> **Example** *Reversion/Reversionary Interest*
>
> Owner Smith established a life estate for his wife on the family homestead, but did not mention any further instructions, namely that Smith's son would ultimately inherit the entire property. When Smith passed away, his wife was granted a life estate in the property. However, upon her death, the interest in this property reverted to Smith's estate and not to the son.

Reference   Reversionary interest should be clearly differentiated from remainder. For additional details, see Remainder.

RIDER

An addition or amendment to a contract.

Application   For real estate practitioners, riders are frequently encountered in lease documents. In fact, the term *rider* is more frequently used in relation to the insurance industry, e.g., a rider on an automobile policy to permit an under age driver to operate the vehicle, or a rider on a homeowner's insurance policy to cover jewelry or art. In real estate, riders are usually referred to as appendices or schedules, such as those in a new home contract or lease.

> **Example** *Rider*
>
> Salesperson Martin is preparing an agreement for Buyer Jones to review involving a new townhouse condominium. In addition to the agreement of purchase and sale, Martin is attaching the following schedules/riders:
>
> • New Home Warranty Program
> • Unit Appointments and Finishes
> • List of Additional Upgrades
> • Deposit Structure and Financing
> • Acknowledgement: Condominium Documents.

RIGHT OF SURVIVORSHIP

(SEE ALSO JOINT TENANCY)

The most important characteristic of a joint tenancy, where if one joint tenant dies, his/her interest does not pass to his/her personal representative or his/her heirs by right of will but passes automatically to the surviving joint tenant or tenants.

A joint tenant may destroy the right of survivorship at any time before his/her death without the consent of the other joint tenant(s). This process, called severance, turns his joint tenancy into a tenancy in common with the other tenant or tenants. Those tenants can remain as joint tenants despite the severance.

A husband and wife often obtain title to a family home as joint tenants. On the death of either spouse, the survivor automatically receives full title to the property because of the right of survivorship. Joint tenancy is an advantage to the surviving spouse because the house does not form part of the deceased's estate thereby avoiding problems of administering and settling the estate.

> **Example** *Right of Survivorship*
>
> Mr. and Mrs. Jones are joint tenants in fee simple. Upon the death of Mrs. Jones, Mr. Jones automatically becomes the owner of the whole interest because of the right of survivorship. This is true, even if Mrs. Jones tried to dispose of the property by will. The right of survivorship takes precedence.

RIGHT-OF-WAY

(SEE ALSO EASEMENT)

The right to pass over another's land, more or less frequently, according to the nature of the easement.

Application   Practitioners may encounter rights-of-way particularly in the listing of rural and recreational properties. An easement can be created whenever an owner decides to grant a privilege called a right-of-way in favour of the adjoining property owner. An easement is obtained for a special purpose rather than for the general use and occupation of the land. The dominant tenement enjoys the right-of-way over the servient tenement to which the easement applies.

An easement expressly granted can be for a limited period (e.g., until completion of a subdivision), or it may be granted forever. In the latter instance, once the right-of-way is granted, it runs with the land and will pass from owner to owner. When listing property, an easement must be clearly identified and described.

RIGHT-OF-WAY ASSOCIATION, INTERNATIONAL

The International Right of Way Association (IRWA) is a non-profit professional association dedicated to the advancement of the right-of-way profession. The Association provides specialized education, a designation, and the opportunity for local, regional, and international professional contact.

The IRWA is an individual membership association for persons involved in the acquisition, management, or disposal of real estate for public agencies and investor-owned companies including:

- Government agencies at all levels, e.g., national, provincial, and local.
- Special authorities, e.g., harbours, ports, districts, airports, and mass transit.
- Investor and publicly owned utility and pipeline companies.
- Private valuation companies and right-of-way contracting companies.

Members are engaged in a wide range of specialty areas including law, appraisal, property management, engineering, relocation assistance, environment, land registration, property acquisition, and management.

Founded in 1934, IRWA has approximately 10,000 members with 75 chapters located throughout the United States and Canada. It is the only professional association representing the right-of-way profession.

RIGHT TO ACCESS

A clause that might be found in an agreement/contract in which the buyer is contemplating the subdividing of the property and/or the erection of some structure(s) and, consequently, requires permission to enter the property for the purpose of surveying and conducting soil tests before the completion of the transaction.

Such permission is normally worded so that the right does not extend to any alteration of the lands, servicing work, removal of trees, soil, or any other activity that would alter the current state of the property.

Example   *Right to Access*

Developer Reed has recently purchased, but not yet closed, the sale for a large tract of vacant land. However, he would like access to the property for purposes of surveying and conducting soil samples. Following is the clause inserted in the offer:

The seller agrees to grant the buyer and his/her authorized agent the right to enter the property for the purpose of surveying and conducting soil tests prior to the completion of this transaction. Such permission does not extend to any alteration of the lands, servicing work, removal of trees, soil, or any other activity which would alter the current state of the property.

RIGHT TO ASSIGN

(SEE ASSIGNMENT)

RIGHT TO DEMOLISH

A right occasionally included in a mortgage document providing that the mortgagor shall have the right to alter or demolish any or all of the existing buildings on the property without such activity constituting waste under the terms of the mortgage, provided that such alteration or demolition meets all applicable by-laws, building codes, or other applicable laws and regulations.

Example   *Right to Demolish*

Smith is selling an older commercial building and will be taking back a mortgage on the property. Reed is buying with the intent of redeveloping the property and building a small neighbourhood mall consisting of seven retail stores on the main level with residential rental units on the upper floor. To redevelop, Reed must first demolish the existing structure, but does not want to create waste under the mortgage document. Waste refers to the destruction of value in the property due to actions of a person that impacts another's interest in that land, for example, the mortgagee.

Accordingly, the following clause is inserted in the mortgage document between Smith and Reed:

This mortgage shall contain a clause providing that the mortgagor shall have the right to alter or demolish any or all of the existing buildings now on the property without such activity constituting waste under the terms of this mortgage, provided that such alteration or demolition shall comply with all applicable by-laws, building codes, or other applicable laws or regulations.

RIPARIAN RIGHTS

The rights of the owners of lands on the banks of watercourses, to take advantageous use of the water on, under, or adjacent to their land.

Application   Real estate practitioners will typically encounter riparian rights in the listing, marketing, and selling of recreational properties. Such rights are deemed to be natural rights by reason of ownership, as they arise from the natural state of the property in conjunction with the abutting watercourse. Riparian rights can be grouped under the following two categories.

R

Rights Concerning the Body of Water

- Right of access to water.
- Direct exclusive access from owned land.
- Right of increase in shore area by natural growth.
- Right of navigation.

Rights Concerning Flow of Water

- Right to enforce water flow.
- Right to unpolluted water.
- Right to use water.

Provincial   See applicable reference materials. Riparian rights are frequently subject to provincial legislation concerning public lands under bodies of water and other environmental legislation impacting shoreline property.

RISK

Most commonly associated with decisions to acquire investment-grade property, but the element of risk applies to all investment decisions. Risk refers to the uncertainty, chance, exposure, and vulnerability imposed on an investor with particular regard to any financial loss that may accrue from an investment. Risk, for real estate purposes, centres on fluctuations in the income stream and the vulnerability of that stream to external influences such as market trends, availability and suitability of financing, degree of positive or negative leverage, and overall economic conditions.

Application   Risk is typically viewed as a primary consideration in any real estate investment. The ability to forecast and in some way quantify the impact of various influences on an investment property is broadly described as risk analysis. Complex risk analysis models and related computer programs do exist, but often go well beyond the practical needs of commercial brokerage. In reality, reliance on intuitive sense, personal experience, and historical market trends is more commonplace.

As a general statement, risk is assessed as either external or internal. Most risk analysts acknowledge *factors beyond the property* as distinct from *factors within the property*. While authoritative texts differ on terms used, most divide risk into several broad segments:

- Financial (e.g., interest rates and purchasing power of future dollars);
- Market (e.g., real estate market trends and occupancy rates);
- Business (e.g., taxation, economic activity, and investment climate); and
- Building risks (e.g., physical calamities).

Variations do exist, e.g., financial risk, business risk, market risk, and purchasing power risk (inflation). Some prefer to combine market and business risks under one category. Regardless, each segment typically contains both general and specific elements. For example, financial risk refers to the ability to preserve principal while ensuring a return on that principal. From a *general* perspective, the availability of finances in the marketplace may dictate ultimate return. However, from a *specific* perspective, the particular leverage used within an individual project will also affect financial risk. With market risk, the property is subject to *general* risks given the ups and downs of the real estate market, while the property itself attracts *specific* risks given its particular use.

Most theorists agree that entrepreneurial ability is a vital dimension in all risk analysis. In other words, the investor's level of sophistication and his/her investment strategy directly affects risk. Financial acumen when securing suitable financing, along with the tax status of the investor, also have a direct bearing on risk. Risk can be reduced through effective business strategy. Obviously, selection of investment properties and proper portfolio diversification can impact risk. The limitation of liability, (e.g., limiting personal covenants on loans and provision for adequate building and liability insurance), and insistence on prudent contracts, (e.g., escalation clauses in tenant leases), are further positive forces in reducing risk.

Risk is also a factor in determining value. Risk in any investment property is ultimately reflected in the value of that property in the marketplace. Appraisers, real estate practitioners, and investors should be particularly sensitive to the type and class of investment opportunity and associated risk. In fact, the discount rate applied when determining the value of a particular property typically includes a risk component, referred to as a *risk premium*.

RISK ANALYSIS

The examination of real estate investments including the assessment of varying degrees of risk associated with such investments. The analysis usually involves a systematic examination of investment options to minimize risk and maximize returns based on investor objectives and levels of risk tolerance. Most discussions of risk centre on two topics: *risk control* techniques typically implemented by the owner, and *risk adjustment* techniques used by investment analysts to quantify risk within investment options.

Risk Control

Investors use a variety of risk control techniques. They may seek to reduce risk through investment portfolio divers-

R

ification involving the distribution of capital between mutual funds, guaranteed investment certificates, cash, real estate, and equity stocks. For those specifically involved in real estate, diversification is typically obtained through various types of properties, ownership options, and geographic locations. Other risk control measures can also apply. The real estate investor may exert some degree of control by means of prudent property selection techniques combined with detailed research to minimize the chance of error when making real estate decisions.

Investors also frequently *hedge* investment decisions by assuring themselves of options while not committing immediately to any particular course of action, e.g., an option for the future purchase of land. The option normally fixes financial commitment while providing sufficient time to fully investigate alternates and/or await some anticipated future event. Hedging can take on many forms. An owner may choose an open-ended mortgage hoping to capitalize on favourable future rates and *lock-in* at the moment interest rates begin to rise. A lessor may seek guarantees from lessees to minimize the impact of default.

Hedging is part of an overall strategy to control or in some way limit risk exposure. Often, a trade-off is required. The landlord may employ a professional property management team to control expenses and minimize financial risks. The savings and peace of mind can effectively balance any increased costs. The business entrepreneur may acquire business loss insurance in addition to fire and theft coverage. The added expense could reduce risk and business calamity in the event of total destruction. The commercial landlord may place stringent requirements on tenants to ensure that most or all costs are passed to the lessee. While potentially limiting the range of possible tenants, the owner limits exposure to unknown variables.

Risk Adjustment

In recent years, risk adjustment techniques have become popular in real estate investment analysis when quantifying risk and assisting rational decision-making. Current literature emphasizes such concepts as payback (breakeven), internal rate of return (IRR) partitioning, certainty-equivalent techniques, sensitivity analysis, and risk analysis based on probabilities. The payback period is simply the number of years required for cash flows to repay initial investment. Shortening the payback period can often limit risks associated with the investment. IRR partitioning involves the division and analysis of components that make up the internal rate of return for a property. The four components normally include cash flows after taxes, sale proceeds after taxes, tax savings (if applicable), and equity buildup. In delineating and examining these sources, the real estate analyst can assess whether the present value of each source is consistent with overall investment objectives. The concept of present value partitioning has also appeared in the marketplace. Just as equity and debt components can be partitioned for valuation purposes, the cash flow after taxes can be partitioned into its component parts (income, operating expense, debt service, and tax savings (if applicable)), and analyzed based on their respective present values. In that way, the investor examines inputs from each source to better evaluate the relevant components in an investment decision.

The certainty-equivalent technique provides a method to discount cash flows in recognition of risk. First, projected cash flows are adjusted for anticipated risk and second, the resulting flows are discounted using a risk-free rate. The investor is presented with a series of risky and risk-free cash flows involving alternate investments. Through deductive analysis and the process of elimination, a risk-free rate is established for decision purposes at the point where the investor becomes indifferent or unconcerned about the difference between the risk and risk-free options. The certainty-equivalent technique, while logically sound, has various limitations for applied use in real estate investment analysis.

The most popular methods of risk adjustment are associated with sensitivity analysis and probability theory. Sensitivity analysis involves the testing of alternate assumptions regarding variables that impact cash flows and provides a broader picture of how various revenues and expenses impact the investment. Probability theory incorporates mathematical probabilities in assessing relative risk associated with the acquisition of real estate.

RISK REDUCTION

Activities that will minimize exposure to risk and associated liability. According to errors and omissions claims research, liability for real estate practitioners is commonly found in three specific areas: unreliable documentation, inaccurate seller representations; and inaccurate and/or unverified published listing information.

False Representations or Misrepresentations

Real estate practitioners are increasingly challenged about what is said, printed, or represented during the listing and selling process. Salespeople must investigate facts before making statements and properly qualify the content of such statements in terms of their knowledge levels, degree of expertise, and other relevant matters. Research should always include direct on-site observations and a thorough review of source documents.

R

Real estate practitioners face litigation under both fraudulent statements, where the person making the statement knows it to be false, and accidental misrepresentations, where the person making the statement should be aware of the facts.

> **Example**   *Risk Reduction—*
> *False Representations or*
> *Misrepresentations*
>
> A salesperson can fraudulently misrepresent if he/she makes a false statement about the condition of a well, while being fully aware that a problem exists. The same salesperson can accidentally misrepresent if he/she assures the buyer that the well is fine, despite the fact that no tests or qualified inspection have been carried out to that effect.
>
> A prudent real estate salesperson would thoroughly discuss the matter with both the seller, (to assess the current circumstances), and the buyer, (to advise alternatives such as bacteriological testing and an inspection by qualified person).

Duty of Care

While agency duties to the client are well defined, legal cases during the past two decades have placed increasing responsibility on the brokerage and salespersons to take particular care when providing information to persons other than the client.

> **Example**   *Risk Reduction—*
> *Duty of Care*
>
> The salesperson gives an assurance to the buyer concerning the condition of the basement (i.e., no leakage problems), without fully investigating the matter. The buyer accepts this unqualified assurance, elects not to include a proper condition in the offer, and ultimately is injured when leakage is discovered after closing that renders the basement area largely unuseable for additional living area contemplated by that buyer.

Latent Defects

Items that are present, but not apparent to the untrained eye, represent a special challenge for real estate practitioners. Latent defects crop up in many errors and omissions claims. Neither reliance on seller representations, nor buyer indifference or ignorance, remove risk associated with latent defects.

Court decisions already exist where salespeople have become embroiled in the nondisclosure of termites, despite the fact that these insects went unnoticed at the time of showing and probably would escape all but the most trained eye. The issue is not the termites but the fact that

termite infestations are common to a specific locale and the real estate professional should be aware of that fact in the normal process of listing and selling property.

Agency

Breach of agency duties and confusion over fiduciary responsibilities to parties in a transaction have caused a great deal of litigation. Real estate practitioners must ensure that proper agency disclosure procedures are followed at all times and agency duties are correctly performed.

> **Example**   *Risk Reduction—Agency*
>
> Salesperson Ward exclusively lists a property for sale and then develops a client relationship with a buyer who expresses an interest in the property. On the one hand, the seller and the brokerage who employs Ward have entered into an express agency relationship. At the same time, the actions and statements of the salesperson toward the buyer have placed the brokerage into an implied agency relationship with the buyer. Consequently, unintended dual agency has arisen without proper disclosure to either principal.

Documentation

Practitioners must be careful in drafting all documents when listing and selling of property. Be careful to avoid confusion in notice periods, improperly drafted conditions, lack of clear intention of the parties to the agreement, and missing and/or inaccurate details about properties.

> **Example**   *Risk Reduction—Documentation*
>
> The buyer purchases an expensive home in a beautiful ravine setting. An existing survey, although available, is not attached or mentioned in the offer and the property measurements lack clarity. The buyer closes the transaction, only to discover that a significant portion of the rear yard is owned by a neighbour. The responsibility of the listing salesperson is a legal issue, but undoubtedly lack of proper documentation will adversely affect his/her position in ensuing litigation.

ROAD ALLOWANCE (PUBLIC ROAD)

A tract of land dedicated for the purposes of public travel. The traditional road allowance within single front townships, double front townships, and sectional systems was 66 feet in width. Road allowances have been expanded dramatically to accommodate major highways, e.g., 100, 200, and 400 feet. Also, in plans of subdivision, developers dedicate certain parts of the draft plan as public roads.

Application   General rules for real estate practitioners concerning public roads follow.

- Unless a road allowance set down originally by Crown surveyors has been closed by municipal decree, the road allowance remains open despite the fact that it has never been used. This also applies to roads accepted and dedicated within a plan of subdivision.
- In the case of subdivisions, the areas dedicated as public roads do not become so until accepted by the municipality.
- Although most roads are declared open by municipal by-law and/or as originally set out by Crown patent, a road may become part of the municipal road system if municipal monies are regularly expended for repair and maintenance. Further, individuals may open road allowances that were originally set out as such (e.g., Crown Patent or plan of subdivision) upon the person meeting certain maintenance standards with the municipality.

Example   Road Allowance (Public Road)

Jones is considering the purchase of a year-round home on Big Lake. Smith, the seller, claims to have used the road throughout the year which according to him is continuously maintained by the township. The salesperson representing Jones in a buyer agency relationship suggests that a condition be placed in the agreement/contract to ensure the accuracy of statements concerning the road. Following is the inserted clause:

This offer is conditional upon the buyer determining, at the buyer's own expense, that access by automobile to the property is by a public road which is maintained throughout the year at public expense. Unless the buyer gives notice in writing delivered to the seller by 12:00 p.m. on the 1st day of May, 20xx that this condition has been fulfilled, this offer shall become null and void and the deposit shall be returned to the buyer in full without deduction. This condition is included for the sole benefit of the buyer and may be waived at the buyer's option by notice in writing to the seller within the time period stated herein.

ROOF

The primary purpose of a roof is to keep the building and its occupants protected from rain, snow, sun, wind, and all combinations thereof. Roofs may also add to or detract from the appearance of a building. Roofs provide some protection against falling objects, although anyone who has seen the damage done by a large tree falling on a house

knows that the strength of the roof is limited. Roof coverings are not intended to keep out the cold and the majority of roofs are extremely poor insulators.

Common Problem Areas

The most vulnerable areas of a roof are where it changes direction, or where a change in materials occurs, such as the roof meeting a chimney or a wall. These areas are flashed on a properly installed roof. In addition to flashings, areas where television antennas or satellite dishes and their supporting wires are attached are potential trouble spots. Areas that have already been repaired are also vulnerable. As a general rule, a roof with a low slope tends to be more vulnerable to wear and leakage.

Ice Damming

Some roofing configurations are more prone to ice damming problems than others. Ice damming occurs when snow and ice collect in a certain area of the roof, often the eaves. Melting snow on the upper portion of the roof cannot drain properly as it is trapped behind the ice dam. If the dam is large enough and enough water collects, it will back up under the shingles and leak into the eaves or worse, into the exterior walls or the building interior.

Ice damming problems do not necessarily occur every winter. They normally occur after periods of heavy snow when day time temperatures are at or slightly above freezing while night time temperatures are below freezing.

Effective solutions to ice damming problems are increased attic insulation and ventilation. These two measures reduce the air temperature in the attic to minimize snow melt over the heated portions of the house.

Tree Branches Touching Roof

Trees should be kept trimmed away from roof and wall surfaces. The abrasive action of branches rubbing against the roof can damage the roof system and shorten its life expectancy. Also, tree limbs touching buildings provide easy access to the home for pests, such as squirrels.

Flashings

Designed to keep water out and are used where dissimilar materials meet, where a material changes direction, or at joints in materials. Most flashings are galvanized steel; however, they can also be tin, aluminum, or copper.

Materials

Although there are many different types of roofing materials on the market today, the following are the most common in provinces throughout Canada.

Asphalt Shingles

Asphalt shingles are the most common roofing material. Shingles consist of asphalt impregnated felt paper, coated with an additional layer of asphalt, and covered with granular material.

Asphalt shingles are classified by weight. The most common type of shingles used today weigh 210 pounds per square and have a life expectancy of 12–15 years (225s, 235s, and 320s are also available).

Most asphalt shingles are self-sealing. A strip of tar is put on the surface of the shingles by the manufacturer. This strip is covered by the shingle installed immediately above. When the sun warms the roof surface, the two shingles stick together. Shingles installed in the late fall or winter do not normally seal themselves until spring.

Wood Shingles and Shakes

Wood shingles are machine cut, while wood shakes are hand split or mechanically split. Wood shakes are thicker and have a much more uneven surface. Most wood shingles are cedar; however, some are redwood. The life expectancy of wood shingles is generally 30 to 40 years. The rate of wear depends largely on exposure (the amount of shingle which is exposed to the weather), the pitch (the steeper the better), the grade of shingle, and the amount of sun and shade. Too much sunlight dehydrates the shingles, causing them to become brittle. Too much shade and moisture causes rot and moss to grow.

Roll Roofing

Roll roofing, sometimes referred to as *selvage roofing*, consists of materials similar to asphalt shingles but is manufactured in 18-inch or 36-inch wide rolls. The surface can be completely covered with granules or only 50 percent covered in the case of two-ply applications. Roll roofing is most appropriate for low pitched roofs and typically has a life expectancy of five to ten years.

Pitch

Roofing systems can be divided into two main categories: sloped roofs and flat roofs. Sloped roofing systems are not watertight per se and shed water much like a pyramid of umbrellas. Flat roofs, on the other hand, are watertight membranes designed to be impervious to water penetration. Flat roofing is actually a misnomer as these roofing systems should never be perfectly flat. They should slope enough to allow water to drain properly, since water standing on the roof for long periods of time will accelerate deterioration of the membrane.

The pitch of a roof is really the slope of the roof. Convention dictates that the slope is defined as a ratio of rise over run. For uniformity, the run is always defined as twelve feet. Therefore, a six in twelve roof would have a vertical rise of six feet, over a horizontal distance of 12 feet. Roofs with a pitch greater than four in twelve are considered conventional roof systems. Roofs with a slope between four in twelve and two in twelve are considered low slope roofs, and roofs with a pitch less than two in twelve are considered flat roofs.

Single ply membranes used for flat roof applications have gained increasing popularity since the early 1980s. Some are a modified bitumen (asphalt) base while others are plastic (primarily PVC) or synthetic rubber. The membranes may be glued, tarred down, or mechanically fastened with strips or buttons. Others are laid loose and held in place with gravel.

Sheathing

Roof sheathing, most commonly wood plank and plywood dating before 1970, has now been largely replaced by wafer board panels. This sheathing performs two functions by supporting the roof covering and transmitting the load of this material as well as the live loads due to snow, ice, and wind to the rafters, trusses, or roof joists.

Practitioners should be aware of certain problems that can arise with roof sheathing.

Condensation   Moisture in an attic can cause considerable problems. Plywood roof sheathing will delaminate and wafer board sheathing will swell. This can cause loss of strength in the sheathing and render the nailing of the sheathing ineffective, as nails are pulled out of the rafters, or through the sheathing. In severe cases, the roof covering has to be removed and the sheathing replaced.

Too Thin   Sheathing that is too thin for the application will deflect under load and result in sagging of the roof line. Aesthetically, this is considered unacceptable although sagging to the point of failure would be unusual.

Edge Support   Unsupported edges of roof sheathing may lead to differential movement between two panels. This can lead to horizontal ridges appearing in the roofing. Seams parallel to rafters in panel roof sheathing should occur only over the rafters and should be staggered. If the sheathing is unusually thick, edge support is not necessary.

Figure R.13 illustrates plank and plywood sheathing in relation to other roof components.

Square

A square is an expression denoting the amount of roofing material required to cover one hundred square feet.

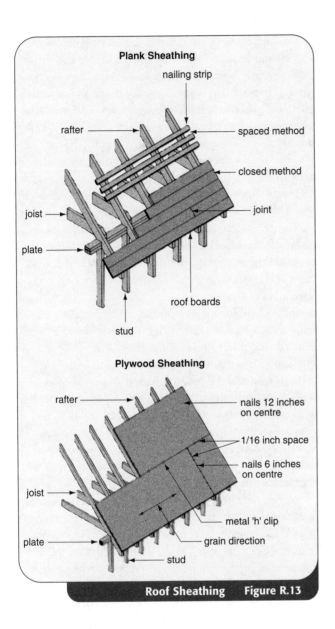

Plank Sheathing

nailing strip

rafter

spaced method

closed method

joist

joint

plate

roof boards

stud

Plywood Sheathing

rafter

nails 12 inches on centre

1/16 inch space

nails 6 inches on centre

joist

metal 'h' clip

grain direction

plate

stud

Roof Sheathing   Figure R.13

Trusses

Roof trusses perform the same function as rafters, collar ties, knee walls, and ceiling joists. The roof truss holds up the roof sheathing and shingles, transferring the roof loads to the outside or bearing walls. The bottom of the truss also supports the ceiling finish, upon which the insulation rests.

Most trusses used in residential construction are made up of wood components. The top and bottom members of the truss are referred to as *chords*, the interior members are called *webs*. Individual wood members are secured with gusset plates and may be made of plywood or steel. Various configurations of trusses have different strengths, and engineers can use the shape and component size that best suits them. Trusses are typically pre-engineered systems and are normally spaced 24 inches apart, but can vary, depending on spans and depth of the desired truss.

Two common types of trusses are used residentially. The *Fink Truss* has web members that form a **W**. The Howe truss can be identified by vertical web members, including a vertical web running up to the peak. The *Howe Truss* is stronger, however if long spans are within the capabilities of the truss, either will perform well. See **Figure R.14**.

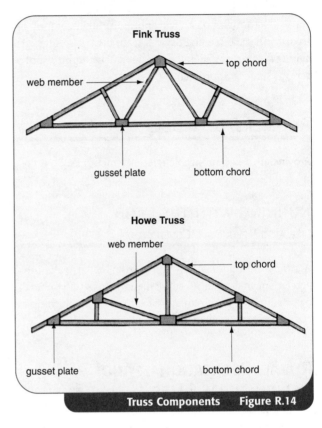

Fink Truss

web member

top chord

gusset plate

bottom chord

Howe Truss

web member

top chord

gusset plate

bottom chord

Truss Components   Figure R.14

Practitioners should be aware of specific problems that can arise with trusses.

Cut   Individual chords or webs that are cut or damaged can be a serious problem. Cutting a truss in one spot may seriously compromise the entire truss structure. Special engineering consideration should be given where trusses have to be cut to accommodate chimneys or other interruptions in the roof line.

Truss Uplift   A phenomenon known as truss uplift is relatively common in new houses and involves the bottom member (chord) of the truss deflecting upward during winter weather. Apparently, the temperature and humidity changes in the attic during the winter months affect the sections of the truss above the insulation level differently than the bottom chord buried in the insulation. This results in an upward bowing of the bottom chord. The result of truss uplift is that the centre section of the bottom chord moves upward and gaps as large as ½ inch appear at the top of the interior walls, where they join the ceiling.

R

The ceiling is picked up by the truss. It is less common but also possible, that the entire wall below will be lifted up, and separation will occur between the bottom of the wall and the floor. At present, a good solution is not known for this problem, and common corrective action is to secure a moulding to the ceiling (but not to the wall). As the ceiling moves up and down, the moulding slides up and down the wall although no gap will appear. Another solution is to disconnect the ceiling drywall from the truss. Alternate ceiling support is generally necessary. Trust uplift is not a serious structural problem.

ROOMERS/BOARDERS

Provincial   See applicable reference materials.

RUNNING WITH THE LAND
(SEE ALSO RESTRICTIVE COVENANTS)

A covenant extending beyond the original parties to the agreement that binds all subsequent owners to liability concerning the requirement to perform, or the right to take advantage of, that covenant.

RURAL, RECREATIONAL, AND AGRICULTURAL SALES

Specializing in one or more areas encompassing the broad category of *rural, recreational, and agricultural sales* is an enormous challenge. In some areas of Canada, depending on local economics and prevalent land uses, real estate practitioners may be able to specialize solely in recreational properties or sales of farms. In other locales, a mixture of rural residential, recreational, and agricultural sales is required to build a worthwhile career. Consequently, it is virtually impossible to identify areas of specialization.

In the western provinces, prime agricultural land and its significant contribution to the provincial economy provides an excellent basis for agricultural sales specialities. In Manitoba, for example, wheat and barley crops account for up to one-half of the harvested crop area. Agricultural and related industries contribute an average of 5 percent to the provincial gross domestic product. Practitioners must have knowledge of farmland tenure and ownership, farm operating agreements, and land leasing arrangements, e.g., crop share lease, cash rent lease, and flexible cash lease. Many other issues come into play including land survey systems, the quality of soils (e.g., texture, fertility, and soil capability), the operation of farm marketing

boards and agencies, quotas and special crop contracts, and various statutes impacting the ownership and operation of farms. Agriculture can also be very diversified with special crops such as sugar beets, dry beans, potatoes, flaxseed, soy, sunflower seeds, buckwheat, and field peas. The livestock industry of cattle, hogs, dairy cows, sheep, and poultry also make significant contributions. The dairy industry represents another important dimension of agricultural production.

Practitioners in other areas of Canada may be involved in the sale of farmland not only for farming purposes but also for redevelopment and hobby/recreational uses. Although most workable land is used for agriculture, the demand for commercial, industrial, and residential development of this land is increasing, especially in heavily populated areas of the country.

Selling land for redevelopment can be lucrative, but requires considerable knowledge. Redevelopment of agricultural land usually takes place close to, or inside, the boundaries of urban centres. It is crucial to know the value of land and the permitted uses. To provide good service to clients, the sales representatives must be familiar with official plans and zoning by-laws. In addition, the sales representative would have to be aware of the saleability and demand for the product, whether that be residential building lots, high-density residential uses, or commercial and industrial uses.

Recreational properties represent a significant portion of activity for many practitioners located in vacation areas. Detailed knowledge of zoning by-laws and restrictions is critical for persons specializing in this field. Cottage and recreational properties fall under statutory requirements, ranging from regulations regarding the installation of wells and septic systems to required permits for construction of waterfront improvements, e.g., wharfs, docks, boathouses, and shoreline alterations. Further, many cottage properties are only accessible by private easements and a knowledge of limitations and potential problems arising from such access systems must be known.

Rural specialists are commonly involved in property types ranging from single-family residential to recreational businesses. In many Canadian areas, the rural economy requires knowledge of different types of business operations. The veteran urban salesperson can be bewildered by unique local customs and practices. Most have little experience in the marketing of worm farms, retreats, marinas, horse farms, and a host of other unique properties. An added difficulty is the sparse availability of comparables when establishing value for such enterprises. As well, distances are greater, access is sometimes limited, and weather conditions are a consideration.

S

National Info Links

Statistics

Statistics Canada

Telephone (800) 263 1163
Web Site www.statcan.ca

For a directory of regional Statistics Canada reference centres visit www.statcan.ca/english/reference/refcentre.html.

Source Deductions

Canada Customs and Revenue Agency

Web Site www.ccra-adrc.gc.ca

See the local telephone directory for addresses and telephone numbers of Tax Services Offices and Tax Centres.

Standards of Business Practice

Canadian Real Estate Association
344 Slater Street, Suite 1600
Canada Building
Ottawa, ON K1R 7Y3

Telephone (613) 237 7111
Web Site www.crea.ca
www.mls.ca

Statutes

For federal statute searches, see the Department of Justice Canada:

Web site www.canada.justice.gc.ca

For provincial statute searches, contact the applicable provincial government office. Links to provincial government web sites can be found at:

Web Site www.canada.gc.ca/othergov/prov_e.html.

SAFE RATE

(SEE ALSO REINVESTMENT RATE)

A term commonly used in the calculation of selected rates of return involving income producing real estate. The safe rate is a rate of interest provided by an investment vehicle, at current market rates, in which funds are highly liquid and may be withdrawn without deduction or penalty involving either principal or interest, for example, treasury bills.

Application The safe rate is used by commercial practitioners when calculating the modified internal rate of return (MIRR) or financial management rate of return (FMRR). Such funds are held until needed to cover negative cash flows when analyzing forecasted variable cash flows in a real estate investment. Use of a safe rate overcomes shortcomings concerning the internal rate of return (IRR).

SAFETY MARGIN (INCOME PROPERTY)

A term used in relation to mortgage lending practices involving investment properties. The safety margin represents either a dollar or percentage factor that serves as a financial cushion for the lender between the obligation of an owner to pay annual debt service and the forecasted net operating income from the property under consideration. In other words, the lender seeks additional security to ensure that not every dollar of net operating income is dedicated to addressing mortgage payments. A safety margin is typically required by a lender when considering income property in commercial mortgage qualification.

Example *Safety Margin (Income Property)*

The Canadian National Bank is concerned about Seller Smith's income stream derived from a multi-residential building located in Anycity. According to the reconstructed worksheet prepared by Salesperson Lane of ABC Realty Inc., the net operating income is $105,256. In theory, this amount could be devoted totally to debt service payments. However, a safety margin of 20% is required by the lender.

Safety Margin/Mortgage Qualification
1937 Lakefront Drive, Anycity

Net Operating Income (Forecasted for Upcoming Year)	$105,256
Lender Safety Margin (20% of Net Operating Income)	21,051
Amount Available for Annual Debt Service (105,256 − 21,051)	84,205
Amount Available for Monthly Debt Service (84,205 ÷ 12)	7,017

Continued...

Assuming that a 7% mortgage can be obtained from the Canadian National Bank with a 25-year amortization, Seller Smith would qualify for a mortgage of approximately $1,001,845. This amount is calculated by referring to the *Mortgage Payment Factors*. The payment factor per $1,000 is 7.004158 for a 7% mortgage with a 25-year amortization. Therefore, the amount of the mortgage can be determined by dividing Smith's amount available for monthly debt service by the factor to arrive at the number of 000s (thousands) in mortgage principal. In this instance, Smith can qualify for 7,017 ÷ 7.004158 = 1001.833 (000s) in mortgage amount which equals $1,001,833 (answer is arrived at by moving the decimal three places to the right).

SALE

Provincial See applicable reference materials for a definition of sale or trade in relation to real property.

SALE OF A BUSINESS

(SEE BUSINESS)

Provincial See applicable reference materials.

SALE PROCEEDS AFTER TAXES

Cash proceeds (cash flow) received from the sale of an investment property following deduction for sale costs less any mortgage balance, and less deductions for tax liability. Real estate investors are concerned with both operations cash flow (arising from the operation of the enterprise), as well as the cash flow realized from the sale (reversion) of the property. Both operations and sale proceeds cash flows are used in the cash flow model when analyzing investment properties.

Application Traditionally, real estate investors treated sale proceeds as a separate and distinct item with emphasis on real estate capital appreciation (or depreciation). However, during recent decades, a more holistic approach has entered both appraisal and commercial brokerage fields as investors sought increased precision in forecasting. Whole cost models (analysis of the entire project), and the use of discounted cash flows arrived from the fields of capital budgeting and financing analysis. Real estate practitioners now routinely review both operations and sale proceeds cash flows from before and after tax positions depending on the circumstances and needs of the client. Advanced calculations have greatly simplified otherwise complex calculations.

S

Three sequential calculations are required to estimate *sale proceeds after taxes*. First the sale price of the property is estimated. Cost of sale items are deducted along with the remaining mortgage balance to arrive at *sale proceeds before taxes*. The tax liability is determined through a complex set of calculations involving recaptured capital cost allowance, the establishment of the adjusted cost base, amount of capital gain, and the resulting tax liability that flows from those calculations. This amount is deducted from the *sale proceeds before taxes* to determine *sale proceeds after taxes*.

Example	Sale Proceeds After Taxes	
Sale Price	$260,000	
Costs of Sale	−15,000	
Mortgage Balance	−100,000	
Proceeds Before Taxes		145,000
Tax Liability on Sale		−20,000
Sale Proceeds After Tax		$125,000

SALE PROCEEDS BEFORE TAXES

Cash proceeds (cash flow) received from the sale of an investment property following deduction for sale costs and less any mortgage balance, but before any deductions for tax liability. In the previous example, the sale proceeds before taxes is $145,000 based on a $200,000 sale price. Sale proceeds before taxes is used in yield capitalization and investment analysis. See **Cash Flow Model**.

SALE PROCESSING

Provincial   See applicable reference materials.

SALE (TRADE) REGISTER

A register, often called the *Deal Book*, summarizing all trade (transaction) activity within a real estate brokerage. Information normally entered includes: trade number, sale date, address of property, selling salesperson, initial/ supplementary deposit(s), conditions and removal dates, closing date, brokerage receivable, and disposition details.

Application   Figure S.1 details typical entries in a manual sale register. During recent years, registers have been included within brokerage software packages in which all management and accounting information is integrated for use by administrative staff and the broker.

SALE/LEASEBACK

The sale of a property by an owner with the lease back of the property to that original owner.

Application   The sale/leaseback arrangement can prove beneficial to both the seller and buyer of property. The seller liquidates his/her equity in the land and building to use for other purposes, while retaining the location under a long-term lease arrangement. The buyer, as an investor, is assured of a long-term cash flow, and the seller may have an option to repurchase the property following the lease. Obviously, certain risks are associated with the sale/leaseback. The investor is relying on the tenant to make regular lease payments, thereby ensuring the anticipated rate of return. Any default can adversely affect investor cash flow. On the converse, the land may appreciate substantially during the lease period with the investor enjoying capital appreciation even though the building may have depreciated significantly during the extended lease period.

				SALE REGISTER				March 20xx
Trade #	Sale Date	Address	Selling Salesperson	Trust Deposits	Conditions	Closing Date	Disposition	Company Receivable
90–012	03/25/xx	123 Main St.	Lee	$2,000–Init $4,000–04/30/xx $8,000–05/30/xx	Financing, 2nd Mtge, Exp 04/30/xx	06/30/xx	Transaction Closed Chq Rec'd 07/07/xx	$1,932.50
90–013	03/27/xx	392 West St.	Warden	$5,000–Init $5,000–05/10/xx	Financing, 1st Mtge, Exp 05/10/xx Sale of House (48 Hr), Exp 07/15/xx		All Conditions Removed	$2,450.00

Figure S.1   Sale (Trade) Register

SALES CONTRACT

A contract by which one party agrees to sell and another agrees to purchase upon the payment of an agreed price.

Provincial   See applicable reference materials concerning agreements involving the purchase and sale of real property.

SALESPERSON, REAL ESTATE

A real estate salesperson is generally described as a person employed, appointed, or authorized by a broker (agent) to trade in real estate. Exact definitions will vary by provincial jurisdiction.

Provincial   See applicable reference materials.

SANDWICH LEASE

A leasehold interest in a property created by means of a sublease from the lessee to a sublessee.

Application   Sandwich leases involve a sublease in which the original lessee conveys part of the leasehold interest, while retaining an interest in the property. A sublease is an arrangement in which the lessee typically collects sublease rent and remits contract rent under the original lease to the landlord. Subleases can result from differential cash flows in which the original lessee gains an economic advantage between contract and market rents and subleases to generate cash flows from this advantage.

Conversely, under adverse market conditions, a lessee may be forced to create a sandwich lease out of necessity and absorb any deficiency between the sublease and the contract rent. The sandwich lease creates three interests in the property: leased fee estate of the landlord (lessor); leasehold estate of the original tenant (lessee), and the interest of the sublessee.

SANDWICH LEASEHOLD VALUATION

The value attributed to an interest or estate in a property that arises from a sandwich lease. A sandwich lease exists when the tenant, as the original lessee, sublets the property to a sublessee. The original lessee becomes *sandwiched* between the landlord and the sublessee. Sandwich leases typically occur when market rents are higher than contracted rent in the original lease.

Example   Sandwich Leasehold Valuation—Sandwich Rent Equal to Market Rent

Tenant Crawford, the original lessee, is paying a contracted rent of $8.50 per square foot for 2,000 square foot premises. The remaining term is four years and the market rent now stands at $14.00 per square foot. The economic advantage is $5.50 per square foot or $11,000 per year for the lease remainder. Crawford sublets the property for $14.00 per square foot to a new tenant. The value of the sandwich lease from the lessee's perspective, assuming a discount rate of 11.50%, is:

Differential: Year 1, $11,000 + Year 2, $11,000 + Year 3, $11,000, and Year 4, $11,000
Discount Rate: 11.50%
Present Value: $33,766

As with all discounted cash flow analysis and valuation, the establishment of the proper discount rate is vital. If greater risk is associated with the sublease, the appraiser may conduct appropriate research and undoubtedly increase the discount rate. Any increase in discount is inversely correlated to value, e.g., a discount rate of 13.5% produces a value of $32,382.

Example   Sandwich Leasehold Valuation—Sandwich Rent Less Than Market But Higher than Contract Rent

Tenant Jarozz, as the original lessee, is paying a contracted rent of $1,200 per month for street level, retail space in an older downtown building. The lease expires in exactly four years and the landlord permits subleasing of space. The current market rent for this space is $1,800 per month. Jarozz locates sublessee Dempster who is prepared to sublease at $1,600 per month for the balance of the lease. Both Jarozz and Dempster derive an economic benefit.

Present Value to the Lessee Jarozz
(difference between contract rent and sandwich rent)

Differential: Year 1, $4,800 + Year 2, $4,800 + Year 3, $4,800 + Year 4, $4,800
Discount Rate: 13.5%
Present Value: $14,130

Present Value to the Sublessee Dempster
(difference between sandwich rent and market rent)

Differential: Year 1, $2,400 + Year 2, $2,400 + Year 3, $2,400 + Year 4, $2,400
Discount Rate: 13.5%
Present Value: $7,065

The same discount rate was used for illustration purposes, but may vary based on the perception of risk associated with either interest. The lessee derives an economic benefit by receiving cash from the sublessee. The sublessee derives an economic benefit through reduced rent in relation to market rates. In other words, the sublessee is getting a rent bargain, sometimes referred to as a *non-marketable interest*.

SCHEMATIC DESIGN

A design, resulting from inspection of the site and conferences with the client, concerning the building program for an industrial, commercial, or investment structure. In developing a design, the client's needs and requirements are carefully analyzed, zoning regulations and codes affecting the work are studied, and sketches and statements of probable construction costs are prepared for client approval.

SECONDARY MORTGAGE MARKET

Market in which existing mortgages are bought and sold based on the value of future cash flows.

SECRETARIAL STAFF
(SEE POLICY MANUAL)

SECTION OF LAND

A division or parcel of land fixed by government survey, comprising one square mile or 640 acres. Each township (6 miles square) is divided by straight lines into 36 sections and these are again divided into half and quarter sections. Sections are most commonly associated with the division of land in western provinces.

Provincial   See applicable reference materials.

SECURITIZATION

A recently coined term (at least for purposes of real estate transactions), referring to the transformation of loans into securities that are subsequently sold to investors. More specifically, loans arranged between lender and borrower in the primary mortgage market are *securitized* or packaged as mortgage investment portfolios and then sold to investor groups on the *secondary market*. Consequently, small investors can participate in the larger mortgage market and receive yields that would otherwise be unavailable to them individually. Typically, a mortgage portfolio that might amount to $5,000,000 in mortgage loans is

divided (securitized) into investment units, e.g., $5,000 per unit, and sold in the financial marketplace.

Application   Securitization of real estate financing is attractive as it expands the range of capital markets beyond large institutions into the world of small investors and increases the availability of capital as well as expanding alternative forms of financing. Securitization through mortgage-backed securities (MBSs) has led to increased funding competition in the marketplace. Proponents point to benefits such as the reduction of yield expectations by traditional lenders given heightened competition and the reduction of commercial mortgage rates.

Mortgage-backed securities have grown tremendously in the residential market, particularly in the United States. Advocates point to the security inherent in standardized housing. Slowly, CMBSs (commercial mortgage-backed securities) are taking hold although the growth has been affected by the heterogeneous nature of industrial, commercial, and investment products and the higher risk traditionally associated with such properties. Mortgage-backed securities can be grouped under two broad categories: The *mega-MBS* refers to the packaging of several very large loans involving substantial borrowers within a portfolio; and the *conduit-MBS* involves numerous smaller loans making up a much more diversified package. Obviously, thorough investigation of credit-related issues is required to assess the quality and corresponding rating of such portfolios.

Securitization, once concentrated in mortgage portfolios, has now overflowed into equity markets. However, the underlying premise is the same: the sale of an interest that is not a security through another type of interest that is a security. Real estate investment trusts (REITs) represent the securitization of equity ownership in large scale projects. Investors now have the option of considering either equity or debt securities based on returns (yields). Obviously, the ultimate decision rests on the performance of the applicable security.

Traditionally, equity markets were relatively closed as investors were forced to participate in publicly traded stock to enjoy equity yields of large corporations with real estate holdings. The REIT provided a framework to transform such ventures into security units managed through trust ownership arrangements and typically regulated under securities legislation. REITs may be focused on a particular class of property, e.g., offices, nursing homes, shopping centres, industrial complexes, or hotels or be diversified across various classes. REITs, as with all mutual fund arrangements, are typically administered by fund managers whose interest is to select and advance equity positions that realize attractive returns to individual investors.

S

SECURITY DEPOSIT

A term typically used in real estate to refer to money advanced by a tenant and held by a landlord for a specific period to cover possible damages and ensure faithful performance of the lease by the tenant.

In residential tenancies, landlords are often governed by provincial legislation and may be limited in terms of the amount of such a deposit, interest paid on the deposit, and situations to which the deposit can be applied, e.g., damages and non payment of rent.

Provincial　See applicable reference materials.

SELLER AGENCY
(SEE AGENCY)

A fiduciary relationship in which the seller is a client.

Provincial　See applicable reference materials.

SELLER PROPERTY INFORMATION STATEMENT
(SEE ALSO PROPERTY CONDITION DISCLOSURE STATEMENT)

A standardized disclosure statement, designed for sellers when offering property for sale, that sets out particulars concerning the offered property.

Provincial　See applicable reference materials.

SELLER TAKE BACK MORTGAGE

Purpose

Acronym: STB　The seller take back mortgage is a popular negotiating tool, particularly when financing proves difficult through conventional lenders and/or seller participation provides a better overall package in negotiations. The buyer may be attracted to this type of financing as it can avoid certain costs, paper work, and regulations of conventional lenders. The seller may be drawn to the STB if his/her property remains unsold. Further, a mortgage might be a worthwhile investment for the seller.

Application　From a real estate practitioner's perspective, the STB is an excellent vehicle provided that the client is given a full explanation before any commitment. STBs may be seriously considered in the following situations:

- The seller is anxious to sell and has no real concerns about taking back a mortgage to hasten the sale of his/her property.
- The market is strong, the equity position of the buyer is adequate (i.e., downpayment), and the buyer can qualify to make the required mortgage payments.
- The property has limited buyer appeal due to age, condition, or location, and financing would improve overall marketing impact.
- The number of competing houses is increasing and a competitive advantage from a financing perspective is required to increase saleability.
- Buyers for the mortgage are available should the seller wish to sell the STB.

Every seller should be given the opportunity to take back a mortgage and, at the same time, be provided with sufficient information to make a well-informed decision on the matter. An example is provided in which the seller is seeking further information when considering a STB.

Example　*Seller Take Back Mortgage (STB)*

Seller Smith is considering a STB with Buyer Jones. The salesperson has explained the basic steps in such an arrangement. Jones requires a $100,000 mortgage and has a downpayment of $80,000 that will come from the sale of his existing home. Accordingly, the salesperson drafted a clause in the agreement concerning the STB but, Smith wants to be assured that he can fully investigate Jones' credit worthiness. An excerpt from that additional clause follows:

> *This offer is conditional upon the seller being satisfied concerning the personal and/or credit worthiness of the buyer by June 15, 20xx. The buyer hereby consents to having the seller conduct or cause to be conducted a personal and/or credit investigation in respect to the buyer…*

Sale of

The range of underwriting criteria used by lenders in buying mortgages is quite broad. Sellers contemplating the sale of a seller take back mortgage should be fully informed concerning lender guidelines on such matters. Yield is usually a major consideration along with information concerning the mortgagor's personal covenant, condition of the property, and general degree of risk associated with the mortgage.

Application　Practitioners should be aware that lenders involved in purchasing STBs will normally require:

- The seller to declare that there is good title other than encumbrances declared in the purchase agreement (e.g., additional mortgages), and allows a time limit to check out that title. It should be noted that title insurance can be required in support of title.

- The seller must normally sell at a discounted value, to increase the rate of return to the investor, unless the mortgage already has terms that are very favourable compared with current market.

- The seller normally supplies a duly executed assignment of mortgage document.

- The seller to supply an affidavit attesting to the balance of the mortgage and that such mortgage is up-to-date and not in default.

- The agreement to be subject to the buyer of the mortgage making an inspection of the property.

Figure S.2 provides an example outlining specific conditions taken from a typical *agreement to purchase mortgage*. The structure normally resembles an agreement/contract. The mortgage is fully described, a deposit is held pending closing, and the seller and buyer warrant and agree to perform certain items. The actual document will vary considerably–some lenders simply use a letter of intent.

Example   *Seller Take Back Mortgage (STB)– Sale of*

Smith is willing to take back a mortgage on Jones' purchase of the property, provided that he can sell the $100,000 mortgage @ 8.5% for a discounted value of $97,000. The salesperson, after fully discussing seller take back mortgages, drafts two clauses as illustrated. The first concerns Jones' co-operation in the sale of the mortgage and the second relates to the actual sale of the mortgage. Exact wordings of clauses will vary by provincial jurisdiction and unique circumstances surrounding individual transactions.

The buyer acknowledges that the mortgage being taken back by the seller may be sold. The buyer agrees to co-operate fully with the seller in connection with the sale of this mortgage, and will provide such personal and financial information together with such documents as the assignee of the mortgage may reasonably require forthwith upon request by the seller, so that the sale of the mortgage may be completed.

Continued....

TYPICAL CONDITIONS
AGREEMENT TO PURCHASE MORTGAGE

1. The title to be good and free from encumbrances save as aforesaid.

2. The Purchaser to be allowed seven days from the date hereof to investigate the title at his/her own expense, and if within that time he/she shall furnish the Vendor in writing with any valid objection to the title which the vendor shall be unable or unwilling to remove, and which the Purchaser will not waive, this agreement shall be null and void, and the deposit money returned to the Purchaser without interest.

3. The Vendor shall supply an Assignment of Mortgage duly executed, and a notice to the mortgagor, together with an acknowledgement or a declaration by the mortgagee verifying the principal outstanding upon the said mortgage, but the Vendor shall not be bound to produce any abstract of title, deeds, copies of deeds, or other evidence of title except such as are in his/her possession or under his/her control.

4. It is understood and agreed by the Vendor, and the Vendor hereby warrants, that the mortgage stands at the sum of about $_____ on account of principal, together with interest thereon at the rate of ____% per annum, repayable $_____ quarter-yearly/monthly, plus/including interest and that the mortgage has about _____ years to run, and is not renewable, and that such mortgage is not in default. In the event that the said mortgage does not comply with these terms, subject to Paragraph 6 below, then this contract is to be null and void and the Purchaser is to have the deposit returned, without interest. The mortgage does_____ contain a prepayment privilege.

5. The Purchaser is to pay his/her own cost of investigating the title and for the registration of his/her documents.

6. The amount of the mortgage is approximate, and any difference in the principal shall be adjusted at the time of closing, upon a pro rata basis, provided that the difference shall not exceed 5% of the amount stated to be correct.

7. Accrued interest upon the mortgage shall be adjusted as of date of closing.

8. This offer upon acceptance shall with such acceptance constitute a binding contract of Purchase and Sale.

9. It is agreed that there is no representation, warranty, collateral agreement or condition affecting this agreement, the mortgage, or the real property or supported hereby other than as expressed herein in writing.

10. The purchaser acknowledges that he/she is relying upon his/her own inspection only as to the nature or condition of the property.

Figure S.2   **Agreement to Purchase Mortgage—Conditions**

> *This offer is conditional upon the seller obtaining, at the seller's own expense, a commitment for the sale of the aforementioned first mortgage for an amount of not less than Ninety-Seven Thousand Dollars ($97,000). Unless the seller gives notice in writing delivered to the buyer or the buyer's address as hereinafter indicated by 4 p.m. on the 1st day of May, 20xx, that this condition is fulfilled, this offer shall be null and void and the deposit shall be returned to the buyer in full without deduction. This condition is included for the sole benefit of the seller and may be waived at the seller's option by notice in writing to the buyer within the time period stated herein.*

Tax Considerations

The seller should be aware that the decision to participate in a STB can affect personal tax position. The real estate salesperson should not provide advice, however, a general knowledge of tax implications is useful. As a guideline, the *Income Tax Act* is quite precise regarding the collection of interest. Normally, it is deemed to be income for the year in which it was received. Consequently, the mortgagee will have to report this interest as income.

If capital gains tax applies in the transaction and part of the gain is involved in the seller take back, then the seller is permitted to set up mortgage reserves. Essentially, the government's position is that part of the gain has not been received but will ultimately be in the seller's possession. The reserve fund takes into account this deferral and delays some tax on the taxable gain. In such circumstances, the seller should contact his/her accountant directly as the reserve structure will impact tax position.

SEMI-VARIABLE EXPENSES
(SEE BUDGETING)

SENSITIVITY ANALYSIS

A technique designed to assess the impact of various assumptions, e.g., an increase in market rents, on an outcome or series of outcomes, e.g., estimated yield from a rental property. Sensitivity analysis is commonly applied to financial strategies through the use of a software spreadsheet program to isolate and examine selected variables and quantify the degree of susceptibility that any investment return has in relation to selected inputs.

Application   Sensitivity analysis has proven valuable for isolating and identifying factors that can significantly impact yield. For example, financial terms can have a direct affect on internal rate, but sensitivity may vary more when applying different loan-to-value ratios or introducing potential rental income fluctuations. This technique isolates variables and their respective impact on forecasted cash flows. Often a single factor is identified that influences cash flow (more so than other variables) and, consequently, is worthy of further investigation given its heightened sensitivity. Sensitivity analysis is an expanding technique in real estate activity.

Example   *Sensitivity Analysis*

Investor McKay is concerned about the impact of cash flow before taxes (CFBT) on internal rate of return (IRR) for an investment property. The original forecast called for CFBT to increase at the rate of 2% per year due to proportionate increases in net operating incomes. The corresponding IRR of 13.50% was calculated based on a three-year holding period. However, Salesperson Lane elects to provide a sensitivity analysis based on incremental CFBT growth forecasts and corresponding impact on IRR.

CFBT FORECASTED INCREASE	INTERNAL RATE OF RETURN
1.0%	12.92%
1.5%	13.42%
2.0%	13.94%
2.5%	14.48%
3.0%	15.04%
3.5%	15.62%

The sensitivity profile generated can be helpful in the decision-making process. Assume that the investor requires a minimum return of 14%. He/she is in a better position to analyze the possibility of obtaining this return based on increases in CFBT. The ultimate decision then rests on whether a 2.5% or higher CFBT increase is realistic given market conditions and the property under investigation.

SEPTIC SYSTEM

The most common private sewer system which includes a septic tank and leaching bed. The septic tank is a watertight container usually made of concrete, steel, or fibreglass. See **Figure S.3**. The tank serves as a holding tank that allows heavy solids to settle to the bottom. Lighter materials that float are also held in the tank. The heavy solids are known as sludge and the lighter floating materials are known as scum.

Most of the material that enters the tank is in a liquid state. Within the tank, most of the solids are broken down to gases and/or liquids. The breakdown takes place as a result of bacteria action, both aerobic and anaerobic. The

S

liquids are discharged from the tank into the tile bed and the gas escapes through the plumbing vents. Variations exist based on the conventional septic tank, including holding tanks that are pumped out on a regular basis and more sophisticated systems that use agitators and aerators to accelerate the chemical decomposition of the solids in the tank.

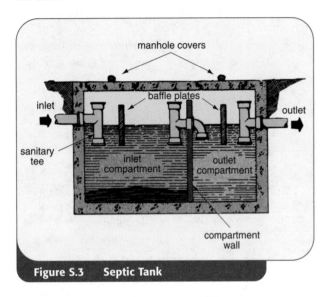

Figure S.3   Septic Tank

Provincial   See applicable reference materials.

SERVANT
(SEE MASTER/SERVANT)

SERVIENT TENEMENT

Land over which an easement exists in favour of a dominant tenement.

Example   *Servient Tenement*

Seller Smith owns a cottage on Big Lake. The listing salesperson noted that access to the property was by way of a private easement over an adjacent property owned by Williams. The right-of-way forms part of the title. In this instance, Williams property is the servient tenement and Smith's property is the dominant tenement. The precise wording for the servient tenement easement follows:

Subject to an easement in, over, and along the most westerly 40 feet of even width through Lot Number 9 and running southerly from the road allowance between Concession IX and X in the said Township of Anytownship to the waters of Big Lake.

SET BACK

A term, not used universally in provincial jurisdictions, but generally referring to the distance from the established lot line within which no buildings may be built according to zoning by-laws. Set backs are normally detailed for front, side, and rear yards in relation to main and accessory structures.

Example   *Set Back*

Buyer Jones has just acquired a building lot to construct a home. Upon visiting the local municipality, he received the requirements for the property currently zoned RES–1 (single-family detached dwellings and uses, buildings and structures consistent with that permitted use). Following are the set back requirements.

Minimum Front Yard: 7.5 metres.

Minimum Side Yard: 1.5 metres except as provided below:

An attached garage or attached carport with no rooms above may be erected at a distance of not less than 1.2 metres from a side lot line that does not abut a public street.

On a corner lot, the minimum side yard abutting a public street shall be 7.5 metres.

Minimum Rear Yard: 10.5 metres.

Provincial   See applicable reference materials.

SEVERANCE (JOINT TENANCY)
(SEE ALSO JOINT TENANT, RIGHT OF SURVIVORSHIP, AND TENANTS IN COMMON)

In common law, an owner in joint tenancy may destroy the right of survivorship at any time before his/her death without the consent of the other joint owners. He/she turns the joint tenancy into a tenancy in common with the other tenant/owners by a procedure called severance. If there are two or more joint tenants remaining, they continue as joint tenants with each other, but are tenants in common with the one who severed the joint tenancy.

Provincial legislation may set out specific limitations or requirements concerning the severance of joint tenancy. For example, the severance of joint tenancy between two or more parties with respect to a title to property might only be permitted with the agreement of all joint tenants, by court order, and/or by following a legislative procedure.

S

SEVERANCE (PLANNING)

Provincial   See applicable reference materials.

SEWAGE SYSTEM

Provincial   See applicable reference materials.

SHELL
(SEE BUILDING SHELL)

SHINGLE

A relatively thin and small unit of roofing, laid in overlapping layers as a roof covering or as cladding on the sides of buildings. See **Figure S.4**.

Application   Asphalt shingles, the most widely used roofing material, are classified by weight. The most common type of shingles used today weigh 210 pounds per square. They have an average life expectancy of 12 to 15 years, while 225s and 235s have an average life expectancy of 15 to 20 years, and 320s are in excess of 25 years. Since the mid-1960s, most asphalt shingles are self sealing. A strip of tar is applied on the surface of the shingles by the manufacturer. The strip is covered by the shingle installed immediately above. When the sun warms the roof surface, the two shingles stick together which helps prevent the shingles from being blown off in a windstorm.

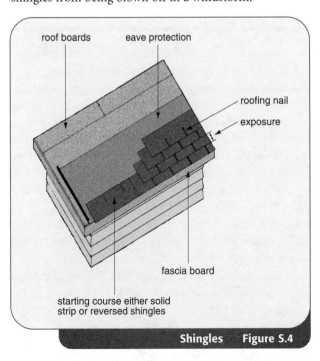

Shingles   Figure S.4

Wood shingles are machine cut, while wood shakes are hand or mechanically split. Wood shakes are thicker and have a more uneven surface. Most are cedar, but some are redwood, and vary in length from 16 to 24 inches. Their life expectancy is generally 30 to 40 years, however low quality shingles have deteriorated in 15 to 20 years.

Other types of shingles include slate, which is a sedimentary rock. High quality slate roofs have an average life expectancy of 60–100 years. Slate roofs weigh three to five times as much as conventional asphalt shingles. Concrete and clay tile roof systems are rare in Canada but are high quality roofing systems with life expectancies of 50–100 years. Like slate, these roofs are heavy, weighing four to five times as much as asphalt shingles.

SHOP DRAWINGS

Drawings made by various trades reflecting construction items detailed on contract documents relating to the building of an industrial, office, retail, or investment property. Shop drawings are a necessary step between the architect's drawings and actual construction. Shop drawings speak not merely the language of the trade, but the language of the shop in which the work is to be done.

SHORELINE/SHORELAND OWNERSHIP

While the water's edge may appear logically to be the extent of ownership, legal complications can arise. In the case of inconsistencies in legal description, the natural boundary between water and land will normally prevail in most instances.

Application   Real estate practitioners, particularly those specializing in recreational property, encounter issues concerning shoreline ownership. Legal advice is strongly recommended and salespersons should avoid making definitive statements about such ownership matters.

When accretion or erosion occurs on a slow gradual basis, usually the rights of ownership are either increased or decreased based on that alteration. Conversely, sudden changes (e.g., improvements made by an owner), will in all likelihood not alter existing boundaries. If the wording of a Crown grant suggests other than the low water mark, a legal opinion should be obtained.

In some areas, property was flooded to expand navigable waterways thereby altering the low water mark. In such instances, the original legal description may describe property now under water. Again, legal advice is essential. Certain cautions are worthy of special attention.

S

- Be careful when inspecting property where shoreline appearance has changed and seller's documents or statements indicate that appropriate approvals have not been obtained.
- Surveys indicating ownership of lands under a water body should be investigated and legal advice sought.
- Location of waterfront improvements may trespass on Crown lands. The timing of such improvements (when located on the land), and the types of improvement are relevant to ownership issues.

Provincial   See applicable reference materials.

SHORT-LIVED ITEMS (APPRAISAL)

Those elements of a structure or items of equipment that are not yet ready to be replaced but whose remaining economic lives are shorter, or are expected to be shorter, than the remaining economic life of the entire structure.

Application   Real estate practitioners commonly encounter short-lived items. Examples would include exterior items such as a swimming pool or garden shed, and interior examples such as mechanical items (stoves, refrigerators, and furnaces), and decorating.

SIDING

External siding (e.g., wood, metal, and vinyl) is frequently used in Canadian residential housing. Siding is installed on top of building paper and over flashings on the exterior walls and is butted against exterior trim. Siding normally has a minimum 6-inch clearance at the bottom above finished grade level.

Application   Practitioners should be aware of problems associated with various types of external siding. In the case of wood siding, rot and water penetration occur most commonly at joints in the siding. Many wood systems require trim to be installed over the joints. Wood-soil contact should be avoided as it promotes rot and provides an ideal environment for wood-boring insects such as termites.

Metal and vinyl sidings have gained the widest popularity in residential construction owing primarily to the low maintenance factor. A variety of metal sidings are available for vertical and horizontal installation. The prevalent materials are aluminum and steel, aluminum being the most common. Metal siding should be ventilated to allow air and moisture pressures to equalize on either side of the metal.

Vinyl sidings are similar to metal in that the majority of problems are associated with installation, as opposed to the material itself. A lack of proper securing, and improper detail work at edges and corners are the most common deficiencies. Some vinyl sidings discolour with age. Most come in a limited colour selection. Vinyl siding can become brittle during cold weather, and can be punctured or cracked.

Figure S.5 demonstrates the process of siding installation for a typical residential wall.

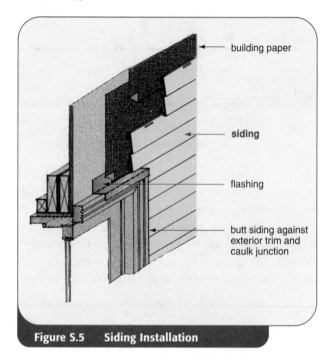

building paper

siding

flashing

butt siding against exterior trim and caulk junction

Figure S.5   Siding Installation

SIGN RESTRICTION

A provision usually found in zoning by-laws limiting the use of outdoor and indoor advertisements and other graphic displays. Sign restrictions are also commonly found in commercial leases. Traditionally, sign restrictions for real estate brokerages relate to office signs and institutional advertising requirements such as billboard advertising restrictions. However, many municipalities have also invoked restrictions regarding *for sale* signs and *open house* signs. Typically, *for sale* signs are limited both as to size and number that can be placed upon residential property. Some municipalities also limit the use of open house directional signs at main intersections as such signs may affect clear vision requirements for traffic. Rural municipalities may have similar restrictions, e.g., number of *for sale* signs that may be placed on large acreages, signage at water's edge for cottages, and placement of directional signs on county and township roads.

S

Example *Sign Restriction—*
Real Estate Signs
(Commercial/Industrial Zones)

Broker/Owner Johnson, of ABC Realty Inc., has investigated sign restrictions in Anycity. He enquires at the municipal office regarding by-laws and necessary permits regarding a new storefront sign for the brokerage. The by-laws for Anycity permit:

…one real estate sign, fascia or free-standing, per lot (i.e., for sale or lease sign), illuminated or non-illuminated, not exceeding 32 square feet in sign surface area, of maximum height not exceeding 20 feet, which sign shall be removed within 15 days of conclusion of the purpose for which the sign is erected.

The by-laws also state that:

…no sign shall be erected, re-erected, or altered which may interfere with, obstruct the view of, or be confused with, any authorized traffic signal or device.

Example *Sign Restriction—*
Real Estate Signs (Residential Zones)

Broker/Owner Brown, of XYZ Real Estate Ltd., wants to ensure compliance regarding real estate signs for the new branch in Southgate. Brown enquires at the municipality regarding applicable by-laws involving sign restrictions. The Southgate sign by-law permits:

- *One ground sign per premise per street frontage except in the case of a co-listing, 2 signs are permitted.*
- *The maximum sign face area shall be 0.7 m² and maximum sign height is 1.5 m.*
- *In regard to location, except for signs in windows, all signs shall be located at a height no greater than the height of the first storey.*
- *Real estate advertising signs in residential areas shall not remain erected for a period longer than 30 days after the subject premises, building, or floor area has been sold, rented, or leased.*

Brown has also investigated sign restrictions in Anytownship adjacent to Southgate. While generally similar, sign face areas and time periods vary slightly.

Example *Sign Restriction—*
Commercial Lease Sign Restrictions

Tenant Jones is signing a commercial lease for a retail unit in the Westgate Plaza in Anycity. The landlord requires full signage compliance for all tenants within the complex and the standard lease provides a boilerplate wording in that regard. The signage restriction in the lease is worded as follows:

The tenant will not place or permit to be placed or maintained on the roof or on any exterior or interior door, wall, or window of the premises any sign, awning, canopy, decoration, lettering, advertising matter, or other thing of any kind and will not place or maintain any decoration, lettering, or advertising matter on the glass of any window or door of the premises without first obtaining the landlord's consent, but this provision has no application to signs, awnings, canopies, decorations, lettering, advertising matter, or other things to be placed inside the premises if of a reasonable standard acceptable to the landlord and not visible from outside the premises. The tenant will maintain every sign, awning, canopy, decoration, lettering, advertising matter, or other thing consented to in good condition and will repair the same at all times. The tenant shall pay all utilities and costs in connection with any signs for the benefit of the premises.

SIGNAL-ZONE CLOSET

A closet that holds communication equipment, for example, telephone, intercom, computer, and related systems pertaining to the building.

SIGNATURE

The signing of documents with the normal signatures of appropriate parties.

Signature lines are inserted in many standard forms used in residential and commercial sales. Forms typically provide for the signatures of the parties to the contract, signatures of witnesses, and the dates on which the contracts were signed. Each party to an agreement or other document should sign with a normal signature and must show the actual date of signing. Each signature should be witnessed by a person who actually sees the person signing the document.

Provincial   See applicable reference materials.

551

SILL

A level, continuous pad between the foundation top and the bottom of the framing system. Typically, the floor joists rest directly on and are secured to the sill. These sills should be anchored to the foundation using bolts fitted into the top of the foundation wall, passing through the sill, and secured with a washer and nut. See Figure S.6.

In new construction, the sill is usually a 2 inch x 4 inch piece of wood laid flat. In older construction, it may be a substantial wood beam, for example, 8 inch x 8 inch. Wood sills support wood framing members, but not masonry, that is, a brick veneer wall sits directly on the foundation, not on a wood sill.

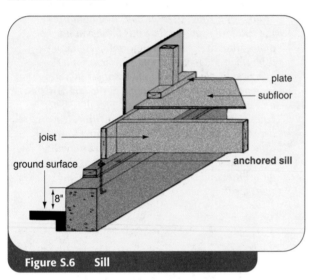

Figure S.6   Sill

Application   Practitioners should be aware of certain problems associated with sills.

Rot and Termites   Wood sills very close to grade level are subject to rot and termite attack. In some older houses, the sills are actually below grade level and may be in constant contact with the soil. Soil contact will undoubtedly lead to rot and the sills can be expected to crush under the weight of the framing system as the rot advances. This phenomenon also applies to beams, posts, and joists.

Point Loads   Sills may be crushed as a result of concentrated loads, for example, steel posts built into walls.

Anchoring   Where the sills are not secured to the foundations, a danger of the building shifting exists during high winds as significant upward and lateral forces are generated.

End Bearing   If the joists are too short, and only the ends rest on the sill (less than one inch, for example), then the concentrated loads may lead to crushing of the sill or joist.

Any wood component in a house is also vulnerable to fire and mechanical damage. Damaged wood sills can usually be replaced readily. Where at or below grade, a material such as concrete would be more suitable. Poorly anchored sills can be secured using bolts.

SINGLE GLAZING

(SEE GLAZING)

SINKING FUND

A fund in which periodic deposits of equal amounts of money are made for the purpose of ultimately paying a debt, or replacing assets. Typically, a sinking fund involves equal annual or monthly deposits which, with compound interest thereon, will accumulate to a pre-determined amount at the end of a stated period.

Application   A sinking fund is sometimes applied to the case of rental properties, where the owner sets aside a specific deduction from income to offset depreciation. The monies are compounded in the fund and then applied to correct the depreciation. A sinking fund is also the basis of reserve funds used by condominiums to set aside funds for the future replacement of common elements.

Example   *Sinking Fund*

Buyer Jones requires a $50,000 downpayment to qualify for a $150,000 conventional mortgage for a home that will be in the $200,000 price range. To ensure that these funds are available in five years' time, Jones establishes a sinking fund in which he places equal payments on a monthly basis over the 60-month period. An investment counsellor at Jones' bank sets up an arrangements in which the downpayment (future value) is $50,000, the interest rate is 5% compounded monthly (end of each period), and the current amount in the account is 0 (present value). Based on a calculation involving compounding, the counsellor determines that Jones must place $735.23 in the account each month over the period in order to accumulate the required downpayment.

Present Value	0
Future Value	$50,000
Payment Amount	$735.23
Deposit Period: Monthly (compounded at end of each month)	
Balance at end of Year One	$9,027.62
Balance at end of Year Two	$18,517.40
Balance at end of Year Three	$28,492.55
Balance at end of Year Four	$38,978.04
Balance at end of Year Five	$50,000.00

SITE

Analysis

Site analysis involves the identification of characteristics that create, enhance, or detract from the utility and marketability of a site.

Application   Practitioners encounter site analysis within specific specialty fields. For example, in an industrial site, the principal physical elements considered in site selection and analysis are usually soil conditions, drainage facilities, water supply, power supply, transportation facilities, and proximity to major centres.

Site analysis also forms part of *Step Three—Data Collection and Analysis* in the appraisal process. Other components in this step include general trends, neighbourhood analysis, and inspection/analysis of improvements.

A comprehensive analysis is basic to valuation and normally involves identifying the highest and best use of the property after examining the site's locational, physical, legal-governmental, and economic attributes; all of which must be analyzed separately. However, before the highest and best use of the site can be estimated and subsequently valued, regional and neighbourhood data are considered. Conclusions drawn from this data are then related to the site analysis, and highest and best use can be estimated.

A brief description of four attributes in a site analysis is provided.

Locational Factors   For example, land use pattern, access, corner influences, hazards, and nuisances.

Physical Factors   For example, site dimensions (frontage, depth, width, shape, and area), soils, topography, plottage, excess land and assembly, climatic conditions, services and utilities, road and street patterns, and landscaping

Legal-Governmental Factors   For example, legal description, title data, easements, zoning, assessment and taxes, and private restrictions.

Economic Factors   For example, prices of comparable sites, tax burden, utility costs, and service costs.

Dimensions

The frontage, depth, and width of a parcel of land. Site dimensions and resulting shape and area create the ultimate desirability, utility, and value of any site. Frontage is that side of a site that abuts a public street or highway. Depth is the distance(s) between the front and rear lot lines. Width is the distance between the side lines of a lot.

The shape of a site is determined by its frontage, depth and width. Area is the size of the site measured in square metres, square feet, hectares, acres, etc.

Site vs. Raw Land

A site is a parcel of land improved to the extent that it is ready for its intended purpose and should be clearly distinguished from raw land. Land includes the surface of the earth, supra surface air space and sub-surface area and is typically referred to as *raw acreage, raw land,* or *unimproved land* because it is unused or in a natural state. A site, on the other hand, is a parcel of land that has been subdivided and serviced to some degree so that it can be used for some purpose, usually as a building site. Generally, the land will have been cleared, graded for drainage, and provided with access to a street or road, together with storm and sanitary sewers, gas, water, electricity, and telephone service. Usually arrangements have been made to ensure that the intended use is legally permitted.

Valuation

Site valuation techniques are outlined under the following topics: Economic Factors, Legal–Governmental Factors, Locational Factors, Physical Factors (Appraisal), Comparative Sales Method–Site Valuation, Abstraction Method–Site Valuation, Land Development Method–Site Valuation, and Land Residual Method–Site Valuation.

SITE PLAN AGREEMENT

A contractual agreement between a municipal authority and a developer of a specific property. In a municipality where an official plan is in effect, the council of that municipality may pass a by-law designating the whole or any part of the area covered by the official plan as a site plan control area. The use of this by-law provides a form of development control by the municipality through a structured site approval process. Essentially, site plan approval allows the council of the municipality to vary or supplement the provisions of its zoning or subdivision control requirements on a site-by-site basis.

The appropriate planning legislation sets out parameters concerning what type of restrictions or controls can be included in site plans. Plans and/or drawings must be approved in a site plan area. The resulting documentation is referred to as a site plan agreement (alternatively referred to a *site plan control agreement* or *site plan development agreement*). Site plan approval is normally required prior to the issuance of a building permit for any development

S

that is subject to site plan approval (certain exceptions may apply in individual municipalities).

Application   Practitioners will encounter various requirements within site plan agreements based on the type of property and specific municipal requirements as set out in appropriate by-laws. In the case of commercial properties, the municipality may require the owner of the land to provide to the satisfaction of, and at no expense to, the municipality any or all of the following:

- Widening or other improvements to roads and/or highways that abut the land.
- Access to and from the land by way of access ramps, curbs, and traffic direction signs.
- Off-street vehicular loading and parking facilities, either covered or uncovered, access driveways, including driveways for emergency vehicles, and the surfacing of such areas and driveways.
- Walkways, including the surfacing thereof, and all other means of pedestrian access.
- Facilities for the lighting, including flood lighting, of the land or of any buildings or structures thereon.
- Walls, fences, hedges, trees, shrubs, or other ground cover and facilities for the landscaping of the lands or the protection of adjoining lands.
- Vaults, central storage and collection areas, and other facilities and enclosures for the storage of garbage and other waste material.
- Easements conveyed to the municipality for the construction, maintenance, or improvement of water courses, ditches, land drainage works, and sanitary sewer facilities on the lands.
- Grading or alterations in elevation or contour of the land and provision for the disposal of storm, surface, and waste water from the land and from any buildings or structures thereon.

A site plan agreement may be registered against the land and enforced against all subsequent owners. In practice, site plan agreements can result in numerous requirements and additional costs for the owner, e.g., deceleration lanes on roads, culverts and drainage requirements, landscaping limitations, and building configuration restrictions owing to building envelope limitations. Opponents argue that site plan agreements affect the flexibility of land use and can reduce long term value. Site plan agreements have traditionally been associated with commercial properties; however, more recently, their use has dramatically expanded particularly with recreational/waterfront developments.

Provincial   See applicable reference materials.

SKYLIGHT

Skylights are frequently installed both in new construction and resale homes and typically made of tempered glass or plastic (flat or bubble shaped). These materials have better resistance to breakage than conventional glass, although they are subject to scratching. Abrasive cleaners should not be used.

Application   Practitioners should be aware of selected problems that can arise. Poorly installed skylights can create a leakage problem due to incorrect flashing. Manufactured skylights should be carefully installed following the manufacturer's recommendations. Flashing kits available from the factory should be used, where appropriate. Most skylights are not operable and are often installed after the house is built. The installation can be tricky, given the need to cut a hole in the roof (and structural considerations related thereto), and ensure that leakage does not occur. This can be difficult, as the skylight usually presents a curb that will collect water. The skylight requires flashing detail that makes a good watertight connection between the roof and the skylight.

SLAB

The reinforced concrete floor between beams, columns, or walls, as well as any large thin area of concrete such as a wall, roof, or balcony. Practitioners most commonly encounter slabs in residential basements. See **Figure S.7**.

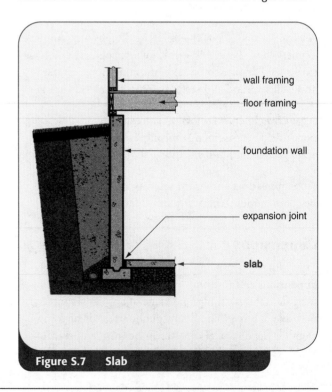

Figure S.7   Slab

Slate

A sedimentary rock used in flooring and occasionally in roofing. High quality slate roofs have an average life expectancy of 60 to 100 years. While providing high durability, slate roofs are particularly susceptible to individual shingle movement (rotting nails holding the shingle), higher cost when flashings with a lower life expectancy have to be removed, and difficulties in finding qualified people to provide maintenance.

Slider (Window)

A type of window normally identified by single panes of glass sliding on a wood or vinyl track with a simple locking device and pull knobs attached to the surface of the glass. The slider window was popular during the 1960s and is generally regarded as a poor quality window. If properly constructed, however, this type of window can perform as well as any other normal household design.

Application   Lower quality sliders have given this style of window a somewhat tarnished reputation, as they suffer from air and water leakage. Better sliders are provided with sashes (metal, vinyl, or wood) around the glass. See Figure S.8. Sliders are relatively inexpensive and typically

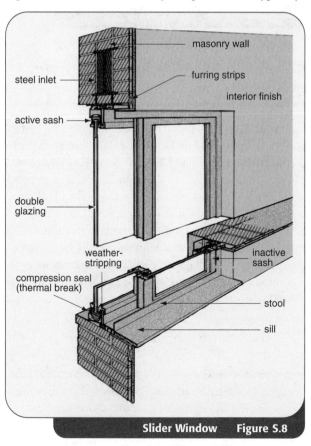

Slider Window   Figure S.8

have very simple locking hardware. If well made, their performance can be as good as any other type of window. Glazing may be single, double, or triple.

Problems include low quality hardware, tracks at the bottom that do not drain water to the outside, poorly fitted slides, and improper joints at corners of the frames. Leaks often result in water damage to wall finishes below the windows, most often at corners. Exterior caulking may help in some cases; in others, storm windows added to the outside improve weather tightness. Where the problem is chronic, replacement windows may be the best answer.

Sliding Glass Door

A popular feature in residential property since the 1950s. Early models were made of metal that often resulted in condensation and ice on inside surfaces. The introduction of thermal breaks between the inner and outer halves, closing/locking hardware, and improved framing have greatly improved the product over the past four decades. In particular, the thermal break was effective in keeping the inside metal part of the frame warmer, thereby reducing condensation and icing problems.

Sliding doors typically have two thicknesses of glass. Each pane can be in a separate sliding door component, or there may be one door sash with a double-glazed or even triple-glazed pane. Better quality sliding glass doors are distinguished by more expensive hardware and sophisticated means of adjustment.

Slope (Pitch)
(see Roof)

Small Business Deduction

A tax deduction provided to qualifying Canadian controlled private corporations carrying on *active* businesses. The term *active* is deemed to refer to any business carried on by a corporation, excluding a specified investment business and a personal service business, e.g., an incorporated employee.

Application   The small business deduction is important when opening a real estate brokerage as it reduces the overall rate of federal and provincial corporate taxes. The tax rate is decreased to approximately 25% of active business income on net earnings up to $200,000 in a year and approximately 46% on the excess (if any). Once net earnings accumulate to $1,000,000 or more, the rate remains constant at the 46% level. The small business deduction provides a worthwhile tax incentive to corporations. As a further benefit, the net business income (after salaries) is taxed at corporate rates, while any salaries of the shareholders are taxed at personal rates.

Figure S.9 illustrates a profit and loss statement for ABC Realty Inc., a Canadian controlled private corporation that would qualify for small business deduction.

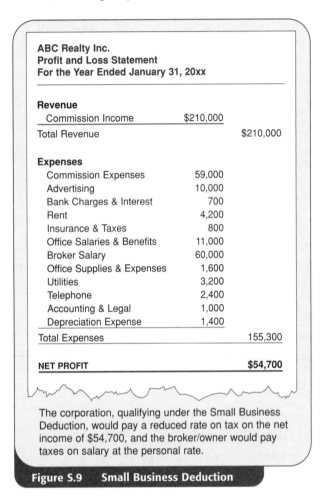

ABC Realty Inc.
Profit and Loss Statement
For the Year Ended January 31, 20xx

Revenue
Commission Income	$210,000	
Total Revenue		$210,000

Expenses
Commission Expenses	59,000	
Advertising	10,000	
Bank Charges & Interest	700	
Rent	4,200	
Insurance & Taxes	800	
Office Salaries & Benefits	11,000	
Broker Salary	60,000	
Office Supplies & Expenses	1,600	
Utilities	3,200	
Telephone	2,400	
Accounting & Legal	1,000	
Depreciation Expense	1,400	
Total Expenses		155,300
NET PROFIT		**$54,700**

The corporation, qualifying under the Small Business Deduction, would pay a reduced rate on tax on the net income of $54,700, and the broker/owner would pay taxes on salary at the personal rate.

Figure S.9   Small Business Deduction

SMOKE CHAMBER

A chamber found above the damper in a fireplace and below the chimney, often covered with a special cement parging to provide a smooth surface. The side walls of the smoke chamber are sloped to direct the smoke from the wide damper opening into the narrow chimney flue. The slope of the smoke chamber wall should not be more than 45 degrees off vertical and should slope evenly from both sides. Brick corbelling is not recommended in a smoke chamber. The smoother the walls of the smoke chamber, the more likely the smoke is to move freely through it. See Figure S.10 for a cross-sectional view of a smoke chamber.

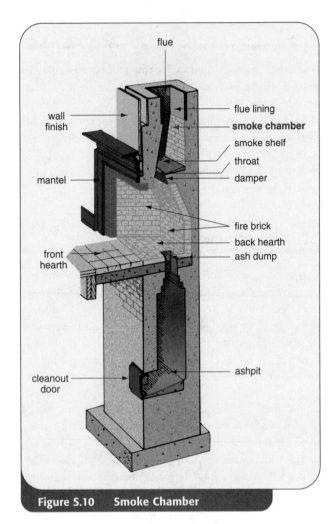

Figure S.10   Smoke Chamber

SOCIETY OF INDUSTRIAL AND OFFICE REALTORS

Acronym: SIOR   The SIOR designation is awarded by the Society of Industrial and Office REALTORS, an affiliate of the National Association of REALTORS in the United States. The Society is dedicated to the maintenance of high professional standards in the fields of industrial and office real estate. The Society offers a candidate status that is designed to provide entry-level real estate practitioners with a meaningful program to motivate and encourage them to work toward obtaining the SIOR designation.

Candidate status identifies those individuals who meet the following criteria:

- Have certifiable full-time employment for a minimum of three years in the commercial real estate business; and

- Receive sponsorship of two active members from the local chapter. At least one active member sponsor must be from a different firm than that of the candidate applicant.

The SIOR designation identifies a broker who:

- Has a minimum of seven years industrial or office real estate experience (unless using experience substitutes as set out by the Society), and is actively engaged as an industrial or office real estate broker or salesperson;

- Maintains a minimum dollar volume of sales per year and a minimum number of transactions or square footage, according to standards set by the local chapter.

- Upholds high ethical standards of practice and has a reputation for sincerity and integrity;

- Pledges to uphold the Society's Code of Ethics and Standards of Business Practice; and

- Proves to be a knowledgeable professional in the industrial or office real estate market as evidenced by passing a written entrance examination or successful completion of specified Society courses.

Experience substitutes are available as set out by the Society. It should be noted that Active Membership–SIOR Designation can be industrial *or* office, or industrial *and* office (dual).

Reference   The SIOR can be contacted at Suite 187, 238 Davenport Road, Toronto, ON M5R 1J6.

The above information was summarized from detailed materials provided by SIOR with no representation concerning its accuracy or completeness.

SOFFIT/FASCIA

The underside of building elements most commonly relating to an architectural feature on the building, such as roof overhangs.

Application   The eave overhang gives some protection to the side wall and forms a connection between the roof and wall. Two major components of this overhang are the fascia board and soffit. The fascia board is simply a board nailed to the end of the joists or trusses running the full length of the roof. The soffit refers to material installed under the eave overhang which closes in the joists and trusses as they project over the edge of the exterior wall. Holes are drilled or vents are installed in the soffit to allow air circulation and reduce wood rot and deterioration in the attic. Metal or vinyl components and coverings are commonly used in both soffit and fascia.

Provincial building codes set out construction standards along with venting requirements and use of noncombustible material, e.g., residential dwelling units sharing a common attic/roof as may be the case in townhouses.

SOFT COSTS
(SEE ALSO HARD COSTS/SOFT COSTS)

Costs of constructing a building or other development project, other than the costs of building the actual physical structure. Soft costs are normally associated with professional fees including architectural, engineering, legal and landscaping expenses.

SOLAR/SUNLIGHT RIGHTS

A right to control or otherwise deal with sunlight as it relates to property ownership. Rights to sunlight do not automatically accrue to owners of property at the present time. Adjacent property owners may agree not to shade or otherwise block one another's sunlight, but this type of agreement is rarely found in Canada. Legally, a property owner does have control over sunlight directly above his/her property as part of the rights that accrue through airspace vertically above the property. This right does not extend to light that passes over the land of others and ultimately reaches the property. Therefore, as most sunlight in Canada is normally at an angle to the property, a vertical right provision has little or no effect in terms of a neighbour who builds a structure that partially shades sunlight to an abutting or adjacent property.

Application   Practitioners will encounter less than unanimous agreement on the entire issue of solar/sunlight rights. Some individuals may refer to an old doctrine of ancient lights and the right to light in which one owner could restrain his neighbour from obstructing sunlight if the sunlight had been enjoyed by that landowner for 20 years. However, this right was abolished in the late 1800s. Generally, current law places a higher value on the economic considerations in developing property than the impact of diminished sunlight on adjacent properties. This stance is already under scrutiny and, as mentioned, it is possible to have a private agreement between owners to limit or in some way define limitations concerning sunlight. As well, restrictive covenants are possible within developments that specifically set out building set-back, height, and related requirements.

Although no natural right to light may exist, unreasonable interference with the use and enjoyment of property might be legally pursued. Undoubtedly, reasonableness of the obstruction, e.g., economic necessity of the improvement, will be a factor. Given that perpetually shadowed land will undoubtedly suffer loss of value, such actions appear both reasonable and logical. Compensation for interference with sunlight has been granted in some jurisdictions.

Given increasing interest in solar power and the economic benefits derived from direct access to such power, this energy source has taken on new prominence. Often referred to as *shade control by-laws* (or shade control or solar control provisions in site plans), municipalities are able to protect solar users from shade caused by vegetation, secondary structures such as signs or walls, and building heights. Similarly, municipal by-laws in large urban areas routinely address sunlight and solar provisions in the construction of large buildings. Often such considerations are set forth in detailed site plan agreements that take into consideration the location of improvements on the property and the placement of vegetation.

Example   Solar/Sunlight Rights

Developer Reed is creating a new residential development that uses both active and passive solar systems to assist in the heating and cooling of homes. The right to solar power must be assured for each landowner within the development. Accordingly, a restrictive covenant has been placed on each title that prevents any alteration to the exterior of the property whatsoever without the express consent of the developer or his nominee and such approvals will only be granted if the property owner does not in any way affect the existing solar/sunlight accessible by abutting and/or adjacent neighbours. Further, the developer retains the right to remove any vegetation that limits solar access/sunlight to abutting and/or adjacent neighbours that affects the operation of both active and passive solar systems throughout the development.

SOLE PROPRIETORSHIP

A sole proprietorship involves a business operation owned by one person who operates individually or with the assistance of employees. The sole proprietor owns all the assets and is:

- Responsible for the debts;
- Entitled to the profits; and
- Accountable for any losses.

Application   Most sole proprietors are permitted under provincial statutes to register a business name with the applicable ministry/department pursuant to appropriate business names registration legislation under a trade name other than a personal name. In the case of real estate brokerages operating as sole proprietorships, such registration must comply with provisions of the applicable real estate act, including how a personal name is used. In most instances, the real estate act requires that the name of the sole proprietor must be exactly as registered and cannot be transferred to another person.

Various advantages exist regarding the use of a sole proprietorship in real estate brokerage. This form of ownership can normally be initiated immediately upon registration and involves little paperwork. Consequently legal and accounting fees can be noticeably less than for other types of business organizations. The sole proprietorship is free from many governmental regulations imposed on corporations within provinces. Tax advantages may also exist, depending on personal levels of income. Finally, a sole proprietorship is easy to establish and relatively inexpensive.

The primary disadvantage is the unlimited liability of the owner. If the business goes bankrupt, the creditors may sue the proprietor and seize personal assets. Growth of a sole proprietorship can also be limited by the amount of the owner's capital resources and individual borrowing power. Also, no separation between the business income and the personal earnings of the owner is possible. Therefore, from a tax perspective, all profits are simply treated as regular income. Of course, business expenses can be deducted from this income. The sole proprietorship lacks any continuity. After the death of the owner, the business would be dissolved by the executor or administrator of the deceased proprietor.

Provincial   See applicable reference materials.

SOLID WASTE PUMP

A pump designed to move solid wastes when conventional gravity flow is not feasible or effective.

Application   Although expensive, this type of pump is found in rural/recreational property where a basement bathroom is below the septic tank level and pumping is required. Solid waste pumps can also be found where municipal sewer lines are higher than the facilities being served.

Provincial   See applicable reference materials.

SOUND BATTS

Soundproofing materials typically associated with commercial buildings but increasingly found in residential co-ownership arrangements, e.g., condominium and co-operatives. Sound batts are usually made of fibreglass or similar sound-limiting batting material that is placed between joists within internal walls or above acoustic ceilings. Sound batts in residential construction reduce noise particularly between floors or between common walls. **Figure S.11** illustrates a sound batt above an acoustic ceiling.

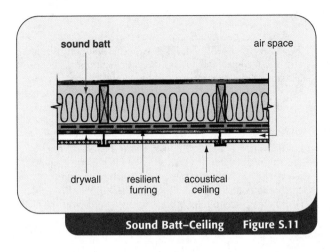

Sound Batt–Ceiling   **Figure S.11**

SOURCE DEDUCTIONS

Selected deductions made by an employer from employees within his/her employ. The Canada Customs and Revenue Agency requires the following:

- Deduct income tax, Canada Pension Plan (CPP) contributions, and Employment Insurance (EI) premiums from amounts paid to employees;

- Remit these amounts along with the employer's share of CPP contributions and Employment Insurance (EI) premiums that have to be paid throughout the year for the employees' benefit; and

- Report all these amounts on an information return by the end of February of the following calendar year.

Application   According to the Canada Customs and Revenue Agency's *Employers' Guide to Payroll Deductions*:

An employer-employee relationship exists if you are in a position to control and direct the person or people who perform the service. Although a written contract might expressly indicate that an individual is self-employed, the Department might not necessarily consider the individual as such. You must examine the written contract and the working conditions to determine if the individual is self-employed. If you cannot determine whether a person is an employee, you can obtain a ruling from the Source Deductions section, CPP/EI unit of your district taxation office.

CPP Deductions

A maximum employee contribution is calculated as a percentage of pensionable earnings to a maximum, set each year. Employer contributions are calculated based on equal contributions deducted from the employees'

remuneration. Employers must deduct and make contributions regardless of prior employers' deductions.

EI Deductions

A maximum employee premium is calculated as a percentage of insurable earnings per pay period to a maximum set each year. Check the *Table for Employment Insurance* in the publication entitled *Information for Employers in* [applicable province], *Payroll Deductions Tables*. See **Reference** below. This table provides individual pay period maximums.

Employer contributions are calculated based on the contributions deducted from the employees' remuneration per pay period. Employers must deduct and make contributions regardless of prior employers' deductions on behalf of employees.

Income Tax

As an employer, income tax deductions are required from remuneration paid to employees. The amount to be deducted is determined through the use of one or more of four forms:

- TD1 for most employees
- TD1X for employees who are paid commission
- TD3 for individuals who receive income other than employment income
- TD3F for fishermen/women.

Based on calculations using these forms, tax tables in the *Payroll Deductions Tables* are provided for weekly, bi-weekly, semi-monthly, and monthly pay periods, and for commission earnings.

Reference   The Canada Customs and Revenue Agency publishes the *Employers' Guide to Payroll Deductions* that includes basic information on how and what to deduct, and how to report and remit deductions. The Guide is published every four years, with updates and required filing forms sent to employers and is available from the local Tax Services Office.

This Guide also provides detailed information on the preparation of T4s. Payroll Deductions Tables are provided by the Canada Customs and Revenue Agency in the guide entitled *Information for Employers in* [applicable province], *Payroll Deductions Tables*. Tables are provided for CPP Contributions, EI Premiums, and Income Tax Deductions.

Issues regarding source deductions in relation to commission salespeople (employees and independent contractors) are addressed in appropriate provincial licensing courses. Specific questions should be directed to the local Canada Customs and Revenue Agency office.

S

SPACE ANALYSIS

An analysis, usually associated with industrial, office, retail, and investment properties, to locate problem areas and to provide a basis for contemplating various changes to better accommodate the user. Space analysis is also associated with planning for new construction and decisions regarding space standards and adequacy requirements. Space planning addresses architectural design of the space with all amenities and mechanical requirements to make the structure more functional for occupants. Space planning also commonly includes analysis of sound and light control within the defined area. Space standards refer to a set of criteria relating to the size of office and work areas in relation to particular functions. The absence of standards leads to space allocation in a haphazard, non-functional manner.

SPECIAL ASSESSMENT

A financial levy made by lawful process against those specific parcels of property that directly benefit from the special assessment.

Application   For real estate practitioners, special assessments are typically encountered in two areas: taxation and condominium property. Under taxation, the taxing authority may levy a special assessment for improvements within a particular area (e.g., installation of curbs and sidewalks), in a residential subdivision. Individual property owners benefiting from this increased utility are levied a special assessment over and above usual property taxes to pay for the expenditure over a pre-determined period.

With condominium property, special assessments are normally levied against all unit owners to make up a deficiency in the reserve fund in contemplation of repair/ replacement concerning the common elements of the condominium corporation.

Example   *Special Assessment-Condominium*

Smith is the owner of a two-bedroom condominium. Currently, the condominium corporation has inadequate reserve funds to cover costly repairs needed to the underground garage. Unfortunately, the waterproof membrane installed during initial construction has deteriorated over a period of time. Consequently, certain landscaped areas and the tennis court above the underground garage have suffered damage, as well as structural components associated with the garage. The estimated repair costs are $180,000.

Continued…

While the condominium corporation has approximately $150,000, the board of directors wish to pay for the repairs and also replenish the fund to its current level. Smith's contribution to common expenses is based on his proportionate ownership within the corporation. The Declaration shows his contribution as to common element expenses as .036911. Consequently, his special assessment amounts to $6,643.98 ($180,000 x .036911). The board of directors, given the size of the assessment, allowed all unit owners the option to pay in six equal installments commencing 30 days following receipt of the notice. Smith questioned the corporation's ability to levy the special assessment. The board of directors referenced the following provision as set out in by-law #1 of the condominium corporation.

> *Where the corporation shall not have sufficient funds to meet extraordinary expenditures not contemplated in any budget or where funds are required to establish or replenish reserves for contingencies and deficits, such funds may be assessed at any time during the year in addition to the annual assessment, by the board giving notice of such further assessment to the owners. Such notice shall include a statement setting out the reasons for the extraordinary assessment, and such extraordinary assessment shall be payable by each owner within ten (10) days after such notice has been given or within such further period of time and in such installments as the board may determine.*

SPECIAL PURPOSE BUILDING
(SEE ALSO INDUSTRIAL BUILDING CATEGORIES)

A structure designed for the particular needs of its occupants.

Application   Practitioners will encounter special purpose buildings throughout the range of real estate uses including multi-residential, retail, office, and industrial properties. Special purposes buildings are particularly evident in the industrial field of specialization as many structures are built to accommodate distinct industrial processes.

SPECIFIC PERFORMANCE
(SEE ALSO CONTRACT)

A remedy in a court of equity compelling a defendant to carry out the terms of an agreement or contract. Specific performance is available only where the remedy of damages cannot afford adequate relief to the plaintiff.

SPECIFICATIONS

A detailed and exacting statement of what is to be done, including requirements, dimensions, and materials as in the case of a proposed building.

SPOUSE

Provincial See applicable reference materials regarding spousal interests in real property.

SPRINKLER SYSTEM
(SEE ALSO FIRE)

A system of interconnected pipes throughout all or a portion of a building that provides water as a fire protection system. Most sprinkler systems can be manually operated or automatically controlled by smoke alarms or other heat sensitive detectors. The term *sprinklered* (often used in building codes), means that a building is equipped with a system of automatic sprinklers. The sprinkler system consists of various pipes, risers, mains, and sprinkler heads.

The term *sprinkler system* may also be used in relation to an underground system of interconnected pipes, together with a timing device, that provides periodic application of water to the grounds surrounding a building.

STABILIZED OPERATING STATEMENT
(SEE ALSO RECONSTRUCTED OPERATING STATEMENT)

An altered profit and loss statement for a specific property that better reflects the ongoing expenses and revenues of a typical property.

Application Appraisers use stabilized statements, also referred to as *adjusted operating statements*, for purposes of both direct and yield capitalization. Commercial practitioners use stabilized amounts for valuation as well for investment comparison purposes. However, forms are typically referred to as worksheets for reconstructing revenues and expenses to establish typical expenses leading to market value, and also for forecasting purposes based on individual investor objectives in order to arrive at investment value.

The term *stabilized* or *adjusted* is not as commonly used as *reconstructed*, given that the process originated in appraisal valuations. Certain terminology differences exist in commercial and appraisal specialty fields in regard to such techniques including related worksheets.

STAGING AREA

A temporary location to store and work with materials and equipment prior to their movement to a final location.

STANDARD CHARGE TERMS

Provincial See applicable reference materials.

STANDARD FORMS

Provincial See applicable reference materials.

STANDARD OF CARE

The standard expected of a reasonably prudent person in a situation that is used in determining negligence concerning a specific act in a similar situation.

Example *Standard of Care*

Salesperson Lee, of ABC Realty Inc., provided full, informed disclosure to the seller when entering into a listing agreement for the marketing of the seller's property. The disclosure met the uniform standard as research indicated that typically prudent real estate practitioners would provide a similar disclosure under like circumstances. Salesperson Lee has accordingly met the standard of care regarding this specific activity.

STANDARDS OF BUSINESS PRACTICE

The Code of Ethics, owned by The Canadian Real Estate Association, embodies various general principles that are detailed at the beginning of the Code. Over the years, these principles required further definition and clarification. Consequently, standards were developed and embodied within the Code of Ethics. These Standards of Business Practice are continuously modified to provide precise guidelines for members and have become the working reference document for professional standards committees and practitioners within organized real estate. See the **Appendix** for a reprint of the Code of Ethics.

STANDBY FEE

A sum of money given by the borrower to the lender to hold a mortgage commitment for a specified period of time. The mortgage commitment, sometimes referred to as a *standby commitment*, is an assurance that the lender has a specified amount of money for lending purposes to that particular borrower on terms as set out in the commitment letter.

STANDBY LOAN

A pre-construction loan commitment arranged between a developer and a lender for preliminary financing as opposed to more permanent, long-term mortgaging.

Application   Practitioners will encounter standby loans most frequently in development projects. The lender is attracted to this arrangement, as the rate charged is normally two to four points higher and an upfront fee (often referred to as a *standby fee*), is normally required. The developer, with a standby commitment, can pursue construction financing and gain additional time to secure a more favourable permanent mortgage arrangement for a particular project.

The standby loan is really a form of guarantee of credit for the project. It is rarely used except when interest rates are high but expected to lower before completion of the project. The standby loan is exercised and then discharged in favour of more attractive rates offered by a permanent lender at some point in the future.

Example   Standby Loan

Developer Reed is concerned with current interest rates at 9% and wants to secure interim financing in hopes that rates will fall before he needs a long-term loan for the project. Reed approaches a private investment group that is willing to advance $300,000 on a six-month, fully open loan with a rate of 11% and a standby fee payable when the funds are advanced. The fee is $2,000 and the interest represents approximately $16,500 for the period (or an approximate annualized yield 12.3%).

STATEMENT OF ADJUSTMENTS

(SEE ALSO ADJUSTMENTS)

A statement, usually prepared by the solicitor for the seller, setting out in balance sheet form, all credits to the seller (e.g., purchase price, prepaid taxes, and prepaid utilities), all credits to the buyer (e.g., deposits and arrears in taxes prior to the date of closing), and the balance due on closing. The statement of adjustments provides all parties to the transaction with a financial breakdown as of the closing date.

STATEMENT OF DISBURSEMENTS

For property management purposes, a statement setting out disbursements made by a real estate brokerage on behalf of a client including the date, description, amount, and balance concerning such disbursements. In fact, this term can apply to any summary of disbursements relating to the usual activities of a real estate brokerage.

Application   In the case of property management, the statement of disbursements represents the primary record produced by the brokerage firm's accounting department for the owner/client. It is essentially a detailed statement of money received and money paid out. A typical ledger for brokerages involved in property management is shown in the following example. Information from this ledger would form the basis of a statement of disbursements.

Requirements concerning disbursements, procedures relating to a property management trust account, and other administrative matters will vary by provincial jurisdiction. The example cited is based on procedures in one particular province.

Example   Statement of Disbursements

Broker/Owner Johnson is managing property for Investor McKay. A ledger is prepared for each individual property that must include all revenue and expense payments along with an appropriate reconciliation at each successive month end.

Single Property Ledger

Property Record: #90-001   Unit: (if appl.)
Property: 123 Main St.

DATE	PARTICULARS	DR	CR	BAL.
May 1	Balance Forward			3,324.03
May 2	Rent (May)		650.00	3,974.03
May 5	Prop. Mgmt. Fee	65.00		3,909.03
May 14	Insurance (Fire)	231.50		3,677.53
May 19	Repairs	400.00		3,277.53
May 31	Closing Balance			$3,277.53

In the above example, the property consisted of one unit at a single address. In the case of small multiple units, individual ledgers can be utilized for each apartment. Alternatively, sub-ledgers could be used for various expense categories with the summary amounts recorded on a single ledger.

Continued…

Multi-Unit Building Ledger

Property Record: #90-002   Units: #101–#131
Property: 125 West St.

DATE	PARTICULARS	DR	CR	BAL.
May 1	Balance Forward			33,324.21
May 2	Rent (May)		18,354.00	51,678.21
May 5	Prop. Mgmt. Fee	1,834.40		49,843.81
May 14	Insurance (Fire)	6,438.90		43,404.91
May 19	Repairs	9,368.00		34,036.91
May 31	Closing Balance			$34,036.91

In this instance, expenditures such as fire insurance would be itemized by individual units and then summarized on the ledger.

Provincial   See applicable reference materials.

STATEMENT OF MORTGAGE

A statement containing details regarding the terms of a mortgage and fees and costs payable by the borrower.

Application   A statement of mortgage (or comparable form depending on the provincial jurisdiction), is typically referenced in provincial legislation. The statement is usually completed, signed, and delivered by a mortgage broker to the borrower for signature before the borrower is asked to sign a mortgage instrument or any commitment to enter into a mortgage. Practitioners will encounter significant provincial variations in regard to requirements concerning mortgages.

Provincial   See applicable reference materials.

STATUTE

A law passed by an act of the legislature. Statutes are enacted pursuant to legislative authority at a provincial or federal level to generally promote the public good. The majority of statutes impacting real property involve provincial legislation and can be broadly grouped under condominium/co-operative, environment, mortgage, taxation, tenancy, planning/development, and title/ownership. Matters relating to the trading of real estate and licensing of salespeople fall to a provincial real estate act.

STATUTE OF FRAUDS

A provincial statute requiring that specific types of contracts, including those involving the sale or lease of real estate, must be in writing in order to be enforced. Most statutes of fraud are based on old English law, but wording differences exist between provinces and, in fact, the original statute of frauds legislation may have been repealed and replaced with other statutes achieving the same basic objective.

Provincial   See applicable reference materials.

STATUTE OF LIMITATIONS

A statute that limits the time period in which legal action can be undertaken to enforce one's rights, e.g., an action for collection of rent in a residential or commercial tenancy, for a covenant in a mortgage, and an action for any penalty imposed under a statute.

Example   Statute of Limitations

Landlord Smith has not made any attempt to recover unpaid rent from a tenant for the past seven years. The statute of limitations for the specific province in which Landlord Smith is resident and in which the owned property is located requires that no person shall bring an action to recover any rent if such action is not brought within ten years from the time at which the landlord had the right to bring such action. Therefore, Smith has approximately three years remaining to commence an action pursuant to the provincial legislation.

Provincial   See applicable reference materials.

STOP CLAUSE
(SEE EXPENSE STOP)

STORE AREA

Store area, for purposes of measurement using the BOMA standard, refers to the square footage of ground floor store area in a commercial building. The measurement of a store area involves establishing the area comprised of the distance from the building line on the store frontage and the inner surface of other outer walls, and from the inner surface of any corridors or other permanent partitions, and to the centre of other partitions that separate the premises from adjoining rentable areas. No deduction is made for vestibules inside the building line or for columns or projections necessary to the building. No addition should be made for bay windows extending outside the building line.

Reference Practitioners interested in obtaining precise definitions and procedures for this and other measurements concerning commercial property should contact the Building Owner and Managers Association International (BOMA). (See also **Boma Standard.**)

STRATA

Provincial See applicable reference materials.

STRIP DEVELOPMENT

A retail centre, normally found in suburban areas, designed as a straight line of stores with retail units possessing narrow storefronts in proportion to overall length. Also traditionally known as a strip mall.

The term has also been used by residential practitioners to describe the development of residential areas along rural roads.

STRUCTURAL INSPECTION

An inspection typically performed on the interior and exterior of a real estate structure with particular regard to deterioration including movement. Since many structural components are buried below grade or behind finishes, much of the structural inspection is necessarily performed by looking for resultant movement. Where no movement has occurred, structural imperfections may go undetected. New interior or exterior finishes and patching work may conceal imperfections over the short term. In this instance, identification of problems is often impossible.

Application Practitioners should understand that structural repairs can be very costly and, in some cases, the problem is so severe that complete renovation is required as opposed to repairs. Usually, a structural engineer should be consulted before making repairs. An incomplete understanding of a problem may lead to incorrect solutions and a possible life-threatening situation.

STRUCTURE

For real estate purposes, the overall skeleton of a home or office that includes the foundation, footings, floors, walls, roof, and related components. The structure is by far the most important part of a residential or commercial building as the safety and useability of that building depends on its sound structural integrity.

STUCCO

Any cement-like material typically used as an exterior covering for walls that is put on wet and dries hard and durable.

Stucco is really the exterior equivalent of plaster, made of cement, lime, aggregate, and water. Stucco can be thought of as a thin coat of concrete, with the cement and lime acting as binders, the aggregate providing the bulk and strength, and the water initiating the chemical reaction.

Application As with all exterior finishes, practitioners should be aware of common problems encountered. Much like plaster, stucco requires periodic maintenance as cracks develop. The amount of maintenance required depends largely on the mix of the stucco, the lath used (if any), and the surface to which the stucco is applied.

Stucco over masonry walls tends to stand up significantly better than stucco over wood-frame construction. The rigidity of a masonry structure allows for virtually no flexing of the stucco, and consequently less cracking and surface separation is likely to occur.

STUDDING
(SEE ALSO FRAMING)

One of the series of vertical wood structural members (usually 2-inch nominal thickness), used as supporting elements in walls and partitions.

SUB-AGENT
(SEE ALSO AGENCY)

A brokerage (agent) authorized by another brokerage (agent) to assist in transacting the affairs of the principal (with express or implied consent of the principal), and having the same duties to the principal as the agent. Sub-agency is traditionally associated with seller agency and the authorization of other brokerages to assist in the sale of a listed property. However, sub-agency can also exist in buyer representation when a brokerage representing the interests of the buyer authorizes other brokerages to assist in seeking out property on behalf of that buyer/principal. The popularity of sub-agency has diminished with the growth of buyer agency.

SUBCONTRACTOR

An individual, corporation, or other entity performing a particular task under the direction and coordination of the general contractor, who has the responsibility of managing a project according to the construction documents.

Example   Subcontractor

Smith wants to have a custom home built and hires Williams Contracting Ltd. as the general contractor to oversee construction. Williams, in turn, hires various subcontractors to complete specific portions of the project: e.g., plumbing, electrical, and roofing.

SUBDIVISION
(SEE PLAN OF SUBDIVISION)

Provincial   See applicable reference materials.

SUBFLOOR

A building component that transmits live loads of people and furnishings to the floor joists. Subflooring may be covered with a finish or may serve as a finished flooring. Historically, one inch thick wood boards were used. More recently, plywood and wafer board have been used. Current standards call for plywood or wafer board to be at least 5/8 inch thick when the floor joists are 16 inches apart. **Figure S.12** illustrates a subfloor along with associated building components.

Application   Practitioners should be aware of selected problems with subflooring.

Springy floors   Wood subflooring (usually found in residential construction), that is too thin will be springy and may fail under concentrated loads such as that of a piano. An overlay is normally required to provide a stiffer subfloor, e.g., the installation of ceramic floor tile.

Squeaky Floors   Subflooring not adequately secured to the floor joists is likely to be squeaky and may be springy. Most floor squeaks are the result of poor contact between the subflooring and joists. The weight of someone walking on a floor will temporarily push the subfloor down onto the joist. When the foot is removed, the subfloor will lift off slightly again. The noise usually results from the wood moving against the nail. Solutions include re-nailing, screwing, and gluing the subfloor to the joists. Shims can also be used between the subfloor and joists.

Water Damage   Wafer board subflooring can be damaged by relatively small amounts of water. The board tends to swell, resulting in floor unevenness. The swelling also pulls the nails out of the joists or through the wafer board. Ultimately, of course, the board can lose its strength.

Uneven   Uneven subflooring can be irritating, although it is rarely a structural problem. Uneven joist installation is a common cause, as is debris on the top of the joists when the subfloor is laid. Swelled wafer board or delaminating plywood can also result in unevenness. Careless joining of tongue and groove sheets can lead to surface irregularity.

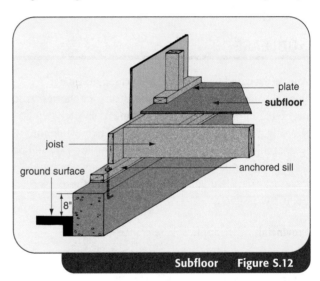

Subfloor   Figure S.12

SUBJECTIVE VALUE

Created and exists only in the minds of the potential buyers and sellers. Subjective value is the price that people will pay for a property, irrespective of its cost, as differentiated from objective value in which value is associated with the cost of production or cost of creating the property.

Application   An appraiser uses subjective value in both the direct comparison approach and the income approach. In fact, the subjective value dominates real estate valuation.

It can matter little what costs are associated with development of a property. Value is measured through the present worth of all the future benefits that likely will accrue through ownership. Future benefits do not necessarily indicate money, e.g., an income stream. Non-monetary benefits, in the case of residential property, may include subjective factors such as pleasurable living, or amenities, e.g., a park or forest reserve.

Example *Subjective Value*

Seller Smith is adamant about the price of his property. According to Smith's figures, a selling price of $169,000 is essential if he is to recapture his investment in the property and pay a commission and associated closing costs. Recent improvements to the house amounted to more than $30,000 and he built the home for $135,000 one year ago. Smith is arguing his position based on objective value; in other words, value is directly tied to the cost of the property and improvements.

Salesperson Lee, however, has completed a residential market comparison guide that clearly shows that comparable homes have been selling in the range of $150,000 – $160,000. Lee's presentation is based on subjective value; the value that exists in the minds of potential buyers.

SUBLEASE

A lease executed by the lessee of a leasehold estate, to a third person, that conveys the same estate for a shorter term, or a portion of the estate for the same or shorter term. A sublease grants the interest to a third person while the lessee retains a reversionary interest. A sublease should be clearly differentiated from an assignment in which the lessee transfers his/her entire interest to a third person, being the assignee.

Provincial   See applicable reference materials.

SUBLETTING

Provincial   See applicable reference materials.

SUBORDINATION

An agreement, by which a lienholder, a lessee, or one having an interest or claim in or against personal or real property, places the interest behind that of another.

Application   Real estate practitioners encounter subordination when a first mortgage expires before a second mortgage on the same property. As a result, upon the first

mortgage becoming due and payable, the second mortgage would move into first mortgage position, leaving the owner with the awkward task of securing a new second mortgage. To avoid that situation, a postponement clause is usually inserted in the second mortgage document that subordinates the second mortgage to a yet to be arranged new first mortgage.

Example   *Subordination*

Seller Smith has an existing first mortgage of $150,000 that expires in one year's time. Currently, he is attempting to arrange a small second mortgage for $15,000 to undertake various home improvements and wishes to repay the loan over a two-year period. When the first mortgage comes due, Smith wants to be able to replace it with a new first mortgage, ensuring that the second mortgage remains in a subordinate position.

A postponement clause is inserted into the second mortgage as follows:

This mortgage shall contain a clause permitting the renewal or replacement of the existing first mortgage at any time, provided that any increase in the principal amount of the new first mortgage over the amount of principal owing under the first mortgage at the time of renewal or replacement shall be applied in reduction of the principal amount of this mortgage; and the mortgagee hereunder shall execute and deliver to the mortgagor such postponement agreement, mortgage statement, or other documents as the first mortgagee may reasonably require, forthwith upon request.

SUBROGATION

The act of replacing one person with another in regard to a legal right, interest, or obligation, e.g., a substitution such as an insured person transferring claim rights to the insurance carrier in return for direct payment of the loss.

Example   *Subrogation–Insurance Claim*

Owner Smith suffered smoke damage as a consequence of a fire that occurred in an adjacent condominium unit within the condominium townhouse development. The fire insurance company who covered Smith's property inspected the damage and provided a cash settlement amounting to $8,500 to pay for cleaning expenses and replacement of various articles. Smith, when signing off on the claim, also provided the insurance company with the right of subrogation to pursue the insurer of the adjacent unit in which the fire started and possibly recover all or part of the money paid to Smith from that insurer.

S

SUBSTITUTION, PRINCIPLE OF
(SEE PRINCIPLES (APPRAISAL))

SUCCESSORS AND ASSIGNS

Heirs, executors, and administrators of the deceased commonly referred to in preprinted agreements/contracts which state that the agreements/contracts are binding upon and shall ensure to the benefit of the buyers and sellers and each of their successors, assigns, and personal representatives.

> **Example** *Successors and Assigns*
> Seller Smith sold his property unconditionally using the standard preprinted agreement/contract and subsequently purchased another home to align with the scheduled sale date. Prior to closing, the buyer passed away; however, based on the 'successors and assigns clause' within the agreement/contract, the estate of the buyer may be obligated to continue with the purchase.

Provincial   See applicable reference materials.

SUMP PUMP

An electric pump, located in a pit (sump) below the basement floor level, used to lift storm water from a low spot into a storm sewer or other discharge point away from the structure. The sump pump is activated by a float when the water level rises in the sump. The sump is typically lined with concrete, but may in some cases consist of dirt walls and floor. Plastic liners are available to prevent dirt from clogging the pump.

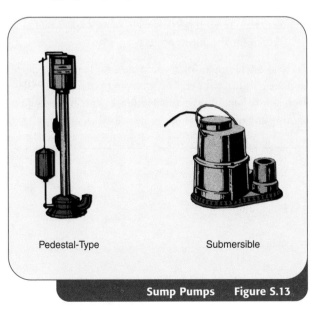

Pedestal-Type   Submersible

Sump Pumps   Figure S.13

SUNLIGHT LAWS
(SEE SOLAR/SUNLIGHT RIGHTS)

SUPERADEQUACY

A greater capacity or quality in the structure, or one of its components, than the typical buyer or owner would include, or would pay for, in that type of structure under current market conditions. A superadequacy does not contribute to value in relation to its cost.

> **Example** *Superadequacy*
> Smith is confident that his new home will be his permanent residence for the remainder of his lifetime. Therefore, he insists that various components be upgraded well beyond normal requirements. For example, while specifications call for a 3" poured concrete slab for the garage floor, Smith insisted that it be 8" in depth. Further, all footings were doubled in size from those in the plans.
> The architectural design called for a two-ton air-conditioner. In true form, Smith doubled the capacity to four. In terms of joists, while most residential specifications require 12 to 24 inch spacing, Smith insisted that all joists be placed 6" apart. His insistence on virtually doubling all building code requirements extended to practically all components of the structure.
> To the casual observer, the interior and exterior of the house looked quite similar to other properties in the area. Smith's cost of construction was almost double that of other homes in the area. Unfortunately, less than one year following construction, Smith had to relocate and placed the home up for sale. Smith wanted to recoup his total investment of $325,000 while comparable properties were selling for approximately $240,000.
> The appraiser, while attributing some additional value due to superior construction, placed the value at $255,000. This figure fell well short of Smith's investment, owing to the concept of superadequacy and the unwillingness of other buyers to pay for the greater quality and building standards within the home.

SUPPLY AND DEMAND
(SEE ECONOMICS)

SUPPLY AND DEMAND, PRINCIPLE OF
(SEE PRINCIPLES (APPRAISAL)

SURETY BOND

Provincial   See applicable reference materials.

SURFACE RIGHTS
(SEE ALSO FRACTIONAL (PARTIAL) INTEREST)

One of several fractional rights (interests) that form part of the total bundle of rights associated with fee simple ownership. Surface rights (also referred to as *ground level rights*), involve the right to use and otherwise alter the surface of real property, as opposed to other fractional or partial rights such as mineral rights and air rights.

SURPLUS PRODUCTIVITY, PRINCIPLE OF
(SEE PRINCIPLES (APPRAISAL))

SURVEY

The accurate mathematical measurements of land and improvements thereon made with the aid of instruments.

Provincial   See applicable reference materials.

SURVIVORSHIP
(SEE ALSO JOINT TENANCY)

The right of a person to secure ownership by reason of outliving someone with whom an interest in the land is shared, by joint tenancy. With tenants in common, the ownership could be acquired by will. In the case of a joint tenancy, the ownership would be automatically and instantaneously transferred upon death.

Example   *Survivorship*

John and Mary Smith own a residential property as joint tenants. The title to the property reads as follows: John Michael Smith and Mary Rose Smith as joint tenants and not as tenants in common. Neither John nor Mary can bequeath the interest in the property by means of a will because the transfer to the other joint tenant is automatic at death. Therefore, upon the death of John, the title to the property will automatically pass to Mary. Effectively, John's joint tenant interest ceases to exist.

SUSPENDED CEILING

A lightweight system that has proven attractive, owing to cost efficiency in installation, the ability to reduce unneeded height within buildings, sound deadening qualities, and ease of access to mechanical parts of the building.

Suspended ceilings are normally built using the exposed T-bar arrangement, but variations exist in which the T-shaped metal framing pieces are either recessed or invisible following final installation of the suspended tiles or panels.

SUSPENSION (REGISTRATION)

Provincial   See applicable reference materials.

SYNDICATION

An association of individuals formed for the purpose of owning, operating, and managing large parcels of real property for the mutual benefit of all, and organized as a corporation, limited partnership, or joint venture.

Application   Real estate registrants must be cautioned concerning transactions involving syndication. Certain real estate transactions could fall under the guidelines of the securities legislation and associated compliance requirements in particular provinces.

- Limited partnerships involving the sale of shares in a corporation.
- Property that is obviously priced well above current values because of representations and future values contingent upon non-owner management expertise.
- Property purchased with a mandatory requirement by the owner to sign management or related agreements/contracts with the owner or a designated agent of the owner.
- Property where warranted cash flows or other financial guarantees are associated with the purchase.
- A project in which rent pooling of all unit owners exists along with participation in an overall rate of return for the entire project.

Real estate practitioners are wise to solicit legal advice and seek additional details concerning provincial legislation before becoming involved in real estate projects containing any or all of the above described characteristics.

T TO U

T TO U

National Info Links

Taxation—Federal (Income)

Canada Customs and Revenue Agency

Web Site   www.ccra-adrc.gc.ca

See the local telephone directory for addresses and telephone numbers of Tax Services Offices and Tax Centres.

For provincial taxation matters involving real property contact the appropriate provincial ministry/department.

T

TARGET MARKET

An identified category of buyers or sellers in a real estate market. Aptly named after the traditional archery target, most target markets are viewed as a single centre point with widening concentric circles. The expanding circles are often geographically defined and identified as primary and secondary markets. The circles can also apply conceptually to types of buyers or sellers, e.g., those closely associated with selected properties or services progressively moving outward to lesser degrees of need and motivation.

Application   While target markets can apply to any real estate specialty, this description relates most commonly to commercial properties. The choice of a target market determines the scope of any marketing proposal and the associated marketing plan that flows from that proposal. While methods to reach target audiences are many, certain tried and true methods are usually employed. Most successful marketing involves the use of target market-related publications and direct mailings. The seller can often provide valuable input to the marketing plan. Frequently the seller, having invested in the property, may have a good feel for the motivations of potential prospects as well as useful contacts to be explored. Targeting usually involves the development of marketing packages and literature for direct distribution or placement in selected publications.

TASK LIGHTING

Overhead lighting systems that provide each work space with individual overhead lighting controls, designed to conserve energy by only lighting work areas occupied at any given time.

TAX

Any charge levied at a municipal, provincial, or federal government upon either things or persons.

Application   Real estate practitioners frequently encounter taxation involving real property either at a municipal level that involves the payment of property taxes based on an

assessed value, the remittance of tax for the transfer of real property, and tax concerning income generated from investment properties. Brokerages are also involved with income tax deductions for employees (see **Source Deductions**), and taxation of brokerage income (see **Taxation (Brokerage)**).

Provincial   See applicable reference materials.

TAX BASE

The total assessed value of property used as the basis for real property taxation. Taxes are calculated based on the tax base multiplied by a tax rate or mill rate.

Provincial   See applicable reference materials.

TAX LIABILITY
(SALE OF INVESTMENT PROPERTY)

Commercial practitioners analyze income property both in terms of operations cash flow after taxes and sale proceeds after taxes to arrive at an accurate basis for comparison. To establish *sale proceeds after tax*, several sequential steps are required including: calculation of an adjusted cost base, resulting gain or capital gain derived from the sale, amount of recaptured capital cost allowance that applies (if any), and establishment of a marginal tax rate that applies to the capital gain.

Example   *Tax Liability*

Following is the calculation of a capital gain and the resulting tax liability for a fictitious income property.

Calculation of Capital Gain

Sale Price	$1,329,684
Adjusted Cost Base	−1,000,000
Cost of Sale	−59,832
Capital Gain Exemption	−0
Capital Gain	$269,852
Taxable Capital Gain (269,852 x .50)	$134,926

Calculation of Tax Liability

Recaptured Capital Cost Allowance	$ 74,861
Taxable Capital Gain	+134,926
Unamortized Expenses	−0
Taxable Income	$209,787
Tax Liability	**$92,306**
(209,787 x .44 (estimated marginal tax rate))	

Calculations for the adjusted cost base and recaptured capital cost allowance are not shown.

TAX RATE
(SEE ALSO TAXATION (REAL PROPERTY))

The rate of tax, that is applied to the assessed value of individual properties to arrive at tax payable.

Provincial   See applicable reference materials.

TAX SHELTER (INVESTMENT PROPERTY)

Broadly viewed as any financial arrangement that results in the reduction or elimination of taxes due. A real estate investment opportunity is normally judged in terms of four characteristics: leverage possible to maximize return on investment, the reliability and durability of the income stream, the opportunity to realize capital appreciation, and tax considerations that apply to that particular property. Taxation considerations include the analysis of tax shelter opportunities.

Application   Practitioners should have a general awareness of significant tax provisions in the *Income Tax Act*. For example, the Act provides for different tax treatment depending on whether a property is used for business/ investment income or as a primary residence. While taxes are payable on the business and investment income, the principal residence is generally excluded from taxation under the Act. Further, the Act also distinguishes between business income and property income when rent is received by an investor from real estate. The differentiation of business income and property income is important as significant distinctions are made concerning the treatment of such income.

The *Income Tax Act* further provides for capital cost allowance (CCA) on income-producing property and generally reduces the taxes payable on operations cash flows as well as impacting final sale proceeds at point of disposition. Advantages can also apply to specific uses. For example, incentives may be provided to stimulate the construction of certain types of residential accommodation. The MURB (Multiple Unit Residential Building) Program of the late 1970s was an excellent example of special tax treatment provided to MURB investors.

TAXABLE INCOME (INVESTMENT PROPERTY)

Cash flows from both the operation of an income-producing property and the sale of that property prior to any tax liability. Tax analysis has become an integral part of cash flow forecasting due to its significant impact on

return generated by investment properties and the analysis of such properties in relation to individual investors. Appropriate expert advice is recommended.

Application   Taxable income on operations cash flow is calculated by deducting interest, capital cost allowance, and selected non-operating expenses from net operating income. The resulting tax liability is deducted from cash flow before taxes to arrive at cash flow after taxes. Taxable income from sale proceeds has a more complex calculation involving four integrated parts: recaptured capital cost allowance, adjusted cost base, gain or capital gain determination, and tax liability on sale. The resulting calculations are then used to determine sale proceeds after tax. Real estate practitioners typically use cash flow worksheets in order to establish taxable income, cash flow after taxes, and sale proceeds after tax.

TAXATION (BROKERAGE)
(SEE ALSO CAPITAL COST ALLOWANCE, CAPITAL GAIN, CAPITAL LOSS, AND SMALL BUSINESS DEDUCTION)

Taxation issues impacting real estate brokerages can be complex. The following summaries are provided for general information purposes only. The Canada Customs and Revenue Agency or a tax expert should be contacted for questions concerning taxation issues.

Allowable and Non-Allowable Expenses

An expense incurred for the purpose of earning income is generally deductible from business income but the onus of proof rests on the taxpayer to prove that such expenses were actually incurred during the activity of earning an income. Any dispute by the Canada Customs and Revenue Agency (CCRA) places the onus of proof on the taxpayer.

When an expense is incurred partially to earn income as well as another purpose, only the income-earning portion is deductible. No deduction is allowed for loss or replacement of capital or depreciation except as expressly provided in the Act. To determine whether an outlay is capital or expense related, the taxpayer must ask: *Did this bring into being an asset of a permanent nature or was it a one-time expenditure?* If the former, it is deemed to be a capital outlay; if the latter, it is deemed to be an expense. Capital expenditures are capitalized and depreciated yearly at rates set out under the Act. Expenses are deductible for the year in which the expenditure occurred.

While there is no legal requirement for the retention of vouchers and receipts to prove expenses, substantiating such payments is virtually impossible unless proper documentation is retained. During a CCRA audit, the auditor will ask for all invoices and receipts. Such documents must have the date of transaction, amount, nature of the expense, supplier (that is the company who is providing the goods or services), name of the taxpayer and, usually, an invoice number. Again, if an expense claim is disputed by the CCRA, the onus of proof is on the taxpayer. Expert advice is required on all such matters.

Example	*Taxation (Brokerage)— Allowable and Non-Allowable Expenses*

Following are selected examples involving typical allowable expenses. The reader is reminded that these will vary substantially, based on the taxpayer's particular situation.

- Selected fees to maintain professional status.
- Automobile expenses, subject to rules concerning business and personal use, additional automobiles owned by the taxpayer, and standby charges.
- Bonuses paid by the employer as additional wages are deductible by the employer.
- Convention expenses relating to the business or profession. Again, several limitations apply.
- Entertainment and meals relating to conduct of business, subject to various limitations.
- Interest on borrowed money used to earn income.
- Legal expenses are generally deductible if incurred in relation to the operation of the business.
- Losses incurred in the ordinary course of business are usually deductible. Capital losses are deductible against taxable capital gains.
- Examples of non-allowable expenses would include the following:
  - Capital outlay for the purchase of a business.
  - Personal expenses.
  - Recreational facilities and club dues whose main purpose is to provide recreational, sporting, or dining facilities.
  - Expenses paid to maintain or use a yacht, camp, golf course, or lodge, other than in the ordinary course of business.

Capital Cost Allowance

The Canada Customs and Revenue Agency recognizes that capital assets, though durable, do have a limited lifetime and at some point will be replaced. Thus, the Act permits a deduction of part of the capital cost against income from the business. Capital cost allowance is the maximum rate set under the *Income Tax Act* that the taxpayer can claim for depreciation.

Capital Gains/Business Income

The debate concerning whether income is a capital gain or business income rests with the taxpayer and the

Canada Customs and Revenue Agency (CCRA). At present, a definite advantage exists for the taxpayer in reporting a transaction as a capital gain as opposed to ordinary business income. The *Income Tax Act*, however, does not detail methods to determine whether a gain or loss is capital in nature. Taxpayers and the CCRA must refer to thousands of Tax Court decisions to make the determination.

It is the taxpayer's responsibility to report the gain as capital or business income. The CCRA will then scrutinize and challenge any submission if sufficient doubt is expressed. The onus of proof is on the taxpayer.

Corporate Year End

In establishing a corporate year end, the fiscal period of a corporation cannot exceed 53 weeks but can be any lesser number of weeks at the option of the owner (applies to the first taxation year only).

Example	*Taxation (Brokerage)— Corporate Year End*

If a real estate brokerage is incorporated on July 25, 20xx, then the corporate year end must fall between that date and July 31 of the following year. The corporate year end can be amended but such a request must be fully documented (including reasons) and subject to approval by the Canada Customs and Revenue Agency.

Small Business Deduction

A Canadian controlled private corporation carrying on an active business can qualify for the small business deduction. This deduction provides a worthwhile tax incentive to corporations as it reduces the overall rate of both federal and provincial corporate taxes. A Canadian controlled private corporation is defined as one that is not controlled by non-residents and whose shares are not publicly traded nor is it controlled by a company whose shares are traded or any combination thereof.

TAXATION (LAND TRANSFER TAX)

Provincial   See applicable reference materials.

TAXATION (REAL PROPERTY)

Municipalities generate revenue by charging a tax to property owners based on the value of their real property. These tax revenues pay for services such as police and fire protection, road construction and maintenance, snow removal, and solid waste collection and disposal. Also, municipalities

are required to collect education funds on behalf of the education authorities.

The value of property for taxation purposes is estimated by the assessing authority in line with regulations set out under the provincial assessment act. The requirement that property tax be paid is one of the basic limitations on the rights of ownership of real property in Canada.

An understanding of the present system of assessing real property for tax purposes is basic to the process of listing, appraising, and showing real property. Each municipality generates most of its operating revenue through the taxation of real property within its boundaries. The basis of the real property tax system is the *ad valorem* or *according to value* system. The amount of property tax to be paid by an owner is simply a percentage of the value of the real property. It follows that a homeowner with more valuable property should pay higher taxes and vice versa. Although this sounds like a straightforward concept, practical implementation is another matter. To apply the system to any individual property, a municipality must be capable of determining two factors: property value (assessment), and the percentage of value to be paid (tax rate).

Provincial   See applicable reference materials concerning specific methods used in individual provinces for assessing value, determining tax rates, and the funding of municipal and educational services.

TENANCY (COMMERCIAL OR RESIDENTIAL)

Provincial   See applicable reference materials.

TENANCY (TYPES)

The relationship of a landlord to a tenant arises from ancient feudal doctrines. Over the years, four major types of tenancy have developed.

Fixed Term

A tenancy in which the tenant has exclusive possession for a specific term, which is normally agreed to in a written contract. In a fixed term lease, both the commencement and expiry dates must be determined before the lease takes effect. In a commercial fixed term tenancy, the tenancy ends on the expiry date and no notice is required, however, it is not unusual for the tenancy to continue on a periodic basis. In residential tenancies, if the tenant remains in possession of the property following the expiry date, the tenancy is deemed to continue on a month-to-month basis pursuant to provincial tenancy legislation.

Periodic Tenancy

A tenancy for a fixed period but indefinite length that can be made certain by notice of termination. In other words, the periodic tenancy automatically renews itself (usually on a weekly, monthly, or yearly basis), unless notice is given to the contrary.

In residential tenancies, a periodic tenancy can be either in writing or oral and may simply state that the tenancy is on a month-to-month basis. If a residential tenant remains in a property following the expiration of a fixed term tenancy, the tenancy relationship normally converts into a periodic tenancy automatically.

> **Example** *Types of Tenancy—Periodic Tenancy*
>
> Owner Smith enters into a commercial tenancy agreement with Jones whereby Jones has a monthly tenancy beginning on the first of each month. This tenancy will automatically renew itself for the same duration as the original period unless either Smith or Jones gives notice to terminate (a notice to quit), to the other.

Tenancy at Will

A tenancy that can arise when, after expiration of a lease, or when no lease exists, the tenant remains in possession with the consent of the landlord or the person entitled to possession.

Real estate practitioners should be aware that a tenancy agreement can occur by contract or by implication from the acts of the parties. An implied tenancy at will may arise when a tenant occupies premises without rent. An express tenancy at will may arise when a real estate transaction does not close on the scheduled date and possession is granted in anticipation of a future closing.

> **Example** *Types of Tenancy—Tenancy at Will*
>
> Seller Smith sells his commercial property to Buyer Jones, but Jones has to wait for the closing of another property on the same day that is now delayed. The solicitors for Jones and Smith agree to allow Jones to take possession of the commercial property, provided that he agrees to vacate the premises without notice if the other transaction does not close in a short period of time.
>
> While there are certain risks involved in such arrangements, the lawyers, as well as Jones and Smith, are confident that closing is a certainty. If this were not the case, Smith could well demand that Jones secure interim financing to close the sale. Further, the parties are comfortable with the arrangement as the property involves commercial usage and does not invoke legislative requirements that would normally be considered in a residential tenancy, e.g., specific notice periods and related requirements. Accordingly, the buyer and seller enter into a tenancy agreement to suit the circumstances.

Tenancy at Sufferance

This type of tenancy (also referred to as an *overholding tenancy*), could occur if a person has possession without the consent of the owner and without paying rent. It arises by implication of law in situations where the tenancy has been terminated but the tenant does not vacate. Tenancy at sufferance might typically arise if the tenant did not vacate after a proper notice to quit, or did not vacate after the fixed term tenancy expired. In certain circumstances, a tenant may be liable for damages or for double rent.

Example   *Types of Tenancy—Tenancy at Sufferance*

Owner Smith, a commercial landlord, gives Tenant Jones a notice to vacate. Jones has occupied the property for several years. Smith, in giving notice, currently resides at a distant location and has no immediate use for the property, which is scheduled for redevelopment. Jones, while accepting the notice, remains on the property without paying any rent.

TENANCY AGREEMENTS

A contract between landlord and tenant setting out the term, the parties, and other particulars relating to the tenancy.

Provincial   See applicable reference materials.

TENANCY LEGISLATION

Provincial   See applicable reference materials.

TENANT MIX

The range of businesses and services that make up a shopping centre or office building, usually identified by specific services offered.

Application   Practitioners specializing in commercial sales encounter retail lease documents setting out specific uses that, in turn, directly impact tenant mix. Each tenant normally operates within a narrowly defined store type, e.g., a shoe store, a hardware store, or a supermarket. The use is clearly and simply defined and precisely limited in scope. Precise limitations of uses are commonly found with smaller tenants to ensure that the retail complex offers a varied, yet complementary range of services and tenant mix for consumers in the identified trading area. Anchor tenants, given their intrinsic strength, can and will demand an extremely broad use definition within leases.

TENANT REPRESENTATION PROPOSAL

The tenant representation proposal, as with buyer representation, is an increasingly important aspect of commercial activity. Exact formats will differ between brokerages but the scope of activity can be generally defined under five primary areas. The explanation is limited to summary points only, given the diversity of approaches found in the market.

Application   In developing a tenant representation proposal, practitioners are best guided by five fundamental questions. The final proposal is largely guided by tenant needs, type of property, and brokerage and/or salesperson creativity.

What goals must be achieved and what tasks are required?
This segment details goals concerning the search for qualified space. Customarily, the scope of work includes a timetable to point of anticipated lease, including a general description of tasks involved.

What location, features, and economic objectives must be addressed?
This stage is similar to the technical review found in a marketing proposal. The search criteria set out parameters for an acceptable lease property based on tenant needs:

Location	Demographics, adjacent facilities and proximity to markets.
Site	Zoning, access/egress, and site services.
Building	Size, ceiling heights, office finishes, utilities, HVAC, sprinkler systems, loading docks, security, building construction, etc.
Economic/Financial	Taxes and financing. Specific investor objectives are also normally outlined.

What properties are best suited to the client?
The practitioner reviews all listed properties based on the search criteria. Solicitation of proposals for leaseable space involving other properties not currently listed for sale may also be required. A comparative summary of all relevant properties is prepared to determine best options for the client, including valuation of those options. Typically commercial practitioners prepare a detailed analysis of lease alternatives including base rent, tenant-paid improvements, operating expenses, additional costs, and landlord concessions to arrive at effective rent comparisons.

How will negotiations be conducted and offers drafted?
For proposal purposes, practitioners normally detail the types of services commonly provided to clients during negotiations and drafting of a commercial agreement to lease.

What follow-up processes and after lease services are provided?
Commercial brokerages promote services to point of, and well beyond, closing. The lease of a property opens other opportunities and aggressive companies have capitalized on this potential. The concluding segment usually includes a detailed resume of both salesperson and brokerage.

TENANTS IN COMMON
(SEE ALSO JOINT TENANCY)

Ownership of land by two or more persons, however, unlike joint tenancy the interest of a deceased person does not pass to the survivor, but is treated as an asset of the deceased's estate.

Application   Tenancy in common requires only the unity of possession as opposed to joint tenancy that has four unities. Each tenant in common is entitled to the same rights over the property and the use of the whole property. Since the only unity that is required is that of possession, tenants in common may hold different interests and acquire those interests in different ways. It is quite possible to have two tenants in common each owning 1/4 of the property and the third tenant in common owning the balance, namely 1/2 of the property.

No right of survivorship exists under a tenancy in common as the tenants/owners hold separate interests. Therefore, upon the death of one of the owners in a tenancy in common arrangement, the interest in the land passes to that individual's estate and does not automatically transfer to the remaining tenants.

Each tenant in common may sell or lease his/her undivided interest to another or dispose of it by will. A tenancy in common arrangement can therefore be terminated by the sale of one tenant's interest to the other tenant(s), the sale of the entire property to another party, or the dissolution of the tenancy in common relationship by a court order.

TERM

A fixed period of time normally associated with mortgages and tenancy agreements.

Application   Practitioners most commonly encounter the word *term* in relation to a mortgage. The term is the actual length of time for which the money is loaned. In a lease, the term is the time period between commencement date and expiry date.

TERMINAL CAPITALIZATION RATE

A capitalization rate that reflects the relationship between forecasted net operating income at the point of disposition and a corresponding sale price. If, for example, an investment analysis covers a 10-year period (EOY10), the value is established at the end of Year 10 based on the projected net operating income (EOY10) along with a suitable terminal cap rate. The assumption made is that the property will sell on or before the end of Year 10. Appraisers may apply the forecasted net operating income for EOY11 in arriving at a value based on the assumption that the actual marketing and sale will occur during the subsequent year.

Application   Commercial brokerages and real estate organizations often produce surveys that include the initial overall capitalization rate (OCR), frequently referred to as a *going-in* rate, and the terminal or reversion capitalization rate. Surveys usually delineate rates by property type (e.g., neighbourhood/regional malls, industrial, power centres, urban/suburban office, apartment, etc.), with separate rates normally provided for Class A, B, and C buildings. In selected instances, expectations of various investor groups are also profiled, e.g., insurance companies, institutional investors, and pension funds.

Risk is a major factor in establishing terminal cap rates and the rates normally reflect that fact. Terminal cap rates are typically higher than the *going-in* OCRs. Research in the Canadian marketplace indicates that the spread between going-in and terminal cap rates ranges from .5 to 2.5%, i.e., if the going-in rate is 9%, the terminal rate will vary from 9.5 to 11.5%. The most significant spreads are found in higher risk properties, e.g., Class C as opposed to Class A. Other factors also contribute to the traditionally higher terminal rate. The building, at the point of disposition, has a shorter economic life and typically has lost some degree of competitive advantage. The reader is reminded that an increase in cap rate results in a decrease in the corresponding estimate of value.

When establishing value based on a terminal cap rate, the net operating income (NOI) must be calculated using the same basic methods as would apply for an NOI during the current period. This requirement, while academically sound, poses certain practical problems regarding a more distant time period, e.g., EOY10. In particular, concerns have been raised given the number of assumptions required. Practitioners and appraisers routinely cite market research and the use of surveys with confidence when arriving at forecasted net operating incomes. However, the reality is that only historical data is available as a benchmark.

Difficulties can also arise in relation to projected net operating incomes for a particular property. For example, net operating income projections may be developed using sequential percentage income/expense increases or decreases, e.g., straight-line (constant amount of change per year), or exponential-curve (constant ratio change per year). This linear approach provides sequential yearly forecasts but may fail to account for unique characteristics in different properties. For example, older buildings typically reach economic obsolescence (assuming no renovations), sooner than newer structures. Forecasts and ultimately the terminal cap rate should reflect this fact both in terms of income (lower revenues due to obsolescence), and expenses (increased repairs).

The growing use of terminal cap rates is largely attributed to discounted cash flow (DCF) analysis and yield capitalization. A reversionary value is usually required to complete present value analysis, net present value (NPV), and internal rate of return (IRR). Terminal cap rates are useful to more accurately forecast value at the point of disposition. Practitioners are reminded that precision is essential as capital appreciation can account for a significant portion of overall cash flow and noticeably impact the amount of projected yield.

Example — *Terminal Capitalization Rate*

Salesperson Warden, of XYZ Real Estate Ltd. has established a *going-in* OCR of 10% based on market-extracted research. The investment property generates a stabilized net operating income (NOI) of $19,319. The terminal cap rate is 11.25% based on market research and brokerage surveys. The NOI is forecasted to increase by 7% over three years following acquisition in Year 1 with a sale at the start of the fifth year.

Year 1 Estimate of Value*	$19,319 ÷ .10	=	$193,190
Year 2 NOI	$19,319 x 1.07	=	$20,671
Year 3 NOI	$20,671 x 1.07	=	$22,118
Year 4 NOI	$22,118 x 1.07	=	$23,666
Year 5 Estimate of Reversionary Value**	$23,666 ÷ .1125	=	$210,364

* Based on going-in OCR ** Based on Terminal OCR

TERMINATION OF AGREEMENT/CONTRACT

Provincial   See applicable reference materials.

TERMITES

Insects that feed on wood, found chiefly in tropical climates but have been known to exist in North America for more than 50 years. Termites live in sophisticated social colonies in the soil, not in the wood. In colder climates, their colonies are usually located below the level of frost penetration, and are typically close to some moisture source. When termites travel, they do so by moving through wood, soil, or shelter tubes that they construct. Termites will not expose themselves to the open air, as their bodies can dry out very quickly.

Shelter tubes are small tunnels that the termites build across any open surface they want to traverse. The shelter tubes are made of earth, debris, and a material they excrete which acts as a binder to hold the tubes together. These tubes are typically sandy in colour and can be readily broken open by hand. An initial tube may be less than one quarter inch in width, although several tubes can be built together over time and the entire grouping may be one or two inches wide.

Since the termites do not like to be exposed to the air, they will typically eat through the inside of a piece of wood, often following the grain. They tend to eat in parallel galleries and leave a smooth honey-combed appearance on the inside of the wood. Termites will eat any kind of wood, although damp or rotted wood is easier for them to break down. Termites need a regular supply of moisture, and workers return to the colony every 24 to 48 hours.

Application   Practitioners should be aware of detection methods along with basic knowledge concerning treatments available for termites.

Detection

The shelter tubes are usually the first indication of infestation. The second indication is typically damaged wood, although often the wood has to be probed to identify damage. An infestation can develop unnoticed behind finished basement floors or walls where shelter tubes are not visible. A small amount of frass is usually found inside the damaged wood consisting of small grey flecks, that differ from the powdery wood (sawdust) generated by carpenter ants. Carpenter ants will tend to push the wood debris out of the tunnels, while termites consume the material.

Wherever termite activity or termite treatment is in evidence, the question is raised as to whether any structural damage has occurred. If none is visible, it may be difficult to know whether damage is concealed or has been repaired. While direct verification can be difficult without disassembling the house, the building should be monitored for

577

sagging structural components, floor springiness, or other signs of structural weakness. It is not unusual for termites to attack a house, passing through the floor and wall systems up into the attic. Wood damage may occur a considerable distance from the point of attack in the basement as the termites move to the centre of wood members.

Treatment

Licensed pest control specialists can eliminate or prevent subterranean termites attacking a building by employing chemicals, which are believed to be effective over a 20–30 year period. The chemical is injected into the soil around the building, through the basement floor and foundations, and through any posts or other penetrations in the basement floor. The objective is to create a chemical envelope around the house. Termites live in a colony in the soil and chemical treatment does not kill the colony, but simply prevents the colony from sending its workers into the building to collect wood to feed the colony. It is also necessary to treat all attached buildings to ensure effectiveness of the treatment. An envelope created around one-half of a semi-detached building will not prevent infestation to the other half and entry of the termites into the treated half through the upper levels. Government grants are available in certain areas for chemical treatment as well as elimination of wood/soil contact.

Detection—Existing Treatment

Plugged holes roughly the size of a quarter, spaced from 12 to 24 inches apart in sidewalks or driveways around the house is usually evidence of chemical treatment. Similar holes may also be found on the exterior foundation walls above grade, on the interior foundation walls, on the basement floor just inside the exterior walls, and on interior walls around the base of columns. Occasionally, the treatment is also injected directly into the columns. Another sign that chemical treatment may have been undertaken is the obvious breakage of wood/soil contact. A wood post with a relatively new concrete base and a concrete pad at the bottom of an old wood basement staircase are typical signs.

TERRITORIAL REAL ESTATE ASSOCIATION

An association formed within a territory in Canada that is a member, along with ten provincial associations, of The Canadian Real Estate Association (CREA) pursuant to CREA By-law No. 1. Currently, the Yukon Real Estate Association is a territorial member of CREA along with ten provincial associations.

Reference   See also **Provincial/Territorial Real Estate Associations.** All general references to provincial associations in this text are deemed to include territorial associations.

THERMOPANE
(SEE ALSO GLAZING)

A brand name (now frequently used in a generic sense), for window-glass construction that has insulating qualities due to two layers of glass separated by an airspace. The type of window construction is also called double-glazing, or insulating glass.

TIME IS OF THE ESSENCE

A term, normally found in an agreement/contract for the sale of real property, requiring punctual performance of the terms of a contract.

Example   *Time is of the Essence*

A typical wording found in a preprinted clause of an agreement/contract is provided for illustration purposes.

> *Time shall in all respects be of the essence hereof provided that the time for doing or completing of any matter provided for herein may be extended or abridged by an agreement in writing signed by Vendor and Purchaser or by their respective lawyers who may be specifically authorized in that regard.*

Provincial   See applicable reference materials.

TIME VALUE OF MONEY (TVM)
(SEE COMPOUNDING AND DISCOUNTING)

TIMESHARE

A relatively new concept in property ownership that generally falls under two broad categories.

Fee Ownership Interest   The right to encumber, convey, or otherwise transfer the interest for all future time.

Right-To-Use Ownership   A non-fee interest in the designated property in which the buyer receives no registrable title. Instead, the owner of this interest has a contractual right to enjoy the use of the property for a specified period.

Provincial   See applicable reference materials if appropriate. Various provinces do not currently have legislation specifically addressing timeshare ownership.

TITLE

The lawful ownership of property, as well as the means of evidence by which the owner has lawful ownership thereof.

Provincial   See applicable reference materials.

TITLE DEFECT

A term commonly used in the United States concerning any encumbrance or claim that affects title to real property. In Canada, an encumbrance or claim relating to title is typically referred to as a *cloud on title*.

Example   *Title Defect*

Mr. and Mrs. James have recently purchased a resale home with a scheduled closing date approximately one month from today's date. The buyers' solicitor, upon completing a title search of the property, discovered several liens registered against the property that affect the marketability of title. Such items would be referred to as *clouds on title* and these unresolved claims would have to be removed prior to closing the transaction.

TITLE INSURANCE

An insured statement of title or ownership of real property provided by a title insurer for a specified, usually onetime, premium. Title insurance is relatively new within the Canadian marketplace, but has flourished for years in the United States. Its growth within the American market appears due in part to more or less ineffective land registration systems in various state jurisdictions, coupled with a dramatic rise in the secondary mortgage market.

The secondary mortgage market involves the sale of title and equitable mortgages in the marketplace. Lenders and investors acquiring this mortgage paper require confirmation of various title matters concerning the property being mortgaged. Title insurance simply offers an expedient and relatively inexpensive method to provide such assurances and furnish appropriate documentation. Insurers normally provide separate policies for commercial and residential properties.

Application   The Canadian experience with title insurance is just now unfolding. The growth of secondary mortgage market activity, certain limitations within the selected provincial land registry systems, and title opinions provided by lawyers have led to increased use of this form of insurance.

Title insurance, according to proponents, can simplify real estate transactions. For example, the title policy may eliminate the need for an up-to-date survey, thereby providing savings to the buyer and possibly avoiding certain delays in closing the transaction. Further, title insurance is often promoted as a method to avoid last minute title defect problems that may destroy the sale. Lastly, advocates cite the benefit of title insurance regarding the lender. Through a title policy, the lending institution receives certain assurances, as do subsequent lending organizations to which the mortgage is assigned such as Canada Mortgage and Housing Corporation.

Provincial   See applicable reference materials.

TITLE SEARCH

A search, for real estate purposes, involves an inspection of records contained within the public land registration office to determine the current state of title to a property including a review of all encumbrances, liens, mortgages and other interests that affect that title.

Provincial   See applicable reference materials.

TOPOGRAPHY

Surface features of land, such as elevation, ridges, slope, and contour.

Application   Topographic maps are of direct benefit to many practitioners as the physical features of land can directly impact the value of one site over another, e.g., development land and large recreational properties. Government agencies typically provide a range of topographical maps.

TORRENS SYSTEM
(SEE ALSO LAND TITLES)

A system of title recording created by provincial law. The Torrens System is a method of registration of land title, indicating the state of the title, including ownership and encumbrances, without the necessity of an additional search of prior public records. The primary objectives of the Torrens System were to provide security within land registration systems and assurances that current entries were valid.

The original Torrens System was introduced in South Australia in the mid-1800s by Robert Torrens. Torrens believed that the system applying to ship registration could in fact be transferred to land ownership. Torrens instituted a system that guaranteed the registered title acquired by an innocent party. As such, the owner of a property as recorded under the Torrens System could not be attacked in terms of the validity of his/her title. In other words, the title was indefeasible (i.e., unable of being attacked or voided by other parties), as recorded.

Provincial land registration statutes, while following the general premises set out in the Torrens System, do have exceptions and limitations to the concept of indefeasibility. Further, methods of land registration will differ both in terms of procedures and forms used in individual provinces.

Provincial   See applicable reference materials.

TORT
(SEE ALSO FIDUCIARY RESPONSIBILITIES)

Tort may be defined as a breach of duty (other than under contract), leading to liability and is a civil wrong for which the remedy is a common law action for damages. The most common tort is the tort of negligence, but others include deceit or fraudulent misrepresentation, nuisance, assault and battery, false imprisonment, malicious prosecution, trespassing, invasion of privacy, and defamation (libel and slander).

Tort law is concerned with the ever-expanding harm suffered by individuals incident to all of the activities carried on in an increasingly complex society. The primary purpose of tort law is to compensate victims of tortious activities, not to punish the wrongdoers. Punishment is left to criminal law when particular tortious conduct also amounts to a criminal offence. Automobile accidents are among the more common causes of harm. For example, when a drunken driver collides with a parked vehicle, its owner may sue the driver in tort for purposes of compensation and the Crown (i.e., the police) may charge him/her with drunken driving and impose penalties under the applicable provincial legislation.

Application   The application of tort law is best seen by viewing the basis for tort liability, the elements of a tort action, duties of professionals, and associated liability.

Basis for Liability

Fault   Blameworthy or culpable conduct, which, in the eyes of the law, is intentional or demonstrates careless disregard for the interests of others.

Strict Liability   A system of strict liability, regardless of fault, already exists under workers compensation legislation. Under this system, industrial accidents are assumed to be the inevitable price of doing business. Employers are compelled to make contributions to a fund which, in turn, compensates victims of industrial accidents, even when the employer has been blameless and the injury has resulted from the employee's own carelessness.

Vicarious Liability   Vicarious liability in the workplace refers to the liability of an employer to compensate persons for harm caused by an employee in the ordinary course of employment. An employer may be held personally at fault for a tort committed by an employee. For example, an employer may knowingly assign an employee a dangerous task for which that individual is not properly trained and thus be liable for injury to others. As another example, in the preparation of a will, a lawyer's legal assistant makes an error that causes a bequest to an intended beneficiary of the client to be void. In such cases, should an employer be liable when not directly at fault, especially if he/she has done the best to train the employee in avoiding anything that might constitute a tort? A consequence of the development of vicarious liability is that employers now insure themselves against such losses.

Real estate brokerages are liable for any harm or losses caused by the tortious acts of any of their employees during the ordinary course of their employment. To offer oneself to the public as a member of a professional organization, which all real estate practitioners do, is to offer a standard of conduct consistent with professional standards and to be accountable for failure to measure up to those standards.

Elements of Tort Action

As a practical matter in establishing the right to recover compensation for a tortious act, a plaintiff must prove three things to the court's satisfaction:

- That the defendant owed the plaintiff a duty to refrain from the injurious conduct in question. This often requires a value judgement. Is the conduct complained of such that it ought to create liability?
- That the defendant broke that duty by acting as he/she did.
- That the defendant's action caused the injury.

Duty in Tort

A duty has meaning only in relation to the class of person to whom it is owed. Defining the scope of a duty becomes essential whenever professional advice is relied upon by persons other than the client who is paying for the services. A client can sue for damages in contract if the breach of a promise contained in the contract results in loss or harm.

In the case of a real estate transaction, an agent has a contractual duty to the person(s) with whom he/she has a listing agreement or a buyer agency relationship. However, this same agent can become liable in tort to others such as prospective buyers if that agent is negligent in performing his/her duties as a real estate practitioner.

An agreement to provide professional services to a client contains a promise, whether expressly stated or not, to perform those services with due care. A breach of that promise is a breach of the contract for professional services, and the client may sue for damages under the contract. *Does the client also have a tort claim for negligence?* Probably.

Even apart from possible tort liability, a professional's duty is not entirely contractual. A principle of equity imposes a fiduciary duty of care on any dominant party in a special relationship of trust. This fiduciary duty arises even when the professional donates his/her services free of charge, so that no contract exists. In fact, a fiduciary duty arising from a relationship of trust may even impose a wider range of duty than is expressly stated in the contract.

Professional Liability

Professionals are highly qualified people whose skills have a significant intellectual content. Members of a profession are usually certified to offer their services to the public under a system of licensing administered by one or more governing bodies. Such is the case with real estate practitioners in provinces whose licensing/registration is administered by a provincial regulatory body. Also, real estate boards and provincial associations have, within their constitutions, the right to administer discipline to members who fail to live up to the established standards of ethical conduct.

Potential third party liability exists for real estate practitioners. Naturally, a contractual duty of a real estate agent is owed to the seller of the property with whom there is a listing contract. However, this same agent owes a duty of care to anyone with whom he/she is in contact regarding the property.

TOTAL DEBT SERVICE RATIO
(SEE ALSO GROSS DEBT SERVICE RATIO)

Acronym: TDS The ratio of annual (or monthly) mortgage charges for principal, interest, and taxes, plus payments on various other debts (normally bank and finance company loans etc.), compared with gross income of the borrower. The TDS ratio should be clearly differentiated from the gross debt service (GDS) ratio that is calculated based on principal, interest, and taxes only.

Application Most lenders require an applicant to meet a particular TDS ratio, in addition to the GDS ratio. As with GDS, required TDS ratios vary from lender to lender but most are in the range of 35% to 40%.

TDS Ratio = (PIT + Loan Payments) ÷ Income

> **Example** *Total Debt Service Ratio*
>
> Assume that the borrower had a payment of $400/month for a car loan, earned $46,000 per year, and contemplated a PIT payment of $9,241.64 per year.
>
> TDS Ratio = (PIT + Loan Payments) ÷ Income
> = [9,241.64 + 4,800 (Annual)] ÷ 46,000
> = 14,041.64 ÷ 46,000
> = 30.53%

The use of total debt service has become increasingly important with the rise in consumer borrowing and special purpose loans. Lenders are concerned that commitments over and above the mortgage payment may cause the applicant to default at some future date. To protect their interest, lenders consider the applicants total financial picture during the loan qualifying process as opposed to qualification based solely on principal, interest, and taxes.

TOWNSHIP LINE

Provincial See applicable reference materials.

TRADE (CONTRACTOR)

A classification of workers based on skills associated with manual or mechanical work, such as sheet-metal workers, carpenters, and electricians.

> **Example** *Trade (Contractor)*
>
> Builder Anderson is constructing new homes on a recently approved plan of subdivision. He intends to build five model homes and hire a real estate broker to operate the sales centre in one of the models. Accordingly, Anderson operates as the general contractor and hires various trades as subcontractors to not only construct the initial models, but also build other homes as they are sold. Anderson's subcontractors include the following trades: carpenters, electricians, roofers, heating system contractors, and concrete specialists.

TRADE (REAL ESTATE)

Broadly described as the act of buying, selling, or exchanging, the term *trade* is often more rigidly defined by provincial real estate legislation. In certain instances, both *trade* and *transaction* are formally defined. While wordings will differ by jurisdiction, the general definition involves the sale, purchase, lease, or other acquisition or disposition of real estate for value.

Practitioners are directed to the appropriate provincial real estate act for a precise definition of a trade and associated terms. The following is an example for illustration purposes.

> *A disposition or acquisition of or transaction in real estate by sale, purchase, agreement for sale, exchange, option, lease, rental or otherwise and any offer or attempt to list real estate for the purpose of such disposition or transaction, and any act, advertisement, conduct or negotiation, directly or indirectly in furtherance of any disposition, acquisition, transaction, offer or attempt, and the verb 'trade' has corresponding meaning.*

Application   Anyone who acquires or disposes of real estate for value is *trading*. Thus, when a house is sold, the seller disposes of an interest in real estate and the buyer acquires one; both are trading. That does not mean that they have to be registered under the appropriate real estate act. Provincial acts typically set out conditions and circumstances under which individuals must be registered in order to trade in real estate and also identify exemptions.

Example   *Trade (Real Estate)*

Salesperson Lee is acting for a buyer, who has just inspected a property for sale with another brokerage through the local real estate board. He obtains an offer from Buyer Williams that is subsequently accepted. Williams, in turn, wanting the property for investment purposes, asks Lee to actively market the property and secure a tenant. Lee obtains an offer to lease from a prospective tenant acceptable to Williams with a planned occupancy date to coincide with the closing date of the property. Lee has engaged in two trades; one for the sale of the property and the other for the rental of that property.

TRADE FIXTURES

Articles installed by a commercial tenant usual to the tenant's business and removable by the tenant before the lease expires. Under the terms of a lease, trade fixtures typically remain personal property and are not true fixtures.

Application   In a commercial lease involving new premises, the landlord will normally have developed the design of the buildings, the landscaping and common areas, and established the elements of the areas to be leased, such as washrooms, electrical devices, HVAC, floor finishes, and store fronts. The balance of the work to be completed is usually at the tenant's cost, subject to the landlord's approval as to design and finish, and of course to building codes and other governmental requirements and restrictions.

All alterations, decorations, additions, and improvements made by the tenant or by the landlord on behalf of the tenant become the property of the landlord, provided that the tenant shall be responsible for the insuring of such affixed alterations, decorations, additions, and improvements. Commonly, the lease specifically references tenant trade fixtures as excluded under the provision and to remain the property of the tenant unless the tenant abandons such fixtures at the expiration of the lease.

Example   *Trade Fixtures*

Developer Reed is negotiating with Tenant Jones concerning a 5,000 square foot retail space for the operation of a restaurant. Given the possibility of a ten-year lease, Reed has agreed to complete various interior improvements for the restaurant, while Jones will install extensive kitchen and related facilities. Under the terms of the lease, all such facilities are deemed to be tenant trade fixtures and as such remain the property of the tenant at the expiration of the lease. Reed and Jones agree to precisely detail such trade fixtures as a schedule to the lease to avoid any future potential confusion.

Following is an excerpt to that effect taken from the lease document:

> *Upon the expiration of this lease, the alterations, decorations, additions and fixed improvements excepting the Tenant's trade fixtures as detailed in Schedule A will remain the property of the landlord as part of the reversion.*

TRADE RECORD

A form, also referred to as a trade record sheet, used for recording real estate trades (transactions) by real estate brokerages as required in specific provinces. Recordkeeping requirements vary across Canada as such matters are dictated by provincial real estate acts and regulatory controls. Typically, trade records must be completed for all trades (e.g., sales and leases) as well as related activities (e.g., referral commissions). See **Figure T.1** as an example.

Provincial   See applicable reference materials.

OREA
Ontario
Real Estate
Association

Ontario Real Estate Association
TRADE RECORD SHEET

Sale No.:

MLS No.:

R
REALTOR

.... Dated .... , ...
(Name of Brokerage Firm)   (year)

I, ..., have today sold (leased or rented, exchanged, optioned) the property
(Name of Salesperson)

known as ....

Owned by ....

Whose address is ....

Tel. No. (............).. to

Now living at ....

at the price (rent, exchange value, option price) of $ ....

transaction to be completed ....

A deposit of $ .... was taken ☐ cash ☐ cheque, payable ...., in trust.

Further deposit of $ .... was taken ☐ cash ☐ cheque, payable ...., in trust.

Total
Commission $ ....

Total
G.S.T. $ ....

Total
Receivable Comm $ ....

(Salesperson) _____   (Salesperson) _____

THE FOLLOWING TO BE COMPLETED BY THE BROKER:

	COMMISSION	GST	TOTAL	DATE PAID	CHEQUE NO.
Total Receivable Commission:					
Listing Broker:					
Listing #1 Salesperson #2					
Selling Broker:					
Selling #1 Salesperson #2					
Referral Fee:					
Real Estate Board:					
Other:					

Received deposit from (Salesperson) .... DATE ....

Further deposit from (Salesperson) .... DATE ....

Deposited in Statutory Trust (Amount) .... DATE .... Statement to Vendor DATE ....

Further deposit to Statutory Trust (Amount) .... DATE ....

Interest bearing deposit transferred to .... DATE .... Cheque # ....

Interest bearing deposit returned to Statutory Trust (Amount) .... DATE .... Cheque # ....

If applicable: Interest earned (Amount) .... Paid to .... Cheque # ....

Remitted to Vendor/Purchaser (Amount) .... DATE .... Cheque # ....

Transferred to Commission Trust (Amount) .... DATE .... Cheque # ....

Transferred Commission to Gen. Acct. (Amount) .... DATE .... Cheque # ....

Vendor's Solicitor ....   Purchaser's Solicitor ....

Address ....   Address ....

Tel. No. (.........)................. Fax No. (.........).........   Tel. No.. (.........)................ Fax No. (.........).........

Additional Necessary Information ....
To the best of my knowledge and belief the above information is correct.

DATED at .... Ontario, this .... day of .... , ...
(year)

_____
(Signature of Broker)

FOR OFFICE USE ONLY

COMMISSION TRUST AGREEMENT

To: The Salesperson(s) shown on the foregoing Trade Record Sheet:
In consideration of the Salesperson(s) having successfully completed a trade in real estate on behalf of the Broker with respect to the property more particularly defined in the foregoing Trade Record Sheet, I hereby declare that all moneys received or receivable by me in connection with the transaction as contemplated in the Office Policy Manual shall be receivable and held in trust. This agreement shall constitute a Commission Trust Agreement as defined in the Office Policy Manual and shall be subject to and governed by the Chapter pertaining to Commission Trust.

DATED as of the date and time of the acceptance of the foregoing Trade Record Sheet.   Acknowledged by:

_____   _____
(Signature of Broker)   (Signature of Salesperson)

OREA Standard Form: Do not alter when printing or reproducing the standard pre-set portion.   Form No. 107   01/99

T TO U

Trade Record Sheet (OREA Standard Form)   Figure T.1

TRAINING PROGRAMS
(BROKERAGE ORIENTATION)

Brokerages often provide training programs for new salespersons in addition to licensing and mandatory continuing education as determined by the provincial regulatory body. Programs for new salespeople can be grouped into two general categories:

- Orientation concerning brokerage policies and sales techniques.
- Continued skills development.

Orientation is generally viewed as a combination of an initial introduction to office systems, combined with an educational program in selling techniques. The ongoing skills training is structured to complement the existing licensing/registration program offered at a provincial level and to build on knowledge already acquired.

Benefits

A structured orientation program for new recruits can provide many benefits for the brokerage.

Smooth Transition for Salespeople   Training offered on a continuous basis can help streamline the entire selection, orientation, and retention process. It provides a quicker start for the new recruit, reduces possible alienation from the rest of the staff, and allows for familiarization with procedures and standards.

Retention   Turnover appears inevitable, but structured training may assist in reducing that turnover. Lack of training can be a major source of dissatisfaction with new recruits.

Structured Development   A real estate career, like any sales position, develops through various skill levels. As people grow in a function, they seek further knowledge to complement their activities. The brokerage can provide useful guidance through proper educational programs. While this is not a guarantee that individuals will remain, training is a further source of employee satisfaction. At the same time, the brokerage is constantly improving skill levels in the sales force.

Well-Trained Sales Team   Underlying the entire discussion of training is a relationship between education, longevity in employment, and skill/experience levels in the sales force. Separating the relative benefits of each is difficult. Education, by itself, will not produce an experienced, knowledgeable sales group. However, in conjunction with other factors training is a major factor in long-term growth.

Orientation Program Structure/Content

An effective orientation program consists of two parts: orientation to rules, procedures and office systems, and sales skills. Guidelines are provided for the practical implementation of both parts.

Brokerage Policies, Procedures, and Office Systems
This first aspect of the program provides the basis for quick assimilation of the new recruit into the office mainstream. A checklist is provided as **Figure T.2** to assist in designing an orientation program.

The brokerage should expand and modify the checklist to suit individual needs. Salespeople should acknowledge having received various items and information detailed in this checklist. Most checklists have space for the manager's or owner's initials and a signature line for the salesperson.

Sales Skills
Transition problems are normally minimized with a complete orientation. Selective sales skills can do much to improve the initial productivity of new recruits and ensure that brokerage standards are clearly understood. Any sales skills course, to be effective, must relate directly to the real world of everyday problems and opportunities. The type of training provided will vary substantially.

Following are a few suggestions for a skills program:

- Develop lists of friends, acquaintances, and business associates to contact;
- Organize list of benefits the salesperson can use when describing the brokerage services for a better, more organized listing presentation;
- Set up a canvassing schedule for a designated area to practice sales prospecting techniques;
- Organize a list for telephone canvassing and techniques to use in telephone prospecting;
- Assemble a structured listing presentation;
- Complete a survey of for sale by owners and expired listings for personal follow-up;
- Prepare and distribute letters to persons already identified as potential customers;
- Schedule open houses for an upcoming period; and
- Identify types of activity that will improve business activity, e.g., time management, showing property, and canvassing.

Continued Skills Training

Many opportunities exist for the creative manager or broker to promote and develop concepts initially introduced in the licensing/registration program. Following is a possible curriculum for introduction following initial orientation for both new and experienced salespeople.

NEW SALESPERSON ORIENTATION CHECKLIST

- ❏ Completion of application.
- ❏ Employee file opened and required employment forms completed.
- ❏ Board membership form completed.
- ❏ Introduction of other employees.
- ❏ Employment contract reviewed/signed and acknowledged.
- ❏ Key to office received/acknowledged.
- ❏ Desk assignment and provision of basic supplies.
- ❏ Order business cards.
- ❏ Photograph/news release.
- ❏ Other promotional items supplied.
- ❏ Office policy manual received/acknowledged.
- ❏ Security/access cards: e.g., photocopier and doors.
- ❏ Procedures for listing property.
- ❏ Filing system and accessibility.
- ❏ Advertising rules and regulations.

- ❏ Use of brokerage provided supplies.
- ❏ Brokerage forms.
- ❏ Use of office equipment and billing systems, if appropriate.
- ❏ Payment of commission and commission related brokerage policies.
- ❏ Duty time procedures, if applicable.
- ❏ Brokerage brochures and promotional items.
- ❏ Processing listings and trades.
- ❏ Procedures for handling calls.
- ❏ Awards programs.
- ❏ Special fees/assessments.
- ❏ MLS procedures.
- ❏ _____
- ❏ _____
- ❏ _____

New Salesperson Orientation Checklist   Figure T.2

Session 1: Approved Forms
   Workshop to review all forms usual to the brokerage.

Session 2: Tenancy Legislation
   Use of guest speaker.

Session 3: Land Registry
   Visit the land registry office and review basic procedures.

Session 4: The Planning Process
   Provide the full picture on local zoning and planning issues and the current activities of the municipal planning department(s) and related organizations.

Session 5: Taxation
   Overview of taxation and capital gains in the sale of property–use a guest speaker.

Session 6: Construction
   On-site instruction relating to house construction, mechanical systems, and layouts.

Session 7: Advertising
   Developing better ads (perhaps use a guest speaker from a local newspaper).

Course 8, 9, and 10
   Utilize video programs on sales skills.

Course 11: Ethics
   Responsibilities to other members and the public.

Other courses may include specific skills relating to specialty fields, e.g., appraisal, property management, rural/recreational, condominium, and commercial activities.

TRAINING PROGRAMS (LICENSING/REGISTRATION)

Provincial   See applicable reference materials.

TRAINING PROGRAMS (PROVINCIAL ASSOCIATIONS/REAL ESTATE BOARDS)

Provincial associations along with real estate boards may provide voluntary education programs, mandatory continuing education programs and, in some instances, educational courses for licensing/registration. The Ontario Real Estate Association, for example, develops and administers educational courses necessary to become licensed/registered in Ontario on behalf of the Real Estate Council of Ontario.

Provincial   See applicable reference materials for services and products provided by provincial associations/real estate boards.

TRANSACTION

(SEE ALSO TRADE)

A transaction, for real estate purposes, involves a contractual arrangement between two or more parties that affects and/or alters the legal relationships between those parties. An agreement/contract for the purchase and sale of real estate is viewed as a real estate transaction. Provincial real estate legislation may more precisely define circumstances giving rise to a real estate transaction for purposes of regulatory issues, e.g., persons licensed/registered and the scope of transactions falling under regulatory control of such persons and exempted transactions (e.g., an owner selling his or her own home).

Provincial   See applicable reference materials.

TRANSACTION BROKER

A person licensed/registered under a regulatory act concerning the trade of real estate who assists one or more parties to the transaction, but is not an agent for the interests of either party.

Application   Transaction brokerages have appeared in various US jurisdictions. Although discussed in regulatory circles in Canada, the concept has not gained significant prominence within the industry. No universally accepted set of duties exist for transaction brokers.

Example   *Transaction Broker*

The following is provided for illustration purposes only, based on procedures in one specific US jurisdiction. A transaction broker has a duty to:

- Account for all monies held in relation to a trade in real estate;
- Act honestly and competently with parties to the transaction;
- Furnish copies of offers and contracts to all parties at the time of signing;
- Comply with all applicable laws, rules, and regulations relating to real estate brokerage;
- Avoid error, exaggeration or concealment of pertinent facts;
- Make no substantial misrepresentation by omission or commission;
- Maintain confidentiality regarding an offer, counter offer or contract during the negotiations for a transaction; and
- Obtain and provide information as necessary to make property disclosures.

Continued…

A transaction broker may not:

- Promote the interests of one party over the interests of the other party;
- Disclose the willingness or ability of the seller to accept less than the asking price, without the seller's express permission;
- Disclose the willingness or ability of the buyer to pay more than has been offered, without the buyer's express permission;
- Disclose negotiating strategy (not disclosed in the offer as terms of the sale), without the express permission of the party making the offer; or
- Disclose the motivation of the seller for selling and the motivation of the buyer for buying without the express permission of the seller or buyer.

TRANSFER TAX (LAND)

A levy on a transfer/deed, signified in certain jurisdictions by affixing stamps to the transfer/deed, that is normally collected at point of registration, although provinces may accept payment in advance of closing.

Provincial   See applicable reference materials.

TRANSFER/DEED OF LAND

More or less common terms used in Canada when referring to a standardized format used in land registration offices for the recording of ownership of real property. Exact terminology will vary by provincial jurisdiction. Transfer is most commonly associated with land titles, and deed with registry.

Provincial   See applicable reference materials.

TRANSFORMER

An electrical device that changes voltage through the transferal of electricity by means of electromagnetic induction, commonly associated with commercial property.

Application   Practitioners will normally encounter three primary types of transformers.

- The *pole* transformer service (resembling a large pot), is located on a pole near the street and is generally used to provide relatively small size services (under 600 amps), to industrial, retail, office, and investment properties.

- The *mat* transformer service is a larger cabinet style unit located on the ground, often directly adjacent to the building.
- The *pad* transformer service, involves several mat transformers located on a pad.

TRAP

Designed to prevent sewer odours from coming back through a fixture drain when not in use. Several different styles of traps are used, e.g., P traps and S traps. P traps are considered best for residential purposes, as they are least vulnerable to siphoning or obstruction problems.

Application Traps are provided below house plumbing fixtures and are designed to hold some water in the waste piping system.

Most fixtures require traps, although a toilet does not, since the water in the toilet bowl creates a natural trap. Dishwashers are usually effectively trapped, although there is no formal fitting. Since the 1960's, basement floor drains have routinely included a priming system in the trap.

Priming is accomplished through a one-quarter inch clear plastic tube connected to a regularly used plumbing fixture. Whenever the fixture is run, a small amount of water is taken off and is carried through the plastic tube to the floor drain. Water is added to the trap on a regular basis to replace any water lost through evaporation.

See **Figure T.3** for a cross-sectional view of a typical P trap in a residential plumbing installation. The figure illustrates the required depth of seal to stop gas odours from rising. **Figure T.4** demonstrates the function of an S trap in relation to a sink fixture.

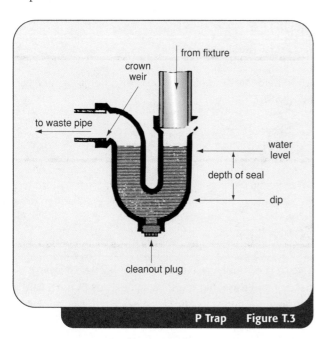

P Trap   Figure T.3

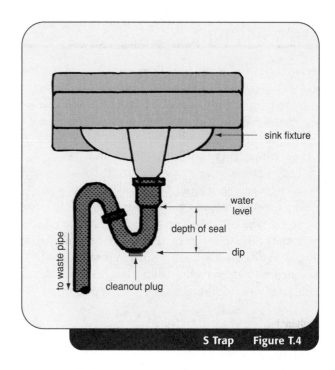

S Trap   Figure T.4

TRIAL BALANCE
(SEE ACCOUNTING SYSTEM)

TRIPLE A TENANT

A term commonly used by real estate practitioners to denote a tenant with excellent credit references.

Example   *Triple A Tenant*

Developer Reed has constructed a neighbourhood retail complex with seven small stores and one large anchor tenant within the development. Reed is prepared to lease property at a base rent of $16.50 per square foot per year for the smaller stores and at a rate of $12.50 for the larger anchor tenant. He will only consider a *Triple A* tenant for the larger space.

TRIPLE NET LEASE
(SEE ALSO BASE RENT AND ADDITIONAL RENT)

A term traditionally referring to a lease arrangement in which the tenant pays a specified rent plus all operating costs. The term *triple net* or *net/net/net lease* is differentiated from variations such as the *net/net* and *net lease* in which the tenant pays varying degrees of operating expenses relating to the property. This terminology was found cumbersome and has gradually given way to *base* and *additional* rent calculations in office leasing.

TRUST ACCOUNT

An account separate and apart from one's personal monies, as required by law. In the case of a real estate brokerage, provincial regulatory bodies set out requirements concerning the establishment of a trust account, methods of disbursement, individuals authorized to sign on behalf of the brokerage, and reconciliation procedures.

Real estate brokerages may be permitted to have more than one real estate trust account. Typically, a second account involves property management. Trust accounts are subject to periodic inspection by representatives of the regulatory body to ensure compliance with statutory and administrative guidelines. Reconciliations are normally required monthly to ensure that brokerage records align with statements furnished by the financial institution.

Provincial   See applicable reference materials.

TRUST ACCOUNT RECONCILIATION
(SEE ALSO BANK RECONCILIATION)

Provincial   See applicable reference materials.

TRUST OWNERSHIP

A special relationship in which one person (often referred to as the *trustor* or *settlor*), by way of an agreement, gives property or other assets to another person (trustee) to manage for the ultimate use or benefit of yet another (the beneficiary). Historically, trust ownership existed when title was in the name of a registered owner who would, in fact, hold the property for the real or beneficial owner. This concept gave rise to the legal concept of *estate to uses* where ownership was held for a future buyer. Although this concept of ownership to uses has been replaced with other concepts, the trust relationship survives.

Application   Practitioners should be aware that trust ownership, over the years, has expanded to address diverse purposes. For example, individuals may wish to protect beneficiaries in the face of creditors, to gain certain tax advantages (e.g., holding funds in trust in a Registered Retirement Savings Plan (RRSP)), or to effectively defer taxes by establishing a trust that will transfer assets from one generation to the next. Trusts are generally identified under two categories: testamentary and inter-vivos. Testamentary trusts take effect upon the death of the trustor; inter-vivos trusts come into effect while the trustor is alive.

The family trust has taken on considerable importance in recent years as individuals seek to protect estates for the benefit of children. As such, the trustor/settlor establishes a trust agreement that sets out administrative responsibilities for the trustee and provides a framework for the disposition of assets and/or income from those assets to the beneficiaries.

Beneficiaries can either be income beneficiaries (receive income from the trust), or capital beneficiaries (receive capital from the sale proceeds of assets), or both. Detailed procedures for establishing a trust go beyond the scope of this reference document. Careful planning is required, both from legal and tax perspectives. Trust agreements can be complex, given the scope of laws that impact their creation and administration. Further, trusts under the *Income Tax Act* are regarded as separate persons for taxation purposes and require the filing of separate returns.

The concept of trust ownership has grown dramatically as the real estate market expands both in depth and complexity. The use of investment trusts is now becoming commonplace with the offering of securities based on equity ownership. Real estate investment trusts (REITs) are now routinely traded on stock exchanges.

Real estate practitioners also encounter the concept of *trust* when a person wishes to avoid unwanted liabilities. For example, a buyer may indicate in an offer that the property is being purchased *in trust for a corporation yet to be formed* or simply *in trust*. The buyer is attempting to remove any liability. Without venturing into the legal merits of a trust, the removal of personal liability is largely determined by the sufficiency of the words used in the agreement, any written agreements underlying such words, and the existence of an intended beneficiary.

TRUSTEE
(SEE ALSO TRUST OWNERSHIP)

An individual who holds property or other assets in trust for another.

TRUSTOR

An individual who gives property or other assets to a trustee.

TURN KEY

A term commonly used when the landlord provides all fixtures and leasehold improvements usual to the tenant's business, save and except for furniture, telephone equipment, goods, and other inventory of the tenant.

UNDER FLOOR DUCTS

An under floor distribution system provided in the structural slab to meet electrical and telephone needs on the floor. Also described as electrical and telephone raceways. The under floor ducting system is typically designed not only to take care of specific arrangements of furniture or equipment, but to provide for a logical rearrangement or reasonable increase in service equipment.

Flexibility in floor, wall, and ceiling systems has become vital to meet the communication needs of advanced companies as well as to address technological requirements for *smart* buildings. Modern structures now require extensive wiring to accommodate computer-driven security, internal communication, and energy conservation systems.

UNDERGROUND STORAGE TANK

Provincial   See applicable reference materials concerning the provincial regulation of underground storage tanks and related issues affecting real estate practitioners when listing, marketing, and selling real property.

UNDIVIDED INTEREST
(SEE ALSO JOINT TENANCY)

A right to use and possess real property in conjunction with other co-owners, in which each owner is entitled to undivided possession of the whole property, such as in the case of joint tenancy.

UNEMPLOYMENT INSURANCE
(SEE SOURCE DEDUCTIONS)

Acronym: UI   Unemployment insurance is now referred to as *employment insurance.*

UNIMPROVED PROPERTY
(SEE RAW LAND)

UNIT

Generally described, for real estate purposes, as a partially or totally self-contained accommodation in the case of residential property, e.g., a dwelling unit; or a particular portion of a large complex that has some degree of independence from other units in the same complex, e.g., an industrial condominium unit in an industrial complex or an office unit within a multi-storey office complex.

UNIT COST

For valuation purposes, the average cost of an item (also referred to by appraisers as the *unit price*), based on the cost of several items of similar quality and design divided by the number of items.

Application   Unit costs can involve both physical items, e.g., furnaces, concrete driveways, and windows, and/or costs associated with the installation/repair of such items. For a furnace, costs may be divided between the device and its installation. For a concrete driveway, the cost (usually per square foot/metre), includes materials and labour.

Unit costs are used in the cost approach to value when estimating the reproduction or replacement cost of a structure by analyzing all unit components making up the improvements.

Example   *Unit Cost*

Salesperson Lee, of ABC Realty Inc. is providing an estimate of value for a residential property that has undergone various renovations. Based on research, he has established various approximate unit costs. A partial list is illustrated.

Upgrade electrical service (new panel and installation)	$1,150
Add 120-volt circuit (circuit and installation)	$175
Add central air (3.0 ton air-conditioner installed on existing furnace)	$2,600
Sand and refinish hardwood floors	$2.30 psf
Insulate open attic area (to current standards)	$1.65 psf
Replace bathtub including ceramic tile	$2,150
Replace basin (basin and installation cost)	$450

UNIT-IN-PLACE METHOD

A method of estimating construction costs that involves determining the unit cost of component sections of the structure installed or in place. The unit cost, in this case, includes both materials and labour.

Application The unit-in-place method, also referred to as the *modified quantity survey method*, involves the pricing of the various units (by area or volume in the structure), such as walls, openings (doors and windows), partitions, and rooms. For example, the average cost of a wall may be a certain amount per square metre of wall surface (the rate applies to one side only), including the studs, interior lath, plastering, painting, assembly, and installation.

The unit-in-place method can also be used in greater detail to estimate the cost-in-place of such items as concrete foundation walls, cement block walls, footings, exterior brickwork, rough framing, roofing, plastering, and wiring.

UNITS OF COMPARISON

The reduction of selling prices to appropriate units, usually determined by a physical attribute, so that standardized comparisons of properties can be made. Appropriate units of comparison can then be applied to individual properties to formulate estimates of value, income, and cost. Ideally, they should represent units in terms of which properties are in fact sold, rented, built, or valued.

Application Common units of comparison specifically relating to the listing and sale of real estate include the following:

Price per Front Foot/Metre

A method of comparison that is regularly used with residential lots. The price per front foot/metre conveys no information about the depth or the width of the lot, but is presumed that the rate takes into consideration these other factors. Care must be exercised in using this unit of comparison, since the value of a site may not continue to increase beyond useful frontage. Extra frontage may, in fact, be an indication of excess land leading to a proportionate reduction in unit value.

> **Example** *Units of Comparison—*
> *Price per Front Foot/Metre—Residential*
>
> Broker Johnson is appraising a serviced building lot and knows that $2,500 per front foot is the prevailing rate for subdivision lots on fully serviced land. Accordingly, the value of a 50-foot lot is $125,000.
>
> A note of caution is necessary. The majority of lots sold at $2,500 per front foot were 40 foot lots ($100,000 per lot). Consequently, the increased size may not reflect a proportionate rise in value. The broker, based on experience and personal judgement, might amend the per front foot value to say $2,200 and arrive at a revised figure of $110,000.

Price per Square Foot/Metre

Often used in the valuation of apartment, commercial, and industrial sites. This measure has validity when used on lots with shapes and depths that are standard for a specific neighbourhood, but can cause difficulties when lots have excessive depths or unusual shapes, since proportional utility must be considered.

> **Example** *Units of Comparison—*
> *Price per Square Foot/Metre—Industrial*
>
> Industrial land (unserviced) is selling for approximately $2.00 per sq. ft. The property being appraised is a normal rectangular tract measuring 300′ by 300′ or a total of 90,000 square feet. The value is estimated to be ($2.00 x 90,000) or $180,000 as the lot was judged typical for the area.

Price Per Lot

Frequently used when all lots are approximately the same size and minor differences do not substantially alter value.

> **Example** *Units of Comparison—*
> *Price Per Lot—Residential*
>
> A subdivision contains 40 lots of which 35 have almost the identical size ranging from 49′ to 51′ frontages and 120′ to 125′ depths, with no outstanding features that would differentiate one from another. Accordingly, the broker in marketing these lots to prospective new home buyers has placed a value of $120,000 per lot. To this point, 10 lots have sold at that price. A lender who is financing a local builder to construct homes on five of the remaining lots wants to establish value. The price per lot figure of $120,000 would be a primary indicator of value as the five lots were judged typical for the area.

Price Per Suite

A unit of comparison most commonly applied in townhouse and highrise condominium developments where groups of units have high degrees of uniformity. Salespeople may sometimes use this measure for basic comparison and add on amounts for special features, i.e., floor level.

> **Example** *Units of Comparison—*
> *Price Per Suite—Condominium*
>
> A new condominium development has groupings of 1, 2, and 3 bedroom units. The smallest unit contains 784 sq. feet. These units are all on the lower 10 floors and all face west. The only differences are minor variations in builder samples for cupboards and carpeting. A price per suite of $148,000 will probably apply to all units at point of initial sale following construction. Some pricing differences may occur based on floor level.

Price Per Acre/Hectare

Found in analyses concerning large industrial tracts and agricultural property.

Example   *Units of Comparison–*
Price Per Acre/Hectare–Agricultural

Vacant land (rural agricultural zoning), has been selling for $1,000 to $1,200 per acre for tracts containing between 35 and 50 acres. A broker is attempting to establish the value of a particular piece of vacant land in that area containing 40 acres. Based on his inspection of relevant market data, a figure of $1,100 per acre is estimated. Therefore, the value is (40 acres x $1,100 per acre) or $44,000.

Example   *Units of Comparison–*
Various

Salesperson Ward is gaining familiarity with approximate costs by using units of comparison based on research of new construction projects. For example, analysis to date reveals that sales of serviced lots between 40 and 50 feet of frontage (assuming a lot depth of approximately 100 feet), range between $1,400 and $1,600 per front foot.

Similarly, building construction costs for new homes built to NHA standards tend to run between $68 and $76 per square foot on the main level. Further investigation reveals that approximately 65% of that figure can be added for the second floor. In the condominium market, she has discovered that prices for two bedroom units between 1,200 and 1,600 square feet normally range from $140 to $160 per square foot unless special features are present, e.g., large number of upgrades, panoramic view, and larger balcony.

UREA FORMALDEHYDE FOAM INSULATION

Acronym: UFFI   Urea formaldehyde is a colourless, chemical compound found in certain resins, glues, and bonding agents and, for real estate practitioners, is most commonly associated with insulation. UFFI is a low density foam made from plastic resins, a foaming agent, and compressed air. At time of installation, UFFI has the appearance and consistency of shaving cream. While normally identified as a white or cream-coloured substance, at least one product contained blue dye.

Application   A controversy arose from the curing process when the product was injected into walls and other areas in residential property, and formaldehyde gas was released. A product ban appeared in 1980 because of potential health concerns, after an estimated 100,000 Canadian homes were insulated, mostly between 1975 and 1979 under government incentive programs for homeowners.

A general consensus now minimizes UFFI as a health concern. However, The Canadian Real Estate Association has strongly urged its members to stay informed, not to treat UFFI as a finalized issue, and maintain UFFI references in listing and sales documents, and more particularly, the agreement/contract.

Example   *Urea Formaldehyde Foam Insulation–*
Clause in Agreement/Contract

A wording similar to the following may be found in recommended or mandated preprinted agreements/contracts.

> *Seller represents and warrants to the buyer that during the time the seller has owned the property, the seller has not caused any building on the property to be insulated with insulation containing urea formaldehyde, and that to the best of the seller's knowledge no building on the property contains or has ever contained insulation that contains urea formaldehyde. This warranty shall survive and not merge on the completion of this transaction, and if the building is part of a multiple unit building, this warranty shall only apply to that part of the building which is the subject of this transaction.*

Note that the above clause relates to continuing concerns regarding urea formaldehyde foam insulation. The seller is warranting that there is no such insulation. Replacing this wording with an appropriate clause concerning testing and an inspection may be necessary. This circumstance could arise when the seller has refused to provide the warranty, i.e., a mortgagee selling under power of sale.

Example   *Urea Formaldehyde Foam Insulation–*
Property Condition Disclosure Statement

The use of disclosure statements by real estate practitioners is becoming more prevalent in Canadian jurisdictions. A typical question that might be found in a Property Condition Disclosure Statement relating to both UFFI and asbestos is illustrated.

> *To your knowledge, do the buildings or other improvements on the property now contain either one or both of urea formaldehyde foam insulation (UFFI) and asbestos, or do you remember ever receiving any information which led you to believe that the buildings or other improvements on the property previously contained either one or both of UFFI and asbestos?*

Provincial   See applicable reference materials.

USEABLE AREA

(SEE ALSO RENTABLE AREA)

Most commonly associated with the measurement of office buildings and more specifically individual tenanted areas. Under the BOMA Standard, the useable area of an office is computed by measuring the total area enclosed by the finished surfaces of the office side of corridor walls and other permanent walls, the centre line of partitions separating individual tenanted areas, and the dominant portion of the vertical perimeter wall. No deduction is made for any supporting columns or projections necessary to the overall building structure. BOMA provides precise guidelines regarding such measurements, particularly when considering the perimeter walls that may have unique glass/masonry/steel configurations. The sum of all useable areas on an individual floor represents the total useable area of that floor.

Application   Practitioners should note that, while the BOMA Standard is widely used in Canada, variations exist in the marketplace. Further wordings for useable and rentable areas, are normally provided in commercial lease agreements.

Reference   For complete details regarding the BOMA Standard, contact the Building Owners and Managers Institute of Canada, 885 Don Mills Road, Suite 106, Don Mills, ON M3C 1V9.

USEFUL LIFE

The period over which a structure or component may reasonably be expected to perform the function for which it was designed or intended.

Application   The useful life, often referred to as *life expectancy*, of a particular component is important for appraisers in determining the amount of depreciation to apply when evaluating properties using the cost approach.

Example   *Useful Life*

Anne Appraiser is attempting to establish the amount of depreciation to deduct when appraising Seller Smith's property. She has already established that the reproduction cost of the bungalow, excluding the land, is $87,500. As part of her calculations, she is analyzing short-lived components, namely, items that will require replacement sometime before the end of the remaining economic life of the structure, or more simply put, items with life expectancy less than that of the building. Two calculations involving useful life follow.

Continued…

- The furnace originally had a life expectancy (useful life) of 20 years, but given its current age and condition, the true effective age is 15 years with a remaining useful life of 5 years. The reproduction cost is $2,000. Therefore, the depreciation charged is:

$$15 \div 20 \times \$2,000 = \$1,500$$

- The built-in appliances originally had a life expectancy (on average) of 15 years, but current condition indicates that the remaining useful life is only 2 years. Given that the reproduction cost is $2,200, then the depreciation charged will be:

$$13 \div 15 \times \$2,200 = \$1,907$$

V TO Z

V TO Z

National Info Links

Waste Management
Most waste management issues fall to provincial legislation. Contact the appropriate provincial ministry/department.

Water Wells
Water wells and water quality fall to provincial jurisdiction:

Installation/Water Well Records
Provincial ministry/department.

Bacteriological Testing
Typically involves the local health department, but procedures may vary in the province.

Waterfront Property

Federal
- Ministry of Fisheries and Oceans (fish habitat protection)
- Parks Canada (heritage rivers and waterways)

Provincial
- Appropriate provincial ministry/department (shoreline abutting public land, flood management, watercourse alterations) and/or conservation authority (if applicable).

Municipal
- Zoning and building requirements.

VACANCY AND CREDIT LOSSES

An allowance, often referred to as *vacancy and bad debts* by appraisers, used in reconstructing owner's operating statements for purposes of real estate valuation and/or investment analysis. Vacancy and credit losses will vary by specific locale, market conditions, and/or type of property and refers to revenue lost due to vacancies in rental units and uncollectible rents from tenants.

Application   Commercial practitioners typically use a property analysis worksheet to develop reconstructed operating statements. The worksheet provides a standardized approach to the analysis of operations cash flows leading to an estimate of value, either market value or investment value. The amount estimated for vacancy and credit losses is deducted from potential rental income when establishing an effective rental income and ultimately leads to gross operating revenue once other income has been added. The practitioner then completes a detailed analysis of expenses which, in turn, leads to an estimate of net operating income (NOI). NOI is used in the income approach to value to arrive at an estimate of value by means of direct capitalization. NOI is also one component in the use of discounted cash flow and yield capitalization.

Example   *Vacancy and Credit Losses*

Salesperson Lee, of ABC Realty Inc., is attempting to establish the value of a 96-unit apartment building through the income approach. Before analyzing expenses, he must first determine the gross operating income and elects to use a property analysis worksheet for calculations.

Excerpt—Property Analysis Worksheet

Potential Rental Income	
18 1-bedroom units ($600/month x 12)	$129,600
78 2-bedroom units ($750/month x 12)	702,000
Effective Rental Income	831,600
Vacancy and Credit Losses (5%)	−41,580
Effective Rental Income	790,020
Other Income	+35,000
Gross Operating Income	$825,020

Terminologies and procedures may differ slightly for appraisers and commercial practitioners when reconstruct-ing financial statements to estimate value or analyze investment opportunities. For details relating to commercial analysis, see **Property Analysis Worksheet**; for an appraiser's perspective, see **Reconstructed Operating Statement**.

VACANCY RATE

A rate calculated by dividing the amount of vacant space by the total inventory of existing space to arrive at a rate expressed as a percentage. A vacancy rate applies to one specific moment in time and is usually analyzed and grouped by type of property. Vacancy rates are most commonly associated with retail and office leasing, but are also frequently referenced in regard to multi-residential properties. Selected organizations and government agencies publish appropriate vacancy statistics.

Example   *Vacancy Rate*

The City of Anycity had a total inventory of office space amounting to 52,068,985 square feet as of a particular year end and the vacant space at that point is 5,180,865 square feet.

$$\text{Vacancy Rate} = 5{,}180{,}865 \div 52{,}068{,}985$$
$$= .0995 \text{ or } 9.95\%$$

VACANT LAND

Land that is not presently being used for a purpose, as opposed to a site with improvements.

Example   *Vacant Land*

Developer Reed is searching for suitable property for the construction of a special purpose industrial building. Salesperson Jamieson has shown Reed various serviced sites including ones with structures. However, following those inspections, it is evident that cleared land with no improvements best suits Reed's purposes. Accordingly, Jamieson locates vacant land that fortunately has services directly adjacent to the property.

VACATION HOME

A residential dwelling, other than the primary residence of an owner, typically used for recreational and/or seasonal purposes.

Application   Real estate practitioners specializing in recreational property are frequently involved with vacation properties. The ownership of such property, typically viewed as a secondary residence, has ramifications from a tax perspective. While a capital gain arising from the sale of an individual's principal residence is typically exempt from taxation (exceptions do apply), a second interest in a vacation home is normally viewed as a taxable event under the *Income Tax Act*.

Reference　Expert advice is required on all matters concerning the disposition of secondary homes.

VALID

Having force or binding force, being legally sufficient, and authorized by law.

> **Example**　*Valid Licence/Registration*
>
> Broker/Owner Johnson must maintain his broker registration under the provincial real estate act in order to trade in real estate. His licence/registration will expire in 60 days. To ensure that the licence/registration remains valid, he must complete the appropriate renewal form, meet other criteria as set out by the provincial regulatory body, pay the current registration fee, and mail or deliver the necessary documents to the required address prior to the expiration date.

VALUABLE CONSIDERATION

(SEE ALSO CONTRACT)

What a person receives or is to receive for what that person does or agrees to do. If a person promises to do something, the law will not enforce that promise unless something is received or promised in exchange. Whatever is given or is to be given is referred to as valuable consideration.

Application　Valuable consideration is anything to which a value can be attached, given by the promisee to the promisor, and may be:

- An act in return for an act;
- A promise in return for a promise;
- An act in return for a promise.

> **Example**　*Valuable Consideration*
>
> Seller Smith and Buyer Jones have entered into an agreement/contract. Jones has agreed to pay $238,000 to Smith for his detached two-storey home at 123 Main Street. The valuable consideration is $238,000 in exchange for title to the property. Consideration received by the seller is $238,000, in the form of a $20,000 deposit and a promise of the balance on completion. Consideration received by the buyer is a promise of title to the property upon final payment.

VALUATION

(SEE ALSO APPRAISAL)

Estimated worth or price. Also, the act of estimating the worth of real property using accepted procedures such as direct comparison approach, cost approach, or income approach (direct or yield capitalization).

VALUE

The quantity of one thing that can be obtained in exchange for another. Money is the common denominator by which real property value is usually measured. The utility of a commodity, such as property, is expressed in the amount of money that would be paid for its acquisition. Value is the present worth of future benefits arising out of ownership to typical users or investors and depends on the need for, and availability of, a commodity; i.e., supply and demand.

Application　Value is the key word used in practically every segment of the real estate business. Its significance and importance would imply a precisely and clearly understood meaning. Unfortunately, this is not often the case. Value is a word for which there are as many definitions as there are types of value in everyday life. For example, the tax assessor usually thinks of value in terms of assessed value, the insurance agent in terms of insurable value, the accountant in terms of book value, the appraiser in terms of market value, and the commercial practitioner in terms of both market value and investment value. Further, the banker or mortgagee is likely to equate value with lending value. A natural tendency exists to attach to the word *value* a variety of descriptive adjectives suggesting a specific kind of value: intrinsic value, sentimental value, salvage value, liquidation value, and appraised value.

A precise meaning has been a life-long study of many economic theorists. Most debates centre on objective versus subjective value. Objective value maintains that value is tied to the cost of reproduction. Subjective value states that value exists only in the minds of buyers and sellers.

Further, one of the most important distinctions for real estate purposes is that value may have one value in exchange and quite a different value in use. A second important distinction arises from activities of commercial practitioners between market value (value based on the actions of typical buyers and sellers), and investment value (value of the subject property based on individual investor needs, goals, and objectives).

For additional discussion relating to differing perspectives on value, see **Investment Value, Market Value, Objective Value** and **Subjective Value.**

VALUE IN EXCHANGE

The amount of goods and services that an informed buyer would offer in exchange for an economic good, under given market conditions. Value in exchange is relative, since there must be comparison with other economic goods and alternatives available from which the potential buyer may choose.

Application Value in exchange is best described as the probable price at which a commodity trades in a free, competitive, and open market and is synonymous with market value.

VALUE IN USE

The value of an economic good to its owner/user or prospective buyer that is based on the productivity of the economic good to that specific individual. This usually consists of market value plus an increment that represents some extra value to the owner/user or prospective buyer.

Application For real estate purposes, value in use is the value given to a property by the owner who is using that property. The property would probably have been designed or used to suit the particular needs and enjoyment of the owner and takes on a special significance that translates into an additional monetary value in the owner's opinion. This type of value is difficult to measure and is normally different in every case. It may often be higher than market value, since it is looked at from the owner's viewpoint only.

Interestingly, buyers considering investment property may perceive special value due to unique circumstances, needs, or uses particular to that individual that can be applied to a property. This uniqueness can translate into value, most commonly referred to as *investment value*. Commercial practitioners often use investment value when analyzing investment-grade properties. However, special value is not limited to commercial property. Residential property may also have additional value to a specific buyer given certain features or amenities.

Example *Value in Use—Owner's Perspective*

Seller Smith, at retirement age, has installed an oversized swimming pool in the rear yard of his new two bedroom, 940 square foot bungalow. As a former athlete, Smith prides himself in his physical prowess, uses the pool every day, and conducts a rigorous exercise program. He took great pains to replicate a lap pool that he once used as a younger man in training for provincial competitions.

Continued…

For Smith, there is considerable value in use that probably exceeds the $38,000 price tag in terms of personal fitness and satisfaction. However, from the standpoint of the average buyer, the unusual shape and size of the pool may in fact add no particular value or, if it did, the value would be considerably less. If Smith elected to sell his home, undoubtedly he would think in terms of value in use as he attaches a high value to the pool. The buyer would negotiate in terms of value in exchange that would typically be a lower amount.

Example *Value in Use—Buyer's Perspective*

Investor Reed is seriously considering a multi-residential property located in Anycity. The market value of the property has been established based on a reconstructed operating statement using data from typical buildings of the same type that are generally comparable to the subject property. The market value of this residential building is estimated at $875,000. Reed, however, has certain managerial abilities, expertise in developing additional income sources from such properties, and can introduce specific cost saving measures through technology that would not be available to smaller investors.

As a consequence, Reed's buyer representative prepares a detailed forecast of cash flows based on those unique factors to arrive at an investment value specific to the client. Using the income approach to value, the buyer representative estimates that the investment value of the property is in the range of $925,000 to $950,000 and will generate a yield of approximately 9.5%. The property would be a sound investment for this particular buyer if acquired for its market value, as the value is clearly higher from the buyer's perspective.

VARIABLE ANNUITY
(SEE ALSO CASH FLOW AND DISCOUNTED CASH FLOW)

An agreement in which regular payments of specified amounts are received. A variable annuity is an annuity with a slightly different income stream pattern in which the amounts are irregular but received on a regular basis.

Application Cash flows generated from an investment property can be viewed as a form of variable annuity in that the rents are normally received on a regular basis (beginning of the month), but may vary due to such factors as escalation clauses and additional rents paid by the tenant. Before tax and after tax cash flows are used by real estate practitioners as the basis for estimating value and analyzing the merits of specific investment properties.

VARIABLE EXPENSES
(SEE ALSO BUDGETING AND FIXED EXPENSES)

From a real estate brokerage perspective, operating costs that fluctuate with sales production (e.g., advertising, and long distance), as opposed to fixed expenses that remain generally stable as production increases or decreases (e.g., rent). The concepts of fixed and variable expenses are commonly used in the budgeting process for brokerages.

VARIABLE RATE MORTGAGE

Acronym: VRM   A mortgage in which the interest rate fluctuates during the term and either payments or balances outstanding are adjusted accordingly. Although the variable rate mortgage is not widely found in Canada at this time. The VRM is normally offered in two standard formats.

Interest Rate and Payment Adjustment

The interest rate is adjusted in line with the rise and fall of the prime lending rate. Payments are, in turn, adjusted on a quarterly, half-yearly, or yearly basis. The system can be cumbersome if payment changes are too frequent and considerable accounting is required when making adjustments. For that reason, annual adjustments for variable rate mortgages have become popular, particularly in the US.

At the anniversary of the mortgage, the rate is established using a pre-determined formula based on the then current prime rate, plus an index factor to arrive at the stated rate. The mortgage payments are then adjusted for the upcoming year based on the new rate.

Interest Rate and Amortization Adjustments

The amortization period of a mortgage is varied to accommodate changes in interest rates. An increase in the mortgage rate is offset by an increase in the amortization of the mortgage. A decrease has the reverse effect.

Variable rate mortgages are attractive from the lender's perspective. The dollars invested in mortgages are always yielding returns consistent with prime rates. The lender is rewarded for periods of tight money when interest rates are rising. The borrower receives the benefit of lower rates when rates are falling.

A popular variation on the variable rate mortgage is the capped mortgage. In other words, certain limitations or caps are placed on interest rate increases or decreases. Most also contain a lock-in provision by which the borrower can fix the interest rate for the duration of the mortgage term.

VARIANCE

Most commonly used in real estate regarding permission by the zoning authority to an owner permitting a minor violation of a zoning requirement for a specific property, e.g., set back requirement, use, or size of structure.

Variance is also used in statistical analysis to measure the amount of variability that exists in a set of numbers (formally referred to as a *frequency distribution*). Variance is one of many statistical techniques gradually being introduced into real estate investment analysis and decision strategies regarding the acquisition and disposition of investment-grade property.

VENDOR

A seller of real property. Traditionally, the terms *vendor* and *purchaser* have been used in preprinted standard forms, however, during recent years, the preference has moved to *seller* and *buyer*.

Application   Practitioners should ensure that, when drafting agreements/contracts, the full names of the seller and buyer are shown. In the case of the seller, a brief examination of the registered title may be necessary to be certain that all sellers are included in the agreement/contract. In the case of companies, the exact corporate name is required. If the owner is deceased, then the personal representatives should be indicated as signing on behalf of the estate.

Most residential properties are owned by both spouses jointly. If the home is a matrimonial (marital) home under provincial legislation, the non-owner spouse will have to consent to the transaction, and only the owner would be shown as the seller. Whenever there is doubt, the salesperson must determine what signatures are required.

VENDOR PROPERTY INFORMATION STATEMENT
(SEE PROPERTY CONDITION DISCLOSURE STATEMENT)

VENDOR TAKE BACK MORTGAGE
(SEE SELLER TAKE BACK MORTGAGE)

VERTICAL ANALYSIS

One of two commonly used methods for analyzing financial statements, the other being horizontal analysis.

V TO Z

Vertical analysis involves the search for significant changes in the chart of accounts in relation to specific time periods (e.g., current year compared with prior year), and expressing such changes in a percentage format. This type of analysis is applied to the profit and loss statement.

Example   *Vertical Analysis*

Broker/Owner Johnson, of ABC Realty Inc., is analyzing the income statement for the past two years and more specifically, advertising expense. By reviewing the two columns of figures, Johnson is able to get a clearer picture of increases and decreases by individual account using vertical analysis. In this example, classified advertising has decreased significantly while remaining categories have increased.

Advertising Expense

	20x1	20x2	DIFF.
Newspaper (Classified)	$98,324	$89,383	($8,941)
Newspaper Institutional	17,183	19,200	2,017
Sign Installations	10,768	11,980	1,212
Radio	8,820	9,271	451

VOID

Having no force or effect. A contract that is void is said to be a nullity at law, with no legal effect. As far as the law is concerned, the agreement does not exist. Neither party can enforce it and neither party has any obligations under it.

Application   The question of void and voidable contracts relates to much larger issues concerning avoidance of a contract. In other words, cases may arise where the elements of a valid contract are present (i.e., not void) but where the promise of one or both parties has been given on the basis of or affected by some misunderstanding, false inducement, force, or the like, so that the offended party has rights of redress. Usually the two types of redress for grievances of this kind are either to allow avoidance of the contract altogether or to obtain damages for the conduct of the other party. Such instances involve voidable contracts as opposed to void contracts, i.e., contracts that do not exist.

Example   *Void*

A void contract can occur when the agreement is impossible to perform. For example, Seller Smith and Buyer Jones enter into an agreement of purchase and sale for the acquisition of an isolated cottage owned by Smith. Unknown to either party, Smith's cottage was destroyed by fire during the winter. All of the elements of the contract are in existence, but the structure is not. Both buyer and seller are mistaken as to this essential fact and the contract is impossible to perform and would undoubtedly be judged void.

VOIDABLE

That which is enforceable, valid, and binding until rendered void. A contract that is voidable is one where the offended party may make a choice. The person may choose to avoid the contract and treat it as being at an end, or to treat it as subsisting and enforce it against the offending party.

Application   Practitioners might encounter the issue of voidable contracts in the case of minors. As a general statement, a minor (the age of majority will vary between provinces), cannot be held liable for contracts unless it can be said that the contract was for necessities, being generally food, clothing, medical services, and lodging. Not only must the item be of a category recognized by the law as being a necessity, but it also must be necessary to that particular infant or minor at that particular time. The category of lodging would not likely be extended by the courts to the purchase of a house since there are many alternative ways to obtain shelter.

Contracts entered into by a minor for the purchase or sale of land are voidable by the minor. If the minor does nothing to avoid the contract within a reasonable time after he/she reaches the age of majority, then the contract becomes binding. However, the minor may repudiate the contract upon reaching the age of majority by notifying the other contracting party. The minor cannot recover what he/she may have paid during minority on account of the contract, but the other contracting party whose contract has been repudiated cannot compel performance of the balance of the contract following repudiation. In many instances, the matter of repudiation is finally resolved in the courts because of the fact that minors may be liable for their contracts where such contracts were for necessities. In making decisions, courts also look at such factors as the knowledge of the infant of his/her rights under the law of contract and whether the minor has acted in any way to indicate that he/she intends to carry out obligations under the contract. However, if the minor acts in any way to indicate that he/she intends to carry out his/her obligations under the contract, such as making payments after reaching the age of majority, then the courts will likely not allow the contract to be repudiated by the minor.

It is immaterial that the minor may have held himself/herself out to be over the age of majority (legal age). Even under such circumstances, the minor has the option of voiding the contract. Another important factor is that an adult representing the minor cannot approach the court to have the contract voided. Such a contract is binding until the minor brings the case to court. If an adult represents the minor by co-signing the contract, the contract cannot be voided even by the minor.

If a real estate salesperson suspects that a potential buyer is under age, it is advisable to request proof of age before proceeding. If in fact the potential buyer is under age, then the salesperson should advise the individual that a guardian or trustee, duly authorized, must sign the contract on his/her behalf so that it will be legally enforceable.

Contracts entered into by others with limited capacity, such as mentally incompetent persons or intoxicated persons, may also be voidable.

Example *Voidable Contract*

An example of a voidable contract involving undue influence can include a situation where one party, by virtue of a special relationship to the other, is in a position of confidence and abuses that position. In cases such as relations between parent and child or solicitor and client, presumption of undue influence may arise that can be rebutted by showing that, in fact, the person susceptible to influence was able to form a decision free of any sort of control.

The fact that the person claiming undue influence received independent legal advice or independent valuations of the property are excellent ways of establishing that no undue influence occurred. Where undue influence is shown, the contract is voidable, not void. That is, the person claiming undue influence must go to court to have the contract adjudged void.

Reference   The issue of void and voidable contracts goes well beyond the normal scope of real estate activities. Legal advice is strongly recommended on such matters.

WAIVER

An intentional relinquishment of some right or interest; the renunciation, abandonment, or surrender of some claim.

Application   A waiver can either be express (in writing) or implied(based on the actions of the applicable party). From a real estate perspective, waivers are most commonly encountered in the removal of conditions by means of a written document in relation to an agreement/contract, e.g., a condition relating to the arranging of mortgage financing, the sale of a buyers property, or an inspection relating to the property under consideration.

WAIVER OF CONDITION

The relinquishment of some right as set out in a condition within an agreement.

Application   Forms specific to provincial jurisdictions have been designed to permit the buyer or seller to waive a condition in an agreement/contract, provided that the right of waiver was included in the original condition. Many agreements/contracts include a condition for the protection and/or benefit of either seller or buyer, however, before the expiration of the time allowed for fulfillment of the condition, circumstances can arise which are different from those contemplated by the condition. In these instances, the protection and/or benefit envisaged by the inclusion of the condition is achieved but not in accordance with the exact terms as expressed in the agreement. The result is the same but the circumstances or terms giving rise to that result are different from those originally contemplated. For example, a buyer makes an agreement conditional on arranging a new mortgage but before arranging that mortgage, receives a windfall and no longer requires the benefit and/or protection of this condition.

The waiver form allows the buyer to waive the condition (again emphasizing that the right of waiver must be part of the original condition), and complete the contract without reference to the fulfillment of the condition. Note that the waiver must be signed by the party seeking the benefit of the waiver and must be received and normally acknowledged by the other party, because the effect of exercising the waiver is to create a binding agreement of purchase and sale.

Provincial   See applicable reference materials.

WAIVER OF LIEN

The intentional or voluntary relinquishment of the right to a lien. A waiver of lien is commonly associated with contractors when they are paid for their work. Waiver of lien forms will vary by provincial jurisdiction.

Example *Waiver of Lien*

Seller Smith is having renovation work completed on his home by a qualified contractor. During the construction process, Smith advances funds to the contractor in three sequential payments that amount to approximately 90% of the agreed price. Smith retains the balance until completion. At that point, Smith pays the contractor the remaining 10%. The contractor provides a receipt for the work completed and also signs a waiver of lien pursuant to applicable provincial legislation.

WALK-UP

An apartment building of two or more floors where the only access to the upper floors is by means of stairways.

WALL SYSTEMS

For descriptions, see under appropriate component: Brick Masonry Wall, Brick Veneer Wall, Framing, and Wood Frame Wall.

WARRANTIES
(SEE REPRESENTATIONS/WARRANTIES)

Provincial   See applicable reference materials.

WASTE SYSTEMS (MUNICIPAL)

Most houses in built-up areas are connected to a municipal sewer system that allows waste from a house to flow by gravity into sewer piping. The waste is carried to a treatment facility where it is cleaned before being released.

Application   Practitioners should be aware of different waste systems found within urban areas. In older neighbourhoods, a combination of storm and sanitary sewers was employed. In modern areas, and where sewer pipes have been replaced, a sanitary sewer carries house waste and a separate storm sewer handles rain and snow run off. Where the street sewers are not deep enough, the main drain pipe from a house must leave the house above the basement floor. This means that plumbing fixtures cannot be put in the basement without the waste being pumped up to the main drain level. A basement floor drain in this situation would also require special attention.

A street with a storm sewer and sanitary sewer is more desirable than a combination sewer. Basement flooding as a result of storm sewer back-up is less likely in a house with separate sewers. With combination sewers, a large volume of storm water may overload the sewers and water (including raw sewage), can back up through basement floor drains. In some areas, this problem is common and some homeowners install one-way valves in their floor drain that allows water down into the drain, but prevents water from coming back up. If pressures are high enough, sewage may back up through basement plumbing fixtures. With separate sewers, floor drains should connect to the sanitary sewer and eavestroughs and downspouts to the storm sewer, or onto the ground several feet away from the building.

WASTE SYSTEMS (ON SITE)

Waste disposal systems, also referred to as *waste management systems,* located on individual sites are governed by provincial environmental regulations.

Provincial   See applicable reference materials.

WATER

Contamination/Testing

Water quality testing can involve a wide array of water sources such as:

- Well water;
- Dugouts, springs, and gravel pits;
- Lakes and rivers;
- Municipal systems and chlorinated water;
- Cisterns and other holding tanks;
- Effluent (sewage, industrial waste, etc.); and
- Swimming pools, whirlpools, and jacuzzis.

Activities of real estate practitioners are generally focused on drinking water and the testing of private well systems when homes are offered for sale. If a supply of drinking water comes from a well or other non-municipal source, then the issue of the quality and safety of the water from that source is an important consideration in both the listing and selling process. Further, every owner should be aware of the quality of water and test it on a regular basis.

Application   Water testing is best viewed from two perspectives: *chemical analysis* and *microbiological analysis* (bacteriological). Both are relevant to water testing, but the latter is most frequently addressed in the sale of property supplied by private wells.

Chemical Analysis

Chemicals in water come from a number of sources, including the geological formations around the well and the leaching of materials that may have been applied to the soils. It is very important for well-owners to be aware of the chemical quality of their water, as the presence of contaminants may not be apparent by taste or appearance.

Some typical situations are listed below:

Metals   Metals such as lead, cadmium, mercury, or arsenic are harmful to health. They may be present naturally in the water or result from the leaching of metals from pipes.

Fluoride   Fluoride can be naturally present in the water of wells. If too high a level exists, mottling of tooth enamel in young children can occur.

Hardness   Often evidenced as mineral scale on kettles and water heaters. Although not a health hazard, hardness can create aesthetic concerns when using soaps.

Red or Black Staining   This type of staining is indicative of the presence of excessive iron or manganese in the water.

Organic Contaminants/Pesticides   The list of organic contaminants that can be present in drinking water is quite extensive. Their presence will depend on the proximity of the well to potential sources of these compounds.

In general, most water quality problems can be treated using treatment systems specifically designed to remove the contaminants.

General Microbiological Analysis

Well-owners should ensure that well water consumed by their families is safe to drink. A general microbiological (bacteriological) analysis can involve several parameters. Testing requirements can differ by provincial jurisdictions and the following is provided for illustration purposes only.

Total Coliform   The coliform group of bacteria, mostly of fecal origin, is the principal indicator of the suitability of water for drinking purposes (potability). The presence of coliform bacteria indicates the existence of pollution and the presence of other harmful bacteria must be assumed until proven otherwise.

Fecal Coliform   Refers to one type of coliform bacteria that is solely of fecal origin. The existence of fecal coliform immediately renders the water unsafe for drinking or any other use.

Heterotrophic Plate Count   A count of the total bacteria population used in assessing the quality of potable water especially where significant changes are noticed in successive samples.

Test for Fecal Streptococcus   The presence of fecal streptococcus is characteristic of fecal population, either human or animal.

Test for Pseudomonas Aeruginosa   The presence of pseudomonas aeruginosa in recreational waters may be related to a high incidence of ear infections and skin rashes that occur during the swimming season, and especially with hot tub use.

Other Parameters   Other bacteriological tests may be performed based on specific needs.

Unacceptable tests on any water supply should be taken very seriously. Chlorination accomplishes immediate well disinfection in certain instances, but is at best a temporary measure. Long term pollution problems such as seepage can still exist and appropriate expert advice is required. Water treatment devices such as reverse osmosis systems are designed to remove various contaminants and are available through private suppliers.

Well systems have caused various litigation problems for real estate practitioners. Avoid representations concerning the quality of water. Buyers and sellers should be fully informed regarding water test procedures. In terms of bacteriological testing, ensure that the parties:

- Clearly understand the need for such testing;
- Are aware that at least three samples are recommended in line with appropriate time frames; and
- Are made aware of the importance of a suitable condition in the agreement.

Provincial   See applicable reference materials.

Distribution System (Residential)

Galvanized steel piping was used almost exclusively until approximately 1950. Depending on the pipe diameter, the water composition, and the amount of use, this piping usually lasts 40 to 60 years. Copper pipes have been in

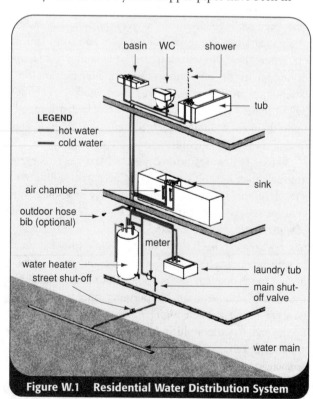

Figure W.1   Residential Water Distribution System

use residentially since approximately 1900. Following the mid-1950s, copper became the predominately used material.

In the 1970s plastic supply piping was approved and is now reasonably prevalent in new home construction. Plumbers still appear to prefer working with copper, and although the plastic pipe is less expensive than copper, the fittings are expensive. Some codes do not allow plastic pipes and some types of plastic pipe are only suitable for waste, underground, or cold water piping. The water distribution system for a typical two-storey residential structure is illustrated in **Figure W.1**.

Drafting Water Supply Conditions

Concerns regarding water supply centre on recreational and rural properties serviced by private water supply sources. Real estate practitioners may be called upon to draft clauses within the agreement/contract that provide a seller's warranty concerning these matters. Alternatively, a condition is inserted in the offer making the agreement/contract conditional on the buyer receiving from the seller a well certificate, prepared by a qualified well driller, attesting that the well is capable of supplying a water volume of not less than a stipulated number of gallons per minute at standing level. Differences exist between wells that are dug, bored, and drilled. Expert advice should be sought by those individuals specializing in properties relying on private water supply sources.

Example   *Water—Drafting Water Supply Conditions*

Buyer Jones is considering the purchase of Smith's rural property but is concerned about water supply. Jones' buyer representative recommends that a clause be inserted in the agreement/contract and provides three alternative clauses for discussion purposes.

Option 1

This offer is conditional upon the buyer determining at the buyer's own expense that there is an adequate and potable water supply, and the pump and all related equipment serving the property are in proper operating condition. Unless the buyer gives notice in writing delivered to the seller by 12 p.m. on the 1st day of May, 20xx that these conditions have been fulfilled, this offer shall become null and void and the deposit shall be returned to the buyer in full without deduction. These conditions are included for the sole benefit of the buyer and may be waived at the buyer's option by notice in writing to the seller within the period stated herein.

Option 2

The seller represents and warrants to the best of the seller's knowledge and belief that during occupancy of the property, the pump and all related equipment serving the said property have performed adequately, and that the well is capable of supplying a water volume of not less than ___ gallons per minute at standing level. The parties agree that this representation and warranty shall survive and not merge on completion of this transaction, but apply only to the state of the property at completion of this transaction.

Option 3

This offer is conditional upon the buyer receiving from the seller a well certificate, prepared by a qualified well driller, attesting that the well is capable of supplying a water volume of not less than ___ gallons per minute at standing level. Unless the seller delivers this well certificate to the buyer at the buyer's address as hereinafter indicated by 12 p.m. on the 1st day of May, 20xx, this offer shall become null and void and the deposit shall be returned to the buyer in full without deduction. This condition is included for the sole benefit of the buyer and may be waived at the buyer's sole option by notice in writing to the seller within the period stated herein.

Jones and his buyer agent decide that Option 1 is most appropriate as it provides maximum latitude to utilize a well inspector as well as other means to be assured that the water supply was both adequate and potable. The reader is reminded that all properties are unique and clauses should be constructed accordingly.

Water Treatment (Municipal)

Municipal water treatment standards are established by both provincial and federal environmental ministries. Water treatment systems vary. Contact the local municipality for detailed information.

Example   *Water—Water Treatment (Municipal)*

The following has been summarized from published material provided by the City of Toronto for illustration purposes only. Procedures will vary by municipality.

Water is pumped from offshore intakes in Lake Ontario with debris extracted by large screens before entry into the treatment plant.

Continued…

V
TO
Z

Stage One   Involves coagulation (chemicals are added to make small particles clump together), and the mixing of the water to promote larger grouping of particles (referenced as flocculation). Aluminum sulphate, polyaluminum chloride and a group of chemicals known as polyelectrolytes are the materials currently used for this purpose. The larger floc (abbreviation for flocculation) settles with the remaining mixture flowing to the second stage.

Stage Two   The remaining floc and other physical impurities, along with most biological (bacterial) impurities are removed through the use of dual media filters that contain layers of sand and anthracite.

Stage Three   Chemical chlorine is added after the filtration process. This is referenced as post-chlorination as pre-chlorination occurs when the water first enters the treatment plant. Occasionally, additional chlorine is added (super-chlorination), given high bacterial presence in incoming water. Sulphur dioxide is then added to reduce chlorine residual in readiness for the last stage.

Stage Four   Fluoridation in low concentrations is added to strengthen enamel and avoid tooth decay. The amount of fluoridation depends on the extent of fluoride that is naturally present in the water. Lastly, ammonia is added to stabilize the remaining chlorine so that it remains dissolved for longer periods, keeping the water safe while in transit through the water distribution system.

WATER RIGHTS
(SEE RIPARIAN RIGHTS)

WATER TABLE

The prevailing level of underground water in a particular location.

Example   *Water Table*

Buyer Jones is concerned about constructing a home in a specific locale given the high water table. During summer months, the water table is well below the depth of his planned basement. However, neighbours report that the water table rises significantly during the spring. Jones raises the basement level several feet to hopefully avoid problems.

WATER WELL (INSTALLATION AND MAINTENANCE)

Provincial   See applicable reference materials.

WATERFRONT PROPERTY SALES
(SEE RURAL, RECREATIONAL, AND AGRICULTURAL SALES)

WATERSHED

All lands drained by a river or stream and its tributaries. Watershed is not be to be confused with flood plain areas defined for purposes of flood control.

Provincial   See applicable reference materials regarding flood plain areas and flood control provisions applicable to a specific province.

WEIGHTED AVERAGE

A mathematical average in which a weighting factor is applied to each component number in a set of numbers. The weighting factor represents the size of the component in relation to the whole.

Application   For real estate practitioners, weighted averages are most commonly associated with the calculation of discount and capitalization rates when estimating value or otherwise analyzing real estate investment property. In determining an overall capitalization rate, for example, the band of investment technique is used when component values along with corresponding cap rates are known for land and building.

Example   *Weighted Average*

Salesperson Lee is attempting to establish an overall capitalization rate. His research indicates that land value is typically 25% of the total value of a property and prevailing capitalization rates on land are 10%. Accordingly, the building value is 75% and building capitalization rates are 12.5%. In order to determine an overall capitalization rate, Lee must apply the band of investment technique and calculate a weighted average rate based on the land and building components in relation to the whole.

Overall Capitalization Rate

Land Ratio x Capitalization Rate
.25   x   .10   =   .02500

Building Ratio x Capitalization Rate
.75   x   .125   =   .09375

Overall (Weighted) Capitalization Rate
                                            .11875
                    (rounded to 0.119 or 11.9%)

WINTERIZATION

In rural and recreational sales, this term most commonly refers to the insulation of a property and its associated mechanical systems for use during the winter period, e.g., a fully winterized cottage. In terms of non-occupied properties, the term can refer to houses that are empty and prepared for vacancy during the winter period, e.g., water lines are drained. This frequently occurs in the case of a corporate guaranteed property in which the employee has vacated the premises and a third party company is handling the listing and selling of the vacant property. Caution is advised as no universally accepted standards exist concerning winterization of structures.

WITNESS

To subscribe one's name to an agreement/contract, will, or other document for the purpose of attesting its authenticity and proving its execution by the party indicated by testifying if required.

Provincial   See applicable reference materials.

WOOD FRAME BRICK VENEER
(SEE BRICK VENEER WALL)

WOOD FRAME WALL
(SEE ALSO FRAMING)

Load-bearing walls that carry the weight of the roof and floors down to the foundations and may be interior or exterior walls. Studs provide space for insulation and surfaces to secure interior and exterior finishes. Some studs are load bearing, others are not. Bearing stud walls should have a double top plate. Non-bearing stud walls may only have a single top plate. A single bottom or sole plate is provided in either case.

Typical materials have been two-by-four studs spaced sixteen inches on centre, although more recently, two-by-six exterior studs have become common in energy efficient homes, as they provide additional space for insulation. Metal studs are not used extensively in single-family homes, although they are common in commercial construction. Metal studs are normally non-load bearing.

Application   Practitioners should be aware of certain problems that can arise with wood frame walls.

Nailings and Openings

Inadequate nailing can lead to difficulties. Openings in walls may not be correctly framed. Wall sections above large openings for picture windows, for example, can sag if the openings are not bridged with appropriate lintels.

Condensation

Condensation damage to studs in exterior walls is a concern, especially where insulation is being upgraded in older houses, and good interior vapour barriers on the warm side of the insulation are not provided. Since the process is largely concealed, it is difficult to spot during a visual inspection and may exist for a long time before the damage is noticed. Occasionally, peeling exterior paint is one indication that wall condensation is a problem.

Condensation is typically a seasonal problem occurring during the winter months. Warm moist air enters the wall from the house. As it passes through, the air cools. Cool air cannot hold as much water as warm air and condensation forms inside the wall as the air cools and gives off its water.

Low Quality Lumber

Poor quality studs or studs that warp and bow shortly after construction can lead to unsightly wall surfaces in new construction. No easy answer to this problem exists–the bowed or twisted studs have to be removed and replaced.

WORK LETTER

A term referring to the quality and extent of standard allowances provided by a landlord to a tenant in a lease agreement. In Canada, commercial leases typically reference such matters in a schedule to the lease under the title *Landlord's and Tenant's Work* setting out the parties' responsibilities.

Example   *Work Letter*

A schedule of landlord's and tenant's work might reference the following:

- The landlord will supply outline drawings showing such things as overall dimensions, cross-sections, location of rear door (if required), and entry points for heat and air-conditioning, water, sewers, electricity, and sprinkler layout.
- The landlord will also specify the extent of structural finishing, e.g., framing, finished roof, concrete floor, party walls, and entrance doors.
- The tenant will submit complete drawings for the finishing of the premises, e.g., underfloor electrical or plumbing systems (if any), floor plan, ceiling plan, ductwork, electrical wiring, distribution panels, washroom facilities, interior partitions, and finishing.

The schedule also sets out any special provisions, e.g., right of first refusal by landlord to complete the tenant's work, limitations on live loads, required completion of work by tenant, compliance with provincial building code, and approval of all improvements by landlord.

WORKING DRAWINGS

(SEE ALSO ARCHITECTURAL DRAWINGS)

Detailed floor space plans that diagrammatically show all improvements to be made and are designed as instructions to the various contractors involved.

YIELD

The return on an investment normally expressed as a percentage per annum of the amount invested.

Example   Yield

Investor Thompson is willing to advance Jones a personal loan for $20,000 for a one-year term at the rate of 10% per annum with no compounding. Thompson, in consideration of risk on this personal loan, requires that a bonus of $500 be deducted from the loan, to increase the yield. Consequently, Jones' yield is as follows:

Loan Amount	$20,000
Loan Advanced	−19,500
Bonus (when mortgage due)	$500
Interest Paid	$2,000
Amount Due at Year End	$20,000

Yield = (Interest Paid + Bonus) ÷ Loan Advanced
     = (2,000 + 500) ÷ 19,500
     = 12.82%

YIELD CAPITALIZATION

One of two methods used to analyze the present value of a future income stream for purposes of investment valuation and comparison. Yield capitalization should be clearly distinguished from direct capitalization. Direct capitalization involves a single year's projected income and expenses to arrive at value. Yield capitalization relies on projected income and expenses over a specified holding period (including operations and sale proceeds cash flows), and an appropriate discount rate to arrive at present value based on those projected cash flows.

Application   Both yield and direct methods fall under the income approach to value. Yield capitalization is associated with value estimates and can be used for estimating either market value or investment value depending on assumptions and criteria used. The duration, timing, and amount of cash flows are critical to establishing present value under this approach. The discounted cash flow approach has become popular with commercial practitioners given the preponderance of irregular income streams in real estate investments. Other yield capitalization models do exist and are widely discussed in appraisal theory, e.g., models based on stable incomes or regular incomes with constant amount changes over forecasted periods. However, most have limited applicability to real estate investment analysis given unpredictability and variability of cash flows. Fortunately, discounted cash flow techniques handle both regular and irregular cash flows.

Yield capitalization can be applied to either before tax or after tax cash flows. Typically, appraisers use cash flows before tax derived from reconstructed operating statements to arrive at market value. Commercial practitioners more frequently gravitate to investment value based on either a before tax or after tax basis. Circumstances may dictate the calculation of both market and investment values. A cash flow model has been developed specifically for commercial practitioners based on after tax operations cash flows and sale proceeds (reversionary) cash flows projected for a specified holding period.

The use of discounted cash flows is generally associated with capital budgeting and the screening/selection of investment opportunities based on investor objectives. Proponents point to the sophistication of this method in deriving detailed cash flow estimates, while opponents reference the various assumptions required for such estimates. Regardless, the use of forecasted cash flows has gained increased popularity with large investors and portfolio managers. The advent of calculators and software programs has served to further promote such techniques.

YIELD RATE

A term referring to the rate of return or yield on capital realized from all future benefits arising out of ownership. For example, a discount rate used in yield capitalization and discounted cash flows is viewed as a yield rate. A mortgage interest rate is also a yield rate as it expresses the rate of return on mortgage funds advanced over a specified period of time.

Application Yield rates should not be confused with income rates. An income rate, such as an overall capitalization rate, expresses a relationship between a single year's income and the capital value of the property. The actual return on that property may be higher, lower, or the same as the capitalization rate used to compute value under direct capitalization. However, no direct link exists between the cap rate and the rate of return. Yield rates reflect the yield on capital, while income rates express mathematical relationships.

Z

ZERO LOT LINE

The construction of a residential, retail, office, industrial or other investment structure on one or more lot lines of the said property. In the case of commercial properties, the zero lot line is most commonly at the front of the structure. In residential, zero lot line homes include the overall structure plus any amenity areas directly associated with the house, e.g., patio, decks, and porches. As with commercial property, the zero lot line need not be on all sides of the property, and will depend on the type of residential development.

ZONING

Rules established by various levels of government dealing with how specific parcels and individual lots of land may be used. The means of controlling land usage is called zoning. Zoning is the setting aside of land for certain predefined purposes and uses. For example, in an urban area, some land falls in residential zones and other land in commercial zones. If one wishes to sell or buy property in an area, how the property is zoned, be it commercial or residential, could be an important part of the sale. Each zone type, sometimes referred to as a *zoning district*, has its own set of restrictions regulating how the land in that zone type may be used. If the property is zoned commercial, one set of restrictions exist; if it is zoned residential, different restrictions apply.

One of the main reasons for zoning requirements is to ensure that adjacent lands have compatible uses. Most people would not want a factory built next to their house. Air pollution, noise, and other undesirable factors make the factory and the house incompatible. To prevent factories from being built next to houses, residential zones are established in which factories cannot be built. Each type of zone has its own restrictions as to the kind of activity that can occur there to ensure that the activities are truly compatible and one does not interfere with the normal use of the other.

The objectives of zoning can be generally described as follows:

- To implement the land use pattern that is in the best interest of the community.
- To serve as a code of preventive nuisance law to protect property values.
- To ensure that there is an adequate supply of land in the future.
- To promote and protect the aesthetic environment of the community.
- To regulate competition and the tax base.
- To prevent over-extension of municipal services.
- To promote the public health and morality of the community.

By-Law

Passed by a municipality to regulate the use of land and specifically limit the use of land in certain areas for any purpose other than as set out in that by-law. Municipalities may enact zoning by-laws that divide the municipality into areas or zones. The by-law defines exactly what can take place on a parcel of land (i.e., within the zone), and how the structures are to be located on the property (e.g., setbacks, coverage, etc.).

An effective set of zoning by-laws will:

- Define zones for various types of uses and establish the specific type of land use in each zone, e.g., residential, commercial, agricultural, industrial, and institutional;
- Set standards for building structures, e.g., minimum lot size, frontage, set-back from street, side yard clearances, building heights, and parking requirements;
- Provide restrictions on use, to ensure land uses are compatible;
- Regulate the construction or alteration of buildings after the passing of the by-law;
- Prescribe the maximum density of population;
- Regulate or prohibit the public display of signs;

V TO Z

- Regulate the amount and nature of sound that may be emitted from a building;
- Reduce costs of operating the municipality by keeping different types of land use in separate areas, thus, for example, reducing the costs of providing an upgraded level of major services to small industrial pockets in the community.

Zoning by-laws essentially set out detailed guidelines for the implementation of the official plan within a particular municipality and the control of permitted uses within individual zones. A range of specialized zoning by-laws may be encountered in addition to those specifically addressing current regulation of land use. For example, a holding by-law sets out future uses and is normally used for areas where municipal services have not yet been supplied. The interim control by-law is a form of zoning by-law used when the municipality wishes to effectively freeze a specific area pending further investigation before deciding upon final designated uses.

By-Law Amendment/Rezoning

A change to an existing zoning by-law to permit the development or use of a property that does not comply with the existing zoning by-law. A public hearing is usually held before adopting, amending, or repealing a zoning by-law. At the public hearing, all those who deem their interest in property to be affected by the proposed by-law are afforded an opportunity to be heard.

Certificate/Memorandum

A zoning compliance certificate or similar memorandum may be issued by a municipality with respect to a specific zoning lot to confirm any of the following:

- That the described use or uses operated or proposed to be operated on the lot comply with the applicable zoning rules, agreements, and orders;
- That the development on the lot complies with all zoning rules, agreements, and orders affecting it; and
- That the location of the building or buildings on the lot complies with the applicable zoning rules, agreements, and orders.

Reference Procedures and terminology regarding certificates will vary both by provincial jurisdictions and individual municipalities.

Classifications/Sub-Classifications

Zones created by the zoning by-law are identified by a series of classifications and sub-classifications. While significant variations exist across Canada, most include the following general classifications:

- Residential;
- Commercial;
- Industrial;
- Agricultural;
- Environmentally Sensitive/Flood Plain; and
- Open Space/Parks/Recreation.

Within each zone type, smaller divisions exist called sub-classifications. For example, under residential, various sub-classifications serve to more precisely define the specific use of the land in the zone and often will set aside parts of a total zone for more exact use as shown in the mix of dwelling types and forms in a total residential zone. (Terminology will differ.) Typical residential sub-classifications might include Residential 1 (R1), Residential 2 (R2), Residential 3 (R3), etc. Just as each zone type has a designated use, each sub-classification also has a designated use. These designated uses are not interchangeable. Without proper authority, one cannot change a property's use from that designated by its zoning type and sub-classification. Figure Z.1 illustrates an excerpt from a typical zoning map identifying various residential sub-classifications.

Non-Conforming Use

When a new zoning by-law is introduced in a community, a number of existing uses of buildings can be caught in a zoning change. There are special provisions for such cases, to the effect that the lawful use of the premises existing at the time of the adoption of a zoning by-law or a building lawfully under construction at the time of the zoning by-law enforcement will be allowed to continue, even if it does not conform to the new regulations. However, it is usual that if such a non-conforming use of premises is discontinued for a specified period, any future use must be in conformity with the new zoning regulations.

Order

The provincial ministry/department responsible for planning has the ultimate authority to zone any property within a province. This is referred to as a *zoning order*. The use of zoning orders is most commonly found in areas that are not currently administered by way of a local municipality and associated zoning by-laws (e.g., remote provincial areas), although technically, a zoning order could be imposed anywhere in the province. In practice, however, all zoning matters are normally handled by local municipalities, pursuant to the provisions of the applicable planning act.

Requirements

Exact zoning requirements concerning specific zones in various municipalities will differ. The range of restrictions are detailed under a more or less standard set of topic areas, e.g., intent and purpose of the applicable zone, permitted and conditional uses, and bulk regulations that apply to all properties within a specific sub-classification, e.g., single-family districts and minimums concerning lot area, lot width, front yard, rear yard, side yard, building height, and lot coverage. The bulk requirements may also detail exceptions, general provisions regarding accessory structures, and permitted projections and obstructions into yards. Further, supplementary regulations may exist for specific uses as defined, e.g., enlargement of existing dwellings, conversions of existing structures, and new construction of accessory buildings.

Variances

A zoning variance may be applied for if the property owner is of the opinion that the regulations of the zoning by-law *injuriously or unnecessarily* affect his/her property.

A zoning variance does not change the rules of the zoning by-law as in the case of rezoning. Rather, a variance *bends* the rules up to the limit applied for. For example, a variance might permit the establishment of a reduced front yard, say 15 feet, for a dwelling where the zoning by-law requires a front yard of 25 feet. This variance would be the subject of a public hearing with representations made by the applicant and adjacent property owners. After hearing representations, the hearing body could do one of three things:

- Approve the variance application, with or without conditions.
- Reject the variance application.
- Approve the application up to a certain limit, for example 20 feet, with or without conditions.

The basic difference between a variance and a rezoning is determined by whether the granting of a zoning variance would *break* the zoning rules rather then merely *bend* them. Clearly, if the rules will be broken, a rezoning application is the more appropriate procedure.

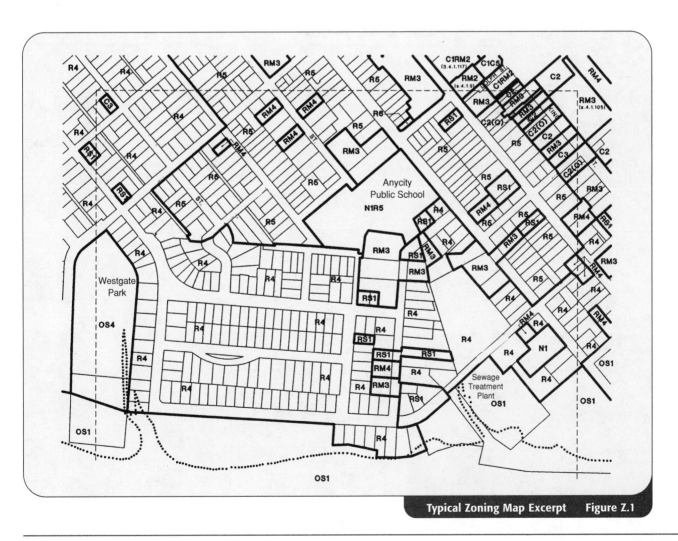

Typical Zoning Map Excerpt   Figure Z.1

APPENDIX

REAL ESTATE
ENCYCLOPEDIA

APPENDIX

Construction Costs, Unit In Place Prices*

Example Only—Southern Ontario Marketplace

	Unit Cost at January, 2000			
	Imperial $/Unit		Metric $/Unit	

GENERAL

Geotechnical and Environmental Investigation for proposed 30,000 SF industrial structure, 22 to 30 ft. ceiling, site area 5 acres. 10 boreholes, 5 m deep and 10 samples tested. Assume routine investigation only.

Item	Imperial $		Metric $	
Geotechnical investigation	2,675.00	E	2,675.00	E
Environmental testing and site history for the above 5 acre site	1,650.00	and up	1,650.00	and up
Site Survey for above 5 acre site and 30,000 SF proposed building	2,550.00	E	2,550.00	E
Routine demolition cost for leasehold improvements including partitions, carpet, doors and general cleaning (excluding removal of contaminated materials)	2.55	SF and up	26.90	m² and up

NON-RESIDENTIAL

Item	Imperial $		Metric $	
Site Services (Site Area)	1.55	SF	16.70	m²
Asphalt paving including granular sub-base	18.90	SY	22.60	m²
Concrete sidewalks including granular base	4.55	SF	49.00	m²
Concrete curbs	12.25	LF	40.20	m
Sodding	4.10	SY	4.90	m²
Ramp for disabled	10,000.00	E and up	10,000.00	E and up
5" (125 mm) reinforced hardened concrete floor with 6" (150 mm) crushed stone base	3.45	SF	37.15	m²
Suspended acoustic tile ceiling	2.85	SF	30.70	m²
Facebrick with 8" (200 mm) block backup	20.90	SF	225.00	m²
Built-up Felt Roofing Complete, Incl. 75 mm Insulation	4.00	SF	43.05	m²
Fluid Applied Roofing Complete, Incl. 75 mm Insulation	4.75	SF	51.15	m²
6" (150 mm) block partition	6.80	SF	73.20	m²
8" (200 mm) block partition	7.25	SF	78.05	m²
10" (250 mm) block partition	8.00	SF	86.10	m²
Insulated steel siding including steel girts	11.00	SF	118.00	m²
Precast concrete panels	25.50	SF	274.00	m²
Medium quality commercial broadloom	22.50	SY and up	26.90	m² and up
2 mm vinyl composite flooring 300 mm x 300 mm	1.60	SF	17.20	m²
Ceramic tile	7.70	SF	82.90	m²
Rubber base–4" (100 mm)	1.50	LF	4.90	m
Carpet base–4" (100 mm)	2.75	LF	9.00	m
Wood base–4" (100 mm) (paint grade, unfinished)	4.60	LF	15.10	m
Raised flooring	11.25	SF and up	121.00	m² and up
Drywall partition	4.20	SF	41.45	m²
Painting	0.60	SF	6.45	m²
Vinyl fabric	3.00	SF	32.30	m²
Rubber base–6" (150 mm)	1.80	LF	5.90	m
Prefinished partition	6.70	SF	72.10	m²
1 ³/₄" (44 mm) commercial hollow core door including hollow metal frames, painting, medium duty hardware and installation	740.00	E and up	740.00	E and up
Narrow line aluminum glazed entrance doors complete	56.00	SF	603.00	m²
Automatic dock leveller	3,500.00	E	3,500.00	E
Door seals 10' x 15' (3.0 m x 4.6 m)	1,800.00	E	1,800.00	E
Shipping door cushions	135.00	E	135.00	E
Fluorescent lighting–80 f.c. (800 lux)	3.70	SF	39.85	m²
(Plant area)–60 f.c. (600 lux)	2.90	SF	31.20	m²
(T8 Lamp/electronic ballast)–30 f.c. (300 lux)	2.15	SF	23.15	m²
H.I.D. (15 to 20 ft. 30 F.C.)	1.85	SF	19.90	m²
Power Outlet—wall mounted	110.00	E	110.00	E
Telephone Outlet—wall mounted	70.00	E	70.00	E

(Non-Residential Cont'd)	Unit Cost at January, 2000			
	Imperial $/Unit		Metric $/Unit	
Relocate 2' x 4' light fixtures	55.00	E	55.00	E
New light fixtures 2' x 4', (4 lamps, lenses)	155.00	E	155.00	E
Light switch	55.00	E	55.00	E
Fluorescent PL down light	165.00	E	165.00	E
Fluorescent PL wall washer	170.00	E	170.00	E
Exit light fixture (LED Type)	220.00	E	220.00	E
300 w battery unit c/w 2 heads emergency lights	500.00	E	500.00	E
Single remote unit—emergency light	85.00	E	85.00	E
Double remote unit—emergency light	115.00	E	115.00	E
100 amp electrical service (factory)	1,300.00	and up	1,300.00	and up
400/300 amp electrical service (factory)	3,000.00	and up	3,000.00	and up
Sub-stations—450 KVA (factory)	20,600.00	and up	20,600.00	and up
F. H. cabinet & pipework system—simple	1,700.00	F. H. C..	1,700.00	F. H. C.
F. H. cabinet & pipework system—medium	2,200.00	F. H. C.	2,200.00	F. H. C.
F. H. cabinet & pipework system—complex	3,250.00	F. H. C.	3,250.00	F. H. C.
Sprinklers—Average overall—open space	1.40	SF	15.05	m^2
Sprinklers—Average overall—partitioned	1.65	SF	17.75	m^2
New sprinkler heads—open space	145.00	E	145.00	E
New sprinkler heads—partitioned	170.00	E	170.00	E
Relocate existing sprinkler heads	90.00	E and up	90.00	E and up
WC—wall mounted, fixture and rough-in only	1,500.00	E	1,500.00	E
Lavatory—wall hung, fixture and rough-in only	1,200.00	E	1,200.00	E
Urinal—wall mounted, fixture and rough-in only	1,400.00	E	1,400.00	E
Office air conditioning—summer cooling	10.75	SF	116.00	m^2
Office air conditioning—year round	14.90	SF	160.00	m^2
Rooftop A/C unit only	1,100.00	TR	313.00	KW
Rooftop unit c/w supply & return ductwork system—simple	1,650.00	TR	469.00	KW
Rooftop unit c/w supply & return ductwork system—medium	2,500.00	TR	711.00	KW
Rooftop unit c/w supply & return ductwork system—complex	3,350.00	TR	953.00	KW
Computer room A/C unit & ductwork	3,350.00	TR and up	953.00	KW & up
Computer room A/C unit & ductwork	65.00	SF and up	700.00	m^2 and up
Gas fired unit heater 48 MBH/HR (14 KW)	1,600.00	E	1,600.00	E
Cabinet/Forceflo/Baseboard heating	210.00	KW	210.00	KW
Shipping door 8' x 10' (2.4 m x 3.0 m) manual wood section	1,700.00	E	1,700.00	E
Chain link fencing 8' (2.4 m) high	18.00	LF	59.05	m
RESIDENTIAL				
Residential garage—single attached	21.75	SF	234.00	m^2
Residential garage—two car, attached	20.50	SF	221.00	m^2
Residential garage—single, attached (10 x 20 ft. or 3.0 m x 6.1 m)	4,350.00	and up	4,350.00	and up
Residential garage—two car, attached (20 x 20 ft. or 6.1 m x 6.1 m)	8,200.00	and up	8,200.00	and up
Fireplaces (each)	2,850.00	and up	2,850.00	and up
Bathrooms (each)	3,100.00	and up	3,100.00	and up
Two piece washrooms	2,850.00	and up	2,850.00	and up
Extra for finishing residential basements—average quality	15.50	SF	167.00	m^2
Extra for finishing residential basements—superior quality	22.75	SF	245.00	m^2
Roofing Shingles—25 year (new roofing only)	1.40	SF	15.05	m^2
Roofing Shingles—25 year (re-roofing)	2.25	SF	24.20	m^2
Hardwood—Parquet flooring	6.15	SF and up	66.20	m^2 and up
Hardwood—Planks	8.25	SF and up	88.80	m^2 and up

* Includes general contractor's overhead and profit

Source: Toronto Real Estate Board

CREA CODE OF ETHICS

INTRODUCTION

It is anticipated that wide use of this manual will result in Members becoming increasingly aware of their ethical obligations and the responsibility of each broker/agent Member for the acts of all licensees affiliated with that broker/agent Member, as well as the responsibilities that each individual Member has.

Questions concerning the meaning or application of the Code of Ethics should always be directed, in the first place, to the Professional Standards Committee of your local board. If the information sought is unavailable at your board, your request should be sent to your provincial association, following which a request, in writing, may be sent to:

The Canadian Real Estate Association
344 Slater Street, Suite 1600
Canada Building
Ottawa, Ontario
K1R 7Y3

PREFACE

The Code of Ethics of The Canadian Real Estate Association is universally recognized by professionals and laymen alike as the measure of professionalism in real estate. It does not, however, describe the lowest common denominator of permissible performance as do the licensing laws of the provinces; rather, it describes the optimum performance the public has a right to expect and makes that performance the "norm" for Members of the Association.

In the same manner that the real estate marketplace is a dynamic, demanding environment, so the Code is, has been, and will continue to be a demanding document; a plan for professionalism in real estate, capable of including and accommodating every change, challenge and controversy which arises.

It is precisely because the Code must continue as a meaningful and relevant standard of professional performance that this manual is especially dedicated to the men and women who serve on Professional Standards Committees, as well as the men and women who, as staff of the Member boards and provincial associations, have the responsibility of working with them. It is these people who are charged with giving early warning of the changes, challenges and controversies which the Code must confront; it is they who must identify the misapplications and misrepresentations of the Code which, if uncorrected or unnoticed, would discredit and ultimately destroy not only it, but also the real estate marketplace.

This manual is published in the hope of providing assistance necessary to carry out these responsibilities.

The Interpretations are supplementary to the Code of Ethics. The Interpretations state general principles relating to an Article of the Code of Ethics to guide Members as to the professional conduct required in a situation covered by a specific Article of the Code.

In filing a charge or defence of an alleged violation of the Code of Ethics by a Member, the charge shall read as an alleged violation of the Code and/or one or more of its Articles. An Interpretation may only be cited in support of the charge or in support of the defence.

The Code of Ethics of
The Canadian Real Estate Association

An Assurance of
Public Service and Protection

The first Code of Ethics was approved in 1913 at the Sixth Annual Convention of the National Association of Real Estate Boards (name changed to National Association of REALTORS® in 1974) held in Winnipeg, Manitoba.

The Code of Ethics of The Canadian Real Estate Association was approved in September 1959.

It has served since then as "the ten commandments of the real estate fraternity", binding Members together in a common continuing quest for professionalism through ethical obligations premised on moral integrity and competent service to clients and customers, and dedication to the interest and welfare of the public. The Code has been amended many times to reflect changes in the real estate marketplace, the needs of property owners and the perceptions and values of society.

But its demand for high standards of professional conduct, which protect the interests of clients and customers and safeguard the rights of consumers of real estate services, remains unchanged.

CODE OF ETHICS (revised 1995)

Under all is the land. Upon its wise utilization and widely allocated ownership depend the survival and growth of free institutions and of our civilization.

Through the REALTOR, the land resource of the nation reaches its highest use and private land ownership its widest distribution. The REALTOR is instrumental in moulding the form of his or her community and the living and working conditions of its people.

Such functions impose grave social responsibilities which REALTORS can meet only by diligent preparation, and considering it a civic duty to dedicate themselves to the fulfilment of a REALTOR's obligations to society.

The REALTOR therefore must be zealous to maintain, and continually strive to improve, the professional standards of his or her calling:

by keeping informed as to developments and trends in real estate,

by endeavouring to protect the public against fraud, misrepresentation or unethical practice in connection with real estate transactions,

by rendering services and opinions based only on the REALTOR's knowledge, training, qualifications and experience in real estate,

by seeking no unfair advantage over, nor injuring directly or indirectly, the reputation of, nor publicly disparaging the business practice of other REALTORS, and

by being loyal to the REALTOR's Real Estate Board and Provincial/Territorial Association and active in their work.

In the interpretation of his or her obligations, the REALTOR can take no safer guide than that which has been embodied in the Golden Rule — "Do unto others as you would have them do unto you".

No inducement of profit and no instructions from clients or customers can ever justify departure from the ideals of fair dealing and high integrity resulting from adherence to a lofty standard of moral conduct in business relations.

Accepting this standard as his or her own, each REALTOR pledges to observe the spirit of the Code in all dealings and to conduct business in accordance with the Standards of Business Practice as adopted by The Canadian Real Estate Association.

INDEX TO
STANDARDS OF BUSINESS PRACTICE

ARTICLE			DUTIES TO CLIENTS AND CUSTOMERS
1			**Informed and up-to-date.**
	Interpretation	1-1	Current and pending legislation
	Interpretation	1-2	Educational courses
	Interpretation	1-3	Financing procedures and requirements
	Interpretation	1-4	Contents of forms
2			**Primary obligation to client, fair treatment to all parties.**
	Interpretation	2-1	Misrepresentation of potential market value
	Interpretation	2-2	Information that could affect successful completion of contract
	Interpretation	2-3	Misleading a customer on matters pertaining to a property
	Interpretation	2-4	Confidential information
	Interpretation	2-5	Competent assistance when dealing with third parties
3			**Disclose role and nature of service.**
	Interpretation	3-1	Application in common law provinces
	Interpretation	3-2	Application in the Province of Québec
4			**Avoid exaggeration and misrepresentation.**
	Interpretation	4-1	Concealing facts
	Interpretation	4-2	Meaning of "pertinent fact"
	Interpretation	4-3	Current and pending legislation
	Interpretation	4-4	Contents of forms
	Interpretation	4-5	Misrepresentation of potential market value
	Interpretation	4-6	Misleading a customer on matters pertaining to a property
	Interpretation	4-7	Confidential information
5			**Written representation agreements.**
6			**Written obligations and commitments pertaining to real estate transactions.**
	Interpretation	6-1	By-laws and rules affecting distribution of contracts
	Interpretation	6-2	Use of written extensions or amendments
7			**Expenses known to all.**
	Interpretation	7-1	Explaining fees for services
8			**Compensation from parties to a transaction.**
9			**Financial benefit from recommending third party services and products.**
	Interpretation	9-1	Disclose interest in recommended/suggested business
	Interpretation	9-2	Meaning of "real estate products or services"
10			**Rebates and profits on expenditures made for clients and customers.**
	Interpretation	10-1	Render proper accounting
	Interpretation	10-2	Disclose interest in recommended/suggested business

STANDARDS OF BUSINESS PRACTICE

DUTIES TO CLIENTS AND CUSTOMERS

ARTICLE 1

REALTORS shall endeavour to be informed regarding the essential facts which affect current market conditions in order to be in a position to counsel their clients and/or to assist customers in a responsible manner.

ARTICLE 2

A REALTOR shall protect and promote the interests of his or her client. This primary obligation does not relieve the REALTOR of the responsibility of dealing fairly with all parties to the transaction.

ARTICLE 3

A REALTOR shall fully disclose in writing to, and is advised to seek written acknowledgement of disclosure from, all parties to a transaction regarding the role and the nature of service the REALTOR will be providing to the client versus the customer or other party to the transaction. The REALTOR shall also disclose his or her role to other REALTORS involved in the transaction.

ARTICLE 4

A REALTOR has an obligation to discover facts pertaining to every property for which the REALTOR accepts an agency which a reasonably prudent REALTOR would discover in order to fulfil the obligation to avoid error, misrepresentation or concealment of pertinent facts.

ARTICLE 5

REALTORS should ensure written representation agreements whenever possible in order to avoid misunderstandings with their clients and customers.

ARTICLE 6

REALTORS shall ensure that agreements regarding real estate transactions are in writing in clear and understandable language, expressing the specific terms, conditions, obligations and commitments of the parties to the agreement. A copy of each final agreement shall be furnished to each party upon their signing or initialing, and shall be dealt with in accordance with the instructions of the parties involved.

ARTICLE 7

The REALTOR shall, prior to the signing of any agreement, fully inform the signing party regarding the type of expenses for which he/she may be normally liable.

ARTICLE 8

A REALTOR shall not accept compensation from more than one party to a transaction without the written consent of his or her client(s).

ARTICLE 9

REALTORS shall disclose to a client or customer if there is any financial benefit the REALTOR or his/her firm may receive as a result of recommending real estate products or services to that party.

ARTICLE 10

A REALTOR shall not accept any rebate or profit on expenditures made for a client without the client's consent or accept any rebate or profit on expenditures for a customer without the customer's knowledge.

ARTICLE 11

The REALTOR shall not discourage parties to a transaction from seeking legal counsel.

ARTICLE 12

The REALTOR shall not knowingly permit any property in his or her charge to be used for unlawful purposes.

ARTICLE 13

A REALTOR shall not present an offer or acquire an interest in property either directly or indirectly for himself or herself, any member of his or her immediate family or any entity in which the REALTOR has a financial interest, without making the REALTOR's position known to the seller in writing. In selling/leasing property owned by the REALTOR, or in which the REALTOR has an interest, the interest shall be revealed to the buyer/tenant in writing.

ARTICLE 14

In providing an opinion of value of real property, a REALTOR shall not undertake to provide such an opinion if it is outside the REALTOR's field of experience to do so, unless this fact is disclosed to the client or unless assistance is obtained from another person who has experience in this area. A REALTOR shall not perform an appraisal contrary to the terms and conditions of any designation the REALTOR holds through The Canadian Real Estate Association. In all other circumstances, the REALTOR shall not provide an opinion of value on property in which the REALTOR has a present or contemplated interest without first disclosing this fact to the client. Fees charged for providing an opinion of value shall not be based on the amount of value reported.

ARTICLE 15

A REALTOR shall present all written offers and counter-offers as objectively and as quickly as possible.

ARTICLE 16

A REALTOR shall not advertise a property if such advertising has been restricted at the request of the seller/landlord. In any advertisement, the advertised or offered price of a property shall not be other than that which was agreed upon with the seller/landlord. (Also applies to Article 25.)

DUTIES TO THE PUBLIC

ARTICLE 17

A REALTOR is obliged to render a skilled and conscientious service, in conformity with standards of competence which are reasonably expected in the specific real estate disciplines in which the REALTOR engages. When a REALTOR is unable to render such service, either alone or with the aid of other REALTORS, the REALTOR should not accept the assignment or otherwise provide assistance in connection with the transaction.

ARTICLE 18

REALTORS shall ensure a true presentation in all advertising. Properties and services shall not be advertised without identifying the firm or, where applicable, the individual practitioner, in accordance with provincial licensing legislation.

ARTICLE 19

The REALTOR shall not deny professional services to any person for reasons of race, creed, colour, sex, familial status, age, or national origin. The REALTOR shall not be party to any plan or agreement to discriminate against a person or persons on the basis of race, creed, colour, sex, familial status, age or national origin.

ARTICLE 20

The REALTOR shall observe the By-Laws, Rules and Regulations established by the REALTOR's Real Estate Board and/or Association, in addition to the regulations, terms and conditions associated with any designation that the REALTOR may hold through membership in The Canadian Real Estate Association.

ARTICLE 21

The business of a REALTOR shall be conducted in strict accordance with all statutory and regulatory requirements that apply to that business.

DUTIES TO REALTORS

ARTICLE 22

The REALTOR shall never publicly discredit a competitor. If the REALTOR's opinion is sought regarding a specific transaction, it should be rendered with strict professional integrity and courtesy.

ARTICLE 23

The agency or other contractual relationship of a competitor shall be respected by all REALTORS. Negotiations concerning exclusively listed property or with any party who is exclusively represented shall be carried on with the client's agent and not with the client directly, except with the consent of the client's agent.

ARTICLE 24

A REALTOR shall not seek information about a competitor's transaction to be used for the purpose of closing a transaction himself or herself, or for the purpose of interfering with any other contractual undertaking.

ARTICLE 25

Signs in respect of the sale, rent, lease, development or exchange should not be placed on any property by other than the listing broker unless authorized by the seller/landlord. REALTORS shall not interfere with another real estate broker's sign.

ARTICLE 26

Should a REALTOR be asked to co-operate in any way in connection with a disciplinary investigation or proceeding pertaining to alleged unethical practice, the REALTOR shall place all pertinent facts before the proper Committee of the Real Estate Board or Association to which the REALTOR belongs.

ARTICLE 27

In the event of a dispute between REALTORS associated with different firms of the same local Board/Association regarding the fee or commission earned or to be earned in connection with a real estate transaction, the dispute shall be submitted for arbitration in accordance with the By-Laws, Rules and Regulations of their local Board/Association.

ARTICLE 28

In the event of a dispute between REALTORS associated with different firms and belonging to different local Boards/Associations, regarding the fee or commission earned or to be earned in connection with a real estate transaction, the dispute shall be submitted to arbitration in accordance with the By-Laws and Rules and Regulations of the appropriate Provincial/Territorial Association. Should the REALTORS belong to different Provincial/Territorial Associations, the dispute shall be arbitrated in accordance with the By-Laws and Rules and Regulations of The Canadian Real Estate Association.

ARTICLE 29

The business of a REALTOR shall be conducted so as to avoid controversies with other REALTORS.

INTERPRETATIONS
STANDARDS OF BUSINESS PRACTICE

DUTIES TO CLIENTS AND CUSTOMERS

ARTICLE 1

REALTORS shall endeavour to be informed regarding the essential facts which affect current market conditions in order to be in a position to counsel their clients and/or to assist customers in a responsible manner.

Interpretations

1-1   A REALTOR should be aware of current legislation and, wherever reasonably possible, be aware of pending legislation (including zoning, government programs, etc.) which could affect trading conditions in the marketplace. (Also applies to Article 4 and Article 14.)

1-2   A REALTOR should attend such educational programs and courses as are made available through his/her Board, Provincial/Territorial Association or CREA, in order to be up-to-date and remain aware of matters that could affect a customer's or client's decisions. (Also applies to Article 14.)

1-3   A REALTOR should be aware of appropriate financing procedures, mortgaging requirements, etc. in order to properly discuss financial obligations on any transaction. (Also applies to Article 14.)

1-4   A REALTOR should be familiar with the contents of forms commonly used in real estate transactions. (Also applies to Article 4.)

ARTICLE 2

A REALTOR shall protect and promote the interests of his or her client. This primary obligation does not relieve the REALTOR of the responsibility of dealing fairly with all parties to the transaction.

Interpretations

2-1   Any REALTOR, in attempting to obtain a listing, should not misrepresent the potential market value of the property to the seller. (Also applies to Article 4.)

2-2   A REALTOR should fully disclose to his or her client, at the earliest opportunity, any information that could affect the successful completion of the contract.

2-3   Any REALTOR, when dealing with a customer, should not mislead the customer as to any matters pertaining to a property. (Also applies to Article 4.)

2-4   A REALTOR should not, during or following the relationship with his/her client, reveal confidential information of the client, use confidential information of the client to the client's disadvantage, or use confidential information of the client for a purpose other than that for which the information was obtained except with the client's consent or as required by law. (Also applies to Article 4.)

2-5   A REALTOR should provide competent assistance when dealing with lawyers, mortgage lenders and other third parties needed to ensure the successful completion of any contract entered into between a seller and a buyer.

ARTICLE 3

A REALTOR shall fully disclose in writing to, and is advised to seek written acknowledgement of disclosure from, all parties to a transaction regarding the role and the nature of service the REALTOR will be providing to the client versus the customer or other party to the transaction. The REALTOR shall also disclose his or her role to other REALTORS involved in the transaction.

Interpretations

3-1   In common law provinces/territories, the requirement to disclose a REALTOR's "role" in a transaction requires the REALTOR to identify if he/she is acting as agent for the seller, and/or the buyer or some other party(ies) to the transaction. The requirement to disclose the "nature of service" requires the REALTOR to explain that his or her primary responsibility is to protect and promote his or her client's best interests, but that this primary obligation does not relieve the REALTOR of the responsibility to deal fairly with all parties to the transaction.

3-2   In the Province of Québec, the requirement to disclose a REALTOR's "role" in a transaction requires the REALTOR to identify if he or she is rendering services on behalf of the seller and/or the buyer or some other party(ies) to the transaction. The requirement to disclose the "nature of service" requires the REALTOR to explain that his or her primary responsibility is to protect and promote the interests of his or her client, but that this does not preclude fair treatment to all parties to a transaction.

ARTICLE 4

A REALTOR has an obligation to discover facts pertaining to every property for which the REALTOR accepts an agency which a reasonably prudent REALTOR would discover in order to fulfil the obligation to avoid error, misrepresentation or concealment of pertinent facts.

Interpretations

4-1   The REALTOR should not be party to any agreement in any way to conceal any facts pertaining to a property.

4-2   Any fact that could affect a reasonable person's decision to buy/lease a property, the price that a reasonable person might pay for a property and/or a reasonable person's ability to resell/sublet a property at a future date is a "pertinent fact" and, unless prohibited by law, should be disclosed.

4-3   Interpretation 1-1 also applies to Article 4.

4-4   Interpretation 1-4 also applies to Article 4.

4-5   Interpretation 2-1 also applies to Article 4.

4-6   Interpretation 2-3 also applies to Article 4.

4-7   Interpretation 2-4 also applies to Article 4.

ARTICLE 5

REALTORS should ensure written representation agreements whenever possible in order to avoid misunderstandings with their clients and customers.

ARTICLE 6

REALTORS shall ensure that agreements regarding real estate transactions are in writing in clear and understandable language, expressing the specific terms, conditions, obligations and commitments of the parties to the agreement. A copy of each final agreement shall be furnished to each party upon their signing or initialing, and shall be dealt with in accordance with the instructions of the parties involved.

Interpretations

6-1   Where the distribution of contracts is regulated by the By-Laws and/or Rules and Regulations of the Board, such distribution shall be in accordance with the requirements of those By-Laws and/or Rules and Regulations.

6-2   REALTORS should use reasonable care to ensure that documents pertaining to the listing, purchase, sale or lease of real estate are kept current through the use of written extensions or amendments.

ARTICLE 7

The REALTOR shall, prior to the signing of any agreement, fully inform the signing party regarding the type of expenses for which he/she may be normally liable.

Interpretation

7-1   In explaining fees for services, the REALTOR shall not state or suggest that the type or level of fees is based on direction from a real estate board, association, institute, society or council to which the REALTOR belongs. (Also applies to Article 14.)

ARTICLE 8

A REALTOR shall not accept compensation from more than one party to a transaction without the written consent of his or her client(s).

ARTICLE 9

REALTORS shall disclose to a client or customer if there is any financial benefit the REALTOR or his/her firm may receive as a result of recommending real estate products or services to that party.

Interpretations

9-1   The REALTOR should not recommend or suggest to a client or a customer the use of services or products of any other organization or business in which the REALTOR has a direct or indirect interest without disclosing such interest in writing at the time of the recommendation or suggestion. (Also applies to Article 10.)

9-2   Without limiting the generality of Article 9, reference to real estate products or services includes lending institutions, solicitors, appraisers and moving companies, but does not include other real estate brokerage firms from which the REALTOR may receive a referral fee.

ARTICLE 10

A REALTOR shall not accept any rebate or profit on expenditures made for a client without the client's consent or accept any rebate or profit on expenditures for a customer without the customer's knowledge.

Interpretations

10-1   A REALTOR should, at all times, be able to render a proper accounting to the REALTOR's client with respect to monies and other properties of the client which have been entrusted to the care of the REALTOR.

10-2   Interpretation 9-1 also applies to Article 10.

ARTICLE 11

The REALTOR shall not discourage parties to a transaction from seeking legal counsel.

Interpretation

11-1   The REALTOR should seek legal assistance for himself or herself and for all other parties to any agreement where it is beyond the expertise of the REALTOR to set out accurately and appropriately any terms or agreement reached by the parties to a transaction.

ARTICLE 12

The REALTOR shall not knowingly permit any property in his or her charge to be used for unlawful purposes.

ARTICLE 13

A REALTOR shall not present an offer or acquire an interest in property either directly or indirectly for himself or herself, any member of his or her immediate family or any entity in which the REALTOR has a financial interest, without making the REALTOR's position known to the seller in writing. In selling/leasing property owned by the REALTOR, or in which the REALTOR has an interest, the interest shall be revealed to the buyer/tenant in writing.

Interpretations

13-1   Where disclosure regarding the acquisition or disposition is also required pursuant to provincial licensing legislation, such additional disclosure shall be made in accordance with that legislation.

13-2   The REALTOR, when acting as a principal in a real estate transaction, remains obligated by the duties imposed by the Code of Ethics and Standards of Business Practice.

13-3   Disclosure pursuant to Article 13 shall be made at the earliest possible opportunity, and in any event not later than the presentation of an offer to purchase.

ARTICLE 14

In providing an opinion of value of real property, a REALTOR shall not undertake to provide such an opinion if it is outside the REALTOR's field of experience to do so, unless this fact is disclosed to the client or unless assistance is obtained from another person who has experience in this area. A REALTOR shall not perform an appraisal contrary to the terms and conditions of any designation the REALTOR holds through The Canadian Real Estate Association. In all other circumstances, the REALTOR shall not provide an opinion of value on property in which the REALTOR has a present or contemplated interest without first disclosing this fact to the client. Fees charged for providing an opinion of value shall not be based on the amount of value reported.

Interpretations

14-1   Interpretation 1-1 also applies to Article 14.

14-2   Interpretation 1-2 also applies to Article 14.

14-3   Interpretation 1-3 also applies to Article 14.

14-4   A REALTOR should not provide services relating to the sale, purchase, appraisal, management, financing or any other involvement pertaining to a real estate transaction where the REALTOR's level of expertise is not on a level that could be reasonably required under the circumstances. Where services are required in such areas and the REALTOR does not have the appropriate level of expertise, such services should not be provided without the aid of another REALTOR who is properly qualified in the area of activity being contemplated. (Also applies to Article 17.)

14-5   Interpretation 7-1 also applies to Article 14.

ARTICLE 15

A REALTOR shall present all written offers and counter-offers as objectively and as quickly as possible.

Interpretations

15-1   The REALTOR in the presentation of an offer or counter-offer should disclose to his/her client all pertinent facts within the REALTOR's possession or knowledge with respect to that offer or counter-offer unless there is a written agreement signed by both parties limiting the disclosure the REALTOR is to make (e.g., dual agency agreement).

15-2   The REALTOR should ensure reception and transmission of all offers and counter-offers, whether such offers or counter-offers are received from another brokerage firm or through the REALTOR's own brokerage firm.

15-3   The REALTOR should not delay the presentation of any offer or counter-offer for the purpose of obtaining another offer or counter-offer without the express consent of the seller.

15-4   The REALTOR should not attempt to dictate to his/her client the price or other terms of an offer or counter-offer that should be accepted by the client but shall give reasonable and competent counselling as to the obligations and privileges that the acceptance of such an offer or counter-offer would impose, while leaving the final decision as to the acceptability of the offer or counter-offer to the client.

15-5   Although there is no obligation to continue to market a property after an unconditional offer or counter-offer has been accepted, any REALTOR acting as a listing agent should continue to submit all offers and counter-offers to the seller until closing, unless the seller has waived this obligation in writing.

15-6   Where there are competing offers or counter-offers, a REALTOR acting as the listing agent should inform the other REALTORS and/or parties involved of the existence of the other offers or counter-offers, without disclosing their specific terms and conditions.

ARTICLE 16

A REALTOR shall not advertise a property if such advertising has been restricted at the request of the seller/landlord. In any advertisement, the advertised or offered price of a property shall not be other than that which was agreed upon with the seller/landlord. (Also applies to Article 25.)

DUTIES TO THE PUBLIC

ARTICLE 17

A REALTOR is obliged to render a skilled and conscientious service, in conformity with standards of competence which are reasonably expected in the specific real estate disciplines in which the REALTOR engages. When a REALTOR is unable to render such service, either alone or with the aid of other REALTORS, the REALTOR should not accept the assignment or otherwise provide assistance in connection with the transaction.

Interpretation

17-1   Interpretation 14-4 also applies to Article 17.

ARTICLE 18

REALTORS shall ensure a true presentation in all advertising. Properties and services shall not be advertised without identifying the firm or, where applicable, the individual practitioner, in accordance with provincial licensing legislation.

Interpretations

18-1   The contents of a REALTOR's advertising, in any form, should accurately reflect the property or services being advertised. (Also applies to Article 25.)

18-2   A REALTOR should not advertise property in any form or in any medium in a manner that is contrary to the requirements of provincial legislation. (Also applies to Article 25.)

18-3   No REALTOR should advertise any property owned by himself or herself or by another person without identifying the REALTOR as a real estate practitioner, and such identification should be in the manner that may be required by the applicable regulatory legislation.

18-4   Interpretation 22-3 also applies to Article 18.

18-5   A REALTOR shall not use as search engine keywords for his/her Internet web sites, the trade names or trade marks of any firm, franchise, board or organization other than those with which the REALTOR is affiliated or otherwise authorized in writing to use.

ARTICLE 19

The REALTOR shall not deny professional services to any person for reasons of race, creed, colour, sex, familial status, age, or national origin. The REALTOR shall not be party to any plan or agreement to discriminate against a person or persons on the basis of race, creed, colour, sex, familial status, age or national origin.

ARTICLE 20

The REALTOR shall observe the By-Laws, Rules and Regulations established by the REALTOR's Real Estate Board and/or Association, in addition to the regulations, terms and conditions associated with any designation that the REALTOR may hold through membership in The Canadian Real Estate Association.

ARTICLE 21

The business of a REALTOR shall be conducted in strict accordance with all statutory and regulatory requirements that apply to that business.

Interpretation

21-1　The REALTOR should not be party to any discussion or agreement where the intent of such discussion or agreement is to circumvent any statutes or regulations affecting the real estate industry.

DUTIES TO THE REALTORS

ARTICLE 22

The REALTOR shall never publicly discredit a competitor. If the REALTOR's opinion is sought regarding a specific transaction, it should be rendered with strict professional integrity and courtesy.

Interpretations

22-1　The REALTOR should not comment in a derogatory manner as to the capacity, integrity, and competence of any other REALTOR.

22-2　Where any REALTOR is asked to comment on the business practices of another REALTOR, such comments should be given with strict professional integrity, objectivity and courtesy.

22-3　This Article does not apply to truthful advertising by REALTORS. Any advertising by a REALTOR which contains seemingly derogatory statements about competitors, their businesses or their business practices may form the basis of an ethics charge only if such statements are false or misleading within the meaning of the Competition Act, are otherwise prohibited by law, or relate to information that was restricted from use at the request of the vendor. (Also applies to Article 18.)

ARTICLE 23

The agency or other contractual relationship of a competitor shall be respected by all REALTORS. Negotiations concerning exclusively listed property or with any party who is exclusively represented shall be carried on with the client's agent and not with the client directly, except with the consent of the client's agent.

Interpretations

23-1　In the Province of Québec, in light of applicable laws, reference to "agent" and "agency" shall be read as if referring to "broker and/or agent" and "brokerage contract", respectively.

23-2　"Exclusively listed property" includes both property listed on MLS® and exclusive listings.

23-3　A REALTOR, whether acting as a buyer's agent or a sub-agent, shall not use the terms of an agreement of purchase and sale or a lease to modify the listing broker's offer of compensation to co-operating brokers, nor make the submission of an executed agreement of purchase and sale contingent on the listing broker's agreement to modify the offer of compensation.

ARTICLE 24

A REALTOR shall not seek information about a competitor's transaction to be used for the purpose of closing a transaction himself or herself, or for the purpose of interfering with any other contractual undertaking.

Interpretation

24-1   A REALTOR should not in any manner, by specific direction or suggestion, advise a party to a contract that the party should attempt to breach the contract.

ARTICLE 25

Signs in respect of the sale, rent, lease, development or exchange should not be placed on any property by other than the listing broker unless authorized by the seller/landlord. REALTORS shall not interfere with another real estate broker's sign.

Interpretation

25-1   It is not considered "interference" for a REALTOR to carefully remove another broker's sign from a property and advise where to pick up where the REALTOR has exclusive advertising right with respect to the sale or lease of that property and the other broker has failed or refused to remove his/her sign after being requested by the seller/lessor to do so.

ARTICLE 26

Should a REALTOR be asked to co-operate in any way in connection with a disciplinary investigation or proceeding pertaining to alleged unethical practice, the REALTOR shall place all pertinent facts before the proper Committee of the Real Estate Board or Association to which the REALTOR belongs.

Interpretations

26-1   A REALTOR who is being investigated for alleged unethical conduct should provide the appropriate Committee, upon request, with all materials and information in the REALTOR's possession in connection with the matter being investigated.

26-2   Where a REALTOR is asked to assist the appropriate Committee in connection with a disciplinary investigation or proceeding involving another REALTOR, the REALTOR should provide all relevant materials and information in that REALTOR's possession, and be prepared to testify at any hearing of the matter. Such assistance should not be deemed a "controversy" within the meaning and intent of Article 29.

26-3   Where a REALTOR is aware that another REALTOR is acting unethically or improperly in any manner, such REALTOR should advise the appropriate Committee of the alleged misconduct.

ARTICLE 27

In the event of a dispute between REALTORS associated with different firms of the same local Board/Association regarding the fee or commission earned or to be earned in connection with a real estate transaction, the dispute shall be submitted for arbitration in accordance with the By-Laws, Rules and Regulations of their local Board/Association.

Interpretations

27-1   A dispute between REALTORS which is properly submitted for arbitration pursuant to this Article should not be deemed a "controversy" within the meaning and intent of Article 29.

27-2   Where a REALTOR fails to submit a dispute to arbitration in accordance with the applicable By-Laws and Rules and Regulations, this Article may be pleaded as a defence in any other action or proceeding.

27-3   This Article does not require REALTORS to arbitrate when all parties to the dispute advise their Board/ Association in writing that they choose not to arbitrate before the Board/Association.

ARTICLE 28

In the event of a dispute between REALTORS associated with different firms and belonging to different local Boards/Associations, regarding the fee or commission earned or to be earned in connection with a real estate transaction, the dispute shall be submitted to arbitration in accordance with the By-Laws and Rules and Regulations of the appropriate Provincial/Territorial Association. Should the REALTORS belong to different Provincial/Territorial Associations, the dispute shall be arbitrated in accordance with the By-Laws and Rules and Regulations of The Canadian Real Estate Association.

Interpretations

28-1   A dispute between REALTORS which is properly submitted for arbitration pursuant to this Article should not be deemed a "controversy" within the meaning and intent of Article 29.

28-2   Where a REALTOR fails to submit a dispute to arbitration in accordance with the applicable By-Laws and Rules and Regulations, this Article may be pleaded as a defence in any other action or proceeding.

28-3   This Article does not require REALTORS to arbitrate when all parties to the dispute advise the appropriate Association in writing that they choose not to arbitrate before that Association.

ARTICLE 29

The business of a REALTOR shall be conducted so as to avoid controversies with other REALTORS.

Interpretations

29-1   Any REALTOR who is aware of or involved in a controversy with another REALTOR, resulting from the alleged misconduct or impropriety of that other REALTOR, should place such matters before the appropriate Committee for resolution in order that the matter may be resolved in accordance with the Rules and Regulations of the Board, Association, Society or Council to which the REALTOR belongs.

29-2   "Controversies", as used in Article 29, does not include aggressive or innovative business practices, which are otherwise ethical and disputes over commissions/fees or the division of commissions/fees.

29-3   REALTORS should not disrupt or obstruct a disciplinary investigation or proceeding relating to the alleged misconduct of another REALTOR.

29-4   REALTORS should not make any unauthorized disclosure or dissemination of allegations, findings or a decision in connection with a disciplinary investigation, hearing or appeal.

29-5   REALTORS should not intentionally impede a disciplinary investigation or proceeding by filing multiple complaints based on the same event or transaction.

CREA PRIVACY CODE

I. INTRODUCTION

In the usual course of real estate transactions, REALTORS and REALTOR organizations often require significant amounts of detailed information about identifiable individuals and companies. Most of this information is considered private under general community standards. The dissemination of information about an individual is not necessarily bad, indeed it is often vital in the conduct of business, but the indiscriminate dissemination of information, even if unintentional, may lead to the loss of privacy of an individual. Buyers and sellers therefore expect that the real estate organizations entrusted with this information will take positive steps to protect it.

In recognition of this fact, the members of The Canadian Real Estate Association must adhere closely to strict rules governing the protection of this information.

The Privacy Code, which applies to all member provincial/territorial associations, real estate boards, brokerage firms, brokers and salespersons, is made up of a set of principles which, if followed, sets in place a solid foundation within which the REALTOR community can protect its customers, clients, and the general public.

The Privacy Code sets a minimum standard. To give life to the principles in this Code, detailed procedures concerning the collection, storage, and distribution of personal information are required to be developed by all REALTOR organizations.

The Canadian Real Estate Association will review this Code at least every two years to ensure it is relevant and up-to-date.

II. SUMMARY OF PRINCIPLES

PRINCIPLE 1 – ACCOUNTABILITY

Members are responsible for the proper management of all personal information under their control, and shall designate one or more persons to be accountable for compliance.

PRINCIPLE 2 – IDENTIFYING THE PURPOSES OF PERSONAL INFORMATION

Members shall identify the purposes of collecting information before or at the time the information is collected.

PRINCIPLE 3 – OBTAINING CONSENT

The knowledge and consent of the consumer are required for the collection, use or disclosure of personal information except where inappropriate.

PRINCIPLE 4 – LIMITING COLLECTION OF PERSONAL INFORMATION

Members shall limit the collection of personal information to that which is necessary for the purposes identified.

PRINCIPLE 5 – LIMITING USE, DISCLOSURE AND RETENTION OF PERSONAL INFORMATION

Members shall use or disclose personal information only for the reason it was collected, except with the consent of the consumer or as required by law.

PRINCIPLE 6 – ACCURACY OF PERSONAL INFORMATION

Members shall keep personal information as accurate, complete, current and relevant as necessary for its identified purpose.

PRINCIPLE 7 – PROTECTING INFORMATION

Members shall protect personal information with safeguards appropriate to the sensitivity of the information.

PRINCIPLE 8 – OPENNESS CONCERNING POLICIES AND PRACTICES

Members shall make readily available to consumers specific information about their policies and practices relating to the management of personal information.

PRINCIPLE 9 – CONSUMER ACCESS TO PERSONAL INFORMATION

Upon request, members shall inform a consumer of the existence, use and disclosure of his or her personal information and shall give the individual access to that information.

PRINCIPLE 10 – CHALLENGING COMPLIANCE

A consumer shall be able to address a challenge concerning compliance with the above principles to the designated accountable person or persons in the member office.

III. DEFINITIONS

Collection	The act of gathering, acquiring, recording, or obtaining personal information from any source, including third parties, by any means.
Consent	Voluntary agreement with the collection, use and disclosure of personal information for defined purposes. Consent can be either express or implied and can be provided directly by the individual or by an authorized representative. Express consent can be given orally, electronically or in writing. Implied consent is consent that can reasonably be inferred from an individual's action or inaction.
Consumer	Any individual or company who consults with or retains in any way the services of a REALTOR, a brokerage or a real estate board or association. A consumer includes both customers and clients.
Disclosure	Making personal information available outside the member organization.
Member	Includes Provincial/Territorial associations, real estate boards, real estate brokerage forms, brokers and salespersons as the context requires.
Personal Information	Means information about an identifiable individual but does not include:

1. the name, title or business address or telephone number of an employee of an organization;
2. aggregated information that cannot be associated with a specific individual.

Reasonable	The standard of conduct which would be expected by a reasonable consumer of real estate services in all of the circumstances.
Third Party	An individual or organization other than the member itself.
Use	The management of personal information by and within the member organization.

IV. THE CREA PRIVACY CODE IN DETAIL

PRINCIPLE 1 – ACCOUNTABILITY

Members are responsible for the proper management of all personal information under their control, and shall designate one or more persons to be accountable for compliance.

1.1 The accountability for the protection of personal information rests with the individual REALTOR for information under his or her control. In the case of Boards/Associations, this refers to the Executive Officer. In the case of brokerages, it refers to the individual designated to be responsible for the brokerage under the provincial licensing legislation.

1.2 The accountable person may delegate the day-to-day procedures of compliance to one or more persons.

1.3 Because of the real cost to organizations of breaches of security and privacy, the designated individual should have an in-depth knowledge of the Privacy Code and should play a part in developing the procedures and ensuring staff conforms to the privacy policies.

1.4 The identity of the designated person will be made known upon request.

1.5 Members are responsible for personal information in their custody, including information transferred to third parties for processing. Each member should use contractual or other means to provide a comparable level of protection in those circumstances.

1.6 Every member shall implement policies and procedures to give effect to this Privacy Code including:
- establishing procedures to protect the privacy of personal information;
- training and communicating to staff about the organization's policies and procedures;
- establishing procedures to receive and respond to complaints;
- developing public information to explain the member's policies and practices

PRINCIPLE 2 – IDENTIFYING THE PURPOSES OF PERSONAL INFORMATION

Members shall identify the purposes of collecting information before or at the time the information is collected.

2.1 Personal information of sellers is used both by the listing brokerage for marketing purposes and the board for purposes relating to the operation of its MLS® system. Both organizations must ensure they have obtained the necessary consents from the consumer.

2.2 Listing agreements must set out all of the potential uses the information will be put to by the board including distributing it to members through the MLS® system, retaining the data indefinitely and publishing it for statistical analysis or otherwise, advertising in board publications, placing the information on the Internet and any other uses the board may make of the data.

2.3 Listing agreements must disclose all classes of potential recipients of information including any non-member individuals or organizations who are allowed some form of access to MLS® information.

2.4 REALTORS must advise buyers and sellers the use that will be made by their brokerage of the information collected. This disclosure must be documented in the listing or buyer agency agreement or in some other document.

2.5 The collection of personal information shall be limited to that which is necessary for the purpose identified in 2.2 and 2.4.

PRINCIPLE 3 – OBTAINING CONSENT

The knowledge and consent of the consumer are required for the collection, use or disclosure of personal information except where inappropriate.

3.1 Each member will make all reasonable efforts to ensure consumers understand how personal information will be used and disclosed by the organization.

3.2 Consent can be expressed orally (when information is collected over the telephone), in writing or electronically. The signing by a consumer of a representation agreement containing the disclosures set out under Principle 2 shall be considered written consent for those identified purposes.

3.3 Generally, the member will seek consent to use and disclose personal information at the time it collects it. However, that consent may be sought after the information has been collected, but before it is used or disclosed for a new purpose.

3.4 Express consent should be obtained whenever practical. However, consent may be implied for the collection, use and disclosure of personal information in accordance with the known expectations of a particular individual or in terms of what a reasonable person in similar circumstances would likely believe necessary, or where express consent is not practical and where the information would not, in the circumstances, be considered sensitive.

3.5 Consent may be given by a consumer, where appropriate, through an authorized representative such as a person with a power of attorney.

3.6 An individual may withdraw consent at any time subject to legal or contractual restrictions and reasonable notice. The organization shall inform the consumer of the implications of such withdrawal.

3.7 Members shall not refuse to represent a consumer for the reason only that the consumer has refused to provide consent for the collection or use of certain information unless that information is required to properly represent the consumer.

3.8 Consent to the collection, use or disclosure of personal information is not required in those circumstances set out in section 7 of the *Personal Information Protection and Electronic Documents Act*. Members may develop policies specifically dealing with these circumstances.

PRINCIPLE 4 – LIMITING COLLECTION OF PERSONAL INFORMATION

Members shall limit the collection of personal information to that which is necessary for the purposes identified.

4.1 Members shall collect from buyers and sellers only the amount and type of information needed for the purposes identified to them.

4.2 Members may also collect personal information from other sources including credit bureaus, public bodies, government agencies and other third parties who represent that they have the right to disclose the information.

4.3 All personal information shall be collected by fair and lawful means.

PRINCIPLE 5 – LIMITING USE, DISCLOSURE AND RETENTION OF PERSONAL INFORMATION

Members shall use or disclose personal information only for the reason it was collected, except with the consent of the consumer or as required by law.

5.1 Personal information will not be disclosed except as is necessary and reasonable to facilitate the real estate transaction unless the written consent of the individual for the extended disclosure is obtained or such disclosure is required by law.

5.2 Buyers and sellers must be informed that the member may be required, as a result of his/her agency obligations, to disclose personal information to other clients in the case of dual agency or where the individual providing the information is a customer and not a client.

5.3 Members shall keep personal information only as long as it remains necessary or relevant for the purposes identified or as required by law.

5.4 Members shall destroy any personal information no longer needed for its identified purposes or for legal requirements.

5.5 Information which has been aggregated so as to make it anonymous (e.g. housing statistics) is not considered personal information.

PRINCIPLE 6 – ACCURACY OF PERSONAL INFORMATION

Members shall keep personal information as accurate, complete, current and relevant as necessary for its identified purpose.

6.1 All reasonable efforts must be made to protect the integrity of the personal information by ensuring that it is relevant and as accurate and complete as possible to minimize the possibility that inappropriate or inaccurate information may be used to make a decision about the consumer.

6.2 Personal information will only be updated if it is necessary for the purposes for which it was collected or if revisions are requested by the consumer.

PRINCIPLE 7 – PROTECTING INFORMATION

Members shall protect personal information with safeguards appropriate to the sensitivity of the information.

7.1 Personal information is considered confidential and due diligence must be exercised to ensure it is not stolen, lost, accessed, copied, used or modified without permission.

7.2 Members shall ensure that all employees and other persons acting on their behalf who have access to such data are required to conform to privacy guidelines.

7.3 The steps taken by Boards/Associations and brokerages to protect personal information in its possession should include, where appropriate:

(a) physical measures, such as locked filing cabinets and restricted access to offices;

(b) technological measures, such as the use of computer passwords and encryption;

(c) organizational measures such as limiting access on a "need-to-know" basis and educating employees and salespersons on the privacy guidelines and procedures.

7.4 Members must establish and implement reasonable record retention and destruction policies consistent with the nature and need for the information and legislative requirements.

PRINCIPLE 8 – OPENNESS CONCERNING POLICIES AND PRACTICES

Members shall make readily available to consumers specific information about their policies and practices relating to the management of personal information.

8.1 Information regarding a member's policies and procedures must be easy to understand, readily available, and will allow consumers to determine:

• the title and office address of the person accountable for the member's compliance with the Privacy Code, and to whom inquiries or complaints can be forwarded;

- the means of gaining access to the personal information held by the member;
- what type of personal information is in the member's control and what it is used for.

8.2   The information described in 8.1 may be made available in a number of ways including brochures, mail information or on-line access.

PRINCIPLE 9 – CONSUMER ACCESS TO PERSONAL INFORMATION

Upon request, members shall inform a consumer of the existence, use and disclosure of his or her personal information and shall give the individual access to that information. The consumer shall be able to challenge the accuracy and completeness of the information and have it amended as appropriate.

9.1   Members shall, on request, inform consumers whether they hold personal information on them. Real estate boards, provincial/territorial associations and brokerages shall develop policies and procedures to allow consumers access to their personal information.

9.2   Policies regarding access to information by the public should be based on openness and ease of use. A sample procedure is as follows:

(a)   One individual in the organization is designated as the person responsible for responding to access requests;

(b)   On written request and appropriate identification satisfactory to the organization, an individual will be advised of personal information about him/her retained in the organization's records;

(c)   Where information cannot be disclosed (for example the information contains reference to other individuals or is subject to solicitor-client privilege) the individual will be given reasons for non-disclosure;

(d)   An individual may correct erroneous or incomplete information and the organization will amend that information;

The information will be supplied at minimal or no cost to the consumer.

PRINCIPLE 10 – CHALLENGING COMPLIANCE

A consumer shall be able to address a challenge concerning compliance with the above principles to the designated accountable person or persons in the member office.

10.1   An individual must be able to put forward a complaint that the principles of this Code have not been adhered to;

10.2   Individuals dissatisfied with the internal complaint resolution of an organization will be advised of the avenues available to direct their complaint, including the office of the Privacy Commissioner of Canada or, if applicable, the appropriate provincial privacy commissioner.

Measurement Guidelines (Residential)

Example 1   One-Storey

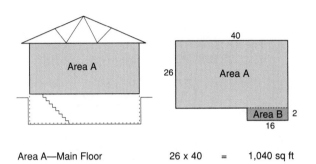

Area A—Main Floor	26 x 40	=	1,040 sq ft
Area B—Main Floor	2 x 16	=	32 sq ft
House area based on guidelines			1,072 sq ft

Measurement Method
Measure exterior dimensions.

Calculation
Length x Width of Exterior +/– Jogs

Exterior Dimensions
Show length and width of exterior dimensions and show length and width of jogs.

Example 2   One and One-Half Storey

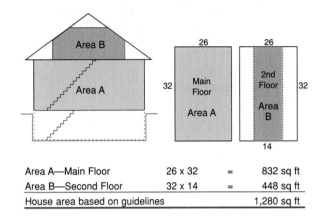

Area A—Main Floor	26 x 32	=	832 sq ft
Area B—Second Floor	32 x 14	=	448 sq ft
House area based on guidelines			1,280 sq ft

Measurement Method
Measure exterior dimensions. Except for ¹/₂ storey.

Calculation
Length x Width (see Areas A & B above)

Exterior Dimensions
Show length and width of exterior dimensions and show length and width of any jogs.

Note: The length of the 2nd floor area will usually be the same as the length of the main floor but the width between vertical interior walls of the 2nd floor can only be obtained by measurement.

Example 3   One and One-Half Storey
(With Dormers)

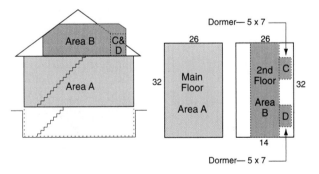

Area A—Main Floor	26 x 32	=	832 sq ft
Area B—Second Floor	32 x 14	=	448 sq ft
Area C&D—Second Floor	2 x (5 x 7)	=	70 sq ft
House area based on guidelines			1,350 sq ft

Measurement Method
Use exterior dimensions only. Except for ¹/₂ storey.

Calculation
Length x Width (see Areas A, B, C, & D above)

Exterior Dimensions
Show length and width of exterior dimensions and show length and width of jogs.

Example 4   Bi-Levels

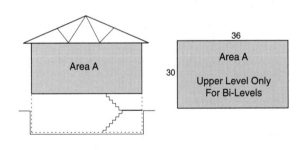

Area A—Upper Level	36 x 30	=	1,080 sq ft
House area based on guidelines			1,080 sq ft

Measurement Method
Use exterior dimensions only.

Calculation
Length x Width of Exterior +/ Jogs of One Level Only

Exterior Dimensions
Show length and width of exterior dimensions and show length and width of any jogs.

Example 5   Three Level Split

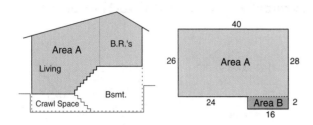

Area A—Main & Upper Floor	26 x 40	=	1,040 sq ft
Area B—Upper Overhang	2 x 16	=	32 sq ft
House area based on guidelines			1,072 sq ft

Measurement Method
Use exterior dimensions.

Calculation
Length x Width of Exterior +/– Jogs of One Level Only

Exterior Dimensions
Show length and width of exterior dimensions and show length and width of jogs.

Example 6   Four Level Split

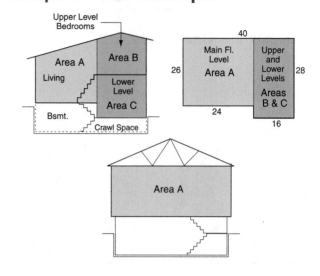

Area A—Main Floor	26 x 24	=	624 sq ft
Area B and Area C	2 x (16 x 28)	=	896 sq ft
House area based on guidelines			1,520 sq ft

Measurement Method
Use exterior dimensions.

Calculation
Length x Width of Exterior For Each Level Totally Above Grade +/- Jogs

Exterior Dimensions
Show length and width of exterior dimensions and show length and width of any jogs.

Example 7   Four Level Split With Built-In Garage

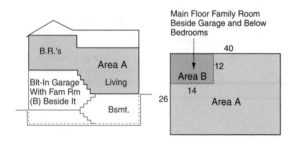

Area A—Main Floor & Bedrooms	26 x 40	=	1,040 sq ft
Area B—Family Room	12 x 14	=	168 sq ft
House area based on guidelines			1,208 sq ft

Measurement Method
Use exterior dimensions.

Calculation
Length x Width of Exterior For Each Level Totally Above Grade +/- Jogs – Garage

Exterior Dimensions
Show length and width of exterior dimensions and show length and width of jogs.

Example 8   Basic Two-Storey

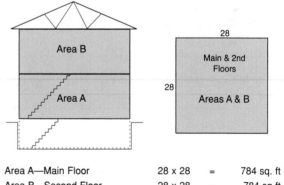

Area A—Main Floor	28 x 28	=	784 sq. ft
Area B—Second Floor	28 x 28	=	784 sq ft
House area based on guidelines			1,568 sq ft

Measurement Method
Use exterior dimensions.

Calculation
Length x Width of Exterior x 2 +/- Jogs

Exterior Dimensions
Show length and width of exterior dimensions and show length and width of jogs.

Example 9 Two-Storey With Built-In Garage

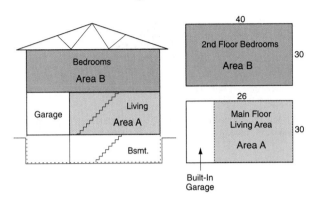

Area A—Main Floor Without Garage	26 x 30	=	780 sq ft
Area B—Bedrooms	30 x 40	=	1,200 sq ft
House area based on guidelines			1,980 sq ft

Measurement Method
Use exterior dimensions.

Calculation
Length x Width of Exterior x 2 +/– Jogs – Garage

Exterior Dimensions
Show length and width of exterior dimensions and show length and width of jogs.

Example 10 Two and One-Half Storey

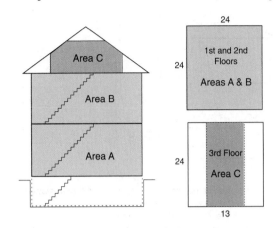

Area A & B—1st & 2nd Floor	2 x (24 x 24)	=	1,152 sq ft
Area C—Third Floor	13 x 24	=	312 sq ft
House area based on guidelines			1,464 sq ft

Measurement Method
Use exterior dimensions. Except for $^1/_2$ storey.

Calculation
Length x Width (see Areas A, B, & C above)

Exterior Dimensions
Show length and width of exterior dimensions and show length and width of any jogs.

Example 11 Two-Storey (Open Two-Storey Foyer/Other, From Main)

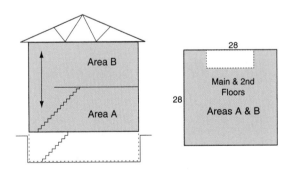

The standard to use when measuring a home with an area open the full two storeys, is to measure the exterior dimensions and double for the two storeys, *minus* the interior open area measurement.

Example 12 Two-Storey With Vault/Slope

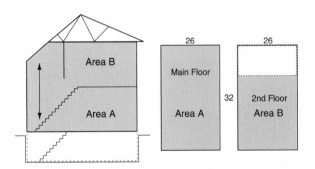

Where the two-storey walls are full height on one side the area should be measured as two floors. The area beneath the slope on the opposite side would be measured as one floor. The vaulted ceiling area should not cause a doubling of the area. Any lofts or catwalks should be measured separately and added to the living area.

APPENDIX

Example 13   Walkout Basement

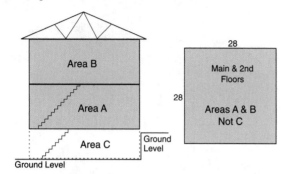

A walkout basement occurs when a home is built on a sloped area so that the main entry is at ground level at the front of the house and the level below that (basement) opens out on the opposite side of the house at the lower ground level. The square footage of this lower basement area is not included in the living area measurement for listing purposes.

Source: Alliance for Canadian Real Estate Education

Example 14   A Frame

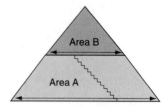

A frame construction with no knee walls should be measured from point to point on both main and second floors.

Caution

These residential measurement guidelines are provided for information purposes only by the Alliance for Canadian Real Estate Education. At the present time, no standard procedures have been approved throughout Canada. Practitioners should fully investigate local practices.

APPENDIX

Metric/Imperial Conversion Factors

Hectare/Acre Conversion

HECTARES TO ACRES
1 Hectare = 2.471 Acres

Hectares x 2.471 = # of Acres

Hectares	Acres	Hectares	Acres
1	2.471	60	148.260
2	4.942	61	150.731
3	7.413	62	153.202
4	9.884	63	155.673
5	12.355	64	158.144
6	14.826	65	160.615
7	17.297	66	163.086
8	19.768	67	165.557
9	22.239	68	168.028
10	24.710	69	170.499
11	27.181	70	172.970
12	29.652	71	175.441
13	32.123	72	177.912
14	34.594	73	180.383
15	37.065	74	182.854
16	39.536	75	185.325
17	42.007	76	187.796
18	44.478	77	190.267
19	46.949	78	192.738
20	49.420	79	195.209
21	51.891	80	197.680
22	54.362	81	200.151
23	56.833	82	202.622
24	59.304	83	205.093
25	61.775	84	207.564
26	64.246	85	210.035
27	66.717	86	212.506
28	69.188	87	214.977
29	71.659	88	217.448
30	74.130	89	219.919
31	76.601	90	222.390
32	79.072	91	224.861
33	81.543	92	227.332
34	84.014	93	229.803
35	86.485	94	232.274
36	88.956	95	234.745
37	91.427	96	237.216
38	93.898	97	239.687
39	96.369	98	242.158
40	98.840	99	244.629
41	101.311	100	247.100
42	103.782	200	494.200
43	106.253	300	741.300
44	108.724	400	988.400
45	111.195	500	1,235.500
46	113.666	600	1,482.600
47	116.137	700	1,729.700
48	118.608	800	1,976.800
49	121.079	900	2,223.900
50	123.550	1000	2,471.000
51	126.021	2000	4,942.000
52	128.492	3000	7,413.000
53	130.963	4000	9,884.000
54	133.434	5000	12,355.000
55	135.905	6000	14,826.000
56	138.376	7000	17,297.000
57	140.847	8000	19,768.000
58	143.318	9000	22,239.000
59	145.789	10000	24,710.000

ACRES TO HECTARES
1 Acre = 0.404686 Hectares

Acres x 0.404686 = # of Hectares

Acres	Hectares	Acres	Hectares
1	0.404686	60	24.281160
2	0.809372	61	24.685846
3	1.214058	62	25.090532
4	1.618744	63	25.495218
5	2.023430	64	25.899904
6	2.428116	65	26.304590
7	2.832802	66	26.709276
8	3.237488	67	27.113962
9	3.642174	68	27.518648
10	4.046860	69	27.923334
11	4.451546	70	28.328020
12	4.856232	71	28.732706
13	5.260918	72	29.137392
14	5.665604	73	29.542078
15	6.070290	74	29.946764
16	6.474976	75	30.351450
17	6.879662	76	30.756136
18	7.284348	77	31.160822
19	7.689034	78	31.565508
20	8.093720	79	31.970194
21	8.498406	80	32.374880
22	8.903092	81	32.779566
23	9.307778	82	33.184252
24	9.712464	83	33.588938
25	10.117150	84	33.993624
26	10.521836	85	34.398310
27	10.926522	86	34.802996
28	11.331208	87	35.207682
29	11.735894	88	35.612368
30	12.140580	89	36.017054
31	12.545266	90	36.421740
32	12.949952	91	36.826426
33	13.354638	92	37.231112
34	13.759324	93	37.635798
35	14.164010	94	38.040484
36	14.568696	95	38.445170
37	14.973382	96	38.849856
38	15.378068	97	39.254542
39	15.782754	98	39.659228
40	16.187440	99	40.063914
41	16.592126	100	40.468600
42	16.996812	200	80.937200
43	17.401498	300	121.405800
44	17.806184	400	161.874400
45	18.210870	500	202.343000
46	18.615556	600	242.811600
47	19.020242	700	283.280200
48	19.424928	800	323.748800
49	19.829614	900	364.217400
50	20.234300	1000	404.686000
51	20.638986	2000	809.372000
52	21.043672	3000	1,214.058000
53	21.448358	4000	1,618.744000
54	21.853044	5000	2,023.430000
55	22.257730	6000	2,428.116000
56	22.662416	7000	2,832.802000
57	23.067102	8000	3,237.488000
58	23.471788	9000	3,642.174000
59	23.876474	10000	4,046.860000

Metre/Foot Conversion

METRES TO FEET
1 Metre = 3.281 Feet

Metres x 3.281 = # of Feet

Metres	Feet	Metres	Feet
1	3.281	60	196.860
2	6.562	61	200.141
3	9.843	62	203.422
4	13.124	63	206.703
5	16.405	64	209.984
6	19.686	65	213.265
7	22.967	66	216.546
8	26.248	67	219.827
9	29.529	68	223.108
10	32.810	69	226.389
11	36.091	70	229.670
12	39.372	71	232.951
13	42.653	72	236.232
14	45.934	73	239.513
15	49.215	74	242.794
16	52.496	75	246.075
17	55.777	76	249.356
18	59.058	77	252.637
19	62.339	78	255.918
20	65.620	79	259.199
21	68.901	80	262.480
22	72.182	81	265.761
23	75.463	82	269.042
24	78.744	83	272.323
25	82.025	84	275.604
26	85.306	85	278.885
27	88.587	86	282.166
28	91.868	87	285.447
29	95.149	88	288.728
30	98.430	89	292.009
31	101.711	90	295.290
32	104.992	91	298.571
33	108.273	92	301.852
34	111.554	93	305.133
35	114.835	94	308.414
36	118.116	95	311.695
37	121.397	96	314.976
38	124.678	97	318.257
39	127.959	98	321.538
40	131.240	99	324.819
41	134.521	100	328.100
42	137.802	200	656.200
43	141.083	300	984.300
44	144.364	400	1,312.400
45	147.645	500	1,640.500
46	150.926	600	1,968.600
47	154.207	700	2,296.700
48	157.488	800	2,624.800
49	160.769	900	2,952.900
50	164.050	1000	3,281.000
51	167.331	2000	6,562.000
52	170.612	3000	9,843.000
53	173.893	4000	13,124.000
54	177.174	5000	16,405.000
55	180.455	6000	19,686.000
56	183.736	7000	22,967.000
57	187.017	8000	26,248.000
58	190.298	9000	29,529.000
59	193.579	10000	32,810.000

FEET TO METRES
1 Foot = 0.3048 Metres

Feet x 0.3048 = # of Metres

Feet	Metres	Feet	Metres
1	0.3048	60	18.2880
2	0.6096	61	18.5928
3	0.9144	62	18.8976
4	1.2192	63	19.2024
5	1.5240	64	19.5072
6	1.8288	65	19.8120
7	2.1336	66	20.1168
8	2.4384	67	20.4216
9	2.7432	68	20.7264
10	3.0480	69	21.0312
11	3.3528	70	21.3360
12	3.6576	71	21.6408
13	3.9624	72	21.9456
14	4.2672	73	22.2504
15	4.5720	74	22.5552
16	4.8768	75	22.8600
17	5.1816	76	23.1648
18	5.4864	77	23.4696
19	5.7912	78	23.7744
20	6.0960	79	24.0792
21	6.4008	80	24.3840
22	6.7056	81	24.6888
23	7.0104	82	24.9936
24	7.3152	83	25.2984
25	7.6200	84	25.6032
26	7.9248	85	25.9080
27	8.2296	86	26.2128
28	8.5344	87	26.5176
29	8.8392	88	26.8224
30	9.1440	89	27.1272
31	9.4488	90	27.4320
32	9.7536	91	27.7368
33	10.0584	92	28.0416
34	10.3632	93	28.3464
35	10.6680	94	28.6512
36	10.9728	95	28.9560
37	11.2776	96	29.2608
38	11.5824	97	29.5656
39	11.8872	98	29.8704
40	12.1920	99	30.1752
41	12.4968	100	30.4800
42	12.8016	200	60.9600
43	13.1064	300	91.4400
44	13.4112	400	121.9200
45	13.7160	500	152.4000
46	14.0208	600	182.8800
47	14.3256	700	213.3600
48	14.6304	800	243.8400
49	14.9352	900	274.3200
50	15.2400	1000	304.8000
51	15.5448	2000	609.6000
52	15.8496	3000	914.4000
53	16.1544	4000	1,219.2000
54	16.4592	5000	1,524.0000
55	16.7640	6000	1,828.8000
56	17.0688	7000	2,133.6000
57	17.3736	8000	2,438.4000
58	17.6784	9000	2,743.2000
59	17.9832	10000	3,048.0000

Square Metre/Square Foot Conversion

SQUARE METRES TO SQUARE FEET
1 Square Metre = 10.76 Square Feet

Square Metres x 10.76 = # of Square Feet

Sq. Metres	Sq. Feet	Sq. Metres	Sq. Feet
1	10.76	60	645.60
2	21.52	61	656.36
3	32.28	62	667.12
4	43.04	63	677.88
5	53.80	64	688.64
6	64.56	65	699.40
7	75.32	66	710.16
8	86.08	67	720.92
9	96.84	68	731.68
10	107.60	69	742.44
11	118.36	70	753.20
12	129.12	71	763.96
13	139.88	72	774.72
14	150.64	73	785.48
15	161.40	74	796.24
16	172.16	75	807.00
17	182.92	76	817.76
18	193.68	77	828.52
19	204.44	78	839.28
20	215.20	79	850.04
21	225.96	80	860.80
22	236.72	81	871.56
23	247.48	82	882.32
24	258.24	83	893.08
25	269.00	84	903.84
26	279.76	85	914.60
27	290.52	86	925.36
28	301.28	87	936.12
29	312.04	88	946.88
30	322.80	89	957.64
31	333.56	90	968.40
32	344.32	91	979.16
33	355.08	92	989.92
34	365.84	93	1,000.68
35	376.60	94	1,011.44
36	387.36	95	1,022.20
37	398.12	96	1,032.96
38	408.88	97	1,043.72
39	419.64	98	1,054.48
40	430.40	99	1,065.24
41	441.16	100	1,076.00
42	451.92	200	2,152.00
43	462.68	300	3,228.00
44	473.44	400	4,304.00
45	484.20	500	5,380.00
46	494.96	600	6,456.00
47	505.72	700	7,532.00
48	516.48	800	8,608.00
49	527.24	900	9,684.00
50	538.00	1000	10,760.00
51	548.76	2000	21,520.00
52	559.52	3000	32,280.00
53	570.28	4000	43,040.00
54	581.04	5000	53,800.00
55	591.80	6000	64,560.00
56	602.56	7000	75,320.00
57	613.32	8000	86,080.00
58	624.08	9000	96,840.00
59	634.84	10000	107,600.00

SQUARE FEET TO SQUARE METRES
1 Square Foot = 0.09290304 Square Metres

Square Feet x 0.09290304 = # of Square Metres

Sq. Feet	Sq. Metres	Sq. Feet	Sq. Metres
1	0.0929030	60	5.5741824
2	0.1858061	61	5.6670854
3	0.2787091	62	5.7599885
4	0.3716122	63	5.8528915
5	0.4645152	64	5.9457946
6	0.5574182	65	6.0386976
7	0.6503213	66	6.1316006
8	0.7432243	67	6.2245037
9	0.8361274	68	6.3174067
10	0.9290304	69	6.4103098
11	1.0219334	70	6.5032128
12	1.1148365	71	6.5961158
13	1.2077395	72	6.6890189
14	1.3006426	73	6.7819219
15	1.3935456	74	6.8748250
16	1.4864486	75	6.9677280
17	1.5793517	76	7.0606310
18	1.6722547	77	7.1535341
19	1.7651578	78	7.2464371
20	1.8580608	79	7.3393402
21	1.9509638	80	7.4322432
22	2.0438669	81	7.5251462
23	2.1367699	82	7.6180493
24	2.2296730	83	7.7109523
25	2.3225760	84	7.8038554
26	2.4154790	85	7.8967584
27	2.5083821	86	7.9896614
28	2.6012851	87	8.0825645
29	2.6941882	88	8.1754675
30	2.7870912	89	8.2683706
31	2.8799942	90	8.3612736
32	2.9728973	91	8.4541766
33	3.0658003	92	8.5470797
34	3.1587034	93	8.6399827
35	3.2516064	94	8.7328858
36	3.3445094	95	8.8257888
37	3.4374125	96	8.9186918
38	3.5303155	97	9.0115949
39	3.6232186	98	9.1044979
40	3.7161216	99	9.1974010
41	3.8090246	100	9.2903040
42	3.9019277	200	18.5806080
43	3.9948309	300	27.8709120
44	4.0877338	400	37.1612160
45	4.1806368	500	46.4515200
46	4.2735398	600	55.7418240
47	4.3664429	700	65.0321280
48	4.4593459	800	74.3224320
49	4.5522490	900	83.6127360
50	4.6451520	1000	92.9030400
51	4.7380550	2000	185.8060800
52	4.8309581	3000	278.7091200
53	4.9238611	4000	371.6121600
54	5.0167642	5000	464.5152000
55	5.1096672	6000	557.4182400
56	5.2025702	7000	650.3212800
57	5.2954733	8000	743.2243200
58	5.3883763	9000	836.1273600
59	5.4812794	10000	929.0304000

General Measurements

DISTANCE	IMPERIAL		METRIC
	1 inch	=	2.540 centimetres
	1 foot	=	0.3048 metres
	1 yard	=	0.9144 metres
	1 rod	=	5.029 metres
	1 mile	=	1.609 kilometres

	METRIC		IMPERIAL
	1 centimetre	=	0.3937 inches
	1 metre	=	3.281 feet
		=	1.094 yards
	1 kilometre	=	0.6214 miles

OTHER

1 link = 7.9 inches = 20.1 centimetres
1 chain= 100 links = 66 feet = 4 rods = 20.1 metres
1 rod = 1 perch = 1 pole = 16.5 feet = 5.0 metres
1 mile = 80 chains = 320 rods = 5,280 feet
       = 1,760 yards = 1.6 kilometres

AREA	IMPERIAL		METRIC
	1 sq. inch	=	6.452 sq. centimetres
	1 sq. foot	=	0.093 sq. metres
	1 sq. yard	=	0.836 sq. metres
	1 acre	=	0.405 hectares
	1 sq. mile	=	2.590 sq. kilometres

	METRIC		IMPERIAL
	1 sq. centimetre	=	0.155 sq. inches
	1 sq. metre	=	10.76 sq. feet
	1 sq. metre	=	1.196 sq. yards
	1 hectare	=	2.471 acres
	1 sq. kilometre	=	0.386 sq. miles
	1 hectare	=	1 sq. hectometre

OTHER

1 acre = 43,560 sq. feet = 10 sq. chains = .4 hectares
1 sq. foot = 0.000023 acres
1 sq. mile = 640 acres = 258.1 hectares

MATHEMATICAL EQUATIONS

l = length   *w = width*   *h = height*
b = base   *p = perpendicular height*

Area of a rectangle or square = l x w

Area of a parallelogram = b x p

(A 4-sided figure with all opposite sides parallel)

Area of a triangle = 1/2 (b x h)

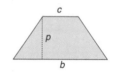

Area of a trapezoid
  = Sum of the 2 parallel sides (b + c) x 1/2 p

(A 4-sided figure with two parallel sides)

Volume (Measuring Cubic Content) = area x h

NOTE In calculating the height it is common practice to include 6 inches for the basement floor.
For houses with gable roofs, include ½ the height of the roof.

1 cubic foot = 12″ × 12″ × 12″
1 cubic yard = 3′ × 3′ × 3′
Cubic ft. to cubic yds., ÷ by 27
   ″   yards   ″   feet , × by 27

$$MPF \times \frac{Mortgage}{1000} = Monthly\ Payment$$

Mortgage Payment Factors (per $1,000 of Loan Amount)

Weekly Payment Factors

Int. Rate	5	10	15	20	25
1.00	3.943244	2.020779	1.380489	1.060742	.869211
1.25	3.967692	2.045628	1.405768	1.086459	.895367
1.50	3.992209	2.070645	1.431313	1.112538	.921982
1.75	4.016796	2.095828	1.457122	1.138977	.949052
2.00	4.041452	2.121178	1.483194	1.165774	.976572
2.25	4.066177	2.146693	1.509426	1.192925	1.004538
2.50	4.090971	2.172373	1.536117	1.220428	1.032945
2.75	4.115832	2.198216	1.562966	1.248279	1.061789
3.00	4.140761	2.224222	1.590070	1.276476	1.091063
3.25	4.165758	2.250390	1.617428	1.305015	1.120762
3.50	4.190821	2.276719	1.645038	1.333891	1.150881
3.75	4.215952	2.303208	1.672897	1.363103	1.181413
4.00	4.241149	2.329856	1.701005	1.392645	1.212352
4.25	4.266412	2.356662	1.729358	1.422515	1.243691
4.50	4.291742	2.383625	1.757955	1.452707	1.275424
4.75	4.317136	2.410745	1.786793	1.483218	1.307543
5.00	4.342596	2.438019	1.815869	1.514043	1.340042
5.25	4.368121	2.465448	1.845183	1.545178	1.372912
5.50	4.393711	2.493030	1.874731	1.576619	1.406147
5.75	4.419364	2.520764	1.904511	1.608361	1.439739
6.00	4.445082	2.548648	1.934520	1.640399	1.473680
6.25	4.470863	2.576683	1.964756	1.672729	1.507963
6.50	4.496708	2.604866	1.995217	1.705345	1.542580
6.75	4.522615	2.633197	2.025900	1.738244	1.577522
7.00	4.548585	2.661674	2.056801	1.771419	1.612781
7.25	4.574617	2.690297	2.087920	1.804867	1.648351
7.50	4.600712	2.719064	2.119252	1.838581	1.684222
7.75	4.626867	2.747974	2.150796	1.872558	1.720386
8.00	4.653084	2.777025	2.182547	1.906791	1.756836
8.25	4.679362	2.806218	2.214505	1.941276	1.793564
8.50	4.705701	2.835550	2.246666	1.976008	1.830560
8.75	4.732100	2.865020	2.279026	2.010981	1.867818
9.00	4.758559	2.894628	2.311584	2.046190	1.905329
9.25	4.785077	2.924371	2.344336	2.081630	1.943086
9.50	4.811654	2.954249	2.377280	2.117296	1.981080
9.75	4.838291	2.984260	2.410413	2.153183	2.019304
10.00	4.864986	3.014404	2.443731	2.189285	2.057750
10.25	4.891739	3.044678	2.477232	2.225598	2.096411
10.50	4.918550	3.075082	2.510913	2.262115	2.135278
10.75	4.945419	3.105614	2.544771	2.298833	2.174345
11.00	4.972345	3.136274	2.578803	2.335746	2.213604
11.25	4.999327	3.167059	2.613007	2.372849	2.253048
11.50	5.026366	3.197969	2.647379	2.410136	2.292670
11.75	5.053461	3.229002	2.681916	2.447604	2.332463
12.00	5.080613	3.260158	2.716615	2.485246	2.372420
12.25	5.107819	3.291433	2.751474	2.523058	2.412534
12.50	5.135081	3.322829	2.786490	2.561036	2.452800
12.75	5.162397	3.354342	2.821659	2.599174	2.493209

Int. Rate	5	10	15	20	25
13.00	5.189768	3.385972	2.856979	2.637467	2.533757
13.25	5.217193	3.417718	2.892446	2.675911	2.574437
13.50	5.244671	3.449578	2.928059	2.714501	2.615243
13.75	5.272203	3.481550	2.963814	2.753233	2.656169
14.00	5.299788	3.513634	2.999707	2.792102	2.697209
14.25	5.327426	3.545829	3.035738	2.831104	2.738358
14.50	5.355116	3.578132	3.071901	2.870233	2.779610
14.75	5.382858	3.610543	3.108195	2.909487	2.820960
15.00	5.410651	3.643060	3.144617	2.948860	2.862404
15.25	5.438496	3.675683	3.181165	2.988348	2.903935
15.50	5.466392	3.708408	3.217834	3.027948	2.945549
15.75	5.494338	3.741237	3.254623	3.067655	2.987241
16.00	5.522335	3.774166	3.291529	3.107465	3.029007
16.25	5.550381	3.807195	3.328548	3.147374	3.070843
16.50	5.578477	3.840322	3.365680	3.187379	3.112743
16.75	5.606623	3.873546	3.402919	3.227475	3.154704
17.00	5.634817	3.906867	3.440265	3.267659	3.196722
17.25	5.663059	3.940281	3.477715	3.307927	3.238793
17.50	5.691350	3.973789	3.515265	3.348277	3.280912
17.75	5.719689	4.007389	3.552914	3.388703	3.323077
18.00	5.748075	4.041079	3.590658	3.429203	3.365284
18.25	5.776508	4.074859	3.628495	3.469774	3.407529
18.50	5.804988	4.108726	3.666424	3.510412	3.449809
18.75	5.833514	4.142681	3.704440	3.551115	3.492122
19.00	5.862087	4.176721	3.742543	3.591878	3.534462
19.25	5.890705	4.210845	3.780729	3.632699	3.576829
19.50	5.919368	4.245051	3.818996	3.673575	3.619219
19.75	5.948077	4.279340	3.857342	3.714503	3.661629
20.00	5.976830	4.313709	3.895764	3.755480	3.704057
20.25	6.005628	4.348157	3.934260	3.796504	3.746499
20.50	6.034469	4.382682	3.972829	3.837572	3.788954
20.75	6.063354	4.417285	4.011467	3.878681	3.831420
21.00	6.092283	4.451962	4.050172	3.919828	3.873893
21.25	6.121254	4.486714	4.088943	3.961011	3.916372
21.50	6.150269	4.521539	4.127777	4.002229	3.958855
21.75	6.179325	4.556436	4.166672	4.043477	4.001339
22.00	6.208423	4.591403	4.205627	4.084755	4.043823
22.25	6.237563	4.626439	4.244638	4.126059	4.086305
22.50	6.266745	4.661543	4.283704	4.167388	4.128783
22.75	6.295967	4.696714	4.322823	4.208739	4.171255
23.00	6.325229	4.731951	4.361994	4.250111	4.213720
23.25	6.354532	4.767253	4.401213	4.291502	4.256176
23.50	6.383875	4.802617	4.440480	4.332908	4.298622
23.75	6.413258	4.838044	4.479793	4.374330	4.341056
24.00	6.442679	4.873532	4.519149	4.415764	4.383477
24.25	6.472140	4.909080	4.558547	4.457210	4.425883
24.50	6.501639	4.944687	4.597985	4.498664	4.468273
24.75	6.531176	4.980351	4.637461	4.540127	4.510647

Bi-Weekly Payment Factors

Int. Rate	\multicolumn{5}{Amortization Period}
	5	10	15	20	25
1.00	7.887244	4.041946	2.761243	2.121687	1.738588
1.25	7.936334	4.091746	2.811874	2.173178	1.790949
1.50	7.985566	4.141884	2.863038	2.225396	1.844230
1.75	8.034939	4.192359	2.914733	2.278337	1.898422
2.00	8.084452	4.243168	2.966955	2.331994	1.953518
2.25	8.134105	4.294310	3.019701	2.386364	2.009508
2.50	8.183896	4.345783	3.072968	2.441440	2.066384
2.75	8.233826	4.397587	3.126752	2.497215	2.124135
3.00	8.283894	4.449718	3.181051	2.553683	2.182751
3.25	8.334099	4.502175	3.235859	2.610839	2.242220
3.50	8.384440	4.554957	3.291174	2.668673	2.302531
3.75	8.434917	4.608062	3.346991	2.727180	2.363671
4.00	8.485530	4.661487	3.403306	2.786352	2.425628
4.25	8.536276	4.715231	3.460115	2.846180	2.488389
4.50	8.587157	4.769291	3.517414	2.906657	2.551940
4.75	8.638172	4.823667	3.575199	2.967775	2.616267
5.00	8.689319	4.878355	3.633464	3.029524	2.681357
5.25	8.740598	4.933354	3.692206	3.091897	2.747193
5.50	8.792008	4.988662	3.751419	3.154884	2.813762
5.75	8.843549	5.044277	3.811099	3.218476	2.881049
6.00	8.895220	5.100196	3.871241	3.282664	2.949037
6.25	8.947021	5.156417	3.931840	3.347438	3.017712
6.50	8.998950	5.212938	3.992890	3.412790	3.087058
6.75	9.051007	5.269757	4.054387	3.478708	3.157059
7.00	9.103192	5.326872	4.116326	3.545184	3.227698
7.25	9.155504	5.384281	4.178701	3.612207	3.298961
7.50	9.207942	5.441980	4.241507	3.679768	3.370830
7.75	9.260505	5.499968	4.304738	3.747856	3.443290
8.00	9.313193	5.558243	4.368390	3.816461	3.516325
8.25	9.366005	5.616802	4.432456	3.885572	3.589918
8.50	9.418941	5.675643	4.496930	3.955181	3.664053
8.75	9.472000	5.734763	4.561809	4.025276	3.738715
9.00	9.525180	5.794160	4.627085	4.095847	3.813887
9.25	9.578482	5.853832	4.692753	4.166883	3.889554
9.50	9.631905	5.913775	4.758807	4.238375	3.965699
9.75	9.685448	5.973989	4.825242	4.310311	4.042308
10.00	9.739110	6.034469	4.892052	4.382682	4.119365
10.25	9.792891	6.095214	4.959230	4.455478	4.196855
10.50	9.846790	6.156222	5.026772	4.528687	4.274762
10.75	9.900806	6.217489	5.094672	4.602300	4.353072
11.00	9.954939	6.279013	5.162923	4.676307	4.431771
11.25	10.009188	6.340792	5.231520	4.750697	4.510843
11.50	10.063552	6.402822	5.300456	4.825461	4.590275
11.75	10.118031	6.465103	5.369727	4.900588	4.670053
12.00	10.172624	6.527630	5.439326	4.976068	4.750162
12.25	10.227330	6.590401	5.509247	5.051892	4.830591
12.50	10.282149	6.653414	5.579484	5.128050	4.911325
12.75	10.337079	6.716667	5.650033	5.204533	4.992352

Int. Rate	\multicolumn{5}{Amortization Period}
	5	10	15	20	25
13.00	10.392121	6.780155	5.720886	5.281330	5.073659
13.25	10.447273	6.843878	5.792038	5.358432	5.155233
13.50	10.502535	6.907832	5.863483	5.435831	5.237064
13.75	10.557906	6.972015	5.935216	5.513516	5.319138
14.00	10.613385	7.036424	6.007231	5.591480	5.401445
14.25	10.668972	7.101057	6.079522	5.669712	5.483974
14.50	10.724667	7.165910	6.152083	5.748204	5.566713
14.75	10.780467	7.230981	6.224909	5.826947	5.649652
15.00	10.836373	7.296268	6.297994	5.905934	5.732780
15.25	10.892384	7.361768	6.371333	5.985155	5.816088
15.50	10.948500	7.427479	6.444919	6.064601	5.899566
15.75	11.004718	7.493397	6.518749	6.144266	5.983205
16.00	11.061040	7.559520	6.592815	6.224141	6.066994
16.25	11.117464	7.625845	6.667113	6.304219	6.150926
16.50	11.173989	7.692371	6.741637	6.384490	6.234992
16.75	11.230615	7.759094	6.816382	6.464949	6.319182
17.00	11.287342	7.826011	6.891342	6.545587	6.403490
17.25	11.344167	7.893121	6.966513	6.626397	6.487908
17.50	11.401092	7.960419	7.041889	6.707373	6.572427
17.75	11.458114	8.027905	7.117466	6.788507	6.657040
18.00	11.515233	8.095575	7.193237	6.869792	6.741741
18.25	11.572450	8.163427	7.269188	6.951222	6.826522
18.50	11.629762	8.231457	7.345344	7.032790	6.911377
18.75	11.687169	8.299665	7.421671	7.114490	6.996300
19.00	11.744671	8.368046	7.498172	7.196315	7.081284
19.25	11.802267	8.436598	7.574844	7.278260	7.166323
19.50	11.859956	8.505320	7.651682	7.360318	7.251412
19.75	11.917736	8.574208	7.728680	7.442885	7.336545
20.00	11.975610	8.643259	7.805835	7.524753	7.421716
20.25	12.033574	8.712472	7.883142	7.607118	7.506922
20.50	12.091629	8.781844	7.960596	7.689573	7.592156
20.75	12.149773	8.851372	8.038193	7.772115	7.677414
21.00	12.208066	8.921054	8.115928	7.854738	7.762691
21.25	12.266328	8.990888	8.193797	7.937436	7.847984
21.50	12.324738	9.060870	8.271797	8.020205	7.933287
21.75	12.383234	9.130999	8.349921	8.103041	8.018597
22.00	12.441816	9.201271	8.428168	8.185938	8.103910
22.25	12.500485	9.271686	8.506532	8.268892	8.189222
22.50	12.559238	9.342240	8.585009	8.351899	8.274530
22.75	12.618075	9.412930	8.663596	8.434954	8.359830
23.00	12.676996	9.483755	8.742288	8.518054	8.445119
23.25	12.736000	9.554713	8.821083	8.601194	8.530393
23.50	12.795086	9.625800	8.899975	8.684370	8.615651
23.75	12.854254	9.697014	8.978961	8.767580	8.700888
24.00	12.913502	9.768354	9.058039	8.850818	8.786102
24.25	12.972831	9.839816	9.137203	8.934082	8.871290
24.50	13.032239	9.911399	9.216451	9.017368	8.956450
24.75	13.091726	9.983100	9.295779	9.100672	9.041580

Semi-Monthly Payment Factors

Int. Rate	5	10	15	20	25
1.00	8.544651	4.378845	2.991394	2.298530	1.883501
1.25	8.597867	4.432814	3.046258	2.354323	1.940234
1.50	8.651237	4.487149	3.101699	2.410903	1.997963
1.75	8.704760	4.541849	3.157715	2.468267	2.056681
2.00	8.758436	4.596912	3.214304	2.526408	2.116378
2.25	8.812263	4.652336	3.271460	2.585320	2.177045
2.50	8.866241	4.708119	3.329181	2.644998	2.238672
2.75	8.920369	4.764261	3.387463	2.705434	2.301247
3.00	8.974647	4.820758	3.446303	2.766622	2.364760
3.25	9.029073	4.877609	3.505695	2.828555	2.429197
3.50	9.083648	4.934811	3.565636	2.891224	2.494547
3.75	9.138371	4.992364	3.626123	2.954621	2.560796
4.00	9.193241	5.050265	3.687149	3.018739	2.627931
4.25	9.248256	5.108511	3.748711	3.083570	2.695937
4.50	9.303418	5.167101	3.810804	3.149104	2.764799
4.75	9.358724	5.226032	3.873424	3.215332	2.834503
5.00	9.414174	5.285303	3.936565	3.282245	2.905033
5.25	9.469767	5.344911	4.000222	3.349834	2.976373
5.50	9.525504	5.404854	4.064391	3.418088	3.048508
5.75	9.581382	5.465130	4.129066	3.486999	3.121420
6.00	9.637402	5.526736	4.194242	3.557556	3.195033
6.25	9.693562	5.586669	4.259913	3.626749	3.269511
6.50	9.749862	5.647929	4.326075	3.697568	3.344656
6.75	9.806302	5.709512	4.392721	3.769002	3.420511
7.00	9.862880	5.771415	4.459845	3.841040	3.497059
7.25	9.919595	5.833637	4.527443	3.913671	3.574282
7.50	9.976448	5.896175	4.595508	3.986886	3.652164
7.75	10.033437	5.959026	4.664035	4.060672	3.730686
8.00	10.090562	6.022188	4.733017	4.135019	3.809831
8.25	10.147821	6.085658	4.802449	4.209916	3.889582
8.50	10.205215	6.149343	4.872325	4.285351	3.969921
8.75	10.262742	6.213513	4.942638	4.361314	4.050831
9.00	10.320402	6.277893	5.013383	4.437793	4.132294
9.25	10.378194	6.342571	5.084553	4.514778	4.214294
9.50	10.436117	6.407544	5.156142	4.592256	4.296814
9.75	10.494170	6.472809	5.228143	4.670217	4.379836
10.00	10.552353	6.538365	5.300552	4.748649	4.463344
10.25	10.610666	6.604207	5.373361	4.827541	4.547322
10.50	10.669106	6.670335	5.446564	4.906883	4.631752
10.75	10.727674	6.736744	5.520155	4.986663	4.716620
11.00	10.786369	6.803432	5.594127	5.066869	4.801910
11.25	10.845190	6.870397	5.668474	5.147492	4.887604
11.50	10.904137	6.937635	5.743191	5.228520	4.973690
11.75	10.963208	7.005144	5.818269	5.309942	5.060150
12.00	11.022403	7.072921	5.893704	5.391748	5.146971
12.25	11.081721	7.140963	5.969489	5.473927	5.234138
12.50	11.141161	7.209267	6.045617	5.556468	5.321637
12.75	11.200723	7.277831	6.122082	5.639362	5.409453

Int. Rate	5	10	15	20	25
13.00	11.260405	7.346652	6.198878	5.722597	5.497574
13.25	11.320208	7.415727	6.275999	5.806163	5.585986
13.50	11.380130	7.485053	6.353438	5.890051	5.674675
13.75	11.440171	7.554628	6.431189	5.974250	5.763629
14.00	11.500330	7.624448	6.509246	6.058751	5.852836
14.25	11.560606	7.694510	6.587603	6.143544	5.942284
14.50	11.620998	7.764812	6.666253	6.228619	6.031960
14.75	11.681506	7.835351	6.745191	6.313968	6.121853
15.00	11.742128	7.906125	6.824410	6.399580	6.211953
15.25	11.802865	7.977129	6.903905	6.485446	6.302248
15.50	11.863715	8.048362	6.983668	6.571559	6.392728
15.75	11.924678	8.119821	7.063695	6.657908	6.483382
16.00	11.985753	8.191502	7.143980	6.744485	6.574200
16.25	12.046938	8.263403	7.224516	6.831282	6.665174
16.50	12.108235	8.335522	7.305297	6.918291	6.756292
16.75	12.169640	8.407854	7.386319	7.005502	6.847548
17.00	12.231155	8.480398	7.467575	7.092909	6.938931
17.25	12.292777	8.553151	7.549060	7.180503	7.030433
17.50	12.354507	8.626109	7.630767	7.268277	7.122046
17.75	12.416344	8.699270	7.712692	7.356222	7.213761
18.00	12.478286	8.772632	7.794828	7.444333	7.305573
18.25	12.540334	8.846191	7.877171	7.532601	7.397472
18.50	12.602486	8.919944	7.959716	7.621019	7.489451
18.75	12.664741	8.993889	8.042455	7.709580	7.581505
19.00	12.727099	9.068023	8.125386	7.798279	7.673625
19.25	12.789560	9.142344	8.208501	7.887107	7.765806
19.50	12.852122	9.216848	8.291797	7.976059	7.858042
19.75	12.914784	9.291533	8.375268	8.065129	7.950326
20.00	12.977546	9.366395	8.458908	8.154309	8.042652
20.25	13.040408	9.441434	8.542714	8.243595	8.135016
20.50	13.103367	9.516644	8.626680	8.332980	8.227411
20.75	13.166425	9.592025	8.710801	8.422459	8.319833
21.00	13.229579	9.667573	8.795073	8.512026	8.412277
21.25	13.292829	9.743285	8.879491	8.601676	8.504738
21.50	13.356175	9.819160	8.964050	8.691403	8.597211
21.75	13.419616	9.895193	9.048746	8.781203	8.689692
22.00	13.483150	9.971383	9.133574	8.871070	8.782177
22.25	13.546777	10.047728	9.218530	8.960999	8.874662
22.50	13.610497	10.124223	9.303610	9.050987	8.967142
22.75	13.674309	10.200868	9.388808	9.141027	9.059615
23.00	13.738212	10.277659	9.474122	9.231116	9.152076
23.25	13.802205	10.354593	9.559547	9.321250	9.244522
23.50	13.866287	10.431669	9.645078	9.411423	9.336950
23.75	13.930458	10.508883	9.730712	9.501633	9.429357
24.00	13.994717	10.586234	9.816446	9.591875	9.521740
24.25	14.059064	10.663718	9.902273	9.682145	9.614095
24.50	14.123497	10.741333	9.988193	9.772439	9.706421
24.75	14.188016	10.819077	10.074199	9.862755	9.798714

Monthly Payment Factors

Int.	Amortization Period				
Rate	5	10	15	20	25
1.00	17.092853	8.759511	5.984032	4.598017	3.767784
1.25	17.200199	8.867930	6.094097	4.709868	3.881475
1.50	17.307863	8.977093	6.205330	4.823308	3.997171
1.75	17.415843	9.086996	6.317724	4.938326	4.114856
2.00	17.524137	9.197636	6.431274	5.054912	4.234512
2.25	17.632745	9.309011	6.545972	5.173052	4.356121
2.50	17.741664	9.421115	6.661811	5.292736	4.479662
2.75	17.850895	9.533946	6.778784	5.413950	4.605115
3.00	17.960435	9.647500	6.896884	5.536680	4.732455
3.25	18.070284	9.761774	7.016102	5.660911	4.861660
3.50	18.180439	9.876762	7.136432	5.786630	4.992703
3.75	18.290900	9.992462	7.257863	5.913820	5.125560
4.00	18.401665	10.108870	7.380387	6.042465	5.260202
4.25	18.512732	10.225981	7.503996	6.172548	5.396602
4.50	18.624102	10.343792	7.628681	6.304052	5.534730
4.75	18.735771	10.462297	7.754431	6.436959	5.674556
5.00	18.847739	10.581483	7.881238	6.571250	5.816050
5.25	18.960005	10.701376	8.009091	6.706908	5.959180
5.50	19.072566	10.821941	8.137981	6.843913	6.103915
5.75	19.185423	10.943184	8.267897	6.982245	6.250221
6.00	19.298572	11.065099	8.398828	7.121884	6.398066
6.25	19.412013	11.187683	8.530764	7.262811	6.547416
6.50	19.525745	11.310931	8.663695	7.405004	6.698238
6.75	19.639766	11.434838	8.797609	7.548443	6.850496
7.00	19.754075	11.559399	8.932494	7.693106	7.004158
7.25	19.868670	11.684610	9.068341	7.838973	7.159187
7.50	19.983549	11.810465	9.205137	7.986021	7.315549
7.75	20.098712	11.936960	9.342870	8.134229	7.473210
8.00	20.214157	12.064090	9.481529	8.283575	7.632135
8.25	20.329883	12.191850	9.621103	8.434037	7.792288
8.50	20.445888	12.320234	9.761579	8.585592	7.953635
8.75	20.562170	12.449238	9.902945	8.738219	8.116142
9.00	20.678729	12.578856	10.045189	8.891895	8.279774
9.25	20.795563	12.709083	10.188298	9.046598	8.444497
9.50	20.912670	12.839914	10.332261	9.202305	8.610276
9.75	21.030049	12.971344	10.477066	9.358995	8.777079
10.00	21.147698	13.103367	10.622699	9.516644	8.944872
10.25	21.262617	13.235979	10.769149	9.675231	9.113622
10.50	21.383803	13.369173	10.916402	9.834734	9.283297
10.75	21.502255	13.502944	11.064446	9.995129	9.453864
11.00	21.620972	13.637287	11.213269	10.156396	9.625292
11.25	21.739952	13.772197	11.362858	10.318512	9.797549
11.50	21.859194	13.907667	11.513201	10.481456	9.970606
11.75	21.978696	14.043693	11.664285	10.645206	10.144431
12.00	22.098457	14.180269	11.816096	10.809741	10.318996
12.25	22.218476	14.317389	11.968624	10.975039	10.494270
12.50	22.338750	14.455048	12.121854	11.141079	10.670227
12.75	22.459278	14.593241	12.275775	11.307841	10.846838

Int.	Amortization Period				
Rate	5	10	15	20	25
13.00	22.580060	14.731961	12.430373	11.475304	11.024075
13.25	22.701092	14.871203	12.585637	11.643447	11.201912
13.50	22.822375	15.010961	12.741554	11.812250	11.380323
13.75	22.943906	15.151230	12.898111	11.981694	11.559282
14.00	23.065685	15.292005	13.055297	12.151759	11.738765
14.25	23.187708	15.433279	13.213098	12.322426	11.918747
14.50	23.309976	15.575047	13.371503	12.493674	12.099205
14.75	23.432486	15.717303	13.530498	12.665487	12.280116
15.00	23.555237	15.860041	13.690073	12.837844	12.461457
15.25	23.678228	16.003257	13.850215	13.010728	12.643207
15.50	23.801457	16.146944	14.010912	13.184121	12.825344
15.75	23.924922	16.291096	14.171253	13.358006	13.007848
16.00	24.048622	16.435709	14.333924	13.532364	13.190699
16.25	24.172556	16.580776	14.496215	13.707180	13.373878
16.50	24.296722	16.726291	14.659014	13.882435	13.557365
16.75	24.421119	16.872250	14.822310	14.058115	13.741144
17.00	24.545744	17.018645	14.986090	14.234202	13.925195
17.25	24.670597	17.165473	15.150344	14.410682	14.109502
17.50	24.795677	17.312727	15.315061	14.587538	14.294049
17.75	24.920981	17.460401	15.480229	14.764755	14.478820
18.00	25.046508	17.608491	15.645837	14.942319	14.663799
18.25	25.172256	17.756990	15.811874	15.120216	14.848971
18.50	25.298225	17.905892	15.978330	15.298430	15.034322
18.75	25.424413	18.055193	16.145194	15.476949	15.219837
19.00	25.550817	18.204887	16.312456	15.655759	15.405505
19.25	25.677437	18.354968	16.480104	15.834845	15.591311
19.50	25.804272	18.505431	16.648129	16.014197	15.777243
19.75	25.931319	18.656270	16.816521	16.193800	15.963289
20.00	26.058577	18.807480	16.985269	16.373642	16.149438
20.25	26.186046	18.959055	17.154364	16.553712	16.335678
20.50	26.313722	19.110990	17.323795	16.733998	16.521998
20.75	26.441605	19.263280	17.493554	16.914489	16.708389
21.00	26.569693	19.415920	17.663630	17.095172	16.894840
21.25	26.697985	19.568903	17.834015	17.276038	17.081342
21.50	26.826480	19.722225	18.004698	17.457076	17.267886
21.75	26.955175	19.875880	18.175672	17.638275	17.454462
22.00	27.084070	20.029863	18.346926	17.819625	17.641063
22.25	27.213162	20.184169	18.518453	18.001117	17.827679
22.50	27.342451	20.338793	18.690242	18.182742	18.014304
22.75	27.471935	20.493729	18.862286	18.364489	12.200930
23.00	27.601613	20.648972	19.034577	18.546351	18.387550
23.25	27.731482	20.804518	19.207105	18.728317	18.574156
23.50	27.861542	20.960361	19.379864	18.910381	18.760742
23.75	27.991791	21.116496	19.552844	19.092533	18.947302
24.00	28.122228	21.272918	19.726037	19.274765	19.133830
24.25	28.252851	21.429622	19.899437	19.457070	19.320319
24.50	28.383658	21.586603	20.073035	19.639441	19.506765
24.75	28.514649	21.743856	20.246823	19.821869	19.693162

INDEX

REAL ESTATE
ENCYCLOPEDIA

A

B

F

J

K

INDEX

INDEX

N

O

T

INDEX

U

Y

Z

Capitalization $\Rightarrow$ $R = I \div V$

$A = P(1+i)^n$ Effective Rate $= (1+i)^n - 1$

Down Payment + Loan = Price Range

Liquid Assets − Costs = Downpayment

GDS × Income = Loan Payments (PIT)

(Loan Payments + Other Debts) ÷ Income = TDS

(Purchase Price + Costs) − Outstanding Mortgage = Assets

Mortgage Averaging

$$\frac{(\text{Amt. of 1st} \times \text{Int. Rate}) + (\text{Amt. of 2nd} \times \text{Int. Rate})}{\text{Total Amt. Being Financed}}$$

Max. Mortgage Amt $= \dfrac{\text{PIT} \times 1000}{\text{Payment Factor}}$

Insurance Premiums

Loan to Value Ratio	Single Advance
Up to + including 65%	0.50%
" " " 75%	0.75%
" " " 80%	1.25%
" " " 85%	2.00%
" " " 90%	2.50%
" " " 95%	3.75%

Limitations of Ownership

1) Easement
2) Restrictive Covenant
3) Dominant Tenement
4) Servient Tenement
5) Escheat
6) Profit a Prendre

Water Damage

1) Flashings
2) Shingles
3) Entire Roof (Age)
4) Ceiling Joists
5) Chimney
6) Wall Cavities
7) Eavestroughs
8) Downspouts
9) Windows

Construction

1) Footings
2) Sills
3) Joists
4) Bridging/Bracing
5) Subfloor
6) Wood Framing
7) Rafters
8) Roof Sheathing
9) Roof Cover
10) Shingles

Listing Concerns

1) Easements/R.O.W.
2) Lot size, shape
3) Rental/Lease
4) Age of Home (Roof)
5) UFFI
6) Heating - Rented?
7) Basement - Zoning
8) Mortgage Info.
9) Remarks
10) Taxes
11) Occupancy - Tenant?
12) Wood Stove
13) Possession Date
14) Condo Fee

Cost Approach

Step 1: Est. Site Value

Sale	Date	Price +/- Time Adj.	Adjusted Price
1	6 months	102,500 + .024 × 102,500	104,960 — Site Valuation

- choose best comparable

* Avg. % Change In Price = $\dfrac{\Sigma \text{ % Change for each sale}}{\text{# of sales}}$

Step 2: Est. RCN

Structure	Measurement	Total Sq. M	Rep. Cost	RCN
House	8.5 × 14m	119m	$550	$65,450
Garage	4.5 × 8.5m	38.25m	$495	$18,933.75

Reproduction Cost New: $84,383.75

Step 3: Est. Accrued Dep.

Structure	Eff. Age / Ec. Life	RCN	Acc. Dep.	Total Acc. Dep.
House	10/40	$65,450	$16,362.50	
Garage	5/30	$18,933.75	$3,155.63	$19,518.13

* Ec. Life = Eff. Age + Remaining Ec. Life

Steps 4+5: Est. Total Dep. Cost + Value of Property

Land Value		$104,960
RCN	$84,384	
Acc. Dep.	− 19,518	
Dep. Cost of Improvements	$64,866	+ 64,866
Indicated Value By Cost Approach		$169,826
	(Rounded	$169,800)

Correcting Offers (Clauses)

1) Postponement
2) Prepayment for STB
3) Oklahoma (New financing + STB)
4) Waivers

Overall Return on Investment = NOI / Capital Invested

Equity Return on Investment = CFBT / Capital Invested

Lender Yield = Interest Payment / Loan Proceeds Received

Debt Coverage Ratio (DCR) = NOI / Annual Debt Service

$$R/U \text{ Factor} = \frac{\text{Rentable Area}}{\text{Usable Area}}$$

Minimum Rent × SF ÷ Percentage Rent = Base Minimum

Rules of Thumb *excludes acquisition costs

1) Cash on Cash = CFBT ÷ Equity Investment*
2) Pay back Period = Equity Investment ÷ CFBT
3) Break Even Ratio = (Op. Expenses + Debt Service) ÷ Gr. Op. Income
4) Gross Income Multiplier = Sale Price ÷ Gr. Op. Income

Modified C.O.C. = (CFAT + Equity Buildup) ÷ Initial Investment*
(Broker's Rate of Return)
↳ Principal Payments

$$OCR = \frac{NOI}{V} \qquad \text{Equity Cap Rate} = \frac{CFBT}{\text{Initial Investment}}$$
(C.O.C)

$$\text{Mortgage Cap Rate} = \frac{\text{Annual Debt Service}}{\text{Principal Amt. Outstanding}}$$

Yr. (Class - %)	CCA Taken	UCC
EOY 1 (half yr. rule)	12,000 (2%)	588,000
EOY 2	23,520 (4%)	564,480
EOY 3	22,579 (4%)	541,801

* Building Allocation - $600,000 (based on acquisition price)
- CCA can only be taken if profit occurs; can't create or increase a loss
- if UCC is negative when asset sold, recapture occurs (declared income)

- IRR is rate when NPV = 0
- NPV doesn't take into account initial investment or holding period

*PV of Discounted NOI : CF for last yr. = NOI for last yr.
  (can use WACC)   + Sale Price (terminal cap rate)
                                          - Cost of Sale

*PV of Discounted CFBT: CF for last Yr. = CFBT for last yr.
                                          + Equity at point of sale

Equity at P.O.S. = Sale Price - Cost of Sale - Mortgage Balance

Est. of Value (based on Discounted CFBT)
   = PV of Equity + PV of Mortgage

* set initial CF to zero